WITHDRAWN
FOR SALE

UNIVERSITY DEGREE
COURSE OFFERS

Choosing Your University And Degree Course...And Completing Your UCAS Application

Why not contact Brian Heap at HEAPS (*Higher Education Advice and Planning Service*) for a telephone consultation for advice on such issues as:

- Choosing A-level subjects (which are the best and required subjects and for which degree courses)
- Degrees and Diploma courses (making the right choice from a list of thousands!)
- Completing your UCAS application (will the admissions tutor remember your personal statement?)
- Choosing the right university or college (the best ones for you and your courses)

For details of services and consultation fees contact:

The Higher Education Advice and Planning Service
Email heapservice@gmail.com

ander Portman Woodward

UNIVERSITY DEGREE COURSE OFFERS

The essential guide to winning
your place at university

Brian Heap

HEAP2015

45th edition

HEAP 2015: UNIVERSITY DEGREE COURSE OFFERS

In order to ensure that *University Degree Course Offers* retains its reputation as the definitive guide for students wishing to study at UK universities and other higher education institutions, hundreds of questionnaires are distributed, months of research and analysis are undertaken, and painstaking data checking and proofing are carried out.

Every effort has been made to maintain absolute accuracy in providing course information and to ensure that the entire book is as up-to-date as possible. However, changes are constantly taking place in higher education so it is important for readers to check carefully with prospectuses and websites before submitting their applications. The author, compilers and publishers cannot be held responsible for any inaccuracies in information supplied to them by third parties or contained in resources and websites listed in the book.

We hope you find this 45th edition useful, and would welcome your feedback as to how we can ensure the 46th edition is even better.

Author Brian Heap
Advertising Sales Crimson Publishing Services.
Contact Lee Scott or Simon Connor on 020 8445 3391 or email info@crimsonpublishingservices.co.uk

This 45th edition published in 2014 by Trotman Publishing an imprint of Crimson Publishing Ltd,
The Tramshed, Walcot Street, Bath BA1 5BB
www.trotman.co.uk

A CIP record for this book is available from the British Library

ISBN 978 1 84455 605 2

Typeset by IDSUK (DataConnection) Ltd
Printed and bound in Italy by L.E.G.O. S.p.A., Lavis TN

Mander Portman Woodward

Founded in 1973, **Mander Portman Woodward (MPW)** is one of the UK's best known groups of independent sixth-form colleges with centres in London, Birmingham and Cambridge. It offers over 40 subjects at AS and A2 with no restrictions on subject combinations and a maximum class size of eight.

MPW has one of the highest numbers of university placements each year of any independent school in the country. It has developed considerable expertise over the years in the field of applications strategy and is frequently consulted by students facing some of the more daunting challenges that may arise in areas such as getting into Oxbridge, Medicine or Law. This expertise is available to a wider audience in the form of **Getting Into** guides on higher education and the seminars that are run for sixth-formers at its London centre. We are grateful to Trotman for publishing the Guides and hope that this latest edition of **University Degree Course Offers** will prove as popular and useful as ever.

If you would like to know more about MPW Courses or Getting Into guides, please telephone us on 020 7835 1355 or visit our website, www.mpw.co.uk.

Exceptional degrees, outstanding career prospects

"For my placement I hope to travel abroad, gaining hands on experience in the maritime industry, an experience I wouldn't be able to have without the help of LJMU."

BSc (Hons) Maritime Business student **Katy Hopkinson** receives an annual LJMU Vice-Chancellor's Scholarship worth £10,000 for every year of her degree.

So whatever your **ambitions** for the **future**, our **degrees** will help you **achieve** more than you ever thought possible.

Contact us now to find out more.
telephone: 0151 231 5090 **website:** www.ljmu.ac.uk
email: courses@ljmu.ac.uk

Study in the heart of London

Regent's University London offers dynamic British and American undergraduate programmes in:

> Business and Management
> Psychology
> Drama, Film and Media
> Arts and Social Sciences
> Fashion and Design

Foundation programmes and scholarships available

Start dates in January and September

Apply direct or via UCAS

T 020 7487 7505   E exrel@regents.ac.uk   W regents.ac.uk

THE LONDON COLLEGE OFFERING A GATEWAY TO SUCCESS

The London College is a stimulating place to further your education.

Among London's longest established independent higher education colleges, it has over 1000 students on campus and is subject to educational oversight by the Quality Assurance Agency for Higher Education (QAA) under the UK Border Agency's Tier 4 sponsorship requirements. The College is also an approved London partner of the University of Derby.

EXCITING LOCATION

The College is located in Notting Hill Gate, one of the most exciting and vibrant areas in London, pulsating with restaurants, pubs, cinemas and other leisure time places.

But the College offers much more than exciting surroundings. Because it is small, it provides the capability for dedicated teachers to work closely with students. This intimate way of teaching has attracted a very experienced faculty to the campus. Each tutor not only has a rich academic background but also extensive practical experience in their fields of study. They offer their in depth knowledge of the workplace in helping career development.

Quote 'Improving the already excellent standard of education at the London College is my burning ambition and I am proud that I am supported in this objective by faculty, staff and indeed the student body itself. Principal Dr Mark Mabey

WIDE RANGE OF COURSES

This depth of talent and knowledge is reflected across a wide range of courses, taught in a range of disciplines from art and design, business, biology, hospitality, travel and tourism and through to electrical and civil engineering.

The student body is made up of an eclectic group of British and international students. Students are encouraged to involve themselves in the social life of the College through the Students' Association. The campus magazine, 'The Gate' is published eight times a year and involves student reporters to cover campus gossip, news, events and critiques of local eating and drinking establishments.

The London College is exciting and stimulating, a place where students can enjoy both social and academic pursuits to the full.

For more information, please visit www.lcuck.ac.uk

Victoria Gardens
London W11 3PE UK
Tel: +44 (0) 207 243 4000
Fax + 44 (0) 207 243 1484
E-Mail admissions@lcuck.ac.uk

Commitment to Excellence

HND / DEGREE TOP-UP

Start JANUARY and SEPTEMBER

• Full-Time • Part-Time • Weekend

- BA (Hons) Business Management
- BA (Hons) Graphic Design
- BSc (Hons) Civil Engineering
- BSc (Hons) Electrical and Electronic Engineering
- BA (Hons) Health and Social Care
- BA (Hons) International Hospitality Management
- BA (Hons) Tourism Management

UNIVERSITY of DERBY®
LONDON PARTNER

THE LONDON COLLEGE

Victoria Gardens
London W11 3PE UK
Tel: +44 (0) 207 243 4000
Fax + 44 (0) 207 243 1484
E-Mail admissions@lcuck.ac.uk

Commitment to Excellence

HNC/HND Programmes

Start JANUARY and SEPTEMBER

• Full-Time • Part-Time • Weekend

- Art and Design
- Biological Sciences for Industry
- Business Management
- Business Accounting
- Business Law
- Computing and Systems Development
- Civil Engineering
- Computer Game Design
- Electrical and Electronic Engineering
- Graphic Design
- Health and Social Care
- Hospitality Management
- Photography
- Travel and Tourism Management

UNIVERSITY
of DERBY®

LONDON PARTNER

THE LONDON COLLEGE

Victoria Gardens
London W11 3PE UK
Tel: +44 (0) 207 243 4000
Fax + 44 (0) 207 243 1484
E-Mail admissions@lcuck.ac.uk

Commitment to Excellence

Tahmid
Law LLB with English
Central Foundation Boys' School

Professor Lawrence Krauss
BSc (Carleton), DPhil (MIT)
Professor of Science Literacy

Catherine
Law LLB with English
Ellesmere College

Where your quick mind **meets** the challenge you deserve.

New College of the Humanities is a meeting
place for some of the world's quickest minds.
You'll be challenged, and you'll be supported.

You'll be part of an enriching undergraduate learning
community. Led by world-class academics teaching and
researching a stimulating breadth of disciplines, you'll learn
through a pioneering programme of small lecture groups,
one to one tutorials and personalised support.

You apply to NCH directly, in addition to your UCAS choices.

**Call 020 7637 4550 or visit www.NCHum.org
to find out more.**

New College
of the Humanities

Where quick minds meet

Economics BSc   English BA   History BA   Law LLB   Philosophy BA   Politics & International Relations BSc

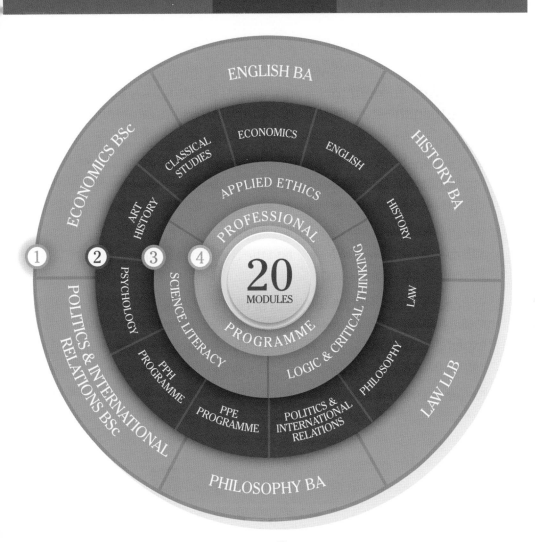

ENGLISH BA

ECONOMICS BSc

HISTORY BA

ECONOMICS

CLASSICAL STUDIES

ENGLISH

APPLIED ETHICS

ART HISTORY

HISTORY

PROFESSIONAL

LAW

LOGIC & CRITICAL THINKING

PSYCHOLOGY

SCIENCE LITERACY

20 MODULES

PROGRAMME

PHILOSOPHY

POLITICS & INTERNATIONAL RELATIONS BSc

PPH PROGRAMME

PPE PROGRAMME

POLITICS & INTERNATIONAL RELATIONS

LAW LLB

PHILOSOPHY BA

(1) **Step one**
Choose **one** undergraduate degree.

(2) **Step two**
Choose **one** Contextual Course.

(3) **Step three**
Study all three compulsory Core Modules.

(4) **Step four**
Complete the compulsory Professional Programme.

Our unique curriculum

New College of the Humanities offers a unique, broader liberal arts curriculum comprising 20 modules – significantly more than the standard 12-module undergraduate degree.

While combining your chosen University of London degree course with another subject of your choice, you will also study Applied Ethics, Logic & Critical Thinking, Science Literacy and the Professional Programme.

To reflect this breadth, you will graduate with the dual award of a University of London degree and the New College of the Humanities Diploma.

With its unparalleled combination of courses and subjects, New College of the Humanities offers you an outstanding intellectual experience, and also prepares you for success in your chosen career path.

Request a prospectus today at www.NCHum.org

New College
of the Humanities

Where quick minds meet

University of Buckingham

Discover the difference: find out why Buckingham has the most satisfied and employable students in the UK

- Two-year undergraduate degrees
- Small-group tutorial teaching with outstanding staff:student ratio
- Leading the National Student Survey since 2006
- Best graduate employability in the UK
- Entry points in January, July and September
- Degrees in Business, Humanities, Law, Medicine and Science

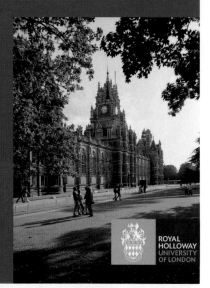

Choosing Your University And Degree Course...And Completing Your UCAS Application

Why not contact Brian Heap at HEAPS (*Higher Education Advice and Planning Service***) for a telephone consultation for advice on such issues as:**

Choosing A-level subjects (which are the best and required subjects and for which degree courses)
Degrees and Diploma courses (making the right choice from a list of thousands!)
Completing your UCAS application (will the admissions tutor remember your personal statement?)
Choosing the right university or college (the best ones for you and your courses)

For details of services and consultation fees contact:

The Higher Education Advice and Planning Service
Email heapservice@gmail.com

HEAP

Degree Course Offers Online!

We've launched a brand new website so students can access the most up-to-date information on degree courses and find the course and university right for them.

The site contains ALL the information you'll find in *HEAP* but delivered in a new and interactive format, enabling students to:

✓ Use UCAS prediction points to search for courses and filter results

✓ Access *HEAP's* unique and invaluable advice to help make their application successful

✓ Search by location, courses or university in an interactive way

✓ Save searches online and access them again at any time

To access *HEAP* online there are a number of flexible subscription options starting from only £99* for multiple users and from only £14.99* for an individual user.

For more information and to subscribe visit www.heaponline.co.uk

OR

Contact us directly by emailing us at heap@trotman.co.uk

Subscription rates are determined by the number of users required.

QUOTES

'*An excellent one-stop shop for finding out information on different universities and courses*'
Oswestry School, 2013

'Degree Course Offers *is my bible and I couldn't be without it ... it gives students focus and saves them time*'
South Thames College, 2013

'Degree Course Offers *remains an essential component of our careers library providing a quick reference to entry requirements and course specific tips for university applications.*'
Mid Kent College, 2013

'Degree Course Offers *... will keep aspirations realistic*'
www.newteachers.tes.co.uk, 2011

'*An extremely useful guide ...*'
Woodhouse Grove School, 2010

'*Look out for Brian Heap's excellent books on choosing higher education courses*'
Carre's Grammar School, 2010

'Degree Course Offers *by Brian Heap – not to be missed. Invaluable*'
Maidstone Grammar School, 2010

'Degree Course Offers *... a really good resource*'
www.positive-parents.com, 2009

'*The guru of university choice*'
The Times, 2007

'*For those of you going through Clearing, an absolute must is the* Degree Course Offers *book. This guide operates subject by subject and gives you each university's requirements, standard offers and, most importantly, "course features"*'
The Independent, August 2007

'*Brian Heap, the guru of university admissions*'
The Independent, September 2007

'*I would like to take this opportunity to congratulate you in maintaining the quality and currency of the information in your guide. We are aware of its wide range and its reputation for impartiality*'
University Senior Assistant Registrar, 2007

'Degree Course Offers *is probably the UK's longest running and best known reference work on the subject*'
www.universityadvice.co.uk, 2005

'*This guide contains useful, practical information for all university applicants and those advising them. I heartily recommend it*'
Dr John Dunford, General Secretary, Association of School and College Leaders, 2005

'*An invaluable guide to helping students and their advisers find their way through the maze of degree courses currently on offer*'
Kath Wright, President, Association for Careers Education and Guidance, 2005

'*No one is better informed or more experienced than Brian Heap in mediating this range of information to university and college applicants*'
Careers Education and Guidance, October 2005

'*The course-listings bible*'
The Guardian, June 2005

CONTENTS

AUTHOR'S ACKNOWLEDGEMENTS

This book and the website www.heaponline.co.uk are a team effort, in which I, my editor Libby Walden and her assistant Bethan Head, and a supporting team at Trotman Publishing make every effort each year to check the contents for accuracy, including all offers from official sources, up to the publication deadline in March. My team's effort throughout the months of preparation therefore deserves my gratitude and praise. In respect of the offers however and the range and abilities of candidates, the reader should recognise that offers are constantly changing and in most cases are shown as 'typical' or target offers.

In the ever-changing world of higher education, research must be on-going and each year many individuals are involved in providing additional up-to-date information. These include Caroline Russell at UCAS, Sarah Hannaford at the Cambridge Admissions Office, Helen Charlesworth at the University of Oxford Public Relations Office and also my daughter Jane Heap (Head of Careers), Putney High School. In addition, deserving of mention are the admissions staff at the many universities who return our annual requests for information and the many teachers and students who furnish me with information on their experiences. To all, I add my grateful thanks.

Finally, I should also add my appreciation to my wife Rita for her 'on the spot' administrative help (and patience!) through 45 years of publication.

Brian Heap BA DA (Manc) ATD
May 2014

ABOUT THIS BOOK

University Degree Course Offers for 45 years has been a first-stop reference for university and college applicants choosing their courses in higher education by providing information from official sources about how to choose courses and how admissions tutors select students.

For 2015/16 higher education applicants, this edition of *University Degree Course Offers* again aims to provide the latest possible information from universities to help equip them to obtain a degree course place in a fiercely competitive applications process. This level of competition will make it essential for every applicant to research carefully courses and institutions.

There are many students who restrict their applications to a small number of well-known universities. They must realise that in doing so they are very likely to receive rejections from all of them. Applicants must spread their choices across a wide range of institutions.

How do applicants decide on a strategy to find a place on a degree course? There are more than 1200 separate degree subjects and over 50,000 Joint and Combined Honours courses so how can applicants choose a course that is right for them, especially at a time of recession and employment difficulties? What can applicants do to find a course place and a university or college that is right for them?

HEAP 2015: University Degree Course Offers is intended to help applicants find their way through these problems by providing the latest possible information about university course offers from official sources, and by giving guidance and information about:

- **Degree courses** – what Honours level courses involve, the range and differences between them, and what applicants need to consider when choosing and deciding on subjects and courses
- **Universities and higher education colleges** – the range and differences between universities and colleges, and the questions applicants might ask when deciding where to study
- **Admissions information** for every university (listed in **Chapter 4**)
- **Target AS/A-level grades/UCAS points offers** (listed in points order in the subject tables in **Chapter 8**) for 2015 entry to Honours degree courses in universities and colleges, with additional Appendix data for applicants with IB, the Progression and Advanced Diplomas, the Extended Project, Scottish Highers, the Welsh Baccalaureate, the Irish Leaving Certificate and international qualifications
- **The UCAS applications process** – what to do, when to do it and how to prepare the personal statement in the UCAS application
- **Universities' and colleges' admissions policies** – how admissions tutors select students
- **Which universities, colleges and courses use admissions tests for entry**
- **Finance, fees and sources of help**
- **Graduate destinations data for each subject area**
- **Action after results day** – and what to do if your grades don't match your offer
- **Entry to UK universities and higher education colleges for international students**

HEAP 2015: *University Degree Course Offers* provides essential information for all students preparing to go into higher education in 2015, covering all stages of researching, planning, deciding and applying to courses and universities. To provide the latest possible information the book is compiled each year between October and March for publication in May and includes important data from the many universities and colleges responding to questionnaires each year.

Every effort is made to ensure the book is as up-to-date as possible. Nevertheless, the increased demand for places and cuts in the number of places available are expected to lead to offers changes during 2015/16, and after prospectuses have been published. Some institutions may also discontinue courses as a result of government cuts and the changes in tuition fees. It will be essential for applicants to check institutions' websites **frequently** to find out any changes in offers, course availability and requirements. If you have any queries, contact admissions staff without delay to find out the latest information as institutions, for many courses, will be looking for a very close, if not precise, match between their requirements and what you offer in your application, qualifications and grades.

Heap 2015: University Degree Course Offers is your starting point for moving on into higher education and planning ahead. Used in conjunction with *Choosing Your Degree Course & University* (see **Appendix 4**) it will take you through all the stages in choosing the course and place of study which is right for you.

Brian Heap
May 2014

Every effort has been made to maintain absolute accuracy in providing course information and to ensure that the entire book is as up-to-date as possible. However, changes are constantly taking place in higher education so it is important for readers to check carefully with prospectuses and websites before submitting their applications.

University College Cork, Ireland
Coláiste na hOllscoile Corcaigh

Founded in 1845, UCC is one of Ireland's most prestigious universities and is among the elite 2% of universities worldwide. UCC is a vibrant university with over 19,000 full-time and part-time students across all disciplines, including over 2,000 international students from 100 countries around the world.

The University's historic city-centre campus is set in mature parklands through which the River Lee meanders, making UCC at once an oasis of learning and calm and a hive of vibrant student activity, in the midst of a bustling city and with the beautiful West Cork region on its doorstep.

Fees
Fees for EU students in 2015 will be €3165 or £2645. This comprises the Student Contribution Charge and Capitation Fee, with Tuition paid by the State for all first-time EU students.

Applying
To be eligible for a place, students must first meet minimum entry and specific subject requirements. Students must also satisfy the points requirements for each programme. Apply through the Central Applications Office by 1st February 2015 for entry in 2015. See www.cao.ie for the application form, and handbook for procedures. Places are offered in August.

A-Level Conversion Table

A2	points	AS	points
A*	150		
A	135	A	65
B	120	B	60
C	100	C	50
D	75	D	35
E	40	E	20

Four subjects are scored – either 4 A Levels or 3 A Levels and a fourth AS subject. Twenty-five bonus points are awarded for A-Level Maths.

www.ucc.ie/study/undergrad/

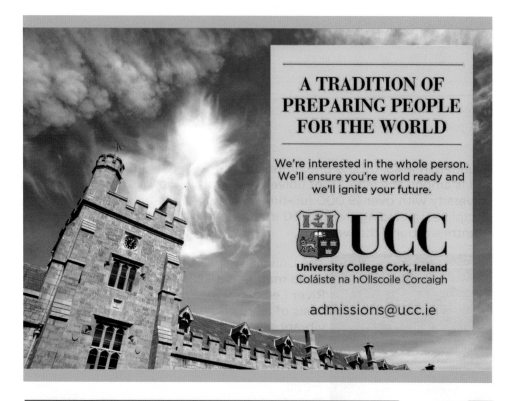

YOUR FIRST DECISIONS

HIGHER EDUCATION OR NOT?

Why do you want to go on to higher education? If you are taking GCE Advanced (AL) and Advanced Subsidiary (AS) qualifications, the International Baccalaureate, Scottish Highers and Advanced Highers, the Welsh Baccalaureate, the Cambridge Pre-U or the Advanced Diploma this is an important question to ask. However, higher education is just one of two options you have. Increasingly, with the competition for university places, full-time employment is the other option and it's important to remember that higher education is not necessarily the best option for everyone, but it should not be rejected lightly. Higher education has the advantage however of opening many doors and giving you opportunities for work and leisure that otherwise you might not have. Also, very often and quite accidentally, it can lead into careers that you might not have considered before.

Choosing your AS/A-levels (or equivalent qualifications) is done on the basis of your best subjects and those which you find most interesting. However, leading universities (and, especially, those with popular and competitive courses) may seek a grouping of subjects with 'academic weight'. Usually at least two AS/A-level 'academic' subjects are preferred.

In some cases the following may not be regarded as strong academic subjects: accounting, art and design, business studies, communication studies, dance, design and technology, drama/theatre studies, film studies, health and social care, home economics, information and communication, leisure studies, media studies, music technology, performance studies, performing arts, photography, physical education, sports studies, technology, travel and tourism.

If you are taking two or more of these subjects at AS/A-level you should check with your preferred universities whether they will be accepted for your chosen course before you apply.

Most courses in higher education lead to a degree or a diploma and for either you will have to make a subject choice. This can be difficult because the universities alone offer over 1200 degree subjects and over 50,000 course combinations within the UCAS scheme. You have two main options:

A Choosing a course that is either similar to, or the same as, one (or more) of your examination subjects, or related to an interest outside the school curriculum, such as Anthropology, American Studies, Archaeology. See **Section A** below.

B Choosing a course in preparation for a future career, for example Medicine, Architecture, Engineering. See **Section B** below and also **Appendix 3**.

SECTION A

Choosing your course by examination subjects

Deciding your degree or diploma course on the basis of your A-level (or equivalent) subjects is a reasonably safe option since you are already familiar with the subjects themselves and what they involve. Inevitably, long-term career prospects will be of some concern, especially in a period of economic recession. However, it is important to remember that a degree in higher education gives you many skills, including, for example, those for critical thinking, assessment and research and, for many occupations, the degree subject is often not as important as the degree itself. If you are taking science subjects, they can lead naturally on to a range of scientific careers, although many scientists follow non-science careers such as law and accountancy. If you are taking arts or social science subjects, remember that specialist training for most non-scientific careers often starts once you have your degree.

When choosing your degree course by examination subjects it is important to consider the subjects you are taking at A-level (or equivalent) as universities may 'require' or 'prefer' certain subjects for entry to some courses. To make sure you have the right subjects, check the course subject requirements in university/college prospectuses and on their websites. Many universities, especially those giving high level offers, have increasingly detailed A-level requirements, so it is very important that you find out the latest information. This also applies to GCSE subjects and grade requirements. When choosing AS-level subjects, students sometimes prefer to select those with a similar subject base, for example four science subjects, or four arts, or four humanities subjects. However, some institutions welcome one, or even two, contrasting subjects, even for specialist courses such as Medicine, providing the required subjects are also offered.

Subjects do not stand on their own, in isolation. Each subject you are taking is one of a much larger family. Each has many similarities to subjects studied in degree and diploma courses that you might never have considered, so before you decide finally on taking a subject to degree level read through the list of A-level subjects below, each followed by examples of degree courses in the same subject field which will give you some idea of degree courses with similarities to the subjects you might be taking. (These lists are also useful if you have to consider alternative courses after the examination results are published!)

Accounting Accountancy, Accounting, Actuarial Mathematics, Banking and Finance, Business Studies (Finance), Economics, Finance Investment and Risk, Financial Mathematics, Financial Software Engineering, Management Sciences, Mathematics. See also **Section B**.

Ancient history Archaeology, Biblical Studies, Classical Greek, Classics and Classical Civilisation, Latin, Middle and Near Eastern Studies.

Arabic Arabic. See also **Languages** below.

Archaeology Ancient History, Anthropology, Archaeological Sciences, Archaeology, Bioarchaeology, Classical Civilisation, Conservation of Objects in Museums and Archaeology, Egyptology, Geology, History, Marine Archaeology, Viking Studies. See also **Section B**.

Art and design Art, Fine Art, Furniture Design, Graphic Design, Photography, Textile Design, Theatre Design, Three-Dimensional Design, Typography and Graphic Communication. See also **Section B**.

Bengali Bengali. See also **Languages** below.

Biblical Hebrew Hebrew, Religious Studies, Theology.

Biology Agricultural Sciences, Animal Behaviour, Audiology, Bioinformatics, Biological Sciences, Biology, Biomedical Sciences, Biotechnology, Dental Hygiene, Ecology and Conservation, Environmental Sciences, Genetics, Human Embryology, Infection and Immunity, Life Sciences, Medicine, Microbiology, Molecular Sciences, Natural Sciences, Physiology, Plant Biology, Plant Science, Veterinary Science, Zoology. See also **Section B**.

Business Accounting, Banking, Business Management, Business Statistics, Computing, Economics, Entrepreneurship, Finance, Hospitality Management, Human Resource Management, Information Systems, Logistics, Management Sciences, Marketing, Mathematics, Publishing, Retail Management, Transport Management, Web Design and Development. See also **Section B**.

Chemistry Biochemistry, Cancer Biology, Chemical Engineering, Chemical Physics, Chemistry, Dentistry, Environmental Sciences, Fire Engineering, Forensic Sciences, Medicinal Chemistry, Medicine, Microbiology, Natural Sciences, Nutritional Biochemistry, Pharmacology, Pharmacy, Veterinary Science, Virology and Immunology. See also **Section B**.

Chinese Chinese. See also **Languages** below.

Classics and classical civilisation Ancient History, Archaeology, Classical Studies, Classics, Greek (Classical), Latin.

Communication studies Advertising, Communication Studies, Drama, Education, English Language, Information and Library Studies, Journalism, Languages, Linguistics, Media and Communications, Psychology, Public Relations, Publishing, Speech Sciences. See also **Section B**.

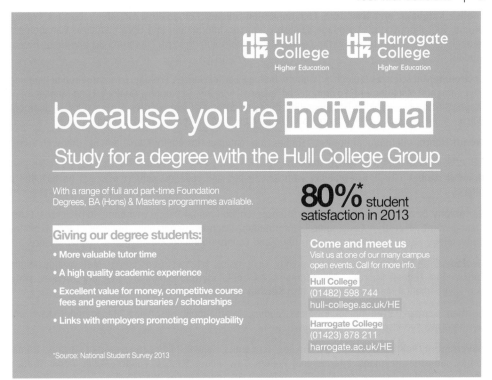

Computing Artificial Intelligence, Business Information Systems, Computer Engineering, Computer Science, Computing, Cybernetics, E-Commerce, Electronic Engineering, Games Technology, Intelligent Product Design, Multimedia Systems Engineering, Network Management and Security, Robotics, Software Engineering. See also **Section B**.

Critical thinking (Check acceptability with universities and colleges: subject may not be included in offers.)

Dance Arts Management, Ballet Education, Choreography, Dance, Drama, Education, Music, Musical Theatre, Performance Management, Performing Arts, Sport and Exercise, Street Arts, Theatre and Performance, Theatre Arts, Writing Directing and Performance. See also **Section B**.

Design technology Food Technology, Manufacturing Engineering, Product Design, Sport Equipment Design, Systems and Control. See also **Section B**.

Drama and theatre studies Acting, Community Drama, Costume Production, Creative Writing, Dance, Drama, Education Studies, English Comedy: Writing and Performance, International Theatre, Music, Performing Arts, Scenic Arts, Scriptwriting, Set Design, Stage Management, Theatre Arts, Theatre Practice. See also **Section B**.

Dutch Dutch. See also **Languages** below.

Economics Accountancy, Banking, Business Administration, Business Economics, Business Studies, Development Studies, Economics, Estate Management, Finance, Management Science, Mathematics, Political Economy, Politics, Quantity Surveying, Sociology, Statistics.

Electronics Computing, Electronics, Engineering (Aeronautical, Aerospace, Communication, Computer, Software, Systems), Mechatronics, Medical Electronics, Multimedia Technology, Technology. See also **Section B**.

English language and literature Communication Studies, Comparative Literature, Creative Writing, Drama, Education, English Language, English Literature, Information and Library Studies/Management, Journalism, Linguistics, Media Writing, Philosophy, Publishing, Scottish Literature, Scriptwriting, Theatre Studies.

Environmental sciences Biological Sciences, Biology, Earth Sciences, Ecology, Environment and Planning, Environmental Management, Environmental Sciences, Forestry, Geography, Geology, Land Management, Marine Biology, Meteorology, Oceanography, Outdoor Education, Plant Sciences, Sustainable Development, Wastes Management, Water Science, Wildlife Biology, Wildlife Conservation, Zoology.

French French, International Business Studies, International Hospitality Management, Law with French Law. See also **Languages** below.

General studies (Check acceptability with universities and colleges: subject may not be included in offers.)

Geography Development Studies, Earth Sciences, Environmental Policy, Environmental Sciences, Estate Management, Forestry, Geographical Information Science, Geography, Geology, Land Economy, Meteorology, Oceanography, Surveying, Town and Country Planning, Urban Studies, Water Science.

Geology Earth Sciences, Geography, Geology, Geophysical Sciences, Geosciences, Meteorology, Mining Engineering, Natural Sciences, Oceanography, Palaeontology and Evolution, Planetary Sciences, Water and Environmental Management. See also **Section B**.

German German, International Business Studies, International Hospitality Management, Law with German Law. See also **Languages** below.

Government/Politics Development Studies, Economics, Global Politics, Government, History, Human Rights, Industrial Relations, International Politics, Law, Peace Studies, Politics, Public Administration, Social and Political Science, Social Policy, Sociology, Strategic Studies, War Studies.

Gujarati Gujarati. See also **Languages** below.

Health and social care Early Childhood Studies, Environmental Health, Health and Social Care, Health Promotion, Health Psychology, Health Sciences, Health Studies, Nursing, Nutrition, Public Health, Social Sciences, Social Work, Sport and Health, Working with Children and Young People, Youth and Community Work. See also **Section B**.

History African Studies, American Studies, Ancient History, Archaeology, Art History, Classical Civilisations, Classical Studies, Education, Egyptology, Fashion and Dress History, History, International Relations, Law, Literature, Medieval Studies, Museum and Heritage Studies, Philosophy, Politics, Russian Studies, Scandinavian Studies, Scottish History, Social and Economic History, Theology and Religious Studies, Victorian Studies.

Home economics Culinary Arts Management, Design and Technology Education, Food and Consumer Management, Food Science, Home Economics (Food Design and Technology), Hospitality Management, Nutrition.

Information and communication technology Business Information Systems, Communications Systems Design, Communications Technology, Digital Communications, Electrical and Electronic Engineering, Geographic Information Science, Information and Library Studies, Information Management, Information Sciences, Information Systems, Internet Engineering, Mobile Computing, Multimedia Computing, Telecommunications Engineering. See also **Section B**.

Italian Italian. See also **Languages** below.

Japanese Japanese. See also **Languages** below.

Languages Languages, Modern Languages, Translating and Interpreting. **NB** Apart from French and German – and Spanish for some universities – it is not usually necessary to have completed an A-level language course before studying the many languages (over 60) offered at degree level. Many universities provide opportunities to study a language in a wide range of degree courses. See also **the Erasmus programme** details in **Chapter 5**.

Law Criminal Justice, Criminology, European Business Law, Human Rights, International Business, International Relations, Law, Legal Studies, Police Sciences, Social Sciences, Sociology, Youth Justice. See also **Section B**.

Leisure studies Adventure Tourism Management, Countryside Recreation and Tourism, Equine Business Management, Events Management, Fitness and Health, Health and Leisure Studies, Hospitality and Leisure Management, Leisure Marketing, Outdoor Leadership, Personal Fitness Training, Sport and Leisure Management, Sport Leisure and Culture, Sports Education, Tourism Management, Tourism Marketing.

Mathematics Accountancy, Actuarial Mathematics, Aeronautical Engineering, Astrophysics, Business Management, Chemical Engineering, Civil Engineering, Computational Science, Computer Systems Engineering, Control Systems Engineering, Cybernetics, Economics, Engineering Science, Ergonomics, Financial Mathematics, Further and Additional Mathematics, Geophysics, Management Science, Materials Science and Technology, Mechanical Engineering, Meteorology, Naval Architecture, Physics, Quantity Surveying, Statistics, Systems Analysis, Telecommunications.

Media studies Advertising, Animation, Broadcasting, Communication Studies, Creative Writing, English, Film and Television Studies, Journalism, Mass Communication, Media courses, Media Culture and Society, Media Production, Media Technology, Multimedia, Photography, Publishing, Radio Production and Communication, Society Culture and Media, Translation Media and French/Spanish, Web and Broadcasting. See also **Section B**.

Modern Greek Greek. See also **Languages** above.

Modern Hebrew Hebrew. See also **Languages** above.

Music Audio and Music Production, Creative Music Technology, Education, Music, Music Broadcasting, Music Informatics, Music Management, Music Systems Engineering, Musical Theatre, Musician, Performance Arts, Popular and World Musics, Sonic Arts. See also **Section B**.

Persian Persian. See also **Languages** above.

Philosophy Classical Studies, Cultural Studies, Divinity, Educational Studies, Ethics, History of Ideas, History of Science, Law, Mathematics, Natural Sciences, Philosophy, Politics Philosophy and Economics, Psychology, Religious Studies, Social Sciences, Theology.

Physics Aeronautical Engineering, Architecture, Astronomy, Astrophysics, Automotive Engineering, Biomedical Engineering, Biophysics, Chemical Physics, Civil Engineering, Communications Engineering, Computer Science, Cybernetics, Education, Electrical/Electronic Engineering, Engineering Science, Ergonomics, Geophysics, Materials Science and Technology, Mechanical Engineering, Medical Physics, Meteorology, Nanotechnology, Naval Architecture, Oceanography, Optometry, Photonics, Planetary Science, Quantum Informatics, Radiography, Renewable Energy, Telecommunications Engineering.

Polish Polish. See also **Languages** above.

Portuguese Portuguese. See also **Languages** above.

Psychology Advertising, Animal Behaviour, Anthropology, Artificial Intelligence, Behavioural Science, Childhood Strudies, Cognitive Science, Counselling Studies, Criminology, Education, Human Resource Management, Marketing, Neuroscience, Nursing, Politics, Psychology, Social Sciences, Sociology, Speech and Language Therapy. See also **Section B**.

Punjabi Punjabi. See also **Languages** above.

Religious studies Abrahamic Religions (Christianity, Islam and Judaism), Anthropology, Archaeology, Biblical Studies, Christian Youth Work, Comparative Religion, Divinity, Education, Ethics, History of Art, International Relations, Islamic Studies, Jewish Studies, Philosophy, Psychology, Religious Studies, Social Policy, Theology.

Russian Russian. See also **Languages** above.

Sport and physical education Chiropractic, Coaching Science, Community Sport Development, Dance Studies, Exercise and Health, Exercise Science, Fitness Science, Football Studies, Golf Studies, Osteopathy,

Outdoor Pursuits, Physical Education, Physiotherapy, Sport and Exercise Science, Sport and Health, Sport Coaching, Sport Equipment Design, Sport Management, Sport Marketing, Teaching (Primary) (Secondary).

Statistics Actuarial Studies, Business Analysis, Business Studies, Informatics, Management Sciences, Statistics. See also Mathematics above and **Section B** Mathematics-related careers.

Travel and tourism See **Section B**.

Turkish Turkish. See also **Languages** above.

Urdu Urdu. See also **Languages** above.

SECTION B
Choosing your course by career interests

An alternative strategy for deciding on the subject of your degree or diploma course is to relate it to your career interests. However, even though you may have set your mind on a particular career, it is important to remember that sometimes there are others which are very similar to your planned career. The following lists give examples of career areas, each followed by examples of degree subjects in the subject field.

Accountancy Accountancy, Accounting, Actuarial Science, Banking, Business Studies, Economics, Finance and Business, Finance and Investment, Financial Services, Management Science, Real Estate Management, Risk Management.

Actuarial work Actuarial Mathematics, Actuarial Science, Actuarial Studies, Financial Mathematics, Risk Analysis and Insurance.

Agricultural careers Agri-Business, Agricultural Engineering, Agriculture, Animal Sciences, Aquaculture and Fishery Sciences, Conservation and Habitat Management, Countryside Management, Crop Science, Ecology, Environmental Science, Estate Management, Forestry, Horticulture, Landscape Management, Plant Sciences, Rural Resource Management, Soil Science, Wildlife Management.

Animal careers Agricultural Sciences, Animal Behaviour and Welfare, Biological Sciences, Bioveterinary Science, Equine Management/Science/Studies, Veterinary Nursing, Veterinary Practice Management, Veterinary Science, Zoology.

Archaeology Ancient History, Anthropology, Archaeology, Bioarchaeology, Classical Civilisation and Classics, Egyptology, Geography, History, History of Art and Architecture, Viking Studies.

Architecture Architectural Design, Architectural Technology, Architecture, Building, Building Conservation, City and Regional Planning, Civil Engineering, Conservation and Restoration, Construction Engineering and Management, Interior Architecture, Stained Glass Restoration and Conservation, Structural Engineering.

Art and Design careers Advertising, Animation, Architecture, Art, Design, Digital Media Design, Education (Art), Fashion and Textiles, Fine Art, Games Art and Design, Glassware, Graphic Design, Illustration, Industrial Design, Jewellery, Landscape Architecture, Photography, Stained Glass, Three-Dimensional Design.

Astronomy Astronomy, Astrophysics, Mathematics, Natural Sciences, Planetary Geology, Physics, Quantum and Cosmological Physics, Space Science, Space Technology and Planetary Exploration.

Audiology Audiology, Education of the Deaf, Human Communication, Nursing, Speech and Language Therapy.

Banking/Insurance Accountancy, Actuarial Sciences, Banking, Business Studies, Economics, Financial Services, Insurance, Real Estate Management, Risk Management.

Biology-related careers Agricultural Sciences, Animal Sciences, Biochemistry, Biological Sciences, Biology, Biomedical Sciences, Biotechnology, Cell Biology, Ecology, Education, Environmental Biology, Environmental Sciences, Freshwater Science, Genetics, Immunology, Life Sciences, Marine Biology, Medical Biochemistry, Medicine, Microbiology, Molecular Biology, Natural Sciences, Oceanography, Pharmacy, Plant Science, Physiology, Wildlife Conservation, Zoology.

Book Publishing Advertising, Business Studies, Communications, Creative Writing, Illustration, Journalism, Media Communication, Photography, Printing, Publishing, Science Communication, Web and Multimedia.

Brewing and Distilling Biochemistry, Brewing and Distilling, Chemistry, Food Science and Technology, Viticulture and Oenology.

Broadcasting Audio Video and Digital Broadcast Engineering, Broadcast Documentary, Broadcast Media, Broadcast Technology and Production, Digital Media, Electronic Engineering (Broadcast Systems), Film and TV Broadcasting, Media and Communications Studies, Media Production, Multimedia, Music Broadcasting, Outside Broadcast Technology, Radio Journalism, Television Studio Production, TV Production, Video and Broadcasting.

Building Architecture, Building Conservation, Building Services Engineering, Building Studies, Building Surveying, Civil Engineering, Estate Management, General Practice Surveying, Land Surveying, Quantity Surveying.

Business Accountancy, Advertising, Banking, Business Administration, Business Analysis, Business Studies, Business Systems, E-Commerce, Economics, Estate Management, European Business, Hospitality Management, Housing Management, Human Resource Management, Industrial Relations, Insurance, Logistics, Management Sciences, Marketing, Property Development, Public Relations, Publishing, Supply Chain Management, Transport Management, Tourism.

Cartography Geographic Information Systems, Geographical Information Science, Geography, Land Surveying.

Catering Consumer Studies, Culinary Arts Management, Dietetics, Food Science, Hospitality Management, International and Hospitality Business Management, Nutrition.

Chemistry-related careers Agricultural Science, Biochemistry, Botany, Ceramics, Chemical Engineering, Chemistry, Colour Chemistry, Education, Environmental Sciences, Geochemistry, Materials Science and Technology, Medical Chemistry, Nanotechnology, Natural Sciences, Pharmacology, Pharmacy, Physiology, Technologies (for example Food, Plastics).

Computing Artificial Intelligence, Bioinformatics, Business Computing, Business Studies, Computer Engineering, Computer Games Development, Computer Science, Computers, Electronics and Communications, Digital Forensics and System Security, Electronic Engineering, Games Design, Information and Communication Technology, Internet Computing, Mathematics, Multimedia Computing, Physics, Software Systems, Telecommunications, Virtual Reality Design.

Construction Architectural Technology, Architecture, Building, Building Services Engineering, Civil Engineering, Construction Management, Fire Risk Engineering, Landscape Architecture, Quantity Surveying, Surveying, Town and Country Planning.

Dance Ballet Education, Choreography, Dance, Drama, Movement Studies, Performance/Performing Arts, Physical Education, Theatre Studies.

Dentistry Biochemistry, Dental Materials, Dental Technician, Dentistry, Equine Dentistry, Medicine, Nursing, Oral Health Sciences, Pharmacy.

Drama Dance, Drama, Education, Movement Studies, Musical Theatre, Scenic Arts, Teaching, Theatre Management.

Education Ballet Education, British Sign Language, Childhood Studies, Coach Education, Deaf Studies, Early Years Education, Education Studies, Education with QTS, Education without QTS, Music Education, Physical Education, Primary Education, Psychology, Secondary Education, Social Work, Special Educational Needs, Speech and Language Therapy, Sport and Exercise, Teaching, Technology for Teaching and Learning, Youth Studies.

Electronics Automotive Electronics, Avionics, Computer Systems, Computer Technology, Computing, Digital Electronics, Digital Media Technology, Electronic Design, Electronic Engineering, Electronics, Information Systems, Internet Engineering, Mechatronics, Medical Electronics, Motorsport Electronic Systems, Multimedia Computing, Software Development, Sound Engineering.

Engineering Engineering (including Aeronautical, Aerospace, Chemical, Civil, Computing, Control, Electrical, Electronics, Energy, Environmental, Food Process, Manufacturing, Mechanical, Motorsport, Nuclear, Product Design, Software, Telecommunications Electronics), Geology and Geotechnics, Horology, Mathematics, Physics.

Estate Management Architecture, Building, Civil Engineering, Economics, Estate Management, Forestry, Housing Studies, Landscape Architecture, Property Development, Real Estate Management, Town and Country Planning.

Food Science and Technology Biochemistry, Brewing and Distilling, Chemistry, Culinary Arts, Dietetics, Food and Consumer Studies, Food Safety Management, Food Science and Technology, Food Supply Chain Management, Fresh Produce Management, Hospitality and Food Management, Nutrition, Public Health Nutrition, Viticulture and Oenology.

Forestry Arboriculture, Biological Sciences, Countryside Management, Ecology, Environmental Science, Forestry, Horticulture, Plant Sciences, Rural Resource Management, Tropical Forestry, Urban Forestry.

Furniture Design Furniture Design, Furniture Production, History of Art and Design, Three-Dimensional Design, Timber Technology.

Geology-related careers Chemistry, Earth Sciences, Engineering (Civil, Minerals), Environmental Sciences, Geochemistry, Geography, Geology, Land Surveying, Oceanography, Soil Science.

Graphic Design Advertising, Graphic Design, Photography, Printing, Web Design.

Health and Safety careers Biomedical Informatics, Biomedical Sciences, Community and Health Studies, Environmental Health, Exercise and Health Science, Fire Science Engineering, Health and Social Care, Health Management, Health Promotion, Health Psychology, Health Sciences, Holistic Therapy, Nursing, Occupational Safety and Health, Paramedic Science, Public Health, Public Services Management. (See also **Medical careers**.)

Horticulture Agriculture, Crop Science, Horticulture, Landscape Architecture, Plant Science, Soil Science.

Hospitality Management Business and Management, Culinary Arts Management, Events and Facilities Management, Food Science, Food Technology, Heritage Management, Hospitality Management, Human Resource Management, International Hospitality Management, Leisure Services Management, Licensed Retail Management, Spa Management, Travel and Tourism Management.

Housing Architecture, Estate Management, General Practice Surveying, Housing, Social Administration, Town and Country Planning.

Law Business Law, Commercial Law, Consumer Law, Criminal Justice, Criminology, European Law, Government and Politics, International History, Land Management, Law, Legal Studies, Politics, Sociology.

Leisure and Recreation Adventure Tourism, Airline and Airport Management, Business Travel and Tourism, Community Arts, Countryside Management, Dance, Drama, Event Management, Fitness Science, Hospitality Management, International Tourism Management, Leisure Management, Movement Studies, Music, Physical Education, Sport and Leisure Management, Sport Development, Sports Management, Theatre Studies, Travel and Tourism.

Library and Information Management Administration, Business Information Systems, Digital Media, Education Studies, Information and Communication Studies, Information and Library Studies, Information Management, Information Sciences and Technology, Management and Marketing, Media and Cultural Studies, Media Communications, Museum and Galleries Studies, Publishing.

Marketing Advertising, Business Studies, Consumer Science, E-Marketing, Health Promotion, International Business, Marketing, Psychology, Public Relations, Retail Management, Sports Development, Travel and Tourism.

Materials Science/Metallurgy Automotive Materials, Chemistry, Engineering, Glass Science and Technology, Materials Science and Technology, Mineral Surveying, Physics, Polymer Science, Sports Materials, Textile Science.

Mathematics-related careers Accountancy, Actuarial Science, Astronomy, Banking, Business Decision Mathematics, Business Studies, Computer Studies, Economics, Education, Engineering, Financial Mathematics, Mathematical Physics, Mathematics, Physics, Quantity Surveying, Statistics.

Media careers Advertising, Broadcasting, Communications, Computer Graphics, Creative Writing, Film/Video Production, Journalism, Media, Multimedia, Photography, Public Relations, Psychology, Visual Communication.

Medical careers Anatomy, Biochemistry, Biological Sciences, Biomedical Sciences, Chiropractic, Dentistry, Genetics, Human Physiology, Immunology, Medical Engineering, Medical Sciences/Medicine, Nursing, Occupational Therapy, Orthoptics, Osteopathy, Pathology and Microbiology, Pharmacology, Pharmacy, Physiotherapy, Psychology, Radiography, Speech and Language Therapy, Sports Biomedicine, Virology.

Music Commercial Music, Creative Music Technology, Digital Music, Drama, Folk and Traditional Music, Music, Music Composition, Music Education, Music Industry Management, Music Performance, Music Production, Music Studies, Musical Theatre, Performance/Performing Arts, Popular Music, Sonic Arts, Sound and Multimedia Technology, Theatre Studies.

Nautical careers Marine Engineering, Marine Studies, Nautical Studies, Naval Architecture, Oceanography, Offshore Engineering, Ship Science.

Naval Architecture Boat Design, Marine Engineering, Marine Studies, Naval Architecture, Offshore Engineering, Ship Science, Yacht and Powercraft Design, Yacht Production.

Nursing Anatomy, Applied Biology, Biochemistry, Biological Sciences, Biology, Dentistry, Education, Environmental Health and Community Studies, Health Studies, Human Biology, Medicine, Midwifery, Nursing, Occupational Therapy, Orthoptics, Physiotherapy, Podiatry, Psychology, Radiography, Social Administration, Speech and Language Therapy, Veterinary Nursing. (See also **Medical careers**.)

Nutrition Dietetics, Food Science and Technology, Health Promotion, Human Nutrition, Nursing, Nutrition, Sport and Fitness.

Occupational Therapy Art, Nursing, Occupational Therapy, Orthoptics, Physiotherapy, Psychology, Social Sciences, Speech and Language Therapy.

Optometry Applied Physics, Optometry, Orthoptics, Physics.

Photography/Film/TV Animation, Communication Studies (some courses), Digital Video Design, Documentary Communications, Film and Media, Graphic Art, Media Studies, Moving Image, Multimedia, Photography.

Physics-related careers Applied Physics, Astronomy, Astrophysics, Avionics and Space Systems, Education, Electronics, Engineering (Civil, Electrical, Mechanical), Laser Physics, Mathematical Physics, Medical Instrumentation, Molecular Physics, Nanotechnology, Natural Sciences, Optometry, Physics, Planetary and Space Physics, Quantum and Cosmological Physics, Theoretical Physics.

Physiotherapy Chiropractic, Exercise Science, Nursing, Orthoptics, Osteopathy, Physical Education, Physiotherapy, Sport and Exercise, Sports Rehabilitation.

Production Technology Engineering (Manufacturing, Mechanical), Materials Science.

Property and Valuation Management Architecture, Building Surveying, Estate Agency, Property Investment and Finance, Property Management and Valuation, Quantity Surveying, Real Estate Management, Residential Property, Urban Land Economics.

Psychology Advertising, Animal Sciences, Anthropology, Applied Social Studies, Behavioural Science, Business, Cognitive Science, Criminology, Early Childhood Studies, Education, Human Resource Management, Human Sciences, Linguistics, Marketing, Neuroscience, Occupational Therapy, Psychology (Clinical, Developmental, Educational, Experimental, Forensic, Health, Occupational, Social, Sports), Psychosocial Sciences, Public Relations, Social Sciences, Sociology.

Public Administration Applied Social Studies, Business Studies, Public Administration, Public Policy Investment and Management, Public Services, Social Administration, Social Policy, Youth Studies.

Quantity Surveying Architecture, Building, Civil Engineering, Construction and Commercial Management, Environmental Construction Surveying, Quantity Surveying, Surveying (Building, Land, Quantity and Valuation), Surveying Technology.

Radiography Anatomy, Audiology, Biological Sciences, Clinical Photography, Diagnostic Imaging, Diagnostic Radiography, Digital Imaging, Imaging Science and Technology, Medical Imaging, Moving Image, Nursing, Orthoptics, Photography, Physics, Physiology, Physiotherapy, Radiography, Radiotherapy, Therapeutic Radiography.

Silversmithing/Jewellery Design Silversmithing and Jewellery, Silversmithing Goldsmithing and Jewellery, Silversmithing Metalwork and Jewellery, Three-Dimensional Design.

Social Work Abuse Studies, Applied Social Science, Community Work, Counselling Studies, Early Childhood Studies, Education, Health and Social Care, Human Rights, Journalism, Law, Nursing, Playwork, Politics and Government, Psychology, Public Administration, Religious Studies, Social Administration, Social Policy, Social Work, Sociology, Town and Country Planning, Youth Studies.

Speech and Language Therapy Audiology, Education (Special Education), Linguistics, Nursing, Occupational Therapy, Psychology, Radiography, Speech and Language Therapy.

Sport and Physical Education Coaching Sciences, Exercise Sciences, Fitness Science, Health and Fitness Management, Leisure and Recreation Management, Physical Education, Sport and Recreational Studies, Sport Journalism, Sports Psychology, Sports Science, Sports Studies.

Statistics Business Studies, Economics, Informatics, Mathematics, Operational Research, Population Sciences, Statistics.

Surveying Building Surveying, General Practice Surveying, Property Development, Quantity Surveying, Real Estate Management.

Technology Audio Technology, Dental Technology, Design Technology, Food Science and Technology, Football Technology, Logistics Technology, Medical Technology, Music Studio Technology, Paper Science, Polymer Science, Product Design Technology, Sports Technology, Technology for Teaching and Learning, Timber Technology.

Textile Design Applied Art and Design, Art, Clothing Studies, Fashion Design, Interior Design, Textile Design (Embroidery, Constructive Textiles, Printed Textiles), Textile Management.

Theatre Design Drama, Interior Design, Leisure and Recreational Studies, Theatre Design, Theatre Management, Theatre Studies.

Three-Dimensional Design Architecture, Industrial Design, Interior Design, Theatre Design, Three-Dimensional Design.

Town and Regional Planning Architecture, Architecture and Planning, City and Regional Planning, Environmental Planning, Estate Management, Geography, Housing, Land Economy, Planning and Development, Population Sciences, Property Planning and Development, Spatial Planning, Statistics, Sustainable Development, Town and Regional Planning, Transport Management, Urban and Regional Planning.

Transport Air Transport Engineering, Air Transport Operations, Air Transport with Pilot Training, Business Studies, Civil and Transportation Engineering, Cruise Operations Management, Industrial Design (Transport), Logistics, Planning with Transport, Supply Chain Management, Sustainable Transport Design, Town and Regional Planning, Urban Planning Design and Management.

Typography and Graphic Communication Design (Graphic and Typographic Design), Digital Graphics, Fine Art (Print and Digital Media), Graphic Communication and Typography, Graphic Design, Illustration, Illustration and Print, Printmaking, Publication Design, Publishing, Visual Communication.

Veterinary careers Agricultural Sciences, Agriculture, Anatomical Science, Animal Behaviour and Welfare, Animal Sciences, Bioveterinary Sciences, Equine Dentistry, Equine Science, Medicine, Pharmacology, Pharmacy, Veterinary Medicine, Veterinary Nursing, Veterinary Practice Management, Zoology.

COURSE TYPES AND DIFFERENCES

You will then need to decide on the type of course you want to follow. The way in which Honours degree courses are arranged differs between institutions. For example, a subject might be offered as a single subject course (a Single Honours degree), or as a two-subject course (a Joint Honours degree), or as one of two, three or four subjects (a Combined Honours degree) or a major/minor degree (75% and 25% of each subject respectively). The chapter **University and College Course Profiles** gives more information about the different types of courses and provides for each university a resumé of the ways their courses are structured and the range of courses they offer.

Courses in the same subject at different universities and colleges can have different subject requirements so it is important to check the acceptability of your GCE A/AS and GCSE subjects (or equivalent) for all your preferred courses. Specific GCE A/AS-levels, and in some cases, GCSE subjects, may be stipulated. (See also **Chapter 7** and **Appendix 1** for information on the International Baccalaureate, Scottish Highers/ Advanced Highers, the Welsh Baccalaureate, the Cambridge Pre-U Diploma, the Advanced Diploma, the Extended Project Qualification and the Irish Leaving Certificate, and **Appendix 2** for international qualifications.)

SANDWICH COURSES AND PROFESSIONAL PLACEMENTS

One variation on Single Honours courses is that of the sandwich course, in which students will spend part of their degree course on professional, industrial or commercial placements. Media coverage on student debt and the introduction of higher tuition fees (see **Chapter 2**) highlight the importance of sandwich courses. Many sandwich and placement courses are on offer, in which industrial, commercial and public sector placements take place, usually, in the third year of a four-year degree course. There is also a Work-Based Learning (WBL) programme, which Chester University established several years ago, with some other institutions following suit, in which students take a WBL module in the second year of their degree course. This involves a placement lasting a few weeks when students can have the opportunity to try out possible careers. Other universities and colleges may offer longer placements of periods of six months with different employers for students taking vocational courses.

However, the most structured arrangements are known as 'professional placements' which a number of universities offer and which are very advantageous to students (see the subject tables in **Chapter 8** and university/college websites and prospectuses). Although placements in some fields such as health, social care, and education may be unpaid, in most cases a salary is paid. Where a placement is unpaid the placement period is shorter – 30 weeks – to allow students time to undertake paid work. It is important to note that during the placement year students' tuition fees will be reduced by 50% except for those on one-year courses on the Erasmus programme (see **Chapter 5**) when no fees are paid but student loans will still apply.

The advantages of sandwich courses are quite considerable although students should be aware that in the present period of recession safeguards are necessary when selecting courses and universities. While students can arrange their own placement, with the approval of their Head of Department, it is more usual for university staff to make contacts with firms and to recommend students. With the present cutbacks, however, some firms may be less likely to take on students or to pay them during their placement. This is an important issue to raise with admissions tutors before applying and it is important also to find out how your studies would continue if placements are not possible. To help you to consider the advantages of sandwich courses, included below are views of some students, employers and university staff. They could well help you decide whether a four-year sandwich course is, for you, preferable to a three-year full-time degree.

Students report ...

'I was able to earn £15,000 during my year out and £4000 during my three-month vacation with the same firm.' (**Bath** Engineering)

'There's really no other better way to find out what you want to do for your future career than having tried it for a year.' (**Aston** Human Resources Management)

'It was a welcome break in formal university education: I met some great people including students from other universities.' (**Kingston** Biochemistry)

'Having experienced a year in a working environment, I am more confident and more employable than students without this experience.' (**Aston** Business Studies)

'At Sanolfi in Toulouse, I learned to think on my feet – no two days were the same.' (**Aston** European Studies)

'I have seen how an organisation works at first-hand, learned how academic skills may be applied in a working environment, become proficient in the use of various software, acquired new skills in interpersonal relationships and communications and used my period away to realign my career perspectives.' (**Aston** European Studies)

'I was working alongside graduate employees and the firm offered me a job when I graduated.' (**Bath** Mathematics)

Employers, too, gain from having students ...
'We meet a lot of enthusiastic potential recruits who bring new ideas into the firm, and we can offer them commercially sponsored help for their final year project.'

'The quality of this student has remained high throughout the year. He will do well for his next employer, whoever that may be. However, I sincerely hope that it will be with us.'

University staff advise ...
'We refer to sandwich courses as professional placements, not "work experience" which is a phrase we reserve for short non-professional experiences, for example summer or pre-university jobs. The opportunity is available to all students but their success in gaining a good placement depends on academic ability.' (**Bath**)

'Where a placement year is optional, those who opt for it are more likely to be awarded a First or an Upper Second compared to those who don't, not because they are given more marks for doing it, but because they always seem to have added context and motivation for their final year.' (**Aston**)

When choosing your sandwich course, check with the university (a) that the institution will guarantee a list of employers, (b) whether placement experience counts towards the final degree result, (c) that placements are paid and (d) that placements are validated by professional bodies. Finally, once you start on the course, remember that your first-year academic performance will be taken into account by potential employers. Now read on!

What do employers require when considering students?
Aston (Biol) Successful second year undergraduates; (Bus) Number of UCAS points, degree programme, any prior experience; (Eng) UCAS points scores and expected degree classification; (Mech Eng) Students interviewed and selected by the company according to student ability, what they are studying and specific needs of the job. **Bath** (Chem) 'Good students': Upper Second or above and non-international students (those without work visas). Students with strong vivisection views rejected; (Mech Elec Eng) Subject-based, eg electronics, aerospace, computing and electrical engineering; (Mech Eng) Good communication, IT and social skills; (Maths) Interest in positions of responsibility, teamwork, integrity, self-motivation, analytical ability, communication, recent work experience, knowledge of the company, desire to work for the company; GCSE maths/English A, AL 360 UCAS points minimum (excluding general studies and critical thinking), predicted 2.1; (Phys) Many organisations have cut-offs regarding students' first-year performance (eg must be heading for a 2.1 although some require better than this), some need students to be particularly good in some areas (eg lab work, computer programming), many require UK nationality with minimum residency condition. **Brunel** Requirements not usually specified except for IT jobs since they need technical skills. **Cardiff Met (UWIC)** (Clsrm Asst) Disclosure and Barring Service (DBS) checks. **Kingston** (Bus Law) Theoretical knowledge and a stated interest in certain areas (eg finance, human resources, marketing, sales, IT), excellent communication skills, teamwork, ability to prioritise, time management and a professional attitude; (Sci) Grades are rarely mentioned: it's usually a specific module or course requirement undertaken by the students that they are looking for, as well as a good attitude, motivation, initiative: a good all-rounder. **Loughborough** (Civ Eng) Target specific courses.

What are the advantages of placements to the students?
Aston (Biol) Many take jobs with their placement employers (eg NHS), gaining valuable research and clinical experience; (Bus) Graduate job offers, sponsorship through the final year of the course, gym

membership, staff discounts; (Eng) Some students are fast-tracked into full-time employment and, in some cases, have been given higher starting salaries as a result of the placement with the company; (Mech Eng) Offers of full-time employment on graduation, bursaries for their final year of study, final year projects following placements, better class of degree. **Bath** (Chem) Sponsorships for final year project work, offers of full-time employment, PhD offers and work-to-study courses, industrial references, establishment of prizes; (Maths) Sponsorship in the second year, graduate employment, bonuses during placement, travel abroad during placement, sponsorship during final year; (Phys) Job offers on graduation, sponsored final year, improved study skills for final year, job market awareness, career decisions. **Brunel** Higher percentage of students get Firsts, many students get a job offer from the placement provider, higher salaries often paid to sandwich course students, some students get exemptions from professional exams, eg ACCA, ACA and IMechE. **Cardiff Met (UWIC)** (Clsrm Asst) Good experience in team work, classroom experience, coaching, mentoring: decisions made whether or not to follow a teaching career. **Kingston** (Bus Law) Sponsorships fewer these days but students return with more confidence and maturity and better able to complete their final year; 60% receive job offers on completion of a successful placement; (Sci) Full-time employment on graduation and occasionally part-time work in the final year; many students are encouraged to write their final year dissertation whilst on placement and benefit from the company's support, subject matter and validation. **Loughborough** (Civ Eng) Most students are sponsored by their firms and perform better in their final examinations; (Prod Des) Final year bursary for some students, offer of employment by the sponsor and a final year design project for the sponsor.

MATURE APPLICANTS
There are a great many mature students following first degree courses in UK universities and colleges. The following is a list of key points a group of mature students found useful in exploring and deciding on a university course.

- Check with your nearest university or college to find out about the courses they can offer, for example degrees, diplomas, full-time, part-time.
- Some institutions will require examination passes in some subjects, others may not.
- An age limit may apply for some vocational courses, for example Medicine, Dentistry and Teaching.
- If entry requirements are an obstacle, prospective students should approach their local colleges for information on Access or Open College courses. These courses are fast-growing in number and popularity, offering adults an alternative route into higher education other than A-levels. They are usually developed jointly by colleges of further education and the local higher education institution.
- Demands of the course – how much time will be required for study? What are the assignments and the deadlines to be met? How is your work assessed – unseen examinations, continuous assessment, practicals?
- The demands on finance – cost of the course – loan needed – loss of earnings – drop in income if changing to another career – travel requirements – accommodation – need to work part-time for income?
- The availability and suitability of the course – geographical location – competition for places – where it will lead – student support services, for example childcare, library.
- What benefits will you derive? Fulfilment, transferable skills, social contacts, sense of achievement, enjoyment, self-esteem, career enhancement?
- Why would employers want to recruit you? Ability to adapt to the work scene, realistic and balanced approach, mature attitude to work?
- Why would employers not want to recruit you? Salary expectations, inability to fit in with younger colleagues, limited mobility? However, some employers particularly welcome older graduates: civil service, local authorities, health service, religious, charitable and voluntary organisations, teaching, social/probation work, careers work, housing.

MODULAR COURSES AND CREDIT ACCUMULATION AND TRANSFER SCHEMES (CATS)
Courses can also differ considerably not only in their content but in how they are organised. Many universities and colleges of higher education have modularised their courses which means you can choose modules of different subjects, and 'build' your course within specified 'pathways' with the help

and approval of your course tutor. It also means that you are likely to be assessed after completing each module, rather than in your last year for all your previous years' learning. In almost every course the options and modules offered include some which reflect the research interests of individual members of staff. In some courses subsidiary subjects are available as minor courses alongside a Single Honours course. In an increasing number of courses these additional subjects include a European language, and the importance of this cannot be over-emphasised with the United Kingdom's membership of the European Union. Such links are also reinforced by way of the Erasmus programme (see **Chapter 5**) which enables university students to apply for courses in Europe for periods of up to a year, some of the courses being taught in English. Many institutions have introduced Credit Accumulation and Transfer Schemes (CATS). These allow students to be awarded credits for modules or units of study they have successfully completed which are accumulated towards a certificate, diploma or degree. They can also put their completed modules towards higher education study in other universities or colleges. Students wanting to transfer their credits should talk to the admissions office of the university they want to enter as there may be additional special subjects or module requirements for the degree they want to study.

FOUNDATION DEGREES AND FOUNDATION COURSES

Foundation courses, not be confused with Foundation degrees, normally require two years' full-time study, or longer for part-time study. They are also often taught in local colleges and may be taken part-time to allow students to continue to work. In comparison a Foundation degree can lead into the second or final year of related Honours degree courses when offered by the university validating the Foundation degree. Two-year Higher National Diplomas will also qualify for entry into the second or final year of degree courses. These, too, are often offered at universities as well as colleges of further education and partnership colleges linked to universities.

Part-time degrees and lifelong learning or distance learning courses are also often available and details of these can be found on university websites and in prospectuses. Some universities publish separate prospectuses for part-time courses.

NEXT STEPS

When choosing your course remember that one course is not better than another – it is just different. The best course for you is the one which best suits you. To give some indication of the differences between courses, see **Chapter 3** and also *Choosing Your Degree Course & University*, the companion book to *Heap 2015: University Degree Course Offers* (see **Appendix 4**). After provisionally choosing your courses, read the prospectuses again carefully to be sure that you understand what is included in the three, four or more years of study. Each institution differs in its course content even though the course titles may be the same and courses differ in other ways, for example:

- methods of assessment (eg unseen examinations, continuous assessment, project work, dissertations)
- contact time with tutors
- how they are taught (for example, frequency and size of lectures, seminars)
- practicals; field work requirements
- library, computing, laboratory and studio facilities
- amount of free study time available.

These are useful points of comparison between courses in different institutions when you are on an Open Day visit or making final course choices. Other important factors to consider when comparing courses include the availability of opportunities for studying and working abroad during your course, professional body accreditation of courses leading to certain professional careers (see **Appendix 3**) and in the career destinations of their graduates.

Once you have chosen your course subject(s) and the type of course you want to follow, the next step is to find out about the universities and colleges offering courses in your subject area, how much a higher education course will cost you and what financial help is available. The next chapter, **University Choice and Finance** provides information to help you do this.

TAKING A GAP YEAR

Choosing your course is the first decision you need to make, the second is choosing your university and then, for an increasing number, the third is deciding whether or not to take a Gap Year. But there lies the problem. Because of the very large number of things to do and places to go, you'll find that you almost need a Gap Year to choose the right one (although a read through *Your Gap Year* by Susan Griffith (see **Appendix 4**) is a good place to start)!

Planning ahead is important but, in the end, bear in mind that you might be overtaken by events, not least in failing to get the grades you need for a place on the course or at the university you were counting on. This could mean repeating A-levels and re-applying, which in turn could mean waiting for interviews and offers and, possibly, deferring the start of your 'gap' until February or March.

Once you have decided to go, however, it's a question of whether you will go under your own steam or through a Gap Year agency. Unless you are streetwise, or preferably 'world wise', then an agency offers several advantages. Some agencies may cover a broad field of opportunities whilst others will focus on a specific region and activity, such as the African Conservation Experience, offering animal and plant conservation work in game and nature reserves in southern Africa.

When making the choice, some students will always prefer a 'do-it-yourself' arrangement. However, there are many advantages to going through specialist agencies. Not only can they offer a choice of destinations and opportunities but also they can provide a lot of essential and helpful advice before your departure on issues such as health precautions and insurance. Support is also available in the case of accidents or illnesses when a link can be established between the agency and parents.

Finally, in order to enhance your next university or college application, applying for a job for the year could be an even better option than spending a year travelling. Not only will it provide you with some financial security but it will also introduce you to the world of work, which could be more challenging than the Inca Trail!

UNIVERSITY CHOICE AND FINANCE

CHOOSING YOUR UNIVERSITY OR COLLEGE

Location, reputation and Open Days

For many applicants the choice of university or college is probably the main priority, with location being a key factor. However, many students have little or no knowledge of regional geography and have no concept of where universities are located: one student thought that Bangor University (situated in North Wales) was located at Bognor on England's south coast!

Some institutions – probably those nearest home or those farthest away – will be rejected quickly. In addition to the region, location and immediate surroundings of a university or college, applicants have their own individual priorities – perhaps a hectic city life or, alternatively, a quiet life in the country! But university isn't all about studying, so it's not a bad idea to link your leisure interests with what the university or college can offer or with the opportunities available in the locality. Many applicants have theatrical, musical or artistic interests while others have sporting interests and achievements ranging from basketball, cricket and football to riding, rowing, sailing, mountaineering, and even fishing for England!

Some other decisions about your choice of university or college, however, could be made for the wrong reasons. Many students, for example, talk about 'reputation' or base their decisions on league tables. Reputations are fairly clear-cut in the case of some institutions. Oxford and Cambridge are both top world-class universities in which all courses have been established for many years and are supported by first class facilities. In other universities certain subjects are predominant, such as the social sciences at the London School of Economics, and the sciences and technologies at Imperial London.

Many other leading universities in the UK are also very strong in some subjects but not necessarily in all. This is why it is wrong to conclude that a 'university has a good reputation' – most universities are not necessarily good at everything! In seeking advice, you should also be a little wary of school staff who will usually always claim that their own university or college has a 'good reputation'. Teachers obviously can provide good advice on the courses and the general atmosphere of their own institution, but they are not in a good position to make comparisons with other universities.

The best way to find out about universities and colleges and the courses that interest you is to visit your preferred institutions. Open Days provide the opportunity to talk to staff and students although, with thousands of students wandering round campuses, it may be difficult to meet and talk to the right people. Also, many institutions hold Open Days during vacations when many students are away which means that you may only hear talks from the staff, and not have any opportunity to meet students. However, it is often possible to visit a university or college in your own time and simply 'walk in'. Alternatively, a letter to the Head of Department requesting a visit could enable you to get a closer look at the subject facilities. But failing this, you will be invited automatically to visit when you receive an offer and then you can meet the students in the department.

ACTION POINTS

Before deciding on your preferred universities and courses check out the following points.

Teaching staff

How do the students react to their tutors? Do staff have a flair and enthusiasm for their subject? Are they approachable? Do they mark your work regularly and is the feedback helpful, or are you left to get on with your own work with very little direction? What are the research interests of the staff?

Teaching styles

How will you be taught, for example, lectures, seminars, tutorials? Are lectures popular? If not, why not? How much online learning will you have? How much time will you be expected to work on your own? If there are field courses, how often are they arranged and are they compulsory? How much will they cost?

Facilities

Are the facilities of a high standard and easily available? Is the laboratory equipment 'state of the art' or just adequate? Are the libraries well-stocked with software packages, books and journals? What are the computing facilities? Is there plenty of space to study or do rooms and workspaces become overcrowded? Do students have to pay for any materials?

New students

Are there induction courses for new students? What student services and facilities are available? Is it possible to buy second-hand copies of set books?

Work placements

Are work placements an optional or compulsory part of the course? Who arranges them? Are the placements popular? Do they count towards your degree? Are work placements paid? How long are they?

Transferable skills

Transferable skills are now regarded as important by all future employers. Does the department provide training in communication skills, teamwork, time-management and information technology as part of the degree course?

Accommodation

How easy is it to find accommodation? Where are the halls of residence? Are they conveniently located for libraries and lecture theatres? Are they self-catering? Alternatively, what is the cost of meals in the university refectory? Which types of student accommodation are the most popular? What is the annual cost of accommodation? If there is more than one campus, is a shuttle-bus service provided?

Costs

Find out the costs of materials, accommodation and travel in addition to tuition fees (see below) and your own personal needs. What are the opportunities for earning money, on or off campus? Does the department or faculty have any rules about part-time employment?

FINANCE: WHAT WILL IT COST AND WHAT HELP IS THERE?

Tuition fees and other costs

Tuition fees are charged for degree courses in England, Wales and Northern Ireland. The level of tuition fees for courses has in the past been decided annually and has varied between institutions. Maintenance grants and loans will still be available.

Specific details of the charges to be made by individual universities for each course will be available on websites, but depending on the popularity of universities and certain courses the maximum charge will be £9000, although some institutions will charge a lower level of fees of up to £6000.

Students starting their courses in 2015 should check university and college websites, and websites listed in this section, for the latest information about fees.

You may also have additional charges, depending on your course of study. For example, studio fees for Art courses could reach £300 per year, while for other courses, such as Architecture, Science and Engineering, there could be charges for equipment. There could also be charges for fieldwork trips, study abroad and vacation courses. To find out your likely yearly course costs, in addition to your tuition fees, check with your subject department.

Also, check your fee status if you are planning a sandwich course involving either unpaid or paid placements. You can receive a salary of up to £12,000 doing a one-year placement but if you earn more than this you'll need to check your fee status carefully with your finance officer and consult the relevant websites listed below.

Loans Students will not have to pay tuition fees before starting their courses or while they are studying. Depending on their household income, students can apply for a tuition fee grant or they will be able to take out a student loan to pay for their fees. Loan repayments are made only after graduation and currently when annual earnings are more than £21,000 per year.

University scholarships These are usually merit-based and are often competitive although some universities offer valuable scholarships to any new entrant who has achieved top grades at A-level. Scholarships vary considerably and are often subject-specific, offered through faculties or departments, so check the availability of any awards with the subject departmental head. Additionally, there are often music, choral and organ awards, and scholarships and bursaries for sporting achievement. Entry scholarships are offered by several universities which normally stipulate that the applicant must place the university as their first choice and achieve the specified high grades. Changes in bursaries and scholarships take place every year so it is important to check university and college websites.

University bursaries These are usually paid in cases of financial need: all universities charging course fees are obliged to offer some bursaries to students receiving maintenance grants. The term 'bursary' is usually used to denote an award to students requiring financial assistance or who are disadvantaged in various ways. Universities are committed to fair access to all students from lower income backgrounds and individual universities and colleges have bursaries, trust funds and sponsorships for those students receiving maintenance grants, although reports suggest that many such students fail to claim the money due to them. These non-repayable awards are linked to the size of the maintenance grant students receive and vary between universities.

Living costs

Most students spend their first year in university accommodation. This is usually the highest single cost in a typical weekly budget and the costs will vary considerably between universities. Rooms may be single or shared and include catering or self-catering arrangements. Outside university in the private sector additional costs are likely to include heating, electricity, hot water and water rates.

In addition, other living expenses will need to be considered. These include insurance, healthcare, food, books and stationery, photocopying, computing and telephone calls, clothes and toiletries, local travel, travel to and from university, entertainment, socialising and sport or leisure activities.

Help towards living costs

Maintenance grants These government grants are available but depend on the student's household income. They are paid on a sliding scale to students, depending on the family income. These grants are not repayable. Loans to help towards living costs are also available, and details of these are found on the websites listed below. In addition, price reductions are often available for students at some shops, restaurants, cinemas, museums and galleries. Contact the University Student Union before or when you arrive to find out more about these arrangements.

Other financial support

Many major organisations also provide financial help to those in various categories. These include the Lawrence Atwell's Charity for refugee young people from low income backgrounds, the Prince's Trust for disadvantaged young people aged between 14 and 25, and grants of up to £2000 for the disabled from the Snowdon Award Scheme.

Similarly, many scholarships are also offered by professional, commercial and other organisations. These include the armed services and the engineering professional organisations, particularly those specialising in civil or mechanical engineering, and also the Institute of Materials, Minerals and Mining. There are also sponsorships in which the student joins a firm on leaving school, combining university study with work experience and with an almost guaranteed offer of full-time employment on graduation. And there is the alternative route of taking a sandwich course and being placed with a firm for a year on full pay, often up to £12,000 (see **Chapter 1**).

Some universities also offer additional bursaries to encourage applications from the locality. These may be available to students applying from partner schools or colleges and living in certain postcode areas, in some cases to the brothers and sisters of current students at the university, or to students who have been in care or are homeless. These awards are not repayable.

In addition, students on some health-related courses, for example Dental Hygiene, Nursing, Occupational Therapy, Physiotherapy, Radiography will be eligible for NHS student bursaries. Other bursaries are also payable for programmes funded through the General Social Care Council and also for shortage subjects for those on teacher training courses.

After starting the course, Access to Learning funds are available to help students in financial hardship or through emergency payments for unexpected financial crises. Hardship funds are also offered in very special cases, particularly to students with children or to single parents, mature students and, in particular, to students with disabilities who may also claim the Personal Independence Payment (which replaced the Disability Living Allowance in April 2013). These payments are made in instalments or as a lump sum or as a short-term loan.

Useful websites   Students from England www.gov.uk/student-finance
Students from Scotland www.saas.gov.uk/student_support
Students from Wales www.studentfinancewales.co.uk
Students from Northern Ireland www.studentfinanceni.co.uk

For comprehensive finance information see the useful websites above, *University Scholarships, Awards and Bursaries* and other sources listed in **Appendix 4**.

INFORMATION SOURCES

Prospectuses, websites and Open Days are key sources of the information you need to decide where to study and at the back of this book a directory of institutions is provided, with full contact details, for you to use in your research. Other sources of information include the books and websites listed in **Appendix 4**, the professional associations listed in **Appendix 3**, and the websites given in the subject tables in **Chapter 8**. It is important to take time to find out as much as you can about your preferred universities, colleges and courses, and to explore their similarities and differences. The following chapter **University and College Course Profiles** gives you information about the types of courses offered by each university and how they are organised. This is important information that you need to know when choosing your university or college because those factors affect, for example, the amount of choice you have in what you study, and the opportunities you have for sandwich placements (see **Chapter 1**). You therefore need to read **Chapter 3** to give you an insight into universities so that you can find the one that is right for you.

UNIVERSITIES, COLLEGES AND THEIR COURSES

Choosing a degree subject is one step of the way to higher education (see **Chapter 1**), choosing a university or college is the next stage (see **Chapters 2** and **10**). However, in addition to such features as location, entry requirements, accommodation, students' facilities and the subjects offered, many universities differ in the way they organise and teach their courses. The course profiles which follow aim to identify the main course features of each of the institutions and to provide some brief notes about the types of courses they offer and how they differ.

Although universities and colleges have their own distinct identities and course characteristics, they have many similarities. Apart from full-time and sandwich courses, one-year Foundation courses are also offered in many subjects which can help the student to either convert or build on existing qualifications to enable them to start an Honours degree programme. All universities and colleges also offer one-year international Foundation courses for overseas students to provide a preliminary introduction to courses and often to provide English language tuition.

Course profiles

Aberdeen Students applying for the MA degree in Arts and Social Sciences are admitted to a degree rather than a subject. Students select from a range of courses in the first year, leading up to the final choice of subject and Honours course in the fourth year. The BSc degree is also flexible but within the Science framework. Engineering students follow a common core course in Years 1 and 2, specialising in Year 3. There is less flexibility, however, in some vocational courses such as Accountancy, Law, Medicine and Dentistry. For some degree programmes, highly qualified applicants may be admitted to the second year of the course. Other courses cover Divinity and Theology, Education and Music.

Abertay Courses have a strong vocational bias and are offered in the Schools of Science, Engineering, Technology, Business, Social and Health Sciences, Media, and Computer Games. Four-year courses are offered on a modular basis.

Aberystwyth The University offers Single, Joint and major/minor Honours courses on a modular basis. In Part 1 (Year 1) core topics related to the chosen subject are studied alongside optional subjects. This arrangement allows some flexibility for change when choosing final degree subjects in Part 2 (Years 2 and 3) provided appropriate pathways and module prerequisites are followed. Some students take a year in industry or commerce between Years 2 and 3. Courses currently available include Accounting and Finance, Agriculture, Business, Celtic Studies, Computer Science, Criminology, Earth Sciences, Economics, Education, French, Geography, German, History, International Politics, Irish, Law, Marketing, Mathematics, Physics, Psychology, Sport and Exercise Science, Theatre and Television Studies, and Welsh and Welsh History.

Anglia Ruskin Courses are modular which enables students to choose from a range of topics in addition to the compulsory subject core modules. Single and Combined Honours courses are offered in the Faculties of Arts, Law and Social Sciences, Science and Technology, Health and Social Care, Education, and in the Business School. Many programmes have a strong vocational focus, with some opportunities to study abroad.

Arts London This university is Europe's largest institution offering courses in Art and Design, Communication and Performing Arts, focusing on creativity and practice in a large number of specialist fields.

Aston The University offers modular courses in Single Honours degrees, Joint Honours (usually in related areas) and in Combined Honours and interdisciplinary studies in which programmes are organised across different subjects. Combined Honours courses may be weighted 50%–50%, and major/minor programmes weighted 67% for the major element and 33% for the minor. Most degrees allow students to spend the third year on a one-year sandwich placement; 70% of students follow sandwich courses or study-abroad programmes, leading to a high percentage of employed graduates. Courses are taught in the Schools of Engineering and Applied Science, Languages and Social Sciences, Life and Health Sciences and in the Aston Business School.

Bangor Modular courses are offered in Single and Joint Honours programmes. A broad and flexible programme is taken in Level 1 (Year 1) with the opportunity to study modules outside the chosen subject, including a language. This is followed by greater specialisation in Levels 2 and 3. Courses include Archaeology, Arts subjects, Biological Sciences, Business and Management, Chemistry, Computer Science and Electronics, Education, Environment, Natural Sciences and Geography subjects, Health Studies, History, Languages, Law, Medical Sciences, Music, Ocean Sciences, Philosophy, Psychology, Social Sciences, Sport and Religion.

Bath The academic year is divided into two semesters with Single and Combined Honours degrees composed of core units and optional units, allowing students some flexibility in shaping their courses with 10–12 units taken each year. A central feature of all programmes is the opportunity to take a professional placement as part of the degree: this is usually taken as either one 12-month placement or two periods of six months. Courses are offered in Engineering, Humanities and Social Sciences, Science, Sport and Management.

Bath Spa Most courses – for Single awards, specialised awards and Combined awards – are part of a flexible modular scheme with students taking six modules each year. Some modules are compulsory but there is a good range of optional modules. The wide range of courses on offer includes Biology, Business and Management, Creative Studies, Cultural Studies, Dance, Drama, Education, English Literature, Food Studies, Geography, Health Studies, History, Media Communications, Music, Psychology, Sociology and Study of Religions.

Bedfordshire The University offers BA and BSc undergraduate, Foundation and Extended degrees in Advertising, Marketing and Communications, Art and Design, Biosciences, Business, Computing, Journalism, Law, Media, Nursing, Psychology, Social Sciences, Sport and Leisure and Tourism. Most of the courses are vocational, some of which offer a placement year in industry or commerce.

Birmingham Courses cover Accounting and Finance, African Studies, American and Canadian Studies, Biochemistry, Biological Sciences, Chemical Engineering, Chemistry, Civil Engineering, Classics, Computer Science, Dentistry, Drama, Earth Sciences, Economics, English, Electrical and Electronic Engineering, Environmental Sciences, Geography, History, History of Art, Human Biology, International Relations, Law, Liberal Arts and Sciences, Management, Mathematics, Mechanical Engineering, Medicine, Metallurgy and Materials, Modern Languages, Music, Nuclear Engineering, Nursing, Pharmacy, Philosophy, Theology and Religion, Physics and Astronomy, Physiotherapy, Policy Politics and Economics, Political Science, Psychology, Social Policy, Social Work, and Sport and Exercise Sciences. Single subject and Joint Honours courses are offered. In Joint Honours courses the two chosen subjects may have common ground or can be disparate, for example Mathematics and a Modern Language. Some major/minor combinations are also possible. The modular system provides opportunities for students to study a subject outside their main degree. An International Foundation Year (Birmingham Foundation Academy) is available for overseas students from 12 year secondary education systems.

Birmingham (UC) University College Birmingham offers degrees within the hospitality and tourism sectors, which are awarded by the University of Birmingham. Students consistently comment on the high levels of study and pastoral support offered by the college. There are excellent international study-exchange opportunities including industrial placement opportunities throughout Europe, USA, Canada and the UK.

Birmingham City Courses are offered through the Birmingham Institute of Art and Design, the Business School, the School of Computing, the School of Jewellery and the Faculties of the Built Environment, Education, Health and Community Care, Law, Humanities and Social Sciences and the Technology Innovation Centre. Many courses have a vocational focus and include sandwich placements. Music is offered through the Birmingham Conservatoire, a music college of international standing. There is also an extensive International Exchange Programme, with many courses abroad being taught in English.

Bishop Grosseteste The University has a strong reputation in Primary Education courses but also offers a varied selection of subjects at Foundation and Single Honours degree level as well as a very large number of joint degrees in subject areas such as psychology, sport and the creative arts. Employability is central to all courses with most incorporating work placements and live projects.

Bolton Modular Single and Combined Honours courses are available, with many offering vocational or professional content and work experience elements. Courses include Accountancy and Law, Art and Design, Biology, Business Management, Civil Engineering and Construction, Community, Youth and Early Years, Complementary Therapies, Creative Technology and Live Events, Education, Engineering, English and Creative Writing, Games, Computing and IT, Health and Social Care, Mathematics, Psychology and Sport, Leisure and Physical Activity. Teaching and learning take place through a mixture of lectures, practicals, seminars and small tutorial groups.

Bournemouth The University offers undergraduate degrees leading to BA, BSc and LLB. The programmes, which are mainly vocational and include sandwich placements, often carry professional recognition. The academic schools cover Arts and Humanities, Business and Management, Design, Food and Nutrition, Law, Media and Communications, Technology, Tourism, Sport and Hospitality.

Bournemouth Arts Arts University Bournemouth (formerly The Arts University College at Bournemouth) was established in 1885 as a specialist institution in art, design, media and performance.

BPP An independent university. Courses are offered in Accountancy, Business, Law and Marketing. Check institution for fee information.

Bradford Single, Joint and major/minor Honours degree courses are offered, many of which are vocational, leading to professional accreditation, and include sandwich placements in industry and commerce. Other courses offer work-shadowing placements. Language options are available to all students irrespective of their chosen degree course. Subjects are taught in the Schools of Computing, Informatics and Media, the School of Engineering Design and Technology, the School of Health Studies, the School of Life Sciences, the School of Management, the School of Social and International Studies and the School of Lifelong Education and Development.

Brighton BA, BSc and BEng courses are offered, 90% with industrial placements including some in Europe, the USA and Canada. Courses include Accounting, Art and Architecture, Business, Education and Sport, Health, Information Studies, Law, and Science and Engineering. Brighton and Sussex Medical School students are based at the Falmer campus for the first two years, with academic and clinical studies integrated from Year 1, and thereafter in the education centre at the Royal Sussex County Hospital in Brighton.

Brighton and Sussex (MS) Students have the ability to use facilities on both the University of Brighton campuses, as well as the University of Sussex, and in Year 1 can choose which campus they would like to live at. All Year 1 Medical School students are guaranteed accommodation as long as they apply by the deadline (some students who live in the immediate local area may not be able to apply for accommodation due to more applicants requiring housing than rooms available). Teaching is 'systems integrated' so students are exposed to the clinical environment from Year 1. Cadaver dissection is also part of the course from Year 1, so students get a real understanding of human anatomy, enhancing their learning experience. As the Medical School is small, so are class sizes, meaning that students have a strong relationship with academic and support staff.

Bristol The University offers Single or Joint Honours degrees. A number of courses include a year of industrial experience or the opportunity to study or work abroad. Most courses take three or four years to complete and are modular in structure. Dentistry, Medicine and Veterinary Science are longer in duration and take five or six years to complete. Most science and engineering courses offer a choice of four-year Integrated master's (MEng, MSci) as well as the three-year bachelor's (BEng, BSc) courses. Also on offer is a two-year Diploma in Dental Hygiene.

Bristol UWE The University offers Single and Joint Honours courses organised on a modular basis which gives flexibility in the choice of options. Many courses include sandwich placements and, in addition, students have the opportunity to undertake a period of study in another EU country. The language centre is open to all students. Courses cover a full range of subjects in the Faculties of Media and Design, Applied Sciences, Built Environment, Computing, Education, Engineering and Mathematical Sciences, Health and Social Care, Humanities, Law, Languages and Social Sciences, the Bristol Business School and Hartpury College (offering Agricultural and Equine Business courses).

Brunel A campus-based university. All courses are made up of self-contained modules enabling students, within their scheme of studies, to choose a broad range of topics or greater specialisation as they prefer. Some modern language modules may be taken, depending on the timetable of the chosen subjects. Almost all degree courses are available in a three-year full-time mode or in four-year thick or thin sandwich courses which combine academic work with industrial experience. Some exchange schemes also operate in Europe and the USA. Degree programmes are offered in the Schools of Arts (Drama, English, Media), Business, Engineering and Design, Health Sciences and Social Care, Information Systems, Law, Social Sciences and Sport and Education. Many courses are accredited by professional institutions recognised by employers.

Buckingham The University is an educational charity with its main income provided by the students who pay full tuition fees. A unique feature is the two-year degree programme which starts in January each year, although some courses may be extended by starting in September; some courses last three years. Courses are offered in Business, Humanities, Law, International Studies and Sciences.

Bucks New Courses are focused on vocational studies in a wide range of subjects in three main groups. These cover Creativity and Culture (Art, Design, Music and Media), Enterprise and Innovation (Business, Computing, Law and Sport) and Society and Health (Health and Social Care and Nursing). There are also several courses focusing on football at their partner college UCFB (Burnley or Wembley).

Cambridge The University offers undergraduate courses in Arts and Sciences and postgraduate degree programmes. Three-year degree courses (Triposes) provide a broad introduction to the subject followed by options at a later stage, and are divided into Part 1 (one or two years) and Part 2. In some Science and Engineering courses there is a fourth year (Part 3). In college-based teaching sessions (supervisions), essays are set for discussion to support university lectures, seminars and practicals.

Canterbury Christ Church A wide range of BA and BSc courses are on offer. Most of these courses are offered at the Canterbury campus and include Primary Education and Law, Arts and Social Science and Science subjects. Nursing and other Paramedical courses are also offered at the Medway campus at Chatham, Visual and Performing Arts are studied at Folkestone and Music and some Business courses are taken at the Broadstairs campus. There is also a wide range of Combined Honours courses available.

Cardiff All students taking the very flexible BA degree study three subjects in the first year and then follow a Single or Joint Honours course in their chosen subject(s). Similarly, BSc Economics courses offer the option to transfer to an alternative degree course at the end of Year 1, depending on the subjects originally chosen. Many degree schemes have a vocational and professional content with a period of attachment in industry, and there are well-established links with universities abroad. Degrees schemes are offered by 26 schools covering Architecture and Planning, Arts and Humanities, Business, Computer Science, Earth and Ocean Sciences, Engineering, Healthcare Studies, Law, Media Studies, Medicine, Dentistry and Nursing, Music, Optometry, Pharmacy, Psychology, Religious Studies, Sciences, Social Sciences and Welsh Studies.

Cardiff Met (UWIC) Cardiff Metropolitan University specialises in courses that are career-orientated and have been designed in conjunction with business and industry. All of the courses are created with the working world in mind and include work placements, visiting lecturers, and options for sandwich courses.

Central Lancashire The University has 16 academic schools: Art, Design and Performance, Built and Natural Environment, Computing, Engineering, and Physical Sciences, Dentistry, Education and Social Sciences, Forensic and Investigative Sciences, Health, Journalism and Digital Communication, Lancashire Business School, Lancashire Law School, Languages, Literature and International Studies, Pharmacy and Biomedical Sciences, Postgraduate Medical and Dental Education, Psychology, Social Work, Sport, Tourism and the Outdoors. Subjects are taught in a series of modules which gives maximum flexibility in the final choice of degree course. Students may specialise or keep their options open with a choice of Single

Honours, Joint or Combined Honours, or they can choose three subjects in Year 1 and reduce to two in the second and third years. Some sandwich courses are offered.

Chester Single and Combined Honours courses are offered in a wide range of subjects on the Chester campus. Subjects offered include Art and Design, Drama and Theatre Studies, Business and Social Studies courses and Nutrition and Health Care. The Warrington campus offers well-established courses in Media (Radio, TV, Music) and Journalism in addition to Computer Science and Sports courses.

Chichester Degree subjects can be studied in major, joint or minor programmes. All undergraduate courses comprise a number of individual short course units/modules, taught and assessed separately. Each degree course consists of compulsory and optional modules enabling students to follow their own interests. BA courses are offered in a range of subjects covering Dance, Education, English, Fine Art, History, Media Studies, Music, Performing Arts, Sports Studies and Theology at Chichester, and Business, Education and Tourism at the Bognor Regis campus.

City The University offers a wide range of three-year and four-year programmes leading to degrees in Business and Management, Communication, Computing, Engineering and Mathematical Sciences, Health Sciences, Law, Nursing and Social Sciences. Some schools and departments provide a common first year, allowing students to make a final decision on their degree course at the end of the first year. Some sandwich courses are optional, others compulsory. Students in some subject areas may apply to study abroad.

Coventry Courses are offered in the Schools of Art and Design, Business, Environment and Society (including Law, Geography and Social Science), Engineering and Computing (including Mathematical Sciences) and Health and Life Sciences. Many courses are industry linked and offer sandwich placements in industry and commerce, with some opportunities to study abroad. Individual programmes of study are usually made up of compulsory modules, core options from a prescribed list and free choice modules.

Creative Arts Foundation and Honours degree courses are offered covering Art and Design, Architecture, Media and Communications.

Cumbria Courses cover Business, Computing, Conservation, Creative Arts, Education, Forestry and Outdoor, Health and Social Care, Humanities, Law and Social Science, Performance, Policing, Science and Engineering and Sport.

De Montfort Courses cover Art and Design, Business and Management, Computing Sciences, Dance and Drama, Engineering, Health and Society, Humanities, Law and Music. Single Honours programmes are offered together with sandwich courses and an extensive Joint Honours programme in which two subjects are chosen to be studied equally. Courses are modular, some assessed by coursework only, or by a combination of coursework and examination, and a few by examination only. It is possible to change a selected module early in the year.

Derby Courses at the Derby campus are offered across three subject areas: Arts, Design and Technology, Business and Education, Health and Sciences, whilst at the Buxton campus Foundation degrees are offered as well as some BA and BSc degrees. There is also a comprehensive Joint Honours programme offering two subjects and Combined Honours courses with a choice of up to three subjects. Major/minor courses are also available.

Dundee Courses are offered in Accountancy, Architecture and Planning, Art and Design, Arts, Education, Engineering, Law, Medicine and Dentistry, Nursing, Sciences and Social Sciences. A flexible modular system is offered in which Arts and Social Science students have a choice of up to three or four subjects in Year 1 leading to greater specialisation as students progress through the next three years. A similar system applies to courses in Life Sciences and Physical Sciences. In Engineering, a common core curriculum operates in Level 1 and in the first half of Level 2.

Durham Degree options include Single and Joint Honours courses to which subsidiary subjects can be added. There are named routes in Natural Sciences and courses in Combined Arts and Social Sciences in which students may design their own degree course by choosing several subjects from a wide range. Courses include the Arts, Business, Computer Science, Education, Engineering, Law, Medicine, Science and Social Science.

East Anglia The University has four faculties (Arts, Humanities, Medicine and Health Science and Science, Social Science). The University maintains an extensive network of international exchanges where students studying certain degree programmes are able to spend up to a year. During these placements, our students are fully integrated into the culture of the host university.

East London The University offers Single Honours and Combined Honours programmes. Courses provide a flexibility of choice and are based on a modular structure with compulsory and optional course units. Courses include Architecture, Art and Design, Business, Computing, Engineering, Health Sciences, Humanities, Law, Media, Social Sciences, Sciences and Sport. A very large number of extended degrees are also available for applicants who do not have the normal university entrance requirements.

Edge Hill The University has three-year programmes including Business, English, Film, Geographical Sciences, History, Law, Media, Midwifery, Nursing, Performance Studies, Social and Psychological Sciences, Sport, and Teacher Training.

Edinburgh Courses are offered in Humanities and the Social Sciences, Medicine and Veterinary Medicine and in Science and Engineering. Depending on the choice of degree, three or more subjects are taken in the first year followed by second level courses in at least two of these subjects in Year 2, thus allowing a range of subjects to be studied at degree level. There is a considerable choice of subjects although there may be restrictions in the case of high-demand subjects such as English, Economics and Psychology. General or Ordinary degrees take three years and Honours degrees take four years. Joint Honours degrees are also offered.

Edinburgh Napier Students choose between Single and Joint degrees and customised degrees which can include a range of subjects. Courses are offered in Accounting, Economics and Financial Services, Business, Management, Languages and Law, Computing, Creative Industries, Engineering and the Built Environment, Life Sciences, Nursing, Social Sciences and Tourism and Hospitality.

Edinburgh Queen Margaret The five main areas covered are Business and Enterprise, Health, Media and Social Sciences, Drama, and the Creative Industries. All courses focus on vocational careers.

Essex Undergraduate departments are grouped in schools of study covering Humanities and Comparative Studies, Social Sciences, Law and Sciences and Engineering. In Year 1 students take four or five courses including modules for their chosen degree. In Year 2 they may follow their chosen degree or choose another degree, including combined and joint courses. The four-year BA and some Law degrees include a year abroad and/or industrial placements. Degree schemes in Health, Business and the Performing Arts are also offered at the Southend campus.

Exeter The University has six colleges: the Business School, the College of Engineering, Maths and Physical Sciences, the College of Humanities, the College of Life and Environmental Sciences, the College of Social Sciences and International Studies, and the University of Exeter Medical School. Most courses include an optional European or international study opportunity. Some subjects, including Biosciences, Geology and Mining Engineering, can be taken at the Cornwall campus at Penryn.

Falmouth The courses focus on Art and Design, Media, Performance and Writing.

Glamorgan The University of Glamorgan and the University of Wales, Newport merged in 2013 to create the University of South Wales. Please see **South Wales** for more information.

Glasgow Applicants choose a faculty and a degree from the Faculties of Arts, Business and Social Sciences, Education, Engineering, Law, Medicine, Science and Veterinary Medicine. Flexible arrangements allow students to build their own degree programme from all the courses on offer. Honours degrees normally take four years, with the decision for Honours taken at the end of Year 2 (not automatic). General degrees take three years except for those involving a foreign language. Creative, Cultural, Environmental, Health and Scottish Studies can also be taken at the Crichton campus in Dumfries.

Glasgow Caledonian The University offers a wide range of vocational full-time and sandwich courses organised in the Schools of the Built and Natural Environment, Computing and Engineering, Health and Social Care, Law and Social Sciences, Life Sciences, Nursing, Midwifery and the Caledonian Business School.

Gloucestershire The University is a teaching-led institution and has been offering high-quality education to students around the world for over 170 years. Located in the county of Gloucestershire in southwest England, Gloucester's Roman and Cheltenham's Regency towns are surrounded by picturesque Cotswold countryside. The University's Employability Hub puts great emphasis on putting theory into practice by offering many work-experience opportunities to prepare its students for life after graduation. Courses are made up of individual study units (modules). Some are compulsory for the chosen course but other modules can be chosen from other subjects. The University has three faculties: Applied Science, Media, Art and Technology, and Business, Education and Professional Studies. All courses have strong employability focus with many opportunities to undertake placements and internships.

Glyndŵr This University in North Wales (Wrexham) offers a range of courses, including many vocational programmes, covering Art and Design, Business, Computing and Communications Technology, Education and Community, Health, Social Sciences, Social Care and Sport and Exercise Sciences, Humanities and Science and Technology.

Greenwich Courses include Architecture and Construction, Business, Chemical and Life Sciences, Computing and Mathematical Sciences, Earth and Environmental Sciences, Education and Training, Engineering, Health and Social Care, Humanities and Social Sciences, Languages and Law. There is also a flexible and comprehensive Combined Honours degree programme offering two joint subjects of equal weight or, alternatively, major/minor combinations.

Heriot-Watt The year is divided into three 10-week terms with four modules taken each term. The six schools cover the Built Environment, Engineering and Physical Sciences, Management and Languages, Mathematical and Computer Sciences, Textiles and Design and Life Sciences.

Hertfordshire Honours degree courses, including sandwich degrees, are offered including Art and Design, Astronomy and Astrophysics, Business, Computer Science, Education, Engineering, Geography, Humanities, Law, Life and Physical Sciences, Music, Nursing and Health subjects, Psychology, Social Studies and Sport. There is also an opportunity to study two subjects together as part of a Joint Honours degree. All Hertfordshire students have a work exposure strand in their degrees and the close links with employers contribute to a consistently good work placement and graduate employment record. The University's Careers and Placements Service offers graduates a central programme of support on employment, entrepreneurial and career development issues for two years. Every student studying anything from Astronomy to Applied Arts has the opportunity to develop self-employment skills through tailor-made packages in addition to their subject expertise and proficiency.

Huddersfield The modular approach to study provides a flexible structure to all courses which are offered as full-time or sandwich options. All students also have the opportunity to study a modern language either as a minor option or by studying part-time through the Modern Languages Centre. Most courses are vocational and include such subjects as Accountancy and Business, Architecture, Art and Design, Computing, Education, Engineering, Geography and Environmental Sciences, Food Sciences, Hospitality and Tourism, Human and Health Sciences, Law, Marketing, Music and Sciences.

Hull All full-time courses are made up of core and optional modules with a free elective scheme which allows students to take one module each year outside their main subject. A 'Languages for All' programme is available for all students irrespective of their degree course subject. The wide range of subjects offered includes Arts and Humanities, Business, Computing, Drama, Economics, Education, Engineering, Law, Medicine (offered at Hull York Medical School), Music, Nursing, Physical Sciences, Social Sciences and Sport. The Scarborough campus also offers a wide range of courses.

ifs (UC) An independent college. Courses focus on financial services and related professions. Check institution for fee details.

Imperial London The College offers world-class programmes in Science, Medicine, Engineering and Management. Joint Honours courses and degree courses with a year abroad are also available. Science courses are offered primarily in one principal subject, but flexibility is provided by the possibility to transfer at the end of the first year and by the choice of optional subjects in the later years of the course. A Humanities programme is also open to all students with a wide range of options, whilst the Tanaka Business School offers Management courses which form an integral part of undergraduate degrees.

Keele Flexibility is provided through either interdisciplinary Single Honours degrees, bringing together a number of topics in an integrated form, or Dual Honours degrees in which two principal subjects are studied to degree level to the same depth as a Single Honours course. In addition, all students take a first-year course in Complementary Studies and may also study a foreign language. Courses are offered in Arts subjects, Biosciences and Physical Sciences, Economics, Education, Law, Management Science, Media, Music and Social Sciences.

Kent The University's main campuses are in Canterbury and Medway in the picturesque southeast of England, and they have specialist centres in Europe where study and research are underpinned by the specialist facilities and resources of these chosen locations: Brussels, Paris, Athens and Rome. Many courses also offer the possibility of a year in industry, giving you valuable practical experience ahead of your final year of study. The majority of programmes offer the opportunity to study or work abroad. By rising to the challenge of spending time in another country, you develop your global outlook, understand and appreciate cultural differences, improve your communication skills and enhance you language. Single Honours courses can include the option of taking up to 25% of the degree in another subject, or to change the focus of a degree at the end of the year. Two subjects are studied on a 50/50 basis in Joint Honours and there are also major/minor Honours degrees.

Kingston Single and Joint Honours courses are offered within a modular structure, with the opportunity to take a language option in French, German, Italian, Japanese, Mandarin Chinese, Russian or Spanish. Several courses are available as a minor field, for example, Business, which adds an extra dimension to the chosen degree. Subjects are offered in Architecture, Art, Design and Music, Arts and Social Sciences, Business, Computing, Earth Sciences, Economics, Education, Engineering, Humanities, Law, Life Sciences, Mathematics, Health and Social Care Sciences, Media, Performance Studies, Pharmacy, Social Sciences and Surveying. Exchange schemes are offered with 72 universities in Europe and five in the USA.

Lancaster Each college has its own social activities and events. The degree programme is split into Part 1 (Year 1) and Part 2 (Years 2 and 3). Students study up to three subjects in Year 1 and then choose to major in one or a combination of subjects in Years 2 and 3. Single and Joint courses are offered in a wide range of subjects, for example, Business, Computer Science, Engineering, Finance, Languages, Mathematics, Medicine, Natural Sciences, Music, Politics and Psychology. There are study opportunities abroad in the USA and Canada, the Far East and Australasia.

Leeds A very wide range of courses is on offer in most subject areas (Leeds is a pioneer of Joint Honours degrees). In the first year, Joint Honours students normally divide their time equally between three subjects, with a wide choice of the third or elective subject in the first year. In many cases, students can transfer to a different course at the end of the first year and delay their final choice of degree. A wide range of subjects is offered in Arts and Humanities, Medicine and Dentistry, Theatre and Performance, Science and Engineering, Social Sciences and in the Business School.

Leeds Beckett Many of the degrees are vocational with links to industry and commerce. Courses are modular with core studies and optional modules. Degree programmes are offered in the Faculties of Arts and Society, Information and Technology, Health, Sport and Recreation, the Leslie Silver International Faculty and the Leeds Business School.

Leeds Trinity This Catholic College was opened in 1966 as a teacher training college. Education still features largely on the list of courses in addition to Faculties of Media, Business and Marketing, and Social Sciences.

Leicester Single Honours courses are offered in all the main disciplines and are taken by 75% of students. The main subject of study may be supported by one or two supplementary subjects taken in the first, and sometimes the second, year. Joint Honours courses are also offered. A three-year Combined Studies degree is also available in which three subjects are studied, one taken for two years only. Apart from Medicine, all programmes have a common modular structure with compulsory modules and a wide choice of optional modules.

Lincoln There are Faculties of Art, Architecture and Design, Business and Law, Health, Life and Social Sciences, Media, Humanities and Technology. Single and Joint subject degrees are offered on a modular basis, with some subjects offering the chance to study abroad.

Liverpool The University offers degrees in the Faculties of Arts, Engineering, Health Sciences, Medicine, Science, Social and Environmental Studies and Veterinary Science. Apart from courses with a clinical component, programmes are modular. In some cases they include placements in industry or in another country whilst a 'Languages for All' scheme offers European languages. Three Combined Honours programmes in Arts, Social and Environmental Sciences, and Science give students the chance to choose up to three subjects in Year 1, reducing to two subjects in Years 2 and 3. A similar Combined Honours course in Social and Environmental Studies is also offered. From 2014 they are offering a much wider range of Joint (50/50) degrees across the Faculty of Humanities and Social Sciences.

Liverpool Hope Liverpool Hope offers a wide range of undergraduate courses both as Single and Combined Honours degrees. The University's excellent academic record and supportive pastoral care are complemented by the beautiful settings of the campuses, making it a very special place to study. Liverpool Hope places great emphasis on bringing together research excellence and top-quality teaching. The aim of this research-informed teaching is to enable students to develop into rounded and employable graduates who can take their place confidently as global citizens in the 21st century.

Liverpool John Moores Courses are offered in the Faculties of Business, Law and Languages, Education, Community and Leisure, Health and Applied Social Sciences, Media, Arts and Social Science, Science and Technology and the Environment. The majority of courses provide the opportunity for work-based learning or for a year-long industrial placement.

London (Birk) Part-time evening courses are offered for mature students wishing to read for first and higher degrees. Courses are offered in the Faculties of Arts, Science, Social Science and Continuing Education.

London (Court) The Institute offers one undergraduate degree programme: BA (Hons) History of Art which is designed to equip students with a detailed knowledge and systematic, historical understanding of Western art from antiquity to the present.

London (Gold) Programmes include Art, Drama and Media, the Arts, Education and Social Sciences. Like most London University degrees, the majority of undergraduate degrees are made up of course units giving some flexibility. Twelve units are taken over three years.

London (Hey) Nine BA courses are offered in Philosophy and Theology and a Foundation degree in Pastoral Mission. Some part-time undergraduate courses are available. The supportive and learning environment is enhanced by one-to-one tutorials for all students throughout their courses.

London (Inst Paris) A Single Honours course in French Studies is offered to 150 students (the majority are British) who study in France for the whole of their course. The course is taught almost entirely in French. Students graduate after their three-year course with a University of London BA.

London (King's) The College offers more than 200 degree programmes in the Faculties of Arts and Humanities, Biomedical and Health Sciences, Law, Nursing and Midwifery, Physical Sciences, Social Science and Public Policy, and Medicine and Dentistry at the Guy's or King's Denmark Hill and St Thomas's campuses. The degree course structure varies with the subject chosen and consists of Single Honours, Joint Honours, Combined Honours (a choice of over 60 programmes) and major/minor courses.

London (QM) The College offers courses in the Arts and Humanities, Biological and Physical Sciences, Business Management and Economics, Computer Science, Engineering, Languages, Materials Science, Mathematics, Medicine and Social Sciences. In most subjects, students choose compulsory and optional course units which allow for some flexibility in planning a course to suit individual interests.

London (RH) The College offers Single, Joint and major/minor Honours degrees in three Faculties: Arts, History and Social Sciences, and Science. Many courses offer the opportunity to study abroad and all students can compete for international exchanges.

London (Royal Central Sch SpDr) The School offers an extensive portfolio of undergraduate and postgraduate courses comprising Acting, Applied Theatre, Theatre Crafts and Making, Design, Dramatherapy, Lighting, Movement, Performance, Puppetry, Performance Research, Scenography, Stage Management, Technical Arts and Production, Voice, Writing, Costume Construction, Stage Design, Prop

Making, Puppetry, Stage Management, Theatre Lighting and Sound Design. The School is the UK's Centre for Excellence in Training for Theatre and students benefit from interaction with industry professionals and opportunities to train within leading theatre practices and technologies.

London (RVC) Courses are offered in Veterinary Medicine and Bioveterinary Sciences; the latter does not qualify graduates to practise as veterinary surgeons. There is also a Veterinary Gateway course and a four-year Veterinary Nursing programme.

London (St George's) Courses are offered in Biomedical Science, Medicine, Paramedic Science, Healthcare Science, Physiotherapy and Diagnostic and Therapeutic Radiography.

London (SOAS) Single subject degrees include compulsory and optional units, with two-thirds of the total units studied in the chosen subject and the remaining units or 'floaters' from a complementary course offered at SOAS or another college of the University. In addition, two-subject degrees give great flexibility in the choice of units, enabling students to personalise their degrees to match their interests.

London (UCL) Subjects are organised in Faculties: Arts and Humanities, Social and Historical Sciences (with a flexible course unit system), Fine Art (the Slade School), Law, Built Environment (the Bartlett), Engineering Sciences, Mathematical and Physical Sciences and Life Sciences. In addition, there is the School of Medicine. The School of Slavonic and East European Studies also offers degrees which focus on developing a high level of proficiency in speaking, writing and understanding the chosen language.

London (UCL Sch Pharm) The School offers the Master of Pharmacy degree. Except for hospital and extra-mural projects, all the teaching takes place on the Bloomsbury campus.

London LSE The School offers courses not only in Economics and Political Science but also in a wide range of other Social Science subjects taught in 19 departments. Programmes are offered as Single Honours, Joint Honours or major/minor courses. All undergraduates study a compulsory course in Year 1 called 'Understanding the causes of things' (LSE 100) which aims to actively challenge them to analyse questions of current public concern and to develop their critical skills.

London Met Single and Joint Honours courses are made up of compulsory and optional modules allowing students some flexibility to follow their particular interests. Courses are offered in Accountancy and Business, Art and Architecture, Arts, Humanities and Languages, Computing, Economics and Finance, Education, Health and Human Sciences and Law.

London NCH The New College of the Humanities offers degrees in BSc Economics, BA English, BA History, LLB Law, BSc Politics and International Relations or BA Philosophy. In addition to studying towards a University of London degree, all students study a contextual subject chosen from one of the other degree subjects alongside four core courses: Logic and Critical Thinking, Science Literacy, Applied Ethics and Professional Skills. To reflect this further study, students are awarded the Diploma of NCH. The College is supported by a stellar professoriate who lecture at the College at times throughout the year. Weekly teaching is by one, one-hour long one-to-one tutorial, one small group tutorial and four participative lectures in the degree subject and seminars and lectures in the Diploma subjects. All students typically receive 12–13 contact hours a week. Scholarships are offered.

London Regent's An independent university offering a wide range of business and other courses. Check institution for fees.

London South Bank Subject areas cover Arts and Human Sciences including Law and Psychology, Business, Computing and Information Management, Engineering, Science and the Built Environment and Health and Social Care. All courses have flexible modes of study and many vocational courses offer sandwich placements.

Loughborough Academic programmes cover Art and Design, Business and Management, Chemistry, Computer Science, Economics, Engineering, Geography, Mathematics, Physics, Politics, History and International Relations, Social Science and Sports Science. Degree programmes combine compulsory and optional modules and some transfers between courses are possible. Sandwich degree courses with a year's paid work experience in industry result in high graduate employment.

Manchester The University offers Single and Joint Honours courses which are divided into course units, some of which are compulsory, some optional, and some are taken from a choice of subjects offered by other Schools and Faculties. A comprehensive Combined Studies degree enables students to choose course units from Arts, Humanities, Social Sciences and Sciences, and this provides the flexibility for students to alter the emphasis of their studies from year to year. Degree programmes are offered in the Faculties of Engineering and Physical Sciences, Humanities, Life Sciences and Medical and Human Sciences.

Manchester Met Degree programmes are offered in the Faculties of Art and Design, Community Studies and Education, Food, Clothing and Hospitality Management, Humanities, Law and Social Science, Science and Engineering and the Manchester Metropolitan Business School. A large number of courses involve industrial and commercial placements. It is also possible to take Combined Honours degrees selecting a combination of two or three subjects. Many programmes have a modular structure with compulsory and optional core modules.

Middlesex Single and Joint Honours courses are offered on a modular basis, most programmes having an optional work placement. Courses cover Art and Design, Arts subjects, Biological and Health Sciences, Business and Management, Computing and IT, Dance, Drama and Music, Social Sciences and Teaching and Education.

Newcastle Degree programmes are available in the Faculties of Humanities Arts and Social Sciences; Science, Agriculture and Engineering and Medical Sciences. Single, Joint and Combined Honours programmes are offered in some cases providing students with the opportunity either to defer their choice of final degree or to transfer to other subjects at a later stage.

Newman A full range of full-time and part-time degree courses can be chosen with a focus on Initial Teacher Training qualifications.

Newport The University of Glamorgan and the University of Wales, Newport merged in 2013 to create the University of South Wales. Please see **South Wales** for more information.

Norwich Arts Courses focus on Art and Design and Media Studies.

Northampton Courses are offered in seven schools: Applied Sciences (Computing, Mechanical and Electrical/Electronic Engineering), Business, Education, Health, Social Sciences, Arts (including Fine Art and Design) and Land-based subjects at Moulton College. Courses are offered as Single, Combined and Joint Honours programmes.

Northumbria A wide range of courses is offered with an emphasis on vocational studies, including Art and Design, Arts subjects, Built Environment, Business and Financial Management, Computing, Education and Sport, Engineering, Health and Social Care, Humanities, Languages, Law, Mathematics, Nursing and Midwifery, Psychology and Sciences. Single and Joint Honours courses are offered, and a Combined Honours course allows a choice of up to three subjects.

Nottingham Single and Joint Honours courses are available, with some industrial placements. Programmes are modular with compulsory and optional modules, the latter giving some flexibility in the selection of topics from outside the chosen subject field. Degree programmes are offered in the Faculties of Arts, Engineering, Medicine and Health Sciences, Science and Social Sciences. The University is committed to operating on a global scale, opening campuses in Malaysia and China in 2000 and 2004, and is able to offer many Nottingham-based students the opportunity to study for part of their degree in Asia. In addition, study-abroad opportunities are offered at over 320 institutions worldwide, through schemes such as Universitas 21 and Erasmus: almost all students can apply to spend a period of time abroad.

Nottingham Trent Degree programmes are offered in a range of subjects covering Animal, Rural and Environmental Sciences, Architecture, Arts and Humanities, Art and Design, Business, Education, Law, Sciences and Technology and Social Sciences. Many courses are vocational with industrial and commercial placements and some students are also able to spend a semester (half an academic year) studying at a partner university in Europe, the USA or Australia.

Open University Degree and diploma courses are offered in the following subject areas: Arts and Humanities, Business and Management, Childhood and Youth, Computing and ICT, Education, Engineering and Technology, Environmental Development and International Studies, Health and Social Care, Languages, Law, Mathematics and Statistics, Psychology, Science and Social Sciences. Students study at home and are sent learning materials by the OU, maintaining contact with their tutors by email, post and telephone. See also **Chapter 1**.

Oxford Candidates apply to a college and for a Single or Joint Honours programme. Courses are offered with a core element plus a variety of options. Weekly contact with a college tutor assists students to tailor their courses to suit personal interests. Arts students are examined twice, once in the first year (Preliminary examinations) and at the end of the course (Final Honours School). Science students are similarly examined although in some subjects examinations also take place in the second year.

Oxford Brookes Single Honours courses are offered with modules chosen from a field of study or, alternatively, Combined Honours courses in which two subjects are chosen. These subjects may be in related or unrelated subjects. There is also a Combined Studies degree in which students 'build' their own degree by taking approved modules from a range of the subjects offered by the University.

Plymouth A broad portfolio of degree courses is available covering Agriculture, Art and Design, Biological and Physical Sciences, Built Environment, Business and Financial Management, Computing, Drama, Education, Engineering, Health and Social Sciences, Humanities, Languages, Law, Marine Studies, Mathematics and Sport Studies. Single Honours courses are offered, with many vocational programmes offering work placements.

Portsmouth The University is a leading modern university with an excellent reputation. Around half of our students are on courses that are accredited or validated by professional organisations and many more of our degrees offer an accelerated route to qualifying with a profession or obtaining chartered status. The Faculties of Creative and Cultural Industries, Humanities and Social Science, Science, Technology and the Portsmouth Business School offer Single and Joint Honours courses. Sandwich programmes are also available in many subjects and there is also an opportunity for all students to learn a foreign language. Many courses are planned on a modular basis, which allows students to defer specialisation until after their first year.

Queen's Belfast The academic year is divided into two semesters of 15 weeks each (12 teaching weeks and three examination weeks), with degree courses (pathways) normally taken over three years of full-time study. Six modules are taken each year (three in each semester) and, in theory, a degree can involve any combination of six Level 1 modules. Single, Joint and Combined Honours courses are offered and, in addition, major/minor combinations; some courses include sandwich placements. Courses cover Agriculture and Food Science, Education, Engineering, Humanities and Social Sciences, Management and Economics, Law and Medicine and Health Sciences.

Reading Faculties of Arts and Humanities and Economics and Social Sciences provide flexible arrangements for students. A teaching system operates in Year 1 in which students can take modules in their chosen subject and in two or three other subjects. At the end of the first year they may transfer from Single Honours to Joint Honours courses or change to another subject. Reading has close links with business and industry through collaborative research projects, the creation of spin-out companies and graduate placement schemes.

Richmond (Am Int Univ) The University runs British and American courses. American courses are accredited by the Middle States Commission on Higher Education, an agency recognised by the US Department of Education. Courses are also approved by the Open University and can lead to Open University Validated Awards.

Robert Gordon The University offers a wide range of vocational courses including Accountancy and Business, Architecture, Art and Design, Computer Science, Engineering, Law, Nursing, Occupational Therapy, Pharmacy, Physiotherapy, Radiography, Sciences, Social Sciences and Sports Science. Many courses offer work placements and there are some opportunities to study abroad in Europe, Canada and the USA.

Roehampton The University manages its academic programmes in eight Schools: Arts and Business, Social Sciences and Computing, Education Studies, English and Modern Languages, Humanities and Cultural Studies, Initial Teacher Education, Sports Science and Psychological and Therapeutic Studies. All programmes operate within a modular and semester-based structure.

St Andrews A very wide range of subjects is offered across the Faculties of Arts, Divinity, Medicine and Science. A flexible programme is offered in the first two years when students take several subjects. The decision of Honours degree subject is made at the end of Year 2 when students choose between Single or Joint Honours degrees for the next two years. A broadly based General degree programme is also offered lasting three years. After two years of a General degree programme students may transfer onto a named Honours degree programme if they meet the requirements of the department(s).

St Mark and St John The University runs 100 plus programmes which place a high emphasis on being relevant to the labour market. Students will be provided with the relevant transferable skills in demand from employers and businesses – key skills that can help put students a step ahead of the competition. Ninety-three per cent of St Mark and St John students are in employment or further study within six months of graduation (HESA, 2013). The University has received 91% for overall student satisfaction in the National Student Survey, 2013, and is ranked equal sixth (with Exeter and Oxford) from 127 Higher Education institutions in England. The University specialises in Sport, Education, Languages and Linguistics, Journalism and Creative Arts.

St Mary's Flexible, modular degree options allow a great deal of choice to both Joint and Single Honours students. Practical and theoretical studies are followed in the Drama course. There are special studies in applied theatre, physical theatre or theatre arts. Applicants must take part in a short practical workshop or perform an audition piece.

Salford The University offers BA, BSc and BEng degrees with teaching methods depending on the degree (it is equally likely to accept students with BTECs and Access qualifications as well as those with A-levels). There is a wide range of professionally accredited programmes many involving work placements. All undergraduates may study a foreign language. Subjects include Accountancy and Business, Art and Design, Computer Science, Drama, Engineering, Humanities, Journalism, Leisure and Tourism, Languages, Music, Nursing, Physiotherapy, Psychology, Sciences, Social Sciences and Sport Science.

Sheffield The teaching year consists of two semesters (two periods of 15 weeks). Courses are fully modular, with the exceptions of Dentistry and Medicine. Students register for a named degree course which has a number of core modules, some optional modules chosen from a prescribed range of topics and some unrestricted modules chosen from any at the University. Programmes offered include Accounting and Business, Arts and Humanities, Computer Science, Engineering and Materials Science, Languages, Law, Nursing, Psychology, Sciences, Social Sciences and Town and Country Planning.

Sheffield Hallam A large number of vocational courses are offered in addition to those in Arts, Humanities and Social Sciences. The University is the largest provider of sandwich courses in the UK with most courses offering work placements, usually between the second and third years. Most students are able to study an additional language from French, German, Italian, Spanish and Japanese.

South Wales Many of the courses are vocational and can be studied as Single or Joint Honours courses or major/minor degrees. Courses are offered in the fields of Art and Design, Built Environment, Business, Computing and Mathematics, Education, Engineering, English and Creative Writing, Geography and the Environment, Health Sciences, Humanities and Social Sciences, Law, Policing and Crime, Media and Drama Studies and Sport.

Southampton A wide range of courses is offered in the Faculties of Law, Arts and Social Sciences, Engineering, Science and Mathematics and Medicine, Health and Life Sciences. Programmes are generally for three years. All students have the chance to study a language as part of their degree and there are many opportunities for students to study abroad or on Erasmus-Socrates exchange programmes whether or not they are studying modern languages.

Southampton Solent Courses are offered in Art and Design, Business and Law, Computing, Construction and Engineering, Fitness, Finance, Human and Social Sciences, Maritime and Geography, Marketing and

HR Management, Media, Film and Journalism, Sport, and Tourism. There are opportunities for students to gain work experience in the form of industrial placements alongside academic study.

Staffordshire The Stafford campus focuses on courses in Computing, Engineering, Technology and Health Studies, whilst at Stoke programmes are offered in Art and Design, Law, Business, Humanities, Social Sciences and Science subjects. Single and Joint Honours are available, some of which are for four years and include a work-placement year. Part-time courses are also offered.

Stirling A flexible system operates in which students can delay their final degree choice until midway through the course. The University year is divided into two 15-week semesters, from September to December and February to May with a reading/study block and exams at the end of each semester. Innovative February entry is possible to some degree programmes. There are 250 degree combinations with the opportunity to study a range of disciplines in the first two years. In addition to Single and Combined Honours degrees, there is a General degree which allows for greater breadth of choice. Subjects range across the Arts, Social Sciences and Sciences.

Stranmillis (UC) The College focuses on teacher training courses with European and International Exchanges as part of the degrees.

Strathclyde A credit-based modular system operates with a good degree of flexibility in course choices. The University offers many vocational courses in the Faculties of Engineering and Science and in the Strathclyde Business School. There are also degree programmes in Arts subjects, Education, Law and the Social Sciences.

Sunderland There are five schools of study: Arts, Media and Culture, Business, Computer Science and Technology. Single and Joint Honours and sandwich courses are offered, with strong links with industry. A modular programme provides maximum flexibility in choosing appropriate subjects. Some placements are possible in Canada, USA, Australia, New Zealand, India and Europe. There is a large number of mature and local students.

Surrey Degree programmes are offered in the Arts, Biomedical Sciences, Electronics and Physical Sciences, Engineering, Health and Medical Sciences and Management. Some 80% of students spend a professional training year as part of their course and in some cases there are placements abroad. There is also a part-time BSc degree in Professional Development through work-based learning.

Sussex Teaching is structured around five schools of study, the Brighton and Sussex Medical School and the Science and Technology Policy Research Unit. Courses cover a wide range of subjects in Humanities, Life Sciences, Science and Technology, Social Sciences and Cultural Studies. Students are registered in a school depending on the degree taken. The flexible structure allows students to interrupt their degree programme to take a year out.

Swansea Courses are offered in Arts and Social Sciences, Business, Economics and Law, Engineering, Languages, Medicine and Health Sciences and Science. Degree courses are modular with the opportunity to take some subjects outside the chosen degree course. Part-time degrees are available and study abroad arrangements are possible in several subject areas.

Teesside Single and Combined Honours degrees are offered with the major subject occupying two-thirds of the course and the minor option one-third. There is a wide choice of vocational courses, many with sandwich arrangements in industry, commerce and the professions. Courses are offered in the Arts, Business, Engineering, Law, Media, Social Sciences and Sport with large Schools of Health and Social Care and Computing and Mathematics. There is a high mature student intake.

Trinity Saint David Courses are offered in the Humanities, Business and Management, Education, Art, Design, the Performing Arts, and the Social Sciences.

Trinity Saint David (Swansea) The University consists of three main faculties: the faculty of Applied Design and Engineering offers a broad spectrum of courses from Automotive Engineering to Multimedia; the Faculty of Art and Design established 150 years ago is a major centre for art and crafts in Wales; the Faculty of Humanities comprises Schools of Business, Education, Health Sciences, Humanities, the Performing Arts, Leisure, Tourism and Recreation.

Ulster The Faculties of Arts, Business and Management, Engineering and Built Environment, Life and Health Sciences and Social Sciences offer a wide range of courses. There are various styles of learning supported by formal lectures and many courses include periods of work placement, eg Communications, Advertising and Marketing, Public Relations, Community Youth Work, Social Policy and Health and Social Care Policy.

Univ Law The University offers specialised law courses across the country with centres in Birmingham, Bristol, Chester, Guildford, London, Manchester and York.

Warwick Courses are offered by Departments in the Faculty of Arts, Science and Social Studies, the Warwick Business School, the Warwick Institute of Education and the Warwick Medical School. Students may choose single-subject degrees or combine several subjects in a Joint degree. Options offered in each course provide flexibility in the choice of subjects, although courses are not fully modularised. Many degrees offer the opportunity to study abroad and work placements on some science courses.

West London Bias towards vocational studies. Subjects offered cover Business, Management and Law, Tourism, Hospitality and Leisure, Music, Media and Creative Technologies and Health and Human Sciences. Credit-rated Single and Joint Honours courses are offered, many with year-long work placements between Years 2 and 3. There are some study-abroad arrangements in Europe, Canada and the USA and there is a large mature student intake.

West Scotland UWS provides a distinctive educational experience through a range of vocationally related courses, supported by strong applied research and knowledge-transfer activities. UWS is widely recognised as a leader in the Scottish university sector for the provision of innovative programmes of study, designed to meet the demands of existing and developing industries. The University has a wide range of undergraduate courses to choose from in the areas of business, computing, creative industries, education, engineering, health, IT, nursing and midwifery, science, social sciences, and sport across all four of its campuses.

Westminster Courses include Architecture and the Built Environment, Biosciences, Business Management, Complementary Therapies, Computer Sciences, Electronics, English and Linguistics, Languages, Law, Media and Arts and Design and Psychology and Social Sciences. Undergraduate courses are modular and taught over two semesters. The University has a broad network of partnerships within the EU which enables students to include a period of study abroad as part of their degree.

Winchester Single and Joint Honours (two subjects studied equally or a 75%–25% split) degrees are available. Courses are offered in American Studies, Archaeology, Business, Dance, Drama and Performance, Education, English and Creative Writing, Film Studies, History, Journalism and Media Studies, Psychology, Sport Science, Theology and Tourism.

Wolverhampton A large number of specialist and Joint Honours degrees are offered and many have work placements at home or abroad. Except for courses linked to specific professional requirements, programmes are modular providing flexibility of choice. Courses include Art and Design, Humanities, Business Studies, Computer Science, Education, Engineering, Environmental Studies, Health Studies, Law, Media, Nursing and Social Studies.

Worcester The courses are grouped into six institutes: Health and Society, Humanities and Creative Arts, Science and the Environment, Sport and Exercise Science, the Worcester Business School, and Education.

York Thirty departments and centres cover a range of subjects in the arts and humanities, sciences, social sciences and medicine. The 'Languages for All' programme enables any student to take a course in any one of a number of languages, in addition to which there are several opportunities to build a period abroad into a degree course. Subjects offered include Archaeology, Biochemistry, Biology, Biomedical Sciences, Chemistry, Computer Science, Economics, Education, Electronics, English and Related Literature, Environment, History, History of Art, Languages, Law, Management, Medicine, Music, Nursing, Midwifery and Healthcare, Philosophy, Physics, Politics, Economics and Philosophy, Psychology, Social Policy and Social Work, Social and Political Sciences, Sociology, Theatre, Film, Television and Interactive Media.

ACTIVATE
LEARNING

GO HIGHER

WITH AN EMPLOYMENT FOCUSED DEGREE AT AN ACTIVATE LEARNING COLLEGE

BANBURY AND BICESTER COLLEGE

CITY OF OXFORD COLLEGE

READING COLLEGE

01865 550 550
HE@activatelearning.ac.uk
www.activatelearning.ac.uk

OXFORD
BROOKES
UNIVERSITY

**ASSOCIATE COLLEGE
PARTNERSHIP**

bucks
new university

WHAT IS ACTIVATE LEARNING?

Activate Learning is a group of education and training providers in Oxfordshire and Berkshire.

Our three colleges – Banbury and Bicester College, City of Oxford College and Reading College – specialise in vocational training in both further and higher education.

Our higher education programmes include HNDs, foundation degrees and honours degrees.

WHY STUDY WITH US?

We know that **employability** – that is, the opportunity to find and sustain employment after study – is very important to you.

Developing employability skills is where we excel. We are vocational specialists, and our teaching and learning is career-focused. We have industry-experienced teachers and professional, industry-standard resources.

All of our foundation degree and honours degree programmes are developed in consultation with employers – such as Thames Valley Police and the NHS – and HE institutions such as Oxford Brookes University and Bucks New University.

All of this means that you graduate with the knowledge, skills and attributes that employers want. You get an employment-focused qualification. Our degrees are accredited and awarded by the universities we partner, and our HNDs are accredited by Edexcel.

One more reason for studying with us is affordability. Our programme fees are lower than universities' fees!

WHAT CAN YOU STUDY?

Our HND, foundation degree and honours programmes cover a broad range of areas:

» ART, DESIGN AND MEDIA PRODUCTION
» BUSINESS AND ENTERPRISE
» CARING AND HEALTH
» COMPUTING
» ENGINEERING
» FURNITURE
» MOTORSPORTS
» MUSIC
» POLICING
» SPORT

We offer HNCs in computing, construction and engineering, and the PGCE in teaching too.

WHERE CAN YOU FIND OUT MORE?

For an overview of all of our HE programmes, go to the **University level** section at:

www.activatelearning.ac.uk

To see which programmes are available at each College, see the **University level** section of each individual college website:

www.banbury-bicester.ac.uk
www.cityofoxford.ac.uk
www.reading-college.ac.uk

GO HIGHER, GO FURTHER …
WITH ACTIVATE LEARNING

York St John The Faculties of Education and Theology, Business and Communication, Health and Life Sciences and Art offer a range of specialist degrees and Joint Honours courses are offered in Business, Counselling, Design, Education, Health Studies, Information Technology, Languages and Linguistics, Management, Occupational Therapy, Physiotherapy, Psychology, Sport and Theology.

OTHER INSTITUTIONS AND THEIR COURSES

In addition to the large numbers of universities and university colleges offering degree courses, there are over 100 colleges admitting several thousands of students, each on full degree courses. These include university centres, colleges of further and higher education and specialist colleges of agriculture and horticulture, art, drama and music: see the directory of institutions at the back of the book (**Chapter 10**). Larger institutions will offer a range of Single subject, Joint and Combined Honours degree courses leading to BA, BSc and BEd degrees whilst the smaller colleges may only offer one or two first degree programmes. Increasingly, a large number are also providing full- or part-time Foundation degrees which can lead to Honours degree courses. These colleges are listed in the subject tables. The next chapter **University and College Admissions** outlines how institutions select applicants for their courses and it provides information relating to key points of their admissions policies.

4

UNIVERSITY AND COLLEGE ADMISSIONS

ADMISSIONS POLICIES

Although the UCAS application process is standard for all undergraduate Honours degree courses (see **Chapter 5**) the admissions policies adopted by individual departments in universities and colleges often differ, depending on the popularity of the course and the quality of applicants. There are, however, common areas of agreement concerning applications, in particular the acceptance of the different qualifying examinations being offered. Apart from a diverse range of international qualifications, A-level grades, the International Baccalaureate (IB) and BTEC have been the common currency of selection linked with the UCAS Tariff points system for many years, although some very popular universities and courses do not make points offers, preferring to set their entry standards in the grades awarded in specific subjects.

Institutions are still making decisions on the timing and introduction of the new A* grades, although this year an A* grade has been stipulated in over 6000 offers. Most, if not all, institutions accept recent qualifications such as the Advanced Diplomas, the Extended Project Qualification and the Cambridge Pre-U Diploma although there may be some additional requirements depending on the degrees applied for when specified subjects may be required. A-levels in general studies and critical thinking are nearly always taken into account when selecting applicants although they rarely form part of an offer. Key Skills may also be noted by selectors and for some courses they could be worth up to 20 Tariff points. BTEC is also acceptable with two passes for some Foundation courses to full distinction for some competitive degree programmes. However, it should also be noted that a number of universities and degree courses also have general entry requirements which include GCSE grade C or above in English and mathematics.

Interview policies vary considerably and, in most cases, offers will simply be based on the information on the UCAS application with the personal statement being highly important for many courses. Candidates receiving offers will be invited to visit their campuses. Interviews are usual for Medicine, Dentistry, Veterinary Science, Art, Social Work and for Teaching courses and inevitable for Dance, Drama and Music (see **Chapter 6**). Mature students (defined as those aged over 21 on entry) are often interviewed. Normal published offers may not apply to mature students. In all institutions certain courses require Disclosure and Barring Service (DBS) checks or medical examinations; students should check these requirements before applying for courses.

Deferred entry is acceptable in almost all cases although many admissions tutors ask that the intention to take a Gap Year be included on the application if firm arrangements have been made. It is worth noting, however, that there may well be fewer places available on a subsequent course for students wanting to defer.

Several universities and colleges advise that if a student fails to achieve the grades required for an offer, they may still be awarded a place; however they may receive a changed offer for an alternative course. Many admissions departments are also prepared to provide feedback on the results of unsuccessful applications.

In addition, all institutions have a number of schemes in place to enable admissions tutors to identify and make offers to applicants who, for example, may have had their education affected by circumstances outside their control. A major initiative is Widening Participation in which various schemes can assist school and college students in getting into university. These programmes focus on specific groups of students and communities including:

- students from low participation areas
- low-performing schools and colleges or those without a strong history of progression to higher education

- students with disabilities
- people living in deprived geographical areas, including deprived rural areas
- students from black or ethnic minority backgrounds
- students from the lower socio-economic groups 4–8 including mature learners
- students requiring financial assistance or who are disadvantaged in various ways
- families with little or no experience of higher education
- students from homes with low household incomes
- students returning to study after a period of time spent away
- students from state schools.

Students who feel that they might qualify for Widening Participation programmes should find out from their school or college about the schemes offered by universities including their local university. In addition to the general information above, universities have emphasised certain aspects of their selection procedures and these are listed below. Even so, applicants are strongly advised to check prospectuses and websites for up-to-date information on admissions and, in particular, any entrance test to be taken (see also **Chapter 6**).

ADMISSIONS INFORMATION

The following information provides a selection of relevant aspects of admissions policies and practice. Where institutions have provided the information, details of courses that were not available through Clearing in 2013 have been provided as well as details of the subjects attracting the highest number of applicants in the 2013 application cycle.

Information on alternative qualifications to A-levels such as the Cambridge Pre-U Diploma, the Advanced Diploma, BTEC qualifications, Key Skills and Access courses is not always published in prospectuses; it is usually available on universities' websites. While it can be assumed that applicants will be considered and accepted with these alternative qualifications, depending on the requirements for individual degree programmes, it is important to check with university admissions staff **before** you make your application that your qualifications will meet their requirements. Applicants whose first language is not English should refer to **Chapter 9** for details of the English Language entry requirements.

Applicants for places at popular universities or for popular courses cannot assume that they will receive an offer even if their predicted grades are the same or higher than a stated standard offer.

Aberdeen Selectors look for evidence of subject knowledge and understanding, commitment, motivation and responsibility, and the ability to cope with a university education.

Abertay Only applicants for courses in Mental Health and Nursing are interviewed.

Aberystwyth Offers are made centrally except for the following academic departments: Art, Biological and Rural Sciences, Geography and Earth Sciences, Welsh. All offers are made on the basis of academic criteria determined by the departments concerned. Personal statements and references are scrutinised by experienced staff in the central office and academic departments. Following unprecedented recruitment of very well-qualified students in recent years, the entry requirements for most study schemes have been reviewed and raised to their current levels. The University states that it is important that applications are made by the initial closing date of 15 January. No guarantee can be made to consider late applications. Offers will be made predominantly on the basis of the application form but interviews are required for some subjects. Candidates will not normally be interviewed unless there are special reasons for doing so – eg the candidate has been away from study for a long time, is not offering the standard qualifications or an interview is requested. Decisions are normally made within four weeks of receiving the application and all those receiving an offer will be invited to visit the University and their chosen academic department. Applicants are advised not to depend on Clearing. If places are available in Clearing, there may be no, or very limited, flexibility on qualifications and grades required for entry. *Most popular subjects 2013* Biology, Drama, English and Creative Writing, Law, Psychology.

Anglia Ruskin The University interviews all shortlisted applicants for Art and Design, Education, Nursing, Social Work and Midwifery. Some applicants are interviewed for Business. Maths and English testing is also used for some Education (ITT), Nursing, Midwifery and Social Work courses. Applicants should visit the University's website regularly to view any changes to entry requirements, and for further information regarding the courses and applications procedures. The University is happy to give advice and guidance about the admissions process.

Arts London In addition to formally qualified applicants, the University welcomes applications from candidates without formal qualifications who can demonstrate equivalent skills, knowledge and ability gained from work or life experience.

Aston Offers are not normally made simply on the basis of UCAS points. Interviews are only used in special cases, for example, mature students, or those with non-standard entry qualifications. Applications from high-achieving students taking Applied A-levels are welcomed and all degree programmes will consider a single award Applied A-level in place of a third A-level subject. For all degree programmes, except those in the School of Health and Life Sciences, a relevant Applied A-level double award plus one relevant A-level will normally be accepted. BTEC awards are acceptable and a mix of BTEC and A-levels welcomed. High-achieving Level 3 Diploma students in relevant subjects will be considered. Key Skills will be taken into account but will not be included in offers; Access programmes are accepted.

Bangor Applications welcomed from students taking validated Access courses and 14–19 Diplomas in specified subjects. *Most popular subjects 2013* Nursing, Psychology.

Bath Some departments interview promising applicants; those not receiving an offer can obtain feedback on the reasons for their rejection. Students are encouraged to take the Extended Project and to provide details on their personal statement.

Bath Spa All eligible candidates are interviewed for the following courses: Art and Design, Broadcast Media, Creative Media Practice, Music and Performing Arts, Publishing. All applicants will be invited to visit the University after receiving an offer. Gap Years are acceptable.

Birmingham Courses are academic and 75% of the personal statement should relate to why the applicant wants to study the subject for which they have applied. The Extended Project will not be included in the University's offers but it welcomes applicants taking this qualification and it may make a difference to a borderline applicant. Some applicants are interviewed, for example for Medicine, Dentistry and for Social Work. The University uses LNAT as its admissions test for Law applicants. Gap Years are acceptable and should be mentioned on the UCAS application or as soon as arrangements have been made. A new admissions policy will be trialled in which unconditional offers will be made to candidates with forecast grades from $A^*A^*A^*$ to AAA in the following subjects: Accountancy and Finance, Business Management, Classics, Economics, International Relations, Mathematics, Metallurgy and Materials, Modern Languages, Philosophy, Political Science, and Sociology. *Most popular subjects 2013* Biosciences, Chemistry, Dentistry, Economics, English, Geography, History, Law, Management, Mathematics, Medicine, Modern Languages, Nursing, Physics, Political Science, Psychology.

Birmingham (UC) Students wishing to apply for part-time courses should apply direct to the college.

Birmingham City Admissions are administered centrally through the Admissions Unit in the Academic Registry. Some applicants will be called to interview and others invited to the department before an offer is made. If the required grades of an offer are not achieved it may still be possible to be accepted on to a course. Deferred entry is acceptable.

Bishop Grosseteste Candidates are advised to attend an Open Day prior to applying. Interview days are a feature of the application process.

Bolton Applicants are advised to apply through UCAS as early as possible. The University welcomes the A-level and AS-level general studies and also Key Skills at Level 3/4. If admissions staff consider that the course applied for is not suitable then an offer for an alternative course may be made. *Most popular subjects 2013* Art and Design, Computing, Media and Creative Technologies, Psychology.

Bournemouth The personal statement is regarded as an important aspect of the application process. Some subject areas may require applicants to attend for interview. Deferred entry is acceptable.

Bradford Candidates will not be accepted on to any degree course purely on the basis of AS-level results (including the double award) although two AS-levels or an AS double award may be accepted instead of a non-essential A-level. Low offers may be made to applicants showing considerable promise in academic or in other areas. Offers are normally based on the UCAS Tariff. The University accepts a range of alternative qualifications and takes a very positive view on the value of the new Advanced Diploma. These qualifications will be considered on a course-by-course basis.

Brighton The University welcomes applications from students with qualifications and experience other than traditional A-levels. The Advanced Diploma, Access courses and BTEC are acceptable alternative qualifications.

Brighton and Sussex (MS) Standard offers usually include three A grades at A level with minimum passes of an A grade in biology and chemistry. The School welcomes candidates offering A*, or predicted to achieve A*. The same policy applies to applicants offering the Extended Project.

Bristol A* grades may be included in the offers for some applicants depending on the application, the subject and the competition for places; if an A* grade is required this will be made clear in the relevant admissions statement and prospectus entry. Students choosing to take the Extended Project may receive two offers, one of which includes the Extended Project, for example, AAA, or AAB plus the Extended Project. Requirements for the Advanced Diploma are detailed in each prospectus entry. Up to two Applied A-levels may be considered with an A-level. Some admissions tutors may take unit grade information into account when making selection decisions. However, as usual, admissions tutors will make decisions within the context of the whole application, and will not disadvantage applicants who are unable to provide unit grade information. If unit grades are to be taken into account, this will be clearly specified in the relevant admissions statement. It is possible that some departments may also wish to specify unit grade achievement in the terms of offers. If so, this information will be published in the relevant prospectus entry and in the admissions statement. In addition, in some marginal cases unit grade information will continue to be used to inform decisions about applicants who have missed the terms of their offers at Confirmation. Deferred entry is acceptable but intention to defer should be indicated in the personal statement, giving information about your plans. However, in some cases the number of places available might be limited and higher offers may be made. An interview is required for an offer for Dentistry, Drama, Engineering Design, Medicine, Veterinary Nursing, and Veterinary Science but not all applicants are interviewed. LNAT (see **Chapter 6**) is used for admission to the Law programmes. Applicants who are re-sitting A-levels or who are re-applying will not be given offers for Dentistry, Law or Medicine. Advice to applicants can be found on www.bristol.ac.uk/study. All programmes at Bristol are extremely competitive with an average of over 10 applicants per place. *Most popular subjects 2013* English, Geography, History, Law, Mathematics, Medicine, Psychology, Veterinary Science.

Bristol UWE Typical offers are made for each degree programme, although these offers may vary between applicants since selection is based on individual merit. Students applying for courses 'subject to approval' or 'subject to validation' will be kept informed of the latest developments. Many offers will be made in terms of Tariff points.

Brunel All applicants are interviewed for Design, Electrical Engineering, Social Work and Education courses. All offers for degree courses are for three A-levels and either one AS-level or the Extended Project. If an applicant has not been able to take a fourth subject at AS-level, or complete a Project, this should be indicated in the application; offers will then be made for three A-levels (or equivalent). For some courses, students who have re-sat A-levels and/or re-applied for the course will be given a higher offer than the standard entry requirements. The University accepts relevant Advanced Diplomas.

Buckingham Candidates apply through UCAS in the normal way or directly with a paper application obtainable from the University. Applicants may be invited for interview.

Bucks New It may be possible to transfer to the University from another university under the Credit Accumulation and Transfer Scheme (CATS), and to gain exemptions from part of the course if the student has CATS credit points from their relevant previous study. Transfer from full-time to part-time study is possible. BTEC qualifications are acceptable. Admissions tests will be used for entry to Nursing and Social Work courses.

Cambridge Currently, the standard offer is A*AA but the subject in which the A* is to be achieved may or may not be specified. Colleges modify offers to take account of individual circumstances. Self-discipline, motivation and commitment are required together with the ability to think critically and independently, plus passion or, at the very least, real enthusiasm for the chosen course. If examination predictions are good then the chance of admission may be better than one in five. Applicants are encouraged to take the Extended Project although it will not be a requirement of any offer. Although AS-level and A-level critical thinking and general studies are acceptable as a fourth AS-level or A-level subject, neither is considered acceptable as a third A-level. For many courses admissions tests are used – and written work may be required – so it is very important to check the University website and prospectus well before completing the application to find out exactly what is needed for entry. Natural Sciences receives the most applications, Classics (four years) receives the lowest. See **Chapter 6**, and also www.cam.ac.uk/ admissions/undergraduate/tests and www.admissionstestingservice.org. *Clearing 2013* The University of Cambridge does not accept applications through Clearing. *Most popular subjects 2013* Natural Sciences.

Canterbury Christ Church The personal statement and school references are regarded as highly important. Applicants for Teaching and Health-related courses must show evidence on their application of relevant experience. If they do not, they will be rejected without interview. Other subjects, including Geography, History and Music, also interview candidates.

Cardiff Applicants are required to take only three A-levels for degree courses. Deferred entry is acceptable. The 14–19 Diploma is an acceptable qualification for entry. Key Skills should be mentioned in an application but will not form part of an offer.

Cardiff Met (UWIC) Students from Foundation degree courses or with HNC/HND qualifications should contact the course director before applying. *Most popular subjects 2013* Business and Management, Educational Studies, Fine Art, Nutrition and Dietetics, Psychology, Social Work, Sport.

Central Lancashire The University looks for grades C/D plus Additional Specialist Learning for applicants with the new Advanced Diplomas. Grades B/C will be required from students with the Progression Diploma.

Chester Interviews and workshops are required for some courses to support applications. General studies at A-level is acceptable for entry to courses in addition to other A-levels.

Chichester Early application is advised for popular courses such as Dance, Physical Education, Primary Education, Teaching and Sports Therapy. Teaching applicants should have spent a minimum of two weeks observing/helping out in a state school within two years of applying. Significant experience is also required for applicants for Social Work courses. Applicants taking a Level 3 Diploma will be considered for entry to the relevant course. Dance, Music and Performing Arts applicants will be required to prepare a set piece in advance and to perform it in front of a group. Decisions on applications are normally made within two weeks, and, except for some courses where interviews are required (see **Chapter 6**) most decisions are made on the basis of the application form. Some applicants will be interviewed for Childhood Studies, Dance, Drama and Performing Arts, Fine Art, Music, Musical Theatre, Physical Education, Social Work and Teacher Training courses. Chichester uses more grade-based offers rather than UCAS Tariff points offers for entry. *Most popular subjects 2013* Adventure Education, Charity Development, Digital Film Production, Media and Cultural Studies, Musical Theatre, Primary Education, Psychology, Sports Therapy, Sports Coaching, Theatre.

City It is hoped that applicants will have taken four AS-level subjects in Year 12, going on to do three at A-level in Year 13.

Coventry The University welcomes applications from those with significant work or life experience who do not necessarily meet the published academic requirements for the course. Applicants will be required to demonstrate evidence of motivation, potential and knowledge of the subject. Some candidates will be required to attend interviews depending on their course choice. Decisions are made centrally, with the exception of applications to courses funded by the NHS and the General Social Care Council where applications are handled by the Admissions Unit in the Faculty of Health and Life Sciences. Applications from international students (including EU) are handled by the International Office. All NHS-funded courses (Nursing, Midwifery, Dietetics, Occupational Therapy, Operating Department Practice, Paramedic Science, Social Work) receive the most applicants and interview in all cases.

Creative Arts Interviews and portfolios are required for all courses. There is no minimum age requirement for entry to undergraduate courses.

Cumbria The University accepts a wide range of qualifications for course entry. Required Tariff points vary across all disciplines and some courses have specific GCSE requirements.

De Montfort Selection criteria depend on the chosen course. Some courses require a personal interview and/or examination of portfolios.

Derby The Level 2 Diploma is regarded as equivalent to GCSEs and the Level 3 Diploma to A-levels. Students without formal qualifications can take an Access course or the Modular Foundation course to gain entry to degree programmes.

Dundee All applications are held until 15 January deadline (except for Medicine and Dentistry: 15 October) before decisions are made. The published grades indicate the minimum which can be accepted at one sitting. The University considers applicants who are re-sitting although offers would be higher than the published grades. All offers are made through the Central Office or devolved to the Departments of Architecture, Community Learning and Development, Education, Dentistry, Medicine, Nursing or Social Work.

Durham The Durham admissions policy reviews the following factors: A-level or equivalent grades; GCSE performance; the personal statement (although students applying for more than one type of course or institution may submit a substitute personal statement of the same length as the original personal statement on the UCAS form; the school/college reference; motivation for the chosen degree programme; independence of thought and working; skills derived from non-academic activities, eg sport, the arts, and voluntary and community work. Admission decisions are made by academic departments. Durham has reviewed its policy towards the A* grade at A-level and will include A* grades in the entry requirements for some of its programmes. Durham University does not use interviews as a means of selection except in those circumstances where external bodies determine that interviewing is compulsory (applicants to Initial Teacher Training and Medicine). Durham also interviews applicants to the Foundation Centre, those applicants whose application does not show adequate evidence of recent and relevant knowledge or who have experienced a break in their study prior to application. This will be determined by academic departments on an individual basis having considered all the information provided in the application. Successful applicants will be informed of the decision on their application before a college is allocated.

East Anglia Offers are normally made in terms of three A-levels although applicants with two A-levels and AS-levels are welcome. Critical thinking and general studies A-levels are not accepted for most courses. Interviews are necessary for some courses. Deferred entry is acceptable.

East London Candidates are advised to apply as soon as possible and results are normally announced within seven days. Some students may be called for interview and in some cases an essay or a portfolio may be required. The interviewers will be looking for evidence of a real interest in the chosen subject. Rejected applicants may receive an offer of a place on an Extended degree or another course.

Edge Hill With the exception of courses in Journalism, Animation, Media (Film and TV), TV Production, Performing Arts, Social and Psychological Sciences, Teacher Training, Nursing and Midwifery, most decisions are made without an interview. Those applicants who receive offers are invited to visit the University. The new Advanced Diploma is accepted as equivalent to three A-levels.

Edinburgh Admission decisions are made by the admissions offices of the University's three colleges: the College of Humanities and Social Science, the College of Science and Engineering and the College of Medicine and Veterinary Medicine. Decisions on the majority of applications will be made after the UCAS deadline, once all applications have been received. All offers will be expressed in grades, not Tariff points.

Edinburgh Napier Offers are made in grades not in the UCAS Tariff system. The normal offers may not apply to candidates aged over 21, who should contact the admissions tutor for details. Interviews may be required for some courses. After an initial application screening, applicants who meet the basic academic criteria will considered by academic staff. Applications are then assessed on other eligibility criteria set by individual departments and before any offer is made all applicants will be interviewed. This applies to the following programmes: Nursing, Vet Nursing, Journalism, Design programmes, Music, Acting for Stage and Screen, Acting and English, Television, Photography, Film. The Health, Life and Social Science Faculty receive the highest number of applicants.

Edinburgh Queen Margaret Applicants are interviewed for some courses including Physiotherapy and Speech Sciences. *Most popular subjects 2013* Diagnostic Radiography, Nursing, Physiotherapy, Psychology.

Essex Candidates are required to have two full A-levels or equivalent – students re-sitting some subjects may get a higher offer. All departments accept general studies and critical thinking. Key Skills at Level 3 can be used as part of the points total providing they do not overlap with other qualifications (eg numeracy or A-level mathematics). Unit grades are not used as standard procedure. Additional aptitude tests are not used. Interviews may be required for some subjects. Admission decisions are made departmentally. *Most popular subjects 2013* Accounting, Acting, Biomedical Science, Business, Economics, Finance, Management, Nursing.

Exeter The University welcomes applications from applicants from all backgrounds. Key indicators include predicted and achieved academic performance in Level 2 and 3 qualifications; candidates would normally be expected to take three A-levels (or the equivalent). Deferred applications are welcome. The subjects interviewing all candidates are Applied Psychology (Clinical), Drama, Medical Imaging, Medicine and Physics. *Most popular subjects 2013* Economics, English, History.

Falmouth For most courses samples of works and/or interviews will be required.

Glasgow Normally all subjects, apart from Dentistry, Education (for the BEd Primary programme), Law, Medicine, Social Sciences and Veterinary Medicine, accept applications after the 15 January deadline, but this is not guaranteed and will depend on the pressure on places and the academic qualifications of the applicant. Offers are made from early to late March. The University does not interview applicants to all faculties, some exceptions being Education and Technological Education, Medical and Veterinary Sciences, and Music. Deferred entry is not guaranteed for all subjects (eg Dentistry, Primary Education and Veterinary Medicine): check with the University. Admissions organised centrally except for Dentistry, Education, Medicine and Veterinary Medicine and the School of Interdisciplinary Studies at the Dumfries campus. *Most popular subjects 2013* Business and Management, Computer Science, Dentistry, Economics, English Literature, History, Mechanical Engineering, Medicine, Primary Education, Psychology, Veterinary Medicine.

Glasgow Caledonian The University accepts a wide range of qualifications for course entry. Selection criteria depend on the chosen course. Some courses require a personal interview and/or examination of portfolios. Nursing and Health courses interview applicants. Applicants who are considering deferred entry should contact the admissions tutor before applying.

Gloucestershire Students failing to meet the UCAS Tariff requirements may be eligible for entry based on life or work experience following an interview. Entry with the Advanced Diploma, BTEC, NVQ Level 3 and Access to Higher Education qualifications is acceptable.

Glyndŵr Offers are made through the Central Office for courses in Sports, Business, Engineering, Communications and Technology, Humanities, Journalism and Media. Enquiries for other courses should be made to the Head of Department. Short-listed candidates are interviewed for Nursing, Social Work, Psychology, Criminal Justice, Education/Families and Childhood Studies. The general requirement for entry to most degree courses is 240–260 UCAS Tariff points and 120 UCAS Tariff points for Foundation degrees. UCAS points may be counted from a wide variety of qualifications but offers are usually made based on points from GCE A-levels or equivalent. Applications are also welcomed from candidates who do not possess the standard qualifications but who can demonstrate their capacity to pursue the course successfully. Entrance can be based on past experience, skills, organisational capabilities and the potential to succeed.

Harper Adams All courses interview all candidates based in the UK.

Heriot-Watt In order to give candidates as much flexibility as possible, many will receive offers for both first and second year entry. Although one of these will be the main offer, candidates accepting this can easily change their main offer to the alternative year if they subsequently want to do so. Applicants are interviewed for some programmes.

Hertfordshire Applicants wanting to take a Gap Year should finalise their arrangements before asking for deferment and accepting a place. Once a place has been accepted for the following year it will not be possible to change their application for entry to the current year. They would need to withdraw their application and apply again through Clearing.

Hull All criteria for selection are set by the academic faculty. A mandatory interview process operates for shortlisted applicants for Nursing, Operating Department Practice, Midwifery, Teaching (QTS), Social Work. Music applicants are invited to a practical session as part of an Open Day. A new course in Chemical Engineering is available, whilst Sport and Leisure Management and Design and Technology have been withdrawn. A wide range of qualifications are accepted for entry to degree courses. Applications are also welcomed from those who can demonstrate Level 3 work-based learning such as Advanced Apprenticeships and NVQ 3. Bridging study may be recommended by way of a Foundation year. Most courses welcome applications for deferred entry although this should be stated on the application. Deferred entry is not available for Nursing courses.

ifs (UC) Applications are submitted through UCAS and the deadline is 15 January 2015. All applications made before the closing date will be considered equally against the stated selection criteria and in the context of the number of available places. The college will consider late applications only for courses where places are still available.

Imperial London Except for courses where three specific A-levels are required for admission, candidates with two A-levels and two AS-levels will normally be considered equally with other candidates offering three A-levels. The College considers candidates with the Advanced Engineering Diploma if they also have A-levels in specified subjects which meet the College's entry requirements. Applicants for entry to Year 2 of some courses can also be considered if they have completed the first year of a comparable degree at another institution with a high level of achievement, but they need to contact the relevant department before applying. A College Admissions and Appeals and Complaints procedure is available to applicants dissatisfied with the way their application has been considered. Applicants should note the College's policy on dress, health and safety published on its website. An offer for an alternative course may be made to rejected applicants.

Keele Conditional offers are normally made in grades for Medicine, Pharmacy and Physiotherapy. For other subjects offers are usually made in Tariff points and include points for Key Skills at Level 3, stand-alone AS-levels and Advanced Extension Awards. The Advanced Diploma is accepted as equivalent to three A-levels and general studies is also accepted as a condition of an offer. Applicants are normally required to be currently undertaking some formal study before starting a course, but if this is not possible the University may make an offer for a Foundation course.

Kent The University accepts a wide range of qualifications. For mature students and those without the required qualifications, Foundation course offers may be made. Applicants returning to study after a long break are advised to contact the admissions staff before making a UCAS application. Deferred entry is acceptable but should be mentioned on the application. The University regards the personal statement as important and recommends that applicants research their chosen courses thoroughly, and show an understanding of the curriculum. *Most popular subjects 2013* Actuarial Science, Business, Law, Mathematics.

Kingston Admissions staff look carefully at each applicant's academic record, references and personal statement. Some courses require interviews where selectors look for evidence of the applicant's intellectual capacity, course knowledge and enthusiasm. Punctuality and a smart appearance could be important.

Lancaster The University welcomes applications from students wishing to defer entry. General studies is acceptable for the majority of courses. Admissions tutors accept a range of qualifications for entry. Some candidates are interviewed before an offer is made, but most are invited to an informal post-offer Open Day which can involve an interview or discussion with an admissions tutor.

Leeds The University welcomes students who do not come straight from school or college or who wish to defer entry. It also welcomes the increased breadth of post-16 qualifications. Some courses do not accept AL general studies or critical thinking.

Leeds Beckett Most offers are made in UCAS Tariff points, and interviews are held before an offer is made for some courses. Deferred entry is acceptable although applicants should be aware that some courses may change slightly each year. Students without the required qualifications may provide a 'portfolio of achievement', giving, for example, information about their work experience and their reasons for applying for the course, and also providing references.

Leeds Trinity All applicants receiving an offer will be invited to an 'Applicants' Day' when they (and families and friends) have the opportunity to visit the campus and receive specific details of their chosen course.

Leicester Most courses do not interview applicants although invitations to visit the University will follow any offers made. Most offers are made on the basis of three A-levels, although in some cases two A-levels and two AS-levels may be accepted. The University welcomes the Extended Project which should be mentioned in the personal statement. The Advanced Diploma and the Cambridge Pre-U Diploma are also acceptable qualifications. Applications from suitably qualified students are also considered for second year entry. Contact the subject department for further information.

Lincoln On some courses, notably Art and Design and Architecture, an interview with a portfolio is sometimes required before an offer can be made. The University accepts a wide range of qualifications but students without the standard entry requirements may still be offered a place on the basis of prior experience and qualifications.

Liverpool Decisions on offers for most schools/departments are made centrally. The exceptions are in the Schools of Medical Education, Dentistry, Health Sciences and the Faculty of Veterinary Science. There are some programmes within the following schools/departments where the decisions are devolved to the school. These are programmes run in conjunction with Carmel College. Most departments will invite applicants to visit the University before or after an offer is made. Some departments require interviews. Offers are normally based on three A-levels or equivalent (a wide range of qualifications is accepted). Some programmes will accept two A-levels and two AS-levels. Irish Studies, Politics, Philosophy, Music and Communication and Media receive the lowest number of applications. *Most popular subjects 2013* Dentistry, Health Sciences, Management, Medicine, Veterinary Science.

Liverpool Hope Their policy is to select those candidates who demonstrate they have an academic ability and personal motivation to succeed in their chosen programme of study. The admissions decision will rest primarily on the qualifications and also on the aspirations of the applicant in relation to their chosen programme of study. They welcome applications from students who meet their academic entry requirements and are looking to be intellectually stretched, stimulated and challenged in their studies, and who will add energy, and bring breath of experience and vitality to the University community.

Liverpool John Moores Admissions decisions are made through the Faculty 'Hubs' (Science; Health and Applied Social Sciences; Technology and Environment; Arts, Professional and Social Studies). The personal statement is regarded as highly important and students are advised to include all relevant interests and work experience. The University welcomes a wide range of entry qualifications. If an applicant fails to receive an offer for their chosen course then an offer for an alternative course may be made. All candidates are interviewed for Drama, Primary Education, Pharmacy (including an admissions test), Nursing, Social Work.

London (Birk) Some applications are made online, direct to the University. For details contact the Registry at www.bbk.ac.uk.

London (Court) History, history of art, English and modern European languages are the most relevant A-level subjects for the one BA course in History of Art, but applications will be considered from those studying other subjects. Art offered at A-level should normally include a history of art paper. The ability to read foreign languages is a particular asset. Candidates will be interviewed.

London (Gold) While offers are stipulated for courses, candidates are assessed individually and may receive an offer lower than the published grades. Some applicants are interviewed, in particular those for Art and Design degrees for which examples of current art and design work are required before interview. Applicants requiring deferred entry (which may or may not be acceptable depending on the course) should contact the admissions tutor before applying. International students applying for the BA in Design, or the MEng/BEng in Design and Innovation are asked to send photographs and explanations of their work.

London (Hey) When considering applications, Heythrop takes note of applicants' current and predicted performance at A-level, their ability to study at the relevant level, to take increasing responsibility for their own learning and their motivation to engage intellectually with issues in theology and philosophy.

London (King's) Applicants will normally have taken four AS-level subjects and pursued three of these at A-level. However, departments will also consider those who have taken five AS-levels and passed only two of these at A-level. Applicants may take all their examinations at the end of Year 13 without prejudice. Conditional offers may include the fourth AS-level, a high grade possibly compensating for a failure to obtain the right grade in one of the A-level subjects. AS and A-level general studies and critical thinking are not accepted although the grade achieved may be considered when the required grades of an offer have not been met. Deferred entry is acceptable.

London (QM) It is possible for students to join undergraduate degree programmes at the beginning of the second and sometimes the third year. Those wishing to transfer their degree studies from another UK higher education institution may be considered but should contact the subject department before applying.

London (RAc Dance) All candidates are interviewed for the BA (Hons) Ballet Education course but not for the degree and diplomas in Dance Education.

London (RH) Applicants likely to meet the entry requirements may be called for interview or invited to an Open Day. International students may be asked to submit an example of academic work or other exercise although it would be preferable if they could visit the campus. Interviews are not intended to be nerve-wracking or daunting but rather a chance to assess the candidate's potential. In Music there may be an audition, in Drama a workshop session, and in Modern Languages some conversation in the appropriate language. Candidates who fail to meet the requirements of their offer may still be offered a place, particularly if they shone at interview.

London (Royal Central Sch SpDr) All candidates are auditioned for entry, or in the case of composition are required to submit a portfolio of their work in advance. All undergraduate candidates are required to undertake musicianship and keyboard skills tests on the day of their audition.

London (RVC) Applications for deferred entry are considered but the offer conditions must be met in the same academic year as the application. Applicants holding offers from RVC who fall slightly below the grades required are always reconsidered and may be offered entry if places are available.

London (St George's) Interviews are required for most courses and admissions tests are required for some courses. Once admitted students are not allowed to change courses. Candidates will be interviewed for all courses in Medicine, Physiotherapy, Paramedic Science, Healthcare Science and Therapeutic and Diagnostic Radiography. *Most popular subjects 2013* Biomedical Science, Medicine 4yr, Medicine 5yr.

London (SOAS) Offers may be made without an interview and particular attention is paid to past and predicted academic performance. SOAS is happy to consider deferred entry, which should be stated on the UCAS application.

London (UCL) UCL welcomes applications from students proposing to spend a pre-university year engaged in constructive activity in the UK or abroad. About 9% of UCL's undergraduates take a Gap Year. Those wanting to enter the second or third year of a degree programme should make early contact with the relevant subject department to obtain approval. Applications are assessed on the basis of the personal statement, the referee's report and the predicted academic performance. UCL is one of the few universities that interviews a significant proportion of its applicants. The programme for the day varies but will include a talk about the subject, a tour of the campus, a discussion with current students and the interview itself. Interviews vary, some being subject-based, others focusing on motivation and communication skills. Decisions on admission are final and there is normally no right of appeal.

London (UCL Sch Pharm) The School looks for students who are intellectually curious, willing to study hard, and who will thrive in a small, friendly environment where the emphasis is on team work and academic achievement. All students who are based in the UK and have educational qualifications which meet or are expected to meet the entry requirements are required to attend an interview before a final decision is taken on their application. Applicants whose UCAS personal statement is aimed at a subject other than Pharmacy are recommended to write a supplementary personal statement which can be sent to the Registry once the UCAS application has been submitted.

London LSE While many other qualifications are considered in the selection of applicants, the vast majority of applicants are expected to have taken four AS-level subjects, followed by three at A-level. Applicants will not be penalised if they have not been able to take the normal number of AS and AL subjects but referees should advise on such circumstances. Applicants normally offer A-levels in LSE's preferred subjects which do not include AS/AL accounting, art and design, business studies, communication studies, design and technology, drama and theatre studies (for some departments), home economics, ICT, law, media studies, music technology, sports studies, travel and tourism. The A* grade is now used in offers for a number of degree courses – applicants should check individual degree course requirements. Competition is particularly high for the Accounting and Finance, Economics, Law, and Management courses. Predicted grades on the application will not guarantee an offer of a place. Applications are often held in a 'gathered field' (candidates are informed) and decisions made only when all on-time applications have been received. Some applicants will be asked to take an entrance examination (held in March each year), which lasts for three hours and consists of a précis of an English language text, essays on general discussion topics and tests of mathematical understanding. Sample papers are available from web pages from January to March. It is unlikely that there will be any course vacancies when A-level results are published. *Most popular subjects 2013* Accounting and Finance, Economics, Government, Law, Management, Statistics.

London Met Applicants may be required to sit a test or to submit a portfolio of work.

London NCH Students must apply to the New College of the Humanities directly rather than through UCAS, and applications can be made any time before term starts. The application form is similar to the traditional UCAS form. NCH will consider applications individually and on their merits. Decisions are quick – usually within four to six weeks. As well as personal details and academic records, applicants are required to supply a reference and piece of written work. An application to NCH can be made in addition to any application made to other universities through UCAS. All shortlisted students are interviewed. NCH accepts deferred entries for those wishing to take a Gap Year.

London South Bank Applicants not achieving the grades required for their chosen course should contact the University which may still be able to make an offer of a place. All applicants are interviewed for Nursing, Allied Health Professions and Architecture courses.

Loughborough The University does not normally differentiate between applicants taking A-levels for the first time or re-sitting subjects. Loughborough University accepts the Advanced Diploma for entry to most of its undergraduate degree programmes, consisting of the Progression Diploma in a relevant line plus an A-level in a specified or relevant subject. The University's admissions and associated policies are available on its website: www.lboro.ac.uk/admin/ar/admissions. All applicants are interviewed prior to being made an offer for courses in Aeronautical, Automotive, Manufacturing, Chemical, Civil and Building Engineering, Information Science, Design and Technology and Art and Design.

Manchester Strong examination results are the main factor in the admission of students to courses and the University accepts a wide range of qualifications. All decisions are made by the academic departments according to their individual requirements. For example, some programmes may require you to have GCSE maths at grade C or above for entry, others may require a compulsory subject at A-level. Other factors that are considered are prior and predicted grades, evidence of knowledge and commitment in your personal statement, and teacher references. Some courses may also take into account performance at interview, aptitude tests and portfolios. Where places are limited, they are offered to those eligible applicants who best meet the selection criteria and who, according to the admissions team, are most likely to benefit from their chosen course and to contribute both to their academic School and the wider University. *Most popular subjects 2013* Business Studies, Dentistry, English Literature, Law, Medicine.

Manchester Met Admissions staff look for personal statements showing evidence of the applicants' motivation and commitment to their chosen courses, work or voluntary experience relevant to any chosen career, and extra-curricular activities, achievements and interests which are relevant to the chosen courses.

Middlesex Some courses start in January (see www.mdx.uk/janstart).

Newcastle They accept a wide range of qualifications offered for degree course entry. All qualifications that are of suitable academic level will be considered. In general, offers will be made in grades, not in Tariff points. *Most popular subjects 2013* Medicine, Law, Business Management, Biomedical Sciences.

Newman Applicants are advised to submit an accurate and well-presented application. Personal statements are applicants' chance to shine, show their qualities and convince admission tutors why they should offer them a place.

Northampton Achievement in Key Skills units counts towards the final UCAS Tariff points score.

Northumbria Interviews are compulsory for courses in Architecture, most courses in Art and Design and courses in Health and Teaching. There are no admissions tests.

Nottingham Although grade predictions may match the offers published for the course there is no guarantee that an offer can be made. There are a number of new courses for 2014 including a new environmental geoscience course in the School of Geography, an accountancy course in the School of Business, a sports rehabilitation and exercise course in the Division of Physiotherapy, two new criminology courses in the School of Sociology and three new courses in the Department of Theology. *Most popular subjects 2013* Economics, Medicine, Veterinary Medicine.

Nottingham Trent The UCAS personal statement is seen as a key part of the application process; the University website provides a guide on its possible content and preparation.

Open University There are no formal entry qualifications for admission to courses. See also **Chapter 1**.

Oxford Entrance requirements range from A*A*A to AAA depending on the course. There are specific subject requirements for some courses, particularly in the sciences. Once any subject requirements are met, any other subjects at A-level are acceptable for admission purposes with the exception of general studies (and both general studies and critical thinking for Medicine). It is generally recommended that students take those subjects which they enjoy the most and those in which they are most likely to achieve top grades. However, as the selection criteria for Oxford University are entirely academic, it is also a good idea for students to consider how best they can demonstrate their academic abilities in their choice of subjects. Admissions tests and written work are often part of the application process. Other equivalent qualifications such as Scottish Advanced Highers, American APs and the International Baccalaureate are also very welcome. Please see www.ox.ac.uk/enreqs for further details. In many subjects, students are required to take an admissions test as part of their application. It is the candidate's responsibility to make sure that they are registered. There are full details at www.ox.ac.uk/tests. For further details contact our website www.ox.ac.uk/study or contact the Admissions Information Centre on 01875 288000 or study@ox.ac.uk.

Oxford Brookes For all applications, considerable emphasis is placed on the personal statement. Fine Art applicants wishing to take a Gap Year should contact the admissions tutor before applying.

Plymouth The University looks for evidence in the UCAS personal statement of your understanding of the course, good numeracy and literacy skills, motivation and commitment, work experience or placement or voluntary work, especially if it is relevant to your course, any sponsorships or placements you have applied for, and your possible plans for a Gap Year.

Portsmouth Decisions on offers are made by the following academic departments: Creative and Cultural Industries, Humanities, Portsmouth Business School, Science and Technology. For some courses, applicants will be expected to attend an interview as part of the selection process. The University accepts the principle of credit transfer and, wherever possible, recognition will be given to prior learning in order to facilitate admission with advanced standing. The Extended Project is not a requirement but may be taken into consideration.

Queen's Belfast Applications for admission to full-time undergraduate courses are made through UCAS, except for courses in Midwifery and Nursing. These should be made direct to the University's School of Nursing and Midwifery (see www.qub.ac.uk). Interviews are essential for Medicine and Dentistry.

Reading Approximately 80% of decisions on applications to undergraduate study are made by the central Admissions Office and 20% of decisions are recommended to the Admissions Office by academic departments/schools. This is agreed on an annual basis according to the requirements of the school or department. In all cases, the criteria on which successful applicants are admitted is agreed with the academic admissions tutor of the relevant school or department, who also maintains oversight of decisions during the year and will be involved in decisions on specific cases. Candidates are interviewed for Accounting and Business, Art, Chemistry, Education, Film and Theatre, Food and Nutritional Sciences, Graphic Communication, Meteorology, Pharmacy and Psychology. Typical offers are presented in terms of A-level grades (or in a few cases UCAS Tariff points), but applications are welcomed from those presenting a wide range of qualifications. For some courses, selection criteria will include interview, portfolio submission or attendance at a selection centre. *Most popular subjects 2013* Biological Sciences, Law, Maths.

Robert Gordon Interviews are held for some courses, for example Social Work.

Roehampton Applicants successfully achieving the new Level 3 Advanced Diplomas will be considered for entry onto degrees in closely related subjects. For entry to other subjects, each application will be judged taking the applicant's entire academic record into account and on its own merit.

St Andrews The University highlights the importance of the personal statement and the quality of this is likely to decide which applicants receive offers. It looks for well-organised, well-written statements which include information about the applicants, their interests, relevant work experience, any voluntary work, ideas about career choice and, importantly, their reasons for their choice of course. Admissions tutors prefer candidates to achieve their grades at the first sitting. Apart from Medicine and Gateway to Physics, no candidates are interviewed.

St Mark and St John The University welcomes applications from students with disabilities, who are well catered for on campus. *Most popular subjects 2013* Primary Education, Secondary Education with Physical Education.

St Mary's Offers are made through the University Registry. Students for over-subscribed courses or programmes of a practical or professional nature may be called for interview and may be required to take tests.

Salford The University is committed to widening participation but it does not make lower offers on the basis of educational or social disadvantage.

Sheffield The University considers qualifications already achieved (including GCSEs), predicted grades and personal statements as the most important parts of an application. Interviews are not a prerequisite of admission; however, some departments do interview to further assess the motivation and personal qualities of applicants. Departments that interview include Medicine, Dentistry, Orthoptics and Human Communication Science (for Speech Science). The Applicant Information Desk (AiD) provides a first point of contact for people who have applied to the University. AiD can help with any questions applicants have about the process of applying to Sheffield and the current status of their application. More information, including contact details, can be found at www.sheffield.ac.uk/aid. (See also Medical Admissions information in **Chapter 8**.)

South Wales Applicants for courses in Art and Design, Teacher Training and Social Work are interviewed. Key Skills points can contribute to the overall Tariff point requirement.

Southampton The University looks for a well-considered personal statement, focusing on your reasons for choosing a particular course, the skills you would bring to it, information about any relevant work experience, your career ideas, your personal interests related to the course, and your thoughts about 'what makes you stand out in a crowd'.

Southampton Solent Admissions staff look for applicants' reasons for their course choice, and for evidence of their abilities and ambitions.

Staffordshire The University provides an online workbook to help applicants prepare their personal statements.

Stirling Admissions are administered through a central office. It is essential to include in the personal statement your reasons for choosing your specified course. The University also looks for evidence of your transferable skills, for example communication skills, teamwork, and how you acquired these, for example through work experience, voluntary work, academic studies, hobbies and general life experience. *Most popular subjects 2013* Nursing and Primary Education.

Stranmillis (UC) Candidates for teacher training courses will be called for interview.

Strathclyde Formal interviews are required for some vocational courses; informal interviews are held by some Science and Engineering courses.

Sunderland The University holds informal interviews for certain courses, when applicants will be asked to present their portfolio, or to give an audition, or to talk about themselves and why they want to study for that particular course.

Surrey The University is willing to consider deferring an application for one year, providing it considers that this will benefit the applicant's studies. Contact the admissions staff if you are considering deferred entry.

Sussex Apart from Social Work and Medicine, interviews at Sussex are increasingly unusual, but some departments may ask for examples of written work or for an additional reference. Mature students submitting a strong application but without the relevant qualifications will probably be asked to attend an interview and submit an essay of up to 1500 words on their chosen subject.

Swansea Selectors take into account the candidate's ability to contribute to the cultural, sporting and social life of the University.

Teesside Interviews are held for a wide range of courses, and successful applicants are given an individualised offer. Each course accepts a minimum of 20 UCAS Tariff points for Level 3 Key Skills.

Trinity Saint David The University guarantees to give equal consideration to all applicants irrespective of when their applications are received. Applicants who successfully complete the residential Wales Summer School at Lampeter, Aberystwyth or Carmarthen are offered a place on an appropriate course of study on completion of their current school or college course. All other candidates will be invited to an interview to discuss their course choice. Entry is based on individual merit.

Trinity Saint David (Swansea) For many courses an interview is an important part of the selection process.

Ulster Applicants seeking admission to any of the following courses should use the University's direct entry form: BSc courses in Community Nursing, Specialist Nursing Practice, Nursing Sciences, and Health Sciences. *Most popular subjects 2013* Accounting, Law, Marketing, Social Work and Sociology.

Univ Law Applications are submitted through UCAS.

Warwick The University welcomes the introduction of the A* grade and is monitoring developments. Students taking the Advanced Diploma will be considered if they are taking subjects closely aligned to the chosen degree courses, and they must also take appropriate additional specialised learning options; they are advised to contact the admissions team before making their application. Advice on the completion of the application is available on www.warwick.ac.uk/go/study. Feedback can be provided if requested for candidates whose application has been rejected. The University welcomes applications for deferred entry in most subjects except for Mathematics and English, in which there is intense competition. Applicants are recommended to maintain and sharpen their competence in the subject during their year out.

West London The University accepts each of the new 14–19 Diplomas as qualification for entry on to all of its undergraduate courses, providing the UCAS Tariff points achieved by applicants match or exceed the UCAS Tariff points listed in the course entry requirements. The University welcomes applicants with the Extended Project, and offers an Extended Project module to students in Years 12 and 13 in the school holidays. It is also possible to transfer credits achieved at another university to a course at this University.

West Scotland Admissions are undertaken by the central office for Engineering, Business, Social Sciences, Computing and Science courses only. Applications to Nursing and Midwifery courses are not made through UCAS but through the Centralised Applications to Nursing and Midwifery Training Clearing House (CATCH): contact the University for details. Interviews are held for applicants for Education, Social Work, Computer Animation, Sports, Engineering (L9), Creative and Cultural Industries, Health, Nursing and Midwifery. These departments will make the decisions independently of the central office.

Westminster Interviews are usually only required for Media, Art and Design and Complementary Therapy courses. The University accepts transfers into Years 1, 2 or 3 of a full-time degree programme if students have studied similar units to the chosen Westminster course, and have passed Year 1 and Year 2, each with 120 credits.

Winchester The following programmes require applicants to take a second subject at Year 1: Childhood, Youth and Community Studies; Education Studies; Education Studies (Early Childhood); Film Studies; Media Studies; Politics and Global Studies; Psychology; Theology and Religious Studies. Second subjects can be contrasting or complementary. Interviews are required for courses in Teaching, Performing Arts and Social Work.

Wolverhampton Admissions staff make decisions on the basis of the application, and may invite applicants for interview or audition. If an applicant cannot meet the entry requirements for the chosen course, the University may offer an alternative course, or give the applicant feedback about why it was unable to offer a place.

Worcester The University advises applicants to consider their personal statements carefully. It advises them to include their reasons for their choice of degree programme, their career plans, their outside interests and work experience, and any other information they consider relevant. Applicants who are not accepted are not necessarily rejected; they may receive a 'changed programme' offer which they need not accept if they prefer to enter Clearing.

York Decisions on offers are made in the following ways. Centralised decision making: Archaeology, Economics, Education, History, History of Art, Language and Linguistic Science, PEP, Philosophy, Politics, Psychology, Social Policy, Social and Political Sciences, Sociology. Semi-centralised decision making: Law, Mathematics, Physics. Devolved decision making in academic departments: Biology, Biochemistry, Chemistry, Computer Science, Electronics, English, Environment, Hull York Medical School, Music, Nursing and Midwifery, Social Work, Theatre Film and Television. The most popular courses are English, Health Sciences, History and Law. Education and Law receive the lowest applications. All candidates are interviewed for Biology, Chemistry, Health Sciences, Law, Medicine and Social Work.

York St John Interviews are compulsory for the following courses: Counselling, Fine Art, Occupational Therapy, Physiotherapy, Primary Education and Product Design.

OXFORD
INTERNATIONAL
COLLEGE

A-Level Study & Retake Courses

Oxford International College offers a home for all. Over the past 12 years the College has created a thriving international community of students. British students benefit greatly from studying with peers from different cultures, and the College prides itself on an extra-curricular programme that enriches students' lives, expanding their horizons and developing their ability to move forward confidently into the world of university and careers.

- Full A-Levels and A-Level retake programmes
- Small groups or individual tuition with Oxford's finest tutors
- Registered examination centre for all British exam boards
- Exam resit places for external candidates
- University preparation, entrance tests and interview practice

Small Group Focus in High Level Study

The College's success is based in offering small group tuition of the highest standard. Students are encouraged to achieve highly at A-Level and move forward to the best universities. Groups, however, remain flexible with a wide choice of subjects on offer. All the while, we ensure that combinations selected will meet the standards top universities expect and that our students are competitive and meet the ever more demanding challenge of university entry with success. There is also provision for individual tuition, and we always aim to help students with any individual needs they may have.

Exceeding Expectations
'Exceeds Expectations' in all categories
Independent School Inspectorate

5

APPLICATIONS

ENTRY REQUIREMENTS

Before applying to universities and colleges, be sure that you have the required subjects and qualifications for entry to your chosen course. Details of entry requirements are available direct from the universities and colleges. You will need to check:

(i) the general entry requirements for courses

(ii) any specific subject requirements to enter a particular course, for example, study of specified GCE A and/or AS-levels, Scottish Highers/Advanced Highers, GCSEs, Scottish Nationals, or BTEC qualifications (for example, Diploma, Certificate). The course requirements are set out in prospectuses and on websites

(iii) any age, health, Disclosure and Barring Service (DBS; formerly CRB) clearance or other requirements for entry to particular courses and universities and colleges. For entry to some specific courses such as Medicine and Nursing, offers are made subject to health screening for hepatitis B, for example, and immunisation requirements. Owing to government regulations, some universities will insist on a minimum age at entry of 18 years. Check university and college websites and prospectuses for these particular course requirements

(iv) admissions tests required by a number of universities for a range of subjects, including Dentistry, Law, Medicine and Veterinary Science/Medicine. Offers of places made by these universities are dependent on an applicant's performance in the relevant test. It is important to find out full details about universities' course requirements for possible admissions tests well before submitting the UCAS application and to make all the necessary arrangements for registering and taking any required admissions tests. See **Chapter 6** and check university/college and admissions tests websites for the latest information.

Potential applicants should ask the advice of teachers, careers advisers and university and college advisers before submitting their application.

APPLICATIONS FOR UNIVERSITY AND COLLEGE COURSES THROUGH UCAS

UCAS, the organisation responsible for managing applications to higher education courses in the UK, deals with applications for admission to full-time and sandwich first degrees, Foundation degrees, Diploma of Higher Education and Higher National Diploma courses and some full-time Higher National Certificate courses in nearly all universities (but not the Open University), university colleges, colleges and institutes of higher education, specialist colleges and some further education colleges.

The UCAS application process

Full details of application procedures and all course information can be found on the UCAS website. Other information is also available in the *UCAS Guide to Getting Into University and College*.

Applications are made online at www.ucas.com using **Apply**. This is a secure web-based application system, which has been designed for all applicants whether they are applying through a UCAS-registered centre, such as a school or college, or applying independently from anywhere in the world.

Applications can be sent to UCAS from mid-September. The first deadline is 15 October for applications to the universities of Oxford or Cambridge and applications for courses in Medicine, Dentistry and Veterinary Science/Medicine. The deadline for UK and EU applicants to apply for all other courses is 15 January, except for some Art and Design courses that have a 24 March deadline. You can still apply after these deadlines up to 30 June, but institutions may not be able to consider you.

On the UCAS application, you have up to five course choices unless you are applying for Dentistry, Medicine or Veterinary Science/Medicine. For these courses only four choices are permitted.

It is important to note that some universities (for example Cambridge) now require their applicants to complete a Supplementary Application Questionnaire after they have received your UCAS application. Check the websites of your listed universities for their latest application information.

Each university or college makes any offer through the UCAS system. UCAS does not make offers, or recruit on behalf of universities and colleges. It does not advise applicants on their choice of subject although it does publish material which applicants may find useful.

Applicants may receive an 'unconditional' offer in the case of those who already hold the required qualifications, or, for those awaiting examination results, a 'conditional' offer or a rejection. When all decisions have been received from universities or colleges, applicants may finally hold up to two offers: a firm choice (first) offer and an insurance offer. Applicants who have made five choices and have no offers or have declined any offers received can use **Extra**. Applicants are told if they become eligible for **Extra** and can apply online for one further course at a time using **Track** at www.ucas.com. **Extra** runs from 25 February until 2 July. Courses available in **Extra** will be highlighted on the course search tool at www.ucas.com. Applicants not placed through this system will be eligible to contact institutions with vacancies in **Clearing** from mid-July.

If you already have your qualifications and are not waiting for any exam results, your place can be confirmed at any time after you send in your application. However, for thousands of applicants confirmation starts on the day when the A-level examination results are released. Full **Clearing** vacancy lists are also published from A-level results day (Scottish vacancy lists are published from Scottish Qualification results day). Applicants meeting the conditions of their offers for their firm choice will receive confirmation from their university or college and may still be accepted even if their results are slightly lower than those stipulated in the original offer. If rejected by their firm choice university/ college, applicants will have their places confirmed by their insurance choice institution providing they have obtained the right grades. Applicants who are unsuccessful with both their institutions will be eligible to go into **Clearing** in which they can select an appropriate course in the same or a different institution where places are available. Last year up to 55,000 applicants obtained places through **Clearing**, and nearly 8000 applicants found a place though **Extra**.

Each year some applicants pass their exams with better results than expected. This may mean that some will not only have met the conditions of their firm choice, but will have exceeded them. UCAS introduced Adjustment for these applicants – it provides an opportunity to reconsider where and what to study whilst holding a confirmed place. The Adjustment process is available from A-level results day (15 August 2015) until 31 August.

UCAS timetable

Mid-September 2014	UCAS begins accepting applications.
15 October	Deadline for UCAS to receive applications to Oxford University or the University of Cambridge, and applications to courses in Medicine, Dentistry or Veterinary Medicine/Science.
15 January 2015	Deadline for UCAS to receive applications from UK and EU applicants for all other courses, except for some Art and Design courses that have a 24 March deadline. Use the course search tool at www.ucas.com to find out whether Art and Design courses have a 15 January or 24 March deadline.
16 January–30 June	Applications received by UCAS are forwarded to the institutions for consideration at their discretion. Applications received after 30 June are processed through **Clearing**.
25 February–2 July	Applicants who have made five choices and have no offers or who have declined any offers received can use **Extra** to apply for one further course at a time on **Track** at www.ucas.com. Institutions will show which courses have vacancies in **Extra** on the UCAS website. Details of the **Extra** service will be included in *Your UCAS Welcome Guide* sent to applicants.
24 March	Deadline for UCAS to receive applications for some Art and Design courses. Use the course search tool at www.ucas.com to find out whether Art and Design courses have a 15 January or 24 March deadline.
7 May	Applicants who have received all their decisions from universities and colleges by the end of March are asked to reply to their offers by this date.
5 June	Applicants receiving decisions from all their choices by 9 May must reply to their offers by this date.

30 June	Last date for receiving applications. Applications received after this date are entered directly into **Clearing**. In mid-July **Clearing** starts.
4 August	Scottish SQA results published. Scottish Clearing vacancy lists available.
14 August	GCE A-level and AS results published. English, Welsh and Northern Ireland Clearing vacancy lists available. (See **What To Do on Results Day ... and After** below.)

PLEASE NOTE

- You are not required to reply to any university/college offers until you have received your last decision.
- Do not send a firm acceptance to more than one offer.
- Do not try to alter a firm acceptance.
- If you decide not to go to university or college this year you can go to **Track** to completely cancel your application. But don't forget, you will not be able to reapply until next year.
- Remember to tell the institutions and UCAS if you change your address, or change your examination board, subjects or arrangements.

Information on the special arrangements for applications for Law, Medicine and Dentistry can be found under separate headings in Chapter 6.

APPLICATIONS FOR ART AND DESIGN COURSES

All art and design courses use one of two application deadlines: 15 January or 24 March. The later closing date is to allow students taking a Diploma in Foundation Studies (Art and Design) time to identify their specialisation and put together a portfolio of work which they will need to present at interview. The deadline for each course is given in the UCAS search tool.

APPLICATIONS FOR MUSIC COURSES AT CONSERVATOIRES

The Conservatoires UK Admissions Service (CUKAS) handles applications for practice-based music, dance and drama courses. Applications can be made simultaneously to a maximum of six of the conservatoires listed below and simultaneous applications can also be made through both UCAS and CUKAS systems. Full details of CUKAS are given on www.cukas.ac.uk. The conservatoires taking part in this online admissions system are:

- Birmingham Conservatoire www.bcu.ac.uk/pme/conservatoire
- Leeds College of Music www.lcm.ac.uk
- Royal Academy of Music www.ram.ac.uk
- Royal College of Music www.rcm.ac.uk
- Royal Northern College of Music www.rncm.ac.uk
- Royal Conservatoire of Scotland www.rcs.ac.uk
- Royal Welsh College of Music and Drama www.rwcmd.ac.uk
- Trinity Laban Conservatoire of Music and Dance www.trinitylaban.ac.uk

APPLICATIONS FOR TEACHER TRAINING COURSES

Applicants intending to start a course of initial teacher training in England leading to Qualified Teacher Status can find information on the Get Into Teaching website www.education.gov.uk/get-into-teaching. See also www.ucas.com/ucas-teacher-training for full details of applying for undergraduate (and postgraduate) training courses. Students in Wales and Northern Ireland should also check with this website; Scottish students should check www.gtcs.org.uk.

THE UCAS APPLICATION

Two important aspects of the UCAS application concern Sections 3 and 10. In the choices section of Apply, all your university/college choices (a maximum of five) are to be listed, but remember that you should not mix your subjects. For example, in popular subject areas such as English, History or Physiotherapy, it is safer to show total commitment by applying for all courses in the same subject and not to include second and/or third subject alternatives on the form. (See advice in separate tables in **Chapter 8** for **Medicine**, **Dentistry** and **Veterinary Science/Medicine**.)

A brief glance at the subject tables in **Chapter 8** will give you some idea of the popularity of various courses. In principle, institutions want the best applicants available so if there are large numbers of applicants the offers made will be higher. For Medicine and a number of other courses, offers in terms of A-level grades are now reaching AAA or A* grades, and often with additional AS-levels. Conversely, for the less popular subjects such as Chemistry or Manufacturing Engineering, the offers can be much lower – down to CCC.

Similarly, some institutions are more popular (not necessarily better) than others. Again, this popularity can be judged easily in the tables in **Chapter 8**: the higher the offer, the more popular the institution. Popular universities often are located in attractive towns or cities such as Bristol, Exeter, Warwick, Bath or York. Additionally, some institutions have established a good 'reputation' for various reasons, for example, Oxford, Cambridge and Durham. Conversely and unfortunately, some universities have confused applicants with unfamiliar names and no immediate identity as to their location, such as De Montfort and Brunel. More students would apply to these excellent institutions if they knew where they were situated! Because of the intense competition for places at the popular universities, applications to five of them could result in rejections from all of them! (If you are not good enough for one of them you won't be good enough for the other four!) Spread your choice of institutions.

When you have chosen your courses and your institutions, look again at the offers made and compare these with the grades projected by your teachers. It is most important to maximise your chances of a place by choosing institutions which might make you a range of offers. When all universities have considered your application you can hold only two offers (one firm and one insurance offer) and naturally it is preferable for one to be lower than the other in case you do not achieve the offer grades or equivalent points for your first choice of university or college.

The other section of the UCAS application that deserves careful thought is Section 10 (the personal statement). This seems simple enough but it is the only part of the application where you can put in a personal bid for a place! In short, you are asked to give relevant background information about yourself, your interests and your choice of course and career. Give yourself plenty of time to prepare your personal statement – if you have a Record of Achievement you could use it as a guide – as this part of your application could make all the difference to getting an offer or not.

Motivation to undertake your chosen course is very important. You can show this by giving details of any work experience and work shadowing you have done (and for History courses, for example, details of visits to places of historical interest). It is a good idea to begin your statement with such evidence and explain how your interest in your chosen subject has developed. In the subject tables in **Chapter 8** under **Advice to applicants and planning the UCAS personal statement**, advice is given on what you might include in your personal statement. You should also include various activities in which you have been involved in the last three or four years. Get your parents and other members of the family to refresh your memory – it is easy to forget something quite important. You might consider planning out this section in a series of sub-sections – and if you have a lot to say, be brief. The sub-sections can include the following.

- **School activities** Are you a prefect, chairperson or treasurer of a society? Are you involved in supervisory duties of any kind? Are you in a school team? Which team? For how long? (Remember, team means any team: sports, chess, debating, even business.)
- **Intellectual activities** Have you attended any field or lecture courses in your main subjects? Where? When? Have you taken part in any school visits? Do you play in the school orchestra or have you taken part in a school drama production – on or off stage? Do you go to the theatre, art galleries or concerts?
- **Out-of-school activities** This category might cover many of the topics above, but it could also include any community or voluntary work you do, or Duke of Edinburgh's Awards, the Combined Cadet Force (CCF), sport, music and drama activities etc. The countries you have visited might also be mentioned – for example, any exchange visits with friends living abroad.
- **Work experience** Details of part-time, holiday or Saturday jobs could be included here, particularly if they have some connection with your chosen course. Some applicants plan ahead and arrange to visit firms and discuss career interests with various people who already work in their chosen field. For some courses such as Veterinary Science, work experience is essential, and it certainly helps for others, for example Medicine and Business courses.

- **Key Skills** These cover numeracy, communication and information technology (the basics) and also advanced skills involving teamwork, problem solving and improving your own learning. If you are not offering the Key Skills Certificate then evidence of your strengths in these areas may be mentioned in the school or college reference or you may include examples in your personal statement relating to your out-of-school activities.

Finally, plan your personal statement carefully. You may write short statements if you wish. It is not essential to write in prose except perhaps if you are applying for English or language courses in which case your statement will be judged grammatically! Take a copy to use as a trial and a copy of your complete application to keep for reference if you are called for interview. Almost certainly you will be questioned on what you have written.

Admissions tutors always stress the importance of the confidential report from your head teacher or form tutors. Most schools and colleges will make some effort to find out why you want to apply for a particular course, but if they do not ask, do not take it for granted that they will know! Consequently, although you have the opportunity to write about your interests on the form, it is still a good idea to tell your teachers about them. Also, if you have to work at home under difficult conditions or if you have any medical problems, your teachers must be told since these points should be mentioned on the report.

Deferred entry

Although application is usually made in the autumn of the year preceding the proposed year of entry, admissions tutors may be prepared to consider an application made two years before entry, so that the applicant can, perhaps, gain work experience or spend a period abroad. Policies on deferred entry may differ from department to department, so you should check with admissions tutors before applying. Simply remember that there is no guarantee that you will get the grades you need or a place at the university of your first choice at the first attempt! If not, you may need to repeat A-levels and try again. It may be better not to apply for deferred entry until you are certain in August of your grades and your place.

APPLICATIONS TO THE UNIVERSITY OF CAMBRIDGE

If you are a UK or EU applicant, you need only complete the UCAS application. You will then receive an email from the University, confirming the arrival of your application and giving you the website address of their online Supplementary Application Questionnaire (SAQ) which you will then need to complete and return by the specified date. Check with the Admissions Office or on www.study.cam.ac.uk/undergraduate/apply for the latest information.

Your UCAS application listing Cambridge as one of your university choices must be sent to UCAS by 15 October. If you are applying for Medicine or Veterinary Medicine you must include your BMAT registration with your application. You can indicate your choice of college or make an Open application if you have no preference. Open applicants are allocated by a computer program to colleges that have had fewer applicants per place for your chosen subject.

The Extenuating Circumstances Form (ECF) has been designed to ensure that the Cambridge colleges have the information they require in order to accurately assess any applicant who has experienced particular personal or educational disadvantage through health, personal problems, disability or difficulties with schooling. The ECF should normally be submitted by the applicant's school/college by 15 October. Further detail can be obtained at www.study.cam.ac.uk/undergraduate/apply/ecf.html.

Interviews take place in Cambridge in the first three weeks of December, although some may be a little earlier. Many of the University's colleges use tests as part of the selection process for specific courses and written work also may be requested before interview. This practice, however, varies between colleges and subjects. See the University website and **Chapter 6** for information you need to know before completing and submitting your application.

In January applicants receive either an offer conditional upon certain grades in examinations to be taken the following summer, or a rejection. Alternatively, you may be placed in a pool for further consideration. Decisions are made on the basis of academic record, reference, personal statement, submitted work/test results and interviews. The conditions set are grades to be obtained in examinations such as A-levels, Scottish Highers/Advanced Highers or the International Baccalaureate. Offers made by some Cambridge colleges may also include Sixth Term Examination Papers (STEP) in mathematics (see **Chapter 6** under

Mathematics). The STEPs are taken in June and copies of past papers and full details are available from www.admissionstestingservice.org.

College policies

All colleges which admit undergraduates use the selection procedures described in **Chapter 6**. However, there will be some minor variations between the various colleges, within each college and also between subjects. Further information about the policies of any particular college can be found in the Cambridge Undergraduate Prospectus and may also be obtained from the admissions tutor of the college concerned. No college operates a quota system for any subject except Medicine and Veterinary Medicine, for which there are strict quotas for the University from which places are allocated to each college.

Full details of the admissions procedures are contained in the current Cambridge Undergraduate Prospectus. Copies of the prospectus are available from Cambridge Admissions Office, Fitzwilliam House, 32 Trumpington Street, Cambridge CB2 1QY, or via the website www.study.cam.ac.uk/undergraduate.

APPLICATIONS TO THE UNIVERSITY OF OXFORD

Oxford University offers a wealth of resources and opportunities to students, including highly personalised teaching in tutorials, where two or three students meet to discuss their work with a tutor. The college system is also a key advantage of an Oxford education, as students gain all the benefits of studying at a large and internationally acclaimed university, as well as the benefits of life in the smaller college community.

Applications for undergraduate courses at Oxford are made through UCAS in the same way as applications to other UK universities but candidates must submit their application by 15 October for entry in the following year.

You can only apply to one undergraduate course at Oxford. You can also express a preference for a particular college if you wish, or you can make an Open application. This is just like saying that you don't mind which college you go to and your application will then be allocated to a college which has relatively fewer applications for your subject in that year. The colleges have far more in common than they have differences, and all offer the same high standard of academic teaching and support, so please do not worry too much about college choice.

Applicants for most courses are required to sit a written test as part of their application, or to submit examples of their written work. See **Chapter 6** for more information and www.ox.ac.uk/apply for full details. Separate registration is required for any tests, so it's really important to check the details for your subject in good time.

When considering your application, tutors will take into account all the information that has been provided, in order to assess your suitability and potential for your chosen course. This includes your academic record, personal statement, academic reference and predicted grades, along with any written tests or written work required. If you haven't done particularly well in one area, you may still be successful if you have performed strongly in other aspects of your application. Each application is considered carefully on its individual merits, including contextual information about candidates' educational background.

A shortlist of the very best candidates will be invited to Oxford for interview, which is an important part of the selection procedure. Candidates will usually be interviewed at their college of preference and also may be interviewed by other colleges. Those from outside Europe who are not able to travel may be interviewed by telephone or Skype or some other remote means. The University works hard to ensure that the best candidates are successful, whichever college you have applied to. Any college may make you an offer of a place.

Successful candidates who have not completed their school-leaving examinations will be made conditional offers based on final grades. This will be probably be between A*A*A and AAA at A-level, 38–40 points in the International Baccalaureate, including core points, or other equivalent qualifications. Decisions are notified to candidates via UCAS by the end of January.

To find out more

The University holds three Open Days a year: two in late June or early July, and one in mid-September. These are highly recommended as a great way to visit the city and the University, meet tutors and current students and find out more. Visit the website at www.ox.ac.uk/study for further information, and details of other events around the UK and beyond.

APPLICATIONS TO IRISH UNIVERSITIES

All applications to universities in the Republic of Ireland are made through the Central Application Office, Tower House, Eglinton Street, Galway, Ireland; see www.cao.ie or telephone 091 509 800. The Central Application Office website gives full details of all 44 institutions and details of the application procedure. Applications are made by 1 February. Individual institutions publish details of their entry requirements for courses, but unlike applications through UCAS in the UK, no conditional offers are made. Applicants are judged purely on their academic ability except for the Royal College of Surgeons which also requires a school reference and a personal statement. The results are published in August when institutions make their offers and when successful students are required to accept or decline the offer.

APPLICATIONS TO COMMONWEALTH UNIVERSITIES

Details of universities in 38 commonwealth countries (all charge fees) are published on www.acu.ac.uk or for those in Australia, on www.australia.idp.com, and for those in Canada, www.studyincanada.com.

APPLICATIONS TO AMERICAN UNIVERSITIES

There are over 2000 universities and colleges offering degree course programmes in the USA; some institutions are independent and others state-controlled. Unlike the UK, however, where UCAS control nearly all university and college applications, it is necessary to apply separately to all American universities. Most American universities will expect applicants to have A-levels or IB qualifications and in addition, usually require students to complete a School Assessment Test (SAT) covering mathematical and verbal reasoning abilities. In some cases applicants may be required to take SAT II tests which are based on specific subjects. Tests can be taken at centres in the UK: see www.collegeboard.org.

Unlike the usual specialised subject degrees at UK universities, 'Liberal Arts programmes' in the USA have considerable breadth and flexibility, although subjects requiring greater specialised knowledge such as Medicine and Law require further study at Medical or Law School.

Because of the complexities of an application to American universities, such as financial implications, visas etc, students should initially refer to www.fulbright.co.uk. It is also important to be able to identify the differences between and the quality of institutions and valuable guides can be sourced through www.petersons.com.

THE ERASMUS PROGRAMME

Many universities in the UK have formal agreements with partner institutions in Europe through the Erasmus programme which enables UK university students to apply for courses in Europe for periods up to one year. Some of these courses are taught in English and students can receive help with accommodation and other expenses through the Erasmus Student Grant scheme.

The Erasmus programme is for undergraduates in all subject areas who would like to study or do a work placement for three to 12 months as part of their degree course in one of 30 other European countries. Most universities offer it although it is not available with every course so students are advised to check with their chosen universities before making an application. Students do not pay any fees to the European university they visit and those who go for the full academic year (24 weeks) have their UK tuition fees waived.

AND FINALLY ... BEFORE YOU SEND IN YOUR APPLICATION

CHECK that you have passes at grade C or higher in the GCSE (or equivalent) subjects required for the course at the institutions to which you are applying. FAILURE TO HAVE THE RIGHT GCSE SUBJECTS OR THE RIGHT NUMBER OF GRADE C PASSES OR HIGHER IN GCSE WILL RESULT IN A REJECTION.

CHECK that you are taking (or have taken) the GCE A and AS-level (or equivalent) subjects required for the course at the institution to which you are applying. FAILURE TO BE TAKING OR HAVE TAKEN THE RIGHT A-LEVELS WILL ALSO RESULT IN A REJECTION.

CHECK that the GCE A-levels and other qualifications you are taking will be accepted for the course for which you are applying. Some subjects and institutions do not stipulate any specific A-levels, only that you are required to offer two or three subjects at GCE A-level. In the view of some admissions tutors NOT ALL GCE A-LEVELS CARRY THE SAME WEIGHT (see **Chapter 1**).

CHECK that you can meet the requirements for all relevant admissions/interview tests.

CHECK that you have made all the necessary arrangements for sitting any required admissions tests.

CHECK that you can meet any age, health and DBS requirements for entry to your listed courses.

WHAT TO DO ON RESULTS DAY … AND AFTER

BE AT HOME! Do not arrange to be away when your results are published. If you do not achieve the grades you require, you will need to follow an alternative course of action and make decisions that could affect your life during the next few years. Do not expect others to make these decisions for you. If you achieve the grades or points which have been offered you will receive confirmation of a place, but this may take a few days to reach you. Once your place is confirmed contact the accommodation office at the university or college and inform them that you will need a place in a hall of residence or other accommodation.

If you achieve grades or points higher than your conditional firm (CF) choice you can reconsider where and what to study by registering with UCAS to use the **Adjustment** process in Track. This is available from A-level results day until 31 August and you have five days to register and secure an alternative course. You must check very carefully all the **Adjustment** information on the UCAS website (www.ucas.com) before changing your CF choice to make sure you are eligible and that a vacancy is available. There is no guarantee of a vacancy on a course you are aiming for, and it is very unlikely that competitive courses will have places. If you decide definitely to change courses advise the university or college immediately, but check with www.ucas.com and your school/college adviser for the latest information.

If your grades or points are higher than you expected and you are not holding any offers you can telephone or email the admissions tutor at the universities and colleges which rejected you and request that they might reconsider you.

If you just miss your offers then telephone or email the universities and colleges to see if they can still offer you a place. ALWAYS HAVE YOUR UCAS REFERENCE NUMBER AVAILABLE WHEN YOU CALL. Their decisions may take a few days. You should check the universities and colleges in your order of preference. Your first choice must reject you before you contact your second choice.

If you have not applied to any university or college earlier in the year then you can apply through the **Clearing** scheme which runs from the middle of July. Check the tables in **Chapter 8** to identify which institutions normally make offers matching your results, then telephone or email the institution to see if they have any vacancies before completing your **Clearing** form.

If you learn finally that you do not have a place because you have missed the grades in your offer you will receive automatically a **Clearing** form to enable you to re-apply. Before you complete this form follow the instructions above.

If an institution has vacancies they will ask you for your grades. If they can consider you they will ask you for your **Clearing** form. You can only be considered by one institution at a time.

If you have to re-apply for a place, check the vacancies on the UCAS website (www.ucas.com), in the national press and through your local careers office. If there are vacancies in your subject, check with the university or college that these vacancies have not been taken.

REMEMBER – There are many thousands of students just like you. Admissions tutors have a mammoth task checking how many students will be taking up their places since not all students whose grades match their offers finally decide to do so!

IF YOU HAVE AN OFFER AND THE RIGHT GRADES BUT ARE NOT ACCEPTING THAT OR AN ALTERNATIVE PLACE – TELL THE UNIVERSITY OR COLLEGE. Someone else is waiting for your place! If you are applying for a place through **Clearing** it may even be late September before you know you have a place so BE PATIENT AND STAY CALM!

Good luck!

6 | ADMISSIONS TESTS, SELECTION OF APPLICANTS AND INTERVIEWS

The selection of applicants by universities and colleges takes many forms. However, with rising numbers of applicants for places (especially in the popular subjects) and increasing numbers of students with high grades, greater importance is now attached not only to applicants' predicted A-level grades and GCSE attainments, but also to other aspects of their applications, especially the school reference and the personal statement and, for some courses and some institutions, performance at interview, and performance in admissions tests.

ADMISSIONS TESTS

Admissions tests are now increasingly used for undergraduate entry to specific courses and specific institutions. These include national subject-based tests such as LNAT, BMAT and UKCAT (see below) which are used for selecting applicants for entry to specified courses at particular institutions in subjects such as Law, Medicine, Dentistry and Veterinary Sciences. Admissions tests are also set by individual universities and colleges (or commercial organisations on their behalf) for entry, again, to particular courses in the individual institutions. Examples of these include the Thinking Skills Assessment (TSA) used by, for example, many Cambridge University colleges, and the Health Professions Aptitude Test (HPAT) used by Ulster University for entry to some health-related courses. Other examples include the subject-based admissions tests used by many universities and colleges for entry to particular courses in subjects such as Art, Dance, Construction, Design, Drama and other Performance-based courses, Education and Teacher Training, Economics, Engineering, Journalism, Languages, Music, Nursing and Social Work.

Admissions tests are usually taken before or at interview and, except for courses requiring auditions or portfolio inspections, they are generally timed, unseen, written, or online tests. They can be used on their own, or alongside other selection methods used by university and college admissions staff, including:

- questionnaires or tests to be completed by applicants prior to interview and/or offer
- examples of school work to be submitted prior to interview and/or offer
- written tests at interview
- mathematical tests at interview
- practical tests at interview
- a response to a passage at interview
- performance-based tests (for example, for Music, Dance, Drama).

Applicants should find out early from university prospectuses and websites whether admissions tests are required for entry to their preferred courses, and if so, what these will be, and the arrangements for taking them. This is important, especially for Oxford and Cambridge applicants as many of their courses and colleges also require submission of marked written work done in Years 12 or 13 at school or college.

Here is a list of commonly used admissions tests, and this is followed by degree subject lists showing subject-based and individual institutions' admissions tests.

English
English Literature Admissions Test (ELAT)
The ELAT is a pre-interview admissions test for applicants to English courses at the University of Oxford (see the ELAT pages on the Admissions Testing Service website www.admissionstestingservice.org).

Health Professions
Health Professions Admissions Test (HPAT)
The HPAT is used by the University of Ulster for entry to Dietetics, Occupational Therapy, Physiotherapy, Podiatry, Radiography and Speech and Language Therapies.

History
History Aptitude Test (HAT)
The HAT is a two-hour test sat by all candidates applying for History courses at Oxford University (see *History* below). See www.history.ox.ac.uk.

Law
Cambridge Law Test
This is a new paper-based, one-hour, one-question test designed and used by most of the Cambridge University colleges with Law applicants who are called for interview. No prior knowledge of law is required for the test. See http://ba.law.com.ac.uk/applying/cambridge_law_test for full details.

National Admissions Test for Law (LNAT)
The LNAT is an on-screen test for applicants to specified undergraduate Law programmes at the Birmingham, Bristol, Durham, Glasgow, London (King's), London (UCL), Nottingham and Oxford universities. (See *Law* below, and **Law** in the subject tables in **Chapter 8**.) Applicants need to check universities' websites and the LNAT website (www.lnat.ac.uk) for the UCAS codes for courses requiring applicants to sit the LNAT. (**NB** Cambridge does not now require Law applicants to take the LNAT but see above and the Cambridge entry under *Law* below.) Details of LNAT (which includes multiple-choice and essay questions), practice papers, registration dates, test dates, test centres and fees are all available on the LNAT website.

Mathematics
Sixth Term Examination Paper (STEP)
Applicants with offers for Mathematics courses at Cambridge and Warwick universities are usually required to take STEP. Bristol and Oxford Universities, and Imperial London also encourage applicants for their Mathematics courses to take STEP. For details, see the STEP pages on the Admissions Testing Service website (www.admissionstestingservice.org).

Medicine, Dentistry, Veterinary Science/Medicine, and related subjects
Most medical schools require applicants to sit the UK Clinical Aptitude Test (UKCAT) or the BioMedical Admissions Test (BMAT) or, for graduate entry, the Graduate Australian Medical Schools Admissions Test (GAMSAT) for specified Medicine courses. Applicants are advised to check the websites of all universities and medical schools offering Medicine for their latest admissions requirements, including admissions and aptitude tests, to check the UKCAT website www.ukcat.ac.uk or the BMAT pages on www.admissionstestingservice.org (and for graduate entry www.gamsat.co.uk) for the latest information.

The BioMedical Admissions Test (BMAT)
This is a pen-and-paper admissions test taken by undergraduate applicants to specified Medicine, Veterinary Science/Medicine courses at Cambridge and Oxford universities, and at Imperial London, London (RVC) and London (UCL). Imperial London also requires BMAT for entry to Biomedical Science, and Pharmacology with Translational Medical Science; BMAT is also a requirement for entry to Biomedical Sciences at Oxford University. A list of the courses requiring BMAT is available on the BMAT pages of the Admissions Testing Service website (www.admissionstestingservice.org) and also on university websites and in their prospectuses. It is important to note BMAT's early closing date for entries and also the test dates. The two-hour test consists of three sections:

- aptitude and skills
- scientific knowledge and application
- writing task.

Applicants sit the test only once and pay one entry fee no matter how many courses they apply for. However, if they re-apply to universities the following year they will need to re-take the BMAT and pay another fee. Past question papers are available (see website) and an official study guide *Preparing for the BMAT* is also available at www.pearsonschoolsandfecolleges.co.uk. Results of the BMAT are first sent to the universities, and then to the BMAT test centres. Candidates need to contact their test centres direct for their results. See *Dentistry*, *Medicine* and *Veterinary Science/Medicine* below and relevant subject tables in **Chapter 8**.

The UK Clinical Aptitude Test (UKCAT)
The UKCAT is a clinical aptitude test used by the majority of medical and dental schools in the selection of applicants for Medicine and Dentistry, alongside their existing selection processes, for undergraduate entry. The tests are not curriculum-based and do not have a science component. No revision is necessary; there is no textbook and no course of instruction. In the first instance, the UKCAT is a test of cognitive skills involving problem-solving and critical reasoning. With over 150 test centres, it is an on-screen test (not paper-based), and is marked electronically. Some bursaries are available to help towards the cost of the test. Further details (including the most recent list of universities requiring applicants to sit the UKCAT) are found on the website www.ukcat.ac.uk. See also the **Dentistry** and **Medicine** subject tables in **Chapter 8**, the entries for *Dentistry* and *Medicine* below, and **Chapter 5** for application details. See www.ukcat.ac.uk.

Modern and Medieval Languages
The Modern and Medieval Languages Test (MML)
This written test is used by the University of Cambridge for selecting applicants for entry to courses involving modern and medieval languages. See www.mml.cam.ac.uk/prospectus/undergrad/test.html.

General Admissions Test
Thinking Skills Assessment (TSA)
The TSA is a 90-minute multiple choice test consisting of 50 questions which test applicants' critical thinking and problem-solving skills. It is used at or before interview by applicants for some courses at Cambridge University by some colleges, by University College London for applicants to European Social and Political Studies, and by Oxford University for entry to several courses (see below and see the TSA web pages on www.admissionstestingservice.org).

LSE Entrance Exam
The LSE Entrance Exam is used for some applicants with non-standard backgrounds. The test is not subject or course specific and consists of English comprehension exercises, essay, questions and mathematical problems.

DEGREE SUBJECT LISTS OF UNIVERSITIES AND COLLEGES USING TESTS AND ASSESSMENTS
Many universities and colleges set their own tests for specific subjects so it is important to check the websites for your preferred institutions and courses for the latest information about their applications and selection processes. The following list provides a guide to the subjects and institutions requiring admissions tests and other forms of assessment.

Accountancy
Lancaster (Acc, Audt Fin) Ernst & Young assessment.
Reading (Acc Bus) Successful candidates at the interview stage will be sent a supplementary application form and an invitation to an assessment day. This is jointly run by the Henley Business School and PwC at the Whiteknights campus in Reading. The assessment centre will involve psychometric testing, a group assessment exercise and a formal interview.

Anglo Saxon, Norse and Celtic
Cambridge *Interview only:* Fitzwilliam, Girton, Murray Edwards, St Edmund's, St John's; *Test at interview:* Hughes Hall, Lucy Cavendish, Wolfson; *School/college essays:* all other colleges offering the subject. Check www.cam.ac.uk/admissions/undergraduate/apply/tests.

Animal Management
Kirklees (Coll) Mature applicants screening test.

Anthropology
Cambridge See **Archaeology**.
Oxford See **Archaeology**.

Arabic
Oxford Language aptitude or translation test.
Salford (Arbc Engl Transl Interp – for native speakers of Arabic) Applicants may be required to sit Arabic or English language tests.

Archaeology
Bournemouth Test for mature applicants.
Cambridge (Arch Anth) *Interview only:* Jesus; *College-set essay:* Newnham, Peterhouse, St Catharine's; *Test at interview:* Clare, Emmanuel, Girton, Hughes Hall, King's, Lucy Cavendish, Robinson, St Edmunds; *Preparatory study/assignment before interview:* Churchill, Robinson, Trinity; *School/college essays:* Christ's, Churchill, Corpus Christi, Downing, Fitzwilliam, Gonville and Caius, Homerton, Magdalene, Murray Edwards, Pembroke, Queens', Robinson, St John's, Selwyn, Sidney Sussex, Trinity Hall. Check www.cam.ac.uk/admissions/undergraduate/apply/tests.
Oxford (Arch Anth) Two recent marked essays are required, preferably in different subjects, plus a statement of no more than 300 words setting out your understanding of the relations between archaeology and social, cultural and biological anthropology required before interview. No written test at interview. Check www.admissions.ox.ac.uk/tests. (Class Arch Anc Hist) Two recent marked essays are required. No written test at interview. Check www.admissions.ox.ac.uk/tests.

Architecture
Cambridge *Interview only:* Downing, Girton, King's, Queens', Robinson, Sidney Sussex, Trinity Hall; *Test at interview:* Jesus, Lucy Cavendish, Pembroke, Trinity; *Preparatory study/assignment at/ before interview:* Clare, Emmanuel, Fitzwilliam, Magdalene, Murray Edwards, St Edmund's, Selwyn, Wolfson; *Project:* Peterhouse; *School/college essays:* Churchill, Clare, Gonville and Caius, Newnham, St John's. **NB** All colleges offering course require a portfolio of recent work at interview. Check www.cam.ac.uk/admissions/undergraduate/apply/tests.
Cardiff (Archit, Archit Eng) Samples of work to be sent before interview.
Dundee Samples of work required before interview.
Huddersfield Portfolio of work required.
Liverpool The interview will be based on the portfolio of work.
London Met Portfolio of work required.
London South Bank Samples of work to be sent before interview.
Nottingham Trent Examples of work are required.
Sheffield Art portfolio required for applicants without A-level art.
Westminster Samples of work required before interview.

Art and Design
Bournemouth (Comp Animat Art) Maths, logic and life-drawing tests at interview, and portfolio of work required.
Bournemouth Arts Practical test.
Creative Arts Tests.
Glyndŵr Portfolios are required for Art and Design courses.
Oxford (Fn Art) No written work required. Portfolio to be submitted by mid-November. Drawing examination. Two drawings in pencil or pencil and ink from a number of possible subjects. Check www.admissions.ox.ac.uk/tests.
Ravensbourne Verbal examination. (Animat) Written test.
Westminster (Fash Mrchnds Mgt) Interview and numeracy test.

Asian and Middle Eastern Studies
Cambridge *Interview only:* St Edmund's; *Test at interview:* Girton (depending on subject), Fitzwilliam, Hughes Hall, Lucy Cavendish, Magdalene (depending on subject), Murray Edwards (depending on

subject), Robinson, Sidney Sussex (depending on subject), Trinity Hall (depending on subject); *Preparatory study at/before interview:* Robinson, St John's, Selwyn; *School/college essays:* Christ's, Churchill, Clare, Corpus Christi, Downing, Emmanuel, Fitzwilliam, Girton, Gonville and Caius, Homerton, Jesus, King's, Magdalene, Murray Edwards, Newnham, Pembroke, Peterhouse, Queens', St Catharine's, St John's, Trinity, Trinity Hall, Wolfson. Check www.cam.ac.uk/admissions/ undergraduate/apply/tests.

Biochemistry
London South Bank Degree subject-based test at interview.

Biological Sciences
London South Bank Degree subject-based test at interview.
Nottingham Trent Essay.

Biomedical Sciences
Hull (Coll) Essay.
Imperial London BMAT.
Nottingham Trent Essay.
Oxford BMAT is required for entry into all colleges. Check www.medsci.ox.ac.uk/study/bms.
Portsmouth Test of motivation and knowledge of the subject, the degree and careers to which it leads.

Bioveterinary Science
London (RVC) BMAT is not required for entry but applicants wanting to be considered for Merit Scholarships will have to take BMAT.

Broadcast Technology
Ravensbourne Written test.

Building/Construction
London South Bank (Bld Serv) Degree subject-based test and numeracy test at interview.

Business Courses
Arts London (CFash) School work to be submitted before interview. Degree subject-based test and numeracy test at interview.
Bolton Literacy and numeracy tests.
Bradford (Coll Univ Centre) Written test.
Newcastle Some short-listed applicants will be given a variety of assessment tests at interview.
Nottingham Trent Short-listed applicants are invited to a day-long business style assessment.
Westminster (Fash Merch Mgt) Interview and numeracy test.

Celtic
Oxford Language aptitude or translation test.

Chemistry
Reading During the interview, applicants will be asked a series of chemistry-related questions from a select list. Applicants are required to discuss these in detail and may be asked to draw molecular formulas.

Classics (see also Archaeology)
Cambridge *Test at interview:* Clare, Corpus Christi, Fitzwilliam, Girton, Hughes Hall, Lucy Cavendish, Newnham, St Catharine's, St Edmund's, St John's, Wolfson; *Preparatory study at/before interview:* Downing, Emmanuel, Jesus, Magdalene, Murray Edwards, Newnham, Peterhouse, Sidney Sussex; *School/college essays:* Christ's, Churchill, Clare, Corpus Christi, Downing, Emmanuel, Fitzwilliam, Girton, Gonville and Caius, Homerton, Jesus, King's, Magdalene, Murray Edwards, Newnham, Pembroke, Peterhouse, Queens', Robinson, St Catharine's, St Edmund's, St John's, Selwyn, Sidney Sussex, Trinity, Trinity Hall. Check www.cam.ac.uk/admissions/undergraduate/apply/tests.
Oxford Two recent, marked essays required, normally in areas related to Classics. Written tests at interview. Check www.admissions.ox.ac.uk/tests.

Classics and English
Oxford The ELAT and the Classics test. Two pieces of written work, relevant to either Classics or English, also required. Check www.admissions.ox.ac.uk/tests.

Classics and Modern Languages
Oxford Classics and Modern Languages tests; two Classics essays and two modern language essays also required, one in the chosen language. Check www.admissions.ox.ac.uk/tests.

Classics and Oriental Studies
Oxford Classics test; also language aptitude test for applicants planning to study Arabic, Hebrew, Persian or Turkish as main language; two pieces written work also required, at least one on classical topic. Check www.admissions.ox.ac.uk/tests.

Computer Science
Abertay (Comp Arts) Portfolio of work required. Practical tests at interview.
Cambridge *Interview only:* Magdalene, Girton, St Catharine's, Sidney Sussex, Wolfson; *Test at interview:* Churchill, Downing, Homerton, Hughes Hall, Peterhouse, Trinity; *Thinking Skills Assessment at interview:* Christ's, Clare, Corpus Christi, Emmanuel, Fitzwilliam, Gonville and Caius, Jesus, King's, Lucy Cavendish, Murray Edwards, Newnham, Pembroke, Peterhouse, Queens', Robinson, St Edmund's, St John's, Selwyn, Trinity Hall; *Preparatory study at/before interview:* Clare, Gonville and Caius, King's, Robinson. **NB** STEP used for conditional offers. Check www.cam.ac.uk/admissions/undergraduate/apply/tests.
Liverpool John Moores Questionnaire before interview. Literacy test at interview.
London (Gold) Degree subject-based test.
London (QM) Mathematical test at interview.
Oxford Maths aptitude test. See also **Mathematics** below. Check www.admissions.ox.ac.uk/tests.

Czech
Oxford Language aptitude or translation test.

Dance
Chichester (Perf Arts) Group practical test.

Dental Nursing
Portsmouth (Dntl Hyg Dntl Thera) Interview.

Dentistry
Glasgow UKCAT.
London (King's) UKCAT.
Manchester UKCAT and interview.

Dietetics
London Met Interview and essay.
Ulster Health Professions Admissions Test: see www.hpat.org.uk and www.ulster.ac.uk before completing the UCAS application.

Drama
De Montfort Written papers and/or tests.
Liverpool (LIPA) (Actg) Applicants will be expected to perform one devised piece, one Shakespearean piece and a song and give a short review of a performance they have seen recently.
London (RH) Written work required at interview. The University looks for students who are mentally agile and versatile who enjoy reading as well as taking part in productions.
London (Royal Central Sch SpDr) Written papers and/or tests.
Reading (Thea) Applicants undertake a practical assessment and an interview.

Economics
Cambridge *Interview only:* Clare, Girton, Selwyn; *Test at interview:* Corpus Christi, Downing (mathematical test), Gonville and Caius, Homerton, Hughes Hall, Lucy Cavendish, Pembroke,

Robinson, Sidney Sussex, Wolfson; *Thinking Skills Assessment:* Fitzwilliam, Jesus, King's, Newnham, Peterhouse, Queens', St Edmund's, St John's; *Preparatory study at/before interview:* Christ's, Churchill, Emmanuel, Fitzwilliam, Jesus, King's, Magdalene, Murray Edwards, Newnham, St Catharine's, St John's; *College-set essay/work:* Peterhouse, St John's, Trinity Hall; *School/college essays:* Christ's, Churchill, Homerton, Magdalene, Newnham, Robinson. Check www.cam.ac.uk/ admissions/undergraduate/apply/tests.

Lancaster Workshop.

Oxford (Econ Mgt) Thinking Skills Assessment. Check www.admissions.ox.ac.uk/tests, and also www. admissionstests.cambridgeassessment.org.uk.

Education Studies *(see also Teacher Training)*

Anglia Ruskin Numeracy tests.

Cambridge *Interview only:* Clare, Fitzwilliam, Girton, Jesus, Murray Edwards, St Edmund's, St John's, Selwyn; *Test at interview:* Churchill (depending on subject), Downing (depending on subject), Homerton (depending on subject), Hughes Hall, Lucy Cavendish, Magdalene (depending on subjects), Trinity Hall, Wolfson; *Preparatory study at/before interview:* Churchill, Emmanuel, Homerton, Magdalene, Robinson, Trinity Hall; *College-set essay:* Emmanuel; *School/college essays:* Christ's, Churchill, Downing, Gonville and Caius, Homerton, Magdalene, Queens', Trinity Hall. Check www.cam.ac.uk/admissions/undergraduate/apply/tests.

Cumbria Literacy test.

Durham Key Skills tests at interview.

Newman Basic numeracy and literacy tests.

Reading Applicants are required to take part in both a group interview and an individual interview as well as completing a short essay-based written test.

Engineering

Birmingham City Mature students without GCSE English and/or mathematics are required to take a literacy and/or numeracy test. (Snd Eng Prod) Mature students to take English and mathematics tests.

Blackburn (Coll) Questionnaire and tests before interview.

Bristol (Eng Des) A-level-based test.

Cambridge *Interview only:* Corpus Christi, Girton, Murray Edwards, St Catharine's; *Test at interview:* Churchill, Downing (mathematical test), Fitzwilliam, Gonville and Caius, Hughes Hall, King's (problem-solving), Lucy Cavendish, Magdalene, Newnham, Peterhouse, Robinson, St John's (mathematical test), Trinity; *Thinking Skills Assessment:* Christ's, Clare, Emmanuel, Gonville and Caius, Homerton, Jesus, King's, Lucy Cavendish, Newnham, Pembroke, Queens', St Edmund's, Selwyn, Sidney Sussex, Trinity Hall, Wolfson; *Preparatory study at/before interview:* Clare, St John's (and possible STEP requirement). Check www.cam.ac.uk/admissions/undergraduate/apply/tests.

Kingston (Aerosp Eng) Numeracy and basic physics test.

London South Bank (Civ Eng; Elec Eng; Mech Eng) Degree subject-based test and numeracy test at interview.

Southampton Literacy and numeracy tests for Foundation course applicants.

Southampton Solent Mathematical test at interview.

English

Anglia Ruskin Samples of written work required.

Bangor (Crea Prof Writ) Applicants are required to submit a portfolio of writing.

Birmingham City Samples of work required.

Blackpool and Fylde (Coll) Samples of work before interview.

Bristol Samples of work required.

Cambridge *Test at interview:* Churchill, Clare, Corpus Christi, Downing, Emmanuel, Fitzwilliam, Girton, Homerton, Hughes Hall, Jesus, King's, Lucy Cavendish, Magdalene, Murray Edwards, Newnham, Pembroke, Peterhouse, Queens', Robinson, St Catharine's, St Edmund's, St John's, Selwyn, Sidney Sussex, Trinity, Trinity Hall, Wolfson; *Preparatory study at/before interview:* Christ's, Churchill, Clare, Corpus Christi, Emmanuel, Fitzwilliam, Jesus, Newnham, Robinson, Selwyn, Sidney Sussex; *School/college essays:* Christ's, Churchill, Clare, Corpus Christi, Emmanuel, Fitzwilliam, Girton,

Homerton, Jesus, King's, Magdalene, Murray Edwards, Newnham, Peterhouse, Queens', Robinson, St Catharine's, St John's, Selwyn, Sidney Sussex, Trinity, Trinity Hall. Check www.cam.ac.uk/admissions/undergraduate/apply/tests.

Cardiff Short essay.

London (UCL) After interview, applicants are asked to write a critical commentary on an unseen passage of prose or verse.

Oxford (Engl Lang Lit) ELAT and one recent marked essay. (Engl Modn Langs) Modern Language(s) test, one recent marked essay. Check www.admissions.ox.ac.uk/tests.

Portsmouth (Crea Writ) All applicants will be required to submit a short piece of creative writing to the admissions office.

Southampton Examples of written work required from Access students.

European and Middle Eastern Languages (see also Modern and Medieval Languages)

Oxford Language aptitude test, modern language test, TSA. Check www.admissions.ox.ac.uk/tests.

Film Production

Bournemouth Arts Portfolio. Practical test of short film stills.

Creative Arts Portfolio at interview.

Westminster Questionnaire to be completed and samples of work required before interview.

Film Studies

Liverpool John Moores Questionnaire and test before interview.

Reading There are three stages to the interview process: a practical, a film seminar and an interview.

Roehampton Essays taken to interview and discussed.

South Wales Portfolio of work at interview.

Food Studies

Reading During the interview, applicants will be given a lead and then asked a specific question tailored to the programme applied for.

Geography

Cambridge *Interview only:* Christ's, Downing, St Edmund's, St John's; *Test at interview:* Hughes Hall, Lucy Cavendish, Murray Edwards, Wolfson; *Preparatory study at/before interview:* Churchill, Clare, Corpus Christi, Emmanuel, Fitzwilliam, Girton, Homerton, King's, Newnham, Robinson, St Catharine's, Selwyn; *School/college essays:* Churchill, Clare, Corpus Christi, Emmanuel, Fitzwilliam, Girton, Gonville and Caius, Homerton, Jesus, King's, Magdalene, Murray Edwards, Newnham, Queens', Robinson, Sidney Sussex, Trinity, Trinity Hall. Check www.cam.ac.uk/admissions/undergraduate/apply/tests.

Cardiff Test for some Joint Honours courses.

Oxford No test. Two pieces of geography-based work to be submitted by mid-November. Check www.admissions.ox.ac.uk/tests.

German (see also Modern and Medieval Languages)

Aston Written test at interview.

History

Bangor Samples of work only required from mature applicants without conventional qualifications.

Cambridge *Test at interview:* Hughes Hall, Lucy Cavendish, Newnham, Pembroke, Peterhouse, Robinson, St Edmund's, St John's, Sidney Sussex, Wolfson; *Thinking Skills Assessment:* St John's; *Preparatory study at/before interview:* Christ's, Churchill, Clare, Corpus Christi, Downing, Emmanuel, Fitzwilliam, Girton, Homerton, Murray Edwards, Newnham, Pembroke, Queens', Robinson, St Catharine's, St John's, Selwyn, Sidney Sussex, Trinity; *School/college essays:* Christ's, Churchill, Clare, Corpus Christi, Downing, Emmanuel, Fitzwilliam, Girton, Gonville and Caius, Homerton, Jesus, King's, Magdalene, Murray Edwards, Newnham, Pembroke, Peterhouse, Queens', Robinson, St Catharine's, Selwyn, Sidney Sussex, Trinity, Trinity Hall, Wolfson. Check www.cam.ac.uk/admissions/undergraduate/apply/tests.

Liverpool Test for mature applicants.

Liverpool John Moores Mature students not in education must submit an essay.
London (Gold) Samples of written work from non-standard applicants and from those without academic qualifications.
Oxford (Hist (Anc Modn); Hist Econ) History Aptitude Test. (Hist Modn Langs) History Aptitude Test and Modern Language Test. (Hist Pol) No test. Those called for interview should send an essay by end of November. Check www.admissions.ox.ac.uk/tests.
Roehampton Essays taken to interview and discussed.

History of Art
Cambridge *Interview only:* Fitzwilliam, Robinson, Selwyn; *Test at interview:* Hughes Hall, Lucy Cavendish, St Edmund's, Wolfson; *School/college essays:* Christ's, Churchill, Clare, Corpus Christi, Downing, Emmanuel, Girton, Gonville and Caius, Homerton, Jesus, King's, Magdalene, Murray Edwards, Newnham, Pembroke, Peterhouse, Queens', St John's, Sidney Sussex, Trinity, Trinity Hall. Check www.cam.ac.uk.admissions/undergraduate/apply/tests.
Oxford Two pieces of work required: (a) a marked essay from an A-level or equivalent course and (b) a brief account of no more than 750 words responding to an item of art or design to which the applicant has had first-hand access with a photograph or photocopy of the item provided if possible. No written test at interview although the applicant may be presented with photographs or artefacts for discussion at interview. Submitted written work may also be discussed at interview. Check www.admissions.ox.ac.uk/tests.

Italian (see also Medieval and Modern Languages)
Cardiff Test for some Joint Honours courses.

Journalism (see also Media Studies)
Brighton (Spo Jrnl) Test for those called to interview: contact admissions tutor.
City Spelling, punctuation, grammar, general knowledge tests and an essay assignment. Tests on current affairs and use of English.
Edinburgh Napier (Jrnl) Samples of work before interview.
Kent English language and academic tests for all candidates, relating to requirements of the accrediting professional bodies.
Portsmouth Candidates are subject to interview and an admissions test.
South Wales Test and interview.

Land Economy
Cambridge *Interview only:* Christ's, Downing, Girton, Gonville and Caius, Pembroke, Queens', St Catharine's, St John's, Selwyn, Sidney Sussex, Trinity Hall; *Test at interview:* Hughes Hall, Lucy Cavendish, Wolfson; *Thinking Skills Assessment:* Jesus, Lucy Cavendish, Newnham, Robinson, St Edmund's; *Preparatory study at/before interview:* Fitzwilliam (written test prior to interview), Jesus, Magdalene, Trinity; *School/college essays:* Clare, Fitzwilliam, Homerton, Magdalene, Murray Edwards, Newnham. Check www.cam.ac.uk/admissions/undergraduate/apply/tests.

Law
Birmingham LNAT.
Birmingham City Questionnaire to be completed and an IQ test.
Bolton Own diagnostic test used (logic and reasoning).
Bradford (Coll Univ Centre) Academic tests at interview for mature students.
Bristol LNAT.
Cambridge *Test at interview:* Churchill, Hughes Hall, St Edmund's, Wolfson; *Cambridge Law Test:* Christ's, Clare, Corpus Christi, Downing, Emmanuel, Fitzwilliam, Girton, Gonville and Caius, Homerton, Jesus, King's, Lucy Cavendish, Magdalene, Murray Edwards, Newnham, Pembroke, Peterhouse, Queens', Robinson, St Catharine's, St John's, Selwyn, Sidney Sussex, Trinity, Trinity Hall; *Preparatory study at/before interview:* Christ's, Corpus Christi, Emmanuel, Homerton, Jesus, King's, Magdalene, Newnham, Pembroke, Selwyn, Sidney Sussex, St John's, Trinity, Trinity Hall. *School/college essays:* Emmanuel, Magdalene, Wolfson. Check www.cam.ac.uk/admissions/undergraduate/apply/tests.

Durham LNAT.
Glasgow LNAT.
Kent Internally devised test for some applicants.
London (King's) LNAT.
London (UCL) LNAT.
Manchester Met LNAT.
Nottingham LNAT.
Oxford All applicants take the LNAT. (Law; Law St Euro) LNAT plus, at interview, a short oral test in the modern language for students taking a joint language, except for those taking European Legal Studies. Check www.admissions.ox.ac.uk/tests.

Linguistics
Cambridge *Interview only:* Christ's, Homerton, King's, Robinson, Wolfson; *Test at interview:* Churchill, Fitzwilliam, Girton, Jesus, Magdalene, St John's; *Preparatory study at/before interview:* Churchill, Robinson, Sidney Sussex, Trinity. *School/college essays:* Churchill, Clare, Corpus Christi, Downing, Emmanuel, Gonville and Caius, Murray Edwards, Newnham, Peterhouse, Selwyn, Sidney Sussex, St John's, Trinity, Trinity Hall; *Contact the College:* Hughes Hall, Lucy Cavendish, Pembroke, Queens', St Catharine's, St Edmund's. Check www.cam.ac.uk/admissions/undergraduate/apply/tests.

Mathematics
Bath STEP.
Cambridge *Test at interview:* Christ's, Churchill, Corpus Christi, Downing, Girton, Homerton, Hughes Hall, King's, Lucy Cavendish, Magdalene, Murray Edwards, Robinson, St Edmund's, St John's, Trinity; *Maths STEP:* Christ's, Churchill, Clare, Corpus Christi, Downing, Emmanuel, Fitzwilliam, Girton, Gonville and Caius, Homerton, Jesus, King's, Lucy Cavendish, Magdalene, Murray Edwards, Newnham, Pembroke, Peterhouse, Queens', Robinson, St Catharine's, St John's, Selwyn, Sidney Sussex, Trinity, Trinity Hall; *Preparatory study at/before interview:* King's, Newnham. Check www.cam.ac.uk/admissions/undergraduate/apply/tests.
Liverpool John Moores Literacy and numeracy tests.
Oxford (Maths; Maths Stats) Mathematics Aptitude Test. Overseas candidates unable to attend for interview may be required to submit written work. (Maths Phil) Mathematics Aptitude Test; two essays showing capacity for reasoned argument and clear writing, not expected to be on a philosophical subject. Check www.admissions.ox.ac.uk/interviews/tests.

Media Studies
Bolton Samples of work at interview.
Bournemouth 250-word essay.
Coventry Interview and portfolio.
Hull (Coll) Essay required before interview.
Liverpool John Moores Questionnaire to be completed before interview. Degree subject-based test at interview.
London Met Mathematics and written English test.

Media Technology
South Wales Portfolio and interview.

Medicine
Cambridge *BMAT:* Christ's, Churchill, Clare, Corpus Christi, Downing, Emmanuel, Fitzwilliam, Girton, Gonville and Caius, Jesus, King's (plus set essay), Lucy Cavendish, Magdalene, Murray Edwards, Newnham, Pembroke, Peterhouse, Queens', Robinson, St Catharine's, St Edmund's, St John's, Selwyn, Sidney Sussex, Trinity, Trinity Hall, Wolfson. Check www.cam.ac.uk/admissions/undergraduate/apply/tests.
Exeter UKCAT and GAMSAT required.
Glasgow UKCAT.
Hull UKCAT.
Imperial London UKCAT.

London (King's) UKCAT.

London (St George's) GAMSAT is required for the four-year Graduate Stream course. UKCAT is required for the five-year course.

London (UCL) (Six-year course) BMAT.

Manchester UKCAT and interview.

Nottingham UKCAT.

Meteorology

Reading (Meteor Clim MMet) All applicants will be asked to attend an interview prior to an offer being made.

Modern and Medieval Languages (see also **Asian and Middle Eastern Studies, Oriental Studies and separate languages**)

Bangor Offer may be lowered after interview.

Cambridge *Test at interview:* Christ's, Churchill, Clare, Corpus Christi, Downing, Emmanuel, Fitzwilliam, Girton, Gonville and Caius, Homerton, Hughes Hall, Jesus, King's, Lucy Cavendish, Magdalene, Murray Edwards, Newnham, Pembroke, Peterhouse, Queens', Robinson, St Catharine's, St Edmund's, St John's, Selwyn, Sidney Sussex, Trinity Hall, Wolfson; *Preparatory study at/before interview:* Churchill, Clare, Emmanuel, Homerton, Jesus, Magdalene, Murray Edwards, Newnham, Pembroke, Peterhouse, Queens', Robinson, St Edmund's, St John's, Selwyn, Trinity, Trinity Hall; *School/college essays:* Christ's, Churchill, Corpus Christi, Downing, Emmanuel, Gonville and Caius, Homerton, Jesus, King's, Magdalene, Murray Edwards, Newnham, Pembroke, Peterhouse, Queens', Robinson, St Catharine's, St Edmund's, St John's, Selwyn, Trinity, Trinity Hall. Check www.cam.ac. uk/admissions/undergraduate/apply/tests.

Oxford (Modn Langs) Modern Languages Test(s). Two marked essays for each language being studied. (Modn Lang Ling) Language Aptitude Test and Modern Language Test. (Euro Mid E Langs) Language Aptitude Test and Modern Language Test. Two recent marked essays, one in the European language. Check course requirements carefully on the University website and check test requirements on www.admissions.ox.ac.uk/tests.

Music

Bangor Candidates offered the option of an audition. Interview requirements include performance, aural and extracts for analysis or 'guessing the composer' dates etc.

Bath Spa Interview requirements include performance, harmony and counterpoint (Written), essay and sight-singing.

Birmingham Interview requirements include harmony and counterpoint (written) and essay.

Birmingham City Some subject-based and practical tests. Interview requirements include performance.

Bristol Interview requirements include performance, sight-singing, keyboard tests, harmony and counterpoint (written), essay, extracts for analysis or 'guessing the composer' dates etc., aural.

Cambridge *Test at interview:* Clare, Downing, Fitzwilliam, Girton, Gonville and Caius, Homerton, Hughes Hall, Jesus, King's, Lucy Cavendish, Magdalene, Murray Edwards, Newnham, Pembroke, Peterhouse, Queens', Robinson, St Catharine's, St Edmund's, St John's (possible keyboard test), Selwyn, Trinity, Trinity Hall; *Preparatory study at/before interview:* Churchill, Clare, Emmanuel, Newnham, Robinson, St Edmund's, Sidney Sussex, Wolfson; *School/college essays:* Christ's, Churchill, Corpus Christi, Downing, Emmanuel, Fitzwilliam, Girton, Gonville and Caius, Homerton, Jesus, King's, Magdalene, Murray Edwards, Newnham, Pembroke, Peterhouse, Queens', Robinson, St Catharine's, St John's, Selwyn, Sidney Sussex, Trinity, Trinity Hall. Check www.cam.ac.uk/ admissions/undergraduate/apply/tests. Interview requirements include aural, harmony and counterpoint (written), essay and extracts for analysis or 'guessing the composer' dates etc.

Cardiff Interview requirements include performance, extracts for analysis or 'guessing the composer' dates etc.

Chichester Interview requirements include performance.

City Interview requirements include performance.

Colchester (Inst) Interview requirements include performance, aural, keyboard skills and essay.

Coventry Music theory exam and audition held alongside an interview. Proforma used prior to interview – some students rejected at this stage.

Derby Interview requirements include performance and essay.

Durham Interview requirements include performance, keyboard tests, aural, extracts for analysis or 'guessing the composer' dates etc.

Edinburgh Interview requirements include performance, harmony and counterpoint (written), essay and sight-singing.

Edinburgh Napier Audition and theory test.

Glasgow Interview requirements include performance and sight-singing.

Guildhall (Sch Mus Dr) Interviews mostly held at the School but also at Newcastle and in the USA.

Huddersfield Interview requirements include performance.

Lancaster Interview requirements include performance, aural and harmony and counterpoint (written).

Leeds Interview requirements include performance.

Leeds (CMus) (Jazz; Mus; Pop Mus St) In-house theory test to determine level of musical theory ability.

Liverpool Candidates may be asked to undertake a variety of aural tests, the performance of a prepared piece of music and some sight-reading when called for interview.

Liverpool Hope Interview requirements include performance, keyboard tests and harmony and counterpoint (written).

London (Gold) Degree subject-based test. Interview requirements include performance and extracts for analysis or 'guessing the composer' dates etc.

London (King's) Only borderline applicants are interviewed. Samples of written work may be requested. Interview requirements include performance, aural, sight-singing and keyboard skills.

London (RAcMus) (Mus) Interview requirements include performance, keyboard skills, harmony and counterpoint (written), and extracts for analysis or 'guessing the composer' dates etc.

London Met Performance tests and essay.

Oxford One marked sample of harmony and/or counterpoint and two marked essays on any areas or aspects of music. Candidates may submit a portfolio of compositions (these are non-returnable). Check www.admissions.ox.ac.uk/tests. Interview requirements include performance, keyboard skills, extracts for analysis or 'guessing the composer' dates etc and sight-singing.

RCMus Interview requirements include performance and sight-singing.

RConsvS Interview requirements include performance, sight-singing and aural.

Royal Welsh (CMusDr) Interview requirements include performance and essay.

Salford Interview requirements include performance, harmony and sight-singing.

Sheffield Interview requirements include performance, essay and aural.

Ulster Interview requirements include performance.

West London Students required to produce a portfolio of work and attend an audition: see www.uwl.ac.uk.

Wolverhampton Interview requirements include performance and essay.

York Interview requirements include performance, aural, keyboard skills and sight-singing.

Natural Sciences (Biological Sciences)

Cambridge *Interview only:* Churchill, Corpus Christi, Downing, Fitzwilliam, Girton, Jesus, King's, Newnham, Pembroke, St Catharine's, Selwyn; *Test at interview:* Homerton, Hughes Hall, Lucy Cavendish, Magdalene, Murray Edwards, Robinson, St Edmund's, St John's, Trinity; *Thinking Skills Assessment:* Clare, Emmanuel, Gonville and Caius, Peterhouse, Queens', St Edmund's, Trinity Hall, Wolfson; *Preparatory study at/before interview:* Emmanuel, Homerton, Magdalene, Robinson; *School/college essays:* Christ's (or project work), Peterhouse, Robinson. Check www.cam.ac.uk/admissions/undergraduate/apply/tests.

Natural Sciences (Physical Sciences)

Cambridge *Interview only:* Christ's, Churchill, Fitzwilliam, Girton, Jesus, Pembroke, St Catharine's, Selwyn; *Test at interview:* Corpus Christi, Downing (mathematical test), Homerton, Hughes Hall, Lucy Cavendish, Magdalene, Robinson, St John's, Trinity; *Thinking Skills Assessment:* Clare, Emmanuel,

Gonville and Caius, King's, Murray Edwards, Newnham, Peterhouse, Queens', St Edmund's, Trinity Hall, Wolfson; *Preparatory study at/before interview:* Emmanuel (for Chemistry), Homerton; *School/college essays:* Murray Edwards. Check www.cam.ac.uk/admissions/undergraduate/apply/tests.

Nursing
Birmingham City Literacy and numeracy tests at interview.
Bristol UWE Questionnaire/test before interview.
Bucks New Tests for BSc Nursing.
City Written test.
Coventry All NHS-funded courses include literacy and numeracy tests.
Cumbria (Nurs; Midwif) Numeracy test.
Derby Literacy and numeracy tests at interview.
East Anglia Tests.
Liverpool A group of candidates are given a task to undertake during which applicants are assessed for their ability to work in a team, maturity, communication skills and their level of involvement.
London South Bank (Nurs A C MH) Literacy and numeracy tests at interview.
Suffolk (Univ Campus) Interview and tests.
West London Numeracy and literacy tests.
Wolverhampton Tests.
York Literacy and numeracy tests.

Occupational Therapy
Bristol UWE Questionnaire/test before interview.
Ulster Health Professions Admissions Test: see www.hpat.org.uk and www.ulster.ac.uk before completing the UCAS application.

Optometry
Bradford (Coll Univ Centre) Literacy and numeracy tests.

Oriental Studies
Cambridge See **Asian and Middle Eastern Studies**.
Oxford Language Aptitude Test. Two essays, preferably of different kinds. Essays in a European language are acceptable. No prior knowledge of Oriental languages required. Occasional written tests. Check the University website and prospectuses and www.admissions.ox.ac.uk/tests.

Osteopathy
BSO All prospective students are required to attend an Interview and Evaluation Day where they are normally required to undertake a range of aptitude tests, a written English test and an interview in order to determine their suitability for the course and the BSO.

Paramedic Science
Coventry Fitness and literacy test.

Pharmacology/Pharmaceutical Sciences
Portsmouth Test of motivation, knowledge of the subject, degree course and the careers to which it leads.

Pharmacy
Liverpool John Moores Literacy and numeracy tests.
Portsmouth (A-level students) Test of motivation and knowledge of pharmacy as a profession. (Other applicants) Test of chemistry and biology, plus literacy and numeracy tests.
Reading A simple numeracy test related to pharmacy.

Philosophy
Cambridge *Test at interview:* Christ's, Churchill, Clare, Corpus Christi, Downing, Emmanuel, Fitzwilliam, Girton, Gonville and Caius, Homerton, Hughes Hall, Jesus, King's, Lucy Cavendish, Magdalene, Newnham, Pembroke, Peterhouse, Queens', Robinson, St Catharine's, St Edmund's, St John's, Selwyn, Sidney Sussex, Trinity, Trinity Hall, Wolfson; *School/college essays:* Churchill, Downing,

Emmanuel, Homerton, Magdalene, Peterhouse, St Catharine's, Trinity. Check www.cam.ac.uk/admissions/undergraduate/apply/tests.

Leeds Written test at interview.

Liverpool Samples of written work may be requested in cases where there is a question of the applicant's ability to cope with the academic skills required of them.

London (UCL) Written test at interview.

Oxford (Phil Modn Langs) Philosophy and Modern Languages tests; two pieces of written work required. (Phil Theol) Philosophy test and two pieces of written work. (Phil Pol Econ (PPE)) Thinking Skills Assessment; no written work required. Check course pages on University website and www.admissions.ox.ac.uk/tests.

Warwick Written test at interview.

Physical Education
Chichester Physical test.
Liverpool John Moores Literacy and numeracy tests and gym assessment.

Physics
Oxford Physics Aptitude test; no written work required. Check www.admissions.ox.ac.uk/tests.

Physiotherapy
East Anglia Tests.
Liverpool A group of candidates are given a task to undertake, during which they are assessed for their ability to work in a team, maturity, communication skills and their level of involvement.
Robert Gordon Practical testing varies from year to year.
Ulster Health Professions Admissions Test: see www.hpat.org.uk and www.ulster.ac.uk before completing the UCAS application.

Podiatry
Ulster Health Professions Admissions Test: see www.hpat.ac.uk and www.ulster.ac.uk before completing the UCAS application.

Policing
Cumbria Constabulary test.

Politics
Cambridge *Test at interview:* Churchill, Jesus, Lucy Cavendish, Robinson, St John's, Sidney Sussex; *Thinking Skills Assessment:* Clare, Gonville and Caius, King's, Newnham, Queens', St John's; *Preparatory work at/before interview:* Emmanuel, Magdalene, Murray Edwards, Newnham, Robinson, Sidney Sussex; *School/college essays:* Christ's, Churchill, Corpus Christi, Downing, Emmanuel, Fitzwilliam, Girton, Gonville and Caius, Homerton, Jesus, King's, Magdalene, Murray Edwards, Newnham, Pembroke, Robinson, St Edmund's, St John's, Selwyn, Sidney Sussex, Trinity, Trinity Hall (College-set essay), Wolfson. Check www.cam.ac.uk/admissions/undergraduate/apply/tests.
Kent (Pol Int Rel Bidiplome) Assessment days run jointly with the IEP Lille.
London (Gold) Essays from current A/AS-level course to be submitted before interview.
Oxford See (Phil Pol Econ (PPE)) under **Philosophy**.

Popular Music
South Wales Audition.

Product Design
Dundee Portfolio and interview will determine the appropriate entry point for candidate (Level 1 or 2).

Psychology
Bangor Access course entry students may be asked to submit an essay.
London (UCL) Questionnaire to be completed.
Oxford (Expmtl Psy) Thinking Skills Assessment test; no written work required. Check www.admissions.ox.ac.uk/tests.
Roehampton Questionnaire before interview; test at interview.

Radiography

Liverpool (Diag Radiog) A group of candidates are given a task to undertake, during which they are assessed for their ability to work in a team, maturity, communication skills and their level of involvement.

Ulster Health Professions Admissions Test: see www.hpat.org.uk and www.ulster.ac.uk before completing the UCAS application.

Social Work

Anglia Ruskin Samples of written work required.

Birmingham Written test at interview.

Birmingham City Some tests are set at interview.

Bristol UWE Questionnaire before interview.

Brunel Written test at interview.

Bucks New Tests.

Cardiff Met (UWIC) Scenario and subject-knowledge tests.

Coventry (Yth Wk) Literacy screening.

De Montfort Written test at interview.

Derby Literacy and numeracy tests at interview.

Dundee Literacy test.

Durham New (Coll) Written test at interview.

East Anglia Test.

Kent Written test followed by an interview and observed group discussions.

London (Gold) Written test at interview. Questions on social work practice and the applicant's experience of working in the social work/social care field.

London Met Pre-interview literacy test and, if successful, an interview.

London South Bank Literacy and numeracy tests.

Manchester Met (Yth Commun Wk) Tests.

Newman (Yth Commun Wk) Written test.

Portsmouth Test.

Suffolk (Univ Campus) Interview and test.

Wolverhampton Tests.

Sociology

Leeds Copy of written work requested.

London Met Where appropriate, separate tests in comprehension and mathematical skills that will be used to help us reach a decision.

Speech Sciences

Manchester Met Two essays and a questionnaire.

Reading A questionnaire is sent to applicants prior to an offer being made.

Sheffield Listening test and problem solving.

Ulster Health Professions Admissions Test: see www.hpat.org.uk and www.ulster.ac.uk before completing the UCAS application.

Teacher Training

Anglia Ruskin Literacy test at interview; maths test for some courses.

Bath Spa Written test at interview.

Bishop Grosseteste Literacy and numeracy tests are part of the selection criteria at interview.

Brighton Written test at interview.

Bristol UWE Literacy and mathematical tests at interview.

Brunel Literacy, mathematical and practical tests depending on subject.

Canterbury Christ Church All candidates are interviewed in groups of 8–10 and assessments are made based on the results of a written English test and performance in the group interview.

Cardiff Met (UWIC) Literacy, numeracy and subject-knowledge tests.

Chester Literacy and numeracy tests.

Chichester Written test at interview.

De Montfort Written test at interview.
Dundee Literacy and numeracy tests.
Durham Key Skills test.
Gloucestershire Mathematical test at interview. Written test at interview.
Liverpool John Moores Written test at interview. Mathematical and diagnostic tests on interview day.
London South Bank Literacy and numeracy tests.
Newman Basic literacy and numeracy tests for QTS and other courses.
Nottingham Trent Practical presentation. Written test at interview.
Plymouth Mathematical test at interview. Written test at interview.
Roehampton Written test at interview.
St Mary's Literacy and mathematical tests at interview. Practical tests for PE applicants.
Sheffield Hallam Interview with numeracy and literary tests.
Winchester Literacy test at interview.
Worcester Written test at interview.

Theatre and Performance
Glyndŵr An audition is required for Theatre and Performance.

Theology and Religious Studies
Cambridge *Test at interview:* Clare, Corpus Christi, Fitzwilliam, Hughes Hall, Lucy Cavendish, St Edmund's; *Preparatory work at/before interview:* Corpus Christi, Emmanuel, Girton, Jesus, Magdalene, Newnham, Selwyn; *School/college essays:* Christ's, Clare, Corpus Christi, Downing, Emmanuel, Fitzwilliam, Girton, Gonville and Caius, Homerton, Jesus, King's, Magdalene, Murray Edwards, Newnham, Pembroke, Peterhouse, Queens', Robinson, St Catharine's, St John's, Selwyn, Sidney Sussex, Trinity, Trinity Hall, Wolfson. Check www.cam.ac.uk/admissions/undergraduate/apply/tests.
Oxford (Theol) No test; two pieces written work required. (Theol Orntl St) Oriental Studies Language Aptitude Test for candidates planning to study Islam or Judaism; two pieces written work required. Check www.admissions.ox.ac.uk/tests.

Veterinary Science/Medicine
Cambridge *BMAT:* Churchill, Clare, Downing, Emmanuel, Fitzwilliam, Girton, Gonville and Caius, Jesus, Lucy Cavendish, Magdalene, Murray Edwards, Newnham, Pembroke, Queens', Robinson, St Catharine's, St Edmund's, St John's, Selwyn, Sidney Sussex, Trinity Hall, Wolfson; *Preparatory work at/before interview:* Emmanuel, Robinson. Check www.cam.ac.uk/admissions/undergraduate/apply/tests.
Liverpool Candidates are asked to write an essay on a veterinary topic prior to interview.
London (RVC) BMAT.
Myerscough (Coll) (Vet Nurs) Subject-based test at interview.

SELECTION OF APPLICANTS
University and college departmental admissions tutors are responsible for selecting candidates, basing their decisions on the policies of acceptable qualifications established by each institution and, where required, applicants' performance in admissions tests. There is little doubt that academic achievement, aptitude and promise are the most important factors although other subsidiary factors may be taken into consideration. The outline which follows provides information on the way in which candidates are selected for degree and diploma courses.

- Grades obtained by the applicant in GCE A-level and AS-level and equivalent examinations and the range of subjects studied may be considered.

- Applicant's performance in aptitude and admissions tests, as required by universities and colleges.

- Academic record of the applicant throughout his or her school career, especially up to A-level and AS-levels, Highers, Advanced Highers or other qualifications and the choice of subjects. If you are taking general studies at A-level or AS-level confirm with the admissions tutor that this is acceptable.

- Time taken by the applicant to obtain good grades at GCSE/Scottish Nationals and A-level and AS-levels/Scottish Highers/Advanced Highers.
- Forecast or the examination results of the applicant at A-level and AS-level (or equivalent) and head teacher's report.
- The applicant's intellectual development; evidence of ability and motivation to follow the chosen course.
- The applicant's range of interests, both in and out of school; aspects of character and personality.
- The vocational interests, knowledge and experience of the applicant particularly if they are choosing vocational courses.

INTERVIEWS

Fewer applicants are now interviewed than in the past but even if you are not called you should make an effort to visit your chosen universities and/or colleges before you accept any offer. Interviews may be arranged simply to give you a chance to see the institution and the department and to meet the staff and students. Alternatively, interviews may be an important part of the selection procedure for specific courses such as Law, Medicine and Teaching. If they are, you need to prepare yourself well. Most interviews last approximately 20–30 minutes and you may be interviewed by more than one person. For practical subjects such as Music and Drama almost certainly you will be asked to perform, and for artistic subjects, to take examples of your work. For some courses you may also have a written or other test at interview (see above).

How best can you prepare yourself?
Firstly, as one applicant advised, 'Go to the interview – at least you'll see the place.'

Secondly, on the question of dress, try to turn up looking smart (it may not matter, but it can't be wrong).

Two previous applicants were more specific: 'Dress smartly but sensibly so you are comfortable for travelling and walking round the campus.'

More general advice is also important
- 'Prepare well – interviewers are never impressed by applicants who only sit there with no willingness to take part.'
- 'Read up the prospectus and course details. Know how their course differs from any others you have applied for and be able to say why you prefer theirs.'
- 'They always ask if you have any questions to ask them: prepare some!' For example, How many students are admitted to the course each year? What are the job prospects for graduates? How easy is it to change from your chosen course to a related course?

Questions which you could ask might focus on the ways in which work is assessed, the content of the course, field work, work experience, teaching methods, accommodation and, especially for vocational courses, contacts with industry, commerce or the professions. However, don't ask questions which are already answered in the prospectus!

These are only a few suggestions and other questions may come to mind during the interview which, above all, should be a two-way flow of information. It is also important to keep a copy of your UCAS application (especially your personal statement) for reference since your interview will probably start with a question about something you have written.

Usually interviewers will want to know why you have chosen the subject and why you have chosen their particular institution. They will want to see how motivated you are, how much care you have taken in choosing your subject, how much you know about your subject, what books you have read. If you have chosen a vocational course they will want to find out how much you know about the career it leads to, and whether you have visited any places of work or had any work experience. If your chosen subject is also an A-level subject you will be asked about your course and the aspects of the course you like the most.

Try to relax. For some people interviews can be an ordeal; most interviewers know this and will make allowances. The following extract from the Oxford prospectus will give you some idea of what admissions tutors look for.

- 'Interviews serve various purposes and no two groups of tutors will conduct them in the same way or give them exactly the same weight. Most tutors wish to discover whether a candidate has done more than absorb passively what he/she has been taught. They try to ascertain the nature and strength of candidates' intellectual interests and their capacity for independent development. They are also likely to ask about applicants' other interests outside their school curriculum. This is partly because between two candidates of equal academic merit, preference will be given to the one who has the livelier interests or activities, and partly because it is easier to learn about candidates when they talk about what interests them most.'
- 'Interviews are in no sense hostile interrogations. Those candidates who show themselves to be honest, thoughtful and unpretentious will be regarded more favourably than those who try to impress or take the view that it is safest to say as little as possible. We do not expect candidates to be invariably mature and judicious.'

In the tables in **Chapter 8** (**Selection interviews**, **Interview advice and questions** and **Reasons for rejection**) you will also find examples of questions which have been asked in recent years for which you might prepare, and non-academic reasons why applicants have been rejected! **Chapter 5**, **Applications**, provides a guide through the process of applying to your chosen universities and courses and highlights key points for your action.

HOW TO USE THE SUBJECT TABLES

The subject tables in the next chapter represent the core of the book, listing degree courses offered by all UK universities and colleges. These tables are designed to provide you with the information you need so that you can match your abilities and interests with your chosen degree subject, prepare your application and find out how applicants are selected for courses.

At the top of each table there is a brief overview of the subject area, together with a selection of websites for organisations that can provide relevant careers or course information. This is then followed by the subject tables themselves in which information is provided in sequence under the following headings.

Course offers information
- Subject requirements/preferences (GCSE/A-level/other requirements)
- NB Offers statement
- Your target offers and examples of courses provided by each institution
- Alternative offers

Examples of Foundation degrees in the subject field

Choosing your course
- Some course features
- Universities and colleges teaching quality
- Top universities and colleges (research)
- Examples of sandwich degree courses

Admissions information
- Number of applicants per place
- Advice to applicants and planning the UCAS personal statement
- Misconceptions about this course
- Selection interviews
- Interview advice and questions
- Reasons for rejection (non-academic)

After-results advice
- Offers to applicants repeating A-levels

Graduate destinations and employment
- Career note

Other degree subjects for consideration

When selecting a degree course it is important to try to judge the points score or grades that you are likely to achieve and compare them with the offers listed under Your target offers and examples of courses provided by each institution. However, even though you might be capable of achieving the indicated grades or UCAS Tariff points, it is important to note that these are likely to be the minimum grades or points required and that there is no guarantee that you will receive an offer: other factors in your application, such as the personal statement, references, and admissions test performance will be taken into consideration (see also **Chapters 4** and **6**).

University departments frequently adjust their offers, depending on the numbers of candidates applying, so you must not assume that the offers and policies published now will necessarily apply to courses starting in 2015 or thereafter. Even though offers may change during the 2014/15 application cycle, you can assume that the offers published in this book represent the typical academic levels at which you should aim.

Below are explanations of the information given under the headings in the subject tables. It is important that you read these carefully so that you understand how they can help you to choose and apply for courses that are right for you.

COURSE OFFERS INFORMATION
Subject requirements/preferences
Brief information is given on the GCSE and A-level requirements. Specific A-level subject requirements for individual institutions are listed separately. Other requirements are sometimes specified, where

these are relevant to the course subject area, for example, medical requirements for health-related courses and Disclosure and Barring Service (DBS) clearance (formerly known as CRB checks). Check prospectuses and websites of universities and colleges for course requirements.

Your target offers and examples of courses provided by each institution
Universities and colleges offering degree courses in the subject area are listed in descending order according to the number of UCAS Tariff points and/or A-level grades they are likely to require applicants to achieve. The UCAS Tariff points total is listed down the left-hand side of the page, and to the right appear all the institutions (in alphabetical order) likely to make offers in this Tariff point range. (Information on the UCAS Tariff is given in **Appendix 1** and guidance on how to calculate your offers is provided on the inside front cover of this book. Please also read the information in the **Important Note** box on page 87.)

The courses included on the offers line are examples of the courses available in the subject field at that university or college. You will need to check prospectuses and websites for a complete list of the institution's Single, Joint, Combined or major/minor degree courses available in the subject. For each institution listed, the following information may be given.

Name of institution
Note that the name of an institution's university college or campus may be given in brackets after the institution title, for example London (King's) or Kent (Medway Sch Pharm). Where the institution is not a university, further information about its status may also be given to indicate the type of college – for example (UC) to mean University College or (CAg) to mean College of Agriculture. This is to help readers to differentiate between the types of colleges and to help them identify any specialisation a college may have, for example art or agriculture. A full list of abbreviations used is given under the heading **INSTITUTION ABBREVIATIONS** later in this chapter.

Grades/points offer
After the institution's name, a line of offers information is given, showing a typical offer made by the institution for the courses indicated in brackets. **Offers, however, may vary between applicants and the published grades and/or points offers should be regarded as targets to aim for and not necessarily the actual grades or points required**. Offers may be reduced after the publication of A-level results, particularly if a university or college is left with spare places. However, individual course offers listed in the tables in **Chapter 8** are abridged and should be used as a first source of reference and comparison only. It is not possible to publish all the variables relevant to each offer: applicants must check prospectuses and websites for full details of all offers and courses.

Depending on the details given by institutions, the offers may provide information as follows.

- **Grades** The specific grades, or average grades, required at GCE A-level or at A-level plus AS-level or, if specified, EPQ for the listed courses. (**NB** Graded offers may require specific grades for specific subjects.) A-level grades are always presented in capital letters; AS-levels and EPQ grades are shown in lower case – so the offer BBBc would indicate three grade Bs at A-level, plus an additional EPQ or AS-level at grade c. Where necessary, the abbreviation 'AL' is used to indicate A-level, 'AS' to indicate AS-level and EPQ to indicate that an Extended Project Qualification is part of the offer. Offers are usually shown in terms of three A-level grades although some institutions accept two grades with the same points total or, alternatively, two A-level grades accompanied by AS-level grades. Two AS-levels may generally be regarded as equivalent to one A-level, and one double award A-level as equivalent to two standard A-levels.

NB Unit grade and module information, now introduced into the admissions system, is most likely to be required by universities where a course is competitive, or where taking a specific unit is necessary or desirable for entry. Check with institutions' websites for their latest information.

- **UCAS Tariff points** A, AS-levels, International Baccalaureate (IB), Scottish Highers, the Advanced Diploma and a range of other qualifications have a unit value in the UCAS Tariff system (see **The UCAS 2015 Entry Tariff Points Tables** in **Appendix 1**). Where a range of Tariff points is shown, for example 220–180 points, offers are usually made within this points range for these specified courses.

Note that, in some cases, an institution may require a points score which is higher than the specified grade offer given. This can be for a number of reasons – for example, you may not be offering the standard subjects that would have been stipulated in a grades offer. In such cases additional points may be added by way of AS-levels, Key Skills etc.

A Tariff points offer will not usually discriminate between the final year exam subjects being taken by the applicant unless otherwise stated, although certain GCSE subjects may be stipulated eg English or mathematics.

Admission tutors have the unenviable task of trying to assess the number of applicants who will apply for their courses against the number of places available and so judging the offers to be made. It is therefore important when reading the offers tables to be aware that variations occur each year. Lower offers or equivalents may be made to disadvantaged students, mature and international applicants.

The offers published in this edition therefore are based on expected admission policies operating from September to January 2014/15. They are targets to be achieved and in the case of popular courses at popular universities they should be regarded as minimum entry qualifications.

See **Chapter 4** for information from universities about their admissions policies including, for example, information about their expected use of A*, unit grades, the Advanced Diploma, the Extended Project and the Cambridge Pre-U in their offers for applicants. See **Appendix 1** for **The UCAS 2015 Entry Tariff Points** tables.

- **Admissions tests for Law, Medicine and Veterinary Science/Medicine** Where admissions tests form part of a university's offer for any of these subjects, this is indicated on the offers line in the subject tables for the relevant university. This is shown by '+LNAT' (for Law), '+BMAT' or '+UKCAT' (for Medicine), and '+BMAT' (for Veterinary Science/Medicine). For example, the offers lines could read as follows:

   Edinburgh – AAAb incl AL chem +1 from maths/phys/biol; AS biol min +UKCAT (Medicine 5/6 yrs) (IB 37 pts HL 766)
   London (King's) – AAAb +LNAT (Law) (IB 38 pts HL 555–554)
   London (RVC) – AAA incl AL chem+biol +1 other +BMAT (Vet Med)

   Entry and admissions tests will be required for 2015 by a number of institutions for a wide range of subjects: see **Chapter 6** and the subject tables in **Chapter 8** for more information and check university websites and prospectuses.

Course title(s)
After the offer, an abbreviated form of the course title(s) to which the offers information refers is provided in brackets. The abbreviations used (see **COURSE ABBREVIATIONS** at the end of this chapter) closely relate to the course titles shown in the institutions' prospectuses. When the course gives the opportunity to study abroad (for example, in Continental Europe, Australia, North America) the abbreviated name of the relevant country is shown after the abbreviated course title. For example:

   Lancaster – AAB 340 pts (Env Sci (N Am/Aus); MChem Env Chem (St Abrd)) (IB 30 pts)

When experience in industry is provided as part of the course (not necessarily a sandwich course) this can be indicated on the offers line by including 'Ind' after the abbreviated course title. For example:

   Bristol – ABB (Pharmacol; Pharmacol (Ind)) (IB 34 pts)

Sometimes the information in the offers line relates to more than one course (see **Plymouth** below). In such cases, each course title is separated with a semicolon.

   Plymouth – 300 pts (MEng Civ Eng; Civ Cstl Eng)

When a number of joint courses exist in combination with a major subject, they may be presented using a list separated by slashes – for example '(Euro Mgt with Fr/Ger/Ital/Span)' indicates European Management with French or German or Italian or Spanish. Some titles may be followed by the word 'courses' – for example, (Geog courses):

St Andrews – AAB (Theol St; Bib St courses) (IB 30 pts)

This means that the information on the offers line refers not only to the Single Honours course in Theological Studies, but also to the range of Biblical Studies courses. For some institutions with extensive Combined Honours programmes, the information given on the offers line may specify (Comb Hons) or (Comb courses).

Courses awaiting validation are usually publicised in prospectuses and on websites. However, these are not included in the tables in **Chapter 8** since there is no guarantee that they will run. You should check with the university that a non-validated course will be available.

To help you understand the information provided under the **Your target offers and examples of courses provided by each institution** heading, the box below provides a few examples with their meaning explained underneath.

OFFERS LINES EXPLAINED

320 pts [University/College name] – BBCc **or** BBccc (Fr Ger)
For the joint course in French and German, the University requires grades of BBC (280 pts) at A-level plus AS-level grade c (40 pts) making a total of 320 points or, alternatively, BB (200 pts) at A-level plus AS-level grades ccc (120 pts), making the same total.

320 pts [University/College name] – 320 pts BBC +AS/EPQ c (Biomed Sci (Genet))
For the Biomedical Sciences course specialising in Genetics the University requires 320 pts, typically from 3 A-levels, together with either one AS-level or Extended Project Qualification (EPQ). The typical offer will be BBC at A-level plus c in either an AS-level or an EPQ.

220 pts [University/College name] – 220–280 pts (Geog)
For Geography, the University usually requires 220 UCAS Tariff points, but offers may range up to 280 UCAS Tariff points.

Alternative offers

In each of the subject tables, offers are shown in A-level grades or equivalent UCAS Tariff points, and in some cases as points offers of the International Baccalaureate Diploma (see below). However, applicants taking Scottish Highers/Advanced Highers, the Welsh Baccalaureate, Advanced Diploma, the IB Diploma, the Irish Leaving Certificate, the Advanced Diploma, the Extended Project and the Cambridge Pre-U should refer to **Appendix 1 – The UCAS 2015 Entry Tariff Points**. For more information, see www.ucas.com/how-it-all-works/explore-your-options/entry-requirements/tariff-tables or contact the institution direct.

IB offers

A selection of IB points offers appears at the end of some university/subject entries. For comparison of entry requirements, applicants with IB qualifications should check the A-level offers required for their course and then refer to **Appendix 1** which gives the revised IB UCAS Tariff points for 2015 entry. The figures under this subheading indicate the number or range of International Baccalaureate (IB) Diploma points likely to be requested in an offer. A range of points indicates variations between Single and Joint Honours courses. Applicants should check with the universities for any requirements for points gained from specific Higher Level (HL) subjects. Applicants offering the IB should check with prospectuses and websites and, if in doubt, contact admissions tutors for the latest information on IB offers.

Scottish offers

Scottish Honours degrees normally take four years. However, students with very good qualifications may be admitted into the second year of courses (Advanced entry). In some cases it may even be possible to enter the third year.

This year we have not included the offers details for Advanced entry. Any student with sufficient A-levels or Advanced Highers considering this option should check with the university to which they are applying. The policies at some Scottish universities are listed below:

Aberdeen Advanced entry possible for many courses, but not for Education, Law or Medicine.
Abertay Possibility of advanced entry largely dependent on content of current course.
Dundee Advanced entry possible for many courses, but not Art, Education, Law or Medicine.
Edinburgh Advanced entry possible for Science, Engineering, and Art and Design courses.
Edinburgh Napier Advanced entry to Stages 2, 3 or 4 of a programme, particularly for those with an HNC/HND or those with (or expecting to obtain) good grades in Advanced Highers or A-levels.
Glasgow Advanced entry possible in a range of subjects, including Neuroscience, Sociology and Civil Engineering.
Glasgow Caledonian Advanced entry available in a wide range of courses, including Business, Civil Engineering, Journalism and Biological Sciences.
Queen Margaret Advanced entry for some courses.
St Andrews Advanced entry for some courses.
Stirling Advanced entry for some courses.
Strathclyde Advanced entry for some courses.
West Scotland Advanced entry for some courses.

For others not on this list, please check individual university and college websites.

Student number controls
Universities and colleges have been given the freedom to expand their number of places for highly qualified applicants – defined as those who hold the following grades at A level, or equivalent, qualifications:

- $A^*A^*A^*$
- A^*A^*A
- A^*AA
- AAA
- A^*AB
- A^*A^*C
- AAB
- A^*A^*D
- A^*AC
- A^*BB
- A^*A and an A at AS-level.

IMPORTANT NOTE ON THE COURSE OFFERS INFORMATION

The information provided in **Chapter 8** is presented as a first reference source as to the target levels required. Institutions may alter their standard offers in the light of the qualifications offered by applicants.

The offers they publish do not constitute a contract and are not binding on prospective students: changes may occur between the time of publication and the time of application in line with market and student demand.

The points levels shown on the left-hand side of the offers listings are for ease of reference for the reader: not all universities will be making offers using the UCAS Tariff points system and it cannot be assumed that they will accept a points equivalent to the grades they have stipulated. Check university and college prospectuses, and also their websites, for their latest information before submitting your application.

EXAMPLES OF FOUNDATION DEGREES IN THE SUBJECT FIELD
This section lists examples of universities and colleges offering Foundation degrees in the subject field. Foundation degrees are employment-related higher education qualifications bringing higher education and business closer together to meet the needs of employers. The degrees are at a lower level than

Honours degrees and can be studied on a part-time basis or full-time over two years. Entry requirements for these courses vary, but many institutions request between 60 and 140 UCAS Tariff points.

CHOOSING YOUR COURSE
The information under this heading (to be read in conjunction with **Chapter 1**) covers factors that are important to consider in order to make an informed decision on which courses to apply for. The information is organised under the following subheadings.

Some course features
The purpose of this section is to alert you to the diversity of courses on offer and the importance of checking the content of your chosen course. It should be noted that many departments provide a common first year in the same subject, for example Biological Sciences, with a choice of specialisation in Year 2. (The courses listed have not been selected on the basis of academic reputation or course quality.)

Universities and colleges teaching quality
The Unistats website (http://unistats.direct.gov.uk) provides official information where available for different subjects and universities and colleges in the UK to help prospective students and their advisers make comparisons between them and so make informed choices about what and where to study. Information is updated annually and is available for each subject taught at each university and college (and for some further education colleges). The Quality Assurance Agency (www.qaa.ac.uk) reviews the quality and standards of all universities and colleges and official reports of their reviews are available on their website but it is important to note their dates of publication.

Top research universities and colleges (RAE 2008)
In December 2008 the latest research assessment exercise took place covering certain subject areas. The leading universities in the relevant subject areas are listed in the order of achievement. It should be noted that not all subjects were assessed.

Examples of sandwich degree courses
This section lists examples of institutions that offer sandwich placements for some of their courses in the subject field shown. The institutions listed offer placements of one-year duration and do not include language courses or work experience or other short-term placements. Check with the institutions too, since new courses may be introduced and others withdrawn depending on industrial or commercial arrangements. Further information on sandwich courses with specific information on the placements of students appears in **Chapter 1**.

NB During a period of recession, universities and colleges may have problems placing students on sandwich courses. Applicants applying for courses are therefore advised to check with admissions tutors that these courses will run, and that placements will be available.

ADMISSIONS INFORMATION
Under this heading, information gathered from the institutions has been provided. This will be useful when planning your application.

Number of applicants per place (approx)
These figures show the approximate number of applicants initially applying for each place before any offers are made. It should be noted that any given number of applicants represents candidates who have also applied for up to four other university and college courses. In some subject areas some universities have provided details of the actual breakdown of numbers of applicants under the following headings: UK, EU (non-UK), non-EU (overseas), mature (over 21).

Advice to applicants and planning the UCAS personal statement
This section offers guidelines on information that could be included in the personal statement section of your UCAS application. In most cases, applicants will be required to indicate why they wish to follow a particular course and, if possible, to provide positive evidence of their interest. See also **Chapters 5** and **6**.

Misconceptions about this course
Admissions tutors are given the opportunity in the research for this book to set the record straight by clarifying aspects of their course they feel are often misunderstood by students, and in some cases, advisers!

Selection interviews
Institutions that normally use the interview as part of their selection procedure are listed here. Those institutions adopting the interview procedure will usually interview only a small proportion of applicants. It is important to use this section in conjunction with **Chapters 4** and **6**.

Interview advice and questions
This section includes information from institutions on what candidates might expect in an interview to cover, and examples of the types of interview questions posed in recent years. Also refer to **Chapters 4** and **6**: these chapters provide information on tests and assessments which are used in selecting students.

Reasons for rejection (non-academic)
Academic ability and potential to suceed on the course are the major factors in the selection (or rejection) of applicants. Under this subheading, admissions tutors give other reasons for rejecting applicants.

AFTER-RESULTS ADVICE
Under this heading, information for helping you decide what to do after the examination results are published is provided (see also the section on **What to do on Results Day ... and After** in **Chapter 5**). Details refer to the main subject area unless otherwise stated in brackets.

Offers to applicants repeating A-levels
This section gives details of whether second-time offers made to applicants repeating their exams may be 'higher', 'possibly higher' or the 'same' as those made to first-time applicants. The information refers to Single Honours courses. It should be noted that circumstances may differ between candidates – some will be repeating the same subjects taken in the previous year, while others may be taking different subjects. Offers will also be dictated by the grades you achieved on your first sitting of the examinations. Remember, if you were rejected by all your universities and have achieved good grades, contact them by telephone on results day – they may be prepared to revise their decision. This applies particularly to medical schools.

GRADUATE DESTINATIONS AND EMPLOYMENT
The information under this heading has been provided by the Higher Education Statistics Agency (HESA) and is taken from their report *Destinations of Leavers from Higher Education 2011/12*. The report can be obtained from www.hesa.ac.uk.

Details are given of the total number of graduates surveyed whose destinations have been recorded – not the total number who graduated in that subject. Employment figures relate to those in full-time permanent paid employment after six months in a variety of occupations not necessarily related to their degree subject (part-time employment figures are not included). Figures are also given for those in voluntary, unpaid work. 'Further study' includes research into a subject-related field, higher degrees, private study or, alternatively, career training involving work and further study. The 'Assumed unemployed' category refers to those students who were believed to be unemployed for various reasons (eg travelling, personal reasons) or those students still seeking permanent employment six months after graduating. The figures given do not equal the total number of graduates surveyed as we have chosen only to include the most relevant or interesting areas.

Career note
Short descriptions of the career destinations of graduates in the subject area are provided.

OTHER DEGREE SUBJECTS FOR CONSIDERATION
This heading includes some suggested alternative courses that have similarities to the courses listed in the subject table.

ABBREVIATIONS USED IN THE SUBJECT TABLES IN CHAPTER 8

INSTITUTION ABBREVIATIONS

The following abbreviations are used to indicate specific institutions or types of institution:

Ac	Academy
AI	Arts Institute
ALRA	Academy of Live and Recorded Arts
AMD	Academy of Music and Drama
Birk	Birkbeck (London University)
BSO	British School of Osteopathy
CA	College of Art(s)
CAD	College of Art and Design
CAFRE	College of Agriculture, Food and Rural Enterprise
CAg	College of Agriculture
CAgH	College of Agriculture and Horticulture
CAT	College of Advanced Technology or Arts and Technology
CComm	College of Communication
CDC	College of Design and Communication
CECOS	London College of IT and Management
CFash	College of Fashion
CHort	College of Horticulture
CmC	Community College
CMus	College of Music
CMusDr	College of Music and Drama
Coll	College
Consv	Conservatoire
Court	Courtauld Institute (London University)
CT	College of Technology
CTA	College of Technology and Arts
Gold	Goldsmiths (London University)
GSA	Guildford School of Acting
Hey	Heythrop College (London University)
IA	Institute of Art(s)
IFHE	Institute of Further and Higher Education
Inst	Institute
King's	King's College (London University)
LIPA	Liverpool Institute of Performing Arts
LSE	London School of Economics and Political Science
Met	Metropolitan
MS	Medical School
NCH	New College of the Humanities
QM	Queen Mary (London University)
RAcMus	Royal Academy of Music
RConsvS	Royal Conservatoire of Scotland
RCMus	Royal College of Music
Reg Coll	Regional College
Reg Fed	Regional Federation (Staffordshire)
RH	Royal Holloway (London University)
RNCM	Royal Northern College of Music
RVC	Royal Veterinary College (London University)
SA	School of Art
SAD	School of Art and Design

Sch	School
Sch SpDr	School of Speech and Drama
SMO	Sabhal Mòr Ostaig
SOAS	School of Oriental and African Studies (London University)
SRUC	Scotland's Rural College
UC	University College
UCFB	University College of Football Business
UCL	University College (London University)
UHI	University of the Highlands and Islands
Univ	University

COURSE ABBREVIATIONS

The following abbreviations are used to indicate course titles:

Ab	Abrahamic	Anat	Anatomy/Anatomical
Abrd	Abroad	Anim	Animal
Acc	Accountancy/Accounting	Animat	Animation
Accs	Accessories	Animatron	Animatronics
Acoust	Acoustics/Acoustical	Anth	Anthropology
Acq	Acquisition	Antq	Antique(s)
Act	Actuarial	App(s)	Applied/Applicable/Applications
Actg	Acting	Appar	Apparel
Actn	Action	Appr	Appropriate
Actr	Actor	Apprsl	Appraisal
Actv	Active	Aqua	Aquaculture/Aquatic
Actvt(s)	Activity/Activities	Ar	Area(s)
Acu	Acupuncture	Arbc	Arabic
Add	Additional	Arbor	Arboriculture
Adlscn	Adolescence	Arch	Archaeology
Adlt	Adult	Archit	Architecture
Admin	Administration/Administrative	Archvl	Archival
Adt	Audit	Aroma	Aromatherapy
Adv	Advertising	Arst	Artist
Advc	Advice	Artfcts	Artefacts
Advnc	Advanced	Artif	Artificial
Advntr	Adventure	As	Asian
Aero	Aeronautical/Aeronautics	Ass	Assessment
Aerodyn	Aerodynamics	Assoc	Associated
Aero-Mech	Aero-mechanical	Asst	Assistant
Aerosp	Aerospace	Assyr	Assyriology
Aeroth	Aerothermal	Ast	Asset
Af	Africa(n)	Astnaut	Astronautics/Astronautical
Affrs	Affairs	Astro	Astrophysics
Age	Ageing	Astron	Astronomy
Agncy	Agency	A-Sxn	Anglo-Saxon
Agric	Agriculture/Agricultural	Ated	Accelerated
Agrofor	Agroforestry	Atel	Atelier
Agron	Agronomy	Atlan	Atlantic
Aircft	Aircraft	Atmos	Atmospheric
Airln	Airline	Attrctns	Attractions
Airpt	Airport	Auc	Auctioneering
Akkdn	Akkadian	Aud	Audio
Am	American	Audiol	Audiology
Amen	Amenity	Audtech	Audiotechnology
Analys	Analysis	Aus	Australia(n)
Analyt	Analytical	Austr	Australasia

Auth	Author/Authoring/Authorship
Auto	Automotive
Autom	Automated/Automation
Automat	Automatic
Autombl	Automobile
Autsm	Autism
AV	Audio Video
Avion	Avionics
Avn	Aviation
Ay St	Ayurvedic Studies
Bank	Banking
Bch	Beach
Bd	Based
Bdwk	Bodywork
Bhv	Behaviourial
Bib	Biblical
Bio Ins	Bio Instrumentation
Bioarch	Bioarchaeology
Bioch	Biochemistry/Biochemical
Biocomp	Biocomputing
Biodiv	Biodiversity
Bioelectron	Bioelectronics
Biogeog	Biogeography
Biogeosci	Biogeoscience
Bioinform	Bioinformatics
Biokin	Biokinetics
Biol	Biological/Biology
Biom	Biometry
Biomed	Biomedical/Biomedicine
Biomol	Biomolecular
Biophys	Biophysics
Bioproc	Bioprocess
Biorg	Bio-organic
Biosci	Bioscience(s)
Biotech	Biotechnology
Biovet	Bioveterinary
Bkbnd	Bookbinding
Bld	Build/Building
Blksmthg	Blacksmithing
Blt	Built
Bngli	Bengali
Braz	Brazilian
Brew	Brewing
Brit	British
Brnd	Brand/Branding
Broad	Broadcast(ing)
Bspk	Bespoke
Bty	Beauty
Bulg	Bulgarian
Burm	Burmese
Bus	Business
Buy	Buying
Byz	Byzantine

Callig	Calligraphy
Can	Canada/Canadian
Cap	Capital
Cardio	Cardiology
Carib	Caribbean
Cart	Cartography
Cat	Catering
CATS	Credit Accumulation and Transfer Scheme
Cell	Cellular
Celt	Celtic
Cent	Century
Ceram	Ceramics
Cert	Certificate
Ch Mgt	Chain Management
Chc	Choice
Chch	Church
Chem	Chemistry
Cheml	Chemical
Chin	Chinese
Chiro	Chiropractic
Chld	Child/Children/Childhood
Chn	Chain
Chng	Change
Choreo	Choreography
Chr	Christian(ity)
Chtls	Chattels
Cits	Cities
Civ	Civilisation/Civil
Class	Classical/Classics
Clim	Climate/Climatic
Clin	Clinical
Cllct	Collect/Collecting
Clnl	Colonial
Cloth	Clothing
Clsrm	Classroom
Cmbt	Combat
Cmdy	Comedy
Cmn	Common
Cmnd	Command
Cmplrs	Compilers
Cmpn	Companion
Cmpsn	Composition
Cmpste	Composite
Cmwlth	Commonwealth
Cncr	Cancer
Cnflct	Conflict
Cnma	Cinema/Cinematics
Cnslg	Counselling
Cnsltncy	Consultancy
Cnt	Central
Cntnt	Content
Cntrms	Countermeasures
Cntry	Country/Countryside
Cntxt	Context

Cnty	Century	**Cur**	Curation
Coach	Coaching	**Cy**	Cyber
Cog	Cognitive	**Cyber**	Cybernetics/Cyberspace
Col	Colour	**Cybertron**	Cybertronics
Coll	Collaborative	**Cym**	Cymraeg
Comb	Combined	**Cz**	Czech
Combus	Combustion		
Comm(s)	Communication(s)	**Dan**	Danish
Commer	Commerce/Commercial	**Decn**	Decision
Commun	Community	**Decr**	Decoration/Decorative
Comp	Computer/Computerised/	**Def**	Defence
	Computing	**Defer**	Deferred Choice
Compar	Comparative	**Deg**	Degree
Complem	Complementary	**Demcr**	Democratic
Comput	Computation/al	**Dept**	Department
Con	Context	**Des**	Design(er)
Concur	Concurrent	**Desr**	Desirable
Cond	Conductive	**Dest**	Destination(s)
Condit	Conditioning	**Dev**	Development/
Cons	Conservation		Developmental
Constr	Construction	**Devsg**	Devising
Consum	Consumer	**Df**	Deaf
Cont	Contour	**Diag**	Diagnostic
Contemp	Contemporary	**Diet**	Diet/Dietetics/Dietitian
Contnl	Continental	**Dif**	Difficulties
Contr	Control	**Dig**	Digital
Conv	Conveyancing	**Dip Ing**	Diplom Ingeneur
Cord	Cordwainers	**Dir**	Direct/Direction/Director/
Corn	Cornish		Directing
Corp	Corporate/Corporation	**Dis**	Diseases
Cos	Cosmetic	**Disab**	Disability
Cosmo	Cosmology	**Disas**	Disaster
Cr	Care	**Discip**	Disciplinary
Crcs	Circus	**Diso**	Disorders
Crdc	Cardiac	**Disp**	Dispensing
Crea	Creative/Creation	**Dist**	Distributed/Distribution
Crfts	Crafts/Craftsmanship	**Distil**	Distillation/Distilling
Crim	Criminal	**Div**	Divinity
Crimin	Criminological/Criminology	**d/l**	distance learning
Crit	Criticism/Critical	**Dlvry**	Delivery
Crm	Crime	**Dnstry**	Dentistry
Cro	Croatian	**Dntl**	Dental
Crr	Career	**Doc**	Document/Documentary
Crs	Course	**Dom**	Domestic/Domesticated
Crsn	Corrosion	**Dr**	Drama
Cru	Cruise	**Drg**	Drawing
Crypt	Cryptography	**Drs**	Dress
Cstl	Coastal	**Dscrt**	Discrete
Cstm	Costume	**Dscvry**	Discovery
Cstmd	Customised	**Dsply**	Display
Ctln	Catalan	**Dtbs**	Databases
Ctlys	Catalysis	**Dth**	Death
Ctzn	Citizenship	**Dvc**	Device
Culn	Culinary	**Dvnc**	Deviance
Cult	Culture/Cultural	**Dynmcs**	Dynamics

Ecol	Ecology/Ecological	**Exer**	Exercise
Ecomet	Econometrics	**Exhib**	Exhibition
e-Commer	E-Commerce	**Exmp**	Exempt(ing)
Econ	Economics	**Exp**	Export
Econy	Economy/ies	**Explor**	Exploration
Ecosys	Ecosystem(s)	**Explsn**	Explosion
Ecotech	Ecotechnology	**Expltn**	Exploitation
Ecotour	Ecotourism	**Expmtl**	Experimental
Ecotox	Ecotoxicology	**Expnc**	Experience
Edit	Editorial	**Expr**	Expressive
Educ	Education	**Ext**	Extended
Educr	Educare	**Extr**	Exterior
Efcts	Effects	**Extrm**	Extreme
EFL	English as a Foreign Language		
Egypt	Egyptian/Egyptology	**Fabs**	Fabric(s)
Elec	Electrical	**Fac**	Faculty
Elecacoust	Electroacoustics	**Facil**	Facilities
Electromech	Electromechanical	**Fash**	Fashion
Electron	Electronic(s)	**Fbr**	Fibre
ELT	English Language Teaching	**Fctn**	Fiction
Ely	Early	**Fd**	Food
Emb	Embryo	**Fdn**	Foundation
Embd	Embedded	**Filmm**	Filmmaking
Embr	Embroidery	**Fin**	Finance/Financial
Emer	Emergency	**Finn**	Finnish
Emp	Employment	**Fish**	Fisheries
Ener	Energy	**Fit**	Fitness
Eng	Engineering	**Fl**	Fluid
Engl	English	**Fld**	Field
Engn	Engine	**Flex**	Flexible
Ent	Enterprise	**Flor**	Floristry
Enter	Entertainment	**FMaths**	Further Mathematics
Entre	Entrepreneur/Entrepreneurship	**Fmly**	Family
Env	Environment/Environmental	**Fn**	Fine
EPQ	Extended Project Qualification	**Foot**	Footwear
Eql	Equal	**For**	Foreign
Eqn	Equine/Equestrian	**Foren**	Forensic
Equip	Equipment	**Foss**	Fossil(s)
Equit	Equitation	**Fr**	French
Ergon	Ergonomics	**Frchd**	Franchised
Est	Estate	**Frcst**	Forecasting
Eth	Ethics	**Frm**	Farm
Ethl	Ethical	**Frmwk**	Framework
Eth-Leg	Ethico-Legal	**Frshwtr**	Freshwater
Ethn	Ethnic	**Frst**	Forest
Ethnol	Ethnology	**Frsty**	Forestry
Ethnomus	Ethnomusicology	**Frtlty**	Fertility
EU	European Union	**Fst Trk**	Fast Track
Euro	European	**Fstvl**	Festival
Eval	Evaluation	**Ftbl**	Football
Evnglstc	Evangelistic	**Ftre**	Feature(s)
Evnt(s)	Event(s)	**Ftwr**	Footwear
Evol	Evolution/Evolutionary	**Furn**	Furniture
Ex	Executing	**Fut**	Futures
Excl	Excellence		

Gael	Gaelic	Hlthcr	Healthcare
Gam	Gambling	Hm	Home
Gdn	Garden	Hnd	Hindi
Gdnc	Guidance	Hol	Holistic
Gem	Gemmology	Hom	Homeopathic
Gen	General	Homin	Hominid
Genet	Genetics	Horol	Horology
Geochem	Geochemistry	Hort	Horticulture
Geog	Geography	Hosp	Hospital
Geoinform	Geoinformatics	Hous	Housing
Geol	Geology	HR	Human Resources
Geophys	Geophysics	Hrdrs	Hairdressing
Geophysl	Geophysical	Hrs	Horse
Geopol	Geopolitics	Hse	House
Geosci	Geoscience	Hspty	Hospitality
Geosptl	Geospatial	Htl	Hotel
Geotech	Geotechnics	Hum	Human(ities)
Ger	German/Germany	Hung	Hungarian
Gerc	Germanic	Hydrog	Hydrography
GIS	Geographical Information Systems	Hydrol	Hydrology
		Hyg	Hygiene
Gk	Greek		
Glf	Golf	Iber	Iberian
Glf Crs	Golf Course	Ice	Icelandic
Gllry	Gallery/Galleries	ICT	Information and Communications Technology
Glob	Global/Globalisation		
Gls	Glass	Id	Ideas
Gmg	Gaming	Idnty	Identity
Gmnt	Garment	Illus	Illustration
Gms	Games	Imag	Image/Imaging/Imaginative
Gmtc	Geomatic	Immun	Immunology/Immunity
Gndr	Gender	Impair	Impairment
Gnm	Genome/Genomics	Incl	Including
Gov	Government	Incln	Inclusion
Govn	Governance	Inclsv	Inclusive
Graph	Graphic	Ind	Industrial/Industry
Grgn	Georgian	Indep St	Independent Study
Grn	Green	Indsn	Indonesian
gs	General Studies	Inf	Information
Guji	Gujerati	Infec	Infectious/Infection
		Infml	Informal
Hab	Habitat	Inform	Informatics
Hack	Hacking	Infra	Infrastructure
Hard	Hardware	Inftq	Informatique
Haz	Hazard	Injry	Injury
Heal	Healing	Innov	Innovation
Heb	Hebrew	Ins	Insurance
Herb	Herbal	Inst	Institution(al)
Herit	Heritage	Instln	Installation
Hisp	Hispanic	Instr	Instrument/Instrumentation
Hist	History/Historical	Int	International
HL	IB Higher level	Integ	Integrated/Integration
Hlcst	Holocaust	Intel	Intelligent/Intelligence
Hlnds	Highlands	Inter	Interior
Hlth	Health	Interact	Interaction/Interactive

Intercult	Intercultural	Lit	Literature/Literary
Interd	Interdisciplinary	Litcy	Literacy
Interp	Interpretation	Lnd	Land(scape)
Intlctl	Intellectual	Lndbd	Land-based
Intnet	Internet	Lns	Lens
Intr	Interest(s)	Log	Logistics
Intrmdl	Intermodal	Lrn	Learn
Inv	Investment	Lrng	Learning
Invstg	Investigating/Investigation	Ls	Loss
IPML	Integrated Professional Master	Lsr	Laser
	in Language	Ltg	Lighting
Ir	Irish	Ltr	Later
Is	Issues	Lv	Live
Isl	Islands	Lvstk	Livestock
Islam	Islamic		
Isrl	Israel/Israeli	Mach	Machine(ry)
IT	Information Technology	Mait	Maitrise Internationale
Ital	Italian	Mak	Making/Maker
ITE	Initial Teacher Education	Mand	Mandarin
ITT	Initial Teacher Training	Manuf	Manufacturing
		Map	Map/Mapping
Jap	Japanese	Mar	Marine
Jew	Jewish	Marit	Maritime
Jewel	Jewellery	Mark	Market(ing)
Jrnl	Journalism	Masch	Maschinenbau
Jud	Judaism	Mat	Materials
Juris	Jurisprudence	Mathem	Mathematical
Just	Justice	Maths	Mathematics
		Mbl	Mobile
Knit	Knit/Knitted	Mdl	Modelling
Kntwr	Knitwear	Measur	Measurement
Knwl	Knowledge	Mech	Mechanical
Kor	Korean	Mecha	Mechatronics
KS	Key Stage	Mechn	Mechanisation
		Mechnsms	Mechanisms
Lab	Laboratory	Med	Medicine/cal
Lang(s)	Language(s)	Medcnl	Medicinal
Las	Laser	Mediev	Medieval
Lat	Latin	Medit	Mediterranean
Lcl	Local	Metal	Metallurgy/Metallurgical
LD	Learning Disabilities	Meteor	Meteorology/Meteorological
Ldrshp	Leadership	Meth	Method(s)
Lea	Leather	Mgr	Manager
Leg	Legal	Mgrl	Managerial
Legis	Legislative	Mgt	Management
Leis	Leisure	Microbiol	Microbiology/Microbiological
Lf	Life	Microbl	Microbial
Lfstl	Lifestyle	Microcomp	Microcomputer/Microcomputing
Lgc	Logic	Microelec	Microelectronics
Lib	Library	Mid E	Middle Eastern
Libshp	Librarianship	Midwif	Midwifery
Lic	Licensed	Min	Mining
Lic de Geog	Licence de Geographie	Miner	Minerals
Lic de Let	Licence de Lettres	Mkup	Make-up
Ling	Linguistics	Mling	Multilingual

Mltry	Military	Nnl	National
MML	Master of Modern Languages	Norw	Norwegian
Mnd	Mind	Npli	Nepali
Mndrn	Mandarin	Nrs	Norse
Mnrts	Minorities	Ntv	Native
Mnstry	Ministry	Nucl	Nuclear
Mnswr	Menswear	Nurs	Nursing
Mntl Hlth	Mental Health	Nursy	Nursery
Mntn	Mountain	Nutr	Nutrition(al)
Mntnce	Maintenance	Nvl	Naval
Mny	Money	NZ	New Zealand
Mod	Modular		
Modl	Modelling/Modelmaking	Objs	Objects
Modn	Modern	Obs	Observational
Modnty	Modernity	Occ	Occupational
Mol	Molecular	Ocean	Oceanography
Monit	Monitoring	Ocn	Ocean
Mov	Movement/Moving	Ocnc	Oceanic
Mrchnds	Merchandise	Oeno	Oenology
Mrchnt	Merchant	Ofce	Office
Mrl	Moral	Off	Offshore
Msg	Massage	Offrd	Off-road
Mslm	Muslim	Okl	Oklahoma
Mtl	Metal(s)	Onc	Oncology
Mtlsmth	Metalsmithing	Onln	Online
Mtn	Motion	Op(s)	Operation(s)
Mtr	Motor	Oph	Ophthamic
Mtrcycl	Motorcycle	Oprtg	Operating
Mtrg	Motoring	Opt	Optical
Mtrspo	Motorsports	Optim	Optimisation
Multid	Multi-disciplinary	Optn/s	Optional/Options
Multim	Multimedia	Optoel	Optoelectronics
Mus	Music(ian)	Optom	Optometry
Muscskel	Musculoskeletal	OR	Operational Research
Musl	Musical	Ord	Ordinary
Musm	Museum	Org	Organisation
Mushp	Musicianship	Orgnc	Organic
		Orgnsms	Organisms
N	New	Orn	Ornithology
N Am	North America	Orntl	Oriental
Nano	Nanoscience	Orth	Orthoptics
Nanoelectron	Nanoelectronics	Orthot	Orthotics
Nanotech	Nanotechnology	Oseas	Overseas
Nat	Nature/Natural	Ost	Osteopathy
Natpth	Naturopathy	Out	Outdoor
Navig	Navigation	Out Act	Outdoor Activity
Nds	Needs	Outsd	Outside
Neg	Negotiated	Ovrs	Overseas
Net	Network		
Neuro	Neuroscience	P	Primary
Neuropsy	Neuropsychology	P Cr	Primary Care
News	Newspaper	Pacif	Pacific
NGO	Non-Governmental	Pack	Packaging
	Organisation(s)	PActv	Physical Activity
NI	Northern Ireland/Northern Irish	Pal	Palaeobiology

Palae	Palaeoecology/Palaeontology	Pop	Popular
Palaeoenv	Palaeoenvironments	Popn	Population
Paramed	Paramedic(al)	Port	Portuguese
Parasit	Parasitology	Postcol	Postcolonial
Parl	Parliamentary	PPE	Philosophy, Politics and
Pat	Patent		Economics or Politics,
Path	Pathology		Philosophy and Economics
Pathobiol	Pathobiological	PPI	Private Pilot Instruction
Pathogen	Pathogenesis	Ppl	People
Patt	Pattern	Ppr	Paper
Pblc	Public	Pptry	Puppetry
Pce	Peace	PR	Public Relations
PE	Physical Education	Prac	Practice/Practical
Ped	Pedagogy	Practnr	Practitioner
Per	Person/Personal	Prchsng	Purchasing
Perf	Performance	Prcrmt	Procurement
Perfum	Perfumery	Prdcl	Periodical
Pers	Personnel	Precsn	Precision
Persn	Persian	Pref	Preferable/Preferred
Petrol	Petroleum	Prehist	Prehistory
PGCE	Postgraduate Certificate in	Prem	Premises
	Education	Proc	Process/Processing
Pharm	Pharmacy	Prod	Product/Production/Produce
Pharmacol	Pharmacology	Prodg	Producing
Pharml	Pharmaceutical	Prof	Professional/Professions
Phil	Philosophy	Prog	Programme/Programming
Philgy	Philology	Proj	Project
Phn	Phone	Prom	Promotion
Phon	Phonetics	Prop	Property/ies
Photo	Photography/Photographic	Pros	Prosthetics
Photojrnl	Photojournalism	Prot	Protection/Protected
Photon	Photonic(s)	Prplsn	Propulsion
Phys	Physics	Prsts	Pursuits
Physio	Physiotherapy	Prt	Print
Physiol	Physiology/Physiological	Prtcl	Particle
Physl	Physical	Prtd	Printed
Pks	Parks	Prtg	Printing/Printmaking
Plan	Planning	Prvntn	Prevention
Planet	Planetary	Pst	Post
Plas	Plastics	Pstrl	Pastoral
Play	Playwork	Psy	Psychology
Plcg	Police/Policing	Psychobiol	Psychobiology
Plcy	Policy	Psyling	Psycholinguistics
Plmt	Placement	Psysoc	Psychosocial
Plnt	Plant	p/t	part-time
Plntsmn	Plantsmanship	Ptcl	Particle
Plt	Pilot	Pub	Publishing
Pltry	Poultry	Pvt	Private
PMaths	Pure Mathematics	Pwr	Power
Pntg	Painting	Pwrcft	Powercraft
Pod	Podiatry/Podiatric		
Pol	Politics/Political	Qntm	Quantum
Polh	Polish	Qry	Quarry
Pollut	Pollution	Qtrnry	Quaternary
Poly	Polymer/Polymeric	QTS	Qualified Teacher Status

Qual	Quality	S	Secondary
Qualif	Qualification	S As	South Asian
Quant	Quantity/Quantitative	Sansk	Sanskrit
		Sat	Satellite
Rad	Radio	Sbstnce	Substance
Radiog	Radiography	Scand	Scandinavian
Radiothera	Radiotherapy	Schlstc	Scholastic
Rbr	Rubber	Schm	Scheme
Rce	Race	Sci	Science/Scientific
Rcycl	Recycling	Scnc	Scenic
Rdtn	Radiation	Scngrph	Scenographic/Scenography
Realsn	Realisation	Scot	Scottish
Rec	Recording	Scr	Secure
Reclam	Reclamation	Script	Scriptwriting
Recr	Recreation	Scrn	Screen
Reg	Regional	Scrnwrit	Sreenwriting
Regn	Regeneration	Scrts	Securities
Rehab	Rehabilitation	Scrty	Security
Rel	Relations	Sctr	Sector
Relgn	Religion	Sculp	Sculpture/Sculpting
Relig	Religious	Sdlry	Saddlery
Reltd	Related	SE	South East
Rem Sens	Remote Sensing	Sec	Secretarial
Ren	Renaissance	Semicond	Semiconductor
Renew	Renewable	SEN	Special Educational
Rep	Representation		Needs
Reqd	Required	Serb Cro	Serbo-Croat
Res	Resources	Serv	Services
Resid	Residential	Set	Settings
Resoln	Resolution	Sfc	Surface
Resp	Response	Sfty	Safety
Respir	Respiratory	Sgnl	Signal
Restor	Restoration	Ship	Shipping
Rev	Revenue	Simul	Simulation
Rflxgy	Reflexology	Sit Lrng	Situated Learning
Rgby	Rugby	Sk	Skills
Rgstrn	Registration	Slav	Slavonic
Rl	Real	Slf	Self
Rlblty	Reliability	Sln	Salon
Rlwy	Railway	Slovak	Slovakian
Rmnc	Romance	Sls	Sales
RN	Registered Nurse	Sml	Small
Rnwl	Renewal	Smt	Smart
Robot	Robotics	Smtc	Semitic
Rom	Roman	Snc	Sonic
Romn	Romanian	Snd	Sound
Rsch	Research	Sndtrk	Soundtrack
Rspnsb	Responsibility	Sndwch	Sandwich
Rsrt	Resort	Sng	Song
Rstrnt	Restaurant	Soc	Social
Rtl	Retail	Sociol	Sociology
Rts	Rights	SocioLeg	Socio-Legal
Rur	Rural	Socling	Sociolinguistics
Russ	Russian	Soft	Software
Rvr	River	Sol	Solution(s)

Soty	Society	TEFL	Teaching English as a Foreign Language
Sov	Soviet		
Sp	Speech	Telecomm	Telecommunications
Span	Spanish	Ter	Terrestrial
Spat	Spatial	TESOL	Teaching English to Speakers of Other Languages
Spc	Space		
SPD	Surface Pattern Design	Testmt	Testament
Spec	Special/Specialisms/Specialist	Tex	Textiles
		Thea	Theatre
Spec Efcts	Special Effects	Theol	Theology
Sply	Supply	Theor	Theory/Theoretical
Spn	Spain	Ther	Therapeutic
Spo	Sports	Thera	Therapy
Spotrf	Sportsturf	Tht	Thought
Spowr	Sportswear	Tiss	Tissue
Spptd	Supported	Tlrg	Tailoring
Sprtng	Supporting	Tm	Time
Sqntl	Sequential	Tmbr	Timber
Srf	Surf/Surfing	Tnnl	Tunnel/Tunnelling
Srgy	Surgery	Tns	Tennis
SS	Solid-state	Topog	Topographical
St	Studies	Tour	Tourism
St Reg	State Registration	Tox	Toxicology
Stats	Statistics	TQ	Teaching Qualification
Std	Studio	Tr	Trade
Stg	Stage	Tr Stands	Trading Standards
Stgs	Settings	Trad	Traditional
Stnds	Standards	Trans	Transport(ation)
STQ	Scottish Teaching Qualification	Transat	Transatlantic
Str	Stringed	Transl	Translation
Strat	Strategic/Strategy	Transnl Med Sci	Translational Medical Science
Strg	Strength	Trav	Travel
Strt	Street	Trfgrs	Turfgrass
Struct	Structural/Structures	Trg	Training
Stry	Story	Trnrs	Trainers
Stt	State	Trpcl	Tropical
Stwdshp	Stewardship	Trpl	Triple
Surf	Surface	Trstrl	Terrestrial
Surv	Surveying	Tstmnt	Testament
Sust	Sustainability/Sustainable	Ttl	Total
Swed	Swedish	Turk	Turkish
Swli	Swahili	Twn	Town
Sxlty	Sexuality	Typo	Typographical/Typography
Sys	System(s)		
Systmtc	Systematic	Ukr	Ukrainian
		Un	Union
Tam	Tamil	Undwtr	Underwater
Tap	Tapestry	Unif	Unified
Tax Rev	Taxation and Revenue	Up	Upland
Tbtn	Tibetan	Urb	Urban
Tcnqs	Techniques	USA	United States of America
Teach	Teaching	Util	Utilities/Utilisation
Tech	Technology/Technician/Technical		
		Val	Valuation
Technol	Technological	Vcl	Vocal

Veh	Vehicle	**Wldlf**	Wildlife
Vert	Vertebrate	**Wls**	Wales
Vet	Veterinary	**Wmnswr**	Womenswear
Vib	Vibration	**Wn**	Wine
Vict	Victorian	**Wrbl**	Wearable
Vid	Video	**Writ**	Writing/Writer
Viet	Vietnamese	**Wrld**	World
Virol	Virology	**Wrlss**	Wireless
Vis	Visual/Visualisation	**Wst**	Waste(s)
Vit	Viticulture	**Wstn**	Western
Vkg	Viking	**Wtr**	Water
Vntr	Venture	**Wtrspo**	Watersports
Vnu	Venue	**Wvn**	Woven
Voc	Vocational	**www**	World Wide Web
Vol	Voluntary		
Vrtl Rlty	Virtual Reality	**Ycht**	Yacht
Vsn	Vision	**Ychtg**	Yachting
Vstr	Visitor	**Yng**	Young
		Yrs	Years
Wdlnd	Woodland	**Yth**	Youth
Welf	Welfare		
Wk	Work	**Zool**	Zoology
Wkg	Working		
Wlbng	Well-being	**3D**	Three-dimensional

Choosing Your University And Degree Course...And Completing Your UCAS Application

Why not contact Brian Heap at HEAPS (*Higher Education Advice and Planning Service*) for a telephone consultation for advice on such issues as:

- Choosing A-level subjects (which are the best and required subjects and for which degree courses)
- Degrees and Diploma courses (making the right choice from a list of thousands!)
- Completing your UCAS application (will the admissions tutor remember your personal statement?)
- Choosing the right university or college (the best ones for you and your courses)

For details of services and consultation fees contact:

The Higher Education Advice and Planning Service
Email heapservice@gmail.com

ACCOUNTANCY/ACCOUNTING

(see also **Finance**)

Accountancy and Accounting degree courses include accounting, finance, economics, law, management, qualitative methods and information technology. Many, but not all, Accountancy and Accounting degrees give exemptions from the examinations of some or all of the accountancy professional bodies. Single Honours courses are more likely to give full exemptions, while Joint Honours courses are more likely to lead to partial exemptions. Students should check with universities and colleges which professional bodies offer exemptions for their courses before applying. Most courses are strongly vocational and many offer sandwich placements or opportunities to study Accountancy/Accounting with a second subject.

Useful websites www.accaglobal.com; www.cimaglobal.com; www.cipfa.org; www.tax.org.uk; www.icaew.com; www.bized.co.uk.

NB The points totals shown to the left of the institutions are for ease of reference only. It must not be assumed that Tariff points are always used by institutions or that they can be substituted for an offer in grades. The level of an offer is not necessarily indicative of the quality of a course.

COURSE OFFERS INFORMATION

Subject requirements/preferences **GCSE** English and mathematics required: popular universities may specify grades. **AL** mathematics or accounting required or preferred for some courses. Business studies accepted for some courses.

Your target offers and examples of courses provided by each institution
380 pts **Exeter** – A*AA–AAB 380–340 pts (Maths Acc) (IB 38–34 pts)
 Warwick – A*AA–AAAb 380 pts (Acc Fin) (IB 38 pts)
360 pts **Bath** – AAA 360 pts (Acc Fin) (IB 38 pts)
 Bristol – AAA–AAB 360–340 pts (Acc Fin; Econ Acc; Acc Mgt) (IB 37–35 pts)
 City – AAA 360 pts (Acc Fin; Econ Acc) (IB 35 pts)
 Edinburgh – AAA–BBB 360–300 pts (Acc Fin; Bus Acc) (IB 37–34 pts)
 Exeter – AAA–AAB 360–340 pts (Bus Acc) (IB 36–34 pts)
 Glasgow – AAA–A*AB (Acc Maths; Acc Fin) (IB 36 pts)
 Lancaster – AAA–A*AB 360 pts (Acc Econ; Acc Fin; Acc Fin Maths; Acc Mgt St) (IB 36 pts)
 Leeds – AAA (Acc Fin) (IB 35 pts HL 17 pts)
 London LSE – AAA (Acc Fin) (IB 38 pts HL 666)
 Newcastle – AAA–AAB 360–340 pts (Bus Acc Fin) (IB 35–38 pts)
 Queen's Belfast – AAA (Acc; Acc Modn Lang (Fr/Ger/Span))
 Southampton – AAA incl maths (Acc Econ) (IB 36 pts HL 18 pts)
 Strathclyde – AAA (Acc; Acc Fin) (IB 36 pts)
340 pts **Aston** – AAB 340 pts (Acc Mgt) (IB 35 pts)
 Birmingham – AAB (Acc Fin) (IB 34–36 pts)
 Brunel – AAB–ABB 340–320 pts (Fin Acc) (IB 35 pts)
 Cardiff – AAB 340 pts (Acc; Acc Mgt; Acc Econ; Acc Fin) (IB 35 pts)
 Durham – AAB 340 pts (Mgt Acc; Acc Fin) (IB 36 pts)
 Exeter – AAA–AAB 360–340 pts (Acc Fin) (IB 36–34 pts)
 Liverpool – AAB (Acc Fin) (IB 35 pts)
 London (QM) – AAB 340 pts (Maths Fin Acc) (IB 34 pts)

Check **Chapter 4** when choosing your university and **Chapter 7** on how to read the subject tables.

London (RH) – AAB (Mgt Acc) (IB 35 pts)
Loughborough – AAA–AAB 340–360 pts (Acc Fin Mgt; Econ Acc) (IB 36 pts)
Manchester – AAB 340 pts (Acc Fin) (IB 35 pts)
Newcastle – AAB–ABB 340–320 pts (Acc Fin) (IB 35 pts)
Nottingham – AAB (Acc Fin Contemp Chin; Fin Acc Mgt) (IB 32–34 pts)
Reading – AAB (Acc Bus; Acc Mgt; Acc Econ; Acc Fin) (IB 35 pts)
Southampton – AAB 340 pts (Acc Fin) (IB 34 pts HL 17 pts)
Surrey – AAB (Acc Fin) (IB 36 pts)
Sussex – AAB–ABB 340–320 pts (Acc Fin) (IB 34 pts)
Ulster – AAB 340 pts (Acc)
York – AAB (Acc Bus Fin Mgt) (IB 34 pts)

320 pts **Bournemouth** – ABB 320 pts (Acc Bus; Acc Law; Acc Fin) (IB 32 pts)
Bradford – ABB 320 pts (Acc Fin)
De Montfort – 320 pts (Acc courses) (IB 30 pts)
East Anglia – ABB (Acc Fin; Econ Acc) (IB 32–31 pts)
Essex – ABB–BBB 320–300 pts (Acc courses; Acc Fin) (IB 29 pts)
ifs (UC) – 320–340 pts (Fin Invest Rk) (IB 32 pts)
Keele – ABB (Acc Law) (IB 28 pts)
Kent – ABB (Acc Fin) (IB 33 pts)
Kingston – ABB 320 pts (Acc Fin) (IB 27 pts)
Lincoln – 320 pts (Acc Fin)
Liverpool – ABB 320 pts (Law Acc Fin) (IB 33 pts)
Northumbria – 320 pts (Acc) (IB 26 pts)
Roehampton – 320 pts (Bus Mgt Acc)
Sheffield – ABB (Acc Fin Mgt) (IB 35 pts)
Swansea – ABB–BBB 320–300 pts (Acc Fin; Fin Econ Acc) (IB 33–32 pts)

300 pts **Aberdeen** – BBB 300 pts (Acc) (IB 30 pts)
Aberystwyth – 300 pts (Acc Fin courses) (IB 27 pts)
Brighton – BBB 300 pts (Acc Fin) (IB 32 pts HL 16 pts)
Bristol UWE – BBB 300 pts (Acc Fin) (IB 26 pts)
Central Lancashire – 300 pts (Acc)
Dundee – BBB (Acc) (IB 30 pts)
Greenwich – 300 pts (Acc Fin)
Heriot-Watt – BBB (Acc Bus Law) (IB 34 pts)
Hertfordshire – 300 pts (Acc; Acc Fin)
Huddersfield – 300 pts (Acc Fin; Acc Law)
Hull – 300 pts (Acc courses) (IB 30 pts)
Keele – ABC (Acc Fin; Fin courses)
Kent – BBB 300 pts (Acc Mgt) (IB 34 pts)
Leeds Beckett – 300 pts (Acc Fin) (IB 26 pts)
Liverpool Hope – 300–320 pts (Acc; Acc Joint Hons)
Middlesex – 300 pts (Acc Fin)
Oxford Brookes – BBB (Acc Fin) (IB 31 pts)
Plymouth – 300 pts (Acc Fin) (IB 26 pts)
Sheffield Hallam – 300 pts (Acc Fin; Foren Acc)
Westminster – BBB (Acc Mgt) (IB 28 pts)

280 pts **Abertay** – BBC (Acc Fin)
Birmingham City – 280 pts (Acc; Acc Joint Hons) (IB 32 pts)
Cardiff Met (UWIC) – 280 pts (Acc)
Central Lancashire – 280 pts (Acc Fin St)
Chichester – 280 pts (Acc Fin) (IB 30 pts)
Coventry – BBC 280 pts (Acc Fin) (IB 29 pts)
Edge Hill – 280 pts (Acc) (IB 26 pts)
Gloucestershire – 280 pts (Acc Fin Mgt)
Liverpool John Moores – 280 pts (Acc Fin) (IB 29 pts)

HOW FAR DO YOU WANT TO GO IN BUSINESS?

THE CHARTERED ACCOUNTANT.
NO ONE'S BETTER QUALIFIED.

London, Shanghai, New York, Singapore? ICAEW Chartered Accountants have the work experience, financial intelligence and skills the business world demands.

Becoming 'chartered' will help start their journey, visit icaew.com/careers

ICAEW

A WORLD LEADER OF THE ACCOUNTANCY AND FINANCE PROFESSION

Kenneth

Capital Markets Group Manager
PwC, London

After graduating with a first-class honours degree in Finance, Accounting and Management from the University of Nottingham, I continued my studies and gained a master's degree in Finance at Warwick Business School.

Upon completing my master's degree, I joined PwC's graduate programme in audit, principally servicing multinational and listed companies in the consumer and industrial products and services sector. Working in audit has helped me to develop my technical ability along with people management skills. You are given responsibility at an early stage of your career in audit, to lead teams and manage others on a day-to-day basis. Opportunities to interact with clients from different roles also enabled me to develop a good overview of how different businesses operate.

I had the opportunity to work on a special project alongside a specialist team from PwC Capital Markets Group. After completing the project, I maintained this internal network within the firm and was offered the option to make an internal transfer after completing the ACA qualification. I currently work as a manager in PwC Capital Markets Group. This role entails providing advice and assurance services to companies looking to raise debt or equity and to listed companies carrying out M&A activities.

It wasn't difficult to make the decision to study for the ACA. ICAEW has a wide global presence and reciprocal memberships with many major accounting bodies around the world. The ACA is not only about the numbers. It equips you well with better commercial sense, and trains you to be a business advisor rather just a financial reporting accountant.

The international recognition enjoyed by ICAEW is the main reason I chose the ACA qualification. If I decide I want to work in Hong Kong, Singapore, China or indeed globally later in my career, I know it will definitely open doors for me!

ICAEW

BUSINESS WITH CONFIDENCE

icaew.com/careers

Be the **one** who **leads** the crowd

**BSc Accounting and Finance
at Leeds University Business School –
an ICAEW Strategic Partnership
degree ranked 5th in the country
(*Complete University Guide, 2014*).**

Find out more:
www.business.leeds.ac.uk/undergraduate/bsc-accounting-and-finance/

EXEMPTIONS

Our BSc Accounting and Finance degree offers the maximum possible exemptions from ICAEW (and ACCA) professional accounting exams – getting you where you want to be, faster.

WORK PLACEMENTS

As part of all of our degrees at Leeds University Business School you have the opportunity to complete a full-year work placement. Our reputation means that many of our students succeed in obtaining competitive placements with the Big Four Accounting firms while others choose to complete a placement with SME accountants or opt to try out alternative career options. It's a great way to gain experience, an income and possibly a job offer at the end of the year.

NURTURING TALENT

We have recruited over 140 skilled professionals from varying industries to act as mentors to our business students. They can pass on their skills, knowledge and experience to help you when searching for internships, placements and graduate opportunities.

CAREERS

A majority of our graduates go on to become qualified accountants with professional firms. However, you will also be well prepared for a career in either retail or investment banking, or indeed a more general management or finance role.

The Business School has built a bridge between academia and the professional world. I'm looking forward to crossing it.

Andrew, Graduate Diploma in Finance, Accounting and Business

#challenging

ncl.ac.uk/nubs

TRANSFORM YOUR FUTURE AT BIRKBECK, UNIVERSITY OF LONDON

Offering a wide range of undergraduate programmes, which can be studied flexibly over 3 or 4 years, the School of Business, Economics and Informatics gives you the chance to gain a prestigious University of London degree through evening study. We are London's only specialist provider of evening higher education taught in a research-intensive institution.

The School of Business, Economics and Informatics is an excellent place for you to start an undergraduate degree, studying alongside part-time students who are working in the city of London.

Our world-class teaching will give you the chance to leave university with a prestigious degree qualification, as well as an excellent network helping you to start your career.

The School of Business, Economics and Informatics includes two departments offering full and part-time courses aimed at students wishing to study financial or accounting related programmes:

Economics, mathematics and statistics

The department brings together research and teaching in economics, finance, mathematics and statistics in a single department, which creates significant inter-disciplinary synergies. Our teaching is informed by the latest research

and by the needs of employers. We offer a wide selection of graduate, undergraduate and "conversion" courses in economics, finance, mathematics and statistics, and also provide customised in-house training to various government departments and city firms.

Management

The Department of Management is an internationally recognised centre of excellence in teaching, research and consultancy in the broad field of management and is the largest department in Birkbeck. We offer an incredibly wide-ranging and flexible set of programmes, taught by leading academics in the field. Our undergraduate degrees include Business, Management and Chartered Institute of Management Accountants (CIMA) accredited Accounting programmes.

To find out more about all our undergraduate courses, please go to www.bbk.ac.uk/business.

Natalie Jackson, BSc Economics and Social Policy
'If I'd been studying during the day then I wouldn't have been able to do the internship during my final year of study ... having both a well-respected degree and the work experience as well meant that I stood out during the recruitment process'

London South Bank – BBC 280 pts (Acc Fin) (IB 25 pts)
Manchester Met – 260–280 pts (Acc Fin) (IB 28 pts)
Nottingham Trent – 280 pts (Acc Fin) (IB 25 pts)
Portsmouth – 280 pts (Acc Fin; Acc Bus)
Salford – 280–320 pts (Fin Acc)
South Wales – BBC 280 pts (Acc Fin)
Stirling – BBC (Acc) (IB 32 pts)
Winchester – 280–320 pts (Acc Fin) (IB 26 pts)
Worcester – 280 pts (Acc) (IB 25 pts)

270 pts **ifs (UC)** – 270–300 pts (Bank Prac Mgt; Fin Acc Fin Serv) (IB 30 pts)
260 pts **Bangor** – 260–300 pts (Acc Fin; Acc Bank; Acc Econ)
Bolton – 260 pts (Acc courses)
BPP – 260 pts (Prof Acc)
Buckingham – BBB–BCC 260–300 pts (Acc Fin Mgt)
Glasgow Caledonian – BCC 260 pts (Acc) (IB 24 pts)
London (Birk) – 240 pts (Acc)
Northampton – 260–300 pts (Acc courses) (IB 24 pts)
Robert Gordon – BCC (Acc Fin) (IB 28 pts)
Sunderland – 260 pts (Acc Fin)

240 pts **Bradford (Coll Univ Centre)** – 240 pts (Law (Acc) LLB)
Canterbury Christ Church – 240 pts (Acc Fin)
Chester – 240–280 pts (Acc Fin) (IB 26 pts)
East London – 240 pts (Acc Fin) (IB 25 pts)
Edinburgh Napier – CCC 240 pts (Acc courses)
Glyndŵr – 240 pts (Bus Acc)
Heriot-Watt – CCC 240 pts (Acc Fin) (IB 24 pts)
Leeds Trinity – 240–260 pts (Acc Bus)
London Met – 240 pts (Acc Fin; Acc Bank)
South Wales – 240 pts (Maths Acc)
Southampton Solent – 240 pts (Acc)
Staffordshire – 240 pts (Acc Fin) (IB 24 pts)
Suffolk (Univ Campus) – 240–280 pts (Acc Fin)
Teesside – 240 pts (Acc Fin) (IB 30 pts)
West Scotland – CCC (Acc)
Wolverhampton – 240 pts (Acc Fin) (IB 24 pts)

230 pts **York St John** – 230–300 pts (Acc Fin)
220 pts **Derby** – 220–300 pts (Acc Joint Hons)
200 pts **Anglia Ruskin** – 200–240 pts (Acc Fin)
Bedfordshire – 200 pts (Acc) (IB 30 pts)
Blackburn (Coll) – 200 pts (Bus Acc)
Bucks New – 200–240 pts (Acc Fin)
Peterborough (Reg Coll) – 200 pts (Acc Fin)
West London – 200 pts (Acc Fin)

160 pts **Kaplan Holborn (Coll)** – 160 pts (Acc Fin)
Trinity Saint David (Swansea) – 160 pts (Acc)
120 pts **Grimsby (Univ Centre)** – 120 pts (Bus Mgt Acc)
Norwich City (Coll) – 120 pts (Bus Mgt (Fin Acc))
80 pts **Farnborough (CT)** – 80–200 pts (Acc)
Greenwich (Sch Mgt) – EE–A*A*80–280 pts (Acc Fin)

Alternative offers
See **Chapter 7** and **Appendix 1** for grades/UCAS Tariff points information for the International Baccalaureate, Scottish Highers/Advanced Highers, the Welsh Baccalaureate, the Irish Leaving Certificate, the Cambridge Pre-U Diploma, the Advanced Diploma and the Extended Project.

EXAMPLES OF FOUNDATION DEGREES IN THE SUBJECT FIELD
Blackburn (Coll); Blackpool and Fylde (Coll); Glyndŵr; Kensington Bus (Coll); London South Bank; Neath Port Talbot (Coll); Nescot; Plymouth; Warwickshire (Coll); West Cheshire (Coll).

CHOOSING YOUR COURSE (SEE ALSO CH.1)
Some course features
Bangor The ACCA-accredited Accounting and Finance course offers training in accounting skills with an emphasis on financial theory and decision-making techniques, providing integration with marketing, economics and banking disciplines. There is an option to change to any other business course up to the start of Year 2.

Bath The three- or four-year Accounting and Finance course is a specialist programme for those aiming for a career in the field of accounting and finance. Economics, law, IT and people and organisations are some of the topics included. The course includes a one-year industrial placement with the opportunity to study abroad.

Birmingham The Accounting and Finance degree emphasises the study of accounting and finance throughout the three years of the course. The course includes business skills, development, computing, economics, industrial relations, law, information technology and marketing. There is also a six-year package which includes a degree course, a professional accountancy qualification and work experience with KMPG paying a salary of £20,000 for working in London, plus all tuition fees and student accommodation costs paid by KMPG.

City (Acc Fin) This course is designed in conjunction with the ICAEW and a good performance will give students exemption of modules or credit towards the ACA, CII, CIMA and CIPFA qualifications. There is also an optional placement year in Year 3 and the opportunity to study abroad is available.

Durham The degrees in Accounting and Finance, Business and Finance and Business share a common first year with the option to transfer at the end of Year 1. The degree in Accountancy leads to exemptions from some professional bodies' exams. There is an optional placement year in Year 3.

Edinburgh A very flexible course in which Accountancy can also be taken with Business, Finance, Economics or Law.

Exeter The Accounting and Finance Single Honours course has a vocational emphasis, and can also be studied as a four-year course with work placement or international study options. Business, Economics, Management and Mathematics are also offered with Accounting. Work experience can be arranged.

Kent In addition to the Single Honours degree in Accounting and Finance (with the option of a year in industry) a degree in Accounting and Finance and Economics is also offered. An important feature of the School of Business is the option of a three-year placement.

Lancaster (Acc Adt Fin) The 60 students on this course spend up to 18 months on salaried placement with Ernst & Young; first-year bursary paid to all students achieving A*AA in A-level examinations.

London LSE A broad course, focusing on both accounting and its applications in different management areas. Options in first year depend on students' level of mathematics.

Newcastle (Bus Acc Fin) Created in collaboration with PwC and accredited by the ICAEW, this course offers each student over 200 days' work experience with PwC across the duration of their degree.

Warwick (Acc Fin) Focusing on the application of mathematics in business, this course also offers flexibility of learning with modules offered in entrepreneurship, HR, law, marketing and strategy, as well as the opportunity to take a 12-month work placement between Years 2 and 3.

Universities and colleges teaching quality See www.qaa.ac.uk; http://unistats.direct.gov.uk.

Top research universities and colleges (RAE 2008) (Accounting and Finance) Bangor; Essex; Exeter; Bristol; Glasgow; Stirling; Bristol UWE; Dundee; Huddersfield.

Examples of sandwich degree courses Aston; Bath; Bedfordshire; Birmingham City; Bournemouth; Bradford; Brighton; Bristol UWE; Brunel; Canterbury Christ Church; Cardiff Met (UWIC); Central Lancashire; Chichester; Coventry; Cumbria; De Montfort; Derby; Durham; Gloucestershire; Greenwich; Hertfordshire; Huddersfield; Hull; Kent; Kingston; Lancaster; Leeds Beckett; Liverpool John Moores; London (RH); Loughborough; Manchester Met; Middlesex; Northumbria; Nottingham Trent; Oxford Brookes; Plymouth; Portsmouth; Reading; Salford; Sheffield Hallam; South Wales; Southampton Solent; Surrey; Sussex; Teesside; Trinity Saint David (Swansea); Ulster; West London; West Scotland; Westminster; Wolverhampton; Worcester; York.

ADMISSIONS INFORMATION

Number of applicants per place (approx) Bath 13; Birmingham 7; Bristol 10; Dundee 5; East Anglia 17; Essex 7; Exeter 18; Glasgow 10; Heriot-Watt 7; Hull 8; Kent 10; Lancaster 20; Leeds 25; London LSE 17; Loughborough 12; Manchester 22; Oxford Brookes 9; Salford 8; Sheffield 40; Southampton 13; Staffordshire 3; Stirling 20; Strathclyde 10; Ulster 10; Warwick 14.

Advice to applicants and planning the UCAS personal statement Universities look for good numerical and communication skills, interest in the business and financial world, teamwork, problem-solving and computing experience. On the UCAS application you should be able to demonstrate your interest and understanding of accountancy and to give details of any work experience or work shadowing undertaken. Try to arrange meetings with accountants, or work shadowing or work experience in accountants' offices, commercial or industrial firms, town halls, banks or insurance companies and describe the work you have done. Obtain information from the main accountancy professional bodies (see **Appendix 3**). Refer to current affairs which have stimulated your interest from articles in the *Financial Times*, *The Economist* or the business and financial sections of the weekend press. **Bath** Gap Year welcomed. Extra-curricular activities are important and should be described on the personal statement. There should be no gaps in your chronological history. **Bristol** Deferred entry accepted. **Brunel** (Bus Mgt (Acc)) Extended Project qualification accepted in place of AS-level; AL critical thinking and general studies acceptable. **Lancaster** (Acc Adt Fin) Selected UCAS applicants complete supplementary application form and online test. They may then be invited to a selection workshop.

Misconceptions about this course Many students believe incorrectly that you need to be a brilliant mathematician. However, you do have to be numerate and enjoy numbers (see **Subject requirements/preferences**). Many underestimate the need for a high level of attention to detail. **Buckingham** Some students think it's a maths course. **Salford** Some applicants believe the course is limited to financial knowledge when it also provides an all-round training in management skills.

Selection interviews Yes Reading, West London; **Some** Abertay, Aberystwyth, Anglia Ruskin, Buckingham, Cardiff, Cardiff Met (UWIC), De Montfort, Dundee, Kent, Lincoln, Liverpool John Moores, London LSE, Southampton, Staffordshire, Stirling, Sunderland, Warwick, Wolverhampton; **No** Birmingham, Bristol, East Anglia, Essex, Surrey.

Interview advice and questions Be prepared to answer questions about why you have chosen the course, the qualities needed to be an accountant, and why you think you have these qualities! You should also be able to discuss any work experience you have had and to describe the differences in the work of chartered, certified, public finance and management accountants. See also **Chapter 6**. **Buckingham** Students from a non-English-speaking background are asked to write an essay. If their maths results are weak they may be asked to do a simple arithmetic test. Mature students with no formal qualifications are usually interviewed and questioned about their work experience.

Reasons for rejection (non-academic) Poor English. Lack of interest in the subject because they realise they have chosen the wrong course! No clear motivation. Course details not researched. **London South Bank** Punctuality, neatness, enthusiasm and desire to come to London South Bank not evident.

AFTER-RESULTS ADVICE

Offers to applicants repeating A-levels Higher Brunel, Glasgow Caledonian, Hull, Manchester Met; **Possibly higher** Brighton, Central Lancashire, East Anglia, Leeds, Newcastle, Oxford Brookes, Sheffield Hallam; **Same** Abertay, Aberystwyth, Anglia Ruskin, Bangor, Birmingham City, Bolton, Bradford, Buckingham, Cardiff, Cardiff Met (UWIC), Chichester, De Montfort, Derby, Dundee, Durham, East London, Edinburgh Napier, Glasgow, Heriot-Watt, Huddersfield, Liverpool John Moores, Loughborough, Northumbria, Portsmouth, Salford, Staffordshire, Stirling, Trinity Saint David (Swansea), West London, West Scotland, Wolverhampton.

GRADUATE DESTINATIONS AND EMPLOYMENT (2011/12 HESA)

Graduates surveyed 4340 **Employed** 2070 **In voluntary employment** 125 **In further study** 1030 **Assumed unemployed** 465

Career note Most Accountancy/Accounting graduates enter careers in finance.

Check **Chapter 4** when choosing your university and **Chapter 7** on how to read the subject tables.

OTHER DEGREE SUBJECTS FOR CONSIDERATION

Actuarial Studies; Banking; Business Studies; Economics; Financial Services; Insurance; International Securities and Investment Banking; Mathematics; Quantity Surveying; Statistics.

ACTUARIAL SCIENCE/STUDIES

Actuaries deal with the evaluation and management of financial risks, particularly those associated with insurance companies and pension funds. Although Actuarial Science/Studies degrees are vocational and give full or partial exemptions from some of the examinations of the Institute and Faculty of Actuaries, students are not necessarily committed to a career as an actuary on graduation. However, many graduates go on to be actuary trainees, leading to one of the highest-paid careers.

Useful websites www.actuaries.org.uk; www.soa.org; www.beanactuary.org.

NB The points totals shown to the left of the institutions are for ease of reference only. It must not be assumed that Tariff points are always used by institutions or that they can be substituted for an offer in grades. The level of an offer is not necessarily indicative of the quality of a course.

COURSE OFFERS INFORMATION

Subject requirements/preferences **GCSE** Most institutions require grades A or B in mathematics. **AL** Mathematics at a specified grade required.

Your target offers and examples of courses provided by each institution

380 pts City – A*AA (Act Sci) (IB 35 pts)
Manchester – A*AA–AAA 380–360 pts (Act Sci Maths) (IB 37 pts)
Queen's Belfast – A*AA–AAAa (Act Sci Rsk Mgt)
Warwick – A*AA (MORSE (Act Fin Maths)) (IB 37 pts HL 7 maths)

360 pts Kent – AAA–AAB (Act Sci) (IB 33 pts HL 6 maths)
Leeds – A*AB–AAA (Act Maths) (IB 35 pts HL 6 maths)
London LSE – AAA incl maths 360 pts (Act Sci) (IB 38 pts HL 766)
Southampton – AAA (Maths Act Sci; Econ Act Sci) (IB 36 pts HL 18 pts)

340 pts East Anglia – AAB incl maths 340 pts (Act Sci; Act Sci (Yr Ind)) (IB 33 pts)
Essex – AAB–ABB (Act Sci) (IB 33 pts)
Leicester – AAB (Maths Act Sci) (IB 34 pts)

320 pts Heriot-Watt – ABB incl maths A (Act Sci)
Liverpool – ABB (Act Maths)

300 pts City – BBB 300 pts (Act Sci 4 yrs incl Fdn)
Kingston – 300 pts (Act Sci)

280 pts Kingston – 280 pts (Act Maths Stats)

Alternative offers

See **Chapter 7** and **Appendix 1** for grades/UCAS Tariff points information for the International Baccalaureate, Scottish Highers/Advanced Highers, the Welsh Baccalaureate, the Irish Leaving Certificate, the Cambridge Pre-U Diploma, the Advanced Diploma and the Extended Project.

CHOOSING YOUR COURSE (SEE ALSO CH.1)

Some course features

City (Act Sci) A course that covers actuarial and financial studies, IT, mathematics and statistics and offers eight exemptions from the Institute and Faculty of Actuaries' professional exams.
Kent A strong mathematical background is required for the Actuarial Science course, which covers economics, computing, probability and inference, mortality, operational research and life contingencies. There is an optional year in industry.
Kingston The Single Honours course in Actuarial Mathematics and Statistics prepares students for the actuarial profession. An optional placement year is available.
Queen's Belfast Nine-month placement in Year 3 in either an actuarial or risk management setting.

Institute
and Faculty
of Actuaries

Analytically minded?
Creative thinker?

Become an Actuary

Actuaries can calculate the probability of future events occurring and quantify those risks to a business.

They are problem solvers and strategic thinkers with a deep understanding of financial systems. They work in a variety of exciting roles internationally. An actuarial career is one of the most diverse and rewarding in the world.

Where could you work?

Every area of business is subject to risks so an actuarial career offers many options. A typical business problem might involve analysing future financial events, especially when the amount or timing of a payment is uncertain. It could also involve assessing when and where devastating storms may hit to help predict risks and their associated costs for investments or insurance.

Salaries for graduate trainee actuaries are around £25,000 – £35,000 and as you become more senior this can rise to well over £150,000. So the rewards are substantial.

How do I find out more?

To find out how to become an actuary, the benefits of studying towards an actuarial qualification and areas that actuaries work in, look at the web link below or find us on Facebook www.be-an-actuary.co.uk.

Find out more:
**www.actuaries.org.uk/
becoming-actuary**

Institute
and Faculty
of Actuaries

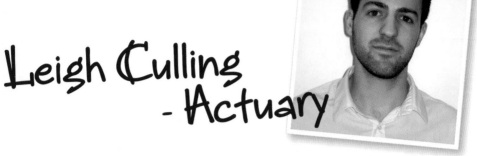

Leigh Culling - Actuary

Leigh Culling from Aon Hewitt talks to the Institute and Faculty of Actuaries (IFoA) about why he enjoys his job as an actuary, what he finds challenging and provides you with some advice if you are considering a career as an actuary.

What do Aon do?

Aon is the leading provider of risk management services, insurance and reinsurance brokerage and a global leader in human capital and management consulting. I work within Aon Hewitt's retirement consulting business in which we provide actuarial services to enable effective and efficient management of retirement plans.

How did you get your job at Aon Hewitt?

I started my career with Aon Hewitt by completing the summer internship program. After completing the internship, I was offered a place on the graduate program following the completion of my degree at the University of Bath.

What do you enjoy most about your job?

I think the great thing about working in pensions is that the retirement landscape is forever changing. It has led actuaries to continually evolve their methods to keep up with their competitors and has provided a wide variety of work.

What are the most stressful parts of the job?

With a lot of actuarial work, you have to meet quite tight deadlines to keep clients happy. This can be quite challenging at times, when you have to meet deadlines for more than one client. It's important to manage your time well and not be afraid to let your team know if you don't have capacity to take on additional work, most people would rather you do this than let your work build up and up.

Do you have any advice for anyone wanting to get into the industry?

An actuarial career can be extremely rewarding if you're willing to work hard. I think the best advice would be to do your research. Decide whether you're willing to commit your time to passing the exams and find out which area suits you best. I chose pensions as it offers more of a consulting role and I like the client-facing side of the work we do.

How do you manage your work/life balance?

The actuarial exams do take up a lot of your spare time. You have to be disciplined and reward yourself with a night off if you have had a good day of study. I have found getting up early and doing some studying in the morning before work has allowed me to free up more of my evenings to relax. In my spare time I like to play sport.

Any advice for the interview process?

I would recommend doing some research into the industry you wish to apply for. I was asked to give a five minute presentation on a pension's related topic. If you do your research you can show that you have a genuine interest in the industry and how new legislation or economic factors may affect the company you are applying for.

What soft skills have you found useful?

I think one of the most important skills I've learnt is the importance of explaining complex ideas in a non-technical way. Most actuaries have very strong technical skills but as a professional it's important that we can also communicate effectively with our clients.

Analytically minded? Creative thinker?
Become an Actuary

www.actuaries.org.uk/becoming-actuary email: **careers@actuaries.org.uk**

Warwick The course is a balance of mathematical theory and its applications between theory and practice.

Universities and colleges teaching quality See www.qaa.ac.uk; http://unistats.direct.gov.uk.

Examples of sandwich degree courses East Anglia; Essex; Heriot-Watt; Kent; Kingston; Queen's Belfast.

ADMISSIONS INFORMATION
Number of applicants per place (approx) City 6; Heriot-Watt 5; Kent 6; London LSE 9; Southampton (Maths Act Sci) 9, (Econ Act Sci) 8.

Advice to applicants and planning the UCAS personal statement Demonstrate your knowledge of this career and its training, and mention any contacts you have made with an actuary. (See **Appendix 3** for contact details of professional associations for further information.) Any work experience or shadowing in insurance companies should be mentioned, together with what you have learned about the problems facing actuaries. It is important to show motivation and sheer determination for training as an actuary as it is long and tough (up to three or four years after graduation). Mathematical flair, an ability to communicate and an interest in business are paramount.

Misconceptions about this course There is a general lack of understanding of actuaries' career training and of the career itself.

Selection interviews **Yes** East Anglia; **Some** Heriot-Watt, Kent, Southampton.

Interview advice and questions In view of the demanding nature of the training, it is important to have spent some time discussing this career with an actuary in practice. Questions, therefore, may focus on the roles of the actuary and the qualities you need to succeed. You should also be ready to field questions about your AL mathematics course and the aspects of it you most enjoy. See also **Chapter 6**.

Reasons for rejection (non-academic) **Kent** Poor language skills.

AFTER-RESULTS ADVICE
Offers to applicants repeating A-levels **Higher** City; **Same** Heriot-Watt, Southampton.

GRADUATE DESTINATIONS AND EMPLOYMENT (2011/12 HESA)
See **Finance**.

Career note Graduates commonly enter careers in finance, many taking further examinations to qualify as actuaries.

OTHER DEGREE SUBJECTS FOR CONSIDERATION
Accountancy; Banking; Business Studies; Economics; Financial Risk Management; Financial Services; Insurance; Mathematics; Money, Banking and Finance; Statistics.

AFRICAN STUDIES
(see also **Languages**)

African Studies courses tend to be multi-disciplinary, covering several subject areas and can include anthropology, history, geography, sociology, social psychology and languages. Most courses focus on Africa and African languages (Amharic (Ethiopia), Hausa (Nigeria), Somali (Horn of Africa), Swahili (Somalia and Mozambique), Yoruba (Nigeria, Sierra Leone, Ghana and Senegal), and Zulu (South Africa)).

Useful websites www.britishmuseum.org; www.africanstudies.org; www.black-history-month.co.uk; www.sasaonline.org.za.

NB The points totals shown to the left of the institutions are for ease of reference only. It must not be assumed that Tariff points are always used by institutions or that they can be substituted for an offer in grades. The level of an offer is not necessarily indicative of the quality of a course.

COURSE OFFERS INFORMATION

Subject requirements/preferences GCSE Grade A–C in mathematics and English may be required. **AL** For language courses a language subject or demonstrated proficiency in a language is required.

Your target offers and examples of courses provided by each institution
380 pts **Exeter** – A*AA–AAB 380–340 pts (Flex Comb Hons Mid E N Af St) (IB 38–34 pts)
        London (UCL) – AAAe 380 pts (Fr As Af Lang) (IB 38 pts)
340 pts **London (SOAS)** – AAB (Af Lang Cult; Af St) (IB 36 pts HL 666)
320 pts **Birmingham** – ABB (Af St Joint Hons)
300 pts **Birmingham** – BBB (Af St; Af St Anth; Af St Dev) (IB 32 pts)

Alternative offers
See **Chapter 7** and **Appendix 1** for grades/UCAS Tariff points information for the International Baccalaureate, Scottish Highers/Advanced Highers, the Welsh Baccalaureate, the Irish Leaving Certificate, the Cambridge Pre-U Diploma, the Advanced Diploma and the Extended Project.

CHOOSING YOUR COURSE (SEE ALSO CH.1)
Some course features
Birmingham A broad multi-disciplinary degree, offering Single and Joint Honours courses.
London (SOAS) Six African languages taught at undergraduate level; students have some flexibility in constructing their own course of study. Languages are supported by studies in anthropology, history, art and archaeology.

Universities and colleges teaching quality See www.qaa.ac.uk; http://unistats.direct.gov.uk.

Top research universities and colleges (RAE 2008) (Middle Eastern and African Studies) Cambridge; Oxford; Edinburgh; London (SOAS); Durham.

ADMISSIONS INFORMATION
Number of applicants per place (approx) Birmingham 5.

Advice to applicants and planning the UCAS personal statement Describe any visits you have made to African countries and why you wish to study this subject. Embassies in London may be able to provide information about the history, geography, politics, economics and the culture of the countries in which you are interested. Keep up-to-date with political developments in African countries. Discuss any aspects which interest you.

Selection interviews No Birmingham.

Interview advice and questions Questions are likely on your choice of country or geographical region, your knowledge of it and your awareness of some of the political, economic and social problems that exist. See also **Chapter 6**.

AFTER-RESULTS ADVICE
Offers to applicants repeating A-levels Higher Information not available from institutions.

GRADUATE DESTINATIONS AND EMPLOYMENT (2011/12 HESA)
Graduates surveyed 25 **Employed** 15 **In voluntary employment** 5 **In further study** 5 **Assumed unemployed** 0

Career note The language skills and knowledge acquired in African Studies courses, particularly when combined with periods of study in Africa, are relevant to a wide range of careers.

OTHER DEGREE SUBJECTS FOR CONSIDERATION
Anthropology; Geography; History; Languages; Sociology.

AGRICULTURAL SCIENCES/AGRICULTURE

(see also **Animal Sciences, Food Science/Studies and Technology, Forestry, Horticulture, Landscape Architecture, Surveying, Zoology**)

Courses in Agriculture recognise that modern farming practice requires sound technical and scientific knowledge, together with appropriate management skills, and most courses focus to a greater or lesser extent on all these requirements. Your choice of course depends on your particular interest and aims: some courses will give greater priority than others to practical application. Most graduates enter the agriculture industry whilst others move into manufacturing, wholesale and retail work.

Useful websites www.defra.gov.uk; www.naturalengland.org.uk; www.ccw.gov.uk; www.rase.org.uk; www.lantra.co.uk; www.nfuonline.com; www.nfyfc.org.uk; www.iagre.org; www.afuturein.com.

NB The points totals shown to the left of the institutions are for ease of reference only. It must not be assumed that Tariff points are always used by institutions or that they can be substituted for an offer in grades. The level of an offer is not necessarily indicative of the quality of a course.

COURSE OFFERS INFORMATION

Subject requirements/preferences **GCSE** English and mathematics usually required; chemistry sometimes required. Practical experience may be required. **AL** One or two maths/biological science subjects may be required or preferred. Geography may be accepted as a science subject. Similar requirements apply for Agricultural Business Management courses. (Crop Sci) Two science subjects may be required. (Cntry Mgt) Geography or biology preferred.

Your target offers and examples of courses provided by each institution
340 pts **Newcastle** – AAB–ABB 320–340 pts (Agri Bus Mgt) (IB 35 pts)
        Reading – AAB–ABBb 340 pts (Rur Prop Mgt) (IB 35 pts)
320 pts **Newcastle** – ABB–BBB 320–300 pts (Cntry Mgt) (IB 32–34 pts)
        Nottingham – ABB–BBB 320–300 pts (Agri; Agric Lvstk Sci; Agri Crop Sci; Agric Env Sci)
          (IB 30–32 pts)
300 pts **Aberdeen** – BBB (Wldlf Mgt)
        CAFRE – BBB incl chem/biol 300 pts (Agric Tech)
        Newcastle – BBB 300 pts (Agri Agron; Frm Bus Mgt) (IB 28–30 pts)
        Queen's Belfast – BBB 300 pts (Lnd Use Env Mgt)
        Reading – BBB–ABC 300 pts (Agric; Agric Bus Mgt) (IB 30 pts)
        Royal Agricultural Univ – 300 pts (Rur Lnd Mgt)
280 pts **Writtle (Coll)** – 280 pts (Agric courses) (IB 24 pts)
260 pts **Bangor** – 260–320 pts (Agric Cons Env) (IB 28 pts)
        Harper Adams – 260–300 pts (Agric Mark; Agric courses)
        Hertfordshire – 260 pts (Sust Agric Fd Sec)
        Myerscough (Coll) – 260 pts (Agric) (IB 24 pts)
        Royal Agricultural Univ – 260 pts (Agric; Agric (Crop); Agric (Cntry Mgt); Agric (Sust Soil
          Mgt); Agric (Frm Mechn Mgt))
240 pts **Aberystwyth** – 240 pts (Cntry Mgt; Cntry Cons; Agric) (IB 28 pts)
        Duchy (Coll) – (Agric Fd)
        Easton Otley (Coll) – 240 pts (Agric)
        Greenwich – 240 pts (Int Agric; Lnd Mgt (Lnd Use)) (IB 24 pts)
        Royal Agricultural Univ – 240 pts (Agric (Agric Sci); Bus Mgt (Int Fd Agri Bus); Int Eqn Agric
          Bus Mgt)
        Sparsholt (Coll) – 240 pts (Aquacult Fish Mgt)
160 pts **SRUC** – CC (Agric Sci)

Alternative offers
See **Chapter 7** and **Appendix 1** for grades/UCAS Tariff points information for the International Baccalaureate, Scottish Highers/Advanced Highers, the Welsh Baccalaureate, the Irish Leaving Certificate, the Cambridge Pre-U Diploma, the Advanced Diploma and the Extended Project.

EXAMPLES OF FOUNDATION DEGREES IN THE SUBJECT FIELD

Aberystwyth; Askham Bryan (Coll); Bishop Burton (Coll); Bournemouth; Bridgend (Coll); Bridgwater (Coll); Bristol UWE; CAFRE; Duchy (Coll); Easton Otley (Coll); Harper Adams; Manchester (Coll); Moulton (Coll); Myerscough (Coll); Nottingham Trent; Oatridge (Coll); Plumpton (Coll); Plymouth; Reaseheath (Coll); Royal Agricultural Univ; South Staffordshire (Coll); Sparsholt (Coll); Suffolk (Univ Campus); Sunderland; Warwickshire (Coll); Wiltshire (Coll); Writtle (Coll).

CHOOSING YOUR COURSE (SEE ALSO CH.1)

Some course features

Universities offer a very wide choice of courses including many specialisms associated with land use including Forest and Woodland Management, Garden Design, and Wildlife Conservation.

Aberystwyth A four-year course in Agriculture is offered with nine months' work experience. From a base of crop science and production, and animal science and production, this modular course covers farm business, management, marketing and crop and animal production in Years 3 and 4. The University has a world-wide reputation for its teaching and research.

Cumbria There are vocational courses in Forestry, Forestry Management and Forestry and Woodland Conservation, with the option of a professional placement year. The University is located on the edge of the Lake District National Park offering extensive opportunities to study these subjects.

Gloucestershire The Garden Design course covers plant sciences and horticulture, the design of formal and informal gardens, and the history of landscapes. There is also a course in Landscape Management and Landscape Architecture.

Harper Adams (Rur Ent Lnd Mgt) Course includes surveying, valuation, law, taxation, the rural economy (including woodlands and field sports management), business finance, and agriculture and the environment. Options include languages and property investment.

Nottingham Trent Opportunities exist to spend a year in placement.

Reading The degree in Agriculture is a unique multi-disciplinary course combining applied studies in the natural and life sciences with economics and management.

Royal Agricultural Univ (Int Eqn Agric Bus Mgt) Twenty-week work placement in second year; links with the Westphalian Riding School.

Universities and colleges teaching quality See www.qaa.ac.uk; http://unistats.direct.gov.uk.

Top research universities and colleges (RAE 2008) (Agriculture, Veterinary and Food Science) Warwick; Aberdeen; Nottingham; Leeds; Reading (Fd Biosci); London (RVC); Aberystwyth; Glasgow; Edinburgh; Stirling; Cambridge; Liverpool; Newcastle; Bristol UWE; Bangor.

Examples of sandwich degree courses Aberystwyth; Askham Bryan (Coll); Bangor; Harper Adams; Hertfordshire; Newcastle; Nottingham Trent; Queen's Belfast; Reading; Royal Agricultural Univ; Ulster.

ADMISSIONS INFORMATION

Number of applicants per place (approx) Aberystwyth (Agric courses) 2–3; Bangor (Agric Cons Env) 4; Newcastle 6; Nottingham 4; Royal Agricultural Univ (Agric) 2.

Advice to applicants and planning the UCAS personal statement First-hand farming experience is essential for most courses and obviously important for all. Check prospectuses and websites. Describe the work done. Details of experience of work with agricultural or food farms (production and laboratory work), garden centres, even with landscape architects, could be appropriate. Keep up-to-date with European agricultural and fishing policies and mention any interests you have in these areas. Read farming magazines and discuss any articles which have interested you. You may even have had first-hand experience of the serious problems facing farmers. Discuss your interest or experience in practical conservation work. Ability to work both independently or as a member of a team is important. (See also **Appendix 3**.)

Selection interviews **Some** Bangor, Bishop Burton (Coll), Derby, Edinburgh, Harper Adams, Queen's Belfast, Royal Agricultural Univ; **No** Reading, Sparsholt (Coll).

Interview advice and questions You should be up-to-date with political and scientific issues concerning the farming community in general and how these problems might be resolved. You are likely to be

questioned on your own farming background (if relevant) and your farming experience. Questions asked in the past have included: What special agricultural interests do you have? What types of farms have you worked on? What farming publications do you read and which agricultural shows have you visited? What is meant by the term 'sustainable development'? Are farmers custodians of the countryside? What are the potential sources of non-fossil-fuel electricity generation? See also **Chapter 6**. **Bangor** (Agric Cons Env) No tests at interview. **Derby** (Cntry Mgt) Discussion about fieldwork experience.

Reasons for rejection (non-academic) Insufficient motivation. Too immature. Unlikely to integrate well. Lack of practical experience with crops or animals.

AFTER-RESULTS ADVICE
Offers to applicants repeating A-levels Possibly higher Newcastle (Agric); **Same** Bangor (Agric Cons Env), Derby, Harper Adams, Nottingham, Royal Agricultural Univ, Writtle (Coll).

GRADUATE DESTINATIONS AND EMPLOYMENT (2011/12 HESA)
Agriculture graduates surveyed 1430 **Employed** 670 **In voluntary employment** 35 **In further study** 385 **Assumed unemployed** 100

Career note The majority of graduates entered the agricultural industry whilst others moved into manufacturing, the wholesale and retail trades and property development.

OTHER DEGREE SUBJECTS FOR CONSIDERATION
Agroforestry; Animal Sciences; Biochemistry; Biological Sciences; Biology; Biotechnology; Chemistry; Conservation Management; Ecology (Biological Sciences); Environmental Sciences; Estate Management (Surveying); Food Science and Technology; Forestry; Horticulture; Land Surveying; Landscape Architecture; Plant Sciences; Veterinary Science; Zoology.

AMERICAN STUDIES

(see also **Latin American Studies**)

Courses normally cover American history, politics and literature, although there are opportunities to study specialist fields such as drama, film studies, history of art, linguistics, politics or sociology. In some universities, a year, term or semester spent in the USA (or Canada) is compulsory or optional whilst at other institutions the course lasts three years without a placement abroad.

Useful websites www.historynet.com; www.americansc.org.uk; www.theasa.net.

NB The points totals shown to the left of the institutions are for ease of reference only. It must not be assumed that Tariff points are always used by institutions or that they can be substituted for an offer in grades. The level of an offer is not necessarily indicative of the quality of a course.

COURSE OFFERS INFORMATION

Subject requirements/preferences **GCSE** Specific grades in some subjects may be specified by some popular universities. **AL** English, a modern language, humanities or social science subjects preferred.

Your target offers and examples of courses provided by each institution

380 pts **Warwick** – AABc (Hist Lit Cult Am) (IB 36 pts)

360 pts **Sussex** – AAA–AAB 360–340 pts (Law Am St; Psy Am St) (IB 35 pts)

340 pts **Birmingham** – AAB–ABB 340–320 pts (Am Can St) (IB 34–36 pts)
   Kent – AAB 340 pts (Engl Am Pstcolnl Lit) (IB 34 pts)
   Loughborough – AAB 340 pts (Engl Am St) (IB 34 pts)
   Sussex – AAB–ABB 340–320 pts (Am St courses) (IB 34 pts)

320 pts **East Anglia** – ABB 320 pts (Am St; Am Engl Lit; Am Hist; Film Am St) (IB 32 pts)
   Essex – ABB–BBB (Am (US) St courses; Am Hist) (IB 32–30 pts)
   Kent – ABB (Am St; Am St (Hist); Engl Lang Ling Eng Am Lit) (IB 34 pts)
   London (Gold) – ABB 320 pts (Engl Am Lit) (IB 34 pts)
   Manchester – ABB 320 pts (Am St) (IB 34 pts)
   Nottingham – ABB 320 pts (Am St Hist; Film TV St Am St; Am St Engl; Am Can Lit Hist Cult; Am St Lat Am St) (IB 32 pts)

300 pts **Hertfordshire** – 300 pts (Hist Am St)
   Keele – BBB 300 pts (Am St) (IB 32 pts)
   Leicester – BBB (Am St) (IB 30 pts)
   Liverpool – BBB (Compar Am St) (IB 30 pts)
   Northumbria – (Am St)

280 pts **Central Lancashire** – 280–320 pts (Engl Am Lit)
   Hull – 280–320 pts (Am St) (IB 28 pts)
   Manchester Met – (Engl Am Lit) (IB 28 pts)
   South Wales – BBC 280 pts (Hist Am St)
   Swansea – BBC 280 pts (Am St; Int Rel Am St) (IB 30 pts)
   Winchester – 280–320 pts (Am St) (IB 26 pts)

260 pts **Manchester Met** – 260–280 pts (Am Hist) (IB 28 pts)

240 pts **Canterbury Christ Church** – 240 pts (Am St courses) (IB 24 pts)
   East London – 240 pts (Anth Ntv Am St) (IB 24 pts)
   Portsmouth – 240–300 pts (Am St Hist; Am St) (IB 28 pts)
   York St John – 240–280 pts (Am St courses) (IB 24 pts)

220 pts **Derby** – 220–260 pts (Am St)

Alternative offers

See **Chapter 7** and **Appendix 1** for grades/UCAS Tariff points information for the International Baccalaureate, Scottish Highers/Advanced Highers, the Welsh Baccalaureate, the Irish Leaving Certificate, the Cambridge Pre-U Diploma, the Advanced Diploma and the Extended Project.

CHOOSING YOUR COURSE (SEE ALSO CH.1)

Some course features

Hull All students on the American Studies course study American history and literature, film and the arts. Special Honours students select one ancillary subject from a wide range on offer. The American Studies course lasts four years (with Year 2 in the USA). There are also seven joint courses. The department is very highly rated for its teaching provision.

Liverpool An interdisciplinary course in Comparative American Studies covering North America, Latin America and the Caribbean. Option to learn Spanish or Portuguese from scratch, or to combine study of AL French, Spanish or Portuguese to degree level.

Manchester (Am St) Course covers the history, literature, film, politics and popular culture of the United States. Year 2 offers the opportunity to study in Manchester or in California for the whole year, or study in Manchester for the first semester followed by a semester in the US.

Nottingham The American Studies course covers history, literature, politics, music and the visual arts. Single Honours students devote two-thirds of the course to American Studies and the remainder to a subsidiary course outside the department. There are optional modules on Canada and Year 2 can be taken in Canada or the US. There are also joint courses with several subjects including English, Chinese Studies, History, or Latin American Studies.

Sussex American Studies may be studied with an emphasis on literature and culture or history and politics. All students take complementary courses within the School of English and American Studies. This is a four-year course with Year 3 spent at a university in the US.

Universities and colleges teaching quality See www.qaa.ac.uk; http://unistats.direct.gov.uk.

Top research universities and colleges (RAE 2008) Sussex; Birmingham; East Anglia; Nottingham; London (King's).

ADMISSIONS INFORMATION

Number of applicants per place (approx) Birmingham 4; Dundee 5; East Anglia 7; Essex 6; Hull 15; Keele 7; Leicester 7; Manchester 6; Nottingham 12; Swansea 2; Warwick 14.

Advice to applicants and planning the UCAS personal statement Visits to America should be described, and any knowledge or interests you have of the history, politics, economics and the culture of the USA should be included on the UCAS application. The US Embassy in London may be a useful source of information. American magazines and newspapers are good reference sources and also give a good insight to life in the USA. Applicants should demonstrate an intelligent interest in both North American literature and history in their personal statement. State why you are interested in the subject and dedicate at least half of your personal statement to how and why your interest has developed – for example through extra-curricular reading, projects, films and academic study. **Manchester** Due to the detailed nature of entry requirements for American Studies courses, we are unable to include full details in the prospectus. For complete and up-to-date information on our entry requirements for these courses, please visit our website at www.manchester.ac.uk/ugcourses.

Misconceptions about this course **Swansea** Some candidates feel that American Studies is a soft option. While we study many topics which students find interesting, we are very much a humanities-based degree course incorporating more traditional subjects such as history, literature and English. Our graduates also find that they are employable in the same jobs as those students taking other degrees.

Selection interviews **Yes** Dundee, Hull, Sussex, Winchester; **Some** Derby, Kent, Warwick; **No** Birmingham, East Anglia, Essex.

Interview advice and questions Courses often focus on history and literature so expect some questions on any American literature you have read and also on aspects of American history, arts and culture. You may also be questioned on visits you have made to America (or Canada) and your impressions. Current political issues might also be raised, so keep up-to-date with the political scene. See also **Chapter 6**. **Birmingham** Access course and mature students are interviewed and also those students with strong applications but whose achieved grades do not meet entrance requirements.

Check **Chapter 4** when choosing your university and **Chapter 7** on how to read the subject tables.

Derby The purpose of the interview is to help applicants understand the interdisciplinary nature of the course. **East Anglia** Admissions tutors want to see how up-to-date is the applicant's knowledge of American culture. **Swansea** Our interviews are very informal, giving students the chance to ask questions about the course.

Reasons for rejection (non-academic) If personal reasons prevent year of study in America. **Birmingham** Lack of commitment to the course. **Swansea** Lack of knowledge covering literature, history and politics.

AFTER-RESULTS ADVICE
Offers to applicants repeating A-levels **Higher** Essex, Warwick, Winchester; **Possibly higher** Nottingham; **Same** Birmingham, Derby, Dundee, East Anglia, Hull, Swansea.

GRADUATE DESTINATIONS AND EMPLOYMENT (2011/12 HESA)
Graduates surveyed 490 **Employed** 240 **In voluntary employment** 25 **In further study** 85 **Assumed unemployed** 55

Career note All non-scientific careers are open to graduates. Start your career planning during your degree course and obtain work experience.

OTHER DEGREE SUBJECTS FOR CONSIDERATION
Business Studies; Cultural Studies; English Literature; Film Studies; Government; History; International History; International Relations; Latin-American Literature/Studies; Politics.

ANATOMICAL SCIENCE/ANATOMY
(including **Neuroscience**; see also **Biological Sciences, Physiology**)

Anatomy is the study of the structures of living creatures, from the sub-cellular level to the whole individual, and relates structure to function in the adult and during embryonic development. Graduates enter careers in various laboratories in the NHS, pharmaceutical and food industries.

Useful websites www.innerbody.com; www.instantanatomy.net.

NB The points totals shown to the left of the institutions are for ease of reference only. It must not be assumed that Tariff points are always used by institutions or that they can be substituted for an offer in grades. The level of an offer is not necessarily indicative of the quality of a course.

COURSE OFFERS INFORMATION
Subject requirements/preferences **GCSE** Mathematics usually required. **AL** One or two mathematics/science subjects usually required; biology and chemistry preferred.

Your target offers and examples of courses provided by each institution
380 pts Cambridge – A*AA (Nat Sci (Neuro)) (IB 40–41 pts HL 776)
London (UCL) – AAAe incl chem (Neuro) (IB 38 pts)
360 pts Edinburgh – AAA–ABB 360–320 pts (Neuro) (IB 37–32 pts)
Manchester – AAA–ABB 360–320 pts (Anat Sci; Anat Sci Modn Lang; Neuro) (IB 37–33 pts)
340 pts Bristol – AAB–ABB incl 2 sci/maths 340–320 pts (Neuro) (IB 35–33 pts HL 666)
Cardiff – AAB–ABB 340–320 pts (Biomed Sci (Anat)) (IB 34 pts)
Dundee – AAB (Anat Sci; Neuro) (IB 34 pts)
Glasgow – AAB (Anat; Neuro) (IB 34 pts)
Leeds – AAB–ABB 340–320 pts (Neuro) (IB 35–34 pts)
Leicester – AAB (Psy Cog Neuro)
Liverpool – AAB–ABB incl biol (Anat Hum Biol) (IB 33–36 pts)
London (King's) – AAB 340 pts (Anat Dev Hum Biol; Neuro) (IB 35 pts HL 665)
Nottingham – AAB 340 pts (Neuro) (IB 34 pts)

St Andrews – AAB 340 pts (Neuro) (IB 35 pts)
Sussex – AAB–ABB (Med Neuro) (IB 34–36 pts)
320 pts **Aberdeen** – ABB 320 pts (Biomed Sci) (IB 34 pts)
Sussex – AAB–ABB (Neuro Cog Sci) (IB 34 pts)
300 pts **Aberdeen** – BBB 300 pts (Neuro Psy) (IB 32 pts)
Keele – BBB 300 pts (Neuro) (IB 32 pts)
260 pts **Central Lancashire** – BCC–BBB 260–300 pts (Neuro)

Alternative offers
See **Chapter 7** and **Appendix 1** for grades/UCAS Tariff points information for the International Baccalaureate, Scottish Highers/Advanced Highers, the Welsh Baccalaureate, the Irish Leaving Certificate, the Cambridge Pre-U Diploma, the Advanced Diploma and the Extended Project.

CHOOSING YOUR COURSE (SEE ALSO CH.1)
Some course features
Cardiff A common Biosciences first-year programme (with the chance to change degrees) with following years centred on human anatomy, with dissection.
Dundee Emphasis on human anatomy.
Glasgow Students may choose to extend programme to an MSci, which includes a one-year research placement.
Liverpool Practical degree involving dissection and module choices from Biomedical and Biological Sciences and Zoology.
Manchester Part of the Life Sciences programme, with a common first year and options to change between degree courses.

Universities and colleges teaching quality See www.qaa.ac.uk; http://unistats.direct.gov.uk.

Top research universities and colleges (RAE 2008) See **Biological Sciences**.

Examples of sandwich degree courses Bath; Bristol; Cardiff; Leeds; Manchester.

ADMISSIONS INFORMATION
Number of applicants per place (approx) Bristol 10; Cardiff 8; Dundee 6; Liverpool 7.

Advice to applicants and planning the UCAS personal statement Give reasons for your interest in this subject (usually stemming from school work in biology). Discuss any articles in medical and other scientific journals which have attracted your attention and any new developments in medicine related to anatomical science.

Selection interviews **Yes** Liverpool; **Some** Cardiff; **No** Bristol, Dundee.

Interview advice and questions Questions are likely on your particular interests in biology and anatomy, why you wish to study the subject and your future career intentions. See also **Chapter 6**.

Reasons for rejection (non-academic) **Liverpool** Unfocused applications with no evidence of basic knowledge of the course.

AFTER-RESULTS ADVICE
Offers to applicants repeating A-levels **Higher** Bristol, Dundee; **Possibly higher** Liverpool; **Same** Cardiff.

GRADUATE DESTINATIONS AND EMPLOYMENT (2011/12 HESA)
Including Pathology and Physiology graduates surveyed 2745 **Employed** 1450 **In voluntary employment** 50 **In further study** 650 **Assumed unemployed** 185

Career note The subject leads to a range of careers in various laboratories, in government establishments, the NHS, pharmaceutical and food industries. It can also lead to postgraduate studies in physiotherapy, nursing, osteopathy and, in exceptional cases, in medicine, dentistry and veterinary science.

OTHER DEGREE SUBJECTS FOR CONSIDERATION
Biological Sciences; Biology; Genetics; Microbiology; Neuroscience; Osteopathy; Physiology; Physiotherapy.

ANIMAL SCIENCES

(including **Equine Science Studies**; see also **Agricultural Sciences/Agriculture, Biological Sciences, Biology, Physiology, Psychology, Veterinary Science/Medicine, Zoology**)

Animal Sciences is a broad-based subject involving both farm and companion animals. The range of specialisms is reflected in the table of courses below and can focus on animal nutrition and health, animal biology, behaviour, ecology and welfare. In addition, many courses specialise in equine science, studies and management. **NB** It is important to note that Bioveterinary Science graduates are not qualified to practise as vets (see **Veterinary Sciences/Medicine**).

Useful websites www.rspca.org.uk; www.iah.bbsrc.ac.uk; www.bhs.org.uk; www.wwf.org.uk; www. bsas.org.uk.

NB The points totals shown to the left of the institutions are for ease of reference only. It must not be assumed that Tariff points are always used by institutions or that they can be substituted for an offer in grades. The level of an offer is not necessarily indicative of the quality of a course.

COURSE OFFERS INFORMATION

Subject requirements/preferences **GCSE** Mathematics/science subjects required. Also check any weight limits on equitation modules. **AL** One or two science subjects required for scientific courses, biology and chemistry preferred.

Your target offers and examples of courses provided by each institution

340 pts **Exeter** – AAB–ABB 320–340 pts (Anim Bhv) (IB 34–32 pts)
Glasgow – AAB 340 pts (Anim Biol) (IB 34 pts)

320 pts **Bristol** – ABB incl biol +sci/maths 320 pts (Anim Bhv Welf Sci) (IB 34 pts HL 665)
Harper Adams – ABB (Vet Physio) (IB 29 pts HL 6 biol)
Kent – ABB 320 pts (Wldlf Cons Prof Pr; Wldlf Cons) (IB 34 pts)
London (QM) – ABB 320 pts (Zool) (IB 34 pts)
Nottingham – ABB–BBB 320–300 pts (Anim Sci) (IB 32–30 pts)

300 pts **Aberdeen** – BBB 300 pts (Anim Ecol) (IB 30 pts)
Gloucestershire – 300 pts (Anim Biol)
Lincoln – 300 pts (Anim Bhv Welf) (IB 30 pts)
Liverpool John Moores – 260–300 pts (Wldlf Cons; Anim Bhv) (IB 25 pts)
Newcastle – ABB–BBB 300–320 pts (Anim Sci) (IB 32–35 pts)
Reading – BBB/ABC 300 pts (Anim Sci) (IB 30 pts)
South Wales – BBB (Int Wldlf Biol; Nat Hist)

280 pts **Aberystwyth** – 280–320 pts (Anim Bhv; Anim Sci)
Bristol UWE – 280 pts (Eqn Sci; Biovet Sci) (IB 24 pts)
Chester – 240–280 pts (Anim Bhv Welf; Anim Bhv)
Oxford Brookes – BBC 280 pts (Anim Biol Cons; Eqn Sci; Eqn Sci Thbred Mgt) (IB 30 pts)
Plumpton (Coll) – (Eqn Spo Perf)
Plymouth – 280 pts (Anim Bhv Welf) (IB 26 pts)
Stirling – BBC (Anim Biol) (IB 32 pts)
Writtle (Coll) – 280 pts (Anim Sci) (IB 24 pts)

260 pts **Aberystwyth** – 260–320 pts (Eqn Sci) (IB 28 pts)
Bangor – 260–320 pts (Zool Anim Bhv) (IB 28 pts)
Bournemouth – 260–320 pts (Ecol Wldlf Cons) (IB 28–32 pts)
Edinburgh Napier – BCC 260 pts (Anim Biol)
Harper Adams – 260–300 pts (Biovet Sci) (IB 26 pts)

Manchester Met – 260–280 pts (Anim Bhv) (IB 27 pts)
Northampton – 260–280 pts (Wldlf Cons) (IB 24 pts)
Nottingham Trent – 260 pts (Wldlf Cons)
Royal Agricultural Univ – 260 pts (Agric (Lvstk))
SRUC – BCC (App Anim Sci)
Worcester – 260–300 pts (Anim Biol) (IB 24 pts)
Writtle (Coll) – 260 pts (Anim Mgt; Eqn Sci (Bhv Nutr); Eqn St Bus Mgt; Eqn Spo Thera) (IB 24 pts)

240 pts **Anglia Ruskin** – 240 pts (Anim Bhv) (IB 24 pts)
Bristol UWE – 240 pts (Anim Sci; Anim Bhv Welf) (IB 24 pts)
CAFRE – 240 pts (Eqn Mgt)
Canterbury Christ Church – CCC 240 pts (Anim Sci) (IB 24 pts)
Chester – 240–280 pts (Wldlf Cons Ecol) (IB 26 pts)
Cumbria – 240 pts (Wldlf Media; Anim Cons Sci) (IB 24 pts)
Easton Otley (Coll) – (Eqn Coach)
Glyndŵr – (Eqn Sci)
Greenwich – 240 pts (App Anim Bhv Sci Wlf; Anim Mgt; Anim Cons Biodivl; Eqn Mgt) (IB 24 pts)
Hadlow (Coll) – 240 pts (Anim Mgt; Eqn Mgt; Anim Cons Biodiv; App Bhv Sci Welf)
Nottingham Trent – 240 pts (Anim Biol; Eqn Spo Sci; Spo Horse Mgt Coach) (IB 29 pts)
Reaseheath (Coll) – 240 pts (Anim Bhv Wlfr; Wldlf Cons Ecol; Eqn Sci) (IB 24 pts)
Royal Agricultural Univ – 240 pts (Eqn Mgt)
Salford – 240–280 pts (Wldlf Cons Zoo Biol) (IB 24 pts)

220 pts **Askham Bryan (Coll)** – 220 pts (Anim Mgt Sci)
Harper Adams – 220–260 pts (Anim Bhv Welf; Anim Hlth Welf)
Moulton (Coll) – 220–260 pts +interview (App Eqn St; App Anim St) (IB 24 pts)

Check **Chapter 4** when choosing your university and **Chapter 7** on how to read the subject tables.

Myerscough (Coll) – 220 pts (Anim Bhv Welf; Eqn Sci Mgt (Physiol); Eqn Sci Mgt (Bhv Welf))
Warwickshire (Coll) – 220 pts (Eqn Hum Spo Sci; Eqn Bus Mgt; Eqn Sci; Eqn St)
West Anglia (Coll) – 220 pts (Eqn St Rehab Thera)

200 pts **Bishop Burton (Coll)** – 200 pts (Eqn St; Eqn Thera Rehab; Eqn Spo Perf; Eqn Spo Coach; App Anim Sci)
Wolverhampton – 200 pts (Anim Bhv Wlf Cons)

180 pts **Warwickshire (Coll)** – 180 pts (Equit Coach)

160 pts **Bolton** – (Anim Biol)
Sparsholt (Coll) – CC 160 pts (Anim Mgt)
Warwickshire (Coll) – 160 pts (Anim Sci Hlth)

120 pts **Anglia Ruskin** – 120 pts (Anim Bhv Welf)
Sparsholt (Coll) – DD 120 pts (Eqn St)

Alternative offers
See **Chapter 7** and **Appendix 1** for grades/UCAS Tariff points information for the International Baccalaureate, Scottish Highers/Advanced Highers, the Welsh Baccalaureate, the Irish Leaving Certificate, the Cambridge Pre-U Diploma, the Advanced Diploma and the Extended Project.

EXAMPLES OF FOUNDATION DEGREES IN THE SUBJECT FIELD
Askham Bryan (Coll); Bedford (Coll); Bishop Burton (Coll); Bristol UWE; Bucks New; Chester; Cornwall (Coll); Craven (Coll); Duchy (Coll); Easton Otley (Coll); Greenwich; Guildford (Coll); Harper Adams; Hertfordshire; Leeds City (Coll); Moulton (Coll); Myerscough (Coll); Nottingham Trent; Oxford Brookes; Plumpton (Coll); Plymouth; South Devon (Coll); Sparsholt (Coll); Suffolk (Univ Campus); Warwickshire (Coll); West Anglia (Coll); Weston (Coll); Wiltshire (Coll); Writtle (Coll).

CHOOSING YOUR COURSE (SEE ALSO CH.1)
Some course features
Aberystwyth After a common first year for all students, one of the four pathways can be chosen: Animal Production Science, Animal Biology, Equine Science or Companion Animal Science. Degrees in Equine Studies and Equine Sciences are also offered. A course is also available in Animal Behaviour, studying farmed and domestic animals with opportunities to observe animals, birds and sea life in their natural habitats.
Chester The course in Animal Behaviour includes theoretical studies and practical modules taken at Reaseheath College, Nantwich and Chester Zoo. There is also a course in Animal Management.
Exeter Two degree schemes are offered, one with Biology. This is an interdisciplinary programme covering zoology, ecology, conservation biology, psychology and neuroscience.
Lancaster Animal Science is taken as a course option in the Biological Science degree.
Oxford Brookes (Eqn Sci) Practical and vocational course with a range of opportunities in the second year to study in Europe, the USA, Canada or Australia.
Wolverhampton The course in Animal Biology and Behaviour has an emphasis on fieldwork and research skills and offers an optional sandwich year or international field courses.

Universities and colleges teaching quality See www.qaa.ac.uk; http://unistats.direct.gov.uk.

Top research universities and colleges (RAE 2008) See **Agricultural Sciences/Agriculture** and **Biological Sciences**.

Examples of sandwich degree courses Aberystwyth; Anglia Ruskin; Cumbria; Greenwich; Harper Adams; Liverpool John Moores; Manchester Met; Nottingham Trent; Royal Agricultural Univ; Warwickshire (Coll).

ADMISSIONS INFORMATION
Number of applicants per place (approx) Aberystwyth 6; Bristol 8; Harper Adams 5; Leeds 6; Newcastle 9; Nottingham 6; Nottingham Trent (Eqn Spo Sci) 4; Reading 10; Royal Agricultural Univ 4.

Advice to applicants and planning the UCAS personal statement Describe any work you have done with animals which generated your interest in this subject. Work experience in veterinary practices, on farms or with agricultural firms would be useful. Read agricultural/scientific journals for updates on animal nutrition or breeding. For equine courses, details of practical experience with horses (eg BHS examinations, Pony Club tests) should be included. **London (RVC)** BMAT is not required for entry but applicants wanting to be considered for the Merit Scholarships will have to take BMAT.

Misconceptions about this course Students are not always aware that equine studies courses cover science, business management, nutrition, health and breeding. **Bishop Burton (Coll)** (Eqn Sci) Some students wrongly believe that riding skills and a science background are not required for this course which, in fact, is heavily focused on the scientific principles and practice of horse management.

Selection interviews Yes Bristol, Cumbria, Lincoln, Newcastle, Royal Agricultural Univ, SRUC, Writtle (Coll); **Some** Anglia Ruskin, Bishop Burton (Coll), Bristol UWE, Harper Adams, Nottingham, Stirling; **No** Plymouth.

Interview advice and questions Questions are likely about your experience with animals and your reasons for wishing to follow this science-based subject. Other questions asked in recent years have included: What do your parents think about your choice of course? What are your views on battery hens and the rearing of veal calves? The causes of blue-tongue disease, foot and mouth disease and BSE may also feature. (Eqn courses) Students should check the level of riding ability expected (eg BHS Level 2 or PC B-test level). Check the amount of riding, jumping and competition work on the course. (See also **Chapter 6**.) **Lincoln** (Eqn Spo Sci) Applicants required to show that they can ride to BHS Level 2. Experience with animals in general.

Reasons for rejection (non-academic) Uncertainty as to why applicants chose the course. Too immature. Unlikely to integrate well.

AFTER-RESULTS ADVICE
Offers to applicants repeating A-levels Possibly higher Nottingham; **Same** Anglia Ruskin, Bishop Burton (Coll), Bristol UWE, Chester, Harper Adams, Liverpool John Moores, Royal Agricultural Univ, Stirling.

GRADUATE DESTINATIONS AND EMPLOYMENT (2011/12 HESA)
Graduates surveyed 1150 **Employed** 450 **In voluntary employment** 40 **In further study** 330 **Assumed unemployed** 105

Career note The majority of graduates obtained work with animals whilst others moved towards business and administration careers. This is a specialised subject area and undergraduates should start early to make contacts with organisations and gain work experience.

OTHER DEGREE SUBJECTS FOR CONSIDERATION
Agriculture; Biological Sciences; Biology; Food Science; Natural Sciences; Veterinary Science; Zoology.

ANTHROPOLOGY

(including **Social Anthropology**; see also **Archaeology, Sociology**)

Anthropology is the study of people's behaviour, beliefs and institutions and the diverse societies in which they live, and is concerned with the biological evolution of human beings. It also involves our relationships with other primates, the structure of communities and the effects of diet and disease on human groups. Alternatively, social or cultural anthropology covers aspects of social behaviour in respect of family, kinship, marriage, gender, religion, political structures, law, psychology and language.

Useful websites www.britishmuseum.org; www.therai.org.uk.

NB The points totals shown to the left of the institutions are for ease of reference only. It must not be assumed that Tariff points are always used by institutions or that they can be substituted for an offer in grades. The level of an offer is not necessarily indicative of the quality of a course.

COURSE OFFERS INFORMATION

Subject requirements/preferences GCSE English and mathematics usually required. A foreign language may be required. **AL** Biology and geography preferred for some biological anthropological courses. (Soc Anth) No specific subjects required.

Your target offers and examples of courses provided by each institution

380 pts **Cambridge** – A*AA 380 pts (Hum Soc Pol Sci (Biol Anth; Soc Anth)) (IB 40–41 pts)
London (UCL) – AAAe–AABe 380–360 pts (Anth) (IB 36–38 pts)

360 pts **Durham** – AAA 360 pts (Anth) (IB 37 pts)
Edinburgh – AAA–BBB 300–360 pts (Soc Anth courses; Persn Soc Anth; Arch Soc Anth) (IB 37–34 pts HL 555)
Exeter – AAA–AAB 360–340 pts (Sociol Anth) (IB 34–36 pts)
London (SOAS) – AAA 360 pts (Soc Anth) (IB 38 pts HL 766)
London (UCL) – AABe 360 pts (Arch Anth) (IB 36 pts)
Oxford – AAA 360 pts (Arch Anth) (IB 38–40 pts)
St Andrews – AAA–AAB (Soc Anth courses) (IB 35–38 pts)

340 pts **Dundee** – AAB (Foren Anth) (IB 34 pts)
Durham – AAB 340 pts (Anth Soc; Anth Arch) (IB 36 pts)
East Anglia – AAB 340 pts (Arch Anth Art Hist (St Abrd)) (IB 33 pts)
Exeter – AAB–ABB 340–320 pts (Anth; Arch Anth) (IB 34–32 pts)
Kent – AAB (Anth (Yr Abrd); Anth; Med Anth) (IB 33 pts)
London LSE – AAB (Soc Anth) (IB 37 pts HL 666)
Manchester – AAB–BBB 300–340 pts (Compar Relgn Soc Anth) (IB 36–31 pts)
Sussex – AAB–ABB 340–320 pts (Anth courses) (IB 35–34 pts)

320 pts **Birmingham** – ABB–BBB (Anth courses) (IB 32–34 pts)
Bristol – ABB–BBB 320–300 pts (Arch Anth) (IB 33–32 pts HL 665)
Brunel – ABB 320 pts (Anth courses; Anth Sociol) (IB 33–35 pts)
East Anglia – ABB 320 pts (Arch Anth Art Hist) (IB 32 pts)
Essex – ABB–BBB 320–300 pts (Sociol Soc Anth) (IB 32–30 pts)
Kent – ABB 320 pts (Soc Anth; Biol Anth) (IB 34 pts)
Liverpool – ABB (Evol Anth) (IB 33 pts)
London (Gold) – ABB 320 pts (Anth courses) (IB 34 pts)
Manchester – ABB (Soc Anth; Soc Anth Sociol; Pol Soc Anth; Arch Anth; Soc Anth Crimin) (IB 34 pts)
Roehampton – 320 pts (Anth) (IB 28 pts)
Southampton – ABB (App Soc Sci (Anth)) (IB 32 pts HL 16 pts)

300 pts **Aberdeen** – BBB (Anth) (IB 30 pts)
Birmingham – BBB (Af St Anth) (IB 32 pts)
Liverpool John Moores – 260–300 pts (Foren Anth) (IB 25 pts)
Queen's Belfast – BBB 300 pts (Soc Anth courses)

280 pts **Central Lancashire** – BBC 280 pts (Foren Sci Anth) (IB 25 pts)
Hull – 280–320 pts (Soc Anth Sociol; Sociol Anth Gndr St) (IB 28 pts)
Oxford Brookes – BBC 280 pts (Anth) (IB 31 pts)

260 pts **Bournemouth** – 260–320 pts (Arch Anth Foren Sci) (IB 28–32 pts)

240 pts **East London** – 240 pts (Anth; Anth Ntv Am St) (IB 24 pts)
Trinity Saint David – 240 pts (Anth) (IB 26 pts)

Alternative offers

See **Chapter 7** and **Appendix 1** for grades/UCAS Tariff points information for the International Baccalaureate, Scottish Highers/Advanced Highers, the Welsh Baccalaureate, the Irish Leaving Certificate, the Cambridge Pre-U Diploma, the Advanced Diploma and the Extended Project.

Cardiff – BBB–BBC 300–280 pts (Arch courses; Arch) (IB 28–36 pts)
Hull – 280–300 pts (Arch courses)
Leicester – BBB 300 pts (Arch) (IB 30 pts)
Queen's Belfast – BBB (Arch; Arch Palae)
Reading – ABC–BBB (Arch courses) (IB 30 pts)
Sheffield – ABB–BBB 300–320 pts (Arch; Arch Sci; Arch Joint Hons) (IB 33–30 pts)
Winchester – 260–300 pts (Arch) (IB 25 pts)

280 pts **Bangor** – 280–300 pts (Arch; Herit Arch Hist; Welsh Hist Arch)
Bradford – 280 pts (Arch courses) (IB 25 pts)
Cardiff – BBC 280 pts (Conserv Obj Mus Arch)

260 pts **Bournemouth** – 260–320 pts (Arch; Arch Anth Foren Sci)
Chester – 260–300 pts (Arch courses) (IB 24 pts)
London (Birk) – 260 pts (Arch)
Portsmouth – 260–320 pts (Palae) (IB 27 pts)
Winchester – 260–300 pts (Arch Prac)
Worcester – 220–260 pts (Arch Herit St courses)

240 pts **Central Lancashire** – CCC 240 pts (Arch) (IB 24 pts)

220 pts **Brighton** – ABB (Geog Arch)

200 pts **Peterborough (Reg Coll)** – 200 pts (Arch Lnd Hist)
Trinity Saint David – 200–260 pts (Arch; Arch Prof Prac) (IB 26 pts)

160 pts **UHI** – CC 160 pts (Scot Hist Arch; Arch; Arch Env St)

Alternative offers
See **Chapter 7** and **Appendix 1** for grades/UCAS Tariff points information for the International Baccalaureate, Scottish Highers/Advanced Highers, the Welsh Baccalaureate, the Irish Leaving Certificate, the Cambridge Pre-U Diploma, the Advanced Diploma and the Extended Project.

EXAMPLES OF FOUNDATION DEGREES IN THE SUBJECT FIELD
Plymouth; Truro (Coll).

CHOOSING YOUR COURSE (SEE ALSO CH.1)
Some course features
Bangor (Herit Arch Hist) Focus on historical and archaeological evidence and its use in the heritage industry.
Bristol The course focuses on the practice, theory and history of archaeology and has a range of options covering European, Aegean and Ancient Mediterranean Studies. Practical units involve site visits, artefacts, environmental archaeology and heritage management. Courses in Archaeology and Anthropology or with Ancient History are also available.
Kent Classical and Archaeological Studies covers literature, art, philosophy, history and archaeology. As the course progresses, students specialise in their preferred interest. Students have the opportunity to learn Latin or Ancient Greek. The course can also be taken as a Joint Honours degree with a humanities subject.
Leicester In the BA Archaeology and Ancient History course one additional subject is taken in Years 1 and 2. The study covers Europe, Western Asia, Africa, Australasia and the Americas and archaeological methodology. Ancient History, History and Geography are also offered with Archaeology and other joint degree programmes are also offered. Scholarships available.
London (King's) The Classical Archaeology course unit structure, covering the art and archaeology of Greece and Rome, allows great flexibility but all students undertake some study of Latin or Greek. (A beginner's level course is an option.)

Universities and colleges teaching quality See www.qaa.ac.uk; http://unistats.direct.gov.uk.

Top research universities and colleges (RAE 2008) Durham; Reading; Oxford; Cambridge; Liverpool; London (UCL); Leicester; Southampton; Sheffield; York; Queen's Belfast; Exeter; Nottingham.

Examples of sandwich degree courses Bradford.

ADMISSIONS INFORMATION

Number of applicants per place (approx) Birmingham 7; Bradford 4; Bristol 7; Cambridge 2; Cardiff 6; Durham 6; Leicester 6; Liverpool 7; London (UCL) 5; Manchester (Anc Hist Arch) 15, (Arch) 4; Newcastle 14; Nottingham 11; Sheffield 5; Southampton 6; Trinity Saint David 2; York 4.

Advice to applicants and planning the UCAS personal statement First-hand experience of digs and other fieldwork should be described. The Council for British Archaeology (see **Appendix 3**) can provide information on where digs are taking place. Describe any interests in fossils and any museum visits as well as details of visits to current archaeological sites. Your local university archaeological department or central library can also provide information on contacts in your local area (each county council employs an archaeological officer). Since this is not a school subject, the selectors will be looking for good reasons for your choice of subject. Gain practical field experience and discuss this in the personal statement. Show your serious commitment to archaeology through your out-of-school activities (fieldwork, museum experience) (see **Chapter 6**). (See also **Anthropology**.) **Bristol** Deferred entry accepted. **Cambridge** Most colleges require a school/college essay.

Misconceptions about this course **Bristol** We are not an elitist course: 75% of applicants and students come from state schools and non-traditional backgrounds. **Liverpool** (Egypt) Some students would have been better advised looking at courses in Archaeology or Ancient History and Archaeology which offer major pathways in the study of Ancient Egypt.

Selection interviews **Yes** Bangor, Bournemouth, Bradford, Cambridge, Glasgow, Liverpool, London (UCL), Newcastle, Oxford (Arch) 30%, (Class Arch Anc Hist) 23%, Southampton, Trinity Saint David; **Some** Bristol, Cardiff, East Anglia, York; **No** Birmingham, Durham, Leicester, Nottingham, Reading.

Interview advice and questions Questions will be asked about any experience you have had in visiting archaeological sites or taking part in digs. Past questions have included: How would you interpret archaeological evidence, for example a pile of flints, coins? What is stratification? How would you date archaeological remains? What recent archaeological discoveries have been made? How did you become interested in archaeology? With which archaeological sites in the UK are you familiar? See also **Chapter 6**. **Birmingham** Questions may cover recent archaeological events. **Cambridge** See **Chapter 6**. **Oxford** Interviews involve artefacts, maps and other material to be interpreted. Successful entrants average 30.7% (see **Chapter 6**). **York** What are your views on the archaeology programmes on TV? What would you do with a spare weekend?

Reasons for rejection (non-academic) (Mature students) Inability to cope with essay-writing and exams. **Bournemouth** Health and fitness important for excavations. **Liverpool** (Egypt) Applicant misguided on choice of course – Egyptology used to fill a gap on the UCAS application.

AFTER-RESULTS ADVICE

Offers to applicants repeating A-levels **Same** Birmingham, Bradford, Cambridge, Chester, Durham, East Anglia, Leicester, Liverpool, London (UCL), Sheffield, Trinity Saint David, Winchester.

GRADUATE DESTINATIONS AND EMPLOYMENT (2011/12 HESA)

Graduates surveyed 720 **Employed** 230 **In voluntary employment** 40 **In further study** 240 **Assumed unemployed** 65

Career note Vocational opportunities closely linked to this subject are limited. However, some graduates aim for positions in local authorities, libraries and museums. A number of organisations covering water boards, forestry, civil engineering and surveying also employ field archaeologists.

OTHER DEGREE SUBJECTS FOR CONSIDERATION

Ancient History; Anthropology; Classical Studies; Classics; Geology; Heritage Studies; History; History of Art and Architecture; Medieval History.

ARCHITECTURE

(including **Architectural Technology, Architectural Engineering** and **Interior Architecture**; see also Art and Design (Product and Industrial Design), Building and Construction)

Courses in Architecture provide a broad education consisting of technological subjects covering structures, construction, materials and environmental studies. Project-based design work is an integral part of all courses and in addition, history and social studies will also be incorporated into degree programmes. After completing the first three years leading to a BA (Hons), students aiming for full professional status take a further two-year course leading to, for example, the BArch, MArch degrees or Diploma, and after a year in an architect's practice, the final professional examinations are taken.

Useful websites www.ciat.org.uk; www.architecture.com; www.rias.org.uk; www.archrecord. construction.com.

NB The points totals shown to the left of the institutions are for ease of reference only. It must not be assumed that Tariff points are always used by institutions or that they can be substituted for an offer in grades. The level of an offer is not necessarily indicative of the quality of a course.

COURSE OFFERS INFORMATION

Subject requirements/preferences GCSE English and mathematics, in some cases at certain grades, are required in all cases. A science subject may also be required. **AL** Mathematics and/or physics required or preferred for some courses. Art and design may be preferable to design and technology. Art is sometimes a requirement and many schools of architecture prefer it; a portfolio of art work is often requested and, in some cases, a drawing test will be set. MEng courses not listed below unless otherwise stated.

Your target offers and examples of courses provided by each institution

380 pts **Bath** – A*AA 380 pts (Archit; Civ Archit Eng MEng) (IB 36 pts HL 6 maths)

Cambridge – A*AA (Archit) (IB 40–41 pts HL 776)

Southampton – A*AA 380 pts (Civ Eng Archit MEng) (IB 36 pts HL 18 pts maths sci)

360 pts **Cardiff** – AAA–AAB 360–340 pts (Archit Eng; Archit) (IB 32–36 pts)

Edinburgh – AAA–BBB 360–300 pts (Archit Crea Cult Env; Archit; Struct Eng Archit) (IB 40–34 pts)

Leeds – AAA incl maths (Archit Eng) (IB 38 pts HL 5 maths)

Liverpool – AAA (Archit) (IB 36 pts)

London (UCL) – AABe +portfolio (Archit) (IB 36 pts HL 17 pts)

Manchester – AAA 360 pts (Archit) (IB 37 pts HL 666)

Manchester Met – AAA (Archit) (IB 36 pts)

Newcastle – AAA +portfolio (Archit) (IB 37 pts)

Nottingham – AAA (Archit Env Des MEng; Archit) (IB 36 pts)

Sheffield – AAA (Archit; Archit Eng Des MEng; Struct Eng Archit) (IB 37 pts)

340 pts **Birmingham City** – AAB 340 pts (Archit) (IB 28 pts)

City – 340 pts (Civ Eng Archit) (IB 30 pts HL maths)

Edinburgh – AAB–BBB 340–300 pts (Archit Hist; Archit Hist Arch) (IB 36–34 pts)

Glasgow – AAB incl maths phys (Civ Eng Archit) (IB 34 pts)

Huddersfield – AAB 340 pts (Archit (Int)) (IB 28–26 pts)

Kent – AAB (Archit) (IB 34 pts HL 17 pts)

London (UCL) – AAB incl art +portfolio (Archit Interd St) (IB 36 pts)

Northumbria – 340 pts (Archit) (IB 28 pts)

Nottingham – AAB–ABB (Archit Env Eng) (IB 32–34 pts)

Oxford Brookes – AAB 340 pts (Archit) (IB 32–34 pts) .

Queen's Belfast – AAB 340 pts (Struct Eng Archit MEng)

Salford – AAB 340 pts (Archit) (IB 28 pts)

Westminster – AAB (Archit) (IB 35 pts)

320 pts **Bournemouth Arts** – ABB (Archit) (IB 32 pts)
Brighton – ABB (Archit) (IB 36 pts)
Bristol UWE – 320 pts (Archit; Archit Plan)
Coventry – ABB 320 pts (Archit) (IB 29 pts)
Creative Arts – 320 pts +portfolio (Archit)
De Montfort – 320 pts +portfolio +interview (Archit) (IB 30 pts)
Glasgow (SA) – ABB (Archit) (IB 30 pts)
Greenwich – 320 pts (Archit)
Kingston – 320 pts (Archit)
Lincoln – 320 pts (Archit)
Newcastle – ABB (Archit Urb Plan) (IB 34–35 pts HL 555)
Northumbria – 320 pts (Archit Eng; Inter Archit) (IB 27 pts)
Nottingham Trent – 320 pts (Archit)
Oxford Brookes – ABB (Inter Archit) (IB 32–34 pts)
Plymouth – 320 pts (Archit) (IB 27 pts)
Queen's Belfast – ABB (Archit)
Strathclyde – ABB 320 pts (Archit St) (IB 34 pts)

300 pts **Archit Assoc Sch London** – BBB 300 pts +portfolio (Archit)
Brighton – BBB +portfolio (Inter Archit) (IB 32 pts)
Bristol UWE – 300 pts (Inter Archit; Archit Env Eng) (IB 26 pts)
Central Lancashire – 300 pts (Archit) (IB 32 pts)
Dundee – BBB (Archit) (IB 30 pts HL 555)
East London – 300 pts (Archit)
Heriot-Watt – ABC–BBB incl maths 300 pts (Archit Eng) (IB 31 pts)
Huddersfield – BBB (Archit Tech)
Leeds Beckett – 300 pts (Archit; Archit Tech; Inter Archit Des) (IB 26 pts)
Liverpool John Moores – 300 pts (Archit) (IB 31 pts)
London Met – 300 pts +portfolio (Inter Archit Des; Archit)
Loughborough – 300 pts (Archit Eng Des Mgt) (IB 32 pts)
Northumbria – 300 pts (Archit Tech) (IB 26 pts)
Nottingham Trent – 300 pts (Inter Archit Des)
Ulster – 300 pts (Archit) (IB 25 pts)
Westminster – BBB (Inter Archit) (IB 28 pts)

280 pts **Birmingham City** – 280 pts (Archit Tech)
Bournemouth Arts – BBC–BBB 280–300 pts +portfolio +interview (Inter Arch Des)
(IB 32 pts)
Bristol UWE – 280 pts (Archit Tech Des) (IB 25 pts)
Cardiff Met (UWIC) – 280 pts (Archit Des Tech)
Coventry – BBC 280 pts (Archit Tech) (IB 29 pts)
Lincoln – 280 pts (Inter Archit Des; Cons Restor)
Norwich Arts – BBC 280 pts (Archit) (IB 25 pts)
Plymouth – 280 pts (Archit Tech Env) (IB 28 pts)
Portsmouth – 280–320 pts (Archit) (IB 29 pts)
Robert Gordon – BBC (Archit) (IB 29 pts)
Sheffield Hallam – 280–320 pts (Archit Env Des; Archit Tech)
Teesside – 280 pts +portfolio (Inter Archit)
Westminster – BBC (Archit Tech) (IB 28 pts)

260 pts **Central Lancashire** – 260 pts (Archit Tech) (IB 26 pts)
Derby – 260 pts (Archit Tech Prac) (IB 28 pts)
Edinburgh Napier – BCC 260 pts (Archit Tech) (IB 26 pts)
Liverpool John Moores – 260 pts (Archit Tech)
London South Bank – BCC–BBB 260–300 pts (Archit)
Northampton – 260–300 pts (Archit Tech)
Nottingham Trent – 260 pts (Archit Tech) (IB 28 pts)

Check **Chapter 4** when choosing your university and **Chapter 7** on how to read the subject tables.

SCHOOL OF ARCHITECTURE

OXFORD
BROOKES
UNIVERSITY

An international reputation for excellence in teaching and research

Founded in 1927, the School of Architecture at Oxford Brookes is one of the largest and most highly regarded architecture schools in the UK.

The location of Oxford offers some of the most historically significant architecture in the world and access to some of the best modern architecture, produced by world-renowned contemporary architects. This highly desirable and rare resource sits right on the doorstep of the School of Architecture at Oxford Brookes University.

Architecture BA (Hons)
Interior Architecture BA (Hons)

/OBUarchitecture

@OBUarchitecture

query@brookes.ac.uk

tde.bz/arch-heap

Salford – 260–300 pts (Archit Des Tech)
Ulster – 260 pts (Archit Tech Mgt) (IB 24 pts)
240 pts   **Anglia Ruskin** – 240 pts +portfolio (Archit) (IB 26 pts)
Bolton – 240 pts (Archit Tech) (IB 24 pts)
Glyndŵr – 240 pts (Archit Des Tech)
Middlesex – 240 pts (Inter Archit)
Ravensbourne – CC–AA (Archit) (IB 28 pts)
Robert Gordon – CCC 240 pts (Archit Tech) (IB 26 pts)
Salford – 240–260 pts (Civ Archit Eng) (IB 30 pts)
Suffolk (Univ Campus) – 240–280 pts (Inter Archit Des)
Writtle (Coll) – 240–280 pts (Inter Archit Des) (IB 24 pts)
220 pts   **Anglia Ruskin** – 220 pts (Archit Tech) (IB 24 pts)
Creative Arts – 220–240 pts +portfolio (Inter Archit Des)
Derby – 220–300 pts (Archit Des Joint Hons)
London South Bank – CCD–CCB 220–260 pts (Archit Tech)
200 pts   **Bedfordshire** – 200 pts (Inter Archit)
Hull (Coll) – 200 pts (Archit)
Southampton Solent – 200 pts (Archit Tech) (IB 24 pts)
West London – 200 pts (Blt Env (Archit Tech))
Wolverhampton – 200 pts (Archit Des Tech; Inter Archit Prop Dev)
80 pts   **Arts London** – 80 pts +portfolio (Arch (Spc Objs))

Alternative offers
See **Chapter 7** and **Appendix 1** for grades/UCAS Tariff points information for the International Baccalaureate, Scottish Highers/Advanced Highers, the Welsh Baccalaureate, the Irish Leaving Certificate, the Cambridge Pre-U Diploma, the Advanced Diploma and the Extended Project.

EXAMPLES OF FOUNDATION DEGREES IN THE SUBJECT FIELD
Anglia Ruskin.

CHOOSING YOUR COURSE (SEE ALSO CH.1)
Some course features
Architecture is a broad subject combining the vocational with the academic. To practise as an architect it is important to check that your chosen courses follow the requirements of the Royal Institute of British Architects (see **Appendix 3**).

Bath Four-year full-time thin sandwich BSc degree with second- and third-year placements, and opportunity for third-year Erasmus exchange at a European school of architecture.

Birmingham City The School of Architecture is one of the largest in the country and draws strength from its association with the Departments of Planning, Landscape and Construction and Surveying. Following the three-year BArch course, a postgraduate diploma course gives complete exemptions from RIBA examinations. Architecture can also be studied with an emphasis on urban design, conservation or regeneration. A BA course in Landscape Architecture is also offered.

De Montfort The three-year Architecture course focusing on studio-based projects is followed by one year of practical study and a further two years leading to the graduate diploma. The course carries exemption from the RIBA Part 1 examination. There is also a course in Architectural Design Technology and Production leading to qualification as an architect technician.

Kingston The Architecture course has design as its principal core element. A particular feature of the course is the use of continuous assessment. Courses in Landscape Architecture and Landscape Planning and Historic Building Conservation are also available.

London (UCL) This three-year Architecture course for a BSc degree is largely based on design projects and provides a very broad academic education for those who are concerned with planning, design and management of the built environment. After completing the degree, most students then undertake a year working in industry in the UK or overseas before proceeding to the two-year diploma programme.

Manchester Met This is a three-year full-time or four-year sandwich course in Architecture with design projects supported by studies in technical and administrative skills. The BArch programme is currently undergoing revalidation, and MArch and MA programmes are offered. There is also a course in Landscape Architecture.

Oxford Brookes (Archit) Wide-ranging three-year full-time course, with teaching centred on the design studio, technology, practice and historical and theoretical approaches to architecture.

Southampton A course is offered in Civil Engineering with Architecture with modules covering architectural principles, acoustics and urban design.

Universities and colleges teaching quality See www.qaa.ac.uk; http://unistats.direct.gov.uk.

Top research universities and colleges (RAE 2008) (Architecture and Built Environment) Cambridge; London (UCL); Sheffield; Liverpool; Loughborough; Bath; Reading; Edinburgh.

Examples of sandwich degree courses Bath; Bristol UWE; City; Coventry; Derby; Dundee; Glasgow (SA); Huddersfield; Leeds Beckett; London South Bank; Northumbria; Nottingham Trent; Sheffield Hallam; Ulster; Wolverhampton.

ADMISSIONS INFORMATION
Number of applicants per place (approx) Archit Assoc Sch London 2; Bath 13; Cambridge 10; Cardiff 12; Cardiff Met (UWIC) 2; Creative Arts 4; Dundee 6; Edinburgh 18; Glasgow 16; London (UCL) 21; London Met 13; Manchester Met 25; Newcastle 11; Nottingham 30; Oxford Brookes 15; Queen's Belfast 9; Robert Gordon 8; Sheffield 20; Southampton 10; Strathclyde 10.

Admissions tutors' advice London (UCL) Selection test and portfolio of work required.

Advice to applicants and planning the UCAS personal statement You should describe any visits to historical or modern architectural sites and give your opinions. Contact architects in your area and try to obtain work shadowing or work experience in their practices. Describe any such work you have done. Develop a portfolio of drawings and sketches of buildings and parts of buildings (you will probably need this for your interview). Show evidence of your reading on the history of architecture in Britain and modern architecture throughout the world. Discuss your preferences among the work of leading 20th century world architects (see **Chapter 5** and also **Appendix 3**). **Cambridge** Check college requirement for preparatory work.

Misconceptions about this course Some applicants believe that Architectural Technology is the same as Architecture. Some students confuse Architecture with Architectural Engineering.

Selection interviews The majority of universities and colleges interview or inspect portfolios for Architecture. **Yes** Archit Assoc Sch London, Birmingham City, Brighton, Cambridge, Coventry, Derby, Dundee, East London, Edinburgh, Huddersfield, Kingston, Liverpool, London (UCL), London South Bank, Newcastle, Sheffield, Ulster; **Some** Anglia Ruskin, Cardiff, Cardiff Met (UWIC); **No** Nottingham, Portsmouth.

Interview advice and questions Most Architecture departments will expect to see evidence of your ability to draw; portfolios are often requested at interview and, in some cases, drawing tests are set prior to the interview. You should have a real awareness of architecture with some knowledge of historical styles as well as examples of modern architecture. If you have gained some work experience then you will be asked to describe the work done in the architect's office and any site visits you have made. Questions in the past have included the following: What is the role of the architect in society? Is the London Eye an eyesore? Discuss one historic and one 20th century building you admire. Who is your favourite architect? What sort of buildings do you want to design? How would you make a place peaceful? How would you reduce crime through architecture? Do you like the university buildings? Do you read any architectural journals? Which? What is the role of an architectural technologist? See also **Chapter 6**. **Archit Assoc Sch London** The interview assesses the student's potential and ability to benefit from the course. Every portfolio we see at interview will be different; sketches, models, photographs and paintings all help to build up a picture of the student's interests. Detailed portfolio guidelines are available on the website. **Cambridge** Candidates who have taken, or are going to take, A-level art should bring with them their portfolio of work (GCSE work is not required). All candidates, including those who are not taking A-level art, should bring photographs of any three-dimensional material. Those not taught art should bring a sketch book (for us to assess drawing abilities) and analytical drawings of a new and an old (pre-1900) building and a natural and human-made artefact. We are interested to see any graphic work in any medium that you would like to show us – please do not feel you should restrict your samples to only those with architectural reference. All evidence of sketching ability is helpful to us. (NB All colleges at Cambridge and other university Departments of Architecture will seek similar evidence.) **Sheffield** Art portfolio required for those without AL/GCSE art.

Reasons for rejection (non-academic) Weak evidence of creative skills. Folio of artwork does not give sufficient evidence of design creativity. Insufficient evidence of interest in architecture. Unwillingness to try freehand sketching. **Archit Assoc Sch London** Poor standard of work in the portfolio.

AFTER-RESULTS ADVICE

Offers to applicants repeating A-levels Higher Huddersfield; **Possibly higher** Brighton, De Montfort, Glasgow, Newcastle; **Same** Archit Assoc Sch London, Bath, Birmingham City, Cambridge, Cardiff, Cardiff Met (UWIC), Creative Arts, Derby, Dundee, Greenwich, Kingston, Liverpool John Moores, London Met, London South Bank, Manchester Met, Nottingham, Nottingham Trent, Oxford Brookes, Queen's Belfast, Robert Gordon, Sheffield.

GRADUATE DESTINATIONS AND EMPLOYMENT (2011/12 HESA)

Graduates surveyed 2560 **Employed** 1365 **In voluntary employment** 135 **In further study** 500 **Assumed unemployed** 280

Career note Further study is needed to enter architecture as a profession. Opportunities exist in local government or private practice – areas include planning, housing, environmental and conservation fields. Architectural technicians support the work of architects and may be involved in project management, design presentations and submissions to planning authorities.

OTHER DEGREE SUBJECTS FOR CONSIDERATION

Building; Building Surveying; Civil Engineering; Construction; Heritage Management; History of Art and Architecture; Housing; Interior Architecture; Interior Design; Landscape Architecture; Property Development; Quantity Surveying; Surveying; Town and Country Planning; Urban Studies.

ART and DESIGN (GENERAL)

(including **Animation, Conservation** and **Restoration**; see also **Art and Design (3d Design), Art and Design (Graphic Design), Combined Courses, Communication Studies/Communication, Drama, Media Studies, Photography**)

Art and Design and all specialisms remain one of the most popular subjects. Many of the courses listed here cover aspects of fine art, graphic or three-dimensional design, but to a less specialised extent than those listed in the other Art and Design tables. Travel and visits to art galleries and museums are strongly recommended by many universities and colleges. Note that for entry to many Art and Design courses it is often necessary to follow an Art and Design Foundation course first: check with your chosen institution.

Art and Design degree courses cover a wide range of subjects. These are grouped together in six tables:

Art and Design (General),
Art and Design (Fashion and Textiles),
Art and Design (Fine Art),
Art and Design (Graphic Design),
Art and Design (Product and Industrial Design),
Art and Design (3D Design).

(History of Art and Photography are listed in separate tables.)

Useful websites www.artscouncil.org.uk; www.designcouncil.org.uk; www.theatredesign.org.uk; www.arts.ac.uk; www.dandad.org; www.csd.org.uk; www.yourcreativefuture.org.uk.

The points total shown to the left of the institutions are for ease of reference only. It must not be assumed that Tariff points are always used by institutions or that they can be substituted for an offer in grades. The level of an offer is not necessarily indicative of the quality of a course.

COURSE OFFERS INFORMATION

Subject requirements/preferences Entry requirements for Art and Design courses vary between institutions and courses (check prospectuses and websites). Most courses require an Art and Design Foundation course and a portfolio of work demonstrating potential and visual awareness. **GCSE** Five subjects at grades A–C, or a recognised equivalent. **AL** Grades or points may be required. (Des Tech) Design technology or a physical science may be required of preferred. (Crea Arts courses) Music/art/drama may be required.

Your target offers and examples of courses provided by each institution
340 pts **Kent** – AAB–ABB 340–320 pts (Art Film) (IB 34 pts HL 17 pts)
　　　　Reading – AAB–ABB 340–320 pts (Art Psy) (IB 35 pts)
320 pts **Dundee** – ABB (Art Phil Contemp Prac) (IB 34 pts)
　　　　Kent – ABB–BBB (Crea Evnts) (IB 33 pts)
　　　　Leeds – ABB (Art Des) (IB 34 pts)
　　　　Reading – ABB–ACC (Art Phil) (IB 32 pts)
300 pts **Cardiff Met (UWIC)** – 300 pts (Maker Art Des)
　　　　Edinburgh (CA) – BBB 300 pts +portfolio (Ptng) (IB 34 pts)
　　　　Huddersfield – BBB +portfolio +interview (Contemp Art)
　　　　Reading – BBB (Art Film Thea) (IB 30 pts)

Check **Chapter 4** when choosing your university and **Chapter 7** on how to read the subject tables.

280 pts **Birmingham City** – (Art Des)
Bournemouth Arts – BBC–BBB 280–300 pts (Arts Evnt Mgt) (IB 32 pts)
Bristol UWE – (Drg App Arts)
Hull – 280 pts (Dig Arts)
Lincoln – 280 pts (Des Exhib Musm)
Manchester Met – 280 pts +portfolio (Interact Arts) (IB 28 pts)
Nottingham Trent – 280 pts +portfolio (Decr Art)
260 pts **Bradford (Coll Univ Centre)** – 260 pts (Vis Arts)
Falmouth – 260–300 pts +portfolio +interview (Drg) (IB 24 pts)
Sheffield Hallam – 260 pts (Crea Art Prac)
Ulster – (Interact Media Arts)
240 pts **Bolton** – 240 pts (Art Des; Animat Illus) (IB 24 pts)
Canterbury Christ Church – 240 pts (Crea Arts)
Chichester – BCD 240 pts Art Fdn (Ptg Drg) (IB 30 pts)
Glyndŵr – 240 pts (Des App Art)
Hertfordshire – 240 pts (Animat; Contemp App Arts)
Portsmouth – 240–300 pts (Animat) (IB 28 pts)
Rose Bruford (Coll) – 240 pts (Scnc Arts)
Ulster – 240 pts (Animat)
220 pts **Creative Arts** – 220–240 pts (Animat) (IB 24 pts)
Worcester – 220–340 pts (Art Des; Animat)
200 pts **Blackburn (Coll)** – 200 pts (Illust Animat)
De Montfort – (Game Art Des)
Hereford (CA) – 200 pts (Contemp App Arts; Illus)
180 pts **Bath Spa** – 180–220 pts (Contemp Arts Prac)
Robert Gordon – BC +portfolio +interview (Contemp Art Prac; Pntg) (IB 24 pts)
West Scotland – (Comput Animat Dig Art)
160 pts **Glasgow Caledonian** – 160 pts (Comput Gms (Art Animat))
120 pts **Bradford (Coll Univ Centre)** – (Art Des)

Alternative offers

See **Chapter 7** and **Appendix 1** for grades/UCAS Tariff points information for the International Baccalaureate, Scottish Highers/Advanced Highers, the Welsh Baccalaureate, the Irish Leaving Certificate, the Cambridge Pre-U Diploma, the Advanced Diploma and the Extended Project.

EXAMPLES OF FOUNDATION DEGREES IN THE SUBJECT FIELD

Anglia Ruskin; Arts London; Barnet and Southgate (Coll); Bath Spa; Bedfordshire; Blackburn (Coll); Bradford (Coll Univ Centre); Brighton; Bristol UWE; Cardiff Met (UWIC); Cleveland (CAD); Cornwall (Coll); Doncaster (Coll Univ Centre); Exeter (Coll); Hertfordshire; Hull (Coll); Kingston (Coll); Llandrillo Cymru (Coll); London UCK (Coll); Manchester (Coll); Menai (Coll); NEW (Coll); North Warwickshire and Hinckley (Coll); Norwich City (Coll); Nottingham New (Coll); Plymouth (CA); South Devon (Coll); Staffordshire; Suffolk (Univ Campus); Sunderland; Truro (Coll); Wolverhampton; Writtle (Coll).

CHOOSING YOUR COURSE (SEE ALSO CH.1)

Top research universities and colleges (RAE 2008) Loughborough (Des Tech); Reading (Typo/Graph Comm); Lancaster; Newcastle; Westminster; London (UCL); Brighton; Bournemouth; Oxford; Cardiff Met (UWIC).

ADMISSIONS INFORMATION

Number of applicants per place (approx) Dundee 5; Manchester Met 10; Portsmouth 3; Southampton Solent 1; Sunderland 8.

Advice to applicants and planning the UCAS personal statement Admissions tutors look for a wide interest in aspects of art and design. Discuss the type of work and the range of media you have explored through your studies to date. Refer to visits to art galleries and museums and give your

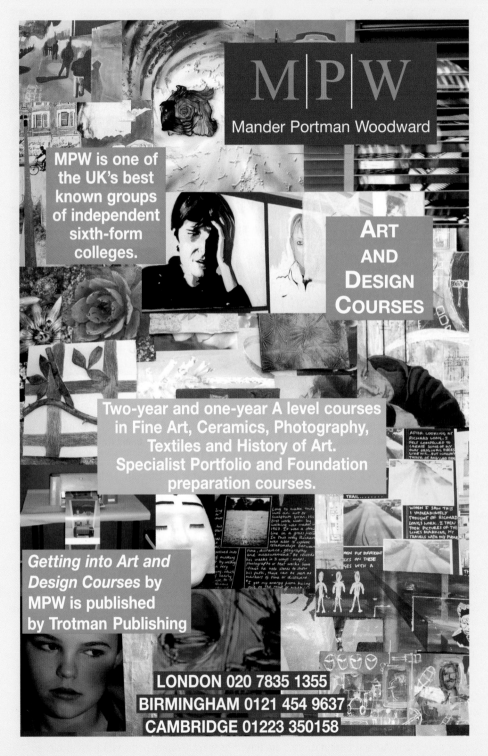

Art & Design

HC UK

Our range of programmes on offer include BA (Hons) in Art & Design disciplines such as Animation, Architecture, Design, Fashion, Film-Making & Creative Media Production, Fine Art, Games Design, Graphic Design, Illustration, Journalism & Digital Media, Photography, Textiles, Web Design, Visual Culture: Theory & Practice* and Event Management, as well as a small number of Masters programmes.

Our courses are validated by The Open University meaning you will receive your degree from one of the country's leading higher education institutions.

"100% of BA (Hons) Graphic Design students said that staff are good at explaining things and are enthusiastic." National Student Survey 2013

Come and meet us
Visit us at one of our campus open events. Call for more info.

Hull School of Art & Design
(01482) 598 744
hull-college.ac.uk/HE

Harrogate School of Art & Design
(01423) 878 211
harrogate.ac.uk/HE

*subject to validation

The Open University

opinions of the styles of paintings and sculpture, both historical and present day. Mention art-related hobbies. Good drawing skills and sketchbook work, creative and analytical thinking will be needed.

Selection interviews Yes Creative Arts, Dundee, Reading; **Some** Portsmouth, Staffordshire.

Interview advice and questions All courses require a portfolio inspection. Admissions tutors will want to see both breadth and depth in the applicant's work and evidence of strong self-motivation. They will also be interested to see any sketchbooks or notebooks. However, they do not wish to see similar work over and over again! A logical, ordered presentation helps considerably. Large work, especially three-dimensional work, can be presented by way of photographs. Video or film work should be edited to a running time of no more than 15 minutes. Examples of written work may also be provided. Past questions have included: How often do you visit art galleries and exhibitions? Discuss the last exhibition you visited. What are the reactions of your parents to your choice of course and career? Do you think that modern art has anything to contribute to society compared with earlier art? Is a brick a work of art? Show signs of life – no apathy! Be eager and enthusiastic.

Reasons for rejection (non-academic) Lack of enthusiasm for design issues or to acquire design skills. Poorly presented practical work. Lack of interest or enthusiasm in contemporary visual arts. Lack of knowledge and experience of the art and design industry.

GRADUATE DESTINATIONS AND EMPLOYMENT (2011/12 HESA)
Graduates surveyed 31340 **Employed** 13270 **In voluntary employment** 1455 **In further study** 5665 **Assumed unemployed** 3270

Career note Many Art and Design courses are linked to specific career paths which are achieved through freelance consultancy work or studio work. Some graduates enter teaching and many find other areas such as retail and management fields. Opportunities for fashion and graphic design specialists exceed those of other areas of art and design. Opportunities in industrial and product design and three-dimensional design are likely to be limited and dependent on the contacts that students establish during their degree courses. Only a very limited number of students committed to painting and sculpture can expect to succeed without seeking alternative employment.

OTHER DEGREE SUBJECTS FOR CONSIDERATION

Animation; Architecture; Art Gallery Management; Communication Studies; Computer Studies; Education; Film Studies; History of Art; Media Studies; Photography; see other **Art and Design** tables.

ART and DESIGN (FASHION and TEXTILES)
(including Surface Design)

Fashion Design courses involve drawing and design, research, pattern cutting and garment construction for clothing for men, women and children. Courses may also cover design for textiles, commercial production and marketing. Some institutions have particularly good contacts with industry and are able to arrange sponsorships for students.

Useful websites www.fashion.net; www.londonfashionweek.co.uk; www.texi.org; www. yourcreativefuture.org.uk.

NB The points totals shown to the left of the institutions are for ease of reference only. It must not be assumed that Tariff points are always used by institutions or that they can be substituted for an offer in grades. The level of an offer is not necessarily indicative of the quality of a course.

COURSE OFFERS INFORMATION

Subject requirements/preferences AL Textiles or textile science and technology may be required.

Your target offers and examples of courses provided by each institution

340 pts **Manchester** – AAB 340 pts (Fash Tex Rtl; Mgt Mark Fash Tex; Tex Des Des Mgt) (IB 35 pts)

320 pts **Brighton** – ABB 320 pts +portfolio +interview (Tex Bus St; Fash Bus St) (IB 34 pts)
  Glasgow (SA) – ABB (Fash Tex Des) (IB 30 pts)
  Leeds – ABB 320 pts (Fash Des) (IB 34 pts)
  Loughborough – ABB 320 pts (Tex Innov Des)
  Manchester – ABB (Tex Sci Tech) (IB 33 pts)
  Northumbria – 320 pts +portfolio +interview (Fash; Fash Mark)
  Southampton (Winchester SA) – ABB (Fash Tex Des; Fash Mark) (IB 32 pts HL 16 pts)

300 pts **Brighton** – BBB 300 pts (Fash Drs Hist) (IB 32 pts)
  Cardiff Met (UWIC) – 300 pts (Tex)
  Edinburgh – BBB 300 pts (Fash) (IB 34 pts)
  Edinburgh (CA) – BBB 300 pts +portfolio (Fash; Jewel Silver; Perf Cstm; Tex) (IB 34 pts)
  Heriot-Watt – BBB (Fash Comm; Fash Wmnswr; Fash Mnswr; Fash Tech; Fash) (IB 28 pts)
  Huddersfield – BBB (Fash Comm Prom; Fash Des Mark Prod; Fash Tex Buy Mgt; Fash Des Tex)
  Leeds – BBB (Tex Des) (IB 30 pts)
  Nottingham Trent – 300 pts (Fash Mark Brnd; Fash Comm Prom) (IB 32 pts)

280 pts **Arts London (CFash)** – 280 pts +portfolio (Fash Mgt)
  Birmingham City – 280 pts (Fash Rtl Mgt; Fash Des courses) (IB 28 pts)
  Bournemouth Arts – BBC–BBB 280–300 pts +portfolio +interview (Mkup Media Perf; Tex)
  Bristol UWE – 280 pts +portfolio (Fash) (IB 25 pts)
  Kingston – +portfolio (Fash)
  Lincoln – 280 pts (Fash St)
  Liverpool John Moores – 280 pts (Fash) (IB 29 pts)

Check **Chapter 4** when choosing your university and **Chapter 7** on how to read the subject tables.

London (Royal Central Sch SpDr) – BBC 280 pts (Thea Prac Cstm Constr)

Manchester Met – 280 pts +portfolio (Fash; Tex Prac) (IB 28 pts)

Norwich Arts – BBC (Tex; Fash) (IB 25 pts)

Nottingham Trent – 280 pts +portfolio (Fash Des; Tex Des)

Sheffield Hallam – 280 pts (Fash Des)

South Wales – BBC (Fash Des; Fash Promo; Fash Mark Rtl Des)

Westminster – BBC 280 pts (Fash Merch Mgt) (IB 29 pts)

260 pts **Bath Spa** – 260–300 pts (Fash Des; Tex Des Fash Inter) (IB 26 pts)

Bradford (Coll Univ Centre) – (Contemp Surf Des Tex; Fash Des)

De Montfort – 260 pts +portfolio +interview (Cont Fash; Fash Buy; Fash Des; Tex Des; Fash Fabs Accs) (IB 28 pts)

Derby – 260 pts +portfolio +interview (Tex Des; Fash St)

Falmouth – 260–300 pts +portfolio +interview (Fash Des; Fash Photo; Perf Spo Des; Tex Des)

Glasgow Caledonian – BCC (Fash Bus)

Northampton – 260–280 pts (Fash Mark; Fash; Fash (Ftwr Accs); Sfc Des Prntd Tex)

Robert Gordon – BCC 260 pts (Fash Mgt) (IB 28 pts)

Sheffield Hallam – 260 pts (Prod Des Jewel Fash)

Southampton Solent – 260 pts (Writ Fash Cult)

Staffordshire – 260 pts +portfolio +interview (Tex Sfc; Sfc Patt Des)

Sunderland – 260 pts (Fash Jrnl)

240 pts **Arts London (CFash)** – 240 pts +portfolio (Cstm Perf; Fash Jrnl (Prt/Broad); Fash PR; Mkup Pros Perf)

Bolton – 240 pts (Tex Sfc Des)

Central Lancashire – 240–260 pts (Fash Brnd Prom Photo)

Cleveland (CAD) – 240 pts (Tex Sfc Des; Fash Ent)

Coventry – CCC 240 pts (Fash) (IB 27 pts)

Hertfordshire – 240 pts +portfolio +interview (Fash)

Leeds (CA) – 240 pts +portfolio (Prtd Tex Surf Patt Des; Fash (Conc Comm); Fash (Des Realsn))

London Met – 240 pts (Fash Mark courses; Fash Buy Rtl)

Manchester Met – 240–280 pts (Int Fash Prom; Fash Buy Merch; Fash Des Tech) (IB 29–30 pts)

Nottingham Trent – 240 pts +portfolio (Fash Kntwr Des Knit Tex; Cstm Des Mak; Fash Accs Des)

Southampton Solent – 240 pts (Fash Graph; Fash Prom Comm; Fash Mgt Mark; Fash courses; Fash Styl)

Ulster – 240 pts (Tex Art Des Fash)

West London – 240 pts (Fash Tex)

220 pts **Blackpool and Fylde (Coll)** – 220 pts (Fash Cstm Perf)

Creative Arts – 220–240 pts +portfolio +interview (Fash Atel; Tex Fash Inter; Fash Prom Imag; Fash Jrnl)

Leeds – ABB (Fash Mark)

Middlesex – 220 pts +portfolio +interview (Fash Tex; Fash Des) (IB 28 pts)

Sunderland – 220 pts (Fash Prod Prom)

200 pts **Anglia Ruskin** – 200–240 pts (Fash Des)

Bedfordshire – 200 pts +portfolio (Fash Des; Fash Tex Des)

Bucks New – 200–240 pts (Fash Des)

Central Lancashire – 200–240 pts (Dig Des Fash; E Fash Des; Fash Prom Styl; Fash Brnd Mgt)

Croydon (Coll) – 200 pts (Fash Des Bus)

Doncaster (Coll Univ Centre) – 200 pts (Fash Tex Des)

East London – 200 pts (Fash Des)

Hereford (CA) – 200 pts (Tex Des; Jewel Des)

Hull (Coll) – 200 pts (Tex; Fash)
Plymouth (CA) – 200 pts (Fash; Print Tex des Surf Patt)
Portsmouth – 200–280 pts (Fash Tex Des Ent)
Salford – 200 pts (Fash) (IB 26 pts)
Trinity Saint David (Swansea) – 200 pts (Sfc Pattn Des (Contemp App Art Prac); Sfc Pattn Des (Tex Inter); Sfc Pattn Des (Tex Fash))
UHI – BB–AA +portfolio (Contemp Tex)
Wolverhampton – 200 pts (Fash Tex)

180 pts **Robert Gordon** – BC (Fash Tex Des) (IB 24 pts)
160 pts **Arts London (CFash)** – 160 pts +portfolio (Bspk Tlrg; Cord Fash Accs Prod Des Dev; Cord Ftwr Prod Des Dev; Crea Dir Fash; Fash Cont; Fash Des Dev; Fash Des Tech Mnswr; Fash Des Tech Wmnswr; Fash Illus; Fash Jewel; Fash Photo; Fash Spowr; Fash Tex)
Colchester (Inst) – 160 pts (Art Des (Fash Tex)) (IB 24 pts)
Northbrook (Coll) – 160 pts +portfolio +interview (Fash Des; Fash Media Prom; Tex Des)
Ravensbourne – CC–AA 160–240 pts (Fash; Fash Accs Des Proto; Fash Prom) (IB 28 pts)
Sir Gâr (Coll) – 160 pts +portfolio +interview (Fash Appar Des Constr)
Somerset (Coll) – 160 pts (Des (Fash/Tex))
South Essex (Coll) – 160 pts (Fash Des)
UHI – CC–AA 160–240 pts +portfolio (Fn Art Tex)
120 pts **Basingstoke (CT)** – 120 pts (Tex Fash)
100 pts and below or other selection criteria (Foundation course, interview and portfolio inspection) Arts London; Arts London (CFash); Arts London (Chelsea CAD); Arts London (Wimb CA); Bath Spa; Birmingham City; Brighton; Bristol UWE; Cardiff Met (UWIC); Chesterfield (Coll); Coventry; East London; Edinburgh (CA); Havering (Coll); Hertfordshire; Kingston; Leeds Beckett; Leicester (Coll); Lincoln; Liverpool John Moores; London Met; London Regent's; Loughborough; Manchester (Coll); Menai (Coll); Middlesex; NEW (Coll); Newcastle (Coll); Nottingham New (Coll); Pembrokeshire (Coll); Plymouth; Robert Gordon; Somerset (Coll); Southampton (Winchester SA); South City Birmingham (Coll); Staffordshire Reg Fed (SURF); Westminster; York (Coll); Yorkshire Coast (Coll)

Alternative offers
See **Chapter 7** and **Appendix 1** for grades/UCAS Tariff points information for the International Baccalaureate, Scottish Highers/Advanced Highers, the Welsh Baccalaureate, the Irish Leaving Certificate, the Cambridge Pre-U Diploma, the Advanced Diploma and the Extended Project.

EXAMPLES OF FOUNDATION DEGREES IN THE SUBJECT FIELD
Arts London (CFash); Barnfield (Coll); Bath City (Coll); Bath Spa; Bedfordshire; Blackburn (Coll); Bournemouth Arts; Bristol UWE; Chesterfield (Coll); Cleveland (CAD); Colchester (Inst); Cornwall (Coll); Creative Arts; Croydon (Coll); Derby; Exeter (Coll); Herefordshire and Ludlow (Coll); Hertfordshire; Hull (Coll); Kent; Kirklees (Coll); Leeds Beckett; Leicester (Coll); Liverpool City (Coll); London Met; Manchester (Coll); Mid-Cheshire (Coll); Newcastle (Coll); Nottingham New (Coll); Plymouth City (Coll); Sheffield (Coll); South Essex (Coll); Suffolk (Univ Campus); West Anglia (Coll).

CHOOSING YOUR COURSE (SEE ALSO CH.1)
Some course features
Universities and colleges offer a very wide range of specialist and individual subjects. In each case programmes will differ, often depending on the specialist interests of teaching staff. When considering specialist courses, eg Fashion Retail Management, Fashion Embroidery, Fashion Journalism, choose only named courses since a number of institutions claim to offer these subjects but only as a minor study.

Universities and colleges teaching quality See www.qaa.ac.uk; http://unistats.direct.gov.uk.

Top research universities and colleges (RAE 2008) See **Art and Design (General)**.

Examples of sandwich degree courses Arts London; Birmingham City; Brighton; Central Lancashire; Coventry; De Montfort; East London; Falmouth; Hertfordshire; Huddersfield; Manchester Met; Northumbria; Nottingham Trent; Portsmouth; South Wales; Southampton Solent; Westminster; Wolverhampton.

ADMISSIONS INFORMATION

Number of applicants per place (approx) Arts London 5; Arts London (CFash) (Fash Mgt) 20; Birmingham City (Tex Des) 4; Bournemouth Arts 6; Brighton 6; Bristol UWE 4; Central Lancashire 4; Creative Arts 8; De Montfort 5; Derby (Tex Des) 2; Essex 2; Heriot-Watt 6; Huddersfield 4; Kingston 5; Leeds (CA) 4; Liverpool John Moores 6; London (Gold) 5; Loughborough 5; Manchester Met 3; Middlesex 5; Northampton 4; Northumbria 8; Nottingham Trent 8, (Tex Des) 3; Southampton 4; Southampton (Winchester SA) 3; Staffordshire 3; Wolverhampton 2.

Advice to applicants and planning the UCAS personal statement A well-written statement is sought, clearly stating an interest in fashion and how prior education and work experience relate to your application. You should describe any visits to exhibitions and, importantly, your views and opinions. Describe any work you have done ('making' and 'doing' skills, if any, for example, pattern cutting, sewing) or work observation in textile firms, fashion houses, even visits to costume departments in theatres can be useful. These contacts and visits should be described in detail, showing your knowledge of the types of fabrics and production processes. Give opinions on trends in haute couture, and show awareness of the work of others. Provide evidence of materials handling (see also **Appendix 3**). Show good knowledge of the contemporary fashion scene. See also **Art and Design (Graphic Design)**.

Misconceptions about this course Some students expect the Fashion degree to include textiles. (Tex) Some applicants feel that it's necessary to have experience in textiles – this is not the case. The qualities sought in the portfolio are analytical drawing, good colour sense and a sensitivity to materials.

Selection interviews Most institutions interview and require a portfolio of work. You should be familiar with current fashion trends and the work of leading designers.

Interview advice and questions Questions mostly originate from student's portfolio. See also **Art and Design (General)** and **Chapter 6**. **Birmingham City** (Tex Des) What do you expect to achieve from a degree in Fashion? **Creative Arts** Describe in detail a specific item in your portfolio and why it was selected.

Reasons for rejection (non-academic) Portfolio work not up to standard. Not enough research. Not articulate at interview. Lack of sense of humour, and inflexibility. Narrow perspective. Lack of resourcefulness, self-motivation and organisation. Complacency, lack of verbal, written and self-presentation skills. Not enough experience in designing or making clothes. See also **Art and Design (General)**.

AFTER-RESULTS ADVICE

Offers to applicants repeating A-levels Same Birmingham City, Bournemouth Arts, Creative Arts, Huddersfield, Manchester Met, Nottingham Trent, South Essex (Coll), Staffordshire.

GRADUATE DESTINATIONS AND EMPLOYMENT (2011/12 HESA)
See **Art and Design (General)**.

Career note See **Art and Design (General)**.

OTHER DEGREE SUBJECTS FOR CONSIDERATION
History of Art; Retail Management; Theatre Design.

ART and DESIGN (FINE ART)

(including **Printing, Printmaking** and **Sculpture**; see also **Art and Design (Graphic Design), Photography**)

Fine Art courses can involve a range of activities such as painting, illustration and sculpture and often fine art media – electronic media, film, video, photography and print – although course options will vary between institutions. As in the case of most Art degrees, admission to courses usually requires a one-year Foundation Art course before applying.

Useful websites www.artcyclopedia.com; www.fine-art.com; www.nationalgallery.org.uk; www.britisharts.co.uk; www.tate.org.uk; www.yourcreativefuture.org.uk.

NB The points totals shown to the left of the institutions are for ease of reference only. It must not be assumed that Tariff points are always used by institutions or that they can be substituted for an offer in grades. The level of an offer is not necessarily indicative of the quality of a course.

COURSE OFFERS INFORMATION

Subject requirements/preferences See **Art and Design (General)**.

Your target offers and examples of courses provided by each institution

360 pts **Oxford** – AAA (Fn Art) (IB 38–40 pts)

340 pts **Lancaster** – AAB 340 pts (Fn Art; Fn Art) (IB 35 pts)
Leeds – AAB–ABB 340–320 pts (Fn Art) (IB 34–35 pts)
London (UCL/Slade SA) – ABBe +interview (Fn Art)
Newcastle – AAB–BBB 340–300 pts (Fn Art) (IB 32–35 pts)

320 pts **Brighton** – ABB (Fn Art Ptg; Fn Art Sculp; Fn Art Crit Prac) (IB 34 pts)
Dundee – ABB (Fn Art) (IB 34 pts HL 665)
Glasgow (SA) – ABB (Fn Art (Sculp Env Art); Fn Art (Pntg/Prtg);
      Fn Art (Photo))
Kent – ABB–BBB 320–300 pts (Fn Art) (IB 33 pts)
London (UCL) – ABB 320 pts (Fn Art) (IB 34 pts)
Loughborough – (Fn Art)
Southampton (Winchester SA) – ABB (Fn Art) (IB 32 pts HL 16 pts)

300 pts **Cardiff Met (UWIC)** – 300 pts (Fn Art)
Edinburgh – BBB 300 pts (Fn Art) (IB 34 pts)
Edinburgh (CA) – BBB 300 pts (Fn Art; Illus) (IB 34 pts)
Leeds Beckett – (Fn Art) (IB 24 pts)
Northumbria – 300 pts +interview (Fn Art) (IB 26 pts)

280 pts **Aberystwyth** – 280 pts (Fn Art; Art Hist Fn Art) (IB 28 pts)
Birmingham City – 280 pts (Fn Art) (IB 28 pts)
Bournemouth Arts – BBC 280 pts (Fn Art)
Bristol UWE – 280 pts (Fn Art)
Gloucestershire – 280 pts +interview +portfolio (Fn Art; Fn Art Photo)
Kingston – 280 pts (Fn Art)
Lincoln – (Fn Art)
Liverpool John Moores – 280–320 pts (Fn Art)
London (Gold) – BBC (Fn Art)
London Met – 280 pts (Fn Art courses)
Manchester Met – 280 pts (Fn Art) (IB 28 pts)
Norwich Arts – BBC (Fn Art) (IB 25 pts)
Oxford Brookes – BBC (Fn Art)
Suffolk (Univ Campus) – 280 pts +interview (Fn Art)
Teesside – 280 pts +portfolio (Fn Art)

260 pts **Bradford (Coll Univ Centre)** – 260 pts (Vis Arts)
Chichester – BCC (Fn Art courses) (IB 28 pts)
De Montfort – 260 pts (Fn Art) (IB 28 pts)

Hertfordshire – 260 pts (Fn Art)
Leeds (CA) – 260 pts (Fn Art)
Liverpool Hope – 260–300 pts (Fn Art) (IB 32 pts)
Northampton – 260–300 pts (Fn Art; Fn Art Pntg Drg)
Plymouth – 260 pts (Fn Art; Fn Art Art Hist) (IB 25–28 pts)
Sheffield Hallam – 260–280 pts (Fn Art)
South wales – BCC 260 pts (Art Prac)
Staffordshire – 260 pts (Fn Art)
York St John – 260–300 pts (Fn Art courses)

240 pts **Bolton** – 240 pts (Fn Art)
Canterbury Christ Church – 240 pts (Art Fn App Arts) (IB 24 pts)
Central Lancashire – (Fn Art)
Chester – 240–280 pts (Fn Art) (IB 26 pts)
Coventry – CCC 240 pts (Fn Art; Fn Art Illus) (IB 27 pts)
Cumbria – 240 pts (Fn Art) (IB 30 pts)
Derby – 240 pts (Fn Art)
Glyndŵr – (Fn Art)
Nottingham Trent – 240 pts +portfolio (Fn Art)
Portsmouth – 240–300 pts (Contemp Fn Art) (IB 28 pts)
South Wales – (Fn Art)
Ulster – 240 pts (Fn Arts)

220 pts **Creative Arts** – (Fn Art courses)
Falmouth – 220 pts (Fn Art)
Middlesex – 220 pts (Fn Art)
Sunderland – 220 pts (Fn Art)
Worcester – 220–260 pts (Fn Art Prac)

205 pts **Reading** – 205 pts +Pass **or** above at Art Foundation (Fn Art (Post Fdn)) (IB 24–35 pts)

200 pts **Anglia Ruskin** – 200–240 pts (Fn Art)
Blackburn (Coll) – 200 pts +interview (Fn Art (Integ Media))
Bucks New – 200–240 pts (Fn Art) (IB 24 pts)
East London – 200 pts (Fn Art)
Grimsby (Univ Centre) – 200 pts (Fn Arts Prac)
Hereford (CA) – 200 pts +portfolio +interview (Fn Art)
Hull (Coll) – 200 pts (Fn Art)
Kirklees (Coll) – 200 pts (Fn Art Des)
Plymouth (CA) – 200 pts (Fn Art)
Southampton Solent – 200 pts (Fn Art)
Trinity Saint David (Swansea) – 200–360 pts +portfolio +interview (Fn Art (Comb Media);
    Fn Art (Pntg Drg))
Yorkshire Coast (Coll) – 200 pts (Fn Art)

160 pts **Blackpool and Fylde (Coll)** – 160 pts (Fine Art Prof Prac)
Colchester (Inst) – 160 pts (Art Des (Fn Art))
Northbrook (Coll) – 160 pts +interview (Fn Art courses)
Sir Gâr (Coll) – 160 pts +interview (Fn Art (Pntg Drg Prtg))
South Essex (Coll) – 160 pts (Fn Art)
UHI – CC–AA 160–240 pts +portfolio (Fn Art; Fn Art Tex)

**100 pts and below or other selection criteria (Foundation course, interview and portfolio
    inspection)** Arts London; Arts London (Camberwell CA); Arts London (Chelsea CAD); Arts
    London (Wimb CA); Barking and Dagenham (Coll); Bath Spa; Bedfordshire; Brighton;
    Bristol UWE; Bucks New; Cardiff Met (UWIC); Central Lancashire; Cornwall (Coll);
    Coventry; Creative Arts; Croydon (Coll); De Montfort; Doncaster (Coll Univ Centre); East
    London; Edinburgh (CA); Glyndŵr; Havering (Coll); Hopwood Hall (Coll); Kingston;
    Kirklees (Coll); Leeds Beckett; Liverpool City (Coll); Liverpool John Moores; London
    (Gold); Middlesex; NEW (Coll); Northbrook (Coll); North Warwickshire and Hinckley (Coll);
    Nottingham; Reading; St Helens (Coll); Salford; Sheffield (Coll); Solihull (Coll);

Staffordshire Reg Fed (SURF); Stourbridge (Coll); Suffolk (Univ Campus); Trinity Saint David; Tyne Met (Coll); Walsall (Coll); West London; Westminster; West Thames (Coll); Wirral Met (Coll).

Alternative offers
See **Chapter 7** and **Appendix 1** for grades/UCAS Tariff points information for the International Baccalaureate, Scottish Highers/Advanced Highers, the Welsh Baccalaureate, the Irish Leaving Certificate, the Cambridge Pre-U Diploma, the Advanced Diploma and the Extended Project.

EXAMPLES OF FOUNDATION DEGREES IN THE SUBJECT FIELD
All are practical workshop courses. Arts London; Bath Spa; Bedfordshire; Blackpool and Fylde (Coll); Brighton; Bristol UWE; Central Bedfordshire (Coll); Cornwall (Coll); Creative Arts; De Montfort; Exeter (Coll); Glyndŵr; Greenwich; Hereford (CA); Huddersfield; Leeds Beckett; Leicester (Coll); Liverpool City (Coll); Llandrillo Cymru (Coll); Newcastle (Coll); Plymouth; Plymouth (CA); Sheffield (Coll); Somerset (Coll); Suffolk (Univ Campus); Sunderland; Sunderland City (Coll); Tyne Met (Coll); West London.

CHOOSING YOUR COURSE (SEE ALSO CH.1)
Universities and colleges teaching quality See www.qaa.ac.uk; http://unistats.direct.gov.uk.

Top research universities and colleges (RAE 2008) See **Art and Design (General)**.

Examples of sandwich degree courses Coventry; Huddersfield; Ulster; Wolverhampton.

ADMISSIONS INFORMATION
Number of applicants per place (approx) Arts London (Chelsea CAD) 5; Arts London (Wimb CA) (Sculp) 3; Bath Spa 8; Birmingham City 6; Bournemouth Arts 6; Bristol UWE 3; Cardiff Met (UWIC) 3; Central Lancashire 4; Cleveland (CAD) 2; Creative Arts 2; Cumbria 4; De Montfort 5; Derby 3; Dundee

5; Gloucestershire 5; Hertfordshire 6; Hull (Scarborough) 2; Hull (Coll) 2; Kingston 9; Lincoln 4; Liverpool John Moores 3; London (Gold) 10; London (UCL) 26; London Met 11; Loughborough 4; Manchester Met 4; Middlesex 3; Newcastle 30; Northampton 3; Northumbria 4; Norwich Arts 3; Nottingham Trent 5; Portsmouth 6; Robert Gordon 5; Sheffield Hallam 4; Solihull (Coll) 4; Southampton 3; Staffordshire 3; Sunderland 3; UHI 2; Wirral Met (Coll) 3.

Advice to applicants and planning the UCAS personal statement Since this is a subject area that can be researched easily in art galleries, you should discuss not only your own style of work and your preferred subjects but also your opinions on various art forms, styles and periods. Keep up-to-date with public opinion on controversial issues. Give your reasons for wishing to pursue a course in Fine Art. Visits to galleries and related hobbies, for example reading, cinema, music, literature should be mentioned. Show the nature of your external involvement in art. (See also **Appendix 3**.) **Oxford** No deferred applications are accepted for this course; successful applicants average 11.5%.

Misconceptions about this course That Fine Art is simply art and design. Sixth-form applicants are often unaware of the importance of a Foundation Art course before starting a degree programme. **Bournemouth Arts** Applicants need to make the distinction between fine art and illustration.

Selection interviews Most institutions interview and require a portfolio of work. **Yes** Arts London (Chelsea CAD), Cardiff Met (UWIC), Kent, Oxford (Fn Art) 12%, Portsmouth.

Interview advice and questions Questions asked on portfolio of work. Be prepared to answer questions on your stated opinions on your UCAS application and on current art trends and controversial topics reported in the press. Discussion covering the applicant's engagement with contemporary fine art practice. Visits to exhibitions, galleries etc. Ambitions for their own work. How do you perceive the world in a visual sense? Who is your favourite living artist and why? See also **Art and Design (General)** and **Chapter 6**. **UHI** Applicants are asked to produce a drawing in response to a set topic.

Reasons for rejection (non-academic) Lack of a fine art specialist portfolio. No intellectual grasp of the subject – only interested in techniques.

AFTER-RESULTS ADVICE
Offers to applicants repeating A-levels Same Anglia Ruskin, Arts London, Birmingham City, Cumbria, Manchester Met, Nottingham Trent, Staffordshire, Sunderland, UHI; **No** Oxford.

GRADUATE DESTINATIONS AND EMPLOYMENT (2011/12 HESA)
Graduates surveyed 3160 **Employed** 1045 **In voluntary employment** 165 **In further study** 545 **Assumed unemployed** 370

Career note See **Art and Design (General)**.

OTHER DEGREE SUBJECTS FOR CONSIDERATION
Art Gallery Management; History of Art; see other **Art and Design** tables.

ART and DESIGN (GRAPHIC DESIGN)

(including **Advertising, Animation, Design, Graphic Communication, Illustration** and **Visual Communication**; see also **Art and Design (Fine Art), Art and Design (General), Film, Radio, Video and TV Studies**)

Graphic Design ranges from the design of websites, books, magazines and newspapers to packaging and advertisements. Visual communication uses symbols as teaching aids and also includes TV graphics. An Art Foundation course is usually taken before entry to degree courses. Graphic Design students are probably the most fortunate in terms of the range of career opportunities open to them on graduation. These include advertising, book and magazine illustration, film, interactive media design, typography, packaging, photography and work in publishing and television.

Useful websites www.graphicdesign.about.com; www.graphic-design.com; www.allgraphicdesign.com; www.yourcreativefuture.org.uk.

NB The points totals shown to the left of the institutions are for ease of reference only. It must not be assumed that Tariff points are always used by institutions or that they can be substituted for an offer in grades. The level of an offer is not necessarily indicative of the quality of a course.

COURSE OFFERS INFORMATION

Subject requirements/preferences See **Art and Design (General)**.

Your target offers and examples of courses provided by each institution

340 pts **Kent** – AAB–ABB 340–320 pts (Vis Perf Arts) (IB 34 pts)
320 pts **Bournemouth** – 320–340 pts (Comp Animat Art; Comp Vis Animat) (IB 32–33 pts)
 Brighton – ABB +portfolio +interview (Graph Des) (IB 34 pts)
 Dundee – ABB (Animat; Graph Des) (IB 34 pts)
 East Anglia – ABB 320 pts (Comp Graph) (IB 32 pts)
 Leeds – ABB 320 pts (Graph Comm Des; Perf Des) (IB 34 pts)
 Northumbria – 320 pts (Comp Animat; Graph Des)
 Southampton (Winchester SA) – ABB (Graph Art) (IB 32 pts HL 16 pts)
300 pts **Birmingham City** – 300 pts (Film Tech Vis Efcts)
 Edinburgh – BBB 300 pts (Graph Des) (IB 34 pts)
 Edinburgh (CA) – BBB 300 pts (Graph Des; Intermed Art) (IB 34 pts)
 Glasgow Caledonian – BBB 300 pts (3D Comp Animat)
 Huddersfield – BBB (Animat; Contemp Art Illus; Graph Des)
 Kent – BBB–BBC (Dig Art) (IB 34 pts)
 Leeds Beckett – 300 pts (Comp Animat Vis Efcts; Graph Art Des; Gms Des) (IB 24–26 pts)
 Reading – BBB (Graph Comm)
 Teesside – 300 pts (Graph Des)
280 pts **Aberystwyth** – 280 pts (Comp Graph Vsn Gms) (IB 24 pts)
 Birmingham City – 280 pts (Animat; Vis Comm (Film Anim); Vis Comm (Photo))
 Bournemouth – 280–300 pts (Dig Media Des) (IB 30–31 pts)
 Bournemouth Arts – BBC 280 pts +portfolio +interview (Graph Des; Animat Prod; Illus; Vis Comm)
 Bradford – 280 pts (Comp Animat)
 Bristol UWE – 280 pts +portfolio (Graph Des; Animat)
 East London – 280 pts (Animat)
 Edge Hill – BBC 280 pts (Animat) (IB 26 pts)
 Greenwich – 280 pts (3D Dig Des Animat; Graph Dig Des)
 Hertfordshire – 280 pts (3D Dig Animat; 2D Dig Animat)
 Kingston – (Graph Des)
 Lincoln – 280 pts (Animat; Graph Des; Illus; Contemp Lns Media)
 Liverpool John Moores – 280 pts (Graph Des Illus; Comp Aid Des; Comp Animat Vis)
 London Met – 280 pts (Graph Des)
 Manchester Met – 280 pts +portfolio (Graph Des; Illus Animat; Crea Multim) (IB 28 pts)
 Norwich Arts – BBC (Graph Comm; Film Mov Imag Prod; Animat; Graph Des; Illus) (IB 25 pts)
 Nottingham Trent – 280 pts (Graph Des)
 Oxford Brookes – BBC (Comp Gms Animat) (IB 30 pts)
 Plymouth – 280 pts (Dig Art Tech; Graph Comm Typo) (IB 28 pts)
 Salford – BBC (Animat) (IB 28 pts)
 Sheffield Hallam – 280 pts (Graph Des)
 South Wales – (Graph Comm; Adv Des)
 Suffolk (Univ Campus) – 280 pts (Graph Des; Graph Des (Graph Illus); Comp Gms Des)
 Teesside – 280 pts (Comp Gms Des; Comp Gms Art; Comp Gms Animat)
260 pts **Bradford (Coll Univ Centre)** – 260 pts (Graph Des Illus Dig Media)
 Canterbury Christ Church – 260 pts (Film Animat)

Derby – 260 pts (Animat; Graph Des; Illus)
Edinburgh Napier – BCC 260 pts (Graph Des)
Falmouth – 260–300 pts +portfolio +interview (Animat Vis Efcts; Graph Des; Illus)
Gloucestershire – 260 pts (Adv; Graph Des)
Hull – 260–300 pts (Des Dig Media)
Salford – 260–300 pts (Graph Des) (IB 28 pts)
Staffordshire – CCC 260 pts (Animat; Graph Des; Crtn Cmc Arts; Illus)
Worcester – 260–380 pts (Graph Des Multim)

240 pts **Anglia Ruskin** – 200–240 pts (Illus)
Bolton – 240 pts (Animat)
Canterbury Christ Church – 240 pts (Graph Des)
Central Lancashire – 240–300 pts (Animat; Adv; Graph Des)
Chester – 240–280 pts (Graph Des) (IB 26 pts)
Coventry – CCC 240 pts (Fn Art Illus; Graph Des; Illus Graph) (IB 27 pts)
Cumbria – 240 pts (Illus; Graph Des)
De Montfort – 240 pts (Graph Des; Graph Des Illus; Animat)
Glyndŵr – 240 pts (Des Animat Vis Efcts Gm Art; Des Graph Des Multim)
Hertfordshire – 240 pts (Graph Des Illus)
Huddersfield – 240 pts (Illus; Adv Des)
Leeds (CA) – 240 pts (Graph Des; Art Des (Interd); Dig Film Gms Animat; Vis Comm)
Portsmouth – 240–300 pts (Illus; Graph Des)
Ravensbourne – AA–CC (Animat; Des Interact; Dig Adv Des; Graph Des; Mtn Graph) (IB 28 pts)
Sheffield Hallam – 240 pts (Animat Vis Efcts; Animat)
Ulster – CC 240 pts (Des Vis Comm; Graph Des Illust)
Westminster – CCC 240 pts (Animat) (IB 26 pts)
West Scotland – CCC 240 pts (Comp Animat) (IB 24 pts)

220 pts **Bath Spa** – 220 pts (Graph Comm)
Creative Arts – 220–240 pts (Graph Des; Graph Comm)
Middlesex – 220 pts (Animat; Graph Des; Illus)
Northampton – 220–260 pts (Graph Comm; Illus)
Sunderland – 220 pts (Graph Comm; Illus Des; Adv Des; Animat Des; Des Multim Graph)
York St John – 220–280 pts (Des Graph)

200 pts **Anglia Ruskin** – 200–240 pts (Illus Animat; Graph Des)
Bedfordshire – +portfolio +interview (Animat)
Blackburn (Coll) – 200 pts +portfolio +interview (Des (Graph Comm); Des (Illus Animat); Des (Mov Imag); Des (N Media))
Bucks New – 200–240 pts (Crea Adv; Graph Arts; Animat Vis Efcts)
Doncaster (Coll Univ Centre) – 200 pts (Graph Des)
Hereford (CA) – 200 pts +portfolio +interview (Graph Media Des)
Hull (Coll) – 200 pts (Graph Des; Illus; Animat)
Leeds Beckett – 200 pts (Animat) (IB 24 pts)
Plymouth (CA) – 200 pts (Animat; Des Gms; Illus; Graph Des)
Salford – 200 pts incl art C (Adv Des)
Southampton Solent – 200 pts (Animat; Graph Des)
Trinity Saint David (Swansea) – 200–360 pts (Graph Des; Gen Illus; 3D Comp Animat)
West London – 200 pts (Adv)
Westminster – BB–CCC 200–240 pts (Illus Vis Comm; Graph Comm Des) (IB 26 pts)
Wolverhampton – 200 pts (Graph Comm; Graph Comm Illus)

180 pts **Coventry** – 180–200 pts (Animat)
Robert Gordon – BC (Comp Graph Animat) (IB 26 pts)

160 pts **Bedfordshire** – 160 pts +portfolio +interview (Graph Des; Adv Des)
Blackpool and Fylde (Coll) – 160 pts (Illus; Graph Des)
Colchester (Inst) – 160 pts (Art Des (Graph Media))
East London – 160 pts (Graph Des; Illus)

Glasgow Caledonian – CC 160 pts (Graph Des Dig Media)

South Essex (Coll) – 160 pts (Graph Des)

Trinity Saint David (Swansea) – 160 pts (Crea Comp Gms Des)

140 pts **Pembrokeshire (Coll)** – 140–200 pts (Des St)

120 pts **Sir Gâr (Coll)** – 120 pts +portfolio +interview (Art Des (Multid); Dig Illus; Graph Comm)

100 pts and below or other selection criteria (Foundation course, interview and portfolio inspection) Arts London; Arts London (Camberwell CA); Arts London (Chelsea CAD); Bath Spa; Bradford; Brighton; Bristol City (Coll); Bristol UWE; Bucks New; Cardiff Met (UWIC); Coventry; Croydon (Coll); Edinburgh (CA); Gloucestershire (Coll); Greenwich; Grimsby (Univ Centre); Havering (Coll); Hertfordshire; Hopwood Hall (Coll); Kent; Kingston; Leeds Beckett; Liverpool John Moores; Loughborough; Manchester (Coll); Mid-Cheshire (Coll); NEW (Coll); Northbrook (Coll); Oxford Brookes; Rotherham (CAT); St Helens (Coll); Solihull (Coll); Somerset (Coll); Southampton (Winchester SA); Southwark (Coll); Stockport (Coll); Suffolk (Univ Campus); Swindon (Coll); Tyne Met (Coll); West London; Westminster; West Thames (Coll); Wigan and Leigh (Coll); Wiltshire (Coll); Worcester; Yorkshire Coast (Coll).

Alternative offers

See **Chapter 7** and **Appendix 1** for grades/UCAS Tariff points information for the International Baccalaureate, Scottish Highers/Advanced Highers, the Welsh Baccalaureate, the Irish Leaving Certificate, the Cambridge Pre-U Diploma, the Advanced Diploma and the Extended Project.

EXAMPLES OF FOUNDATION DEGREES IN THE SUBJECT FIELD

Arts London; Barking and Dagenham (Coll); Barnet and Southgate (Coll); Bath Spa; Bedfordshire; Blackburn (Coll); Bournemouth; Brighton; Bristol City (Coll); Bucks New; Cardiff Met (UWIC); Central Lancashire; Chichester; Cleveland (CAD); Cornwall (Coll); Creative Arts; Cumbria; Durham New (Coll); Exeter (Coll); Farnborough (CT); Greenwich; Hertfordshire; Hugh Baird (Coll); Kingston; Kirklees (Coll); Leeds (CA); Leicester (Coll); Mid-Cheshire (Coll); Middlesex; Newcastle (Coll); Northampton; Northbrook (Coll); Norwich Arts; Nottingham New (Coll); Plymouth (CA); Rotherham (CAT); St Helens (Coll); Salford; Sheffield (Coll); Somerset (Coll); South Cheshire (Coll); Southwark (Coll); Staffordshire Reg Fed (SURF); Suffolk (Univ Campus); Teesside; Truro (Coll); Wigan and Leigh (Coll).

CHOOSING YOUR COURSE (SEE ALSO CH.1)

Some course features

These courses offer a wide range of specialisms; check the course contents before selecting.

Universities and colleges teaching quality See www.qaa.ac.uk; http://unistats.direct.gov.uk.

Top research universities and colleges (RAE 2008) See **Art and Design (General)**.

Examples of sandwich degree courses Aberystwyth; Arts London; Birmingham Met (Coll); Central Lancashire; Coventry; Hertfordshire; Huddersfield; Kingston; Loughborough; Middlesex; Northumbria; Portsmouth; South Wales; Ulster; Wolverhampton.

ADMISSIONS INFORMATION

Number of applicants per place (approx) Anglia Ruskin (Illus) 3; Arts London 4; Bath Spa 9; Blackburn (Coll) 2; Bournemouth Arts 6; Bristol UWE 4; Cardiff Met (UWIC) 5; Central Lancashire 5; Colchester (Inst) 3; Coventry 6; Creative Arts 5; Derby 5; Edinburgh Napier 7; Hertfordshire 6; Kingston 8; Lincoln 5; Liverpool John Moores 7; Loughborough 5; Manchester Met 8; Middlesex 3; Northampton 3; Northumbria 8; Norwich Arts 4; Nottingham Trent 6; Ravensbourne 9; Solihull (Coll) 3; South Essex (Coll) 2; Southampton 6; Staffordshire 3; Teesside 5; Trinity Saint David (Swansea) 10; Wolverhampton 5.

Advice to applicants and planning the UCAS personal statement Discuss your special interest in this field and any commercial applications that have impressed you. Discuss the work you are enjoying at present and the range of media that you have explored. Show your interests in travel, architecture, the arts, literature, film, current affairs (see also **Appendix 3** for contact details of relevant professional associations). Have an awareness of the place of design in society.

Misconceptions about this course Bath Spa Some students think that they can start the course from A-levels; that a course in Illustration is simply 'doing small drawings'; and that Graphic Design is a soft option with little academic work.

Selection interviews All institutions interview and require a portfolio of work.

Interview advice and questions Questions may be asked on recent trends in graphic design from the points of view of methods and designers and, particularly, art and the computer. Questions are usually asked on applicant's portfolio of work. See also **Art and Design (General)** and **Chapter 6**. **Nottingham Trent** Why Graphic Design? Why this course? Describe a piece of graphic design which has succeeded.

Reasons for rejection (non-academic) Not enough work in portfolio. Inability to think imaginatively. Lack of interest in the arts in general. Lack of drive. Tutor's statement indicating problems. Poorly constructed personal statement. Inability to talk about your work. Lack of knowledge about the chosen course. See also **Art and Design (General)**.

AFTER-RESULTS ADVICE
Offers to applicants repeating A-levels Same Bath Spa, Blackpool and Fylde (Coll), Bournemouth Arts, Cardiff Met (UWIC), Creative Arts, Lincoln, Manchester Met, Nottingham Trent, Salford, South Essex (Coll), Staffordshire.

GRADUATE DESTINATIONS AND EMPLOYMENT (2011/12 HESA)
See **Art and Design (General)**.

Career note See **Art and Design (General)**.

OTHER DEGREE SUBJECTS FOR CONSIDERATION
Art Gallery Management; Film and Video Production; History of Art; Multimedia Design, Photography and Digital Imaging. See also other **Art and Design** tables.

ART and DESIGN (PRODUCT and INDUSTRIAL DESIGN)

(including **Design Technology, Footwear Design, Furniture Design, Product Design, Theatre Design** and **Transport Design**; see also **Architecture, Art and Design (3d Design)**)

The field of industrial design is extensive and degree studies are usually preceded by an Art Foundation course. Product Design is one of the most common courses in which technological studies (involving materials and methods of production) are integrated with creative design in the production of a range of household and industrial products. Other courses on offer include Furniture Design, Interior, Theatre, Museum and Exhibition, Automotive and Transport Design. It should be noted that some Product Design courses have an engineering bias: see **Subject requirements/preferences** below. These are stimulating courses but graduate opportunities in this field are very limited. Good courses will have good industrial contacts for sandwich courses or shorter work placements – check with course leaders (or students) before applying.

Useful websites www.ergonomics.org.uk; www.yourcreativefuture.org.uk; www.productdesignforums.com; www.carbodydesign.com; www.shoe-design.com.

NB The points totals shown to the left of the institutions are for ease of reference only. It must not be assumed that Tariff points are always used by institutions or that they can be substituted for an offer in grades. The level of an offer is not necessarily indicative of the quality of a course.

COURSE OFFERS INFORMATION

Subject requirements/preferences AL Check Product Design, Industrial Design and Engineering Design course requirements since these will often require mathematics and/or physics.

Your target offers and examples of courses provided by each institution

380 pts **Glasgow** – A*AA 380 pts (Prod Des Eng MEng) (IB 36 pts)

360 pts **Leeds** – AAA 360 pts (Prod Des) (IB 35 pts HL 18 pts)

340 pts **Glasgow** – AAB 340 pts (Prod Des Eng BEng) (IB 34 pts)

Queen's Belfast – AAB 340 pts (Prod Des Dev MEng)

Strathclyde – AAB (Prod Des Eng MEng; Prod Eng Mgt MEng) (IB 36 pts)

Swansea – AAB–ABB 340–320 pts (Prod Des Eng MEng) (IB 34–33 pts)

320 pts **Brighton** – ABB 320 pts (Prod Des Prof Expnc; Prod Des courses) (IB 34 pts)

Brunel – ABB 320 pts (Prod Des; Prod Des Eng; Ind Des Tech) (IB 33 pts)

Glasgow (SA) – ABB 320 pts (Prod Des; Inter Des) (IB 30 pts)

Leeds – ABB (Ind Des Inv)

Liverpool – ABB 320 pts (Ind Des Eng) (IB 35 pts)

Strathclyde – ABB 320 pts (Prod Des Innov; Prod Eng Mgt BEng) (IB 34 pts)

Sussex – ABB–BBB (Prod Des) (IB 32 pts)

300 pts **Aston** – BBB–ABB 300–320 pts (Trans Prod Des; Ind Prod Des) (IB 32 pts)

Brighton – ABB–BBB 300–320 pts (Prod Des Tech (Yr Ind); Spo Prod Des (Yr Ind)) (IB 32 pts)

Edinburgh – BBB 300 pts (Prod Des) (IB 34 pts)

Edinburgh (CA) – BBB 300 pts (Inter Des; Prod Des) (IB 34 pts)

Huddersfield – 300 pts (Prod Des (3D Animat); Exhib Rtl Des; Prod Des (Child Prod Toys/Sust Des); Prod Innov Des Dev; Trans Des)

Leeds Beckett – 300 pts (Des Prod) (IB 26 pts)

Loughborough – BBB (Prod Des Tech; Ind Des Tech) (IB 32 pts)

Nottingham – BBB (Prod Des Manuf) (IB 30 pts)

Plymouth – 300 pts (3D Des courses) (IB 28 pts)

Queen's Belfast – BBB 300 pts (Prod Des Dev)

Swansea – BBB 300 pts (Prod Des Eng BEng) (IB 32 pts)

280 pts **Birmingham City** – 280 pts (Prod Des)

Bournemouth – 280–300 pts (Prod Des; Ind Des)

Bradford – 280 pts (Prod Des)

Bristol UWE – 280 pts (Crea Prod Des; Prod Des Tech)

Cardiff Met (UWIC) – 280 pts (Prod Des)

De Montfort – 280 pts +portfolio (Inter Des) (IB 28 pts)

Kingston – 280 pts +portfolio (Prod Furn Des)

Lincoln – 280 pts (Prod Des)

London (Royal Central Sch SpDr) – BBC 280 pts (Thea Prac Stg Des; Thea Prac Prod Ltg; Thea Prac Prop Mak; Thea Prac Scnc Art; Thea Prac Ltg Des)

London Met – 280 pts (Furn Prod Des)

Manchester Met – 280 pts +portfolio (Inter Des) (IB 28 pts)

Nottingham Trent – 280 pts (Furn Prod Des; Prod Des)

Sheffield Hallam – 280 pts (Inter Des)

Staffordshire – 280 pts (Prod Des Tech)

Teesside – 280 pts +portfolio (Prod Des; Inter Des)

260 pts **De Montfort** – 260 pts (Prod Des; Ftwr Des; Prod Furn Des; Furn Des)

Derby – 260 pts (Prod Des)

Dundee – BCC (Prod Des)

Liverpool John Moores – 260 pts (Spat Des) (IB 27 pts)

Northampton – 260–280 pts (Prod Des)

Northumbria – 260 pts (Prod Des Tech)

Sheffield Hallam – 260–280 pts (Prod Des)

Staffordshire – 260 pts +portfolio +interview (Prod Des)

Check **Chapter 4** when choosing your university and **Chapter 7** on how to read the subject tables.

Trinity Saint David (Swansea) – 260 pts (Prod Des)
240 pts Abertay – CCC 240 pts (Fd Prod Des)
Central Lancashire – 240–300 pts (Prod Des; Inter Des)
Coventry – CCC 240 pts (Inter Des; Prod Des) (IB 27 pts)
East London – 240 pts (Prod Des; Prod Des Fut)
Edinburgh Napier – CCC (Prod Des)
Hertfordshire – 240 pts (Prod Des; Ind Des)
Liverpool John Moores – 240 pts (Inter Des)
Manchester Met – 240–280 pts (Prod Des Tech) (IB 28 pts)
Nottingham Trent – 240 pts +portfolio (Thea Des)
Portsmouth – 240–280 pts (Prod Des Innov) (IB 26 pts)
Ravensbourne – CC–AA (Des Prod; Inter Des Env Archit) (IB 28 pts)
Rose Bruford (Coll) – 240 pts (Ltg Des)
Salford – 240–280 pts (3D Des Prod Des) (IB 26 pts)
Sheffield Hallam – 240 pts (Prod Des Furn)
Southampton Solent – 240 pts (Prod Des)
Staffordshire – CCC 240 pts (Trans Des)
Ulster – 240 pts +portfolio +interview (Prod Furn Des) (IB 24 pts)
220 pts Creative Arts – 220–240 pts (Prod Des Interact; Prod Des)
Falmouth – 220 pts +portfolio (Inter Des)
Moulton (Coll) – 220 pts +portfolio +interview (Inter Des)
Northampton – 220–260 pts (Inter Des)
Portsmouth – 220–320 pts (Inter Des) (IB 28 pts)
Trinity Saint David (Swansea) – 220 pts (Auto Des)
York St John – 220–280 pts (Des Inter)
200 pts Bangor – 200–220 pts (Prod Des)
Bucks New – 200–240 pts (Furn)
Hull (Coll) – 200 pts (Des (Inter, Prod, Des Mak))
London South Bank – CDD 200 pts (Prod Des)
Plymouth (CA) – 200 pts (Sculp Mtl)
Portsmouth – 200 pts (Prod Des Modn Mat)
Southampton Solent – 200 pts (Inter Des (Decr))
Wolverhampton – 200 pts (Inter Des; Prod Des)
York St John – 200–280 pts (Des Prod)
160 pts Glasgow Caledonian – 160 pts (Comput Gms (Art Animat))
Liverpool (LIPA) – 160–280 pts (Thea Perf Des; Thea Perf Tech)
London Regent's – CC 160 pts (Inter Des)
**100 pts and below or other selection criteria (Foundation course, interview and portfolio
inspection)** Arts London; Arts London (Chelsea CAD); Arts London (Wimb CA); Barking
and Dagenham (Coll); Bath Spa; Bolton; Bournemouth Arts; Brighton; Bucks New; Cardiff
Met (UWIC); De Montfort; Dundee; Easton Otley (Coll); Edinburgh (CA); Forth Valley
(Coll); Glasgow Caledonian; Glasgow City (Coll); Heriot-Watt; Hertfordshire; Kingston;
Kirklees (Coll); Lincoln; London South Bank; NEW (Coll); Royal Welsh (CMusDr);
Shrewsbury (CAT); Southampton Solent; South Essex (Coll).

Alternative offers

See **Chapter 7** and **Appendix 1** for grades/UCAS Tariff points information for the International
Baccalaureate, Scottish Highers/Advanced Highers, the Welsh Baccalaureate, the Irish Leaving
Certificate, the Cambridge Pre-U Diploma, the Advanced Diploma and the Extended Project.

EXAMPLES OF FOUNDATION DEGREES IN THE SUBJECT FIELD

Arts London; Barking and Dagenham (Coll); Bath Spa; Bedfordshire; Bishop Burton (Coll); Blackburn
(Coll); Bournemouth Arts; Bristol City (Coll); Bristol UWE; Bucks New; Cornwall (Coll); Croydon (Coll);
Greenwich; Kirklees (Coll); Leeds (CA); Leicester (Coll); London Met; Plymouth (CA); Rose Bruford
(Coll); Somerset (Coll); South Devon (Coll); Trinity Saint David (Swansea); West London.

CHOOSING YOUR COURSE (SEE ALSO CH.1)

Some course features
Note that there is an engineering element in some Product Design courses, and several specifically lead to an Engineering degree. Many are accredited by the Institution of Engineering Designers (see **Appendix 3**).
Ulster Live projects undertaken in all three years of course. Furniture Design covers public, contract, domestic and street furniture.

Universities and colleges teaching quality See www.qaa.ac.uk; http://unistats.direct.gov.uk.

Top research universities and colleges (RAE 2008) See **Art and Design (General)**.

Examples of sandwich degree courses Aston; Bournemouth; Bradford; Brighton; Bristol UWE; Brunel; Central Lancashire; De Montfort; East London; Huddersfield; Lincoln; Liverpool John Moores; London South Bank; Loughborough; Manchester Met; Middlesex; Northumbria; Nottingham Trent; Portsmouth; Queen's Belfast; Sheffield Hallam; Staffordshire; Sussex; West Scotland; Wolverhampton.

ADMISSIONS INFORMATION

Number of applicants per place (approx) Arts London 2; Arts London (Chelsea CAD) 2; Arts London (Wimb CA) 2; Aston 6; Bath Spa 4; Birmingham City (Inter Des) 9; Bolton 1; Brunel 4; Cardiff Met (UWIC) 6; Central Lancashire 7; Colchester (Inst) 4; Coventry 5; Creative Arts 4; De Montfort 5; Derby 2; Edinburgh Napier 6; Loughborough 9; Manchester Met 2; Middlesex (Inter Archit Des) 4; Northampton (Prod Des) 2; Northumbria 4; Nottingham Trent (Inter Archit Des) 7, (Prod Des) 5; Portsmouth 3; Ravensbourne (Inter Des) 4, (Prod Des) 7; Salford 6; Sheffield 4; Shrewsbury (CAT) 6; Staffordshire 3; Teesside 3; Trinity Saint David (Swansea) 3.

Advice to applicants and planning the UCAS personal statement Your knowledge of design in all fields should be described, including any special interests you may have, for example in domestic, rail and road aspects of design, and visits to exhibitions, motor shows. **School/college reference:** tutors should make it clear that the applicant's knowledge, experience and attitude match the chosen course – not simply higher education in general. Admissions tutors look for knowledge of interior design and interior architecture, experience in three-dimensional design projects (which include problem-solving and sculptural demands), model-making experience in diverse materials, experience with two-dimensional illustration and colour work, and knowledge of computer-aided design. Photography is also helpful, and also CAD/computer skills. See also **Art and Design (Graphic Design)**.

Misconceptions about this course Theatre Design is sometimes confused with Theatre Architecture or an academic course in Theatre Studies. **Birmingham City** (Inter Des) Some applicants believe that it is an interior decorating course (carpets and curtains). **Lincoln** (Musm Exhib Des) This is a design course, not a museum course. **Portsmouth** (Inter Des) Some students think that this is about interior decorating after Laurence Llewelyn-Bowen!

Selection interviews Most institutions will interview and require a portfolio of work. **Yes** Brunel, Cardiff Met (UWIC), Dundee, Portsmouth; **Some** Salford, Staffordshire.

Interview advice and questions Applicants' portfolios of artwork form an important talking-point throughout the interview. Applicants should be able to discuss examples of current design and new developments in the field and answer questions on the aspects of industrial design which interest them. See also **Art and Design (General)** and **Chapter 6**. **Creative Arts** No tests. Discuss any visits to modern buildings and new developments, eg British Museum Great Court or the Louvre Pyramid.

Reasons for rejection (non-academic) Not hungry enough! Mature students without formal qualifications may not be able to demonstrate the necessary mathematical or engineering skills. Poor quality and organisation of portfolio. Lack of interest. Inappropriate dress. Lack of enthusiasm. Insufficient portfolio work (eg exercises instead of projects). Lack of historical knowledge of interior design. Weak oral communication. See also **Art and Design (General)**. **Creative Arts** Not enough three-dimensional model-making. Poor sketching and drawing.

AFTER-RESULTS ADVICE
Offers to applicants repeating A-levels Same Birmingham City, Bournemouth, Creative Arts, Nottingham Trent, Salford, Staffordshire.

GRADUATE DESTINATIONS AND EMPLOYMENT (2011/12 HESA)
See **Art and Design (General)**.

Career note See **Art and Design (General)**.

OTHER DEGREE SUBJECTS FOR CONSIDERATION
Architectural Studies; Architecture; Art Gallery Management; Design (Manufacturing Systems); History of Art; Manufacturing Engineering; Multimedia and Communication Design and subjects in other **Art and Design** tables.

ART and DESIGN (3D DESIGN)

(including **Ceramics, Design Crafts, Glassmaking, Jewellery, Metalwork, Silversmithing, Plastics** and **Woodwork**; see also **Art and Design (General), Art and Design (Product and Industrial Design)**)

This group of courses covers mainly three-dimensional design work, focusing on creative design involving jewellery, silverware, ceramics, glass, wood and plastics. Some institutions offer broad three-dimensional studies courses while others provide the opportunity to study very specialised subjects such as stained glass, gemology and horology. Students normally take an Art Foundation course before their degree level studies.

Useful websites www.ergonomics.org.uk; www.yourcreativefuture.org.uk; www.top3D.net; www.glassassociation.co.uk; www.bja.org.uk; www.cpaceramics.com.

NB The points totals shown to the left of the institutions are for ease of reference only. It must not be assumed that Tariff points are always used by institutions or that they can be substituted for an offer in grades. The level of an offer is not necessarily indicative of the quality of a course.

COURSE OFFERS INFORMATION
Subject requirements/preferences See **Art and Design (General)**.

Your target offers and examples of courses provided by each institution

320 pts **Dundee** – ABB 320 pts (Jewel Metal Des) (IB 34 pts)
Glasgow (SA) – ABB 320 pts (Silver Jewel Des)

300 pts **Cardiff Met (UWIC)** – 300 pts (Ceram)
Edinburgh (CA) – BBB 300 pts (Sculp) (IB 34 pts)
Plymouth – 300 pts (3D Des courses) (IB 28 pts)

280 pts **Birmingham City** – 280 pts (Horol; Jewel Silver) (IB 28 pts)
Bournemouth Arts – BBC–BBB 280–300 pts +interview (Mdl)
Greenwich – 280 pts (3D Dig Des Animat)
Hertfordshire – 280 pts (3D Dig Animat)
Lincoln – (Jewel Obj)
London Met – 280 pts (Jewel Silver)
Manchester Met – 280 pts (3D Des) (IB 28 pts)
Northumbria – 280 pts (3D Des)

260 pts **Falmouth** – 260–300 pts +interview (Contemp Crfts)
Liverpool Hope – 260–300 pts (Des)
Stranmillis (UC) – BCC (Tech Des Educ)

240 pts **Cleveland (CAD)** – 240 pts (Enter Des Crfts)
De Montfort – 240–260 pts (Des Crafts)

Glyndŵr – 240 pts (App Arts)
Oldham (Univ Campus) – 240 pts (Dig Art Prac)
Sheffield Hallam – 240–260 pts (Mtl Jewel)
220 pts **Creative Arts** – 220–240 pts (Contemp Jewel; Silver Gold Jewel; 3D Des)
Falmouth – 220 pts (3D Des)
Sunderland – 220 pts (Glass Ceram)
200 pts **Bucks New** – 200–240 pts (3D Contemp Crfts Prods)
Hereford (CA) – 200 pts (Arst Blksmthg; Jewel Des)
Plymouth (CA) – 200 pts (Ceram; Contemp Cfts; Gls; Jewel Silver)
Portsmouth – 200–280 pts (3D Des)
Trinity Saint David (Swansea) – 200–360 pts (Fn Art (3d Sculp Prac))
Wolverhampton – 200 pts (App Arts)
180 pts **Robert Gordon** – BC 180 pts (3D Des) (IB 24 pts)
160 pts **Colchester (Inst)** – 160 pts (Art Des 3D Des Crft)
120 pts **Havering (Coll)** – 120 pts (3D Des Crft)
Sir Gâr (Coll) – 120 pts +portfolio +interview (Ceram Jewel; Sculp)
100 pts and below or other selection criteria (Foundation course, interview and portfolio inspection) Anglia Ruskin; Arts London; Arts London (Camberwell CA); Barking and Dagenham (Coll); Bath Spa; Bedfordshire; Brighton; Bucks New; Central Lancashire; Cornwall (Coll); Dundee; East London; Edinburgh (CA); Greenwich; Hertfordshire; Lincoln; Loughborough; Manchester (Coll); Menai (Coll); Middlesex; NEW (Coll); Northampton; Northbrook (Coll); Northumbria; Nottingham New (Coll); Plymouth; Staffordshire Reg Fed (SURF); York St John.

Alternative offers
See **Chapter 7** and **Appendix 1** for grades/UCAS Tariff points information for the International Baccalaureate, Scottish Highers/Advanced Highers, the Welsh Baccalaureate, the Irish Leaving Certificate, the Cambridge Pre-U Diploma, the Advanced Diploma and the Extended Project.

EXAMPLES OF FOUNDATION DEGREES IN THE SUBJECT FIELD
Barking and Dagenham (Coll); Bedfordshire; Bournemouth and Poole (Coll); Bournemouth Arts; Brighton; Cleveland (CAD); Croydon (Coll); Cumbria; East Anglia; East London; Hereford (CA); Hertfordshire; London Met; Manchester (Coll); Newcastle (Coll); Plymouth; Plymouth (CA); South Devon (Coll); South Essex (Coll); Truro (Coll); Writtle (Coll).

CHOOSING YOUR COURSE (SEE ALSO CH.1)
Some course features
Courses available specialise in ceramics, glassware, jewellery and silversmithing.
Manchester Met Three-year course offers a study exchange to Norway.
Plymouth Opportunity for European study exchange or work placement for 12 weeks in Year 2.
Staffordshire Three-dimensional Design courses cover ceramics, crafts and jewellery.
Wolverhampton A combination of theory and practice is offered.

Universities and colleges teaching quality See www.qaa.ac.uk; http://unistats.direct.gov.uk.

Top research universities and colleges (RAE 2008) See **Art and Design (General)**.

ADMISSIONS INFORMATION
Number of applicants per place (approx) Arts London (Ceram) 2; Arts London (Camberwell CA) 2, (Ceram) 3, (Jewel) 2; Bath Spa 3; Birmingham City 4, (Jewel) 5; Brighton 3; Creative Arts 4; De Montfort 3; Dundee 5; Manchester Met 5; Middlesex (3D Des) 4, (Jewel) 4; Portsmouth 3; Ravensbourne 110 total applicants.

Advice to applicants and planning the UCAS personal statement Describe your art studies and your experience of different types of materials used. Discuss your special interest in your chosen field. Compare your work with that of professional artists and designers and describe your visits to museums, art galleries, exhibitions etc. Submit a portfolio of recent work to demonstrate drawing skills, visual awareness, creativity and innovation, showing examples of three-dimensional work in photographic or model form. See also **Art and Design (Graphic Design)**.

Selection interviews All institutions will interview and require a portfolio of work.

Interview advice and questions Questions focus on the artwork presented in the student's portfolio. See also **Art and Design (General)** and **Chapter 6**.

Reasons for rejection (non-academic) Lack of pride in their work. No ideas. See also **Art and Design (General)**.

AFTER-RESULTS ADVICE
Offers to applicants repeating A-levels **Same** Brighton, Creative Arts, Dundee, Manchester Met.

GRADUATE DESTINATIONS AND EMPLOYMENT (2011/12 HESA)
See **Art and Design (General)**.

Career note See **Art and Design (General)**.

OTHER DEGREE SUBJECTS FOR CONSIDERATION
Design Technology; see other **Art and Design** tables.

ASIA-PACIFIC STUDIES

(including **East** and **South Asian Studies**; see also **Chinese, Japanese, Languages**)

These courses focus on the study of the cultures and the languages of this region of the world, such as Korean, Sanskrit, Thai, Vietnamese. Work experience during undergraduate years will help students to focus their interests. Many courses have a language bias or are taught jointly with other subjects.

Useful websites www.dur.ac.uk/oriental.museum; www.asia-alliance.org; www.bacsuk.org.uk.

NB The points totals shown to the left of the institutions are for ease of reference only. It must not be assumed that Tariff points are always used by institutions or that they can be substituted for an offer in grades. The level of an offer is not necessarily indicative of the quality of a course.

COURSE OFFERS INFORMATION
Subject requirements/preferences **GCSE** A language at grade A–C. **AL** A language may be required.

Your target offers and examples of courses provided by each institution
380 pts **Cambridge** – A*AA (As Mid E St) (IB 40–41 pts HL 776)
360 pts **Oxford** – AAA (Orntl St) (IB 38–40 pts)
340 pts **London (SOAS)** – AAB 340 pts (S As St 3/4 yrs; SE As St courses; Viet Joint Hons 3/4 yrs) (IB 36 pts HL 666)
　　　　Nottingham – AAB 340 pts (Mgt Chin St) (IB 34 pts)
320 pts **Leeds** – ABB 320 pts (As Pacif St (Int); Thai S E As St; As Pacif St; Int Rel Thai St)
　　　　Sheffield – ABB 320 pts (E As St; Jap St; Kor St; Kor St Joint Hons; Jap St Joint Hons) (IB 34 pts)
280 pts **Central Lancashire** – BBC–ABB 280–320 pts (As Pacif St)

Alternative offers
See **Chapter 7** and **Appendix 1** for grades/UCAS Tariff points information for the International Baccalaureate, Scottish Highers/Advanced Highers, the Welsh Baccalaureate, the Irish Leaving Certificate, the Cambridge Pre-U Diploma, the Advanced Diploma and the Extended Project.

CHOOSING YOUR COURSE (SEE ALSO CH.1)

Some course features

Central Lancashire A sandwich course covering business, politics and Asian languages – Chinese and Japanese.

Leeds (As Pacif St courses) Courses deal mainly with the region's politics, economics and culture. Single Honours, major and Joint courses available.

Universities and colleges teaching quality See www.qaa.ac.uk; http://unistats.direct.gov.uk.

Top research universities and colleges (RAE 2008) London (SOAS); Oxford; Cambridge; Leeds; Sheffield.

Examples of sandwich degree courses Central Lancashire.

ADMISSIONS INFORMATION

Number of applicants per place (approx) London (SOAS) 4, (Thai) 2, (Burm) 1.

Advice to applicants and planning the UCAS personal statement Connections with, and visits to, South and South East Asia should be mentioned. You should give some indication of what impressed you and your reasons for wishing to study these subjects. An awareness of the geography, culture and politics of the area also should be shown on the UCAS application. Show your skills in learning a foreign language (if choosing a language course), interest in current affairs of the region, experience of travel and self-discipline.

Selection interviews **Yes** Cambridge, Oxford (Orntl St) 26%.

Interview advice and questions General questions are usually asked that relate to applicants' reasons for choosing degree courses in this subject area and to their background knowledge of the various cultures. See also **Chapter 6**.

GRADUATE DESTINATIONS AND EMPLOYMENT (2011/12 HESA)

South Asian Studies graduates surveyed 25 **Employed** 15 **In voluntary employment** 0 **In further study** 0 **Assumed unemployed** 10

Other Asian Studies graduates surveyed 35 **Employed** 10 **In voluntary employment** 0 **In further study** 10 **Assumed unemployed** 5

Career note Graduates enter a wide range of careers covering business and administration, retail work, education, transport, finance, community and social services. Work experience during undergraduate years will help students to focus their interests. Graduates may have opportunities of using their languages in a range of occupations.

OTHER DEGREE SUBJECTS FOR CONSIDERATION

Anthropology; Development Studies; Far Eastern Languages; Geography; History; International Relations; Politics; Social Studies.

ASTRONOMY and ASTROPHYSICS

(including **Planetary Science** and **Space Science**; see also **Geology/Geological Sciences, Physics**)

All Astronomy-related degrees are built on a core of mathematics and physics which, in the first two years, is augmented by an introduction to the theory and practice of astronomy or astrophysics. Astronomy emphasises observational aspects of the science and includes a study of the planetary system whilst Astrophysics tends to pursue the subject from a more theoretical standpoint. Courses often combine Mathematics or Physics with Astronomy.

Useful websites www.ras.org.uk; www.scicentral.com; www.iop.org

NB The points totals shown to the left of the institutions are for ease of reference only. It must not be assumed that Tariff points are always used by institutions or that they can be substituted for an offer in grades. The level of an offer is not necessarily indicative of the quality of a course.

COURSE OFFERS INFORMATION

Subject requirements/preferences GCSE English and a foreign language may be required by some universities; specified grades may be stipulated for some subjects. **AL** Mathematics and physics usually required.

Your target offers and examples of courses provided by each institution

400 pts **Manchester** – A*A*A-A*AA 400–380 pts (Phys Astro) (IB 39–38 pts HL 766 incl maths phys)

380 pts **Cambridge** – A*AA 380 pts (Nat Sci (Astro)) (IB 40–41 pts HL 776)

Durham – A*AA 380 pts (Phys Astron) (IB 38 pts HL 766 maths phys)

Lancaster – A*AA 380 pts (Phys Astro Cosmo MPhys; Phys Ptcl Phys Cosmo MPhys) (IB 38 pts HL 17 pts)

Nottingham – A*AA-AAA 380–360 pts (Phys Theor Astro; Phys Astron) (HL 665)

360 pts **Birmingham** – AAA 360 pts (Phys Astro) (IB 36 pts)

Cardiff – AAA-ABB 360–320 pts (Astro; Astro MPhys; Phys Astron MPhys; Phys Astron) (IB 32–34 pts)

Edinburgh – AAA-ABB incl maths phys 360–320 pts (Astro) (IB 37–32 pts)

Exeter – AAA-ABB 360–320 pts (Phys Astro) (IB 36–32 pts)

Lancaster – AAA 360 pts (Phys Ptcl Phys Cosmo; Phys Astro Cosmo) (IB 36 pts HL 16 pts)

Liverpool John Moores – AAA 360 pts (Astro MPhys)

London (UCL) – AAA-AAB (Astro) (IB 36–38 pts HL 17–18 pts incl 6 maths phys)

St Andrews – AAA (Astro) (IB 38 pts)

Southampton – AAA 360 pts (Maths Astron) (IB 36 pts HL 18 pts)

Sussex – AAA-AAB incl phys maths (Astro) (IB 32–36 pts)

340 pts **Bristol** – AAB-ABB 340–320 pts (Phys Astro) (IB 35–33 pts HL 6 maths 6 phys)

Leeds – AAB (Phys Astro) (IB 34 pts HL 5 maths phys)

Liverpool – AAB 340 pts (Phys Astron) (IB 35 pts HL 6 maths phys)

London (QM) – AAB-ABB (Astro MSci; Astro) (IB 30–34 pts HL 6 maths 6 phys)

Queen's Belfast – AAB (Phys Astro MSci)

Sheffield – AAB 340 pts (Phys Astro) (IB 35 pts HL 6 maths phys)

Southampton – AAB incl maths phys (Phys Astron) (IB 34 pts HL 17 pts)

Sussex – AAB-ABB (Phys Astro) (IB 34 pts HL 5 maths 5 phys)

York – AAB-AAA 340–360 pts (Phys Astro) (IB 36–35 pts)

320 pts **Glasgow** – ABB (Astron Phys; Phys Astro) (IB 32 pts)

Hertfordshire – 320 pts (Astro)

Kent – ABB 320 pts (Astron Spc Sci Astro; Phys Astro)

Kingston – 320 pts (Aerosp Eng Astnaut Spc Tech MEng)

Leicester – ABB (Phys Astro; Phys Planet Sci; Phys Spc Sci Tech) (IB 24–34 pts)

London (RH) – ABB 320 pts (Astro) (IB 35 pts HL 5 maths phys)

Loughborough – ABB 320 pts (Phys Cosmo) (IB 34 pts)

Manchester – ABB 320 pts (Geol Planet Sci) (IB 33 pts)

Surrey – ABB (Phys Astron) (IB 34 pts)

Swansea – ABB (Phys Ptcl Phys Cosmo)

300 pts **Keele** – BBB (Astro) (IB 31 pts HL 6 phys maths)

Liverpool John Moores – 300–340 pts (Phys Astron) (IB 24–28 pts)

London (Birk) – BBB 300 pts (Planet Sci Astron)

Queen's Belfast – BBB 300 pts (Phys Astro) (HL 665 incl maths physics)

280 pts **Aberystwyth** – 280 pts (Spc Sci Robot) (IB 27 pts)

Central Lancashire – BBC-ABB 280–320 pts (Astro)

Hull – BBC-BBB 280–300 pts (Phys Astro)

Kingston – 280 pts (Aerosp Eng Astnaut Spc Tech)
Nottingham Trent – 280 pts (Phys Astro)
240 pts **South Wales** – CCC 240 (Obs Astro)

Alternative offers
See **Chapter 7** and **Appendix 1** for grades/UCAS Tariff points information for the International Baccalaureate, Scottish Highers/Advanced Highers, the Welsh Baccalaureate, the Irish Leaving Certificate, the Cambridge Pre-U Diploma, the Advanced Diploma and the Extended Project.

CHOOSING YOUR COURSE (SEE ALSO CH.1)
Some course features
Aberystwyth New Astrophysics course designed for students with a general interest in astronomy; it includes core physics modules and broader modules in cosmology and galactic astronomy; progression possible to MPhys degree.
Durham Three- and four-year courses are offered in Physics and Astronomy, with theoretical studies in physics, stars and galaxies and materials for sustainable energy supported by laboratory sessions.
Hertfordshire In addition to degrees in Astronomy and Astrophysics, both are offered within the University's combined modular scheme with an industrial placement option prior to the final year, or alternatively a year in Europe or North America. There is a well-equipped teaching observatory.
Kent Course includes involvement in space missions and work on Hubble Telescope data and an exchange programme in Year 3 in the USA.
Lancaster Three-year BSc and four-year MPhys courses are available. Students can use the on-site observatory, which contains a 356mm Schmidt-Cassegrain reflecting telescope.
South Wales Course provides practical experience of observational astronomy and training in astrophysical techniques, with astronomy field schools in Poland, La Palma, Andalusia and other overseas locations.

Universities and colleges teaching quality See www.qaa.ac.uk; http://unistats.direct.gov.uk.

Top research universities and colleges (RAE 2008) See **Physics**.

Examples of sandwich degree courses Cardiff; Hertfordshire; Kingston; Surrey.

ADMISSIONS INFORMATION
Number of applicants per place (approx) Bristol 8; Cardiff 6; Durham 3; Hertfordshire 5; Leicester 7; London (QM) 6; London (RH) 6; London (UCL) 5; Newcastle 7; Southampton 6.

Advice to applicants and planning the UCAS personal statement Books and magazines you have read on astronomy and astrophysics are an obvious source of information. Describe your interests and why you have chosen this subject. Visits to observatories would also be important. (See also **Appendix 3**.) **Bristol** Deferred entry accepted. **York** Advanced Diploma not generally accepted.

Misconceptions about this course Career opportunities are not as limited as some students think. These courses involve an extensive study of maths and physics, opening many opportunities for graduates such as geodesy, rocket and satellite studies and engineering specialisms.

Selection interviews **Yes** Bristol, Cambridge, London (QM), London (UCL), Newcastle; **Some** Cardiff.

Interview advice and questions You will probably be questioned on your study of physics and the aspects of the subject you most enjoy. Questions in the past have included: Can you name a recent development in physics which will be important in the future? Describe a physics experiment, indicating any errors and exactly what it was intended to prove. Explain weightlessness. What is a black hole? What are the latest discoveries in space? See also **Chapter 6**. **Southampton** Entrance examination for year-abroad courses.

AFTER-RESULTS ADVICE
Offers to applicants repeating A-levels **Higher** St Andrews; **Same** Cardiff, Durham, London (UCL), Newcastle; **No** Cambridge.

GRADUATE DESTINATIONS AND EMPLOYMENT (2011/12 HESA)
Graduates surveyed 310 **Employed** 90 **In voluntary employment** 5 **In further study** 100 **Assumed unemployed** 25

Career note The number of posts for professional astronomers is limited although some technological posts are occasionally offered in observatories. However, degree courses include extensive mathematics and physics so many graduates can look towards related fields including telecommunications and electronics.

OTHER DEGREE SUBJECTS FOR CONSIDERATION
Aeronautical/Aerospace Engineering; Computer Science; Earth Sciences; Geology; Geophysics; Mathematics; Meteorology; Mineral Sciences; Oceanography; Physics.

BIOCHEMISTRY

(see also **Biological Sciences, Chemistry, Food Science/Studies and Technology, Pharmacy and Pharmaceutical Sciences**)

Biochemistry is the study of life processes at molecular level. Most courses are extremely flexible and have common first years. Modules could include genetics, immunology, blood biochemistry, physiology and biotechnology. The option to choose other courses in the subject field features at many universities. Many courses allow for a placement in industry in the UK or in Europe or North America.

Useful websites www.biochemistry.org; www.bioworld.com; www.annualreviews.org; see also **Biological Sciences** and **Biology**.

NB The points totals shown to the left of the institutions are for ease of reference only. It must not be assumed that Tariff points are always used by institutions or that they can be substituted for an offer in grades. The level of an offer is not necessarily indicative of the quality of a course.

COURSE OFFERS INFORMATION
Subject requirements/preferences **GCSE** English, mathematics and science usually required; leading universities often stipulate A–B grades. **AL** Chemistry required and biology usually preferred; one or two mathematics/science subjects required.

Your target offers and examples of courses provided by each institution

380 pts **Cambridge** – A*AA (Nat Sci (Bioch)) (IB 40–41 pts HL 776)
London (UCL) – AAAe 380 pts (Bioch) (IB 38 pts HL 18 pts incl chem)
Oxford – A*AA (Bioch (Mol Cell)) (IB 39 pts HL 7 chem)

360 pts **Bristol** – AAA–AAB 360–340 pts (Bioch; Bioch Med Bioch; Bioch Mol Biol Biotech) (IB 37–35 pts)
Edinburgh – AAA–ABB 360–320 pts (Bioch) (IB 37–32 pts)
Imperial London – AAA (Bioch; Bioch (Yr Ind/Rsch); Bioch courses) (IB 38 pts HL 6 biol chem)
Leeds – AAA–ABB 360–320 pts (Bioch; Bioch; Med Bioch) (IB 35–34 pts HL 18–16 pts incl 6 chem)
Manchester – AAA–ABB 320–360 pts (Bioch; Bioch (Yr Ind); Med Bioch) (IB 37–33 pts)
Southampton – AAA–ABB (Bioch) (IB 36–32 pts HL 18–16 pts incl 6 chem)
York – AAA–ABB 320–360 pts (Chem Biol Medcnl Chem) (IB 32–34 pts)

340 pts **Bath** – AAB 340 pts (Bioch) (IB 35 pts)
Birmingham – AAB–ABB (Bioch; Bioch Biotech; Bioch (Genet); Bioch Mol Cel Biol; Med Bioch) (IB 32–35 pts)
Cardiff – AAB–ABB incl chem 340 pts (Bioch) (IB 34 pts)
Dundee – AAB (Bioch) (IB 34 pts)
East Anglia – AAB incl chem (Bioch (Yr Ind)) (IB 33 pts HL 6 chem)
Exeter – AAB–BBB (Bioch) (IB 34–30 pts)

Glasgow – AAB 340 pts (Bioch) (IB 34 pts)
Lancaster – AAB (Bioch Biomed/Genet; Bioch) (IB 35 pts)
London (King's) – AAB incl chem biol (Bioch) (IB 35 pts HL 665 incl chem biol)
Nottingham – AAB-ABB 340-320 pts (Bioch; Bioch Mol Med; Bioch Biol Chem; Bioch Genet) (IB 34-32 pts)
St Andrews – AAB (Bioch) (IB 35 pts)
Sheffield – AAB (Bioch; Bioch Joint Hons; Med Bioch) (IB 35 pts)
Warwick – AAB-ABB (Bioch; Cheml Biol) (IB 34-36 pts)
York – AAB-ABB (Bioch) (IB 35 pts)

320 pts Brunel – ABB 320 pts (Biomed Sci (Bioch)) (IB 33 pts)
East Anglia – ABB incl chem (Bioch) (IB 32 pts HL 555)
Essex – ABB-BBB 320-300 pts (Bioch) (IB 32-30 pts)
Leicester – ABB (Biol Sci (Bioch); Med Bioch) (IB 32-34 pts)
Liverpool – ABB 320 pts (Bioch; Bioch (Yr Ind/Rsch)) (IB 33 pts)
Strathclyde – ABB-BBB 320-300 pts (Bioch courses) (IB 32-28pts)
Surrey – ABB 320 pts (Bioch) (IB 34 pts)
Sussex – ABB incl biol chem (Bioch) (IB 34 pts)
Warwick – ABB incl chem 320 pts (Biomed Chem) (IB 34 pts)

300 pts Aberdeen – BBB (Bioch courses) (IB 32 pts)
Aston – BBB-ABB 300-320 pts (Biol Chem) (IB 32 pts)
Heriot-Watt – BBB (Chem Bioch) (IB 29 pts)
Keele – BBB (Bioch courses) (IB 32 pts)
Kent – BBB (Bioch) (IB 31-33 pts HL 14-15 pts)
London (QM) – 300 pts incl chem biol (Bioch) (IB 32 pts HL 5 chem biol)
London (RH) – 300-320 pts (Mol Biol; Med Bioch; Bioch) (IB 34 pts)
Portsmouth – 300 pts (Bioch) (IB 27 pts)
Queen's Belfast – BBB/BBCd (Biochem) (IB 28 pts HL 555)
Reading – ABC-BBB (Bioch) (IB 30 pts)
Swansea – BBB-ABB 300-320 pts (Bioch; Bioch Genet) (IB 32-33 pts)

280 pts Aberystwyth – 280-320 pts (Bioch; Genet Bioch)
Hertfordshire – 280 pts (Bioch; Bioch (St Abrd)) (IB 25 pts)
Huddersfield – 280 pts (Bioch; Med Bioch)
Lincoln – (Bioch)
Nottingham Trent – 280 pts incl biol (Bioch)
Sheffield Hallam – 280 pts incl biol+chem (Bioch)

260 pts Bradford – 260 pts (Biomed Sci)
Kingston – 260-280 pts (Bioch; Med Bioch)
Liverpool John Moores – 260-300 pts (Bioch) (IB 25 pts)
Manchester Met – 260-280 pts (Medcnl Biol Chem) (IB 28 pts)
Salford – 260-300 pts (Bioch; Bioch St USA) (IB 28 pts)

240 pts East London – 240 pts (Bioch)
London Met – 240 pts (Bioch) (IB 24 pts)
Westminster – CCC (Bioch) (IB 26 pts)

200 pts London South Bank – 200 pts (Bioch)
Wolverhampton – 200 pts (Bioch) (IB 24 pts)

Alternative offers
See **Chapter 7** and **Appendix 1** for grades/UCAS Tariff points information for the International Baccalaureate, Scottish Highers/Advanced Highers, the Welsh Baccalaureate, the Irish Leaving Certificate, the Cambridge Pre-U Diploma, the Advanced Diploma and the Extended Project.

EXAMPLES OF FOUNDATION DEGREES IN THE SUBJECT FIELD
Truro (Coll).

Check **Chapter 4** when choosing your university and **Chapter 7** on how to read the subject tables.

CHOOSING YOUR COURSE (SEE ALSO CH.1)

Some course features

Cardiff Biochemistry is taught as a modular course in the School of Biosciences. There is a common first-year course after which students make a choice. Separate degree courses are offered in Anatomy, Neuroscience, Physiology and Pharmacology. A four-year course including a year in industry is available.

Durham First-year Molecular Biology and Biochemistry students follow courses in botany, zoology and chemistry, and go on to specialist areas that include genetics, virology and immunology. A compulsory field course is included.

Edinburgh There is a common first year for all Biochemistry students entering courses in the School of Biology, covering cell formation, components and interaction.

Leeds Accredited by the Society of Biology, the Biochemistry course covers a wide variety of topics such as cancer and oncogenes, enzyme design and evolution, genomics and bioinformatics, and molecular machines in action and viruses. There is also the option to study abroad.

Newcastle The Biochemistry degree shares a common first year with Genetics and covers DNA synthesis and repair, immunology, virus and plant biology. Students may then change courses after stage 1. A three-year full-time course in Biochemistry and Immunology is also offered.

Universities and colleges teaching quality See www.qaa.ac.uk; http://unistats.direct.gov.uk.

Top research universities and colleges (RAE 2008) See **Biological Sciences**.

Examples of sandwich degree courses Aberdeen; Aston; Bath; Bristol; Brunel; Cardiff; Coventry; De Montfort; East London; Essex; Hertfordshire; Huddersfield; Imperial London; Kent; Kingston; Leeds; Lincoln; Liverpool John Moores; London South Bank; Manchester; Manchester Met; Nottingham Trent; Queen's Belfast; Sheffield Hallam; Surrey; Sussex; Teesside; York.

ADMISSIONS INFORMATION

Number of applicants per place (approx) Aberystwyth 5; Bath 7; Birmingham 5; Bradford 7; Bristol 10; Cardiff 6; Dundee 6; Durham 6; East Anglia 10; East London 5; Edinburgh 8; Essex 5; Imperial London 6; Keele 7; Leeds 10; Leicester (Med Bioch) 5; London (RH) 8; London (UCL) 8; Newcastle 7; Nottingham 14; Salford 4; Southampton 8; Staffordshire 6; Strathclyde 7; Surrey 3; Warwick 6; York 6.

Advice to applicants and planning the UCAS personal statement It is important to show by reading scientific journals that you have interests in chemistry and biology beyond the exam syllabus. Focus on one or two aspects of biochemistry that interest you. Attend scientific lectures (often arranged by universities on Open Days), find some work experience if possible, and use these to show your understanding of what biochemistry is. Give evidence of your communication skills and time management. (See **Appendix 3**.) **Bristol** Deferred entry accepted. **Oxford** No written or work tests; successful entrants 42.7%. Further information may be obtained from the Institute of Biology and the Royal Society of Chemistry.

Misconceptions about this course **York** Students feel that being taught by two departments could be a problem but actually it increases their options.

Selection interviews **Yes** Bradford, Brunel, Cambridge, East London, Essex, Kingston, Leeds, London (RH), London (UCL), London South Bank, Oxford (38%), Warwick; **Some** Aberystwyth (mature students only), Bath, Birmingham (Clearing only), Cardiff, East Anglia, Keele (mature students only), Liverpool John Moores, Portsmouth (mature students only), Salford, Sheffield, Staffordshire, Surrey, Wolverhampton; **No** Dundee.

Interview advice and questions Questions will be asked on your study of chemistry and biology and any special interests. They will also probe your understanding of what a course in Biochemistry involves and the special features offered by the university. In the past questions have been asked covering Mendel, genetics, RNA and DNA. See also **Chapter 6**. **Liverpool John Moores** Informal interviews. It would be useful to bring samples of coursework to the interview.

Reasons for rejection (non-academic) Borderline grades plus poor motivation. Failure to turn up for interviews or answer correspondence. Inability to discuss subject. Not compatible with A-level predictions or references. **Birmingham** Lack of total commitment to Biochemistry, for example intention to transfer to Medicine without completing the course.

AFTER-RESULTS ADVICE

Offers to applicants repeating A-levels **Higher** East Anglia, Leeds, Leicester, Nottingham, St Andrews, Strathclyde, Surrey, Warwick; **Possibly higher** Bath, Bristol, Brunel, Keele, Kent, Lancaster, Newcastle; **Same** Aberystwyth, Birmingham, Bradford, Cardiff, Dundee, Durham, Heriot-Watt, Hull, Liverpool, Liverpool John Moores, London (RH), London (UCL), Salford, Sheffield, Staffordshire, Wolverhampton, York; **No** Cambridge.

GRADUATE DESTINATIONS AND EMPLOYMENT (2011/12 HESA)

Biochemistry, Biophysics and Molecular Biology graduates surveyed 1735 **Employed** 580 **In voluntary employment** 45 **In further study** 670 **Assumed unemployed** 180

Career note Biochemistry courses involve several specialities which offer a range of job opportunities. These include the application of biochemistry in industrial, medical and clinical areas with additional openings in pharmaceuticals and agricultural work, environmental science and in toxicology.

OTHER DEGREE SUBJECTS FOR CONSIDERATION

Agricultural Sciences; Agriculture; Biological Sciences; Biology; Biotechnology; Botany; Brewing; Chemistry; Food Science; Genetics; Medical Sciences; Medicine; Microbiology; Neuroscience; Nursing; Nutrition; Pharmaceutical Sciences; Pharmacology; Pharmacy; Plant Science.

BIOLOGICAL SCIENCES

(including **Biomedical Science, Cosmetic Science, Forensic Science, Immunology** and **Virology**; see also **Anatomical Science/Anatomy, Animal Sciences, Biochemistry, Biology, Biotechnology, Environmental Sciences/Studies, Genetics, Medicine, Microbiology, Natural Sciences, Nursing and Midwifery, Pharmacology, Plant Sciences, Psychology, Zoology**)

Biological Science (in some universities referred to as Biosciences) is a fast-moving, rapidly expanding and wide subject area, ranging from, for example, conservation biology to molecular genetics. Boundaries between separate subjects are blurring and this is reflected in the content and variety of the courses offered. Many universities offer a common first year allowing final decisions to be made later in the course. Since most subjects are research-based, students undertake their own projects in the final year.

Useful websites bsi.immunology.org; www.ibms.org; www.scicentral.com; www.bbsrc.ac.uk; see also **Biochemistry** and **Biology**.

NB The points totals shown to the left of the institutions are for ease of reference only. It must not be assumed that Tariff points are always used by institutions or that they can be substituted for an offer in grades. The level of an offer is not necessarily indicative of the quality of a course.

COURSE OFFERS INFORMATION

Subject requirements/preferences **GCSE** English, mathematics and science usually required. Grades AB often stipulated by popular universities. **AL** Chemistry required plus one or two other mathematics/science subjects, biology preferred. (Ecol) Biology and one other science subject may be required or preferred. (Neuro) Mathematics/science subjects with chemistry and/or biology required or preferred.

London (St George's) (Biol Inform) Computer science, mathematics and/or science advantageous.

Your target offers and examples of courses provided by each institution
410 pts **Imperial London** – AAAb (Biomed Sci) (IB 38 pts HL 6 chem 6 biol)
380 pts **Cambridge** – A*AA (Nat Sci (Biol Biomed Sci); Nat Sci (Path); Nat Sci (Neuro); Educ Biol Sci) (IB 40–41 pts HL 776)
        London (UCL) – AAAe (Biol Sci; Biomed Sci) (IB 38 pts HL 18 pts)
        Oxford – A*AA (Biol Sci; Biomed Sci) (IB 38–40 pts)

360 pts **Durham** – AAA 360 pts (Biomed Sci) (IB 37 pts)

Edinburgh – AAA-ABB 360-320 pts (Neuro; Dev Cell Biol; Infec Dis; Biol Sci; Biol Sci Mgt; Immun; Biol Sci courses) (IB 37-32 pts)

Leeds – AAA-AAB 360-340 pts (Biol Sci; Med Sci) (IB 35-34 pts)

London (UCL) – A*AAe-AABe (Bioproc N Med (Bus Mgt); Bioproc N Med (Sci Eng)) (IB 36-39 pts HL 17-19 pts)

Manchester – AAA-ABB 360-320 pts (Biomed Sci; Cog Neuro Psy; Neuro) (IB 37-33 pts)

Newcastle – AAA-BBB (Biomed Sci; Biomed Genet; Med Sci) (IB 34-35 pts)

Southampton – AAA-ABB 360-320 pts (Biomed Sci) (IB 36-32 pts HL 18-16 pts)

340 pts **Aberdeen** – AAB 340 pts (Biol Sci) (IB 36 pts HL 666)

Bath – AAB incl biol chem sci 340 pts (Biomed Sci) (IB 35 pts HL 6 chem 6 biol)

Birmingham – AAB-ABB 340-320 pts (Biol Sci (Genet); Biol Sci; Biol Sci (Biotech)) (IB 34-35 pts)

Bristol – AAB-ABB 340-320 pts (Cell Mol Med; Palae Evol; Virol Immun; Cncr Biol Immun) (IB 35-33 pts)

Cardiff – AAB-ABB 340-320 pts (Mol Biol; Biomed Sci (Physiol); Biomed Sci (Neuro); Biomed Sci (Anat); Biomed Sci; Ecol) (IB 34 pts)

Dundee – AAB (Biol Sci; Foren Anth)

East Anglia – AAB (Biol Sci (St Abrd); Biol Sci (Yr Ind)) (IB 33-34 pts)

Exeter – AAB-BBB (Biol Sci; Hum Biosci) (IB 34-30 pts)

Glasgow – AAB (Immun) (IB 32 pts)

Lancaster – AAB-ABB (Biomed Sci; Biol Sci Biomed; Biol Sci courses) (IB 32-34 pts)

London (King's) – AAB incl chem/biol (Biomed Sci) (IB 35 pts HL 6 chem biol)

London (QM) – AAB incl biol chem (Biomed Sci) (IB 34 pts)

Newcastle – AAB-BBB (Biol (Cell Mol Biol); Biol Psy) (IB 32 pts)

Nottingham – AAB 340 pts (Neuro) (IB 34 pts)

St Andrews – AAB 340 pts (Neuro) (IB 35 pts)

Sheffield – AAB (Ecol Cons Biol; Biomed Sci; Med Bioch; Biol Chem MChem) (IB 35 pts)

Sussex – AAB-ABB 340-320 pts (Biomed Sci; Neuro) (IB 34-35 pts)

Warwick – AAB-ABB 340-320 pts (Biol Sci; Biomed Sci; Biol Sci Cell Biol; Biol Sci Env Res) (IB 34-36 pts)

York – AAB 340 pts (Biomed Sci) (IB 35 pts)

320 pts **Aston** – ABB-BBB 320-300 pts (Biomed Sci; Biol Sci) (IB 33 pts)

Birmingham – ABB (Med Sci) (IB 32-34 pts)

Brighton – ABB 320 pts (Biol Sci; Biomed Sci) (IB 34 pts)

Brunel – ABB 320 pts (Biomed Sci; Biomed Sci (Bioch); Biomed Sci (Genet); Biomed Sci (Foren); Biomed Sci (Hum Hlth)) (IB 33 pts)

East Anglia – ABB 320 pts (Biol Sci; Ecol; Biomed) (IB 32 pts)

Essex – ABB-BBB 320-300 pts (Biol Sci; Biomed Sci) (IB 32-30 pts)

Kent – ABB (Biomed Sci) (IB 34 pts)

Leicester – ABB (Med Genet; Chem Foren Sci; Biol Sci (Genet); Biol Sci (Bioch); Biol Sci (Physiol Pharmacol); Biol Sci courses) (IB 32 pts)

Liverpool – ABB 320 pts (Biol Sci) (IB 33 pts)

London (RH) – ABB (Biomed Sci) (IB 34 pts)

London (St George's) – ABB (Biomed Sci) (IB 31 pts HL 655 chem biol)

Manchester – AAA-ABB 360-320 pts (Biomed Sci (Yr Ind)) (IB 37-33 pts)

Queen's Belfast – ABB/BBBb (Biomed Sci)

Reading – ABB-AAC 320 pts (Biol Sci; Biol Sci Ind; Biomed Sci) (IB 30-32 pts)

Roehampton – 320 pts (Hum Sci; Biomed Sci)

Surrey – ABB (Biomed Sci) (IB 34 pts)

Swansea – ABB-BBB 320-300 pts (Biol Sci courses) (IB 33-32 pts)

300 pts **Aberdeen** – BBB 300 pts (Immun) (IB 32 pts)

Bournemouth – 300 pts (Foren Sci; Biol Sci)

Bradford – 300 pts (Clin Sci) (IB 26 pts) optional transfer for some students to Medicine at **Leeds**

University *of* Hertfordshire — UH

School of
Life and Medical Sciences

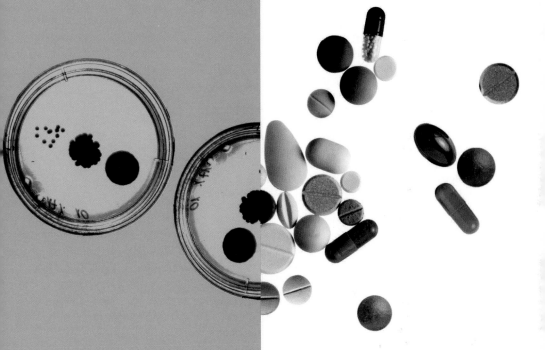

Experimentation that supports innovation

Our Bioscience courses examine the fundamental processes of life in all its diverse forms – from how organisms function at a molecular level, to the whole being – providing advanced knowledge of human health, disease and treatment.

Numerate, scientifically literate graduates are valued by a wide variety of employers. With first-class teaching and advanced facilities, we will provide you with the technical, analytical and practical skills needed to pursue a range of careers in areas such as the NHS, pharmaceuticals and food and drink manufacturing.

Indulge your curiosity as you seek to answer questions about life, health and the world around us, with a broad range of courses which include:

- BSc (Hons) Biomedical Science
- BSc (Hons) Pharmaceutical Science
- BSc (Hons) Pharmacology
- BSc (Hons) Healthcare Science (Life Sciences)

Become more.

Find out more about our range of courses at:

go.herts.ac.uk/biosciences

Bristol UWE – 300 pts (Biol Sci; Biomed; Foren Sci)
Dundee – BBB (Mol Genet) (IB 30 pts)
Edinburgh – BBB 300 pts (Med Sci) (IB 36 pts)
Greenwich – 300 pts (App Biomed Sci; Biol Sci; Foren Sci; Foren Sci Crim; Biomed Sci)
Heriot-Watt – BBB 300 pts (Biol Sci (Fd Bev Sci); Biol Sci) (IB 27 pts)
Keele – BBB 300 pts (Biomed Sci; Foren Sci) (IB 32 pts)
Kent – BBB (Foren Sci) (IB 33 pts)
Leeds Beckett – 300 pts (Biomed Sci courses) (IB 26 pts)
London (RH) – 300–320 pts (Mol Biol) (IB 34 pts)
London Met – 300 pts (Biomed Sci)
Northumbria – 300 pts (Biomed Sci) (IB 26 pts)
Plymouth – 300 pts (Biomed Sci) (IB 28 pts)
Portsmouth – BBB 300 pts (Biomed Sci) (IB 30 pts)
Queen's Belfast – BBB–BBC (Biol Sci) (IB 28 pts)
South Wales – 300 pts (Med Sci)
Strathclyde – BBB 300 pts (Biomed Sci) (IB 28 pts)
Ulster – 300 pts incl 2 sci (Strtf Med)

280 pts   **Anglia Ruskin** – 280 pts (Foren Sci) (IB 26 pts)
Bangor – 280–320 pts (Biomed Sci) (IB 28 pts)
Derby – 280 pts (Foren Sci Crimin; Foren Sci)
Hertfordshire – 280 pts (Biol Sci; Biomed Sci)
Huddersfield – 280 pts (Foren Analyt Sci; Med Bioch)
Hull – 280–320 pts (Biomed Sci)
Kingston – 280–320 pts (Biomed Sci)
Lincoln – 280 pts (Foren Sci; Biomed Sci)
Manchester Met – 280 pts (Ecol Cons (St Abrd); Biomed Sci) (IB 28 pts)
Middlesex – 280 pts (Biomed Sci) (IB 28 pts)
Northampton – 280 pts (Hum Biosci) (IB 24 pts)
Northumbria – 280 pts (Foren Sci) (IB 25 pts)
Nottingham Trent – 280 pts (Biomed Sci) (IB 28 pts)
Oxford Brookes – BBC (Biomed Sci; Biol Sci)
Plymouth – 280 pts (Hum Biosci; Biol Sci) (IB 26 pts)
Portsmouth – 280–300 pts (Foren Biol)
South Wales – 280 pts (Foren Sci)
Stirling – BBC (Cell Biol) (IB 32 pts)
Teesside – 280 pts (Foren Biol; Biol Sci)
Ulster – 280 pts (Biomed Sci)

260 pts   **Bradford** – 260 pts (Biomed Sci; Foren Sci; Foren Med Sci)
Cardiff Met (UWIC) – 260 pts (Biomed Sci)
Central Lancashire – BCC–BBB 260–300 pts (Neuro)
De Montfort – 260 pts (Med Sci)
Dundee – BCC (Biomed Sci) (IB 30 pts)
Edinburgh Napier – BCC 260 pts (Biomed Sci; Biol Sci; Foren Biol)
Glasgow Caledonian – BCC 260 pts (Biomed Sci)
Kingston – 260–280 pts (Foren Sci; Biol Sci)
Liverpool John Moores – 260–300 pts (Foren Sci; Biomed Sci) (IB 25 pts)
Northampton – 260–300 pts (Hum Biosci courses)
Nottingham Trent – 260 pts (Foren Biol; Foren Sci (Physl); Foren Sci)
Robert Gordon – BCC (App Biomed Sci) (IB 28 pts)
Sheffield Hallam – 260 pts (Foren Sci; Biomed Sci)
SRUC – BCC (App Anim Plnt Sci)
Staffordshire – 260 pts (Biomed Sci; Foren Biol) (IB 28 pts)
Sunderland – 260 pts (Biomed Sci)
West Scotland – BCC (Biomed Sci) (IB 24 pts)

240 pts **Abertay** – CCC (Biomed Sci; Foren Sci)
Anglia Ruskin – 240 pts (Biomed Sci)
Canterbury Christ Church – CCC 240 pts (Biosci; Foren Invstg) (IB 24 pts)
Central Lancashire – 240–260 pts (Biomed Sci; Biol Sci; Foren Sci)
Chester – 240–280 pts (Biomed Sci; Foren Biol) (IB 26–30 pts)
Coventry – CCC 240 pts (Biomed Sci; Biol Foren Sci) (IB 27 pts)
De Montfort – 240–260 pts (Biomed Sci) (IB 28 pts)
East Anglia – CCC (Biol Sci Fdn Yr)
East London – 240 pts (Biomed Sci)
Hertfordshire – 240 pts (Biol (Yr Abrd))
London Met – 240 pts (Biol Sci) (IB 28 pts)
Nottingham Trent – 240 pts (Biol Sci) (IB 28 pts)
Robert Gordon – CCC (Foren Analyt Sci) (IB 26 pts)
Salford – 240–280 pts (Biomed Sci) (IB 28 pts)
Westminster – CCC (Biol Sci; Biomed Sci) (IB 26 pts)
West Scotland – CCC (App Biosci; App Biosci Zool; Foren Sci)
Wolverhampton – 240 pts (Biomed Sci) (IB 24 pts)
220 pts **Moulton (Coll)** – 220 pts +interview (App Cons Biol)
South Wales – 220–260 pts (Comb Sci)
200 pts **Bedfordshire** – 200 pts (Biol Sci)
East London – 200 pts (Foren Sci)
London South Bank – 200 pts (Bioscience) (IB 24 pts)
Wolverhampton – 200 pts (Foren Sci; Foren Sci Crimin)
160 pts **Abertay** – CC 160 pts (Foren Psychobiol) (IB 26 pts)

Alternative offers
See **Chapter 7** and **Appendix 1** for grades/UCAS Tariff points information for the International Baccalaureate, Scottish Highers/Advanced Highers, the Welsh Baccalaureate, the Irish Leaving Certificate, the Cambridge Pre-U Diploma, the Advanced Diploma and the Extended Project.

EXAMPLES OF FOUNDATION DEGREES IN THE SUBJECT FIELD
Aston; Brighton; Bristol UWE; Cornwall (Coll); Glyndŵr; Hertfordshire; Hull (Coll); Kent; London (QM); Myerscough (Coll); Nescot; Nottingham Trent; Petroc; Plymouth; Plymouth City (Coll); Preston (Coll); Riverside Halton (Coll); Sheffield (Coll); Staffordshire; Truro (Coll); West London; Weymouth (Coll); Wigan and Leigh (Coll); Worcester; Writtle (Coll); York (Coll).

CHOOSING YOUR COURSE (SEE ALSO CH.1)
Some course features
Brighton (Biol Sci) A sandwich placement in Year 3 is optional. Specialist fields include animal sciences, ecology, forestry and countryside management.
Durham (Biomed Sci) Accredited by the Institute of Biomedical Science, this course covers a core set of modules including haematology, immunology and medical microbiology. Students can also elect to take part in projects with Biological Enterprise.
Imperial London Biomedical Science may be studied as a Single Honours degree or Joint Honours when combined with Management.
Liverpool (Biol Sci) A broad programme, with option in first two years to specialise by transferring to any one of a range of courses in the subject field, eg Ecology, Genetics, Molecular Biology.
Northumbria Biomedical Sciences is a three-year full-time or four-year sandwich course available as a Single Honours (including an optional year abroad) or combined with Chemistry. There are also degrees in Applied Sciences, Forensic Science, Biotechnology and Human Biosciences.
Surrey The course in Biomedical Science includes biochemistry, physiology and pharmacology, with practical training in clinically relevant techniques. Optional subjects such as microbiology, nutrition and food science can also be studied. Courses involving Microbiology are offered with specialisms in medicine, food science and genetics. There are also Food Science and Biotechnology degrees.
Warwick (Biol Sci) Specialisations in biochemistry, cell biology, biological sciences, environmental biology, microbiology and virology.

Westminster Biological Sciences subjects share common modules, with specialism possible in biomedical science, biotechnology, biochemistry, or microbiology. There is also a course in Biomedical Science and a BEng in Biochemical Engineering.

Universities and colleges teaching quality See www.qaa.ac.uk; http://unistats.direct.gov.uk.

Top research universities and colleges (RAE 2008) Oxford (Bioch); Manchester; Sheffield; Dundee; Bristol (Bioch); London (RH); York; Imperial London; London (King's); Leeds; Cambridge; Edinburgh.

Examples of sandwich degree courses See **Biology**.

ADMISSIONS INFORMATION

Number of applicants per place (approx) Aston (Biomed Sci) 8; Bristol 8, (Neuro) 10; Cardiff 5; Durham 11; East Anglia (Biol Sci) 15; Edinburgh 8; Essex 8; Lancaster (Biol Sci) 12; Leeds (Med Sci) 25; Leicester 8; London (King's) 7; London (QM) 8; London (St George's) 15; London (UCL) (Biomed Sci) 15, (Biol Sci) 8, (Neuro) 10;Newcastle 14; Nottingham 11; Southampton 8; Stirling 7; York 9.

Advice to applicants and planning the UCAS personal statement Read scientific journals and try to extend your knowledge beyond the A-level syllabus. Discuss your special interests, for example, ecology, microbiology, genetics or zoology (read up thoroughly on your interests since questions could be asked at interview). Mention any voluntary attendance on courses, work experience, voluntary work, or holiday jobs. Demonstrate good oral and written communication skills and be competent at handling numerical data. Interest in the law for Forensic Science courses. See **Appendix 3**.

Misconceptions about this course **Anglia Ruskin** (Foren Sci) Some students are not aware that modules in management and quality assurance are taken as part of the course. **Birmingham** We offer a range of degree labels each with different UCAS codes, for example Biological Sciences Genetics, Biological Sciences Microbiology: all have the same first year and students can freely transfer between them. (Med Sci) Applicants often use this course as an insurance for a vocational course (usually Medicine). If they are unsuccessful for their first choice, they occasionally find it difficult to commit themselves to Medical Sciences and do not perform as well as their academic performance would predict. **Cardiff** Some students mistakenly believe that they can transfer to Medicine. **De Montfort** (Foren Sci) Students are often unaware of how much of the work is analytical biology and chemistry: they think they spend their time visiting crime scenes. **London (St George's)** It is not possible to transfer to Medicine after the first year of the Biomedical Science course. Students may be able to transfer to Year 3 of the Medical course on completion of the BSc degree. **Swansea** (Med Sci Hum) Some applicants think the course is a form of medical training – it isn't, but it is relevant to anyone planning graduate entry for courses in Medicine or paramedical careers. (Biol Sci deferred entry) Some applicants think that this is a degree in its own right. In fact, after the first year, students have to choose one of the other degrees offered by the School of Biological Sciences. This course allows students an extra year in which to consider their final specialisation.

Selection interviews **Yes** Bangor, Bristol UWE, Essex, Greenwich, Hull, London (RH), London (St George's), London (UCL), London South Bank, Manchester, Newcastle, Nottingham Trent, Oxford (Biol Sci) 38%, Oxford Brookes, Reading, Stirling, Strathclyde, Sunderland, Sussex, Swansea (Med Sci Hum), Warwick; **Some** Anglia Ruskin, Aston, Bristol, Cardiff, Cardiff Met (UWIC), De Montfort, Derby, East Anglia, Kent, Liverpool John Moores, Roehampton, Salford, Sheffield, Sheffield Hallam, Staffordshire, Surrey (Biomed Sci), Wolverhampton, York; **No** Birmingham, Dundee, Durham, Nottingham.

Interview advice and questions You are likely to be asked about your main interests in biology and your choice of specialisation in the field of biological sciences or, for example, about the role of the botanist, specialist microbiologist in industry, your understanding of biotechnology or genetic engineering. Questions likely to be asked on any field courses attended. If you have a field course workbook, take it to interview. See also **Chapter 6**. **London (St George's)** (Biomed Sci) What career path do you envisage for yourself with this degree? **Oxford** No written or work tests. Interviews are rigorous but sympathetic; successful entrants average 38.8%. Applicants are expected to demonstrate their ability to understand whatever facts they have encountered and to discuss a particular aspect of biology in which they are interested. What problems does a fish face under water? Are humans still evolving?

Reasons for rejection (non-academic) **Oxford** Applicant appeared to have so much in his head that he tended to express his ideas in too much of a rush. He needs to slow down a bit and take more time to select points that are really pertinent to the questions.

AFTER-RESULTS ADVICE

Offers to applicants repeating A-levels **Higher** Bristol, Bristol UWE, Glasgow Caledonian, Hull, London (St George's), Newcastle, St Andrews, Sheffield; **Possibly higher** Aston, Essex, Lancaster, Manchester Met; **Same** Abertay, Aberystwyth, Anglia Ruskin, Birmingham, Birmingham City, Bolton, Cardiff, Cardiff Met (UWIC), Chester, Chichester, De Montfort, Derby, Durham, East Anglia, East London, Edinburgh Napier, Exeter, Glasgow, Harper Adams, Heriot-Watt, Huddersfield, Kingston, Leeds, Lincoln, Liverpool Hope, Liverpool John Moores, London (RH), Oxford Brookes, Plymouth, Portsmouth, Robert Gordon, Roehampton, Salford, Sheffield Hallam, Stirling, West London, West Scotland, Wolverhampton, Worcester, York; **No** Cambridge.

GRADUATE DESTINATIONS AND EMPLOYMENT (2011/12 HESA)

See also **Biology**

Biological Science graduates surveyed 1270 **Employed** 460 **In voluntary employment** 25 **In further study** 470 **Assumed unemployed** 95

Career note Degrees in biological science subjects often lead graduates into medical, pharmaceutical, veterinary, food and environmental work, research and education, in both the public and private sectors (see also **Biology**). Sandwich courses are offered at a number of institutions enabling students to gain paid experience in industry and commerce, often resulting in permanent employment on graduation. In recent years there has been a considerable increase in the number of Biomedical Science courses designed for students interested in taking a hands-on approach to studying the biology of disease. However, students should be warned that the ever-popular Forensic Science courses may not always pave the way to jobs in this highly specialised field.

OTHER DEGREE SUBJECTS FOR CONSIDERATION

Biochemistry; Biology; Biotechnology; Botany; Chemistry; Consumer Sciences; Ecology; Environmental Health; Environmental Science; Genetics; Genomics; Immunology; Microbiology; Pharmaceutical Sciences; Pharmacology; Pharmacy; Physiology; Plant Sciences; Psychology; Sport and Exercise Science; Toxicology; Virology; Zoology.

BIOLOGY

(see also **Animal Sciences, Biological Sciences, Biotechnology, Environmental Sciences/Studies, Microbiology, Plant Sciences, Zoology**)

The science of biology is a broad and rapidly developing subject that increasingly affects our lives. Biologists address the challenges faced by human populations such as disease, conservation and food production, and the continuing advances in such areas as genetics and molecular biology that have applications in medicine and agriculture.

Useful websites www.societyofbiology.org; www.mba.ac.uk; www.bbsrc.ac.uk; see also **Biochemistry**.

NB The points totals shown to the left of the institutions are for ease of reference only. It must not be assumed that Tariff points are always used by institutions or that they can be substituted for an offer in grades. The level of an offer is not necessarily indicative of the quality of a course.

COURSE OFFERS INFORMATION

Subject requirements/preferences **GCSE** Mathematics and English stipulated in some cases. **AL** Biology and chemistry important, other science subjects may be accepted. Two and sometimes three mathematics/science subjects required including biology.

182 | Biology

Your target offers and examples of courses provided by each institution

380 pts Oxford – A*AA (Biol Sci) (IB 38–40 pts)

360 pts Durham – AAA 360 pts (Biol) (IB 37 pts)

Edinburgh – AAA–ABB 360–320 pts (Med Biol; Evol Biol; Repro Bio) (IB 37–32 pts)

Imperial London – AAA 360 pts (Biol; Biol Ger Sci; Ecol Env Biol) (IB 38 pts)

Manchester – AAA–ABB 360–320 pts (Biol; Cell Biol; Dev Biol; Biol Sci Soty; Biol (Yr Ind);
Biol Modn Lang; Cell Biol (Yr Ind); Cell Biol Modn Lang; Mol Biol) (IB 37–33 pts)

Sheffield – AAA incl biol sci (Biol (Yr Abrd); Biol MBiolSci) (IB 37 pts)

Southampton – AAA–ABB (Biol; Mar Biol; Mar Biol Ocean) (IB 36–32 pts HL 18–16 pts)

340 pts Bath – AAB 340 pts (Biol; Mol Cell Biol) (IB 34–35 pts)

Birmingham – AAB–ABB 340–320 pts (Hum Biol; Biol Sci (Env Biol)) (IB 34–35 pts)

Bristol – AAB–ABB (Biol) (IB 35–33 pts)

Cardiff – AAB–ABB 340–320 pts (Biol)

Exeter – AAB–BBB (Evol Biol; Flex Comb Hons Mol Cell Biol) (IB 34–29 pts)

Glasgow – AAB (Hum Biol; Biol courses; Mar Frshwtr Biol) (IB 34 pts)

Lancaster – AAB–ABB 340–320 pts (Biol courses) (IB 36–32 pts)

Leeds – AAA–ABB 360–320 pts (App Biol) (IB 38–34 pts)

Newcastle – AAB–ABB 320–340 pts (Biol (Ecol Env Biol); Biol; Mar Biol Ocean)
(IB 34–35 pts)

Nottingham – AAB–ABB (Microbiol; Biol) (IB 32–34 pts)

St Andrews – AAB (Biol courses) (IB 35–38 pts)

Sheffield – AAB incl biol sci (Biol BSc) (IB 35 pts)

Sussex – AAB–ABB 340–320 pts (Biol) (IB 34 pts)

Warwick – AAB (Biol Sci Cell Biol; Cheml Biol) (IB 36–34 pts)

York – AAB (Biol; Biol (Yr Abrd); Mol Cell Biol) (IB 35 pts)

320 pts Aston – ABB–BBB 320–300 pts (Cell Mol Biol) (IB 33 pts)

Bristol UWE – 320 pts (Hum Biol) (IB 32 pts)

East Anglia – ABB (Mol Biol Genet) (IB 32 pts)

Essex – ABB–BBB (Mar Biol) (IB 32–30 pts)

Leeds – ABB (Biol Hist Phil Sci) (IB 34 pts HL 16 pts incl 6 hist)

Liverpool – ABB (Trpcl Dis Biol; Biol (Yr Ind/Rsch); Mar Biol) (IB 33 pts)

London (QM) – ABB (Biol) (IB 34 pts HL 5 biol)

London (RH) – ABB (Biol; Biol Sci Comm) (IB 34 pts)

Newcastle – AAB–ABB 320–340 pts (Mar Biol) (IB 34–35 pts)

Nottingham – ABB–BBB 300–320 pts (App Biol) (IB 30–32 pts)

Plymouth – 320 pts (Biol courses) (IB 28 pts)

Queen's Belfast – ABB/BBBb (Hum Biol)

Strathclyde – ABB (Microbiol) (IB 32 pts)

Swansea – ABB–BBB (Biol) (IB 33–32 pts)

300 pts Aberdeen – BBB (Biol; Cons Biol; Mar Biol) (IB 32 pts)

Aston – ABB–BBB 320–300 pts (Microbiol Immun; Hum Biol) (IB 33 pts)

Bristol UWE – 300 pts (Foren Biol) (IB 32 pts)

Dundee – BBB–BCC 280–300 pts (Mathem Biol; Mol Biol) (IB 32 pts)

Edge Hill – 300 pts (Biol) (IB 26 pts)

Gloucestershire – 300 pts (Anim Biol; Biol)

Heriot-Watt – BBB (App Mar Biol)

Keele – BBB (Hum Biol) (IB 32 pts)

Kent – BBB (Biol courses) (IB 33 pts HL 5 biol)

London (RH) – 300–320 pts (Mol Biol) (IB 34 pts)

Loughborough – ABB–BBB 320–300 pts (Hum Biol) (IB 32–34 pts)

Nottingham – ABC/BBB–BCC (Env Biol) (IB 34–26 pts)

Portsmouth – 300 pts (Biol) (IB 27 pts)

Queen's Belfast – BBB (Env Biol; Mar Biol; Mol Biol)

South Wales – BBB (Int Wldlf Biol) (IB 28 pts)

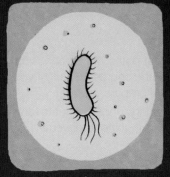  

  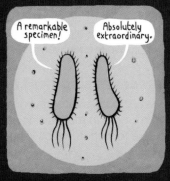

SUPPORTING LIFE SCIENCES

As the leading professional body for the biosciences, the Society of Biology is commited to recognising professional excellence.

Degree accreditation

Our Degree Accreditation Programme has been designed to address the skills gap between academic study and employment in the biosciences, and help employers to identify research-ready graduates, with a known profile of skills and knowledge.

Professional registers

Through a scheme licensed by the Science Council, members can apply to become *Registered Science Technician*, *Registered Scientist* and *Chartered Scientist*, in addition to *Chartered Biologist* (which is exclusive to the Society of Biology).

Join today

We offer a number of membership categories to ensure that anyone with an interest in biology can become a member and access a range of valuable benefits, including discounted training courses, a free subscription to our award-winning magazine, *The Biologist*.

For more information (including a list of accredited degrees) visit
www.societyofbiology.org/supporting-life-sciences

SOCIETY OF
Biology

SUPPORTING YOU
THROUGHOUT YOUR CAREER

Degree accreditation and careers resources

Biology is a very broad subject, and can lead to very diverse career paths. When choosing your degree you might have a lot of questions, such as how long the course will last, if you can combine it with another subject, and what sort of career it will prepare you for.

Our career resources are designed to support you through secondary, undergraduate, and postgraduate education, and beyond. You will find information about going to unversity, applying for jobs, and finding relevant work experience.

If you are already thinking of a career in research, then you might want to consider what practical experience and opportunities a degree offers. Degrees accredited by the Society of Biology will provide you with the opportunity to conduct your own research in a working environment for at least six months. This will help you to start building your confidence and ability to work effectively as a research scientist.

Career development and professional recognition

As you progress through your career, you will want to demonstrate your professionalism and commitment to maintaining your expertise. As a member of the Society of Biology, you will be able to work towards joining one of our professional registers.

Through a licence from the Science Council, we are able to offer three professional registers, Registered Science Technician, Registered Scientist, and Chartered Scientist, in addition to our own Chartered Biologist register.

Our continuing professional development (CPD) programme goes hand-in-hand with the registers, and helps you to demonstrate the competencies and abilities you have gained through your work and interests. In addition to your own activities, we offer a full schedule of training events and CPD approved external events that will strengthen your CV and contribute to your development.

Join today

We offer several membership grades, depending on how much experience you have and where you are in you career. As a student affiliate member, you will show potential employers that you are serious about your career as a biologist.

You will be able to access our network of experienced biologists, receive *The Biologist*, our award-winning magazine, and apply for the Society's travel grants; as well as saving money on life science text books and attending the Life Science Careers Conferences for free.

Once you graduate, you can become an associate (AMSB) member, and then after three years of relevant experience, you can apply to be a full member of the Society (MSB). Graduates from Society of Biology accredited degrees can apply for MSB status after only one year of professional experience.

Go to www.societyofbiology.org/students to find out more

The Degree Accreditation Programme has received co-investment from the UK Commission for Employment and Skills through the Growth and Innovation Fund.

University of
South Wales
Prifysgol
De Cymru

Science at the University of South Wales

At the University of South Wales we're serious about science. We have invested £15m in facilities to offer our students an exceptional science education.

Our impressive George Knox science laboratories have been purpose-built to ensure our students are taught in a modern learning environment. In these labs, you will develop the important practical skills that graduate employers are looking for. Many of our science courses are accredited by the relevant professional bodies, so students can apply for membership when they graduate.

Course areas:
- Astronomy
- Biology
- Chemistry and Pharmaceutical Science
- Forensic Science
- Geography and Geology
- Medical Sciences
- Sustainable Energy

Book your place at an Open Day to find out more:
08455 76 77 78
www.southwales.ac.uk/science

Start your career in science with us

The University of South Wales has many highly regarded science degrees in specialist areas. These range from Forensic Science to International Wildlife Biology. No matter what you choose to study, you can be sure you'll gain the right skills, knowledge and practical experience to make you an attractive candidate to employers.

Facilities

We value a hands-on approach to study, so you'll undertake practical work in our specialist laboratories. This will allow you to enter the workplace with hands-on experience of industry equipment and techniques, which will be an advantage when you apply for graduate jobs.

We're also proud of our facilities for forensic sciences students. Our new analytical and forensic evidence laboratories allow you to gain the practical skills that employers demand. You'll also learn in our unique, multi-room crime scene house.

Astronomy students can use a number of telescopes on campus, and are also trained in digital photography, CCD imaging and a range of data analysis techniques such as astrometry, photometry and spectroscopy. That's in addition to regular access to the two-metre Faulkes Telescopes in Australia and Hawaii.

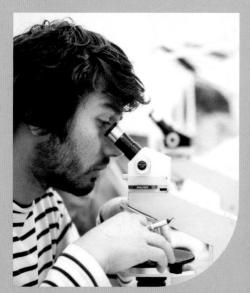

"I chose the University because the facilities for studying science are superb. We do various experiments and get to use the high-spec instrumentation. This is really good, as having a working knowledge of these will considerably enhance my career prospects."

**Lydia Yip,
BSc (Hons) Forensic Chemistry**

Employability

Many of our degrees are accredited by professional bodies. For example, our BSc (Hons) Chemistry degree is accredited by the Royal Society of Chemistry (RSC), the professional body for chemists, which means that graduates are eligible for RSC professional membership, eg, AMRSC.

Our forensic science degrees are accredited by the Forensic Science Society, making us the only university in Wales with this accreditation.

All our biology courses have been granted Recognised Programme status by the Society of Biology, the professional body for biologists. As a graduate from one of our biology degrees, you would be eligible for Associate Membership of the Society, and entitled to use the letters AMSB after your name.

All our courses allow you to gain valuable experience in the workplace. By the end of your placement, you'll be able to apply what you've learned to real-life situations which can help your studies when you return to university.

Field courses

Our science courses offer exciting fieldwork opportunities. As well as making use of the varied habitats on our doorstep in south Wales, our students also have the opportunity to visit locations much further afield. In recent years, these have included Honduras, Cuba, Indonesia and South Africa.

Careers

Skilled science graduates are in demand by employers. By delivering specialist subject knowledge, laboratory and field skills, our courses will unlock career opportunities throughout the sector. Our graduates have an excellent track record of securing employment within their specialist fields, while many choose to continue their studies and research at postgraduate level.

The best way to find out if a university is right for you is to come to an Open Day. We have events throughout the year, so visit **www.southwales.ac.uk/science** or call **08455 76 77 78** for further information.

Crime scene house

George Knox laboratories

280 pts **Aberystwyth** – 280–320 pts (Biol; Mar Frshwtr Biol; Env Biosci; Plnt Biol)
Bangor – 280–320 pts (App Mar Biol; Mar Biol; Mar Biol Zool; Mar Biol Ocean)
Brighton – BBC 280 pts (Hum Biol Educ) (IB 30 pts)
Hertfordshire – 280 pts (Hum Biol)
Huddersfield – 280 pts (Med Biol; Hum Biol; Biol (Mol Cell))
Hull – 280 pts (Biol; Hum Biol)
Lincoln – 280 pts (Biol)
Manchester Met – 280–300 pts (Biol Joint Hons)
Northumbria – 280 pts (App Biol; Biol Foren Biol)
Oxford Brookes – BBC (Biol; Hum Biol) (IB 30 pts)
Plymouth – 280 pts (Env Biol; Hum Biosci) (IB 26 pts)
Portsmouth – 280–300 pts (Foren Biol; Mar Biol)
Sheffield Hallam – 280 pts (Hum Biol; Biol)
Staffordshire – 280 pts (Biol Microbiol)
Stirling – BBC 280 pts (Biol) (IB 32 pts)
Teesside – 280 pts (Foren Biol)

260 pts **Bangor** – 260–320 pts (App Ter Mar Ecol; Biol Biotech; Biol) (IB 28 pts)
Bath Spa – 260–300 pts (Biol) (IB 26 pts)
Bradford – 260 pts (Med Cell Biol)
Brighton – BCC–CCC (Biol)
Derby – 260 pts (Biol)
Edinburgh Napier – BCC 260 pts (Mar Frshwtr Biol; Anim Biol)
Glasgow Caledonian – BCC 260 pts (Cell Mol Biol; Hum Biol Sociol Psy; Foren Invstg)
   (IB 24 pts)
Hull – 260 pts (Cstl Mar Biol)
Kingston – 260–280 pts (Foren Biol)
Liverpool Hope – 260–320 pts (Biol; Hum Biol)
Liverpool John Moores – 260–300 pts (Biol) (IB 25 pts)
Manchester Met – 260–280 pts (Biol; Hum Biol) (IB 27 pts)
Northampton – 260–300 pts (Biol)
Nottingham Trent – 260 pts (Foren Biol; Zoo Biol)
South Wales – BCC 260 pts (Biol; Hum Biol; Foren Biol)
Staffordshire – 260 pts (Hum Biol) (IB 28 pts)
Ulster – 260 pts (Biol) (IB 28 pts)
Worcester – 260–300 pts (Biol) (IB 25 pts)

240 pts **Anglia Ruskin** – 240 pts (Biol courses)
Bolton – 240 pts (Biol; Biol (Mol Sci))
Canterbury Christ Church – 240 pts (Env Biol) (IB 24 pts)
Chester – 240–280 pts (Foren Biol; Biol courses) (IB 24–26 pts)
Cumbria – 240 pts (Cons Biol) (IB 24 pts)
De Montfort – 240–260 pts (Foren Sci) (IB 24 pts)
East London – 240 pts (App Biol; Hum Biol)
Northampton – 240–280 pts (App Cons Biol) (IB 24 pts)
Nottingham Trent – 240 pts (Anim Biol) (IB 29 pts)
Salford – 240–280 pts (Biol courses)
Westminster – CCC 240 pts (Biol Sci (Mol Biol Genet)) (IB 26 pts)
Wolverhampton – 240 pts (Hum Biol) (IB 24 pts)
Worcester – 240–280 pts (Biol courses) (IB 24 pts)

220 pts **West London** – 220–240 pts (Foren Sci)
Westminster – CCD (Foren Biol) (IB 28 pts)

200 pts **Glyndŵr** – 200 pts (Foren Sci; Foren Sci Crim Just)
London South Bank – 200 pts (Biosci (Hum Biol); App Sci)
Staffordshire – 200–260 pts (Biol) (IB 28 pts)
Wolverhampton – 200 pts (App Microbiol; Genet Mol Biol)

For a quick reference offers calculator, fold out the inside front cover.

160 pts **Edinburgh Queen Margaret** – 160 pts (Hum Biol) (IB 26 pts)
120 pts **Blackpool and Fylde (Coll)** – 120 pts (App Biol)

Alternative offers
See **Chapter 7** and **Appendix 1** for grades/UCAS Tariff points information for the International Baccalaureate, Scottish Highers/Advanced Highers, the Welsh Baccalaureate, the Irish Leaving Certificate, the Cambridge Pre-U Diploma, the Advanced Diploma and the Extended Project.

EXAMPLES OF FOUNDATION DEGREES IN THE SUBJECT FIELD
Anglia Ruskin; Bedfordshire; Blackpool and Fylde (Coll); Bournemouth; Cornwall (Coll); Harlow (Coll); Nottingham Trent; Truro (Coll).

CHOOSING YOUR COURSE (SEE ALSO CH.1)
Some course features
Bath A flexible programme is offered covering Biology and Molecular and Cellular Biology, and Biochemistry, with three-year or four-year courses and possible placements or overseas study in industry in the UK or Europe and at universities in the US. (High research rating.)
London (UCL) The course provides a broad and flexible Biology programme and also acts as an entry route for those who decide to transfer to more specialised degrees including Cellular and Molecular Biology, Environmental Biology and the Biology of Fertility and Embryo Development.
Loughborough Degree courses are offered in Human Biology, with modules in genetics, psychology and nutrition, and Ergonomics (Human Factors Design) which includes psychology, anatomy and physiology.
Manchester Biology is offered with industrial experience, a modern language or Science and Society, or as a Single Honours course. Biology is also part of the Life Sciences programme. Courses are also available in Anatomical Sciences and Developmental Biology.
Southampton Biology is offered as a Single Honours subject or Joint Honours when combined with Marine Biology. It is an interdisciplinary programme, with the opportunity to personalise learning, and opportunities for overseas field trips.

Universities and colleges teaching quality See www.qaa.ac.uk; http://unistats.direct.gov.uk.

Top research universities and colleges (RAE 2008) See **Biological Sciences**.

Examples of sandwich degree courses Aston; Bath; Birmingham; Bristol; Bristol UWE; Brunel; Cardiff; Cardiff Met (UWIC); Coventry; De Montfort; Dundee; East London; Edinburgh Napier; Greenwich; Hertfordshire; Huddersfield; Kent; Kingston; Leeds; Lincoln; Liverpool John Moores; London South Bank; Loughborough; Manchester; Manchester Met; Newcastle; Northumbria; Nottingham Trent; Plymouth; Queen's Belfast; Reading; Sheffield Hallam; South Wales; Surrey; Sussex; Teesside; Ulster; York.

ADMISSIONS INFORMATION
Number of applicants per place (approx) Aberdeen 8; Aberystwyth 5; Aston 6; Bath 7; Bath Spa 8; Birmingham 3; Bradford 7; Bristol 9; Cardiff 8; Dundee 6; Durham 11; Exeter 6; Hull 4; Imperial London 4; Kent 10; Leeds 6; Leicester 15; London (RH) 5; Newcastle (Mar Biol) 15; Nottingham 9; Oxford Brookes 13; Salford 3; Southampton (Mar Biol Ocean) 6, (Biol) 7; Stirling 15; Sussex 4; Swansea (Mar Biol) 8, (Biol) 4; York 8.

Advice to applicants and planning the UCAS personal statement See **Biochemistry**, **Biological Sciences** and **Appendix 3**. **York** Advanced Diploma not generally accepted.

Misconceptions about this course **Sussex** Many students think that a Biology degree limits you to being a professional scientist which is not the case. **York** Some fail to realise that chemistry beyond GCSE is essential. Mature students often lack the confidence to consider the course.

Selection interviews **Yes** Bangor, Bath, Birmingham, Bradford (informal, after offer), Cambridge, Durham, East Anglia, Essex, Hertfordshire, Imperial London, Kent, Kingston, London (RH), London (UCL), London South Bank, Sheffield Hallam, Southampton, SRUC, Staffordshire, Surrey, Swansea, Writtle (Coll); **Some** Anglia Ruskin, Aston, Bath Spa, Derby, Liverpool John Moores, Roehampton, Salford, Sheffield, Stirling, Wolverhampton, York; **No** Dundee, Nottingham.

190 | Biotechnology

Interview advice and questions Questions are likely to focus on your studies in biology, on any work experience or any special interests you may have in biology outside school. In the past, questions have included: Is the computer like a brain and, if so, could it ever be taught to think? What do you think the role of the environmental biologist will be in the next 40–50 years? Have you any strong views on vivisection? You have a micro-organism in the blood: you want to make a culture. What conditions should be borne in mind? What is a pacemaker? What problems will a giraffe experience? How does water enter a flowering plant? Compare an egg and a potato. Discuss a family tree of human genotypes. Discuss fish farming in Britain today. What problems do fish face underwater? See also **Chapter 6**. **Liverpool John Moores** Informal interview. It is useful to bring samples of coursework to the interview. **York** Why Biology? How do you see your future?

Reasons for rejection (non-academic) Bath Spa Poor mathematical and scientific knowledge.

AFTER-RESULTS ADVICE
Offers to applicants repeating A-levels Higher Cardiff, East London, St Andrews, Strathclyde; **Possibly higher** Aston, Bath, Bradford, Durham, Leeds, London (RH), Nottingham, Portsmouth; **Same** Aberystwyth, Anglia Ruskin, Bangor, Bedfordshire, Brunel, Chester, Derby, Dundee, Edinburgh Napier, Heriot-Watt, Hull, Liverpool John Moores, London (UCL), London South Bank, Loughborough, Manchester Met, Newcastle, Oxford Brookes, Plymouth, Roehampton, Salford, Sheffield, Southampton, Staffordshire, Stirling, Teesside, Ulster, Wolverhampton, York.

GRADUATE DESTINATIONS AND EMPLOYMENT (2011/12 HESA)
Graduates surveyed 3910 **Employed** 1450 **In voluntary employment** 150 **In further study** 1200 **Assumed unemployed** 415

Career note Some graduates go into research, but many will go into laboratory work in hospitals, food laboratories, agriculture, the environment and pharmaceuticals. Others go into teaching, management and other professional and technical areas.

OTHER DEGREE SUBJECTS FOR CONSIDERATION
Anatomy; Biochemistry; Biological Sciences; Biotechnology; Chemistry; Dentistry; Ecology; Environmental Health; Environmental Science/Studies; Food Science; Genomics; Health Studies; Medicine; Midwifery; Nursing; Nutrition; Optometry; Orthoptics; Pharmaceutical Sciences; Pharmacology; Pharmacy; Physiology; Physiotherapy; Plant Sciences; Radiography; Speech and Language Therapy; Zoology.

BIOTECHNOLOGY

(see also **Biological Sciences, Biology, Engineering (Medical), Microbiology**)

Biotechnology is a multi-disciplinary subject which can include chemistry, biological sciences, microbiology, genetics and chemical engineering. Medical engineering involves the design, installation, maintenance and provision of technical support for diagnostic, therapeutic and other clinical equipment used by doctors, nurses and other clinical healthcare workers.

Useful websites www.bbsrc.ac.uk; www.bioindustry.org; www.abcinformation.org.

NB The points totals shown to the left of the institutions are for ease of reference only. It must not be assumed that Tariff points are always used by institutions or that they can be substituted for an offer in grades. The level of an offer is not necessarily indicative of the quality of a course.

COURSE OFFERS INFORMATION
Subject requirements/preferences GCSE Mathematics and science subjects required. **AL** Courses vary but one, two or three subjects from chemistry, biology, physics and mathematics may be required.

Your target offers and examples of courses provided by each institution

360 pts **Bristol** – AAA–AAB 360–340 pts (Bioch Mol Biol Biotech) (IB 37–35 pts)
Edinburgh – AAA–ABB 360–320 pts (Biotech) (IB 37–32 pts)
Imperial London – AAA (Biomat Tiss Eng; Biotech; Biotech (Yr Ind/Rsch)) (IB 38 pts HL 66)
Leeds – AAA 360 pts (Med Eng MEng/BEng) (IB 35 pts HL 18 pts)
London (UCL) – AAAe incl chem (Biotech) (IB 38 pts HL 18 pts)
Manchester – AAA–ABB (Biotech; Cheml Eng Biotech) (IB 37–33 pts)
Nottingham – AAA–AAB 360–320 pts (Biomed Mat Sci) (IB 34–36 pts)

340 pts **Cardiff** – AAB–ABB 340–320 pts (Biotech) (IB 34 pts)
Glasgow – AAB 340 pts (Mol Cel Biol (Biotech)) (IB 34 pts)
Sheffield – AAB (Cheml Eng Biotech) (IB 35 pts)
York – AAB–ABB (Biotech Microbiol) (IB 35 pts)

320 pts **Birmingham** – ABB (Biomed Mat Sci) (IB 34 pts)
Kent – ABB incl maths bio +sci/tech 320 pts (Bioeng)
Liverpool – ABB (Microbl Biotech) (IB 33 pts HL 6 biol)
Nottingham – ABB–BBB 320–300 pts (Biotech; Biotech Cert Euro St) (IB 32–30 pts)
Salford – 320 pts (Pros Orthot) (IB 27 pts)
Strathclyde – ABB (Pros Orthot) (IB 34 pts)
Surrey – AAB–ABB 340–320 pts (Biotech) (IB 34 pts)

300 pts **Aberdeen** – BBB (Biotech App Mol Biol) (IB 30 pts)
Greenwich – 300 pts (Biotech) (IB 26 pts)
Northumbria – 300 pts (Biotech) (IB 26 pts)

260 pts **Bangor** – 260–320 pts (Biol Biotech) (IB 28 pts)
Edinburgh Napier – BCC 260 pts (Microbiol Biotech)

240 pts **East London** – 240 pts (Med Biotech) (IB 24 pts)
London Met – 240 pts (Biotech) (IB 28 pts)
Westminster – CCC (Biol Sci (Biotech)) (IB 26 pts)

200 pts **Wolverhampton** – 200 pts (Biotech) (IB 24 pts)

Alternative offers

See **Chapter 7** and **Appendix 1** for grades/UCAS Tariff points information for the International Baccalaureate, Scottish Highers/Advanced Highers, the Welsh Baccalaureate, the Irish Leaving Certificate, the Cambridge Pre-U Diploma, the Advanced Diploma and the Extended Project.

EXAMPLES OF FOUNDATION DEGREES IN THE SUBJECT FIELD
Edinburgh Napier.

CHOOSING YOUR COURSE (SEE ALSO CH.1)
Some course features

Leeds (Med Eng) The course combines engineering science, biological science and medicine. It has study-abroad and work-placement opportunities and strong links with industry.
Manchester (Biotech) A common first year covering several life science subjects provides the opportunity to change at a later stage.
Northumbria (Biotech) Main focus of course is on molecular biotechnology, including molecular biology, immunology and bioinformatics.
Surrey The course in Biotechnology is offered with the option of a year-long professional training placement. The courses within the microbiology programmes are flexible and students are able to transfer if they wish to specialise in Microbiology, Microbiology (Medical) or Food Science and Microbiology later on.
Swansea Students on the four-year course in Clinical Technology spend 50% of the time on paid hospital placements (salary currently £17,000). No fees are paid for this course.

Universities and colleges teaching quality See www.qaa.ac.uk; http://unistats.direct.gov.uk.

Examples of sandwich degree courses Aberdeen; Bristol; Cardiff; Imperial London; Manchester; Northumbria; Surrey; Sussex.

ADMISSIONS INFORMATION

Number of applicants per place (approx) Birmingham 6; Bristol 9; Cardiff 4; Imperial London 4; Leeds 7; London (UCL) 4; Strathclyde 4.

Advice to applicants and planning the UCAS personal statement See **Biological Sciences**, **Biochemistry** and **Appendix 3**.

Selection interviews Yes Leeds, Strathclyde, Surrey; **Some** Cardiff, Wolverhampton; **No** Dundee, Imperial London.

Interview advice and questions See **Biology**, **Biological Sciences** and **Chapter 6**.

AFTER-RESULTS ADVICE

Offers to applicants repeating A-levels Possibly higher Nottingham; **Same** Cardiff, Leeds, Liverpool John Moores, Wolverhampton.

GRADUATE DESTINATIONS AND EMPLOYMENT (2011/12 HESA)

Biotechnology graduates surveyed 25 **Employed** 5 **In voluntary employment** 0 **In further study** 5 **Assumed unemployed** 5

Medical Technology graduates surveyed 1340 **Employed** 1065 **In voluntary employment** 10 **In further study** 100 **Assumed unemployed** 90

Career note Biotechnology, biomedical and biochemical engineering opportunities exist in medical, agricultural, food science and pharmaceutical laboratories. Some Bioengineering graduates apply for graduate medical courses and obtain both engineering and medical qualifications.

OTHER DEGREE SUBJECTS FOR CONSIDERATION

Agriculture; Biochemistry; Biological Sciences; Biomedicine; Chemistry; Food Technology; Genetics; Materials Science and Technology; Microbiology; Molecular Biology; Pharmacology.

BUILDING and CONSTRUCTION

(including **Building Design, Building Services Engineering, Building Surveying, Construction, Fire Risk Engineering** and **Fire Safety Management**; see also **Architecture, Engineering (Civil), Housing, Surveying**)

The building and construction industry covers a wide range of activities and is closely allied to civil, municipal and structural engineering and quantity surveying. One branch of the industry covers building services engineering, a career which involves specialised areas such as heating, acoustics, lighting, refrigeration and air conditioning. Many Building, Construction, Building Surveying and Building Services Engineering courses include industrial placements and are accredited by professional bodies such as the Chartered Institute of Building, the Royal Institution of Chartered Surveyors and the Engineering Council.

Useful websites www.ciob.org.uk; www.cibse.org; www.citb.co.uk.

NB The points totals shown to the left of the institutions are for ease of reference only. It must not be assumed that Tariff points are always used by institutions or that they can be substituted for an offer in grades. The level of an offer is not necessarily indicative of the quality of a course.

COURSE OFFERS INFORMATION

Subject requirements/preferences GCSE English, mathematics and science usually required. **AL** Physics, mathematics or a technical subject may be required for some courses.

Your target offers and examples of courses provided by each institution
340 pts Brunel – AAB 340 pts (Mech Eng Bld Serv) (IB 35 pts)
        London (UCL) – ABBe (Proj Mgt Constr) (IB 34 pts)

OXFORD
BROOKES
UNIVERSITY

BSc CONSTRUCTION STUDENT PROFILE
Ross Dunford

Ross studied BSc (Hons) Construction Project Management with the Department of Real Estate and Construction and took a work placement with Leadbitter in Abingdon, Oxfordshire

Before you came to Brookes what did you study and where?
A Level Art, Environmental Science and English Language at Norton Hill School near Bath then a Diploma in Architecture at Dundee University.

What made you choose Brookes as a place to study?
I chose Brookes as it catered for the course content I was looking for and also due to the department's good reputation.

What do/did you think of the course while studying here?
I have enjoyed the course in general as most subjects covered interest me, but especially the fact that I am able to do a year out in industry as I feel that you learn a lot more getting your hands dirty rather than just reading about what is done on a construction site.

How did your scholarship or bursary enhance your experience of the course?
It made my standard of living a lot more comfortable as a student, and mainly helped cover the cost of my rent.

What are the best bits of studying at Brookes?
A good level of teaching and support as well as Oxford being a nice place to live and be in.

What do you think of the industrial placement aspect of your course?
I think that this is definitely the best aspect of the course as it is where you can put the theory into practice and you get to see the industry in a different light.

What advice do you have for others?
I would recommend this course to others as I feel it has taught me a lot about the industry and its affiliation with construction companies is what enabled me to gain my placement opportunity.

What are your plans for when you've completed your course, for work or further study?
Once I graduate I would ideally like to gain a position with a construction company as a Site or Project Manager.

tde.bz/rec-heap

320 pts **Newcastle** – ABB–BBB 320–300 pts (Surv Map Sci) (IB 32–34 pts HL 5 maths)
Reading – ABB/AAC 320 pts (Bld Surv) (IB 32 pts)
300 pts **Brighton** – BBB 300 pts (Bld Surv; Constr Mgt) (IB 32 pts)
Bristol UWE – 300 pts (Bld Surv)
Heriot-Watt – BBB 300 pts (Constr Proj Mgt) (IB 29 pts)
Leeds Beckett – 300 pts (Constr Mgt) (IB 26 pts)
Loughborough – 300 pts (Commer Mgt Quant Surv) (IB 32 pts)
Northumbria – 300 pts (Bld Surv)
Plymouth – BBB 300 pts (Bld Surv Env) (IB 30 pts)
Reading – 300–320 pts (Bld Constr Mgt)
Ulster – 300 pts (Bld Surv; Constr Eng Mgt) (IB 25–32 pts)
285 pts **Glasgow Caledonian** – 285 pts (Bld Surv; Constr Mgt)
280 pts **Aston** – 280–300 pts (Constr Proj Mgt) (IB 29 pts)
Birmingham City – 280 pts (Bld Surv)
Bristol UWE – 280 pts (Constr Mgt)
Kingston – 280–300 pts (Bld Surv)
Leeds Beckett – 280 pts (Bld Surv; Quant Surv) (IB 25 pts)
Loughborough – 280 pts (Constr Eng Mgt) (IB 30 pts)
Nottingham – BBC (Sust Blt Env) (IB 28 pts)
Nottingham Trent – 280 pts (Prop Fin Inv; Bld Surv)
Oxford Brookes – BBC-BCC 280–260 pts (Cnstr Proj Mgt) (IB 30–31 pts)
Plymouth – 280 pts (Constr Mgt Env) (IB 28 pts)
Sheffield Hallam – 280 pts (Constr Proj Mgt; Bld Surv)
Westminster – BBC 280 pts (Bld Surv; Constr Mgt) (IB 28 pts)
270 pts **Anglia Ruskin** – 270 pts (Bld Surv)
Liverpool John Moores – 270 pts (Bld Serv Eng; Bld Surv)
260 pts **Coventry** – BCC 260 pts (Bld Surv) (IB 29 pts)
Derby – 260 pts (Constr Mgt) (IB 26 pts)
Greenwich – 260 pts (Des Constr Mgt)
Liverpool John Moores – 260 pts (Constr Mgt)
Salford – 260–300 pts (Constr Proj Mgt; Bld Surv)
South Wales – BCC 260 pts (Proj Mgt (Surv))
240 pts **Anglia Ruskin** – 240 pts (Constr Mgt) (IB 24 pts)
Bolton – 240 pts (Bld Surv Prop Mgt)
Central Lancashire – 240 pts (Constr Proj Mgt; Bld Serv Sust Eng; Fire Sfty Risk Mgt)
(IB 24 pts)
Edinburgh Napier – CCC 240 pts (Bld Surv; Constr Proj Mgt)
Glyndŵr – 240 pts (Bld St (Constr Mgt))
Hull (Coll) – 240 pts (Constr Mgt)
Kingston – 240 pts (Constr Mgt) (IB 24 pts)
Northumbria – 240–280 pts (Bld Des Mgt; Constr Mgt; Bld Proj Mgt) (IB 25 pts)
Nottingham Trent – 240 pts (Constr Mgt)
Plymouth – 240 pts (Env Constr Surv) (IB 24 pts)
South Wales – 240–280 pts (Bld St; Bld Serv Eng)
Ulster – 240 pts (Bld Eng Mat) (IB 24 pts)
Wolverhampton – CCC (Bld Surv) (IB 26 pts)
220 pts **London South Bank** – 220 pts (Constr Mgt; Prop Mgt (Bld Surv)) (IB 24 pts)
200 pts **Huddersfield** – 200 pts (Constr Proj Mgt)
Portsmouth – 200–260 pts (Constr Eng Mgt) (IB 24 pts)
Sheffield Hallam – 200 pts (Blt Env)
Southampton Solent – 200 pts (Constr Mgt)
West London – 200 pts (Blt Env (Constr Mgt); Blt Env (Archit Tech))
Wolverhampton – 200 pts (Constr Mgt) (IB 24 pts)
180 pts **Glasgow Caledonian** – BC 180 pts (Bld Serv Eng)
Kingston – 180 pts (Hist Bld Cons)

160 pts   **Trinity Saint David (Swansea)** – 160 pts (Proj Constr Mgt) (IB 24 pts)
120 pts   **Colchester (Inst)** – 120 pts (Constr Mgt (Commer Mgt); Constr Mgt (Site Mgt))

Alternative offers

See **Chapter 7** and **Appendix 1** for grades/UCAS Tariff points information for the International Baccalaureate, Scottish Highers/Advanced Highers, the Welsh Baccalaureate, the Irish Leaving Certificate, the Cambridge Pre-U Diploma, the Advanced Diploma and the Extended Project.

EXAMPLES OF FOUNDATION DEGREES IN THE SUBJECT FIELD

Bedfordshire; Blackburn (Coll); Bolton; Bournemouth; Bradford; Brighton; Central Lancashire; Colchester (Inst); Cornwall (Coll); Cumbria; Derby; Ealing, Hammersmith and West London (Coll); East London; Glyndŵr; Greenwich; Huddersfield; Kent; Kingston; Northampton; Northumbria; Suffolk (Univ Campus); Trinity Saint David (Swansea); West London; West Nottinghamshire (Coll); Westminster City (Coll); Weymouth (Coll); Wolverhampton.

CHOOSING YOUR COURSE (SEE ALSO CH.1)

Some course features

Aston Construction and Construction Project Management courses have a common first year; sandwich course has good industrial contacts.

Kingston Courses offered associated with Building in the School of Surveying include Building and Quantity Surveying, which is RICS- and CIOB-accredited and is available as a four-year sandwich course, Construction Management and Property Planning and Development.

London (UCL) The Project Management for Construction BSc degree is offered either as a three-year course or a four-year sandwich course, where the third year is spent in industry. Both degrees provide full exemption from the professional examinations of both the CIOB and the RICS.

Loughborough (Constr Eng Mgt) Course sponsored by industry. Two six-month placements of industrial training.

Newcastle The Surveying and Mapping Science degree has a practical focus with the opportunity to attend field courses in and around Newcastle. The degree is accredited by the RICS and the Chartered Institution of Civil Engineers (CICE).

Northumbria The Construction Management course focuses on site construction with supporting studies in financial control and management.

Reading Students taking Construction Management, Quantity Surveying and Building Surveying follow the same course for two years, choosing the specialism in Year 3. All three programmes are accredited by the RICS and CIOB.

South Wales Courses offered include Construction Management, Architectural Technology, Quantity Surveying and Building Services Engineering. Sandwich courses with placements in industry are also available.

Universities and colleges teaching quality See www.qaa.ac.uk; http://unistats.direct.gov.uk.

Top research universities and colleges (RAE 2008) See **Architecture**.

Examples of sandwich degree courses Aston; Brighton; Bristol UWE; Brunel; Central Lancashire; Coventry; Glasgow Caledonian; Greenwich; Heriot-Watt; Huddersfield; Kingston; Leeds Beckett; Liverpool John Moores; London Met; London South Bank; Loughborough; Northumbria; Nottingham Trent; Sheffield Hallam; Ulster; Wolverhampton.

ADMISSIONS INFORMATION

Number of applicants per place (approx) Bristol UWE (Constr Mgt) 5; Edinburgh Napier 8; Glasgow Caledonian 6; Heriot-Watt 6; Kingston 4; London (UCL) 6; Loughborough 4; Northumbria 6; Salford (Bld Surv) 6; Strathclyde 5.

Advice to applicants and planning the UCAS personal statement Details of work experience with any levels of responsibility should be included. Make contact with any building organisation to arrange a meeting with staff to discuss careers in building. Give evidence of your ability to work in a team and give details of any personal achievements in technological areas and work experience. Building also covers civil engineering, surveying, quantity surveying etc and these areas should also be explored. See also **Appendix 3**.

Misconceptions about this course Loughborough Some students fail to realise that the degree includes law, finance, economics and management plus constructional technology.

Selection interviews Yes Brunel, Derby, Glasgow Caledonian, Greenwich, Kingston, Liverpool John Moores, London South Bank, Loughborough, Oxford Brookes, Plymouth, Robert Gordon, Sheffield Hallam, Staffordshire, Westminster; **Some** Anglia Ruskin, Birmingham City, Brighton, Salford; **No** Nottingham, Reading.

Interview advice and questions Work experience in the building and civil engineering industries is important and you could be expected to describe any building project you have visited and any problems experienced in its construction. A knowledge of the range of activities to be found on a building site will be expected, for example the work of quantity and land surveyors and of the various building trades. See also **Chapter 6**. **Loughborough** The applicant should show an understanding of the role of the quantity surveyor.

Reasons for rejection (non-academic) Inability to communicate. Lack of motivation. Indecisiveness about reasons for choosing the course. **Loughborough** Applicant more suited to a hands-on course rather than an academic one.

AFTER-RESULTS ADVICE
Offers to applicants repeating A-levels Higher Liverpool John Moores, Strathclyde; **Possibly higher** Bristol UWE; **Same** Birmingham City, Bolton, Brighton, Coventry, Heriot-Watt, Huddersfield, Kingston, London (UCL), Loughborough, Northumbria, Robert Gordon, Trinity Saint David (Swansea).

GRADUATE DESTINATIONS AND EMPLOYMENT (2011/12 HESA)
Building graduates surveyed 4155 **Employed** 2760 **In voluntary employment** 20 **In further study** 710 **Assumed unemployed** 245

Career note There is a wide range of opportunities within the building and construction industry for building technologists and managers. This subject area also overlaps into surveying, quantity surveying, civil engineering, architecture and planning and graduates from all these subjects commonly work together as members of construction teams.

OTHER DEGREE SUBJECTS FOR CONSIDERATION
Architectural Technology; Architecture; Civil Engineering; Property Planning and Development; Quantity Surveying; Surveying.

BUSINESS and MANAGEMENT COURSES

(see also **Business and Management Courses (International and European), Business and Management Courses (Specialised), Economics, Hospitality and Event Management, Human Resource Management, Leisure and Recreation Management/Studies, Marketing, Retail Management, Tourism and Travel**)

Business degrees attract more applicants than any other degree subject, with a further rise in the past year for places on a wide range of programmes. Financial studies form part of most courses, in addition to sales, marketing, human resources management and general management. Since this is a vocational subject, some work experience in the field is generally required prior to application. Many courses offer industrial placements, in some cases in the USA, Australia and New Zealand and, for those students with an A-level in a language (and in some cases a good GCSE), placements in Europe are possible.

Useful websites www.faststream.civilservice.gov.uk; www.bized.co.uk; www.icsa.org.uk; www.oft.gov.uk; www.adassoc.org.uk; www.cipr.co.uk; www.ismm.co.uk; www.export.org.uk; www.ipsos-mori.com; www.capitaresourcing.co.uk; www.tax.org.uk; www.hmrc.gov.uk; www.camfoundation.com; www.shell-livewire.org; www.iconsulting.org.uk; www.managers.org.uk; www.cipd.co.uk; www.instam.org.

Check **Chapter 4** when choosing your university and **Chapter 7** on how to read the subject tables.

NB The points totals shown to the left of the institutions are for ease of reference only. It must not be assumed that Tariff points are always used by institutions or that they can be substituted for an offer in grades. The level of an offer is not necessarily indicative of the quality of a course.

COURSE OFFERS INFORMATION

Subject requirements/preferences **GCSE** Mathematics and English often at grade A or B required. **AL** Mathematics required for some courses. In some cases grades A, B or C may be required.

Your target offers and examples of courses provided by each institution

380 pts **Durham** – A*AA incl maths 380 pts (Econ Mgt) (IB 38 pts HL 666)
Exeter – A*AA-AAB 380-340 pts (Maths Mgt) (IB 38-34 pts)
Warwick – A*AA-AABc (Law Bus St; Mgt; Phys Bus St) (IB 36-38 pts)

360 pts **Bath** – AAA/A*AB (Mgt courses) (IB 38 pts)
Bristol – AAA-AAB 360-340 pts (Acc Mgt) (IB 37-35 pts)
City – AAA 360 pts (Mgt) (IB 35 pts)
Edinburgh – AAA-BBB 360-300 pts (Bus Acc; Econ Hist Bus) (IB 40-34 pts)
Exeter – AAA-ABB (Bus Acc; Bus Mgt) (IB 36-34 pts)
Huddersfield – 360 pts (Bus Law)
Lancaster – AAA-ABB (Acc Mgt St; Mgt courses; Bus St courses; Fin Mgt St; Mgt Org) (IB 32-36 pts)
Leeds – AAA 360 pts (Bus Econ; Econ Mgt; Mgt Mark) (IB 35 pts)
London (King's) – AAA (Bus Mgt) (IB 35 pts HL 666)
London LSE – AAA (Bus Maths Stats) (IB 38 pts)
Newcastle – AAA-AAB 360-340 pts (Bus Mgt) (IB 35-37 pts)
St Andrews – AAA (Mgt Span; Mgt courses; Mgt Sci) (IB 38 pts)
Southampton – AAA incl maths (Econ Mgt Sci) (IB 36 pts HL 18 pts)

For a quick reference offers calculator, fold out the inside front cover.

Surrey – AAA–AAB (Bus Econ) (IB 37–35 pts)
Sussex – AAA–AAB (Law Bus) (IB 35–36 pts)
340 pts **Aston** – AAB–AAA 340–360 pts (Acc Mgt; Bus Mgt) (IB 35 pts)
Birmingham – AAB 340 pts (Bus Mgt courses; Civ Eng Bus Mgt; Maths Bus Mgt)
(IB 35–36 pts)
Brunel – AAB (Bus Mgt (Mark); Bus Mgt; Bus Mgt (Acc)) (IB 35 pts)
Cardiff – AAB 340 pts (Fin Mgt; Bus Mgt (Mark); Bus Mgt) (IB 35 pts)
City – AAB 340 pts (Bus St) (IB 35 pts)
Durham – AAB 340 pts (Bus Mgt; Mgt Acc) (IB 36 pts)
Kent – AAB–ABB (Bus Admin courses) (IB 33 pts HL 15 pts)
Leeds – AAB (Mgt) (IB 35 pts)
Leicester – AAB (Mgt St courses; Mgt St)
Liverpool – AAB (Bus St; Bus St Ind) (IB 35 pts)
London (RH) – AAB (Mgt; Mgt Acc; Econ Mgt) (IB 35 pts)
London LSE – AAB (Mgt; Mgt Sci) (IB 37 pts HL 766)
Loughborough – AAB–AAA 340–360 pts (Mgt Sci; Maths Mgt) (IB 36 pts)
Manchester – AAB (Bus St; Bus St Econ; Mgt courses; Bus St Pol; Bus St Sociol; Comp Sci
Bus Mgt) (IB 35 pts)
Nottingham – AAB–ABB 320–340 pts (Bus Econy Contemp Chin; Mgt St) (IB 32–34 pts)
Nottingham Trent – AAB (Bus Mgt)
Queen's Belfast – AAB–ABBa (Bus Mgt)
Reading – AAB 340 pts (Bus Mgt; Acc Bus; Acc Mgt) (IB 35 pts)
Sheffield – AAB (Bus Mgt Joint Hons) (IB 35 pts)
Southampton – AAB 340 pts (Mgt; Mgt Sci; Mgt Sci Acc; Mus Mgt Sci) (IB 34 pts HL 17 pts)
Strathclyde – AAB (Bus; Bus Ent courses) (IB 32 pts)
Surrey – AAB (Bus Mgt Engl Int Comm; Bus Mgt) (IB 35 pts)
Sussex – AAB–ABB 340–320 pts (Bus Mgt St; Fin Bus; Econ Mgt St; Mark Mgt; Int Bus)
(IB 34–35 pts)
Warwick – AAB (Chem Mgt; Comp Bus St; Eng Bus St) (IB 36 pts)
York – AAB (Mgt) (IB 35 pts)
320 pts **Aston** – ABB–AAB 320–340 pts (Psy Bus) (IB 33 pts)
Birmingham – ABB (Electron Eng Bus Mgt) (IB 32–34 pts)
Bournemouth – ABB 320–340 pts (Acc Bus; Bus St) (IB 32–33 pts)
Bradford – 320 pts (Bus Mgt St) (IB 26 pts)
Brighton – ABB (Bus Mgt Mark; Fash Bus St)
Cardiff – ABB 320 pts (Bus Inf Sys; Bus St Jap) (IB 33–35 pts)
East Anglia – ABB (Bus Econ; Fr Lang Mgt St; Span Lang Mgt St; Mgt; Jap Lang Mgt St; Fr
Span Lang Mgt St (4 yrs)) (IB 32 pts)
Essex – ABB–BBB 320–300 pts (Bus Mgt; Sociol Mgt) (IB 32–30 pts)
Glasgow – ABB (Bus Mgt Joint Hons) (IB 36 pts)
Kingston – 320 pts (Bus St) (IB 27 pts)
Liverpool – ABB (Maths Bus St) (IB 33 pts HL 6 maths)
London (QM) – ABB 320 pts (Bus Mgt) (IB 34 pts)
Northumbria – ABB 320 pts (Bus St; Bus Mgt)
Nottingham – ABB 320 pts (Modn Langs Bus) (IB 32 pts)
Roehampton – 320 pts (Bus Mgt Acc)
Sheffield – ABB (Sociol Bus Mgt; Bus Mgt) (IB 33 pts)
Sussex – ABB 320 pts (Comp Bus Mgt) (IB 34 pts)
300 pts **Aberdeen** – BBB (Mgt St) (IB 30 pts)
Bristol UWE – 300 pts (Bus courses; Mgt; Bus Ent; Bus Mgt (Ldrshp Chng Org); Bus Mgt
courses)
Buckingham – BBB 300 pts (Law Mgt St) (IB 34 pts)
Cardiff Met (UWIC) – 300 pts (Bus Mgt St HR Mgt; Bus Mgt Fin; Bus Mgt St Law; Bus Mgt
St courses)
Coventry – 300 pts (Glob Bus Mgt)

De Montfort – 300 pts (Bus Inf Sys)
Edinburgh – BBB-AAA 300-360 pts (Bus St) (IB 34-42 pts)
Heriot-Watt – BBB (Bus Mgt HR Mgt; Bus Mgt Mark) (IB 29 pts)
Hertfordshire – 300 pts (Bus St; Mgt) (IB 30 pts)
Huddersfield – BBB 300 pts (Bus St Env Mgt; Bus Mgt; Bus; Bus Mgt Fin; Bus St)
Hull – BBB 300 pts (Bus Fin Mgt)
Keele – ABC 300 pts (Bus Mgt) (IB 32 pts)
Kent – BBB 300 pts (Acc Mgt) (IB 34 pts)
Leicester – BBB (Comp Mgt)
Liverpool Hope – 300 pts (Bus Mgt)
London (QM) – 300-340 pts (Bus Comp; Comp ICT Bus Mgt) (IB 32-34 pts)
Northumbria – BBB 300 pts (Bus Econ; Bus Mark Mgt; Bus Log Sply Chn Mgt; Bus Tour Mgt) (IB 26 pts)
Nottingham Trent – 300 pts (Bus Mgt courses; Bus; Mgt Joint Hons)
Oxford Brookes – BBB (Bus Mgt (Comb)) (IB 31 pts)
Plymouth – 300 pts (Law Bus) (IB 26 pts)
Salford – 300 pts (Bus St HR Mgt)
Sheffield Hallam – 300 pts (Bus Econ; Bus courses; Bus St)
Swansea – BBB-BCC 300-260 pts (Bus Mgt; Bus Mgt (Fin)) (IB 32-30 pts)
Westminster – BBB 300 pts (Bus Mgt courses; Bus St courses) (IB 28 pts)

280 pts **Abertay** – BBC (Bus St)
Aberystwyth – 280 pts (Bus Mgt) (IB 28 pts)
Birmingham City – 280 pts (Bus courses; Fash Rtl Mgt)
Brighton – BBC 280 pts (Maths Bus; Bus Mgt Fin; Law Bus; Bus Mgt courses) (IB 30 pts)
Bristol UWE – 280 pts (Spo Bus Mgt) (IB 24 pts)
Central Lancashire – BBC-ABB 280-320 pts (Bus Mgt Chin) (IB 25 pts)
De Montfort – 280 pts (Bus courses) (IB 28 pts)
Derby – 280 pts (Bus St) (IB 26 pts)
East London – 280 pts (Bus Mgt) (IB 25 pts)
Edge Hill – BBC 280 pts (Bus Mgt) (IB 26 pts)
Gloucestershire – 280-300 pts (Bus Mgt)
Greenwich – 280 pts (PR; Bus Mgt; Bus Law)
Hull – 280 pts (Bus courses) (IB 28 pts)
Kingston – 280 pts (Bus Mgt) (IB 25 pts)
Leeds Beckett – 280 pts (Int Tour Mgt) (IB 25 pts)
Leeds Trinity – 280 pts (Bus Mark; Bus; Bus Mgt)
Liverpool John Moores – 280 pts (Bus Mgt; Bus St) (IB 29 pts)
Loughborough – 280 pts (Trans Bus Mgt) (IB 30 pts)
Manchester Met – 280 pts (Spo Mgt; Bus Econ Inter Bus; Bus Ent HR Mgt; Bus Mgt; Bus Joint Hons; Bus; PR Dig Comms Mgt; Bus Econ) (IB 28 pts)
Newman – 280 pts (Bus Mgt) (IB 26 pts)
Northumbria – 280-300 pts (Ger Bus) (IB 26 pts)
Nottingham Trent – 280 pts (Bus Educ Dev)
Oxford Brookes – BBC (Bus Mgt) (IB 30 pts)
Portsmouth – 280 pts (Fin Mgt Bus; Bus Mgt; Econ Mgt)
Roehampton – 280 pts (Bus Mgt Dig Media) (IB 25 pts)
Salford – ABB 280-320 pts (Bus Fin Mgt; Bus Mgt St; Bus Econ) (IB 27 pts)
South Wales – 280 pts (Bus Mgt; Bus Mgt (Top Up); Bus St)
Stirling – BBC (Bus St; Mgt; Mgt Sci) (IB 32 pts)
West London – 280 pts (Bus St; Bus St Fin; Bus St HR Mgt; Bus St Mark)
Winchester – 280-320 pts (Bus Mgt courses) (IB 26 pts)
Worcester – 280 pts (Bus courses) (IB 25 pts)

260 pts **Bangor** – 260-300 pts (Bus St courses; Admin Mgt; Mgt Acc)
Bath Spa – 260-300 pts (Bus Mgt (Mark); Bus Mgt HR Mgt; Bus Mgt courses)

Bolton – 260 pts (Bus Mgt; Bus Inf Sys)
BPP – BCC 260 pts (Bus Mgt Psy; Bus Mgt)
Coventry – BBC–BCC 260–280 pts (Bus St; Bus Mgt; Span Bus) (IB 28 pts)
Derby – 260 pts (Bus Mgt) (IB 28 pts)
Dundee – BCC (Bus Mgt) (IB 30 pts)
Edinburgh Napier – BCC 260 pts (Bus Mgt)
Edinburgh Queen Margaret – 260 pts (Bus Mgt) (IB 28 pts)
Glasgow Caledonian – BCC–CCC 260–240 pts (Bus St) (IB 24 pts)
Greenwich – 260 pts (Bus Admin; Bus Entre Innov; Bus Prchsg Sply Chn Mgt)
Heriot-Watt – BCC (Bus Mgt Ind Expnc)
Kingston – 260–280 pts (Pharmacol Bus)
Lincoln – 260 pts (Bus Mgt; Bus St; Mgt)
Liverpool John Moores – 260 pts (Bus Comm) (IB 28 pts)
Northampton – 260–300 pts (Bus Comp (Sys); Bus Entre; Bus St) (IB 24–25 pts)
Plymouth – 260 pts (Bus St; Bus Ent) (IB 26 pts)
Portsmouth – 260–300 pts (Law Bus; Bus Ent Dev)
Robert Gordon – BCC (Mgt) (IB 27 pts)
SRUC – BCC (Rur Bus Mgt)
Staffordshire – BCC (Bus Mgt)
Sunderland – 260 pts (Bus HR Mgt; App Mgt; Bus Mark Mgt; Bus Fin Mgt; Bus Mgt)
Westminster – BCC (Bus; Bus Mgt (Mark)) (IB 28 pts)

240 pts **Birmingham (UC)** – 240 pts (Hspty Bus Mgt) (IB 24 pts)
BPP – 240 pts (Bus Mgt Fin)
Bradford – 240 pts (Psy Mgt) (IB 24 pts)
Bradford (Coll Univ Centre) – 240 pts (Bus Admin; Bus St)
Buckingham – 240 pts (Bus Mgt courses; Bus Ent)
Canterbury Christ Church – 240 pts (Bus St; Bus Mgt) (IB 24 pts)
Central Lancashire – 240–280 pts (Bus St courses)
Chester – 240–280 pts (Bus Mgt; Bus; Bus Mgt Entre) (IB 26 pts)
Chichester – CCC (Bus St) (IB 26 pts)
Cumbria – 240 pts (Bus Mgt)
Edinburgh Napier – CCC 240 pts (Bus St)
Glasgow Caledonian – CCC 240 pts (Bus Mgt) (IB 24 pts)
Greenwich (Sch Mgt) – 240 pts (Law Mgt)
Kensington Bus (Coll) – 240 pts (Bus St)
Kingston – 240 pts (Bus Inf Tech) (IB 24 pts)
Leeds Trinity – 240–260 pts (Acc Bus)
London Met – 240 pts (Bus Admin; Bus Econ; Mgt)
London Regent's – CCC 240 pts (Glob Mgt) (IB 32 pts)
Manchester Met – 240–280 pts (Spo Mark Mgt) (IB 28 pts)
Middlesex – 240–280 pts (Bus Admin; Bus Mark)
Oldham (Univ Campus) – 240 pts (Bus Mgt)
Roehampton – 240 pts (Bus Mgt) (IB 24 pts)
Royal Agricultural Univ – 240 pts (Bus Mgt)
Southampton Solent – 240 pts (Bus Mgt)
Suffolk (Univ Campus) – 240–280 pts (Bus Mgt Fin; Bus Mgt Mark; Psy Bus Mgt; Bus Mgt)
Teesside – 240 pts (Bus Mgt; Bus Law)
Ulster – 240–280 pts (Bus courses; Bus St courses)
West Scotland – CCC (Bus)
York St John – 240–300 pts (Bus Mgt courses; Bus Mgt HR Mgt; Bus IT; Bus Mgt Ger)

220 pts **Harper Adams** – 220–260 pts (Bus Mgt Mark)
Leeds Beckett – 220 pts (Int Bus; Bus St; Bus Mgt) (IB 24 pts)
St Mary's – 220 pts (Bus Law; Mgt St) (IB 28 pts)
Wolverhampton – 220 pts (Bus Mgt)

200 pts **Anglia Ruskin** – 200–240 pts (Bus Econ; Bus Mgt)

Check **Chapter 4** when choosing your university and **Chapter 7** on how to read the subject tables.

Bedfordshire – 200 pts (Bus Mgt; Bus St) (IB 24 pts)
Blackburn (Coll) – 200 pts (Bus HR Mgt; Bus St; Bus Acc)
Bucks New – 200–240 pts (Bus Ent; Bus Mgt)
Croydon (Coll) – 200 pts (Bus Fin; Fash Des Bus; Bus Mark)
Doncaster (Coll Univ Centre) – 200 pts (Bus Mgt)
Glyndŵr – 200 pts (Bus Mgt)
London (Birk) – 200 pts (Mgt)
Middlesex – 200–300 pts (Bus Mgt)
Writtle (Coll) – 200–360 pts (Bus Mgt) (IB 28 pts)

180 pts **Abertay** – DDD (Mark Bus) (IB 24 pts)
Greenwich – 180–160 pts (Bus St) (IB 24 pts)
West Anglia (Coll) – 180 pts (Bus Mgt)

160 pts **Greenwich (Sch Mgt)** – 160 pts (Bus Mgt IT; Bus Mgt; Comp Sci Bus Inform)
Kaplan Holborn (Coll) – 160 pts (Bus Mgt)
London South Bank – 160 pts (Bus St; Bus Admin; Mgt Comb courses) (IB 24 pts)
Peterborough (Reg Coll) – 160 pts (Bus Mgt)
South Essex (Coll) – 160 pts (Bus St)
Trinity Saint David (Swansea) – 160 pts (Mgt Ldrshp; Bus; Bus Fin)

140 pts **Trinity Saint David** – 140–360 pts (Bus Mgt)

120 pts **Colchester (Inst)** – 120 pts (Mgt)
Croydon (Coll) – 120 pts (Bus Mgt)
Grimsby (Univ Centre) – 120 pts (Bus Mgt Acc; Bus courses)
Kaplan Holborn (Coll) – 120 pts (Bus Mgt Fin)
Llandrillo Cymru (Coll) – 120 pts (Mgt Bus) (IB 24 pts)
Norwich City (Coll) – 120 pts (Bus Mgt (Fin Acc); Bus Mgt)

80 pts **Greenwich (Sch Mgt)** – 80 pts (Mgt HR Mgt)
Sir Gâr (Coll) – 80 pts (Bus Mgt)
Trinity Saint David – 80 pts (Bus IT)

Open University – contact +44 (0)845 300 6090 **or** www.openuniversity.co.uk/you
(Bus St)

Alternative offers

See **Chapter 7** and **Appendix 1** for grades/UCAS Tariff points information for the International Baccalaureate, Scottish Highers/Advanced Highers, the Welsh Baccalaureate, the Irish Leaving Certificate, the Cambridge Pre-U Diploma, the Advanced Diploma and the Extended Project.

EXAMPLES OF FOUNDATION DEGREES IN THE SUBJECT FIELD

Askham Bryan (Coll); Bedfordshire; Bexley (Coll); Birmingham (UC); Blackburn (Coll); Blackpool and Fylde (Coll); Bolton; Bournemouth; Bournemouth and Poole (Coll); Bradford; Brighton; Bristol City (Coll); Bristol UWE; Central Lancashire; Central Nottingham (Coll); Colchester (Inst); Cornwall (Coll); Croydon (Coll); De Montfort; Doncaster (Coll Univ Centre); Duchy (Coll); Durham New (Coll); Ealing, Hammersmith and West London (Coll); East London; Edge Hill; Farnborough (CT); Gloucestershire; Glyndŵr; Greenwich; Grimsby (Univ Centre); Harper Adams; Hertfordshire; Kirklees (Coll); Knowsley (CmC); Lakes (Coll); Leeds Beckett; Liverpool John Moores; London South Bank; Manchester (Coll); Mid-Cheshire (Coll); Middlesex; NEW (Coll); Newcastle (Coll); North Lindsey (Coll); Northampton; Northbrook (Coll); Nottingham New (Coll); Plymouth; Riverside Halton (Coll); Royal Agricultural Univ; St Helens (Coll); Sheffield (Coll); Sheffield Hallam; Somerset (Coll); South Devon (Coll); South Essex (Coll); South Wales; Southampton Solent; Suffolk (Univ Campus); Wakefield (Coll); Warwickshire (Coll); Westminster Kingsway (Coll); Writtle (Coll); York (Coll).

CHOOSING YOUR COURSE (SEE ALSO CH.1)

Some course features

Bath (Bus Admin) A popular and highly respected sandwich course with placements in the UK and abroad.

Birmingham Courses are offered with a year in industry, in European Business and with Communications. The three-year specialist programme in Business Administration leads to a BCom degree and provides a window on the modern world of business. French, German, Italian, Japanese, Portuguese and Spanish and 12 engineering subjects are also offered with Business Studies.

Bristol UWE A large number of courses are offered in Business. These include Business Studies linked with Financial Management, Accountancy, Marketing, Tourism Management, Human Resources and Property. Also offered are International Business and Languages with placements in France, Germany or Spain and Business Mathematics combining business topics and mathematics. Modern language options support some of these courses.

Brunel Courses are offered in Business and Management, with an optional placement year and pathways in accountancy, e-business systems and marketing. Business Studies is also offered with Sports Sciences. There are also three-year and four-year (sandwich) courses in International Business, without a language requirement.

Kent Business Administration can be studied with a year in industry. Courses are also offered in Accounting and Management, Industrial Relations and Human Resource Management and in Business Studies or Business Economics.

Nottingham All business courses include a study of how organisations are run, their management styles and how societal, industry and environmental changes affect them. There are also opportunities to study abroad at partner universities in China and Malaysia.

Universities and colleges teaching quality See www.qaa.ac.uk; http://unistats.direct.gov.uk.

Top research universities and colleges (RAE 2008) (Business and Management Studies) Imperial London; Cambridge; Cardiff; Bath; London (King's); London LSE; Oxford; Lancaster; Warwick; Manchester; Strathclyde; Leeds; Nottingham; Aston; Loughborough; Sheffield.

Examples of sandwich degree courses Abertay; Aston; Bath; Bedfordshire; Birmingham (UC); Birmingham City; Bournemouth; Bradford; Brighton; Bristol UWE; Brunel; CAFRE; Cardiff Met (UWIC); Central Lancashire; Chester; City; Coventry; De Montfort; Derby; Glasgow Caledonian; Gloucestershire; Greenwich; Harper Adams; Hertfordshire; Huddersfield; Hull; Kingston; Liverpool John Moores; Loughborough; Manchester Met; Newcastle; Nottingham Trent; Oxford Brookes; Plymouth; Portsmouth; Royal Agricultural Univ; Sheffield Hallam; Staffordshire; Surrey; Teesside; Trinity Saint David (Swansea); Ulster; Warwickshire (Coll); West Scotland; Westminster; Wolverhampton.

ADMISSIONS INFORMATION

Number of applicants per place (approx) Abertay (Bus St) 4; Aberystwyth 3; Anglia Ruskin 5; Aston (Bus Mgt) 12, (Mgt) 5; Bangor 4; Bath (Bus Admin) 7; Birmingham 28; Birmingham (UC) 5; Blackpool and Fylde (Coll) 2; Bolton 3; Bournemouth 30; Bradford 12; Bristol 2; Brunel 12; Canterbury Christ Church 20; Cardiff 8; Central Lancashire 15; City (Bus St) 17, (Mgt Sys) 6; Colchester (Inst) 2; De Montfort (Bus Mgt) 5; Edge Hill 4; Glasgow Caledonian 18; Heriot-Watt 5; Hertfordshire 10; Huddersfield 5; Hull (Bus St) 19, (Mgt) 10; Hull (Coll) 3; Kent 30; Kingston 50; Leeds 27, (Mgt St) 16; Leeds Trinity 3; Liverpool 9; Llandrillo Cymru (Coll) 2; London (King's) 25, (Mgt Sci) 12; London (RH) 9; London LSE 18; London Met 10; London Regent's 25; London South Bank 4; Loughborough 5; Manchester Met (Bus St) 26; Middlesex 12; Newcastle 27, (Bus Mgt) 40; Northumbria 10; Oxford Brookes 40; Plymouth 4; Portsmouth 10, (Bus Admin) 7, (Bus St) 6; Robert Gordon 5; Salford (Bus St) 9, (Mgt Sci) 2; Southampton Solent 13; Strathclyde 12; Sunderland 20; Surrey (Bus Mgt) 6; Teesside (Bus St) 4; Trinity Saint David (Swansea) 7; Warwick 22; West London 4; West Scotland 5; Westminster 12; Winchester 4; Wolverhampton 7; York 6; York St John 3.

Advice to applicants and planning the UCAS personal statement There are many different kinds of businesses and any work experience is almost essential for these courses. This should be described in detail: for example, size of firm, turnover, managerial problems, sales and marketing aspects, customers' attitudes. Any special interests in business management should also be included, for example, personnel work, purchasing, marketing. Give details of travel or work experience abroad and, for international courses, language expertise and examples of leadership and organising skills. Reference can be made to any particular business topics you have studied in the *Financial Times*, *The Economist* and the business sections in the weekend press. Applicants need to be sociable, ambitious, team players. Say why you are interested in the course, identify your academic strengths, your personal strengths and interests. Check information on the websites of the Chartered Institute of Public Relations, the Chartered Institute of Marketing and the Chartered Institute of Personnel and Development. See **Appendix 3**; see also **Accountancy/Accounting**.

Misconceptions about this course **Aberystwyth** Students are unaware that the course addresses practical aspects of business. **Salford** (Mgt Sci) Students should appreciate that the courses are fairly mathematical. **York** A previous study of management, IT or languages at A-level is necessary.

Selection interviews **Yes** Birmingham City, Bradford, Coventry, Doncaster (Coll Univ Centre), Durham, Edge Hill, Essex, Euro Bus Sch London, Glasgow Caledonian, Hull, London Met, Middlesex, Northumbria, Nottingham Trent, Plymouth, Portsmouth, Robert Gordon, Roehampton, Sheffield Hallam, Sir Gâr (Coll), South Wales, Strathclyde, Swansea, Teesside, Trinity Saint David, West London, West Thames (Coll), York; **Some** Abertay, Aberystwyth, Anglia Ruskin, Bath, Bath Spa, Blackpool and Fylde (Coll), Brighton, Buckingham, Cardiff Met (UWIC), City, De Montfort, Derby (Int Bus), East Anglia, Greenwich, Kent (mature and Access students), Leeds, Lincoln, Liverpool John Moores, Manchester Met, Salford, Southampton, Staffordshire, Stirling, Sunderland, Warwick, Winchester, Wolverhampton; **No** Birmingham, Chichester, Dundee, Nottingham, West Scotland.

Interview advice and questions Any work experience you describe on the UCAS application probably will be the focus of questions which could include topics covering marketing, selling, store organisation and management and customer problems. Personal qualities are naturally important in a career in business, so be ready for such questions as: What qualities do you have which are suitable and important for this course? Describe your strengths and weaknesses. Why should we give you a place on this course? Is advertising fair? What qualities does a person in business require to be successful? What makes a good manager? What is a cash-flow system? What problems can it cause? How could supermarkets improve customer relations? See also **Chapter 6**. **Buckingham** Why Business? How do you see yourself in five years' time? Have you had any work experience? If so, discuss. **Wolverhampton** Mature students with no qualifications will be asked about their work experience.

Reasons for rejection (non-academic) Hadn't read the prospectus. Lack of communication skills. Limited commercial interest. Weak on numeracy and problem-solving. Lack of interview preparation (no questions). Lack of outside interests. Inability to cope with a year abroad. The candidate brought his parent who answered all the questions. See also **Marketing**. **Aberystwyth** Would have trouble fitting into the unique environment of Aberystwyth. Casual approach to learning. **Bournemouth** The Business Studies course is very popular. **Surrey** Hesitation about the period abroad.

AFTER-RESULTS ADVICE

Offers to applicants repeating A-levels **Higher** Bradford, Bristol UWE, Brunel, Greenwich, Hertfordshire, Kingston, Lancaster, Liverpool, Manchester Met, St Andrews, Sheffield, Strathclyde, Teesside; **Same** Abertay, Aberystwyth, Anglia Ruskin, Aston, Bath, Bath Spa, Birmingham City, Bolton, Bournemouth, Brighton, Brunel, Buckingham, Cardiff, Cardiff Met (UWIC), Chester, Chichester, De Montfort, Derby, Durham, East Anglia, East London, Glasgow, Gloucestershire, Harper Adams, Huddersfield, Hull, Kent, Leeds, Lincoln, Liverpool Hope, Liverpool John Moores, Loughborough, Newman, Northumbria, Oxford Brookes, Portsmouth, Robert Gordon, Roehampton, Royal Agricultural Univ, Salford, Sheffield Hallam, Staffordshire, Stirling, Suffolk (Univ Campus), Sunderland, Surrey, Trinity Saint David, Ulster, West London, West Scotland, Winchester, Wolverhampton, Worcester, York, York St John.

GRADUATE DESTINATIONS AND EMPLOYMENT (2011/12 HESA)
Business Studies graduates surveyed 12750 **Employed** 6985 **In voluntary employment** 245 **In further study** 2445 **Assumed unemployed** 1175

Management Sciences graduates surveyed 6840 **Employed** 4265 **In voluntary employment** 130 **In further study** 1150 **Assumed unemployed** 435

Career note The majority of graduates enter trainee management roles in business-related and administrative careers, many specialising in some of the areas listed in **Other degree subjects for**

consideration below. The main graduate destinations are in finance, property development, wholesale, retail and manufacturing.

OTHER DEGREE SUBJECTS FOR CONSIDERATION

Accountancy; Banking; Business Information Technology; E-Business; Economics; Estate Management; Finance; Hospitality Management; Housing Management; Human Resource Management; Insurance; Leisure Management; Logistics; Marketing; Public Administration; Retail Management; Sports Management; Surveying.

BUSINESS and MANAGEMENT COURSES (INTERNATIONAL and EUROPEAN)

(including **Business** and **Management Courses with Languages**; see also **Business and Management Courses, Business and Management Courses (Specialised), Hospitality and Event Management, Human Resource Management, Leisure and Recreation Management/Studies, Marketing, Retail Management, Tourism and Travel**)

Similar to Business and Management Courses, this subject area focuses on business but with more of an international theme. Studying or taking part in an industrial placement abroad is another higlight of this subject area.

Useful websites See **Business and Management Courses**.

NB The points totals shown to the left of the institutions are for ease of reference only. It must not be assumed that Tariff points are always used by institutions or that they can be substituted for an offer in grades. The level of an offer is not necessarily indicative of the quality of a course.

COURSE OFFERS INFORMATION

Subject requirements/preferences GCSE Mathematics and English often at grade A or B required. **AL** A language will be stipulated for most courses in this subject area. In some cases grades A, B or C may be required.

Your target offers and examples of courses provided by each institution

410 pts **Warwick** – AAAb–A*AA (Int Bus (Yr Abrd); Int Mgt (Yr Abrd)) (IB 38 pts)

380 pts **London (UCL)** – AAAe incl maths (Econ Bus E Euro St) (IB 38 pts HL 18 pts)

360 pts **Bath** – AAA/A*AB 360 pts (Int Mgt) (IB 38 pts)

Edinburgh – AAA–BBB 360–300 pts (Int Bus; Int Bus Fr/Ger/Span) (IB 37–34 pts HL 666–555)

Leeds – AAA 360 pts (Int Bus) (IB 36 pts HL 17 pts)

Newcastle – AAA–AAB (Int Bus Mgt) (IB 35–37 pts)

340 pts **Aston** – AAB–ABB 340–320 pts (Int Bus Fr/Ger/Span) (IB 34 pts HL 665)

Bath – AAB (Int Bus Span; Int Mgt Fr; Int Bus Ger) (IB 34–36 pts)

Birmingham – AAB (Int Bus Lang; Int Bus) (IB 35 pts)

Cardiff – AAB 340 pts (Bus Mgt (Int Mgt); Bus Mgt Euro Lang) (IB 35 pts)

Liverpool – AAB (Int Bus) (IB 35 pts)

London (King's) – AAB 340 pts (Fr Mgt) (IB 35 pts)

London (RH) – AAB–ABB 340–320 pts (Mgt Fr/Ger/Ital/Span; Mgt Int Bus) (IB 35–34 pts)

London (SOAS) – AAB (Int Mgt) (IB 36 pts HL 666)

Loughborough – AAB–AAA 340 pts (Int Bus) (IB 36 pts)

Manchester – AAB (Int Mgt; Int Mgt Am Bus St) (IB 35 pts)

Newcastle – AAB 340 pts (Mgt St Fr) (IB 34 pts)

Nottingham – AAB (Mgt St Fr/Ger/Span; Mgt Chin St) (IB 34 pts)

Reading – AAB (Int Mgt Bus Admin Fr/Ger/Ital) (HL 666)

Southampton – AAB–ABB 340–320 pts (Mgt Sci Fr/Ger/Span) (IB 34 pts)

Surrey – AAB (Bus Mgt Fr/Ger/Span) (IB 35 pts)

Sussex – AAB (Int Bus) (IB 35 pts)

320 pts **Bournemouth** – 320–340 pts (Int Bus St) (IB 32–33 pts HL 555)

Bradford – 320 pts (Int Bus Mgt)

Essex – ABB–BBB 320–300 pts (Int Bus Entre) (IB 33–32 pts)

Kent – ABB (Int Bus) (IB 33 pts)

Oxford Brookes – ABB (Int Bus Mgt) (IB 33 pts)

Queen's Belfast – ABB/BBBb (Int Bus Fr/Ger) (IB 32 pts)

Sheffield – ABB (Int Bus Mgt (Yr Abrd); Kor St Joint Hons) (IB 34 pts)

Swansea – ABB–BBB (Int Bus; Int Mgt Sci (Lang); Int Bus Mgt (St Abrd); Int Mgt Sci (St Abrd)) (IB 33 pts)

300 pts **Anglia Ruskin** – 300 pts (Int Bus (Berlin))

Brighton – BBB 300 pts (Int Bus)

Bristol UWE – 300 pts (Int Bus St)

Brunel – AAB–BBB 340–300 pts (Int Bus) (IB 35 pts)

Cardiff Met (UWIC) – 300 pts (Int Bus Mgt) (IB 24 pts)

Coventry – BBB 300 pts (Int Bus Mgt) (IB 28 pts)

Dundee – BBB–BCC (Int Bus; Int Bus Ger; Int Bus Mark)

Heriot-Watt – BBB (Int Bus Mgt Fr/Ger/Span) (IB 30 pts)

Hertfordshire – 300 pts (Int Mgt) (IB 30 pts)

Huddersfield – 300 pts (Int Bus)

Hull – BBB 300 pts (Bus Econ (Int)) (IB 30 pts)

Keele – ABC (Int Bus) (IB 26 pts)

Liverpool – BBB (Bus St Modn Lang) (IB 30 pts HL 6 lang)

London (QM) – BBB–ABB 300–320 pts (Russ Bus Mgt) (IB 32 pts)

Northumbria – 300 pts (Int Bus Mgt) (IB 26 pts)

Nottingham Trent – 300 pts (Int Bus Joint Hons) (IB 24 pts)

Portsmouth – 300 pts (Int Bus St) (IB 29 pts)

Sheffield Hallam – 300 pts (Int Bus St)

Westminster – BBB 300 pts (Int Bus Ger; Int Bus (Arbc/Chin/Fr/Russ/Span); Int Bus) (IB 28 pts)

280 pts **De Montfort** – 280 pts (Int Bus Glob) (IB 24 pts)

Gloucestershire – 280 pts (Bus Mgt (Int Bus))

Greenwich – 280 pts (Int Bus) (IB 24 pts)

Kingston – 280–320 pts (Int Bus; Int Bus Fr/Span) (IB 25 pts)

Manchester Met – 280 pts (Int Bus Lang (Fr/Ger/Ital/Span); Int Bus)

Portsmouth – 280 pts (Euro Bus) (IB 29 pts HL 16 pts incl 5 Fren/Ger/Span)

Roehampton – 280 pts (Int Bus) (IB 25 pts)

Sheffield Hallam – 280 pts (Int Htl Mgt; Tour Mgt (Int); Int Bus St Lang; Tour Hspty Bus Mgt (Int))

Staffordshire – BBC–BB (Int Bus Mgt) (IB 24 pts)

Stirling – BBC (Int Mgt St Intercult St; Int Mgt St Euro Lang Soty) (IB 32 pts)

260 pts **Central Lancashire** – 260–300 pts (Int Bus)

Derby – 260 pts (Int Spa Mgt) (IB 26 pts)

Hertfordshire – 260 pts (Int Bus; Bus Mand Chin/Euro Langs)

Lincoln – 260 pts (Int Bus Mgt)

Middlesex – 260–300 pts (Bus Mgt Fr/Ger/Ital/Span; Int Bus)

Robert Gordon – BCC (Int Bus Mgt) (IB 28 pts)

Salford – 260–300 pts (Int Bus) (IB 27 pts)

240 pts **Chester** – 240–280 pts (Int Bus) (IB 26 pts)

East London – 240 pts (Int Bus) (IB 24 pts)

Euro Bus Sch London – 240 pts (Int Bus; Int Bus Lang; Int Bus Span; Int Bus Mark Lang; Int Bus HR Mgt 2 Langs)

Glasgow Caledonian – CCC 240 pts (Int Bus) (IB 24 pts)

Hull – 240 pts (Int Bus)

London Met – 240 pts (Bus Mgt (Int Bus)) (IB 28 pts HL 15 pts)

London Regent's – CCC 240 pts (Glob Mgt; Int Bus)
Middlesex – 240 pts (Int Tour Mgt Span)
Plymouth – 240 pts (Int Bus; Int Bus (Fr); Int Bus Span) (IB 24 pts)
Salford – 240–260 pts (Bus St Int Bus Mgt) (IB 28 pts)
Southampton Solent – 240 pts (Int Bus Mgt)
Teesside – 240 pts (Int Mgt)
Ulster – CCC–BBC 240–280 pts (Bus Int Dev; Bus St Fr/Ger/Span) (IB 24 pts)
York St John – CCC 240–300 pts (Int Bus Mgt)

220 pts **Leeds Beckett** – 220 pts (Langs Int Bus) (IB 24 pts)
Wolverhampton – 220 pts (Int Bus Mgt)

200 pts **Anglia Ruskin** – 200–240 pts (Int Bus Strat) (IB 24 pts)
Bedfordshire – 200 pts (Bus St (Int)) (IB 24 pts)
Bucks New – 200–240 pts (Int Bus) (IB 24 pts)

Open University – contact +44 (0)845 300 6090 **or** www.openuniversity.co.uk/you (Bus St Fr/Span)

Alternative offers
See **Chapter 7** and **Appendix 1** for grades/UCAS Tariff points information for the International Baccalaureate, Scottish Highers/Advanced Highers, the Welsh Baccalaureate, the Irish Leaving Certificate, the Cambridge Pre-U Diploma, the Advanced Diploma and the Extended Project.

EXAMPLES OF FOUNDATION DEGREES IN THE SUBJECT FIELD
Askham Bryan (Coll); Bedfordshire; Bexley (Coll); Birmingham (UC); Blackburn (Coll); Blackpool and Fylde (Coll); Bolton; Bournemouth; Bradford; Brighton; Bristol City (Coll); Bristol UWE; Central Lancashire; Colchester (Inst); Cornwall (Coll); Croydon (Coll); De Montfort; Doncaster (Coll Univ Centre); Duchy (Coll); Durham New (Coll); Ealing, Hammersmith and West London (Coll); East London; Edge Hill; Farnborough (CT); Gloucestershire; Glyndŵr; Greenwich; Grimsby (Univ Centre); Harper Adams; Hertfordshire; Kirklees (Coll); Knowsley (CmC); Lakes (Coll); Leeds Beckett; Liverpool John Moores; London South Bank; Manchester (Coll); Mid-Cheshire (Coll); Middlesex; NEW (Coll); Newcastle (Coll); North Lindsey (Coll); Northampton; Northbrook (Coll); Nottingham New (Coll); Plymouth; Riverside Halton (Coll); Royal Agricultural Univ; St Helens (Coll); Sheffield (Coll); Sheffield Hallam; Somerset (Coll); South Devon (Coll); South Essex (Coll); South Wales; Southampton Solent; Suffolk (Univ Campus); Wakefield (Coll); Warwickshire (Coll); Westminster Kingsway (Coll); Writtle (Coll); York (Coll).

CHOOSING YOUR COURSE (SEE ALSO CH.1)
Some course features
Bath For students preparing for placements abroad, language tuition is provided in French, German, Greek, Russian, Spanish, Japanese and Mandarin Chinese.

Universities and colleges teaching quality See www.qaa.ac.uk; http://unistats.direct.gov.uk.

Top research universities and colleges (RAE 2008) See **Business and Management Courses**.

Examples of sandwich degree courses Anglia Ruskin; Aston; Bath; Bournemouth; Bradford; Brighton; Brunel; Cardiff Met (UWIC); De Montfort; Greenwich; Hertfordshire; Kingston; Leeds Beckett; Loughborough; Manchester Met; Middlesex; Northumbria; Nottingham Trent; Oxford Brookes; Plymouth; Portsmouth; Sheffield Hallam; Staffordshire; Teesside.

ADMISSIONS INFORMATION
Number of applicants per place (approx) Abertay (Bus St) 4; Aberystwyth 3; Anglia Ruskin 5; Aston (Int Bus) 6, (Int Bus Econ) 8; Bangor 4; Bath (Int Mgt Lang) 14; Birmingham 28; Birmingham (UC) 5; Blackpool and Fylde (Coll) 2; Bolton 3; Bradford 12; Bristol 28; Brunel 12; Canterbury Christ Church 20; Cardiff 8; Central Lancashire 15; Colchester (Inst) 2; Derby (Int Bus) 4; Edge Hill 4; Glasgow Caledonian 18; Heriot-Watt 5; Hertfordshire 10; Huddersfield 5; Hull (Scarborough) 3; Hull (Coll) 3; Kent 30; Kingston 50; Leeds 27; Leeds Trinity 3; Liverpool John Moores (Int Bus) 16; Llandrillo Cymru

(Coll) 2; London (King's) 25; London (RH) 9; London Met 10; London Regent's 25; London South Bank 4; Loughborough 5; Manchester Met (Int Bus) 8; Middlesex 12; Newcastle 27, (Int Bus Mgt) 25; Northumbria 10; Oxford Brookes 40; Plymouth 4; Portsmouth 10, (Int Bus) 5; Robert Gordon 5; Sheffield Hallam (Int Bus) 6; Southampton Solent 13; Strathclyde 12, (Int Bus Modn Lang) 6; Sunderland 20; Trinity Saint David (Swansea) 7; Warwick 22; West London 4; West Scotland 5; Westminster 12; Winchester 4; Wolverhampton 7; York 6; York St John 3.

Advice to applicants and planning the UCAS personal statement See **Business and Management Courses**.

Misconceptions about this course Aston (Int Bus Fr) Not two separate disciplines – the two subjects are integrated involving the study of language in a business and management context.

Selection interviews Yes Birmingham City, Bradford, Coventry, Doncaster (Coll Univ Centre), Durham, Edge Hill, Euro Bus Sch London, Glasgow Caledonian, Hull, London Met, Middlesex, Northumbria, Nottingham Trent, Plymouth, Robert Gordon, Roehampton, Sheffield Hallam, Sir Gâr (Coll), Strathclyde, Swansea, Teesside, Trinity Saint David, West London, West Thames (Coll), York; **Some** Abertay, Aberystwyth, Anglia Ruskin, Bath, Bath Spa, Blackpool and Fylde (Coll), Brighton, Buckingham, Cardiff Met (UWIC), Chichester, City, De Montfort, Derby (Int Bus), East Anglia, Greenwich, Kent (mature and Access students), Leeds, Lincoln, Liverpool John Moores, Manchester Met, Salford, Staffordshire, Stirling, Sunderland, Warwick, Winchester, Wolverhampton; **No** Birmingham.

Interview advice and questions See **Business and Management Courses**. **Wolverhampton** Mature students with no qualifications will be asked about their work experience.

Reasons for rejection (non-academic) See **Business and Management Courses**. **Bournemouth** The Business Studies course is very popular. **Surrey** Hesitation about the period abroad.

AFTER-RESULTS ADVICE
Offers to applicants repeating A-levels Higher Bradford, Bristol UWE, Brunel, Greenwich, Hertfordshire, Kingston, Lancaster, Liverpool, Manchester Met, St Andrews, Sheffield, Strathclyde, Teesside; **Same** Aberystwyth, Anglia Ruskin, Aston, Bath, Birmingham City, Bournemouth, Brighton, Buckingham, Cardiff, Cardiff Met (UWIC), Chester, Chichester, De Montfort, Derby, Durham, East Anglia, Gloucestershire, Huddersfield, Hull, Kent, Leeds, Lincoln, Liverpool Hope, Liverpool John Moores, Loughborough, Northumbria, Oxford Brookes, Robert Gordon, Roehampton, Royal Agricultural Univ, Salford, Sheffield Hallam, Staffordshire, Stirling, Suffolk (Univ Campus), Sunderland, Surrey, Ulster, West London, Winchester, Wolverhampton, Worcester, York, York St John.

GRADUATE DESTINATIONS AND EMPLOYMENT (2011/12 HESA)
See **Business and Management Courses**.

Career note See **Business and Management Courses**.

OTHER DEGREE SUBJECTS FOR CONSIDERATION
Accountancy; Banking; Business Information Technology; E-Business; Economics; Estate Management; Finance; Hospitality Management; Housing Management; Human Resource Management; Insurance; Leisure Management; Logistics; Marketing; Public Administration; Retail Management; Sports Management; Surveying.

BUSINESS and MANAGEMENT COURSES (SPECIALISED)

(including **Advertising, E-Commerce, Entrepreneurship, Operations Management, Public Relations** and **Publishing**; see also **Business and Management Courses, Business and Management Courses (International and European), Hospitality and Event Management, Human Resource Management, Leisure and Recreation Management/Studies, Marketing, Retail Management, Tourism and Travel**)

This subject table contains courses that are business and management related but which allow students to focus on business within a particular area, such as agriculture, media, extreme sports or leisure and recreation, to give a few examples.

Useful websites See **Business and Management Courses**.

NB The points totals shown to the left of the institutions are for ease of reference only. It must not be assumed that Tariff points are always used by institutions or that they can be substituted for an offer in grades. The level of an offer is not necessarily indicative of the quality of a course.

COURSE OFFERS INFORMATION

Subject requirements/preferences GCSE Mathematics and English often at grade A or B required. **AL** Mathematics required for some courses. In some cases grades A, B or C may be required. (Publ) English required for some courses.

Your target offers and examples of courses provided by each institution

380 pts London (UCL) – AAAe–ABBe (Chem Mgt St) (IB 34–38 pts HL 16–18 pts)
Southampton – A*AA 380 pts (Aero Astnaut (Eng Mgt)) (IB 38 pts HL 18 pts)

360 pts Edinburgh – AAA–ABB 360–320 pts (Ecol Env Sci Mgt) (IB 37–32 pts)
Ulster – AAA 360 pts (Comm Adv Mark) (IB 27 pts)

340 pts Cardiff – AAB 340 pts (Bus Mgt (Log Ops)) (IB 35 pts)
Lancaster – AAB (Adv Mark; Euro Amer Mgt) (IB 35 pts HL 16 pts)
Leeds – AAB 340 pts (Env Bus) (IB 35 pts)
London (SOAS) – AAB (S E As St Intl Mgt)
Manchester – AAB (Tex Des Des Mgt; Mgt Mark Fash Tex) (IB 35 pts)
Newcastle – AAB–ABB 320–340 pts (Agri Bus Mgt) (IB 35 pts)
Warwick – AAB (Eng Bus Mgt) (IB 36 pts HL 5 maths phys)

320 pts Bournemouth – 320 pts (Fin Bus) (IB 32 pts)
Essex – ABB–BBB (Lat Am St Bus Mgt) (IB 32–30 pts)
London (Birk) – ABB 320 pts (Env Mgt)
Loughborough – ABB (Inf Mgt Bus St) (IB 34 pts)
Northumbria – ABB 320 pts (Adv Mgt)
Nottingham Trent – 320 pts (Fash Mgt)
Reading – ABB–BBB 320–300 pts (Fd Sci Bus)

300 pts Bournemouth – 300 pts (Des Bus Mgt)
East Anglia – BBB (Cr-Cult Comm Bus Mgt) (IB 31 pts)
Heriot-Watt – BBB 300 pts (Bus Fin) (IB 29 pts)
Hertfordshire – (Mus Ent Ind Mgt)
Huddersfield – 300 pts (PR)
Loughborough – 300 pts (Pub Engl) (IB 32 pts HL 5 Engl)
Newcastle – BBB 300 pts (Frm Bus Mgt) (IB 28–30 pts)
Royal Agricultural Univ – 300 pts (Rur Lnd Mgt)
Sheffield Hallam – BBB 300 pts (Bus Fin Mgt)

280 pts Arts London – (PR)
Arts London (CFash) – 280 pts +portfolio (Fash Mgt)
Bournemouth – 280–300 pts (PR) (IB 30–31 pts HL 555)
Bucks New – 280 pts (Int Ftbl Bus) (IB 24 pts)

Cardiff Met (UWIC) – 280 pts (Food Prod Mgt)
Coventry – BBC–BCC 280–260 pts (Adv Bus; Disas Mgt) (IB 28–29 pts)
De Montfort – 280 pts (Adv; Mark Mgt)
Harper Adams – 280 pts (Agric Frm Bus Mgt)
Huddersfield – 280 pts (Adv Mark Comm; Adv Media)
Kingston – 280 pts (Web Dev Bus)
Leeds Beckett – 280 pts (Spo Bus Mgt) (IB 25 pts)
Liverpool John Moores – 280 pts (Marit Bus Mgt)
London (Royal Central Sch SpDr) – BBC 280 pts (Thea Prac Stg Mgt; Thea Prac Tech Prod
  Mgt)
Loughborough – 280 pts (Air Trans Mgt) (IB 30 pts)
Middlesex – 280 pts (Adv PR Media; Mus Bus Arts Mgt)
Nottingham Trent – 280 pts (Quant Surv Constr Commer Mgt)
Oxford Brookes – BBC–BCC 280–260 pts (Quant Surv Commer Mgt) (IB 30–31 pts)
Plymouth – 280 pts (Marit Bus Log; Marit Bus Marit Law) (IB 25 pts)
Sheffield Hallam – 280 pts (Tour Mgt (Int))
Ulster – 280 pts (Eng Mgt)
Worcester – 280 pts (Bus Mark PR)

260 pts **Central Lancashire** – 260–300 pts (PR)
Coventry – BCC–BBC 260–280 pts (Adv Media; Disas Mgt Emer Plan) (IB 28–29 pts)
Derby – 260–280 pts (Cntry Mgt; Int Spa Mgt; Mark Adv Mgt; Tour Mgt)
Edinburgh Queen Margaret – BCC (PR Media; PR Mark) (IB 28 pts)
Glasgow Caledonian – BCC (Spo Mgt)
Huddersfield – BCC 260 pts (Air Trans Log Mgt) (IB 26 pts)
Leeds Beckett – 260 pts (PR) (IB 26 pts)
Liverpool John Moores – 260 pts (Mgt Trans Log)
Northampton – 260–300 pts (Bus Entre) (IB 24 pts)
Portsmouth – 260–300 pts (Bus Ent Dev; Bus Ent Sys)
Robert Gordon – BCC 260 pts (Fash Mgt) (IB 28 pts)
Royal Agricultural Univ – 260 pts (Agric (Frm Mechn Mgt))
Sheffield Hallam – 260 pts (PR)
Sunderland – 260 pts (PR; Tour Mgt)
West London – 260 pts (Airln Airpt Mgt)

240 pts **Arts London (CFash)** – 240 pts +portfolio (Fash PR)
Birmingham (UC) – 240 pts (Culn Arts Mgt; Fd Consum Mgt; Spa Mgt) (IB 24 pts)
Canterbury Christ Church – CCC 240 pts (Bus Fin) (IB 24 pts)
Central Lancashire – 240–300 pts (Adv; Fire Sfty Risk Mgt)
Cumbria – 240 pts (Bus Entre Comp)
East London – 240 pts (Adv) (IB 24 pts HL 15 pts)
Edinburgh Napier – CCC 240 pts (Econ Mgt)
Glasgow Caledonian – CCC (Risk Mgt)
Leeds Beckett – 240 pts (Spo Evnt Mgt) (IB 24 pts)
London Met – 240 pts (Adv Mark Comm; Arts Mgt Joint Hons; Bus Mgt (Avn Mgt))
London South Bank – CCC 240 pts (Arts Fstvl Mgt)
Manchester Met – 240–280 pts (Adv Mgt Brnd Mgt; Evnts Mgt) (IB 26–29 pts)
Nottingham Trent – 240 pts (Constr Mgt)
Plymouth – 240 pts (Cru Mgt) (IB 24 pts)
Royal Agricultural Univ – 240 pts (Bus Mgt (Int Fd Agri Bus))
St Mark and St John – 240 pts (Int Spo Evnt Mgt)
Sheffield Hallam – 240–280 pts (Hspty Bus Mgt; IT Mgt)
Southampton Solent – 240 pts (Evnts Mgt; Cru Ind Mgt; Fash Mgt Mark; Fd Mgt Prom;
  Advntr Extrm Spo Mgt)
Sparsholt (Coll) – 240 pts (Aquacult Fish Mgt)

230 pts **CEM** – 230 pts (Est Mgt)
220 pts **Derby** – 220–300 pts (Bus Mgt Thea Sci) (IB 26 pts)

Edge Hill – 220–260 pts (PR)
Glyndŵr – 220 pts (Fest Evnt Mgt)
Staffordshire – 220 pts (Adv Brnd Mgt)
Warwickshire (Coll) – 220 pts (Eqn Bus Mgt)

200 pts Bedfordshire – 200 pts (PR; Adv Mark Comm)
Birmingham (UC) – 200 pts (Ent Mgt)
Bucks New – 200–240 pts (Airln Mgt; Airpt Mgt; Airln Airpt Mgt)
Coventry – 200 pts (Bus Inf Tech) (IB 24 pts)
Salford – 200 pts incl art C (Adv Des)
Southampton Solent – 200 pts (Bus Inf Tech)
West London – 200 pts (Culn Art Mgt; Adv; PR)

180 pts Abertay – DDD 180 pts (Fin Bus)
West Scotland – BC (Eng Mgt)

160 pts Greenwich (Sch Mgt) – 160 pts (Bus Mgt (Trav Tour))
Liverpool (LIPA) – 160–280 pts (Mus Thea Enter Mgt)
SRUC – CC (Rur Bus Mgt (Fd))
Trinity Saint David (Swansea) – 160–360 pts (Int Trav Tour Mgt; Tour Mgt; Spo Mgt; Evnt
Mgt; Mtrspo Mgt)
UHI – CC–AA (Glf Mgt)

120 pts Colchester (Inst) – 120 pts (Constr Mgt (Site Mgt))
80 pts Greenwich (Sch Mgt) – 80–120 pts (Oil Gas Mgt) (IB 24 pts)
60 pts UHI – D (Mus Bus)

Open University – contact +44 (0)845 300 6090 **or** www.openuniversity.co.uk/you
(Bus Law)

Alternative offers
See **Chapter 7** and **Appendix 1** for grades/UCAS Tariff points information for the International
Baccalaureate, Scottish Highers/Advanced Highers, the Welsh Baccalaureate, the Irish Leaving
Certificate, the Cambridge Pre-U Diploma, the Advanced Diploma and the Extended Project.

EXAMPLES OF FOUNDATION DEGREES IN THE SUBJECT FIELD
Askham Bryan (Coll); Bedfordshire; Bexley (Coll); Birmingham (UC); Blackburn (Coll); Blackpool and
Fylde (Coll); Bolton; Bournemouth; Bradford; Brighton; Bristol City (Coll); Bristol UWE; Central Lancashire;
Colchester (Inst); Cornwall (Coll); Croydon (Coll); De Montfort; Doncaster (Coll Univ Centre); Duchy (Coll);
Durham New (Coll); Ealing, Hammersmith and West London (Coll); East London; Edge Hill; Exeter (Coll);
Farnborough (CT); Gloucestershire; Glyndŵr; Greenwich; Grimsby (Univ Centre); Harper Adams;
Hertfordshire; Kirklees (Coll); Knowsley (CmC); Lakes (Coll); Leeds Beckett; Liverpool John Moores;
London South Bank; Manchester (Coll); Mid-Cheshire (Coll); Middlesex; NEW (Coll); Newcastle (Coll);
North Lindsey (Coll); Northampton; Northbrook (Coll); Nottingham New (Coll); Plymouth; Riverside
Halton (Coll); Royal Agricultural Univ; St Helens (Coll); Sheffield (Coll); Sheffield Hallam; Somerset (Coll);
South Devon (Coll); South Essex (Coll); South Wales; Southampton Solent; Suffolk (Univ Campus); Truro
(Coll); Wakefield (Coll); Warwickshire (Coll); Westminster Kingsway (Coll); Writtle (Coll); York (Coll).

CHOOSING YOUR COURSE (SEE ALSO CH.1)
Some course features
Birmingham (UC) Marketing is offered with Hospitality, Events and Tourism. Salon Business and Spa
Management are also offered.
Manchester Management is offered alongside Accounting and Finance, HR, Innovation, Sustainability
and Entrepreneurship, International Business Economics, International Studies, Leisure and Marketing.
St Mark and St John There are minor combined courses with Management in either Applied Sports
Science or Outdoor Adventure. A course in Applied Professional Studies (Leadership and Management)
is also available.
Winchester (Bus Mgt) Optional pathway to BA in Business Management with Public Service
Management. Modules include quality management and customer care, local government, public
administration and European culture and institutions.

Check **Chapter 4** when choosing your university and **Chapter 7** on how to read the subject tables.

Universities and colleges teaching quality See www.qaa.ac.uk; http://unistats.direct.gov.uk.

Top research universities and colleges (RAE 2008) See **Business and Management Courses**.

Examples of sandwich degree courses Abertay; Aberystwyth; Aston; Bath; Birmingham (UC); Birmingham City; Bournemouth; Bradford; Brighton; Bristol UWE; Brunel; Central Lancashire; City; Coventry; De Montfort; Edinburgh Napier; Glasgow Caledonian; Gloucestershire; Greenwich; Harper Adams; Hertfordshire; Huddersfield; Hull; Kingston; Lancaster; Leeds Beckett; Lincoln; Liverpool John Moores; London (QM); Loughborough; Manchester; Manchester Met; Middlesex; Newcastle; Northumbria; Nottingham Trent; Oxford Brookes; Plymouth; Portsmouth; Reading; Royal Agricultural Univ; Sheffield Hallam; Southampton Solent; Staffordshire; Surrey; Teesside; Trinity Saint David (Swansea); Ulster; Warwickshire (Coll); West Scotland; Westminster; Wolverhampton.

ADMISSIONS INFORMATION

Number of applicants per place (approx) Abertay (Bus St) 4; Aberystwyth 3; Anglia Ruskin 5; Aston (Bus Mgt) 12, (Int Bus) 6, (Mgt) 5, (Int Bus Econ) 8; Bangor 4; Bath (Bus Admin) 7, (Int Mgt Lang) 14; Birmingham 28; Birmingham (UC) 5; Blackpool and Fylde (Coll) 2; Bolton 3; Bournemouth (PR) 10; Bradford 12; Bristol 28; Brunel 12; Canterbury Christ Church 20; Cardiff 8; Central Lancashire 15; Colchester (Inst) 2; Edge Hill 4; Edinburgh Napier (Pub) 7; Glasgow Caledonian 18; Heriot-Watt 5; Hertfordshire 10; Huddersfield 5; Hull (Coll) 3; Kent 30; Kingston 50; Leeds 27; Leeds Trinity 3; Llandrillo Cymru (Coll) 2; London (King's) 25; London (RH) 9; London Met 10; London Regent's 25; London South Bank 4; Loughborough 5; Middlesex 12; Newcastle 27; Northumbria 10; Oxford Brookes 40; Plymouth 4; Portsmouth 10; Robert Gordon 5; Southampton Solent 13; Strathclyde 12; Sunderland 20; Trinity Saint David (Swansea) 7; Warwick 22; West London 4; West Scotland 5; Westminster 12; Winchester 4; Wolverhampton 7; York 6; York St John 3.

Advice to applicants and planning the UCAS personal statement See **Business and Management Courses**.

Misconceptions about this course Loughborough (Pub Engl) That this is a course in Journalism: it is not!

Selection interviews Yes Birmingham City, Bradford, Coventry, Doncaster (Coll Univ Centre), Durham, Edge Hill, Euro Bus Sch London, Glasgow Caledonian, Hull, London Met, Middlesex, Northumbria, Nottingham Trent, Plymouth, Robert Gordon, Roehampton, Sheffield Hallam, Sir Gâr (Coll), Strathclyde, Swansea, Teesside, Trinity Saint David, West London, West Thames (Coll), York; **Some** Abertay, Aberystwyth, Anglia Ruskin, Bath, Bath Spa, Blackpool and Fylde (Coll), Brighton, Buckingham, Cardiff Met (UWIC), Chichester, City, De Montfort, Derby (Int Bus), East Anglia, Greenwich, Kent (mature and Access students), Leeds, Lincoln, Liverpool John Moores, Manchester Met, Salford, Staffordshire, Stirling, Sunderland, Warwick, Winchester, Wolverhampton; **No** Birmingham.

Interview advice and questions See **Business and Management Courses**. **Loughborough** (Pub Engl) No tests at interview. We seek students with an interest in information issues within society.

Reasons for rejection (non-academic) See **Business and Management Courses**. **Bournemouth** The Business Studies course is very popular.

AFTER-RESULTS ADVICE

Offers to applicants repeating A-levels Higher Bradford, Bristol UWE, Brunel, Greenwich, Hertfordshire, Kingston, Lancaster, Liverpool, Manchester Met, Sheffield, Strathclyde, Teesside; **Same** Aberystwyth, Anglia Ruskin, Aston, Bath, Birmingham City, Bournemouth, Brighton, Buckingham, Cardiff, Cardiff Met (UWIC), Chester, Chichester, De Montfort, Derby, Durham, East Anglia, Gloucestershire, Huddersfield, Hull, Kent, Leeds, Lincoln, Liverpool Hope, Liverpool John Moores, Loughborough, Northumbria, Oxford Brookes, Robert Gordon, Roehampton, Royal Agricultural Univ, Salford, Sheffield Hallam, Staffordshire, Stirling, Suffolk (Univ Campus), Sunderland, Surrey, Ulster, West London, Winchester, Wolverhampton, Worcester, York, York St John.

GRADUATE DESTINATIONS AND EMPLOYMENT (2011/12 HESA)
See **Business and Management Courses**.

Career note See **Business and Management Courses**.

OTHER DEGREE SUBJECTS FOR CONSIDERATION
Accountancy; Banking; Business Information Technology; E-Business; Economics; Estate Management; Finance; Hospitality Management; Housing Management; Human Resource Management; Insurance; Leisure Management; Logistics; Marketing; Public Administration; Retail Management; Sports Management; Surveying.

CELTIC, IRISH, SCOTTISH and WELSH STUDIES

(including Cornish Studies and Gaelic Studies)

Irish, Scottish, Gaelic, Welsh, Breton, Manx, Cornish, Gaulish and Celtiberian languages are all included in this subject area. Courses may also include the history and civilisation of the Celtic peoples.

Useful websites www.webarchive.org.uk; new.wales.gov.uk; www.bbc.co.uk/wales; www.daltai.com; www.eisteddfod.org.uk; www.digitalmedievalist.com; www.gaelic-scotland.co.uk.

NB The points totals shown to the left of the institutions are for ease of reference only. It must not be assumed that Tariff points are always used by institutions or that they can be substituted for an offer in grades. The level of an offer is not necessarily indicative of the quality of a course.

COURSE OFFERS INFORMATION
Subject requirements/preferences **GCSE** A foreign language or Welsh may be required. **AL** Welsh may be required for some courses.

Your target offers and examples of courses provided by each institution
380 pts **Cambridge** – A*AA (A-Sxn Nrs Celt) (IB 40–41 pts HL 776)
360 pts **Edinburgh** – AAA–BBB 360–300 pts (Scot Hist; Engl Scot Lit; Scot Lit) (IB 40–34 pts HL 666–555)
  Oxford – AAA (Celt courses) (IB 38–40 pts)
  St Andrews – AAA (Phil Scot Hist; Scot Hist courses) (IB 36 pts)
340 pts **Edinburgh** – AAB–BBB 340–300 pts (Celt Arch; Celt Scot Hist; Celtic Engl Lit; Celt; Scot St; Celt Scot Lit; Scot Ethnol; Celt Ling) (IB 36–34 pts HL 665–555)
  Glasgow – AAB (Scot Lit; Celt St courses) (IB 34 pts)
  Liverpool – AAB (Ir St Joint Hons) (IB 33 pts)
320 pts **Cardiff** – ABB 320 pts (Sociol Welsh; Welsh)
  Glasgow – ABB (Scot Hist; Celt Civ; Gael Joint Hons) (IB 34 pts)
  Liverpool – ABB (Ir St) (IB 33 pts)
300 pts **Aberdeen** – BBB (Celt Civ; Celt St; Engl Scot Lit; Celt Civ Engl; Gael St)
  Aberystwyth – 300 pts (Hist Welsh Hist) (IB 29 pts)
  Queen's Belfast – BBB/BBCb (Irish Celt St)
  Swansea – BBB (Int Rel Welsh; Welsh courses)
280 pts **Stirling** – BBC (Scot Hist) (IB 32 pts)
  Ulster – BBC 280 pts (Irish Hist Soc; Dr Ir)
260 pts **Aberystwyth** – 260 pts (Celt St; Ir Joint Hons; Welsh courses) (IB 24 pts)
  Bangor – 260–300 pts (Welsh Hist)
  Cardiff Met (UWIC) – 260 pts (Educ St Welsh)
  Ulster – BCC 260 pts (Ir Mus; Ir Lang Lit; Ir courses) (IB 24 pts)
240 pts **Ulster** – CCC 240 pts (Sociol Ir) (IB 24 pts HL 12 pts)
200 pts **South Wales** – 200–240 pts (Welsh; Welsh Educ)
160 pts **UHI** – CC 160 pts (Gael Trad Mus; Gael Media St; Scot Cult St; Scot Hist; Gael Dev; Scot Hist Arch)

Check **Chapter 4** when choosing your university and **Chapter 7** on how to read the subject tables.

Alternative offers
See **Chapter 7** and **Appendix 1** for grades/UCAS Tariff points information for the International Baccalaureate, Scottish Highers/Advanced Highers, the Welsh Baccalaureate, the Irish Leaving Certificate, the Cambridge Pre-U Diploma, the Advanced Diploma and the Extended Project.

CHOOSING YOUR COURSE (SEE ALSO CH.1)
Some course features
Aberystwyth There are beginners' courses for those with no previous knowledge of Welsh or Celtic languages. (Welsh Celt Langs) One or more Celtic languages, together with Welsh, are studied, with a semester spent in Brittany or Ireland.
Bangor (Welsh Hist Arch) The course focuses on the development of Wales over the centuries, the changing nature of society and settlements, and the historical context of contemporary Wales.
Edinburgh In addition to studying the cultures of Ireland and Wales, Scottish Gaelic is offered on the course in Celtic Studies.
Queen's Belfast (Ir Celt) The course focuses on modern Irish language and literature and contemporary Irish culture and society, but also provides a study of Old and Middle Irish, Scottish Gaelic, Welsh and Cornish. Students spend at least six weeks in the Gaeltacht.
UHI The only degree in Scotland delivered entirely through Gaelic.

Universities and colleges teaching quality See www.qaa.ac.uk; http://unistats.direct.gov.uk.

Top research universities and colleges (RAE 2008) (Celtic studies) Cambridge; Ulster; Aberystwyth; Swansea; Cardiff; Glasgow; Bangor; Edinburgh.

ADMISSIONS INFORMATION
Number of applicants per place (approx) Aberystwyth 6; Bangor 8; Cambridge 2; Cardiff 2; Exeter 5; Swansea 7.

Advice to applicants and planning the UCAS personal statement Interests in this field largely develop through literature, museum visits or archaeology which should be fully described in the UCAS application.

Selection interviews **Yes** Aberystwyth, Cardiff Met (UWIC).

Interview advice and questions Past questions have included: Why do you want to study this subject? What specific areas of Celtic culture interest you? What do you expect to gain by studying unusual subjects? See **Chapter 6**.

AFTER-RESULTS ADVICE
Offers to applicants repeating A-levels **Higher** Glasgow (AAA); **Same** Aberystwyth, Bangor, Cardiff, Swansea.

GRADUATE DESTINATIONS AND EMPLOYMENT (2011/12 HESA)
Celtic Studies graduates surveyed 170 **Employed** 50 **In voluntary employment** 0 **In further study** 65 **Assumed unemployed** 5

Career note See **Combined Courses** and **Languages**.

OTHER DEGREE SUBJECTS FOR CONSIDERATION
Anthropology; Archaeology; History.

CHEMISTRY

(see also **Biochemistry, Engineering (Chemical), Pharmacy and Pharmaceutical Sciences**)

There is a shortage of applicants for this subject despite the fact that it is the basis of a wide range of careers in the manufacturing industries. These focus on such areas as pharmaceuticals, medicine, veterinary science and health, agriculture, petroleum, cosmetics, plastics, the food industry, colour chemistry and aspects of the environment such as pollution and recycling.

Useful websites www.rsc.org; www.chem.ox.ac.uk/vrchemistry.

NB The points totals shown to the left of the institutions are for ease of reference only. It must not be assumed that Tariff points are always used by institutions or that they can be substituted for an offer in grades. The level of an offer is not necessarily indicative of the quality of a course.

COURSE OFFERS INFORMATION

Subject requirements/preferences GCSE English, mathematics/science subjects usually required. A/B grades often stipulated by popular universities. **AL** Two science subjects including chemistry required.

Your target offers and examples of courses provided by each institution

380 pts **Cambridge** – A*AA (Nat Sci (Chem)) (IB 40–41 pts HL 776)

Durham – A*AA 380 pts (Chem) (IB 38 pts)

Imperial London – A*AA–AAA (Chem Fr/Ger/Span Sci; Chem Medcnl Chem; Chem Mol Phys; Chem courses) (IB 38 pts HL 7 chem 6 maths)

London (UCL) – AAAe–ABBe (Chem; Chem Maths; Chem Mgt St) (IB 34–38 pts HL 16–18 pts)

Oxford – A*AA (Chem) (IB 38–40 pts)

360 pts **Bristol** – AAA–AAB 360–340 pts (Chem) (IB 37–35 pts HL 666)

Edinburgh – AAA–ABB 360–320 pts (Chem Env Sust Chem; Medcnl Biol Chem; Cheml Phys) (IB 37–32 pts HL 555)

London (UCL) – AAA–ABB (Chem Euro Lang; Cheml Phys; Medcnl Chem) (IB 34–38 pts HL 16–18 pts)

Nottingham – AAA–ABB 320–360 pts (Chem; Chem Eng Env Eng (Yr Ind); Medcnl Biol Chem) (IB 36–32 pts)

Southampton – AAA–ABB 360–320 pts (Ocn Chem; Chem Maths; Chem courses; Chem Medcnl Sci) (IB 34 pts HL 18 pts)

York – AAA–ABB 320–360 pts (Chem; Chem Biol Medcnl Chem; Chem Mgt Ind; Chem Res Env) (IB 32–36 pts)

340 pts **Bath** – AAB 340 pts (Chem Educ; Chem courses) (IB 35 pts HL 6 chem 55)

Birmingham – AAB–ABB 340–320 pts (Chem; Chem Modn Lang; Chem Pharmacol) (IB 32–36 pts)

East Anglia – AAB incl chem (Biol Medcnl Chem MChem; Foren Invest Chem MChem) (IB 33 pts HL 6 chem)

London (King's) – AAB (Chem Biomed) (IB 35 pts HL 665 incl chem maths)

Nottingham – AAB (Bioch Biol Chem; Chem Mol Phys) (IB 34 pts)

St Andrews – AAB (Chem; Chem Medcnl Chem) (IB 35–37 pts)

Sheffield – AAB (Cheml Phys) (IB 35 pts)

Surrey – AAB (Chem Foren Invstg; Medcnl Chem) (IB 35 pts)

Warwick – AAB (Chem Mgt; Chem Medcnl Chem; Chem) (IB 36 pts)

320 pts **Aberdeen** – ABB–BBB (Biomed Mat Chem; Chem Off Ind; Env Chem)

Brighton – ABB (Pharml Cheml Sci) (IB 34 pts)

Cardiff – ABB–BBB 320–300 pts (Chem)

East Anglia – ABB incl chem (Biol Medcnl Chem; Chem) (IB 32 pts HL 5 chem +sci/maths)

Edinburgh – ABB–AAA incl chem maths 320–360 pts (Chem Mat Chem) (IB 37–32 pts)

Glasgow – ABB (Chem; Chem Medcnl Chem) (IB 32 pts)

Leeds – ABB (Chem Phys; Chem Analyt Chem; Chem Col Sci; Medcnl Chem; Chem Joint Hons; Chem courses) (IB 34 pts HL 6 chem)

Check **Chapter 4** when choosing your university and **Chapter 7** on how to read the subject tables.

Leicester – ABB (Chem; Chem Foren Sci) (IB 32 pts)
Liverpool – ABB (Medcnl Chem; Chem; Chem (Yr Ind); Chem Nanotech) (IB 33 pts HL 6 chem)
Loughborough – ABB–BBB 320 pts (Medcnl Pharml Chem) (IB 32–34 pts)
Manchester – ABB (Chem; Chem Foren Analyt Chem; Chem Medcnl Chem) (IB 33 pts)
Newcastle – ABB 320 pts (Chem (Ind Yr); Chem Medcnl Chem; Chem; Chem MChem) (IB 34 pts HL 6 chem)
Reading – ABB–BBB (Chem courses)
Sheffield – ABB (Chem) (IB 33 pts)
Strathclyde – ABB (Chem Teach) (IB 34 pts)
Surrey – ABB (Chem) (IB 35 pts)
Sussex – ABB (Chem) (IB 34 pts HL 5 chem)
Warwick – ABB incl chem 320 pts (Biomed Chem) (IB 34 pts)

300 pts Aberdeen – BBB (Chem; Medcnl Chem)
Aston – BBB–ABB 300–320 pts (App Chem; Chem courses)
Birmingham – ABB–BBB (Chem Biorg Chem)
Bradford – 300 pts (Chem) (IB 28 pts)
Dundee – BBB (Biol Chem Drug Dscvry) (IB 30 pts)
East Anglia – BBB (Biol Chem) (IB 31 pts)
Heriot-Watt – BBB (Chem Mat; Chem Bioch; Chem courses) (IB 29 pts)
Kent – 300 pts (Foren Chem) (IB 33 pts)
Leicester – BBB (Pharml Chem) (IB 32 pts HL 5 chem)
London (QM) – 300 pts (Pharml Chem; Chem) (IB 32 pts)
Loughborough – 300–320 pts (Chem; Chem Analyt Chem; Chem MChem) (IB 32–34 pts)
Plymouth – 300 pts (Chem) (IB 28 pts)
Queen's Belfast – BBB–BBCd (Chem; Chem Euro; Medcnl Chem; Chem Foren Analys)

280 pts Huddersfield – 280 pts (Chem courses)
Hull – 280–300 pts incl 100 pts from chem (Chem) (IB 30 pts HL chem)
Keele – 280–300 pts (Chem) (IB 26–28 pts)
Manchester Met – 280 pts (Chem) (IB 28 pts)
Northumbria – 280 pts (Chem Foren Chem; App Chem; Pharml Chem) (IB 25 pts)
Nottingham Trent – 280 pts (Chem MChem)
Strathclyde – BBC (Chem; Chem Analyt Chem; Foren Chem) (IB 28 pts)

260 pts Bangor – 260–320 pts (Chem; Chem Biomol Sci; Mar Chem)
Central Lancashire – BCC 260 pts (Chem; Foren Chem)
Greenwich – 260 pts (Chem) (IB 26 pts)
Kingston – 260 pts (Chem)
Liverpool John Moores – 260 pts (App Cheml Pharml Sci) (IB 25 pts)
Manchester Met – 260–280 pts (Foren Chem; Medcnl Biol Chem; Pharml Chem) (IB 28 pts)
Nottingham Trent – 260 pts (Pharml Medcnl Chem; Chem)
Reading – 260–300 pts (Chem BSc; Chem Educ)
Sheffield Hallam – 260 pts (Chem)
South Wales – BCC 260 pts (Chem; Foren Chem) (IB 30 pts)
Teesside – 260–280 pts (Chem) (IB 30 pts HL chem)

240 pts Coventry – CCC 240 pts (Analyt Chem Foren Sci) (IB 27 pts HL chem/biol)
London Met – 240 pts incl 80 pts from chem (Chem) (IB 28 pts)
West Scotland – CCC (Chem)

80 pts London (Birk) – p/t, for under 21s (over 21s varies) (Chem)

Open University – contact +44 (0)845 300 6090 **or** www.openuniversity.co.uk/you (Nat Sci)

Alternative offers
See **Chapter 7** and **Appendix 1** for grades/UCAS Tariff points information for the International Baccalaureate, Scottish Highers/Advanced Highers, the Welsh Baccalaureate, the Irish Leaving Certificate, the Cambridge Pre-U Diploma, the Advanced Diploma and the Extended Project.

ChemNet

What do these
have in common?
...Chemistry!

Are you a 14–18 year
old chemistry student?
Join **ChemNet** to discover
the chemistry in your life

Find out:
• how the latest advances in
  chemistry could change your world
• where chemistry could take you
• how to get help with your studies
and much more...

http://my.rsc.org/chemnet

ROYAL SOCIETY
OF **CHEMISTRY**

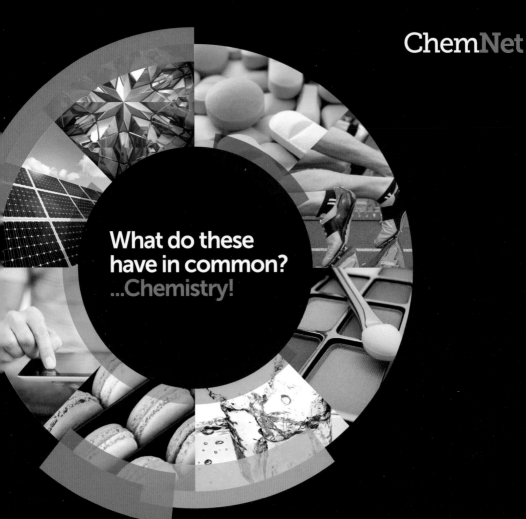

ChemNet

What do these have in common?
...Chemistry!

Are you a 14-18 year old chemistry student? Join **ChemNet** to discover the chemistry in your life

You can:
- Explore what a career in chemistry and university has to offer
- Seek guidance with study/further education choices
- Visit industry, labs and universities
- Attend events such as Meet the Universities
- Read *The Mole*, our student chemistry magazine
- Get help with studies from Dr ChemNet

http://my.rsc.org/chemnet

ROYAL SOCIETY OF **CHEMISTRY**

Registered Charity Number 207890

EXAMPLES OF FOUNDATION DEGREES IN THE SUBJECT FIELD
London Met.

CHOOSING YOUR COURSE (SEE ALSO CH.1)
Some course features
Bath There are 18 different courses offered within the chemistry department, including Chemistry for Drug Discovery and Chemistry with Education, as well as options for study abroad and a year in industrial placement.
Cambridge Chemistry is offered as a speciality within the Natural Sciences degree. Options within the subject include atmospheric science, chemical biology and synthetic organic chemistry.
Cardiff Degrees in Chemistry, Chemistry and Physics, and Chemistry with Bioscience or Chemistry with Industrial Experience (BSc and MChem; Year 3 in industry or a year abroad (MChem only)) are available. Optional modules in Year 1 of the Chemistry course include biochemistry, biology, geology, physics and languages. The MChem scheme follows the same syllabus in Years 1 and 2.
Glasgow Chemistry is a broad course that provides a basis of the principles of chemical science in the early years and leads to special topics at Honours level in the fourth year. The BSc course is RSC-recognised and the MSci is accredited. Chemistry with Medicinal Chemistry, Forensic Studies, Chemistry and Mathematics and Environmental Chemistry are also offered.
Heriot-Watt Fifteen Chemistry courses are offered including BSc and MChem options, with the choice of degree being deferred up to the end of Year 3. There are options in Biochemistry, Computer Science, Materials, Environmental Economics, Forensic Science, Industrial Experience, Management, Pharmaceutical Chemistry and Education. Scholarships available.
Keele Chemistry and Medicinal Chemistry are offered as dual Honours courses with a large number of combinations from science, social science and humanities subjects. A semester abroad and sandwich placement year are offered.
London (UCL) MSc and BSc courses are common in the first two years after which a choice can be made. MSc courses provide greater depth and are aimed at those wishing to follow a scientific career.
Loughborough Strong links with industry for sandwich courses.
Nottingham Options within the subject include the chance to study abroad in Australia, Canada, Hong Kong, Ireland, New Zealand, Singapore or the USA. There is also an option to include a year's placement within the industry.
South Wales The RSC-accredited Chemistry course includes physical, inorganic, organic and analytical chemistry with specialisms in Years 3 and 4 in pharmaceutical, agrochemistry and food chemistry. The study of a foreign language can be continued throughout the course. Several joint courses are offered along with Combined Science and Combined Studies programmes. There are also degrees in Forensic Science and Forensic Chemistry.
Warwick MSc and BSc courses are common in the first two years after which a choice can be made. MSc courses provide greater depth and are aimed at those wishing to follow a scientific career.

Universities and colleges teaching quality See www.qaa.ac.uk; http://unistats.direct.gov.uk.

Top research universities and colleges (RAE 2008) Cambridge; Nottingham; Oxford; Edinburgh; St Andrews; Bristol; Imperial London; Leeds; Warwick; York; Liverpool; Manchester; Sheffield.

Examples of sandwich degree courses Aston; Bangor; Bath; Cardiff; Cardiff Met (UWIC); Dundee; East Anglia; Hertfordshire; Huddersfield; Kent; Kingston; Liverpool John Moores; Loughborough; Manchester; Manchester Met; Northumbria; Nottingham Trent; Queen's Belfast; St Andrews; Sheffield Hallam; South Wales; Surrey; Teesside; West Scotland; York.

ADMISSIONS INFORMATION
Number of applicants per place (approx) Bangor (Mar Chem) 3, (Chem) 6; Bath 7; Bradford (Chem Pharml Foren Sci) 10; Bristol 5; Cardiff 4; Durham 6; Edinburgh 5; Heriot-Watt 6; Hull 7; Imperial London 3; Kingston 4; Leeds 3; Leicester 9; Liverpool 6; London (QM) 3; London (UCL) 8; Newcastle 5; Nottingham (Chem Mol Phys) 4, (Chem) 8; Oxford (success rate 63%); Southampton 7; Surrey 3; York 5.

Advice to applicants and planning the UCAS personal statement Extend your knowledge beyond your exam studies by reading scientific journals and keeping abreast of scientific developments in the news. Discuss any visits to chemical firms and laboratories, for example, pharmaceutical, food science, rubber and plastic, paper, photographic, environmental health. See also **Appendix 3**. **Bristol** Deferred entry accepted.

Misconceptions about this course Many students do not fully appreciate the strengths of a Chemistry degree for any career despite the fact that graduates regularly go into a diverse range of careers. **Durham** Students fail to realise that they require mathematics and that physics is useful.

Selection interviews Yes Bangor, Bath, Birmingham, Bristol, Cambridge, Coventry, Durham, Greenwich, Huddersfield, Hull, Imperial London, Kingston, Leicester, London (QM), London (UCL), London Met, Loughborough, Newcastle, Northumbria, Nottingham, Nottingham Trent, Oxford (success rate 39%), Reading, Sheffield, Surrey, Warwick, York; **Some** Aston, Cardiff, Dundee, East Anglia, Keele (mature students only), Liverpool John Moores, Plymouth; **No** Bristol UWE, Southampton.

Interview advice and questions Be prepared for questions on your chemistry syllabus and aspects that you enjoy the most. In the past a variety of questions have been asked, for example: Why is carbon a special element? Discuss the nature of forces between atoms with varying intermolecular distances. Describe recent practicals. What is acid rain? What other types of pollution are caused by the human race? What is an enzyme? What are the general properties of benzene? Why might sciences be less popular among girls at school? What can a mass spectrometer be used for? What would you do if a river turned bright blue and you were asked how to test a sample? What would be the difference between metal and non-metal pollution? What is 'turning you on' in chemistry at the moment? See also **Chapter 6**. **Bath** Why Chemistry? Discuss the practical work you are doing. **Oxford** No written or work tests. Evidence required of motivation and further potential and a capacity to analyse and use information to form opinions and a willingness to discuss them. **York** Discuss your favourite areas of chemistry, some of your extra-curricular activities, your preferred learning styles – for example, small tutorials of four or fewer, or lectures.

Reasons for rejection (non-academic) Didn't attend interview. Rude and uncooperative. Arrived under influence of drink. Poor attitude and poor commitment to chemistry. Incomplete, inappropriate, illegible, illiterate personal statements. **Southampton** Applicants called for interview are not normally rejected.

AFTER-RESULTS ADVICE
Offers to applicants repeating A-levels Higher Bangor, Dundee, Hull, Leeds, Northumbria, Nottingham, St Andrews, Warwick; **Possibly higher** Coventry, Edinburgh, Newcastle; **Same** Aston, Bath, Bristol, Cardiff, Durham, East Anglia, Greenwich, Heriot-Watt, Huddersfield, Keele, Kingston, Liverpool John Moores, London (UCL), London Met, Loughborough, Plymouth, Sheffield, Surrey; **No** Cambridge.

GRADUATE DESTINATIONS AND EMPLOYMENT (2011/12 HESA)
Graduates surveyed 2650 **Employed** 1035 **In voluntary employment** 40 **In further study** 985 **Assumed unemployed** 250

Career note A large number of Chemistry graduates choose to go on to further study as well as into scientific careers in research, analysis or development. Significant numbers also follow careers in a wide range of areas in management, teaching and retail work.

OTHER DEGREE SUBJECTS FOR CONSIDERATION
Agriculture; Biochemistry; Biological Sciences; Biomedical Science; Chemical Engineering; Environmental Science; Forensic Science; Genetics; Materials Science; Medicine; Microbiology; Oceanography; Pharmacology; Pharmacy.

CHINESE
(including **Korean**; see also **Asia-Pacific Studies, Languages**)

Oriental languages are not necessarily difficult languages but they differ considerably in their writing systems which present their own problems for the new student. Even so, Chinese is not a language to be chosen for its novelty and students should have a strong interest in China and its people.

Useful websites www.cilt.org.uk; www.iol.org.uk; www.bbc.co.uk/languages; www.china.org.cn/english; www.languageadvantage.com; www.languagematters.co.uk; www.chineseculture.about.com.

NB The points totals shown to the left of the institutions are for ease of reference only. It must not be assumed that Tariff points are always used by institutions or that they can be substituted for an offer in grades. The level of an offer is not necessarily indicative of the quality of a course.

COURSE OFFERS INFORMATION

Subject requirements/preferences GCSE A language is required. **AL** A modern language is usually required.

Your target offers and examples of courses provided by each institution

380 pts Cambridge – A*AA (As Mid E St) (IB 40–41 pts HL 776)
Nottingham – A*AA–AAA incl maths 380–360 pts (Econ Chin St) (IB 38–36 pts)

360 pts Edinburgh – AAA–BBB 360–300 pts (Chin) (IB 37–34 pts HL 666–555)
Oxford – AAA (Ornt St (Chin)) (IB 38–40 pts)

340 pts Durham – AAB 340 pts (Chin St) (IB 36 pts)
Leeds – AAB–ABC (Chin Joint Hons) (IB 34 pts)
London (SOAS) – AAB (Chin (Modn Class); Chin St; Kor Joint Hons) (IB 36 pts HL 666)
Manchester – AAB–ABB 340–320 pts (Chin Jap; Russ Chin) (IB 32–36 pts)
Newcastle – AAB–ABB 340–320 pts (Ling Chin/Jap) (IB 34 pts)
Nottingham – AAB–ABB (Contemp Chin St BA/MSci; Geog Chin St; Mgt Chin St; Span Contemp Chin St) (IB 32–34 pts)

320 pts Leeds – ABB (Chin Pol; Chin (Modn)) (IB 34 pts)
Manchester – ABB–BBB 320–300 pts (Chin St; Chin courses) (IB 34–32 pts HL 655–555)
Newcastle – ABB 320 pts (Chin St Jap St) (IB 34 pts)
Nottingham – ABB (Hist Contemp Chin St) (IB 32 pts HL 6 hist)
Sheffield – ABB (Chin St courses) (IB 33 pts)

280 pts Central Lancashire – BBC–ABB 280–320 pts (Bus Mgt Chin) (IB 25 pts)
Hull – 280 pts (Chin St)
Salford – 280–320 pts (Transl Interp Chin) (IB 27 pts)
Westminster – BBC (Contemp Chin St)

260 pts Westminster – BCC (Chin Engl Lang) (IB 30 pts)

240 pts Chester – 280–240 pts (Chin St) (IB 26 pts)
Middlesex – 240 pts (Trad Chin Med)
Trinity Saint David – 240 pts (Chin St courses) (IB 26 pts)

Alternative offers
See **Chapter 7** and **Appendix 1** for grades/UCAS Tariff points information for the International Baccalaureate, Scottish Highers/Advanced Highers, the Welsh Baccalaureate, the Irish Leaving Certificate, the Cambridge Pre-U Diploma, the Advanced Diploma and the Extended Project.

CHOOSING YOUR COURSE (SEE ALSO CH.1)

Some course features
Edinburgh (Chin) This is an intensive language course in Mandarin Chinese and Modern Standard (colloquial) Chinese. Year 3 is spent in China.
Leeds (Chin Int Rel) Year 2 spent in China taking language courses at a university in Beijing, Tianjin or Taipei. Students expected to reach a high standard of language ability.
London (SOAS) (Chin (Modn Class)) Course designed to give broad understanding of Chinese culture, past and present, through its language, history and literature. In Years 3 and 4 students can choose to specialise in either modern or classical China.
Manchester (Chin St) Course covers both language (Mandarin) and culture, society, economics, politics and international relations.
Oxford Chinese is offered as a speciality with the Oriental Studies degree. Students study classical and contemporary Chinese language with module options including art, history, literature and philosophy, and spend their second year in China attending a course at Peking University. There is also the option of studying Japanese, Korean or Tibetan as a subsidiary language.

Sheffield (Mus Chin St) Dual Honours course allows students to design their own Music programme, specialising in composition, dissertation or performance. Chinese Studies involves intensive language learning (from scratch or with some prior knowledge). Year 2 at Nanjing University, and modules in Chinese business, literature, history and the environment.

Universities and colleges teaching quality See www.qaa.ac.uk; http://unistats.direct.gov.uk.

Top research universities and colleges (RAE 2008) (Asian Studies) London (SOAS); Oxford; Cambridge; Leeds; Manchester; Nottingham; Westminster.

Examples of sandwich degree courses Westminster.

ADMISSIONS INFORMATION

Number of applicants per place (approx) Leeds 5; London (SOAS) 8; Westminster 18.

Advice to applicants and planning the UCAS personal statement It will be necessary to demonstrate a knowledge of China, its culture, political and economic background. Visits to the Far East should be mentioned, with reference to any features which have influenced your choice of degree course. See also **Appendix 3** under Languages.

Selection interviews Yes Cambridge, Oxford; **Some** Leeds, London (SOAS).

Interview advice and questions You will be expected to convince the admissions tutor why you want to study the language. Your knowledge of Chinese culture, politics and society in general, and of Far Eastern problems, could also be tested. See also **Chapter 6**.

Reasons for rejection (non-academic) Oxford Applicant's language background seemed a little weak and his written work not as strong as that of other applicants. At interview he showed himself to be a dedicated hard-working young man but lacking in the imagination, flexibility and the intellectual liveliness needed to succeed on the course.

AFTER-RESULTS ADVICE

Offers to applicants repeating A-levels Higher Leeds; **No** Cambridge.

GRADUATE DESTINATIONS AND EMPLOYMENT (2011/12 HESA)

Graduates surveyed 155 **Employed** 75 **In voluntary employment** 10 **In further study** 40 **Assumed unemployed** 15

Career note China is a country with a high economic growth rate and there are good opportunities for graduates, an increasing number being recruited by firms based in East Asia. Other opportunities exist in diplomacy, aid work and tourism throughout China, Taiwan and Mongolia as well as most non-scientific career areas in the UK. See also **Languages**.

OTHER DEGREE SUBJECTS FOR CONSIDERATION

Traditional Chinese Medicine; other Oriental languages.

CLASSICAL STUDIES/CLASSICAL CIVILISATION

(see also **Archaeology, Classics, Greek, History (Ancient), Latin**)

Classical Studies and Classical Civilisation courses cover the literature, history, philosophy and archaeology of Ancient Greece and Rome. A knowledge of Latin or Greek is not necessary for many courses, but check subject requirements carefully.

Useful websites www.britishmuseum.org; see also **History** and **History (Ancient)**.

NB The points totals shown to the left of the institutions are for ease of reference only. It must not be assumed that Tariff points are always used by institutions or that they can be substituted for an offer in grades. The level of an offer is not necessarily indicative of the quality of a course.

COURSE OFFERS INFORMATION

Subject requirements/preferences **GCSE** English and a foreign language often required. **AL** A modern language is required for joint language courses. Relevant subjects include classical civilisation, English literature, archaeology, Latin, Greek.

Your target offers and examples of courses provided by each institution

380 pts **Warwick** – AABc (Class Civ) (IB 36 pts)

360 pts **Bristol** – AAA-AAB 360-340 pts (Engl Class St) (IB 37-35 pts HL 666 incl Engl)
Edinburgh – AAA-BBB 360-300 pts (Anc Medit Civ; Class St; Class Mid E St; Class Arch Gk) (IB 40-34 pts HL 666-555)
Exeter – AAA-ABB 360-320 pts (Class St; Class St Engl) (IB 32-36 pts)
London (King's) – AAA (Class St Engl) (IB 35 pts HL 666 Engl)
London (UCL) – AABe-ABBe (Class Arch Class Civ) (IB 34-36 pts HL 16-17 pts)
St Andrews – AAA-AAB 360-340 (Class St courses) (IB 36-38 pts)

340 pts **Bristol** – AAB-ABB (Class St) (IB 35-33 pts HL 666)
Exeter – AAB-ABB (Class St Modn Lang) (IB 34-32 pts)
Leeds – AAB (Class Civ) (IB 36 pts)
London (King's) – AAB (Class St; Class St Byz Modn Gk St) (IB 35 pts HL 665)
Nottingham – AAB (Class Civ; Class Civ Engl; Class Civ Phil) (IB 32-34 pts)
St Andrews – AAB (Art Hist Class St; Class St Lat) (IB 36 pts)

320 pts **Birmingham** – ABB 320 pts (Class Lit Civ) (IB 34 pts)
Kent – ABB (Class Arch St) (IB 33 pts)
Leeds – ABB 320 pts (Class Lit courses) (IB 35 pts HL 16 pts)
Liverpool – ABB (Class St; Egypt) (IB 33 pts)
London (RH) – ABB (Class St; Class St Ital) (IB 34 pts)
Manchester – ABB-BBB 300-320 pts (Class St) (IB 34-31 pts)
Newcastle – AAB-ABB 320-340 pts (Class St) (IB 32 pts)
Nottingham – ABB-AAC (Arch Class Civ; Class Civ Fr/Ger; Class Civ Art Hist) (IB 32 pts)
Reading – ABB (Class St; Class Mediev St) (IB 32 pts)
Sheffield – ABB 320 pts (Class Hist Arch) (IB 34 pts)
Warwick – ABB (Class Civ Phil) (IB 36 pts)

300 pts **Roehampton** – 300 pts (Class Civ) (IB 26 pts)

280 pts **Swansea** – BBC (Class Civ; Class Civ Lat) (IB 30 pts)

240 pts **Trinity Saint David** – 240-260 pts (Class St; Anc Civ) (IB 26 pts)

Alternative offers

See **Chapter 7** and **Appendix 1** for grades/UCAS Tariff points information for the International Baccalaureate, Scottish Highers/Advanced Highers, the Welsh Baccalaureate, the Irish Leaving Certificate, the Cambridge Pre-U Diploma, the Advanced Diploma and the Extended Project.

CHOOSING YOUR COURSE (SEE ALSO CH.1)

Some course features

Birmingham (Class Lit Civ) Broad course covering literature, history, drama, politics, philosophy, art, religion and science.
Durham Three courses, Classical Past, Ancient History and Classics, have a common first year.
London (King's) The course is designed for those wishing to study the classical world as a whole covering the Greek and Roman empires.
London (RH) The course covers all aspects of the classical world – literature, history, philosophy and archaeology with options to study Greek and Latin.
Manchester (Class St) Greek or Latin options available including beginners' courses.

Universities and colleges teaching quality See www.qaa.ac.uk; http://unistats.direct.gov.uk.

Top research universities and colleges (RAE 2008) See **Classics**.

ADMISSIONS INFORMATION

Number of applicants per place (approx) Birmingham 3; Bristol 9; Durham (Class Past) 10; Exeter 3; Leeds 7; London (RH) 4; Manchester (Class St) 4; Newcastle 8; Nottingham 6; Reading 10; Swansea 5; Trinity Saint David 2; Warwick 23.

Advice to applicants and planning the UCAS personal statement Discuss any A-level work and what has attracted you to this subject. Describe visits to classical sites or museums and what impressed you.

Misconceptions about this course Birmingham (Class Lit Civ) A study of classics at school is not necessary although while many people catch the classics bug by doing classical civilisation at A-level, others come to classics through reading the myths or seeing the plays and being fascinated by them. For others the interdisciplinary nature of the subject attracts them – literature, drama, history, politics and philosophy. **Exeter** (Class St) This is not a language degree. There is no requirement for either A-level Latin or Greek.

Selection interviews Yes Durham, Kent, Newcastle, Nottingham; **Some** Bristol, London (RH), Trinity Saint David, Warwick; **No** Birmingham.

Interview advice and questions In the past, questions have included: What special interests do you have in Classical Studies/Classics? Have you visited Greece, Rome or any other classical sites or museums and what were your impressions? These are the types of questions to expect, along with those to explore your knowledge of the culture, theatre and architecture of the period. See also **Chapter 6**. **Birmingham** (Class Lit Civ) The programme includes some language study and, if applicants do not have a GCSE in a foreign language, we ask them to do a short language aptitude test. Interview questions are likely to focus on your reading interests (not necessarily classical texts!) and your own reflections on them. We are interested in your ability to think for yourself and we want to be sure that you are someone who will enjoy three years of reading and talking about books. **Swansea** Reasons for choosing the subject and how the student hopes to benefit from the course.

Reasons for rejection (non-academic) Birmingham Lukewarm interest in the subject. Lack of clear idea why they wanted to do this degree.

AFTER-RESULTS ADVICE

Offers to applicants repeating A-levels Higher Glasgow (AAA), Nottingham, St Andrews, Warwick; **Same** Birmingham, Bristol, Durham, Exeter, Leeds, London (RH), Newcastle.

GRADUATE DESTINATIONS AND EMPLOYMENT (2011/12 HESA)

Classical Studies graduates surveyed 945 **Employed** 360 **In voluntary employment** 40 **In further study** 285 **Assumed unemployed** 75

Career note As with other non-vocational subjects, graduates enter a wide range of careers. In a small number of cases this may be subject-related with work in museums and art galleries. However, much will depend on how the student's interests develop during the undergraduate years and career planning should start early.

OTHER DEGREE SUBJECTS FOR CONSIDERATION

Archaeology; Ancient History; Classics; Greek; History; History of Art; Latin; Philosophy.

CLASSICS

(see also **Classical Studies/Classical Civilisation, Greek, Latin**)

Classics courses focus on a study of Greek and Latin but may also include topics related to ancient history, art and architecture, drama and philosophy. These subjects are also frequently offered in joint courses.

Useful websites www.classicspage.com; www.classics.ac.uk; www.cambridgescp.com; www.bbc.co.uk/history/ancient/greeks; www.bbc.co.uk/history/ancient/romans.

NB The points totals shown to the left of the institutions are for ease of reference only. It must not be assumed that Tariff points are always used by institutions or that they can be substituted for an offer in grades. The level of an offer is not necessarily indicative of the quality of a course.

COURSE OFFERS INFORMATION

Subject requirements/preferences GCSE English and a foreign language usually required. Grades A*/A/B may be stipulated. **AL** Check courses for Latin/Greek requirements.

Your target offers and examples of courses provided by each institution
380 pts **Cambridge** – A*AA 380 pts (Class; Educ Class) (IB 40–41 pts HL 776)
360 pts **Bristol** – AAA–AAB 360–340 pts (Class) (IB 37–35 pts HL 666)
        Durham – AAA 360 pts (Class; Class Past) (IB 37 pts HL 666)
        Edinburgh – AAA–BBB 360–300 pts (Class; Class Engl Lang; Class Ling) (IB 40–34 pts HL 666–555)
        Exeter – AAA–AAB (Class) (IB 36–34 pts HL 6 Lat/Gk)
        London (King's) – AAA (Class) (IB 38 pts HL 666)
        London (UCL) – AABe (Class) (IB 34 pts)
        Oxford – AAA (Class Engl; Class; Class Modn Langs; Class Orntl St) (IB 39 pts HL 766)
340 pts **London (UCL)** – AAB (Class (Yr Abrd)) (IB 36 pts)
        Nottingham – AAB (Class) (IB 34 pts)
        St Andrews – AAB (Class) (IB 36 pts)
        Warwick – AAB (Class) (IB 36 pts)
320 pts **Birmingham** – ABB 320 pts (Class Lit Civ) (IB 34 pts)
        Edinburgh – ABB (Div Class) (IB 36 pts)
        Leeds – ABB 320 pts (Class Lit courses) (IB 35 pts HL 16 pts)
        Liverpool – ABB (Class) (IB 33 pts)
        London (RH) – ABB (Class) (IB 34 pts)
        Manchester – ABB–BBB (Class) (IB 34–31 pts)
        Newcastle – AAB–ABB 320–340 pts (Class) (IB 35 pts HL 555)
        Reading – ABB 320 pts (Classics) (IB 32 pts)
280 pts **Swansea** – BBC (Class) (IB 30 pts)
200 pts **Trinity Saint David** – 200 pts (Class) (IB 26 pts)

Alternative offers
See **Chapter 7** and **Appendix 1** for grades/UCAS Tariff points information for the International Baccalaureate, Scottish Highers/Advanced Highers, the Welsh Baccalaureate, the Irish Leaving Certificate, the Cambridge Pre-U Diploma, the Advanced Diploma and the Extended Project.

CHOOSING YOUR COURSE (SEE ALSO CH.1)

Some course features
Bristol (Class) Greek and Latin languages are studied for the first two years plus option topics from literature, art, philosophy, political, social and cultural history.
Cambridge (Class Gk Lat) Latin or Greek A-levels not required for the four-year course.
Liverpool (Class) Language study (Greek or Latin), including beginners' level, comprises 50% of the course. The remainder is a study of literature, art, history and archaeology.
Newcastle (Class) A concentration on the study of Greek and Latin languages and literature.
St Andrews (Class) A wide range of related subjects is offered as part of the Single Honours course and a wide choice of complementary courses from other departments.
Swansea The department offers a wide range of courses in Classics, Classical Civilisation, Latin and Greek or Roman Studies, Ancient History and Medieval Studies and Egyptology.

Universities and colleges teaching quality See www.qaa.ac.uk; http://unistats.direct.gov.uk.

Top research universities and colleges (RAE 2008) (Including Classics, Ancient History, Byzantine and Modern Greek Studies) Cambridge; Oxford; London (UCL); London (King's); Durham; Warwick; Exeter; Manchester; Bristol; St Andrews.

ADMISSIONS INFORMATION

Number of applicants per place (approx) Bristol 14; Cambridge 2; Durham (Class) 8, (Class Past) 10; Leeds 4; London (King's) 6; London (RH) 6; Manchester (Class) 10, (Class Anc Hist) 8; Newcastle 14; Nottingham 6; Oxford 2; Swansea 6; Trinity Saint David 5.

Advice to applicants and planning the UCAS personal statement Describe any visits made to classical sites or museums, or literature which you have read and enjoyed. Discuss any significant aspects which impressed you. Classics is an interdisciplinary subject and universities are looking for people who are versatile, imaginative and independently minded, so all types of extra-curricular activities (drama, music, philosophy, creative arts, politics, other languages and cultures) will be relevant. See also **Classical Studies/Classical Civilisation**.

Misconceptions about this course While Classics can appear irrelevant and elitist, universities aim to assist students to leave with a range of transferable skills that are of importance to employers.

Selection interviews Yes Cambridge, London (RH), London (UCL), Newcastle, Oxford (Class) 45%, (Class Eng) 20%, (Class Mod Lang) 33%, Swansea; **Some** Bristol (mature students), Warwick; **No** Dundee, Durham, Leeds, Nottingham, Reading, St Andrews.

Interview advice and questions What do you think it means to study Classics? Do you think Classics is still a vital and central cultural discipline? What made you apply to study Classics at this university? There are often detailed questions on the texts which the students have read, to find out how reflective they are in their reading. See also **Classical Studies/Classical Civilisation** and **Chapter 6**. **Cambridge** What would happen if the Classics department burned down? Do you think feminism is dead? Emma has become a different person since she took up yoga. Therefore she is not responsible for anything she did before she took up yoga. Discuss. **Oxford** Written tests to demonstrate ability in linguistics, competence in translation. Use of dictionaries not permitted. Classics and English applicants take the English Admissions Test.

Reasons for rejection (non-academic) Did not demonstrate a clear sense of why they wanted to study Classics rather than anything else.

AFTER-RESULTS ADVICE

Offers to applicants repeating A-levels Higher Leeds, Nottingham, St Andrews; **Same** Cambridge, Durham, Newcastle, Swansea.

GRADUATE DESTINATIONS AND EMPLOYMENT (2011/12 HESA)
See **Classical Studies/Classical Civilisation**.

Career note See **Classical Studies/Classical Civilisation**.

OTHER DEGREE SUBJECTS FOR CONSIDERATION
See **Classical Studies/Classical Civilisation**.

COMBINED COURSES

(see also Art and Design (General), Social Sciences/Studies)

Many different subjects are offered in combined or modular arrangements. These courses are particularly useful for those applicants who have difficulty in deciding on one specialist subject to follow, allowing students to mix and match according to their interests and often enabling them to embark on new subjects.

Useful websites www.artscouncil.org.uk; www.scottisharts.org.uk; www.artsprofessional.co.uk.

NB The points totals shown to the left of the institutions are for ease of reference only. It must not be assumed that Tariff points are always used by institutions or that they can be substituted for an offer in grades. The level of an offer is not necessarily indicative of the quality of a course.

COURSE OFFERS INFORMATION

Subject requirements/preferences The offers listed below are average offers. Specific offers will vary depending on the relative popularity of each subject. Check with the admissions tutor of your selected institution. **GCSE** English, mathematics or science and foreign language may be required by some universities. **AL** Some joint courses may require a specified subject.

Your target offers and examples of courses provided by each institution

380 pts **Bath** – A*AA (Nat Sci) (IB 38 pts HL 766)
Cambridge – A*AA 380 pts (Nat Sci) (IB 40–41 pts HL 776)
Durham – A*AA 380 pts (Comb Hons Arts; Comb Hons Soc Sci) (IB 38 pts)
Exeter – A*AA–AAB 380–340 pts (Flex Comb Hons Mid E N Af St; Flex Comb Hons) (IB 38–34 pts)

360 pts **Birmingham** – AAA–A*AA 360–380 pts (Lib Arts Sci) (IB 36–38 pts)
Exeter – AAA–A*AA 360–380 pts (Lib Arts)
Imperial London – AAA 360 pts (Bioch courses) (IB 38 pts HL 6 biol chem)
Lancaster – AAA 360 pts (Nat Sci) (IB 36 pts)
London (King's) – AAA 360 pts (Librl Arts) (IB 35 pts HL 666)
Newcastle – AAA (Phil Comb Hons) (IB 32 pts HL 555)
St Andrews – AAA–BBB (General Arts Sci) (IB 32 pts)

340 pts **Cardiff** – ABB–BBB 340–300 pts (Anc Hist Joint Hons) (IB 30–32 pts)
Durham – AAB 340 pts (Mus) (IB 36 pts)
East Anglia – AAB (Lib Art) (IB 33 pts)
Kent – AAB (Lib Arts) (IB 34 pts)
Liverpool – AAB–ABB 340–320 pts (Comb Hons)
London (QM) – AAB (Econ Joint Hons) (IB 36 pts HL 5 maths)
Newcastle – AAB 340 pts (Hist Art Comb Hons; Lit Comb Hons; Film St Comb Hons; Comb Hons) (IB 35 pts)
Sheffield – AAB–BBB (Fr St Joint Hons; Hisp St Joint Hons; Hist Joint Hons; Ger St Joint Hons; Phys Joint Hons; Maths Joint Hons; Econ Joint Hons; Bus Mgt Joint Hons; Bioch Joint Hons) (IB 35–32 pts)

320 pts **East Anglia** – ABB 320 pts (Int Rel Joint Hons; Film courses) (IB 32 pts)
Heriot-Watt – ABB (Comb St)
Hull – 280–320 pts (Comb Lang)
Kent – ABB (Cult St Comb) (IB 33 pts)
Liverpool – ABB 320 pts (Comb Hons Film St (Euro); Comb Hons (Engl)) (IB 30–36 pts)
Sheffield – AAB–ABB 320–340 pts (Phil Joint Hons; Ling Joint Hons; Mus Joint Hons; Russ St Joint Hons)

300 pts **Aberystwyth** – BBB 300 pts (Euro St Joint Hons) (IB 28 pts)
Aston – 300–320 pts (Comb Hons)
Cardiff – BBB–BBC 300–280 pts (Welsh Joint Hons)
Hertfordshire – 300 pts (Joint Comb Hons)

280 pts **Bath Spa** – 280–300 pts (Psy Comb Hons)
Essex – 280 pts (Hum)
Hull – 280–320 pts (Am St) (IB 28 pts)
Kingston – 280 pts (Cyb Scrty Comp Foren Joint Hons)
Winchester – 280–320 pts (Modn Lib Arts)

260 pts **Bath Spa** – 260–300 pts (Sociol Comb courses)
Hertfordshire – 260 pts (Comb courses)
Hull – 260–340 pts (Relgn Joint courses) (IB 28–30 pts)
Kingston – 260–360 pts (Mus Joint Hons)

Check **Chapter 4** when choosing your university and **Chapter 7** on how to read the subject tables.

Nottingham – BCC 260 pts (Hum)
Nottingham Trent – 260 pts (Euro St Joint Hons)
South Wales – 260 pts (Comb St)
240 pts **Aberdeen** – CCC (Arts Soc Sci) (IB 28 pts)
Leeds (CMus) – 240 pts (Mus (Comb))
Manchester Met – 240–280 pts (Comb Hons)
220 pts **Bradford** – 220 pts (Comb St)
120 pts **Wirral Met (Coll)** – DD 120 pts (Cult St (Comb))

Open University – contact +44 (0)845 300 6090 **or** www.openuniversity.co.uk/you
(Hum Engl/Fr/Ger/Span)

Alternative offers
See **Chapter 7** and **Appendix 1** for grades/UCAS Tariff points information for the International Baccalaureate, Scottish Highers/Advanced Highers, the Welsh Baccalaureate, the Irish Leaving Certificate, the Cambridge Pre-U Diploma, the Advanced Diploma and the Extended Project.

EXAMPLES OF FOUNDATION DEGREES IN THE SUBJECT FIELD
Bedfordshire; Canterbury Christ Church; Colchester (Inst); Norwich Arts; Suffolk (Univ Campus); Truro (Coll).

CHOOSING YOUR COURSE (SEE ALSO CH.1)
Some course features
Bath (Nat Sci) Offers a choice from biology, chemistry, education, environmental sciences, languages and management
Birmingham (Nat Sci) The course covers biochemistry, biology, chemistry, computer science and earth science, mathematics and physics.
East London (Cult St) Exploration of social and political issues and the media.
London (King's) The Liberal Arts BA offers a wide choice of subjects.
Winchester The Modern Liberal Arts course enables students to make an initial choice of subjects, deciding on their specialist degree later.

Universities and colleges teaching quality See www.qaa.ac.uk; http://unistats.direct.gov.uk.

Top research universities and colleges (RAE 2008) (Cultural Studies) See **Communication Studies/ Communication**.

ADMISSIONS INFORMATION
Number of applicants per place (approx) Birmingham 9; Dundee 13 ave; Durham (Comb Arts) 7; Heriot-Watt 3; Leeds 15; Liverpool 6; Newcastle 7; Strathclyde 9.

Advice to applicants and planning the UCAS personal statement Refer to tables for those subjects you've chosen. **Bath Spa** (Crea Arts) Looks for personal statements which clarify relevant work done outside the school syllabus (eg creative writing). **De Montfort** Give information about practical experience and a personal interest in one or more areas of the arts. Show a mature attitude on arts/ culture and be an original thinker. **Liverpool** (Comb Hons) We look for evidence of a broad interest across a range of subjects.

Misconceptions about this course **Bath Spa** (Crea Arts) Some applicants wish to specialise in one subject not realising it is a Joint Honours course. **Liverpool** (Comb Hons) Some students deterred because they believe that the course is too general. This is not so. The degree certificate shows the names of the two subjects taken to Honours degree level.

Selection interviews Yes Aberdeen, Bristol UWE, De Montfort, Dundee, Durham, London Met, Manchester Met, Roehampton, Worcester; **Some** Bath Spa, Bournemouth Arts, Liverpool.

Interview advice and questions Questions will focus on your chosen subjects. See under individual subject tables. See also **Chapter 6**. **De Montfort** What do you understand to be the role of the Arts Council of England? What recent arts events have you seen/enjoyed?

Reasons for rejection (non-academic) Lack of clarity of personal goals.

AFTER-RESULTS ADVICE
Offers to applicants repeating A-levels **Higher** St Andrews; **Possibly higher** Bristol UWE, Leeds, Newcastle, Roehampton, St Mary's; **Same** Bath Spa, Birmingham, De Montfort, Derby, Durham, Greenwich, Leicester, Liverpool, London Met, Manchester Met, Worcester.

GRADUATE DESTINATIONS AND EMPLOYMENT (2011/12 HESA)
Career note Graduates enter a wide range of careers covering business and administration, retail work, education, transport, finance, community and social services. Work experience during undergraduate years will help students to focus their interests.

OTHER DEGREE SUBJECTS FOR CONSIDERATION
See **Social Sciences/Studies**.

COMMUNICATION STUDIES/COMMUNICATION

(including **Advertising, Communications, Information Studies, Public Relations** and **Telecommunications**; see also **Art and Design (General), Computer Courses, Engineering (Communications), Film, Radio, Video and TV Studies, Journalism, Media Studies, Speech Pathology/Sciences/Therapy**)

Some courses combine academic and vocational studies, whilst others may be wholly academic or strictly vocational. The subject thus covers a very wide range of approaches concerning communication which should be carefully researched before applying. Graduates have developed a range of transferable skills in their courses which open up opportunities in several areas. There are obvious links with openings in the media, public relations and advertising.

Useful websites www.camfoundation.com; www.aejmc.org.

NB The points totals shown to the left of the institutions are for ease of reference only. It must not be assumed that Tariff points are always used by institutions or that they can be substituted for an offer in grades. The level of an offer is not necessarily indicative of the quality of a course.

COURSE OFFERS INFORMATION
Subject requirements/preferences **GCSE** English and mathematics grade A–C may be required. **AL** No specific subjects required.

Kingston GCSE Five subjects including mathematics and English (grade A*–C required). **AL** English language/literature/related subject (80 points required), general studies accepted when one of three A-levels or equivalent.

Your target offers and examples of courses provided by each institution
360 pts **City** – AAA–ABB 360–320 pts (Hum Comm)
　　　　Ulster – AAA 360 pts (Comm Adv Mark) (IB 27 pts)
340 pts **Leeds** – AAB 340 pts (Comms Media) (IB 35 pts)
　　　　London (Gold) – AAB–ABB 340–320 pts (Media Comm) (IB 34 pts)
　　　　Newcastle – AAB–ABB 340–320 pts (Media Comm Cult St) (IB 34–35 pts)
320 pts **East Anglia** – ABB (Hum Comm Sci)
　　　　Leeds – ABB 320 pts (Graph Comm Des) (IB 34 pts)
　　　　Leicester – ABB 320 pts (Comms Media Soty) (IB 32 pts)
　　　　Liverpool – ABB 320 pts (Comm Media; Engl Comm St; Comm St Joint Hons; Pol Comm St)
　　　　　　(IB 33 pts)
　　　　London (King's) – ABB (Engl Lang Comm) (IB 34 pts HL 6 Engl)
　　　　Northumbria – 320 pts +interview (Fash Comm) (IB 25 pts)
　　　　Nottingham – ABB 320 pts (Span Int Media Comms St) (IB 32 pts)

300 pts **Aberystwyth** – 300–320pts (Media Comms)
Bristol UWE – 300 pts (Mark Comm) (IB 36 pts)
Brunel – BBB 300 pts (Comm Media St) (IB 32 pts)
Buckingham – BBB–BBC (Mark Media Comm)
East Anglia – BBB (Cr-Cult Comm Bus Mgt) (IB 31 pts)
Hertfordshire – 300 pts (Mass Comm)
Leeds Beckett – 300 pts (Media Comm Cult) (IB 26 pts)
Liverpool Hope – 300 pts (Media Comm)
Loughborough – BBB–ABB (Comm Media St) (IB 32 pts)
Sheffield Hallam – 300 pts (Mark Comm Adv)

280 pts **Bath Spa** – 280–320 pts (Media Comms) (IB 26 pts)
Birmingham City – BBC 280 pts (Media Comm) (IB 28 pts)
Bournemouth – 280–300 pts (Comm Media) (IB 30–31 pts)
Glasgow Caledonian – BBC (Media Comm) (IB 24 pts)
Greenwich – 280 pts (Media Comm) (IB 28 pts)
Keele – BBC (Media Comm Cult) (IB 30 pts)
London Met – 280 pts (Comms) (IB 28 pts)
Oxford Brookes – BBC 280 pts (Comm Media Cult; Engl Lang Comm) (IB 30 pts)
Swansea – BBC 280 pts (Lang Comm; Pol Comm) (IB 30 pts)

260 pts **Central Lancashire** – 260–300 pts (Comm St Pop Cult) (IB 28 pts)
Coventry – BCC 260 pts (Media Comm)
De Montfort – 260 pts (Media Comm) (IB 28 pts)
Keele – 260–300 pts (Media Comm)
Liverpool John Moores – 260 pts (Bus Comm) (IB 28 pts)
Manchester Met – 260–280 pts (Dig Media Comm; Inf Comm)
Nottingham Trent – 260 pts (Comm Soty)
Robert Gordon – BCC (PR) (IB 27 pts)
Sheffield Hallam – 260 pts (PR Media)
Sunderland – 260 pts (Mass Comm)
Ulster – 260 pts (Comm courses; Ling Comm) (IB 24 pts)

240 pts **Abertay** – CCC 240 pts (Web Des Commun)
Buckingham – CCC 240 pts (Comm Media St; Comm Media Jrnl)
Canterbury Christ Church – CCC 240 pts (Media Comm) (IB 24 pts)
East London – 240 pts (Comm St) (IB 24 pts)
Glyndŵr – 240 pts (Media Comms)
Kingston – 240–360 pts (Engl Lang Comm courses)
Southampton Solent – 240 pts (Dig Cult Comms)
Westminster – CCC–AA 240 pts (Comp Net Comm) (IB 28 pts)

220 pts **Sunderland** – 220 pts (Graph Comm)

200 pts **Bedfordshire** – 200 pts (Media Prac (Mass Comm))
Wolverhampton – 200 pts (Media Comm St)

Alternative offers
See **Chapter 7** and **Appendix 1** for grades/UCAS Tariff points information for the International Baccalaureate, Scottish Highers/Advanced Highers, the Welsh Baccalaureate, the Irish Leaving Certificate, the Cambridge Pre-U Diploma, the Advanced Diploma and the Extended Project.

EXAMPLES OF FOUNDATION DEGREES IN THE SUBJECT FIELD
See also **Film, Radio, Video and TV Studies** and **Media Studies**. Blackpool and Fylde (Coll); Oxford Brookes; Ravensbourne; Truro (Coll).

CHOOSING YOUR COURSE (SEE ALSO CH.1)
Some course features
Birmingham City (Media Comm) Students can opt for a general course or degree specific courses.
Keele (Media Cult) An interdisciplinary course covering relevant aspects in English, sociology, visual arts, music and music technology.

Leeds (Comm Media) Core modules in media industries and cultures. Options to choose from political journalism, public relations, film or photography.

Nottingham Trent (Comm Soc) A broad course covering unconscious and non-verbal communication, the history of communication, psychology, anthropology and sociological aspects.

Universities and colleges teaching quality See www.qaa.ac.uk; http://unistats.direct.gov.uk.

Top research universities and colleges (RAE 2008) (Communication, Cultural and Media Studies) Westminster; East Anglia; London (Gold); Cardiff; East London; London (RH); Sussex; Nottingham Trent; Ulster; Lincoln; Sunderland; Stirling.

Examples of sandwich degree courses Arts London (Central St Martins CAD); Birmingham City; Bournemouth; Brunel; Central Lancashire; Coventry; Leeds Beckett; Liverpool John Moores; Loughborough; Nottingham Trent; Southampton Solent; Ulster; Westminster.

ADMISSIONS INFORMATION
Number of applicants per place (approx) Brunel 9; Cardiff 6; Leicester 15; Liverpool 6; Manchester 5.

Advice to applicants and planning the UCAS personal statement Applicants should be able to give details of any work experience/work shadowing/discussions they have had in the media including, for example, in newspaper offices, advertising agencies, local radio stations or film companies (see also **Media Studies**). **Huddersfield** Critical awareness. Willingness to develop a range of communication skills including new technologies. **London (Gold)** Interest in a study in depth of media theory plus some experience in media practice. **Manchester Met** Motivation more important than grades.

Selection interviews **Yes** Brunel, Buckingham, Coventry, Glasgow Caledonian, Leicester, Middlesex, Southampton Solent, Ulster; **Some** Anglia Ruskin, Chester, Huddersfield (rarely), London (Gold) (mature students), Sheffield Hallam (mature students).

Interview advice and questions Courses differ in this subject and, depending on your choice, the questions will focus on the type of course, either biased towards the media, or towards human communication by way of language, psychology, sociology or linguistics. See also separate subject tables and **Chapter 6**.

Reasons for rejection (non-academic) Unlikely to work well in groups. Poor writing. Misguided application, for example more practical work wanted. Poor motivation. Inability to give reasons for choosing the course. More practice needed in academic writing skills. Wrong course choice, wanted more practical work.

AFTER-RESULTS ADVICE
Offers to applicants repeating A-levels **Possibly higher** Coventry; **Same** Brunel, Cardiff, Chester, Huddersfield, Loughborough, Nottingham Trent, Robert Gordon, Sheffield Hallam.

GRADUATE DESTINATIONS AND EMPLOYMENT (2011/12 HESA)
See **Business and Management Courses (Specialised)**, **Marketing** and **Media Studies**.

Career note Graduates have developed a range of transferable skills in their courses which open up opportunities in several areas. There are obvious links with openings in the media, public relations and advertising.

OTHER DEGREE SUBJECTS FOR CONSIDERATION
Advertising; Art and Design; Cultural Studies; Digital Communications; English; Film, Radio, Video and TV Studies; Information Studies; Journalism; Languages; Linguistics; Marketing; Media Studies; Psychology; Public Relations; Speech Sciences.

Check **Chapter 4** when choosing your university and **Chapter 7** on how to read the subject tables.

COMMUNITY STUDIES/DEVELOPMENT

(see also **Health Sciences/Studies, Nursing and Midwifery, Social and Public Policy and Administration, Social Work**)

These courses cover aspects of community social issues, for example housing, food, health, the elderly, welfare rights and counselling and features of community development such as education, arts, sport and leisure. Work experience is very important. Most courses will lead to professional qualifications.

Useful websites www.csv.org.uk; infed.org/mobi/developing-community.

NB The points totals shown to the left of the institutions are for ease of reference only. It must not be assumed that Tariff points are always used by institutions or that they can be substituted for an offer in grades. The level of an offer is not necessarily indicative of the quality of a course.

COURSE OFFERS INFORMATION

Subject requirements/preferences **GCSE** English and mathematics grade A–C may be required at some institutions. **AL** No specific subjects required. **Other** Minimum age 19 plus youth work experience for some courses. Health and Disclosure and Barring Service (DBS) checks required for some courses.

Your target offers and examples of courses provided by each institution

320 pts **Sussex** – ABB 320 pts (Chld Yth Theor Prac) (IB 34 pts)

300 pts **Birmingham** – BBB 300 pts (Soc Pol Hous Commun) (IB 32 pts)
Edinburgh – BBB 300 pts (Commun Educ) (IB 34 pts)
Glasgow – BBB 300 pts (Commun Dev) (IB 30 pts)

280 pts **Huddersfield** – 280 pts (Yth Commun Wk)
Hull – 280 pts (Commun Yth Wk St)
London Met – BBC 280 pts (Commun Dev Ldrshp)
Newman – 280 pts (Yth Commun Wk)

260 pts **Sunderland** – 260 pts (Pblc Hlth; Commun Yth St)
West Scotland – BCC 260 pts (Commun Lrng Part)
Winchester – 260–300 pts (Chld Yth Commun St) (IB 25 pts)

240 pts **Bolton** – 240 pts (Commun St)
Dundee – AB–CCC (Commun Lrng Dev)
Glyndŵr – 240 pts (Yth Commun Wk)
Leeds Beckett – 240 pts (Yth Wrk Commun Dev) (IB 24 pts)
Manchester Met – 240–280 pts (Yth Commun Wk) (IB 26 pts)
Oldham (Univ Campus) – 240 pts (Hlth Commun St)

220 pts **Coventry** – CCD (App Commun Soc St) (IB 26 pts)
Sunderland – 220 pts (Commun Mus)
Worcester – 220–240 pts (Yth Commun Serv)

200 pts **Bedfordshire** – 200 pts (Yth Commun St)
Cardiff Met (UWIC) – 200 pts (Yth Commun Educ)
East London – 200 pts (Commun Serv Ent; Yth Commun Wk)
Gloucestershire – 200 pts (Yth Wk)
St Mark and St John – 200 pts (Yth Commun Wk)
Ulster – 200 pts (Commun Yth Wk)

180 pts **Bradford (Coll Univ Centre)** – 180 pts (Yth Commun Dev)
St Mark and St John – 180 pts (Commun Soc; Commun Dev)
Sheffield Hallam – 180 pts (Yth Commun Wk)

160 pts **De Montfort** – 160 pts (Yth Commun Dev) (IB 28 pts)
London (Gold) – CC (App Soc Sci Commun Dev Yth Wk)
Trinity Saint David – 160 pts (Yth Commun Wk)

120 pts **South Wales** – 120 pts (Comm Hlth Wlbng)

80 pts **Cumbria** – 80 pts (Yth Commun Wk)
London (Birk) – for under 21s (over 21s varies) (Commun Dev Pblc Plcy)

For a quick reference offers calculator, fold out the inside front cover.

Alternative offers
See **Chapter 7** and **Appendix 1** for grades/UCAS Tariff points information for the International Baccalaureate, Scottish Highers/Advanced Highers, the Welsh Baccalaureate, the Irish Leaving Certificate, the Cambridge Pre-U Diploma, the Advanced Diploma and the Extended Project.

EXAMPLES OF FOUNDATION DEGREES IN THE SUBJECT FIELD
Cornwall (Coll); De Montfort; Derby; Durham New (Coll); Glyndŵr; Grimsby (Univ Centre); Kent; Leeds Beckett; Lincoln; Llandrillo Cymru (Coll); Newcastle (Coll); Northampton; Northumberland (Coll); Norwich Arts; Sheffield Hallam; Somerset (Coll); South Devon (Coll); South Wales; Staffordshire Reg Fed (SURF); Truro (Coll); Walsall (Coll); Warwickshire (Coll); Wirral Met (Coll); Wolverhampton; Worcester; York (Coll).

CHOOSING YOUR COURSE (SEE ALSO CH.1)
Some course features
Birmingham Modules offered in criminology, youth and children, political history, the family, migration and faith. A year in industry is also offered.
Coventry A professional training route for careers in community and charity work and urban regeneration.
Edinburgh Course focuses on adult education, community work, community arts and youth work and people's participation in all aspects of community life. Practice placement blocks in Years 2 and 3, and concurrent practice placements in Year 4.
Hull A professional training for practitioners in youth and community work.
Sussex In the Social Work degree, 170 days of placement take place in Years 2 and 3.

Universities and colleges teaching quality See www.qaa.ac.uk; http://unistats.direct.gov.uk.

ADMISSIONS INFORMATION
Number of applicants per place (approx) Liverpool John Moores 2; Manchester Met 8; St Mark and St John 7.

Advice to applicants and planning the UCAS personal statement You should describe work you have done with people (elderly or young), particularly in a caring capacity, such as social work, or with the elderly or young children in schools, nursing, hospital work, youth work, community or charity work. You should also describe any problems arising and how staff dealt with them. See **Appendix 3**. **St Mark and St John** Strong multicultural policy. English as a Foreign Language teaching offered.

Selection interviews **Yes** Huddersfield (in groups), Manchester Met; **Some** Cardiff Met (UWIC), Liverpool John Moores.

Interview advice and questions This subject has a vocational emphasis and work experience, or even full-time work in the field, will be expected. Community work varies considerably, so, depending on your experiences, you could be asked about the extent of your work and how you would solve the problems which occur. See also **Chapter 6**. **Derby** Take us through your experience of youth and community work. What are the problems facing young people today?

Reasons for rejection (non-academic) Insufficient experience. Lack of understanding of community and youth work. Uncertain career aspirations. Incompatibility with values, methods and aims of the course. No work experience.

AFTER-RESULTS ADVICE
Offers to applicants repeating A-levels **Same** Liverpool John Moores, St Mark and St John.

GRADUATE DESTINATIONS AND EMPLOYMENT (2011/12 HESA)
See **Social Work**.

Career note Social and welfare areas of employment provide openings for those wanting to specialise in their chosen field of social work. Other opportunities will also exist in educational administration, leisure and outdoor activities.

OTHER DEGREE SUBJECTS FOR CONSIDERATION

Communication Studies; Education; Health and Social Care; Nursing; Politics; Psychology; Social Policy and Administration; Social Work; Sociology; Youth Studies.

COMPUTER COURSES

(including **Artificial Intelligence, Computing, Computer Networks, Computer Science, Games Technology** and **Web Management**; see also **Communication Studies/Communication, Information Management and Librarianship, Media Studies**)

Computer courses are popular and provide graduates with good career prospects. Courses vary in content and in the specialisations offered, which may include software engineering, programming languages, artificial intelligence, data processing and graphics. Many universities offer sandwich placements in industry and commerce.

Useful websites www.bcs.org; www.techuk.org; www.e-skills.com; www.iap.org.uk.

NB The points totals shown to the left of the institutions are for ease of reference only. It must not be assumed that Tariff points are always used by institutions or that they can be substituted for an offer in grades. The level of an offer is not necessarily indicative of the quality of a course.

COURSE OFFERS INFORMATION

Subject requirements/preferences **GCSE** Mathematics usually required. A*/A/B grades may be stipulated for some subjects. **AL** Mathematics, a science subject or computer science required for some courses.

Cambridge (Churchill, Magdalene) STEP used as part of the offer; (Gonville and Caius) AEA mathematics required (see **Chapter 6**).

Your target offers and examples of courses provided by each institution

420 pts **London (UCL)** – A*AAc incl maths/fmaths (Mathem Comp) (IB 39 pts)

400 pts **Imperial London** – A*A*A (Maths Mathem Comp) (IB 39 pts HL 7 maths)

380 pts **Bristol** – A*AA–AAB 380–320 pts (Comp Sci; Comp Sci (St Abrd); Comp Sci Electron; Maths Comp Sci) (IB 38–35 pts HL 665)

Cambridge – A*AA 380 pts (Comp Sci) (IB 40–41 pts HL 766–777)

Imperial London – A*AA 380 pts (Comp; Comp (Artif Intel); Comp (Gms Vis Interact); Comp (Comp Biol Med); Comp (Soft Eng)) (IB 39–42 pts)

London (UCL) – A*AA incl maths 380 pts (Comp Sci) (IB 39 pts)

Oxford – A*AA 380 pts (Comp Sci) (IB 39 pts)

Southampton – A*AA incl maths phys 380 pts (Electron Eng Comp Sys) (IB 38 pts HL 18 pts)

360 pts **Bath** – AAA–A*AB 360 pts (Comp Sci) (IB 38–34 pts)

City – 360 pts (Comp Sci) (IB 29 pts)

Durham – AAA 360 pts (Comp (Euro St)) (IB 37 pts)

Edinburgh – AAA–ABB incl maths 360–320 pts (Comp Sci courses; Artif Intel; Inform) (IB 37–32 pts)

Exeter – AAA–ABB (Comp Sci; IT Mgt Bus) (IB 36–32 pts)

Leeds – AAA (Artif Intel; Comp Sci Maths; Comp Sci) (IB 35–38 pts)

Queen's Belfast – A*AB–AAA 360 pts (Maths Comp Sci MSci)

St Andrews – AAA–AAB 360 pts (Comp Sci courses; Comp Sci Psy; Comp Sci Phys) (IB 36–40 pts)

Southampton – AAA incl maths 360 pts (Comp Sci; Comp Sci Artif Intel; Maths Comp Sci; Comp Sci Imag Multim Sys; Comp Sci Dist Sys Net; Comp Sci Mbl Scr Sys)

Warwick – AAA (Comp Sci; Comp Sys; Comp Mgt Sci) (IB 38 pts)

York – AAA (Comp Sci courses) (IB 36 pts)

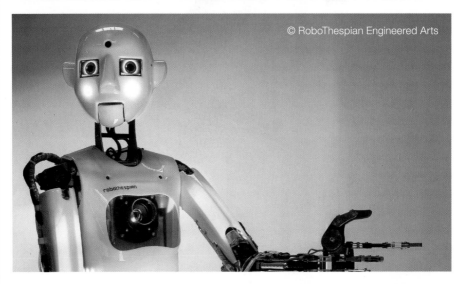
Check **Chapter 4** when choosing your university and **Chapter 7** on how to read the subject tables.

A Guide to Uni Life

The one-stop guide
to what student life is <u>REALLY</u> like

LUCY TOBIN

ISBN: 978 1 84455 216 0

£9.99

Fresh from graduation, Lucy Tobin gives you the lowdown on everything you need to know to have a brilliant time at uni and get a great degree!

trotman t

The UK's leading education publisher

Computing at Brunel

At Brunel, you can expect:

- £27,000 average salary six months after the course

- 89% of 2012 graduates went on to work and/or study six months after completing their studies

Courses available include:
Business Computing BSc
Computer Science BSc
(with optional specialisms)

Brunel
UNIVERSITY
L O N D O N

OPEN DAYS & CAMPUS TOURS' BOOKING
🖥 www.brunel.ac.uk/openday
📞 +44(0)1895 265595

340 pts **Aston** – AAB–AAA 340–360 pts (Bus Comp IT) (IB 35 pts HL 665)
Birmingham – AAB (Comp Sci) (IB 34–36 pts)
Durham – AAB 340 pts (Comp Sci) (IB 36 pts)
East Anglia – AAB (Comp Sci MComp) (IB 33 pts)
Kent – AAB (Comp Sci courses) (IB 33 pts)
Liverpool – AAB (Electron Commer Comp; Intnet Comp; Comp Inf Sys; Comp Sci (Yr Ind); Comp Sci) (IB 33 pts HL 5 maths)
London (King's) – AAB 340 pts (Comp Sci Robot; Comp Sci (St Abrd/Yr Ind); Comp Sci Mgt; Comp Sci Intel Sys) (IB 35 pts)
London (QM) – 340 pts (Comp Sci MSc) (IB 34 pts)
Loughborough – AAB–AAA (Comp Sci MSci) (IB 34 pts HL 5 maths)
Manchester – AAB (Comp Sci Maths; Artif Intel; Comp Sci; Comp Sci Bus Mgt) (IB 35 pts)
Newcastle – AAB–ABB 340–320 pts (Comp Sci Courses) (IB 34–35 pts)
Nottingham – AAB (Comp Sci) (IB 36–34 pts HL 6 maths)
Queen's Belfast – AAB 340 pts (Comp Sci MEng)
Sheffield – AAB (Comp Sci; Ent Comp IT Mgt Bus; Comp Sci Maths) (IB 35 pts HL 6 maths)
Surrey – 340 pts (Comp IT; Comp Sci) (IB 34 pts)
Sussex – AAB–ABB 340–320 (Comp Sci; Comp Sci Artif Intel; Gms Multim Env) (IB 34 pts)
Warwick – AAB (Comp Bus St) (IB 36 pts)
320 pts **Bournemouth** – 320–340 pts (Comp Animat Art; Comp Vis Animat) (IB 32–33 pts)
Bristol UWE – 320 pts (Comp Sci Gms Tech; Comp courses)
Brunel – ABB–BBB 320–300 pts (Comp Sci (Artif Intel); Comp Sci (Soft Eng); Comp Sci; Comp Sci (Net Comp); Comp Sci (Dig Media Gms); Maths Comp Sci) (IB 33 pts)
Cardiff – ABB 320 pts (Comp Sci; Comp Sci Vis Comp; Comp Sci Hi Perf Comp; Comp Sci Scrty Foren; Comp Maths) (IB 33 pts)
City – 320–280 pts (Inf Sys) (IB 28 pts)

Check **Chapter 4** when choosing your university and **Chapter 7** on how to read the subject tables.

East Anglia – ABB (Comp Graph; Comp Sci BSc; Comp Sci Imag Multim; Comp Bus) (IB 32 pts)

Essex – ABB–BBB (Comp courses; Comp Net; Comp Gms) (IB 32–30 pts)

Glasgow – ABB (Comp Sci courses) (IB 32 pts)

Huddersfield – ABB 320 pts (Comp Gms Prog)

Kent – ABB (Web Comp) (IB 33 pts)

Lancaster – ABB (Comp Sci courses; Acc Fin Comp Sci)

Leicester – ABB (Comp Sci)

Loughborough – ABB–AAB (Comp Sci; Comp Sci Artif Intel) (IB 32 pts)

Northumbria – 320 pts (Comp Sci; Web Des Dev) (IB 26 pts)

Nottingham – ABB (Comp Sci; Comp Sci Artif Intel) (IB 32 pts)

Reading – 320 pts (Cyber) (IB 33 pts)

Strathclyde – ABB 320 pts (Comp Sci) (IB 34 pts)

Sussex – ABB (Comp Bus Mgt; Comp Dig Media) (IB 34 pts)

Swansea – ABB 280–320 pts (Comp Sci) (IB 33 pts)

300 pts **Aberdeen** – BBB 300 pts (Comp Sci) (IB 32 pts)

Aston – BBB–ABB 300–320 pts (Comp Sci courses; Comp Bus) (IB 32 pts)

Bournemouth – 300 pts (Web Des; Comp)

Bristol UWE – 300 pts (Comp Sci; Gms Tech) (IB 26 pts)

Buckingham – BBB–BBC 300–280 pts (Comp courses)

Central Lancashire – 300 pts (Web Multim)

De Montfort – 300 pts (Bus Inf Sys)

Greenwich – 300 pts (Maths Comp)

Heriot-Watt – BBB 300 pts (Comp Sci) (IB 29 pts)

Huddersfield – BBB (Comp Sci; Comp)

Keele – BBB 300 pts (Comp Sci) (IB 30 pts)

Leeds Beckett – 300 pts (Gms Des) (IB 26 pts)

Leicester – BBB (Comp; Comp Mgt)

London (Gold) – BBB (Crea Comp; Comp Sci; Interact Des)

London (QM) – 300–340 pts (Bus Comp; Comp Sci courses; Comp ICT; Comp ICT Bus Mgt) (IB 32–34 pts)

London (RH) – ABC–BBB 300 pts (Comp Sci) (IB 32 pts)

Loughborough – BBB (Inf Mgt Web Dev) (IB 32 pts HL 5 maths)

Northumbria – 300 pts (Comp Gms Des Prod; Ethl Hack Comp Scrty) (IB 26 pts)

Plymouth – BBB 300 pts (Comp Inf Scrty; Comp Net; Comp Gms Dev; Comp Sci) (IB 30 pts)

Queen's Belfast – BBB 300 pts (Comp Sci courses)

Reading – 300–340 pts (Comp Sci courses)

Salford – 300 pts (Comp sci)

South Wales – 300pts (Comp Sci)

Teesside – 300 pts +interview (Comp Gms Prog)

280 pts **Abertay** – BBC (Comp Arts; Comp Gms Tech)

Aberystwyth – 280 pts (Intnet Comp Sys Admin; Bus Inf Tech; Comp Graph Vsn Gms; Comp Sci Artif Intel; Comp Sci) (IB 24 pts)

Brighton – BBC 280 pts (Web Des; Comp Sci (Gms); Comp Sci Gms Tech; Bus Comp Sys; Dig Media; Comp Sci) (IB 28 pts)

Central Lancashire – 280–300 pts (Comp Gms Dev)

City – 280–320 pts (Comp Sci Gms Tech) (IB 28 pts)

Coventry – BBC 280 pts (Comp Sci) (IB 29 pts)

Derby – 280 pts (Comp Gms Modl Animat; IT; Comp Foren Inv; Comp Gms Prog; Net Scrty; Comp Sci)

Hertfordshire – 280 pts (Comp Maths)

Kingston – 280 pts (Web Dev Bus; Inf Sys; Cyb Scrty Comp Foren Joint Hons; Comp Sci)

Leeds Beckett – 280 pts (Comp Foren Scrty; Comp; Comp Foren) (IB 25 pts)

Lincoln – 280 pts (Comp Gms Prod; Comp Inf Sys; Comp Sci; Gms Dev)

Liverpool John Moores – 280 pts (Comp St; Comp Animat Vis; Comp Foren; IT Multim Comp; Comp Gms Tech)

Manchester Met – 280 pts (Comp Net Tech; Comp Sci; Gms Des Dev; Multim Web Comp; Comp Foren Scrty; Comp Gms Tech; Comp; Web Mob App Dev) (IB 28 pts)

Norwich Arts – BBC 280 pts (Gms Art Des) (IB 25 pts)

Nottingham Trent – 280 pts (Comp Sci courses; Comp Sys (Foren/Net))

Oxford Brookes – BBC (Comp Gms Animat; Comp Sci; Net Comp) (IB 30 pts)

Sheffield Hallam – 280 pts (Comp Sci)

South Wales – 280 pts (Comp Gms Des)

Stirling – BBC 280 pts (Comp Sci; Bus Comp) (IB 32 pts)

Suffolk (Univ Campus) – 280 pts (Comp Gms Des)

Teesside – 280 pts (Comp Dig Foren; Comp Chrctr Animat; Comp Gms Animat; Comp Sci; Comp; Crea Dig Media; ICT; Web Multim Des; Comp Gms Des; Comp Gms Art)

Ulster – 280–300 pts (Comp Sci; Comp Sci (Soft Sys Dev); Comp Gms Dev)

260 pts **Bolton** – 260 pts (Gms Des)

De Montfort – 260 pts (Comp courses; Gms Tech)

Derby – 260 pts (Maths Comp Sci)

Gloucestershire – 260 pts (Comp)

Greenwich – 260 pts (Comp Sys Net)

Hertfordshire – 260 pts (Multim Sys Tech)

Hull – 260–280 pts (Comp Sci; Comp Gms; Web Des Dev)

Liverpool Hope – 260–300 pts (Comp Sci; Comp)

Liverpool John Moores – 260 pts (Cy Scrty) (IB 24 pts)

Northampton – 260–280 pts (Comp courses)

Portsmouth – 260–300 pts (Comp; Comp Sci; Web Tech) (IB 26 pts)

Sunderland – 260 pts (Comp Sci; Net Comp; Bus Comp; Comp Foren; Comp; ICT)

West Scotland – BCC 260 pts (Comp Gms Tech) (IB 24 pts)

240 pts **Aberdeen** – CCC (Artif Intel)

Abertay – CCC 240 pts (Web Des Commun)

Bangor – 240–300 pts (Comp Sci; Comp Sci Bus)

Bolton – 240 pts (Comp Net Scrty)

Bradford – 240–260 pts (Comp courses; Comp Sci Gms; Web Des Tech)

Canterbury Christ Church – CCC 240 pts (Comp; Web Des)

Cardiff Met (UWIC) – 240 pts (Comp)

Central Lancashire – 240–280 pts (Comp)

Chester – 240–280 pts (Comp Sci) (IB 26 pts)

Colchester (Inst) – 240–120 pts (Comp Sol (Intnet); Comp Sol (Net))

Cumbria – 240 pts (Bus Entre Comp)

East Anglia – CCC (App Comp Sci incl Fdn Yr) (IB 28 pts)

East London – 240 pts (Comp Net; Comp Gms Dev)

Edge Hill – 240 pts (Comp courses)

Edinburgh Napier – CCC 240 pts (Comp; Web Tech)

Glyndŵr – 240 pts (Comp Net Mgt Scrty)

Hertfordshire – 240 pts (Web Des; IT; Comp Sci)

Manchester Met – 240–280 pts (Artif Intel; Web Dev; Comp Comm Eng) (IB 28 pts)

Middlesex – 240 pts (Comp Net Comm)

Nottingham Trent – 240 pts (Comp St; Inf Sys)

Ravensbourne – AA–CC (Web Media) (IB 28 pts)

Sheffield Hallam – 240 pts (Comp; Net Mgt Des; Web Sys Des)

Staffordshire – 240 pts (Comp Sci; Dig Foren)

Westminster – CCC-AA 240 pts (Comp Net Comm; Comp Sci) (IB 28 pts)

West Scotland – CCC 240 pts (Web Mbl Dev) (IB 24 pts)

Worcester – 240 pts (Comp Gms Des Dev; Comp)

York St John – 240–300 pts (Bus IT)

220 pts **Dundee** – CCD (Comp Sci) (IB 28 pts)

Check **Chapter 4** when choosing your university and **Chapter 7** on how to read the subject tables.

      London Met – 220 pts (Comp courses; Comp Gms Prog)
      London South Bank – 220 pts (Comp courses)
      Wolverhampton – 220 pts (Comp Sci courses; Comp Sci (Gms Dev))
200 pts **Anglia Ruskin** – 200 pts (Comp Sci; Comp Gmg Tech)
      Bedfordshire – 200 pts (Comp Sci; Comp Maths; Comp Net; Gms Dev)
      Birmingham City – 200–280 pts (Comp Net Scrty; Comp Sci; Gms Tech; Web Des)
      Bucks New – 200–240 pts (Comp courses; Gms Dev)
      East London – 200 pts (Comp)
      Grimsby (Univ Centre) – 200 pts (Gms Des)
      Kingston – 200 pts (Comp St)
      Middlesex – 200–280 pts (Comp Gms; Comp Net; Comp Sci)
      Robert Gordon – BB–CCC (Comp Sci)
      Southampton Solent – 200 pts (Comp Gms Dev; Web Des; Net Scrty Mgt)
      Staffordshire – 200–240 pts (Comp Gms Des)
      Trinity Saint David (Swansea) – 200 pts (Comp Net; Comp Gms Dev; Comp Inf Sys)
      West Anglia (Coll) – 200 pts (Comp Sci)
      West London – 200 pts (Comp Inf Sys; Net Mbl Comp; Comp Sci; Inf Sys Bus)
180 pts **Bradford (Coll Univ Centre)** – 180 pts (Comp Net Sys Sprt; Comp Inf Sys)
      Sir Gâr (Coll) – 180 pts (Intnet Comp)
      West Scotland – BC 180 pts (Comp Net; Comp Gms Dev; Comp; IT) (IB 24 pts)
      Wolverhampton – 180 pts (Comp; IT Scrty)
160 pts **Farnborough (CT)** – 160 pts (Comp; Comp Gmg; Comp Netwrkg)
      Glasgow Caledonian – CC 160 pts (Comp Gms)
      Greenwich (Sch Mgt) – 160 pts (Bus Mgt IT; Comp Sci; Comp Sci Bus Inform)
      Peterborough (Reg Coll) – 160 pts (Comp Inf Sys)
      South Essex (Coll) – 160 pts (Comp Gms Des)
      Trinity Saint David (Swansea) – 160 pts (Web Dev; Crea Comp Gms Des)
140 pts **Trinity Saint David** – 140–360 pts (Comp)
120 pts **East London** – 120 pts (Comp Gms Des (Stry Dev))
  80 pts **Greenwich (Sch Mgt)** – 80 pts (HR Mgt Inform Sys)
      UHI – C (Comp)

      Open University – contact +44 (0)845 300 6090 **or** www.openuniversity.co.uk/you (Comp IT; Comp Bus/Des/Maths/Psy/Stats; ICT)

Alternative offers
See **Chapter 7** and **Appendix 1** for grades/UCAS Tariff points information for the International Baccalaureate, Scottish Highers/Advanced Highers, the Welsh Baccalaureate, the Irish Leaving Certificate, the Cambridge Pre-U Diploma, the Advanced Diploma and the Extended Project.

EXAMPLES OF FOUNDATION DEGREES IN THE SUBJECT FIELD
Central Nottingham (Coll); Chesterfield (Coll); Colchester (Inst); Cornwall (Coll); Croydon (Coll); Cumbria; Doncaster (Coll Univ Centre); Durham New (Coll); Ealing, Hammersmith and West London (Coll); East Berkshire (Coll); Edge Hill; Kent; Kingston; Kirklees (Coll); Lakes (Coll); Leeds (CA); Llandrillo Cymru (Coll); London Met; Manchester (Coll); Mid-Cheshire (Coll); NEW (Coll); Newcastle (Coll); Northbrook (Coll); Nottingham New (Coll); Ravensbourne; Riverside Halton (Coll); St Helens (Coll); Sheffield (Coll); Shrewsbury (CAT); Somerset (Coll); South Devon (Coll); South Essex (Coll); South Wales; Southampton Solent; Staffordshire Reg Fed (SURF); Stockport (Coll); Stockton Riverside (Coll); Stoke-on-Trent (Coll); Suffolk (Univ Campus); Truro (Coll); Tyne Met (Coll); Warrington (Coll); West Cheshire (Coll); Westminster Kingsway (Coll); Wigan and Leigh (Coll); Wiltshire (Coll); York (Coll).

CHOOSING YOUR COURSE (SEE ALSO CH.1)
Some course features
Lancaster and Morecambe (Coll) The degree in Computer Science has a strong emphasis on practical computing with a balance between hardware and software aspects. A common first-year

course leads to specialisms in Software Engineering, Multimedia Systems or Embedded Systems. There is also an option to study abroad or spend a year in industry.

Leicester Courses are offered with sandwich and European placements.

Reading A course is offered in Computer Science and Cybernetics involving applications with human activities and systems.

Southampton All computer courses are accredited by the British Computer Society.

Surrey The first two years of the Computer Science programme offer a wide range of modules and are followed by an optional placement in Year 3. Three- or four-year courses are offered in Computer Modelling and Simulation, Computer Science Engineering, and Computing and Information Technology.

Warwick (Comp Sci) The course places strong emphasis on physical science, mathematics and computing principles. Accredited by the British Computer Society, it offers modules in computer security, machine learning and artificial intelligence, and the option to extend to a master's degree after the first two years.

Universities and colleges teaching quality See www.qaa.ac.uk; http://unistats.direct.gov.uk.

Top research universities and colleges (RAE 2008) (Computer Science and Informatics) Cambridge; Imperial London; Southampton; Edinburgh; Oxford; London (UCL); Manchester; Nottingham; Glasgow; Liverpool; Lancaster; Leeds.

Examples of sandwich degree courses Aberystwyth; Aston; Bath; Birmingham City; Bournemouth; Bradford; Brighton; Bristol UWE; Brunel; Cardiff; Cardiff Met (UWIC); City; Coventry; De Montfort; Derby; East Anglia; Edinburgh Napier; Gloucestershire; Greenwich; Hertfordshire; Huddersfield; Kent; Kingston; Leeds Beckett; Lincoln; Liverpool John Moores; London (QM); London (RH); London South Bank; Loughborough; Manchester; Manchester Met; Middlesex; Newcastle; Northumbria; Nottingham Trent; Oxford Brookes; Plymouth; Portsmouth; Queen's Belfast; Reading; Sheffield Hallam; South Wales; Southampton Solent; Staffordshire; Sunderland; Surrey; Teesside; Ulster; Westminster; Wolverhampton; York.

ADMISSIONS INFORMATION

Number of applicants per place (approx) Abertay 2; Aberystwyth 8; Aston (Bus Comp IT) 12; Bath 9; Birmingham 7; Bournemouth 8; Bradford 13; Bristol 8; Bristol UWE 4; Brunel 10; Buckingham 6; Cambridge 5; Cardiff 5; City 10; Coventry 10; Derby 3; Dundee 6; Durham 10; East Anglia (Maths Comp) 7; Edinburgh 4; Essex 2; Exeter 10; Glasgow Caledonian 8; Glyndŵr 3; Heriot-Watt 6; Hull (Comp Sci) 6; Imperial London 6; Kent 8; Kingston 10; Lancaster 5; Leeds 10; Leicester 13; Lincoln 5; Liverpool 7; Liverpool John Moores 3; London (King's) 20; London (QM) 6; London (RH) 5; London (UCL) 15; Loughborough 2; Manchester Met 10, (Bus IT) 8; Newcastle 7; Northumbria 4; Nottingham 8; Nottingham Trent 4; Oxford Brookes 18; Plymouth 12; Portsmouth 6; Robert Gordon 3; Roehampton 3; Sheffield Hallam 5; Southampton 9; Staffordshire 4; Stirling 6; Strathclyde 16; Surrey 9; Swansea 5; Teesside 4; Warwick 11; York 6.

Advice to applicants and planning the UCAS personal statement Your computer and programming interests in and outside school or college should be described. It is also useful to give details of any visits, work experience and work shadowing relating to industrial or commercial organisations and their computer systems. (See **Appendix 3**.) Give details of your interests in, and knowledge of computer hardware, software and multimedia packages. Contact the Chartered Institute for IT for information. **Bristol** Deferred entry accepted.

Misconceptions about this course That anyone who plays computer games or uses a word processor can do a degree in Computer Studies. Some think Computing degrees are just about programming; in reality, programming is only one, albeit essential, part of computing. **Aston** (Bus Comp IT) 60% business, 40% computing and IT; compulsory placement year in industry. **City** (Bus Comp Sys) Some applicants think that it is a Business degree: it is a Computing degree focused on computing in business. **London (QM)** There are many misconceptions – among students, teachers and careers advisers – about what computer science entails. The main one is to confuse it with what schools call information and communication technology which is about the use of computer applications. Computer science is all about software – ie programming – and will generally only cover a limited study of hardware.

Check **Chapter 4** when choosing your university and **Chapter 7** on how to read the subject tables.

Selection interviews Yes Abertay, Bath, Blackburn (Coll), Bradford, Bristol UWE, Brunel, Buckingham, Cambridge, Cardiff, City, Coventry, Cumbria, Durham, Edinburgh, Edinburgh Napier, Hertfordshire, Hull, Kent, Kingston, Liverpool Hope, London (Gold), London (QM), London (UCL), London South Bank, Loughborough, Newcastle, Northampton, Northbrook (Coll), Nottingham Trent, Oxford (Comp Sci) 20%, Plymouth, Portsmouth, Sheffield Hallam, Southampton, Surrey, West London, Wigan and Leigh (Coll), York; **Some** Aberystwyth, Anglia Ruskin, Birmingham City, Blackpool and Fylde (Coll), Brighton, Chichester, East Anglia, Exeter, Imperial London, Liverpool John Moores, London Met, Manchester Met, Salford, South Wales, Staffordshire, Sunderland, Warwick (5%–10%); **No** Dundee, Nottingham, West Scotland.

Interview advice and questions While A-level computer studies is not usually required, you will be questioned on your use of computers and aspects of the subject which interest you. How do you organise your homework/social life? What are your strengths and weaknesses? Do you have any idea of the type of career you would like? See also **Chapter 6**. **City** The aim of the interview is to obtain a full picture of the applicant's background, life experiences etc, before making an offer. **York** No tests. Questions for discussion at the whiteboard are usually mathematical or are about fundamental computer science such as sorting.

Reasons for rejection (non-academic) Little practical interest in computers/electronics. Inability to work as part of a small team. Mismatch between referee's description and performance at interview. Unsatisfactory English. Can't communicate. Inability to convince interviewer of the candidate's worth. Incoherent, unmotivated, arrogant and without any evidence of good reason. **London (QM)** Misunderstanding of what computer science involves as an academic subject – especially in personal statements where some suggest that they are interested in a course with business and administrative skills. Lack of sufficient mathematics. Computer science is a mathematical subject and we cannot accept applicants who are unable to demonstrate good mathematical skills. **Southampton** Lack of motivation; incoherence; carelessness.

AFTER-RESULTS ADVICE
Offers to applicants repeating A-levels Higher Brighton, De Montfort, Greenwich, Kingston, St Andrews, Surrey, Sussex, Warwick; **Possibly higher** Bath, Bristol UWE, Edinburgh, Lancaster, Leeds, Newcastle, Oxford Brookes, Portsmouth, Sheffield, Teesside; **Same** Abertay, Aberystwyth, Anglia Ruskin, Aston, Blackpool and Fylde (Coll), Brunel, Buckingham, Cambridge, Cardiff, Cardiff Met (UWIC), Chichester, City, Derby, Dundee, Durham, East Anglia, East London, Exeter, Farnborough (CT), Huddersfield, Hull, Kent, Lincoln, Liverpool, Liverpool Hope, Liverpool John Moores, London (RH), London (UCL), London South Bank, Loughborough, Manchester Met, Newman, Northumbria, Nottingham Trent, Robert Gordon, Salford, Sheffield Hallam, Staffordshire, Suffolk (Univ Campus), Sunderland, Ulster, West London, Wolverhampton, Worcester, York.

GRADUATE DESTINATIONS AND EMPLOYMENT (2011/12 HESA)
Computer Science graduates surveyed 7740 **Employed** 4175 **In voluntary employment** 170 **In further study** 1275 **Assumed unemployed** 1125

Information Systems graduates surveyed 2660 **Employed** 1275 **In voluntary employment** 40 **In further study** 670 **Assumed unemployed** 315

Artificial Intelligence graduates surveyed 70 **Employed** 40 **In voluntary employment** 0 **In further study** 10 **Assumed unemployed** 5

Career note A high proportion of graduates go to work in the IT sector with some degrees leading towards particular fields (usually indicated by the course title). Significant areas include software design and engineering, web and internet-based fields, programming, systems analysis and administration.

OTHER DEGREE SUBJECTS FOR CONSIDERATION
Business Studies; Communications Engineering; Computer Engineering; Electrical and Electronic Engineering; Geographical Information Systems; Information Studies; Mathematics; Physics; Software Engineering.

CONSUMER STUDIES/SCIENCES

(including **Consumer Product Design** and **Trading Standards**; see also **Food Science/Studies and Technology, Hospitality and Event Management**)

Consumer Studies courses involve topics such as food and nutrition, shelter, clothing, community studies and consumer behaviour and marketing. Trading Standards courses focus on consumer law, contract law, food law, weights and measures, criminal investigation, fraud, counterfeiting, and fair trading. Accredited by the Trading Standards Institute, they can lead to careers as trading standards officers.

Useful websites www.which.co.uk; www.tradingstandards.gov.uk.

NB The points totals shown to the left of the institutions are for ease of reference only. It must not be assumed that Tariff points are always used by institutions or that they can be substituted for an offer in grades. The level of an offer is not necessarily indicative of the quality of a course.

COURSE OFFERS INFORMATION

Subject requirements/preferences GCSE Mathematics and English usually required. **AL** No specific subjects required.

Your target offers and examples of courses provided by each institution
320 pts **Reading** – ABB–BBB 320–300 pts (Nutr Fd Consum Sci; Consum Bhv Mark)
260 pts **Ulster** – BCC 260 pts (Consum St)
240 pts **Abertay** – CCC 240 pts (Fd Consum Sci)
    Birmingham (UC) – 240 pts (Fd Consum Mgt) (IB 24 pts)
    Edinburgh Napier – CCC 240 pts (Mark Mgt Consum St)
220 pts **Harper Adams** – 220–260 pts (Fd Consum St)

Alternative offers
See **Chapter 7** and **Appendix 1** for grades/UCAS Tariff points information for the International Baccalaureate, Scottish Highers/Advanced Highers, the Welsh Baccalaureate, the Irish Leaving Certificate, the Cambridge Pre-U Diploma, the Advanced Diploma and the Extended Project.

EXAMPLES OF FOUNDATION DEGREES IN THE SUBJECT FIELD
Leeds Beckett.

CHOOSING YOUR COURSE (SEE ALSO CH.1)
Some course features
Harper Adams The Course in Food and Consumer Studies covers aspects of the food industry from processing to retail in relation to the consumer. Paid work placements are an option.
Reading (Consum Bhv Mark) Course focuses on marketing, psychology, economics and research methods, with a wide range of optional modules from across the University including management, languages, politics and sociology.

Universities and colleges teaching quality See www.qaa.ac.uk; http://unistats.direct.gov.uk.

Examples of sandwich degree courses Birmingham (UC); Harper Adams.

ADMISSIONS INFORMATION
Number of applicants per place (approx) Birmingham (UC).

Advice to applicants and planning the UCAS personal statement Relevant work experience or work shadowing in, for example, business organisations, restaurants, cafes, or the school meals service, would be appropriate. See also **Hospitality and Event Management** and **Dietetics** and **Appendix 3**.

Interview advice and questions Questions will stem from your special interests in this subject and in the past have included: What interests you in consumer behaviour? What are the advantages and disadvantages of measuring consumer behaviour? What is ergonomics? What do you understand by the term sustainable consumption? What world or national news has annoyed, pleased or upset you? What relevance do textiles and dress have to home economics? How would you react in a room full of fools? See also **Chapter 6**.

AFTER-RESULTS ADVICE
Offers to applicants repeating A-levels **Same** Ulster.

GRADUATE DESTINATIONS AND EMPLOYMENT (2011/12 HESA)
Career note The various specialisms involved in these courses allow graduates to look for openings in several other career areas, for example, food quality assurance, consumer education and advice. Many graduates enter business administration and careers in retailing, evaluating new products and liaising with the public.

OTHER DEGREE SUBJECTS FOR CONSIDERATION
Biological Sciences; Business Studies; Dietetics; Environmental Health; Food Science; Health Studies; Hospitality Management; Marketing; Nutrition; Psychology; Retail Management.

DANCE/DANCE STUDIES
(see also **Drama**)

Every aspect of dance can be studied in the various courses on offer as well as the theoretical, educational, historical and social aspects of the subject.

Useful websites www.arts.org.uk; www.cdet.org.uk; www.ballet.co.uk; www.ndta.org.uk.

NB The points totals shown to the left of the institutions are for ease of reference only. It must not be assumed that Tariff points are always used by institutions or that they can be substituted for an offer in grades. The level of an offer is not necessarily indicative of the quality of a course.

COURSE OFFERS INFORMATION
Subject requirements/preferences **GCSE** English usually required. **AL** No specific subjects required. **Other** Disclosure and Barring Service (DBS) checks required for some courses: check websites. Practical dance experience essential.

Your target offers and examples of courses provided by each institution

340 pts **Brighton** – AAB 340 pts +interview +portfolio (Perf Vis Arts (Dance))
Roehampton – 340 pts (Dance St) (IB 28 pts)
320 pts **Edge Hill** – 320 pts (Dance; Dance Dr) (IB 27 pts) offer may be altered based on audition
Lancaster – ABB 320 pts (Thea) (IB 32 pts)
Surrey – ABB (Dance Cult Choreo) (IB 34 pts)
300 pts **Chichester** – BBB–BBC 280–300 pts (Dance) (IB 30 pts)
Kingston – BBB 300–360 pts (Dance) (IB 26 pts)
Leeds Beckett – 300 pts (Dance) (IB 26 pts)
West London – 300 pts (Musl Thea)
280 pts **Cardiff Met (UWIC)** – 280 pts (Dance) (IB 25 pts)
Cumbria – 280 pts (Dance Perf Dr Perf; Dance Perf Musl Thea Perf)
De Montfort – 280 pts (Dance) (IB 28 pts)
Lincoln – 280 pts (Dance)
Liverpool John Moores – 280 pts (Dance Prac)
London (RAc Dance) – 280 pts (Ballet Educ)
Middlesex – 280–300 pts (Dance) (IB 24 pts)
Suffolk (Univ Campus) – 280 pts (Dance)
Teesside – 280 pts (Dance) (IB 25 pts)

Winchester – 280–320 pts (Choreo Dance) (IB 25 pts)

260 pts Bath Spa – 260–300 pts (Dance) (IB 26 pts)
Central Lancashire – 260–300 pts (Dance Perf Teach)
Chester – 260–300 pts +audition (Dance) (IB 28 pts)
Greenwich – 260 pts (Prof Dance Musl Thea) (IB 28 pts)
Liverpool Hope – 260–280 pts (Dance) (IB 25 pts)
Northampton – 260–300 pts (Dance) (IB 24 pts)
Plymouth – 260 pts (Dance Thea) (IB 28 pts)
Salford – BCC–BBB 260–300 pts (Perf Dance Thea) (IB 31 pts)

240 pts Bedfordshire – 240 pts (Dance Prof Prac)
Birmingham City – 240 pts (App Perf (Commun Educ))
Canterbury Christ Church – 240 pts (Dance Educ; Perf Arts (Dance))
Coventry – CCC 240 pts (Dance) (IB 27 pts)
East London – 240 pts (Dance Urb Prac; Prof Dance Musl Thea)
London Met – 240 pts (Spo Dance Thera)
Manchester Met – 240–280 pts (Dance) (IB 28 pts)
Ulster – BCD–CCC 240 pts (Dance Dr; Dance); Dance Mus; Dance Ir) (IB 24 pts)
Wolverhampton – 240 pts (Dance Dr; Dance)
York St John – 200–240 pts (Dance) (IB 24 pts)

220 pts Brooksby Melton (Coll) – 220 pts +interview (Perf Arts)
Derby – 220–300 pts (Dance Mov St Joint Hons) (IB 26 pts)
Falmouth – 220 pts (Dance; Choreo) (IB 24 pts)
South Wales – 220–180 pts (Crea Thea Arts)
Sunderland – 220 pts (Dance)

200 pts Bucks New – 200–240 pts (Dance Perf) (IB 24 pts)
Doncaster (Coll Univ Centre) – 200 pts +interview +audition (Dance Prac)

Check **Chapter 4** when choosing your university and **Chapter 7** on how to read the subject tables.

Grimsby (Univ Centre) – 200 pts (Perf (Dance))
Hull (Coll) – 200 pts (Dance)
Middlesex – 200–300 pts (Dance St) (IB 24 pts)
180 pts **Liverpool (LIPA)** – 180 pts (Dance)
160 pts **London (RAc Dance)** – 160 pts Dist learn (Dance Educ) (IB 24 pts)
 80 pts **Northern (Sch Contemp Dance)** – 80 pts check with School (Contemp Dance)

RConsvS – +audition (Modn Ballet) check with School
Trinity Laban Consv – +audition (Contemp Dance) check with School

Alternative offers
See **Chapter 7** and **Appendix 1** for grades/UCAS Tariff points information for the International Baccalaureate, Scottish Highers/Advanced Highers, the Welsh Baccalaureate, the Irish Leaving Certificate, the Cambridge Pre-U Diploma, the Advanced Diploma and the Extended Project.

EXAMPLES OF FOUNDATION DEGREES IN THE SUBJECT FIELD
Bournemouth; Bristol City (Coll); Farnborough (CT); Hull (Coll); Leeds City (Coll); Manchester (Coll); Newcastle (Coll); Northbrook (Coll); Nottingham New (Coll); Truro (Coll).

CHOOSING YOUR COURSE (SEE ALSO CH.1)
Some course features
Chichester Modules include choreography, stage and screen, improvisation, teaching and dance management therapy.
Kingston (Dance) Two themes: technique and expression and a study of British dance in modern muticultural Britain.
Roehampton The course involves an intensive programme of in-house performances and dance events. Strong links with ballet and contemporary dance companies.
Surrey (Dance Cult) Focus on dance of the 20th and 21st centuries, on dance techniques (including ballet, kathak, contemporary, and African people's dance), together with choreography and dance policy and practice.

Universities and colleges teaching quality See www.qaa.ac.uk; http://unistats.direct.gov.uk.

Top research universities and colleges (RAE 2008) See **Drama**.

Examples of sandwich degree courses Coventry; Staffordshire; Surrey.

ADMISSIONS INFORMATION
Number of applicants per place (approx) Chichester 6; De Montfort (Dance) 13, (Perf Arts) 9; Derby 12; Liverpool (LIPA) 24; Liverpool John Moores 3; Middlesex 12; Northern (Sch Contemp Dance) 6; Roehampton 17; Surrey 5; Trinity Laban Consv 5; York St John 3.

Advice to applicants and planning the UCAS personal statement Full details should be given of examinations taken and practical experience in contemporary dance or ballet. Refer to your visits to the theatre and your impressions. You should list the dance projects in which you have worked, productions in which you have performed and the roles. State any formal dance training you have had and the grades achieved. Applicants need to have dedication, versatility, inventiveness and individuality, practical experience of dance, theoretical ability and language competency. **Bath Spa** Dance experience outside education should be mentioned.

Misconceptions about this course That Performing Arts is only an acting course: it also includes music.

Selection interviews **Yes** Birmingham City, Cardiff Met (UWIC).

Interview advice and questions Nearly all institutions will require auditions or interviews or attendance at a workshop. The following scheme required by **Liverpool (LIPA)** may act as a guide:

1   Write a short essay (500 words) on your own views and experience of dance. You should take into account the following.

(i)   Your history and how you have developed physically and intellectually in your run-up to applying to LIPA.
(ii) Your main influences and what inspires you.
(iii) What you want to gain from training as a dancer.
(iv) Your ideas on health and nutrition as a dancer, taking into account gender and physicality.
2   All candidates must prepare **two** practical audition pieces.
(i)   Whatever you like, in whatever style you wish, as long as the piece does not exceed two minutes (please note: panel will stop anyone exceeding this time limit). There will be no pianist at this part of the session, so if you're using music please bring it with you. This devised piece should be created by you and this means that you should feel comfortable with it and that it expresses something personal about you. You should wear your regular practice clothes for your presentation.
(ii) You are asked to sing a musical theatre solo as part of the audition and will be accompanied by a pianist. An accompanist is provided, but you must provide the sheet music for your song, fully written out for piano accompaniment and in the key you wish to sing (the accompanist will **not** transpose at sight). **Important** Do NOT choreograph your song. You should expect to sit on a high stool or stand when singing for the audition.
3   Additionally, all candidates will participate in a class given on the day of audition.
(i)   Please ensure that you are dressed appropriately for class with clothing you are comfortable in but allows your movement to be seen. In preparing the practical elements of the audition, please remember that audition panels are not looking for a polished performance. The panel will be looking for candidates' ability to make a genuine emotional and physical connection with the material that they are presenting which shows clear intent and focus.

Remember that it is in your best interest to prepare thoroughly. Nerves inevitably play a part in any audition and can undermine even the best-prepared candidate. Your best defence is to feel confident in your preparation. See also **Chapter 6**. **Chichester** Applicants will be asked to prepare a set-piece in advance and to perform the piece in front of a group. **De Montfort** (Perf Arts) Practical workshops in dance and theatre plus a written paper. **Salford** (Perf Arts) Audition and interview. **Surrey** Applicants invited to spend a day at the University for interview and a practical class to assess dance skills. An audition fee may be charged. **Wolverhampton** Audition in the form of a dance class

Reasons for rejection (non-academic) Applicants more suitable for an acting or dance school course than a degree course. No experience of dance on the UCAS application. Limited dance skills. **Surrey** Inadequate dance background. Had not seen/read about/done any dance.

AFTER-RESULTS ADVICE
Offers to applicants repeating A-levels Same Chester, Chichester, De Montfort (Perf Arts), Liverpool John Moores, Salford, Surrey, Trinity Laban Consv, Winchester, Wolverhampton, York St John.

GRADUATE DESTINATIONS AND EMPLOYMENT (2011/12 HESA)
Graduates surveyed 1010 **Employed** 400 **In voluntary employment** 20 **In further study** 245 **Assumed unemployed** 70

Career note Teaching is the most popular career destination for the majority of graduates. Other opportunities exist as dance animators working in education or in the community to encourage activity and participation in dance. There is a limited number of openings for dance or movement therapists who work with the emotionally disturbed, the elderly or physically disadvantaged.

OTHER DEGREE SUBJECTS FOR CONSIDERATION
Arts Management; Drama; Education (Primary); Music; Performance Studies; Physical Education; Sport and Exercise Science.

DENTISTRY

(including **Dental Technology, Dental Hygiene** and **Oral Health Science**)

Dentistry involves the treatment and prevention of a wide range of mouth diseases from tooth decay and gum disease to mouth cancer. Courses in Dentistry/Dental Surgery cover the basic medical sciences, human disease, clinical studies and clinical dentistry. The amount of patient contact will vary between institutions but will be considerable in all dental schools. Intercalated courses in other science subjects are offered on most courses.

Useful websites www.bda.org; www.bsdht.org.uk; www.dla.org.uk.

NB The points totals shown to the left of the institutions are for ease of reference only. It must not be assumed that Tariff points are always used by institutions or that they can be substituted for an offer in grades. The level of an offer is not necessarily indicative of the quality of a course.

COURSE OFFERS INFORMATION

Subject requirements/preferences GCSE English, mathematics and science subjects required in most cases for Dentistry courses. A*/A/B grades stipulated in certain subjects by many dental schools. **AL** Chemistry plus biology or a science subject usually required for Dentistry: see offers lines below. (Dntl Tech, Oral Hlth Sci) Science subject required or preferred. **Other** Many dental schools use admissions tests (eg UKCAT: see **Chapter 6**). Evidence of non-infectivity or hepatitis B immunisation required and all new dental students screened for hepatitis C. Disclosure and Barring Service (DBS) check at enhanced level is also required.

London (King's) GCSE English and maths grade B.
Manchester GCSE 6 subjects at grade A.

Your target offers and examples of courses provided by each institution
420 pts **Birmingham** – AAAa–AAAb (Dnstry) (IB 36 pts)
        London (King's) – AAAa +UKCAT contact Health Schools Admissions for further information (Dnstry) (IB 35 pts HL 666 biol chem)
        Queen's Belfast – AAAa incl AL/AS chem A +1 from biol/maths/phys +UKCAT (Dnstry) (IB 36 pts HL 666)
410 pts **London (QM)** – AAAb incl biol+chem +UKCAT (Dnstry) (IB 38 pts HL 666)
360 pts **Bristol** – AAA incl chem +biol/phys (Dnstry) (IB 37 pts HL 666)
        Cardiff – AAA incl chem+biol 360 pts +UKCAT (Dnstry) (IB 36 pts HL 6 chem 6 biol)
        Dundee – AAA incl biol +2 from chem/phys/maths +UKCAT (Dnstry) (IB 37 pts)
        Leeds – AAA incl chem+biol (Dntl Srgy) (IB 37 pts HL 6 chem biol)
        Liverpool – AAA incl chem/biol (Dntl Srgy) (IB 36 pts HL 6 chem biol)
        Manchester – AAA +UKCAT (Dnstry) (IB 34 pts)
        Newcastle – AAA incl chem+biol +UKCAT (Dnstry) (IB 35 pts HL 6 chem biol)
        Sheffield – AAA +UKCAT (Dntl Srgy) (IB 37 pts HL 6 chem biol)
340 pts **Buckingham** – AAB incl chem+biol (Dntl Srgy)
        Glasgow – AAB incl chem +sci/maths +UKCAT (Dnstry) (IB 36 pts)
320 pts **Birmingham** – ABB (Dntl Hyg Thera) (IB 32–34 pts)
300 pts **Cardiff** – BBB 300 pts (Dntl Thera Hyg)
        Dundee – BBB (Oral Hlth Sci) (IB 30 pts HL 555)
        Edinburgh – BBB incl biol 300 pts (Oral Hlth Sci) (IB 32 pts)
        London (QM) – BBB 300 pts (Dntl Mat) (IB 26–28 pts)
        Portsmouth – 300 pts (Dntl Hyg Dntl Thera) (IB 29 pts HL 16 pts)
260 pts **Manchester Met** – 260–280 pts (Dntl Tech) (IB 27 pts)
        Teesside – 260 pts +interview (Dntl Hyg Dntl Thera) (IB 24 pts)
        UHI – BCC 260 pts (Oral Hlth Sci)
240 pts **Cardiff Met (UWIC)** – CCC incl 1 sci subj 240 pts (Dntl Tech) (IB 24 pts)
        Glasgow Caledonian – 240 pts (Oral Hlth Sci)

Alternative offers
See **Chapter 7** and **Appendix 1** for grades/UCAS Tariff points information for the International Baccalaureate, Scottish Highers/Advanced Highers, the Welsh Baccalaureate, the Irish Leaving Certificate, the Cambridge Pre-U Diploma, the Advanced Diploma and the Extended Project.

EXAMPLES OF FOUNDATION DEGREES IN THE SUBJECT FIELD
Bedfordshire; Essex; London (QM); Northampton.

CHOOSING YOUR COURSE (SEE ALSO CH.1)
Some course features
Birmingham Basic sciences are covered in Years 1 and 2, and clinical studies in Years 3, 4 and 5.
Bristol This is a six-year course, academically able students are encouraged to intercalate.
Cardiff Clinical teaching starts at an early stage.
Leeds Focus on clinical dentistry from the outset.
Liverpool Clinical skills introduced from Year 2.
London (King's) Main components cover the basic sciences, diagnosis and treatment of oral and dental conditions and clinical dentistry. These are vertically integrated with a larger component of basic sciences at the beginning and a larger clinical component at the end.
London (QM) Clinical skills introduced from Year 2.
Manchester Clinical skills introduced from Year 2.
Newcastle Basic sciences are covered in Years 1 and 2, and clinical studies in Years 3, 4 and 5.
Queen's Belfast Basic sciences are covered in Years 1 and 2, and clinical studies in Years 3, 4 and 5.
Sheffield Main components cover the basic sciences, diagnosis and treatment of oral and dental conditions and clinical dentistry. These are vertically integrated with a larger component of basic sciences at the beginning and a larger clinical component at the end.

Universities and colleges teaching quality See www.qaa.ac.uk; http://unistats.direct.gov.uk.

Top research universities and colleges (RAE 2008) Manchester; London (QM); London (King's); Sheffield; Bristol; Cardiff; Leeds; Newcastle; London (UCL).

ADMISSIONS INFORMATION
Number of applicants per place (approx) Birmingham 10, (Dntl Hyg Thera) 17, International applicants 129 (no quota); Bristol 9, (Pre-Dntl) 22; Cardiff 4; Cardiff Met (UWIC) (Dntl Tech) 1; Dundee 8, (Pre-Dntl) 5; Edinburgh (Oral Hlth Sci) 10 places every 2nd yr; Glasgow 7; Leeds 11; Liverpool 15; London (King's) 128 (offers to 1 in 5); London (QM) 18, (300 interviewed, 200 offers); Manchester 11, (Pre-Dntl) 21, (Oral Hlth Sci) 18, (Dnstry) 10; Manchester Met 16; Newcastle 12; Portsmouth 2; Queen's Belfast 5; Sheffield 16.

Numbers of applicants (a UK b EU (non-UK) c non-EU d mature) Bristol a633 b633 c83 d148; Glasgow a437 b45 c70 d79; Leeds a877 b42 c97 d158; Liverpool a704 b46 c73 d143; London (King's) a137 b137 c25; Manchester a1290 b81 c152 d331; Sheffield c3 accepted each year.

Admissions tutors' advice **Buckingham** The course is specially designed for the international student market and takes place at the Leicester Dental Academy and Clinic. Applications go through UCAS and should be submitted in June (check with University) for a September entry. Results of Medical or Dental examinations taken in the applicant's country should also be submitted, eg the All India Pre-Medical Test (AIPMT) for Indian applicants.

Advice to applicants and planning the UCAS personal statement UCAS applications listing four choices only should be submitted by 15 October. Applicants may add one alternative (non-Dentistry) course. However, if they receive an offer for this courses and are rejected for Dentistry, they will not be considered for Dentistry courses in Clearing if they perform better than expected in the examinations. On your UCAS application show evidence of your manual dexterity, work experience and awareness of problems experienced by dentists. Details should be provided of discussions with dentists and work shadowing in dental surgeries. Employment (paid or voluntary) in any field, preferably dealing with people in an environment widely removed from your home or school, could be described. Discuss any specialised fields of dentistry in which you might be interested. See also **Appendix 3**. **Bristol** Applications are not segregated by type of educational institution. Candidates are assessed on general presentation. At least 20 days of work experience is expected, if possible in different fields of dentistry. Re-sit candidates only considered if they failed to get the grades by a small margin and they had originally placed Bristol as their first firm choice. **Cardiff** Applicants must be able to demonstrate: (a) evidence of, and potential for, high academic achievement, (b) an understanding of the demands of dental training and practice, (c) a caring and committed attitude towards people, (d) a willingness to accept resonsibility, (e) an ability to communicate effectively, (f) evidence of broad social, cultural or sporting interests. **Glasgow** Applicants invited to submit a portfolio as evidence of their suitability. This will be assessed against the BDS Person Specification available from the Dental School. Candidates who do not submit a portfolio are not invited to selection interview. **London (King's)** School activities desirable, for example, general reading, debating, theological interests. Community activities very desirable. General activities desirable, for example, sport, first-aid, handiwork (which can be shown at interview to demonstrate manual dexterity). Work shadowing and paid or voluntary work very desirable (check website). **Manchester** Re-sit offers normally only made to students who firmly accepted an offer the previous year. Re-sit offers AAA. Applicants are required to have observed a general dental practitioner at work before applying; a minimum of two weeks is expected. **Newcastle** Applications from students with disabilities welcomed.

Misconceptions about this course **Cardiff Met (UWIC)** (Dntl Tech) Some think that the course allows them to practise as a dentist. Some think the degree is entirely practical.

Selection interviews Most dental schools will interview candidates. **Yes** Birmingham (400–450 applicants; 50% get through initial sort), Bristol, Cardiff, Dundee, Glasgow, Leeds, Liverpool, London (King's), London (QM), London (St George's), Newcastle, Portsmouth, Sheffield; **Some** Cardiff Met (UWIC).

Interview advice and questions Dental work experience or work shadowing is essential (check with university websites) and, as a result, questions will be asked on your reactions to the work and your understanding of the different types of treatment that a dentist can offer. In the past, questions at interview have included: What is conservative dentistry? What does integrity mean? Do you think the first-year syllabus is a good one? What qualities are required by a dentist? What are prosthetics, periodontics, orthodontics? What causes tooth decay? Questions asked on the disadvantages of being a dentist, the future of dentistry and how you could show that you are manually dexterous. Other questions on personal attributes and spare time activities. What are the careers within the profession open to dentists? Questions on the future of dentistry (preventative and cosmetic dentistry), the problems facing dentists, the skills needed and the advantages and disadvantages of fluoride in water. How do you relax? How do you cope with stress? See also **Chapter 6**. **Bristol** All candidates called for interview must attend in order to be considered for a place; 200 are selected for interview for the five-year course and 15 for the six-year course. Offers are made to 180 and six respectively. An essay is set on a dental subject and will be assessed for spontaneity, written content and clear thought processes. Candidates at interview are assessed on general presentation, response to questions, knowledge of dentistry, evidence of teamwork, leadership, general interests, manual dexterity and good eyesight (a practical test is taken). Examples of practical work, for example, art work, needlework etc may be taken to interview as evidence of manual dexterity. **Leeds** The interview assesses personality, verbal and communication skills and knowledge of dentistry. **London (King's)** 220 applicants are interviewed of whom 180 will receive offers. All applicants receiving offers will have been interviewed. Applicants complete a questionnaire prior to interview and the interviews last about 20 minutes. Applicants may take to interview any examples of practical work, for example, art, woodwork, needlework etc as evidence of manual dexterity.

Reasons for rejection (non-academic) Lack of evidence of a firm commitment to dentistry. Lack of breadth of interests. Lack of motivation for a health care profession. Unprofessional attitude. Poor manual dexterity. Poor communication skills. Poor English. Lack of evidence of ability to work in groups. Not for the faint-hearted! More interested in running a business and making money than in caring for people. **Cardiff Met (UWIC)** (Dntl Tech) Target numbers need to be precise so the course fills at a late stage.

Mature students The following universities/dental schools offer shortened (usually four years) courses in Dentistry/Dental Surgery for graduates with at least 2.1 degrees in specified subjects. GCE A-level subjects and grades are also specified. Check with universities: Liverpool, London (King's), (QM).

AFTER-RESULTS ADVICE

Offers to applicants repeating A-levels **Higher** Bristol (AAA), Cardiff (preference given to students who previously applied), Dundee, Leeds (very few), Manchester (AAA for applicants who firmly accepted offer of a place); **Same** Cardiff Met (UWIC) (Dntl Tech), Queen's Belfast.

GRADUATE DESTINATIONS AND EMPLOYMENT (2011/12 HESA)

Clinical Dentistry graduates surveyed 830 **Employed** 770 **In voluntary employment** 0 **In further study** 25 **Assumed unemployed** 5

Career note The great majority of Dental Technology graduates gain employment in this career with job opportunities excellent in both the UK and Europe. There are openings in the NHS, commercial dental laboratories and the armed services.

OTHER DEGREE SUBJECTS FOR CONSIDERATION

Anatomy; Biochemistry; Biological Sciences; Biomedical Materials Science; Chemistry; Medical Sciences; Medicine; Nursing; Optometry; Pharmacy; Physiology; Physiotherapy; Radiography; Speech Therapy/Sciences; Veterinary Medicine/Science.

DEVELOPMENT STUDIES

(see also **International Relations, Politics, Town and Country Planning**)

Development Studies courses are multi-disciplinary and cover a range of subjects including economics, geography, sociology, social anthropology, politics, natural resources, with special reference to countries overseas.

Useful websites www.devstud.org.uk; www.gov.uk/government/organisations/department-for-international-development; www.ids.ac.uk; see also **Politics**.

NB The points totals shown to the left of the institutions are for ease of reference only. It must not be assumed that Tariff points are always used by institutions or that they can be substituted for an offer in grades. The level of an offer is not necessarily indicative of the quality of a course.

COURSE OFFERS INFORMATION

Subject requirements/preferences **GCSE** Mathematics, English and a foreign language may be required. **AL** Science or social science subjects may be required or preferred for some courses.

Your target offers and examples of courses provided by each institution

340 pts **London LSE** – AAB (Env Dev) (IB 37 pts HL 666)
Manchester – AAB 340 pts (Dev St) (IB 35 pts)
Sussex – AAB–ABB (Econ Int Dev; Int Dev; Int Rel Dev) (IB 34–35 pts)

320 pts **Birmingham** – ABB 320 pts (Plan Econ) (IB 34 pts HL 665)
East Anglia – ABB 320 pts (Int Dev Soc Anth Pol; Int Dev) (IB 32 pts)
Leeds – ABB (Int Dev courses) (IB 34 pts)
London (Birk) – 320 pts p/t (Dev St Env)
London (QM) – 320–340 pts (Glob Chng Env Econ Dev) (IB 32 pts)
Reading – ABB–AAC 320 pts (Int Dev) (IB 32 pts)
Sussex – ABB–BBB (Sociol Int Dev) (IB 32 pts)

300 pts **Birmingham** – BBB (Af St Dev) (IB 32 pts)

280 pts **Bradford** – 280 pts (Econ Dev St) (30 pts)
Leeds Beckett – 280 pts (Int Rel Glob Dev) (IB 25 pts)

Check **Chapter 4** when choosing your university and **Chapter 7** on how to read the subject tables.

260 pts **Bath Spa** – 260–300 pts (Glob Dev Sust)
Derby – 260–300 pts (Int Rel Glob Dev Joint Hons; Thrd Wrld Dev Joint Hons)
Northampton – 260–300 pts (Int Dev courses)
240 pts **Bradford** – 240–280 pts (Dev Pce St)
East London – 240 pts (Int Dev Wrld NGO Mgt) (IB 24 pts)
London Met – 240 pts (Int Dev; Int Dev Int Rel)
220 pts **Ulster** – 220–260 pts (Geog Int Dev) (IB 24 pts)
200 pts **Portsmouth** – 200–280 pts (Int Dev St) (IB 28 pts)
160 pts **UHI** – CC 160 pts (Gael Dev; Sust Dev)

Alternative offers
See **Chapter 7** and **Appendix 1** for grades/UCAS Tariff points information for the International Baccalaureate, Scottish Highers/Advanced Highers, the Welsh Baccalaureate, the Irish Leaving Certificate, the Cambridge Pre-U Diploma, the Advanced Diploma and the Extended Project.

CHOOSING YOUR COURSE (SEE ALSO CH.1)
Some course features
Bradford Development Studies is offered with Economics or Peace Studies.
Derby (Int Rel Glob Dev) Course explores environmental, geographical, political, social, cultural and economic aspects of international relations and global development. Visits to key development organisations.
Leeds This is an interdisciplinary degree course with opportunity to study a language alongside. There are opportunities to spend a year abroad.
Manchester (Dev St) Students start to specialise in Year 2, choosing options from 10 study areas; in Year 3 they take a single or a joint specialisation with another area of study, for example, politics, economics.
Sussex International Development is also offered with French, Spanish or Italian, Geography, Economics, Anthropology, International Relations and Sociology.

Universities and colleges teaching quality See www.qaa.ac.uk; http://unistats.direct.gov.uk.

Top research universities and colleges (RAE 2008) Oxford; Manchester; East Anglia; Bath; London (SOAS); Birmingham.

Examples of sandwich degree courses Bath.

ADMISSIONS INFORMATION
Number of applicants per place (approx) Bradford 6; East Anglia 8; Leeds 8.

Admissions tutors' advice Discuss aspects of development studies which interest you, for example in relation to geography, economics, politics. Interests in Third World countries should be mentioned. Knowledge of current events.

Advice to applicants and planning the UCAS personal statement Some students think that Development Studies has something to do with property, with plants or with childhood. It is none of these and is about international processes of change, development, progress and crisis.

Interview advice and questions Since this is a multi-disciplinary subject, questions will vary considerably. Initially they will stem from your interests and the information given on your UCAS application and your reasons for choosing the course. In the past, questions at interview have included: Define a Third World country. What help does the United Nations provide in the Third World? Could it do too much? What problems does the United Nations face in its work throughout the world? Why Development Studies? What will you do in your Gap Year, and what do you want to achieve? See also **Chapter 6**.

AFTER-RESULTS ADVICE
Offers to applicants repeating A-levels **Same** East Anglia.

GRADUATE DESTINATIONS AND EMPLOYMENT (2011/12 HESA)
Career note The range of specialisms offered on these courses will encourage graduates to make contact with and seek opportunities in a wide range of organisations, not necessarily limited to the Third World and government agencies.

OTHER DEGREE SUBJECTS FOR CONSIDERATION
Economics; Environmental Science/Studies; Geography; Government; International Relations; Politics; Sociology; Sustainable Development.

DIETETICS
(see also **Food Science/Studies and Technology, Health Sciences/Studies, Nutrition**)

In addition to the scientific aspects of dietetics covering biochemistry, human physiology, food and clinical medicine, students are also introduced to health promotion, psychology, counselling and management skills. (See **Appendix 3**.)

Useful websites www.nutrition.org; www.bda.uk.com; www.dietetics.co.uk.

NB The points totals shown to the left of the institutions are for ease of reference only. It must not be assumed that Tariff points are always used by institutions or that they can be substituted for an offer in grades. The level of an offer is not necessarily indicative of the quality of a course.

COURSE OFFERS INFORMATION
Subject requirements/preferences **GCSE** English, mathematics and science usually required. **AL** Biology and/or chemistry may be required. **Other** Health and Disclosure and Barring Service (DBS) checks required and possible immunisation against hepatitis B for practice placements.

Your target offers and examples of courses provided by each institution
340 pts **London (King's)** – AAB (Nutr Diet) (IB 35 pts HL 665 chem biol)
Nottingham – AAB-ABB 340-320 pts (Nutr (Diet) MNutr) (IB 32-34 pts)
320 pts **Leeds** – ABB 320 pts (Fd Sci Nutr) (IB 34 pts)
Surrey – ABB 320 pts (Nutr Diet) (IB 34 pts)
300 pts **Cardiff Met (UWIC)** – 300 pts (Hum Nutr Diet) (IB 26 pts)
Coventry – BBB incl biol 300 pts (Diet) (IB 32 pts)
Hertfordshire – 300 pts incl B chem B biol (Diet)
Leeds Beckett – BBB incl chem 300 pts (Diet) (IB 26 pts HL 6 chem)
London Met – 300 pts (Diet Nutr)
Plymouth – 300 pts (Diet) (IB 31 pts)
Ulster – 300 pts +HPAT (Diet)
280 pts **Chester** – 280-300 pts (Nutr Diet) (IB 28 pts)
260 pts **Bath Spa** – 260-300 pts (Hum Nutr) (IB 26 pts)
Glasgow Caledonian – BCC incl chem 260 pts (Hum Nutr Diet) (IB 24 pts)
Robert Gordon – BCC 260 pts (Nutr Diet) (IB 27 pts)
200 pts **Edinburgh Queen Margaret** – BB 200 pts (Diet) (IB 26 pts)

Alternative offers
See **Chapter 7** and **Appendix 1** for grades/UCAS Tariff points information for the International Baccalaureate, Scottish Highers/Advanced Highers, the Welsh Baccalaureate, the Irish Leaving Certificate, the Cambridge Pre-U Diploma, the Advanced Diploma and the Extended Project.

CHOOSING YOUR COURSE (SEE ALSO CH.1)
Some course features
Bath Spa (Hum Nutr) Course focuses on the impact of diet, nutrition and lifestyle on health. It is not a Dietetics course and is aimed at students without a science background. There are scholarships of £1000 available.

University of Hertfordshire
UH

School of
Life and Medical Sciences

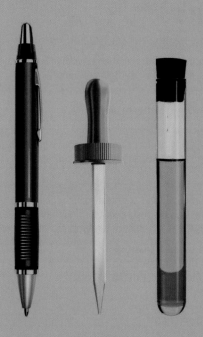

Develop the expertise to inspire healthier lives

Nutrition and diet are inextricably linked with good health. An understanding of a number of subjects – including human physiology, metabolism and cell biology, food preparation and hygiene, psychology and public health policy – will allow you to deliver advice and care to improve the wellbeing of individuals, groups or even populations throughout the lifecycle.

Our nutrition and dietetics focused courses will give you an in-depth knowledge of the science of nutrition and how food can be used to maintain health, as well as its role in the prevention and management of issues such as obesity, diabetes, cardiovascular disease and cancer.

Through a combination of theoretical study and practical placements, we will prepare you for employment in an area that presents a diverse range of career opportunities – such as dietitian, nutrition scientist, food manufacturing, education, public health and the food and leisure industry to name but a few.

Become more.

Find out more about our range of courses at:

go.herts.ac.uk/nutrition

Hertfordshire Three-year course leading to registration with the Health Professions Council to practise as a dietitian.
London (King's) Clinical placements in Years 2, 3 and 4.
Nottingham This is a four-year Master of Nutrition course which includes three integrated clinical placements.
Plymouth Supervised clinical practice in Year 2.
Surrey A professional training year is included.

Universities and colleges teaching quality See www.qaa.ac.uk; http://unistats.direct.gov.uk.

Examples of sandwich degree courses Cardiff Met (UWIC); Glasgow Caledonian; Leeds Beckett; Manchester Met; Surrey; Teesside; Ulster.

ADMISSIONS INFORMATION
Number of applicants per place (approx) Edinburgh Queen Margaret 5; Glasgow Caledonian 11; Nottingham 7; Surrey 1.

Advice to applicants and planning the UCAS personal statement Discuss the work with a hospital dietitian and describe fully work experience gained in hospital dietetics departments or with the schools meals services, and the problems of working in these fields. Admissions tutors expect applicants to have at least visited a dietetics department, and to be outgoing with good oral and written communication skills. Contact the British Dietetic Association (see **Appendix 3**).

Selection interviews **Yes** Coventry, Ulster.

Interview advice and questions Your knowledge of a career in dietetics will be fully explored and questions will be asked on your work experience and how you reacted to it. See also **Chapter 6**.

AFTER-RESULTS ADVICE
Offers to applicants repeating A-levels **Possibly higher** Glasgow Caledonian.

GRADUATE DESTINATIONS AND EMPLOYMENT (2011/12 HESA)
See **Nutrition**.

Career note Dietitians are professionally trained to advise on diets and aspects of nutrition and many degree courses combine both subjects. They may work in the NHS as hospital dietitians collaborating with medical staff on the balance of foods for patients, or in local health authorities working with GPs, or in health centres or clinics dealing with infant welfare and ante-natal problems. In addition, dietitians advise consumer groups in the food industry and government and may be involved in research. Courses can lead to professional registration: check with admissions tutors.

OTHER DEGREE SUBJECTS FOR CONSIDERATION
Biological Sciences; Biochemistry; Biology; Consumer Studies; Food Science; Health Studies; Hospitality Management; Human Nutrition; Nursing; Nutrition.

DRAMA

(including **Performing Arts/Studies, Theatre Arts, Theatre Studies** and **Theatre Design**; see also **Art and Design (General), Dance/Dance Studies)**

Drama courses are popular, with twice as many women as men applying each year. Lack of confidence in securing appropriate work at the end of the course, however, tends to encourage many applicants to bid for joint courses although these are usually far more competitive since there are fewer places available. Most schools of acting and drama provide a strong vocational bias whilst university drama departments offer a broader field of studies combining theory and practice. The choice of course will depend on personal preferences, either practical or theoretical, or a combination of both.

Useful websites www.equity.org.uk; www.abtt.org.uk; www.thestage.co.uk; www.uktw.co.uk; www.ukperformingarts.co.uk; www.arts.org.uk; www.stagecoach.co.uk.

NB The points totals shown to the left of the institutions are for ease of reference only. It must not be assumed that Tariff points are always used by institutions or that they can be substituted for an offer in grades. The level of an offer is not necessarily indicative of the quality of a course.

COURSE OFFERS INFORMATION

Subject requirements/preferences GCSE English usually required. **AL** English, drama, theatre studies may be required or preferred. (Thea Arts) English, theatre studies or drama may be required for some courses. **Other** Disclosure and Barring Service (DBS) clearance required for some courses: check websites.

Your target offers and examples of courses provided by each institution
390 pts Warwick – AABb (Thea Perf St; Engl Thea St) (IB 36 pts)
380 pts Cambridge – A*AA (Educ Engl Dr) (IB 40–41 pts HL 776)
360 pts Bristol – AAA-AAB 360–340 pts (Thea Engl) (IB 37–35 pts HL 666 incl Engl)
          Exeter – AAA-ABB 360–320 pts (Dr) (IB 36–32 pts)
          Lancaster – AAA 360 pts (Thea Engl Lit) (IB 36 pts)
          Leeds – AAA-ABB 360–320 pts (Thea Perf) (IB 34 pts)
340 pts Birmingham – AAB-ABB 340–320 pts (Dr Thea Art) (IB 34–36 pts)
          Bristol – AAB-ABB 340–320 pts (Thea Perf St; Thea courses) (IB 35–33 pts)
          Brunel – AAB-ABB 340–320 pts (Thea Engl) (IB 35 pts)
          East Anglia – AAB (Dr; Script Perf) (IB 33 pts)
          Kent – AAB-ABB 340–320 pts (Dr Thea; Vis Perf Arts; Dr courses)
          Kingston – 340–360 pts (Dr)
          London (RH) – AAB-ABB 340–320 pts (Dr Thea St; Engl Dr; Dr Crea Writ; Dr Mus; Dr Ger/
              Ital; Dr Phil; Fr Dr) (IB 35–34 pts)
          Loughborough – AAB (Engl Dr) (IB 34 pts)
          Manchester – AAB (Dr; Dr Engl/Scrn St/Mus) (IB 35 pts)
          Sheffield – AAB 340 pts (Engl Thea) (IB 35 pts)
          Surrey – AAB (Thea St) (IB 35–34 pts)
          Sussex – AAB-BBB (Dr courses; Dr St Film St; Dr St Span) (IB 34–36 pts)
          York – AAB 340 pts (Writ Dir Perf) (IB 35 pts)
320 pts Birmingham – ABB (Span Thea St) (IB 32 pts)
          Brunel – ABB 320 pts (Thea Crea Writ) (IB 33 pts)
          Edge Hill – ABB 320 pts (Dr) (IB 27 pts)
          Essex – ABB-BBB 320–300 pts (Dr Lit) (IB 32–30 pts)
          Glasgow – ABB (Thea St) (IB 36 pts)
          Huddersfield – ABB (Mus Dr)
          Lancaster – ABB 320 pts (Thea) (IB 32 pts)
          London (Gold) – ABB (Dr Thea Arts)
          London (QM) – ABB-BBB 320–340 pts (Dr; Fr/Ger/Russ Dr) (IB 34 pts)
          Loughborough – ABB-AAB 320–340 pts (Dr) (IB 34 pts)
          Reading – ABB-AAC 320 pts (Engl Lit Film Thea; Thea) (IB 32 pts)

THEATRE TRAINING
AT ITS FINEST

Short Courses · Foundation · Diploma · BA (Hons) · MA

ACTING | ACTOR MUSICIAN | MUSICAL THEATRE
THEATRE DIRECTING | MUSICAL DIRECTION
THEATRE PRODUCTION ARTS

MOUNTVIEW.ORG.UK

Mountview is one of the UK's leading drama schools with an outstanding reputation for training actors, musical theatre performers and theatre technicians.

INTRODUCTION TO DRAMA SCHOOL

Two-week summer courses in acting and musical theatre for students aged 17+ who love to perform or are planning on applying for drama school.

FOUNDATION COURSES

Want to take it further? Mountview's one-year foundation courses in acting and musical theatre provide a thorough grounding in acting skills for students seeking a career in performance.

FURTHER TRAINING AT MOUNTVIEW

FDA / BA (HONS) / POSTGRADUATE DIPLOMA IN THEATRE PRODUCTION ARTS

Technical theatre training offering specialist study in production and stage management, lighting, sound and digital design and set, prop and wardrobe design.

BA (HONS) / MA / POSTGRADUATE DIPLOMA IN PERFORMANCE

ACTING | ACTOR MUSICIAN | MUSICAL THEATRE | THEATRE DIRECTING | MUSICAL DIRECTION

The highest quality drama training with over 30 hours' contact teaching time per week preparing students for a successful and diverse career.

MOUNTVIEW.ORG.UK | @MOUNTVIEWLDN | 020 8881 2201

TAKE TO THE STAGE WITH RICHMOND

Find out more about our BA Degree
in Performance & Theatre Arts

+44 208 332 9000
enrol@richmond.ac.uk
www.richmond.ac.uk/theatre

RICHMOND
THE AMERICAN INTERNATIONAL
UNIVERSITY
IN LONDON

EXPERIENCE THE PERFORMING ARTS AT RICHMOND

Study BA Performance & Theatre Arts at Richmond, the American International University in London.

We provide a practical acting experience, a comprehensive knowledge of theatre history, scriptwriting and current performance and theatre practices.

Cast and crew of *Beyond Therapy* by Christopher Durang

7 reasons to study Performance & Theatre Arts

1. Participate in workshops and student showcase productions at a leading London theatre.

2. Participate in intensive acting, movement, stage fighting, voice and screen acting classes.

3. Acquire skills in preparing for auditions and how to respond to constructive critique.

4. Learn how to translate a play from the page to the stage.

5. Visit and critique plays in London's West End and Stratford-upon-Avon.

6. Write, produce or act in a play in a London theatre for the final project.

7. A high proportion of classes are practice-based.

Develop the professional competencies required of performers, actors, writers and directors.

Students will hone their creative skills as actors, performers, directors, writers and devisors, and their critical analytical abilities to enable them to appreciate drama, both as text and in performance.

Our performance facilities afford students the opportunity to act in a wide range of plays, from the classical repertoire to contemporary plays and performance pieces. Students are encouraged to devise their own scripts, creating new and imaginative theatre and performance work, crossing genres. Graduating students will present their final work in a public performance in a London Theatre.

To experience it for yourself, get in touch.

+44 208 332 9000
enrol@richmond.ac.uk
www.richmond.ac.uk/theatre

RICHMOND
THE AMERICAN INTERNATIONAL
UNIVERSITY
IN LONDON

GSA
/est. 1935

UNIVERSITY OF SURREY

GSA HAS BUILT AN INTERNATIONAL REPUTATION FOR EXCELLENCE IN TRAINING FOR ACTORS AND TECHNICIANS IN ALL AREAS OF THEATRE AND THE RECORDED MEDIA.

Situated in brand new building where it is part of the School of Arts at the University of Surrey, GSA offers quality vocational training in Acting, Musical Theatre and Professional Production Skills with courses ranging from National Diplomas and Foundation Degrees through to Post Graduate qualifications in Acting, Musical Theatre and Practice of Voice and Singing.

We currently offer both funded places as well as private ones. The opening of the Ivy Arts centre in 2011 has ensured new state of the art facilities for Professional Production Skills training and a versatile theatre space for productions. An excellent film and TV department and access to a number of other local theatres and a very special creative community make GSA a top choice amongst candidates wishing to train for the performing arts industry.

GSA also offers the only full-time Foundation Course in Musical Theatre at an accredited drama school. In addition GSA offers a Part-time evening course for students who intend to complete their A Levels prior to applying for full-time training. These new courses complement GSA's existing Saturday School and well subscribed Summer Schools.

Current high profile graduates include Tom Chambers, Brenda Blethyn OBE, Celia Imrie, Michael Ball, Bill Nighy, Chloe Hart, Chris Geere, Ellie Paskell, Claire Cooper, Rob Kazinsky, Ian Kelsey and Justin Fletcher MBE. Virtually every West End show features performers who trained at GSA. Current students have performed at the Olivier Awards ceremony, the opening of G-Live, Guildford, The Festival of Remembrance aat The Royal Albert Hall and numerous other prestigious events.

Guildford School of Acting   t: +44 (0)1483 684040
Stag Hill Campus,   f: +44 (0)1483 684070
Guildford, Surrey   e: gsaenquiries@gsa.surrey.ac.uk
GU2 7XH, UK   w: www.gsauk.org

Accredited

COURSES FOR 2015 ENTRY

GSA /est.1935
UNIVERSITY OF SURREY

UNDERGRADUATE COURSES
- BA (HONS) ACTING
- BA (HONS) MUSICAL THEATRE
- BA (HONS) PRODUCTION SKILLS

POSTGRADUATE COURSES
- MA ACTING
- MA MUSICAL THEATRE
- MA CONTEMPORARY THEATRE MAKING
- MA PRACTICE OF VOICE AND SINGING

WE ALSO OFFER
- FOUNDATION COURSE
- PART-TIME COURSE
- SUMMER SCHOOLS
- SATURDAY SCHOOL

For an application form/further details contact:

t: +44 (0)1483 684040
f: +44 (0)1483 684070
e: gsaenquiries@gsa.surrey.ac.uk
w: www.gsauk.org

drama uk
Accredited

Guildford School of Acting
Stag Hill Campus,
Guildford, Surrey
GU2 7XH, UK

TRINITY
COLLEGE LONDON

UNIVERSITY OF
SURREY

300 pts **Aberystwyth** – 300–320 pts (Dr Thea St; Perf St Joint Hons) (IB 30 pts)
Bristol UWE – 300–340 pts (Dr; Dr courses)
Brunel – BBB 300 pts (Thea Film TV St; Thea) (IB 32 pts)
Edinburgh Queen Margaret – 300 pts (Dr Perf)
Essex – 300 pts (Dr) (IB 32 pts)
GSA Consv – BBB +audition (Actg; Musl Thea) (IB 32 pts)
Leeds Beckett – 300 pts (Perf) (IB 26 pts)
London (Birk) – 300 pts p/t, for under 21s (over 21s varies) (Thea Dr St)
London (Royal Central Sch SpDr) – BBB 300 pts (Dr App Thea Educ)
Northumbria – 300 pts (Dr; Perf)
Queen's Belfast – BBB/BBCb (Dr courses)
West London – 300 pts (Musl Thea)

280 pts **Bangor** – 280–300 pts (Engl Thea Perf) (IB 26 pts)
Birmingham City – 280 pts (Engl Dr; Thea Perf Evnt Des)
Brighton – BBC +interview +portfolio Fdn Dip required (Perf Vis Arts (Thea))
Chichester – BBC–BCC +interview (Thea) (IB 30 pts)
Cumbria – 280 pts (Perf Art; Dr Perf Musl Thea Perf)
De Montfort – 280 pts (Perf Arts) (IB 28 pts)
Derby – 280 pts (Thea Arts) (IB 26 pts)
Edge Hill – BBC 280 pts (Mus Snd Dr)
GSA Consv – BBC +audition (Prof Prod Sk) (IB 30 pts)
Huddersfield – 280 pts (Dr; Dr Engl)
Hull – 280–320 pts (Dr Engl; Dr Thea Prac)
Lincoln – 280 pts (Dr) (IB 25 pts)

For a quick reference offers calculator, fold out the inside front cover.

London (Royal Central Sch SpDr) – BBC 280 pts (Thea Prac Thea Snd; Thea Prac Stg Des; Thea Prac Perf Arts; Thea Prac Prod Ltg; Thea Prac Pptry; Thea Prac Prop Mak; Thea Prac Scnc Art; Thea Prac Scnc Constr; Thea Prac Stg Mgt; Thea Prac Tech Prod Mgt; Thea Prac Ltg Des; Thea Prac Cstm Constr)

London Met – 280 pts (Thea Perf Prac)

Middlesex – 280 pts (Thea Arts (Perf); Thea Arts)

Oxford Brookes – BBC (Dr) (IB 29 pts)

Roehampton – 280 pts (Dr Thea Perf St) (IB 25 pts)

South Wales – BBC 280 pts (Thea Dr; Perf Media) (IB 25 pts)

Teesside – 280 pts +audition (Perf Lv Rec Media)

Ulster – BBC 280 pts (Dr; Dr Ir; Dr Mark; Dr Psy)

260 pts   **Cardiff Met (UWIC)** – 260 pts (Engl Dr)

Central Lancashire – BCC-BBB 260–300 pts (Mus Thea)

Chester – 260–300 pts (Dr Thea St courses) (IB 28 pts)

De Montfort – 260 pts (Dr St) (IB 28 pts)

Greenwich – 260 pts (Dr)

Liverpool Hope – 260–280 pts (Dr Thea St; Crea Perf Arts; Dr)

Liverpool John Moores – 260 pts (Dr) (IB 28 pts)

Newman – 260 pts (Dr courses)

Northampton – 260–300 pts (Dr courses; Actg)

Plymouth – 260 pts (Thea Perf)

St Mary's – (Dr; Dr Thea Arts; Dr App Thea) (IB 28 pts)

Salford – 260–300 pts (Engl Dr; Perf Actg)

Sunderland – 260 pts (Dr Engl)

Winchester – 260–300 pts (Strt Arts; Dr Perf Arts; Dr) (IB 26 pts)

240 pts   **Bath Spa** – 240–300 pts (Dr St; Perf Arts) (IB 24 pts)

Birmingham (UC) – 240 pts (Arts Ent Mgt)

Birmingham City – 240 pts (Stg Mgt)

Bishop Grosseteste – 240 pts (App Dr Mus)

Bournemouth Arts – 240–280 pts (Actg)

Canterbury Christ Church – 240 pts (Perf Arts (Dr)) (IB 24 pts)

Central Lancashire – 240–280 pts (Contemp Thea Perf; Actg)

Coventry – CCC 240 pts (Thea Prof Prac) (IB 27 pts)

Cumbria – 240 pts (Dr)

East London – 240 pts (Prof Dance Musl Thea; Thea St)

Glyndŵr – 240 pts (Thea TV Perf)

London South Bank – 240 pts (Engl Dr Perf; Dr Perf St; Thea Prac Crea Prodg)

Manchester Met – 240–280 pts (Dr; Contemp Thea Perf; Actg) (IB 28 pts)

Portsmouth – 240–300 pts (Engl Dr; Dr Perf; Crea Perf Arts)

Rose Bruford (Coll) – 240–280 pts (Am Thea Arts; Euro Thea Arts; Stg Mgt; Cstm Prod)

Royal Welsh (CMusDr) – 240–360 pts (Actg; Stg Mgt; Thea Des)

St Mark and St John – 240 pts (Actg)

Sheffield Hallam – 240 pts (Perf Stg Scrn)

Southampton Solent – 240 pts (Perf)

Staffordshire – 240–200 pts (Thea St Tech Stg Prod)

Ulster – CCC 240 pts (Dance Dr) (IB 24 pts)

Wolverhampton – 240 pts (Dance Dr)

Worcester – 240–300 pts (Dr Perf)

220 pts   **Anglia Ruskin** – 220–260 pts (Dr; Dr Engl Lit) (IB 24 pts)

Bishop Grosseteste – 220 pts (App Dr Vis Art)

Blackpool and Fylde (Coll) – 220 pts (Musl Thea)

Brooksby Melton (Coll) – 220 pts +interview (Perf Arts)

Derby – 220–300 pts (Thea St Joint Hons)

Falmouth – 220 pts (Mus Thea; Thea)

Sunderland – 220 pts (Dr; Perf Arts)

Check **Chapter 4** when choosing your university and **Chapter 7** on how to read the subject tables.

Wolverhampton – 220 pts (Dr) (IB 24 pts)

200 pts **Bedfordshire** – 200 pts (Thea Prof Prac)
Bucks New – 200–240 pts (Perf Arts)
Doncaster (Coll Univ Centre) – 200 pts +audition +interview (Contemp Perf Prac)
Hull (Coll) – 200 pts (Musl Thea; Tech Thea Prod)
Staffordshire – 200–240 pts (Dr Perf Thea Arts)
Trinity Saint David (Swansea) – 200 pts (Dr Educ St)
West London – 200 pts (Actg Stg)
York St John – 200–240 pts (Thea)

180 pts **Manchester (Coll)** – 180 pts (Actg Media)
Trinity Saint David (Swansea) – 180 pts (Cnslg Dr; Perf Arts)

160 pts **Birmingham City** – 160 pts audition (Actg)
Colchester (Inst) – 160 pts (Musl Thea; Crea Perf; Tech Thea)
Grimsby (Univ Centre) – 160 pts interview +audition (Perf (Dr))
Liverpool (LIPA) – 160–280 pts (Mus Thea Enter Mgt; Commun Dr; Actg; Thea Perf Des; Thea Perf Tech)
London (Royal Central Sch SpDr) – CC (Act (Mus Thea); Actg (Coll Devsd Thea); Actg)
London Regent's – CC 160 pts (Actg Glob Thea)
Reading – 160 pts (Thea Arts Educ Df St)
Rose Bruford (Coll) – 160–280 pts (Actr Mushp; Actg)
Trinity Saint David – 160–360 pts +audition individual offers made after audition (Actg) (IB 26 pts)

120 pts **Blackpool and Fylde (Coll)** – 120–360 pts (Actg)
100 pts **Guildhall (Sch Mus Dr)** – 100 pts (Stg Mgt Tech Thea; Actg)
80 pts **Croydon (Coll)** – 80–100 pts (Des Crft Stg Scrn)
Essex – EE 80 pts +audition (Actg; Actg Contemp Thea)
RConsvS – 80 pts (Contemp Perf Prac; Actg; Tech Prod Arts)

ALRA – +audition (Actg)
Arts Educ Sch – +audition; contact admissions tutor (Actg Film TV; Musl Thea)
Arts London – +interview +portfolio +audition (Actg; Dir; Perf Des Prac)
Bristol Old Vic (Thea Sch) – +audition +interview (Prof Actg; Prof Stg Mgt)
LAMDA – +audition (Prof Actg; Stg Mgt Tech Thea)
London (RADA) – +audition +interview (Actg; Tech Thea Stg Mgt)
London Mountview (Ac Thea Arts) – +audition +interview +portfolio (Thea Prod Arts; Perf (Musl Thea); Perf (Actg))

Alternative offers
See **Chapter 7** and **Appendix 1** for grades/UCAS Tariff points information for the International Baccalaureate, Scottish Highers/Advanced Highers, the Welsh Baccalaureate, the Irish Leaving Certificate, the Cambridge Pre-U Diploma, the Advanced Diploma and the Extended Project.

EXAMPLES OF FOUNDATION DEGREES IN THE SUBJECT FIELD
Blackpool and Fylde (Coll); Bournemouth; Bournemouth and Poole (Coll); Bournemouth Arts; Bradford; Bristol City (Coll); Chichester; Colchester (Inst); Cornwall (Coll); Craven (Coll); Exeter (Coll); Farnborough (CT); Hereford (CA); Hertfordshire; Hull (Coll); Kirklees (Coll); Leeds City (Coll); NEW (Coll); Newcastle (Coll); Northbrook (Coll); Norwich City (Coll); Nottingham New (Coll); Rose Bruford (Coll); Rotherham (CAT); St Helens (Coll); Sheffield (Coll); South Devon (Coll); South Essex (Coll); Staffordshire Reg Fed (SURF); Suffolk (Univ Campus); Sunderland; Truro (Coll); Wigan and Leigh (Coll).

CHOOSING YOUR COURSE (SEE ALSO CH.1)
Some course features
Anglia Ruskin (Dr) The course content depends on the options chosen, for example dramatic performance, technical theatre, drama in theory and practice, directing and TV drama.
Brunel (Thea) A strong practical emphasis.

De Montfort (Perf Arts) A highly practical programme covering acting, directing, dance, film, arts management and community education.

Hull The Drama course offers a study of drama in all its aspects – literary, historical, aesthetic and presentational – with equal stress on formal teaching and practical work. Performance Studies is also offered with Drama, Music or Theatre.

London (Gold) The Drama and Theatre Arts course provides a broad study of theatre, radio, film and TV as well as drama in the community. It has a good balance of practical experience and theatrical study.

Loughborough (Dr) Throughout the course, theoretical studies support the practical aspects with historical and analytical elements of European and American Theatre.

Universities and colleges teaching quality See www.qaa.ac.uk; http://unistats.direct.gov.uk.

Top research universities and colleges (RAE 2008) (Drama, Dance and Performing Arts) Warwick (Film TV St); Roehampton (Dance); London (QM); St Andrews; Manchester; Bristol; Glasgow; Exeter; London (RH).

ADMISSIONS INFORMATION

Number of applicants per place (approx) Aberystwyth 10; Arts London (Actg) 32, (Dir) 10; Bath Spa (Dr) 10, (Actg) 13; Birmingham 15; Bishop Grosseteste 4; Bristol 19; Brunel 9; Chester 14; Cumbria 4; De Montfort (Perf Arts) 5; East Anglia 13; Edge Hill 8; Edinburgh Queen Margaret 4; Essex 15; Exeter 20; Huddersfield 5; Hull 16, (Scarborough) 2; Hull (Coll) 2; Kent 24; Lancaster 18; Leeds 10; Liverpool (LIPA) (Perf Arts (Actg)) 48; Liverpool John Moores 10; London (Gold) 28; London (RH) 10; London (Royal Central Sch SpDr) (Thea Prac) 5; London Met 20; London Mountview (Ac Thea Arts) (Musl Thea) 8; Loughborough 6; Manchester (Dr) 6, (Dr Engl Lit) 8; Manchester (Coll) 10; Manchester Met 48; Middlesex 26; Northampton 3; Northumbria 25; Nottingham Trent 4; Reading 17; Roehampton 6; Royal Welsh (CMusDr) (Actg) 50, (Stg Mgt) 10; Warwick 18; Winchester (Dr) 6; Worcester 4; York 4; York St John 9.

Advice to applicants and planning the UCAS personal statement List the plays in which you have performed and specify the characters played. Indicate any experience in other areas of theatre, especially directing or writing. Add any information on projects you have initiated or developed or worked on in theatre craft, such as set design, costume design, lighting design, prop-making, scene painting. List any community arts projects such as work with youth clubs, hospital radio, amateur dramatics, music/drama workshops and voluntary work within the arts. Show your strengths in dance and theatre, and your commitment to drama in all its aspects. See **Chapter 6** and also **Appendix 3**. **Bristol** Deferred entry accepted. **London (Royal Central Sch SpDr)** (Dr App Thea Educ) We look for an interest in theatre and performance in different social and cultural settings, for example, community, schools, prisons. We also look for an enquiring mind, practical drama skills, flexibility and focus. **Manchester** Due to the detailed nature of entry requirements for Drama courses, the University is unable to include full details in the prospectus. For complete and up-to-date information on the entry requirements for these courses, please visit the website at www.manchester.ac.uk/ugcourses. **Warwick** Gap Year only acceptable in exceptional circumstances. **York** (Writ Dir Perf) Strong analytical ability plus experience in a related field, eg stage management/design, drama, writing are important factors.

Misconceptions about this course That a Theatre Studies course is a training for the stage: it is not. **Arts London** Provides a long-established classical conservatoire-type training for actors, and not Theatre Studies or Performance Arts courses, contrary to the views of some students. It is no longer a private school and home and EU students pay the standard degree fee. **De Montfort** (Perf Arts) Students are unaware that the course involves music. **Kent** This is not like an acting school. **Staffordshire** We stress to applicants that this is not a drama school course. **Winchester** This is not an Acting course although practical work is involved. **York St John** This is not a course for intending actors.

Selection interviews Most institutions, usually with auditions which are likely to involve solo and group tests. **Yes** East Anglia, Essex, Portsmouth; **Some** Anglia Ruskin, Bristol, Bucks New, Chester, St Mary's.

Interview advice and questions See also **Chapter 6**. **Arts London** (Actg) Two three-minute speeches or scenes, one of which must be from the classical repertoire. (Dir) Interview and practical workshop which may involve directing actors. **Bristol** Assesses each case on its merits, paying attention to candidate's educational and cultural opportunities. Particularly interested in applicants who have already shown some evidence of commitment in their approach to drama in practical work, theatre-going, film viewing or reading. One fifth of applicants are called for interview and take part in practical sessions. They may present any art work, photography or similar material. (London Board Practical Music not acceptable for Drama/Music unless offered with theoretical music plus one other A-level.) **Brunel** All applicants to whom an offer may be made will be auditioned, involving a practical workshop, voice, movement improvisation and a short prepared speech. Offers unlikely to be made to those with less than a grade B in drama or theatre studies. **Chichester** Applicants will be asked to prepare a set-piece in advance and to perform it before a group. **De Montfort** (Perf Arts) What do you hope to gain on a three-year course in Performing Arts? Interviews involve practical workshops in drama and theatre and a written paper. **East Anglia** Looks for candidates with a sound balance of academic and practical skills. Applicants will be expected to analyse performance and to understand what is entailed in the production of a drama. **Hull** Interviews two groups of 18 for whole day which presents a mini-version of the course, with entire staff and a number of current students present. Offers then made to about half. Selection process is all-important. More applicants for the Joint Honours courses with English, Theology, American Studies or a modern language, who have a conventional half-hour interview. Drama/English is the most popular combination and the offer includes a B in English. **Kent** No Single Honours candidate accepted without interview. Emphasis equally on academic and practical abilities. Questions asked to probe the applicant's creative and analytical grasp of theatre. **Lancaster** (Thea St) Candidates invited for interview and should be prepared to take part in a workshop with other candidates. We are just as interested in backstage people as actors and now have an arts administration option. **Loughborough** Candidates judged as individuals. Applicants with unconventional subject combinations and mature students considered. Final selection based on interview and audition. Applicants ought to show experience of practical drama, preferably beyond school plays. **Royal Welsh (CMusDr)** (Actg) audition; (Stg Mgt) interview; (Thea Des) interview and portfolio presentation. All applicants are charged an audition/interview fee. **Warwick** Interview is important to assess academic potential and particularly commitment to, and suitability for, teaching; offers therefore variable.

Reasons for rejection (non-academic) Poor ambition. Wrong expectations of the course. Several students clearly want drama school acting training rather than a degree course. Not enough background reading. **Arts London** Insufficient clarity about career aims. **De Montfort** (Perf Arts) Candidate more suitable for a drama or dance school than for a degree course. No genuine engagement with the subject. Evidence of poor attendance at school.

AFTER-RESULTS ADVICE
Offers to applicants repeating A-levels Higher Bristol, Glasgow (AAA), Hull, Warwick; **Possibly higher** London (RH); **Same** Brunel, Chichester, De Montfort (Perf Arts), East Anglia, GSA Consv, Huddersfield, Kent, Leeds (further audition required), Liverpool Hope, Liverpool John Moores, Loughborough, Manchester (Coll), Newman, Nottingham Trent, Roehampton, Royal Welsh (CMusDr), St Mary's, Staffordshire, Sunderland, Winchester, York St John.

GRADUATE DESTINATIONS AND EMPLOYMENT (2011/12 HESA)
Graduates surveyed 4850 **Employed** 2215 **In voluntary employment** 175 **In further study** 835 **Assumed unemployed** 440

Career note Some graduates develop careers in performance, writing, directing and producing as well as wider roles within the theatre. Others go on to careers such as teaching, media management and retail where their creativity and communication skills are valued.

OTHER DEGREE SUBJECTS FOR CONSIDERATION
Art and Design (Costume Design, Stage Design); Arts Management; Dance; Education (Primary); English; Performance Studies.

ECONOMICS

(see also **Business and Management Courses, Mathematics, Statistics**)

Economics is about how society makes good use of the limited resources available. Degree courses cover all aspects of finance, taxation and monetary union between countries, aiming to equip the student to analyse economic problems in a systematic way and thus acquire an understanding of how economic systems work. Economics involves mathematics and statistics, and applicants without economics at A or AS-level should be prepared for this.

Useful websites www.bized.co.uk; www.iea.org.uk; www.res.org.uk; www.economist.com; www.neweconomics.org; see also **Finance**.

NB The points totals shown to the left of the institutions are for ease of reference only. It must not be assumed that Tariff points are always used by institutions or that they can be substituted for an offer in grades. The level of an offer is not necessarily indicative of the quality of a course.

COURSE OFFERS INFORMATION

Subject requirements/preferences GCSE English, mathematics and occasionally a foreign language required. A*/A/B may be stipulated by some universities. **AL** Mathematics, economics or business studies may be required or preferred. Business studies may be preferred if economics is not offered. Applicants should note that many courses will accept students without economics (check prospectuses and websites).

Your target offers and examples of courses provided by each institution

440 pts **Warwick** – A*AAa (Econ; Econ Ind Org; Econ Pol Int St) (IB 38 pts HL 6 maths)

430 pts **Warwick** – A*AAb (PPE) (IB 38 pts)

400 pts **London (UCL)** – A*AAe–AAAe incl maths (Econ; Econ Stats; Stats Econ Fin) (IB 38–39 pts HL 18–19 pts incl 7 maths)

380 pts **Bath** – A*AA incl maths (Econ Pol; Econ) (IB 38 pts HL 766)

Bristol – A*AA–AAB (Econ courses) (IB 38–35 pts)

Cambridge – A*AA (Econ; Lnd Econ) (IB 40–41 pts HL 776)

Durham – A*AA incl maths 380 pts (Econ Mgt; PPE; Econ) (IB 38 pts HL 666)

Exeter – A*AA–AAB (Econ; Bus Econ; Maths Econ; Econ Ecomet; Econ Fin; Econ Fin Int St) (IB 38–34 pts)

London (UCL) – AAAe–AABe (Econ Bus E Euro St; Econ Geog) (IB 36–38 pts)

London LSE – A*AA incl maths (Econ; Ecomet Mathem Econ; Maths Econ) (IB 38 pts HL 766)

Nottingham – A*AA–AAA 380–360 pts (Econ Ger; Econ Fr; Econ Chin St; Econ Phil; Econ courses) (IB 38–36 pts)

Oxford – A*AA (Econ Mgt) (IB 38–40 pts)

York – A*AA–AAA 380–360 pts (PPE) (IB 37 pts)

360 pts **Birmingham** – AAA incl maths (Econ; Econ Lang; Mathem Econ Stats) (IB 36–38 pts)

Bristol – AAA–AAB 360–340 pts (Phil Econ; Econ Acc) (IB 37–35 pts)

City – AAA 360 pts (Econ; Fin Econ; Econ Acc) (IB 35 pts)

Durham – AAA 360 pts (Econ Pol) (IB 37 pts)

Edinburgh – AAA–BBB 360–300 pts (Econ Fin; Econ Stats; Econ courses) (IB 37–34 pts)

Exeter – AAA–AAB 360–340 pts (PPE) (IB 36–34 pts)

Lancaster – AAA–A*AB 360 pts (Acc Econ; Econ (St Abrd)) (IB 36 pts HL 16 pts)

Leeds – AAA (Bus Econ; Econ Mgt; Econ Fin; Econ Trans St; Econ)

London (SOAS) – AAA (Econ courses) (IB 38 pts HL 766)

London LSE – AAA (Geog Econ; Gov Econ; Phil Econ) (IB 38 pts HL 766)

Newcastle – AAA–ABB (Econ Fin; Pol Econ) (IB 34–37 pts)

Nottingham – A*AA–AAA 380–360 pts (Econ Hisp St) (IB 38–36 pts)

Oxford – AAA (Hist Econ; PPE) (IB 38–40 pts)

St Andrews – AAA (Anc Hist Econ; Econ Psy; Arbc Econ; Fin Econ; Econ courses) (IB 36–38 pts)

Southampton – AAA incl maths (Econ; Econ Fin; Econ Mgt Sci; Acc Econ; Econ Act Sci; Maths OR Stats Econ) (IB 36 pts HL 18 pts)

Surrey – AAA–AAB (Bus Econ) (IB 37–35 pts)
York – AAA–AAB 360–340 pts (Econ Econ Hist; Econ Fin) (IB 36–35 pts HL 666)

340 pts **Aston** – AAB 340 pts (Econ Mgt) (IB 35 pts HL 665)
Brunel – AAB–ABB 320–340 pts (Pol Econ) (IB 35 pts)
Cardiff – AAB 340 pts (Bus Econ; Econ; Bus Econ Euro Lang) (IB 35 pts)
Essex – AAB–ABB (PPE) (IB 33–32 pts)
Exeter – A*AA–AAB (Econ Pol Euro St; Bus Econ Euro St) (IB 38–34 pts)
Lancaster – AAB 340 pts (Econ; Econ Geog/Int Rel/Maths/Pol; Fin Econ; PPE) (IB 34–35 pts)
Liverpool – AAB (Econ; Bus Econ) (IB 35 pts)
London (QM) – AAB (Econ; Econ Fin Mgt; Econ Joint Hons) (IB 36 pts HL 5 maths)
London (RH) – AAB (Econ; Econ Pol Int Rel; Econ Maths; Fin Bus Econ; Econ Mgt; Pol Phil Econ) (IB 35–34 pts)
London LSE – AAB (Env Plcy Econ; Econ Hist; Soc Plcy Econ) (IB 37 pts)
Loughborough – AAB (Geog Econ; Bus Econ Fin; Econ; Econ Pol; Econ Acc) (IB 34–36 pts)
Manchester – AAB 340 pts (PPE; Bus St Econ; Econ; Econ Pol; Econ Sociol; Econ courses) (IB 35 pts)
Newcastle – AAB (Econ; Econ Bus Mgt) (IB 34 pts)
Nottingham – AAB (Ind Econ; Ind Econ Ins) (IB 34 pts)
Queen's Belfast – AAB 340 pts (PPE) (IB 35 pts HL 666)
Reading – AAB (Acc Econ) (IB 35 pts)
Sheffield – AAB (Econ Joint Hons; Econ) (IB 35 pts)
Southampton – AAB (Econ Phil) (IB 34 pts HL 17 pts)
Strathclyde – AAB (Econ; Econ Psy)
Surrey – AAA–AAB 340–360 pts (Econ Fin; Econ) (IB 36–35 pts)
Sussex – AAB–ABB (Econ; Econ Int Rel; Econ Mgt St; Econ Pol; Econ Int Dev) (IB 34–35 pts)
York – AAB–AAA (Econ Ecomet Fin; Econ; Econ Maths) (IB 36 pts HL 666)

320 pts **Birmingham** – ABB (Pol Econ) (IB 34 pts)
Birmingham (UC) – ABB (Geog Econ) (IB 32–34 pts)
Bournemouth – 320 pts (Fin Econ; Econ) (IB 32 pts)
Brunel – ABB 320 pts (Econ; Econ Bus Fin) (IB 33 pts)
East Anglia – ABB 320 pts (Econ; Econ Acc; Bus Econ; PPE) (IB 32 pts)
Essex – 320 pts (Econ Fr; Econ; Fin Econ; Int Econ; Mgt Econ; Econ Langs)
Glasgow – ABB (Econ Joint Hons) (IB 36 pts)
Hull – ABB 320 pts (Econ; Econ (Int))
Kent – ABB 320 pts (Euro Econ; Fin Econ; Econ) (IB 34 pts)
Leicester – ABB 320 pts (Econ Courses) (IB 32 pts)
London (QM) – 320–340 pts (Glob Chng Env Econ Dev) (IB 32 pts)
Queen's Belfast – ABB 320 pts (Econ courses) (IB 33 pts)
Reading – 320–340 pts (Bus Econ; Econ)
Southampton – ABB–BBB (Pol Econ) (IB 32 pts HL 16 pts)
Swansea – ABB–BBC 320–280 pts (Fin Econ Acc; PPE; Econ courses) (IB 30–33 pts)

300 pts **Aberdeen** – BBB 300 pts (Econ) (IB 32 pts)
Aberystwyth – 300 pts (Econ; Bus Econ)
Bristol UWE – 300 pts (Econ) (IB 24–28 pts)
Buckingham – BBB 300 pts (Law Econ) (IB 34 pts)
Cardiff Met (UWIC) – 300 pts (Econ; Int Econ Fin)
Coventry – BBB 300 pts (Bus Econ; Int Econ Tr)
Dundee – BBB (Bus Econ Mark; Bus Econ Mark Hist; Spat Econ)
East Anglia – BBB (Bus Fin Econ) (IB 32 pts)
Essex – 300–320 pts (Econ Pol) (IB 32–36 pts)
Greenwich – 300 pts (Econ; Econ Bank)
Heriot-Watt – ABC–BBB (Econ)
Hertfordshire – 300 pts (Econ; Bus Econ) (IB 26 pts)
Huddersfield – BBB 300 pts (Econ; Econ courses)
Hull – BBB 300 pts (Bus Econ; Bus Econ (Int); PPE)

Keele – ABC 300 pts (Bus Econ; Econ courses) (IB 32 pts)
London (Birk) – 300 pts p/t, for under 21s (over 21s varies) (Econ Soc Pol)
Reading – BBB–ABC 300 pts (Fd Mark Bus Econ)
Sheffield Hallam – 300 pts (Bus Econ)
Strathclyde – BBB (Maths Stats Econ) (IB 32 pts)
Swansea – BBB–BCC 300–260 pts (Econ; Bus Econ) (IB 32–30 pts)
Westminster – BBB (Bus Econ) (IB 28 pts)

280 pts **Birmingham City** – 280 pts (Econ Fin)
Bradford – 280–320 pts (Econ; Fin Econ; Econ Mark; Econ Int Rel)
Coventry – BBC 280 pts (Econ courses) (IB 29 pts)
De Montfort – 280 pts (Econ Fin)
Kingston – 280 pts (Fin Econ) (IB 25 pts)
Manchester Met – 280 pts (Econ Joint Hons) (IB 28 pts)
Middlesex – 280 pts (Bus Econ) (IB 28 pts)
Nottingham Trent – 280 pts (Econ; Bus Econ; Econ Fin Bank)
Plymouth – 280 pts (Econ courses)
Portsmouth – 280–320 pts (Econ; Econ Mgt) (IB 29 pts)
Sheffield Hallam – 280 pts (Int Fin Econ)
South Wales – 280 pts (Bus Econ) (IB 28 pts)
Stirling – BBC (PPE; Econ) (IB 32 pts)
Worcester – 280 pts (Bus Econ Adv; Bus Econ PR)

260 pts **Bangor** – 260–300 pts (Bus Econ; Econ Joint Hons) (IB 28 pts)
Central Lancashire – 260–300 pts (Econ courses)
Dundee – BCC (Econ St) (IB 30 pts)
Kaplan Holborn (Coll) – 260 pts (Econ Fin)
Kingston – 260 pts (Bus Econ; Econ) (IB 24 pts)
Manchester Met – 260–280 pts (Econ) (IB 26 pts)
Northampton – 260–300 pts (Econ courses)
Plymouth – 260 pts (Fin Econ; Int Bus Econ; Bus Econ courses)
Portsmouth – 260–300 pts (Econ Fin Bank; Bus Econ) (IB 28 pts)
Salford – BCC 260–300 pts (Bus Econ) (IB 27 pts)

240 pts **East London** – 240 pts (Bus Econ) (IB 24 pts)
Edinburgh Napier – CCC 240 pts (Econ Mgt)
Leeds Beckett – 240 pts (Econ Bus) (IB 24 pts)
London Met – 240 pts (Bus Econ; Econ)

200 pts **Anglia Ruskin** – 200–240 pts (Bus Econ) (IB 24 pts)

80 pts **Greenwich (Sch Mgt)** – 80–120 pts (Econ)

Abertay – check with School (Int Econ Mgt)
Open University – contact +44 (0)845 300 6090 **or** www.openuniversity.co.uk/you (Econ Mathem Sci; PPE; Soc Sci Econ)

Alternative offers
See **Chapter 7** and **Appendix 1** for grades/UCAS Tariff points information for the International Baccalaureate, Scottish Highers/Advanced Highers, the Welsh Baccalaureate, the Irish Leaving Certificate, the Cambridge Pre-U Diploma, the Advanced Diploma and the Extended Project.

CHOOSING YOUR COURSE (SEE ALSO CH.1)
Some course features
Birmingham There is a new Single Honours course in Policy, Politics and Economics covering real-world issues. Mathematical Economics and Statistics is also a Single Honours course. Joint Honours courses are offered with several subjects including Politics and modern languages.
Brunel The Economics course focuses on the applications of economics to business, finance, industry and government. Joint courses are also offered with accountancy, business and management with placements.

Cardiff The course involves compulsory and optional modules. The latter include economy of the EU, money banking and finance, international trade and economic development.

Durham Single and Joint Honours Economics students follow the same first-year course in economics. This allows flexibility in the choice of combined degree at the end of the first year, leading on to courses in Economics, Business Economics or Economics with French or Politics. There is also a course in PPE and a Combined Honours programme in Social Sciences.

Hull All students taking the BSc Economics degree follow a largely common course and a definitive choice of specialism need not be made until the beginning of the second year. Various streams are offered including mainstream economics, business economics, finance and development, accountancy and economic history. Joint, combined and major/minor options are offered, as well as a Foundation year with Politics and Philosophy. BA students choose their specialism in Year 3.

Liverpool John Moores The Business and Economics course offers modules in finance in organisations and an introduction to accounting. The Economics course focuses on political economy. Economics can also be studied with History or Politics.

London (RH) The Economics course deals with all aspects of the subject including financial and industrial economics, and analytical political economy. Ten courses are also offered with economics as a major subject and there is a separate degree in Financial and Business Economics.

Middlesex There are degrees in Business Economics, Business Economics and Statistics, and Money, Banking and Finance, each with optional work placements. Special options can be chosen in the third year of each course. An industrial placement year is optional.

Northumbria Economics is offered as a specialism within the Business degree. There is also a degree in Business with International Trade. A four-year sandwich course is offered.

Nottingham The first two years of all School of Economics degrees provide a basic foundation of theoretical and applied knowledge. Specialist options are chosen in Year 3. Economics is also offered with Philosophy, Modern Languages, European Union Studies and Chinese Studies. There are also courses in Industrial and International Economics.

Universities and colleges teaching quality See www.qaa.ac.uk; http://unistats.direct.gov.uk.

Top research universities and colleges (RAE 2008) (Economics and Econometrics) London LSE; London (UCL); Essex; Oxford; Warwick; Bristol; Nottingham; London (QM); Cambridge; Manchester; Glasgow; London (RH); Southampton.

Examples of sandwich degree courses Aston; Bath; Birmingham City; Bournemouth; Brighton; Bristol UWE; Brunel; Cardiff Met (UWIC); Coventry; De Montfort; Essex; Gloucestershire; Greenwich; Hertfordshire; Kingston; Leeds Beckett; Loughborough; Newcastle; Nottingham Trent; Oxford Brookes; Plymouth; Portsmouth; Salford; Sheffield Hallam; Staffordshire; Surrey; Teesside; Ulster; Westminster; Worcester.

ADMISSIONS INFORMATION

Number of applicants per place (approx) Aberystwyth 3; Anglia Ruskin 10; Aston 8; Bangor 4; Bath 7; Birmingham 10; Birmingham City 16; Bradford 5; Bristol 41; Brunel 12; Buckingham 4; Cambridge (Econ) 8 (Land Econ) 5; Cardiff 8; Central Lancashire 5; City 18, (Econ Acc) 12; Coventry 10; Dundee 5; Durham (Econ) 10; East Anglia 15; Essex 6; Exeter 12; Greenwich 8; Heriot-Watt 4; Hull 15; Kent 11; Kingston 9; Lancaster 14; Leeds 16; Leicester 10; Liverpool 4; Liverpool John Moores 8; London (UCL) 12; London LSE (Econ) 15, (Econ Econ Hist) 8, (Ecomet Mathem Econ) 20; Loughborough 15; Manchester (Econ) 8, (Econ Fin) 9, (Econ Pol) 27, (Econ Sociol) 27; Manchester Met 5; Middlesex 8; Newcastle 11, (Econ Bus Mgt) 27; Northampton 8; Northumbria 16; Nottingham (Econ Chin) 8; Nottingham Trent 2; Oxford Brookes 51; Plymouth 4; Portsmouth 6; Queen's Belfast 10; St Andrews 5; Salford 6; Sheffield 10; Southampton 8; Staffordshire 4; Stirling 6; Surrey 5; Swansea 7; Warwick 16; West Scotland 7; York 4.

Numbers of applicants (**a** UK **b** EU (non-UK) **c** non-EU **d** mature) Aston **a**300 **b**30 **c**50 **d**20; Leeds **b**5 **c**70 **d**33.

Advice to applicants and planning the UCAS personal statement Visits, work experience and work shadowing in banks, insurance companies, accountants' offices etc should be described. Keep up-to-date with economic issues by reading *The Economist* and the *Financial Times* and find other sources of information. Describe any particular aspects of economics which interest you – and why. Make it clear on the statement that you know what economics is and why you want to study it. Give evidence of your interest in economics and your reasons for choosing the course and provide information about your sport/extra-curricular activities and positions of responsibility.

Misconceptions about this course **Bradford** That the Economics course is very mathematical and that students will not get a good job, eg management. **Kent** That the Economics course is mathematical, has a high failure rate and has poorer job prospects than Business Studies courses. **London (UCL)** Some think the Economics course is a Business course.

Selection interviews **Yes** Birmingham, Bristol UWE, Brunel, Cambridge, Coventry, East Anglia, East London, Edinburgh, Essex, Keele, London (RH), London (UCL), Manchester Met, Middlesex, Nottingham, Nottingham Trent, Oxford (Econ Mgt) 16%, Reading, Southampton (Acc Econ), Surrey; **Some** Aberystwyth, Anglia Ruskin, Bangor, Buckingham, Dundee, Kent, Leeds, London Met (mature students), Loughborough, Staffordshire, Swansea; **No** Bristol, London LSE.

Interview advice and questions If you have studied economics at A-level or in other examinations, expect to be questioned on aspects of the subject. This is a subject which is constantly in the news, so keep abreast of developments and be prepared to be asked questions such as: What is happening to sterling at present? What is happening to the dollar? How relevant is economics today? What are your views on the government's economic policy? Do you think that the family is declining as an institution? Discuss Keynesian economics. Is the power of the Prime Minister increasing? What is a recession? How would you get the world out of recession? What causes a recession? See also **Chapter 6**. **Cambridge** What is the point of using NHS money to keep old people alive? **Oxford** (Econ Mgt) 'I was asked questions on a newspaper article I had been given to read 45 minutes beforehand, followed by a few maths problems and an economics question.' Explain why teachers might be changing jobs to become plumbers. (Econ Mgt) What is the difference between the buying and selling of slaves and the buying and selling of football players? Should a Wal-Mart store be opened in the middle of Oxford?

Reasons for rejection (non-academic) Lack of knowledge about the course offered and the subject matter; lack of care in preparing personal statement; poor written English; the revelation on the statement that they want a course different from that for which they have applied! **Aberystwyth** Would have trouble fitting into the unique environment at Aberystwyth.

AFTER-RESULTS ADVICE
Offers to applicants repeating A-levels **Higher** Birmingham City, City, East Anglia, Essex, Leeds, Newcastle, Northumbria, Nottingham, Queen's Belfast, St Andrews, Warwick, York; **Possibly higher** Bradford, Brunel, Durham, Lancaster, Oxford Brookes; **Same** Aberystwyth, Anglia Ruskin, Bangor, Bath, Buckingham, Cambridge, Cardiff, Coventry, Dundee, East London, Edinburgh Napier, Heriot-Watt, Hull, Kingston, Liverpool, Liverpool John Moores, London (RH), London Met, Loughborough, Nottingham Trent, Salford, Sheffield, Staffordshire, Surrey, Swansea, Ulster.

GRADUATE DESTINATIONS AND EMPLOYMENT (2011/12 HESA)
Graduates surveyed 4360 **Employed** 2285 **In voluntary employment** 145 **In further study** 1015 **Assumed unemployed** 445

Career note Most graduates work within areas of business and finance, and in a range of jobs including management and administration posts across both public and private sectors.

OTHER DEGREE SUBJECTS FOR CONSIDERATION
Accountancy; Actuarial Studies; Administration; Banking; Business Studies; Development Studies; Estate Management; Financial Services; Government; Politics; Management Sciences/Studies; Property Development; Quantity Surveying; Social Sciences; Sociology; Statistics.

Check **Chapter 4** when choosing your university and **Chapter 7** on how to read the subject tables.

EDUCATION STUDIES

(see also **Physical Education, Social Sciences/Studies, Teacher Training**)

There are two types of degree course in Education – those which cover the history, philosophy and theory of education but which are not necessarily teacher training courses, and those which prepare the student for a career in the teaching profession. This subject table contains courses that are related to the study of education. For teacher training please see **Teacher Training**. Interview panels look for candidates with confidence in their own ability, a lively personality, patience and optimism. Experience of working with children is important. Students planning to follow a degree with a Postgraduate Certificate in Education (PGCE) are advised that problems may arise if their first degree subject is not a National Curriculum subject.

Two-year BEd courses are also offered for holders of HND or equivalent qualifications (minimum age in some cases 23-25) in the following subject areas (P – Primary; S – Secondary): Business Studies (S); Chemistry (S); Design and Technology (S); English (P); French (S); General Primary; German (S); Language Studies (P); Mathematics (S); Music (S); Physics (S); Science (S); Spanish (S); Welsh (S).

Useful websites www.gtcs.org.uk; www.gttr.ac.uk; teachertrainingcymru.org; www.education.gov.uk.

NB The points totals shown to the left of the institutions are for ease of reference only. It must not be assumed that Tariff points are always used by institutions or that they can be substituted for an offer in grades. The level of an offer is not necessarily indicative of the quality of a course.

COURSE OFFERS INFORMATION

Subject requirements/preferences **GCSE** English, mathematics and a science subject for those born after 1 September 1979. **AL** One A-level is usually required in the main subject of choice plus one or two other subjects. **Other** Disclosure and Barring Service (DBS) enhanced level clearance and health checks required.

Your target offers and examples of courses provided by each institution

380 pts **Cambridge** – A*AA (Educ Biol Sci; Educ Class; Educ Engl Dr; Educ Engl/Geog/Hist/Lang/
Mus/Phys/Relig St) (IB 40–41 pts HL 776)

360 pts **Durham** – AAA 360 pts (Educ St (Biol Sci/Engl St/Geog/Hist/Phil/Psy/Sociol/Theol))
(IB 37 pts)

340 pts **Bath** – AAB 340 pts (Chem Educ) (IB 35 pts HL 655 incl HL 6 chem)
London (King's) – AAB 340 pts (Sci Comm)

320 pts **Bath** – ABB 320 pts (Chld Yth Educ St) (IB 35 pts)
Birmingham – ABB 320 pts (Educ) (IB 32–34 pts)
Brighton – ABB 320 pts (Educ) (IB 34 pts)
Bristol – ABB–BBB 320–300 pts (Chld St) (IB 33–32 pts)
Cardiff – ABB–BBB 320–300 pts (Educ) (IB 32–34 pts)
Leeds – ABB 320 pts (Child St; Eng Lang Educ)
Manchester – ABB–BBB 300–320 pts (Lrng Disab St) (IB 31–35 pts)
Southampton – ABB (Educ St) (IB 32 pts HL 16 pts)
York – ABB (Sociol Educ) (IB 34 pts)

300 pts **Aberdeen** – BBB 300 pts (P Educ) (IB 30 pts)
Brunel – BBB 300 pts (Contemp Educ) (IB 32 pts)
Cardiff – BBB 300 pts (Educ Sociol; Educ Welsh) (IB 32 pts)
Chichester – 300–340 pts (P Educ (Engl))
De Montfort – 300 pts (Educ St Psy)
Derby – 300 pts (Educ)
East Anglia – BBB (Educ St) (IB 31 pts)
Edinburgh – BBB 300 pts (Commun Educ) (IB 34 pts)
Glasgow – BBB (Technol Educ; Educ P QTS) (IB 32 pts)
Leeds – BBB (Chld St) (IB 30 pts)
Newman – 300 pts (P Educ)
Sheffield – BBB (Educ Cult Chld) (IB 32 pts)

Warwick – BBB (Chld Educ Soc) (IB 34 pts)
York – BBB 300 pts (Engl Educ; Educ St) (IB 31 pts)
280 pts **Aberystwyth** – 280 pts (Educ Joint Hons) (IB 28 pts)
Brighton – BBC 280 pts (Hum Biol Educ) (IB 30 pts)
Bristol UWE – 280 pts (Educ St)
Cardiff Met (UWIC) – 280 pts (Educ St)
Cumbria – 280 pts (Ely Yrs Educ QTS) (IB 28 pts)
De Montfort – 280 pts (Educ St) (IB 28 pts)
Edge Hill – 280 pts (Chld Yng Ppl Lrng Dev)
Gloucestershire – 280–300 pts (Spo Educ; Educ P)
Hertfordshire – 280 pts (Educ St)
Huddersfield – BBC 280 pts (Relgn Educ)
Keele – BBC 280 pts (Educ St) (IB 28–30 pts)
Leeds Trinity – BBC (P Educ (7–11) BA)
Liverpool John Moores – 280 pts (Educ St PE)
London (Gold) – BBC 280 pts (Educ Cult Soty) (IB 32 pts)
London Met – BBC 280 pts (Educ St) (IB 28 pts)
Manchester Met – 280 pts (Educ St)
Newman – 280 pts (Phil Relgn Educ)
Northumbria – 280 pts (Ely P Educ)
Nottingham Trent – 280 pts (Bus Educ Dev; Ely Yrs Educ Dev; Ely Yrs Spec Inclsv Educ; Spec Incl Educ Educl Dev)
Oxford Brookes – BBC 280 pts (Educ St) (IB 30 pts)
Reading – 280 pts (P Ed Mus; P Educ Engl)
Roehampton – 280 pts (Educ) (IB 25 pts)
South Wales – 280 pts (Ely Yrs; Educ; Sociol Educ) (IB 25 pts)
Suffolk (Univ Campus) – 280 pts (Ely Chld St)
Winchester – 280–320 pts (Educ St courses; Educ St (Ely Child)) (IB 26 pts)
260 pts **Bath Spa** – 260–300 pts (Educ St courses; Yth Commun St)
Birmingham (UC) – 260 pts (Chld St) (IB 24 pts)
Canterbury Christ Church – 260 pts (Educ P)
Cardiff Met (UWIC) – 260 pts (Educ St Spo Physl Actvt; Educ St Engl; Educ St Modn Hist; Educ St Ely Chld St; Educ St Welsh)
Central Lancashire – BCC 260 pts (Df St Educ; Educ courses)
Derby – 260 pts (Ely Chld St; Maths Educ)
Hull – 260 pts (Educ courses)
Liverpool Hope – 260–300 pts (Chld Yth; Educ; Spec Educ Nds)
Liverpool John Moores – 260 pts (Educ St Ely Yrs; Ely Chld St; Out Educ; Educ St Spec Inclsv Nds)
Northampton – 260–280 pts (Educ St courses; Ely Chld St; Chld Yth)
Nottingham Trent – 260–300 pts (Chld St)
Sheffield Hallam – 260 pts (Educ Psy Cnslg)
Stranmillis (UC) – BCC (Tech Des Educ)
Sunderland – 260 pts (Educ; Chld St)
West Scotland – BCC–CDDd (P Educ)
240 pts **Aberystwyth** – 240 pts (Chld St) (IB 28 pts)
Bangor – 240 pts (Chld St; Astudiaethau Plentyndod Joint Hons)
Bishop Grosseteste – 240 pts (Educ St courses; Spec Educl Nds Incln courses)
Canterbury Christ Church – 240 pts (Chld St; Educ St)
Chester – 240–280 pts (Educ St Courses) (IB 26 pts)
Chichester – CCC (Ely Chld St) (IB 28 pts)
East London – 240 pts (Educ St; Ely Chld St; Spec Educ)
Gloucestershire – 240–300 pts (Ely Chld St; Educ St courses)
Glyndŵr – 240 pts (Educ)
Greenwich – 240 pts (Chld St)

Check **Chapter 4** when choosing your university and **Chapter 7** on how to read the subject tables.

    Manchester Met – 240–280 pts (Chld Yth St) (IB 28 pts)
    Middlesex – 240 pts (Educ St; Ely Chld St)
    Newman – 240–280 pts (Educ St courses; Ely Chld Educ Care) (IB 26 pts)
    Oldham (Univ Campus) – CCC 240 pts (Ely Yrs) (IB 25 pts)
    Plymouth – 240 pts (Ely Chld St; Educ St)
    Portsmouth – 240–300 pts (Ely Chld St) (IB 28 pts)
    St Mary's – 240 pts (Educ Soc Sci) (IB 28 pts)
    Sheffield Hallam – 240 pts (Educ Disab St; Educ St)
    Staffordshire – 240 pts (Ely Chld St)
    Worcester – 240–260 pts (Educ courses)

220 pts **Bath Spa** – 220–280 pts (Ely Yrs Educ courses; Int Educ)
    Chichester – 220–280 pts (Advntr Educ)
    Kent – CCD (Autsm St)
    Leeds Beckett – 220 pts (Chld St) (IB 24 pts)
    Nottingham Trent – 220 pts (Ely Yrs Psy Educ; Psy Spec Incl Educ)
    St Mark and St John – 220 pts (Educ St courses; Spec Educ Nds)
    Teesside – 220 pts (Ely Chld St; Chld Yth St)
    Ulster – 220–300 pts (Educ courses)
    Worcester – 220 pts (Educ St) (IB 24 pts)

200 pts **Anglia Ruskin** – 200 pts (Educ St)
    Blackburn (Coll) – 200 pts (Educ St)
    Cardiff Met (UWIC) – 200 pts (Yth Commun Educ)
    Greenwich – 200 pts (Educ P BA QTS)
    Leeds Trinity – 200 pts (Educ)
    South Wales – 200–240 pts (Welsh Educ)
    Trinity Saint David (Swansea) – 200 pts (Educ St Psy; Educ St; Cnslg St Educ St;
      Dr Educ St)
    Wolverhampton – 200–260 pts (Cond Educ)

180 pts **Bedfordshire** – 180–220 pts (Educ St; Ely Yrs Educ)
    Bradford (Coll Univ Centre) – 180 pts (Educ St)
    Leeds Trinity – 180 pts (Ely Yrs Educ St)
    Trinity Saint David – 180–360 pts (Ely Yrs Educ; P Educ St)

160 pts **South Essex (Coll)** – 160 pts (Ely Yrs Educ)
    Stockport (Coll) – 160 pts (Chld St)

140 pts **Queen's Belfast** – concurrent option available at St Mary's (UC) **or** Stranmillis (UC); check
      with admissions tutor (Educ)

    Open University – contact +44 (0)845 300 6090 **or** www.openuniversity.co.uk/you
      (Chld Yth St; Ely Yrs)

EXAMPLES OF FOUNDATION DEGREES IN THE SUBJECT FIELD

Bath City (Coll); Blackburn (Coll); Blackpool and Fylde (Coll); Bournemouth and Poole (Coll); Bradford; Bristol City (Coll); Bucks New; Cornwall (Coll); Doncaster (Coll Univ Centre); Duchy (Coll); Exeter (Coll); Farnborough (CT); Grimsby (Univ Centre); Guildford (Coll); Havering (Coll); Hopwood Hall (Coll); Kirklees (Coll); Lakes (Coll); Leeds City (Coll); Loughborough (Coll); Manchester (Coll); Mid-Cheshire (Coll); Northbrook (Coll); Norwich City (Coll); Peterborough (Reg Coll); Petroc; Plymouth City (Coll); Riverside Halton (Coll); St Mary's; Sheffield (Coll); South Cheshire (Coll); South Devon (Coll); Stratford-upon-Avon (Coll); Truro (Coll); Wakefield (Coll); Warrington (Coll); West Anglia (Coll); Wigan and Leigh (Coll); Wirral Met (Coll).

CHOOSING YOUR COURSE (SEE ALSO CH.1)

Some course features

Birmingham Psychology, sociology, philosophy and social policy are disciplines studied in the Childhood, Culture and Education degree. Education programmes are offered in Childhood Studies, English Language and Literature, Sport, and Physical Education.

Bristol (Chld St) This new course is provided in the Department of Social Policy and Social Work. It focuses on children, their communities and on the political and economic environment. A study of children, social policy and psychology (not a teacher training course).

Chichester Courses in Education include Adventure Education and Childhood Studies including health, child development and special needs.

East Anglia The Educational Studies degree offers a flexible pathway enabling students to tailor their degree to their own interests. It involves a balance between theory and practical experience and a study of the whole field of education in the UK and abroad including modules in teaching, learning and assessment.

Leeds There is a course in Childhood Studies covering education, sociology and psychology.

Liverpool Hope Single and Combined Honours degrees are offered in Education Studies, Inclusive Education, Special Educational Needs and Early Childhood Studies, focusing on Early Years education and childcare provision. There are Single and Combined Honours degrees in Childhood and Youth Studies.

Universities and colleges teaching quality See www.qaa.ac.uk; http://unistats.direct.gov.uk.

Top research universities and colleges (RAE 2008) London (Inst Ed); Oxford; Cambridge; London (King's); Bristol; Leeds; Exeter; Manchester Met; Warwick; York; Durham; Sussex; Stirling.

ADMISSIONS INFORMATION

Number of applicants per place (approx) Aberystwyth 6; Anglia Ruskin 1; Bangor 5; Bath 17; Bath Spa 5; Birmingham 8; Bishop Grosseteste 12; Bristol (Chld St) 6; Bristol UWE 20; Brunel (PE) 5; Cambridge 2.5; Canterbury Christ Church 15; Cardiff (Educ) 8; Cardiff Met (UWIC) 3; Central Lancashire 5; Chester 25; Chichester 12; Cumbria 5; Derby 13; Dundee 5; Durham 8; Edge Hill 17; Gloucestershire 20; Glyndŵr 15; Greenwich 3; Hull 7; Hull (Coll) 4; Kingston 9; Leeds 4; Liverpool Hope 5; Liverpool John Moores 3; London (Gold) 5, (Des Tech) 4; Manchester 2 (Lrn Disab St); Manchester Met 23; Middlesex 7; Northampton 7; Northumbria 8; Nottingham Trent 11; Oxford Brookes 6; Plymouth 14; Roehampton 6; St Mark and St John 5; St Mary's 19; Sheffield Hallam 7; Strathclyde 7; Trinity Saint David (Swansea) 10; West Scotland 7; Winchester 4; Wolverhampton 4; Worcester 21; York 3.

Advice to applicants and planning the UCAS personal statement **Chichester** Applicants should have spent a minimum of two weeks observing/helping out in a state school.

Misconceptions about this course That Childhood Studies is a childcare, child health or teaching course: it is not. That Educational Studies leads to a teaching qualification – it does not. **Bath Spa** (Educ St) Applicants should note that this is not a teacher training course – it leads on to PGCE teacher training (this applies to other Education Studies courses). **UHI** Candidates are unaware that on-line methods form a significant part of the course delivery.

Selection interviews **Yes** Birmingham City, Bishop Grosseteste, Brighton, Bristol UWE, Brunel, Cambridge, Cardiff Met (UWIC), Chichester, Derby, Durham, Glyndŵr, Kingston, Liverpool John Moores, London (Gold), Manchester Met (group interviews), Newman, Nottingham, Nottingham Trent, Oxford Brookes, Plymouth, Reading, Stirling, Stockport (Coll), West Scotland, Worcester, York St John; **Some** Anglia Ruskin, Bangor, Cardiff, Dundee, Lincoln, Roehampton, St Mark and St John, Winchester, York; **No** East Anglia.

Interview advice and questions **Cambridge** The stage is a platform for opinions or just entertainment? **Derby** Applicants are asked about an aspect of education. **Liverpool John Moores** Discussion regarding any experience the applicant has had with children. **Worcester** Interviewees are asked to write a statement concerning their impressions of the interview.

Reasons for rejection (non-academic) Unable to meet the requirements of written standard English. Ungrammatical personal statements. Lack of research about teaching at primary or secondary levels. Lack of experience in schools. Insufficient experience of working with people; tendency to be racist.

AFTER-RESULTS ADVICE

Offers to applicants repeating A-levels **Higher** Oxford Brookes, Warwick; **Possibly higher** Cumbria; **Same** Anglia Ruskin, Bangor, Bishop Grosseteste, Brighton, Brunel, Cambridge, Canterbury Christ Church, Cardiff, Chester, Chichester, De Montfort, Derby, Dundee, Durham, East Anglia, Lincoln,

Liverpool Hope, Liverpool John Moores, London (Gold), Manchester Met, Newman, Northumbria, Nottingham Trent, Roehampton, St Mark and St John, St Mary's, Stirling, Sunderland, UHI, Winchester, Wolverhampton, Worcester, York, York St John; **No** Kingston.

GRADUATE DESTINATIONS AND EMPLOYMENT (2011/12 HESA)
Academic Studies in Education graduates surveyed 10435 **Employed** 4135 **In voluntary employment** 125 **In further study** 3670 **Assumed unemployed** 345

Career note Education Studies degrees prepare graduates for careers in educational administration although many will move into more general areas of business or into aspects of work with Social Services. If courses in Education include Qualified Teacher Status (QTS), graduates can enter the teaching profession. Prospects are generally good. Courses in Childhood Studies could lead to work in health or childcare-related posts, in social work or administration.

OTHER DEGREE SUBJECTS FOR CONSIDERATION
Psychology; Social Policy; Social Sciences; Social Work.

ENGINEERING/ENGINEERING SCIENCES

(including **General Engineering, Integrated Engineering, Engineering Design** and **Product Design**; see also **Engineering (Manufacturing), Transport Management and Planning**)

Many of the Engineering courses listed below enable students to delay their decision of their final engineering specialism. Mathematics and physics provide the basis of all Engineering courses although several universities and colleges now provide one-year Foundation courses for applicants without science A-levels. Many institutions offer sandwich courses and firms also offer sponsorships. In prospectuses it will be noted that some courses are subject to approval. The problem which can arise is that the examinations taken on these courses may not be accepted by the professional body overseeing that particular branch of engineering and examinations set by those professional bodies (see **Appendix 3**) will have to be taken in order that graduates can obtain Chartered Engineer status.

Engineering Council UK (ECUK) Statement
Recent developments in the engineering profession and the regulations that govern registration as a professional engineer (UK-SPEC) mean that MEng and bachelor's degrees are the typical academic routes to becoming registered.

Chartered Engineers (CEng) develop solutions to engineering problems, using new or existing technologies, through innovation, creativity and change. They might develop and apply new technologies, promote advanced designs and design methods, introduce new and more efficient production techniques, marketing and construction concepts, and pioneer new engineering services and management methods.

Incorporated Engineers (IEng) act as exponents of today's technology through creativity and innovation. They maintain and manage applications of current and developing technology, and may be involved in engineering design, development, manufacture, construction and operation. Both Chartered and Incorporated Engineers are variously engaged in technical and commercial leadership and possess effective interpersonal skills.

You should confirm with universities whether their courses are accredited for CEng or IEng by relevant professional engineering institutions. To become a Chartered or Incorporated Engineer, you will have to demonstrate competence and commitment appropriate to the registration category. On top of your academic knowledge, you will also need to demonstrate your professional development and experience. Most of this will come after you graduate but placements in industry during your degree course are also available. Both Chartered and Incorporated Engineers usually progress to become team leaders or to take other key management roles. For full information check www.engc.org.uk/ukspec.

Engineering is a fascinating, multi-faceted industry, integral to society and driving forward advances in lifestyle and decreasing our impact on the environment.

Engineers are now needed within a multitude of businesses so our graduates are able to work within a variety of sectors and locations around the world.

We have close ties with local industry through our Northants Engineering Training Partnership (NETP) scheme. Consequently, our undergraduate programmes are highly industry-focussed with opportunities for students to undertake paid placements as part of their course, either part-time in conjunction with their studies or as a year-long option. We offer a range of entry and study options to suit a wide range of people and circumstances.

Our programmes aim to equip students with the skills, confidence and in-depth understanding that is necessary for this fast-paced industry. You are able to tailor your qualification to suit your needs and interests as our programmes are flexible and can be tailored to you.

When you come to the University of Northampton you will work within our recently refurbished premises, including our state-of-the-art computer simulations facilities and thermo-fluids laboratory.

By studying Engineering with us, you will gain valuable skills and contacts that you can utilise throughout your career. Our team of academics are internationally recognised for their research as well as being experience in industry.

We carry out cutting edge research and encourage you to join us extend engineering expertise now and for the future.

WE ARE **NORTHAMPTON.AC.UK**

Study Engineering at the University of Northampton. To find out more about Engineering courses Call **0800 358 2232** Email **study@northampton.ac.uk** or Visit **www.northampton.ac.uk/ engineering**

Construction & Engineering

at Hull & Harrogate College

Our Engineering and Construction options at Higher Education level include HNC/HND Construction & the Built Environment, BSc (Hons) Construction Management, BSc Sustainability and Environmental Management*, FdSc Engineering Technology and BEng (Hons) Engineering Technology.

Our courses are validated by The Open University and other professional bodies meaning you will receive your degree from one of the country's leading higher education institutions.

"89% of FdSc Engineering students were satisfied overall with the programme." National Student Survey 2013

Come and meet us
Visit us at one of our campus open events. Call for more info.

Hull Campus	**Harrogate Campus**
(01482) 598 744	(01423) 878 211
hull-college.ac.uk/HE	harrogate.ac.uk/HE

*subject to validation

The Open University

Useful websites www.scicentral.com; www.engc.org.uk; www.epsrc.ac.uk; www.etrust.org.uk.

NB The points totals shown to the left of the institutions are for ease of reference only. It must not be assumed that Tariff points are always used by institutions or that they can be substituted for an offer in grades. The level of an offer is not necessarily indicative of the quality of a course.

COURSE OFFERS INFORMATION

Subject requirements/preferences GCSE English, mathematics and a science subject required. **AL** Mathematics and/or physics, engineering or another science usually required. Design technology may be acceptable or in some cases required. Offers shown below refer to BEng or BSc courses unless otherwise stated.

Cambridge (Churchill, Peterhouse) STEP may be used as part of conditional offer; (Trinity) if student does not have AL further mathematics, AEA mathematics is required.
Oxford AL Mathematics and mechanics modules are recommended, further mathematics is helpful.

Your target offers and examples of courses provided by each institution

400 pts **London (UCL)** – A*AAe-AAAe (Eng (Mech Bus Fin) MEng) (IB 38-39 pts HL 18-19 pts incl 6 maths phys)

380 pts **Bristol** – A*AA-AAB incl maths 380-340 pts (Eng Des St Ind MEng) (IB 38 pts)
Cambridge – A*AA 380 pts (Eng) (IB 40-41 pts HL 776)
London (UCL) – A*AA-AAA 380-360 pts (Env Eng) (IB 38-39 pts)
Nottingham – A*AA-AAA 380-360 pts (Maths Eng) (IB 36-38 pts HL 7/6 maths)
Oxford – A*AA (Eng Sci) (IB 38-40 pts)

360 pts **Birmingham** – AAA-BCC 360-260 pts (Eng incl Fdn Yr) (IB 25-36 pts)
Bristol – AAA-AAB incl maths 360-340 pts (Eng Maths) (IB 37-35 pts)
Durham – AAA 360 pts (Gen Eng) (IB 37 pts)

Edinburgh – AAA–ABB incl maths 360–320 pts (Eng; Eng Sust Ener) (IB 37–32 pts)
Exeter – AAA–AAB 360–340 pts (Eng Mgt MEng; Eng MEng; Eng; Eng Mgt; Eng Maths)
Lancaster – AAA (Eng (St Abrd) MEng) (IB 36 pts)
Nottingham – AAA 360 pts (Env Eng; Chem Eng Env Eng (Yr Ind)) (IB 36 pts)

340 pts **City** – 340 pts (Eng Mgt Entre) (IB 30 pts HL 5 maths)
Lancaster – AAB (Sust Eng)
Leicester – AAB–ABB 340–320 pts (Gen Eng MEng)
Liverpool – AAB incl maths phys (Eng MEng) (IB 35 pts HL 5 maths phys)
Loughborough – AAB (Prod Des Eng MEng) (IB 34 pts)
Newcastle – AAB–ABB 340–320 pts (Mar Tech Off Eng) (IB 34–35 pts HL 5 maths phys)
Strathclyde – AAB (Prod Des Eng MEng; Prod Eng Mgt MEng) (IB 36 pts)
Swansea – AAB–ABB 340–320 pts (Prod Des Eng MEng) (IB 34–33 pts)
Warwick – AAB 340 pts (Eng Bus Mgt; Eng Bus St; Eng) (IB 36 pts)

320 pts **Brunel** – ABB 320 pts (Prod Des Eng) (IB 33 pts)
Cardiff – ABB 320 pts (Integ Eng) (IB 32–36 pts)
Lancaster – ABB (Eng) (IB 32 pts)
Leeds – ABB (Ind Des Inv)
Leeds Beckett – ABB 320 pts (Env Des Eng) (IB 34 pts)
Liverpool – ABB 320 pts (Eng; Ind Des Eng) (IB 33 pts HL 5 maths phys)
Loughborough – ABB 320 pts (Eng Mgt) (IB 33 pts HL 665)
Strathclyde – ABB 320 pts (Prod Des Eng; Prod Des Innov; Prod Eng Mgt) (IB 34 pts)

300 pts **Aberdeen** – BBB (Eng) (IB 30 pts)
Aston – BBB–ABB 300–320 pts (Trans Prod Des; Des Eng) (IB 32 pts)
Bristol UWE – 300 pts (Archit Env Eng) (IB 26 pts)
Heriot-Watt – BBB 300 pts (Eng) (IB 29 pts)
Huddersfield – 300 pts (Prod Des (Child Prod Toys/Sust Des))
Leicester – BBB 300 pts (Gen Eng)
Loughborough – BBB (Prod Des Eng; Prod Des Tech) (IB 32 pts)
Queen's Belfast – BBB 300 pts (Prod Des Dev)
Strathclyde – BBB (Eng MEng)
Swansea – BBB 300 pts (Prod Des Eng) (IB 32 pts)

280 pts **Bournemouth** – 280–300 pts (Des Eng)
Bristol UWE – 280 pts (Prod Des Tech) (IB 25 pts)
Cardiff Met (UWIC) – 280 pts (Prod Des)
Central Lancashire – 280–320 pts (Robot Eng)
Huddersfield – 280 pts (Eng Tech Mgt)
Liverpool John Moores – 280 pts (Prod Innov Dev)
Manchester Met – 280 pts (Autom Contr; Auto Eng; Eng) (IB 28 pts)
Nottingham Trent – 280 pts (Prod Des)
Plymouth – 280 pts (Robot) (IB 28 pts)
Ulster – 280 pts (Eng Mgt)

260 pts **Derby** – 260 pts (Prod Des)
Hull – 260 pts (Prod Innov)
Robert Gordon – BCC (Eng) (IB 24 pts)
Staffordshire – 260 pts +portfolio +interview (Prod Des)

240 pts **De Montfort** – 240 pts (Eng Des)
East London – 240 pts (Prod Des)
Hertfordshire – 240 pts (Ind Des)
Hull (Coll) – 240 pts (Eng Tech)
Northampton – 240–280 pts (Eng)
Portsmouth – 240–280 pts (Prod Des Innov) (IB 26 pts)
Salford – 240–280 pts (3D Des Prod Des) (IB 26 pts)
Swansea – CCC (Eng) (IB 26 pts)

200 pts **London South Bank** – 200 pts (Eng Prod Des)
Wolverhampton – 200 pts (Eng Des Mgt)

Check **Chapter 4** when choosing your university and **Chapter 7** on how to read the subject tables.

60 pts UHI – D (Ener Eng)

Open University – contact +44 (0)845 300 6090 **or** www.openuniversity.co.uk/you (Eng)

Alternative offers
See **Chapter 7** and **Appendix 1** for grades/UCAS Tariff points information for the International Baccalaureate, Scottish Highers/Advanced Highers, the Welsh Baccalaureate, the Irish Leaving Certificate, the Cambridge Pre-U Diploma, the Advanced Diploma and the Extended Project.

EXAMPLES OF FOUNDATION DEGREES IN THE SUBJECT FIELD
Blackburn (Coll); Bolton; Bristol City (Coll); Greenwich; Harper Adams; Hull (Coll); London Met; Manchester (Coll); Mid-Cheshire (Coll); Middlesex; Newcastle (Coll); Newman; Northumbria; Oxford Brookes; Sheffield Hallam; Somerset (Coll); Suffolk (Univ Campus); Tyne Met (Coll); Warwickshire (Coll); West Thames (Coll).

CHOOSING YOUR COURSE (SEE ALSO CH.1)
Some course features
Birmingham There are courses on offer which cover Chemical, Biomedical, Civil, Electronic and Electrical, Mechanical and Materials, and Computer and Communications Systems Engineering. Three-year and four-year programmes are offered and in each discipline the first two years are common to both the BEng and MEng programmes. Civil Engineering can also be studied with Business Management. A year of industrial training in the UK or abroad is optional. Scholarships available.
Lancaster All students follow a common first year followed by a choice from six engineering specialisations.
London (QM) (Des Innov MEng/BEng) The course is run jointly by the Engineering Department at London (QM) and the Department of Design at London (Goldsmiths). It consists of core studio practice (at QM), design context study (at Goldsmiths) and design engineering (at QM). Applications are to London (QM), via UCAS.
Warwick All engineering courses share the first two years, with the choice of specialisation made in Year 3.

Universities and colleges teaching quality See www.qaa.ac.uk; http://unistats.direct.gov.uk.

Top research universities and colleges (RAE 2008) (General, Mineral and Mining Engineering) Cambridge; Oxford; Nottingham; Leeds; Imperial London; Swansea; Manchester; Surrey; Warwick.

Examples of sandwich degree courses Aston; Bath; Bradford; Bristol UWE; Brunel; Cardiff; Central Lancashire; Coventry; De Montfort; East London; Huddersfield; Leicester; London South Bank; Loughborough; Manchester Met; Middlesex; Nottingham; Nottingham Trent; Portsmouth; Sheffield Hallam; Southampton; Staffordshire; Ulster; Wolverhampton.

ADMISSIONS INFORMATION
Number of applicants per place (approx) Aberdeen 6; Aston 8; Bath 15; Birmingham 6; Bournemouth 5; Bristol (Eng Des) 3, (Eng Maths) 5; Brunel (Ind Des Eng) 10; Cambridge 4; Cardiff 5; City 3; Coventry 6; Durham 9; Edinburgh 5; Exeter 6; Hull 6; Lancaster 15; Leicester 10; London (UCL) 5; Loughborough 9; Manchester Met 2; Northampton 3; Robert Gordon 2; Salford (Pros Orthot) 3; Sheffield Hallam 6; Strathclyde 5; Warwick 10.

Advice to applicants and planning the UCAS personal statement Details of careers in the various engineering specialisms should be obtained from the relevant engineering institutions (see **Appendix 3**). This will enable you to describe your interests in various aspects of engineering. Contact engineers to discuss their work with them. Try to visit an engineering firm relevant to your choice of specialism.

Selection interviews **Yes** Bristol, Brunel, Cambridge, Coventry, Lancaster, London (QM), London (UCL), Loughborough, Manchester Met, Oxford, Oxford Brookes, Robert Gordon, Salford, Sheffield Hallam, Strathclyde, West Scotland; **Some** Cardiff, Leicester (mature students only); **No** Dundee, Durham.

Interview advice and questions Since mathematics and physics are important subjects, it is probable that you will be questioned on the applications of these subjects too, for example, the transmission of electricity, nuclear power, aeronautics, mechanics etc. Past questions have included: Explain the theory of an arch; what is its function? What is the connection between distance and velocity and acceleration and velocity? How does a car ignition work? See also separate **Engineering** tables and **Chapter 6**. **Nottingham Trent** What is Integrated Engineering?

Reasons for rejection (non-academic) Made no contribution whatsoever to the project discussions during the UCAS interview. Forged reference! Poor work ethic. Lack of motivation towards the subject area. Better suited to an alternative Engineering course. Failure to attend interview. Poor interview preparation.

AFTER-RESULTS ADVICE

Offers to applicants repeating A-levels Higher Loughborough, Warwick; **Possibly higher** Coventry, Edinburgh, Lancaster, Manchester Met, Robert Gordon, Sheffield Hallam; **Same** Birmingham City, Brunel (good reasons needed for repeating), Cambridge, Cardiff, Derby, Durham, Edinburgh Napier, Exeter, Heriot-Watt, Hull, Liverpool, London (UCL), Nottingham Trent.

GRADUATE DESTINATIONS AND EMPLOYMENT (2011/12 HESA)

Graduates surveyed 1640 **Employed** 1065 **In voluntary employment** 30 **In further study** 305 **Assumed unemployed** 95

Career note A high proportion of Engineering graduates go into industry as engineers, technicians, IT specialists or managers, irrespective of their engineering speciality. However, the transferable skills gained during their courses are also valued by employers in other sectors.

OTHER DEGREE SUBJECTS FOR CONSIDERATION

Computer Science; Materials Science; Mathematics; Physics; Technology; all branches of Engineering (see also following **Engineering** tables).

ENGINEERING (ACOUSTICS and SOUND)

(including **Audio Engineering** and **Sound Technology**; see also **Engineering (Electrical and Electronic), Film, Radio, Video and TV Studies, Media Studies, Music**)

Apart from the scientific aspect of sound, these courses also involve the measurement of sound, hearing, environmental health and legal aspects of sound and vibration. Acoustics topics are also included in some Music and Media Technology courses.

Useful websites www.ioa.org.uk; www.engc.org.uk.

NB The points totals shown to the left of the institutions are for ease of reference only. It must not be assumed that Tariff points are always used by institutions or that they can be substituted for an offer in grades. The level of an offer is not necessarily indicative of the quality of a course.

COURSE OFFERS INFORMATION

Subject requirements/preferences AL Mathematics and physics usually required; music is also required for some courses. See also **Engineering/Engineering Sciences**. Offers shown below refer to BEng or BSc courses unless otherwise stated.

Your target offers and examples of courses provided by each institution
380 pts Glasgow – A*AA 380 pts (Electron Mus MEng) (IB 36 pts)
360 pts Surrey – AAA 360 pts (Mus Snd Rec (Tonmeister)) (IB 37 pts HL 666)
340 pts Glasgow – AAB 340 pts (Electron Mus)
  London (QM) – AAB 340 pts (Aud Sys Eng MEng) (IB 32–34 pts)
  Southampton – AAB–ABB 340–320 pts (Acoust Eng) (IB 34 pts HL 17 pts)
  York – AAB 340 pts (Mus Tech Sys MEng; Electron Eng Mus Tech MEng) (IB 35 pts)

320 pts **Southampton** – ABB 320 pts +gr 8 (Acoust Mus) (IB 32 pts HL 16 pts)
300 pts **Brunel** – BBB incl mus 300 pts (Snc Arts) (IB 32 pts)
           Huddersfield – BBB 300 pts (Mus Tech courses)
           London (QM) – BBB 300 pts (Aud Sys Eng) (IB 36–34 pts)
           Salford – 300 pts (Dig Broad Tech; Acoust; Aud Tech)
           York – BBB 300 pts (Mus Tech Sys; Electron Eng Mus Tech) (IB 32 pts)
280 pts **Birmingham City** – 280 pts (Snd Multim Tech; Snd Eng Prod)
           Bournemouth – 280–300 pts (Mus Aud Tech; Mus Snd Prod Tech) (IB 30–31 pts)
           Liverpool John Moores – 280 pts (Aud Mus Prod)
           London (Royal Central Sch SpDr) – BBC 280 pts (Thea Prac Thea Snd)
           London Met – 280 pts (Mus Tech (Aud Sys/Snd Media))
           Oxford Brookes – BBC 280 pts (Snd Tech Dig Mus) (IB 30 pts)
           South Wales – BBC (Snd Tech)
260 pts **Bolton** – BCC 260 pts (Snd Eng Des) (IB 24 pts HL 544)
           De Montfort – 260 pts (Aud Rec Tech)
           Lincoln – 260 pts (Aud Prod)
           Salford – 260–280 pts (Phys Acoust)
240 pts **Glyndŵr** – 240 pts (Snd Tech)
           Hertfordshire – 240 pts (Snd Des Tech; Aud Rec Prod)
           London South Bank – 240 pts (Mus Sonic Med) (IB 24 pts)
           Portsmouth – 240–300 pts (Comp Dig Snd; Mus Snd Tech) (IB 28 pts)
           Ravensbourne – AA–CC (Snd Des; Broad Aud Tech; Broad Inf Tech; Broad Tech; Outsd Broad Tech) (IB 28 pts)
           Southampton Solent – 240 pts (Pop Mus Prod)
           West London – 240 pts (App Snd Eng)
220 pts **Derby** – 220 pts (Snd Lgt Lve Evnt Tech)
200 pts **Rose Bruford (Coll)** – 200 pts (Perf Snd)
           Southampton Solent – 200 pts (Aud Tech; Snd Eng; Liv Std Snd; Mus Std Tech)
160 pts **Liverpool (LIPA)** – 160–280 pts (Snd Tech)
 80 pts **Arts London** – 80 pts (Snd Arts Des)
 60 pts **UHI** – D 60 pts (Aud Eng)

Alternative offers
See **Chapter 7** and **Appendix 1** for grades/UCAS Tariff points information for the International Baccalaureate, Scottish Highers/Advanced Highers, the Welsh Baccalaureate, the Irish Leaving Certificate, the Cambridge Pre-U Diploma, the Advanced Diploma and the Extended Project.

EXAMPLES OF FOUNDATION DEGREES IN THE SUBJECT FIELD
St Helens (Coll).

CHOOSING YOUR COURSE (SEE ALSO CH.1)
Some course features
Salford (Acoust) Course includes electronics, computing, maths and specialist acoustic topics, for example musical acoustics, psychoacoustics and acoustics of performance spaces.
Southampton (Acoust Eng) The course involves engineering design to minimise noise and vibration, ocean acoustics and sonar and sound reproduction and musical instrument acoustics. There are 10-week industrial placements. The Acoustics and Music degree allows students to weight their studies in favour of either subject 75/25 or 25/75.
Surrey (Mus Snd Rec (Tonmeister)) This well-established course comprises three areas of study: the technical aspects of audio, practical experience of recording, and music theory and practice.

Universities and colleges teaching quality See www.qaa.ac.uk; http://unistats.direct.gov.uk.

Examples of sandwich degree courses Birmingham City; De Montfort; Huddersfield; Portsmouth; Surrey; York.

ADMISSIONS INFORMATION

Number of applicants per place (approx) Anglia Ruskin 5; Salford 4; Southampton 4.

Advice to applicants and planning the UCAS personal statement See **Engineering/Engineering Sciences**. See also **Appendix 3**.

Misconceptions about this course Anglia Ruskin Failure to appreciate the emphasis that the course gives to science and technology.

Selection interviews Yes Salford, Southampton; **Some** Anglia Ruskin.

Interview advice and questions What interests you about acoustics engineering? What career do you have in mind on graduating? See also **Chapter 6**.

Reasons for rejection (non-academic) See **Engineering/Engineering Sciences**.

AFTER-RESULTS ADVICE

Offers to applicants repeating A-levels Same Anglia Ruskin, Salford.

GRADUATE DESTINATIONS AND EMPLOYMENT (2011/12 HESA)

See **Engineering/Engineering Sciences**.

Career note Specialist topics on these courses will enable graduates to make decisions as to their future career destinations.

OTHER DEGREE SUBJECTS FOR CONSIDERATION

Audiology; Broadcast Engineering; Communications Engineering; Computer Engineering; Computer Science; Media Technology; Music; Radio and TV; Technology; Telecommunications Engineering and Electronic Engineering.

ENGINEERING (AERONAUTICAL and AEROSPACE)

(see also **Engineering (Electrical and Electronic)**)

Courses cover the manufacture of military and civil aircraft, theories of mechanics, thermodynamics, electronics, computing and engine design. Avionics courses include flight and energy control systems, airborne computing, navigation, optical and TV displays, airborne communications, and radar systems for navigation and power.

Engineering Council statement See **Engineering/Engineering Sciences**.

Useful websites aerosociety.com; www.engc.org.uk.

NB The points totals shown to the left of the institutions are for ease of reference only. It must not be assumed that Tariff points are always used by institutions or that they can be substituted for an offer in grades. The level of an offer is not necessarily indicative of the quality of a course.

COURSE OFFERS INFORMATION

Subject requirements/preferences See **Engineering/Engineering Sciences**. Offers shown below refer to BEng or BSc courses unless otherwise stated.

Your target offers and examples of courses provided by each institution

400 pts **Imperial London** – A*A*A incl phys maths 400 pts (Aero Eng MEng; Aero Eng (Yr Abrd))
(IB 40 pts)

380 pts **Bath** – A*AA 380 pts (Aerosp Eng) (IB 36 pts HL 6 maths phys)
Bristol – A*AA–AAA 380–360 pts (Aerosp Eng; Aerosp Eng (St Abrd) MEng) (IB 38 pts)
Cambridge – A*AA 380 pts (Aerosp Aeroth Eng) (IB 40–41 pts HL 776)
Glasgow – A*AA 380 pts (Aero Eng MEng; Aerosp Sys MEng) (IB 36 pts)

The facts

» One of Europe's leading Schools of Engineering

» Eighty teaching staff, with up to 350 undergraduate places each year

» Seventy percent of graduates are awarded First or Upper Second Class Honours degrees

Your experience

From the flexible, 24/7 learning environment of the Alan Gilbert Learning Commons to the personal development opportunities and specialist support services we offer, we will empower you to be your best. We're well underway with the biggest investment programme ever seen in UK higher education, having invested £750 million in our facilities since 2004, with another £1 billion to follow. Away from your studies you'll have access to the UK's largest student union, almost 300 student societies, and excellent sports and fitness facilities. The only thing you won't experience is boredom.

Nine reasons we should be your number one choice

1. Professionally accredited courses
2. Top-rated for graduate employment
3. Student clubs and groups
4. Strong industrial partnerships
5. Peer Assisted Study Scheme (PASS)
6. Excellent research rankings
7. Extensive laboratory facilities
8. Cross-disciplinary
9. Teamwork

Courses

Aerospace Engineering

SWL 3.21

Civil Engineering

Mechanical Engineering

BEng   MEng

School of Mechanical, Aerospace and Civil Engineering

Profile

Katherine Woolley
MEng(Hons) Civil Engineering
Senior Tunnel Engineer, AECOM

"A good degree in engineering from Manchester impresses the employers. My MEng degree has given me a great benchmark. It also meant that I've been able to get chartered without a Masters

degree. After University I worked for Mott MacDonald in Croydon, UK as a tunnel engineer. I moved to Auckland in New Zealand in July 2011 to work for AECOM as a senior tunnel engineer. My main responsibilities are management, design and construction supervision of tunnels. "

MEng or BEng?

We offer a range of degree courses at both MEng (Master of Engineering) or BEng (Bachelor of Engineering) level. The most obvious difference between these is duration: four or five years for MEng, and three years for BEng. Transfer between BEng and MEng is possible. The first three years cover most of the engineering science whereas the fourth year looks in more depth at particular applications. But what else could influence your choice?

Many students studying for a degree in engineering aim to become Chartered Engineers, and accredited MEng courses give you the required educational base to achieve this. Accredited BEng courses require you to complete further study in order to achieve the same status.

Student Recruitment and Admissions

School of Mechanical, Aerospace and Civil Engineering

Pariser Building, Sackville Street, Manchester, M13 9PL

Tel +44 (0) 161 306 9210
email ug-mace@manchester.ac.uk

www.manchester.ac.uk/mace/undergraduate

Southampton – A*AA 380 pts (Aero Astnaut (Aerodyn); Aero Astnaut (Struct Des); Mech Eng (Aerosp); Aero Astnaut MEng; Aero Astnaut BEng; Aero Astnaut (Airvhcl Sys Des); Aero Astnaut (Eng Mgt)) (IB 38 pts HL 18 pts)

360 pts
Bath – AAA 360 pts (Electron Eng Spc Sci Tech MEng) (IB 36 pts HL 6 maths phys)

Brunel – AAA 360 pts (Aerosp Eng MEng; Mech Eng Aero MEng; Avn Eng MEng) (IB 37 pts)

City – 360 pts (Aero Eng MEng) (IB 32 pts)

Imperial London – AAA incl maths phys 360 pts (Aerosp Mat) (IB 38 pts HL 6 maths phys)

Leeds – AAA 360 pts (Aero Aerosp Eng) (IB 35 pts HL 18 pts)

Liverpool – AAA 360 pts (Aerosp Eng Plt St MEng; Aerosp Eng MEng) (IB 35 pts)

London (QM) – AAA 360 pts (Aerosp Eng MEng)

Loughborough – AAA–ABB (Aero Eng) (IB 34 pts)

Manchester – AAA (Aerosp Eng MEng; Aerosp Eng Mgt) (IB 37 pts)

Nottingham – AAA–AAB (Mech Eng Aerosp) (IB 36 pts HL 5 maths phys)

Sheffield – AAA incl maths phys (Aero Eng (Yr Ind); Aerosp Eng (PPI) MEng; Aerosp Eng MEng) (IB 37 pts HL 6 maths phys)

Southampton – AAA incl maths phys (Sp Sys Eng) (IB 36 pts HL 18 pts)

Strathclyde – AAA 360 pts (Aero Mech Eng MEng; Mech Eng Aero MEng) (IB 36 pts)

Surrey – AAA (Aerosp Eng MEng) (IB 36 pts)

340 pts
Brunel – AAB 340 pts (Aerosp Eng; Avn Eng; Avn Eng Plt St; Mech Eng Aero) (IB 35 pts)

City – 340 pts (Aero Eng; Air Trans Eng) (IB 30–32 pts)

Glasgow – AAB (Aero Eng; Aerosp Sys) (IB 34 pts)

Hertfordshire – 340 pts (Aerosp Eng MEng; Aerosp Sys Eng Plt St MEng; Aerosp Sys Eng MEng)

Leeds – AAA incl maths+phys (Avn Tech Mgt; Avn Tech Plt St) (IB 35 pts HL 18 pts incl 5 phys/maths)

Leicester – AAB–ABB 340–320 pts (Aerosp Eng MEng) (IB 34–32 pts)

Manchester – AAB (Aerosp Eng) (IB 35 pts)

Queen's Belfast – AAB 340 pts (Prod Des Dev MEng; Aerosp Eng MEng)

Sheffield – AAB incl maths phys (Aerosp Eng; Aerosp Eng (PPI)) (IB 35 pts HL 6 maths phys)

Southampton – AAB 340 pts (Aero Astnaut (Spcrft Eng)) (IB 38 pts HL 18 pts)

Strathclyde – AAB 340 pts (Aero Mech Eng) (IB 32 pts)

Surrey – AAB (Aerosp Eng) (IB 34 pts)

Swansea – AAB 340 pts (Aerosp Eng MEng) (IB 34 pts)

York – AAB–ABB (Avion MEng) (IB 34 pts)

320 pts
Brighton – ABB 320 pts (Aero Eng) (IB 34 pts)

Kingston – 320 pts (Aerosp Eng MEng; Aerosp Eng Astnaut Spc Tech MEng)

Liverpool – ABB 320 pts (Aerosp Eng; Aerosp Eng Plt St; Avion Sys; Avion Sys MEng; Avion Sys Plt St MEng) (IB 33 pts HL 5 maths phys/electron)

London (QM) – ABB 320 pts (Aerosp Eng)

300 pts
Bristol UWE – 300 pts (Aerosp Sys Eng)

Coventry – BBB 300 pts (Avn Mgt; Aerosp Sys Eng) (IB 29 pts)

Leicester – BBB 300 pts (Aerosp Eng) (IB 30 pts)

Queen's Belfast – BBB (Aero Eng; Aerosp Eng)

Sheffield Hallam – BBB 300 pts incl maths (Aerosp Eng MEng)

Swansea – BBB 300 pts (Aerosp Eng) (IB 32 pts)

280 pts
Bristol UWE – 280 pts (Aerosp Des Eng; Aerosp Manuf Eng)

Glyndŵr – 280 pts (Aero Mech Eng)

Hertfordshire – 280 pts (Aerosp Eng; Aerosp Sys Eng Plt St; Aerosp Sys Eng)

Kingston – 280 pts (Aerosp Eng; Aerosp Eng Astnaut Spc Tech)

Loughborough – 280 pts (Air Trans Mgt) (IB 30 pts)

Salford – 280–300 pts (Aero Eng MEng)

South Wales – 280 pts (Aero Eng)
Teesside – 280 pts (Aerosp Eng)
260 pts **Hertfordshire** – 260 pts (Aerosp Tech Mgt; Aerosp Tech Plt St)
Salford – 260–280 pts (Aero Eng; Aircft Eng Plt St)
Sheffield Hallam – 260 pts (Aerosp Eng)
240 pts **Farnborough (CT)** – 240 pts (Aero Eng)
South Wales – 240 pts (Aircrft Mntnc Eng)
200 pts **Sheffield Hallam** – 200 pts incl AL maths (Aero Eng)
60 pts **UHI** – (Aircrft Eng)

Alternative offers
See **Chapter 7** and **Appendix 1** for grades/UCAS Tariff points information for the International Baccalaureate, Scottish Highers/Advanced Highers, the Welsh Baccalaureate, the Irish Leaving Certificate, the Cambridge Pre-U Diploma, the Advanced Diploma and the Extended Project.

EXAMPLES OF FOUNDATION DEGREES IN THE SUBJECT FIELD
Bristol City (Coll); Bristol UWE; Farnborough (CT); Glyndŵr; Hertfordshire; Kingston; London Met; Sheffield Hallam.

CHOOSING YOUR COURSE (SEE ALSO CH.1)
Some course features
Brunel Pilot Studies available with Aviation Engineering.
Durham A common course for Years 1 and 2 and then two years specialising in the chosen discipline.
Hertfordshire Pilot Studies available with Aerospace Systems Engineering.
Imperial London Fourth-year students may take the option of spending four months researching in universities in the UK or Europe.
Liverpool Pilot Studies available in some Aeronautical or Aerospace Engineering courses.
Loughborough The first two years are common for all BEng and MEng students allowing the former to transfer to the MEng course at the end of the second year.
Manchester A year out in industry or in Europe are options.
Sheffield Pilot Studies available in some Aeronautical or Aerospace Engineering courses.
Swansea Aerospace Engineering can be taken as a BEng or MEng or with a year in industry.
York All Electronics courses have a common first year with specialisation following in Avionics in Year 2 or allowing students to transfer to one of eight Electronics courses.

Universities and colleges teaching quality See www.qaa.ac.uk; http://unistats.direct.gov.uk.

Top research universities and colleges (RAE 2008) See **Engineering (Mechanical)**.

Examples of sandwich degree courses Bath; Brighton; Bristol UWE; Brunel; City; Coventry; Hertfordshire; Kingston; Loughborough; Queen's Belfast; Sheffield Hallam; Surrey.

ADMISSIONS INFORMATION
Number of applicants per place (approx) Bath 13, (MEng) 18; Bristol 7; Bristol UWE 4; City 17; Coventry 7; Farnborough (CT) 7; Glyndŵr 5; Hertfordshire 17; Kingston 9; London (QM) 8; Loughborough 10; Queen's Belfast 6; Salford 6; Southampton 10; York 3 av.

Advice to applicants and planning the UCAS personal statement Interest in engineering and aerospace. Work experience in engineering. Flying experience. Personal attainments. Relevant hobbies. Membership of Air Training Corps. See also **Engineering/Engineering Sciences**. **Bristol** Deferred entry accepted. **Imperial London** Deferred entry acceptable.

Misconceptions about this course That Aeronautical Engineering is not a highly analytical subject: it is.

Selection interviews **Yes** Bristol, Cambridge, Farnborough (CT), Hertfordshire, Imperial London, Kingston, London (QM), Loughborough, Salford, Southampton.

296 | Engineering (Chemical)

Interview advice and questions Why Aeronautical Engineering? Questions about different types of aircraft and flight principles of helicopters. Range of interests in engineering. See also **Chapter 6**.

Reasons for rejection (non-academic) See **Engineering/Engineering Sciences**.

AFTER-RESULTS ADVICE

Offers to applicants repeating A-levels Higher Bristol, Queen's Belfast; **Possibly higher** Hertfordshire; **Same** Bath, City, Farnborough (CT), Kingston, Liverpool, Loughborough, Salford, Southampton, York; **No** Cambridge.

GRADUATE DESTINATIONS AND EMPLOYMENT (2011/12 HESA)

Aerospace Engineering graduates surveyed 1030 **Employed** 545 **In voluntary employment** 10 **In further study** 300 **Assumed unemployed** 100

Career note Specialist areas of study on these courses will open up possible career directions. See also **Engineering/Engineering Sciences**.

OTHER DEGREE SUBJECTS FOR CONSIDERATION

Astronomy; Astrophysics; Computer Science; Electronics and Systems Engineering; Materials Science; Mathematics; Naval Architecture; Physics.

ENGINEERING (CHEMICAL)

(including **Fire Engineering, Fire Safety** and **Nuclear Engineering**; see also **Chemistry**)

Courses involve chemistry, microbiology, physics and mathematics. Management, economics, process dynamics, process design and safety are introduced in Years 2 and 3.

Engineering Council statement See **Engineering/Engineering Sciences**.

Useful websites www.icheme.org; www.engc.org.uk; www.whynotchemeng.com.

NB The points totals shown to the left of the institutions are for ease of reference only. It must not be assumed that Tariff points are always used by institutions or that they can be substituted for an offer in grades. The level of an offer is not necessarily indicative of the quality of a course.

COURSE OFFERS INFORMATION

Subject requirements/preferences AL Mathematics and chemistry required. See also **Engineering/ Engineering Sciences**. Offers shown below refer to BEng or BSc courses unless otherwise stated.

Your target offers and examples of courses provided by each institution

380 pts **Cambridge** – A*AA 380 pts (Cheml Eng) (IB 40–41 pts HL 776)
Imperial London – A*AA 380 pts (Cheml Nucl Eng MEng; Cheml Eng) (IB 41 pts HL 776)
London (UCL) – A*AA–AAB 380–340 pts (Cheml Eng) (IB 36–39 pts)
Oxford – A*AA 380 pts (Cheml Eng) (IB 38–40 pts)
360 pts **Bath** – AAA 360 pts (Bioch Eng MEng; Cheml Eng BEng/MEng) (IB 36 pts HL 6)
Birmingham – AAA–AAB 360–340 pts (Cheml Eng; Cheml Eng (Int St); Cheml Eng MEng; Nucl Eng MEng) (IB 35–36 pts)
Edinburgh – AAA–ABB 360–320 pts (Cheml Eng; Cheml Eng Mgt) (IB 37–32 pts)
Lancaster – AAA 360 pts (Nucl Eng) (IB 36 pts)
Leeds – AAA 360 pts (Petrol Eng; Cheml Eng courses) (IB 35 pts HL 18 pts)
London (UCL) – AAA–AAB (Bioch Cheml Eng MEng; Bioch Eng MEng; Bioch; Bioch Eng Bioproc Mgt) (IB 36–38 pts)
Manchester – AAA (Cheml Eng Biotech; Cheml Eng Env Tech; Cheml Eng (Bus Mgt); Cheml Eng) (IB 37 pts)
Nottingham – AAA 360 pts (Cheml Eng BEng/MEng; Cheml Eng Env Eng) (IB 36 pts)
Strathclyde – AAA 360 pts (Cheml Eng MEng) (IB 36 pts)

why not CHEMENG
shape the future...

Engineering your future —
why chemical is the
way to go...

By Matt Stalker

Chemical engineers are considered to be the problem-solvers of the science and engineering community. Whether it's working out how to make industrial processes more environmentally friendly or deciding which fuels are best suited to Formula One racing cars, chemical engineers have usually got the answers.

If you're reading this, you're probably already thinking about studying chemical engineering at university.

It's a career path that offers variety, travel and outstanding earning potential with graduates earning £28,992 on average – the second highest in the UK.

Chemical engineers understand how to alter the chemical, biochemical or physical state of a substance, to create everything from face creams to fuels. For example, did you know that petrol, plastics and synthetic fibres such as polyester and nylon, all come from oil? www.whynotchemeng.com is a website that's full of information about chemical engineering. Whether you're trying to better understand what chemical engineers do on a day-to-day basis, which companies employ chemical engineers, or which universities offer chemical engineering degree courses, whynotchemeng can help.

Since the campaign's launch, volunteers have visited hundreds of schools and colleges throughout the UK and played a key role in the staggering rise in number of students choosing to study chemical engineering at UK universities. Last year, a record intake of over 2200 students chose to start studying the subject at university.

Companies such as BP, Shell, Sellafield, Davy Process Technology, Foster Wheeler, KBR, ReAgent and British Sugar all employ chemical engineering graduates in a wide range of roles.

Because the skills of a chemical engineer are so transferable, international travel is a very real possibility for chemical engineers.

Sheida Khajavi studied chemical engineering at Delft University in the Netherlands, and now works as an oil markets analyst for Shell: "Chemical engineering is a really exciting subject and there are many different aspects to it. It's not just about the sciences, you need to be analytical too and there is lots of variety within the profession. Just about everything we see and touch throughout our lives has at some point, been touched by chemical engineering", she explained.

Al Sacco is another chemical engineer and he's got further than most...much further. Al spent time working for NASA and has been into space, spending three weeks doing research into Earth's orbit! "When people ask how far chemical engineering has taken me, I can tell them that it's taken me into space – it doesn't get much further than that!" said Al.

Whilst a chemical engineering degree isn't certain to take you as far as Al, it's a door-opening degree that equips graduates with an outstanding grasp of project management, design and how industrial processes operate. So maybe it's time to think... whynotchemeng?

whynotchemeng.com

0862_13

Chemical Engineering

at the University of Leeds

We have an established reputation for teaching and research, in the UK and overseas, across the entire spectrum of chemical, energy, petroleum and nuclear engineering.

An active research environment allows us to offer a range of exciting degree courses taught by experts who are leaders in their fields.

Visit our website to find out about our undergraduate degrees.

- **Chemical Engineering**
- **Chemical and Energy Engineering**
- **Chemical and Materials Engineering**
- **Chemical and Nuclear Engineering**
- **Food Process Engineering**
- **Petroleum Engineering**

Careers in the field of chemical engineering are wide ranging, and employment prospects are excellent. Recent graduates have successfully secured positions in chemical and pharmaceutical companies, renewable energy plants, mineral processing and metals recycling operations.

www.engineering.leeds.ac.uk/chemical

f www.facebook.com/
facultyofengineeringleeds

Why study Chemical Engineering at Leeds

- 3rd in the UK for Chemical Engineering – The Good University Guide 2014.
- Our courses are integrated masters (MEng, BEng) degrees, which provide the most direct route to becoming a Chartered Engineer (CEng), a vital distinguishing qualification in the UK job market.
- All courses are professionally accredited by the Institution of Chemical Engineers (IChemE) or the Energy Institute.
- Highly employable graduates - 100% of our graduates are in a professional or managerial role within 6 months of graduating (Unistats 2013).
- Our ground-breaking research feeds directly into our teaching.
- All of our courses offer you the opportunity to study abroad or undertake a placement year.
- Strong industrial links with top graduate recruiters.
- Taught by academics at the forefront of their subjects.
- Access to specialist facilities and laboratories equipped with the latest technology.

Come along to a University Open Day to find out more: www.leeds.ac.uk/openday

UNIVERSITY OF LEEDS

340 pts **Liverpool** – AAB–BBB (Phys Nucl Sci) (IB 33 pts HL 6 maths phys)
Loughborough – 340 pts (Cheml Eng Mgt (4 yrs); Cheml Eng MEng; Cheml Eng Mgt) (IB 36 pts HL maths phys chem)
Manchester – AAB 340 pts (Petrol Eng) (IB 35 pts HL 17 pts)
Newcastle – AAB (Cheml Eng MEng; Bioproc Eng) (IB 36 pts HL 5 maths chem)
Queen's Belfast – AAB 340 pts (Cheml Eng MEng)
Sheffield – AAB (Cheml Eng; Cheml Eng Joint Hons; Cheml Eng Biotech) (IB 35 pts)
Strathclyde – AAB 340 pts (Cheml Eng) (IB 32 pts)
Surrey – AAB 340 pts (Cheml Eng MEng) (IB 35 pts HL 11 pts)

320 pts **Edinburgh** – AAA–ABB incl maths 320–360 pts (Struct Fire Sfty Eng) (IB 37–32 pts)
Lancaster – ABB (Cheml Eng)
Sheffield – ABB (Cheml Proc Eng) (IB 33 pts)
Surrey – ABB (Cheml Eng) (IB 34 pts)

300 pts **Aberdeen** – BBB 300 pts (Cheml Eng; Petrol Eng) (IB 34 pts)
Aston – BBB–ABB 300–320 pts (Cheml Eng MEng; Cheml Eng)
Heriot-Watt – BBB (Cheml Eng; Cheml Eng Ener Eng; Cheml Eng Oil Gas Tech; Cheml Eng Pharml Chem)
Queen's Belfast – BBB 300 pts (Cheml Eng)
Swansea – BBB (Cheml Eng)
Teesside – 300 pts (Cheml Eng)

280 pts **Hull** – 280 pts (Cheml Eng)
Teesside – 280 pts (Cheml Eng)

270 pts **Glasgow Caledonian** – 270 pts (Fire Risk Eng)

260 pts **Bradford** – 260 pts (Cheml Eng)
Central Lancashire – BCC 260 pts (Fire Eng BEng/MEng)
Huddersfield – 260 pts (Chem Cheml Eng)
South Wales – 260 pts (Fire Sfty Eng)

240 pts **Central Lancashire** – CCC 240 pts (Fire Sfty Risk Mgt)
London South Bank – 240 pts (Cheml Proc Eng)
Portsmouth – 240–280 pts (Petrol Eng) (IB 26 pts)
West Scotland – CCC 240 pts (Cheml Eng) (IB 24 pts)

Alternative offers
See **Chapter 7** and **Appendix 1** for grades/UCAS Tariff points information for the International Baccalaureate, Scottish Highers/Advanced Highers, the Welsh Baccalaureate, the Irish Leaving Certificate, the Cambridge Pre-U Diploma, the Advanced Diploma and the Extended Project.

CHOOSING YOUR COURSE (SEE ALSO CH.1)
Some course features
Aberdeen Close contacts with the oil and gas industries. Years 1 and 2 have a common core structure with students specialising in Year 3.
Birmingham One-third of the course focuses on Business Management and is devoted to management subjects.
Heriot-Watt Direct entry to Year 2 depending on A-level results. Courses have a common structure up to Year 3 allowing for a change in specialisation.
London (UCL) The MEng course leads directly to Chartered Engineer status. Students taking the BEng course will need to complete a period of further training to achieve this.
Newcastle Stages 1 and 2 are common for all nine courses in the department.
Nottingham Chemical Engineering can be combined with Environmental Engineering with fully paid placements at the end of Year 2.

Universities and colleges teaching quality See www.qaa.ac.uk; http://unistats.direct.gov.uk.

Top research universities and colleges (RAE 2008) Cambridge; Imperial London; Manchester; London (UCL); Birmingham; Sheffield; Newcastle; Bath.

Examples of sandwich degree courses Aston; Bath; Bradford; Huddersfield; London South Bank; Loughborough; Manchester; Queen's Belfast; Surrey; Teesside.

ADMISSIONS INFORMATION

Number of applicants per place (approx) Aston 4; Bath 9; Birmingham 8; Heriot-Watt 8; Huddersfield 7; Imperial London 4, (MEng) 4; Leeds 9; London (UCL) 8; Loughborough 7; Newcastle 6; Nottingham 6; Sheffield 14; Strathclyde 6; Surrey 5; Swansea 3.

Misconceptions about this course **Surrey** That chemical engineering is chemistry on a large scale: physics is as applicable as chemistry.

Selection interviews **Yes** Bath, Birmingham, Cambridge, Imperial London, Leeds, London (UCL), London South Bank, Loughborough, Newcastle, Oxford, Surrey, Sussex, Teesside; **No** Nottingham.

Interview advice and questions Past questions have included the following: How would you justify the processing of radioactive waste to people living in the neighbourhood? What is public health engineering? What is biochemical engineering? What could be the sources of fuel and energy in the year 2020? Discuss some industrial applications of chemistry. Regular incidents occur in which chemical spillage and other problems affect the environment – be prepared to discuss these social issues. See also **Chapter 6**. **Imperial London** Interviews can be conducted in South East Asia if necessary.

Reasons for rejection (non-academic) See **Engineering/Engineering Sciences**.

AFTER-RESULTS ADVICE

Offers to applicants repeating A-levels **Higher** Swansea; **Possibly higher** Bath, Leeds, London South Bank, Queen's Belfast; **Same** Aston, Birmingham, Cambridge, Loughborough, Newcastle, Nottingham, Sheffield, Surrey, Teesside.

GRADUATE DESTINATIONS AND EMPLOYMENT (2011/12 HESA)

Chemical, Process and Energy Engineering graduates surveyed 755 **Employed** 435 **In voluntary employment** 10 **In further study** 185 **Assumed unemployed** 75

Career note Chemical engineering is involved in many aspects of industry and scientific development. In addition to the oil and chemical-based industries, graduates enter a wide range of careers including the design and construction of chemical process plants, food production, pollution control, environmental protection, energy conservation, waste recovery and recycling, medical science, health and safety, and alternative energy sources.

OTHER DEGREE SUBJECTS FOR CONSIDERATION

Biochemistry; Biotechnology; Chemistry; Cosmetic Science; Environmental Science; Food Science and Technology; Materials Science; Mathematics; Nuclear Engineering; Physics.

ENGINEERING (CIVIL)

(including **Architectural, Coastal, Disaster Management, Environmental, Offshore, Structural** and **Transportation Engineering**; see also **Building and Construction, Environmental Sciences/Studies**)

Civil engineering is concerned with the science and art of large-scale projects. This involves the planning, design, construction, maintenance and environmental assessment of roads, railways, bridges, airports, tunnels, docks, offshore structures, dams, high-rise buildings and other major works. Specialist courses may also involve water, drainage, irrigation schemes and waste engineering, traffic and coastal engineering.

Engineering Council statement See **Engineering/Engineering Sciences**

Useful websites www.ice.org.uk; www.engc.org.uk.

Find out more about a future in civil engineering

China Central TV Headquarters

Image courtesy of Arup

USAID water pump, Ghana

Burj Khalifa, Dubai

Where will a career in civil

Why study civil engineering?

A world of civil engineering

Civil engineers shape the world around us. Each time you turn on a tap, enter a building, catch a train or cross a road, you're benefiting from civil engineering. Without civil engineers the world as we know it would not exist.

A world of opportunities

Choose to study engineering and you'll be taking the first step on an exciting journey. Around the world, today's engineers have created iconic towers in Dubai, stunning structures in China and are building a new high-capacity passenger service for London. Imagine where you could go.

A better world

By building bridges that connect people, providing remote communities with clean drinking water and protecting us from the elements, civil engineers build a better world.

Engineers are needed to help local people rebuild after earthquakes or wars and during droughts. There are real opportunities to make a difference, by helping societies to develop and tackle poverty.

Find out where a future in civil engineering could take you at ice.org.uk/future

Choose a future in civil engineering. There's no telling where it could take you

Registered charity number 210252. Charity registered in Scotland number SC038629.

ice
Institution of Civil Engineers

Image courtesy of Crossrail

Crossrail, London (under construction) Worldwide opportunities

engineering take you?

Civil
Engineering
at the University of Leeds

Globally renowned for our teaching and research, we are one of the largest and longest established civil engineering schools in the country.

A cutting-edge, vibrant research environment enables us to offer a range of exciting degree courses taught by experts who are national and global leaders in their fields.

Visit our website to find out about our undergraduate degrees.

- **Architectural Engineering**
- **Civil and Environmental Engineering**
- **Civil and Structural Engineering**
- **Civil Engineering with Project Management**

Graduates are highly sought after and gain professional positions in the engineering sector, with contractors, consultants, government agencies and utilities, both in the UK and abroad.

www.engineering.leeds.ac.uk/civil

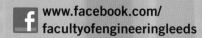 **www.facebook.com/ facultyofengineeringleeds**

Why study Civil Engineering at Leeds

- All courses are professionally accredited by the Institution of Civil Engineers, the Institution of Structural Engineers, the Chartered Institution of Highways and Transportation and the Institute of Highway Engineering.

- Our courses are integrated masters (MEng, BEng) degrees, which provide the most direct route to becoming a Chartered Engineer (CEng), a vital distinguishing qualification in the UK job market.

- Our ground-breaking research feeds directly into our teaching.

- Highly employable graduates - 90% of our graduates are employed or in further study within six months of graduating (Unistats 2013).

- All of our courses offer you the opportunity to study abroad or undertake a placement year.

- Industry-sponsored fieldwork allows you to gain hands-on experience investigating and applying material from your lectures and tutorials to real-life work situations.

- Strong industrial links with top graduate recruiters including Arup, Atkins, White Young Green, Balfour Beatty, Rolls-Royce and Shepherd Construction.

- Taught by academics at the forefront of their subjects.

- Access to specialist facilities and laboratories equipped with the latest technology.

Come along to a University Open Day to find out more: **www.leeds.ac.uk/openday**

 **UNIVERSITY OF LEEDS**

Engineer your future with undergraduate study at Ulster...

Fees only £6000 for GB Students

Top 20 University for UCAS applications

Largest University on the island of Ireland

BSc Hons
BEng Hons
MEng
degree options

Civil Engineering & Energy and Building Services Engineering

Engineering Council Accredited Courses

Full-time and Part-time study options

Professional Education for a Professional Future

study.ulster.ac.uk
adbe.ulster.ac.uk

University of ULSTER

Your future, make it happen

ENGINEERING AT ULSTER

BSc Hons / BEng Hons / MEng

Have you considered studying Engineering at Ulster? The university is based in Belfast, the most student friendly city in the UK, with some of the best value student accommodation, a vibrant nightlife and only one hour away from most major cities in Great Britain. The School of the Built Environment offers courses in energy, building services and civil engineering.

Would you like to be involved in design, construction and maintenance of bridges, airports, seaports and other major structures? Would you like a career in an innovative profession that is essential to the operation of a modern society?

Yes? Then come and study Civil Engineering at Ulster.

Ulster offers a suite of Civil Engineering courses including MEng Civil Engineering, BEng (Hons) Civil Engineering and the BSc (Hons) Civil Engineering (Geoinformatics) and covers a wide range of subjects that allow you to develop abilities you will use throughout your working life.

The teaching is delivered by qualified Civil Engineers who have over 500 research publications between them. Ulster offers a blend the blend of industry and research experience and lecturers have industry experience and most are Chartered Engineers. The courses are accredited by the relevant professional bodies: Institution of Civil Engineers (ICE), Institution of Structural Engineers (IStructE), the Chartered Institution of Highways and Transportation (CIHT), and the Institute of Highway Engineers (IHE).

Interested in renewable energy systems or engineering low and zero carbon buildings? These are the main aims of the Energy and Building Services Engineering course at Ulster.

50% of UK energy demand is consumed in buildings. To meet climate change targets, address fuel poverty and reduce the size of fuel bills we need to decarbonise through alternative energy sources, new building design or deep building retrofit. The challenge is large; there are fewer than 19 million minutes to upgrade 25 million UK homes by 2050.

"This course has provided me with an excellent foundation in this engineering discipline and opened an insight into opportunities that exist in this field. I believe the course offers a broad range of teaching in relevant subject areas and maintains a balanced approach to individual and team activities."

Donal Cotter (graduate from MEng Energy & Building Services Engineering)

The course is professionally accredited and won the Happold Brilliant Award 2010/11 awarded from the Chartered Institution of Building Services Engineers for excellence in teaching and research for building services engineering.

Visit **study.ulster.ac.uk** for more information including entry requirements. We hope to see you on an Engineering course at Ulster soon.

UCAS

BSc Hons Civil Engineering	H202
BEng Hons / MEng Civil Engineering	H200
BEng Hons / MEng Energy and Building Services Engineering	KH22

University of ULSTER

Your future, make it happen

NB *The points totals shown to the left of the institutions are for ease of reference only. It must not be assumed that Tariff points are always used by institutions or that they can be substituted for an offer in grades. The level of an offer is not necessarily indicative of the quality of a course.*

COURSE OFFERS INFORMATION

Subject requirements/preferences See **Engineering/Engineering Sciences**. Offers shown below refer to BEng or BSc courses unless otherwise stated.

Your target offers and examples of courses provided by each institution

400 pts **Imperial London** – A*A*A 400 pts (Civ Eng MEng) (IB 39 pts HL 7 maths 6 phys)
London (UCL) – A*AAe–AAAe 400 pts (Eng (Civ)) (IB 38–39 pts)

380 pts **Bath** – A*AA 380 pts (Civ Archit Eng MEng; Civ Eng) (IB 36 pts HL 6 maths)
Bristol – A*AA–AAA 380–360 pts (Civ Eng BEng/MEng) (IB 38–35 pts)
Cambridge – A*AA 380 pts (Civ Eng) (IB 40–41 pts)
Durham – A*AA 380 pts (Civ Eng MEng) (IB 38 pts)
Oxford – A*AA 380 pts (Civ Eng MEng) (IB 38–40 pts)
Southampton – A*AA 380 pts (Civ Eng BEng/MEng; Civ Eng Archit MEng) (IB 36 pts HL 18 pts)

360 pts **Brunel** – AAA 360 pts (Civ Eng MEng) (IB 37 pts)
Cardiff – AAA–AAB 360–340 pts (Archit Eng; Civ Eng; Civ Env Eng) (IB 32–36 pts)
Edinburgh – AAA–ABB incl maths 360–320 pts (Civ Eng; Struct Eng Archit) (IB 37–32 pts)
Exeter – AAA–AAB 360–340 pts (Civ Eng MEng) (IB 36–32 pts)
Leeds – AAA (Civ Eng courses) (IB 38 pts HL 18 pts)
Manchester – AAA (Civ Struct Eng MEng) (IB 37 pts)
Newcastle – AAA 360 pts (Civ Struct Eng; Civ Eng) (IB 37 pts)
Nottingham – AAA (Civ Eng BEng/MEng) (IB 36 pts)
Sheffield – AAA incl maths sci (Civ Struct Eng; Civ Eng; Civ Eng Modn Lang; Struct Eng Archit) (IB 37 pts HL 6 maths sci)
Strathclyde – AAA–AAB (Civ Eng BEng/MEng)
Swansea – AAA–AAB incl maths (Civ Eng MEng) (IB 34 pts)

340 pts **Birmingham** – AAB 340 pts (Civ Eng; Civ Eng MEng; Civ Eng Bus Mgt; Civ Ener Eng MEng) (IB 35–36 pts)
Brunel – AAB 340 pts (Mech Eng Bld Serv MEng) (IB 35 pts)
City – 340 pts (Civ Eng; Civ Eng Archit) (IB 30 pts HL maths)
Exeter – AAB–ABB 340–320 pts (Civ Eng) (IB 36–32 pts)
Glasgow – AAB (Civ Eng Archit; Civ Eng MEng) (IB 34 pts)
Liverpool – AAB incl maths 340 pts (Civ Struct Eng; Civ Eng MEng) (IB 35 pts)
Manchester – AAB (Civ Eng) (IB 35 pts)
Newcastle – AAB (Mar Tech Off Eng MEng) (IB 37 pts HL 5 maths phys)
Queen's Belfast – AAB 340 pts (Civ Eng MEng; Env Civ Eng; Struct Eng Archit MEng)
Surrey – AAB–ABB (Civ Eng BEng/MEng)
Swansea – AAB–ABB incl maths (Civ Eng) (IB 32 pts)
Warwick – AAB 340 pts (Civ Eng) (IB 36 pts)

320 pts **Brighton** – ABB (Civ Eng MEng) (IB 28 pts)
Brunel – ABB 320 pts (Civ Eng; Civ Eng Sust) (IB 33–35 pts)
Coventry – ABB 320 pts (Civ Eng MEng) (IB 27 pts)
Dundee – ABB (Civ Eng) (IB 32 pts)
Glasgow – ABB incl maths phys (Civ Eng) (IB 32 pts)
Liverpool – ABB incl maths (Civ Eng) (IB 32 pts HL 5 maths)
Liverpool John Moores – 320 pts (Civ Eng MEng) (IB 27 pts)
Loughborough – ABB 320 pts (Civ Eng) (IB 34–36 pts)
Northumbria – 320 pts (Archit Eng) (IB 27 pts)

300 pts **Aberdeen** – BBB 300 pts (Civ Eng; Civ (Struct) Eng; Civ Env Eng) (IB 34 pts)
Brighton – BBB (Civ Eng; Civ Env Eng) (IB 32 pts)
Heriot-Watt – BBB (Civ Eng; Civ Eng Int St)

Check **Chapter 4** when choosing your university and **Chapter 7** on how to read the subject tables.

Portsmouth – 300–360 pts (Civ Eng)
Queen's Belfast – BBB 300 pts (Civ Eng)
Teesside – 300 pts (Civ Eng MEng)

280 pts **Bristol UWE** – 280 pts (Civ Environ Eng) (IB 25 pts)
East London – 280 pts (Civ Eng)
Edinburgh Napier – BBC 280 pts (Civ Eng MEng)
Kingston – 280 pts (Civ Eng)
Plymouth – 280 pts (Civ Eng; Civ Cstl Eng)
South Wales – BBC 280 pts (Civ Eng)
Teesside – 280 pts (Civ Eng; Civ Eng Disas Mgt) (IB 30 pts)

270 pts **Glasgow Caledonian** – 270 pts (Env Civ Eng)
Liverpool John Moores – 270 pts (Civ Eng; Bld Serv Eng)
Ulster – 270 pts (Civ Eng)

260 pts **Bolton** – 260 pts (Civ Eng)
Bradford – 260 pts (Civ Struct Eng) (IB 28–32 pts)
Coventry – BCC 260 pts (Civ Eng) (IB 28 pts)
Greenwich – 260–300 pts (Civ Eng; Civ Eng Wtr Env Mgt; Civ Eng Proj Mgt)
Leeds Beckett – 260 pts (Civ Eng) (IB 25 pts)
Salford – 260 pts (Civ Eng) (IB 30 pts)

240 pts **Coventry** – CCC 240 pts (Civ Eng BSc) (IB 27 pts)
East London – 240 pts (Civ Eng Surv Surv Map Sci)
Edinburgh Napier – CCC 240 pts (Civ Eng; Civ Trans Eng)
London South Bank – 240 pts (Civ Eng) (IB 24 pts)
Salford – 240–260 pts (Civ Archit Eng) (IB 30 pts)
Ulster – 240 pts (Civ Eng (Geoinform))
West London – 240 pts (Civ Env Eng)
West Scotland – CCC 240 pts (Civ Eng) (IB 24 pts)

230 pts **Wolverhampton** – 230 pts (Civ Eng)

225 pts **Anglia Ruskin** – 225 pts (Civ Eng) (IB 26 pts)

220 pts **Abertay** – CCD 220 pts (Civ Eng) (IB 26 pts)
Derby – 220 pts (Civ Eng)
Edinburgh Napier – CCD 220 pts (Civ Tmbr Eng)
Nottingham Trent – 220 pts (Civ Eng)

180 pts **West Scotland** – BC (Civ Eng) (IB 24 pts)

160 pts **Trinity Saint David (Swansea)** – 160 pts (Civ Eng Environ Mgt)

Alternative offers

See **Chapter 7** and **Appendix 1** for grades/UCAS Tariff points information for the International Baccalaureate, Scottish Highers/Advanced Highers, the Welsh Baccalaureate, the Irish Leaving Certificate, the Cambridge Pre-U Diploma, the Advanced Diploma and the Extended Project.

EXAMPLES OF FOUNDATION DEGREES IN THE SUBJECT FIELD

Bedfordshire; Blackburn (Coll); Bolton; Bristol UWE; Derby; Kent; Kingston; Northampton; Nottingham Trent; Somerset (Coll); Suffolk (Univ Campus); Trinity Saint David (Swansea).

CHOOSING YOUR COURSE (SEE ALSO CH.1)

Some course features

Cardiff The first and second year is common to all nine Engineering programmes.
Durham A common course for Years 1 and 2 and then two years specialising in the chosen discipline.
Exeter A multi-disciplinary first year before specialising in Year 2.
Liverpool John Moores Projects include highways, railways, airports, flood control and sports stadia.
Portsmouth The course leads to a professional qualification in civil engineering.
Southampton Options to take a year in industry or Europe.

Universities and colleges teaching quality See www.qaa.ac.uk; http://unistats.direct.gov.uk.

Top research universities and colleges (RAE 2008) Imperial London; Swansea; Cardiff; Nottingham; Newcastle; Southampton; Sheffield; Bristol; Dundee.

Examples of sandwich degree courses Bath; Bradford; Brighton; Bristol UWE; Cardiff; City; Coventry; East London; Kingston; Liverpool John Moores; London South Bank; Loughborough; Nottingham Trent; Plymouth; Portsmouth; Queen's Belfast; Salford; Surrey; Teesside; Ulster; West Scotland; Wolverhampton.

ADMISSIONS INFORMATION

Number of applicants per place (approx) Abertay 8; Bath 13; Birmingham 6; Bradford 5; Bristol 10; Brunel 4; Cardiff 5; City 11; Coventry 10, (Civ Eng) 11; Dundee 5; Durham 8; Edinburgh Napier 4; Glasgow Caledonian 4; Greenwich 11; Heriot-Watt 7; Imperial London 4; Kingston 8; Leeds 10; Liverpool John Moores 16; London (UCL) 5; London South Bank 5; Loughborough 6; Newcastle 11, (Off Eng) 9; Nottingham 6; Nottingham Trent 11; Plymouth 3; Portsmouth 3; Queen's Belfast 6; Salford 5; Sheffield 7; South Wales 6; Southampton 8; Strathclyde 4; Surrey 5; Swansea 3; Teesside 6; West Scotland 4; Wolverhampton 3.

Advice to applicants and planning the UCAS personal statement See **Engineering/Engineering Sciences**. Also read the magazine *The New Civil Engineer* and discuss articles which interest you on your application. See also **Appendix 3**. **Bristol** Deferred entry accepted.

Selection interviews **Yes** Bath, Birmingham, Brighton, Bristol, Brunel, Cambridge, Coventry, Durham, Edinburgh Napier, Greenwich, Heriot-Watt, Imperial London, Kingston, Leeds, London (UCL), London South Bank, Loughborough, Newcastle, Oxford, Queen's Belfast, South Wales, Southampton, Surrey, Sussex, Warwick; **Some** Abertay, Anglia Ruskin, Cardiff, Dundee, Nottingham Trent, Salford; **No** Nottingham.

Interview advice and questions Past questions have included: Why have you chosen Civil Engineering? Have you contacted the Institution of Civil Engineers/Institution of Structural Engineers? How would you define the difference between the work of a civil engineer and the work of an architect? What would happen to a concrete beam if a load were applied? Where would it break and how could it be strengthened? The favourite question: Why do you want to be a civil engineer? What would you do if you were asked to build a concrete boat? Do you know any civil engineers? What problems were faced in building the Channel Tunnel? See also **Chapter 6**. **Cambridge** Why did they make mill chimneys so tall?

Reasons for rejection (non-academic) Lack of vitality. Lack of interest in buildings, the built environment or in civil engineering. Poor communication skills. See also **Engineering/Engineering Sciences**.

AFTER-RESULTS ADVICE

Offers to applicants repeating A-levels **Higher** East London, Kingston, Liverpool John Moores, Nottingham, Queen's Belfast, Teesside, Warwick; **Possibly higher** Portsmouth, Southampton; **Same** Abertay, Bath, Birmingham, Bradford, Brighton, Bristol, Cardiff, City, Coventry, Dundee, Durham, Greenwich, Heriot-Watt, Leeds, London (UCL), London South Bank, Loughborough, Newcastle, Nottingham Trent, Salford, Sheffield, Wolverhampton; **No** Cambridge.

GRADUATE DESTINATIONS AND EMPLOYMENT (2011/12 HESA)

Graduates surveyed 2780 **Employed** 1765 **In voluntary employment** 30 **In further study** 515 **Assumed unemployed** 215

Career note The many aspects of this subject will provide career directions for graduates with many openings with local authorities and commercial organisations.

OTHER DEGREE SUBJECTS FOR CONSIDERATION

Architecture; Building; Surveying; Town and Country Planning.

ENGINEERING (COMMUNICATIONS)

(including **Mobile Communications**; see also **Communication Studies/Communication, Engineering (Electrical and Electronic)**)

Communications Engineering impacts on many aspects of the engineering and business world. Courses overlap considerably with Electronic, Computer, Digital, Media and Internet Engineering and provide graduates with expertise in such fields as telecommunications, mobile communications and microwave engineering, optoelectronics, radio engineering and internet technology. Sandwich courses and sponsorships are offered by several universities.

Engineering Council statement See **Engineering/Engineering Sciences**.

Useful websites See **Computer Courses** and **Engineering (Electrical and Electronic)**.

NB The points totals shown to the left of the institutions are for ease of reference only. It must not be assumed that Tariff points are always used by institutions or that they can be substituted for an offer in grades. The level of an offer is not necessarily indicative of the quality of a course.

COURSE OFFERS INFORMATION

Subject requirements/preferences See **Engineering/Engineering Sciences**. Offers shown below refer to BEng or BSc courses unless otherwise stated.

Your target offers and examples of courses provided by each institution

380 pts **London (UCL)** – AAAe (Eng (Electron Elec) Comms) (IB 38 pts)
Southampton – A*AA incl maths phys 380 pts (Electron Eng Wrlss Comms)

360 pts **Bath** – AAA 360 pts (Electron Comm Eng MEng) (IB 36 pts HL 6 maths phys)
Birmingham – AAA 360 pts (Comp Sys Eng MEng) (IB 36 pts)
Bristol – AAA–AAB 360–340 pts (Electron Comm Eng MEng; Electron Comm Eng) (IB 37–35 pts)
Edinburgh – AAA–ABB incl maths 360–320 pts (Electron Elec Eng (Comms)) (IB 37–32 pts)
Nottingham – AAA–ABB incl maths +sci/electron 360–320 pts (Electron Comms Eng; Electron Comms Eng MEng) (IB 32–36 pts)
Surrey – AAA 360 pts (Electron Eng Comm MEng) (IB 37 pts)
York – AAA 360 pts (Electron Comm Eng MEng) (IB 36 pts)

340 pts **Birmingham** – AAB 340 pts (Comp Sys Eng) (IB 35 pts)
Cardiff – AAB–ABB 340–320 pts (Electron Comm Eng; Electron Comm Eng MEng) (IB 32–36 pts)
City – AAB 340 pts (Telecomm) (IB 30 pts)
Leicester – AAB–ABB 340–320 pts (Comms Electron Eng MEng) (IB 34–32 pts)
London (QM) – AAB 340 pts (Electron Eng Telecomm MEng) (IB 32–34 pts)
Newcastle – AAB–ABB 340–320 pts (Electron Comm) (IB 35 pts)
Sheffield – AAB incl maths (Electron Comms Eng MEng) (IB 35 pts)
Surrey – AAB 340 pts (Electron Eng Comm) (IB 35 pts)
Swansea – AAB–ABB 340–320 pts (Telecomm Eng MEng) (IB 33 pts)

320 pts **Bath** – ABB 320 pts (Electron Comm Eng) (IB 34 pts HL 6 maths phys)
Kent – ABB 320 pts (Electron Comm Eng MEng) (IB 34 pts HL 15 pts)
Lancaster – ABB–BBB (Comm Sys Electron) (IB 32 pts)
Liverpool – ABB (Electron Comm Eng) (IB 30 pts HL 5 maths phys/elec)
Sheffield – ABB incl maths (Electron Comms Eng) (IB 33 pts)
York – ABB 320 pts (Electron Comm Eng) (IB 32 pts)

300 pts **Aston** – 300–320 pts (Comm Eng)
Birmingham City – 300 pts (Telecomm Net Eng)
Bradford – BBB 300 pts (Electron Telecomm Intnet Eng MEng) (IB 28–32 pts)
Brunel – BBB 300 pts (Electron Comm Eng) (IB 32 pts HL 5 maths)
Essex – BBB 300 pts (Telecomm Eng) (IB 29 pts)

Huddersfield – BBB 300 pts (Electron Comm Eng)
Kent – BBB 300 pts (Electron Comm Eng) (IB 34 pts HL 15 pts)
Leicester – BBB 300 pts (Comms Electron Eng) (IB 30 pts)
London (QM) – BBB 300 pts (Electron Eng Telecomm) (IB 32–34 pts)
Swansea – BBB 300 pts (Telecomm Eng) (IB 30–36 pts)
280 pts **Hertfordshire** – 280 pts (Dig Comm Electron)
South Wales – BBC 280 pts (Electron Comm Eng)
260 pts **Greenwich** – 260 pts (Inf Comm Tech)
Portsmouth – 260–300 pts (Comm Sys)
240 pts **London South Bank** – 240 pts (Telecomm Comp Net Eng)
Manchester Met – 240–280 pts (Comp Comm Eng) (IB 28 pts)
Middlesex – 240 pts (Mob Sys Comm Eng)
220 pts **London Met** – 220 pts (Electron Comm Eng) (IB 24 pts)
200 pts **Wolverhampton** – 200 pts (Electron Comm Eng)
80 pts **Bedfordshire** – 80 pts (Telecomm Net Eng)

Alternative offers
See **Chapter 7** and **Appendix 1** for grades/UCAS Tariff points information for the International Baccalaureate, Scottish Highers/Advanced Highers, the Welsh Baccalaureate, the Irish Leaving Certificate, the Cambridge Pre-U Diploma, the Advanced Diploma and the Extended Project.

EXAMPLES OF FOUNDATION DEGREES IN THE SUBJECT FIELD
Plymouth.

CHOOSING YOUR COURSE (SEE ALSO CH.1)
Some course features
Durham A common course for Years 1 and 2 and then two years specialising in the chosen discipline.
Leicester Communications and Electronic Engineering combined. Options to study for a year in industry or in Europe.
London (QM) There are a range of degree programmes offered in the Department of Electronic Engineering, and there is some flexibility and overlap.
York The Electronic and Communications Engineering course has options in electronics for medicine, mobile communications, wireless and sensor networks, radio programming and many others.

Universities and colleges teaching quality See www.qaa.ac.uk; http://unistats.direct.gov.uk.

Examples of sandwich degree courses Aston; Bath; Bradford; Brunel; Coventry; Glasgow Caledonian; Kent; Kingston; Manchester Met; Northumbria; Portsmouth; Wolverhampton; York.

ADMISSIONS INFORMATION
Number of applicants per place (approx) Birmingham 10; Bradford 9; Bristol 2; Coventry 7; Hull 8; London Met 5; London South Bank 3; Northumbria 7; Plymouth 4; York 8 av.

Advice to applicants and planning the UCAS personal statement See **Engineering (Electrical and Electronic)** and **Appendix 3**.

Selection interviews **Yes** Bradford, Bristol, Hertfordshire, Kent, London Met, London South Bank, Sunderland.

Interview advice and questions See **Engineering (Electrical and Electronic)**.

Reasons for rejection (non-academic) See **Engineering (Electrical and Electronic)**.

AFTER-RESULTS ADVICE
Offers to applicants repeating A-levels **Same** Loughborough.

GRADUATE DESTINATIONS AND EMPLOYMENT (2011/12 HESA)
See **Engineering (Electrical and Electronic)** and **Engineering/Engineering Sciences**.

Career note Many commercial organisations offer opportunities in the specialist areas described at the top of this table. Work placements and sandwich courses have, in the past, resulted in over 60% of graduates gaining employment with their firms.

OTHER DEGREE SUBJECTS FOR CONSIDERATION

Computer Science; Engineering (Computer, Control, Electrical, Electronic, Systems); Physics.

ENGINEERING (COMPUTER, CONTROL, SOFTWARE and SYSTEMS)

The design and application of modern computer systems is fundamental to a wide range of disciplines which also include electronic, software and computer-aided engineering. Most courses give priority to reinforcing the essential transferable skills consisting of management techniques, leadership skills, literacy, presentation skills, business skills and time management. At many universities Computer Engineering is offered as part of a range of Electronics degree programmes where the first and even the second year courses are common to all students, who then choose to specialise later. A year in industry is a common feature of many of these courses.

Engineering Council statement See **Engineering/Engineering Sciences**.

Useful websites See **Computer Courses** and **Engineering/Engineering Sciences**.

NB The points totals shown to the left of the institutions are for ease of reference only. It must not be assumed that Tariff points are always used by institutions or that they can be substituted for an offer in grades. The level of an offer is not necessarily indicative of the quality of a course.

COURSE OFFERS INFORMATION

Subject requirements/preferences See **Engineering/Engineering Sciences**. Offers shown below refer to BEng or BSc courses unless otherwise stated.

Your target offers and examples of courses provided by each institution

380 pts **Cambridge** – A*AA 380 pts (Eng (Inf Comp Eng)) (IB 40–41 pts)

Imperial London – A*AA 380 pts (Comp (Soft Eng); Electron Inf Eng; Electron Inf Eng (St Abrd)) (IB 38–42 pts)

Oxford – A*AA 380 pts (Inf Eng) (IB 38–40 pts)

360 pts **Bath** – AAA 360 pts (Comp Sys Eng MEng) (IB 36 pts HL 6 maths phys)

Birmingham – AAA 360 pts (Comp Sys Eng MEng) (IB 36 pts)

Edinburgh – AAA–ABB incl maths 360–320 pts (Electron Comp Sci MEng; Electron Soft Eng Meng; Soft Eng) (IB 37–32 pts)

Lancaster – AAA 360 pts (Comp Sys Eng MEng) (IB 36 pts)

Nottingham – AAA–ABB 360–320 pts (Soft Eng) (IB 34 pts HL 5 maths)

Southampton – AAA incl maths 360 pts (Soft Eng; Comp Sci Artif Intel; Comp Sci)

Strathclyde – AAA 360 pts (Comp Electron Sys MEng) (IB 36 pts)

Warwick – AAA (Comp Sys) (IB 38 pts)

340 pts **Aberystwyth** – 340 pts (Soft Eng MEng) (IB 28 pts)

Birmingham – AAB 340 pts (Comp Sys Eng) (IB 35 pts)

City – AAB 340 pts (Comp Sys Eng) (IB 30 pts)

Glasgow – AAB (Microcomp Sys Eng MEng) (IB 34 pts)

Lancaster – AAB 340 pts (Comp Sys Eng) (IB 35 pts)

Leicester – AAB–ABB 340–320 pts (Soft Electron Eng MEng) (IB 34 pts)

Liverpool – AAB 340 pts (Soft Dev) (IB 35 pts HL 5 maths)

London (QM) – 340 pts (Comp Eng MEng) (IB 34 pts)

Loughborough – AAB (Sys Eng MEng) (IB 34–36 pts)
Manchester – AAB 340 pts (Comp Sys Eng) (IB 35 pts)
Newcastle – AAB–ABB 340–320 pts (Electron Comp Eng) (IB 35 pts)
Sheffield – AAB incl maths (Comp Sys Eng MEng; Soft Eng; Sys Cntrl Eng (Eng Mgt) MEng; Sys Cntrl Eng MEng) (IB 35 pts HL 6 maths)
Strathclyde – AAB 340 pts (Comp Electron Sys) (IB 32 pts)
Sussex – AAB–BBB incl maths (Comp Eng) (IB 32–35 pts HL 5/6 maths)
Warwick – AAB (Sys Eng) (IB 36 pts)
York – AAB–ABB (Comp Sci Embd Sys)

320 pts **Bath** – ABB 320 pts (Comp Sys Eng) (IB 34 pts HL 6 maths phys)
Brunel – ABB–BBB 320–300 pts (Comp Sci (Soft Eng)) (IB 33 pts)
Cardiff – ABB 320 pts (Soft Eng) (33 pts)
East Anglia – ABB (Soft Eng; Comp Sys Eng; Comp Sys Eng (Yr Ind)) (IB 32 pts)
Essex – ABB–BBB (Comp Electron; Comp Net; Comp Sys Eng) (IB 32–30 pts)
Glasgow – ABB (Microcomp Sys Eng; Electron Soft Eng) (IB 32 pts)
Kent – ABB (Comp Sys Eng MEng) (IB 33 pts)
Lancaster – ABB 320 pts (Soft Eng) (IB 32 pts)
Liverpool – ABB (Comp Sci Electron Eng MEng) (IB 33 pts HL 5 maths phys elec)
Reading – 320 pts (Cyber) (IB 33 pts)
Sheffield – ABB 320 pts (Sys Cntrl Eng; Comp Sys Eng; Sys Cntrl Eng (Eng Mgt); Mecha Robot Eng) (IB 34 pts)
Strathclyde – ABB 320 pts (Soft Eng) (IB 34 pts)
300 pts **Aberdeen** – BBB (Electron Comp Eng) (IB 30 pts)
Bangor – 300–320 pts (Comp Sys Eng MEng)
Bradford – BBB 300 pts (Electron Telecomm Intnet Eng MEng) (IB 28–32 pts)

Check **Chapter 4** when choosing your university and **Chapter 7** on how to read the subject tables.

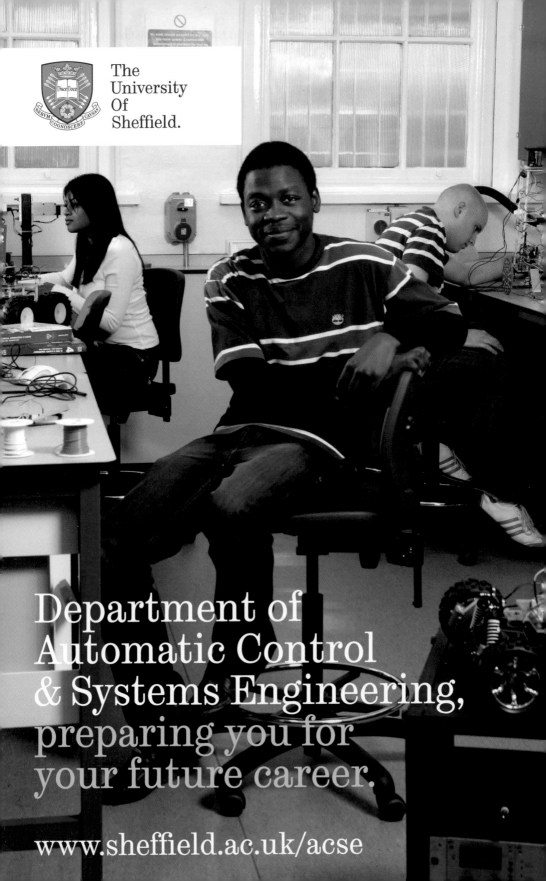

The
University
Of
Sheffield.

Department of
Automatic Control
& Systems Engineering,
preparing you for
your future career.

www.sheffield.ac.uk/acse

The University Of Sheffield.

Automatic Control & Systems Engineering.

We are the largest Control and Systems Engineering Department in Europe and one of the best in the world.

Our high calibre graduates are hired by companies in a wide range of sectors including Rolls Royce, Jaguar Land Rover, HSBC, BAE Systems, IBM, Shell, Siemens and the Ministry of Defence.

What is control and systems engineering?

Control and systems engineering is an interdisciplinary approach to solving some of today's complex technical challenges. It not only provides key enabling technology for aerospace, robotics, autonomous vehicles, manufacturing and renewable energy, but also provides a systematic way to solve biological, medical, social and financial system problems.

A system engineer's role is to design and develop highly sophisticated systems that integrate all key elements needed to achieve optimum performance, including electronics, software, sensors and other hardware. With unlimited imagination a system engineer can revolutionise the way we interact with each other and perform everyday tasks.

Why study with us?

Our degrees provide a multi/interdisciplinary perspective at the core of recent developments in engineering, finance, medicine, biology, drug discovery and the environment. By studying with us you will gain the knowledge, understanding and skills that will enable you to make a real difference to society, now and in the future.

Our research and industrial collaborations strongly inform our degree programmes, ensuring we produce industry ready graduates with maximum prospects across a wide range of career opportunities. Our graduates are in high demand and earn substantial salaries. They work in many different sectors and have gone on to make a significant impact in their chosen fields.

A unique place to study

We are home to Rolls Royce's University Technology Centre in Control Systems and have research contracts with major institutions like the European Space Agency.

These connections mean our teaching is based on the latest thinking.

Our facilities include two new undergraduate teaching laboratories, robotics lab, smart-grid lab and flight simulator.

A year in industry

You can combine most of our courses with a year in industry. Working in an engineering or technology company will put your academic studies into context, improve your skills and enhance your employment prospects when you graduate.

What next?

Visit us at one of our open days which run throughout the year or arrange an informal visit. Contact us and we'll arrange a date that's convenient for you.

For more about courses and modules, see our online prospectus: www.sheffield.ac.uk/undergraduate

Contact

Department of Automatic Control and Systems Engineering

T: +44 (0)114 222 5647
E: adacse@sheffield.ac.uk

Bristol UWE – BBB 300 pts (Comp Sys Integ) (IB 26 pts)
Brunel – BBB–ABB 300–320 pts (Electron Comp Eng; Gms Des; Snc Arts; Gms Des Film TV St; Comp Sys Eng courses) (IB 32 pts)
Heriot-Watt – BBB 300 pts (Comp Electron) (IB 29 pts)
Huddersfield – BBB (Comp Sys Eng)
Kent – BBB (Comp Sys Eng) (IB 33 pts)
Kingston – 300 pts (Soft Eng)
Leicester – BBB 300 pts (Soft Electron Eng) (IB 32 pts)
Liverpool – BBB (Comp Sci Electron Eng) (IB 30 pts HL 5 maths phys elec)
London (QM) – 300 pts (Comp Eng) (IB 28 pts)
Loughborough – BBB (Electron Comp Sys Eng; Sys Eng) (IB 32 pts)
Plymouth – BBB 300 pts (Comp Sys Net) (IB 30 pts)
Portsmouth – 300–360 pts (Comp Eng MEng) (IB 30 pts)
Reading – 300–340 pts (Comp Eng) (IB 30 pts)
Sheffield Hallam – 300 pts (Soft Eng MEng)
Teesside – 300 pts (Instr Contr Eng MEng)
Westminster – BBB (Comp Sys Eng MEng) (IB 32 pts)
280 pts **Aberystwyth** – 280 pts (Soft Eng; Intnet Eng; Spc Sci Robot)
Central Lancashire – 280 pts (Comp Aid Eng MEng)
Hull – 280 pts (Comp Sys Eng)
Northumbria – 280 pts (Comp Net Tech)
Nottingham Trent – 280 pts (Comp Sys Eng; Soft Eng)
Oxford Brookes – BBC 280 pts (Soft Eng) (IB 30 pts)
South Wales – BBC 280 pts (Comp Sys Eng)
Stirling – BBC (Soft Eng) (IB 32 pts)
Teesside – 280 pts (Instr Contr Eng)
Westminster – BBC (Comp Sys Eng) (IB 30 pts)
260 pts **Bournemouth** – 260–300 pts (Soft Eng Mgt; Soft Eng)
Bradford – 260 pts (Soft Eng)
Greenwich – 260–300 pts (Comp Sys Soft Eng)
Liverpool John Moores – 260 pts (Soft Eng) (IB 24 pts)
Northampton – 260–300 pts (Comp (Comp Sys Eng))
Portsmouth – 260–300 pts (Comp Eng)
Sheffield Hallam – 260 pts (Gms Soft Dev)
Sunderland – 260 pts (Gms Soft Dev)
240 pts **Bangor** – 240–260 pts (Comp Sys Eng)
Bolton – 240 pts (Comp Aid Eng)
Cardiff Met (UWIC) – 240 pts (Soft Eng)
Central Lancashire – 240–280 pts (Comp Aid Eng)
Coventry – 240 pts (Soft Eng)
East London – 240 pts (Soft Eng)
Edinburgh Napier – CCC 240 pts (Comp Sys Net)
Greenwich – 240 pts (Soft Eng)
London South Bank – 240 pts (Comp Sys Net; Telecomm Comp Net Eng)
Manchester Met – 240–280 pts (Soft Eng) (IB 28 pts)
Middlesex – 240 pts (Comp Net Comm)
Sheffield Hallam – 240 pts (Soft Eng; Comp Net Eng)
220 pts **London Met** – 220 pts (Comp Sys Eng)
Robert Gordon – 220–240 pts (Comp Net Mgt Des)
Wolverhampton – 220 pts (Comp Sci (Soft Eng); Comp Sys Eng)
200 pts **Bedfordshire** – 200 pts (Comp Sys Eng)
Coventry – 200 pts (Comp Hard Soft Eng; Sys Eng; Vrtl Eng)
Hertfordshire – 200–240 pts (Comp Sci (Soft Eng))
Southampton Solent – 200 pts (Comp Sys Net)

180 pts **Glasgow Caledonian** – BC 180 pts (Comp Eng) (IB 24 pts)
170 pts **Glasgow Caledonian** – CC 170 pts (Comp Aid Mech Eng)
160 pts **Accrington and Rossendale (Coll)** – 160 pts (Soft Eng)
        Farnborough (CT) – 160 pts (Soft Eng)
120 pts **Trinity Saint David (Swansea)** – 120 pts (Soft Eng; Comp Sys Eng)
 80 pts **Bedfordshire** – 80–120 pts (Comp Sci Soft Eng)

Alternative offers

See **Chapter 7** and **Appendix 1** for grades/UCAS Tariff points information for the International Baccalaureate, Scottish Highers/Advanced Highers, the Welsh Baccalaureate, the Irish Leaving Certificate, the Cambridge Pre-U Diploma, the Advanced Diploma and the Extended Project.

EXAMPLES OF FOUNDATION DEGREES IN THE SUBJECT FIELD
Bedfordshire; Bournemouth; Manchester (Coll); Trinity Saint David (Swansea).

CHOOSING YOUR COURSE (SEE ALSO CH.1)
Some course features
Bristol UWE (Comp Sys Integ) A practical course covering all aspects of computer systems, but also focuses on networks, CPU architecture and embedded systems development.
Cardiff The first year is common to all nine Engineering programmes.
Durham (MEng courses) A common course for Years 1 and 2 and then two years specialising in one of four streams, with a major design project (from design to manufacture) in Year 3.
Heriot-Watt The Software Engineering course involves a study of computer science in the first three years followed in Year 4 and 5 by specialist studies in software technology.
London (QM) The MEng programme covers all the material of the BEng programme with more time spent on professional development and advanced studies.
Plymouth Four final-year pathways from which to choose your specialisation.

Universities and colleges teaching quality See www.qaa.ac.uk; http://unistats.direct.gov.uk.

Top research universities and colleges (RAE 2008) See **Computer Courses**.

Examples of sandwich degree courses Aberystwyth; Aston; Bath; Bradford; Brighton; Bristol UWE; Brunel; Cardiff; Cardiff Met (UWIC); City; Greenwich; Huddersfield; Kent; London South Bank; Loughborough; Manchester; Manchester Met; Northumbria; Nottingham Trent; Plymouth; Portsmouth; Reading; Sheffield Hallam; South Wales; Westminster; York.

ADMISSIONS INFORMATION
Number of applicants per place (approx) Birmingham 10; Birmingham City 6; Bournemouth 3; Bristol 4; Bristol UWE 12; Cardiff 6; Central Lancashire 12; Coventry 2; Durham 6; East Anglia 4; Edinburgh 3; Huddersfield 2; Imperial London 5; Kent 5; Lancaster 12; Liverpool John Moores 2; London South Bank 3; Loughborough 17; Sheffield 10; Sheffield Hallam 8; Southampton 4; Staffordshire 5; Stirling 7; Strathclyde 7; Surrey 3; Teesside 3; Trinity Saint David (Swansea) 4; Westminster 5; York 3 ave.

Advice to applicants and planning the UCAS personal statement See **Computer Courses**, **Engineering (Electrical and Electronic)** and **Appendix 3**.

Selection interviews **Yes** Bradford, East Anglia, Hertfordshire, Huddersfield, Kent, London South Bank, Manchester, Nottingham Trent, Sheffield Hallam, Trinity Saint David (Swansea), Westminster, York; **Some** Exeter, Loughborough; **No** Bath, Cardiff, Durham, Liverpool John Moores, Reading.

Interview advice and questions See **Computer Courses**, **Engineering (Electrical and Electronic)** and **Chapter 6**.

Reasons for rejection (non-academic) Lack of understanding that the course involves engineering. See also **Computer Courses** and **Engineering (Electrical and Electronic)**.

322 | Engineering (Electrical and Electronic)

AFTER-RESULTS ADVICE

Offers to applicants repeating A-levels **Higher** Bristol, Strathclyde, Warwick, York; **Possibly higher** City, Huddersfield, Sheffield; **Same** Bath, Birmingham, Coventry, East Anglia, Exeter, Lancaster, Liverpool John Moores, London South Bank, Loughborough, Salford, Teesside, Ulster; **No** Cambridge.

GRADUATE DESTINATIONS AND EMPLOYMENT (2011/12 HESA)

Software Engineering graduates surveyed 705 **Employed** 420 **In voluntary employment** 15 **In further study** 70 **Assumed unemployed** 95

Career note Career opportunities extend right across the whole field of electronics, telecommunications, control and systems engineering.

OTHER DEGREE SUBJECTS FOR CONSIDERATION

Computer Science; Computing; Engineering (Aeronautical, Aerospace, Communications, Electrical and Electronic); Mathematics; Media (Systems/Engineering/Technology); Physics.

ENGINEERING (ELECTRICAL and ELECTRONIC)

(see also **Engineering (Acoustics and Sound)**, **Engineering (Aeronautical and Aerospace)**, **Engineering (Communications)**)

Electrical and Electronic Engineering courses provide a sound foundation for those looking for a career in electricity generation and transmission, communications or control systems, including robotics. All courses cater for students wanting a general or specialist engineering education and options should be considered when choosing degree courses. These could include optoelectronics and optical communication systems, microwave systems, radio frequency engineering and circuit technology. Many courses have common first years, allowing transfer in Year 2. Most institutions have good industrial contacts and can arrange industrial placements, in some cases abroad.

Engineering Council statement See **Engineering/Engineering Sciences**.

Useful websites www.theiet.org; www.engc.org.uk.

NB The points totals shown to the left of the institutions are for ease of reference only. It must not be assumed that Tariff points are always used by institutions or that they can be substituted for an offer in grades. The level of an offer is not necessarily indicative of the quality of a course.

COURSE OFFERS INFORMATION

Subject requirements/preferences See **Engineering/Engineering Sciences**. Offers shown below refer to BEng or BSc courses unless otherwise stated.

Your target offers and examples of courses provided by each institution

380 pts **Bristol** – A*AA–ABB 380–320 pts (Comp Sci Electron) (IB 37–35 pts HL 665)

Cambridge – A*AA (Eng (Elec Inf Sci/Elec Electron Eng)) (IB 40–41 pts HL 776)

Durham – A*AA 380 pts (Electron Eng MEng) (IB 38 pts)

Glasgow – A*AA 380 pts (Electron Mus MEng) (IB 36 pts)

Imperial London – A*AA incl maths 380 pts (Elec Electron Eng Mgt; Elec Electron Eng; Electron Inf Eng; Electron Inf Eng (St Abrd)) (IB 38 pts HL 6 maths 6 phys)

London (UCL) – AAAe (Eng (Electron Elec) Comp Sci; Eng (Electron Elec) Nanotech; Eng (Electron Elec) Comms; Eng (Electron Elec)) (IB 38 pts)

Oxford – A*AA (Elec Eng Sci) (IB 38–40 pts)

Southampton – A*AA incl maths phys 380 pts (Electron Eng Mbl Scr Sys; Electron Eng Comp Sys; Electron Eng Wrlss Comms) (IB 38 pts HL 18 pts)

360 pts **Bath** – AAA 360 pts (Electron Elec Eng MEng; Electron Eng Spc Sci Tech MEng; Electron Comm Eng MEng; Elec Pwr Eng MEng) (IB 36 pts HL 6 maths phys)

Your **sparkling**
engineering career
starts here

Achieve either:

- 3 'A's at A Level, or
- 3 'A' grade Advanced Highers or
- 5 'A' grade Highers or
- International Diploma at 36 points or above or
- HND Diploma with distinction

and join an IET accredited BEng/MEng engineering or technology degree course in Autumn 2014* and you could be awarded a **Diamond Jubilee Scholarship worth £1,000** per year.

Applications must be submitted online at www.theiet.org/diamond by **29 August 2014**.

*Please see a list of IET accredited courses on our website

www.**theiet**.org/diamond

The Institution of
Engineering and Technology

High flyers start their career at the IET

Join Europe's largest and most influential membership organisation for engineers and technicians and prepare for even greater academic and professional success.

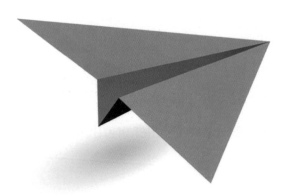

We can take you further

Your journey is just beginning - join the IET as a Student Member and you'll be joining people who share your enthusiasm and drive for success.

Call on the resources of the IET to give you a competitive advantage. You will benefit from:

- **Student web zone resources**
  Giving you revision, study and technical support and guidance

- **IET Library and Archives**
  Offering over 68,500 books and journals as well as thousands of online resources available 24/7 with a free global postal loan service

- **E&T Magazine**
  Award winning monthly magazine available in print, online and on tablet

- **Scholarships and travel bursaries**
  A range of annual scholarships and awards from £500 to £10,000

- **Lifeskills courses**
  Free workshops run by Local Networks (LNs) to help you get ahead in your professional life and give you the skills you need to make you more employable

- **IET.tv**
  Allowing you to watch live or archived events and seminars as well as accessing over 5,000 multimedia presentations.

We would be delighted if you were to become a member of the IET.

"In today's dynamic job market, membership of a professional organisation can be the one constant you can rely on for support throughout your career. So it's good to know, no matter where you are in your career, what challenges you are facing or where you want to be, the IET can provide you with a Professional Home for Life® which can help you achieve your career goals."

Nigel Fine BSc MBA CEng FICE FIET, Chief Executive and Secretary

Take your first step towards career success at www.theiet.org/join and make the IET your Professional Home for Life®.

www.**theiet**.org/join

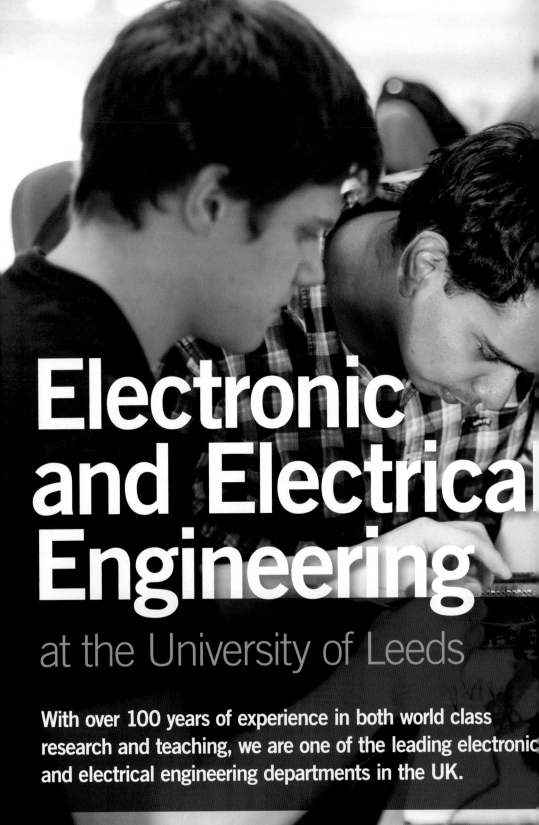

Electronic and Electrical Engineering

at the University of Leeds

With over 100 years of experience in both world class research and teaching, we are one of the leading electronic and electrical engineering departments in the UK.

An active research environment enables us to offer a range of exciting degree courses taught by experts who are leaders in their fields.

Visit our website to find out about our undergraduate degrees.

- **Electronic and Communications Engineering**
- **Electronic and Electrical Engineering**
- **Electronic Engineering**
- **Electronics and Nanotechnology**
- **Electronics and Renewable Energy Systems**
- **Mechatronics and Robotics**
- **Music Multimedia and Electronics**

Our reputation with industry ensures that we maintain close working relationships with companies who actively recruit Leeds graduates. Recent graduates have secured positions with organisations such as Agilent Technologies, Filtronics, O2, Farnell, Motorola, Siemens and Radio Design.

www.engineering.leeds.ac.uk/electronic

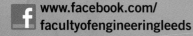 **www.facebook.com/ facultyofengineeringleeds**

Why study Electronic and Electrical Engineering at Leeds

- 7th in the UK for Electronic and Electrical Engineering - The Complete University Guide 2014.
- Our courses are integrated masters (MEng, BEng) degrees, which provide the most direct route to becoming a Chartered Engineer (CEng), a vital distinguishing qualification in the UK job market.
- All courses are professionally accredited by the Institution of Engineering and Technology (IET).
- 92% of students satisfied with the quality of their course (NSS).
- Hands-on learning with extensive project work in every year of study.
- All of our degree courses offer you the opportunity to study abroad or undertake a placement year.
- Taught by world leading research experts.
- Highly employable graduates - 90% of our graduates are employed or in further study within six months of graduating (Unistats 2013).
- Access to specialist facilities and laboratories equipped with the latest technology.

Come along to a University Open Day to find out more: **www.leeds.ac.uk/openday**

UNIVERSITY OF LEEDS

UNIVERSITY *of York*
Department of Electronics

☏ 01904 322365   ✉ *elec-ug-admissions@york.ac.uk*   💻 *www.elec.york.ac.uk/ugrad/*

The Department of Electronics at the University of York has been consistently ranked amongst the best electronics departments in the country for its teaching quality and world-leading research in electromagnetic compatibility, biologically-inspired computing, music technology, wireless communications and nanotechnology. Programmes include:

- **Electronic Engineering**: provides a very wide range of knowledge and techniques in modern electronics.
- **Electronic and Communication Engineering**: gives students a strong electronics background with an emphasis on application to communication technologies.
- **Electronic and Computer Engineering**: a Computer Systems Engineering programme combining the use of electronics and computer hardware/software.
- **Music Technology Systems**: focuses on the internal design and function of contemporary music technology systems within an electronic engineering programme.
- **Music Technology**: a creative music technology programme for students who are not taking Mathematics at a higher level.
- **Electronic Engineering with Nanotechnology**: gives students a strong electronics background with an emphasis on its application to nanotechnologies.
- **Electronic Engineering with Business Management**: comprises 35 percent business management, 65 percent electronics. It meets the needs of those with ambitions to progress to a management position.
- **Avionics**: an electronics degree with an emphasis on the design and application of equipment for the aerospace industries.
- **Foundation Year**: an entry route for those who do not have relevant qualifications, particularly mature students.

The Department has a wide range of facilities used to support the teaching and research activities. Most of these facilities are also available in collaboration with industry, allowing direct input to project work.

Facilities include: interactive BioWall; Nanotechnology Clean Room; Computing Labs; Electromagnetic Test Facilities; FPGA and ARM-based Development Systems; Audio Recording Studios; Teaching Laboratories for practical work, project work and iPad/iPhone workstations. Also, the Department's Technical Support provide design and construction facilities, including PCB design and manufacture, digital manufacturing technology 3D printing and a surface-mount assembly line.

Check **Chapter 4** when choosing your university and **Chapter 7** on how to read the subject tables.

Studying Nanotechnology and Electronic Engineering

Stories about nanotechnology are commonplace, from current uses in CPU design to very speculative ideas. But what does it mean to study the engineering of nanotechnology?

At the University of York, students study nanotechnology in all 3 or 4 years of an electronic engineering degree. The applications vary widely, but to carry out such engineering it is necessary to acquire the complex fundamental knowledge. This ranges from core electronic engineering through to aspects of physics and chemistry.

The practical skills also required are considerable – at York students are taken into the clean room fabrication facilities from their First Year on. They carry out full fabrication exercises to become familiar with the many stages required to build electronic devices starting with pristine silicon wafers and finishing with devices that can be measured in a normal electronics laboratory or imaged in one of the electron microscopes.

But on top of the fundamentals, there is often surprise due to the range of applications the students may study in their course. Some applications are to core aspects of electronics – improving the performance of processors and memory. The fabrication and use of nano-wires can be studied to improve the speed of such devices. Imaging of nano-devices is challenging, so novel electron sources within electron microscopes can be investigated – perhaps using beams of electrons from carbon nano-tubes to probe the magnetic structure of devices.

Using small (10 nanometre) nano-particles within nano-fluids can give interesting effects. The physical properties of such materials can be controlled by magnetic or electric fields. Students have investigated these fluids in shock absorbers for cars – behaving fluidly or stiffly by applying voltage, giving shock absorbers with smoothly varying properties depending on the driver or the road.

Many potential medical applications exist to extend the major impact electronics has on diagnostics and treatment. Integrated electronic sensors can detect proteins, enzymes and small molecule biomarkers. With nanoelectronic devices, such as single-electron transistors, not only large samples but the properties of individual molecules can be investigated.

The diversity of nanotechnology applications is growing rapidly – what is required to sustain this are good engineering graduates with the knowledge and practical skills to push these forward!

📞 *01904 322365*   ✉ *elec-ug-admissions@york.ac.uk*   💻 *www.elec.york.ac.uk/ugrad/*

For a quick reference offers calculator, fold out the inside front cover.

The University Of Sheffield.

WORLD-CLASS FACILITIES

STRONG INDUSTRIAL LINKS

Choose from a range of BEng and MEng degrees.

- Electronic Engineering
- Electrical Engineering
- Electrical & Electronic Engineering
- Electronic & Communications Engineering
- Digital Electronics
- Microelectronics
- Electronic & Electrical Engineering with a Modern Language
- Foundation Year

Include a Year in Industry option or you might want to take a Study Abroad year - the choice is yours.

DEPARTMENT OF ELECTRONIC & ELECTRICAL ENGINEERING
Website: www.sheffield.ac.uk/eee **Email:** eee-rec@sheffield.ac.uk
Accredited by the Institution of Engineering and Technology

The
University
Of
Sheffield.

To
Discover
And
Understand.

ELECTRONIC ENGINEER OR ELECTRICAL ENGINEER?

We are often asked what the difference is between the two professions. Electronic Engineers are concerned with the design, manufacture and management of the circuits and systems that contribute to almost all areas of our technological lives. Think of lap tops, mobile phones, communication satellites. Perhaps less well known to you are semiconductors, nanotechnology and bio-electronics.

Electrical Engineers design systems that generate and move power between distances of just a few millimetres up to miles. They need to know how to use the laws governing electromagnetics to convert energy into motion and back. Their products include machines such as rotary electric motors, power transformers, heaters and lighting. But they also develop fault tolerant actuators for use in aerospace, electrically powered transport and natural energy converters.

Although there are differences as well as overlaps, our electronics graduates are competent electrical engineers and vice-versa. We will teach you all the theories and tools necessary to prepare you for an exciting career in a profession that touches all areas of human civilisation.

Flexibility and Choice

You can tailor your degree to suit your interests. Our flexible course structure means you can transfer from one EEE specialisation to another. For most of our degrees, the first two years offer a common core, giving you a broad educational base in the subject. You can then make an informed decision on your future specialisations.

Taught by Experts

You'll learn from internationally acclaimed academics in a creative and supportive environment. We work with industry to develop our courses so you acquire the knowledge and skills employers are looking for. The world-leading research we're doing feeds directly into your learning, so you understand the very latest innovations in the field of electrical science.

Our courses are very practical and you'll get to grips with the sort of challenges that professionals face, exploring your ideas using the latest test facilities.

We are home to a number of research centres, including the Rolls-Royce University Technology Centre for Advanced Electrical Machines and Drives, the Sheffield-Siemens Wind Power Research Centre and the EPSRC National Centre for III-V Technologies.

Year in Industry Options

Put theory into practice and gain industrial experience as part of your degree course. It will improve your employment prospects and, of course, you will benefit financially from earning!

What Next?

Find out more about us by booking online for a University Open Day, (June to October) or visit us on one of our own Departmental Visit Days, (November to March).
For more about courses and modules, see the online prospectus:
www.sheffield.ac.uk/undergraduate

DEPARTMENT OF ELECTRONIC & ELECTRICAL ENGINEERING
Website: www.sheffield.ac.uk/eee **Email:** eee-rec@sheffield.ac.uk
Telephone: 0114 2225382

Electrical **and Electronic** Engineering at Nottingham

The University of **Nottingham**

UNITED KINGDOM · CHINA · MALAYSIA

Providing a strong foundation for your future career...

Courses

Electrical and Electronic Engineering is a broad field ranging from the equipment associated with electrical power transmission and distribution through to nanoscale technologies associated with future information and communication technologies. We offer a wide range of degrees so that you can specialise or keep a broad base to your skills and knowledge, but we understand that making the decision as to which course to choose can be challenging. We have structured our courses so that you can keep your options open for as long as possible. Our first and second years are structured to enable you to transfer between most of our electrical and electronic degree courses. This gives you the opportunity to discover both electrical and electronic engineering before committing to your final degree programme. The final years of our courses allows flexibility in your module options and project choices, so you can follow your interests.

Links with Industry

The Department of Electrical and Electronic Engineering is recognised by industry as one of the best. We maintain strong links with over 30 top companies; some companies support student projects and laboratories, others sponsor students. For example the E3 academy offers sponsorship (for the full length of their degree course) from UK based companies to students interested in electrical energy engineering, and is endorsed by the Insitution of Engineering and Technology (IET). The UK Electronics Skills Foundation links students with companies in the electronics sector for sponsorship over the duration of the course. Both of these schemes provide students with valuable industrial experience, together with strong financial support.

There are many opportunities to pursue a year in industry with an added incentive: The Industrial Placement Award. Students may postpone a year of their course and spend the year working in industry which allows them to apply knowledge gained in academic studies to problem solving in a 'real life' industrial situation - and they graduate with engineering work experience. Upon successful completion and meeting the University requirements, degree certificates are endorsed with "Industrial Placement Award" in recognition of this achievement. Many opportunities also exist to spend a summer placement with a company. The department's Industrial Liaison Officer helps students to find placements.

It is our priority to prepare you for future success. Each year we organise an exclusive careers event specifically for electrical and electronic engineering students. The following companies are typical of those attending to recruit our students: Atkins, British Nuclear Group, Control Techniques Ltd, DESG, John G Peck Ltd, Lintott Control Systems, Matchtech Group plc, Metronet Rail, Royal Navy, Royal Marines, Siemens, Spirent Enterprises Ltd, Royal Air Force, BAE Systems, National Grid UK, Texas Instruments.

Sean Loddick, manager of Power Electrical Centres of Excellence for Marine Electrical Systems at Rolls-Royce Plc. believes that the Department of Electrical and Electronic Engineering at The University of Nottingham is one of the best. He says:

"We're looking for young people with an enthusiasm and an ability to learn. It's because of the good foundation they've learned at somewhere like The University of Nottingham that we have something to build on."

www.nottingham.ac.uk/go/eee

Birmingham – AAA 360 pts (Electron Elec Eng MEng)

Bristol – AAA–AAB 360–340 pts (Electron Comm Eng MEng; Electron Comm Eng; Elec Electron Eng) (IB 37–35 pts)

Brunel – AAA 360 pts (Electron Comp Eng MEng; Electron Elec Eng MEng) (IB 32 pts)

Edinburgh – AAA–ABB 360–320 pts (Elec Mech Eng; Electron Elec Eng; Electron; Electron Elec Eng (Comms); Electron Soft Eng MEng; Electron Elec Eng MEng) (IB 37–32 pts)

Exeter – AAA–ABB incl maths+sci 360–320 pts (Electron Eng Comp Sci) (IB 36–32 pts HL 5 maths 5 sci)

Lancaster – AAA 360 pts (Electron Elec Eng MEng) (IB 36 pts HL 16 pts)

Leeds – AAA 360 pts (Elec Eng courses; Electron Nanotech BEng/MEng; Electron Eng BEng/MEng) (IB 35 pts HL 18 pts)

Manchester – AAA (Elec Electron Eng MEng) (IB 37 pts)

Nottingham – AAA–AAB 320–360 pts (Elec Eng; Elec Eng Renew Ener Sys; Electron Eng; Elec Electron Eng Maths; Electron Comp Eng; Electron Comms Eng BEng/MEng) (IB 36 pts)

Southampton – AAA incl maths phys (Electron Eng; Electron Eng Nanotech) (IB 36 pts HL 18 pts)

Strathclyde – AAA (Electron Dig Sys MEng) (IB 36 pts)

Surrey – AAA (Electron Eng Comm MEng; Electron Eng MEng; Electron Eng Comp Sys MEng) (IB 37 pts)

York – AAA 360 pts (Electron Comm Eng MEng) (IB 36 pts)

340 pts **Aston** – AAB–AAA 340–360 pts (Elec Electron Eng MEng) (IB 34 pts)

Birmingham – AAB 340 pts (Electron Elec Eng) (IB 35 pts)

Cardiff – AAB–ABB 340–320 pts (Elect Electron Eng MEng; Electron Comm Eng; Electron Comm Eng MEng) (IB 32–36 pts)

City – AAB 340 pts (Elec Electron Eng) (IB 30 pts)

Check **Chapter 4** when choosing your university and **Chapter 7** on how to read the subject tables.

Glasgow – AAB (Electron Mus; Elec Electron Eng MEng) (IB 34 pts)
Leicester – AAB–ABB (Electron Elec Eng; Elec Electron Eng MEng; Soft Electron Eng MEng) (IB 34–32 pts)
London (QM) – AAB–ABB 340–320 pts (Electron Eng Telecomm MEng; Electron Eng MEng courses) (IB 34–32 pts)
Loughborough – AAB (Electron Elec Eng MEng; Electron Comp Sys Eng MEng; Electron Elec Sys Eng MEng) (IB 34–36 pts)
Manchester – AAB 340 pts (Comp Sys Eng; Elec Electron Eng) (IB 35 pts)
Newcastle – AAB–ABB 340–320 pts (Electron Comm; Electron Comp Eng; Elec Electron Eng) (IB 35 pts)
Reading – AAB 340 pts (Cyber MEng) (IB 35 pts)
Sheffield – AAB incl maths (Dig Electron; Electron Comms Eng MEng; Electron Elec Eng Modn Lang; Microelec; Elec Eng MEng; Electron Eng MEng) (IB 35 pts)
Southampton – AAB incl maths phys (Elec Eng; Electromech Eng) (IB 34 pts HL 17 pts)
Strathclyde – AAB 340 pts (Electron Elec Eng) (IB 32 pts)
Surrey – AAB 340 pts (Electron Comp Eng; Electron Eng; Electron Eng Comm) (IB 35 pts)
Sussex – AAB 340 pts (Elec Electron Eng) (IB 35 pts HL 5/6 maths)
Warwick – AAB (Electron Eng) (IB 36 pts)
York – AAB–ABB (Electron Eng MEng; Electron Eng Nanotech MEng)

320 pts **Bath** – ABB 320 pts (Electron Comm Eng; Elec Electron Eng; Elec Pwr Eng) (IB 34 pts HL 6 maths phys)
Birmingham – ABB (Electron Eng Bus Mgt; Elec Ener Eng) (IB 32–34 pts)
Dundee – ABB (Electron Eng Mgt MEng) (IB 32 pts)
Edinburgh – AAA–ABB 320–360 pts (Elec Eng Renew Ener) (IB 37–32 pts)
Essex – ABB–BBB 320–300 pts (Comp Electron; Electron Eng) (IB 32–30 pts)
Glasgow – ABB (Elec Electron Eng) (IB 32 pts)
Kent – ABB 320 pts (Electron Comm Eng MEng) (IB 34 pts HL 15 pts)
Liverpool – ABB (Elec Eng Electron (Yr Ind); Electron Comm Eng MEng; Electron MEng; Elec Eng Electron MEng; Med Electron Instr MEng) (IB 33 pts HL 5 maths phys/elec)
Plymouth – 320 pts (Elec Electron Eng MEng) (IB 32 pts)
Queen's Belfast – ABB (Elec Electron Eng MEng) (IB 31–32 pts)
Sheffield – ABB incl maths (Electron Comms Eng; Electron Eng; Elec Eng) (IB 33 pts)
Sussex – ABB–BBB incl maths (Electron Eng) (IB 32–35 pts HL 5/6 maths)
York – ABB 320 pts (Electron Comm Eng) (IB 32 pts)

300 pts **Aberdeen** – BBB 300 pts (Elec Electron Eng) (IB 34 pts)
Aston – BBB–ABB 300–320 pts (Electron Eng Comp Sci; Electromech Eng) (IB 32 pts)
Bangor – 300–320 pts (Electron Eng MEng)
Birmingham City – 300 pts (Electron Elec Eng)
Brighton – BBB 300 pts (Elec Electron Eng) (IB 32 pts)
Cardiff – BBB 300 pts (Elec Electron Eng) (IB 28 pts)
Chester – 300 pts (Electron Elec Eng) (IB 28 pts)
Coventry – BBB 300 pts (Elec Electron Eng) (IB 29 pts)
Dundee – BBB (Electron Elec Eng MEng) (IB 32 pts)
Heriot-Watt – BBB 300 pts (Comp Electron) (IB 29 pts)
Huddersfield – BBB 300 pts (Electron Comm Eng)
Hull – 300 pts (Electron Eng MEng) (IB 30 pts)
Kent – BBB 300 pts (Electron Comm Eng) (IB 34 pts HL 15 pts)
Leicester – BBB 300 pts (Comms Electron Eng; Elec Electron Eng; Soft Electron Eng)
Liverpool – BBB (Electron; Med Electron Instr; Elec Eng Electron) (IB 30 pts HL 5 maths phys/elec)
London (QM) – BBB 300–340 pts (Elect Electron Eng; Electron Eng Telecomm) (IB 32–34 pts)
Loughborough – BBB (Electron Comp Sys Eng) (IB 32 pts)
Portsmouth – 300 pts (Electron Elect Eng MEng)

Queen's Belfast – BBB–AAB 300–340 pts (Electron Eng courses) (IB 32–34 pts)
Reading – 300 pts (Electron Eng; Electron Eng courses MEng) (IB 29–32 pts)
Sheffield Hallam – 300 pts (Elec Electron Eng MEng)
Swansea – BBB 300 pts (Electron Elect Eng) (IB 32 pts)
Westminster – BBB (Electron Eng MEng) (IB 32 pts)
York – BBB–BBC (Electron Eng; Electron Eng Mus Tech; Electron Eng Nanotech)
       (IB 32 pts)

280 pts Bristol UWE – 280pts (Electron Eng) (IB 28–30 pts)
Heriot-Watt – BBC 280 pts (Elec Electron Eng courses)
Hertfordshire – 280 pts (Dig Comm Electron; Elec Electron Eng) (IB 26–28 pts)
Liverpool John Moores – 280 pts (Elec Electron Eng MEng)
London (QM) – 280 pts (Electron Eng courses) (IB 28 pts)
Northumbria – 280 pts (Elec Electron Eng)
South Wales – BBC 280–320 pts (Electron Comm Eng; Elec Electron Eng; Ltg
       Des Tech)
Southampton – A*AA incl maths phys 380 pts (Electron Eng Artif Intel) (IB 38 pts
       HL 18 pts)
Teesside – 280–300 pts (Elec Electron Eng BEng/MEng) (IB 30 pts)
Westminster – BBC (Electron Eng)

260 pts Bangor – 240–260 pts (Electron Eng)
De Montfort – 260 pts (Electron Eng)
Derby – 260 pts (Elec Electron Eng) (IB 26 pts)
Greenwich – 260–280 pts (Electron Eng)
Huddersfield – 260 pts (Electron Eng MEng)
Liverpool John Moores – 260 pts (Elec Electron Eng)
Plymouth – 260 pts (Elec Electron Eng)
Portsmouth – 260–300 pts (Elect Electron Eng)
Robert Gordon – BCC (Electron Elec Eng MEng)
Sheffield Hallam – 260 pts (Elec Electron Eng)
Sunderland – 260 pts (Electron Elec Eng)
Ulster – 260 pts (Electron Comp Sys; Electron Eng)

240 pts Blackburn (Coll) – 240 pts (Elec Electron Eng)
Bradford – 240 pts (Elec Electron Eng; Med Eng)
Central Lancashire – CCC–BBC 240–280 pts (Electron Eng) (IB 24 pts)
Dundee – CCC (Electron Elec Eng; Electron Eng Mgt) (IB 28 pts)
Edinburgh Napier – CCC 240 pts (Elec Eng; Electron Elec Eng)
Glyndŵr – 240 pts (Elec Electron Eng)
Greenwich – 240 pts (Elec Eng)
Huddersfield – 240 pts (Electron Des; Electron Eng)
Hull – 240–260 pts (Electron Eng)
London South Bank – BCD 240 pts (Elec Electron Eng) (IB 24 pts)
Manchester Met – 240–280 pts (Elec Electron Eng) (IB 28 pts)
Staffordshire – 240 pts (Elec Eng; Electron Eng)

220 pts East London – 220 pts (Elec Electron Eng; Elec Electron Eng (Contr/Pwr))
London Met – 220 pts (Electron Comm Eng) (IB 24 pts)
Robert Gordon – 220–240 pts (Electron Elec Eng) (IB 26 pts)
Sheffield Hallam – 220 pts (Electron Eng)

200 pts Bedfordshire – 200 pts (Electron Eng)
Peterborough (Reg Coll) – 200 pts (Elec Electron Eng)
Southampton Solent – 200 pts (Electron Eng)
Wolverhampton – 200 pts (Electron Comm Eng)

180 pts Glasgow Caledonian – BC 180 pts (Elec Pwr Eng)
60 pts UHI – D 60 pts (Elec Electron Eng)

Alternative offers
See **Chapter 7** and **Appendix 1** for grades/UCAS Tariff points information for the International Baccalaureate, Scottish Highers/Advanced Highers, the Welsh Baccalaureate, the Irish Leaving Certificate, the Cambridge Pre-U Diploma, the Advanced Diploma and the Extended Project.

EXAMPLES OF FOUNDATION DEGREES IN THE SUBJECT FIELD
Bedfordshire; Bolton; Bournemouth; Bournemouth and Poole (Coll); Brighton; De Montfort; Exeter (Coll); Farnborough (CT); Greenwich; Havering (Coll); Hertfordshire; Leeds Beckett; London South Bank; Manchester (Coll); Newcastle (Coll); Northbrook (Coll); Plymouth; Ravensbourne; St Helens (Coll); South Cheshire (Coll); South Wales; Southampton Solent; Trinity Saint David (Swansea); Walsall (Coll); West London; York (Coll).

CHOOSING YOUR COURSE (SEE ALSO CH.1)
Some course features
Bath After a common two-year introduction covering electronics, communications, electrical engineering, mathematics and design, students specialise in Years 3 and 4, choosing from a range of optional and core modules. Individual and group project and design work and placement opportunities are key features of these modular courses.
Exeter A multi-disciplinary first year before specialising in Year 2.
Leicester Options to study for a year in industry, in Europe or the USA.
London (QM) The MEng and BEng courses include modules on telecoms, programming, digital systems, multimedia systems, wireless networks and video and image processing.
London (UCL) (Electron Eng Nanotech) Course has solid foundation of traditional electronics and specialisation in Years 3 and 4 in fast-developing field of nanotechnology (a research specialisation at UCL).
Loughborough There is a common first year for all students in the Department, followed by a choice of five degrees.
Manchester (Comp Sys Eng) Course focuses on embedded computer systems, for example in engine management systems, MP3 players and mobile phones, with emphasis on system design.

Universities and colleges teaching quality See www.qaa.ac.uk; http://unistats.direct.gov.uk.

Top research universities and colleges (RAE 2008) Leeds; Surrey; Bangor; Manchester; Imperial London; Sheffield (Automatic Control and Systems Engineering); Southampton; London (UCL); Glasgow; Bath.

Examples of sandwich degree courses Aston; Bath; Birmingham City; Bradford; Brighton; Bristol UWE; Brunel; Cardiff; Central Lancashire; City; Coventry; De Montfort; East London; Glasgow Caledonian; Greenwich; Hertfordshire; Huddersfield; Kent; Leicester; Liverpool John Moores; London South Bank; Loughborough; Manchester Met; Middlesex; Northumbria; Plymouth; Portsmouth; Queen's Belfast; Reading; Sheffield Hallam; South Wales; Staffordshire; Sunderland; Surrey; Teesside; Ulster; Westminster; Wolverhampton; York.

ADMISSIONS INFORMATION
Number of applicants per place (approx) Aston 6; Bath 8; Birmingham 18; Birmingham City 11; Bolton 3; Bournemouth 3; Bradford (Elec Electron Eng) 8; Bristol 5; Bristol UWE 8; Cardiff 7; Central Lancashire 4; City 10; Coventry 8; De Montfort 1; Derby 8; Dundee 5; Edinburgh Napier 8; Glasgow Caledonian 5; Greenwich 10; Heriot-Watt 6; Hertfordshire 7; Huddersfield 5; Hull 8; Kent 5; Kingston 8; Lancaster 7; Leeds 15; Leicester 15; Lincoln 8; Liverpool John Moores 2; London (UCL) 9; London South Bank 5; Manchester Met 5; Newcastle 9; Northumbria 7; Nottingham 8; Plymouth 22; Portsmouth 4; Robert Gordon 3; Salford 5; Sheffield 15; Sheffield Hallam 2; South Wales 2; Southampton 8; Staffordshire 7; Strathclyde 7; Sunderland 6; Surrey (BEng) 6, (MEng) 3; Swansea 3; Teesside 4; Warwick 8; Westminster 5; York 5.

Advice to applicants and planning the UCAS personal statement Enthusiasm for the subject, for example career ambitions, hobbies, work experience, attendance at appropriate events, competitions etc. Evidence of good ability in mathematics and also a scientific mind. Applicants should show that they can think creatively and have the motivation to succeed on a demanding course. See also **Engineering/Engineering Sciences** and **Appendix 3**. **Bristol** Deferred entry accepted.

Selection interviews Yes Aston, Bangor (Electron Eng), Bath, Birmingham, Bournemouth, Bradford, Bristol, Bristol UWE, Brunel, Cambridge, Central Lancashire, De Montfort, Derby, Durham, Essex, Heriot-Watt, Hertfordshire, Huddersfield, Hull, Imperial London, Kingston, Lancaster, Liverpool, London (UCL), London South Bank, Newcastle, Nottingham, Oxford, Plymouth, Portsmouth, Queen's Belfast, Southampton, Strathclyde, Sunderland, Surrey, West London, Westminster, York; **Some** Anglia Ruskin, Brighton, Cardiff, Dundee, Kent, Leicester, Loughborough, Salford, Staffordshire; **No** Liverpool John Moores.

Interview advice and questions Past questions have included: How does a combustion engine work? How does a trumpet work? What type of position do you hope to reach in five to 10 years' time? Could you sack an employee? What was your last physics practical? What did you learn from it? What are the methods of transmitting information from a moving object to a stationary observer? Wire bending exercise – you are provided with an accurate diagram of a shape that could be produced by bending a length of wire in a particular way. You are supplied with a pair of pliers and the exact length of wire required and you are given 10 minutes to reproduce as accurately as possible the shape drawn. A three-minute talk had to be given on one of six subjects (topics given several weeks before the interview); for example, 'The best is the enemy of the good'. Is there a lesson here for British industry? 'I was asked to take my physics file and discuss some of my conclusions in certain experiments.' Explain power transmission through the National Grid. How would you explain power transmission to a friend who hasn't done physics? See also **Chapter 6**. **York** Questions based on a mathematical problem.

Reasons for rejection (non-academic) Poor English. Inability to communicate. Frightened of technology or mathematics. Poor motivation and work ethic. Better suited to a less specialised engineering/science course. Some foreign applicants do not have adequate English. See also **Engineering/Engineering Sciences**. **Surrey** Can't speak English (it has happened!).

AFTER-RESULTS ADVICE
Offers to applicants repeating A-levels Higher Brighton, Central Lancashire, Greenwich, Huddersfield, Kingston, Newcastle, Queen's Belfast, Strathclyde, Warwick; **Possibly higher** Aston, City, De Montfort, Derby, Glasgow, Hertfordshire, London Met, Portsmouth, Sheffield; **Same** Anglia Ruskin, Bangor, Bath, Birmingham, Bolton, Bradford, Cardiff, Coventry, Dundee, Durham, Hull, Kent, Leeds, Liverpool, Liverpool John Moores, London South Bank, Loughborough, Northumbria, Nottingham (usually), Nottingham Trent, Robert Gordon, Salford, Southampton, Staffordshire, Surrey, West London, Wolverhampton, York; **No** Cambridge.

GRADUATE DESTINATIONS AND EMPLOYMENT (2011/12 HESA)
Graduates surveyed 3225 **Employed** 1815 **In voluntary employment** 70 **In further study** 685 **Assumed unemployed** 315

Career note Electrical and Electronic Engineering is divided into two main fields – heavy current (electrical machinery, distribution systems, generating stations) and light current (computers, control engineering, telecommunications). Opportunities exist with many commercial organisations.

OTHER DEGREE SUBJECTS FOR CONSIDERATION
Computer Science; Engineering (Aeronautical, Communications, Computer, Control); Mathematics; Physics.

ENGINEERING (MANUFACTURING)

(see also Engineering/Engineering Sciences)

Manufacturing engineering is sometimes referred to as production engineering. It is a branch of the subject concerned with management aspects of engineering such as industrial organisation, purchasing, and the planning and control of operations. Manufacturing Engineering courses are therefore geared to providing the student with a broad-based portfolio of knowledge in both the technical and business areas.

Engineering Council statement See **Engineering/Engineering Sciences**.

Useful websites www.engc.org.uk; www.imeche.org.

NB The points totals shown to the left of the institutions are for ease of reference only. It must not be assumed that Tariff points are always used by institutions or that they can be substituted for an offer in grades. The level of an offer is not necessarily indicative of the quality of a course.

COURSE OFFERS INFORMATION

Subject requirements/preferences See **Engineering/Engineering Sciences**. Offers shown below refer to BEng or BSc courses unless otherwise stated.

Your target offers and examples of courses provided by each institution

380 pts **Bath** – A*AA 380 pts (Mech Eng Manuf Mgt MEng) (IB 36 pts HL 6 maths phys)

Cambridge – A*AA 380 pts (Eng (Manuf Eng)) (IB 40–41 pts HL 776)

Durham – A*AA 380 pts (Des Ops Eng) (IB 38 pts)

Glasgow – A*AA 380 pts (Prod Des Eng MEng) (IB 36 pts)

360 pts **Loughborough** – AAA 360 pts (Innov Manuf Eng MEng) (IB 35 pts)

Newcastle – AAA 360 pts (Mech Des Manuf Eng MEng) (IB 37 pts)

Nottingham – AAA 360 pts (Manuf Eng MEng) (IB 36 pts)

340 pts **Newcastle** – AAB 340 pts (Mech Des Manuf Eng) (IB 35 pts HL 5 maths phys)

Nottingham – AAB (Manuf Eng Mgt) (IB 32–30 pts)

Strathclyde – AAB (Prod Des Eng MEng) (IB 36 pts)

Warwick – AAB (Manuf Mech Eng) (IB 36 pts)

320 pts **Liverpool** – ABB 320 pts (Ind Des Eng MEng) (IB 35 pts)

Strathclyde – ABB 320 pts (Prod Des Eng) (IB 34 pts)

300 pts **Aston** – BBB–ABB 300–320 pts (Prod Des Mgt) (IB 32 pts)

Loughborough – BBB (Manuf Eng) (IB 32 pts)

280 pts **Bristol UWE** – 280 pts (Aerosp Manuf Eng)

Queen's Belfast – BBC–BCC (Manuf Eng) (IB 29–30 pts)

South Wales – BBC 280 pts (Mech Manuf Eng) (IB 24 pts)

260 pts **Bradford** – 260 pts (Ind Eng) (IB 25 pts)

220 pts **Derby** – 220 pts (Manuf Prod Eng)

Plymouth – 220 pts (Mech Des Manuf) (IB 26 pts)

200 pts **Southampton Solent** – 200 pts (Eng Des Manuf) (IB 24 pts)

Alternative offers

See **Chapter 7** and **Appendix 1** for grades/UCAS Tariff points information for the International Baccalaureate, Scottish Highers/Advanced Highers, the Welsh Baccalaureate, the Irish Leaving Certificate, the Cambridge Pre-U Diploma, the Advanced Diploma and the Extended Project.

EXAMPLES OF FOUNDATION DEGREES IN THE SUBJECT FIELD

Blackpool and Fylde (Coll); Brighton; Bristol City (Coll); Exeter (Coll); Havering (Coll); Myerscough (Coll); Somerset (Coll); Sunderland; Trinity Saint David (Swansea); York (Coll).

For a quick reference offers calculator, fold out the inside front cover.

CHOOSING YOUR COURSE (SEE ALSO CH.1)

Some course features

Greenwich The degree programme in Manufacturing Systems Engineering shares the first two years with Mechanical Engineering, opening doors to a wide range of engineering technologies, eg aeronautical, automotive and process engineering.

Loughborough Courses include an industrial placement year leading to both a degree and a Diploma in Industrial Studies.

Newcastle Mechanical or Manufacturing Engineering is an option which is chosen after the first two years.

Nottingham (Manuf Eng Mgt) Management and business modules support studies in engineering science and design.

Universities and colleges teaching quality See www.qaa.ac.uk; http://unistats.direct.gov.uk.

Top research universities and colleges (RAE 2008) See **Engineering (Mechanical)**.

Examples of sandwich degree courses Aston; Bath; Bournemouth; Bradford; Brighton; Brunel; Liverpool John Moores; London South Bank; Loughborough; Portsmouth; Queen's Belfast; Staffordshire; Ulster.

ADMISSIONS INFORMATION

Number of applicants per place (approx) Aston 6; Bath 18; Huddersfield 1; Loughborough 6; Nottingham 5; Strathclyde 8; Warwick 8.

Advice to applicants and planning the UCAS personal statement Work experience or work shadowing in industry should be mentioned. See **Engineering/Engineering Sciences** and **Appendix 3**.

Selection interviews **Yes** Cambridge, Loughborough, Nottingham, Strathclyde.

Interview advice and questions Past questions include: What is the function of an engineer? Describe something interesting you have recently done in your A-levels. What do you know about careers in manufacturing engineering? Discuss the role of women engineers in industry. Why is a disc brake better than a drum brake? Would you be prepared to make people redundant to improve the efficiency of a production line? See also **Chapter 6**.

Reasons for rejection (non-academic) Mature students failing to attend interview are rejected. One applicant produced a forged reference and was immediately rejected. See also **Engineering/ Engineering Sciences**.

AFTER-RESULTS ADVICE

Offers to applicants repeating A-levels **Higher** Strathclyde; **Same** Cambridge, Huddersfield, Loughborough, Nottingham.

GRADUATE DESTINATIONS AND EMPLOYMENT (2011/12 HESA)

Production and Manufacturing Engineering graduates surveyed 650 **Employed** 415 **In voluntary employment** 5 **In further study** 100 **Assumed unemployed** 45

Career note Graduates with experience in both technical and business skills have the flexibility to enter careers in technology or business management.

OTHER DEGREE SUBJECTS FOR CONSIDERATION

Business Studies; Computer Science; Engineering (Electrical, Mechanical); Physics; Technology.

ENGINEERING (MECHANICAL)

(including Agricultural Engineering, Automotive Engineering and Motorsport Engineering)

Mechanical Engineering is one of the most wide-ranging engineering disciplines. All courses involve the design, installation and maintenance of equipment used in industry. Several universities include a range of Engineering courses with a common first year allowing students to specialise from Year 2. Agricultural Engineering involves all aspects of off-road vehicle design and maintenance of other machinery used in agriculture.

Engineering Council statement See **Engineering/Engineering Sciences**.

Useful websites www.imeche.org; www.engc.org.uk; www.iagre.org.

NB The points totals shown to the left of the institutions are for ease of reference only. It must not be assumed that Tariff points are always used by institutions or that they can be substituted for an offer in grades. The level of an offer is not necessarily indicative of the quality of a course.

COURSE OFFERS INFORMATION

Subject requirements/preferences (Prod Des courses) Design technology or art may be required or preferred. See also **Engineering/Engineering Sciences**. Offers shown below refer to BEng or BSc courses unless otherwise stated.

Your target offers and examples of courses provided by each institution

400 pts **Imperial London** – A*A*A 400 pts (Mech Eng) (IB 40 pts HL 6 maths phys)

380 pts **Bath** – A*AA 380 pts (Auto Eng; Mech Eng MEng) (IB 36 pts HL 6 maths phys)

Bristol – A*AA–AAB 380–340 pts (Mech Eng) (IB 38–35 pts)

Cambridge – A*AA (Eng (Mech Eng) MEng) (IB 40–41 pts HL 776)

Durham – A*AA 380 pts (Mech Eng MEng) (IB 38 pts)

Leeds – A*AA 380 pts (Mech Eng) (IB 35 pts HL 18 pts)

London (UCL) – AAAe–AABe incl maths+phys (Eng (Mech)) MEng) (IB 36–38 pts HL 17–18 pts)

Loughborough – A*AA 380 pts (Mech Eng MEng) (IB 36 pts HL 666 maths phys)

Oxford – A*AA (Mech Eng) (IB 38–40 pts)

Southampton – A*AA 380 pts (Mech Eng (Aerosp); Mech Eng (Advnc Mat) MEng) (IB 38 pts HL 18 pts)

360 pts **Bath** – AAA 360 pts (Integ Mech Elec Eng) (IB 36 pts HL 6 maths phys)

Birmingham – AAA 360 pts (Mech Eng MEng) (IB 36 pts HL 6 maths phys)

Brunel – AAA 360 pts (Mech Eng Bld Serv; Mtrspo Eng; Mech Eng Auto Des; Mech Eng Aero; Mech Eng Auto Des MEng; Mech Eng MEng; Mtrspo Eng MEng; Mech Eng Aero MEng; Mech Eng Bld Serv MEng; Mech Eng) (IB 37 pts)

Cardiff – AAA–AAB 360–320 pts (Mech Eng) (IB 32–36 pts HL 5 maths)

City – 360 pts (Auto Mtrspo Eng MEng) (IB 32 pts HL 6 maths)

Durham – AAA 360 pts (Gen Eng) (IB 37 pts)

Edinburgh – AAA–ABB 360–320 pts (Mech Eng; Mech Eng Mgt; Mech Eng Renew Ener; Elec Mech Eng) (IB 37–32 pts)

Exeter – AAA–AAB (Mech Eng MEng) (IB 36–34 pts)

Leeds – AAA 360 pts (Auto Eng; Mecha Robot) (IB 35 pts HL 18 pts)

London (UCL) – AAA–AAB 360–340 pts (Eng (Mech Bus Fin)) (IB 36–38 pts)

Loughborough – AAA (Auto Eng MEng) (IB 36 pts)

Manchester – AAA (Mech Eng MEng) (IB 37 pts)

Newcastle – AAA 360 pts (Mech Eng Bioeng MEng; Mech Des Manuf Eng MEng; Mech Eng MEng; Mech Eng Microsys MEng; Mech Low Carbon Trans Eng MEng) (IB 37 pts)

Nottingham – AAA (Mech Eng MEng) (IB 36–34 pts)

Sheffield – AAA 360 pts (Mech Eng; Mech Eng (Ind Mgt); Mech Eng Fr/Ger/Ital) (IB 37 pts HL 6 maths sci)

Southampton – AAA incl maths phys (Mech Eng; Mech Eng (Bioeng); Mech Eng (Auto); Mech Eng (Eng Mgt); Mech Eng (Mecha); Mech Eng (Nvl Eng); Mech Eng (Sust Ener Sys)) (IB 36 pts HL 18 pts)

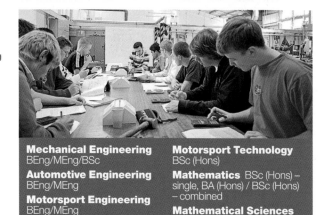

Strathclyde – AAA 360 pts (Mech Eng Mat Eng MEng; Mech Eng MEng; Mech Eng Aero MEng; Mech Eng Fin Mgt MEng) (IB 36 pts)

Surrey – AAA 360 pts (Mech Eng MEng) (IB 34 pts)

Warwick – AAA (Mech Eng) (IB 36 pts)

340 pts **Aston** – AAB–AAA 340–360 pts (Mech Eng MEng) (IB 34 pts)

Birmingham – AAB (Mech Eng; Mech Eng (Auto/Biomed)) (IB 34–36 pts)

City – 340–360 pts (Mech Eng) (IB 32 pts)

Durham – AAB 340 pts (Mech Eng)

Exeter – AAB–BBB 340–300 pts (Min Eng) (IB 34–30 pts)

Glasgow – AAB (Mech Eng MEng; Mech Eng Aero MEng; Mech Des Eng MEng) (IB 34 pts)

Huddersfield – AAB 340 pts (Mech Eng MEng)

Lancaster – AAB (Eng (Mech) MEng; Mech Eng)

Liverpool – AAB incl maths (Mech Eng MEng; Mech Eng Bus MEng; Mech Mat Eng MEng) (IB 35 pts HL 5 maths)

London (QM) – 340 pts (Mech Eng MEng; Des Innov MEng) (IB 34 pts)

London (UCL) – AAB–ABB incl maths +phys (Mech Eng) (IB 34–36 pts)

Manchester – AAB 340 pts (Mech Eng Mgt; Mech Eng; Mecha Eng) (IB 35 pts)

Newcastle – AAB–ABB (Mech Eng; Mech Des Manuf Eng) (IB 35 pts HL 5 maths phys)

Nottingham – AAB (Mech Eng) (IB 32–30 pts)

Queen's Belfast – AAB (Mech Manuf Eng MEng) (IB 31–32 pts)

Strathclyde – AAB (Mech Eng) (IB 32 pts)

Surrey – AAB (Mech Eng) (IB 27 pts)

Swansea – AAB 340 pts (Mech Eng MEng) (IB 34 pts)

Warwick – AAB (Manuf Mech Eng; Auto Eng) (IB 36 pts)

320 pts **Brighton** – ABB 320 pts (Auto Eng) (IB 34 pts)
Bristol UWE – 320 pts (Mech Eng) (IB 28–30 pts)
Exeter – ABB–BBB 320–300 pts (Mech Eng) (IB 32–29 pts)
Glasgow – ABB (Mech Eng; Mech Des Eng; Mech Eng Aero) (IB 32 pts)
Glasgow (SA) – ABB (Prod Des Eng)
Hertfordshire – 320 pts (Auto Eng MEng; Auto Eng Mtrspo MEng) (IB 30 pts)
Hull – 320 pts (Mech Eng MEng)
Leicester – AAB–ABB 340–320 pts (Mech Eng MEng) (IB 34–32 pts)
Liverpool – ABB incl maths (Mech Mat Eng; Mecha Robot Sys MEng; Mech Eng Bus) (IB 33 pts HL 5 maths)
Liverpool John Moores – 320 pts (Mech Mar Eng MEng; Mech Eng MEng; Auto Eng MEng)
Loughborough – ABB (Mech Eng; Auto Eng) (IB 32 pts)
Northumbria – 320 pts (Mech Eng) (IB 27 pts)
Oxford Brookes – ABB 320 pts (Auto Eng MEng; Mtrspo Eng MEng; Mech Eng MEng) (IB 33 pts)
Sussex – ABB–BBB incl maths (Auto Eng; Mech Eng) (IB 32–34 pts HL 5/6 maths)
Swansea – ABB–BBB (Mech Eng)
300 pts **Aberdeen** – BBB 300 pts (Mech Eng; Mech Eng Mgt; Eng (Mech Oil Gas St); Eng (Mech Euro St)) (IB 32 pts)
Aston – BBB–ABB 300–320 pts (Electromech Eng; Mech Eng) (IB 32 pts)
Bradford – 300 pts (Mech Eng MEng) (IB 28–32 pts)
Brighton – BBB (Mech Eng) (IB 32 pts)
Coventry – BBB 300 pts (Mtrspo Eng; Mech Eng) (IB 29 pts)
Harper Adams – 300 pts (Agric Eng) (IB 30 pts)
Heriot-Watt – BBB (Mech Eng Ener Eng; Mech Eng)
Hull – 300 pts (Mech Med Eng MEng) (IB 30 pts)
Liverpool – BBB incl maths (Mech Eng) (IB 32 pts HL 5 maths)
London (QM) – 300 pts (Des Innov) (IB 28 pts)
Loughborough – BBB 280–300 pts (Des Ergon)
Oxford Brookes – BBB (Mech Eng; Mtrspo Eng; Auto Eng) (IB 30 pts)
Plymouth – 300 pts (Mech Eng MEng) (IB 30 pts)
Queen's Belfast – BBB (Mech Eng) (IB 31–32 pts)
Sheffield Hallam – 300 pts (Mech Eng MEng)
Ulster – 300 pts (Mech Eng MEng) (IB 25 pts)
280 pts **Birmingham City** – 280 pts (Mech Eng; Auto Eng; Mtrspo Tech)
Bristol UWE – 280–300 pts (Mtrspo Eng) (IB 28–30 pts)
City – BBC 280 pts (Auto Mtrspo Eng) (IB 28 pts)
Derby – 280 pts (Mech Eng; Mtrcycl Eng; Mtrspo Eng)
Dundee – BBC 280 pts (Mech Eng)
Edinburgh Napier – BBC (Mech Eng MEng)
Glyndŵr – 280 pts (Aero Mech Eng)
Heriot-Watt – BBC (Auto Eng)
Hertfordshire – 280 pts (Auto Eng; Mech Eng; Auto Eng Mtrspo) (IB 26–28 pts)
Hull – 280 pts (Mech Med Eng) (IB 27 pts)
Leicester – BBB–BBC (Mech Eng) (IB 30 pts)
London (QM) – 280 pts (Mech Eng) (IB 28 pts)
Manchester Met – 280 pts (Mech Eng; Mech Des Tech) (IB 28 pts)
Oxford Brookes – BBC 280 pts (Mtrspo Tech) (IB 30 pts)
Plymouth – 280 pts (Mech Eng; Mech Eng Cmpsts) (IB 28 pts)
Robert Gordon – BBC (Mech Elec Eng MEng; Mech Eng MEng) (IB 28 pts)
Salford – 280–300 pts (Mech Eng MEng) (IB 35 pts)
South Wales – BBC 280 pts (Mech Manuf Eng) (IB 24 pts)
Staffordshire – 280 pts (Mtrspo Tech; Mech Eng) (IB 24 pts)
Teesside – 280 pts (Mech Eng) (IB 30 pts)
Ulster – 280 pts (Mech Eng)

260 pts **Bradford** – 260 pts (Mech Eng; Mech Auto Eng)
De Montfort – 260 pts (Mech Eng; Mecha) (IB 28 pts)
Greenwich – 260–280 pts (Mech Eng)
Hull – 260–320 pts (Mech Eng)
Lincoln – 260–300 pts (Mech Eng)
Liverpool John Moores – 260 pts (Auto Eng; Mech Mar Eng; Mech Eng)
Robert Gordon – BCC (Mech Off Eng; Mech Eng; Mech Elec Eng) (IB 27 pts)
Salford – 260 pts (Mech Eng) (IB 30 pts)
Sheffield Hallam – 260 pts (Mech Eng; Auto Eng)
Sunderland – 260 pts (Mech Eng) (IB 32 pts)

240 pts **Bolton** – 240 pts (Auto Eng; Mech Eng)
Central Lancashire – CCC–BBC 240–280 pts (Mtr Spo Eng) (IB 24 pts)
Edinburgh Napier – CCC (Mech Eng)
Harper Adams – 240 pts (Offrd Veh Des)
Huddersfield – 240 pts (Mech Eng) (IB 26 pts)
Kingston – 240 pts (Mtrspo Eng (Mtrcycl); Mtrspo Eng; Mech Eng)
London South Bank – CCC 240 pts (Mech Eng; Mecha)
Portsmouth – 240–280 pts (Mech Eng) (IB 28 pts)
Sheffield Hallam – 240 pts (Auto Des Tech)
Trinity Saint David (Swansea) – 240 pts (Auto Eng; Mtrspo Eng Des; Mtrcycl Eng)
West Scotland – CCC 240 pts (Mech Eng; Mtrspo Des Eng) (IB 24 pts)

230 pts **Glasgow Caledonian** – AB incl maths phys 230 pts (Mech Electron Sys Eng)

220 pts **Plymouth** – 220 pts (Mech Des Manuf) (IB 26 pts)
Sunderland – 220 pts (Auto Eng) (IB 32 pts)

200 pts **Portsmouth** – 200–240 pts (Mech Manuf Eng) (IB 24 pts)
Southampton Solent – 200 pts (Eng Des Manuf) (IB 24 pts)
Staffordshire – 200–240 pts (Mecha)
Trinity Saint David (Swansea) – 200 pts (Mtrspo Eng)
Wolverhampton – 200 pts (Mech Eng) (IB 24 pts)

180 pts **Harper Adams** – 180–220 pts (Offrd Veh Des Mark Mgt; Agric Eng Mark Mgt) (IB 26 pts)

150 pts **Anglia Ruskin** – 150 pts (Mech Eng)

120 pts **Blackburn (Coll)** – 120 pts (Mech Eng)

Alternative offers
See **Chapter 7** and **Appendix 1** for grades/UCAS Tariff points information for the International Baccalaureate, Scottish Highers/Advanced Highers, the Welsh Baccalaureate, the Irish Leaving Certificate, the Cambridge Pre-U Diploma, the Advanced Diploma and the Extended Project.

EXAMPLES OF FOUNDATION DEGREES IN THE SUBJECT FIELD
Bath; Blackburn (Coll); Blackpool and Fylde (Coll); Brighton; Bristol City (Coll); Bristol UWE; Derby; Exeter (Coll); Glyndŵr; Greenwich; Harper Adams; Havering (Coll); Kingston; Loughborough (Coll); Myerscough (Coll); Oxford Brookes; Plymouth; Queen's Belfast; Sheffield Hallam; Somerset (Coll); South Cheshire (Coll); Staffordshire; Sunderland; Trinity Saint David (Swansea); Warwickshire (Coll).

CHOOSING YOUR COURSE (SEE ALSO CH.1)
Some course features
Brunel (Mech Eng) Course combines fundamental elements of mechanical engineering and design with study in associated disciplines including computing, electronics, environment and energy systems. All courses emphasise importance of industrial and commercial insight and awareness.
Cardiff The first year is common to all Engineering programmes. Core subjects include mathematics, dynamics, properties of materials, electrical engineering, electronics and business management.
Durham A common course for Years 1 and 2 and then two years specialising in the chosen discipline.
Exeter A multi-disciplinary first year before specialising in Year 2. Emphasis on design skills, practice and development.

Leicester Options to study for a year in industry, in Europe or the USA.
Lincoln The Mechanical Engineering programme has options in Power and Energy or Control Systems.
Newcastle Ten Mechanical Engineering options with common first and second years for all students.
Salford (MEng Mech Eng) Programme has broad engineering themes and the option to spend a year in industry.
Strathclyde Four- and five-year degrees offered in Mechanical Engineering.
Surrey Mechanical, medical and aerospace programmes have a common first year allowing for a final choice of degree in Year 2.

Universities and colleges teaching quality See www.qaa.ac.uk; http://unistats.direct.gov.uk.

Top research universities and colleges (RAE 2008) (Mechanical, Aeronautical and Manufacturing Engineering) Imperial London; Sheffield; Bristol (Aerosp Eng); Greenwich; Nottingham; Leeds; Loughborough; Birmingham; Cardiff.

Examples of sandwich degree courses Aston; Bath; Birmingham City; Bradford; Brighton; Bristol UWE; Brunel; Cardiff; Central Lancashire; City; Coventry; De Montfort; Glasgow Caledonian; Harper Adams; Hertfordshire; Huddersfield; Kingston; Leicester; Liverpool John Moores; London South Bank; Loughborough; Manchester Met; Northumbria; Oxford Brookes; Plymouth; Portsmouth; Queen's Belfast; Salford; Sheffield Hallam; South Wales; Staffordshire; Sunderland; Surrey; Teesside; Ulster; West Scotland; Wolverhampton.

ADMISSIONS INFORMATION

Number of applicants per place (approx) Abertay 4; Aston 8; Bath (MEng) 13; Birmingham 6; Bradford 4; Brighton 10; Bristol 8; Bristol UWE 17; Brunel 12; Cardiff 8; City 13; Coventry 8; Dundee 5; Durham 8; Glyndŵr 4; Heriot-Watt 9; Hertfordshire 10; Huddersfield 1; Hull 11; Kingston 8; Lancaster 8; Leeds 15; Leicester 11; Liverpool 6; Liverpool John Moores (Mech Eng) 2; London (QM) 6; London South Bank 4; Loughborough 8, (Mech Eng) 12, (Auto Eng) 7; Manchester Met 6, (Mech Eng) 6; Newcastle 10; Northumbria 4; Nottingham 8; Plymouth 6; Portsmouth 6; Sheffield 10; South Wales 6; Southampton 8; Staffordshire 6; Strathclyde 6; Surrey 9; Teesside 7; Warwick 8; Westminster 11.

Advice to applicants and planning the UCAS personal statement Work experience; hands-on skills. An interest in solving mathematical problems related to physical concepts. Enjoyment in designing mechanical devices or components. Interest in engines, structures, dynamics or fluid flow and efficient use of materials or energy. Apply to the Year in Industry Scheme (www.etrust.org.uk) for placement. Scholarships are available to supplement the scheme. See **Engineering/Engineering Sciences** and **Appendix 3**.

Misconceptions about this course Loughborough Although organised by the Wolfson School of Manufacturing and Mechanical Engineering, the degree does not include manufacturing.

Selection interviews Yes Aston, Birmingham, Bolton, Bradford, Brighton, Bristol, Brunel, Cambridge, Cardiff, Durham, Harper Adams, Hertfordshire, Huddersfield, Imperial London, Kingston, Lancaster, Leeds, Leicester, Liverpool John Moores, London (QM), London South Bank, Loughborough (Auto Eng), Manchester Met, Newcastle, Nottingham, Oxford, Queen's Belfast, Sheffield, Sheffield Hallam, Strathclyde, Sunderland, Surrey, Sussex; **Some** Blackpool and Fylde (Coll), Dundee, Liverpool, Staffordshire.

Interview advice and questions Past questions include: What mechanical objects have you examined and/or tried to repair? How do you see yourself in five years' time? What do you imagine you would be doing (production, management or design engineering)? What engineering interests do you have? What qualities are required to become a successful mechanical engineer? Do you like sixth-form work? Describe the working of parts on an engineering drawing. How does a fridge work? What is design in the context of mechanical engineering? What has been your greatest achievement to date? What are your career plans? See also **Engineering/Engineering Sciences** and **Chapter 6**. **Hertfordshire** All interviewees receive a conditional offer. Provide an example of working as part of a team, meeting a deadline, working on your own.

Reasons for rejection (non-academic) See **Engineering/Engineering Sciences**.

AFTER-RESULTS ADVICE

Offers to applicants repeating A-levels **Higher** Brighton, Dundee, Kingston, Newcastle, Queen's Belfast, Swansea, Warwick; **Possibly higher** City, Huddersfield; **Same** Aston, Bath, Bradford, Bristol, Brunel, Coventry, Derby, Durham, East London, Edinburgh Napier, Harper Adams, Heriot-Watt, Leeds (usually), Lincoln, Liverpool, Liverpool John Moores, London South Bank, Loughborough, Manchester Met, Northumbria, Nottingham, Nottingham Trent, Oxford Brookes, Sheffield, Sheffield Hallam, Southampton, Staffordshire, Sunderland, Surrey, Teesside, Wolverhampton; **No** Cambridge.

GRADUATE DESTINATIONS AND EMPLOYMENT (2011/12 HESA)

Graduates surveyed 3275 **Employed** 2100 **In voluntary employment** 45 **In further study** 605 **Assumed unemployed** 255

Career note Mechanical Engineering graduates have a wide choice of career options. Apart from design and development of plant and machinery, they are also likely to be involved in production processes and working at various levels of management. Mechanical engineers share interests such as structures and stress analysis with civil and aeronautical engineers, and electronics and computing with electrical and software engineers.

OTHER DEGREE SUBJECTS FOR CONSIDERATION

Engineering (Aeronautical/Aerospace, Building, Computer (Control, Software and Systems), Electrical/ Electronic, Manufacturing, Marine); Materials Science; Mathematics; Physics; Product Design; Technologies.

ENGINEERING (MEDICAL)

(including **Clinical Engineering, Medical Electronics** and **Instrumentation, Mechanical** and **Medical Engineering, Medical Physics, Medical Product Design, Product Design for Medical Devices** and **Rehabilitation Engineering**; see also **Biotechnology**)

Biomedical Engineering lies at the interface between engineering, mathematics, physics, chemistry, biology and clinical practice. This makes it a branch of engineering that has the most direct effect on human health. It is a rapidly expanding interdisciplinary field that applies engineering principles and technology to medical and biological problems. Biomedical engineers work in fields as diverse as neuro-technology, fluid mechanics of the blood and respiratory systems, bone and joint biomechanics, biosensors, medical imaging, synthetic biology and biomaterials. These can lead to novel devices such as joint replacements and heart valves, new surgical instruments, rehabilitation protocols and even prosthetic limbs.

NB The points totals shown to the left of the institutions are for ease of reference only. It must not be assumed that Tariff points are always used by institutions or that they can be substituted for an offer in grades. The level of an offer is not necessarily indicative of the quality of a course.

COURSE OFFERS INFORMATION

Subject requirements/preferences **GCSE/AL** Subjects taken from mathematics, physics, chemistry and biology. Offers shown below refer to BEng or BSc courses unless otherwise stated.

Your target offers and examples of courses provided by each institution

380 pts **Glasgow** – A*AA incl maths phys 380 pts (Biomed Eng MEng) (IB 36 pts HL 6 maths phys)

Imperial London – A*AA incl maths phys 380 pts (Biomed Eng) (IB 38 pts HL 766 incl maths phys)

360 pts **Cardiff** – AAA–AAB 360–340 pts (Med Eng) (IB 32–36 pts)

Leeds – AAA 360 pts (Med Eng BEng/MEng) (IB 35 pts HL 18 pts)

London (King's) – AAA–A*AB (Biomed Eng; Phys Med Apps) (IB 35 pts HL 666 maths phys)

London (QM) – AAA 360 pts (Med Eng MEng) (IB 34 pts)

London (UCL) – AAA–ABB 360–320 pts (Med Phys) (IB 34–38 pts HL 16–18 pts incl maths phys)

Manchester – AAA–ABB 360–320 pts (Biomed Sci) (IB 37–33 pts)

Surrey – AAA 360 pts (Med Eng MEng) (IB 37 pts)

340 pts **City** – AAB 340 pts (Biomed Eng) (IB 30 pts)

Glasgow – AAB 340 pts (Biomed Eng) (IB 34 pts)

Queen's Belfast – AAB (Phys Med Apps MSci) (IB 34 pts HL 666 maths phys)

Sheffield – AAB 340 pts (Bioeng MEng) (IB 35 pts)

Surrey – AAB 340 pts (Med Eng) (IB 35 pts)

Swansea – AAB–ABB 340–320 pts (Med Eng MEng) (IB 34–33 pts)

320 pts **London (QM)** – ABB 320 pts (Med Eng) (IB 34 pts)

Sheffield – ABB 320 pts (Bioeng) (IB 34 pts)

300 pts **Hull** – 300 pts (Mech Med Eng MEng) (IB 30 pts)

Queen's Belfast – BBB (Phys Med Apps) (IB 32 pts HL 665 incl maths physics)

Swansea – BBB 300 pts (Med Eng) (IB 32 pts)

280 pts **Hull** – 280 pts (Mech Med Eng) (IB 27 pts)

Alternative offers

See **Chapter 7** and **Appendix 1** for Grades/UCAS Tariff points information for the International Baccalaureate, Scottish Highers/Advanced Highers, the Welsh Baccalaureate, the Irish Leaving Certificate, the Cambridge Pre-U Diploma, the Advanced Diploma and the Extended Project.

CHOOSING YOUR COURSE (SEE ALSO CH.1)

Some course features

Cardiff A long-standing Medical Engineering course blending engineering knowledge with biomechanical applications. Lectures delivered by research-active biomechanists, clinicians and industrialists. One year paid employment. MEng students have the opportunity to spend a year in a European university.

London (UCL) (Med Phys) Graduates have an Institute of Physics accredited degree with a range of careers open to students not committed to a career in medical physics. Those taking this subject usually train to be an NHS medical physicist, seek a position in industry or take a higher degree.

Swansea BEng and MEng courses are offered with the fourth year of the MEng course covering advanced studies. Courses are accredited by the Institute of Mechanical Engineers.

Universities and colleges teaching quality See www.qaa.ac.uk; http://unistats.direct.gov.uk.

Examples of sandwich degree courses Cardiff; City; Surrey.

ADMISSIONS INFORMATION

Number of applicants per place (approx) Cardiff 4; London (UCL) 6; Swansea 5.

Advice to applicants and planning the UCAS personal statement **Cardiff** An appreciation of the typical careers available within medical engineering and an interest in engineering and anatomy would be preferable. **London (UCL)** Evidence of interest in medical physics/physics, eg visits to hospitals or internships.

Selection interviews **Yes** Cardiff (all applicants), London (UCL); **Some** Swansea.

Interview advice and questions **London (UCL)** Searching questions at interview. Test may be included.

AFTER-RESULTS ADVICE

Offers to applicants repeating A-levels **Same** Cardiff, Liverpool, London (UCL), Swansea.

GRADUATE DESTINATIONS AND EMPLOYMENT (2011/12 HESA)

See **Biotechnology**.

Career note High rate of graduate employment. *Money* magazine ranks Biomedical Engineering number 1 for job growth prospects for the next 10 years.

OTHER DEGREE SUBJECTS FOR CONSIDERATION

Biological Sciences; Prosthetic; Orthotics.

ENGLISH

(including **Creative Writing**; see also **Journalism, Languages, Linguistics, Literature**)

English courses continue to be extremely popular and competitive. They are an extension of school studies in literature and language and may cover topics ranging from Anglo-Saxon literature to writing in the present day. Most courses, however, will focus on certain areas such as the Medieval or Renaissance periods of literature or on English language studies. Admissions tutors will expect students to have read widely outside their A-level syllabus.

Useful websites www.bl.uk; www.lrb.co.uk; www.literature.org; www.bibliomania.com.

NB The points totals shown to the left of the institutions are for ease of reference only. It must not be assumed that Tariff points are always used by institutions or that they can be substituted for an offer in grades. The level of an offer is not necessarily indicative of the quality of a course.

COURSE OFFERS INFORMATION

Subject requirements/preferences GCSE English language and English literature required and a foreign language may be preferred. Grades may be stipulated. **AL** English with specific grades usually stipulated. Modern languages required for joint courses with languages.

Your target offers and examples of courses provided by each institution

380 pts **Bristol** – A*AA–AAB 380–340 pts (Engl) (IB 38–35 pts HL 666 incl Engl)
Cambridge – A*AA (Educ Engl Dr; Engl; A-Sxn Nrs Celt) (IB 40–41 pts HL 776)
Durham – A*AA 380 pts (Engl Lit) (IB 38 pts)
Exeter – A*AA–AAB 380–340 pts (Engl) (IB 38–34 pts)
London (UCL) – AAAe (Engl) (IB 38 pts HL 18 pts)

360 pts **Birmingham** – AAA 360 pts (Engl Crea Writ) (IB 38–36 pts HL 6 Engl)
Bristol – AAA–AAB 360–340 pts (Thea Engl; Engl Class St) (IB 37–35 pts HL 666 incl Engl)
Edinburgh – AAA–BBB 360–300 pts (Engl Lang; Engl Lit; Engl Scot Lit; Class Engl Lang) (IB 40–34 pts HL 666–555)
Exeter – AAA–AAB (Engl (St Abrd)) (IB 36–33 pts)
Lancaster – AAA 360 pts (Engl Lang Lit; Engl Lang; Engl Lang Crea Writ; Mediev Ren St; Engl Lit) (IB 36 pts HL 16 pts)
London (King's) – AAA 360 pts (Class St Engl; Engl Lang Lit; Gk Engl; Compar Lit; Engl Film St) (IB 35 pts HL 666 Engl)
London (QM) – 360 pts (Engl) (IB 32 pts)
London NCH – AAA 360 pts (Engl) (IB 36 pts HL 666 Engl)
Nottingham – AAA–AAB 340–360 pts (Engl Crea Writ; Engl St; Engl Lang Lit) (IB 34–36 pts)
Oxford – AAA (Engl Lang Lit; Engl Modn Langs) (IB 38–40 pts)
St Andrews – AAA (Engl courses) (IB 36–38 pts)
Sussex – AAA–AAB (Engl; Engl Lang Lit; Engl Joint Hons; Engl Lang) (IB 35–36 pts)
Warwick – AAA (Engl Lit; Engl Fr; Engl Lit Crea Writ) (IB 38 pts)
York – AAA–AAB 360–340 pts (Engl; Engl Hist; Engl courses) (IB 36 pts HL 6 Engl)

340 pts **Birmingham** – AAB 340 pts (Engl; Engl Lang) (IB 35 pts HL 6 Engl)
Brunel – AAB–ABB 340–320 pts (Engl; Engl Crea Writ; Engl Film TV St; Thea Engl) (IB 35 pts)
Cardiff – AAB 340 pts (Engl Lit) (IB 34 pts)
East Anglia – AAB 340 pts (Script Perf; Engl Lit) (IB 33 pts HL 5 Engl)
Essex – AAB–ABB 340–320 pts (Engl Lit; Crea Writ; Lit Myth) (IB 33–32 pts)
Leeds – AAB (Engl Lang Lit; Engl Lang) (IB 35 pts HL 6 Engl)
Leicester – AAB–ABB 340–320 pts (Engl courses) (IB 34–32 pts)
Liverpool – AAB–ABB (Engl; Engl Joint Hons) (IB 35–33 pts HL 6 Engl)
London (Gold) – AAB (Engl Crea Writ)
London (RH) – AAB–ABB 340–320 pts (Engl; Engl Dr) (IB 35–34 pts)
Loughborough – AAB 340 pts (Engl; Engl Spo Sci; Engl Am St) (IB 34 pts)
Manchester – AAB 340 pts (Engl Lit courses) (IB 35 pts)
Newcastle – AAB 340 pts (Engl Lang Lit) (IB 35 pts)

Nottingham – AAB (Engl Phil; Class Civ Engl; Engl Lat) (IB 34 pts)

Reading – A*BB–AAB (Engl Lit courses) (IB 35 pts)

Sheffield – AAB–ABB 340–320 pts (Engl Lang Lit; Engl Lit; Engl Lang Ling; Engl Joint Hons) (IB 35–33 pts)

Southampton – AAB (Engl Fr/Ger/Span; Film Engl; Engl; Engl Hist; Phil Engl; Engl Mus) (IB 34 pts HL 17 pts)

Surrey – AAB–ABB (Engl Lit; Engl Lit Crea Writ; Engl Lit Fr/Span) (IB 35–34 pts)

Sussex – AAB–ABB 340–320 pts (Am St courses) (IB 34 pts)

Warwick – AAB 340 pts (Engl Lat Lit; Engl Ital Lit; Engl Ger Lit) (IB 36 pts)

York – AAB (Engl Ling; Engl Phil; Engl Hist Art; Engl Pol) (IB 35 pts)

320 pts   **Aston** – ABB 320 pts (Engl Lang; Int Rel Engl Lang; Engl Lang Fr/Ger; Pol Engl Lang) (IB 32–34 pts)

Bournemouth – 320 pts (Engl)

Brighton – ABB (Engl Lit) (IB 34 pts)

Bristol – 320 pts (Engl Lang Ling) (IB 27 pts)

Brunel – ABB 320 pts (Thea Crea Writ) (IB 33 pts)

Cardiff – ABB 320 pts (Engl Lang; Engl Lang Lit)

Central Lancashire – ABB–BBC 320–280 pts (Engl Lit) (IB 25 pts)

East Anglia – ABB–AAB 320–340 pts (Am Engl Lit; Engl Lit Joint Hons; Film Engl St) (IB 32–33 pts HL 5 Engl)

Essex – ABB–BBB 320–300 pts (Engl Lang; Engl Lang Lit) (IB 32–30 pts)

Glasgow – ABB (Engl Lit; Engl Lang) (IB 36 pts)

Gloucestershire – 320 pts (Engl Lit)

Huddersfield – (Engl Lit)

Keele – ABB–BBB 320–300 pts (Engl courses) (IB 34–32 pts)

Kent – ABB 320 pts (Engl Lang Ling; Engl Lang Ling Engl Am Lit) (IB 34 pts)

Liverpool – ABB 320 pts (Engl Comm St) (IB 33 pts)

London (Birk) – ABB 320 pts (Engl)

London (Gold) – ABB 320 pts (Engl; Engl Compar Lit) (IB 34 pts)

London (King's) – ABB (Engl Lang Comm) (IB 34 pts HL 6 Engl)

London (QM) – ABB–AAB 320–340 pts (Engl Lang Ling; Engl Lit Ling) (IB 34 pts)

Loughborough – ABB–AAB 320–340 pts (Hist Engl) (IB 32–34 pts)

Manchester – AAA–ABB 320–360 pts (Engl Lang courses) (IB 33–37 pts)

Newcastle – ABB 320 pts (Engl Lang) (IB 34 pts)

Nottingham – ABB 320 pts (Am St Engl; Art Hist Engl; Engl E Euro Cult St; Engl Serb/Cro; Engl Theol) (IB 32 pts)

Queen's Belfast – ABB/BBBb (Engl courses)

Sheffield – ABB (Engl Lang Sociol) (IB 33 pts)

Strathclyde – ABB 320 pts (Engl courses) (IB 34 pts)

Swansea – ABB–BBB (Engl courses; Engl Lit Lang St)

Winchester – 320–360 pts (Engl Lit Am Lit) (IB 27 pts)

300 pts   **Aberdeen** – BBB (Engl; Engl Scot Lit; Celt Civ Engl) (IB 30 pts)

Aberystwyth – 300 pts (Engl Lit) (IB 30 pts)

Bristol UWE – 300 pts (Engl; Engl Jrnl) (IB 26 pts)

Buckingham – 300 pts (Engl Lit courses)

Chichester – BBB–BCC 300–260 pts (Engl; Engl Crea Writ) (IB 30 pts)

Dundee – BBB (Engl Film St; Engl) (IB 30 pts)

Gloucestershire – 280–300 pts (Engl Lang; Crea Writ)

Hertfordshire – 300 pts (Engl Lit) (IB 24–26 pts)

Huddersfield – 300 pts (Engl St; Engl Lang)

Hull – 300–340 pts (Engl)

Leeds Beckett – BBB 300 pts (Engl Lit) (IB 26 pts)

Loughborough – 300 pts (Pub Engl) (IB 32 pts HL 5 Engl)

Northumbria – 300 pts (Engl Lit; Engl Lang Lit; Engl Lit Crea Writ)

Nottingham – BBB (Engl Span) (IB 26 pts)

Oxford Brookes – BBB 300 pts (Engl) (IB 32 pts)
Plymouth – BBB 300 pts (Engl Fr; Engl Span) (IB 26 pts)
Reading – 300–360 pts (Engl Lang courses) (IB 31–32 pts)
Roehampton – 300 pts (Engl Lit; Crea Writ; Engl Lang Ling)
Sheffield Hallam – 300 pts (Engl; Crea Writ; Engl Lang; Engl Lit)
Winchester – 300–340 pts (Engl courses)
York – BBB 300 pts (Engl Educ) (IB 31 pts)

280 pts **Bangor** – 280–300 pts (Engl Thea Perf; Engl Lit Engl Lang) (IB 26 pts)
Bath Spa – 280–320 pts (Engl Lit; Crea Writ)
Birmingham City – 280 pts (Engl Crea Writ; Engl Lang Engl Lit; Engl) (IB 26 pts)
Edge Hill – 280 pts (Engl Media; Engl Hist; Engl; Crea Writ; Engl Lang; Engl Lit)
Edinburgh Napier – BBC 280 pts (Engl Film; Engl)
Greenwich – (Phil Crea Writ)
Huddersfield – 280 pts (Dr Engl)
Hull – 280–320 pts (Dr Engl)
Liverpool John Moores – 280 pts (Crea Writ Flm St) (IB 29 pts)
London Met – 280 pts (Crea Writ; Engl Lit)
Manchester Met – 280 pts (Engl Am Lit; Creat Writ; Engl) (IB 28 pts)
Newman – 280 pts (Engl; Phil Relgn Engl)
Oxford Brookes – BBC 280 pts (Engl Lang Comm) (IB 30 pts)
Reading – 280 pts (P Educ Engl) (IB 28 pts)
South Wales – BBC 280 pts (Engl Lit; Crea Prof Writ; Engl Lang)
Stirling – BBC (Engl St) (IB 32 pts)
Teesside – 280 pts (Engl St; Engl St Crea Writ)
Westminster – BBC (Engl Lang courses) (IB 30 pts)
Winchester – 280–320 pts (Crea Writ courses) (IB 24–26 pts)
Worcester – 280–380 pts (Engl Lit St courses)

260 pts **Bangor** – 260–300 pts (Mus Crea Writ)
Cardiff Met (UWIC) – 260 pts (Engl Contemp Media; Engl Crea Writ; Engl Dr; Educ St Engl)
Central Lancashire – 260–280 pts (Engl Lang St)
Chester – 260–300 pts (Engl; Engl Lang) (IB 28 pts)
Coventry – BCC 260 pts (Engl; Engl Jrnl; Fr Engl) (IB 28 pts)
De Montfort – 260 pts (Engl; Engl Lang; Crea Writ)
Derby – 260 pts (Engl; Crea Writ)
Liverpool Hope – 260–300 pts (Engl Lit; Engl Lang) (IB 26 pts)
Liverpool John Moores – 260 pts (Hist Engl; Crea Writ; Engl) (IB 28 pts)
Manchester Met – 260–280 pts (Am Hist) (IB 28 pts)
Middlesex – 260 pts (Crea Writ Jrnl; Engl Lang Media)
Northampton – 260–280 pts (Engl courses; Crea Writ courses)
Nottingham – BCC 260 pts (Crea Prof Writ) (IB 28 pts)
Nottingham Trent – 260 pts (Engl; Engl Crea Writ)
Plymouth – 260 pts (Crea Writ; Engl courses)
Salford – 260–300 pts (Engl Dr; Engl Crea Writ; Engl Lit; Engl Lit Engl Lang) (IB 26 pts)
Sheffield Hallam – 260 pts (Engl Hist)
South Wales – 260 pts (Engl Crea Writ)
Sunderland – 260 pts (Engl; Engl Crea Writ; Dr Engl; Engl Lang Ling; Engl Film; Engl Lang Lit)
Ulster – BCC 260 pts (Engl courses)
Westminster – BCC (Chin Engl Lang) (IB 30 pts)
York St John – 260–300 pts (Engl Lang Ling)

240 pts **Anglia Ruskin** – 240–280 pts (Writ Engl Lit) (IB 28 pts)
Arts London – 240 pts (Mag Pub)
Bangor – 240–300 pts (Engl courses; Engl Lang courses)
Bishop Grosseteste – 240 pts (Engl courses)
Bolton – 240 pts (Crea Writ; Engl) (IB 24 pts)
Bradford – 240 pts (Engl)

Canterbury Christ Church – 240 pts (Engl; Engl Lang Comm)
Chester – 240–280 pts (Crea Writ) (IB 26 pts)
Cumbria – 240 pts (Engl Crea Writ; Engl)
East London – 240 pts (Engl Lit)
Glyndŵr – 240 pts (Engl; Engl Crea Writ)
Greenwich – 240 pts (Crea Writ; Eng Lang ELT)
Kingston – 240–360 pts (Engl Lang Comm courses)
London South Bank – 240 pts (Engl Dr Perf; Engl Crea Writ)
Portsmouth – 240–300 pts (Engl Lang courses; Crea Writ; Engl Dr; Engl Hist)
St Mary's – 240 pts (Engl; Crea Writ) (IB 28 pts)
Southampton Solent – 240 pts (Engl; Jrnl Engl Media; Engl Film)
Staffordshire – 240 pts (Engl Lit) (IB 28 pts)
Suffolk (Univ Campus) – 240–280 pts (Engl)
Worcester – 240–340 pts (Engl Lang St courses)
York St John – 240–280 pts (Engl Lit Crea Writ; Engl Lit courses)

220 pts   **Anglia Ruskin** – 220–260 pts (Engl Lang Engl Lang Teach)
Derby – 220–300 pts (Prof Writ Joint Hons)
Falmouth – 220 pts (Engl Crea Writ; Engl)
Kingston – 220–360 pts (Crea Writ)
Leeds Trinity – 220–260 pts (Engl Hist; Engl; Engl Writ; Engl Film St; Engl Media)
St Mark and St John – 220 pts (Engl Lit; Crea Writ; Ling Engl Lang)
Wolverhampton – 220 pts (Engl courses)

200 pts   **Anglia Ruskin** – 200–280 pts (Engl)
Bedfordshire – 200 pts (Engl courses; Crea Writ)
Blackburn (Coll) – 200 pts (Engl Lang Lit St; Engl Lang)
Blackpool and Fylde (Coll) – 200 pts (Engl Lang Lit Writ)
Bucks New – 200–240 pts (Crea Writ; Script)
Doncaster (Coll Univ Centre) – 200 pts (Engl)
East London – 200 pts (Engl Lang; Crea Prof Writ)
Grimsby (Univ Centre) – 200 pts (Engl St)
Leeds Trinity – 200–260 pts (Engl Jrnl)

180 pts   **Bradford** – 180–220 pts (Crea Writ)
Leeds Beckett – 180 pts (Engl Hist) (IB 24 pts)
West Anglia (Coll) – 180 pts (Engl Hist)

160 pts   **Norwich City (Coll)** – 160 pts (Engl Psy Soc; Engl Cult St)
Peterborough (Reg Coll) – 160 pts (Engl)
UHI – CC 160 pts (Lit)
Wolverhampton – 160–220 pts (Crea Prof Writ courses)

120 pts   **Anglia Ruskin** – DD (Sociol Engl; Hist Engl)
Trinity Saint David – 120–360 pts (Crea Writ; Engl)

80 pts   **Newham (CFE)** – 80 pts (Engl courses)

Alternative offers

See **Chapter 7** and **Appendix 1** for grades/UCAS Tariff points information for the International Baccalaureate, Scottish Highers/Advanced Highers, the Welsh Baccalaureate, the Irish Leaving Certificate, the Cambridge Pre-U Diploma, the Advanced Diploma and the Extended Project.

EXAMPLES OF FOUNDATION DEGREES IN THE SUBJECT FIELD
Greenwich; Plymouth.

CHOOSING YOUR COURSE (SEE ALSO CH.1)
Some course features
Birmingham Single Honours students choose between literature and some language or literature and language equally. Joint Honours students choose between all literature or all language. English can also be taken as a major or minor subject with American Literature or Creative Writing.

Durham English Literature is a wide-ranging course focusing on poetry, drama and the novel in Year 1 with modules on selected themes. Years 2 and 3 enable students to follow their special interest. Joint courses are offered with History and Philosophy and the subject can be studied in Combined Honours in Arts.

East Anglia The School of English Literature and Creative Writing offers a wide range of courses including American and English Literature, English Literature and Drama. There are also courses in English Literature with Creative Writing, English and Comparative Literature, and Literature and joint courses with History, Drama, American Literature, Politics, Film, Philosophy and Art History. Degree courses in Linguistics are also offered.

Exeter The English course provides a knowledge of the major texts, literary forms and periods of English literature and allows for considerable specialisation. The basic courses are the Renaissance, Shakespeare, the Restoration and the 18th century, and the 19th and 20th centuries. In Levels 2 and 3, specialisation takes place, with options including creative writing, American literature and postcolonial studies. English can also be taken with study in North America, or with Film Studies.

Leicester English is a diverse and flexible course with lectures and small-group teaching. A modular course is provided with a chronological approach to the major periods of English literature. Language is part of the curriculum in Years 1 and 2 and there is an optional year in Europe. Optional modules from other departments include Film Studies, Languages and History of Art.

Liverpool English Language and Literature can be studied from its origins in the Anglo-Saxon period to the modern period, covering all the major literary and linguistic developments. Optional courses are available in the second and third years. There are also seven joint courses with English including Communication Studies, languages, History and Philosophy.

London NCH This course consists of 12 modules; four modules are taken each year, including introduction to creative writing. In addition to degree subject modules, students study four modules in another degree subject and compulsory core modules in applied ethics, logic and critical thinking to make up the NCH diploma which is awarded alongside a degree.

Swansea In the English Literature syllabus, tragic drama, lyric poetry, theories and monsters (Dracula and Frankenstein) are studied in Part I. For Single Honours during Years 2 and 3 there are two core courses – literature from Chaucer to the present day and criticism – plus a choice of options. English with Gender covers the representation of gender in literary culture. English Language is also offered in a wide range of joint courses including with Welsh, Politics, European Languages and Geography. Language Studies courses are offered with subjects such as Latin, Ancient History and Italian.

Universities and colleges teaching quality See www.qaa.ac.uk; http://unistats.direct.gov.uk.

Top research universities and colleges (RAE 2008) (English Language and Literature) York; London (QM); Edinburgh; Manchester; Exeter; Oxford; Nottingham; Cambridge; De Montfort; Leeds; Warwick; Glasgow; St Andrews; Queen's Belfast; Liverpool; Newcastle.

Examples of sandwich degree courses Aston; Brighton; Coventry; Hertfordshire; Huddersfield; Loughborough; Southampton Solent; Surrey.

ADMISSIONS INFORMATION

Number of applicants per place (approx) Bangor 5; Bath Spa 8; Birmingham 7, (Engl Educ) 4; Birmingham City 9; Blackpool and Fylde (Coll) 2; Bristol 18; Bristol UWE 4; Brunel 10; Buckingham 2; Cambridge (A-Sxn Nrs Celt) 2, (Engl) 4.9; Cardiff (Engl Lit) 6; Central Lancashire 10; Chester 20; Chichester 4; Cumbria 24; De Montfort 7; Derby 6; Dundee 6; Durham 20; East Anglia (Engl Lit Dr) 22, (Engl Lit Crea Writ) 17, (Engl St) 12; Edge Hill 4; Exeter 13; Gloucestershire 35; Glyndŵr 2; Hertfordshire 6; Huddersfield 5; Hull 14; Hull (Coll) 1; Kingston 6; Lancaster 12; Leeds 10; Leeds Trinity 7; Leicester 6; Liverpool (Engl Comm St) 7; London (Gold) 9; London (King's) (Engl Film) 15; London (QM) 9; London (RH) 9; London (UCL) 13; London South Bank 5; Loughborough 40; Manchester (Engl Lit) 11, (Engl Lang) 7; Manchester Met 7; Middlesex 8; Newman 3; Northampton 3; Nottingham 22; Nottingham Trent 21; Oxford (success rate 25%), (Magdalen) 15; Oxford Brookes 15; Portsmouth 8; Reading 11; Roehampton 5; Salford 12; Sheffield 12; Sheffield Hallam 4; South Wales 8; Southampton 4; Stirling 9; Sunderland 10; Teesside 5; Trinity Saint David (Swansea) 4; Warwick 15, (Engl Thea) 26; Winchester 3; York 8; York St John 3.

Advice to applicants and planning the UCAS personal statement Applicants should read outside their subject. Details of any writing you have done (for example poetry, short stories) should be provided. Theatre visits and play readings are also important. Keep up-to-date by reading literary and theatre reviews in the national newspapers (keep a scrapbook of reviews for reference). Evidence is needed of a good writing style. Favourite authors, spare-time reading. Ability to write lucidly, accurately and succinctly. Evidence of literary enthusiasm. General interest in communications – verbal, visual, media. **Bristol** Deferred entry accepted in some cases. Late applications may not be accepted. **Manchester** Due to the detailed nature of entry requirements for English Literature and American Studies courses, we are unable to include full details in the prospectus. For complete and up-to-date information on our entry requirements for these courses, please visit our website at www.manchester.ac.uk/ugcourses.

Misconceptions about this course Birmingham City The study of English language means descriptive linguistics – the course won't necessarily enable students to speak or write better English. **Buckingham** Native speakers of English often do not realise that the EFL degree courses are restricted to non-native speakers of English. **East Anglia** (Engl Lit Crea Writ) This is not simply a creative writing course: English literature is the predominant element. **Liverpool** (Engl Comm St) The course is not a training in journalism, although some students go on to work in the press, radio or TV.

Selection interviews Yes Bangor (mature students), Birmingham, Brunel, Cambridge, Canterbury Christ Church, Chichester, East Anglia, Essex, Exeter, Gloucestershire, Huddersfield, Hull, Hull (Coll), Kingston, Lancaster, Leeds Trinity, London (Gold), London (RH), London South Bank, Middlesex, Newcastle, Nottingham, Oxford (Engl) 27%, (Engl Econ Mgt) 11%, (Engl Lang Lit) 21%, (Engl Mod Lang) 16%, Portsmouth, Reading, Roehampton, Trinity Saint David, Warwick; **Some** Bangor, Bath Spa, Birmingham City, Blackburn (Coll), Blackpool and Fylde (Coll), Bristol, Cardiff Met (UWIC), Chester, De Montfort, Derby, Dundee, Leeds, Liverpool (Engl Comm St), London (King's), London Met, Loughborough, Salford, Southampton, Trinity Saint David (Swansea), Truro (Coll), Wolverhampton.

Interview advice and questions Questions will almost certainly be asked on set A-level texts and any essays which have been submitted prior to the interview. You will also be expected to have read outside your A-level subjects and to answer questions about your favourite authors, poets, dramatists etc. Questions in the past have included: Do you think that class discussion plays an important part in your English course? What is the value of studying a text in depth rather than just reading it for pleasure? What is the difference between satire and comedy? Are books written by women different from those written by men? Why would you go to see a production of *Hamlet*? What are your views on the choice of novels for this year's Booker Prize? What books are bad for you? If you could make up a word, what would it be? Short verbal tests and a précis may be set. See also **Chapter 6**. **Buckingham** It is useful to know if there is any particular reason why students want a particular programme; for example, for the TEFL degree is a member of the family a teacher? **Cambridge** We look for interviewees who respond positively to ideas, can think on their feet, engage intelligently with critical issues and sustain an argument. If they don't evince any of these we reject them. What books are bad for you? **East Anglia** (Engl Lit Dr) How do you reconcile yourself to an academic interest in literature on the one hand and the belief in practical performance on the other? Interviews are accompanied by auditions. **Leeds** Interview questions based on information supplied in the personal statement. One third of the applicants are interviewed. Academic ability; current reading interests. **Liverpool** (Engl Comm St) General questions only. Reading interests, general interests, career ambitions. **London (King's)** Interview questions are based on the information in the personal statement. Applicants are asked to prepare a short literary text which will be discussed at interview. **London (UCL)** The interview will focus on an ability to discuss literature in terms of language, plot, characters and genre. Following the interview applicants will be asked to write a critical commentary on an example of unseen prose or verse. **Oxford** Is there a difference between innocence and naivety? If you could make up a word, what would it be? Why? Do you think *Hamlet* is a bit long? No? Well I do. Is the Bible a fictional work? Was Shakespeare a rebel? **Roehampton** Samples of work taken to interview and discussed. **Warwick** We may ask students to sight-read or to analyse a text. **York** Written essays are required to be submitted at interview.

Check **Chapter 4** when choosing your university and **Chapter 7** on how to read the subject tables.

Reasons for rejection (non-academic) Some are well-informed about English literature – others are not. Inability to respond to questions about their current studies. Lack of enthusiasm for the challenge of studying familiar subjects from a different perspective. Must be able to benefit from the course. Little interest in how people communicate with each other. They don't know a single thing about our course. **Bangor** We reject those who decline interviews. **Bristol** Not enough places to make offers to all those whose qualifications deserve one. **Cambridge** See Interview advice and questions. **East Anglia** (Engl Am Lit) Personal statement unconvincing in its commitment to American literature. (Other courses) Poor examples of work submitted. **Leeds** Unsuitable predictions. **Liverpool** (Engl Comm St) Student more suited to a practical course. Ungrammatical personal statement. **Oxford** (1) The essay she submitted was poorly written, careless and reductive and, in general, lacking in attention to the subject. She should be encouraged to write less and think more about what she is saying. She seems to put down the first thing that comes into her head. (2) We had the feeling that he rather tended to dismiss texts which did not satisfy the requirements of his personal canon and that he therefore might not be happy pursuing a course requiring the study of texts from all periods. (3) In her essay on Bronte she took a phrase from Arnold which was metaphorical (to do with hunger) and applied it literally, writing at length about the diet of the characters. **Reading** None. If they have reached the interview we have already eliminated all other factors. **Sheffield Hallam** Apparent lack of eagerness to tackle all three strands of the course (literature, language and creative writing). **Southampton** Insufficient or patchy academic achievement. Applicants coming from non-standard academic backgrounds are assessed in terms of their individual situations.

AFTER-RESULTS ADVICE
Offers to applicants repeating A-levels Higher Sheffield Hallam, Southampton (varies), Warwick; **Possibly higher** Lancaster, Newcastle, Oxford Brookes; **Same** Bangor, Birmingham City, Blackpool and Fylde (Coll), Bristol, Cambridge, Cardiff, Cardiff Met (UWIC), Chester, Chichester, Cumbria, De Montfort, Derby, Dundee, Durham, East Anglia, Edge Hill, Hull, Leeds, Leeds Trinity, Liverpool, Liverpool Hope, London (Gold), London (RH), Loughborough, Manchester Met, Newman, Nottingham, Nottingham Trent, Portsmouth, Reading, Roehampton, St Mary's, Salford, Sheffield, Staffordshire, Stirling, Suffolk (Univ Campus), Trinity Saint David, Ulster, Winchester, Wolverhampton, York, York St John.

GRADUATE DESTINATIONS AND EMPLOYMENT (2011/12 HESA)
English Studies graduates surveyed 9395 **Employed** 3920 **In voluntary employment** 470 **In further study** 2430 **Assumed unemployed** 815

Career note English graduates work in the media, management, public and social services, business, administration and IT, retail sales, the cultural industries and the teaching profession. Those who have undertaken courses in creative writing could aim for careers in advertising, public relations, journalism or publishing.

OTHER DEGREE SUBJECTS FOR CONSIDERATION
Communication Studies; Drama; Language courses; Linguistics; Literature; Media Studies.

ENVIRONMENTAL SCIENCES/STUDIES

(including **Conservation, Ecology, Environmental Health, Environmental Management** and **Meteorology**; see also **Biological Sciences, Biology, Engineering (Civil), Geography, Geology/Geological Sciences, Health Sciences/Studies, Marine/Maritime Studies, Town and Country Planning**)

Environmental Science/Studies courses need to be considered with care as, depending on their content and specialisms, they lead to very different careers. Environmental Health courses usually focus on the training of environmental health officers whilst Environmental Studies or Science degrees cover a range of subjects with options which may include biology, geography, geology, oceanography, chemistry, legal, social and political issues.

University of Hertfordshire

School of
Life and Medical Sciences

Innovative thinking for a more sustainable future

Understanding the relationship between society and the environment is ever more important in helping us manage our rapidly changing world. With a range of courses designed to place you at the forefront of this agenda, we will empower you to respond to challenges such as climate change, food security, biodiversity loss and urban change.

Our pioneering research has already made significant contributions to sustainability worldwide and our courses all uphold a strong tradition of practical experience and fieldwork. With access to our specialist field station, dedicated laboratories and facilities for geographical information analysis, you will gain the scientific and analytical skills that are highly sought after in this ever expanding area for employment.

Our range of courses include:

- BSc (Hons) Environmental Management
- BSc (Hons) Environmental Management with Agriculture
- BSc (Hons) Geography
- BSc (Hons) Human Geography
- BSc (Hons) Human Geography and Environmental Studies
- BSc (Hons) Physical Geography
- BSc (Hons) Sustainable Agriculture and Food Security (New for 2014)

Become more.

Find out more about our range of courses at:

go.herts.ac.uk/GEA

Useful websites www.cieh.org; www.ends.co.uk; www.enn.com; www.iagre.org.uk; www.defra.gov.uk; www.socenv.org.uk; www.ies-uk.org.uk; www.noc.soton.ac.uk.

NB The points totals shown to the left of the institutions are for ease of reference only. It must not be assumed that Tariff points are always used by institutions or that they can be substituted for an offer in grades. The level of an offer is not necessarily indicative of the quality of a course.

COURSE OFFERS INFORMATION

Subject requirements/preferences GCSE English, mathematics and a science (often chemistry or biology) usually required. **AL** One or two science subjects are usually stipulated; mathematics may be required. (Meteor) Mathematics, physics and another science may be required sometimes with specified grades, eg **Reading** mathematics and physics grade B.

Your target offers and examples of courses provided by each institution

380 pts London (UCL) – AAAe–AABe 380–360 pts (Env Geog) (IB 36–38 pts)

360 pts Edinburgh – AAA–BBB 360–300 pts (Env Arch; Chem Env Sust Chem; Ecol Env Sci Mgt; Ecol Env Sci; Env Geosci; Ecol; Geophys Meteor; Phys Meteor) (IB 37–34 pts)

Imperial London – AAA 360 pts (Ecol Env Biol) (IB 38 pts HL 6 biol chem/maths)

Leeds – AAA (Meteor Clim Sci (Int))

Sheffield – AAA incl biol+sci 360 pts (Ecol Cons Biol MBiolSci) (IB 37 pts)

York – AAA–ABB 320–360 pts (Chem Res Env) (IB 35–36 pts)

340 pts Birmingham – AAB–ABB 340–320 pts (Biol Sci (Env Biol)) (IB 34–35 pts)

Bristol – AAB–ABB 320–340 pts (Env Geosci) (IB 35–33 pts)

Cardiff – AAB–ABB 340–320 pts (Ecol) (IB 34 pts)

Durham – AAB 340 pts (Env Geosci) (IB 36 pts)

East Anglia – AAB–ABB (Env Earth Sci MSci; Clim Sci MSci; Env Sci MSci; Clim Sci (St Abrd); Env Geog Clim Chng; Env Earth Sci (St Abrd); Meteor Ocean) (IB 33 pts)

Exeter – AAB–BBB 340–300 pts (Cons Biol Ecol; Renew Ener MEng; Env Sci; Renew Ener) (IB 34–30 pts)

Glasgow – AAB 340 pts (Earth Sci) (IB 34 pts)

Lancaster – AAB (Env Sci (St Abrd); Sust Eng; Env Chem (St Abrd); Env Biol (St Abrd); Env Maths)

Leeds – AAB 340 pts (Env Bus) (IB 35 pts)

London (RH) – AAB 340 pts (Ecol Env) (IB 34 pts)

London LSE – AAB incl maths (Env Plcy Econ) (IB 37 pts HL 666)

Newcastle – AAB (Env Sci) (IB 30 pts)

St Andrews – AAB 340 pts (Geol; Env Earth Sci; Ecol Cons) (IB 35 pts)

Sheffield – AAB (Ecol Cons Biol) (IB 35 pts)

Warwick – AAB–ABB 340 pts (Biol Sci Env Res) (IB 34–36 pts)

York – AAB 340 pts (Ecol) (IB 35 pts)

320 pts Birmingham – ABB (Env Mgt; Pal Palaeoenv; Env Sci) (IB 32–34 pts)

Cardiff – ABB 320 pts (Env Geosci) (IB 30–32 pts)

East Anglia – ABB 320 pts (Meteor Ocean BSc; Env Sci; Env Geog Int Dev; Int Dev Env; Env Geophys; Env Earth Sci; Ecol; Clim Sci) (IB 32 pts)

Kent – ABB 320 pts (Env St; Env St Prof Pr) (IB 34 pts)

Lancaster – ABB (Env Chem; Env Biol; Env Sci; Ecol Cons) (IB 32 pts)

Leeds – ABB 320 pts (Sust Env Mgt; Env Sci) (IB 34 pts)

Leeds Beckett – ABB 320 pts (Env Des Eng) (IB 34 pts)

Leicester – ABB 320 pts (App Env Geol) (IB 32 pts)

Liverpool – ABB (Ecol Env; Env Sci) (IB 33 pts)

London (Birk) – ABB 320 pts (Env Mgt)

Manchester – ABB 320 pts (Env Sci; Env Res Geol) (IB 33 pts)

Nottingham – ABB–BBC 280–320 pts (Env Sci) (IB 32–38 pts)

Plymouth – ABB 320–360 pts (Mar Biol Cstl Ecol) (IB 24 pts)

Reading – 320 pts (Meteor; App Ecol Cons; Env Sci; Env Phys) (IB 31 pts)

Sheffield – ABB–BBB 320–300 pts (Lnd Archit) (IB 34 pts)

Southampton – ABB 320 pts +interview (Env Sci) (IB 34–32 pts HL 17–16 pts)
Sussex – ABB (Ecol Cons) (IB 32 pts)
York – ABB (Env Geog; Env Sci; Env Econ Env Mgt) (IB 34 pts)
300 pts Aberdeen – BBB 300 pts (Env Sci; Ecol) (IB 32 pts)
Bournemouth – 300 pts (Env Sci) (IB 31 pts)
Brighton – BBB (Ecol; Env Haz; Env Sci) (IB 32 pts)
Dundee – BBB-BCC 300–260 pts (Env Sci; Env Sust; Renew)
Edge Hill – 300 pts (Env Sci)
Glasgow – BBB 300 pts (Env Stwdshp (Dumfries Campus)) (IB 30 pts)
Gloucestershire – 300 pts (Ecol Env Sci)
Greenwich – 300 pts (Env Sci)
Huddersfield – BBB 300 pts (Bus St Env Mgt)
Keele – BBB 300 pts (Env Sust; App Env Sci courses) (IB 32 pts)
Liverpool – BBB (Env Plan) (IB 31 pts)
Liverpool Hope – 300–320 pts (Env Sci)
London (QM) – 300–340 pts (Env Sci) (IB 30–34 pts)
Manchester – BBB (Env Mgt)
Northumbria – BBB 300 pts (Env Mgt; Geog Env Mgt) (IB 26 pts)
Nottingham – ABC/BBB-BCC (Env Biol) (IB 34–26 pts)
Plymouth – BBB 300 pts (Bld Surv Env) (IB 30 pts)
Queen's Belfast – BBB 300 pts (Lnd Use Env Mgt; Env Biol)
Reading – 300 pts (Env Cntry Mgt; Meteor Clim)
285 pts Glasgow Caledonian – 285 pts (Env Mgt Plan)
280 pts Aberystwyth – 280–320 pts (Ecol; Env Biosci)
Bangor – 280–320 pts (Mar Env St; Env Sci)
Bristol UWE – 280 pts (Env Sci) (IB 27 pts)
Coventry – 280–300 pts (Clim Chng Sust)
Essex – BBB-BBC 280–300 pts (Ecol) (IB 26–28 pts)
Hertfordshire – 280 pts (Env St)
Leeds Beckett – 280 pts (Env Hlth) (IB 25 pts)
Manchester Met – 280 pts (Clim Chng; Env Ent (St Abrd); Ecol Cons (St Abrd); Env Mgt Sust (St Abrd); Env Sci (St Abrd); Physl Geog) (IB 28 pts)
Oxford Brookes – BBC 280 pts (Env Sci) (IB 30 pts)
Plymouth – 280 pts (Env Sci; Env Biol; Archit Tech Env)
Sheffield – 280 pts (Env Sci)
Staffordshire – 280 pts (Env Sust) (IB 24 pts)
Stirling – BBC (Env Sci; Ecol; Cons Biol Mgt; Env Sci Out Educ) (IB 32 pts)
Ulster – 280 pts (Env Hlth)
260 pts Bangor – 260–320 pts (Env Cons; Env Sci; Ecol; Env Mgt; Agric Cons Env; App Ter Mar Ecol) (IB 28 pts)
Bradford – 260 pts (Env Sci)
Derby – 260–300 pts (Cntry Mgt; Env Haz Joint Hons)
Greenwich – 260–300 pts (Civ Eng Wtr Env Mgt)
Hertfordshire – 260 pts (Env Mgt)
Hull – 260 pts (Env Sci)
Liverpool John Moores – 260 pts (Env Hlth) (IB 24 pts)
Northampton – 260–300 pts (Env Sci courses)
Portsmouth – 260–320 pts (Mar Env Sci) (IB 26 pts)
Sheffield Hallam – 260 pts (Env Cons; Env Sci)
Teesside – 260–280 pts (Env Sci; Env Hlth)
240 pts Canterbury Christ Church – 240 pts (Env Sci; Ecol Cons)
Chester – 240–280 pts (Nat Haz Mgt) (IB 26 pts)
East Anglia – CCC (Env Sci Fdn Year)
Glyndŵr – 240 pts (Geog Ecol Env; Env Sci)
Kingston – 240–280 pts (Env Mgt; Env Sci)

Middlesex – 240 pts (Env Pblc Hlth)
Northampton – 240–280 pts (App Cons Biol) (IB 24 pts)
Nottingham Trent – 240 pts (Env Cons; Env Sci)
Plymouth – 240 pts (Env Constr Surv) (IB 24 pts)
Salford – 240 pts (Env Geog) (IB 24 pts)
Sparsholt (Coll) – 240–280 pts (Cons Wldlf Mgt)
Worcester – 240–280 pts (Env Mgt; Cons Ecol; Env Sci; Ecol)
220 pts **Bath Spa** – 220–280 pts (Env Sci)
Cardiff Met (UWIC) – 220–240 pts (Env Hlth)
Ulster – 220 pts (Env Sci courses) (IB 24 pts)
200 pts **Bishop Burton (Coll)** – 200 pts (Env Cons)
Central Lancashire – 200–240 pts (Env Mgt; Env Haz Sci Plcy Mgt)
Glyndŵr – 200 pts (Sust Dev)
Salford – 200 pts (Env Mgt) (IB 24 pts)
Southampton Solent – 200 pts (Geog Env St)
Wolverhampton – 200 pts (Env Hlth)
160 pts **Trinity Saint David (Swansea)** – 160 pts (Env Cons)
UHI – CC–AA 160–240 pts (Env Sci; Nat Env Sci; Arch Env St)
120 pts **Bournemouth** – 120 pts (Mar Ecol Cons) (IB 24 pts)

Open University – contact +44 (0)845 300 6090 **or** www.openuniversity.co.uk/you (Env St)

Alternative offers
See **Chapter 7** and **Appendix 1** for grades/UCAS Tariff points information for the International Baccalaureate, Scottish Highers/Advanced Highers, the Welsh Baccalaureate, the Irish Leaving Certificate, the Cambridge Pre-U Diploma, the Advanced Diploma and the Extended Project.

EXAMPLES OF FOUNDATION DEGREES IN THE SUBJECT FIELD
Askham Bryan (Coll); Bournemouth; Cumbria; Glyndŵr; Leeds City (Coll); Manchester (Coll); Nottingham Trent; Suffolk (Univ Campus); Writtle (Coll).

CHOOSING YOUR COURSE (SEE ALSO CH.1)
Some course features
Birmingham Specialisation in four pathways (applied ecology, water in the environment, atmospheric processes and earth surface processes) follows a broad first year Environmental Science course. There is also a course in Environmental Geoscience.
Brighton The Environmental Sciences course involves a study of the human and physical environment, ecology, energy and pollution. There are also degrees in Environmental Hazards, covering geography, health, pollution and human hazards, and Earth and Ocean Science, Environmental Biology and Ecology.
Keele The Applied Environmental Science Joint Honours course covers biology, geology and chemistry and is taken with Physical Geography. Over 20 Joint Honours combinations are possible. An optional field trip to the European Alps is offered in Year 2.
Kingston Pathways in Environmental Science include ecology, conservation and resource management. Options include languages, business and human geography. Environmental Studies is offered with a range of subjects including Business Management. There are also degree courses in Natural History, Sustainable Development, Environmental Hazards and Disaster Management.
Manchester The Environmental Science degree programme enables students to specialise in their particular fields of interest within biology, earth sciences, chemistry or biology. Entrance scholarships available.
Newcastle The Environmental Science course covers management, ecology, tropical environments, marine sciences and biological conservation. Courses are also offered in Countryside Management and Rural Studies.

Universities and colleges teaching quality See www.qaa.ac.uk; http://unistats.direct.gov.uk.

Top research universities and colleges (RAE 2008) (Geography and Environmental Studies) Bristol; Cambridge; Durham; Oxford; London (QM); Leeds; London (King's); London (UCL); London LSE; Sheffield; London (RH); Aberystwyth; London (Birk); Reading; East Anglia; Manchester; Southampton. (Earth Systems and Environmental Sciences) Cambridge; Oxford; London (UCL); Bristol; London (RH).

Examples of sandwich degree courses Brighton; Bristol UWE; Coventry; Glasgow Caledonian; Greenwich; Hertfordshire; Kingston; Liverpool John Moores; Manchester Met; Middlesex; Nottingham Trent; Reading; Salford; Teesside; Ulster.

ADMISSIONS INFORMATION

Number of applicants per place (approx) Abertay 5; Aberystwyth 3; Bangor 3; Bath Spa 2; Birmingham 5; Bournemouth 4; Bradford 3; Bristol 7; Bristol UWE 1; Cardiff Met (UWIC) 4; Coventry 9; De Montfort 9; Dundee 6; Durham 5; East Anglia 7; Edinburgh 1; Essex 3; Glasgow Caledonian 1; Gloucestershire 11; Glyndŵr 3; Greenwich 2; Harper Adams 5; Hertfordshire 5; Hull 8; Kingston 3; Lancaster 11; Leeds (Env Sci Ener) 2; Liverpool John Moores 5; London (King's) 5; London (RH) 8; London LSE 7; Manchester Met (Env Sci) 5; Northampton 4; Northumbria 8; Nottingham 6; Nottingham Trent 3; Oxford Brookes 13; Plymouth 8; Portsmouth 5; Roehampton 3; Salford 8; Sheffield Hallam 8; Southampton 5; Stirling 10; Strathclyde 1; Trinity Saint David 3; Ulster 16; Wolverhampton 2; Worcester 7; York 4.

Advice to applicants and planning the UCAS personal statement 'We want doers, not just thinkers' is one comment from an admissions tutor. Describe any field courses which you have attended; make an effort to visit one of the National Parks. Discuss these visits and identify any particular aspects which impressed you. Outline travel interests. Give details of work as a conservation volunteer and other outside-school activities. Strong communication skills, people-oriented work experience. Watch your spelling and grammar! What sparked your interest in Environmental Science? Discuss your field trips. (Env Hlth courses) A basic knowledge of environmental health as opposed to environmental sciences. Work experience in an environmental health department is looked upon very favourably. See also **Appendix 3**. **Lancaster** Two A-level subjects required from biology, chemistry, computing, environmental science, geography or geology.

Misconceptions about this course **Bangor** Students should note that only simple mathematical skills are required for this course. **Leeds** (Ener Env Sci) Note that the course is closer to environmental technology than to environmental science. **Southampton** This is not just a course for environmentalists, for example links with BP, IBM etc. **Wolverhampton** This is a course in Environmental Science, not Environmental Studies: there is a difference. **York** (Env Econ Env Mgt) Some students worry that the economics part of the course will be too difficult, which is not the case.

Selection interviews **Yes** Bradford, Bristol UWE, Cambridge, Coventry, Durham, Gloucestershire, Greenwich, Harper Adams (advisory), Hertfordshire, Kingston, Manchester Met, Newcastle, Nottingham, Nottingham Trent, Oxford Brookes, Sheffield Hallam, Strathclyde, Sussex, Trinity Saint David; **Some** Anglia Ruskin, Bangor, Bath Spa, Birmingham, Cardiff Met (UWIC), Derby, East Anglia, London (King's), Plymouth, Salford, Southampton, Staffordshire, York; **No** Dundee.

Interview advice and questions Environmental issues are constantly in the news, so keep abreast of developments. You could be asked to discuss any particular environmental problems in the area in which you live and to justify your stance on any environmental issues on which you have strong opinions. See also **Chapter 6**. **Bath Spa** Questions on school work, current affairs and field courses. **East Anglia** Can you display an informed interest in any aspect of environmental science?

Reasons for rejection (non-academic) Inability to be aware of the needs of others.

AFTER-RESULTS ADVICE

Offers to applicants repeating A-levels **Higher** Greenwich, Lancaster, London (King's), Nottingham, Nottingham Trent, Strathclyde; **Possibly higher** Aberystwyth, Bradford, Northumbria; **Same** Bangor, Birmingham, Brighton, Cardiff Met (UWIC), Derby, Dundee, East Anglia, Leeds, Liverpool John Moores, Manchester Met, Plymouth, Salford, Southampton, SRUC, Ulster, Wolverhampton.

Check **Chapter 4** when choosing your university and **Chapter 7** on how to read the subject tables.

GRADUATE DESTINATIONS AND EMPLOYMENT (2011/12 HESA)
See **Biological Sciences**.

Career note Some graduates find work with government departments, local authorities, statutory and voluntary bodies in areas like land management and pollution control. Others go into a range of non-scientific careers.

OTHER DEGREE SUBJECTS FOR CONSIDERATION
Biological Sciences; Biology; Chemistry; Earth Sciences; Environmental Engineering; Geography; Geology; Meteorology; Ocean Sciences/Oceanography; Town and Country Planning.

EUROPEAN STUDIES

(see also **French, German, International Relations, Languages, Russian and East European Studies**)

European Studies is a popular subject and in many cases offers the language student an opportunity to study modern languages within the context of a European country (covering economics, politics, legal, social and cultural aspects). In these courses there is usually a strong emphasis on the written and spoken word. It is important to note, also, that many courses in other subjects offer the opportunity to study in Europe.

Useful websites www.europa.eu; www.britishcouncil.org/erasmus; see also **Languages**.

NB The points totals shown to the left of the institutions are for ease of reference only. It must not be assumed that Tariff points are always used by institutions or that they can be substituted for an offer in grades. The level of an offer is not necessarily indicative of the quality of a course.

COURSE OFFERS INFORMATION
Subject requirements/preferences **GCSE** English and a foreign language for all courses and possibly mathematics. Grades may be stipulated. **AL** A modern language usually required.

Your target offers and examples of courses provided by each institution

400 pts **London (UCL)** – A*AAe 400 pts (Euro Soc Pol St) (IB 39 pts)

380 pts **Durham** – A*AA 380 pts (Maths (Euro St)) (IB 38 pts)
London (UCL) – AAAe 380 pts (Pol E Euro St) (IB 38 pts)

360 pts **London (King's)** – AAA–AAB 360–340 pts (Euro St (Fr/Ger/Span)) (IB 33–35 pts)
London (UCL) – AABe 360 pts (Lang Cult) (IB 36 pts)
Newcastle – AAA–ABB 360–320 pts (Gov EU St) (IB 34–37 pts)

340 pts **Exeter** – A*AA–AAB 380–340 pts (Econ Pol Euro St) (IB 38–34 pts)
Glasgow – AAB 340 pts (Cnt E Euro St) (IB 34 pts)
Southampton – AAB 340 pts (Langs Contemp Euro St) (IB 34 pts HL 17 pts)

320 pts **Bath** – ABB–AAA 320–360 pts (Modn Langs Euro St) (IB 34–36 pts)
Birmingham – ABB (Modn Langs Euro St; Euro Pol Soty Econ)
Essex – ABB–BBB (Euro St; Euro St Fr/Ger/Ital/Span) (IB 32–30 pts)
Kent – ABB (Euro Econ; Euro St (Soc Sci); Euro St (Hum); Euro St Hum Comb Lang courses) (IB 33 pts)
Leeds – ABB (Euro St Lang)
Leicester – ABB 320 pts (Euro St)
London (RH) – ABB 320 pts (Euro St Fr/Ger/Ital/Span) (IB 34 pts)
Northumbria – ABB (Euro St Lang)
Nottingham – ABB 320 pts (Modn Euro St) (IB 32 pts)
Swansea – ABB–BBB 320–300 pts (Geog Euro St) (IB 33–32 pts)

300 pts **Aberdeen** – BBB 300 pts (Euro St) (IB 32 pts)
Aberystwyth – BBB 300 pts (Euro St Joint Hons) (IB 28 pts)

Dundee – BBB 300 pts (Euro St) (IB 30 pts)
Reading – ABC–BBB 300 pts (Euro St) (IB 30 pts)
280 pts **Stirling** – BBC 280 pts (Euro Film Media) (IB 32 pts)
260 pts **Nottingham Trent** – 260 pts (Euro St Joint Hons)
200 pts **Portsmouth** – 200–280 pts (Euro St Int Rel) (IB 28 pts)

Open University – contact +44 (0)845 300 6090 **or** www.openuniversity.co.uk/you (Euro St)

Alternative offers
See **Chapter 7** and **Appendix 1** for grades/UCAS Tariff points information for the International Baccalaureate, Scottish Highers/Advanced Highers, the Welsh Baccalaureate, the Irish Leaving Certificate, the Cambridge Pre-U Diploma, the Advanced Diploma and the Extended Project.

CHOOSING YOUR COURSE (SEE ALSO CH.1)
Some course features
Aberystwyth The four-year BA course in European Studies combines a European language (French, German or Spanish) with a study of European economic, political and legal institutions. There are also separate degree courses in European Languages, European History and European Politics.
Essex European Studies is offered with a range of subjects including French, German, Italian, Spanish, and Politics and Economics. Beginners' courses are possible and it is possible to transfer between courses. Previous language skills are not a necessity as the year abroad is taught in English.
London (UCL) European Social and Political Studies is a four-year degree that combines the study of one or two European languages (from Dutch, French, German, Italian, Russian, Scandinavian languages and Spanish) with a chosen humanities or social science specialisation including Anthropology, Economics, Geography, History, Law, Philosophy or Politics. The third year is spent abroad. Degree courses are also offered in East European Studies with Bulgarian, Czech, Slovak, Finnish, Hungarian, Polish, Romanian, Serbian, and Ukrainian.
Northumbria The European Studies courses cover the Humanities and Social Sciences plus French or Spanish languages expertise. An additional European or Oriental language can be studied.
Portsmouth The course in European Studies and International Relations focuses on the changes now taking place in Europe covering historical, economic, political, legal and cultural aspects.
Southampton The Contemporary Europe degree comprises a study of the history and politics of Europe and European Union institutions, with options in economics, history, law or politics. Two European languages are studied from French, German or Spanish. Portuguese is offered as a minor language. Scholarships available.

Universities and colleges teaching quality See www.qaa.ac.uk; http://unistats.direct.gov.uk.

Top research universities and colleges (RAE 2008) Southampton; Sussex; Birmingham; Portsmouth; Cardiff; Bath; Liverpool; Aberystwyth.

ADMISSIONS INFORMATION
Number of applicants per place (approx) Aberystwyth 10; Aston 5; Cardiff 5; Dundee 6; Durham 2; East Anglia 11; Hull 6; Kent 11; Lancaster 9; Leicester 15; London (King's) 7; London (UCL) 2; London South Bank 6; Loughborough 4; Northumbria 7; Nottingham 6; Nottingham Trent 12; Portsmouth 5.

Advice to applicants and planning the UCAS personal statement Try to identify an interest you have in the country relevant to your studies. Visits to that country should be described. Read the national newspapers and magazines and keep up-to-date with political and economic developments. Show your interest in the culture and civilisation of Europe as a whole, through, for example, European travel. Show your motivation for choosing the course and give details of your personal achievements and any future career plans, showing your international awareness and perspective.

Selection interviews **Yes** Durham, East Anglia, Hull, London Met, London South Bank; **Some** Cardiff, Dundee, Kent (not usually), Liverpool John Moores; **No** Essex, Portsmouth, Reading.

Interview advice and questions Whilst your interest in studying a language may be the main reason for applying for this subject, the politics, economics and culture of European countries are constantly in the news. You should keep up-to-date with any such topics concerning your chosen country and be prepared for questions. A language test may occupy part of the interview. See also **Chapter 6**. **Loughborough** No tests. Interview designed to inform students about the course.

Reasons for rejection (non-academic) Poor powers of expression. Lack of ideas on any issues. Lack of enthusiasm.

AFTER-RESULTS ADVICE
Offers to applicants repeating A-levels **Higher** Aberystwyth, East Anglia; **Same** Aston, Cardiff, Dundee, Liverpool John Moores, London South Bank, Loughborough.

GRADUATE DESTINATIONS AND EMPLOYMENT (2011/12 HESA)
Graduates surveyed 210 Employed 95 In voluntary employment 20 In further study 65 Assumed unemployed 10

Career note See **Languages**.

OTHER DEGREE SUBJECTS FOR CONSIDERATION
Business and Management; History; International Relations; Politics; Language courses.

FILM, RADIO, VIDEO and TV STUDIES

(see also **Art and Design (Graphic Design), Communication Studies/Communication, Engineering (Acoustics and Sound), Media Studies, Photography**)

A wide range of courses in this field are on offer although applicants should be aware that many courses cover theoretical or historical aspects of the subject. Students wishing to follow courses with practical applications must check with the institution beforehand to determine how much time in the course is spent on actual film-making or video production.

Useful websites www.bfi.org.uk; www.film.com; www.allmovie.com; www.bksts.com; www.imdb.com; www.fwfr.com; www.bafta.org; www.movingimage.us; film.britishcouncil.org; www.filmsite.org; www.festival-cannes.com/en; www.bbc.co.uk/careers/home; www.rogerebert.com.

NB The points totals shown to the left of the institutions are for ease of reference only. It must not be assumed that Tariff points are always used by institutions or that they can be substituted for an offer in grades. The level of an offer is not necessarily indicative of the quality of a course.

COURSE OFFERS INFORMATION
Subject requirements/preferences **GCSE** English usually required. Courses vary, check prospectuses. **AL** English may be stipulated for some courses.

Your target offers and examples of courses provided by each institution
380 pts **London (UCL)** – AAAe–ABBe (Mod Lang Film St) (IB 34–38 pts)
360 pts **Lancaster** – AAA 360 pts (Film Engl Lit) (IB 36 pts HL 16 pts)
       London (King's) – AAA 360 pts (Compar Lit Film St; Engl Film St) (IB 35 pts)
       St Andrews – AAA–AAB 360–340 pts (Film St courses) (IB 35–36 pts)
340 pts **Brunel** – AAB 340 pts (Engl Film TV St) (IB 35 pts)
       Exeter – AAB–ABB 340–320 pts (Film St)
       Kent – AAB–ABB 340–320 pts (Film St courses; Art Film; Film) (IB 34 pts HL 17 pts)
       Lancaster – AAB 340 pts (Film; Film Sociol) (IB 35 pts)
       London (King's) – AAB 340 pts (Film St) (IB 35 pts HL 6 Engl)
       Manchester – AAB–BBB (Scrn St courses) (IB 31–36 pts)

Newcastle – AAB 340 pts (Film St Comb Hons) (IB 35 pts)

Southampton – AAB 340 pts (Film St; Film Engl; Film Phil; Film Hist; Film Fr/Ger/Span) (IB 34 pts HL 17 pts)

Sussex – AAB–ABB (Film St; Dr St Film St; Am St courses) (IB 34–36 pts)

Warwick – AAB (Film Lit; Film St) (IB 36 pts)

York – AAB 340 pts (Film TV Prod) (IB 35 pts)

320 pts **Birmingham** – ABB (Film St courses) (IB 32 pts)

Bournemouth – 320 pts (Film Prod Cnma) (IB 32 pts)

East Anglia – ABB (Fr Film TV; Span Film TV; Jap Film TV; Film courses; Film Am St; Film TV St; Film Engl St) (IB 32 pts)

Essex – ABB–BBB 320–300 pts (Film St Lit) (IB 32–30 pts)

Glasgow – ABB (Film TV St Joint Hons) (IB 36 pts)

Leeds – ABB (Wrld Cnma courses) (IB 34 pts HL 16 pts)

Leicester – ABB (Film Media St)

Liverpool – ABB 320 pts (Comb Hons Film St (Euro)) (IB 30–35 pts)

London (QM) – 320 pts (Film St) (IB 32 pts)

London (RH) – ABB–ABbb (Film TV St) (IB 34 pts)

Nottingham – ABB 320 pts (Film TV St Cult Sociol; Film TV St Am St; Film TV Hisp St; Film TV St; Film TV St Fr) (IB 32 pts)

Reading – ABB–AAC 320 pts (Film; Engl Lit Film Thea; Film Thea) (IB 32 pts)

Surrey – ABB 320 pts (Film St; Film St Crea Writ)

Westminster – ABB (Film TV Prod) (IB 30 pts)

300 pts **Aberdeen** – BBB (Film Vis Cult) (IB 28 pts)

Aberystwyth – 300–320 pts (Scngrph Thea Des; Film TV St) (IB 30 pts)

Birmingham City – 300 pts (Film Prod Tech; Film Tech Vis Efcts)

Bournemouth – 300–320 pts (TV Production) (IB 31–32 pts HL 555)

Brighton – (Film Scrn St) (IB 32 pts)

Bristol – (Film St)

Bristol UWE – 300 pts (Film) (IB 26 pts)

Brunel – BBB 300 pts (Film TV St; Thea Film TV St; Gms Des Film TV St) (IB 32 pts)

Dundee – BBB (Engl Film St) (IB 30 pts)

Edinburgh (CA) – BBB 300 pts +portfolio (Film TV) (IB 34 pts)

Edinburgh Queen Margaret – BBB 300 pts (Thea Film St) (IB 30 pts)

Essex – ABB–BBB 320–300 pts (Film St) (IB 32–30 pts)

Hertfordshire – 280–300 pts (Film TV (Fctn/Doc/Enter); Engl Lang Comm Film)

Keele – BBB 300 pts (Film St) (IB 32 pts)

Northumbria – 300 pts (Film TV St)

Queen's Belfast – BBB/BBCb (Film St courses)

Reading – BBB (Art Film Thea) (IB 30 pts)

280 pts **Bournemouth Arts** – BBC 280 pts +portfolio +interview (Animat Prod)

Bradford – 280 pts (Film St; TV Prod)

Edge Hill – 280 pts (Film TV Prod; Media Film TV; Film St)

Edinburgh Napier – BBC 280 pts (Engl Film)

Gloucestershire – 280–300 pts (Film St; Dig Film Prod; Film St Media Writ)

Greenwich – 280 pts (Film St; Film TV Prod; Dig Film Prod)

Hull – 280 pts (Film St)

Leeds Trinity – 280 pts (Film St; Film TV St; TV)

Lincoln – 280 pts (Film TV; Film TV Jrnl Joint Hons)

Liverpool John Moores – 280 pts (Film St; Crea Writ Flm St) (IB 29 pts)

London Met – 280 pts (Film Broad Prod; Jrnl Film TV St)

Manchester Met – 280 pts (Film TV Cult St; Filmm; St Film) (IB 28 pts)

Norwich Arts – BBC (Film Mov Imag Prod) (IB 25 pts)

Oxford Brookes – BBC (Film St) (IB 30 pts)

Roehampton – 280 pts (Film)

Sheffield Hallam – 280 pts (Film Media Prod)

South Wales – 280-300 pts (Film St; Film Vid)
Stirling – BBC (Film Media; Glob Cnma Cult) (IB 32 pts)
Suffolk (Univ Campus) – 280 pts (Film)
Teesside – 280 pts +interview (TV Film Prod)
Ulster – BBC 280 pts (Film St courses)

260 pts **Bangor** – 260-300 pts (Mus Film St; Film St courses)
Bath Spa – 260-300 pts (Film Scrn St courses)
Bournemouth Arts – BCC-BBC 260-280 pts +portfolio +interview (Film Prod)
Canterbury Christ Church – BCC 260 pts (Film Rad TV St courses) (IB 24 pts)
Central Lancashire – 260-300 pts (TV Prod; Film Prod Scrnwrit)
Chester – 260-300 pts (Rad Prod courses; Rad; TV Prod) (IB 28 pts)
De Montfort – 260 pts (Film St Media Comm; Aud Rec Tech; Film St Joint Hons)
Derby – 260 pts (Film Vid Prod; Media Prod)
Edinburgh Queen Margaret – 260 pts (Film Media)
London Met – 260 pts (Film St)
Northampton – 260-280 pts (Film TV St courses)
Nottingham Trent – 260 pts (Film TV Joint Hons)
Salford – 260-300 pts (Film St) (IB 31 pts)
Sunderland – 260 pts (Film Media; Media Prod (TV Rad); Dig Film Prod; Engl Film; Media Prod (Vid N Media))
Winchester – 260-300 pts (Film St courses)
York St John – 260-300 pts (Film TV Prod)

240 pts **Arts London** – 240 pts (Film TV)
Central Lancashire – 240-260 pts (Film Prod; Film Media)
Chester – 240-280 pts (Film St) (IB 26 pts)
Chichester – BBC-CCC 280-240 pts (Film TV St)
Cumbria – 240 pts (Film TV Prod)
Derby – 240 pts (Film TV St; Film St)
Glyndŵr – 240 pts (Std Rec Perf Tech)
Huddersfield – 240 pts (Dig Film Vis Efcts Prod; Film Animat Mus Enter)
Kingston – 240 pts (Film St)
Leeds Beckett – 240 pts (Film Mov Imag Prod) (IB 24 pts)
London South Bank – 240 pts (Film St; Dig Film Vid)
Manchester Met – 240-280 pts (Film Media St) (IB 28 pts)
Nottingham Trent – 240 pts (Des Film TV; Dig Media Tech; Dig Media Tech)
Portsmouth – 240-300 pts (Film St courses)
Ravensbourne – CC-AA 160-240 pts (Dig Film Prod) (IB 28 pts)
St Mary's – 240 pts (Film Pop Cult) (IB 28 pts)
Sheffield Hallam – 240 pts (Film St; Film Scrnwrit)
Southampton Solent – 240 pts (Film TV St; Film; Engl Film; Scrnwrit; TV Vid Prod; TV Std Prod)
Staffordshire – 240 pts (Film TV Rad St; Media (Film) Prod)
West London – 240 pts (Film Prod)
West Scotland – CCC 240 pts (Film Scrnwrit; Broad Prod) (IB 24 pts)
Worcester – 240-300 pts (Film St Scrn Writ)

220 pts **Anglia Ruskin** – 220-260 pts (Film St)
Creative Arts – 220 pts (Film Prod) (IB 30 pts)
Derby – 220-300 pts (Film TV St Joint Hons)
Falmouth – 220 pts (Film)
Leeds Trinity – 220-260 pts (TV Prod; Engl Film St)
Sunderland – 220 pts (Photo Vid Dig Imag)
Wolverhampton – 160-220 pts (Film St courses)
Worcester – 220-260 pts (Dig Film Prod)

200 pts **Anglia Ruskin** – 200-240 pts (Film TV Prod)
Bedfordshire – 200 pts (TV Prod)

Check **Chapter 4** when choosing your university and **Chapter 7** on how to read the subject tables.

Bucks New – 200–240 pts (Film TV Prod)
Doncaster (Coll Univ Centre) – 200 pts (Mov Imag Prod)
East London – 200 pts (Film St; Film Vid (Theor Prac))
Hull – 200 pts (TV Film Des)
Hull (Coll) – 200 pts (TV Film Des)
Middlesex – 200–300 pts (Film St; Film Media Cult St)
Plymouth (CA) – 200 pts (Film)
Trinity Saint David (Swansea) – 200 pts (Vid Art; Doc Vid; Vid)
Wolverhampton – 200 pts (Film Media Cult St)
160 pts **Colchester (Inst)** – 160 pts (Film Mus Sndtrk Prod)
80 pts **RConsvS** – 80 pts (Dig Film TV)

Alternative offers
See **Chapter 7** and **Appendix 1** for grades/UCAS Tariff points information for the International Baccalaureate, Scottish Highers/Advanced Highers, the Welsh Baccalaureate, the Irish Leaving Certificate, the Cambridge Pre-U Diploma, the Advanced Diploma and the Extended Project.

EXAMPLES OF FOUNDATION DEGREES IN THE SUBJECT FIELD
Accrington and Rossendale (Coll); Barking and Dagenham (Coll); Bournemouth and Poole (Coll); Bradford (Coll Univ Centre); Brooksby Melton (Coll); Cleveland (CAD); Colchester (Inst); Cornwall (Coll); Croydon (Coll); East Surrey (Coll); Exeter (Coll); Farnborough (CT); Grimsby (Univ Centre); Manchester (Coll); Nescot; SAE Inst; Solihull (Coll); Truro (Coll); Warwickshire (Coll).

CHOOSING YOUR COURSE (SEE ALSO CH.1)
Some course features
Bradford Film Studies is a largely theoretical course; 20% of the time is spent on practical work. The degree is also offered as a sandwich course, with students being given the opportunity to work in industry for a year.
Bucks New The Film and TV Production course covers camera work, lighting, sound and editing. A creative production-based course is also offered in Digital Film Art. There is also a scriptwriting course.
East Anglia Emphasis on the history and theory of film with practical units offered in Years 2 and 3. Study abroad available in Europe, USA and Australia.
Essex Film Studies is a broad course focusing on the social and historical aspects of the media. It is offered as a joint programme with Creative Writing, History of Art, Literature or History and American Studies, and a year abroad is available.
Hertfordshire These degrees are offered in Film and Television specialising in Fiction Documentary or Entertainment. There are also degrees in Screen Cultures with Media. There is also a course in Special Effects.
Manchester Theoretical and academic courses are offered in Film Studies which can be combined with Media and Cultural Studies, Creative Writing or Video. There are also courses in TV Journalism and Production.
Manchester Met Practical work is the main focus of the Studies in Film programme whilst the Film and Media Studies course is a predominantly critical and textual academic study.
Oxford Brookes The Film Studies course comprises theoretical and practical work covering production, script-writing and film projects.
Reading The Film, Theatre and Television course integrates practical work, a critical study of film and theatre and the historical and social significance of television.
Surrey The course covers the study of contemporary film-making, the film industry, film history, aesthetics and theory.
York (Film TV Prod) This new BSc course combines practical production work with theoretical and historical understanding, involving students in a wide range of technical roles.

Universities and colleges teaching quality See www.qaa.ac.uk; http://unistats.direct.gov.uk.

Top research universities and colleges (RAE 2008) See **Drama**.

Examples of sandwich degree courses Aberystwyth; Birmingham City; Bradford; Bristol UWE; Hertfordshire; Huddersfield; Leeds Beckett; Portsmouth; Southampton Solent; Surrey; Teesside; Wolverhampton.

ADMISSIONS INFORMATION

Number of applicants per place (approx) Bournemouth 30; Bournemouth Arts 9; Brunel 10; Canterbury Christ Church 50; Cardiff 11; Central Lancashire 5; East Anglia (Film Engl St) 7, (Film Am St) 5; Kent 30; Leicester 9; Leicester (Coll) 5; Liverpool John Moores 17; London Met 7; Portsmouth 20; Sheffield Hallam 60; Southampton 5; Southampton Solent 7; Staffordshire 31; Stirling 12; Warwick 18; Westminster 41; York 4; York St John 6.

Advice to applicants and planning the UCAS personal statement **Bournemouth Arts** Any experience in film-making (beyond home videos) should be described in detail. Knowledge and preferences of types of films and the work of some producers should be included on the UCAS application. Read film magazines and other appropriate literature to keep informed of developments. Show genuine interest in a range of film genres and be knowledgeable about favourite films, directors and give details of work experience or film projects undertaken. You should also be able to discuss the ways in which films relate to broader cultural phenomena, social, literary, historical.

Misconceptions about this course That an A-level in film or media studies is required; it is not. That it's Film so it's easy! That the course is all practical work. Some applicants believe that these are Media courses. Some applicants believe that Film and TV Studies is a training for production work. **Bournemouth Arts** (Animat Prod) This is not a Film Studies course but a course based on traditional animation with supported computer image processing. **De Montfort** Some believe that this is a course in practical film-making: it is not, it is for analysts and historians. **Winchester** That graduation automatically leads to a job in broadcasting!

Selection interviews Most institutions will interview applicants in this subject. **Yes** Birmingham City, Bournemouth, Bournemouth Arts, Brunel, Canterbury Christ Church, Chichester, Reading, York, York St John; **Some** East Anglia, Southampton, Staffordshire, Wolverhampton; **No** Essex, Liverpool John Moores, Nottingham.

Interview advice and questions Questions will focus on your chosen field. In the case of films be prepared to answer questions not only on your favourite films but on the work of one or two directors you admire and early Hollywood examples. See also **Chapter 6**. **Bournemouth** (TV Script Film) Successful applicants will be required to submit a 20-page screenplay. A good applicant will have the ability to discuss media issues in depth, to have total commitment to TV and video production and will have attempted to make programmes. **Bournemouth Arts** Written piece prior to interview. Questions at interview relevant to the portfolio/reel. **Staffordshire** We assess essay-writing skills.

Reasons for rejection (non-academic) Not enough drive or ambition. No creative or original ideas. Preference for production work rather than practical work. Inability to articulate the thought process behind the work in the applicant's portfolio. Insufficient knowledge of media affairs. Lack of knowledge of film history. Wrong course choice, wanted more practical work.

AFTER-RESULTS ADVICE

Offers to applicants repeating A-levels **Higher** Bournemouth Arts, Glasgow, Manchester Met; **Same** De Montfort, East Anglia, Liverpool Hope, St Mary's, Staffordshire, Stirling, Winchester, Wolverhampton, York St John.

GRADUATE DESTINATIONS AND EMPLOYMENT (2011/12 HESA)
See **Media Studies**.

Career note Although this is a popular subject field, job opportunities in film, TV and radio are limited. Successful graduates frequently have gained work experience with companies during their undergraduate years. The transferable skills (verbal communication etc) will open up other career opportunities.

Check **Chapter 4** when choosing your university and **Chapter 7** on how to read the subject tables.

OTHER DEGREE SUBJECTS FOR CONSIDERATION
Animation; Communication Studies; Creative Writing; Media Studies; Photography.

FINANCE

(including **Banking, Financial Services** and **Insurance**; see also **Accountancy/Accounting**)

Financial Services courses provide a comprehensive view of the world of finance and normally cover banking, insurance, investment, building societies, international finance, accounting and economics. Major banks offer sponsorships for some of the specialised Banking courses.

Useful websites www.cii.co.uk; www.secinst.co.uk; www.financialadvice.co.uk; www.efinancialnews. com; www.worldbank.org; www.ifslearning.ac.uk; www.ft.com.

NB The points totals shown to the left of the institutions are for ease of reference only. It must not be assumed that Tariff points are always used by institutions or that they can be substituted for an offer in grades. The level of an offer is not necessarily indicative of the quality of a course.

COURSE OFFERS INFORMATION
Subject requirements/preferences **GCSE** Most institutions will require English and mathematics grade C minimum. **AL** Mathematics may be required or preferred.

Your target offers and examples of courses provided by each institution

400 pts **Imperial London** – A*A*A (Maths Stats Fin) (IB 39 pts HL 7 maths)
 London (UCL) – A*AAe-AAAe (Stats Econ Fin) (IB 38-39 pts HL 18-19 pts incl 7 maths)

380 pts **Exeter** – A*AA-AAB 380-340 pts (Econ Fin; Econ Fin Int St) (IB 38-34 pts)
 Nottingham – A*AA-AAA (Fin Maths) (IB 38-36 pts HL 6 maths)
 Warwick – A*AA-AAAb 380 pts (Acc Fin) (IB 38 pts)

360 pts **Bath** – AAA 360 pts (Acc Fin) (IB 38 pts)
 Birmingham – AAA 360 pts (Mny Bank Fin; Mny Bank Fin courses) (IB 36-38 pts)
 Bristol – AAA-AAB 360-340 pts (Acc Fin) (IB 37-35 pts)
 City – AAA 360 pts (Bank Int Fin; Inv Fin Risk Mgt; Fin Econ) (IB 35 pts)
 Edinburgh – AAA-BBB 360-300 pts (Acc Fin; Econ Fin) (IB 37-34 pts)
 Glasgow – AAA-A*AB (Acc Fin; Fin Stats) (IB 36 pts)
 Lancaster – AAA-A*AB 360 pts (Acc Fin; Fin Maths; Acc Fin Maths; Fin) (IB 36-34 pts)
 Leeds – A*AB-AAA (Maths Fin; Acc Fin; Int Bus Fin; Econ Fin) (IB 35 pts HL 17 pts)
 London (UCL) – AAA-AAB 360-340 pts (Eng (Mech Bus Fin) BEng) (IB 36-38 pts)
 London LSE – AAA (Acc Fin; Stats Fin) (IB 38 pts HL 666)
 Manchester – A*AB-AAB 340-360 pts (Maths Fin; Maths Fin Maths) (IB 36 pts)
 Newcastle – AAA-AAB 360-340 pts (Bus Acc Fin; Econ Fin) (IB 35-38 pts)
 St Andrews – AAA (Fin Econ) (IB 36 pts)
 Southampton – AAA incl maths (Maths Fin; Econ Fin) (IB 36 pts HL 18 pts)
 Strathclyde – AAA (Acc Fin; Mech Eng Fin Mgt MEng) (IB 36 pts)
 York – AAA-AAB (Econ Fin) (IB 36 pts HL 666)

340 pts **Aston** – AAB 340 pts (Fin) (IB 35 pts)
 Birmingham – AAB (Acc Fin) (IB 34-36 pts)
 Brunel – AAB-ABB 340-320 pts (Fin Acc) (IB 35 pts)
 Cardiff – AAB 340 pts (Acc Fin; Bank Fin; Bank Fin Euro Lang; Fin Mgt) (IB 35 pts)
 Durham – AAB 340 pts (Acc Fin) (IB 36 pts)
 Exeter – AAA-AAB 360-340 pts (Acc Fin) (IB 36-34 pts)
 Lancaster – AAB 340 pts (Fin Econ) (IB 34 pts)
 Leicester – AAB (Fin Maths; Bank Fin) (IB 28-32 pts)
 Liverpool – AAB (Acc Fin; e-Fin) (IB 35 pts)
 London (QM) – AAB 340 pts (Maths Fin Acc) (IB 34 pts)
 London (RH) – AAB (Fin Bus Econ) (IB 35 pts)

Loughborough – AAA-AAB 340-360 pts (Acc Fin Mgt; Bank Fin Mgt; Bus Econ Fin) (IB 36 pts)

Manchester – AAB (Acc Fin; Fin) (IB 35 pts)

Newcastle – AAB-ABB 340-320 pts (Acc Fin; Fin Maths Mgt; Fin Maths) (IB 35-37 pts)

Nottingham – AAB (Acc Fin Contemp Chin; Fin Acc Mgt) (IB 32-34 pts)

Reading – AAB (Invest Fin Bank; Acc Fin; Fin Inv Bank) (IB 35 pts)

Sheffield – AAB incl maths (Fin Math) (IB 35 pts HL 6 maths)

Southampton – AAB 340 pts (Acc Fin) (IB 34 pts HL 17 pts)

Surrey – AAA-AAB 340-360 pts (Acc Fin; Econ Fin; Fin Maths) (IB 36-35 pts)

Sussex – AAB-ABB 340-320 pts (Fin Bus; Acc Fin) (IB 34 pts)

York – AAB-AAA (Econ Ecomet Fin; Acc Bus Fin Mgt) (IB 36-34 pts HL 666)

320 pts **Bournemouth** – 320 pts (Acc Fin; Fin Bus; Fin Econ) (IB 32 pts)

Bradford – ABB 320 pts (Acc Fin; Fin Plan)

Brunel – ABB 320 pts (Econ Bus Fin) (IB 33 pts)

Essex – ABB-BBB 320-300 pts (Acc Fin; Fin Mgt; Fin; Fin Econ)

ifs (UC) – 320-340 pts (Fin Invest Rk) (IB 32 pts)

Kent – ABB (Acc Fin; Fin Econ) (IB 34 pts)

Kingston – ABB 320 pts (Acc Fin) (IB 27 pts)

Lancaster – ABB (Acc Fin Comp Sci)

Lincoln – 320 pts (Acc Fin)

Liverpool – ABB 320 pts (Law Acc Fin; Maths Fin) (IB 33 pts)

Northumbria – 320 pts (Fin Inv Mgt)

Plymouth – 320 pts (Maths Fin) (IB 30 pts)

Queen's Belfast – ABB/BBBb (Fin) (IB 32 pts)

Sheffield – ABB (Acc Fin Mgt) (IB 35 pts)

Strathclyde – ABB 320 pts (Fin courses) (IB 33 pts)

Swansea – ABB-BBB 320-300 pts (Fin Econ Acc; Acc Fin) (IB 33-32 pts)

300 pts **Aberdeen** – BBB (Int Rel Fin; Fin) (IB 28 pts)

Aberystwyth – 300 pts (Bus Fin; Acc Fin courses) (IB 27 pts)

Brighton – BBB 300 pts (Acc Fin; Fin Inv) (IB 32 pts)

Bristol UWE – BBB 300 pts (Acc Fin; Bank Fin) (IB 26 pts)

Buckingham – 300 pts (Law Bus Fin)

Cardiff Met (UWIC) – 300 pts (Bus Mgt Fin; Int Econ Fin)

Coventry – BBB 300 pts (Fin Econ)

Dundee – BBB 300 pts (Fin; Int Fin; Int Bus Fin) (IB 30 pts)

East Anglia – BBB (Bus Fin Econ) (IB 32 pts)

Greenwich – 300 pts (Econ Bank; Acc Fin)

Heriot-Watt – BBB 300 pts (Bus Fin) (IB 29 pts)

Hertfordshire – 300 pts (Acc Fin)

Huddersfield – BBB 300 pts (Acc Fin; Bus Fin Serv)

Hull – BBB 300 pts (Bus Fin Mgt; Fin Mgt)

Keele – ABC (Acc Fin; Fin courses)

Leeds Beckett – 300 pts (Acc Fin) (IB 26 pts)

Middlesex – 300 pts (Acc Fin)

Oxford Brookes – BBB (Acc Fin) (IB 31 pts)

Plymouth – 300 pts (Acc Fin) (IB 26 pts)

Portsmouth – 300 pts (Fin)

Sheffield Hallam – BBB 300 pts (Acc Fin; Bus Fin Mgt)

South Wales – BBB 300 pts (Fin Maths)

Swansea – BBB-BCC 300-260 pts (Bus Mgt (Fin)) (IB 32-30 pts)

280 pts **Abertay** – BBC (Acc Fin)

Birmingham City – 280 pts (Acc Fin; Bus Fin; Econ Fin)

Brighton – BBC (Maths Fin) (IB 28 pts)

Central Lancashire – 280 pts (Acc Fin St)

Chichester – 280 pts (Fin Econ) (IB 30 pts)

Check **Chapter 4** when choosing your university and **Chapter 7** on how to read the subject tables.

ifs University College
Incorporated by Royal Charter

Professional degrees for careers in financial services

Based in the heart of the City of London, **ifs** *University College* provides the essential knowledge that you'll need for a wide range of careers in the financial sector.

ifs *University College* programmes have been specifically created to develop the key skills that employers are looking for in the next generation of financial services professionals.

With unrivalled links to the financial services industry, **ifs** *University College* places employability at the heart of all of its degree programmes and its alumni can be found working for many of the world's largest financial institutions.

BSc (Hons) in Banking Practice and Management	**UCAS Code N310**
BSc (Hons) in Finance and Accounting for Financial Services	**UCAS Code NN34**
BSc (Hons) in Finance, Investment and Risk	**UCAS Code N300**
BSc (Hons) in Business, Enterprise and Finance	**UCAS Code 4K25**
BSc (Hons) in Politics, Finance and Economics	**UCAS Code TBC**

ifs *University College* is a registered charity, incorporated by Royal Charter.

Coventry – BBC 280 pts (Acc Fin; Fin Inv) (IB 29 pts)
De Montfort – 280 pts (Fin; Fin Mgt; Econ Fin)
Gloucestershire – 280 pts (Acc Fin Mgt; Bus Fin Mgt)
Hertfordshire – 280 pts (Fin Maths)
Lincoln – 280 pts (Bus Fin)
Liverpool John Moores – 280 pts (Acc Fin) (IB 29 pts)
London South Bank – BBC 280 pts (Acc Fin) (IB 25 pts)
Manchester Met – 260–280 pts (Acc Fin; Fin Mgt; Fin Serv Plan Mgt) (IB 28 pts)
Nottingham Trent – 280 pts (Acc Fin; Fin Maths; Econ Fin Bank)
Oxford Brookes – BBC (Econ Fin Int Bus) (IB 30 pts)
Portsmouth – 280 pts (Acc Fin; Fin Mgt Bus)
Salford – 280–320 pts (Bus Fin Mgt; Fin Acc)
Sheffield Hallam – 280 pts (Int Fin Econ; Int Fin Invest; Int Fin Bank)
South Wales – BBC 280 pts (Acc Fin)
Stirling – BBC (Fin) (IB 32 pts)
West London – 280 pts (Bus St Fin)
Westminster – BBC (Fin Mgt)
Winchester – 280–320 pts (Acc Fin) (IB 26 pts)
270 pts **ifs (UC)** – 270–300 pts (Bank Prac Mgt; Fin Acc Fin Serv) (IB 30 pts)
260 pts **Bangor** – 260–300 pts (Acc Fin; Bank Fin; Mgt Bank Fin)
Buckingham – BBB–BCC 260–300 pts (Acc Fin Mgt)
Greenwich – 260 pts (Bus Fin; Fin Maths)
Hertfordshire – 260 pts (Fin)
Kaplan Holborn (Coll) – 260 pts (Econ Fin)
Northampton – 260–280 pts (Fin Serv Mgt)
Plymouth – 260 pts (Fin Econ) (IB 24 pts)
Portsmouth – 260–300 pts (Econ Fin Bank; Maths Fin Mgt; Int Fin Tr)
Robert Gordon – BCC (Acc Fin) (IB 28 pts)
Sunderland – 260 pts (Bus Fin Mgt; Acc Fin)
240 pts **Bradford (Coll Univ Centre)** – 240 pts (Fin Serv)
Canterbury Christ Church – CCC 240 pts (Acc Fin; Bus Fin) (IB 24 pts)
Chester – 240–280 pts (Acc Fin) (IB 26 pts)
East London – 240 pts (Acc Fin) (IB 25 pts)
Edinburgh Napier – CCC 240 pts (Fin Serv) (IB 26 pts)
Glasgow Caledonian – CCC 240 pts (Fin Inv Risk)
Heriot-Watt – CCC 240 pts (Acc Fin) (IB 24 pts)
London Met – 240 pts (Acc Fin; Bank Fin)
London Regent's – CCC 240 pts (Glob Mgt) (IB 32 pts)
Plymouth – 240 pts (Int Fin)
Staffordshire – 240 pts (Acc Fin) (IB 24 pts)
Suffolk (Univ Campus) – 240–280 pts (Bus Mgt Fin; Acc Fin)
Teesside – 240 pts (Acc Fin) (IB 30 pts)
Ulster – 240 pts (Bank Fin)
Wolverhampton – 240 pts (Acc Fin) (IB 24 pts)
230 pts **York St John** – 230–300 pts (Acc Fin)
200 pts **Bedfordshire** – 200 pts (Int Fin; Bus St (Fin))
Bucks New – 200–240 pts (Ftbl Bus Fin; Acc Fin; Bus Fin)
Croydon (Coll) – 200 pts (Bus Fin)
East London – 200 pts (Fin Mny Bank)
Kingston – 200 pts (Bank Fin)
London Met – 200 pts (Fin Maths)
Middlesex – 200–280 pts (Bank Fin)
Peterborough (Reg Coll) – 200 pts (Acc Fin)
West London – 200 pts (Acc Fin)
York St John – 200–240 pts (Bus Mgt (Fin))

180 pts **Abertay** – DDD 180 pts (Fin Bus)
160 pts **Kaplan Holborn (Coll)** – 160 pts (Acc Fin)
Trinity Saint David (Swansea) – 160 pts (Bus Fin)
120 pts **Kaplan Holborn (Coll)** – 120 pts (Bus Mgt Fin)
Norwich City (Coll) – 120 pts (Bus Mgt (Fin Acc))
80 pts **Greenwich (Sch Mgt)** – A*A*-EE 80–280 pts (Acc Fin)

Alternative offers
See **Chapter 7** and **Appendix 1** for grades/UCAS Tariff points information for the International Baccalaureate, Scottish Highers/Advanced Highers, the Welsh Baccalaureate, the Irish Leaving Certificate, the Cambridge Pre-U Diploma, the Advanced Diploma and the Extended Project.

EXAMPLES OF FOUNDATION DEGREES IN THE SUBJECT FIELD
Blackburn (Coll); Chichester (Coll); Cornwall (Coll); Croydon (Coll); Dudley (Coll); Hertfordshire; Hopwood Hall (Coll); Loughborough (Coll); Manchester (Coll); Newcastle (Coll); Nottingham New (Coll); St Mark and St John; Truro (Coll).

CHOOSING YOUR COURSE (SEE ALSO CH.1)
Some course features
Brighton (Fin Invest) The course in Finance and Investment shares a common first year with the Economics and Finance degree, making transfers possible.
Durham A course in Business Finance covering economics, management, marketing and international money. It shares a first year with Accountancy and Business degrees with options to transfer at the end of the year.
Reading Courses are offered in Finance and Investment Banking or Property Investment. Internships can be arranged during summer vacations.
Surrey The course in Financial Mathematics is designed to match the needs of industry and can be taken to include a Professional Training year adding considerably to employment prospects.

Universities and colleges teaching quality See www.qaa.ac.uk; http://unistats.direct.gov.uk.

Top research universities and colleges (RAE 2008) See **Accountancy/Accounting**.

Examples of sandwich degree courses Abertay; Aston; Bath; Birmingham City; Bournemouth; Bradford; Brighton; Bristol UWE; Brunel; Cardiff Met (UWIC); Chichester; City; Coventry; De Montfort; Derby; Durham; Gloucestershire; Greenwich; Heriot-Watt; Hertfordshire; Huddersfield; Kent; Kingston; Lancaster; Leeds Beckett; Liverpool John Moores; London Met; Loughborough; Manchester Met; Middlesex; Nottingham Trent; Oxford Brookes; Plymouth; Portsmouth; Queen's Belfast; Salford; Sheffield Hallam; Surrey; Sussex; Teesside; Trinity Saint David (Swansea); West London; Westminster; Wolverhampton; Worcester; York.

ADMISSIONS INFORMATION
Number of applicants per place (approx) Aberystwyth 4; Bangor 10; Birmingham 3; Birmingham City 13; Bristol UWE 4; Buckingham 4; Cardiff 10; Central Lancashire 6; City 10; Dundee 5; Durham 4; Loughborough 35; Manchester 22; Middlesex 3; Northampton 3; Portsmouth 4; Sheffield Hallam 4.

Advice to applicants and planning the UCAS personal statement Visits to banks or insurance companies should be described, giving details of any work experience or work shadowing done in various departments. Discuss any particular aspects of finance etc which interest you. See also **Appendix 3**.

Misconceptions about this course Many applicants believe that they can only enter careers in banking and finance when they graduate. In fact, business and industry provide wide-ranging opportunities.

Selection interviews **Yes** Huddersfield; **Some** Buckingham, Dundee, Staffordshire, Stirling; **No** City.

Interview advice and questions Banking involves both high street and merchant banks, so a knowledge of banking activities in general will be expected. In the past mergers have been discussed and also the role of the Bank of England in the economy. The work of the accountant may be discussed. See also **Chapter 6**.

Reasons for rejection (non-academic) Lack of interest. Poor English. Lacking in motivation and determination to complete the course.

AFTER-RESULTS ADVICE
Offers to applicants repeating A-levels **Higher** Glasgow; **Possibly higher** Bangor; **Same** Birmingham, Birmingham City, Bradford, Cardiff, City, Dundee, Edinburgh Napier, London Met, Loughborough, Northumbria, Stirling.

GRADUATE DESTINATIONS AND EMPLOYMENT (2011/12 HESA)
Graduates surveyed 1780 **Employed** 950 **In voluntary employment** 40 **In further study** 400 **Assumed unemployed** 165

Career note Most graduates enter financial careers. Further study is required to qualify as an accountant and to obtain other professional qualifications, eg Institute of Banking.

OTHER DEGREE SUBJECTS FOR CONSIDERATION
Accountancy; Actuarial Studies; Business Studies; Economics.

FOOD SCIENCE/STUDIES and TECHNOLOGY

(see also **Agricultural Sciences/Agriculture, Biochemistry, Consumer Studies/Sciences, Dietetics, Hospitality and Event Management, Nutrition**)

Biochemistry, microbiology, dietetics, human nutrition, food processing and technology are components of Food Science courses as well as being degree courses in their own right (and appropriate alternative courses). The study depends on a secure foundation of several pure sciences: chemistry and two subjects from physics, mathematics, biology, botany or zoology. Only students offering subjects from these fields are likely to be considered. Food Technology covers the engineering aspects of food processing and management. A number of bursaries are offered by the food industry. Check with admissions tutors. See also **Appendix 3**.

Useful websites www.sofht.co.uk; www.ifst.org; www.defra.gov.uk; www.iagre.org.

NB The points totals shown to the left of the institutions are for ease of reference only. It must not be assumed that Tariff points are always used by institutions or that they can be substituted for an offer in grades. The level of an offer is not necessarily indicative of the quality of a course.

COURSE OFFERS INFORMATION
Subject requirements/preferences **GCSE** English, mathematics and a science. **AL** One or two mathematics/science subjects; chemistry may be required.

Your target offers and examples of courses provided by each institution
340 pts **Newcastle** – AAB–ABB 340–320 pts (Fd Mark Nutr) (IB 34–35 pts)
320 pts **Leeds** – ABB 320 pts (Fd Sci; Fd Sci Nutr) (IB 34 pts)
Newcastle – ABB 320 pts (Fd Hum Nutr) (IB 34 pts)
Nottingham – ABB–BBB 320–300 pts (Fd Sci; Nutr Fd Sci) (IB 30–32 pts)
Reading – ABB–BBB 320–300 pts (Fd Sci Bus; Fd Sci; Nutr Fd Sci; Fd Tech Bioproc)
Surrey – ABB 320 pts (Nutr Fd Sci; Fd Sci Microbiol) (IB 34 pts)
300 pts **Heriot-Watt** – BBB 300 pts (Biol Sci (Fd Bev Sci); Brew Distil) (IB 27 pts)
Queen's Belfast – BBB 300 pts (Fd Qual Sfty Nutr)
Reading – BBB–ABC 300 pts (Fd Mark Bus Econ)

280 pts **Brighton** – BBC (Vit Oeno) (IB 30 pts)
Cardiff Met (UWIC) – 280 pts (Food Prod Mgt)
Leeds Trinity – 280 pts (Nutr Fd)
Northumbria – 280 pts (Fd Sci Nutr)
Sheffield Hallam – 280 pts (Fd Nutr; Fd Mark Mgt)

260 pts **Bath Spa** – 260–300 pts (Fd Nutr)
Derby – 260–280 pts (Culn Art)
Glasgow Caledonian – BCC 260 pts (Fd Biosci)
Huddersfield – BCC 260 pts (Fd Nutr Hlth)
Liverpool John Moores – 260 pts (Fd Nutr; Fd Des Tech)
Teesside – 260–280 pts (Fd Nutr)

240 pts **Abertay** – CCC 240 pts (Fd Consum Sci; Fd Nutr Hlth; Fd Prod Des)
Birmingham (UC) – 240 pts (Fd Mark Mgt; Culn Arts Mgt; Fd Consum Mgt) (IB 24 pts)
CAFRE – 240 pts (Fd Des Nutr; Food Tech)
Cardiff Met (UWIC) – 240 pts (Fd Sci Tech)
Coventry – CCC 240 pts (Fd Sci Nutr) (IB 27 pts)
Reaseheath (Coll) – 240 pts (Fd Tech)
Royal Agricultural Univ – 240 pts (Fd Prod Sply Mgt; Bus Mgt (Int Fd Agri Bus))
Ulster – 240 pts (Fd Nutr)

220 pts **Harper Adams** – 220–260 pts (Agri-Fd Mark Bus St; Fd Consum St)
200 pts **London South Bank** – CDD 200 pts (Fd Nutr)

Alternative offers
See **Chapter 7** and **Appendix 1** for grades/UCAS Tariff points information for the International Baccalaureate, Scottish Highers/Advanced Highers, the Welsh Baccalaureate, the Irish Leaving Certificate, the Cambridge Pre-U Diploma, the Advanced Diploma and the Extended Project.

EXAMPLES OF FOUNDATION DEGREES IN THE SUBJECT FIELD
Bridgwater (Coll); Brighton; Duchy (Coll); Grimsby (Univ Centre); Leeds City (Coll); Loughborough (Coll); Middlesex; Neath Port Talbot (Coll); Nottingham New (Coll); Oxford Brookes; Plymouth; Warwickshire (Coll); Worcester.

CHOOSING YOUR COURSE (SEE ALSO CH.1)
Some course features
Coventry The Food Science and Nutrition course deals with food analysis, food safety and human nutrition. There is also a four-year Dietetics course in which they seek 'strong interpersonal skills, adaptability and flexibility'.
Heriot-Watt The course in Biological Science (Food and Beverage) is biology-based with an emphasis on food and nutrition as well as aspects of beverage science, including brewing and distilling.
Liverpool John Moores The Home Economics (Food Design Technology) course qualifies graduates to work in the consumer and services industries, including food product development, journalism and product development.
Reading (Fd Tech) The course focuses on food products manufacture, food engineering and food materials, chemicals and microbiology (with bioprocessing).

Universities and colleges teaching quality See www.qaa.ac.uk; http://unistats.direct.gov.uk.

Top research universities and colleges (RAE 2008) See **Agricultural Sciences/Agriculture** and **Nutrition**.

Examples of sandwich degree courses Birmingham (UC); Cardiff Met (UWIC); Coventry; Huddersfield; Kingston; London South Bank; Northumbria; Queen's Belfast; Reading; Sheffield Hallam.

ADMISSIONS INFORMATION
Number of applicants per place (approx) Bath Spa 4; Cardiff Met (UWIC) 1; Huddersfield 4; Leeds 5; Liverpool John Moores 2; London South Bank 3; Newcastle 13; Nottingham 7; Oxford Brookes 20; Queen's Belfast 10; Sheffield Hallam 4; Surrey 17.

Advice to applicants and planning the UCAS personal statement Visits, work experience or work shadowing in any food manufacturing firm, or visits to laboratories, should be described on your UCAS application. Keep up-to-date with developments by reading journals relating to the industry.

Misconceptions about this course Some applicants confuse food technology with catering or hospitality management. Applicants under-estimate the job prospects. **Leeds** Food Science is not food technology, catering or cooking. It aims to understand why food materials behave in the way they do, in order to improve the nutritive value, safety and quality of the food we eat.

Selection interviews Yes London South Bank, Queen's Belfast, Reading; **Some** Abertay, Bath Spa, Leeds, Nottingham, Salford, Surrey; **No** Liverpool John Moores.

Interview advice and questions Food science and technology is a specialised field and admissions tutors will want to know your reasons for choosing the subject. You will be questioned on any experience you have had in the food industry. More general questions may cover the reasons for the trends in the popularity of certain types of food, the value of junk food and whether scientific interference with food is justifiable. See also **Chapter 6**. **Leeds** Questions asked to ensure that the student understands, and can cope with, the science content of the course.

Reasons for rejection (non-academic) Too immature. Unlikely to integrate well. Lack of vocational commitment.

AFTER-RESULTS ADVICE
Offers to applicants repeating A-levels Higher Heriot-Watt, Leeds; **Possibly higher** Nottingham; **Same** Abertay, Liverpool John Moores, Queen's Belfast, Salford, Sheffield Hallam, Surrey.

GRADUATE DESTINATIONS AND EMPLOYMENT (2011/12 HESA)
Food and Beverage Studies graduates surveyed 455 **Employed** 240 **In voluntary employment** 0 **In further study** 115 **Assumed unemployed** 25

Career note Employment levels for food graduates are high mainly in manufacturing and retailing and increasingly with large companies.

OTHER DEGREE SUBJECTS FOR CONSIDERATION
Biochemistry; Biological Sciences; Biology; Biotechnology; Chemistry; Consumer Studies; Crop Science; Dietetics; Health Studies; Hospitality Management; Nutrition; Plant Science.

FORESTRY
(see also **Agricultural Sciences/Agriculture**)

Forestry is concerned with the establishment and management of woodlands and forests for timber production, environmental, conservation and amenity purposes.

Useful websites www.iagre.org.uk; www.forestry.gov.uk; www.rfs.org.uk; www.charteredforesters.org; www.iom3.org/content/wood-technology; www.woodlandtrust.org.uk/learn/british-trees.

NB The points totals shown to the left of the institutions are for ease of reference only. It must not be assumed that Tariff points are always used by institutions or that they can be substituted for an offer in grades. The level of an offer is not necessarily indicative of the quality of a course.

COURSE OFFERS INFORMATION
Subject requirements/preferences GCSE English, mathematics or science usually required. Check prospectuses. **AL** Two science subjects are usually stipulated which can include mathematics, geography or geology.

Your target offers and examples of courses provided by each institution
300 pts **Aberdeen** – BBB 300 pts (Frsty; Frst Sci) (IB 32 pts)
260 pts **Bangor** – 260–320 pts (Frsty; Cons Frst Ecosys)
Myerscough (Coll) – 260 pts (Arbor Urb Frsty) (IB 24 pts)
240 pts **Cumbria** – 240 pts (Frst; Wdlnd Cons)
Sparsholt (Coll) – 240–280 pts (Wdlnd Cons Mgt)
60 pts **UHI** – D–A 60–120 pts (Sust Frst Mgt)

Alternative offers
See **Chapter 7** and **Appendix 1** for grades/UCAS Tariff points information for the International Baccalaureate, Scottish Highers/Advanced Highers, the Welsh Baccalaureate, the Irish Leaving Certificate, the Cambridge Pre-U Diploma, the Advanced Diploma and the Extended Project.

EXAMPLES OF FOUNDATION DEGREES IN THE SUBJECT FIELD
Brighton; Sparsholt (Coll).

CHOOSING YOUR COURSE (SEE ALSO CH.1)
Some course features
Aberdeen Accredited by the Institute of Chartered Foresters, the Forestry degree gives students full exemption from Part I examinations, as well as the opportunity to travel with overseas field trips.
Bangor Students on the four-year Conservation and Forest Ecosystems course spend 7–12 months of practical work with a forestry organisation.
UHI This applied fieldwork-based course focuses on the practical aspects of either forest or arboricultural conservation and management. It provides a technical management qualification and includes wood technology, woodland ecology and conservation, environmental economics, environmental change and capital project planning.

Universities and colleges teaching quality See www.qaa.ac.uk; http://unistats.direct.gov.uk.

Examples of sandwich degree courses Bangor; Cumbria.

ADMISSIONS INFORMATION
Number of applicants per place (approx) Bangor 2.

Advice to applicants and planning the UCAS personal statement Contact the Forestry Commission and the Woodland Trust and try to arrange visits to forestry centres, local community woodlands and forests and to the Woodland Trust's sites. Discuss the work with forest officers and learn about future plans for specific forest areas and describe any visits made. Mention any experience of forestry or wood processing industries (for example, visits to forests and mills, work experience in relevant organisations). See also **Appendix 3**.

Misconceptions about this course **Bangor** That the course provides practical training in forestry (for example, in the use of chainsaws and pesticides) or wood processing. It does not: it is intended to educate future managers, for example; not to train forestry or mill workers.

Selection interviews Most institutions.

Interview advice and questions Work experience or field courses attended are likely to be discussed and questions asked such as: What is arboriculture? On a desert island how would you get food from wood? How do you see forestry developing in the next hundred years? What aspects of forestry are the most important? See also **Chapter 6**. **Bangor** Why are you interested in forestry?

AFTER-RESULTS ADVICE
Offers to applicants repeating A-levels **Same** Bangor.

GRADUATE DESTINATIONS AND EMPLOYMENT (2011/12 HESA)
Graduates surveyed 125 **Employed** 65 **In voluntary employment** 5 **In further study** 20 **Assumed unemployed** 10

Career note Opportunities exist with the Forestry Commission as supervisors, managers and in some cases, scientists. Other employers include private landowners (especially in Scotland), co-operative forest societies, local authorities and commercial firms.

OTHER DEGREE SUBJECTS FOR CONSIDERATION

Agriculture; Biological Sciences; Countryside Management; Crop Science; Ecology; Environmental Sciences; Woodland and Wildlife Management.

FRENCH

(see also **European Studies, Languages**)

Applicants should select courses according to the emphasis which they prefer. Courses could focus on literature or language (or both), or on the written and spoken word, as in the case of interpreting and translating courses, or on the broader study of French culture, political and social aspects found on European Studies courses.

Useful websites http://europa.eu; www.visavis.org; www.bbc.co.uk/languages; www. languageadvantage.com; www.languagematters.co.uk; www.iol.org.uk; www.reed.co.uk/multilingual; www.cilt.org.uk; www.lemonde.fr; www.institut-francais.org.uk; www.academie-francaise.fr; www. institut-de-france.fr; www.sfs.ac.uk; http://fs.oxfordjournals.org.

NB The points totals shown to the left of the institutions are for ease of reference only. It must not be assumed that Tariff points are always used by institutions or that they can be substituted for an offer in grades. The level of an offer is not necessarily indicative of the quality of a course.

COURSE OFFERS INFORMATION

Subject requirements/preferences **GCSE** French, mathematics (for business courses), grade levels may be stipulated. **AL** French is usually required at a specific grade and in some cases a second language may be stipulated.

Your target offers and examples of courses provided by each institution
380 pts **Imperial London** – A*AA–AAA (Chem Fr/Ger/Span Sci) (IB 38 pts HL 7 chem 6 maths)
London (King's) – AABc (Fr 3/4 yrs) (IB 36 pts)
London (UCL) – AAAe 380 pts (Fr; Fr As Af Lang) (IB 38 pts)
Nottingham – A*AA–AAA 380–360 pts (Econ Fr) (IB 38–36 pts)
360 pts **Durham** – AAA 360 pts (Modn Langs) (IB 37 pts)
Edinburgh – AAA 360 pts (Int Bus Fr/Ger/Span) (IB 37 pts HL 666–555)
London (King's) – AAA–AAB 360–340 pts (Euro St (Fr/Ger/Span); Fr Hist; Fr Phil)
    (IB 33–35 pts)
Newcastle – AAA (Comb Hons Fr)
Oxford – AAA (Fr) (IB 38–40 pts)
Southampton – AAB (Ocean Fr; Maths Fr/Ger/Span) (IB 36–32 pts HL 18–16 pts)
340 pts **Aston** – AAB–ABB 340–320 pts (Int Bus Fr/Ger/Span) (IB 34 pts HL 665)
Bath – AAB (Int Mgt Fr) (IB 34–36 pts)
Birmingham – AAB 340 pts (Fr St Joint Hons) (IB 36 pts)
Bristol – AAB–ABB (Fr courses) (IB 33–30 pts)
East Anglia – AAB (Modn Lang Fr) (IB 33 pts)
Exeter – AAB–ABB (Fr courses; Modn Lang) (IB 34–32 pts)
Lancaster – AAB 340 pts (Fr St) (IB 35 pts)
Leeds – AAB (Fr Maths) (IB 36 pts HL 17 pts incl 6 Fr maths)
London (King's) – AAB 340 pts (Fr Hisp St; Fr Modn Gk St; Fr Mgt; Fr Ger) (IB 35 pts)
London (RH) – AAB–ABB 340–320 pts (Fr Dr; Mgt Fr/Ger/Ital/Span) (IB 35–34 pts)
Manchester – AAB–ABB 320–340 pts (Fr courses) (IB 33–36 pts)
Newcastle – AAB 340 pts (Mgt St Fr) (IB 34 pts)

Nottingham – AAB-BBB (Fr Joint Hons; Mgt St Fr/Ger/Span)
St Andrews – AAA-AAB (Fr courses) (IB 35-38 pts)
Sheffield – AAB-BBB (Fr St; Fr St Joint Hons) (IB 35-32 pts)
Southampton – AAB 340 pts (Fr; Film Fr/Ger/Span; Engl Fr/Ger/Span) (IB 34 pts HL 17 pts)
Warwick – AAB (Fr St; Fr Joint Hons) (IB 36 pts)
York – AAB-ABB 340-320 pts (Fr Ger Lang; Fr Ling; Fr Ital Lang; Fr Sp Lang) (IB 34 pts)

320 pts Aston – ABB 360-320 pts (Fr courses) (IB 33-34 pts)
Bath – ABB-AAA 320-360 pts (Modn Langs Euro St) (IB 34-36 pts)
Birmingham – ABB (Fr St) (IB 32 pts)
Cardiff – AAB-ABB 340-320 pts (Fr courses) (IB 34 pts)
Dundee – ABB 320 pts (Law Lang) (IB 32 pts)
East Anglia – ABB (Fr Film TV; Transl Med Fr; Fr Span Lang Mgt St 4 yrs; Fr Lang Mgt St; Fr Int Dev St) (IB 32 pts)
Essex – 320 pts (Econ Fr)
Glasgow – ABB (Fr Joint Hons) (IB 36 pts)
Kent – ABB (Fr (Lic de Let); Fr) (IB 33 pts)
Leeds – ABB 320 pts (Fr) (IB 34 pts HL 6 Fr)
Leicester – ABB (Fr Joint Hons)
Liverpool – ABB-BBB (Fr Joint Hons) (IB 33-30 pts)
London (Inst Paris) – ABB 320 pts (Fr St)
London (QM) – ABB-BBB 300-320 pts (Fr courses; Fr/Ger/Russ Dr) (IB 34-32 pts)
London (RH) – ABB-BBB (Fr; Euro St Fr/Ger/Ital/Span)
Newcastle – ABB 320 pts (Fr Joint Hons) (IB 32 pts)
Nottingham – ABB 320 pts (Fr St; Film TV St Fr) (IB 32 pts)
Reading – ABB 320 pts (Fr courses) (IB 32 pts)
Strathclyde – ABB (Fr courses)
Surrey – AAB-ABB (Fr courses)
Sussex – ABB-BBB (Fr courses) (IB 32-34 pts)
Warwick – ABB 320 pts (Fr St Ger/Ital) (IB 34 pts)

300 pts Aberdeen – BBB 300 pts (Fr) (IB 32 pts)
Bath – AAA-BBB 300-360 pts (Modn Lang) (IB 34 pts HL 6 lang)
Buckingham – 300 pts (Law Fr)
Edinburgh – AAA-BBB 300-360 pts (Fr) (IB 34-42 pts)
Essex – 300 pts (Fr St Modn Langs) (IB 30 pts)
Heriot-Watt – BBB 300 pts (App Langs Transl (Fr/Ger)) (IB 30 pts)
Liverpool – BBB (Fr) (IB 30 pts HL 6 Fr)
Northumbria – 300 pts (Int Bus Mgt Fr)
Plymouth – BBB 300 pts (Engl Fr) (IB 26 pts)
Queen's Belfast – BBB 300 pts (Fr Joint Hons; Fr)
Swansea – ABB-BBB 300 pts (Fr)

280 pts Aberystwyth – 280 pts (Fr Joint Hons) (IB 28 pts)
Hull – 280-300 pts (Fr; Fr/Ger/Ital/Span Hist; Fr Joint Hons)
Leeds Beckett – 280 pts (Fr courses; Lang St) (IB 25 pts)
Oxford Brookes – BBC (Fr St) (IB 31 pts)
Stirling – BBC (Fr) (IB 32 pts)

260 pts Bangor – 260-320 pts (Fr courses)
Central Lancashire – 260-300 pts (Fr (Comb))
Coventry – BCC 260 pts (Fr courses; Fr Engl) (IB 28 pts)
Greenwich – 260 pts (Fr)
Manchester Met – 260-280 pts (Fr St; Ling Lang (Fr/Ger/Ital/Span)) (IB 28 pts)
Middlesex – 260 pts (Bus Mgt Fr/Ger/Ital/Span)
Northampton – 260-280 pts (Fr courses)
Nottingham Trent – 260 pts (Fr Joint Hons)

      Plymouth – 260 pts (Int Rel Fr) (IB 26 pts)
      Sunderland – 260 pts (Fr courses)
      Westminster – BCC (Fr courses) (IB 28 pts)
      Winchester – 260–300 pts (Fr P Teach)
240 pts **Canterbury Christ Church** – 240 pts (Fr) (IB 24 pts)
      Chester – 240–280 pts (Fr) (IB 26 pts)
      Plymouth – 240 pts (Pol Fr) (IB 26 pts)
      Ulster – CCC–BBC 240–280 pts (Bus St Fr/Ger/Span; Fr courses) (IB 24 pts)
200 pts **Portsmouth** – 200–280 pts (Fr St) (IB 28 pts HL 15 pts)
 80 pts **Kingston** – 80 pts (Fr)
      London (Birk) – p/t, for under 21s (over 21s varies) (Modn Langs Euro St (Fr, Ger, Jap, Port, Span); Fr Mgt; Fr St)

Alternative offers

See **Chapter 7** and **Appendix 1** for grades/UCAS Tariff points information for the International Baccalaureate, Scottish Highers/Advanced Highers, the Welsh Baccalaureate, the Irish Leaving Certificate, the Cambridge Pre-U Diploma, the Advanced Diploma and the Extended Project.

CHOOSING YOUR COURSE (SEE ALSO CH.1)

Some course features

Bangor A three-language Honours course is offered with languages chosen from French, German, Italian or Spanish. This is an exclusively practical language course, two semesters being spent at universities appropriate to the languages chosen.

Bath (Modn Langs Euro St) French is studied with a second, equally weighted, language. The course has a contemporary focus and a wide range of options.

Cardiff (Fr) The course has a vocational emphasis, and the opportunity to sit the Paris Chamber of Commerce examination and to gain a French language qualification recognised in France. The year abroad offers the opportunity to work as a teaching assistant in a French school.

Chester French can be studied as a Single Honours degree or as part of a Combined Honours programme.

Heriot-Watt (Langs (Interp Transl) (App Langs Transl)) Both degrees enable two main foreign languages to be studied to the same level throughout the course: the second language can be studied either from beginners' or post-beginners' level.

Leeds A large department offering a range of Single, Combined and major/minor courses. Students can spend a year in France.

Salford (Modn Langs Transl Interp St) Three languages are chosen from French, German, Italian, Portuguese, Spanish, and English as a Foreign Language. Modern languages are also available with TESOL (Teaching English to Speakers of Other Languages).

Universities and colleges teaching quality See www.qaa.ac.uk; http://unistats.direct.gov.uk.

Top research universities and colleges (RAE 2008) Oxford; London (King's); Warwick; Cambridge; Aberdeen; St Andrews; Sheffield; Nottingham; Kent; Leeds; Exeter; London (UCL).

ADMISSIONS INFORMATION

Number of applicants per place (approx) Aston 6; Bangor 4; Bath (Euro St Modn Langs) 6; Birmingham 5; Bradford 3; Bristol 7; Cardiff 6; Central Lancashire 5; Durham 8; Exeter 8; Huddersfield 3; Hull 12; Kent 10; Kingston 4; Lancaster 7; Leeds (Joint Hons) 8; Leicester (Fr Ital) 5; Liverpool 5; Liverpool John Moores 8; London (Inst Paris) 9; London (King's) 9; London (RH) 5; London (UCL) 8; Manchester Met 13; Middlesex 6; Newcastle 17; Northampton 3; Nottingham 16; Oxford Brookes 8; Portsmouth 20; Roehampton 5; Warwick 7; York 8.

Advice to applicants and planning the UCAS personal statement Visits to France (including exchange visits) should be described, with reference to any particular cultural or geographical features of the region visited. Providing information about your contacts with French friends and experience in speaking the language are also important. Express your willingness to work/live/travel abroad and show your interests in French life and culture. Read French newspapers and magazines and keep up-to-date with news stories etc. See also **Appendix 3**. **Bristol** Deferred entry accepted in some cases. Late applications may not be accepted.

Misconceptions about this course **Leeds** See **Languages**. **Swansea** Some applicants are not aware of the range of subjects which can be combined with French in our flexible modular system. They sometimes do not know that linguistics and area studies options are also available as well as literature options in French.

Selection interviews **Yes** Bangor, Birmingham, Cambridge, Durham, East Anglia (after offer), Essex, Exeter, Heriot-Watt, Huddersfield, Hull, Kingston, Lancaster, Liverpool, Liverpool John Moores, London (RH), London (UCL), Oxford, Surrey, Sussex, Warwick; **Some** Brighton, Canterbury Christ Church (mature students), Leeds; **No** Nottingham, Portsmouth, Reading.

Interview advice and questions Questions will almost certainly be asked on your A-level texts, in addition to your reading outside the syllabus – books, magazines, newspapers etc. Part of the interview may be conducted in French and written tests may be involved. See also **Chapter 6**. **Leeds** See **Languages**.

Reasons for rejection (non-academic) Unstable personality. Known alcoholism. Poor motivation. Candidate unenthusiastic, unmotivated, ill-informed about the nature of the course (had not read the prospectus). Not keen to spend a year abroad.

AFTER-RESULTS ADVICE
Offers to applicants repeating A-levels **Higher** Aberystwyth, Bristol (Fr), Glasgow, Leeds, Oxford Brookes, Warwick; **Possibly higher** Aston (Fr; Fr Ger); **Same** Aston, Bradford, Brighton, Bristol (Phil Fr; Fr Lat), Chester, Durham, East Anglia, Lancaster, Liverpool, London (RH), Newcastle, Nottingham (Fr Ger; Fr Lat), Sheffield, Surrey, Sussex, Ulster; **No** Cambridge.

GRADUATE DESTINATIONS AND EMPLOYMENT (2011/12 HESA)
Graduates surveyed 1700 **Employed** 795 **In voluntary employment** 70 **In further study** 375 **Assumed unemployed** 125

Career note See **Languages**.

OTHER DEGREE SUBJECTS FOR CONSIDERATION
European Studies; International Business Studies; Literature; other language.

GENETICS
(see also Biological Sciences, Microbiology)

Over the years, genetics, the science of heredity, has developed into a detailed and wide-ranging science. It involves, on the one hand, population genetics, and on the other, molecular interactions. Studies may therefore cover microbial, plant, animal and human genetics.

Useful websites www.genetics.org; www.nature.com/genetics; www.genetics.org.uk; see also **Biological Sciences**.

NB The points totals shown to the left of the institutions are for ease of reference only. It must not be assumed that Tariff points are always used by institutions or that they can be substituted for an offer in grades. The level of an offer is not necessarily indicative of the quality of a course.

COURSE OFFERS INFORMATION
Subject requirements/preferences **GCSE** English, mathematics and science subjects. **AL** Chemistry and/or biology are usually required or preferred.

Your target offers and examples of courses provided by each institution
380 pts   Cambridge – A*AA (Nat Sci (Genet)) (IB 40–41 pts HL 776)

London (UCL) – AAAe (Biol Sci (Genet)) (IB 38 pts HL 18 pts)

360 pts **Manchester** – AAA–ABB 360–320 pts (Genet; Genet (Yr Ind); Genet Modn Lang; Genet Prof Expnc) (IB 37–33 pts)

Newcastle – AAA–AAB 360–340 pts (Biomed Genet) (IB 34–35 pts HL 5 biol chem)

Sheffield – AAA–AAB 360–340 pts (Genet Microbiol; Genet; Genet Mol Cell Biol; Med Genet) (IB 37–35 pts)

340 pts **Bath** – AAB 340 pts (Mol Cell Biol) (IB 34 pts)

Birmingham – AAB–ABB (Biol Sci (Genet); Bioch (Genet)) (IB 34–35 pts)

Cardiff – AAB–ABB 340–320 pts (Genet) (IB 34 pts)

Lancaster – AAB (Bioch Biomed/Genet) (IB 35 pts)

London (King's) – AAB (Mol Genet; Pharmacol Mol Genet) (IB 35 pts HL 665)

Nottingham – AAB–ABB 340–320 pts (Bioch Genet; Genet) (IB 32–34 pts)

Warwick – AAB (Biol Sci (Mol Genet)) (IB 36 pts)

York – AAB (Genet) (IB 32 pts)

320 pts **Brunel** – ABB 320 pts (Biomed Sci (Genet)) (IB 33 pts)

East Anglia – ABB (Mol Biol Genet) (IB 32 pts)

Essex – ABB–BBB 320–300 pts (Genet) (IB 32–30 pts)

Glasgow – ABB (Genet) (IB 32 pts)

Leicester – ABB (Med Genet) (IB 32 pts)

Liverpool – ABB 320 pts (Genet) (IB 33 pts HL 6 biol)

Swansea – ABB 320 pts (Genet; Med Genet)

York – ABB (Genet Euro) (IB 32 pts)

300 pts **Aberdeen** – BBB 300 pts (Genet; Genet (Immun)) (IB 32 pts)

Dundee – BBB (Mol Genet) (IB 30 pts)

Leeds – AAB–BBB (Genet) (IB 34–38 pts HL 15–16 pts)

London (QM) – 300 pts (Genet) (IB 28 pts)

Swansea – BBB–ABB 300–320 pts (Bioch Genet) (IB 32–33 pts)

280 pts **Aberystwyth** – 280–320 pts (Genet) (IB 26 pts)

Bradford – BBC (Hlth Care Sci (Genet))

Hertfordshire – 280 pts (Mol Biol Genet)

Huddersfield – BBC 280 pts (Med Genet)

240 pts **Westminster** – CCC 240 pts (Biol Sci (Mol Biol Genet)) (IB 26 pts)

200 pts **Wolverhampton** – 200 pts (Genet Mol Biol) (IB 24 pts)

Alternative offers

See **Chapter 7** and **Appendix 1** for grades/UCAS Tariff points information for the International Baccalaureate, Scottish Highers/Advanced Highers, the Welsh Baccalaureate, the Irish Leaving Certificate, the Cambridge Pre-U Diploma, the Advanced Diploma and the Extended Project.

CHOOSING YOUR COURSE (SEE ALSO CH.1)

Some course features

Liverpool Modules are offered in genetic engineering, human and medical genetics. The year in industry/research enables students to work in the UK, Europe or the USA, and a field course in Uganda is offered.

London (UCL) After a common first year for all Biological Sciences students, Genetics and Human Genetics are two of the degree specialisms offered for the following years of the BSc and MSci courses. The Genetics programme focuses on genomic, evolutionary and population genetics, while cytology, pre-natal diagnosis and genetic counselling are options in the Human Genetics programme.

Manchester Transfer possible between most life sciences degree programmes at the end of the first year; students can also opt on, or off, sandwich placement year, and a Foundation year is also available. A programme is offered in Genetics with a Modern Language.

Nottingham Human Genetics is offered as a three- or four-year programme.

Swansea After a first year covering genetics and biological subjects, second year specialisms include human genetics, forensic and medical genetics. There is also a Joint Honours programme with Biochemistry.

York Genetics is available as a specialist degree programme in the Biology degree programme, with an opportunity to spend a year abroad or in industry.

Universities and colleges teaching quality See www.qaa.ac.uk; http://unistats.direct.gov.uk.

Top research universities and colleges (RAE 2008) See **Biological Sciences**.

Examples of sandwich degree courses See also **Biological Sciences**. Brunel; Cardiff; Glasgow; Huddersfield; Liverpool; Manchester; York.

ADMISSIONS INFORMATION
Number of applicants per place (approx) Cardiff 8; Dundee 5; Leeds 7; Leicester (all Biol Sci courses) 10;Newcastle 8; Nottingham 6; Swansea 7; Wolverhampton 4; York 9.

Advice to applicants and planning the UCAS personal statement See **Biological Sciences**.

Misconceptions about this course York Some fail to realise that chemistry (beyond GCSE) is essential to an understanding of genetics.

Selection interviews Yes Cambridge, Liverpool, Swansea, Wolverhampton; **Some** York; **No** Cardiff, Dundee.

Interview advice and questions Likely questions will focus on your A-level science subjects, particularly biology, why you wish to study genetics, and on careers in genetics. See also **Chapter 6**.

AFTER-RESULTS ADVICE
Offers to applicants repeating A-levels Higher Aberystwyth, Leeds, Newcastle, Nottingham, Swansea; **Same** Cardiff, Dundee, London (UCL), Wolverhampton, York; **No** Cambridge.

GRADUATE DESTINATIONS AND EMPLOYMENT (2011/12 HESA)
Graduates surveyed 290 **Employed** 85 **In voluntary employment** 5 **In further study** 115 **Assumed unemployed** 30

Career note See **Biological Sciences**.

OTHER DEGREE SUBJECTS FOR CONSIDERATION
Biochemistry; Biological Sciences; Biology; Biotechnology; Human Sciences; Immunology; Life Sciences; Medical Biochemistry; Medical Biology; Medicine; Microbiology; Molecular Biology; Natural Sciences; Physiology; Plant Sciences.

GEOGRAPHY
(see also **Environmental Sciences/Studies**)

Students following BA and BSc Geography courses often choose options from the same range of modules, but the choice of degree will depend on the arts or science subjects taken at A-level (or equivalent). The content and focus of courses will vary between universities and could emphasise the human, physical, economic or social aspects of the subject.

Useful websites www.metoffice.gov.uk; www.ccw.gov.uk; www.rgs.org; www.ordnancesurvey.co.uk; www.geographical.co.uk; www.nationalgeographic.com; www.cartography.org.uk; www.naturalengland.org.uk; www.geography.org.uk; www.thepowerofgeography.co.uk; www.publicprofiler.org; www.esri.com/what-is-gis.

NB The points totals shown to the left of the institutions are for ease of reference only. It must not be assumed that Tariff points are always used by institutions or that they can be substituted for an offer in grades. The level of an offer is not necessarily indicative of the quality of a course.

COURSE OFFERS INFORMATION

Subject requirements/preferences **GCSE** Geography usually required. Mathematics/sciences often required for BSc courses. **AL** Geography is usually required for most courses. Mathematics/science subjects required for BSc courses. (Meteor) Mathematics, physics and another science may be required sometimes with specified grades, eg **Reading**: mathematics and physics grade B.

Your target offers and examples of courses provided by each institution

380 pts **Cambridge** – A*AA (Geog) (IB 40–41 pts HL 776)

Durham – A*AA 380 pts (Geog; Comb Hons Soc Sci) (IB 38 pts)

Exeter – A*AA–AAB 380–340 pts (Flex Comb Hons Geog) (IB 38–34 pts)

London (UCL) – AAAe–AABe 380–360 pts (Econ Geog; Geog; Env Geog) (IB 36–38 pts)

360 pts **Bristol** – AAA–AAB 360–340 pts (Geog) (IB 37–35 pts HL 666)

Edinburgh – AAA–ABB 360–320 pts (Geol Physl Geog) (IB 37–32 pts)

Exeter – AAA–AAB 360–340 pts (Geog BSc; Geog BA) (IB 36–34 pts)

Leeds – AAA (Geog (BA))

London LSE – AAA 360 pts (Geog; Geog Econ) (IB 38 pts HL 766)

Manchester – AAA 360 pts (Geog Int St) (IB 36 pts)

Nottingham – AAA (Geog) (IB 36–38 pts)

Oxford – AAA (Geog) (IB 38–40 pts)

St Andrews – AAA 360 pts (Geog Psy; Geog; Geog Scot Hist; Geog Lang; Geog Int Rel) (IB 36 pts)

340 pts **Birmingham** – AAB (Geog) (IB 34–36 pts)

Cardiff – AAB–ABB 340–320 pts (Geog (Hum) Plan; Hum Geog)

East Anglia – AAB–ABB (Env Geog Clim Chng) (IB 33 pts)

Lancaster – AAB (Geog; Geog Earth Sci; Physl Geog) (IB 34 pts)

Leeds – AAB (Geog (BSc); Geog Pol)

Liverpool – AAB (Geog) (IB 35 pts)

London (King's) – AAB (Geog) (IB 35 pts HL 665)

London (SOAS) – AAB (Geog Joint Hons) (IB 36 pts HL 666)

Loughborough – AAB–ABB (Geog Spo Mgt; Hist Geog; Geog Econ; Geog Spo Sci) (IB 36–32 pts)

Manchester – AAB 340 pts (Geog) (IB 35 pts)

Newcastle – AAB–ABB 340–320 pts (Geog) (IB 32 pts HL 6 geog)

Nottingham – AAA–AAB 340–360 pts (Geog Bus; Geog Chin St) (IB 34 pts)

Sheffield – AAB–ABB (Geog) (IB 33–35 pts)

Southampton – AAB–ABB incl geog (Arch Geog; Geog Ocean; Geog; Geog Geol; Geol Physl Geog; Popn Geog; Ocean Physl Geog) (IB 34–32 pts HL 17–16 pts)

Sussex – AAB 340 pts (Geog; Geog Anth) (IB 35 pts)

320 pts **Birmingham** – ABB (Geol Geog) (IB 32–34 pts)

Birmingham (UC) – ABB (Geog Econ; Geog) (IB 32–34 pts)

Brighton – ABB 320 pts (Geog; Geog Arch) (IB 34 pts)

Cardiff – ABB 320 pts (Mar Geog) (IB 30–32 pts)

East Anglia – ABB (Env Geog Int Dev) (IB 32 pts)

Edinburgh – AAA–ABB 360–320 pts (Geog Soc Plcy; Geog) (IB 37–32 pts)

Glasgow – ABB (Geog) (IB 32 pts)

Lancaster – ABB (Span St Geog) (IB 32 pts)

Leicester – ABB 320 pts (Geog; Hum Geog; Physl Geog) (IB 32 pts)

Liverpool – ABB (Ocns Clim Physl Geog) (IB 33 pts)

London (Birk) – ABB 320 pts (Geog)

London (QM) – 320–340 pts (Geog; Cits Econ Soc Chng) (IB 32 pts)

London (RH) – ABB 320 pts (Geog; Hum Geog; Physl Geog; Geog Pol Int Rel) (IB 37 pts HL 666)

Manchester – ABB 320 pts (Geog Geol) (IB 33 pts)

Newcastle – ABB–BBB 320–300 pts (Geog Plan; Physl Geog) (IB 30–34 pts)

Nottingham – ABB–BBB 300–320 pts (Arch Geog) (IB 30–32 pts)

Reading – 320 pts (Hum Geog; Physl Geog; Geog Econ (Reg Sci); Hum Physl Geog) (IB 34–31 pts)

Sheffield – ABB (Geog Plan)

Strathclyde – 320 pts (Geog)

Swansea – ABB–BBB 320–300 pts (Geog; Geog Geoinform; Geog Euro St) (IB 33–32 pts)

York – ABB (Env Sci; Env Geog) (IB 34 pts)

300 pts **Aberdeen** – 300 pts (Geog (Arts/Sci))

Aberystwyth – 280–300 pts (Physl Geog; Geog; Hum Geog) (IB 29 pts)

Brighton – BBB 300 pts (Physl Geog Geol) (IB 30–32 pts)

Dundee – BBB (Geopol; Geog Plan) (IB 30 pts)

Edge Hill – 300 pts (Geog; Physl Geog Geol) (IB 26 pts)

Greenwich – 300 pts (Geog)

Keele – 300 pts (Geog; Physl Geog; Hum Geog) (IB 26–28 pts)

Leeds Beckett – 300 pts (Hum Geog Plan; Hum Geog)

London (QM) – BBB–AAB 300–340 pts (Hum Geog) (IB 30–34 pts)

Newcastle – AAB–BBB 300–320 pts (GIS) (IB 32 pts)

Northumbria – BBB 300 pts (Geog Env Mgt) (IB 26 pts)

Queen's Belfast – BBB 300 pts (Geog (St Abrd); Geog)

Sheffield Hallam – 300 pts (Geog)

280 pts **Bangor** – 280–320 pts (Cstl Geog)

Bournemouth – 280 pts (App Geog) (IB 30–32 pts)

Bristol UWE – 280–300 pts (Geog) (IB 26–32 pts)

Coventry – BBC–BCC 280–260 pts (Geog; Disas Mgt) (IB 28–30 pts)

Gloucestershire – 280–300 pts (Geog courses)

Hull – 280–320 pts (Geol Physl Geog; Physl Geog; Hum Geog; Geog)

Manchester Met – 280 pts (Geog (St Abrd); Physl Geog) (IB 28 pts)

Northumbria – 280 pts (Geog) (IB 28 pts)

Oxford Brookes – BBC 280 pts (Geog) (IB 30 pts)

Plymouth – 280–320 pts (Geog BA/BSc; Geog Media Arts; Geog Lang; Physl Geog Geol) (IB 28–30 pts)

Portsmouth – 280 pts (Geog BA/BSc; Hum Geog; Physl Geog; Geog GIS) (IB 26 pts)

Sheffield Hallam – 280 pts incl geog (Geog Plan; Hum Geog)

South Wales – 280 pts (Geog; Physl Geog)

Staffordshire – 280 pts (Geog; Geog Mntn Ldrshp) (IB 24 pts)

Stirling – BBC (Geog) (IB 32 pts)

260 pts **Bangor** – 260–320 pts (Geog) (IB 28 pts)

Bath Spa – 260–300 pts (Geog)

Bradford – 260 pts (Geog; Env Sci; Physl Env Geog)

Chester – 260–300 pts (Geog) (IB 28 pts)

Coventry – BCC–BBC 260–280 pts (Disas Mgt Emer Plan) (IB 28–29 pts)

Dundee – BCC (Geog) (IB 29 pts)

Hertfordshire – 260–280 pts (Hum Geog; Geog)

Liverpool Hope – 260–300 pts (Geog) (IB 26 pts)

Liverpool John Moores – 260–300 pts (Geog) (IB 25 pts)

Manchester Met – 260–280 pts (Hum Geog (St Abrd)) (IB 28 pts)

Northampton – 260–280 pts (Physl Geog; Geog)

Nottingham Trent – 260 pts (Geog (Physl))

Worcester – 260–300 pts (Geog; Hum Geog; Geog courses) (IB 24 pts)

240 pts **Aberdeen** – 240 pts (GIS)

Canterbury Christ Church – CCC 240 pts (Geog) (IB 24 pts)

Central Lancashire – CCC 240 pts (Geog)

Derby – 240 pts (Geog)

Edge Hill – 240 pts (Hum Geog; Physl Geog)

Check **Chapter 4** when choosing your university and **Chapter 7** on how to read the subject tables.

– 240 pts (Geog Ecol Env)

Kingston – 240–280 pts (Geog Joint Hons; Hum Geog; Geog Inf Sys)

Nottingham Trent – 240 pts (Geog) (IB 24 pts)

St Mary's – 240 pts (Geog) (IB 28 pts)

Salford – 240–280 pts (Geog) (IB 30 pts)

220 pts **Ulster** – 220–260 pts (Geog Int Dev; Geog Joint Hons)

200 pts **Southampton Solent** – 200 pts (Geog Env St; Geog Mar St)

Open University – contact +44 (0)845 300 6090 **or** www.openuniversity.co.uk/you (Soc Sci Geog)

Alternative offers

See **Chapter 7** and **Appendix 1** for grades/UCAS Tariff points information for the International Baccalaureate, Scottish Highers/Advanced Highers, the Welsh Baccalaureate, the Irish Leaving Certificate, the Cambridge Pre-U Diploma, the Advanced Diploma and the Extended Project.

EXAMPLES OF FOUNDATION DEGREES IN THE SUBJECT FIELD
Bournemouth.

CHOOSING YOUR COURSE (SEE ALSO CH.1)
Some course features

East Anglia A strong department of Environmental Sciences incorporating courses in Geography with opportunities to study abroad and in industry. Specialised courses are offered with International Development and in Environmental Georgraphy and Climate Change.

Lancaster The Geography degree schemes are flexible so students can specialise in human geography, physical geography, or geography, or study an outside related subject, in the second and third years. There are study abroad opportunities in Canada, North America, New Zealand and Australia, and an option to teach geography in a local school.

Newcastle Geography can be taken in the BA Combined Studies degree with three other subjects in Stage 1 and two in Stage 2.

Reading A leading university for the study of meteorology with opportunities for placement at the University of Oklahoma, equally renowned for this subject.

St Mary's A flexible modular scheme allowing a choice of specialisms.

Universities and colleges teaching quality See www.qaa.ac.uk; http://unistats.direct.gov.uk.

Top research universities and colleges (RAE 2008) See **Environmental Science/Studies**.

Examples of sandwich degree courses Brighton; Bristol UWE; Cardiff; Coventry; Hertfordshire; Kingston; Loughborough; Manchester Met; Northumbria; Nottingham Trent; Plymouth; Sheffield Hallam; Ulster.

ADMISSIONS INFORMATION
Number of applicants per place (approx) Aberystwyth 3; Birmingham 6; Bristol 15; Bristol UWE 10; Cambridge 3; Cardiff 5; Central Lancashire 3; Chester 10; Coventry 12; Derby 4; Dundee 5; Durham 8; East Anglia (Meteor Ocean) 7; Edge Hill 8; Edinburgh 8; Exeter 10; Gloucestershire 40; Greenwich 2; Hull 10; Kent 15; Kingston 7; Lancaster 13; Leeds 12; Leicester 5; Liverpool 3; Liverpool John Moores 6; London (King's) 5; London (QM) 5; London (RH) 7; London (SOAS) 5; London (UCL) 5; London LSE 8; Loughborough 6, (Geog Spo Sci) 20; Newcastle 14; Newman 2; Northampton 4; Northumbria 16; Nottingham 7; Portsmouth (Geog) 5; St Mary's 4; Salford 3; Sheffield (BA) 13, (BSc) 10; South Wales 5; Southampton (Geog) 7; Staffordshire 10; Strathclyde 8; Swansea 5; Wolverhampton 2; Worcester 5.

Advice to applicants and planning the UCAS personal statement Visits to, and field courses in, any specific geographical region should be fully described. Study your own locality in detail and get in touch with the area planning office to learn about any future developments. Read geographical magazines and describe any special interests you have – and why. Awareness of world issues and travel experience. **Bristol** Deferred entry accepted.

Misconceptions about this course **Birmingham** Some students think that the BA and BSc Geography courses are very different; in fact they do not differ from one another. All course options are available for both degrees. **Liverpool** Some applicants assume that a BSc course restricts them to physical geography modules. This is not so since human geography modules can be taken. Some students later specialise in human geography.

Selection interviews **Yes** Bristol UWE, Cambridge, Canterbury Christ Church, Central Lancashire, Coventry, Durham (essential for overseas applicants), Edge Hill, Greenwich, Kingston, London (King's), London (QM), London (RH), London (UCL), Manchester Met, Northumbria, Oxford (Geog) 27%; **Some** Bath Spa, Bristol, Cardiff, Dundee, East Anglia, Liverpool, London (SOAS), Loughborough, Newcastle, Salford, Southampton, Staffordshire; **No** Birmingham, Nottingham, Reading.

Interview advice and questions Geography is a very broad subject and applicants can expect to be questioned on their syllabus and those aspects which they find of special interest. Some questions in the past have included: What fieldwork have you done? What are your views on ecology? What changes in the landscape have you noticed on the way to the interview? Explain in simple meteorological terms today's weather. Why are earthquakes almost unknown in Britain? What is the value of practical work in geography to primary school children? (BEd course) What do you enjoy about geography and why? Are there any articles of geographical importance in the news at present? Discuss the current economic situation in Britain and give your views. Questions on the Third World, on world ocean currents and drainage and economic factors world-wide. What do you think about those people who consider global warming nonsense? Expect to comment on local geography and on geographical photographs and diagrams. See also **Chapter 6**. **Cambridge** Are Fairtrade bananas really fair? Imagine you are hosting the BBC radio show on New Year's day, what message would you send to listeners? **Liverpool** Looks for why students have chosen Geography and the aspects of the subject they enjoy. **Oxford** Is nature natural? **Southampton** Applicants selected on academic ability only.

Reasons for rejection (non-academic) Lack of awareness of the content of the course. Failure to attend interview. Poor general knowledge. Lack of geographical awareness. **Hull** (BSc) Usually insufficient science background. **Liverpool** Personal statement gave no reason for choosing Geography.

AFTER-RESULTS ADVICE
Offers to applicants repeating A-levels **Higher** Bournemouth, Glasgow, Hull, Kingston, Nottingham, St Andrews, Sussex (Geog Lang); **Possibly higher** Edinburgh; **Same** Aberystwyth, Birmingham, Bradford, Brighton, Bristol, Cardiff, Chester, Coventry, Derby, Dundee, Durham, East Anglia, Edge Hill, Lancaster, Leeds, Liverpool, Liverpool Hope, Liverpool John Moores, London (RH), London (SOAS), Loughborough, Manchester Met, Newcastle, Newman, Northumbria, Oxford Brookes, St Mary's, Salford, Southampton, Staffordshire, Ulster, Wolverhampton; **No** Cambridge.

GRADUATE DESTINATIONS AND EMPLOYMENT (2011/12 HESA)
Human and Social Geography graduates surveyed 2135 **Employed** 1015 **In voluntary employment** 110 **In further study** 530 **Assumed unemployed** 150

Physical Geographical Studies graduates surveyed 2960 **Employed** 1340 **In voluntary employment** 115 **In further study** 755 **Assumed unemployed** 255

Career note Geography graduates enter a wide range of occupations, many in business and administrative careers. Depending on specialisations, areas could include agriculture, forestry, hydrology, transport, market research and retail. Teaching is also a popular option.

OTHER DEGREE SUBJECTS FOR CONSIDERATION
Agriculture; Anthropology; Civil Engineering; Countryside Management; Development Studies; Environmental Engineering/Science/Studies; Forestry; Geology; Geomatic Engineering; Surveying; Town Planning; Urban Land Economics; Urban Studies.

GEOLOGY/GEOLOGICAL SCIENCES

(including **Earth Sciences**, **Geophysics** and **Geoscience**; see also **Astronomy and Astrophysics**, **Environmental Sciences/Studies**)

Topics in Geology courses include the physical and chemical constitution of the earth, exploration geophysics, oil and marine geology (oceanography) and seismic interpretation. Earth Sciences cover geology, environmental science, physical geography and can also include business studies and language modules. No previous knowledge of geology is required for most courses.

Useful websites www.geolsoc.org.uk; www.bgs.ac.uk; www.noc.soton.ac.uk; www.scicentral.com.

NB The points totals shown to the left of the institutions are for ease of reference only. It must not be assumed that Tariff points are always used by institutions or that they can be substituted for an offer in grades. The level of an offer is not necessarily indicative of the quality of a course.

COURSE OFFERS INFORMATION

Subject requirements/preferences GCSE English, mathematics and a science required. **AL** One or two mathematics/science subjects usually required. Geography may be accepted as a science subject.

Your target offers and examples of courses provided by each institution

380 pts **Cambridge** – A*AA (Nat Sci (Earth Sci)) (IB 40–41 pts HL 776)

Leeds – A*AA 380 pts (Geophysl Sci (Int); Geol Sci (Int)) (IB 35 pts HL 19 pts)

London (UCL) – AAAe–ABBe 380–340 pts (Earth Sci (Int); Earth Sci; Env Geosci; Geophys; Geol) (IB 34–38 pts HL 16–18 pts)

Oxford – A*AA (Earth Sci (Geol)) (IB 38–40 pts)

360 pts **Cardiff** – AAA 360 pts (Env Geosci (Int); Explor Res Geol (Int); Geol (Int)) (IB 34 pts)

Durham – AAA 360 pts (Earth Sci; Geosci; Geol; Geophys Geol) (IB 37 pts)

Edinburgh – AAA–ABB 360–320 pts (Geol Physl Geog; Geophys; Geophys Meteor; Geophys Geol; Geol) (IB 37–32 pts)

Imperial London – AAA 360 pts (Geol; Geol Geophys; Petrol Geosci MSci; Geophys) (IB 38 pts)

Leicester – AAA 360 pts (Geol MGeol; Geol Pal MGeol) (IB 36 pts)

St Andrews – AAA–AAB (Geosci courses) (IB 35–38 pts)

Southampton – AAA–ABB (Geol; Geophys; Geophys Sci; Ocn Earth Clim Sci) (IB 36–32 pts HL 18–16 pts)

340 pts **Bristol** – AAB–ABB 340–320 pts (Geol) (IB 35–33 pts HL 666)

Cardiff – AAB 340 pts (Earth Sci; Explor Res Geol MESci; Geol MESci) (IB 32–34 pts)

East Anglia – AAB–ABB (Clim Sci (St Abrd); Env Earth Sci MSci; Clim Sci MSci; Geophys Sci (Yr Abrd)) (IB 33 pts)

Exeter – AAB–ABB 340–320 pts (App Geol; Geol courses (Cornwall)) (IB 34–30 pts)

Glasgow – AAB 340 pts (Earth Sci) (IB 34 pts)

Leeds – AAB 340 pts (Geol Sci) (IB 35 pts HL 17 pts)

Liverpool – AAB (Geol MSci; Geol Geophys MESci; Geol Physl Geog MESci) (IB 35 pts)

Manchester – AAB 340 pts (Earth Sci) (IB 35 pts)

St Andrews – AAB 340 pts (Geol; Env Earth Sci) (IB 36 pts)

Southampton – AAB incl geog (Geol Physl Geog; Geog Geol) (IB 34 pts HL 17 pts)

320 pts **Birmingham** – ABB (Geol (St Abrd); Geol Arch; Geol) (IB 32–34 pts)

Brighton – ABB 320 pts (Geol) (IB 34 pts)

Cardiff – ABB 320 pts (Explor Res Geol; Geol) (IB 30–32 pts)

East Anglia – ABB 320 pts (Env Geophys; Env Earth Sci; Clim Sci; Env Geophys) (IB 32 pts)

Lancaster – ABB (Earth Env Sci) (IB 32 pts)

Leicester – ABB 320 pts (Geol BSc; App Env Geol; Geol Geophys) (IB 32 pts)

Liverpool – ABB (Geol; Geol Physl Geog) (IB 33 pts)

London (RH) – ABB (Geol; Geosci) (IB 34 pts HL 6 sci)

Manchester – ABB 320 pts (Geol; Geol Planet Sci; Env Res Geol; Geochem; Geog Geol) (IB 33 pts)

Southampton – ABB (Geol Mar Biol) (IB 36–32 pts HL 18–16 pts)
Swansea – ABB (Physl Earth Sci)
300 pts **Aberdeen** – ABB-BBB 320–300 pts (Geol Petrol Geol) (IB 32 pts HL 5)
Brighton – BBB 300 pts (Physl Geog Geol) (IB 30–32 pts)
Edge Hill – 300 pts (Physl Geog Geol) (IB 26 pts)
Keele – BBB (Geol) (IB 26–30 pts)
London (Birk) – BBB 300 pts (Geol)
280 pts **Aberystwyth** – 280 pts (Env Earth Sci) (IB 28–30 pts)
Bangor – 280–320 pts (Geol Ocean)
Hull – 280–320 pts (Geol Physl Geog)
Plymouth – 280–320 pts (App Geol; Geol Ocn Sci; Physl Geog Geol) (IB 28–32 pts)
Portsmouth – 280–340 pts (Eng Geol Geotech) (IB 28 pts)
260 pts **Derby** – 260 pts (Geol) (IB 28 pts)
Portsmouth – 260–320 pts (Geol; Geol Haz) (IB 28 pts)
240 pts **Kingston** – 240–280 pts (Geol)
South Wales – CCC 240 pts (Geol) (IB 28 pts)

Open University – contact +44 (0)845 300 6090 **or** www.openuniversity.co.uk/you (Geol St)

Alternative offers
See **Chapter 7** and **Appendix 1** for grades/UCAS Tariff points information for the International Baccalaureate, Scottish Highers/Advanced Highers, the Welsh Baccalaureate, the Irish Leaving Certificate, the Cambridge Pre-U Diploma, the Advanced Diploma and the Extended Project.

CHOOSING YOUR COURSE (SEE ALSO CH.1)
Some course features
Cardiff (Explor Res Geol) Course provides a grounding in applied geology and the evaluation and exploration of the Earth's natural resources. During the second summer, an industrial placement is offered with an exploration company in the UK or overseas. Option to spend Year 3 in the USA or Australia on the MESci courses.
East Anglia A strong department of Environmental Sciences incorporating courses in Geophysical Sciences with opportunities to study abroad and in industry. A new range of integrated master's degrees were introduced in 2010, including an MSci in Climate Science.
Exeter Camborne School of Mines is a leader in the field of Engineering Geology and Geotechnics and Mining Engineering. £2000 scholarships are offered on the basis of academic excellence, together with some sponsorships.
Leeds Geological and Geophysical Sciences can be studied with placements in Europe or worldwide or with industrial placement. From 2012 there will be no additional charges for fieldwork programmes.

Universities and colleges teaching quality See www.qaa.ac.uk; http://unistats.direct.gov.uk.

Top research universities and colleges (RAE 2008) See **Environmental Science/Studies**.

Examples of sandwich degree courses Brighton; Cardiff; East Anglia; Kingston; London (RH); Portsmouth.

ADMISSIONS INFORMATION
Number of applicants per place (approx) Aberystwyth 5; Bangor 4; Birmingham 4; Bristol 7; Cardiff 5; Derby 4; Durham 4; East Anglia 7; Edinburgh 5; Exeter 5; Imperial London 5; Kingston 19, (Earth Sys Sci) 3; Leeds 8; Leicester 5; Liverpool 5; London (RH) 5; London (UCL) 3; Oxford 1.2; Plymouth 7; Portsmouth (Eng Geol Geotech) 2, (Geol) 2; Southampton 5.

Advice to applicants and planning the UCAS personal statement Visits to any outstanding geological sites and field courses you have attended should be described in detail. Apart from geological formations, you should also be aware of how geology has affected humankind in specific areas in the architecture of the region and artefacts used. Evidence of social skills could be given. See also **Appendix 3**. **Bristol** Only accepting a limited number of deferred applicants in fairness to next year's applicants. Apply early.

Misconceptions about this course East Anglia Many applicants fail to realise that environmental earth science extends beyond geology to the links between the solid earth and its behaviour and society in general. **London (UCL)** Environmental geoscience is sometimes mistaken for environmental science; they are two different subjects.

Selection interviews Yes Cambridge, Durham, Kingston, Liverpool, London (RH), Oxford (Geol) 46%, Southampton; **Some** Aberystwyth (mature students only), Derby; **No** Birmingham, East Anglia, Edinburgh.

Interview advice and questions Some knowledge of the subject will be expected and applicants could be questioned on specimens of rocks and their origins. Past interviews have included questions on the field courses attended, and the geophysical methods of exploration in the detection of metals. How would you determine the age of this rock (sample shown)? Can you integrate a decay curve function and would it help you to determine the age of rocks? How many planes of crystallisation could this rock have? What causes a volcano? What is your local geology? See also **Chapter 6**. **Oxford** (Earth Sci) Candidates may be asked to comment on specimens of a geological nature, based on previous knowledge of the subject.

Reasons for rejection (non-academic) Exeter Outright rejection uncommon but some applicants advised to apply for other programmes.

AFTER-RESULTS ADVICE
Offers to applicants repeating A-levels Higher Bristol, St Andrews; **Possibly higher** Cardiff, Portsmouth; **Same** Aberystwyth, Derby, Durham, East Anglia, Leeds, London (RH), Plymouth, Southampton; **No** Cambridge.

GRADUATE DESTINATIONS AND EMPLOYMENT (2011/12 HESA)
Graduates surveyed 1140 **Employed** 505 **In voluntary employment** 30 **In further study** 325 **Assumed unemployed** 95

Career note Areas of employment include mining and quarrying, the oil and gas industry, prospecting and processing.

OTHER DEGREE SUBJECTS FOR CONSIDERATION
Archaeology; Civil and Mining Engineering; Environmental Science; Geography; Meteorology; Oceanography; Physics.

GERMAN

(see also European Studies, Languages)

Language, literature, practical language skills or a broader study of Germany and its culture (European Studies) are alternative study approaches. See also **Appendix 3** under Languages.

Useful websites www.cilt.org.uk; www.goethe.de; www.bbc.co.uk/languages; www.iol.org.uk; www.languageadvantage.com; www.languagematters.co.uk; www.faz.net; www.sueddeutsche.de; www.europa.eu; www.gslg.org.uk; www.amgs.org.uk; www.wigs.ac.uk.

NB The points totals shown to the left of the institutions are for ease of reference only. It must not be assumed that Tariff points are always used by institutions or that they can be substituted for an offer in grades. The level of an offer is not necessarily indicative of the quality of a course.

COURSE OFFERS INFORMATION
Subject requirements/preferences GCSE English and German are required. **AL** German required usually at a specified grade.

Your target offers and examples of courses provided by each institution

380 pts **Cambridge** – A*AA 380 pts (Modn Mediev Lang) (IB 40-41 pts HL 776)
Imperial London – A*AA-AAA (Chem Fr/Ger/Span Sci) (IB 38 pts HL 7 chem 6 maths)
London (UCL) – AAAe-ABBe 380-340 pts (Modn Lang) (IB 34-38 pts)
Nottingham – A*AA-AAA 380-360 pts (Econ Ger) (IB 38-36 pts)

360 pts **Birmingham** – AAA 360 pts +LNAT (Law Ger) (IB 36 pts)
Bristol – AAA-AAB incl Ger 360-340 pts +LNAT (Law Ger) (IB 37-35 pts HL 666 incl Ger)
Durham – AAA 360 pts (Modn Langs (Ger)) (IB 37 pts)
Edinburgh – AAA 360 pts (Int Bus Fr/Ger/Span) (IB 37 pts HL 666-555)
Imperial London – AAA 360 pts (Biol Ger Sci) (IB 38 pts)
London (King's) – AAA-AAB 360-340 pts (Ger Mus; Euro St (Fr/Ger/Span))
(IB 33-35 pts)
Oxford – AAA (Ger courses) (IB 38-40 pts)
St Andrews – AAA-AAB (Ger courses) (IB 35-38 pts)

340 pts **Aston** – AAB-ABB 340-320 pts (Int Bus Fr/Ger/Span) (IB 34 pts HL 665)
Bristol – AAB-BBB 340-300 pts (Ger courses) (IB 35-32 pts)
Exeter – AAB-ABB 340-320 pts (Ger) (IB 34-32 pts)
Lancaster – AAB 340 pts (Ger St courses) (IB 34 pts)
London (King's) – AAB 340 pts (Fr Ger; Ger courses) (IB 35 pts)
London (RH) – AAB-ABB 340-320 pts (Mgt Fr/Ger/Ital/Span; Dr Ger/Ital; Ger courses)
(IB 35-34 pts)
Manchester – AAB-BBB 300-340 pts (Ger courses) (IB 31-36 pts)
Nottingham – AAB (Mgt St Fr/Ger/Span) (IB 34 pts)
Sheffield – AAB-BBB (Ger St Joint Hons) (IB 35-32 pts)
Southampton – AAB (Engl Fr/Ger/Span; Ger courses) (IB 34 pts HL 17 pts)
Warwick – AAB-ABB 340-320 pts (Ger Joint Hons; Ger St Ital; Engl Ger Lit)
York – AAB-ABB 340-320 pts (Fr Ger Lang; Ger courses) (IB 34 pts)

320 pts **Aston** – ABB-BBB (Ger) (IB 32-34 pts)
Bath – ABB (Modn Langs Euro St) (IB 34 pts)
Bristol – ABB-BBB 320-300 pts (Ger) (IB 33-32 pts)
Dundee – ABB 320 pts (Law Lang) (IB 32 pts)
Glasgow – ABB (Ger Joint Hons) (IB 36 pts)
Kent – ABB (Ger courses; Ger Joint Hons) (IB 33 pts)
London (QM) – ABB-BBB 300-320 pts (Fr/Ger/Russ Dr) (IB 34 pts)
London (RH) – ABB 320 pts (Euro St Fr/Ger/Ital/Span) (IB 34 pts)
Nottingham – ABB-BBB (Ger Joint Hons) (IB 32 pts)
Surrey – ABB-BBB (Ger courses) (IB 32 pts)
Warwick – ABB 320 pts (Ger St; Fr St Ger/Ital) (IB 34 pts)

300 pts **Aberdeen** – BBB (Ger) (IB 28 pts)
Birmingham – BBB (Ger St courses) (IB 30 pts)
Cardiff – BBB 300 pts (Ger)
Dundee – BBB-BCC (Int Bus Ger; Phil Ger)
Edinburgh – BBB-AAA 300-360 pts (Ger) (IB 34-37 pts)
Heriot-Watt – BBB 300 pts (App Langs Transl (Fr/Span) (Ger/Span); App Langs Transl
(Fr/Ger)) (IB 30 pts)
Hertfordshire – 300 pts (Ger courses)
Leeds – ABC-BBB (Ger courses)
Liverpool – BBB (Ger courses) (IB 30 pts HL 6 Ger)
London (Birk) – 300 pts (Ger)
London (QM) – BBB-ABB 300-320 pts (Ger Compar Lit; Ger Ling; Ger courses)
(IB 32-34 pts)
Manchester – BBB 300 pts (Ger St) (IB 31 pts)
Nottingham – ABC-BBB (Ger; Film TV St Ger) (IB 30 pts)
Reading – BBB/ABC 300 pts (Ger courses) (IB 30 pts)
Sheffield – BBB incl Ger (Ger St) (IB 32 pts)

Check **Chapter 4** when choosing your university and **Chapter 7** on how to read the subject tables.

Swansea – BBB (Ger courses)
Westminster – BBB 300 pts (Int Bus Ger) (IB 28 pts)
280 pts **Aberystwyth** – 280–320 pts (Ger courses)
Hull – 280–300 pts (Ger; Fr/Ger/Ital/Span Hist)
Northumbria – 280–300 pts (Int Bus Mgt Ger; Ger Bus) (IB 26 pts)
Salford – 320–280 pts (Modn Lang Transl Interp St (Fr/Ger/Port/Span))
Westminster – BBC (Int Rel Ger)
260 pts **Central Lancashire** – 260–300 pts (Ger (Comb); Ger Bus Ger)
Dundee – BCC (Ger)
Hull – 260–300 pts (Ger Joint Hons; Ger Transl St) (IB 28 pts)
Manchester Met – 260–280 pts (Ling Lang (Fr/Ger/Ital/Span)) (IB 28 pts)
Middlesex – 260 pts (Bus Mgt Fr/Ger/Ital/Span)
Nottingham Trent – 260 pts (Ger Joint Hons) (IB 24 pts)
Sunderland – 260 pts (Ger (Comb))
Ulster – BCC 260 pts (Ger courses)
Westminster – BCC 260 pts (Ger courses) (IB 30 pts)
240 pts **Bangor** – 240–260 pts (Ger courses)
Chester – 240–280 pts (Ger courses) (IB 26 pts)
Ulster – CCC–BBC 240–280 pts (Bus St Fr/Ger/Span) (IB 24 pts)
York St John – 240–300 pts (Bus Mgt Ger) (IB 24 pts)
200 pts **Portsmouth** – 200–280 pts (Ger St) (IB 28 pts)
80 pts **London (Birk)** – p/t, for under 21s (over 21s varies) (Modn Langs Euro St (Fr, Ger, Jap, Port, Span))

Alternative offers
See **Chapter 7** and **Appendix 1** for grades/UCAS Tariff points information for the International Baccalaureate, Scottish Highers/Advanced Highers, the Welsh Baccalaureate, the Irish Leaving Certificate, the Cambridge Pre-U Diploma, the Advanced Diploma and the Extended Project.

CHOOSING YOUR COURSE (SEE ALSO CH.1)
Some course features
Bangor German is offered with two other languages from Dutch, French, Italian and Spanish.
Durham (Modn Lang) Students take core language module each year and options from a range of modules, including film, history, literature, translation, interpreting and cultural studies.
East Anglia German can be taken as part of the Law course with European Legal Systems.
Heriot-Watt The course focuses on practical language skills, linguistics and translation studies, communication studies and European studies.
Salford The only university to offer a course combining media, a language and business studies.

Universities and colleges teaching quality See www.qaa.ac.uk; http://unistats.direct.gov.uk.

Top research universities and colleges (RAE 2008) (German, Dutch and Scandinavian languages) Oxford; Cambridge; London (King's); Leeds; London (UCL); Durham; London (RH); St Andrews; Manchester; Birmingham.

ADMISSIONS INFORMATION
Number of applicants per place (approx) Aston 4; Bangor 6; Birmingham 6; Bradford 6; Bristol 7; Cardiff 6; Central Lancashire 2; Durham 4; East Anglia 4; Exeter 4; Heriot-Watt 10; Hull 12; Kent 10; Lancaster 7; Leeds (Joint Hons) 8; Leicester 4; London (King's) 5; London (QM) 6; London (RH) 5; London (UCL) 4; Newcastle 6; Nottingham 5; Portsmouth 5; Salford 5; Staffordshire 5; Stirling 6; Surrey 2; Swansea 4; Warwick (Ger Bus St) 16, (Ger) 8; York 6.

Advice to applicants and planning the UCAS personal statement Describe visits to Germany or a German-speaking country and the particular cultural and geographical features of the region. Contacts with friends in Germany and language experience should also be mentioned, and if you are bilingual, say so. Read German newspapers and magazines and keep up-to-date with national news.

Misconceptions about this course Leeds See **Languages**. **Swansea** Some students are afraid of the year abroad, which is actually one of the most enjoyable parts of the course.

Selection interviews Yes Bangor, Birmingham, Cambridge, Durham, East Anglia, Exeter, Heriot-Watt, Hull, Liverpool, London (RH), London (UCL), Newcastle, Oxford, Sheffield, Southampton, Surrey; **Some** Cardiff, Leeds, Portsmouth, Swansea; **No** Nottingham.

Interview advice and questions Questions asked on A-level syllabus. Part of the interview may be in German. What foreign newspapers and/or magazines do you read? Questions on German current affairs, particularly politics and reunification problems, books read outside the course, etc. See also **Chapter 6**. **Leeds** See **Languages**.

Reasons for rejection (non-academic) Unstable personality. Poor motivation. Insufficient commitment. Unrealistic expectations. Not interested in spending a year abroad.

AFTER-RESULTS ADVICE
Offers to applicants repeating A-levels Higher Birmingham, Glasgow, Leeds, Warwick; **Same** Aston, Cardiff, Chester, Durham, East Anglia, London (RH), Newcastle (not always), Nottingham, Salford, Surrey, Swansea, Ulster, York; **No** Cambridge.

GRADUATE DESTINATIONS AND EMPLOYMENT (2011/12 HESA)
Graduates surveyed 600 **Employed** 305 **In voluntary employment** 30 **In further study** 135 **Assumed unemployed** 50

Career note See **Languages**.

OTHER DEGREE SUBJECTS FOR CONSIDERATION
East European Studies; European Studies; International Business Studies.

GREEK
(see also Classical Studies/Classical Civilisation, Classics, Languages, Latin)

Courses are offered in Ancient and Modern Greek, covering the language and literature from ancient times to the present day. Classics and Classical Studies courses (see separate tables) also focus on Greek language and literature, and many provide the opportunity to learn Greek (and/or Latin) from scratch.

Useful websites www.greek-language.com; www.arwhead.com/Greeks; www.greekmyth.org; www.fhw.gr; www.culture.gr; www.greeklanguage.gr.

NB The points totals shown to the left of the institutions are for ease of reference only. It must not be assumed that Tariff points are always used by institutions or that they can be substituted for an offer in grades. The level of an offer is not necessarily indicative of the quality of a course.

COURSE OFFERS INFORMATION
Subject requirements/preferences GCSE English and a foreign language required. Greek required by some universities. **AL** Latin, Greek or a foreign language may be specified by some universities.

Your target offers and examples of courses provided by each institution
380 pts **Cambridge** – A*AA 380 pts (Class; Modn Mediev Lang (Class Gk)) (IB 40–41 pts HL 776)
360 pts **Edinburgh** – AAA–BBB 360–300 pts (Gk St courses; Anc Hist Gk) (IB 40–34 pts)
　　　　　　Oxford – AAA 360 pts (Modn Lang (Gk)) (IB 38–40 pts)
340 pts **Leeds** – AAB (Gk) (IB 33 pts)
　　　　　　London (King's) – AAB 340 pts (Modn GK; GK Engl; Mod Gk Byz St; Class St Byz Modn Gk St; Turk Modn Gk St; Fr Modn Gk St) (IB 35 pts HL 665)

Check **Chapter 4** when choosing your university and **Chapter 7** on how to read the subject tables.

      London (UCL) – AAB (Lat Gk) (IB 36 pts)
      Nottingham – AAB (Gk (Anc)) (IB 34 pts)
      St Andrews – AAB 340 pts (Gk courses) (IB 36 pts)
320 pts **Glasgow** – ABB (Gk) (IB 36 pts)
      London (RH) – ABB 320 pts (Gk) (IB 34 pts)
280 pts **Swansea** – BBC 280 pts (Gk courses) (IB 30 pts)
200 pts **Trinity Saint David** – 200 pts (Lat Gk) (IB 26 pts)

Alternative offers
See **Chapter 7** and **Appendix 1** for grades/UCAS Tariff points information for the International Baccalaureate, Scottish Highers/Advanced Highers, the Welsh Baccalaureate, the Irish Leaving Certificate, the Cambridge Pre-U Diploma, the Advanced Diploma and the Extended Project.

CHOOSING YOUR COURSE (SEE ALSO CH.1)
Some course features
Edinburgh (Gk St) The course covers archaeology, art, literature of Greek civilisation, with an intensive Greek course in the first term for beginners. Greek can be taken for one or two years as part of almost any Arts degree.
London (King's) The Modern Greek with English course focuses on studying the classical world through reading ancient texts in Greek. A-level Greek is required for entry.
Nottingham (Gk (Anc)) The course combines Greek language learning throughout (no prior knowledge required) with a study of Greek literature, history, society and culture. Intensive language study is provided so at each level of the course students can read texts in the original Greek.

Universities and colleges teaching quality See www.qaa.ac.uk; http://unistats.direct.gov.uk.

Top research universities and colleges (RAE 2008) See **Classics**.

ADMISSIONS INFORMATION
Number of applicants per place (approx) Leeds 2; London (King's) 3.

Advice to applicants and planning the UCAS personal statement See **Classical Studies/Classical Civilisation**.

Selection interviews Yes Cambridge, London (RH).

Interview advice and questions Questions asked on A-level syllabus: Why do you want to study Greek? What aspects of this course interest you? (Questions will develop from answers.) See also **Chapter 6**.

Reasons for rejection (non-academic) Poor language ability.

AFTER-RESULTS ADVICE
Offers to applicants repeating A-levels Higher St Andrews; **Same** Leeds; **No** Cambridge.

GRADUATE DESTINATIONS AND EMPLOYMENT (2011/12 HESA)
Classical Greek graduates surveyed 10 **Employed** 0 **In voluntary employment** 0 **In further study** 5 **Assumed unemployed** 0

Career note See **Languages**.

OTHER DEGREE SUBJECTS FOR CONSIDERATION
Ancient History; Classical Studies; Classics; European Studies; Philosophy.

HEALTH SCIENCES/STUDIES

(including **Audiology, Chiropractic, Orthoptics, Osteopathy** and **Paramedic Science**; see also **Community Studies/Development, Dietetics, Environmental Sciences/Studies, Nursing and Midwifery, Nutrition, Pharmacology, Pharmacy and Pharmaceutical Sciences, Physiotherapy, Radiography, Social Sciences/Studies, Speech Pathology/Sciences/Therapy**)

Health Sciences/Studies is a broad subject field which offers courses covering both practical applications concerning health and well-being (some of which border on nursing) and also the administrative activities involved in the promotion of health in the community. Also included are some specialised careers which include chiropractic, involving the healing process by way of manipulation, mainly in the spinal region, and osteopathy in which joints and tissues are manipulated to correct abnormalities. Audiology is concerned with the treatment and diagnosis of hearing and balance disorders while prosthetics involves the provision and fitting of artificial limbs and orthotics is concerned with making and fitting braces, splints and special footwear to ease pain and to assist movement.

Useful websites www.rsph.org.uk; www.bmj.com; www.reflexology.org; www.baap.org.uk; www.chiropractic-uk.co.uk; www.osteopathy.org.uk; www.who.int; www.csp.org.uk; www.intute.ac.uk.

NB The points totals shown to the left of the institutions are for ease of reference only. It must not be assumed that Tariff points are always used by institutions or that they can be substituted for an offer in grades. The level of an offer is not necessarily indicative of the quality of a course.

COURSE OFFERS INFORMATION

Subject requirements/preferences GCSE English, mathematics and a science important or essential for some courses. **AL** Mathematics, chemistry or biology may be required for some courses. **Other** Health checks and Disclosure and Barring Service (DBS) clearance required for many courses.

Your target offers and examples of courses provided by each institution

340 pts **Exeter** – AAB–ABB 340–320 pts (Med Sci) (IB 34–32 pts)
Southampton – AAB (Hlthcr Sci (Audiol); Hlthcr Mgt Plcy Rsch) (IB 34 pts HL 17 pts)

320 pts **Bristol UWE** – 320 pts (Hlthcr Sci (Physiol Sci); Hlthcr Sci (Lf Sci)) (IB 27 pts)
Durham – ABB 320 pts (Hlth Hum Sci) (IB 34 pts)
Salford – 320 pts (Pros Orthot) (IB 27 pts)
Sheffield – ABB (Hlth Hum Sci) (IB 34 pts)
Southampton – ABB (Hlthcr Sci (Cardio Respir Slp Sci)) (IB 32 pts HL 16 pts)
Strathclyde – ABB (Pros Orthot) (IB 34 pts)
Surrey – ABB (Midwif; Paramed Prac)

300 pts **Anglo-Euro (Coll Chiro)** – BBB +DBS check (Chiro) (IB 26 pts)
Bradford – 300 pts (Clin Med Sci; Clin Sci (optional transfer for some students to Medicine at **Leeds**))
Brunel – BBB 300 pts (Occ Thera) (IB 32 pts)
Cardiff Met (UWIC) – 300 pts (Hlthcr Sci) (IB 26 pts HL 15 pts incl chem biol)
Dundee – BBB (Oral Hlth Sci) (IB 30 pts HL 555)
Essex – 300–280 pts (Hlth Hum Sci) (IB 32–30 pts)
Glasgow – BBB (Hlth Soc Plcy (Dumfries)) (IB 30 pts)
Hertfordshire – 300 pts (Paramed Sci) (IB 28–30 pts)
Liverpool – BBB (Orth) (IB 30 pts HL 5 biol)
London (St George's) – BBB (Hlthcr Sci (Physiol Sci))
Manchester – BBB (Oral Hlth Sci) (IB 30 pts)
Sheffield – BBB 300 pts (Orth) (IB 32 pts)
Swansea – BBB (Ost)

280 pts **Bradford** – BBC (Hlth Care Sci (Genet))
Brit Coll Ost Med – BBC incl biol+chem 280 pts (Ost (MOst))

Study public health or health and well-being at the University of Greenwich

If you are looking for a rewarding career in this area, there are many great reasons to choose to study these programmes at the University of Greenwich, including:

- We offer a curriculum that has been mapped to meet competencies of the UK Public Health Register

- The majority of research is rated of an internationally excellent standard

- Our students are very satisfied – 91% of 2013 graduates were satisfied overall with their course *

- We have high employment rates – 90% of our students are in employment or postgraduate education, 6 months after graduating *

- You will be taught by a team of highly qualified, committed academics

- You will enjoy an attractive campus university experience only 20 minutes from central London

*Unistats

What some of our students have to say:

"The work experience I embarked on as part of my degree gave me an insight into the broader spectrum of the prison health system and the importance of their health needs. The recent initiation of public health improvement in local communities has been placed high on the Government agenda to improve the health and well-being of society as a whole.

Studying at the University of Greenwich has been an exceptionally rewarding experience. I would highly recommend it to anyone wishing to have an inspiring, exciting and worthwhile experience whilst gaining knowledge and understanding in preventing, promoting and improving the health of the population."

Sonia Kirkland,
BSc Hons Public Health, graduated 2013

"It's not every day young adults like me make decisions that we are proud of, but so far after my first academic year of studying at the University of Greenwich, I am sure and proud to say anytime, any day that this has been one of the best decisions and choices I have made .

I am an optimistic person and always interested in learning new things. In studying health and well-being I have acquired new knowledge that has changed me as an individual. I have developed my thinking and can now understand different perspectives towards health, well-being, lifestyle, the community and the society we live in as a whole."

Sandra Egbobawaye,
BSc Hons Health and Well-Being, Year 2

Entry requirements: 280 UCAS points from at A-Levels and/or BTEC **OR** Access Course in a relevant subject (Merit or Distinction)

Health
Sciences

UNIVERSITY OF
Southampton

The University of Southampton offers you more than just a degree. We're training the next generation of health professionals in a supportive and friendly environment.

Health Sciences is nationally regarded as a pioneering centre of excellence for developing innovative Health Science roles. We enable practitioners to combine clinically focused research with developing advanced clinical skills, as part of the modernisation of health care professional careers and the drive to deliver patient-focused translational research.

Our vision is to create a world-class environment of learning and discovery. Improving health outcomes and transforming health care drives our ambitions locally, nationally and globally. Practitioners who train at Southampton are well-placed to become expert clinicians and leaders across health and social care.

Our academic staff work together in multidisciplinary research groups tackling challenging issues such as cancer, palliative and end of life care, rehabilitation and the organisation of care.

www.southampton.ac.uk/healthsciences

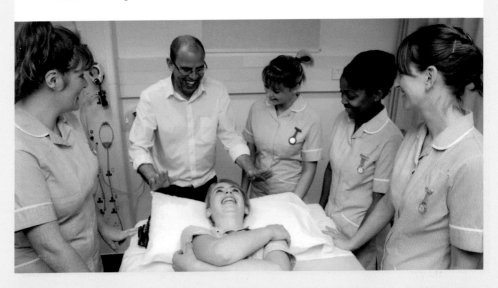

BSO – BBC incl biol+sci 280 pts (Ost) (IB 28 pts)

Greenwich – 280 pts (Hlth Wlbng)

Hertfordshire – 280 pts (Hlth St Joint Hons; Hlthcr Sci (Lf Sci))

Kent – BBC (Hlth Soc Cr) (IB 33 pts)

London Met – 280 pts (Hlth Soc Plcy; Hlth Soc Cr)

Manchester Met – 280 pts (Hlthcr Sci) (IB 28 pts)

Northampton – 280 pts (Hum Biosci) (IB 24 pts)

Plymouth – 280–300 pts (Pblc Hlth Nutr)

Portsmouth – BBC (Hlthcr Sci)

Sheffield Hallam – 280 pts (Pblc Hlth Nutr)

Swansea – 280 pts (Hlth Soc Cr; Med Sci)

Ulster – 280 pts (Hlth Soc Cr Plcy) (IB 24 pts HL 12 pts)

260 pts **Anglo-Euro (Coll Chiro)** – 260 pts incl biol/chem (Exer Hlth (Hlth Rehab))

Central Lancashire – 260–300 pts (Hlth St courses; Df St Educ)

Derby – 260 pts (Hlth Soc Cr)

Edge Hill – 260 pts (Hlth Soc Wlbng)

European Sch Ost – BCC 260 pts (Ost)

Greenwich – 260 pts (Pblc Hlth)

Kingston – 260–360 pts (Exer Nutr Hlth)

Lincoln – 260 pts (Hlth Soc Cr)

Liverpool Hope – 260–300 pts (Hlth Wlbng Nutr) (IB 26 pts)

Liverpool John Moores – 260 pts (Hlth Soc Cr Fmly Indiv Comm)

Northampton – 260–280 pts (Hlth St courses)

Nottingham Trent – 260 pts (Exer Nutr Hlth)

Sunderland – 260 pts (Pblc Hlth; Hlth Soc Cr; Hlthcr Sci (Physiol Sci/Lf Sci/Audiol))

UHI – BCC 260 pts (Oral Hlth Sci)

240 pts **Bangor** – 240–260 pts (Hlth Soc Cr)

Birmingham City – 240 pts (Hlth Wlbng)

Canterbury Christ Church – 240 pts (Hlth St) (IB 24 pts)

Cardiff Met (UWIC) – 240 pts (Hlth Soc Cr)

Chester – 240–280 pts (Hlth Soc Cr)

East London – 240 pts (Hlth Prom)

Leeds Beckett – 240 pts (Ost) (IB 24 pts)

Leeds Trinity – 240–280 pts (Nutr Fd Hlth)

Middlesex – 240 pts (Trad Chin Med)

Nescot – 240 pts (Ost Med)

Nottingham Trent – 240 pts (Hlth Soc Cr)

Oldham (Univ Campus) – 240 pts (Hlth Commun St)

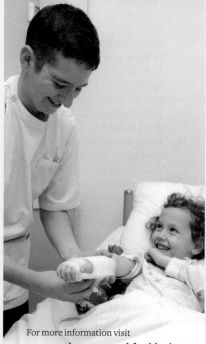

UNIVERSITY OF
Southampton

Leading healthcare. Learn with the best

The University of Southampton, Faculty of Health Sciences is one of the leading universities for nursing, midwifery, healthcare science, occupational therapy, physiotherapy and podiatry, offering:

– Cutting edge, research led teaching

– Excellent connections with the NHS

– Varied and interesting practice experiences

– Supportive and friendly environment

For more information visit
www.southampton.ac.uk/healthsciences
Tel: +44 (0)23 8059 5500
www.facebook.com/healthsciences

Check **Chapter 4** when choosing your university and **Chapter 7** on how to read the subject tables.

Health & Science

at Hull & Harrogate College

We offer students the opportunity to study towards a Certificate in Education, Professional Graduate Certificate in Education, Foundation Degrees and BA (Hons) Degrees. Areas of study include Certificate in Education & PGCE, Professional Development in Education, Young Children's Learning & Development, Sport Studies, Sport & Health Sciences, Criminology and Travel & Tourism Management.

Our courses are validated by either The Open University or the University of Huddersfield meaning you will receive your degree from one of the country's leading higher education institutions.

Come and meet us
Visit us at one of our campus open events. Call for more info.

Hull Campus	**Harrogate Campus**
(01482) 598 744	(01423) 878 211
hull-college.ac.uk/HE	harrogate.ac.uk/HE

The Open University

University of HUDDERSFIELD

Plymouth – 240 pts (Hlth Soc Cr St)
St Mark and St John – 240 pts (Hlth Exer Physl Actvt)
Salford – 240-280 pts (Exer Physl Actvt Hlth) (IB 29 pts)
Southampton Solent – 240 pts (Psy (Hlth Psy); Hlth Exer Physl Actvt) (IB 24 pts)
Suffolk (Univ Campus) – 240 pts (Hlth Wlbng)
Westminster – CCC (Chin Med Acu) (IB 26 pts)
West Scotland – CCC (Env Hlth) (IB 24 pts)

220 pts **Anglo-Euro (Coll Chiro)** – 220 pts (Comm Hlth Rehab)
St Mary's – 220 pts (Hlth Exer Physl Actvts) (IB 28 pts)
Westminster – CCD (Hlth Sci (Complem Med)) (IB 26 pts)

200 pts **Bedfordshire** – 200 pts (Disab St)
Central Lancashire – 200 pts (Sex Hlth St)
Middlesex – 200-300 pts (Acu; Herb Med) (IB 28 pts)
West London – 200 pts (Hlth St)
Wolverhampton – 200 pts (Soc Cr Hlth St; Hlth St; Df St Soc Pol)

160 pts **Accrington and Rossendale (Coll)** – 160 pts (Hlth App Soc St)
Anglia Ruskin – 160 pts (Pblc Hlth)
Stockport (Coll) – 160 pts (Hlth Soc Cr)
UHI – CC–AA (Hlth St Rur Hlth/Hlth Welf; Hlth St)

140 pts **Bradford (Coll Univ Centre)** – 140 pts (Hlth Soc Welf)
120 pts **Cumbria** – 120 pts (Hlth Cr Prac)

Brighton – individual offers may vary (Acu St; Ost)
Open University – contact +44 (0)845 300 6090 **or** www.openuniversity.co.uk/you (Hlth Soc Cr)
Trinity Saint David – entry is based on individual merit (Hlth Nutr Lfstl)

For a quick reference offers calculator, fold out the inside front cover.

Alternative offers
See **Chapter 7** and **Appendix 1** for grades/UCAS Tariff points information for the International Baccalaureate, Scottish Highers/Advanced Highers, the Welsh Baccalaureate, the Irish Leaving Certificate, the Cambridge Pre-U Diploma, the Advanced Diploma and the Extended Project.

EXAMPLES OF FOUNDATION DEGREES IN THE SUBJECT FIELD
See also **Social and Public Policy and Administration** Blackburn (Coll); Blackpool and Fylde (Coll); Bolton; Brighton; Bucks New; Croydon (Coll); Cumbria; Duchy (Coll); Durham New (Coll); Exeter (Coll); Grimsby (Univ Centre); Havering (Coll); Hopwood Hall (Coll); Lakes (Coll); Llandrillo Cymru (Coll); Manchester (Coll); Neath Port Talbot (Coll); North Lindsey (Coll); Norwich City (Coll); Oxford Brookes; Petroc; St Helens (Coll); Somerset (Coll); Stockport (Coll); Truro (Coll); Wakefield (Coll); Walsall (Coll); West Cheshire (Coll); Worcester (CT).

CHOOSING YOUR COURSE (SEE ALSO CH.1)
Some course features
Aberdeen The Health Sciences programme is based in the Medical School and combines courses in social, life and medical sciences. In the third year students are attached to a health or social care agency in the community.
Bath Spa Health Studies is a part of the Combined Honours programme. In addition to health subjects the course focuses on social, cultural, economic and environmental factors.
Brunel Degrees are offered in Occupational Therapy and Physiotherapy. Both courses place an emphasis on preparing students for working life by promoting autonomy and clinical practice.
Hertfordshire (Paramed Sci) Full paramedic training leading to a degree combined with vocational placement with the London Ambulance Service.
Strathclyde (Pros Orthot) A highly practical course covering human biology and the design and engineering applications dealing with patients who have lost the use of limbs.

Universities and colleges teaching quality See www.qaa.ac.uk; http://unistats.direct.gov.uk.

Top research universities and colleges (RAE 2008) (Allied Health Professions and Studies) London (UCL); Lancaster; Surrey; Bristol UWE; Hull; Cardiff; Swansea; Glasgow; Strathclyde; Queen's Belfast.

ADMISSIONS INFORMATION
Number of applicants per place (approx) Anglo-Euro (Coll Chiro) 1; Bangor 2; Bath Spa 1; Bournemouth 4; Bristol (Audiol) 5, (Df St) 2; Brit Coll Ost Med 5; Brunel 2; Central Lancashire 6; Chester 6; Chichester 5; Cumbria 4; European Sch Ost 3; Liverpool John Moores 10; London Met 7; Manchester 18; Manchester Met 10; Middlesex 4; Northampton 3; Portsmouth 12; Roehampton 10; Salford 8; Southampton 4; Swansea 1; Worcester 3.

Admissions tutors' advice You should describe any work with people you have done, particularly in a caring capacity, for example, working with the elderly, nursing, hospital work. Show why you wish to study this subject. You should give evidence of your ability to communicate and to work in a group. Evidence needed of applicants' understanding of the NHS and health care systems. Osteopathy applicants should provide clear evidence of why they want to work as an osteopath: work shadowing in an osteopath's practice is important and should be described. Give details of any work using your hands.

Misconceptions about this course There is a mistaken belief that Health Science courses include nursing. **Bangor** (Hlth Soc Cr) This is an administration course, not a nursing course. **Brit Coll Ost Med** Some students think that we offer an orthodox course in medicine. **European Sch Ost** Some applicants think we teach in French: we do not although we do have a franchise with a French school based in St Etienne and a high percentage of international students. All lectures are in English. Applicants should note that cranial osteopathy – one of our specialisms – is only one aspect of the programme.

Selection interviews Yes Birmingham, Central Lancashire, Chichester, Coventry, European Sch Ost, London (St George's), Middlesex, Nottingham Trent, Portsmouth, Southampton, West Scotland,

Worcester, York; **Some** Abertay, Bath Spa, Canterbury Christ Church, Cardiff Met (UWIC) (Complem Thera), Derby, Huddersfield (mature students), Liverpool John Moores, Salford, Swansea; **No** Dundee.

Interview advice and questions Courses vary considerably and you are likely to be questioned on your reasons for choosing the course at that university or college. If you have studied biology then questions are possible on the A-level syllabus and you could also be asked to discuss any work experience you have had. (Ost) What personal qualities would you need to be a good osteopath? What have you done that you would feel demonstrates a sense of responsibility? What would you do if you were not able to secure a place on an Osteopathy course this year? See also **Chapter 6**. **Liverpool John Moores** Interviews are informal. It would be useful for you to bring samples of coursework to the interview.

Reasons for rejection (non-academic) Some students are mistakenly looking for a professional qualification in, for example, occupational therapy, nursing. **Coventry** Inadequate mathematics knowledge.

AFTER-RESULTS ADVICE
Offers to applicants repeating A-levels **Same** Abertay, Aston, Bangor, Brighton, Chester, Derby, European Sch Ost, Huddersfield, Lincoln, Liverpool John Moores, Nottingham Trent (Hlth Env), Roehampton, Salford, Surrey, Swansea.

GRADUATE DESTINATIONS AND EMPLOYMENT (2011/12 HESA)
See also **Biotechnology**, **Dentistry**, **Medicine**, **Nursing and Midwifery**, **Nutrition** and **Optometry**.

Complementary Medicine graduates surveyed 900 **Employed** 400 **In voluntary employment** 5 **In further study** 145 **Assumed unemployed** 55

Aural and Oral Sciences graduates surveyed 670 **Employed** 440 **In voluntary employment** 20 **In further study** 55 **Assumed unemployed** 35

Career note Graduates enter a very broad variety of careers depending on their specialism. Opportunities exist in the public sector, for example, management and administrative positions with health and local authorities and in health promotion.

OTHER DEGREE SUBJECTS FOR CONSIDERATION
Audiology; Biological Sciences; Biology; Community Studies; Consumer Studies; Dentistry; Dietetics; Medicine; Environmental Health; Nursing; Nutrition; Occupational Therapy; Optometry; Physiotherapy; Psychology; Podiatry; Radiography; Speech Therapy; Sport Science.

HISTORY

(including **Heritage Management** and **Medieval Studies**; see also **History (Ancient)**, **History (Economic and Social)**, **History of Art**)

Degrees in History cover a very broad field with many courses focusing on British and European history. However, specialised History degrees are available which cover other regions of the world and, in addition, all courses will offer a wide range of modules.

Useful websites www.english-heritage.org.uk; www.historytoday.com; www.archives.com; www.historynet.com; www.archives.org.uk; www.royalhistoricalsociety.org; www.nationalarchives.gov.uk; www.historesearch.com.

NB The points totals shown to the left of the institutions are for ease of reference only. It must not be assumed that Tariff points are always used by institutions or that they can be substituted for an offer in grades. The level of an offer is not necessarily indicative of the quality of a course.

A PLACE TO INSPIRE YOU/AN APPROACH TO CHALLENGE YOU

The School of History at the University of Kent combines research excellence with inspirational teaching to offer a superb student experience.

- Ranked 2nd in the UK for research excellence (RAE 2008)
- Offering flexible, research-led teaching
- Programmes include; medieval, early modern, modern British and European, American, imperial and colonial, military, scientific and medical history
- Scored 95% for student satisfaction in the most recent National Student Survey (*NSS 2013*)
- Based in the historic cathedral city of Canterbury, across 300 acres of parkland
- Outstanding employability support – 91% of History graduates go on to employment or further study after six months

To find out more go to
www.kent.ac.uk/history,
or come along to an Open Day
www.kent.ac.uk/opendays
01227 827272

University of **Kent**

50
1965-2015
THE UK'S
EUROPEAN
UNIVERSITY

COMBINING RESEARCH EXCELLENCE WITH INSPIRATIONAL TEACHING

The School of History at the University of Kent is recognised as one of the leading history departments in the country. Ranked second nationally in the most recent Research Assessment Exercise, students are taught by world-class academics, actively working at the forefront of their fields.

The School prides itself on its flexible programmes, offering students the opportunity to tailor their degree to their own interests. Undergraduate students have access to over 70 modules covering British, Irish, European, American, South Asian and African history. An unparalleled range of joint honours degrees are also on offer, for those wishing to pursue a cross-disciplinary programme.

For the past five years, the School of History has consistently scored over 90% for student satisfaction in the National Student Survey – reflecting its inspiring teaching, lively and engaging student body and fantastic student support. A student-led History Society maintains a vibrant undergraduate community, organising extra-curricular lectures, field trips to places such as Rome and Vienna, and a host of social events.

The School is situated on Canterbury's leafy campus, where students have access to the University library, which holds over one million items, as well as the British Cartoon Archive. The medieval city provides a dramatic backdrop to the study of history, and students have privileged access to the Canterbury Cathedral Library and archives. High-speed trains link Canterbury to London and the continent, placing many of the most influential and historic sites in Europe a stone's throw away.

The School of History also has strong and established links with institutions across Europe as well as in Canada, the United States and South Africa allowing for a truly global outlook and opportunities to study abroad.

The strength of the School's degrees means that graduates are highly sought after; in 2012 91% of students were in employment or further study shortly after graduation.

A superb student experience

"I came to an Open Day at Kent and loved it, I met a professor who teaches the subject who really sold the course to me, and of course, Canterbury's a beautiful city.

My course is going really well, it's a lot of work, but I love it. For my 15,000-word dissertation I'm researching the treatment of shell shock in the First World War and the differentiation of treatment depending on class and rank. That's the beauty is this degree – you can do whatever interests you.

The group of students is small so you get more personalised teaching and you really get to know your lecturers. I'm currently applying for work in MGOs, charities and campaigning organisations, but the truth is that I love University so much I don't want to leave! I've learnt so much and made some great friends."

Lisa Whitehead
War Studies

"I was attracted to Kent after coming to an Open Day, I liked the fact that everything was contained and everyone was really friendly and enthusiastic. The facilities are great, especially the library, and my course had a lot of modules to choose form.

The highlight of my degree has been my third year when I went to France – it was so much fun. It was a very different teaching method in France, and it was interesting learning history from a French perspective!

The one characteristic all the lecturers have in common is that you can talk to them. If you are struggling over something, you can email them and they respond very quickly. I find the idea of teaching quite rewarding and I have been accepted to study a PGCE to teach history at secondary school level."

Jonathan Brown
European History with a Year Abroad

Further details

For more information please contact:
history@kent.ac.uk
01227 823710
www.kent.ac.uk/history

COURSE OFFERS INFORMATION

Subject requirements/preferences GCSE English and a foreign language may be required or preferred. **AL** History usually required at a specified grade. (Mediev St) History or English literature required for some courses. (Vkg St) English or history.

Your target offers and examples of courses provided by each institution

400 pts   **London (UCL)** – A*AAe–AAAe 400–380 pts (Hist; Hist Euro Lang; Hist (St Abrd)) (IB 38–39 pts HL 18–19 pts)

Warwick – AAAc (Hist (Ren/Modn Modn)) (IB 38 pts HL 6 hist)

380 pts   **Cambridge** – A*AA (Hist) (IB 40–41 pts HL 776)

Durham – A*AA 380 pts (Hist) (IB 38 pts HL 666)

Exeter – A*AA–AAB (Hist) (IB 38–34 pts)

360 pts   **Bristol** – AAA–AAB (Hist) (IB 35–37 pts HL 666)

Durham – AAA 360 pts (Modn Langs Hist) (IB 37 pts)

Edinburgh – AAA–BBB 360–300 pts (Hist; Hist Pol; Scot Hist) (IB 42–34 pts)

Exeter – AAA–AAB (Hist Joint Hons; Hist Int Rel (St Abrd); Hist Int Rel) (IB 36–34 pts)

Lancaster – AAA (Hist Pol; Hist; Mediev Ren St) (IB 36 pts)

Leeds – AAA (Hist) (IB 35–37 pts)

Liverpool – AAA (Hist) (IB 36 pts HL 6 hist)

London (King's) – AAA (Hist; Fr Hist; War St Hist) (IB 35 pts HL 666)

London (QM) – AAA 340 pts (Hist) (IB 32 pts)

London (UCL) – AABe–ABBe incl hist 360–340 pts (Russ Hist) (IB 34–36 pts)

London LSE – AAA (Gov Hist; Int Rel Hist; Hist) (IB 38 pts HL 766)

London NCH – AAA 360 pts (Hist) (IB 36 pts HL 666)

Manchester – AAA–AAB 340–360 pts (Hist) (IB 37 pts)

Newcastle – AAA–AAB 340–360 pts (Hist) (IB 37–35 pts HL 6 hist)

Nottingham – AAA (Hist Pol; Hist) (IB 36 pts)

Oxford – AAA (Hist Pol; Hist Modn Langs; Hist Econ; Class Arch Anc Hist; Persn Islam St/Hist; Anc Modn Hist; Hist) (IB 38–40 pts)

St Andrews – AAA–AAB (Mediev Hist Arch; Mediev Hist courses; Scot Hist courses; Modn Hist courses) (IB 35–36 pts)

Sussex – AAA–ABB 360–320 pts (Hist Joint Hons) (IB 35–34 pts)

York – AAA (Hist; Fr Hist; Engl Hist)

340 pts   **Birmingham** – AAB (Hist) (IB 36 pts)

Brunel – AAB–ABB 340 pts (Hist) (IB 35 pts HL 6)

Cardiff – AAB incl hist 340 pts (Hist; Modn Hist Pol)

East Anglia – AAB incl hist (Hist; Hist Hist Art) (IB 33 pts HL 5 hist)

Edinburgh – AAB–BBB 340–300 pts (Celt Scot Hist; Archit Hist) (IB 36–34 pts)

Glasgow – AAB (Hist) (IB 34 pts)

Lancaster – AAB (Hist Int Rel; Hist Phil) (IB 35 pts HL 16 pts)

Leicester – AAB (Hist) (IB 34 pts)

London (RH) – AAB (Hist) (IB 36 pts)

London (SOAS) – AAB (Hist) (IB 30–32 pts)

London (UCL) – AAB–ABB 340–320 pts (Hist Phil Sci; Jew Hist; Scand St Hist) (IB 34–36 pts)

Loughborough – AAB–ABB (Hist Int Rel; Hist Geog) (IB 34–32 pts)

Manchester – AAB–ABB (Pol Modn Hist; Hist courses) (IB 36–33 pts)

Newcastle – AAB–ABB (Herit Hist Arch) (IB 35 pts HL 555)

Nottingham – AAB (Hisp St Hist; Anc Hist Hist; Engl St Hist) (IB 34 pts)

Reading – AAB–A*BB (Hist) (IB 35 pts HL 5 hist)

Sheffield – AAB–ABB 340–320 pts (Hist Joint Hons; Hist; Hist Pol) (IB 35–34 pts HL 6 hist)

Southampton – AAB (Hist; Engl Hist; Modn Hist; Phil Hist; Film Hist; Modn Hist Pol) (IB 34 pts HL 17 pts)

Sussex – AAB (Hist) (IB 35 pts)

320 pts   **Aberystwyth** – 320 pts (Hist) (IB 32 pts)

Birmingham – ABB–AAB 320–340 pts (Hist Joint Hons)

Bristol UWE – 320 pts (Hist) (IB 27 pts)
East Anglia – ABB (Am Hist; Modn Hist; Hist Pol; Lit Hist; Phil Hist) (IB 32 pts)
Essex – ABB–BBB (Hist; Phil Hist; Am Hist) (IB 32–30 pts)
Glasgow – ABB (Scot Hist) (IB 34 pts)
Gloucestershire – 320 pts (Engl Lit Hist)
Keele – ABB 320 pts (Hist) (IB 34 pts)
Kent – ABB (Hist courses; War St; Am St (Hist)) (IB 33 pts)
Leeds – ABB (Hist Phil Sci courses; Biol Hist Phil Sci) (IB 34 pts HL 16 pts incl 6 hist)
Leicester – ABB (Int Rel Hist; Anc Hist Hist; Hist Am St; Contemp Hist; Hist courses)
Liverpool – ABB (Comb Hons (Hist)) (IB 33–36 pts)
London (Birk) – ABB 320 pts (Hist)
London (Gold) – ABB (Hist; Hist Hist Ideas) (IB 34 pts)
London (QM) – ABB (Hist Pol; Hist Compar Lit; Mediev Hist) (IB 34–32 pts)
Loughborough – ABB–AAB (Hist Pol; Hist; Hist Engl) (IB 32–34 pts)
Northumbria – 320 pts (Hist) (IB 26 pts)
Nottingham – ABB (Am St Hist; Am Can Lit Hist Cult; Hist Contemp Chin St Hist Art Hist; Hist Russ) (IB 32 pts)
Queen's Belfast – ABB (Hist)
Reading – ABB 320 pts (Hist Art Hist) (IB 32 pts)
Sheffield – ABB 320 pts (Jap St Joint Hons) (IB 34 pts)
Southampton – ABB (Arch Hist) (IB 32 pts HL 16 pts)
Strathclyde – ABB (Hist) (IB 34 pts)
Swansea – ABB–BBB (Euro Hist; Mediev St courses)

300 pts **Aberdeen** – BBB 300 pts (Hist) (IB 32 pts)
Aberystwyth – 300 pts (Hist Archvl St; Hist Welsh Hist; Mediev Ely Modn Hist; Modn Contemp Hist) (IB 29 pts)
Brighton – BBB (Hist Cult Lit) (IB 32 pts)
Buckingham – BBB 300 pts (Engl Lit Hist) (IB 34 pts)
Dundee – BBB (Hist; Bus Econ Mark Hist; Scot Hist St) (IB 30 pts HL 555)
Essex – 300–320 pts (Modn Hist) (IB 32 pts)
Gloucestershire – 300 pts (Hist)
Hertfordshire – 300 pts (Hist Ital; Hist)
Huddersfield – BBB 300 pts (Hist Pol Contemp Hist)
Hull – 300–340 pts (Hist; Hist Marit Hist)
Northumbria – 300 pts (Hist Pol) (IB 26 pts)
Oxford Brookes – BBB (Hist) (IB 32 pts)
Queen's Belfast – BBB 300 pts (Fr Joint Hons)
Roehampton – 300 pts (Hist) (IB 26 pts)
Swansea – ABB–BBB 300 pts (Hist)

280 pts **Bangor** – 280–300 pts (Herit Arch Hist; Hist; Mediev Ely Modn Hist; Modn Contemp Hist) (IB 28 pts)
Brighton – BBC (Sociol Soc Hist) (IB 30 pts)
Chichester – BBC–BCC 260–280 pts (Hist) (IB 30 pts)
Edge Hill – 280 pts (Hist; Engl Hist; Hist Sociol)
Greenwich – 280 pts (Phil Hist) (IB 28 pts)
Hull – 280 pts (Fr/Ger/Ital/Span Hist) (IB 30 pts)
Lincoln – 280 pts (Hist)
Liverpool John Moores – 280 pts (Hist) (IB 28 pts)
Manchester Met – 280 pts (Hist Joint Hons) (IB 29 pts)
Nottingham Trent – 280 pts (Hist)
Salford – 280 pts (Contemp Mltry Int Hist) (IB 25–27 pts)
South Wales – BBC 280 pts (Hist Am St)
Stirling – BBC (Scot Hist; Hist) (IB 32 pts)
Teesside – 280 pts (Hist) (IB 24 pts)
Ulster – BBC 280 pts (Irish Hist Soc)

Check **Chapter 4** when choosing your university and **Chapter 7** on how to read the subject tables.

Westminster – BBC 280 pts (Engl Lit Hist) (IB 30 pts HL 5 Engl)
Worcester – 280–380 pts (Hist courses) (IB 24 pts)

260 pts **Bangor** – 260–300 pts (Welsh Hist)
Bath Spa – 260–300 pts (Hist) (IB 26 pts)
Cardiff Met (UWIC) – 260 pts (Educ St Modn Hist)
Central Lancashire – BCC 260 pts (Hist Musm Herit; Modn Wrld Hist; Hist) (IB 24 pts)
Chester – 260–300 pts (Hist) (IB 28 pts HL 5 hist)
Coventry – BCC (Hist courses; Pol Hist)
De Montfort – 260 pts (Hist) (IB 24 pts)
Derby – 260 pts (Hist)
Greenwich – 260 pts (Hist)
Liverpool Hope – 260–320 pts (Hist)
Liverpool John Moores – 260 pts (Hist Engl) (IB 28 pts)
Newman – 260 pts (Hist) (IB 24 pts)
Northampton – 260–280 pts (Hist courses) (IB 24 pts)
Nottingham Trent – 260 pts (Pol Hist)
Plymouth – 260 pts (Hist courses) (IB 27 pts)
St Mary's – 260 pts (Hist) (IB 28 pts)
Sheffield Hallam – 260 pts (Engl Hist; Hist)
South Wales – 260 pts (Hist)
Sunderland – 260 pts (Hist courses)
Ulster – 260–280 pts (Hist courses) (IB 24 pts)
Westminster – BCC (Modn Hist) (IB 28 pts)
Winchester – 260–300 pts (Hist; Hist Mediev Wrld) (IB 24 pts)

240 pts **Bishop Grosseteste** – 240 pts (Vis Art Hist)
Bradford – 240 pts (Modn Euro Hist)
Canterbury Christ Church – 240 pts (Hist Arch; Hist) (IB 24 pts)
Glyndŵr – 240 pts (Hist)
Kingston – 240 pts (Hist)
Leeds Beckett – 240 pts (Hist) (IB 24 pts)
Manchester Met – 240–260 pts (Mediev Modn Hist; Modn Hist; Pol Hist; Hist) (IB 28 pts)
Portsmouth – 240–300 pts (Am St Hist; Hist; Engl Hist)
Staffordshire – 240 pts (Modn Hist)
Suffolk (Univ Campus) – 240–280 pts (Hist) (IB 28 pts)

220 pts **Anglia Ruskin** – 220–260 pts (Hist)
Bishop Grosseteste – 220 pts (Herit St; Hist courses)
Leeds Trinity – 220–260 pts (Hist; Engl Hist) (IB 24 pts)
Wolverhampton – 220 pts (Pol Hist)
York St John – 220–260 pts (Hist courses) (IB 24 pts)

200 pts **Blackburn (Coll)** – 200 pts (Hist)
East London – 200 pts (Hist)
Trinity Saint David – 200–300 pts (Hist courses; Mediev St) (IB 26 pts)

180 pts **Kingston** – 180 pts (Hist Bld Cons)
West Anglia (Coll) – 180 pts (Engl Hist)

160 pts **UHI** – CC 160 pts (Scot Hist Arch; Scot Hist; Hist Pol)
Wolverhampton – 160–220 pts (Hist)

120 pts **Anglia Ruskin** – DD (Hist Engl)

Alternative offers

See **Chapter 7** and **Appendix 1** for grades/UCAS Tariff points information for the International Baccalaureate, Scottish Highers/Advanced Highers, the Welsh Baccalaureate, the Irish Leaving Certificate, the Cambridge Pre-U Diploma, the Advanced Diploma and the Extended Project.

EXAMPLES OF FOUNDATION DEGREES IN THE SUBJECT FIELD
Blackpool and Fylde (Coll); Harper Adams; Petroc; Truro (Coll).

CHOOSING YOUR COURSE (SEE ALSO CH.1)
Some course features
Kent History can be taken with an optional deferred subject. The Single Honours programme provides the opportunity of a work placement in a museum, a cathedral workshop or a year abroad in Europe.
Leicester A very large department offering specialisms in a wide range of subjects. The subject is also part of the Combined Studies programme with a choice of 17 subjects including Politics, Ancient History, Archaeology and International Relations.
London NCH Twelve modules are taken over three years and in Year 3 students choose a special subject which requires a 10,000 word dissertation. In addition to degree subject modules students study four modules in another degree subject and compulsory core modules in applied ethics, logic and critical thinking to make up the NCH diploma which is awarded alongside a degree.
Manchester The History programme enables students to study course units across the whole range of history topics including the history of science. There are opportunities to spend part of the course studying abroad.
Ulster In addition to the Single Honours course, History is offered as a joint course (two subjects) or under the Combined Arts programme when students choose three subjects in Year 1 continuing with a study of two subjects or one major and one minor subject.

Universities and colleges teaching quality See www.qaa.ac.uk; http://unistats.direct.gov.uk.

Top research universities and colleges (RAE 2008) Imperial London; Essex; Kent; Liverpool; Oxford; Warwick; Cambridge; London (UCL); London (Birk); Southampton; Hertfordshire; London LSE; Sheffield.

ADMISSIONS INFORMATION
Number of applicants per place (approx) Aberystwyth 6; Anglia Ruskin 4; Bangor 6; Bath Spa 6; Birmingham 8, (E Medit Hist) 3, (War St) 4; Bournemouth (Herit Cons) 3; Bristol 13; Bristol UWE 6; Brunel 6; Buckingham 10; Cambridge 3; Cardiff 7; Central Lancashire 5; Chichester 4; Cumbria 5; De Montfort 10; Dundee 6; Durham 15; East Anglia 8; Edge Hill 8; Exeter 9; Gloucestershire 26; Glyndŵr 2; Huddersfield 4; Hull 5; Kent 12; Kingston 6; Lancaster 11; Leeds 12; Leeds Trinity 14; Leicester 7; Liverpool 6; London (Gold) 6; London (King's) 10; London (QM) 5; London (RH) 9; London (UCL) 8; London LSE 19; London Met 2; Manchester 5; Manchester Met 8; Middlesex 10; Newcastle 13; Newman 2; Northampton 4; Nottingham 20; Oxford Brookes 25; Portsmouth 5; Roehampton 3; St Mary's 5; Sheffield Hallam 21; Southampton 5; Staffordshire 8; Stirling 2; Teesside 4; Trinity Saint David 6; Warwick 17; York 5; York St John 3.

Advice to applicants and planning the UCAS personal statement Show your passion for the past! Visits to places of interest should be mentioned, together with any particular features which impressed you. Read historical books and magazines outside your A-level syllabus. Mention these and describe any special areas of study which interest you. (Check that these areas are covered in the courses for which you are applying!) **Bristol** Only accepting a limited number of deferred applicants in fairness to next year's applicants. Apply early. **Manchester** Due to the detailed nature of entry requirements for History courses, we are unable to include full details in the prospectus. For complete and up-to-date information on our entry requirements for these courses, please visit our website at www.manchester.ac.uk/ugcourses.

Misconceptions about this course Students sometimes underestimate the amount of reading required. **Lincoln** Some students expect the subject to be assessed only by exams and essays. It is not – we use a wide range of assessment methods. **Liverpool John Moores** Some applicants think that they have to study ancient and medieval history as well as modern; we actually only cover post-1750 history. **Stirling** Some applicants think that we only teach British history. We also cover European, American, African and environmental history.

Selection interviews Yes Bangor, Birmingham, Bishop Grosseteste, Brighton, Brunel, Cambridge, Canterbury Christ Church, Chichester, Edge Hill, Hertfordshire, Hull, Lancaster, Leeds Trinity, Lincoln (Cons Restor), London (King's), London (QM), London (RH), London (UCL), London Met, London South

Bank, Middlesex, Oxford (Hist) 29% (Hist Mod Lang) 18%, Oxford Brookes, Portsmouth, Roehampton, Sussex, Warwick; **Some** Anglia Ruskin, Bath Spa, Buckingham, Cardiff, De Montfort, East Anglia, Exeter, Huddersfield, Kent, Lincoln, Liverpool, London LSE (rarely), Salford, Sheffield Hallam, Staffordshire, Trinity Saint David, Winchester, Wolverhampton, York; **No** Bristol, Dundee, Essex, Nottingham, Reading, Southampton.

Interview advice and questions Questions are almost certain to be asked on those aspects of the history A-level syllabus which interest you. Examples of questions in previous years have included: Why did imperialism happen? If a Martian arrived on Earth what aspect of life would you show him/her to sum up today's society? Has the role of class been exaggerated by Marxist historians? What is the difference between power and authority and between patriotism and nationalism? Did Elizabeth I have a foreign policy? What is the relevance of history in modern society? Who are your favourite monarchs? How could you justify your study of history to the taxpayer? What are the origins of your Christian name? See also **Chapter 6**. **Cambridge** How would you compare Henry VIII to Stalin? In the 1920s did the invention of the Henry Ford car lead to a national sub-culture or was it just an aspect of one? Is there such a thing as 'race'? Should historians be allowed to read sci-fi novels? **Cumbria** Questions about interest in research, analysis, argument, information gathering, future plans after study, motivation. **De Montfort** Why History? Why is history important? **Oxford** Questions on submitted work and the capacity to think independently. What are the origins of your name? Why are you sitting in this chair? **Sheffield** Written work may be required. **Swansea** We ask applicants to explain something – a hobby, an historical problem or a novel. The subject is less important than a coherent and enthusiastic explanation.

Reasons for rejection (non-academic) Personal statements which read like job applications, focusing extensively on personal skills and saying nothing about the applicant's passion for history. Poor use of personal statement combined with predicted grades. Little commitment and enthusiasm. No clear reason for choice of course. Little understanding of history. Absence or narrowness of intellectual pursuits. Deception or concealment on the UCAS application. Knowledge of 19th century history (chosen subject) did not have any depth. Unwillingness to learn. Narrow approach to subject. Failure to submit requested information. **Birmingham** Commitment insufficient to sustain interest over three years. **London (King's)** Inability to think analytically and comparatively. **London (UCL)** The vast majority of applications are of a very high standard, many applicants being predicted AAA grades. We view each application as a complete picture, taking into account personal statement, reference and performance at any interview as well as actual and predicted academic performance. There is no single rule by which applicants are selected and therefore no single reason why they are rejected. **Nottingham** No discrimination against Oxbridge applicants.

AFTER-RESULTS ADVICE
Offers to applicants repeating A-levels Higher Exeter, Glasgow, Huddersfield, Leeds, Liverpool, St Andrews, Trinity Saint David, Warwick; **Possibly higher** Aberystwyth, Birmingham, Cambridge, Portsmouth; **Same** Anglia Ruskin, Bangor, Bristol, Buckingham, Cardiff, Chester, Chichester, De Montfort, Dundee, Durham, East Anglia, Edge Hill, Hull, Kent, Lancaster, Lincoln, Liverpool Hope, Liverpool John Moores, London (QM), London (RH), London (SOAS), Newcastle, Newman, Nottingham Trent, Oxford Brookes, Roehampton, St Mary's, Staffordshire, Stirling, Suffolk (Univ Campus), Winchester, Wolverhampton, York, York St John.

GRADUATE DESTINATIONS AND EMPLOYMENT (2011/12 HESA)
Graduates surveyed 8790 **Employed** 3580 **In voluntary employment** 445 **In further study** 2410 **Assumed unemployed** 765

Career note Graduates enter a broad spectrum of careers. Whilst a small number seek positions with museums and galleries, most will enter careers in management, public and social services and retail as well as the teaching profession.

OTHER DEGREE SUBJECTS FOR CONSIDERATION
Ancient History; Anthropology; Archaeology; Economic and Social History; Government; History of Art; International Relations; Medieval History; Politics.

HISTORY (ANCIENT)

(see also **Arabic and Ancient Near and Middle Eastern Studies, Archaeology, Classical Studies/ Classical Civilisation, History**)

Ancient History covers the Greek and Roman world, the social, religious, political and economic changes taking place in the Byzantine period and the medieval era which followed.

Useful websites www.royalhistoricalsociety.org; www.guardians.net; www.arwhead.com/Greeks; www.ancientworlds.net; www.bbc.co.uk/history/ancient; www.historesearch.com/ancient.html.

NB The points totals shown to the left of the institutions are for ease of reference only. It must not be assumed that Tariff points are always used by institutions or that they can be substituted for an offer in grades. The level of an offer is not necessarily indicative of the quality of a course.

COURSE OFFERS INFORMATION

Subject requirements/preferences GCSE A foreign language or classical language may be required. **AL** History or classical civilisation may be preferred subjects.

Your target offers and examples of courses provided by each institution

400 pts **London (UCL)** – A*AAe–AAAe (Anc Hist; Anc Hist Egypt) (IB 38–39 pts)

380 pts **Cambridge** – A*AA 380 pts (Hum Soc Pol Sci (Assyr Egypt)) (IB 40–41 pts HL 776)

360 pts **Durham** – AAA 360 pts (Anc Hist) (IB 37 pts)

Edinburgh – AAA–BBB 360–300 pts (Anc Hist; Anc Medit Civ; Anc Hist Gk; Anc Hist Class Arch; Anc Hist Lat) (IB 40–34 pts)

London (UCL) – AABe (Anc Wrld) (IB 36 pts)

Oxford – AAA (Anc Modn Hist) (IB 38–40 pts)

St Andrews – AAA (Anc Hist Econ) (IB 38 pts)

340 pts **Bristol** – AAB–ABB (Anc Hist) (IB 35–33 pts HL 666)

Cardiff – ABB–BBB 340–300 pts (Anc Hist Joint Hons) (IB 30–32 pts)

Exeter – AAA–ABB 360–320 pts (Anc Hist) (IB 36–32 pts)

Kent – AAB (Anc Hist) (IB 33 pts)

London (King's) – AAB (Anc Hist) (IB 35 pts HL 665)

London (RH) – AAB–ABB (Anc Hist Phil)

Nottingham – AAB (Anc Hist Hist; Anc Hist Lat) (IB 34 pts)

St Andrews – AAB (Anc Hist Arch; Anc Hist Film St) (IB 36 pts)

320 pts **Birmingham** – ABB (Arch Anc Hist; Hist Anc Mediev; Anc Hist) (IB 32–34 pts)

Leeds – ABB (Gk Civ Hist) (IB 34 pts)

Leicester – ABB (Anc Hist Hist; Anc Hist Arch)

Liverpool – ABB 320 pts (Anc Hist; Arch Anc Civ; Anc Hist Arch) (IB 33 pts)

London (RH) – ABB (Anc Hist) (IB 34 pts)

Manchester – ABB–BBB 320–300 pts (Anc Hist) (IB 34–31 pts HL 666–555)

Nottingham – ABB–AAC 320 pts (Anc Hist Arch) (IB 32 pts)

Warwick – ABB (Anc Hist Class Arch) (IB 34 pts)

280 pts **Swansea** – BBC (Anc Hist; Anc Mediev Hist; Egypt Anc Hist) (IB 30 pts)

180 pts **Trinity Saint David** – 180–200 pts (Anc Mediev Hist; Anc Hist) (IB 26 pts)

Alternative offers

See **Chapter 7** and **Appendix 1** for grades/UCAS Tariff points information for the International Baccalaureate, Scottish Highers/Advanced Highers, the Welsh Baccalaureate, the Irish Leaving Certificate, the Cambridge Pre-U Diploma, the Advanced Diploma and the Extended Project.

CHOOSING YOUR COURSE (SEE ALSO CH.1)

Some course features

Birmingham (Anc Hist) Course focuses on social history and the lives, work, trade and leisure of everyday people from around 1000BC to AD1500.

Cardiff (Anc Hist) Archaeological modules can be studied as well as language modules in Greek or Latin at beginners and advanced levels.

Leicester (Anc Hist Arch) The course centres on Ancient Greece and Rome, with particular reference to the interpretation of classical texts and material remains. There is an optional module in classical and post-classical Latin.

Swansea Egyptian language study is essential for Egyptology students but optional for the Ancient History and Egyptology course. Students use the resources of the Egypt Centre, with over 3000 Egyptian antiquities.

Universities and colleges teaching quality See www.qaa.ac.uk; http://unistats.direct.gov.uk.

Top research universities and colleges (RAE 2008) See **Classics**.

ADMISSIONS INFORMATION
Number of applicants per place (approx) Birmingham 7; Bristol 12; Cardiff 4; Durham 12; Leicester 32; London (RH) 3; Manchester 6; Nottingham 10; Oxford 2.

Advice to applicants and planning the UCAS personal statement Any information about experience of excavation or museum work should be given. Visits to Greece and Italy to study archaeological sites should be described. Show how your interest in, for example, Ancient Egypt developed through, for example, reading, television and the internet. Be aware of the work of the career archaeologist, for example, sites and measurement officers, field officers and field researchers (often specialists in pottery, glass, metalwork). See also **History**.

Misconceptions about this course **Liverpool** (Egypt) Some students would have been better advised looking at V400 Archaeology or VV16 Ancient History and Archaeology, both of which offer major pathways in the study of Ancient Egypt.

Selection interviews **Yes** Durham, Leeds, London (RH), Oxford (Anc Hist) 21%; **Some** Cardiff; **No** Birmingham.

Interview advice and questions See **History**.

Reasons for rejection (non-academic) **Liverpool** (Egypt) Egyptology used to fill a gap on the UCAS application. Applicant misguided in choice of subject.

AFTER-RESULTS ADVICE
Offers to applicants repeating A-levels **Same** Birmingham, Cardiff, Durham, Newcastle.

GRADUATE DESTINATIONS AND EMPLOYMENT (2011/12 HESA)
See **History**.

Career note See **History**.

OTHER DEGREE SUBJECTS FOR CONSIDERATION
Anthropology; Archaeology; Classical Studies; Classics; Greek; History of Art; Latin.

HISTORY (ECONOMIC and SOCIAL)
(see also **History**)

Economic and Social History is a study of societies and economies and explores the changes that have taken place in the past and the causes and consequences of those changes. The study can cover Britain, Europe and other major powers.

Useful websites www.royalhistoricalsociety.org; www.ehs.org.uk; see also **Economics** and **History**.

NB The points totals shown to the left of the institutions are for ease of reference only. It must not be assumed that Tariff points are always used by institutions or that they can be substituted for an offer in grades. The level of an offer is not necessarily indicative of the quality of a course.

COURSE OFFERS INFORMATION

Subject requirements/preferences **GCSE** Mathematics usually required and a language may be preferred. **AL** History preferred.

Your target offers and examples of courses provided by each institution

360 pts **Edinburgh** – AAA-BBB 360-300 pts (Sociol Soc Econ Hist) (IB 37-34 pts HL 666-555)
York – AAA-AAB 360-340 pts (Econ Econ Hist) (IB 36-35 pts HL 666)
340 pts **London LSE** – AAB incl maths (Econ Hist) (IB 37 pts HL 666)
320 pts **Birmingham** – ABB (Econ Soc Hist) (IB 34 pts)
Glasgow – ABB (Econ Soc Hist) (IB 36 pts)
Liverpool – ABB (Hist (Soc Econ)) (IB 33 pts)
Manchester – ABB (Hist Sociol) (IB 34 pts)
300 pts **Aberdeen** – BBB 300 pts (Econ Hist)
Aberystwyth – 300-320 pts (Econ Soc Hist) (IB 30-32 pts)
Edinburgh – BBB-AAA 300-360 pts (Soc Hist) (IB 34-42 pts)
Essex – ABB-BBB 320-300 pts (Soc Cult Hist) (IB 32-30 pts)
Manchester Met – 300-320 pts (Soc Hist) (IB 28 pts)
280 pts **Hull** – 280-320 pts (Hist Soc Hist) (IB 30 pts)

Alternative offers

See **Chapter 7** and **Appendix 1** for grades/UCAS Tariff points information for the International Baccalaureate, Scottish Highers/Advanced Highers, the Welsh Baccalaureate, the Irish Leaving Certificate, the Cambridge Pre-U Diploma, the Advanced Diploma and the Extended Project.

CHOOSING YOUR COURSE (SEE ALSO CH.1)

Some course features

Birmingham (Econ Soc Hist) The course offers a study of modern and medieval historical periods in relation to social development and current economic practice.
Manchester (Hist Sociol) A flexible course with a large choice of modules offered every year in history and sociology, with the option to study abroad and/or study a language.

Universities and colleges teaching quality See www.qaa.ac.uk; http://unistats.direct.gov.uk.

ADMISSIONS INFORMATION

Number of applicants per place (approx) Birmingham 3; Liverpool 3; London LSE (Econ Hist) 3, (Econ Hist Econ) 5; York 8.

Advice to applicants and planning the UCAS personal statement See **History**.

Selection interviews **Yes** Aberystwyth, Birmingham, Liverpool.

Interview advice and questions See **History**.

AFTER-RESULTS ADVICE

Offers to applicants repeating A-levels **Higher** Warwick, York; **Possibly higher** Liverpool.

GRADUATE DESTINATIONS AND EMPLOYMENT (2011/12 HESA)

See **History**.

Career note See **History**.

OTHER DEGREE SUBJECTS FOR CONSIDERATION

Economics; Government; History; Politics; Social Policy and Administration; Sociology.

HISTORY OF ART

(see also History)

History of Art (and Design) courses differ slightly between universities although most will focus on the history and appreciation of European art and architecture from the 14th to 20th centuries. Some courses also cover the Egyptian, Greek and Roman periods and at London (SOAS), Asian, African and European Art. The history of all aspects of design and film can also be studied in some courses. There has been an increase in the popularity of these courses in recent years.

Useful websites www.artchive.com; www.artcyclopedia.com; theartguide.com; www.galleries.co.uk; www.fine-art.com; www.nationalgallery.org.uk; www.britisharts.co.uk; www.tate.org.uk.

NB The points totals shown to the left of the institutions are for ease of reference only. It must not be assumed that Tariff points are always used by institutions or that they can be substituted for an offer in grades. The level of an offer is not necessarily indicative of the quality of a course.

COURSE OFFERS INFORMATION

Subject requirements/preferences GCSE English required and a foreign language usually preferred. **AL** History is preferred for some courses.

Your target offers and examples of courses provided by each institution

380 pts **Cambridge** – A*AA (Hist Art) (IB 40–42 pts HL 776–777)
360 pts **Bristol** – AAA–AAB 360–340 pts (Hist Art) (IB 37–35 pts HL 666)
 Edinburgh – AAA–BBB 360–300 pts (Hist Art Hist Mus) (IB 37–34 pts)
 London (UCL) – AABe (Hist Art) (IB 36 pts HL 17 pts)
 Oxford – AAA (Hist Art) (IB 38–40 pts)
 St Andrews – AAA (Art Hist Psy; Art Hist Mid E St) (IB 36 pts)
340 pts **Bristol** – AAB–ABB (Hist Art Modn Lang) (IB 35–33 pts HL 666)
 East Anglia – AAB (Arch Anth Art Hist (St Abrd); Hist Art; Hist Hist Art) (IB 33 pts)
 Kent – AAB–ABB (Art Hist) (IB 33 pts)
 Leeds – AAB–ABB (Hist Art Musm St) (IB 35 pts)
 London (Court) – AAB 340 pts (Hist Art) (IB 30 pts)
 Manchester – ABB (Hist Social) (IB 34 pts)
 Newcastle – AAB (Hist Art Comb Hons) (IB 35 pts HL 665)
 St Andrews – AAB (Art Hist Class St; Art Hist; Art Hist Lang) (IB 36 pts)
 Sussex – AAB–ABB (Art Hist) (IB 34 pts)
 York – AAB (Engl Hist Art; Hist Hist Art) (IB 35 pts)
320 pts **Birmingham** – ABB (Span Hist Art; Hist Art) (IB 32 pts)
 East Anglia – ABB (Art Hist Lit; Hist Art Gllry Musm St) (IB 32 pts)
 Glasgow – ABB (Hist Art) (IB 36 pts)
 Kent – ABB (Hist Phil Art courses) (IB 33 pts)
 Leeds – ABB (Hist Art) (IB 32 pts)
 London (Gold) – ABB (Hist Art) (IB 34 pts)
 London (SOAS) – ABB (Hist Art Arch courses; Hist Art; Hist Art (As Af Euro)) (IB 34 pts HL 555)
 Manchester – ABB–BBB 300–320 pts (Arch Art Hist) (IB 33–32 pts)
 Nottingham – ABB–AAC (Art Hist; Class Civ Art Hist) (IB 32 pts)
 Nottingham – ABB–BBB (Arch Art Hist) (IB 30–32 pts)
 Nottingham – ABB (Art Hist Engl; Hist Art Hist) (IB 32 pts)
 Reading – ABB (Art Hist; Hist Art Hist)
 Sussex – ABB–BBB (Art Hist Lang) (IB 32–34 pts)
 Warwick – ABB (Hist Art) (IB 34 pts)
 York – ABB (Hist Art) (IB 32–34 pts)
300 pts **Aberdeen** – BBB (Hist Art; Phil Hist Art) (IB 32 pts HL 555)
 Brighton – BBB (Musm Herit St; Hist Decr Arts Crfts; Fash Drs Hist; Hist Des) (IB 32 pts)
 Buckingham – BBB (Art Hist Herit Mgt) (IB 32 pts)

Edinburgh – BBB–AAA 300–360 pts (Hist Art) (IB 42–34 pts HL 555)
Essex – ABB–BBB 300–320 pts (Hist Art) (IB 34–32 pts)
Leicester – BBB (Hist Art)
London (Birk) – ABC 300 pts (Hist Art)
280 pts **Aberystwyth** – 280 pts (Art Hist Fine Art; Art Hist) (IB 28 pts)
Hull – 280–320 pts (Hist Hist Art)
Kingston – 280–300 pts (Art Mark)
Liverpool John Moores – 280 pts (Hist Art) (IB 28 pts)
260 pts **Plymouth** – 260 pts (Art Hist; Fn Art Art Hist)
240 pts **Kingston** – 240 pts (Hist Art Des Film) (IB 25 pts)
Manchester Met – 240–280 pts (Art Hist) (IB 28 pts)
180 pts **Essex** – DD 180 pts (Lit Art Hist (incl Fdn Yr)) (IB 24 pts)

Alternative offers
See **Chapter 7** and **Appendix 1** for grades/UCAS Tariff points information for the International
Baccalaureate, Scottish Highers/Advanced Highers, the Welsh Baccalaureate, the Irish Leaving
Certificate, the Cambridge Pre-U Diploma, the Advanced Diploma and the Extended Project.

CHOOSING YOUR COURSE (SEE ALSO CH.1)
Some course features
Aberystwyth (Art Hist) The course combines the study of art history and visual culture. In the second
and third years students choose from a wide range of core and optional modules, including history of
graphic art, history of photography, contemporary art and Renaissance art.
Kent (Hist Phil Art) The course has streams in art history, contemporary arts, philosophy of art or
photographic studies.
Kingston The course focuses on the appraisal of art and artefacts for sale and auction. It is accredited
by the Royal Institution of Chartered Surveyors.
Leeds (Hist Art Musm St) An unusual course focusing on art history, fine art and museum and gallery
collections and country houses, with opportunities for related work experience.
Leicester (Hist Art) A wide range of supplementary subjects (including languages) can be studied
including practical art which explores artistic techniques and problems.
Manchester (Hist Art) A study of art history, visual culture, architecture and theory from antiquity to
the present day. The course focuses mainly on European art but there are opportunities to study non-
Western cultures.

Universities and colleges teaching quality See www.qaa.ac.uk; http://unistats.direct.gov.uk.

Top research universities and colleges (RAE 2008) (History of Art, Architecture and Design)
Glasgow; London (Court); East Anglia; Sussex; Manchester; York; Birmingham; London (UCL); Essex;
Nottingham; London (Birk); Warwick.

ADMISSIONS INFORMATION
Number of applicants per place (approx) Aberystwyth 9; Birmingham 14; Brighton 8; Bristol 8;
Cambridge 4; East Anglia 7; Essex 5; Kent 3; Kingston 4; Leeds 29; Leicester 6; London (Gold) 10;
London (SOAS) 4; Manchester 3; Manchester Met 10; Nottingham 10; York 4.

Advice to applicants and planning the UCAS personal statement Applicants for History of Art
courses should have made extensive visits to art galleries, particularly in London, and should be
familiar with the main European schools of painting. Evidence of lively interest required. Discuss your
preferences and say why you prefer certain types of work or particular artists. You should also
describe any visits to museums and any special interests in furniture, pottery or other artefacts.
Bristol Deferred entry may be considered. **London (Court)** A-levels in history, history of art, English,
and modern European languages are the most relevant; however, other subjects are considered. Art
offered as an A-level should include a history of art paper.

Misconceptions about this course **Kent** The History of Art is not a practical course in fine arts. **York**
Students do not need a background in art or art history. It is not a course with a studio element in it.

Selection interviews Yes Brighton, Cambridge, Essex, London (Court), London (UCL), Manchester Met, Oxford (Hist Art) 16%; **Some** Bristol, Buckingham, Kent, Warwick, York; **No** Birmingham, East Anglia, Nottingham.

Interview advice and questions Some universities set slide tests on painting and sculpture. Those applicants who have not taken history of art at A-level will be questioned on their reasons for choosing the subject, their visits to art galleries and museums and their reactions to the art work which has impressed them. See **Chapter 6**. **Kent** Do they visit art galleries? Have they studied art history previously? What do they expect to get out of the degree? Sometimes they are given images to compare and discuss.

Reasons for rejection (non-academic) Poorly presented practical work. Students who do not express any interest or enthusiasm in contemporary visual arts are rejected.

AFTER-RESULTS ADVICE
Offers to applicants repeating A-levels Possibly higher St Andrews; **Same** Aberystwyth, East Anglia, Kent, Leeds, Warwick, York; **No** Cambridge.

GRADUATE DESTINATIONS AND EMPLOYMENT (2011/12 HESA)
Career note Work in galleries, museums and collections will be the objective of many graduates, who should try to establish contacts by way of work placements and experience during their undergraduate years. The personal skills acquired during their studies, however, open up many opportunities in other careers.

OTHER DEGREE SUBJECTS FOR CONSIDERATION
Art; Archaeology; Architecture; Classical Studies; Photography.

HORTICULTURE

(including **Garden Design**; see also **Agricultural Sciences/Agriculture, Landscape Architecture, Plant Sciences**)

Horticulture is a broad subject area covering amenity or landscape horticulture, production horticulture and retail horticulture.

Useful websites www.iagre.org; www.rhs.org.uk; www.horticulture.org.uk.

NB The points totals shown to the left of the institutions are for ease of reference only. It must not be assumed that Tariff points are always used by institutions or that they can be substituted for an offer in grades. The level of an offer is not necessarily indicative of the quality of a course.

COURSE OFFERS INFORMATION
Subject requirements/preferences GCSE Mathematics sometimes required. **AL** A science subject may be required or preferred for some courses.

Your target offers and examples of courses provided by each institution
260 pts **SRUC** – BCC (Hort Plntsmn; Hort)
240 pts **Greenwich** – 240 pts (Hort) (IB 24 pts)
       Hadlow (Coll) – 240 pts (Hort; Gdn Des)
       Writtle (Coll) – 240–280 pts (Hort) (IB 24 pts)
160 pts **Warwickshire (Coll)** – 160 pts (Hort)
       Worcester – 160 pts (Hort) (IB 24 pts)
120 pts **Nottingham Trent** – 120 pts (Hort Gard Des)

Alternative offers
See **Chapter 7** and **Appendix 1** for grades/UCAS Tariff points information for the International Baccalaureate, Scottish Highers/Advanced Highers, the Welsh Baccalaureate, the Irish Leaving Certificate, the Cambridge Pre-U Diploma, the Advanced Diploma and the Extended Project.

EXAMPLES OF FOUNDATION DEGREES IN THE SUBJECT FIELD

Askham Bryan (Coll); Bishop Burton (Coll); CAFRE; Duchy (Coll); Glyndŵr; Greenwich; Guildford (Coll); Harper Adams; Moulton (Coll); Myerscough (Coll); Nottingham Trent; Plymouth; Warwickshire (Coll); Writtle (Coll).

CHOOSING YOUR COURSE (SEE ALSO CH.1)

Some course features

SRUC (Hort Plntsmn) The course combines a study of the diversity of plants and their cultivation, with practical horticultural skills, and is delivered in partnership with the Royal Botanic Garden, Edinburgh.

Worcester (Hort) Course based at Pershore College and enables students to gain practical experience in the horticultural industry in the UK at the end of the first and second years.

Writtle (Coll) The College, the largest provider of horticultural education in the country, encourages students to take a sandwich placement during their course, in the UK or overseas. Twelve-month practical training placements are available with the Royal Horticultural Society.

Universities and colleges teaching quality See www.qaa.ac.uk; http://unistats.direct.gov.uk.

Examples of sandwich degree courses Writtle (Coll).

ADMISSIONS INFORMATION

Number of applicants per place (approx) Greenwich 4; SRUC 1; Writtle (Coll) 3.

Advice to applicants and planning the UCAS personal statement Practical experience is important and visits to botanical gardens (the Royal Botanic Gardens, Kew or Edinburgh and the Royal Horticultural Society gardens at Wisley) could be described. Contact your local authority offices for details of work in parks and gardens departments. See also **Appendix 3**.

Misconceptions about this course Greenwich (Hort) Students are unaware of the scope of this degree. The course covers commercial horticulture, nursery retail and production, commercial and medicinal crop production, horticultural chemistry, plant physiology, hydroponics and fruit practice and production.

Selection interviews Yes Worcester; **Some** Greenwich, SRUC.

Interview advice and questions Past questions have included: How did you become interested in horticulture? How do you think this course will benefit you? Could you work in all weathers? What career are you aiming for? Are you interested in gardening? Describe your garden. What plants do you grow? How do you prune rose trees and fruit trees? Are there any EU policies at present affecting the horticulture industry? Topics relating to the importance of science and horticulture. See also **Chapter 6**.

AFTER-RESULTS ADVICE

Offers to applicants repeating A-levels Same Greenwich, SRUC.

GRADUATE DESTINATIONS AND EMPLOYMENT (2011/12 HESA)

See **Agricultural Sciences/Agriculture**.

Career note Graduates seeking employment in horticulture will look towards commercial organisations for the majority of openings. These will include positions as growers and managers with fewer vacancies for scientists involved in research and development and advisory services.

OTHER DEGREE SUBJECTS FOR CONSIDERATION

Agriculture; Biology; Crop Science; Ecology; Forestry; Landscape Architecture; Plant Sciences.

Check **Chapter 4** when choosing your university and **Chapter 7** on how to read the subject tables.

HOSPITALITY and EVENT MANAGEMENT

(see also **Business and Management Courses, Business and Management Courses (International and European), Business and Management Courses (Specialised), Consumer Studies/Sciences, Food Science/Studies and Technology, Leisure and Recreation Management/Studies, Tourism and Travel)**

Courses cover the full range of skills required for those working in the industry. Specific studies include management, food and beverage supplies, equipment design, public relations and marketing. Depending on the course, other topics may include events management, tourism and the international trade.

Useful websites www.thebapa.org.uk; www.cordonbleu.net; www.instituteofhospitality.org; www.people1st.co.uk.

NB The points totals shown to the left of the institutions are for ease of reference only. It must not be assumed that Tariff points are always used by institutions or that they can be substituted for an offer in grades. The level of an offer is not necessarily indicative of the quality of a course.

COURSE OFFERS INFORMATION

Subject requirements/preferences GCSE English and mathematics usually required together with a foreign language for International Management courses. **AL** No specified subjects.

Your target offers and examples of courses provided by each institution

320 pts   Kent – ABB–BBB (Crea Evnts) (IB 33 pts)
Strathclyde – ABB 320 pts (Mgt Hspty Tour) (IB 33 pts)
Surrey – ABB (Int Hspty Mgt) (IB 34 pts)

300 pts   Brighton – BBB (Int Hspty Mgt; Int Evnt Mgt) (IB 32 pts)
Hertfordshire – BBB 300 pts (Evnt Mgt Lang)
Sheffield Hallam – 300 pts (Evnt Mngt; Evnts Mgt Art Enter)

280 pts   Birmingham City – BBC 280 pts (Media Comm (Evnt Exhib Ind)) (IB 28 pts)
Bournemouth – 280–320 pts (Evnt Mgt) (IB 30–32 pts HL 555)
Bournemouth Arts – BBC–BBB 280–300 pts (Arts Evnt Mgt) (IB 32 pts)
De Montfort – 280 pts (Arts Fstvl Mgt) (IB 28 pts)
Gloucestershire – 280 pts (Evnt Mgt Hspty Mgt)
Liverpool John Moores – 280 pts (Evnt Mgt) (IB 28 pts)
Oxford Brookes – BBC (Int Hspty Mgt) (IB 30 pts)
Plymouth – 280 pts (Evnt Mgt) (IB 25 pts)
Salford – BBC–BBB 240–300 pts (Hspty Mgt) (IB 29 pts)
Sheffield Hallam – 280 pts (Evnts Mgt Tour)
South Wales – BBC (Evnt Mgt)
Suffolk (Univ Campus) – 280 pts (Evnt Mgt; Hspty Mgt)
Ulster – 280 pts (Int Htl Tour Mgt; Int Hspty Mgt)

260 pts   Birmingham (UC) – 260 pts (Evnt Mgt)
Coventry – 260 pts (Evnt Mgt; Hspty Mgt)
Derby – 260–280 pts (Hspty Joint Hons; Evnt Mgt)
Edinburgh Queen Margaret – BCC (Evnt Mgt) (IB 28 pts)
Glasgow Caledonian – BCC 260 pts (Bus (Evnt Mgt)) (IB 24 pts)
Greenwich – 260 pts (Evnt Mgt)
Huddersfield – 260 pts (Evnt Mgt)
Northampton – 260–300 pts (Evnt Mgt; Evnt Mgt Joint Hons)
Robert Gordon – BCC (Evnt Mgt) (IB 27 pts)
Staffordshire – (Evnt Mgt)
Sunderland – 260 pts (Int Tour Hspty Mgt)
Winchester – 260–300 pts (Evnt Mgt)

240 pts   Birmingham (UC) – 240 pts (Spa Mgt; Culn Arts Mgt; Hspty Bus Mgt; Hosp courses)
Canterbury Christ Church – 240 pts (Evnt Mgt)

Cardiff Met (UWIC) – 240 pts (Int Tour Hspty Mgt; Evnts Mgt)
Central Lancashire – 240–280 pts (Hspty Mgt; Int Hspty Mgt; Evnt Mgt)
Chester – 240–280 pts (Evnts Mgt) (IB 26 pts)
Chichester – CCC (Evnt Mgt) (IB 28 pts)
East London – 240 pts (Hspty Int Tour Mgt) (IB 24 pts)
Edinburgh Napier – CCC 240 pts (Hspty Mark Mgt)
Glyndŵr – 240 pts (Bus Evnt Mgt)
London Met – 240 pts (Evnts Mgt Mark; Evnts Mgt PR; Int Hspty Mgt; Arts Mgt
   Evnts Mgt)
Manchester Met – 240–280 pts (Evnts Mgt; Hspty Mgt) (IB 29 pts)
Plymouth – 240 pts (Int Hspty Mgt; Hspty Mgt; Cru Mgt) (IB 24 pts)
Robert Gordon – CCC (Int Hspty Mgt) (IB 26 pts)
Sheffield Hallam – 240–280 pts (Hspty Bus Mgt)
Southampton Solent – 240 pts (Evnts Mgt)
West Scotland – CCC (Evnt Mgt) (IB 24 pts)
Writtle (Coll) – 240 pts (Evnt Mgt)

220 pts   Huddersfield – 220 pts (Hspty Mgt)
Lincoln – 220 pts (Evnt Mgt)
Portsmouth – 220 pts (Hspty Mgt; Hspty Mgt Tour)

200 pts   Bedfordshire – 200 pts (Evnt Mgt)
Blackpool and Fylde (Coll) – 200 pts (Hspty Mgt)
Bucks New – 200–240 pts (Evnt Fstvl Mgt; Mus Live Evnt Mgt)
CAFRE – 200 pts (Fd Mgt Mark)
West London – 200 pts (Hspty Mgt; Evnts Mgt) (IB 28 pts)
Wolverhampton – 200 pts (Evnt Vnu Mgt) (IB 24 pts)

160 pts   London Regent's – CC 160 pts (Int Evnts Mgt)

120 pts   Colchester (Inst) – 120 pts (Mgt Hspty)
Llandrillo Cymru (Coll) – 120 pts (Hspty Mgt) (IB 24 pts)

100 pts   Cumbria – 100 pts (Evnt Mgt)

80 pts   UHI – C–A 80–140 pts (Tour Hosp Mgt)

Alternative offers

See **Chapter 7** and **Appendix 1** for grades/UCAS Tariff points information for the International Baccalaureate, Scottish Highers/Advanced Highers, the Welsh Baccalaureate, the Irish Leaving Certificate, the Cambridge Pre-U Diploma, the Advanced Diploma and the Extended Project.

EXAMPLES OF FOUNDATION DEGREES IN THE SUBJECT FIELD

Askham Bryan (Coll); Bedford (Coll); Bishop Burton (Coll); Blackburn (Coll); Blackpool and Fylde (Coll); Bolton; Bournemouth and Poole (Coll); Bradford (Coll Univ Centre); Chichester; Colchester (Inst); Cornwall (Coll); Craven (Coll); Durham New (Coll); Ealing, Hammersmith and West London (Coll); Farnborough (CT); Glasgow Caledonian; Greenwich; Grimsby (Univ Centre); Guildford (Coll); Harper Adams; Highbury Portsmouth (Coll); Hopwood Hall (Coll); Liverpool City (Coll); Loughborough (Coll); Middlesex; Neath Port Talbot (Coll); NEW (Coll); Newcastle (Coll); North Lindsey (Coll); Northumbria; Norwich City (Coll); Nottingham New (Coll); South Cheshire (Coll); South Devon (Coll); Stratford-upon-Avon (Coll); Suffolk (Univ Campus); UHI; West Cheshire (Coll); West Scotland; Westminster Kingsway (Coll); Worcester.

CHOOSING YOUR COURSE (SEE ALSO CH.1)

Some course features

Edinburgh Napier (Fstvl Evnts Mgt courses) Students learn how to plan, design, market, operate and develop events and how they can be used to help local economies. There are opportunities to study a European language and to study abroad.

Manchester Met The wide range of courses includes options in International Hospitality Management and Events Management.

Oxford Brookes (Int Hspty Mgt) A Single Honours course with a paid placement year and opportunities to study abroad. There is an emphasis on professional and personal development.

Surrey Opportunities for professional training places with leading UK and overseas companies.

Universities and colleges teaching quality See www.qaa.ac.uk; http://unistats.direct.gov.uk.

Examples of sandwich degree courses Birmingham (UC); Bournemouth; Brighton; Cardiff Met (UWIC); Central Lancashire; Derby; Gloucestershire; Huddersfield; Leeds Beckett; London Met; Manchester Met; Oxford Brookes; Plymouth; Portsmouth; Salford; Sheffield Hallam; Staffordshire; Sunderland; Surrey; Ulster; West London; Wolverhampton.

ADMISSIONS INFORMATION

Number of applicants per place (approx) Bournemouth 9; Cardiff Met (UWIC) 12; Central Lancashire 8; Edinburgh Napier 17; London Met 10; Manchester Met (Hspty Mgt) 12, (Hspty Mgt Tour) 20; Middlesex 4; Oxford Brookes 9; Portsmouth 10; Robert Gordon 3; Strathclyde 8; Surrey 12.

Advice to applicants and planning the UCAS personal statement Experience in dealing with members of the public is an important element in this work which, coupled with work experience in cafés, restaurants or hotels, should be described fully. All applicants are strongly recommended to obtain practical experience in catering or hotel work. Admissions tutors are likely to look for experience in industry and for people who are ambitious, sociable and team players. See also **Appendix 3**.

Misconceptions about this course Cardiff Met (UWIC) (Hspty Mgt) The course is not about cooking! We are looking to create managers, not chefs.

Selection interviews Some Cardiff Met (UWIC), Manchester Met, Robert Gordon; **No** Bucks New, Portsmouth, Salford, Surrey.

Interview advice and questions Past questions have included: What books do you read? What do you know about hotel work and management? What work experience have you had? What kind of job do you have in mind when you have qualified? How did you become interested in this course? Do you eat in restaurants? What types of restaurants? Discuss examples of good and bad restaurant organisation. What qualities do you have which make you suitable for management? See also **Chapter 6**.

Reasons for rejection (non-academic) Lack of suitable work experience or practical training. Inability to communicate. Lack of awareness of workload, for example shift working, weekend work. **Cardiff Met (UWIC)** Students looking specifically for licensed trade courses or a cookery course. **Oxford Brookes** Lack of commitment to the hotel and restaurant industry.

AFTER-RESULTS ADVICE

Offers to applicants repeating A-levels Higher Bournemouth, Huddersfield, Oxford Brookes, Surrey; **Same** Brighton, Cardiff Met (UWIC), Manchester Met, Salford, Strathclyde, Suffolk (Univ Campus), Ulster, West London, Wolverhampton.

GRADUATE DESTINATIONS AND EMPLOYMENT (2011/12 HESA)

Including Leisure, Tourism and Transport graduates surveyed 5000 **Employed** 2720 **In voluntary employment** 100 **In further study** 890 **Assumed unemployed** 365

Career note These business-focused hospitality programmes open up a wide range of employment and career opportunities in both hospitality and other business sectors. The demand for employees has been high in recent years. Events Management is currently a growth area with graduates working in sports and the arts, tourist attractions, hospitality, business and industry.

OTHER DEGREE SUBJECTS FOR CONSIDERATION

Business; Consumer Studies; Dietetics; Food Science; Health Studies; Leisure and Recreation Management; Management; Tourism and Travel.

HOUSING

(see also **Building and Construction, Surveying, Town and Country Planning**)

These courses prepare students for careers in housing management although topics covered will also be relevant to other careers in business and administration. Modules will be taken in housing, law, finance, planning policy, public administration and construction.

Useful websites www.gov.uk/government/topics/housing; www.rtpi.org.uk; www.freeindex.co.uk/categories/property/construction/Property_Development.

NB The points totals shown to the left of the institutions are for ease of reference only. It must not be assumed that Tariff points are always used by institutions or that they can be substituted for an offer in grades. The level of an offer is not necessarily indicative of the quality of a course.

COURSE OFFERS INFORMATION

Subject requirements/preferences GCSE English and mathematics required. **AL** No specified subjects.

Your target offers and examples of courses provided by each institution
300 pts Birmingham – BBB 300 pts (Soc Pol Hous Commun) (IB 32 pts)
240 pts Central Lancashire – CCC 240 pts (Commun Soc Care (Plcy Prac))
　　　　　London South Bank – CCC 240 pts (Hous St; Sust Commun)
　　　　　Ulster – CCC 240 pts (Hous Mgt)
180 pts Cardiff Met (UWIC) – 180 pts (Hous (Supptd Hous/Hous Plcy Prac))

Alternative offers
See **Chapter 7** and **Appendix 1** for grades/UCAS Tariff points information for the International Baccalaureate, Scottish Highers/Advanced Highers, the Welsh Baccalaureate, the Irish Leaving Certificate, the Cambridge Pre-U Diploma, the Advanced Diploma and the Extended Project.

EXAMPLES OF FOUNDATION DEGREES IN THE SUBJECT FIELD
Blackburn (Coll); St Helens (Coll); Truro (Coll).

CHOOSING YOUR COURSE (SEE ALSO CH.1)
Some course features
Cardiff Met (UWIC) (Hous (Supptd Hous)) The course involves social, emotional and/or lifestyle support for a variety of client needs, for example, learning disabilities, mental health, vulnerable people.
London South Bank (Hous St) The course focuses on the policy, management and economic aspects of housing, and on housing in the European context.
Ulster (Hous Mgt) The course, involving research, practical placements and links with practitioners, focuses on how housing management affects individuals in society, on the built environment, housing needs and the development and implementation of housing policy. The course links to others in the built environment, including Environmental Health, Construction Engineering and Management.

Universities and colleges teaching quality See www.qaa.ac.uk; http://unistats.direct.gov.uk.

Examples of sandwich degree courses Ulster.

ADMISSIONS INFORMATION
Number of applicants per place (approx) Cardiff Met (UWIC) 1.

Advice to applicants and planning the UCAS personal statement An interest in people, housing problems, social affairs and the built environment is important for this course. Contacts with local housing managers (through local authority offices or housing associations) are important. Describe any such contacts and your knowledge of the housing types and needs in your area. The planning department in your local council office will be able to provide information on the various types of developments taking place in your locality and how housing needs have changed during the past 50 years. See also **Appendix 3**.

Misconceptions about this course Applicants do not appreciate that the course is very close to social work/community work and is most suitable for those wishing to work with people.

Selection interviews Yes Cardiff Met (UWIC).

Interview advice and questions Since the subject is not studied at school, questions are likely to be asked on reasons for choosing this degree. Other past questions include: What is a housing association? Why were housing associations formed? In which parts of the country would you expect private housing to be expensive and, by comparison, cheap? What is the cause of this? Have estates of multi-storey flats fulfilled their original purpose? If not, why not? What causes a slum? What is an almshouse? See also **Chapter 6**.

Reasons for rejection (non-academic) Lack of awareness of current social policy issues.

AFTER-RESULTS ADVICE
Offers to applicants repeating A-levels Same Cardiff Met (UWIC), London South Bank.

GRADUATE DESTINATIONS AND EMPLOYMENT (2011/12 HESA)
See **Building and Construction**.

Career note Graduates aiming for openings in housing will be employed mainly as managers with local authorities; others will be employed by non-profit-making housing associations and trusts and also by property companies owning blocks of flats.

OTHER DEGREE SUBJECTS FOR CONSIDERATION
Architecture; Building; Business Studies; Community Studies; Environmental Planning; Estate Management; Property Development; Social Policy and Administration; Social Studies; Surveying; Town Planning; Urban Regeneration.

HUMAN RESOURCE MANAGEMENT

(see also **Business and Management Courses, Business and Management Courses (International and European), Business and Management Courses (Specialised)**)

This is one of the many branches of the world of business and has developed from the role of the personnel manager. HR managers may be involved with the induction and training of staff, disciplinary and grievance procedures, redundancies and equal opportunities issues. In large organisations some HR staff may specialise in one or more of these areas. Work experience dealing with the public should be stressed in the UCAS personal statement.

Useful websites www.hrmguide.co.uk; www.humanresourcemanagement.co.uk.

NB The points totals shown to the left of the institutions are for ease of reference only. It must not be assumed that Tariff points are always used by institutions or that they can be substituted for an offer in grades. The level of an offer is not necessarily indicative of the quality of a course.

COURSE OFFERS INFORMATION
Subject requirements/preferences GCSE English and mathematics at C or above. **AL** No subjects specified.

Your target offers and examples of courses provided by each institution
340 pts Aston – AAB 340 pts (HR Mgt) (IB 35 pts)
       Cardiff – AAB 340 pts (Bus Mgt (HR)) (IB 35 pts)
       Lancaster – AAB (Mgt Org (HR Mgt)) (IB 35 pts)
       Leeds – AAB (HR Mgt) (IB 35 pts HL 17 pts)
       London (RH) – AAB 340 pts (Mgt HR) (IB 35 pts)

	Manchester – AAB 340 pts (Mgt HR) (IB 35 pts)
320 pts	**Bournemouth** – 320–340 pts (Bus St (HR Mgt))
	Northumbria – ABB 320 pts (HR Mgt) (IB 27 pts)
	Strathclyde – ABB 320 pts (HR Mgt) (IB 33 pts)
300 pts	**Bradford** – 300 pts (HR Mgt)
	Brighton – BBB (Bus HR Mgt) (IB 32 pts)
	Cardiff Met (UWIC) – 300 pts (Bus Mgt St HR Mgt)
	Heriot-Watt – BBB (Bus Mgt HR Mgt) (IB 29 pts)
	Hertfordshire – 300 pts (Bus HR)
	Huddersfield – BBB 300 pts (Bus HR Mgt)
	Keele – ABC 280–340 pts (HR Mgt Comb) (IB 28–30 pts)
	Leeds Beckett – 300 pts (Bus HR Mgt) (IB 26 pts)
	Middlesex – 300 pts (Psy HR Mgt) (IB 28 pts)
	Nottingham Trent – 300 pts (Bus Mgt HR)
	Salford – 300 pts (Bus St HR Mgt)
	Sheffield Hallam – 300 pts (Bus HR Mgt)
	Ulster – BBB (Law HR Mgt) (IB 25 pts)
280 pts	**Birmingham City** – 280 pts (Bus HR Mgt) (IB 32 pts)
	Chichester – 280 pts (HR Mgt) (IB 30 pts)
	De Montfort – 280 pts (HR Mgt) (IB 28 pts)
	Greenwich – 280 pts (HR Mgt)
	Hertfordshire – 280 pts (HR Mgt)
	Kingston – 280 pts (HR Mgt) (IB 31 pts)
	Manchester Met – 280 pts (HR Mgt) (IB 28 pts)
	Portsmouth – 280 pts (HR Mgt; HR Mgt Psy)
	South Wales – BBC 280 pts (HR Mgt)
	Stirling – BBC (HR Mgt) (IB 32 pts)
	Suffolk (Univ Campus) – 280 pts (Bus HR Mgt)
	West London – 280 pts (Bus St HR Mgt)
	Worcester – 280 pts (HR Mgt courses; Bus Mark HR Mgt)
260 pts	**Bath Spa** – 260–300 pts (Bus Mgt HR Mgt)
	Coventry – BCC 260 pts (HR Mgt)
	Derby – 260–300 pts (HR Mgt)
	Gloucestershire – 260–300 pts (Bus Mgt (HR Mgt))
	Liverpool John Moores – 260 pts (Mgt HR Mgt; HR Mgt) (IB 28 pts)
	Northampton – 260–280 pts (HR Mgt courses)
	Robert Gordon – BCC 260 pts (Mgt HR Mgt)
	Staffordshire – (HR Mgt)
	Sunderland – 260 pts (Bus HR Mgt; HR Mgt)
	Westminster – BCC 260 pts (Bus HR Mgt) (IB 28 pts)
240 pts	**Canterbury Christ Church** – 240 pts (HR Mgt Bus; HR Mgt Mark)
	Central Lancashire – 240–280 pts (HR Mgt (Comb)) (IB 28 pts)
	East London – 240 pts (HR Mgt)
	Euro Bus Sch London – 240 pts (Int Bus HR Mgt 2 Langs)
	London Met – 240 pts (HR Mgt)
	Ulster – 240–260 pts (Adv HR Mgt; HR Mgt Mark)
	West Scotland – CCC (HR Mgt)
	York St John – 240–300 pts (Bus Mgt HR Mgt)
220 pts	**Wolverhampton** – 220 pts (HR Mgt)
200 pts	**Anglia Ruskin** – 200–240 pts (HR Mgt)
	Bedfordshire – 200 pts (HR Mgt)
	Bucks New – 200–240 pts (HR Mgt; Bus HR Mgt)
	Middlesex – 200–300 pts (Bus HR Mgt)
160 pts	**Trinity Saint David (Swansea)** – 160 pts (HR Mgt)

Check **Chapter 4** when choosing your university and **Chapter 7** on how to read the subject tables.

120 pts Norwich City (Coll) – 120 pts (Bus Mgt (HR Mgt))
 80 pts Greenwich (Sch Mgt) – 80 pts (HR Mgt Inform Sys; Mgt HR Mgt)

Alternative offers
See **Chapter 7** and **Appendix 1** for grades/UCAS Tariff points information for the International Baccalaureate, Scottish Highers/Advanced Highers, the Welsh Baccalaureate, the Irish Leaving Certificate, the Cambridge Pre-U Diploma, the Advanced Diploma and the Extended Project.

EXAMPLES OF FOUNDATION DEGREES IN THE SUBJECT FIELD
Ealing, Hammersmith and West London (Coll); Newcastle (Coll); North Lindsey (Coll); Petroc; Plymouth; Southampton Solent.

CHOOSING YOUR COURSE (SEE ALSO CH.1)
Some course features
Cardiff Human Resources is an option within the Business programme which offers several specialist routes. The course provides the flexibility for students to transfer between degree programmes in the first year.
Lancaster (Mgt Org (HR Mgt)) The course focuses on social scientific concepts and an analysis of HR techniques, including recruitment, motivation, development and strategic planning. Students can opt to spend third year in industry.
Portsmouth Optional industrial placement year between Year 2 and the final year.

Universities and colleges teaching quality See www.qaa.ac.uk; http://unistats.direct.gov.uk.

Examples of sandwich degree courses Aston; Bath; Bath Spa; Bedfordshire; Birmingham City; Bournemouth; Bradford; Brighton; Bristol UWE; Cardiff Met (UWIC); Central Lancashire; Chichester; Coventry; De Montfort; Gloucestershire; Hertfordshire; Huddersfield; Leeds Beckett; Liverpool John Moores; Manchester Met; Northampton; Northumbria; Portsmouth; Sheffield Hallam; Sussex; Trinity Saint David (Swansea); Ulster; West Scotland; Westminster; Wolverhampton; Worcester.

ADMISSIONS INFORMATION
Number of applicants per place (approx) Anglia Ruskin 10; Aston 10; (see also **Business and Management Courses**).

Advice to applicants and planning the UCAS personal statement See **Business and Management Courses**.

Selection interviews **Yes** De Montfort; **Some** Anglia Ruskin (See **Business and Management Courses**).

Interview advice and questions See **Business and Management Courses**.

Reasons for rejection (non-academic) See **Business and Management Courses**.

AFTER-RESULTS ADVICE
Offers to applicants repeating A-levels **Higher** Anglia Ruskin.

GRADUATE DESTINATIONS AND EMPLOYMENT (2011/12 HESA)
Graduates surveyed 835 **Employed** 470 **In voluntary employment** 20 **In further study** 150 **Assumed unemployed** 65

Career note See under **Business and Management Courses**.

OTHER DEGREE SUBJECTS FOR CONSIDERATION
Business Studies; Information Systems; Management Studies/Sciences; Marketing; Psychology; Retail Management; Sociology; Sports Management.

HUMAN SCIENCES/HUMAN BIOSCIENCES

(see also **Medicine**)

Human Sciences is a multi-disciplinary study relating to biological and social sciences and focuses on social and cultural behaviour. Topics range from genetics and evolution to health, disease, social behaviour and industrial societies.

Useful websites www.bbsrc.ac.uk; www.becominghuman.org; see also **Biology** and **Geography**.

NB The points totals shown to the left of the institutions are for ease of reference only. It must not be assumed that Tariff points are always used by institutions or that they can be substituted for an offer in grades. The level of an offer is not necessarily indicative of the quality of a course.

COURSE OFFERS INFORMATION

Subject requirements/preferences **GCSE** Science essential and mathematics usually required. **AL** Chemistry/biology usually required or preferred for some courses.

Your target offers and examples of courses provided by each institution

380 pts London (UCL) – AAA (Hum Sci) (IB 38 pts)

360 pts Oxford – AAA (Hum Sci) (IB 38–40 pts)

340 pts Exeter – AAB–ABB 340–320 pts (Hum Sci) (IB 34–32 pts)
Sussex – AAA–AAB (Psy Cog Sci; Psy Neuro) (IB 35 pts)

320 pts Durham – ABB 320 pts (Hlth Hum Sci) (IB 34 pts)
East Anglia – ABB (Hum Comm Sci)
Sheffield – ABB (Hlth Hum Sci) (IB 34 pts)
Swansea – ABB 320 pts (Med Sci Hum)

300 pts Anglo-Euro (Coll Chiro) – 300 pts (Hum Sci (Chiro))

280 pts Loughborough – BBC 280–300 pts (Ergon (Hum Fact Des)) (IB 30–32 pts)
Manchester Met – 280 pts (Hum Nutr) (IB 28 pts)
Northumbria – 280 pts (Hum Biosci) (IB 24 pts)
Plymouth – 280 pts (Hum Biosci) (IB 26 pts)

260 pts Glasgow Caledonian – BCC 260 pts (Hum Biosci) (IB 24 pts)
Manchester Met – 260–280 pts (Hum Biol; Hum Geog (St Abrd)) (IB 28 pts)
Northampton – 260–300 pts (Hum Biosci courses)
West Scotland – BCC (App Biomed Sci; Biomed Sci) (IB 24 pts)

240 pts Coventry – CCC 240 pts (Hum Biosci)
Manchester Met – 240–280 pts (Nutr Sci) (IB 29 pts)
Westminster – CCC (Hum Med Sci) (IB 26 pts)
West Scotland – CCC (Foren Sci) (IB 24 pts)

180 pts Bradford – 180–220 pts (Interd Hum St)

Alternative offers
See **Chapter 7** and **Appendix 1** for grades/UCAS Tariff points information for the International Baccalaureate, Scottish Highers/Advanced Highers, the Welsh Baccalaureate, the Irish Leaving Certificate, the Cambridge Pre-U Diploma, the Advanced Diploma and the Extended Project.

EXAMPLES OF FOUNDATION DEGREES IN THE SUBJECT FIELD
Petroc.

CHOOSING YOUR COURSE (SEE ALSO CH.1)
Some course features
Bradford (Interd Hum St) The course covers philosophy, psychology and sociology.
Exeter The subject is taught equally between the Schools of Biosciences and Sport and Health Sciences and has a strong scientific element.
London (UCL) (Hum Sci) The course combines biological and social studies and covers such topics as anatomy, physiology, genetics, anthropology, geography and psychology.

Loughborough (Ergon (Hum Fact Des)) The course deals with human reactions to technical and social environments, and includes anatomy, physiology, bio-mechanics, human psychology, the principles of design and organisational behaviour.

Oxford (Hum Sci) The degree focuses on the biological, social and cultural aspects of human life. A-level or AS-level biology or mathematics may be helpful but are not a requirement.

Universities and colleges teaching quality See www.qaa.ac.uk; http://unistats.direct.gov.uk.

ADMISSIONS INFORMATION
Number of applicants per place (approx) Bradford 7; Oxford 4–5.

Advice to applicants and planning the UCAS personal statement See **Biology** and **Anthropology**.

Selection interviews **Yes** London (UCL), Oxford (Hum Sci) 31%.

Interview advice and questions Past questions have included: What do you expect to get out of a degree in Human Sciences? Why are you interested in this subject? What problems do you think you will be able to tackle after completing the course? Why did you drop PE as an A-level given that it's relevant to Human Sciences? How do you explain altruism, given that we are surely programmed by our genes to be selfish? How far is human behaviour determined by genes? What do you think are the key differences between animals and human beings? See also **Chapter 6**. **Oxford** Are there too many people in the world?

GRADUATE DESTINATIONS AND EMPLOYMENT (2011/12 HESA)
See **Biology**.

Career note As a result of the multi-disciplinary nature of these courses, graduates could focus on openings linked to their special interests or look in general at the scientific and health sectors. Health administration and social services work and laboratory-based careers are some of the more common career destinations of graduates.

OTHER DEGREE SUBJECTS FOR CONSIDERATION
Anthropology; Biology; Community Studies; Environmental Sciences; Life Sciences; Psychology; Sociology.

INFORMATION MANAGEMENT and LIBRARIANSHIP

(including **Business Information Systems, Information Technology** and **Library Studies**; see also **Computer Courses, Media Studies**)

Information Management and Library Studies covers the very wide field of information. Its organisation, retrieval, indexing, computer and media technology, classification and cataloguing are all included in these courses.

Useful websites www.aslib.co.uk; www.ukoln.ac.uk; www.cilip.org.uk; www.bl.uk.

NB The points totals shown to the left of the institutions are for ease of reference only. It must not be assumed that Tariff points are always used by institutions or that they can be substituted for an offer in grades. The level of an offer is not necessarily indicative of the quality of a course.

COURSE OFFERS INFORMATION
Subject requirements/preferences **GCSE** English, mathematics and occasionally a foreign language. **AL** No specified subjects.

Your target offers and examples of courses provided by each institution

360 pts **Bath** – A*AB-AAA (Comp Inf Sys)
Edinburgh – AAA-ABB incl maths 360-320 pts (Inform) (IB 37-32 pts)
Exeter – AAA-AAB 360-340 pts (IT Mgt Bus) (IB 36-34 pts)
Leeds – AAA 360 pts (IT) (IB 35 pts)

340 pts **Lancaster** – AAB (Mgt IT) (IB 35 pts)
London (UCL) – AAB 340 pts (Inf Mgt Bus) (IB 36 pts)
Manchester – AAB (IT Mgt Bus (Yr Ind); IT Mgt Bus) (IB 35 pts)
Reading – AAB (Mgt IT) (IB 35 pts)
Sheffield – AAB (IT Mgt Bus) (IB 35 pts)
Southampton – AAB (IT Org) (IB 34 pts HL 17 pts)

320 pts **Loughborough** – ABB-AAB (IT Mgt Bus; Inf Mgt Bus St) (IB 34 pts)
Sheffield – ABB (Inform) (IB 34 pts)

300 pts **Aberdeen** – 300 pts (Inf Sys)
Aberystwyth – 300 pts (Hist Archvl St) (IB 29 pts)
Bradford – 300 pts (Op Inf Mgt)
Brighton – BBB (Bus Inf Sys; Musm Herit St) (IB 32 pts)
Bristol UWE – 300 pts (IT Mgt Bus)
Heriot-Watt – BBB (Inf Sys courses) (IB 28 pts)
Hertfordshire – 300 pts (Inf Sys Mark)
Huddersfield – 300 pts (ICT)
Keele – BBB (Inf Sys) (IB 30 pts)

280 pts **Birmingham City** – 280 pts (ICT)
Chichester – BBC (IT Mgt Bus) (IB 30 pts)
Hull – 280-300 pts (Inf Sys)
Kent – 280 pts (IT courses) (IB 33 pts)
Kingston – 280 pts (Inf Sys)
Northumbria – 280 pts (Inf Lib Mgt) (IB 24 pts)
Oxford Brookes – BBC (IT Mgt Bus)
Plymouth – 280 pts (IT Mgt)
South Wales – 280 pts (ICT)
Stirling – BBC (Inf Sys) (IB 32 pts)

260 pts **Bournemouth** – 260-300 pts (IT Mgt) (IB 28-30 pts)
De Montfort – 260 pts (ICT)
Liverpool Hope – 260-300 pts (IT)
Manchester Met – 260-280 pts (Inf Comm) (IB 28 pts)

240 pts **Aberystwyth** – 240 pts (Inf Mgt) (IB 24 pts)
Cardiff Met (UWIC) – 240 pts (Bus Inf Sys)
Central Lancashire – 240-280 pts (Inf Sys Des)
Chester – 240-280 pts (Inf Sys Mgt) (IB 26 pts)
Edge Hill – 240 pts (IT Mgt Bus)
Gloucestershire – 240 pts (Bus Inf Sys)
Greenwich – 240 pts (IT Scrty)
Kingston – 240 pts (Musm Gllry St)
Liverpool John Moores – 240 pts (Inf Sys)
Middlesex – 240 pts (Bus Inf Sys)
Nottingham Trent – 240 pts (ICT; Inf Sys)
Westminster – CCC-AA (Bus Inf Sys) (IB 26 pts)

220 pts **Edinburgh Napier** – CCD 220 pts (Inf Tech)

200 pts **Anglia Ruskin** – 200 pts (Bus Inf Sys)
Bangor – 200 pts (Comp Inf Sys)
Bedfordshire – 200 pts (Inf Sys)
Northumbria – 200 pts (IT Mgt)
Southampton Solent – 200 pts (Bus Inf Tech)

160 pts **Southampton Solent** – 160 pts (ICT)
Wolverhampton – 160 pts (Bus Inf Sys courses)
140 pts **Blackpool and Fylde (Coll)** – 140–360 pts (IT)

Alternative offers

See **Chapter 7** and **Appendix 1** for grades/UCAS Tariff points information for the International Baccalaureate, Scottish Highers/Advanced Highers, the Welsh Baccalaureate, the Irish Leaving Certificate, the Cambridge Pre-U Diploma, the Advanced Diploma and the Extended Project.

EXAMPLES OF FOUNDATION DEGREES IN THE SUBJECT FIELD

Birmingham City; Blackburn (Coll); Glyndŵr; Greenwich; Hertfordshire; Huddersfield; Kent; Llandrillo Cymru (Coll); Nottingham New (Coll); South Essex (Coll); Truro (Coll).

CHOOSING YOUR COURSE (SEE ALSO CH.1)

Some course features

Aberystwyth This leading department offers courses in Information and Library Studies by way of 10 specialist joint subjects. There is also a unique course in Historical and Archival Studies in addition to courses in Museum and Gallery Studies.

Edge Hill Information Technology for Business is a highly rated computer course with a focus on practical work-based learning.

Hertfordshire Information Systems can be combined with Accountancy, Business, Economics, European Studies, Event Management and Human Resources Management.

Manchester Met Information and Communications is a modular course, and offers the basic core subjects covering management, information systems, retrieval and information technology. Special studies in Year 3 provide flexibility to cover areas of special interest to students. These include working in academic, business and commercial communities. Students are required to undertake placements.

Universities and colleges teaching quality See www.qaa.ac.uk; http://unistats.direct.gov.uk.

Top research universities and colleges (RAE 2008) Sheffield; London (King's); London (UCL); Wolverhampton; City; Robert Gordon; Glasgow; Brunel; Loughborough; Edinburgh Napier.

Examples of sandwich degree courses Birmingham City; Bournemouth; Bradford; Bristol UWE; De Montfort; Gloucestershire; Hertfordshire; Huddersfield; Kent; Kingston; Lancaster; Liverpool John Moores; Loughborough; Manchester; Northumbria; Nottingham Trent; Plymouth; Reading; Staffordshire; Sunderland.

ADMISSIONS INFORMATION

Number of applicants per place (approx) Aberystwyth 4; London (UCL) 7; Loughborough 5; Manchester Met 4; Sheffield 30; Southampton 5.

Advice to applicants and planning the UCAS personal statement Work experience or work shadowing in local libraries is important but remember that reference libraries provide a different field of work. Visit university libraries and major reference libraries and discuss the work with librarians. Describe your experiences in the personal statement. See also **Appendix 3**.

Misconceptions about this course Read the prospectus carefully. The course details can be confusing. Some courses have a bias towards the organisation and retrieval of information, others towards information systems technology.

Selection interviews **Yes** London (UCL), Southampton; **Some** Loughborough.

Interview advice and questions Past questions include: What is it about librarianship that interests you? Why do you think you are suited to be a librarian? What does the job entail? What is the role of the library in school? What is the role of the public library? What new developments are taking place in libraries? Which books do you read? How often do you use a library? What is the Dewey number for the history section in the library? (Applicant studying A-level history.) See also **Chapter 6**.

AFTER-RESULTS ADVICE

Offers to applicants repeating A-levels **Higher** Loughborough; **Same** Sheffield.

GRADUATE DESTINATIONS AND EMPLOYMENT (2011/12 HESA)

Career note Graduates in this subject area and in communications enter a wide range of public and private sector jobs where the need to process information as well as to make it easily accessible and user-friendly, is very high. Areas of work could include web content, design and internet management and library management.

OTHER DEGREE SUBJECTS FOR CONSIDERATION

Business Information Systems; Communication Studies; Computer Science; Geographic Information Systems; Media Studies.

INTERNATIONAL RELATIONS

(including **International Development, Peace Studies** and **War Studies**; see also **Development Studies, European Studies, Politics**)

A strong interest in international affairs is a prerequisite for these courses which often allow students to focus on a specific area such as African, Asian, West European politics.

Useful websites www.sipri.org; www.un.org; www.un.int; www.irc-online.org; see also **Politics**.

NB The points totals shown to the left of the institutions are for ease of reference only. It must not be assumed that Tariff points are always used by institutions or that they can be substituted for an offer in grades. The level of an offer is not necessarily indicative of the quality of a course.

COURSE OFFERS INFORMATION

Subject requirements/preferences **GCSE** English; a foreign language usually required. **AL** No specified subjects. (War St) History may be required.

Your target offers and examples of courses provided by each institution

440 pts **Warwick** – A*AAa (Econ Pol Int St) (IB 38 pts HL 6 maths)

380 pts **Cambridge** – A*AA (Hum Soc Pol Sci (Pol Int Rel)) (IB 40–41 pts HL 776)

360 pts **Bath** – AAA (Pol Int Rel) (IB 38 pts HL 666)
 Bristol – AAA–AAB (Pol Int Rel) (IB 37–35 pts HL 666)
 Durham – AAA 360 pts (Int Rel) (37 pts)
 Edinburgh – AAA–BBB 360–300 pts (Int Rel; Int Rel Law) (IB 40–34 pts)
 Exeter – AAA–ABB 360–340 pts (Int Rel Modn Lang; Hist Int Rel; Pol Int Rel (Cornwall); Hist Int Rel (St Abrd)) (IB 36–32 pts)
 London (King's) – AAA (War St Phil; War St; War St Hist) (IB 35 pts HL 666)
 London (QM) – AAA 360 pts (Int Rel) (IB 32 pts)
 London LSE – AAA (Int Rel Hist; Int Rel) (IB 38 pts HL 766)
 Nottingham – AAA (Int Rel Glob Is; Int Rel) (IB 36 pts)
 St Andrews – AAA (Geog Int Rel; Int Rel courses) (IB 38 pts)
 Sussex – AAA–AAB (Law Int Rel) (IB 35–36 pts)

340 pts **Aston** – AAB–ABB 340–320 pts (Pol Int Rel) (IB 34–35 pts)
 Birmingham – AAB (Int Rel) (IB 34 pts)
 Brunel – AAB–ABB 320–340 pts (Int Pol) (IB 35 pts)
 Cardiff – AAB 340 pts (Euro Pol Int Rel)
 Essex – AAB–ABB 340–320 pts (Int Rel) (IB 33–32 pts)
 Lancaster – AAB (Hist Int Rel; Pce St Int Rel; Pol Int Rel) (IB 35 pts)
 Leeds – AAB (Int Rel) (IB 34 pts HL 16 pts)
 London (Gold) – AAB (Int St) (IB 28 pts)
 London (RH) – AAB 340 pts (Econ Pol Int Rel; Int Rel Pol) (IB 32–35 pts)
 Loughborough – AAB–ABB (Hist Int Rel) (IB 34–32 pts)
 Manchester – AAB (Pol Int Rel) (IB 35 pts)
 Sheffield – AAB (Int Rel Pol; Int Pol Scrty St; Hist Pol) (IB 35 pts)

Southampton – AAB 340 pts (Int Rel) (IB 34 pts HL 17 pts)
Surrey – AAB (Law Int St) (IB 35 pts)
Sussex – AAB (Econ Int Rel; Int Rel; Int Rel Dev) (IB 35 pts)
York – AAB (Pol Int Rel) (IB 35 pts)

320 pts **Aston** – ABB 320 pts (Int Rel Bus; Int Rel Engl Lang) (IB 32–34 pts)
Birmingham – AAB–ABB (Int Rel Joint Hons; Int Rel Pol Sci; War St) (IB 34 pts)
Brighton – ABB (Hum: War Cnflct Modnty) (IB 34 pts)
Bristol UWE – 320 pts (Int Rel courses)
East Anglia – ABB (Int Rel; Int Rel Joint Hons; Jap Int Dev St; Fr Int Dev St; Span Int Dev St) (IB 32 pts)
Essex – ABB–BBB 320–300 pts (Pol Hum Rts; Sociol Hum Rts) (IB 33–32 pts)
Kent – ABB (Int Rel Fr/Ger/Ital) (IB 33 pts)
Leeds – ABB 320 pts (Int Rel Thai St)
Leicester – ABB (Int Rel Hist; Int Rel)
London (RH) – ABB 320 pts (Geog Pol Int Rel) (IB 37 pts HL 666)
London Met – 320 pts (Law Int Rel)
Reading – ABB–AAC 320 pts (Int Dev; Pol Int Rel; War Pce Int Rel) (IB 32 pts)
Southampton – ABB–BBB (Pol Int Rel) (IB 32 pts HL 16 pts)

300 pts **Aberdeen** – BBB (Int Rel Mgt St; Int Rel Fin) (IB 28 pts)
Aberystwyth – 300 pts (Int Pol; Int Pol Strat St)
Dundee – BBB (Pol Int Rel) (IB 30 pts)
Heriot-Watt – BBB (Civ Eng Int St) (IB 35 pts)
Hull – 300–320 pts (Pol Int Rel) (IB 34 pts)
Keele – ABC 300–320 pts (Int Rel) (IB 28–30 pts)
Loughborough – BBB–ABB 300–320 pts (Int Rel) (IB 32–34 pts)
Plymouth – 300 pts (Int Rel Law)
Queen's Belfast – BBB/BBCb (Int Pol Cnflct St)
Reading – 300–320 pts (Int Rel courses)
Swansea – BBB (Int Rel; Int Rel Welsh)

280 pts **Bradford** – 280–320 pts (Econ Int Rel)
De Montfort – 280 pts (Int Rel Pol)
Greenwich – 280 pts (Lang Int Rel) (IB 28 pts)
Leeds Beckett – 280 pts (Int Rel Glob Dev) (IB 25 pts)
Lincoln – 280 pts (Int Rel)
London Met – 280 pts (Int Rel Pce Cnflct St) (IB 28 pts)
Manchester Met – 280 pts (Int Pol Phil; Int Pol Lang (Fr/Ger/Ital/Span)) (IB 28 pts)
Nottingham Trent – 280 pts (Int Law)
Oxford Brookes – BBC (Int Rel) (IB 31 pts)
Portsmouth – BBC 280 pts (Law Int Rel) (IB 29 pts)
Sheffield Hallam – 280 pts (Int Fin Bank)
Stirling – BBC (Pol (Int Pol)) (IB 32 pts)
Swansea – BBC–BBB (Int Rel Am St; War Soty) (IB 30 pts)
Westminster – BBC (Int Rel Ger; Int Rel courses)
Winchester – 280–320 pts (Pol Glob St courses) (IB 26 pts)

260 pts **Coventry** – BBC–BCC 260–280 pts (Int Rel; Span Int Rel) (IB 28 pts)
De Montfort – 260 pts (Int Rel)
Derby – 260–300 pts (Int Rel Glob Dev Joint Hons; Thrd Wrld Dev Joint Hons)
Liverpool Hope – 260–320 pts (Int Rel)
London (Birk) – 260 pts (Glob Pol Int Rel)
Nottingham Trent – 260 pts (Glob St Joint Hons; Int Rel Joint Hons)
Plymouth – 260 pts (Int Rel; Int Bus Econ; Int Rel Fr; Int Rel Pol) (IB 26 pts)

240 pts **Bradford** – 240–280 pts (Pce St; Dev Pce St; Int Rel Scrty St)
Buckingham – 240 pts (Int St)
Canterbury Christ Church – CCC 240 pts (Pol Int Rel; Int Rel) (IB 24 pts)
Chester – 240–280 pts (Int Dev St) (IB 26 pts)

LEEDS METROPOLITAN UNIVERSITY

BA (Hons) International Relations and Global Development

This course will enable you to develop an understanding of the critical challenges facing the world. You will study poverty, distribution of resources, inequality, trade, environmental issues and international relations. You will also learn skills in development practice and project management.

BA (Hons) International Relations and Peace Studies

This course will challenge you to think critically about complex international and local problems, developing a theoretical and practical understanding of International Relations, conflict resolution, reconciliation and peace building.

All of our students undertake a voluntary work placement, in the UK or abroad, which will increase your employability.

To find out more visit: **www.leedsmet.ac.uk**

LEEDS
METROPOLITAN
UNIVERSITY

LEEDS
BECKETT
UNIVERSITY | From September 2014 Leeds Metropolitan University will become Leeds Beckett University

Leeds Beckett – 240 pts (Int Rel Pce St) (IB 24 pts)
London Met – 240 pts (Int Dev Int Rel; Int Rel)
London South Bank – 240 pts (Int Pol)
Middlesex – 240 pts (Int Pol) (IB 28 pts)
Nottingham Trent – 240 pts (Pol Int Rel)
Plymouth – 240 pts (Pol Int Rel) (IB 26 pts)
Portsmouth – 240–300 pts (Int Rel) (IB 28 pts)
Salford – 240–280 pts (Int Rel Pol) (IB 25 pts)
220 pts Wolverhampton – 220 pts (War St courses; War St Phil)
200 pts Portsmouth – 200–280 pts (Euro St Int Rel) (IB 28 pts)

Open University – contact +44 (0)845 300 6090 **or** www.openuniversity.co.uk/you (Int St)

Alternative offers

See **Chapter 7** and **Appendix 1** for grades/UCAS Tariff points information for the International Baccalaureate, Scottish Highers/Advanced Highers, the Welsh Baccalaureate, the Irish Leaving Certificate, the Cambridge Pre-U Diploma, the Advanced Diploma and the Extended Project.

CHOOSING YOUR COURSE (SEE ALSO CH.1)

Some course features

De Montfort International Relations and Journalism. Two subjects taught equally with 50% of modules chosen from each course.

East Anglia International Development is offered with overseas experience.

East London (Int Dev: Thrd Wrld NGO Mgt) An interdisciplinary course, this draws on economics, politics, sociology, history and cultural studies to focus on the role of NGOs, their functions and relationships. Students are encouraged to travel to Africa, Asia, Central and Latin America; there is also a final-year work placement scheme.

Check **Chapter 4** when choosing your university and **Chapter 7** on how to read the subject tables.

Kent The degree in Conflict Peace and Security is a flexibile programme covering European integration, ethnic conflict, terrorism, international relations and politics. There is a year-out option in countries world-wide some of which offer courses taught in English.

Universities and colleges teaching quality See www.qaa.ac.uk; http://unistats.direct.gov.uk.

Top research universities and colleges (RAE 2008) See **Politics**.

Examples of sandwich degree courses Aston; Bath; Brunel; Coventry; Nottingham Trent; Oxford Brookes; Plymouth; Portsmouth; Westminster.

ADMISSIONS INFORMATION

Number of applicants per place (approx) Aberystwyth 6; Birmingham 10; De Montfort 6; Derby 3; Exeter 8; Leeds 13; London (King's) 6; London LSE (Int Rel) 21; Nottingham 5; Portsmouth 2; Reading 5; Southampton (Int Rel) 6.

Advice to applicants and planning the UCAS personal statement Describe any special interests you have in the affairs of any particular country. Contact embassies for information on cultural, economic and political developments. Follow international events through newspapers and magazines. Give details of any voluntary work you have done. **London (King's)** Substantial experience required in some area of direct relevance to War Studies. **St Andrews** Give reasons for choice of course and evidence of your interest.

Misconceptions about this course Some students think that this degree will give direct entry into the Diplomatic Service.

Selection interviews Yes London (King's), London Met; **Some** De Montfort, East Anglia, Kent, Nottingham Trent, Wolverhampton; **No** Birmingham, Nottingham.

Interview advice and questions Applicants are likely to be questioned on current international events and crises between countries. See also **Chapter 6**. **Nottingham Trent** Be prepared to be challenged on your existing views!

AFTER-RESULTS ADVICE

Offers to applicants repeating A-levels Same Chester, De Montfort, Exeter, Lincoln, Wolverhampton.

GRADUATE DESTINATIONS AND EMPLOYMENT (2011/12 HESA)
See **Politics**.

Career note See **Politics**.

OTHER DEGREE SUBJECTS FOR CONSIDERATION
Development Studies; Economics; European Studies; Government; Politics.

ITALIAN
(see also Languages)

The language and literature of Italy will feature strongly on most Italian courses. The majority of applicants have no knowledge of Italian. They will need to give convincing reasons for their interest and to show that they have the ability to assimilate language quickly. See also **Appendix 3** under Languages.

Useful websites www.europa.eu; www.italia.gov.it; www.bbc.co.uk/languages; www.languageadvantage.com; www.italianstudies.org; www.languagematters.co.uk; see also **Languages**.

NB The points totals shown to the left of the institutions are for ease of reference only. It must not be assumed that Tariff points are always used by institutions or that they can be substituted for an offer in grades. The level of an offer is not necessarily indicative of the quality of a course.

COURSE OFFERS INFORMATION

Subject requirements/preferences **GCSE** English and a foreign language required. **AL** Italian may be required for some courses.

Your target offers and examples of courses provided by each institution
380 pts **Cambridge** – A*AA 380 pts (Modn Mediev Lang) (IB 40–41 pts HL 776)
360 pts **Durham** – AAA 360 pts (Modn Langs) (IB 37 pts)
        Edinburgh – AAA–BBB 360–300 pts (Ital Ling; Ital) (IB 37–34 pts)
        London (UCL) – AAB (Ital) (IB 36 pts)
        Oxford – AAA 360 pts (Ital courses) (IB 38–40 pts)
340 pts **Exeter** – AAB–ABB 340–320 pts (Ital) (IB 34–32 pts)
        London (RH) – AAB–ABB 340–320 pts (Mgt Fr/Ger/Ital/Span; Dr Ger/Ital) (IB 35–34 pts)
        St Andrews – AAB–AAA 340–360 pts (Ital courses) (IB 35–36 pts)
        Sussex – AAB–ABB 340–320 pts (Ital courses) (IB 35–34 pts)
        Warwick – AAB 340 pts (Engl Ital Lit; Ger St Ital) (IB 36 pts)
        York – AAB–ABB 340–320 pts (Fr Ital Lang) (IB 34 pts)
320 pts **Bath** – ABB–AAA 320–360 pts (Modn Langs Euro St) (IB 34–36 pts)
        Birmingham – ABB (Ital St Joint Hons) (IB 32 pts)
        Bristol – ABB–BBB (Ital) (IB 33–32 pts)
        Glasgow – ABB (Ital Joint Hons) (IB 36 pts)
        Kent – ABB (Ital courses) (IB 33 pts)
        Leicester – ABB (Ital Joint Hons) (IB 30 pts)
        London (RH) – ABB (Class St Ital; Ital Joint Hons)
        Strathclyde – ABB (Ital courses)
        Warwick – ABB (Ital; Ital Joint Hons; Fr St Ger/Ital) (IB 32–34 pts)
300 pts **Cardiff** – BBB 300 pts (Ital) (IB 34 pts)
        Hertfordshire – 300 pts (Phil Ital; Hist Ital; Engl Lit Ital)
        Leeds – ABC–BBB (Ital; Ital Joint Hons) (IB 34 pts HL 16 pts)
        Liverpool – BBB (Hisp St Ital) (IB 30 pts)
        Manchester – BBB 300 pts (Ital courses; Ital St) (IB 31 pts)
        Reading – ABC–BBB (Ital) (IB 30 pts)
        Swansea – BBB (Ital courses)
280 pts **Hull** – 280–320 pts (Ital Joint courses; Fr/Ger/Ital/Span Hist)
260 pts **Manchester Met** – 260–280 pts (Ling Lang (Fr/Ger/Ital/Span)) (IB 28 pts)
        Nottingham Trent – 260 pts (Ital Joint Hons)
240 pts **Bangor** – 240–260 pts (Ital Joint Hons)

Alternative offers
See **Chapter 7** and **Appendix 1** for grades/UCAS Tariff points information for the International Baccalaureate, Scottish Highers/Advanced Highers, the Welsh Baccalaureate, the Irish Leaving Certificate, the Cambridge Pre-U Diploma, the Advanced Diploma and the Extended Project.

CHOOSING YOUR COURSE (SEE ALSO CH.1)

Some course features
Bangor Italian can be studied with two other languages or with Law, Journalism or Media Studies.
Bath Italian is taken with a second European language as part of the European Studies course.
Hull In addition to modern language combinations, Italian can be studied with a choice from 17 other subjects.
Reading Single and Joint Honours courses are offered, the latter with up to 15 subjects. Exchange agreements in Florence, Rome, Bologna and Venice. There is an option to take half your courses in subjects outside Italian.

Universities and colleges teaching quality See www.qaa.ac.uk; http://unistats.direct.gov.uk.

Top research universities and colleges (RAE 2008) Cambridge; Leeds; Warwick; Reading; Oxford; Bristol; Manchester; Birmingham; London (UCL); Exeter.

ADMISSIONS INFORMATION

Number of applicants per place (approx) Birmingham 5; Bristol 8; Cardiff 3; Hull 8; Leeds 3; London (RH) 4.

Advice to applicants and planning the UCAS personal statement Describe any visits to Italy and experience of speaking the language. Interests in Italian art, literature, culture, society and architecture could also be mentioned. Read Italian newspapers and magazines and give details if you have a bilingual background. Give evidence of your interest and your reasons for choosing the course. See also **Appendix 3** under Languages.

Misconceptions about this course Leeds See **Languages**.

Selection interviews Yes Birmingham (majority receive offers), Cambridge, London (RH), Oxford; **No** Reading.

Interview advice and questions Past questions include: Why do you want to learn Italian? What foreign newspapers or magazines do you read (particularly if the applicant has taken A-level Italian)? Have you visited Italy? What do you know of the Italian people, culture, art? See also **Chapter 6**. **Leeds** See **Languages**.

AFTER-RESULTS ADVICE

Offers to applicants repeating A-levels Higher Birmingham, Glasgow, Warwick; **Same** Cardiff, Hull, Leeds.

GRADUATE DESTINATIONS AND EMPLOYMENT (2011/12 HESA)

Graduates surveyed 360 **Employed** 145 **In voluntary employment** 15 **In further study** 70 **Assumed unemployed** 15

Career note See **Languages**.

OTHER DEGREE SUBJECTS FOR CONSIDERATION

European Studies; International Business Studies; other languages.

JAPANESE

(see also Asia-Pacific Studies, Languages)

A strong interest in Japan and its culture is expected of applicants. A number of four-year joint courses are now offered, all of which include a period of study in Japan. Potential employers are showing an interest in Japanese. Students report that 'it is not a soft option'. They are expected to be firmly committed to a Japanese degree (for example, by listing only Japanese on the UCAS application), to have an interest in using their degree in employment and to be prepared for a lot of hard work. See **Appendix 3** under Languages.

Useful websites www.cilt.org.uk; www.iol.org.uk; www.bbc.co.uk/languages; www.languageadvantage.com; www.languagematters.co.uk; www.japanese-online.com; www.gojapango.com; www.thejapanesepage.com; www.japanesestudies.org.uk.

NB The points totals shown to the left of the institutions are for ease of reference only. It must not be assumed that Tariff points are always used by institutions or that they can be substituted for an offer in grades. The level of an offer is not necessarily indicative of the quality of a course.

COURSE OFFERS INFORMATION

Subject requirements/preferences GCSE A foreign language usually required. **AL** Modern language required for some courses.

Your target offers and examples of courses provided by each institution
380 pts Cambridge – A*AA (As Mid E St) (IB 40–41 pts HL 776)
360 pts Edinburgh – AAA–BBB 360–300 pts (Jap Ling; Jap) (IB 40–34 pts)

Manchester – AAA (Russ Jap IPML) (IB 37 pts)

Oxford – AAA (Orntl St; Class Orntl St) (IB 38–40 pts)

340 pts Birmingham – AAB (Modn Lang) (IB 36 pts)

Leeds – AAB 340 pts (Jap courses) (IB 35 pts HL 16 pts)

Manchester – AAB–ABB 340–320 pts (Jap Scrn St; Chin Jap; Russ Jap) (IB 36–33 pts)

320 pts Cardiff – ABB 320 pts (Bus St Jap) (IB 35 pts)

Central Lancashire – ABB (Fr/Ger/Span/Jap) (IB 25 pts)

East Anglia – ABB (Jap Film TV; Modn Lang Jap; Jap Lang Mgt St; Jap Int Dev St; Transl Media Jap) (IB 32 pts)

Manchester – ABB 320 pts (Jap St) (IB 34 pts)

Newcastle – ABB 320 pts (Chin St Jap St) (IB 34 pts)

Sheffield – ABB 320 pts (Jap St; Jap St Joint Hons; Kor St Joint Hons) (IB 34 pts)

80 pts London (Birk) – p/t, for under 21s (over 21s varies) (Modn Langs Euro St (Fr, Ger, Jap, Port, Span))

Alternative offers

See **Chapter 7** and **Appendix 1** for grades/UCAS Tariff points information for the International Baccalaureate, Scottish Highers/Advanced Highers, the Welsh Baccalaureate, the Irish Leaving Certificate, the Cambridge Pre-U Diploma, the Advanced Diploma and the Extended Project.

CHOOSING YOUR COURSE (SEE ALSO CH.1)

Some course features

Cardiff Courses are offered with Business or a choice of four European languages.

Manchester (Jap Scrn St) The course combines Japanese language and culture with core course units in understanding film, its history and pre-history, and its development across other media including television, DVD and the internet. The third year is spent abroad.

Sheffield Japanese taught from scratch. Modules in contemporary society, politics, economics, international relations and business management.

Universities and colleges teaching quality See www.qaa.ac.uk; http://unistats.direct.gov.uk.

ADMISSIONS INFORMATION

Number of applicants per place (approx) Cardiff 8; Sheffield 10.

Advice to applicants and planning the UCAS personal statement Discuss your interest in Japan and your reasons for wishing to study the language. Know Japan, its culture and background history. Discuss any visits you have made or contacts with Japanese nationals. See also **Appendix 3** under Languages. **Leeds** See **Languages**.

Selection interviews **Yes** Cambridge, Oxford; Southampton; **Some** Leeds.

Interview advice and questions Japanese is an extremely demanding subject and applicants are most likely to be questioned on their reasons for choosing this degree. They will be expected also to have some knowledge of Japanese culture, history and current affairs. See also **Chapter 6**.

Reasons for rejection (non-academic) Insufficient evidence of genuine motivation.

AFTER-RESULTS ADVICE

Offers to applicants repeating A-levels **No** Cambridge.

GRADUATE DESTINATIONS AND EMPLOYMENT (2011/12 HESA)

Graduates surveyed 140 **Employed** 65 **In voluntary employment** 5 **In further study** 20 **Assumed unemployed** 15

Career note See **Languages**.

OTHER DEGREE SUBJECTS FOR CONSIDERATION

Asia-Pacific Studies; International Business Studies; Oriental Languages; South East Asia Studies.

JOURNALISM

(see also **Communication Studies/Communication, English, Media Studies**)

A passion for writing, good spelling, grammar and punctuation and the ability to work under pressure are some of the qualities which all journalists require. The opportunities within journalism range from covering day-to-day news stories in the local and national press to periodicals and magazines covering specialist subjects. Journalism is also the foundation for work in local radio.

Useful websites www.journalism.co.uk; www.wannabehacks.co.uk

The points totals shown to the left of the institutions are for ease of reference only. It must not be assumed that Tariff points are always used by institutions or that they can be substituted for an offer in grades. The level of an offer is not necessarily indicative of the quality of a course.

COURSE OFFERS INFORMATION

Subject requirements/preferences GCSE English and maths often required. **AL** No specific subjects required.

Your target offers and examples of courses provided by each institution

360 pts **City** – AAA 360 pts (Jrnl) (IB 35 pts)

340 pts **Cardiff** – AAB 340 pts (Jrnl Media Engl Lit) (IB 34 pts)
London (Gold) – AAB-ABB 340–300 pts (Jrnl) (IB 34 pts)

320 pts **Brunel** – ABB-BBB 320 pts (Jrnl) (IB 33 pts)
Cardiff – ABB 320 pts (Jrnl Media Cult St; Jrnl Media Sociol)
Central Lancashire – ABB-BBC (Jrnl; Spo Jrnl)
Kent – ABB (Jrnl) (IB 33 pts HL 16 pts)
Kingston – ABB 320 pts (Jrnl; Pol Jrnl)
Leeds – ABB (Broad Jrnl) (IB 35 pts)
Northumbria – 320 pts incl 100 pts from Engl (Jrnl Engl Lit; Jrnl) (IB 27 pts)
Sheffield – ABB (Jrnl St) (IB 34 pts)
Strathclyde – ABB (Jrnl Crea Writ) (IB 34 pts)
Winchester – 320–360 pts (Jrnl) (IB 27 pts HL 5)

300 pts **Bournemouth** – 300–320 pts (Multim Jrnl) (IB 31–32 pts)
Brighton – BBB 300 pts (Spo Jrnl) (IB 32 pts)
Bristol UWE – 300 pts (Jrnl PR; Jrnl) (IB 26 pts)
Leeds Beckett – 300 pts (Photo Jrnl; Jrnl)
Lincoln – 300 pts (Jrnl)
Nottingham Trent – 300 pts (Prnt Jrnl; Broad Jrnl)
Staffordshire – 300–260 pts (Jrnl)
Westminster – BBB (Jrnl) (IB 30 pts)

280 pts **Birmingham City** – BBC 280 pts (Media Comm Jrnl) (IB 28 pts)
Brighton – BBC (Multim Broad Jrnl) (IB 30 pts)
Bristol UWE – 280–320 pts (Crimin Jrnl)
Buckingham – BBC-BCC (Jrnl Comm St)
East London – 280 pts (Spo Jrnl)
Glasgow Caledonian – BBC (Multim Jrnl)
Gloucestershire – 280–300 pts (Jrnl; Photojrnl Doc Photo)
Huddersfield – BBC (Jrnl; Spo Jrnl) (IB 28 pts)
Leeds Trinity – 240–280 pts (Spo Jrnl)
Liverpool John Moores – 280 pts (Jrnl) (IB 29 pts)
London Met – 280 pts (Jrnl; Jrnl Film TV St)
Robert Gordon – BBC incl Engl (Jrnl)
Roehampton – 280 pts (Jrnl) (IB 25 pts)
Salford – 280–320 pts (Jrnl (News/Multim/Broad)) (IB 31 pts)
South Wales – BBC (Jrnl) (IB 26 pts)
Stirling – BBC (Jrnl St) (IB 32 pts)

Bournemouth University

Launch your
**journalism
career** at BU

Study BA (Hons) Multimedia Journalism

To find out more, please visit
www.bournemouth.ac.uk/journalism-heap

Accredited by:

Bournemouth University

Study **BA (Hons) Multimedia Journalism** at BU

Now, more than ever, journalists need to be versatile and flexible to succeed. In the age of convergence, it is likely that they will be expected to transfer their work from one medium to another. So, for example, a print journalist can be expected to produce a piece for camera and write for the website as well.

Additional abilities, such as digital skills and being able to film, or record and edit audio as well as write, are prized by employers. Having such a portfolio of skills helps journalists build up their career and that is a key principle of the Multimedia Journalism course at Bournemouth University (BU), which combines multi-disciplinary training in television, radio, newspaper, magazine and online journalism. The course is accredited by all three industry councils: the National Council for the Training of Journalists (NCTJ), the Broadcast Journalism Training Council (BJTC) and the Periodicals Training Council (PTC).

As graduate Stuart James explains, "The beauty of the course is its multimedia aspect. Through the course at BU you come away with experience of using a camera, operating a radio mic and recording and mixing sound. The course is excellent as it doesn't rush you to narrow your options…initially I thought I wanted to concentrate on broadcast, but it wasn't until I had a chance to try radio, TV and print that I realised I wanted to focus on a career in print."

Live radio broadcast

Mirroring professional practice

As well as the opportunity to explore various media, another element of the course is the emphasis we place on professional practice and preparing you for your future career.

A professional working environment is created in dedicated newsrooms and digitally equipped studios, and practical work is project-based. You will write copy for online, newspapers and magazines as well as producing radio and television bulletins to industry standards and deadlines. The course also produces BU's own student and community newspaper, which allows for hands-on journalism experience to be gained.

Frequent visits from leading journalists and editors who give guest lectures at BU also provide important networking opportunities for you and enable you to develop key contacts in industry.

BU newsroom

To find out more about studying BA (Hons) Multimedia Journalism at BU, visit

www.bournemouth.ac.uk/journalism-heap

Teesside – 280 pts +interview (Broad Media Prod; Multim Jrnl)
Ulster – BBC–BBB 280–300 pts (Jrnl courses)
Worcester – 280–340 pts (Jrnl) (IB 25 pts)
260 pts **Canterbury Christ Church** – BCC (Multim Jrnl)
Chester – 260–300 pts (Spo Jrnl; Law Jrnl/Crimin; Jrnl) (IB 28 pts)
Coventry – BCC 260 pts (Jrnl; Engl Jrnl)
Derby – 260 pts (Jrnl)
Edinburgh Napier – BCC incl Engl 260 pts (Jrnl) (IB 28 pts HL 5 Engl)
Middlesex – 260 pts (Crea Writ Jrnl)
Northampton – 260–300 pts incl Engl (Multim Jrnl)
Sunderland – 260 pts (Mag Jrnl; Jrnl; Broad Jrnl; Fash Jrnl; Spo Jrnl)
Winchester – 260–300 pts (Jrnl Media St)
240 pts **Bangor** – 240–260 pts (Jrnl Media St)
Cumbria – 240 pts (Jrnl)
East London – 240 pts (Jrnl)
Glyndŵr – 240 pts (Broad Jrnl Media Comms)
Grimsby (Univ Centre) – 240 pts (Multim Jrnl)
Leeds Trinity – 240–280 pts (Broad Jrnl; Jrnl)
London Met – 240 pts (Fash Mark Jrnl)
Portsmouth – 240–300 pts (Jrnl)
St Mark and St John – 240 pts (Spo Jrnl; Jrnl)
Southampton Solent – 240 pts (Jrnl; Jrnl Engl Media)
Staffordshire – CCC 240 pts (Photojrnl) (IB 24 pts)
West Scotland – CCC (Jrnl; Spo Jrnl) (IB 24 pts)
220 pts **Creative Arts** – 220–240 pts (Jrnl; Mus Jrnl; Fash Jrnl)
200 pts **Bedfordshire** – 200 pts (Jrnl)
Leeds Trinity – 200–260 pts (Engl Jrnl)
Middlesex – 200–300 pts (Jrnl Media)
Trinity Saint David (Swansea) – 200–360 pts (Photojrnl) (IB 24 pts)
Wolverhampton – 200 pts (Broad Jrnl)
160 pts **Arts London** – 160 pts (Jrnl)
Peterborough (Reg Coll) – 160 pts (Jrnl)

Alternative offers
See **Chapter 7** and **Appendix 1** for grades/UCAS Tariff points information for the International Baccalaureate, Scottish Highers/Advanced Highers, the Welsh Baccalaureate, the Irish Leaving Certificate, the Cambridge Pre-U Diploma, the Advanced Diploma and the Extended Project.

EXAMPLES OF FOUNDATION DEGREES IN THE SUBJECT FIELD
Anglia Ruskin; Chesterfield (Coll); Cornwall (Coll); Darlington (Coll); Doncaster (Coll Univ Centre); Exeter (Coll); Glyndŵr; Milton Keynes (Coll); Nottingham New (Coll); Teesside; Wolverhampton.

CHOOSING YOUR COURSE (SEE ALSO CH.1)
Some course features
Birmingham City A highly vocational course covering newspaper, magazine, TV and radio news media.
Bournemouth A highly practical course in multimedia journalism focusing on newspaper, magazine, TV, radio and online journalism.
City A highly regarded School of Journalism offering additional studies in shorthand, media law and government studies.
Leeds (Broad Jrnl) Course covers all relevant aspects of news production. It offers a range of technical skills and theoretical studies, such as media law and journalistic ethics. A year in industry is also offered.

Universities and colleges teaching quality See www.qaa.ac.uk; http://unistats.direct.gov.uk.

Examples of sandwich degree courses City; Coventry; Hertfordshire; Huddersfield; Kingston; Southampton Solent.

ADMISSIONS INFORMATION

Selection interviews Most institutions will interview candidates, some requiring auditions and/or a portfolio. **Some**

GRADUATE DESTINATIONS AND EMPLOYMENT (2011/12 HESA)

Graduates surveyed 1995 **Employed** 1065 **In voluntary employment** 115 **In further study** 195 **Assumed unemployed** 225

LANDSCAPE ARCHITECTURE

(including **Garden Design** and **Landscape Design** and **Management**; see also **Agricultural Sciences/Agriculture, Horticulture**)

Landscape architects shape the world you live in, they are responsible for urban design and the integration of ecology and the quality of the built environment. Courses in Landscape Architecture include project-based design, landscape theory, management, planning and design, ecology, construction, plant design and design practice. After completing the first three years leading to a BSc (Hons) or BA (Hons), students aiming for full professional status take a further one year in practice and one year to achieve their Master of Landscape Architecture (MLA).

Useful websites www.landscapeinstitute.org; www.iwanttobealandscapearchitect.com.

NB The points totals shown to the left of the institutions are for ease of reference only. It must not be assumed that Tariff points are always used by institutions or that they can be substituted for an offer in grades. The level of an offer is not necessarily indicative of the quality of a course.

COURSE OFFERS INFORMATION

Subject requirements/preferences GCSE English, geography, art and design, mathematics and at least one science usually required. **AL** Preferred subjects for some courses include biology, geography, environmental science. A portfolio may also be required.

Sheffield Art and design or design technology at A-level required.

Your target offers and examples of courses provided by each institution
360 pts **Sheffield** – AAA (Archit Lnd) (IB 37 pts)
340 pts **Edinburgh** – AAB–BBB 340–300 pts (Lnd Archit) (IB 36–34 pts HL 665)
320 pts **Greenwich** – 320 pts (Lnd Archit)
        Sheffield – ABB–BBB 320–300 pts (Lnd Archit) (IB 34 pts)
300 pts **Edinburgh (CA)** – BBB 300 pts (Lnd Archit) (IB 34 pts)
        Leeds Beckett – 300 pts (Lnd Archit Des) (IB 26 pts)
280 pts **Birmingham City** – 280 pts (Land Archit) (IB 28 pts)
        Gloucestershire – 280–300 pts (Lnd Archit)
        Manchester Met – 280 pts +portfolio (Lnd Archit) (IB 28 pts)
        Writtle (Coll) – 280 pts (Lnd Gdn Des; Gdn Des Restor Mgt; Lnd Archit) (IB 24 pts)
240 pts **Greenwich** – 240 pts (Gdn Des)
        Hadlow (Coll) – 240 pts (Lnd Mgt; Gdn Des)

Alternative offers
See **Chapter 7** and **Appendix 1** for grades/UCAS Tariff points information for the International Baccalaureate, Scottish Highers/Advanced Highers, the Welsh Baccalaureate, the Irish Leaving Certificate, the Cambridge Pre-U Diploma, the Advanced Diploma and the Extended Project.

EXAMPLES OF FOUNDATION DEGREES IN THE SUBJECT FIELD

Brighton; Brooksby Melton (Coll); Guildford (Coll); Harper Adams; Kingston; Moulton (Coll); Sparsholt (Coll); SRUC; Suffolk (Univ Campus); Writtle (Coll).

The
University
Of
Sheffield.

Sheffield. Inspiration for the spaces you'll transform.

Landscape Architecture
Undergraduate Courses

BA Hons or BSc Hons in
Landscape Architecture

shef.ac.uk/landscape

The
University
Of
Sheffield.

Department
Of
Landscape

Studying Landscape Architecture
at Sheffield

The Department of Landscape at the University of Sheffield is one of the leading university to study Landscape Architecture in the UK. We are one of the largest academic institution in our field and offer research and taught courses with an international reputation spanning arts, design, social sciences, geography, planning, ecology and management.

Come to the Department of Landscape and you will be joining one of the world's leading departments for landscape education and research. Our staff are involved in some of the most exciting contemporary landscape design projects through their practice and consultancy and they are strongly committed to excellence in research and practice led teaching.

93%
of our 2011 graduates got jobs.
(GEMS 2012)

BA/BSc (Hons) Landscape Architecture

The BA(Hons) (UCAS code: K3K4) in **Landscape Architecture with Planning** aims to educate Landscape Architects who combine design skills with a sound understanding of urban design theory, planning and practice. If you enjoy subjects such as geography, politics, economics or history you will appreciate the scope and challenge of this course in addressing issues which examine the role of the environment in meeting the changing needs of individuals and societies. Students completing this course are in a strong position to appreciate the planning context in which design takes place and the wider implications of their landscape design proposals.

The BSc(Hons) (UCAS code: KC39) in **Landscape Architecture with Ecology** aims to educate Landscape Architects who have a more in-depth understanding of ecology and habitat creation. If you enjoy subjects related to biology or environmental sciences, or have a keen interest in the natural world, this course will equip you to combine a more detailed appreciation of ecological processes and how they work within the designed landscape. Through their specialist training in ecology graduates are able to assist in the restoration of degraded environments and also to understand the wider implications of design proposals on existing habitats.

The
University
Of
Sheffield.

Department
Of
Landscape

Study
Landscape Architecture
at the University of Sheffield

The Department of Landscape at the University of Sheffield is one of the leading universities to study Landscape Architecture in the UK. We are one of the largest academic institutions in our field and offer research and taught courses with an international reputation. Our course spans art, design, social sciences, geography, planning, ecology and management.

What is a Landscape Architect?

Landscape architecture is the planning, design and management of places for people and nature; both special and everyday places. Landscape Architects design spaces between buildings that are imaginative yet functional. They also shape and design elements of natural and semi- natural landscapes to help restore ecological processes and enable people in cities to engage with nature. Every public environment in the UK has had some element of design: whether it is a local park, a school playground, a green space between offices or a National Park like the Peak District. They have all been influenced by a Landscape Architect.

To be a Landscape Architect requires artistic flair, a passion for improving environmental quality and people's lives, and an ability to fuse diverse knowledge to produce inventive yet workable solutions. This requires the ability to blend applied geography and arts with social science and the built environment.

Our students are highly sought after within the Landscape profession. At Sheffield, we aim to develop graduates with outstanding skills, who will be able to take key roles in multidisciplinary projects with an underlying commitment to care for the landscape and the people who live within it. This fusion of attributes ensures that you will be highly employable, ready for professional practice and a committed lifelong learner.

As a Sheffield Graduate you develop a proficiency in design, and understand the cultural, social and ecological drivers that underpin successful landscapes. Our courses equip students with excellent transferable skills, which are also highly relevant beyond the landscape profession. Through working in teams, solving complex problems, undertaking live projects for community groups, and developing your own personal portfolio you will acquire

Complex landform and built structures represent the depository of natural elements. A large compost heap collects waste ready to create gardens for the oncoming housing.

professional standards in communication, graphic design, report writing and verbal presentation. Skills that will allow you to become adept at presenting your ideas and visions in a coherent and highly- effective manner.

You will also gain an aptitude for combining your creative skills with research and analytical capabilities. Our teaching strategies encourage you to think independently and develop innovative and imaginative solutions to the complex issues concerning landscape design. Indeed, because we provide a robust education covering key elements of design, art, social science and natural science, you will have a comprehensive understanding of the landscape, and retain a critical but open mind to how environments could be developed in the future.

Graduates from the Department of Landscape work in the private sector where many have set up their own companies. Others work in the public or Third sectors, helping to improve local communities. A number of graduates have gone on to become consultants – advising Governments on how landscapes should be designed and managed, for example, setting up new National Parks. Some have achieved the highest levels of recognition, for example President of the Landscape Institute (UK) or President of the International Federation of Landscape Architects (IFLA). In the recent National Student Survey the Department of Landscape achieved the highest UK graduate employment rate of 90% for all UK Landscape Design courses. Many of our alumni now run their own national and international practices, it is not uncommon for them to come back to Sheffield to recruit new staff for their firms.

Contact us

Email: landscape@sheffield.ac.uk   **Telephone:** +44 (0)114 222 0600

Visit our website for more information www.sheffield.ac.uk/landscape

For more information about our profession visit
www.landscapeinstitute.org   www.iwanttobealandscapearchitect.com

CHOOSING YOUR COURSE (SEE ALSO CH.1)

Some course features

Birmingham City (Land Archit) The course is accredited by the Landscape Institute and combines a strong study of design with a focus on environmental and cultural issues and technical skills.

Gloucestershire Students have access to dedicated landscape studios as part of this vocational course studied at Francis Close Hall.

Manchester Met The three-year BA course can be followed by an MA in Landscape Architecture for those wanting to enter the profession of landscape architecture. The course focuses on the design of outdoor space and includes a European study tour and offers study opportunities in European universities.

Sheffield A multi-disciplinary course providing a comprehensive training in landscape architecture with a specialism in either planning or ecology. The Ecology pathway focuses on habitat restoration, urban regeneration and green technologies, while the Planning pathway centres on the political, social and economic facors of urban and rural environments.

Universities and colleges teaching quality See www.qaa.ac.uk; http://unistats.direct.gov.uk.

Examples of sandwich degree courses Edinburgh; Writtle (Coll).

ADMISSIONS INFORMATION

Number of applicants per place (approx) Edinburgh (CA) 7; Gloucestershire 9; Greenwich 3; Manchester Met 9; Writtle (Coll) 5.

Advice to applicants and planning the UCAS personal statement Knowledge of the work of landscape architects is important. Arrange a visit to a landscape architect's office and try to organise some work experience. Read up on historical landscape design and visit country house estates with examples of outstanding designs. Describe these visits in detail and your preferences. Membership of the National Trust could be useful. See also **Appendix 3**.

Selection interviews **Yes** Gloucestershire, Greenwich, Manchester Met, Sheffield, Writtle (Coll); **Some** Birmingham City.

Interview advice and questions Applicants will be expected to have had some work experience and are likely to be questioned on their knowledge of landscape architectural work and the subject. Historical examples of good landscaping could also be asked for. See also **Chapter 6**.

Reasons for rejection (non-academic) Lack of historical knowledge and awareness of current developments. Poor portfolio.

AFTER-RESULTS ADVICE

Offers to applicants repeating A-levels **Same** Birmingham City, Edinburgh (CA), Greenwich, Manchester Met.

GRADUATE DESTINATIONS AND EMPLOYMENT (2011/12 HESA)

Landscape Design graduates surveyed 215 **Employed** 75 **In voluntary employment** 5 **In further study** 70 **Assumed unemployed** 15

Career note Opportunities at present in landscape architecture are good. Openings exist in local government or private practice and may cover planning, housing, and conservation.

OTHER DEGREE SUBJECTS FOR CONSIDERATION

Architecture; Art and Design; Environmental Planning; Forestry; Horticulture.

LANGUAGES

(including **British Sign Language, European Language Studies, Modern Languages** and **Translation Studies; see separate language tables;** see also **African Studies, Asia-Pacific Studies, Chinese, English, European Studies, French, German, Greek, Italian, Japanese, Latin, Linguistics, Russian and East European Studies, Scandinavian Studies, Spanish**)

Modern Language courses usually offer three main options: a single subject degree commonly based on literature and language, a European Studies course, or two-language subjects which can often include languages different from those available at school (such as Scandinavian Studies, Russian and the languages of Eastern Europe, the Middle and Far East).

Useful websites www.iol.org.uk; www.iti.org.uk; www.europa.eu; www.cilt.org.uk; www.bbc.co.uk/ languages; www.languageadvantage.com; www.omniglot.com; www.languagematters.co.uk.

NB The points totals shown to the left of the institutions are for ease of reference only. It must not be assumed that Tariff points are always used by institutions or that they can be substituted for an offer in grades. The level of an offer is not necessarily indicative of the quality of a course.

COURSE OFFERS INFORMATION

Subject requirements/preferences GCSE English and a modern language required. In some cases grades A and/or B may be stipulated. **AL** A modern foreign language required usually with a specified grade.

Your target offers and examples of courses provided by each institution

400 pts **London (UCL)** – A*AAe–AAAe 400–380 pts (Hist Euro Lang) (IB 38–39 pts HL 666)

380 pts **Cambridge** – A*AA (Modn Mediev Lang; As Mid E St; As Mid E St; Ling) (IB 40–41 pts HL 776)

Imperial London – A*AA–AAA (Chem Fr/Ger/Span Sci) (IB 38 pts HL 7 chem 6 maths)

London (UCL) – AAAe–ABBe (Mod Lang Film St; Modn Lang) (IB 34–38 pts)

Nottingham – A*AA–AAA 380–360 pts (Phys Euro Lang) (IB 24 pts HL 665)

360 pts **Birmingham** – AAA incl maths (Econ Lang) (IB 36–38 pts)

Durham – AAA 360 pts (Modn Langs; Modn Langs Hist) (IB 37 pts)

Exeter – AAA–ABB 360–340 pts (Int Rel Modn Lang) (IB 36–32 pts)

London (UCL) – AABe 360 pts (Lang Cult) (IB 36 pts)

Manchester – AAA–ABB 360–320 pts (Biol Modn Lang; Genet Modn Lang; Zool Modn Lang; Plnt Sci Modn Lang; Anat Sci Modn Lang) (IB 37–33 pts)

Oxford – AAA (Modn Langs; Class Modn Langs; Phil Modn Langs; Hist Modn Langs; Engl Modn Langs; Orntl St; Modn Lang Ling) (IB 38–40 pts)

St Andrews – AAA–AAB (Modn Lang courses; Maths Langs; Heb courses) (IB 38–36 pts)

Sheffield – AAA incl maths sci (Civ Eng Modn Lang) (IB 37 pts HL 6 maths sci)

340 pts **Birmingham** – AAB (Modn Lang) (IB 36 pts)

Bristol – AAB–BBB 340–300 pts (Modn Lang courses; Span Modn Lang; Mus Modn Lang; Phil Modn Lang; Hist Art Modn Lang; Pol Modn Lang) (IB 35–32 pts)

Exeter – AAB–ABB (Modn Lang) (IB 34–32 pts)

Lancaster – AAB (Euro Langs; Modn Langs; Mgt St Euro Langs) (IB 35 pts)

London (King's) – AAB (Port Braz St) (IB 36 pts HL 6 hist)

London (RH) – AAB–ABB 340–320 pts (Mus Fr/Ger/Ital/Span) (IB 35–34 pts)

London (SOAS) – AAB (Burm (Myan) courses; Hausa Joint Hons; Indsn Joint Hons; Kor Joint Hons; Swli Joint Hons; Thai Joint Hons; Turk; Akkdn/Aram/Bngli/Guji/Heb/Hnd/Tbtn/ Npli/Sansk/Tam/Urdu/Viet) (IB 36 pts HL 666)

Manchester – AAB–ABB 320–340 pts (Euro St Modn Lang) (IB 33–36 pts)

St Andrews – AAB (Art Hist Lang) (IB 36 pts)

Sheffield – AAB incl maths (Electron Elec Eng Modn Lang) (IB 35 pts)

Southampton – AAB–ABB 340–320 pts (Langs Contemp Euro St; Mgt Sci Fr/Ger/Span) (IB 34 pts)

Check **Chapter 4** when choosing your university and **Chapter 7** on how to read the subject tables.

Surrey – AAB (Bus Mgt Engl Int Comm; Langs St) (IB 35 pts)

York – AAB (Modn Lang Ling courses) (IB 35 pts)

320 pts **Bath** – ABB–AAA 320–360 pts (Modn Langs Euro St) (IB 34–36 pts)

Birmingham – ABB (Port Joint Hons; Modn Langs Euro St; Film St courses) (IB 32 pts)

Bristol – ABB–BBB 320–300 pts (Russ (Cz/Port)) (IB 32–33 pts)

Cardiff – ABB 320 pts (Euro Lang)

East Anglia – ABB (Jap Lang Mgt St; Fr Lang Mgt St; Span Lang Mgt St; Transl Interp Langs; Modn Langs 4 yrs dbl Hons) (IB 32 pts)

Essex – ABB–BBB (Euro St; Euro St Fr/Ger/Ital/Span) (IB 32–30 pts)

Hull – 280–320 pts (Comb Lang)

Leeds – ABB (Port Russ)

Liverpool – ABB (Modn Euro Langs; Comb Hons Lat Am Hisp St; Mathem Sci Euro Lang) (IB 33 pts)

London (RH) – ABB–BBB (Mling St Int Rel) (IB 34–32 pts)

London (SOAS) – ABB (Bngli) (IB 30 pts)

Manchester – AAA–ABB 320–360 pts (Microbiol Modn Langs; Span Port) (IB 37–33 pts)

Newcastle – ABB–AAB 320–340 pts (Modn Lang Ling; Modn Langs; Mod Lang Transl Interp) (IB 34 pts)

Nottingham – ABB 320 pts (Modn Euro St; Modn Langs Bus; Modn Lang St (Fr/Ger/Russ/Span/Cro/Serb/Port/Slovak)) (IB 32 pts)

Sheffield – ABB (Modn Langs) (IB 33 pts HL 6 lang)

300 pts **Aberdeen** – BBB 300 pts (Euro St; Lang Ling) (IB 32 pts)

Aston – 300–320 pts (Transl St (Fr/Ger/Span); Modn Langs courses) (IB 32–34 pts)

Bath – AAA–BBB 300–360 pts (Modn Lang) (IB 34 pts HL 6 lang)

Dundee – BBB 300 pts (Euro St) (IB 30 pts)

Edinburgh – AAA–BBB 300–360 pts (Span Port) (IB 34–37 pts)

Essex – ABB–BBB 300–320 pts (Span St Modn Langs; Modn Langs; Lang St; Port St Modn Langs) (IB 32–30 pts)

Heriot-Watt – BBB 300 pts (Langs (Interp Transl); Langs (Interp Transl) (Fr/Ger) (Ger/Span); App Langs Transl (Fr/Span) (Ger/Span); App Langs Transl (Fr/Ger); Brit Sign Lang) (IB 30 pts)

Liverpool – BBB (Bus St Modn Lang) (IB 30 pts HL 6 lang)

Roehampton – 300 pts (Modn Langs Transl; Modn Lang)

Salford – 300 pts (Modn Lang courses)

Strathclyde – BBB (Modn Langs)

280 pts **Aberystwyth** – 280 pts incl B modn lang (Euro Lang; Rmnc Langs) (IB 28 pts)

Chester – 280 pts (Modn Langs)

Greenwich – 280 pts (Lang Int Rel) (IB 28 pts)

Hull – 280–320 pts (Modn Langs Transl St)

London (Birk) – BBC 280 pts (Ling Lang)

Salford – 320–280 pts (Modn Lang Transl Interp St (Fr/Ger/Port/Span))

Stirling – BBC (Int Mgt St Euro Lang Soty; Mod Lang) (IB 32 pts)

Swansea – BBC (Pol Langs; Modn Lang Transl Inter) (IB 30 pts)

260 pts **Edinburgh Napier** – BCC 260 pts (Lang Joint Hons)

London Met – 260 pts (Transl)

Nottingham Trent – 260 pts (Modn Langs; Fr Joint Hons)

Westminster – BCC (Transl St (Fr); Transl St (Span)) (IB 28 pts)

240 pts **Central Lancashire** – 240 pts (Modn Langs)

London Met – 240 pts (App Transl)

Plymouth – 240 pts (Int Bus (Fr)) (IB 24 pts)

Portsmouth – 240–300 pts (Modn Langs) (IB 28 pts)

York St John – 240–300 pts (Lang) (24 pts)

220 pts **Middlesex** – 220 pts (Transl)

200 pts **Trinity Saint David** – 200 pts (Lat Gk) (IB 26 pts)

160 pts **Wolverhampton** – 160–220 pts (Interp (Brit Sign Lang/Engl)) (IB 24 pts)

Open University – no formal entry requirements contact +44 (0)845 300 6090 **or** www.openuniversity.co.uk/you (Modn Lang St)

Alternative offers
See **Chapter 7** and **Appendix 1** for grades/UCAS Tariff points information for the International Baccalaureate, Scottish Highers/Advanced Highers, the Welsh Baccalaureate, the Irish Leaving Certificate, the Cambridge Pre-U Diploma, the Advanced Diploma and the Extended Project.

CHOOSING YOUR COURSE (SEE ALSO CH.1)
Some course features
See separate language tables.
Central Lancashire The Modern Language degree covers French, German, Spanish, Arabic, Chinese and Japanese offered with a wide range of combinations and options.
Edinburgh Language courses are offered in Arabic, Celtic, Chinese, French, German, Italian, Japanese, Persian, Russian, Scandinavian Studies (Danish, Swedish, Norwegian) and Hispanic Studies. There is also an Islamic Studies and Middle Eastern Studies course.
Exeter A flexible Modern Language degree with one, two or three language choices. One year spent abroad teaching English, or in work placement or university study.
Portsmouth The Combined Modern Language degree offers year abroad placement for French students in France, African French-speaking countries, for Spanish students in Spain, Latin American countries or Central America.

Universities and colleges teaching quality See www.qaa.ac.uk; http://unistats.direct.gov.uk.

Top research universities and colleges (RAE 2008) See separate language tables.

ADMISSIONS INFORMATION
Number of applicants per place (approx) Aston 4; Bangor 5; Bath 6; Birmingham 5; Brighton 4; Bristol 15; Cambridge 3; Cardiff 6; Durham 6; East Anglia 15; Heriot-Watt 5; Huddersfield 12; Lancaster 10; Leeds (Joint Hons) 8; Leicester 6; Liverpool 5; Newcastle 22; Northumbria 4; Roehampton 3; Salford 6; Swansea 4; Wolverhampton 10; York 4.

Advice to applicants and planning the UCAS personal statement Discuss any literature studied outside your course work. Students applying for courses in which they have no previous knowledge (for example, Italian, Portuguese, Modern Greek, Czech, Russian) would be expected to have done a considerable amount of language work on their own in their chosen language before starting the course. See also **Appendix 3**.

Misconceptions about this course Leeds (Joint Hons) Some applicants think that studying languages means studying masses of literature – wrong. At Leeds, generally speaking, it's up to you; you study as much or as little literature as you choose. Residence abroad does not inevitably mean a university course (except where you are taking a language from scratch). Paid employment is usually another option.

Selection interviews Yes Aston, Cambridge, Coventry, Durham, Heriot-Watt, Hertfordshire, Huddersfield, Liverpool, London (RH), Oxford (Modn Lang) 32%, (Modn Lang Ling) 27%, Roehampton; **Some** Brighton, Leeds, Salford, Swansea; **No** Dundee, East Anglia.

Interview advice and questions See also **Chapter 6**. **Bangor** All applicants are invited for interview after an initial offer; a lower offer may subsequently be made. **Cambridge** Think of a painting of a tree. Is the tree real? **Leeds** (Joint Hons) Give an example of something outside your studies that you have achieved over the past year. **London (RH)** Conversation in the appropriate language.

Reasons for rejection (non-academic) Lack of commitment to spend a year abroad. Poor references. Poor standard of English. No reasons for why the course has been selected. Poor communication skills. Incomplete applications, for example missing qualifications and reference.

AFTER-RESULTS ADVICE

Offers to applicants repeating A-levels **Higher** Bristol UWE; **Possibly higher** Aston; **Same** Bangor (usually), Birmingham, Bristol, Durham, East Anglia, Leeds, Liverpool, Newcastle, Nottingham Trent, Salford, Stirling, Wolverhampton, York; **No** Cambridge.

GRADUATE DESTINATIONS AND EMPLOYMENT (2011/12 HESA)

See separate language tables.

Career note The only career-related fields for language students are teaching, which attracts some graduates, and the demanding work of interpreting and translating, to which only a small number aspire. The majority will be attracted to work in management and administration, financial services and a host of other occupations which may include the social services, law and property development.

OTHER DEGREE SUBJECTS FOR CONSIDERATION

Communication Studies; Linguistics; Modern Languages Education/Teaching.

LATIN

(see also **Classical Studies/Classical Civilisation, Classics, Greek, Languages**)

Latin courses provide a study of the language, art, religion and history of the Roman world. This table should be read in conjunction with the **Classical Studies/Classical Civilisation** and **Classics** tables.

Useful websites www.thelatinlibrary.com; www.la.wikipedia.org; www.arlt.co.uk.

NB The points totals shown to the left of the institutions are for ease of reference only. It must not be assumed that Tariff points are always used by institutions or that they can be substituted for an offer in grades. The level of an offer is not necessarily indicative of the quality of a course.

COURSE OFFERS INFORMATION

Subject requirements/preferences **GCSE** English, a foreign language and Latin may be stipulated. **AL** Check courses for Latin requirement.

Your target offers and examples of courses provided by each institution
380 pts **Cambridge** – A*AA 380 pts (Class; Modn Mediev Lang (Class Lat)) (IB 40–41 pts HL 776)
360 pts **Edinburgh** – AAA–BBB 360–300 pts (Anc Hist Lat) (IB 40–34 pts)
　　　　 St Andrews – AAA (Lat Mediaev Hist) (IB 36 pts)
340 pts **Exeter** – AAB–ABB (Modn Lang) (IB 34–32 pts)
　　　　 London (UCL) – AAB (Lat Gk) (IB 36 pts)
　　　　 Nottingham – AAB 340 pts (Lat courses) (IB 34 pts)
　　　　 St Andrews – AAB–AAA (Lat courses) (IB 35–36 pts)
　　　　 Warwick – AABc 340 pts (Engl Lat Lit) (IB 36 pts)
320 pts **Glasgow** – ABB (Latin Joint courses) (IB 36 pts)
　　　　 Leeds – ABB 320 pts (Lat Joint courses)
　　　　 London (RH) – ABB (Fr Lat; Ger Lat; Lat) (IB 34 pts)
300 pts **Edinburgh** – BBB–AAA 300–360 pts (Lat St) (IB 34–40 pts)
280 pts **Swansea** – BBC (Lat Joint Hons) (IB 30 pts)
200 pts **Trinity Saint David** – 200 pts (Lat Gk) (IB 26 pts)

Alternative offers
See **Chapter 7** and **Appendix 1** for grades/UCAS Tariff points information for the International Baccalaureate, Scottish Highers/Advanced Highers, the Welsh Baccalaureate, the Irish Leaving Certificate, the Cambridge Pre-U Diploma, the Advanced Diploma and the Extended Project.

CHOOSING YOUR COURSE (SEE ALSO CH.1)

Some course features

Edinburgh An intensive Latin course is offered to beginners.

Exeter (Lat) The Combined Honours course focuses on the language and society of Rome, with modules in literature, history and culture, and translation from set books from and into Latin.

Leeds Joint Honours Latin students focus on Latin language and literature, and do intensive beginners' Latin course. There may be opportunities for study abroad.

St Andrews Latin is available as a Single Honours degree or in a wide range of Joint Honours courses. The Single Honours course combines Latin language study (beginners' and post A-level/ Highers) with an in-depth reading and understanding of Latin classics and other texts.

Swansea Latin is offered as a Joint Honours course with History, Medieval Studies, Classical Civilisation or Modern Languages.

Trinity Saint David Latin is offered at beginners', intermediate and advanced levels.

Universities and colleges teaching quality See www.qaa.ac.uk; http://unistats.direct.gov.uk.

Top research universities and colleges (RAE 2008) See **Classics**.

ADMISSIONS INFORMATION

Number of applicants per place (approx) Leeds 2; Nottingham 6; Trinity Saint David 6.

Advice to applicants and planning the UCAS personal statement See **Classical Studies/Classical Civilisation** and **Classics**.

Selection interviews **Yes** Cambridge, Exeter, London (RH), London (UCL), Nottingham, Oxford, Trinity Saint David.

Interview advice and questions See **Classical Studies/Classical Civilisation** and **Classics**.

AFTER-RESULTS ADVICE

Offers to applicants repeating A-levels **Higher** Leeds, St Andrews, Warwick.

GRADUATE DESTINATIONS AND EMPLOYMENT (2011/12 HESA)

Graduates surveyed 20 **Employed** 10 **In voluntary employment** 0 **In further study** 5 **Assumed unemployed** 0

Career note Graduates enter a broad range of careers within management, the media, commerce and tourism as well as social and public services. Some graduates choose to work abroad and teaching is a popular option.

OTHER DEGREE SUBJECTS FOR CONSIDERATION

Ancient History; Archaeology; Classical Studies; Classics.

LATIN AMERICAN STUDIES

(including **Hispanic Studies**; see also **American Studies, Spanish**)

Latin American courses provide a study of Spanish and of Latin American republics, covering both historical and present-day conditions and problems. Normally a year is spent in Latin America.

Useful websites www.iol.org.uk; www.bbc.co.uk/languages; www.languageadvantage.com; www. languagematters.co.uk; www.cilt.org.uk; www.latinworld.com; www.wola.org; www.latinamericalinks. com; www.thelaa.org; see also **Languages** and **Spanish**.

NB The points totals shown to the left of the institutions are for ease of reference only. It must not be assumed that Tariff points are always used by institutions or that they can be substituted for an offer in grades. The level of an offer is not necessarily indicative of the quality of a course.

COURSE OFFERS INFORMATION

Subject requirements/preferences GCSE English and a foreign language required by most universities. **AL** Spanish may be required for some courses.

Aberdeen English, mathematics or science and a foreign language.

Your target offers and examples of courses provided by each institution
400 pts **London (UCL)** – A*AAe (Law Hisp Law) (IB 39 pts)
360 pts **London (UCL)** – AABe (Span Lat Am St) (IB 36 pts)
         Nottingham – A*AA–AAA 380–360 pts (Econ Hisp St) (IB 38–36 pts)
340 pts **Birmingham** – AAB (Hisp St Hist) (IB 36 pts)
         Glasgow – AAB (Hisp St) (IB 34 pts)
         London (King's) – AAB (Port Braz St; Hisp St) (IB 36 pts)
         Manchester – AAB–ABB (Span Port Lat Am St) (IB 33–37 pts)
         Nottingham – AAB (Hisp St Hist) (IB 34 pts)
         Sheffield – AAB–BBB (Hisp St Joint Hons) (IB 35–32 pts)
         Southampton – AAB–ABB (Pol Span/Port Lat Am St; Span Lat Am St) (IB 34 pts)
320 pts **Birmingham** – AAB–ABB (Hisp St) (IB 36–34 pts)
         Bristol – ABB–BBB (Hisp St) (IB 33 pts HL 665 incl Span)
         Essex – ABB–BBB 320–300 pts (Lat Am St courses) (IB 32–30 pts)
         Kent – ABB (Hisp St courses) (IB 35 pts)
         Liverpool – ABB (Comb Hons Lat Am Hisp St) (IB 33–36 pts HL 6 lang)
         London (RH) – ABB–BBB (Comp Lit Cult Span)
         Nottingham – ABB (Am St Lat Am St; Hisp St Russ) (IB 32 pts)
         Sheffield – ABB (Hisp St) (IB 34 pts HL 6 Span)
         Warwick – ABB 320 pts (Hisp St) (IB 34 pts HL 6 modn lang)
300 pts **Aberdeen** – BBB (Hisp St (Lat Am/Spn)) (IB 30 pts)
         London (QM) – BBB–AAB 300–340 pts (Hisp St; Hisp St courses) (IB 32–34 pts HL 5 lang)
         Manchester – BBB–AAB 300–340 pts (Lat Am St Scrn St) (IB 31–36 pts)
280 pts **Hull** – 280–320 pts (Hisp St Relgn Joint Hons) (IB 28 pts)
         Stirling – BBC (Span Lat Am St) (IB 32 pts)
200 pts **Portsmouth** – 200–280 pts (Span Lat Am St) (IB 28 pts)

Alternative offers
See **Chapter 7** and **Appendix 1** for grades/UCAS Tariff points information for the International Baccalaureate, Scottish Highers/Advanced Highers, the Welsh Baccalaureate, the Irish Leaving Certificate, the Cambridge Pre-U Diploma, the Advanced Diploma and the Extended Project.

CHOOSING YOUR COURSE (SEE ALSO CH.1)

Some course features
Birmingham (Hisp St) The first two years of the course focus on Spanish language skills and Hispanic literature and culture. The third year is spent in Spain or Latin America while the fourth year centres on students' individual programme interests, for example advanced translation skills or cultural studies.
Liverpool (Hisp St) Three Iberian Romance languages (Catalan, Portuguese or Galician) are studied in addition to the main degree of Spanish. The degree programme also focuses on Spanish, Portuguese, Galician and Latin American culture.
London (UCL) (Hisp St) Course combines a study of Spanish language with courses in film history and literature. (Lat Am St) The course focuses on a study of Spanish and Portuguese and the literature and history of Spain, Portugal and Latin America.
Portsmouth (Span Lat Am St) Students study the language and culture of contemporary Latin American societies, taking Spanish throughout the course. Half the placement year is in Spain and the other half at a partner institution in Latin America.

Universities and colleges teaching quality See www.qaa.ac.uk; http://unistats.direct.gov.uk.

Top research universities and colleges (RAE 2008) See **Spanish**.

ADMISSIONS INFORMATION

Number of applicants per place (approx) Essex 3; Liverpool 3; Nottingham 7; Portsmouth 5.

Advice to applicants and planning the UCAS personal statement Visits and contacts with Spain and Latin American countries should be described. An awareness of the economic, historical and political scene of these countries is also important. Information may be obtained from respective embassies.

Selection interviews No Portsmouth.

Interview advice and questions Past questions include: Why are you interested in studying Latin American Studies? What countries related to the degree course have you visited? What career are you planning when you finish your degree? Applicants taking Spanish are likely to be asked questions on their syllabus and should also be familiar with some Spanish newspapers and magazines. See also **Chapter 6**.

AFTER-RESULTS ADVICE

Offers to applicants repeating A-levels Higher Essex; **Same** Portsmouth.

GRADUATE DESTINATIONS AND EMPLOYMENT (2011/12 HESA)

See **American Studies**.

Career note See **Languages**.

OTHER DEGREE SUBJECTS FOR CONSIDERATION

American Studies; Portuguese; Spanish.

LAW

(including **Law** and **Criminology**; see also **Social Sciences/Studies**)

Law courses are usually divided into two parts. Part I occupies the first year and introduces the student to criminal and constitutional law and the legal process. Thereafter, many different specialised topics can be studied in the second and third years. The course content is very similar for most courses. Applicants are advised to check with universities for their current policies concerning their use of the National Admissions Test for Law (LNAT). See **Subject requirements/preferences** below and also **Chapter 6**.

Useful websites www.barcouncil.org.uk; www.cilex.org.uk; www.lawcareers.net; www.lawsociety.org. uk; www.cps.gov.uk; www.justice.gov.uk/about/hmcts; www.lawscot.org.uk; www.lawsoc-ni.org; www.rollonfriday.com; www.lnat.ac.uk.

NB The points totals shown to the left of the institutions are for ease of reference only. It must not be assumed that Tariff points are always used by institutions or that they can be substituted for an offer in grades. The level of an offer is not necessarily indicative of the quality of a course.

COURSE OFFERS INFORMATION

Subject requirements/preferences GCSE Many universities will expect high grades. **AL** Arts, humanities, social sciences and sciences plus languages for courses combined with a foreign language. **All universities** Applicants offering art and music A-levels should check whether these subjects are acceptable.

Manchester Requirements are often higher than normal – minimum of five A grades at GCSE.

Your target offers and examples of courses provided by each institution
440 pts London (King's) – A*AAa +LNAT (Law; Engl Law Fr Law/Ger Law/H K Law) (IB 35–39 pts HL 766)

400 pts **London (UCL)** – A*AAe incl Fr/Ger/Span +LNAT (Law; Law Fr Law/Ger Lat/Hisp Law) (IB 39 pts HL 6 Fr/Ger/Span)

Warwick – AAAc (Law; Euro Law; Law (St Abrd)) (IB 38 pts)

380 pts **Cambridge** – A*AA (Lnd Econ; Law) (IB 40–41 pts HL 776)

Durham – A*AA 380 pts (Law) (IB 38 pts)

London (King's) – A*AA +LNAT (Pol Phil Law) (IB 35 pts HL 766)

London (QM) – A*AA (Law) (IB 36 pts HL 666)

London (SOAS) – A*AA (Law) (IB 38 pts HL 766)

London LSE – A*AA (Law) (IB 38 pts HL 766/666)

Nottingham – A*AA +LNAT (Law) (IB 38 pts)

Warwick – AABc (Law Bus St; Law Sociol) (IB 36 pts)

360 pts **Birmingham** – AAA 360 pts +LNAT (Law Ger) (IB 36 pts)

Birmingham – A*AB–AAA +LNAT (Law; Law Bus St) (IB 36 pts)

Bristol – AAA–AAB +LNAT (Law; Law Fr; Law Ger) (IB 37–35 pts HL 666)

Cardiff – AAA 360 pts (Law) (IB 36 pts)

City – AAA 360 pts (Law) (IB 35 pts)

East Anglia – AAA (Law Am Law) (IB 34 pts)

Edinburgh – AAA–BBB 360–300 pts (Acc Law; Law courses) (IB 34–42 pts)

Exeter – AAA–AAB (Law; Law (Euro) (Fr/Ger)) (IB 36–34 pts)

Glasgow – AAA +LNAT (Law Joint Hons) (IB 39 pts incl Engl)

Huddersfield – AAA 360 pts (Law (Exmpt); Bus Law; Law)

Lancaster – AAA (Law Crimin; Law (Int); Law) (IB 36 pts HL 16 pts)

Leeds – AAA (Law; Law Mgt) (IB 38 pts HL 18 pts)

London (QM) – AAA (Law Pol) (IB 36 pts)

London NCH – AAA–AAB 340–360 pts (Law) (IB 37–38 pts HL 77)

Manchester – AAA (Law) (IB 37 pts)

Newcastle – AAA (Law) (IB 34 pts)

Nottingham – AAA incl Fr/Ger/Span +LNAT (Law Fr Fr Law/Ger Ger Law/Span Span Law) (IB 38 pts HL 7 Fr/Ger/Span)

Oxford – AAA +LNAT (Law; Law Euro Law) (IB 39 pts)

Queen's Belfast – AAA/AABa (Law) (IB 34 pts HL 666)

Reading – AAA (Law; Law Leg St Euro)

Sheffield – AAA (Law; Law (Euro Int)) (IB 37 pts HL 666)

Southampton – AAA–AAB (Law; Law (Euro Leg St); Law (Int Leg St)) (IB 36 pts HL 18 pts)

Sussex – AAA–AAB (Law Am St; Law Pol; Law Int Rel; Law Fr/Ital/Span (Yr Abrd); Law) (IB 35–36 pts)

York – AAA (Law) (IB 36 pts)

340 pts **Aberystwyth** – 340 pts (Law; Crimin Law; Euro Law) (IB 28 pts)

Aston – AAB 340 pts (Law Mgt) (IB 34 pts HL 665)

Bournemouth – 340 pts (Law; Law Tax; Bus Law; Enter Law)

Brunel – AAB 340 pts (Law) (IB 35 pts)

Cardiff – AAB 340 pts (Law Crimin)

Durham – AAB 340 pts (Crimin) (IB 36 pts)

East Anglia – AAB (Law; Law Fr Law Lang) (IB 32–33 pts)

Essex – AAB–BBB (Law; Engl Fr Law (Mait)) (IB 32–30 pts)

Glasgow Caledonian – AAB 340 pts (Law)

Kent – AAB (Law Joint Hons; Law; Engl Fr Law/Ger Law/Ital Law/Span Law) (IB 33 pts)

Leicester – AAB (Law; Maîtrise Engl Fr Law; Law Modn Lang (Fr/Span/Ital))

London LSE – AAB (Anth Law) (IB 37 pts)

Manchester – AAB (Law Pol) (IB 35 pts HL 665)

Sheffield – AAB (Law Crimin) (IB 35 pts HL 665)

Strathclyde – AAB (Scots Law LLB) (IB 38 pts)

Surrey – AAB (Law Int St; Law Crimin; Law) (IB 35 pts)

Swansea – AAB 340 pts (Law Bus) (IB 34 pts)

Westminster – AAB 340 pts (Soli Exmpt LLB) (IB 32 pts)

For a quick reference offers calculator, fold out the inside front cover.

The University of **Law**
incorporating The College of Law

Professional law degrees for ambitious people

Find out about our full range of law degrees – you can study full-time over two or three years, or part-time over four years.

Book your open day now:
law.ac.uk/heapllb

0800 289 997

'I chose The University of Law because it's so **focused**. It's almost vocational. You're learning to think like a lawyer rather than learning law.'

Matthew Hooker, LL.B student, London Bloomsbury

Birmingham   Bristol   Chester   Guildford   London Bloomsbury   Leeds   Manchester

Professional law degrees for ambitious people

Professional undergraduate law degrees

Our professionally focused LL.B law degrees enable you to learn the law in a truly realistic context - how the law affects clients, and how lawyers think about and use the law to represent their clients' interests.

Whether you're considering a career in law, business or a related field, our law degrees will equip you with the all-important business skills you need to succeed.

Through our focus on how the law actually affects people and businesses, and how it's used in the real world, you'll develop a range of transferable skills – commercial, analytical, negotiation and decision-making – to get where you want to be.

The University's law degree is academically challenging and set in a real-world context from the start, so you can best understand how the law applies to individuals and businesses.

For 2015, you there are four options: LL.B (Hons) Law, LL.B (Hons) Law Accelerated, LL.B (Hons) Law – International, LL.B (Hons) Law – International – Accelerated.

Our new LL.B (Hons) Law – International is the world's first specialist law degree for future international lawyers. The course reflects the predominance of English law in international business, the increasingly international needs of clients and the global dimensions involved in many areas of law. It is designed to be the most relevant and rounded degree-level education available to prepare you for a career in a modern legal and business environment. It can be studied over two or three years.

About The University of Law

The University of Law is the world's leading professional law school. With many years of experience and unrivalled contacts within the legal profession, no other law school can match The University of Law for its reputation and commitment to preparing future lawyers for the dynamic world of law.

More than 7,500 students study our postgraduate courses each year – the Graduate Diploma in Law – a conversion course for non-law graduates, the LL.M Legal Practice Course for aspiring solicitors and the Bar Professional Training Course for prospective barristers. Our unique mix of face-to-face teaching in small group workshops which reflect working in legal practice, along with market- leading online learning, delivers better results. All of the University's tutors are qualified lawyers who can pass on their experience of working in practice. This combination ensures that you will get the best possible preparation for a career in law.

The University of Law develops self-reliant, confident future lawyers for the legal profession. Our Bachelor of Laws (LL.B) degree is the first step. Find out more: **www.law.ac.uk/undergraduate**

The University of Law's specialist law careers service

Employability is at the heart of everything The University of Law does. The University understands that you want the best possible chance of securing a job in your chosen profession. We have the best team of specialist legal careers advisors in the business, offering personalised, face-to-face guidance on the recruitment process and how to succeed. It's no surprise that 97%* of Legal Practice Course students who graduated in summer 2012 were in work, legal positions or continuing education 9 months after graduation.

based on known records of students successfully completing their studies in 2012

Seriously well connected

The legal services sector is one of the most dynamic parts of the economy, offering a wide range of careers whether as a solicitor or barrister, in-house legal advisor, business manager or legal service entrepreneur.

The University of Law works with over 90 of the top 100 UK firms and four out of five of the top global firms, and has thriving relationships with hundreds of regional firms.

The University enjoys close working relationships with a number of key international organisations. We work with the International Bar Association to deliver our international Masters degree programme, and have close links with IE Law School in Spain, the Singapore Institute of Legal Education and the Nigerian Law School. We also work in association with the British Council and The College of Law Australia.

A choice of locations

The University of Law has centres across the country - Birmingham, Bristol, Chester, Guildford, London Bloomsbury, Leeds and Manchester - offering you the widest choice of location of any law school.

Whichever centre you choose you can be sure of the same high standards of tuition, support and facilities. Find out about each of the centres on our website: **www.law.ac.uk/uglocations**

Accommodation

The University of Law has reserved accommodation for our students with some of the UK's leading student accommodation providers, who pride themselves on ensuring you have a safe, comfortable place to live while you're studying with us.

We guarantee an offer of accommodation to all first year LL.B students who have made us their firm choice by 31 March.

The Future Lawyers Network

The University's Future Lawyers Network is a unique, free-to-join resource for aspiring lawyers over the age of 16. You will get access to useful information on a career in law and what you need to do to succeed.
law.ac.uk/futurelawyers2

Do you want to be a lawyer?

Study with the Chartered Institute of Legal Executives

- Earn as you learn
- No UCAS points needed
- Degree equivalent qualifications
- Study in your own time, at your own pace
- Fully-funded apprenticeships available
- Starting salaries of up to £20,000 a year

Contact us today for more information

E: membership@cilex.org.uk | W: www.cilexcareers.org.uk | T: (0)1234 845777

CILEx CHARTERED INSTITUTE OF LEGAL EXECUTIVES

 Search Groups 'CILEx'

 CILExfan

 @CILExLawyers

The CILEx route to a career in law

The Chartered Institute of Legal Executives (CILEx) is unique in that you can become a qualified lawyer without needing a university degree.

A career in law is a popular choice with many school leavers, offering a worthwhile, interesting and varied job, an excellent salary and the possibility of career advancement. Become a Chartered Legal Executive lawyer and you could reach the very top of the legal profession.

Nick Read – Legal Services Apprentice working at Kennedys LLP

"I turned down offers from two top fifteen universities in order to accept a place as a Legal Services Apprentice at Kennedys. It was an invaluable opportunity to learn from experienced partners, solicitors and Chartered Legal Executives while developing my own experience."

Apprenticeships

An Apprenticeship in Legal Services is a full-time job that comes with a structured training programme. You will be employed, by a law firm or company, receive a salary and you gain a nationally-recognised qualification.

Anyone living in England or Wales, aged over 16 and not in full-time education can be an apprentice.

Choose an apprenticeship in legal services instead of university and you can:

- Earn as you learn

- Take paid holiday

- Have fully-funded training if you are aged under 19

- Gain valuable and relevant work experience

- Continue studying with CILEx to become a lawyer

Flexible learning

If you want to attain legal qualifications without completing an apprenticeship, CILEx offers a flexible route which allows you to fit study around your personal and work life.

When you're fully qualified you'll still have gained a degree-equivalent qualification and you'll also get to attend your own graduation ceremony.

> " I'm working whilst I'm learning; this allows me to put what I'm learning into practice and also witness real life examples. I'm gaining a lot of experience which I wouldn't have been able to get right from the beginning if I went to university. "

Damilola Muyi-Opaleye – School leaver taking the CILEx route whilst working at Field Fisher Waterhouse LLP

Entry requirements

To study with CILEx there are no formal entry requirements and we don't require you to collect UCAS points. We do however, strongly recommend that you have a minimum of four GCSE grades C or above, including English Language or Literature, or qualifications at an equivalent level.

If you already have some legal qualifications, including AS and A2 level Law, you may be exempt from some CILEx exams.

Benefits

CILEx is a professional association and as a student you will become a member. Being a member of CILEx gives you access to free careers advice at every stage of your learning, a monthly magazine keeping you up to date with current news in the legal sector and you can also get your own NUS card, which gives you savings with over 160 brands.

Find out more

If you want to find out more about studying law as an apprentice or becoming a Chartered Legal Executive then contact us today.

E: membership@cilex.org.uk
W: www.cilexcareers.org.uk
T: +44 (0)1234 845777

 Search Groups 'CILEx'

 CILExfan

@CILExLawyers

Check **Chapter 4** when choosing your university and **Chapter 7** on how to read the subject tables.

COME TO KENT/
STUDY AT A TOP 10 LAW SCHOOL

Choose from a range of professionally qualifying law degrees and develop your experience of the law by representing real clients at our award-winning Law Clinic at Kent Law School; ranked 10th in the UK for Law in the *Times Good University Guide 2014.*

- Discuss the role of law in contemporary society with our distinctive approach to studying law
- Join an active and international community with extensive opportunities to study abroad
- Represent real clients at our award-winning Kent Law Clinic
- Learn from world-leading researchers in an exciting academic environment with outstanding student satisfaction
- Benefit from excellent graduate prospects, extensive professional connections, with opportunities to develop your legal skills

www.kent.ac.uk/law
admissionslaw@kent.ac.uk
Twitter: @kentlawschool
Facebook: /kentlawschool

University of Kent

50
1965-2015
THE UK'S
EUROPEAN
UNIVERSITY

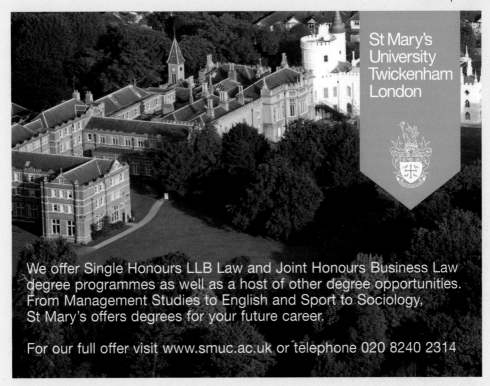

St Mary's
University
Twickenham
London

We offer Single Honours LLB Law and Joint Honours Business Law
degree programmes as well as a host of other degree opportunities.
From Management Studies to English and Sport to Sociology,
St Mary's offers degrees for your future career.

For our full offer visit www.smuc.ac.uk or telephone 020 8240 2314

320 pts **Aberdeen** – ABB (Law) (IB 34 pts HL 5)
Bournemouth – 320 pts (Acc Law) (IB 32 pts)
Bristol UWE – 320 pts (Law; Crimin Law) (IB 27 pts)
De Montfort – 320 pts (Law)
Dundee – ABB (Law Lang; Law (Scot); Law (Engl/NI); Law (Scot Engl))
Durham – ABB 320 pts (Sociol Law)
Essex – ABB–BBB 320–300 pts (Law Hum Rts (LLB); Phil Law) (IB 32–30 pts)
Hertfordshire – 320 pts (Law; Law Fr)
Hull – ABB (Law Phil; Law; Law Pol; Law Lit) (IB 30 pts)
Keele – ABB (Acc Law; Law courses) (IB 28 pts)
Kingston – 320 pts (Law; Law Crimin)
Leicester – ABB (Crimin) (IB 32 pts)
Lincoln – (Law)
Liverpool – ABB (Law; Law Acc Fin) (IB 33 pts)
Manchester – ABB (Law Crimin)
Northumbria – ABB 320 pts (Law (Exmp)) (IB 32 pts)
Oxford Brookes – ABB (Law) (IB 33 pts)
Portsmouth – 320 pts (Law; Law Crimin)
Stirling – ABB (Law LLB) (IB 36 pts)
Ulster – ABB (Law; Law Ir) (IB 26 pts)
Univ Law – ABB 320 pts (LLB Law; LLB Law Int) (IB 31 pts)
Westminster – ABB–ABC (Commer Law; Euro Leg St; Law) (IB 32 pts)
300 pts **Bradford** – 300 pts (Bus St Law; Law)
Buckingham – 300 pts (Law Bus Fin; Law; Law Fr; Law Econ; Law Mgt St; Law Pol)
Bucks New – 300–340 pts (Law; Bus Law) (IB 25 pts)

Cardiff Met (UWIC) – 300 pts (Bus Mgt St Law)
Central Lancashire – BBB (Law Hum Rts (LLB); Law Crimin; Law)
Coventry – BBB 300 pts (Law) (IB 30 pts)
Derby – 300 pts (Law LLB; Law Crimin)
Edge Hill – 300 pts (Law; Law Crimin)
Greenwich – 300 pts (Law LLB) (IB 28 pts)
Heriot-Watt – BBB 300 pts (Bus Law) (IB 29 pts)
Leeds Beckett – 300 pts (Law) (IB 28 pts)
Lincoln – (Crimin)
Liverpool Hope – 300–320 pts (Law Comb Hons)
Liverpool John Moores – 300 pts (Law Crim Just; Law) (IB 30 pts)
London (Birk) – BBB (Crimin Crim Just; Law)
London Met – 300 pts (Law LLB)
Middlesex – 300 pts (Law LLB) (IB 28 pts)
Nottingham Trent – 300 pts (Law) (IB 24 pts)
Plymouth – 300 pts (Law; Int Rel Law; Law Bus)
Sheffield Hallam – 300 pts (Law; Law Crimin; Law Maîtrise Fr; Bus Law)
Ulster – BBB (Law HR Mgt; Law Mark) (IB 25 pts)
West London – 300 pts (Law; Commer Law)
Westminster – ABC (Law Fr) (IB 30 pts)
280 pts **Bangor** – 280–320 pts (Law Crimin; Law courses)
Birmingham City – 280 pts (Law; Law Am Leg St; Law Hum Rts; Law Crimin; Sociol Crimin) (IB 26 pts)
Brighton – BBC 280 pts (Law Bus) (IB 30 pts)
Cumbria – 280 pts (Law)
De Montfort – 280 pts (Law Hum Rts Soc Just) (IB 30 pts)
Edge Hill – BBC 280 pts (Crimin Crim Just)
Gloucestershire – 280–300 pts (Law)
Greenwich – 280 pts (Bus Law)
Kingston – 280–320 pts (Crimin courses)
Manchester Met – BBC–BBB 280–300 pts (Law; Crimin) (IB 30 pts)
Northampton – 280–320 pts (Law courses) (IB 24 pts)
Nottingham Trent – 280 pts (Law Bus; Law Crimin) (IB 24 pts)
Plymouth – 280 pts (Marit Bus Marit Law) (IB 25 pts)
Portsmouth – BBC 280 pts (Law Int Rel) (IB 29 pts)
Robert Gordon – BBC (Law) (IB 28 pts HL 5 Engl)
Roehampton – 280 pts (Crimin) (IB 25 pts)
Salford – BBC (Law Span; Law Crimin)
South Wales – 280 pts (Law; Bus Law; Crimin Law)
Staffordshire – 280 pts (Law (Crim) LLB) (IB 26 pts)
Stirling – BBC (Law BA) (IB 32 pts)
Sunderland – 280 pts (Law LLB)
Winchester – 280–320 pts (Law LLB; Law (Comb)) (IB 26 pts)
260 pts **Abertay** – BCC (Law) (IB 26 pts)
BPP – 260 pts (Law Psy; Bus Law; Law)
Canterbury Christ Church – BCC 260 pts (Law) (IB 24 pts)
Chester – 260–300 pts (Law LLB; Law Jrnl/Crimin) (IB 28 pts)
Coventry – BCC 260 pts (Sociol Crimin)
De Montfort – 260 pts (App Crimin; App Crimin Foren Sci)
Derby – 260–300 pts (Law Joint Hons)
Edinburgh Napier – BCC 260 pts (Crimin; Law LLB)
Greenwich – 260 pts (Crimin)
London South Bank – 260 pts (Law LLB)
Middlesex – 260 pts (Crimin courses)

Nottingham Trent – 260 pts (Law Psy)
Oldham (Univ Campus) – 260 pts (Law)
Portsmouth – 260–300 pts (Law Euro St; Law Bus)
St Mary's – 260 pts (Law) (IB 28 pts)
Salford – 260 pts (Law) (IB 32 pts)
Sunderland – 260 pts (Law (Comb))
Teesside – 260 pts (Law)
West London – 260 pys (Crimin)
245 pts Glasgow Caledonian – CCC 245 pts (Soc Sci (Crimin))
240 pts Anglia Ruskin – 240–280 pts (Law)
Bradford – 240 pts (App Crim Just St)
Bradford (Coll Univ Centre) – 240 pts (Law (Acc) LLB; Law courses)
Canterbury Christ Church – 240 pts (Leg St)
Chester – 240–280 pts (Law (Comb)) (IB 26 pts)
East London – 240 pts (Law)
Glyndŵr – 240 pts (Crimin Crim Just)
Greenwich (Sch Mgt) – 240 pts (Law Mgt; Law LLB)
London Met – 240 pts (Bus Law) (IB 28 pts)
Southampton Solent – 240 pts (Crimin; Law) (IB 24 pts)
Teesside – 240 pts (Crimin courses; Bus Law)
West Scotland – CCC (Law Bus) (IB 24 pts)
220 pts Blackburn (Coll) – (Law) (IB 26 pts)
Kaplan Holborn (Coll) – 220 pts (Law) (IB 24 pts)
St Mary's – 220 pts (Bus Law) (IB 28 pts)
200 pts Bedfordshire – 200 pts (Law; Crimin)
Bolton – 200 pts (Law; Law (Comb))
Bucks New – 200–240 pts (Crimin) (IB 24 pts)
Croydon (Coll) – 200 pts (Law)
Cumbria – 200 pts (Crimin Law)
Doncaster (Coll Univ Centre) – 200 pts (Crim Just)
Wolverhampton – 200 pts (Law; Law Phil)

Open University – contact +44 (0)845 300 6090 or www.openuniversity.co.uk/you
(Law)

Alternative offers
See **Chapter 7** and **Appendix 1** for grades/UCAS Tariff points information for the International Baccalaureate, Scottish Highers/Advanced Highers, the Welsh Baccalaureate, the Irish Leaving Certificate, the Cambridge Pre-U Diploma, the Advanced Diploma and the Extended Project.

EXAMPLES OF FOUNDATION DEGREES IN THE SUBJECT FIELD
Bournemouth; Hertfordshire; Leeds City (Coll); Nottingham New (Coll); South Devon (Coll); Sunderland; Truro (Coll).

CHOOSING YOUR COURSE (SEE ALSO CH.1)
Some course features
Anglia Ruskin An integrated LLB degree is available for students seeking to qualify as a solicitor which aims to combine the academic and practical aspects of law to prepare students to enter a legal career.
Aston The Law with Management programme is a qualifying Law degree focusing on business skills.
Bournemouth All Law degrees have a common first year, with specialisation options made at the end. A minimum of 40 weeks is spent in industry.
Chester Core subjects are offered to fulfil the requirements for a Qualifying Law Degree, covering contract, land, European Union, constitutional and administrative law, crime and tort. Students studying combined law can apply for partial exemption.

Dundee English Law and Scots Law are both offered.

Edinburgh Over 12 joint courses with Law are offered including accountancy, business studies and languages.

Exeter (Law (Euro)) The fourth year is spent either at Rennes following a French Maîtrise en Droit programme or at Saabrucken following the German Magister programme. Graduates obtain a dual qualification, are exempt from the academic stages of UK professional training and are ready for the aptitude test to practise as a lawyer in France or Germany.

Huddersfield There is a Law (Exempting) course enabling students to qualify as a solicitor by incorporating the legal practice course in Years 3 and 4 (subject to an appropriate training contract). Degree courses are also offered in Law and Accountancy and Business.

Kent The Law course is designed to enable students to gain the necessary exemptions from the Law Society examinations. Other Law courses include English and French/German/Spanish/Italian Law. There is a law clinic enabling students to practise law under the supervision of solicitors.

London (King's) A long established leading law school, courses include English and French Law, English and Hong Kong Law and Law and German Law.

London (UCL) Law can be studied with another legal system with a year spent at a host university in Australia or Singapore.

London NCH The first year of this course is comprised of four compulsory modules, while Years 2 and 3 give a choice of two modules plus two compulsory modules. In addition to degree subject modules students study four modules in another degree subject and compulsory core modules in applied ehtics, logic and critical thinking to make up the NCH diploma which is awarded alongside a degree.

Universities and colleges teaching quality See www.qaa.ac.uk; http://unistats.direct.gov.uk.

Top research universities and colleges (RAE 2008) London LSE; London (UCL); Oxford; Durham; Nottingham; Kent; Cambridge; Cardiff; Queen's Belfast; Edinburgh; London (QM); Reading; Strathclyde; Ulster; Birmingham.

Examples of sandwich degree courses Aston (compulsory); Bournemouth; Bradford; Brunel; Coventry; De Montfort; Greenwich; Hertfordshire; Huddersfield; Kingston; Lancaster; Newcastle; Nottingham Trent; Plymouth; Portsmouth; Surrey; Teesside; West Scotland; Westminster.

ADMISSIONS INFORMATION

Number of applicants per place (approx) Abertay 3; Aberystwyth 8; Anglia Ruskin 10; Aston 10; Bangor 3; Birmingham 4; Birmingham City 20; Bournemouth 9; Bradford 2; Bristol 9; Bristol UWE 27; Brunel 2; Buckingham 3; Cambridge 7; Cardiff 12; Central Lancashire 36; City 23; Coventry 15; De Montfort 6; Derby 7; Dundee 6; Durham 14; East Anglia 14; East London 13; Edinburgh 5; Edinburgh Napier 7; Essex 26; Exeter 15; Glasgow 8; Glasgow Caledonian 10; Huddersfield 10; Hull 15; Kent 11; Kingston 25; Lancaster 8; Leeds 15; Leicester 9; Liverpool 10; Liverpool John Moores 10; London (King's) 14; London (QM) 17; London (SOAS) 8; London (UCL) 21; London LSE 14; London Met 13; London South Bank 4; Manchester 8; Manchester Met 21; Middlesex 25; Newcastle 13; Northampton 4; Northumbria 12; Nottingham 9; Nottingham Trent 15; Oxford Brookes 18; Plymouth 14; Robert Gordon 4; Sheffield 16; Sheffield Hallam 6; Southampton 7; Southampton Solent 5; Staffordshire 16; Strathclyde (Law) 10; Sussex 10; Teesside 3; Warwick 20; West London 18; Westminster 29; Wolverhampton 12; York 8.

Advice to applicants and planning the UCAS personal statement Visit the law courts and take notes on cases heard. Follow leading legal arguments in the press. Read the law sections in the *Independent*, *The Times* and the *Guardian*. Discuss the career with lawyers and, if possible, obtain work shadowing in lawyers' offices. Describe these visits and experiences and indicate any special areas of law which interest you. (Read *Learning the Law* by Glanville Williams.) Commitment is essential to the study of law as an academic discipline, not necessarily with a view to taking it up as a career.

When writing to admissions tutors, especially by email, take care to present yourself well: text language is not acceptable. You should use communication as an opportunity to demonstrate your skill in the use of English. Spelling mistakes, punctuation errors and bad grammar suggest that you will struggle to develop the expected writing ability (see **Misconceptions about this course**) and may lead to your application being rejected. When writing to an admissions tutor do not demand an answer immediately or by return or urgently. If your query is reasonable the tutor will respond without such urging. Adding these demands is bad manners and suggests that you are doing everything at the last minute and increases your chances of a rejection.

The criteria for admission are: motivation and capacity for sustained and intense work; the ability to analyse and solve problems using logical and critical approaches; the ability to draw fine distinctions, to separate the relevant from the irrelevant; the capacity for accurate and critical observation, for sustained and cogent argument; creativity and flexibility of thought and lateral thinking; competence in English; the ability to express ideas clearly and effectively, a willingness to listen and to be able to give considered responses. See also **Appendix 3**. **Deferred entry** Check with your university choices since deferred entry will not necessarily be accepted. **Bristol** Deferred entry is limited. **Manchester** Deferred entry is not accepted. **Warwick** Deferred entry is usually acceptable.

Misconceptions about this course **Aberystwyth** Some applicants believe that all Law graduates enter the legal profession – this is incorrect. **Birmingham** Students tend to believe that success in the law centres on the ability to learn information. Whilst some information does necessarily have to be learnt, the most important skills involve (a) developing an ability to select the most relevant pieces of information and (b) developing the ability to write tightly argued, persuasively reasoned essays on the basis of such information. **Bristol** Many applicants think that most of our applicants have been privately educated: the reverse is true. **Derby** Many applicants do not realise the amount of work involved to get a good degree classification.

Selection interviews Approximately four well-qualified candidates apply for every place on undergraduate Law courses in the UK and the National Admissions Test for Law (LNAT) is used by a number of universities (see **Your target offers and examples of courses provided by each institution** and **Chapter 6**). **Yes** Aberystwyth, Anglia Ruskin, Buckingham, Cambridge, Canterbury Christ Church, Central Lancashire, Coventry, Durham, East London, Edinburgh Napier, Essex, Exeter, Glasgow, Kent, Lancaster, Liverpool, London (King's), London (UCL), London South Bank, Oxford (Course 1) 18%, (Course 2) 10%, Queen's Belfast, Teesside, York; **Some** Bangor, Bristol UWE, Cardiff, Derby, Huddersfield, Liverpool John Moores, Northumbria, Nottingham Trent (mature students), Oxford Brookes (mature students), Sheffield Hallam, Southampton (mature students), Staffordshire, Sunderland, Surrey, Warwick; **No** Birmingham, Bristol, Dundee, East Anglia, Nottingham, Reading, Southampton Solent, Sussex.

Interview advice and questions Law is a highly competitive subject and applicants will be expected to have a basic awareness of aspects of law and to have gained some work experience, on which they are likely to be questioned. It is almost certain that a legal question will be asked at interview and applicants will be tested on their responses. Questions in the past have included: What interests you in the study of law? What would you do to overcome the problem of prison overcrowding if you were (a) a judge, (b) a prosecutor, (c) the Prime Minister? What legal cases have you read about recently? What is jurisprudence? What are the causes of violence in society? A friend bought a bun which, unknown to him, contained a stone. He gave it to you to eat and you broke a tooth. Could you sue anyone? Have you visited any law courts? What cases did you see? A person arrives in England unable to speak the language. He lights a cigarette in a restaurant where smoking is not allowed. Can he be charged and convicted? What should be done in the case of an elderly person who steals a bar of soap? What, in your opinion, would be the two basic laws in Utopia? Describe, without using your hands, how you would do the butterfly stroke. What would happen if there were no law? Should we legalise euthanasia? If you could change any law, what would it be? How would you implement the changes? If a person tries to kill someone using black magic, are they guilty of attempted murder? If a jury uses a ouija board to reach a decision, is it wrong? If so, why? Jane attends a university interview. As she enters the building she sees a diamond brooch on the floor. She hands it to the interviewer who hands it to the police. The brooch is never claimed. Who is entitled to it? Jane? The interviewer? The police? The University authorities? The Crown? Mr Grabbit who owns the building? Where does honesty fit into Law? For joint courses: what academic skills are needed to succeed? Why have you applied for a joint degree? Where does honesty fit into law? See also **Chapter 6**. **Cambridge** Logic questions. If I returned to the waiting room and my jacket had been taken and I then took another one, got home and actually discovered it was mine, had I committed a crime? If the interviewer pulled out a gun and aimed it at me, but missed as he had a bad arm, had he committed a crime? If the interviewer pulled out a gun and aimed it at me, thinking it was loaded but, in fact, it was full of blanks and fired it at me with the intention to kill, had he committed a crime? Which of the three preceding situations are similar and which is the odd one out? If a law is immoral, is it still a law and must people abide by it? For example, when Hitler legalised the systematic killing of Jews, was it still law? **Oxford** Should the use of mobile phones be banned on public transport? Is wearing school uniform a breach of human rights? If you could go back in time to any period of time, when would it be and why? Would you trade your scarf for my bike, even if you have no idea what state it's in or if I even have one? Is someone guilty of an offence if they did not set out to commit a crime but ended up doing so? Does a girl who joins the Scouts have a political agenda?

Reasons for rejection (non-academic) 'Dreams' about being a lawyer! Poorly informed about the subject. Badly drafted application. Underestimated workload. Poor communication skills. **Manchester Met** Some were rejected because they were obviously more suited to Psychology.

AFTER-RESULTS ADVICE
Offers to applicants repeating A-levels Higher Aberystwyth, Bristol UWE, Coventry, Dundee, Essex, Glasgow, Hull, Leeds, London Met, Manchester Met, Newcastle, Nottingham, Oxford Brookes, Queen's Belfast, Sheffield, Sheffield Hallam, Strathclyde, Warwick; **Possibly higher** Liverpool; **Same** Anglia Ruskin, Bangor, Birmingham, Bradford, Brighton, Bristol, Brunel, Cardiff, De Montfort, Derby, Durham, East Anglia, Huddersfield, Kingston, Lincoln, Liverpool Hope, Liverpool John Moores, Northumbria, Nottingham Trent, Staffordshire, Stirling, Sunderland, Surrey, Wolverhampton; **No** Cambridge.

GRADUATE DESTINATIONS AND EMPLOYMENT (2011/12 HESA)
Graduates surveyed 11550 **Employed** 4070 **In voluntary employment** 420 **In further study** 4610 **Assumed unemployed** 800

Career note Recent reports (Oct 2013) suggest that at the present time there are too many students training to be lawyers at a time when jobs in the legal profession are scarce. Thus, applicants intending to aim for a career in the profession should note that at the present time training places for the bar and solicitors' examinations are in short supply. There are, however, alternative legal careers such as legal journalism, patent law, legal publishing and teaching. The course also proves a good starting point for careers in industry, commerce and the public service, whilst the study of consumer protection can lead to qualification as a Trading Standards officer.

OTHER DEGREE SUBJECTS FOR CONSIDERATION
Criminology; Economics; Government; History; International Relations; Politics; Social Policy and Administration; Sociology.

LEISURE and RECREATION MANAGEMENT/STUDIES

(see also **Business and Management Courses, Business and Management Courses (International and European), Business and Management Courses (Specialised), Hospitality and Event Management, Sports Sciences/Studies, Tourism and Travel**)

The courses cover various aspects of leisure and recreation. Specialist options include recreation management, tourism and countryside management, all of which are offered as individual degree courses in their own right. There is also an obvious link with Sports Studies, Physical Education and Tourism and Travel courses. See also **Appendix 3**.

Useful websites www.cimspa.co.uk; www.bized.co.uk; www.leisuremanagement.co.uk; www.thebapa. org.uk; www.leisureopportunities.co.uk; www.recmanagement.com; www.uksport.gov.uk.

NB The points totals shown to the left of the institutions are for ease of reference only. It must not be assumed that Tariff points are always used by institutions or that they can be substituted for an offer in grades. The level of an offer is not necessarily indicative of the quality of a course.

COURSE OFFERS INFORMATION

Subject requirements/preferences **GCSE** Normally English and mathematics grades A–C. **AL** No specified subjects. **Other** Disclosure and Barring Service (DBS) clearance and health checks required for some courses.

Your target offers and examples of courses provided by each institution

320 pts **Manchester** – ABB–BBB 320 pts (Mgt Leis) (IB 31–34 pts)
300 pts **Brighton** – BBB (Spo St) (IB 32 pts)
280 pts **Sheffield Hallam** – 280 pts (Evnts Mgt Tour)
         South Wales – BBC (Spo Mgt)
         Stirling – BBC (Env Sci Out Educ) (IB 32 pts)
260 pts **Cumbria** – 260 pts (Out St; Out Ldrshp; Out St (Env))
         Derby – 260–280 pts (Out Recr Advntr Tour; Out Actv Ldrshp Coach)
         Gloucestershire – (Leis Spo Mgt)
         Stranmillis (UC) – BCC +interview (Hlth Leis St)
240 pts **Birmingham (UC)** – 240 pts (Spa Mgt)
         Bournemouth – 240–280 pts (Leis Mark)
         Canterbury Christ Church – CCC 240 pts (Spo Leis Mgt) (IB 24 pts)
         Central Lancashire – 240–280 pts (Out Ldrshp)
         Cumbria – 240 pts (Advntr Media)
         Hull – 240 pts (Spo Leis Mgt)
         Manchester Met – 240–280 pts (Out St) (IB 28 pts)
         Southampton Solent – 240 pts (Advntr Extrm Spo Mgt)
         Suffolk (Univ Campus) – 240–280 pts (Leis Mgt) (IB 28 pts)
         Ulster – 240 pts (Leis Evnts Mgt)
         Worcester – 240 pts (Out Advntr Ldrshp Mgt)
220 pts **Leeds Beckett** – 220 pts (Enter Mgt) (IB 24 pts)
200 pts **Bucks New** – 200–240 pts (Spo Bus Mgt) (IB 20 pts)
160 pts **SRUC** – CC (Spo Recr Mgt)
         Trinity Saint David (Swansea) – 160 pts (Leis Mgt)
         UHI – CC 160 pts (Advntr Tour Mgt)

Alternative offers

See **Chapter 7** and **Appendix 1** for grades/UCAS Tariff points information for the International Baccalaureate, Scottish Highers/Advanced Highers, the Welsh Baccalaureate, the Irish Leaving Certificate, the Cambridge Pre-U Diploma, the Advanced Diploma and the Extended Project.

EXAMPLES OF FOUNDATION DEGREES IN THE SUBJECT FIELD

See also **Tourism and Travel**. Bath Spa; Birmingham (UC); Bournemouth; Cornwall (Coll); Cumbria; Derby; Duchy (Coll); Edge Hill; Hertfordshire; Liverpool City (Coll); Loughborough (Coll); Norwich City (Coll); Nottingham New (Coll); Pembrokeshire (Coll); Plymouth; Teesside; Truro (Coll); Warwickshire (Coll); West London.

CHOOSING YOUR COURSE (SEE ALSO CH.1)

Some course features

Birmingham (UC) The Adventure Tourism Management course involves studies in commercial and risk management, options include modern languages, international sports and nature tourism.
Brighton (Spo Leis Mgt) The course has options in sport psychology, performance and marketing.
Cumbria (Out St; Out Ldrshp) The courses involve climbing, canoeing, sailing and mountaineering and are based in the centre of the Lake District.
Derby (Out Rec Advntr Tour; Out Actv Ldrshp Coach) These courses are physically demanding, involving climbing, canoeing, kayaking and trekking, and include modules on leadership, practical skills and outdoor education.

Manchester Met The degree course in Outdoor Studies is available with a Foundation year and offers modules in developing outdoor performance, managing risk, and living landscapes, with field trips to Snowdonia, Scotland and the French Alps taken throughout the course.

Southampton Solent (Advntr Extrm Spo Mgt) As well as academic credentials, students are assessed on their practical coaching throughout the course. An outdoor residential course is taken in the first year and a field trip is offered in Year 2. During the second year students will undertake practical work experience to develop and transfer their skills into a work environment.

Stirling (Env Sci Out Educ) Alongside a study in environmental science, this course offers practical training in designing outdoor ecological programmes, navigation, mountain hazards and outdoor safety. Students will also work towards a certificate in summer mountain leadership.

Trinity Saint David (Swansea) A broad course is available which includes work placement.

Universities and colleges teaching quality See www.qaa.ac.uk; http://unistats.direct.gov.uk.

Top research universities and colleges (RAE 2008) See **Sports Sciences/Studies**.

Examples of sandwich degree courses Bournemouth; Gloucestershire; Ulster.

ADMISSIONS INFORMATION

Number of applicants per place (approx) Brighton 10; Gloucestershire 7; Hull 3; SRUC 4.

Advice to applicants and planning the UCAS personal statement Work experience, visits to leisure centres and national parks and any interests you have in particular aspects of leisure should be described, for example, art galleries, museums, countryside management, sport. An involvement in sports and leisure as a participant or employee is an advantage. See also **Appendix 3**.

Misconceptions about this course The level of business studies in leisure management courses is higher than many students expect.

Interview advice and questions In addition to sporting or other related interests, applicants will be expected to have had some work experience and can expect to be asked to discuss their interests. What do you hope to gain by going to university? See also **Chapter 6**.

Reasons for rejection (non-academic) Poor communication or presentation skills. Relatively poor sporting background or knowledge.

GRADUATE DESTINATIONS AND EMPLOYMENT (2011/12 HESA)
See **Hospitality and Event Management**.

Career note Career opportunities exist in public and private sectors within leisure facilities, health clubs, the arts, leisure promotion, marketing and events management. Some graduates work in sports development and outdoor activities.

OTHER DEGREE SUBJECTS FOR CONSIDERATION
Business Studies; Events Management; Hospitality Management; Sports Studies; Tourism.

LINGUISTICS

(see also English, Languages)

Linguistics covers the study of language structure and function, and also includes areas such as children's language, slang, language handicap, advertising language, language styles and the learning of foreign languages.

Useful websites www.iol.org.uk; www.cal.org; www.applij.oxfordjournals.org; www.linguisticsociety. org; www.sil.org; www.baal.org.uk.

NB The points totals shown to the left of the institutions are for ease of reference only. It must not be assumed that Tariff points are always used by institutions or that they can be substituted for an offer in grades. The level of an offer is not necessarily indicative of the quality of a course.

COURSE OFFERS INFORMATION

Subject requirements/preferences **GCSE** English required and a foreign language preferred. **AL** English may be required or preferred for some courses.

Your target offers and examples of courses provided by each institution

380 pts **Cambridge** – A*AA 380 pts (Ling; Modn Mediev Lang) (IB 40–41 pts HL 776)
London (UCL) – AAA-ABB (Ling) (IB 34–38 pts)

360 pts **Edinburgh** – AAA-BBB 360–300 pts (Ling Engl Lang; Ital Ling; Ling; Class Ling; Jap Ling; Phil Ling) (IB 40–34 pts)
Oxford – AAA (Modn Lang Ling) (IB 38–40 pts)

340 pts **Edinburgh** – AAB-BBB 340–300 pts (Celt Ling) (IB 36–34 pts HL 665–555)
Lancaster – AAB (Ling Psy; Ling (St Abrd); Ling; Ling Phil) (IB 35 pts)
Leeds – AAB-ABB (Ling Joint Hons; Ling Phon)
London (SOAS) – AAB (Ling) (IB 36 pts HL 666)
Manchester – AAB-BBB 340–300 pts (Ling courses) (IB 31–36 pts)
Newcastle – AAB-ABB 340–320 pts (Ling Chin/Jap) (IB 34 pts)
Sheffield – AAB (Engl Lang Ling) (IB 35 pts)
Southampton – AAB (Lang Soc) (IB 34 pts HL 17 pts)
York – AAB (Modn Lang Ling courses; Ling; Fr Ling; Phil Ling) (IB 35 pts)

320 pts **Bristol** – 320 pts (Engl Lang Ling) (IB 27 pts)
Kent – ABB 320 pts (Engl Lang Ling; Engl Lang Ling Eng Am Lit) (IB 34 pts)
London (QM) – ABB-AAB 320–340 pts (Engl Lang Ling; Engl Lit Ling) (IB 34 pts)
Newcastle – ABB-AAB 320–340 pts (Ling; Modn Lang Ling) (IB 34 pts HL 5)
Queen's Belfast – ABB (Engl Ling) (IB 34 pts)
Sheffield – ABB (Ling Joint Hons) (IB 33 pts)

300 pts **Aberdeen** – BBB (Lang Ling) (IB 32 pts)
Bristol UWE – 300 pts (Engl Lang Ling) (IB 26–32 pts)
Essex – ABB-BBB 300–320 pts (Ling) (IB 30–32 pts)
London (QM) – 300 pts (Ger Ling) (IB 32 pts)
Roehampton – 300 pts (Engl Lang Ling)

280 pts **Brighton** – BBC (Engl Lang Ling) (IB 28 pts)
London (Birk) – BBC 280 pts (Ling Lang)
Westminster – BBC (Engl Lang Ling) (IB 30 pts)

260 pts **Bangor** – 260–320 pts (Ling; Ling Engl Lit; Ling Engl Lang) (IB 28 pts)
Central Lancashire – 260–300 pts (Engl Lang Ling)
Manchester Met – 260–280 pts (Ling Lang (Fr/Ger/Ital/Span)) (IB 28 pts)
Nottingham Trent – 260 pts (Ling Joint Hons)
Sunderland – 260 pts (Engl Lang Ling)
Ulster – 260–280 pts (Ling Comm; Lang Ling Adv; Lang Ling courses) (IB 24–25 pts)
Westminster – BCC 260 pts (Arbc Ling) (IB 30 pts)

220 pts **Anglia Ruskin** – 220–260 pts (Eng Lang Ling) (IB 24 pts)
St Mark and St John – 220 pts (Ling Engl Lang)

200 pts **Wolverhampton** – (Ling courses)

Alternative offers

See **Chapter 7** and **Appendix 1** for grades/UCAS Tariff points information for the International Baccalaureate, Scottish Highers/Advanced Highers, the Welsh Baccalaureate, the Irish Leaving Certificate, the Cambridge Pre-U Diploma, the Advanced Diploma and the Extended Project.

CHOOSING YOUR COURSE (SEE ALSO CH.1)

Some course features

Edinburgh The University is regarded as a world leader in the study of linguistics. Opportunity to take an MA in Linguistics or as the lead subject combined with a second subject.
Lancaster (Ling N Am) The course focuses on the sound, grammar and meaning systems of different languages, and has a wide range of options. Study in a North American institution may be possible.

Check **Chapter 4** when choosing your university and **Chapter 7** on how to read the subject tables.

Leeds Linguistics and Phonetics can be taken as a single subject with opportunities to take electives from outside the subject area.

London (QM) (Compar Lit Ling) Students divide their time between the two subjects, the former making connections with literature and film, music, the visual arts and popular culture.

Oxford The Modern Languages and Linguistics course couples the study of a modern language with the analysis of the nature and structure of language. Linguistic topics include the formation of words and sentences, how gender/age/class affects the use of language, and how language is used in literature.

Universities and colleges teaching quality See www.qaa.ac.uk; http://unistats.direct.gov.uk.

Top research universities and colleges (RAE 2008) London (QM); Edinburgh; York; Essex; Sheffield; Wolverhampton; London (UCL); Manchester; Lancaster; Central Lancashire; Cambridge; Bristol UWE.

Examples of sandwich degree courses Nottingham Trent; Wolverhampton.

ADMISSIONS INFORMATION

Number of applicants per place (approx) Bangor 3; Essex 1; Lancaster 12; Leeds 12; York 11.

Advice to applicants and planning the UCAS personal statement Give details of your interests in language and how it works, and about your knowledge of languages and their similarities and differences.

Selection interviews Yes Brighton, Cambridge, Essex, Lancaster; **Some** Newcastle, Reading, Sheffield.

Interview advice and questions Past questions include: Why do you want to study linguistics? What does the subject involve? What do you intend to do at the end of your degree course? What answer do you give to your parents or friends when they ask why you want to study the subject? How and why does language vary according to sex, age, social background and regional origins? See also **Chapter 6**.

Reasons for rejection (non-academic) Lack of knowledge of linguistics. Hesitation about the period to be spent abroad.

AFTER-RESULTS ADVICE

Offers to applicants repeating A-levels Higher Essex; **Same** Brighton, Leeds, Newcastle, York.

GRADUATE DESTINATIONS AND EMPLOYMENT (2011/12 HESA)

Graduates surveyed 560 **Employed** 265 **In voluntary employment** 25 **In further study** 135 **Assumed unemployed** 40

Career note Students enter a wide range of careers, with information management and editorial work in publishing offering some interesting and useful outlets.

OTHER DEGREE SUBJECTS FOR CONSIDERATION

Cognitive Science; Communication Studies; Education Studies; English; Psychology; Speech Sciences.

LITERATURE

(see also **English**)

This is a very broad subject introducing many aspects of the study of literature and aesthetics. Courses will vary in content. Degree courses in English and foreign languages will also include a study of literature.

Useful websites www.lrb.co.uk; www.literature.org; www.bibliomania.com; www.bl.uk; www.acla.org.

NB *The points totals shown to the left of the institutions are for ease of reference only. It must not be assumed that Tariff points are always used by institutions or that they can be substituted for an offer in grades. The level of an offer is not necessarily indicative of the quality of a course.*

COURSE OFFERS INFORMATION

Subject requirements/preferences GCSE English and a foreign language usually required. **AL** English may be required or preferred for some courses.

Ulster (Ir Lang Lit) Applicants need at least grade B (or equivalent) in A-level Irish.

Your target offers and examples of courses provided by each institution
380 pts **Durham** – A*AA 380 pts (Engl Lit Hist; Engl Lit; Engl Lit Phil) (IB 38 pts)
360 pts **Edinburgh** – AAA–BBB 360–300 pts (Scot Lit; Engl Lit) (IB 40–34 pts)
  Lancaster – AAA 360 pts (Engl Lit; Film Engl Lit; Thea Engl Lit; Engl Lang Lit) (IB 36 pts)
  London (King's) – AAA 360 pts (Compar Lit; Compar Lit Film St) (IB 35 pts HL 666 Engl)
  Newcastle – AAA–AAB 360–340 pts (Engl Lit) (IB 35–36 pts)
  Nottingham – AAA–AAB 340–360 pts (Engl Lang Lit) (IB 36–34 pts)
  Oxford – AAA 360 pts (Engl Lang Lit) (IB 38–40 pts)
  Sussex – AAA–AAB (Engl Lang Lit) (IB 35–36 pts)
  Warwick – AAA (Engl Lit; Engl Lit Crea Writ) (IB 38 pts)
340 pts **Birmingham** – AAB (Engl Lit Hisp St) (IB 36 pts)
  Cardiff – AAB 340 pts (Jrnl Media Engl Lit; Engl Lit) (IB 34 pts)
  East Anglia – AAB (Am Lit Crea Writ; Engl Lit) (IB 33 pts HL 5 Engl)
  Edinburgh – AAB–BBB 340–300 pts (Celt Scot Lit) (IB 36–34 pts HL 665–555)
  Essex – AAB–ABB 340–320 pts (Engl Lit; Lit Myth) (IB 33–32 pts)
  Glasgow – AAB (Scot Lit) (IB 34 pts)
  Kent – AAB 340 pts (Engl Am Pstcolnl Lit) (IB 34 pts)
  Leeds – AAB (Engl Lang Lit) (IB 35 pts HL 6 Engl)
  Manchester – AAB 340 pts (Engl Lit courses) (IB 35 pts)
  Newcastle – AAB 340 pts (Engl Lang Lit; Lit Comb Hons) (IB 35 pts)
  Reading – A*BB–AAB (Engl Lit courses) (IB 35 pts)
  Sheffield – AAB (Bib Lit Engl; Engl Lang Lit; Engl Lit) (IB 35 pts)
  Surrey – AAB–ABB (Engl Lit; Engl Lit Crea Writ) (IB 35–34 pts)
  Warwick – AAB 340 pts (Engl Ital Lit; Engl Ger Lit; Film Lit) (IB 36 pts)
320 pts **Brighton** – ABB (Engl Lit) (IB 34 pts)
  Cardiff – ABB 320 pts (Engl Lang Lit)
  Central Lancashire – ABB–BBC 320–280 pts (Engl Lit) (IB 25 pts)
  East Anglia – ABB–AAB 320–340 pts (Am Engl Lit; Engl Lit Joint Hons; Art Hist Lit; Lit Hist; Cult Lit Pol) (IB 32–33 pts HL 5 Engl)
  Essex – ABB–BBB 320–300 pts (Film St Lit; Dr Lit; Engl Lang Lit) (IB 32–30 pts)
  Glasgow – ABB (Engl Lit; Compar Lit Joint Hons) (IB 36 pts)
  Gloucestershire – 320 pts (Engl Lit Hist; Engl Lit; Engl Lit Lang)
  Huddersfield – (Engl Lit; Engl Lit Crea Writ)
  Hull – ABB (Law Lit) (IB 30 pts)
  Kent – ABB 320 pts (Engl Lang Ling Eng Am Lit; Compar Lit St courses) (IB 34 pts)
  Leeds – ABB 320 pts (Class Lit courses) (IB 35 pts HL 16 pts)
  London (Gold) – ABB 320 pts (Eng Compar Lit; Engl Am Lit) (IB 34 pts)
  London (QM) – ABB–AAB 320–340 pts (Engl Lit Ling; Hist Compar Lit) (IB 34 pts)
  London (RH) – ABB–BBB (Compar Lit Cult) (IB 32 pts)
  Northumbria – 320 pts (Engl Lit Hist; Jrnl Engl Lit) (IB 26 pts)
  Nottingham – ABB 320 pts (Am Can Lit Hist Cult) (IB 32 pts)
  Reading – ABB–AAC (Engl Lit Euro Lit Cult; Engl Lit Film Thea) (IB 32 pts HL 5 Engl)
  Swansea – ABB–BBB (Engl Lit Lang St)

Winchester – 320–360 pts (Engl Lit Am Lit) (IB 27 pts)
300 pts **Aberdeen** – BBB (Engl Scot Lit; Langs Lit Scot; Lit Wrld Cntxt courses) (IB 30 pts)
Aberystwyth – 300 pts (Engl Crea Writ; Engl Lit; Engl Wrld Lit) (IB 30 pts)
Brighton – BBB (Media Engl Lit; Hist Cult Lit) (IB 32 pts)
Buckingham – BBB 300 pts (Engl Lit Hist; Engl Lit courses) (IB 34 pts)
Hertfordshire – 300 pts (Engl Lit; Engl Lit Ital)
Hull – 300 pts (Engl Lit Cult) (30 pts)
Kingston – 300 pts (Engl Lit) (IB 30 pts)
Leeds Beckett – BBB 300 pts (Engl Lit) (IB 26 pts)
London (QM) – BBB 300 pts (Ger Compar Lit; Compar Lit courses) (IB 32 pts)
Northumbria – 300 pts (Engl Lit; Engl Lang Lit; Engl Lit Crea Writ)
Roehampton – 300 pts (Engl Lit)
Sheffield Hallam – 300 pts (Engl Lit)
York – BBB 300 pts (Engl Educ) (IB 31 pts)
280 pts **Bangor** – 280–300 pts (Engl Lit Engl Lang) (IB 26 pts)
Bath Spa – 280–320 pts (Engl Lit) (IB 27 pts)
Birmingham City – 280 pts (Engl Lit courses)
Central Lancashire – 280–320 pts (Engl Am Lit)
Edge Hill – 280 pts (Engl Lit)
Greenwich – (Phil Engl Lit)
London Met – 280 pts (Engl Lit)
Manchester Met – (Engl Am Lit) (IB 28 pts)
South Wales – BBC 280 pts (Engl Lit) (IB 25 pts)
Westminster – BBC 280 pts (Engl Lit Hist) (IB 30 pts HL 5 Engl)
Worcester – 280–380 pts (Engl Lit St courses)
260 pts **Bangor** – 260–320 pts (Ling Engl Lit) (IB 28 pts)
Liverpool Hope – 260–300 pts (Engl Lit) (IB 26 pts)
Middlesex – 260 pts (Engl Lang Media)
Salford – 260–300 pts (Engl Lit; Engl Lit Engl Lang) (IB 26 pts)
Sunderland – 260 pts (Engl Lang Lit)
Ulster – BCC 260 pts (Ir Lang Lit) (IB 24 pts HL 12 pts)
240 pts **Anglia Ruskin** – 240–280 pts (Writ Engl Lit) (IB 28 pts)
Bishop Grosseteste – 240 pts (Engl courses)
East London – 240 pts (Engl Lit)
Greenwich – 240 pts (Engl Lit)
Portsmouth – 240–300 pts (Engl Lit courses)
Staffordshire – 240 pts (Engl Lit) (IB 28 pts)
York St John – 240–280 pts (Engl Lit Crea Writ; Engl Lit courses)
220 pts **Anglia Ruskin** – 220–260 pts (Phil Engl Lit; Dr Engl Lit)
St Mark and St John – 220 pts (Engl Lit)
200 pts **Blackburn (Coll)** – 200 pts (Engl Lit)
Blackpool and Fylde (Coll) – 200 pts (Engl Lang Lit Writ)
180 pts **Essex** – DD 180 pts (Lit Art Hist (incl Fdn Yr)) (IB 24 pts)
West Anglia (Coll) – 180 pts (Engl Hist; Sociol Engl Lit)
160 pts **UHI** – CC 160 pts (Lit)

Alternative offers
See **Chapter 7** and **Appendix 1** for grades/UCAS Tariff points information for the International Baccalaureate, Scottish Highers/Advanced Highers, the Welsh Baccalaureate, the Irish Leaving Certificate, the Cambridge Pre-U Diploma, the Advanced Diploma and the Extended Project.

EXAMPLES OF FOUNDATION DEGREES IN THE SUBJECT FIELD
Bath Spa; Truro (Coll); Winchester.

CHOOSING YOUR COURSE (SEE ALSO CH.1)

Some course features

Glasgow (Scot Lit) Course covers poetry, drama, fiction and prose of Scotland in English and Scots from the 14th century to the present day.

London (Gold) (Engl Compar Lit) There is an option to specialise in the literature of other countries, for example America, Europe, the Caribbean.

Reading (Engl Lit Euro Lit Cult) The course explores the inter-relationship between the literatures and cultures of different European countries to gain a comparative perspective on English literature, culture and history. All works are in translation for those without foreign language skills.

Ulster (Ir Lang Lit) Course focuses on an in-depth study of the literary and historical traditions of Gaelic Ireland from the Early Modern period (1200–1650) to the present day and gaining a high level of competence in written and spoken Irish.

Universities and colleges teaching quality See www.qaa.ac.uk; http://unistats.direct.gov.uk.

Top research universities and colleges (RAE 2008) See **English**.

ADMISSIONS INFORMATION

Number of applicants per place (approx) East Anglia 12; Essex 4.

Advice to applicants and planning the UCAS personal statement See **English**. **Kent** Interest in literatures other than English.

Misconceptions about this course **Kent** Some students think that a foreign language is required – it is not.

Interview advice and questions See **English**. See also **Chapter 6**. **Kent** Which book would you take on a desert island, and why? What is the point of doing a Literature degree in the 21st century?

Reasons for rejection (non-academic) **Kent** Perceived inability to think on their feet.

GRADUATE DESTINATIONS AND EMPLOYMENT (2011/12 HESA)

See **English**.

Career note Students enter a wide range of careers, with information management and editorial work in publishing offering some interesting and useful outlets. See also **English**, **Linguistics** and **Celtic, Irish, Scottish and Welsh Studies**.

MARINE/MARITIME STUDIES

(including **Marine Engineering** and **Oceanography**; see also **Environmental Sciences/Studies, Naval Architecture**)

Marine and Maritime Studies can involve a range of subjects such as marine business, technology, navigation, nautical studies, underwater rescue and transport.

Useful websites www.bized.co.uk; www.ukchamberofshipping.com; uksa.org; www.rya.org.uk; www.royalnavy.mod.uk; www.sstg.org; www.noc.soton.ac.uk; www.nautinst.org; www.mcsuk.org; www.nmm.ac.uk; www.imo.org; www.mcga.gov.uk.

NB The points totals shown to the left of the institutions are for ease of reference only. It must not be assumed that Tariff points are always used by institutions or that they can be substituted for an offer in grades. The level of an offer is not necessarily indicative of the quality of a course.

COURSE OFFERS INFORMATION

Subject requirements/preferences **GCSE** Mathematics and science are required for several courses. **AL** Science or mathematics will be required or preferred for some courses.

360 pts **Cardiff** – AAA 360 pts (Mar Geog (Int)) (IB 34 pts)

Southampton – AAA-ABB (Mar Biol; Mar Biol Ocean; Ocean; Ocn Chem; Ocean Fr) (IB 36–32 pts HL 18–16 pts)

340 pts **Cardiff** – AAB 340 pts (Mar Geog MESci) (IB 32–33 pts)

East Anglia – AAB 340 pts (Meteor Ocean (Yr Abrd); Meteor Ocean MSci) (IB 33 pts)

Glasgow – AAB (Mar Frshwtr Biol) (IB 34 pts)

Newcastle – AAB-ABB 320–340 pts (Mar Biol Ocean; Mar Tech Sml Crft Tech; Mar Tech Mar Eng) (IB 34–35 pts)

Newcastle – AAB (Mar Tech Mar Eng MEng; Mar Tech Sml Crft Tech MEng; Mar Tech Off Eng MEng) (IB 37 pts HL 5 maths phys)

St Andrews – AAB 340 pts (Mar Biol) (IB 35 pts)

Southampton – AAB-ABB incl geog (Geog Ocean; Ocean Physl Geog) (IB 34–32 pts HL 17–16 pts)

Strathclyde – AAB (Nvl Archit Ocn Eng MEng) (IB 36 pts)

320 pts **Cardiff** – ABB 320 pts (Mar Geog) (IB 30–32 pts)

East Anglia – ABB (Meteor Ocean BSc) (IB 32 pts)

Essex – ABB-BBB (Mar Biol) (IB 32–30 pts)

Liverpool – ABB (Ocns Clim Physl Geog; Phys Ocn Clim St; Ocn Sci; Mar Biol Ocean) (IB 33 pts)

Newcastle – AAB-ABB 320–340 pts (Mar Biol) (IB 34–35 pts)

Plymouth – ABB 320–360 pts (Mar Biol Cstl Ecol; Mar Biol Ocean) (IB 24 pts)

Southampton – ABB (Geol Mar Biol) (IB 36–32 pts HL 18–16 pts)

Stirling – ABB 320 pts (Mar Biol) (IB 35 pts)

Strathclyde – ABB (Nvl Archit Mar Eng; Nvl Archit Ocn Eng) (IB 32 pts)

300 pts **Aberdeen** – BBB (Mar Biol) (IB 32 pts)

Heriot-Watt – BBB (App Mar Biol)

Plymouth – 300 pts (Ocn Explor) (IB 28 pts)

Queen's Belfast – BBB (Mar Biol)

280 pts **Aberystwyth** – 280–320 pts (Mar Frshwtr Biol)

Bangor – 280–320 pts (App Mar Biol; Mar Env St; Mar Biol Zool; Mar Biol Ocean; Ocn Sci; Geol Ocean; Cstl Geog)

Hull – 280 pts (Mar Frshwtr Biol; Aqua Zool)

Liverpool John Moores – 280 pts (Marit Bus Mgt; Port Marit Mgt; Marit St)

Plymouth – 280 pts (Marit Bus Log; Marit Bus Marit Law; Mar Tech) (IB 25 pts)

Portsmouth – 280–300 pts (Mar Biol)

260 pts **Bangor** – 260–320 pts (Mar Chem; Mar Vert Zool; App Ter Mar Ecol)

Edinburgh Napier – BCC 260 pts (Mar Frshwtr Biol)

Falmouth – 260–300 pts +portfolio +interview (Mar Nat Hist Photo) (IB 24 pts)

Hull – 260 pts (Cstl Mar Biol)

Portsmouth – 260–320 pts (Mar Env Sci) (IB 26 pts)

UHI – BCC (Mar Sci)

240 pts **Aberdeen** – 240 pts (Mar Coast Res Mgt Mar Biol)

Anglia Ruskin – 240 pts (Mar Biol Cons Biodiv) (IB 24 pts)

Plymouth – 240–280 pts (Env Sci (Marit Cons); Ocn Sci)

Southampton Solent – 240 pts (Ycht Des Prod)

220 pts **Bangor** – 220–260 pts (Ocean Comp) (IB 28 pts)

Plymouth – 220 pts (Mar Cmpstes Tech) (IB 26 pts)

Ulster – 220–260 pts (Mar Sci) (IB 24 pts)

200 pts **Plymouth** – 200 pts (Mar St (Navig Marit Sci)) (IB 28 pts)

Southampton Solent – 200 pts (Geog Mar St; Ship Port Mgt) (IB 24 pts)

180 pts **Southampton Solent** – 180 pts (Mar Ops)

120 pts **Bournemouth** – 120 pts (Mar Ecol Cons) (IB 24 pts)

Plymouth – 120–180 pts (Mar Eng) (IB 24 pts)

Alternative offers
See **Chapter 7** and **Appendix 1** for grades/UCAS Tariff points information for the International Baccalaureate, Scottish Highers/Advanced Highers, the Welsh Baccalaureate, the Irish Leaving Certificate, the Cambridge Pre-U Diploma, the Advanced Diploma and the Extended Project.

EXAMPLES OF FOUNDATION DEGREES IN THE SUBJECT FIELD
Blackpool and Fylde (Coll); Bournemouth; Cornwall (Coll); Plymouth; South Tyneside (Coll); Southampton Solent; Sparsholt (Coll).

CHOOSING YOUR COURSE (SEE ALSO CH.1)
Some course features
Bangor A leading department of Marine Sciences offering courses in Marine Biology, Chemistry, Ecology, Environmental Science, Zoology, Coastal Geography and Ocean Sciences. It has an underwater nature trail along the Menai Strait.
Liverpool John Moores (Marit St) A broad-based programme for students with a general interest in ships and sea, with a wide range of optional maritime subjects (for example, maritime and port operations, navigation and meteorology, international trade and finance). Students can build their own degree course as their interests develop, based on core modules such as port and cargo operations, management of people and goods, management science and law. The course can be studied with a year in work placement.
Plymouth (App Mar Spo Sci) A unique course involving the study of human performance, equipment use and design, the nature of the marine environment and practical work. An optional professional diving module is available in the second year.
Southampton Solent Unique courses in Yacht and Powercraft Design and Yacht Production and Surveying.

Universities and colleges teaching quality See www.qaa.ac.uk; http://unistats.direct.gov.uk.

Examples of sandwich degree courses Bangor; Blackpool and Fylde (Coll); Bournemouth; Cardiff; Cornwall (Coll); Greenwich; Liverpool John Moores; Plymouth; Southampton Solent.

ADMISSIONS INFORMATION
Number of applicants per place (approx) Glasgow 2; Liverpool John Moores (Marit St) 3; Southampton 6; Southampton Solent (Ocean) 6, (Ocn Chem) 6.

Advice to applicants and planning the UCAS personal statement This is a specialised field and, in many cases, applicants will have experience of marine activities. Describe these experiences, for example, sailing, snorkelling, fishing. See also **Appendix 3**.

Selection interviews Yes Southampton, UHI; **No** Dundee.

Interview advice and questions Most applicants will have been stimulated by their studies in science or will have strong interests or connections with marine activities. They are likely to be questioned on their reasons for choosing the course. See also **Chapter 6**.

AFTER-RESULTS ADVICE
Offers to applicants repeating A-levels Same Bangor, Liverpool John Moores, Plymouth, UHI.

GRADUATE DESTINATIONS AND EMPLOYMENT (2011/12 HESA)
Maritime Technology graduates surveyed 270 **Employed** 155 **In voluntary employment** 0 **In further study** 55 **Assumed unemployed** 25

Career note This subject area covers a wide range of vocational courses, each offering graduates an equally wide choice of career openings in either purely scientific or very practical areas.

OTHER DEGREE SUBJECTS FOR CONSIDERATION
Biology; Civil Engineering; Environmental Studies/Sciences; Geography; Marine Engineering; Marine Transport; Naval Architecture; Oceanography.

MARKETING

(including **Public Relations**; see also **Business and Management Courses, Business and Management Courses (International and European), Business and Management Courses (Specialised), Retail Management)**

Marketing courses are very popular and applications should include evidence of work experience or work shadowing. Marketing is a subject also covered in most Business Studies courses and in specialist (and equally relevant) courses such as Leisure Marketing and Food Marketing, for which lower offers are often made. Most courses offer the same subject content.

Useful websites www.adassoc.org.uk; www.cim.co.uk; www.camfoundation.com; www.ipa.co.uk; www.ipsos-mori.com; www.marketingstudies.net; www.marketingtoday.com.

NB The points totals shown to the left of the institutions are for ease of reference only. It must not be assumed that Tariff points are always used by institutions or that they can be substituted for an offer in grades. The level of an offer is not necessarily indicative of the quality of a course.

COURSE OFFERS INFORMATION

Subject requirements/preferences GCSE English and mathematics. **AL** No specified subjects required.

Your target offers and examples of courses provided by each institution

380 pts **Lancaster** – A*AA 380 pts (Mark (St Abrd); Mark Mgt (St Abrd))

360 pts **Exeter** – AAA–AAB (Mgt Mark) (IB 36–34 pts)
Leeds – AAA 360 pts (Mgt Mark) (IB 35 pts HL 17 pts)
Loughborough – AAA–AAB (Rtl Mark Mgt) (IB 36 pts)
Ulster – AAA 360 pts (Comm Adv Mark) (IB 27 pts)

340 pts **Aston** – AAB 340 pts (Mark) (IB 35 pts)
Cardiff – AAB 340 pts (Bus Mgt (Mark)) (IB 35 pts)
Essex – AAB–ABB 340–320 pts (Mgt Mark) (IB 33–32 pts)
Lancaster – AAB 340 pts (Mark Des; Mark; Mark Mgt; Adv Mark) (IB 35 pts)
Liverpool – AAB (Mark) (IB 35 pts)
London (RH) – AAB (Mgt Mark) (IB 35 pts)
Newcastle – AAB (Mark; Mark Mgt) (IB 34 pts)
Southampton – AAB (Int Mark; Mark) (IB 34 pts HL 17 pts)
Sussex – AAB (Mark Mgt) (IB 35 pts)

320 pts **Durham** – ABB 320 pts (Mark) (IB 34 pts)
Essex – ABB–BBB (Mark) (IB 32–30 pts)
Kent – ABB–BBB (Crea Evnts) (IB 33 pts)
Northumbria – ABB 320 pts (Adv Mgt; Mark Mgt; Fash Mark)
Reading – ABB 320 pts (Consum Bhv Mark)
Southampton (Winchester SA) – ABB (Fash Mark) (IB 32 pts HL 16 pts)
Strathclyde – ABB (Mark courses)

300 pts **Aberystwyth** – 300 pts (Mark) (IB 28 pts)
Bournemouth – 300–320 pts (Adv; Mark) (IB 30–32 pts)
Bradford – 300 pts (Mark)
Bristol UWE – 300 pts (Mark Comm) (IB 36 pts)
Buckingham – BBB–BBC (Mark Psy; Mark Media Comm; Mark Span)
Dundee – BBB (Bus Econ Mark Hist; Bus Econ Mark; Int Bus Mark) (IB 30 pts)
Edge Hill – BBB 300 pts (Mark) (IB 26 pts)
Heriot-Watt – BBB (Bus Mgt Mark) (IB 29 pts)
Hertfordshire – 300 pts (Mark Span; Mark)
Huddersfield – BBB 300 pts (Adv Mark Comm; Mark; Mark PR; Spo Prom Mark; Fash Comm Prom)
Hull – (Mark)

Keele – ABC 300 pts (Mark) (IB 32 pts)

Kent – BBB (Bus Admin (Mark)) (IB 33 pts)

Northumbria – BBB 300 pts (Bus Mark Mgt) (IB 26 pts)

Nottingham Trent – 300 pts (Mark Des Comm; Fash Mark Brnd; Fash Comm Prom)
(IB 32 pts)

Oxford Brookes – BBB (Bus Mark Mgt) (IB 31 pts)

Reading – BBB–ABC 300 pts (Fd Mark Bus Econ)

Salford – 300 pts (Mark)

Sheffield Hallam – 300 pts (Mark; Mark Comm Adv; Bus Mark)

Swansea – BBB–BCC 300–260 pts (Bus Mgt (Mark)) (IB 33 pts)

Ulster – BBB (Law Mark) (IB 25 pts)

280 pts **Aberystwyth** – 280 pts (Mark Int Pol) (IB 27 pts)

Bournemouth – 280–300 pts (PR) (IB 30–31 pts HL 555)

Bradford – 280–320 pts (Econ Mark)

Cardiff Met (UWIC) – 280 pts (Mark Mgt)

Coventry – BBC 280 pts (Mark; Adv Mark) (IB 29 pts)

De Montfort – 280 pts (Mark Mgt; Mark; Int Mark Bus; Adv)

Greenwich – 280 pts (Adv Mark Comm; Mark)

Huddersfield – 280 pts (Adv Mark Comm; Spo Mark PR)

Hull – 280 pts (Mgt Mark)

Kingston – 280 pts (Mark Mgt) (IB 31 pts)

Leeds Beckett – 280 pts (Spo Mark) (IB 24 pts)

Lincoln – 280 pts (Bus Mark)

Liverpool John Moores – 280 pts (Mark; Bus PR) (IB 29 pts)

Manchester Met – 280 pts (Mark Mgt; Rtl Mark Mgt; Mark Comb Hons) (IB 28 pts)

Middlesex – 280 pts (Adv PR Media)

Portsmouth – 280 pts (Mark; Mark Psy) (IB 29 pts)

Roehampton – 280 pts (Mark; Mark Multim)

Sheffield Hallam – 280 pts (Mark Lang)

South Wales – BBC (Mark; Fash Promo)

Stirling – BBC (Mark; Rtl Mark) (IB 32 pts)

Ulster – BBC 280 pts (Mark; Dr Mark)

West London – 280 pts (Bus St Mark) (IB 28 pts)

Westminster – BBC (Mark Mgt) (IB 28 pts)

Worcester – 280 pts (Bus Mark PR; Bus Mark HR Mgt; Mark courses; Bus Econ Adv;
Adv courses)

260 pts **Bangor** – 260–300 pts (Mark)

Bath Spa – 260–300 pts (Bus Mgt (Mark))

Birmingham City – 260–280 pts (Mark; Mark Adv PR) (IB 24 pts)

Coventry – BCC (Spo Mark) (IB 28 pts)

Derby – 260 pts (Mark Adv Mgt)

Edinburgh Queen Margaret – BCC (PR Mark) (IB 28 pts)

Gloucestershire – 260 pts (Adv)

Harper Adams – 260–300 pts (Agric Mark)

Leeds Beckett – 260 pts (PR Mark) (IB 26 pts)

Lincoln – 260–280 pts (Mark; Mark PR; Adv Mark)

Liverpool Hope – 260–300 pts (Mark) (IB 26 pts)

Manchester Met – 260–280 pts (Dig Media Mark)

Middlesex – 260 pts (Mark)

Northampton – 260–300 pts (Adv courses; Fash Mark; Adv; Mark; Mark Psy;
Mark Joint Hons)

Plymouth – 260 pts (Mark) (IB 26 pts)

Robert Gordon – 260 pts (Mgt Mark)

Sunderland – 260 pts (Bus Mark Mgt)

Check **Chapter 4** when choosing your university and **Chapter 7** on how to read the subject tables.

Ulster – 260-280 pts (Lang Ling Adv) (IB 24 pts)
Westminster – BCC (Bus Mgt (Mark); Mark Comms) (IB 28 pts)

240 pts **Bournemouth** – 240-280 pts (Leis Mark)
Bradford (Coll Univ Centre) – 240 pts (Mark Sls)
Canterbury Christ Church – CCC (Mark)
Central Lancashire – BCC-BBB 260-300 pts (Mark Mgt; Mark Mgt Fash) (IB 28 pts)
Chester – 240-280 pts (Mark; Adv; Mark PR) (IB 26 pts)
Chichester – CCC (Mark) (IB 28 pts)
East London – 240 pts (Adv) (IB 24 pts HL 15 pts)
Edinburgh Napier – CCC 240 pts (Mark Mgt Consum St; Mark Mgt; Mark Dig Media)
Euro Bus Sch London – 240 pts (Int Bus Mark Lang)
Farnborough (CT) – BCD 240 pts (Psy Mark)
Glasgow Caledonian – CCC-CCD 240-220 pts (Mark)
Glyndŵr – 240 pts (Bus Mark)
Leeds (CA) – 240 pts (Crea Adv)
London Met – 240 pts (Mark; Fash Mark courses; PR; Evnts Mgt Mark; Fash
    Mark Jrnl)
Manchester Met – 240-280 pts (Int Fash Prom; Spo Mark Mgt) (IB 29-30 pts)
Southampton Solent – 240 pts (PR Comm; Adv; Fash Prom Comm)
Suffolk (Univ Campus) – 240-280 pts (Bus Mgt Mark)
Teesside – 240 pts (Mark Adv) (IB 24-28 pts)
Ulster – 240-260 pts (Adv courses; Adv HR Mgt; HR Mgt Mark)
West Scotland – CCC (Mark)
Wolverhampton – CCC (PR)
York St John – 240-300 pts (Tour Mgt Mark; Mark Mgt)

220 pts **Creative Arts** – 220-240 pts (Adv Brnd Comm; Fash Prom Imag; Fash Mgt Mark)
    (IB 24 pts)
Derby – 220-300 pts (Mark courses)
Falmouth – 220 pts (Adv)
Harper Adams – 220-260 pts (Bus Mgt Mark; Agri-Fd Mark Bus St)
Leeds Beckett – 220 pts (Mark; Mark Adv Mgt)
Leeds Trinity – 220-260 pts (Media Mark)
London South Bank – 220 pts (Mark Comb courses)
Northampton – 220-260 pts (Spo Mark)
Southampton Solent – 220-240 pts (Mark; Mark Adv Mgt; Mark Evnt Mgt)
Sunderland – 220 pts (Adv Des; Fash Prod Prom)
Wolverhampton – 220 pts (Mark Mgt)

200 pts **Anglia Ruskin** – 240-200 pts (Mark)
Bedfordshire – 200 pts (Mark; Mark Media Prac; PR; Adv Mark Comm)
Birmingham (UC) – 200 pts (Mark Mgt; Mark Evnts Mgt)
Bucks New – 200-240 pts (PR Mark Comm; Mark; Bus Mark Mgt) (IB 24 pts)
Croydon (Coll) – 200 pts (Bus Mark)
East London – 200 pts (Mark)
Peterborough (Reg Coll) – 200 pts (Mark)
Staffordshire – BB-BCC (Mark Mgt)

180 pts **Abertay** – DDD (Mark Bus) (IB 24 pts)

160 pts **Ravensbourne** – CC-AA 160-240 pts (Fash Prom) (IB 28 pts)
Trinity Saint David (Swansea) – 160 pts (Mark Mgt) (IB 24 pts)

120 pts **Grimsby (Univ Centre)** – 120 pts (Mark)

Alternative offers
See **Chapter 7** and **Appendix 1** for grades/UCAS Tariff points information for the International
Baccalaureate, Scottish Highers/Advanced Highers, the Welsh Baccalaureate, the Irish Leaving
Certificate, the Cambridge Pre-U Diploma, the Advanced Diploma and the Extended Project.

EXAMPLES OF FOUNDATION DEGREES IN THE SUBJECT FIELD

Arts London; Bedfordshire; Birmingham (UC); Bournemouth; Cornwall (Coll); Glyndŵr; Harper Adams; Hertfordshire; Hull (Coll); Manchester (Coll); Middlesex; Newcastle (Coll); Northbrook (Coll); Nottingham New (Coll); Petroc; Plymouth; South Devon (Coll); Truro (Coll); Warwickshire (Coll); West London; West Thames (Coll); Worcester (CT); York (Coll).

CHOOSING YOUR COURSE (SEE ALSO CH.1)

Some course features

Bournemouth The course covers advertising communications, media and marketing methods. The Marketing Communications course involves a 40-week placement.

Brunel Marketing is offered as a pathway in the Business and Management programme and can be taken as a three-year full-time or four-year sandwich course.

Lancaster (Mark Mgt) There is a one-year work placement between the second and third years.

Loughborough (Rtl Mark Mgt) The third year is spent on a salaried business placement as a trainee manager in a UK retail or marketing organisation.

Manchester Met A full-time or sandwich course, the latter with placements in the UK and abroad. Special features include a study of the fashion business, fashion products and the world-wide fashion industry.

Northumbria The course integrates fashion design with the fashion business and marketing.

Portsmouth (Mark) The course is recognised by the Chartered Institute of Marketing. The four-year sandwich course involves a paid marketing placement.

Westminster Students are expected to find employment for a period during the course, ideally abroad. Work placement officers have contacts with institutions overseas.

Universities and colleges teaching quality See www.qaa.ac.uk; http://unistats.direct.gov.uk.

Examples of sandwich degree courses Abertay; Arts London (Camberwell CA); Aston; Bath Spa; Bedfordshire; Birmingham City; Bournemouth; Bradford; Brighton; Bristol UWE; Brunel; Cardiff Met (UWIC); Central Lancashire; Chichester; Coventry; De Montfort; Derby; Durham; Gloucestershire; Greenwich; Harper Adams; Hertfordshire; Huddersfield; Kingston; Lancaster; Leeds Beckett; Liverpool John Moores; London (RH); London South Bank; Loughborough; Manchester Met; Newcastle; Northumbria; Nottingham Trent; Oxford Brookes; Plymouth; Portsmouth; Salford; Sheffield Hallam; Southampton Solent; Staffordshire; Sussex; Teesside; Trinity Saint David (Swansea); Ulster; Westminster; Wolverhampton; Worcester.

ADMISSIONS INFORMATION

Number of applicants per place (approx) Abertay 6; Aberystwyth 3; Anglia Ruskin 5; Aston 9; Birmingham City 4; Bournemouth 10; Brunel 10; Central Lancashire 13; De Montfort 3; Derby 5; Glasgow Caledonian 15; Harper Adams 3; Huddersfield 7; Lancaster 28; Lincoln 3; London Met 10; Northampton 4; Northumbria 8; Nottingham Trent 2; Plymouth 12; Portsmouth 4; Staffordshire 6; Stirling 10; Teesside 3.

Advice to applicants and planning the UCAS personal statement See **Business and Management Courses** and **Appendix 3**.

Selection interviews **Yes** Harper Adams, Middlesex; **Some** Abertay, Aberystwyth, Anglia Ruskin, Aston, Buckingham, De Montfort, Edinburgh Queen Margaret, Manchester Met, Staffordshire; **No** Essex.

Interview advice and questions Past questions include: What is marketing? Why do you want to take a Marketing degree? Is sales pressure justified? How would you feel if you had to market a product which you considered to be inferior? See also **Chapter 6**. **Buckingham** What job do you see yourself doing in five years' time?

Reasons for rejection (non-academic) Little thought of reasons for deciding on a Marketing degree. Weak on numeracy and problem-solving. Limited commercial awareness. Poor inter-personal skills. Lack of leadership potential. No interest in widening their horizons, either geographically or intellectually. 'We look at appearance, motivation and the applicant's ability to ask questions.' Not hungry enough. Limited understanding of the career. No clear reasons for wishing to do the course.

AFTER-RESULTS ADVICE

Offers to applicants repeating A-levels Same Abertay, Aberystwyth, Anglia Ruskin, Aston, Buckingham, De Montfort, Edinburgh Queen Margaret, Lincoln, Manchester Met, Staffordshire.

GRADUATE DESTINATIONS AND EMPLOYMENT (2011/12 HESA)

Graduates surveyed 3055 **Employed** 1975 **In voluntary employment** 130 **In further study** 265 **Assumed unemployed** 285

Career note See **Business and Management Courses**.

OTHER DEGREE SUBJECTS FOR CONSIDERATION

Advertising; Art and Design; Business courses; Communications; Graphic Design; Psychology; Public Relations.

MATERIALS SCIENCE/METALLURGY

Materials Science is a broad subject which mainly covers physics, chemistry and engineering at one and the same time! From its origins in metallurgy, materials science has now moved into the processing, structure and properties of materials – ceramics, polymers, composites and electrical materials. Materials science and metallurgy are perhaps the most misunderstood of all careers and applications for degree courses are low with very reasonable offers. Valuable bursaries and scholarships are offered by the Institute of Materials, Minerals and Mining (check with Institute – see **Appendix 3**). Polymer Science is a branch of materials science and is often studied in conjunction with Chemistry and covers such topics as polymer properties and processing relating to industrial applications with, for example, plastics, paints, adhesives. Other courses under this heading include Fashion and Leather Technology. See also **Appendix 3**.

Useful websites www.eef.org.uk/uksteel; www.iom3.org; www.epsrc.ac.uk; www.imm.org.

NB The points totals shown to the left of the institutions are for ease of reference only. It must not be assumed that Tariff points are always used by institutions or that they can be substituted for an offer in grades. The level of an offer is not necessarily indicative of the quality of a course.

COURSE OFFERS INFORMATION

Subject requirements/preferences GCSE (Eng/Sci courses) Science/mathematics subjects. **AL** Mathematics, physics and/or chemistry required for most courses. (Poly Sci) Mathematics and/or physics usually required; design technology encouraged.

Your target offers and examples of courses provided by each institution

380 pts Cambridge – A*AA (Nat Sci (Mat Sci)) (IB 40–41 pts HL 776)

Oxford – A*AA (Mat Sci) (IB 40 pts)

Southampton – A*AA A* in maths **or** phys (Mech Eng (Advnc Mat) MEng) (IB 38 pts HL 18 pts)

360 pts Birmingham – AAA (Mat Eng; Mat Sci Eng Bus Mgt MEng) (IB 36 pts)

Exeter – AAA–ABB 360–320 pts (Mat Eng; Mat Eng MEng) (IB 36–32 pts)

Imperial London – AAA incl maths phys (Aerosp Mat; Mat courses; Mat Mgt; Mat Sci Eng; Biomat Tiss Eng) (IB 38 pts HL 6 maths phys)

London (QM) – AAA (Dntl Mat MEng; Mat Sci Eng MEng; Mat Sci MEng) (IB 36 pts)

Nottingham – AAA–AAB 360–320 pts (Biomed Mat Sci) (IB 34–36 pts)

Southampton – AAA incl maths phys (Ship Sci (Advncd Mat)) (IB 36 pts HL 18 pts)

Strathclyde – AAA 360 pts (Mech Eng Mat Eng MEng) (IB 36 pts)

340 pts Birmingham – AAB (Mat Sci Eng Bus Mgt BEng; Spo Mat Sci; Metal) (IB 35 pts)

Exeter – AAB–BBB 340–300 pts (Min Eng) (IB 34–30 pts)

Liverpool – AAB incl maths (Mech Mat Eng MEng) (IB 35 pts HL 5 maths)

Loughborough – AAB 340 pts (Des Eng Mat MEng; Mat Eng MEng; Auto Mat MEng) (IB 34–36 pts)

Manchester – AAB (Mat Sci Eng; Biomat Sci Tiss Eng) (IB 35 pts)
St Andrews – AAB (Mat Chem) (IB 35 pts)
Sheffield – AAB (Mat Sci Eng (Biomat) MEng; Mat Sci Eng (Ind Mgt) MEng; Mat Sci Eng
(Modn Lang); Mat Sci Eng MEng; Metal) (IB 35 pts)

320 pts **Birmingham** – ABB (Mat Sci Ener Eng) (IB 32 pts)
Edinburgh – ABB–AAA incl chem maths 320–360 pts (Chem Mat Chem) (IB 37–32 pts)
Liverpool – ABB incl maths (Mech Mat Eng) (IB 33 pts HL 5 maths)
Loughborough – ABB–ACC 320 pts (Auto Mat; Mat Eng) (IB 32 pts)
Sheffield – ABB (Mat Sci Eng) (IB 34 pts)
Swansea – ABB (Mat Sci Eng MEng)

300 pts **Birmingham** – BBB (Metal Mat Eng) (IB 32 pts)
Heriot-Watt – BBB (Chem Mat) (IB 29 pts)
London (QM) – BBB 300 pts (Mat Des; Dntl Mat; Mat Sci Eng; Med Mat; Med Mat Sci) (IB
26–28 pts)
Sheffield – ABC/BBB (Mat Sci Eng (Biomat); Mat Sci Eng (Ind Mgt); Aerosp Mat) (IB 32 pts)
Swansea – BBB 300 pts (Mat Sci Eng)

260 pts **Northampton** – 260–280 pts (Lea Tech) (IB 24 pts)

240 pts **Edinburgh Napier** – CCC 240 pts (Poly Eng)
Ulster – 240 pts (Bld Eng Mat) (IB 24 pts)

220 pts **Sheffield Hallam** – 220 pts incl maths+chem (Mat Eng)

Alternative offers
See **Chapter 7** and **Appendix 1** for grades/UCAS Tariff points information for the International
Baccalaureate, Scottish Highers/Advanced Highers, the Welsh Baccalaureate, the Irish Leaving
Certificate, the Cambridge Pre-U Diploma, the Advanced Diploma and the Extended Project.

EXAMPLES OF FOUNDATION DEGREES IN THE SUBJECT FIELD
Blackburn (Coll); Bradford; Loughborough; Manchester Met.

CHOOSING YOUR COURSE (SEE ALSO CH.1)
Some course features
Birmingham Courses are offered in Mechanical and Materials Science, Metallurgy/Materials
Engineering, Materials Science and Technology. There is also a course in Sports Science and Materials
Technology.
Imperial London The Department offers three-year BEng courses in Materials Science and Engineering,
Materials with Management, and Materials with a year abroad, and four-year courses in Aerospace
Materials, and Materials Science and Engineering. Students are encouraged to gain practical experience
during two summer vacations; some are spent abroad. There are also opportunities for industrial
sponsorship. A course in Biomaterials and Tissue Engineering is also offered.
London (QM) The course in Materials Science and Engineering provides a bridge between pure and
applied sciences and covers polymers, biomaterials, metals and ceramics. There are also courses in
Biomedical, Aerospace, Dental and Environmental Materials Science.
Loughborough The Materials Engineering programme allows students to develop either Materials
Engineering or Business Management options in the final year. There is an optional third year in
Europe or in industry. There are also courses in Automotive Materials. Scholarships available.
Manchester The Materials Science and Engineering programme focuses on engineering aspects whilst
the Biomedical Materials Science programme can be taken with or without industrial experience. The
Biomedical Materials Science course covers cell structure, anatomy, tissue interaction and drug release
systems. There are also courses in Textile Sciences and Technology. Entrance scholarships.
Northampton (Mat Tech (Lea)) This course is unique. The University is the UK's leading provider of
leather technology courses, and is the only one to have a tannery.
Sheffield In this Materials Science and Engineering course modules are offered in biomaterials,
mathematics and material chemistry. Admission can also be by way of Physical Sciences since final
degree course decisions between Materials Science or Physics or Chemistry can be delayed. Various
Engineering courses are also available.

Universities and colleges teaching quality See www.qaa.ac.uk; http://unistats.direct.gov.uk.

Top research universities and colleges (RAE 2008) (Metallurgy and Materials) Cambridge; Liverpool; Oxford; Manchester; Birmingham; Sheffield; Imperial London; Swansea; London (QM).

Examples of sandwich degree courses Bradford; Exeter; London (QM); Loughborough; Manchester; Plymouth; St Andrews; Sheffield Hallam.

ADMISSIONS INFORMATION
Number of applicants per place (approx) Birmingham 8; Imperial London 3; Liverpool 3; Manchester Met 7; Nottingham 7; Southampton 8; Swansea 4.

Advice to applicants and planning the UCAS personal statement Read scientific and engineering journals and describe any special interests you have. Try to visit chemical or technological installations (rubber, plastics, glass etc) and describe your visits. See also **Appendix 3**.

Misconceptions about this course Students are generally unaware of what this subject involves or the opportunities within the industry.

Selection interviews Yes Birmingham, Imperial London, Nottingham, Oxford (Mat Sci) 44%; (Mat Sci Econ Mgt) 44%; **Some** Leeds.

Interview advice and questions Questions are likely to be based on A/AS-level science subjects. Recent examples include: Why did you choose Materials Science? How would you make each part of this table lamp (on the interviewer's desk)? Identify this piece of material. How was it manufactured? How has it been treated? (Questions related to metal and polymer samples.) What would you consider the major growth area in materials science? See also **Chapter 6**. **Birmingham** We try to gauge understanding; for example, an applicant would be unlikely to be questioned on specific facts, but might be asked what they have understood from a piece of coursework at school. **Oxford** Tutors look for an ability to apply logical reasoning to problems in physical science and an enthusiasm for thinking about new concepts in science and engineering.

AFTER-RESULTS ADVICE
Offers to applicants repeating A-levels Higher Swansea; **Same** Birmingham, Leeds (CA), Liverpool, Manchester Met; **No** Cambridge.

GRADUATE DESTINATIONS AND EMPLOYMENT (2011/12 HESA)
Metallurgy graduates surveyed 10 **Employed** 0 **In voluntary employment** 0 **In further study** 5 **Assumed unemployed** 0

Polymers and Textiles graduates surveyed 230 **Employed** 135 **In voluntary employment** 5 **In further study** 35 **Assumed unemployed** 20

Materials Science graduates surveyed 220 **Employed** 80 **In voluntary employment** 0 **In further study** 95 **Assumed unemployed** 20

Career note Materials scientists are involved in a wide range of specialisms in which openings are likely in a range of industries. These include manufacturing processes in which the work is closely linked with that of mechanical, chemical, production and design engineers.

OTHER DEGREE SUBJECTS FOR CONSIDERATION
Aerospace Engineering; Biotechnology; Chemistry; Dentistry; Engineering Sciences; Mathematics; Mechanical Engineering; Medical Engineering; Plastics Technology; Physics; Product Design and Materials; Prosthetics and Orthotics; Sports Technology.

MATHEMATICS

(including **Mathematical Sciences/Studies**; see also **Economics, Statistics**)

Mathematics at degree level is an extension of A-level mathematics, covering pure and applied mathematics, statistics, computing, mathematical analysis and mathematical applications. Mathematics is of increasing importance and is used in the simplest of design procedures and not only in applications in the physical sciences and engineering. It also plays a key role in management, economics, medicine and the social and behavioural sciences.

Useful websites www.ima.org.uk; www.orsoc.org.uk; www.m-a.org.uk; www.mathscareers.org.uk; www.imo.math.ca; www.bmoc.maths.org; www.maths.org; www.ukmt.org.uk.

NB The points totals shown to the left of the institutions are for ease of reference only. It must not be assumed that Tariff points are always used by institutions or that they can be substituted for an offer in grades. The level of an offer is not necessarily indicative of the quality of a course.

COURSE OFFERS INFORMATION

Subject requirements/preferences GCSE English often required and mathematics is obviously essential at a high grade for leading universities. **AL** Mathematics, in several cases with a specified grade, required for all courses. **AS** Further mathematics may be required. **Other** Mathematics AEA or STEP papers may be required by some universities (eg Imperial, Warwick). See also **Chapter 5**. NB The level of an offer may depend on whether an applicant is taking A/AS further maths; check websites.

Imperial London 5 A/A* grades at GCSE.

Your target offers and examples of courses provided by each institution

460 pts   **Warwick** – A*A*Aa–A*AA 460–380 pts (Maths MMaths; Maths Joint Hons) (IB 39 pts HL 6 maths)

420 pts   **London (UCL)** – A*AAc incl maths/fmaths (Maths; Mathem Comp) (IB 39–40 pts)
        Manchester – A*A*A*–A*AA (Maths Phys) (IB 39–38 pts HL 776–766)

400 pts   **Imperial London** – A*A*A (Maths Stats; Maths Stats Fin; PMaths; Maths Optim Stats; Maths Mathem Comp) (IB 39 pts HL 7 maths)
        London (King's) – A*AAe (Maths; Maths Phys; Maths Phil) (IB 35 pts)
        London (UCL) – A*AA+AS (Maths courses) (IB 39–40 pts HL 766)
        Oxford – A*A*A (Maths; Maths Phil; Maths Stats) (IB 39 pts)

380 pts   **Bath** – A*AA (Mathem Sci) (IB 39 pts HL 6 maths)
        Bristol – A*AA–AAA 380–360 pts (Maths; Maths Comp Sci) (IB 38–37 pts HL 666)
        Cambridge – A*AA +STEP (Maths; Maths Phys) (IB 40–42 pts HL 766–777)
        Durham – A*AA 380 pts (Maths (Euro St); Maths) (IB 38 pts)
        Exeter – A*AA–AAB (Maths; Maths Fin; Maths Phys; Maths Econ; Maths Acc) (IB 38–34 pts)
        Imperial London – A*AA (Maths) (IB 39 pts HL 7 maths)
        London (UCL) – AAAe–ABBe (Chem Maths) (IB 36–38 pts HL 17–19 pts)
        London LSE – A*AA incl maths (Ecomet Mathem Econ; Maths Econ) (IB 38 pts HL 766)
        Manchester – A*AA–AAA (Act Sci Maths; Maths Phil) (IB 37 pts)
        Nottingham – A*AA–AAA (Maths; Fin Maths; Maths Eng; Mathem Phys) (IB 38–36 pts HL 6 maths)
        Southampton – A*AA (Maths; Maths MMaths) (IB 37 pts HL 18 pts)
        Warwick – A*AA (Maths; Discr Maths; MORSE (Act Fin Maths)) (IB 39–37 pts)

360 pts   **Bath** – AAA (Maths Phys) (IB 36 pts HL 6 maths)
        Birmingham – AAA–AAB (Maths) (IB 36–38 pts HL 6 maths)
        Bristol – AAA–AAB incl maths 360–340 pts (Eng Maths; Maths Phil) (IB 37–35 pts)
        Cardiff – AAA incl maths 360 pts (Maths MMaths) (IB 35 pts)
        City – AAA 360 pts (Maths Fin; Mathem Sci; Mathem Sci Stats) (IB 32 pts)
        Edinburgh – AAA–ABB 360–320 pts (Maths Stats; Maths Mus; App Maths; Maths; Maths Mgt; Maths MA; Mathem Phys) (IB 37–32 pts)
        Exeter – AAA–AAB 360–340 pts (Eng Maths)

Glasgow – AAA-A*AB (Acc Maths) (IB 36 pts)

Lancaster – AAA 360 pts (Acc Fin Maths; Fin Maths; Theor Phys Maths) (IB 36 pts)

Leeds – A*AB-AAA (Act Maths; Maths Fin; Maths Stats) (IB 35 pts HL 6 maths)

Leeds – AAA-AAB (Maths) (IB 34 pts HL 6 maths)

London (QM) – 360 pts (Maths Stats MSci; Maths MSci) (IB 34 pts HL 6 maths)

Loughborough – AAA-AAB (Maths; Maths Maths Educ) (IB 36 pts)

Manchester – A*AB-AAB 340-360 pts (Maths; Maths Fin; Maths Fin Maths) (IB 36 pts)

Queen's Belfast – A*AB-AAA (Maths MSci; Maths Stats OR MSci; App Maths Phys MSci; Maths Comp Sci MSci) (IB 34 pts)

St Andrews – AAA (Anc Hist Maths; App Maths; Maths; PMaths; Maths Langs; Arbc Maths; Maths Span) (IB 36 pts)

Sheffield – AAA (Maths MMaths; Maths (Yr Abrd)) (IB 37 pts HL 6 maths)

Southampton – AAA (Maths Fin; Maths Biol; Maths Comp Sci; Maths Stats; Maths OR Stats Econ; Mathem St; Maths Fr/Ger/Span; Maths Mus; Maths Act Sci; Maths Phys; Maths Astron) (IB 36 pts HL 18 pts)

Surrey – AAA-AAB (Maths courses)

Sussex – AAA-AAB incl maths (Maths MMaths; Maths Econ; Maths courses) (IB 35 pts)

York – AAA (Maths Stats)

340 pts **Birmingham** – AAB 340 pts (Maths Bus Mgt) (IB 35-36 pts)

Cardiff – AAB 340 pts (Maths Relig St; Maths; Maths Apps; Maths OR Stats; Maths Welsh) (IB 33 pts)

East Anglia – AAB (Maths BSc; Maths MMath) (IB 33 pts)

Essex – AAB-ABB 320-340 pts (Maths) (IB 33-32 pts)

Glasgow – AAB (Maths/App Maths/PMaths) (IB 34 pts)

Lancaster – AAB (Maths Stats; Maths Phil; Maths) (IB 34 pts)

Leicester – AAB (Maths; Fin Maths; Maths Mgt; Maths Econ) (IB 28-32 pts)

Liverpool – AAB (Mathem Phys MMath) (IB 35 pts HL 6 maths)

London (QM) – AAB 340 pts (Maths Stats Fin Econ; Maths; Maths Fin Acc) (IB 36 pts HL 6 maths)

London (RH) – AAB (Maths; Econ Maths) (IB 35 pts)

Loughborough – AAB-AAA 340-360 pts (Maths Mgt) (IB 36 pts)

Manchester – AAB (Comp Sci Maths) (IB 35 pts)

Newcastle – AAB (Acc Maths; Maths MMaths; Maths; Mathem Sci; Maths Stats; Fin Maths Mgt; Fin Maths) (IB 34-37 pts HL 6 maths)

Nottingham – AAB (Comp Sci) (IB 36-34 pts HL 6 maths)

Sheffield – AAB incl maths (Comp Sci Maths; Fin Math; Maths; Maths Joint Hons) (IB 35 pts HL 6 maths)

Southampton – AAB incl maths (Phil Maths) (IB 34 pts HL 17 pts)

Strathclyde – AAB-ABB (Maths courses)

Surrey – AAB 340 pts (Maths Stats; Fin Maths) (IB 35 pts)

Swansea – AAB-ABB 340-320 pts (Maths MMaths) (IB 34-33 pts)

York – AAB-AAA (Maths; Maths courses; Maths Phys; Econ Maths) (IB 36-35 pts)

320 pts **Aberystwyth** – 280-320 pts (App Maths Stats; App Maths PMaths) (IB 28 pts)

Aston – ABB-AAB 320-340 pts (Maths; Maths Joint Hons) (IB 32 pts)

Brunel – ABB 320 pts (Maths Stats Mgt; Maths; Maths Comp Sci; Fin Maths MMaths) (IB 33 pts)

Kent – ABB (Fin Maths; Maths; Maths Stats) (IB 33 pts)

Liverpool – ABB (Maths; Mathem Sci Euro Lang; PMaths; Maths Bus St; Econ Maths; Maths Fin; Maths Stats) (IB 33 pts HL 6 maths)

London (RH) – ABB (Maths Stats) (IB 33 pts HL 6 maths)

Loughborough – ABB (Phys Maths) (IB 34 pts)

Northumbria – 320 pts (Maths) (IB 28 pts)

Plymouth – 320 pts (Maths Fin) (IB 30 pts)

Queen's Belfast – ABB (App Maths Phys; Maths Comp Sci; Maths; Maths (St Abrd); Maths Stats OR)

Maths at Brunel

At Brunel, you can expect:

- 93% overall student satisfaction
- £22,000 average salary six months after the course
- 90% of 2012 graduates went on to work and/or study six months after completing their studies

For an exciting, innovative course selection

- Financial Mathematics BSc/MMath
- Mathematics BSc/MMath
- Mathematics and Statistics with Management BSc
- Mathematics with Computer Science BSc

Brunel
UNIVERSITY
L O N D O N

OPEN DAYS & CAMPUS TOURS' BOOKING
🐭 www.brunel.ac.uk/openday
📞 +44(0)1895 265595

Reading – 320–340 pts (Maths; Maths App Stats; Maths Meteor; Maths Stats Comput Maths)

Swansea – ABB–BBB (Maths) (IB 33–32 pts)

300 pts **Aberdeen** – BBB 300 pts (App Maths; Maths)

Bristol UWE – 300 pts (Maths) (IB 26 pts)

De Montfort – 300 pts (Maths) (IB 30 pts)

Dundee – BBB–BCC 280–300 pts (Mathem Biol) (IB 32 pts)

Greenwich – 300 pts (Maths Comp)

Heriot-Watt – BBB (Maths; Maths Joint Hons; Maths Span)

Keele – ABC incl maths A 300 pts (Maths) (IB 32 pts)

Oxford Brookes – BBB–BBC (Maths courses) (IB 31–32 pts)

Roehampton – 300–360 pts (P Educ (Maths))

South Wales – BBB 300 pts (Fin Maths; Maths)

Strathclyde – BBB (Maths Stats Econ) (IB 32 pts)

280 pts **Aberystwyth** – 280–320 pts (Maths) (IB 28 pts)

Brighton – BBC (Maths Fin; Maths; Maths Bus) (IB 28 pts)

Canterbury Christ Church – 280 pts (Maths Educ QTS)

Central Lancashire – 280 pts (Maths)

Hertfordshire – 280 pts (Comp Maths; Maths; Fin Maths)

Kingston – 280 pts (Act Maths Stats; Maths)

Liverpool John Moores – 280 pts (Maths) (IB 24 pts)

Manchester Met – 280 pts (Maths) (IB 28 pts)

Northampton – 280–320 pts (P Ed Maths) (IB 26 pts)

Nottingham Trent – 280 pts (Maths; Spo Sci Maths)

Oxford Brookes – BBC (Mathem Sci) (IB 31 pts)

Sheffield Hallam – 280 pts (Maths)

For a quick reference offers calculator, fold out the inside front cover.

Staffordshire – 280 pts (Maths Stats) (IB 24 pts)
Stirling – BBC (Maths App) (IB 32 pts)
260 pts **Bolton** – 260 pts (Maths)
Bradford – 260 pts (Comput Maths) (IB 24 pts)
Chichester – BCC–CCC incl maths 260–240 pts (Maths Math Learn) (IB 28 pts HL 4 maths)
Coventry – 260 pts (Maths courses)
Derby – 260 pts (Maths Comp Sci; Maths Educ; Maths)
Dundee – BCC 260 pts (Maths)
Greenwich – 260 pts (Fin Maths; Maths)
Liverpool Hope – 260–320 pts (Maths)
Portsmouth – 260–300 pts (Maths; Maths Fin Mgt; Maths Stats)
240 pts **Bishop Grosseteste** – 240 pts (Spo Maths) (IB 24 pts)
Chester – 240–280 pts (Maths) (IB 26 pts)
Coventry – CCC 240 pts (Maths Stats) (IB 27 pts)
South Wales – 240 pts (Maths Acc)
200 pts **Bedfordshire** – 200 pts (Comp Maths) (IB 24 pts)
London Met – 200 pts (Fin Maths; Maths; Mathem Sci; Maths Stats)
Wolverhampton – 200 pts (Maths) (IB 24 pts)
80 pts **London (Birk)** – p/t, for under 21s (over 21s varies) (Maths Stats)

Open University – contact +44 (0)845 300 6090 **or** www.openuniversity.co.uk/you (Maths)

Alternative offers
See **Chapter 7** and **Appendix 1** for grades/UCAS Tariff points information for the International Baccalaureate, Scottish Highers/Advanced Highers, the Welsh Baccalaureate, the Irish Leaving Certificate, the Cambridge Pre-U Diploma, the Advanced Diploma and the Extended Project.

CHOOSING YOUR COURSE (SEE ALSO CH.1)
Some course features
Aston There is an emphasis on Applied Mathematics relevant to business, industry and computing in addition to combinations with Economics and Languages. There are sandwich placement opportunities allowing students to spend the third year gaining experience in paid work.
Bradford There is a course in Computational Mathematics with a Foundation year in Informatics for applicants with non-standard qualifications.
Coventry Courses focus on the applications of mathematics in engineering, finance, computing, business and statistics.
Exeter Most first-year modules are common to all Single Honours courses. Transfers to other courses are possible from Year 2. There is a wide range of degrees including combinations with Management, languages, Physics and Finance and Accounting. Optional summer industrial placements are possible as part of the degree course.
Imperial London Twelve courses are offered with considerable flexibility to transfer between courses and between BSc and MSci options including Applied Maths, Statistics, Computer Science and a year in Europe.
Lancaster The Mathematics degree course is for those students wanting to specialise in pure mathematics whilst having the option to include some statistics or another subject.
Leicester BA, BSc and MMaths courses are offered in Mathematics, Financial Mathematics, Mathematics with Economics and Mathematics with Management. The MMath Mathematics degree course is an opportunity to study abroad. Options for a year in Europe or USA.
London (QM) A wide range of joint courses are available offering specialisms in accounting, business, computing and finance.
London (UCL) A range of courses, including Economics, Statistical Science and Theoretical Physics, is offered with Mathematics and some sponsorships are possible. Small group tutorials and computer-assisted learning are important features of this course. There are a range of options in Years 3 and 4. There are several also Statistics degree courses.
Plymouth Five Mathematics courses are offered including combinations with Statistics, Education, Computing and Finance. Applied Statistics can also be taken with Management Science.

Universities and colleges teaching quality See www.qaa.ac.uk; http://unistats.direct.gov.uk.

Top research universities and colleges (RAE 2008) (Pure Maths) Imperial London; Warwick; Oxford; Cambridge; Bristol; Edinburgh; Heriot-Watt; Bath; Aberdeen; London (King's); Manchester; London (UCL); Durham; East Anglia; Sheffield; London (QM).

(Applied Maths) Cambridge; Oxford; Bristol; St Andrews; Bath; Portsmouth; Warwick; Manchester; Imperial London; Durham; Southampton; Nottingham; Surrey.

Examples of sandwich degree courses Aston; Bath; Bradford; Brighton; Bristol UWE; Brunel; Cardiff; Coventry; East Anglia; Greenwich; Hertfordshire; Kent; Kingston; Lancaster; Liverpool John Moores; Loughborough; Northumbria; Nottingham Trent; Portsmouth; Reading; Staffordshire; Surrey; Teesside; Wolverhampton; York.

ADMISSIONS INFORMATION

Number of applicants per place (approx) Aberystwyth 8, (App Maths) 5; Anglia Ruskin 6; Aston 8; Bangor 4; Bath 6; Birmingham 4; Bristol UWE 7; Brunel 5; Cambridge 4; Cardiff 5; Central Lancashire 7; City 6; Coventry 8; Cumbria 9; Derby 4; Dundee 5; Durham 5; East Anglia 5; East London 2; Edinburgh 4; Exeter 6; Greenwich 2; Heriot-Watt 5; Hertfordshire 9; Kent 8; Lancaster 12; Leeds (Maths) 5, (Maths Fin) 4; Leicester 14; Liverpool 5; London (Gold) 5; London (King's) 8; London (QM) 5; London (RH) 8; London (UCL) 8; London LSE (Maths) 11, (Bus Maths Stats) 10; London Met 3; Manchester Met 3; Middlesex 5; Newcastle 7; Northumbria 7; Nottingham Trent 7; Oxford Brookes 21; Plymouth 8; Portsmouth 7; Sheffield 5; Sheffield Hallam 3; Southampton 9–10; Strathclyde 6; Surrey 7; Warwick 6; York 6.

Advice to applicants and planning the UCAS personal statement Any interests you have in careers requiring mathematical ability could be mentioned, for example, engineering, computers (hardware and software) and business applications. Show determination, love of mathematics and an appreciation of the rigour of the course. Give details of your skills, work experience, positions of responsibility. A variety of non-academic interests to complement the applicant's academic abilities preferred. For non-UK students fluency in oral and written English required. **Manchester** Unit grades may form part of an offer. **Warwick** Offers for courses in Statistics (MORSE, Mathematics and Statistics) include achievement requirements in STEP and other requirements. Check university websites for latest information. See also **Appendix 3**.

Misconceptions about this course London (QM) Some believe that a study of mechanics is compulsory – it is not. **Surrey** Maths is not just about calculations: it focuses on reasoning, logic and applications. **York** Further maths is not required.

Selection interviews Yes Aberystwyth, Bath, Bristol UWE, Cambridge, Central Lancashire, City, Coventry, Durham, Exeter, Imperial London, Kingston, Lancaster, Leeds, London (King's), London (RH), Northampton, Nottingham, Oxford (Maths) 20%, (Maths Comp Sci) 31%, (Maths Phil) 25%, (Maths Stats) 17%, Sheffield, Southampton, Sussex, Warwick, York; **Some** Brighton, Bristol, Cardiff, East Anglia, Greenwich, Heriot-Watt, Kent, London (UCL), London LSE (rarely), London Met, Loughborough, Manchester Met, Newcastle, Salford; **No** Birmingham, Brunel, Dundee, Essex, Liverpool, Liverpool John Moores, Reading.

Interview advice and questions Questions are likely to be asked arising from the information you have given in your UCAS application and about your interests in the subject. Questions in recent years have included: How many ways are there of incorrectly setting up the back row of a chess board? A ladder on a rough floor leans against a smooth wall. Describe the forces acting on the ladder and give the maximum possible angle of inclination possible. There are three particles connected by a string; the middle one is made to move – describe the subsequent motion of the particles. What mathematics books have you read outside your syllabus? Why does a ball bounce? Discuss the work of any renowned mathematician. Balance a pencil on your index fingers and then try to move both towards the centre of the pencil. Explain what is happening in terms of forces and friction. See also **Chapter 6**. **Cambridge** If you could spend half an hour with any mathematician past or present, who would it be? **Oxford** (2011 Stats/Maths) Intake 174, 51% interviewed, 15.3% successful. (Maths Phil)

What makes you think I'm having thoughts? What was the most beautiful proof in A-level mathematics? I am an oil baron in the desert and I need to deliver oil to four different towns which happen to lie in a straight line. In order to deliver the correct amount to each town I must visit each town in turn, returning to my warehouse in between each visit. Where would I position my warehouse in order to drive the shortest possible distance? Roads are no problem since I have a friend who will build me as many roads as I like for free. **Southampton** Personal statements generate discussion points. Our interviews are informal chats and so technical probing is kept low key.

Reasons for rejection (non-academic) Usually academic reasons only. Lack of motivation. We were somewhat uneasy about how much mathematics he will remember after a Gap Year running a theatre in South Africa. **Birmingham** A poorly written and poorly organised personal statement.

AFTER-RESULTS ADVICE
Offers to applicants repeating A-levels **Higher** Brighton, Coventry, Essex, Glasgow, London Met, Salford, Strathclyde, Surrey, Swansea, Warwick; **Possibly higher** Cambridge (Hom), Durham, Lancaster, Leeds, Newcastle, Sheffield; **Same** Aberystwyth, Aston, Bath, Birmingham, Bristol, Brunel, Chester, East Anglia, Liverpool, Liverpool Hope, London (RH), Loughborough (usually), Manchester Met, Nottingham, Nottingham Trent, Oxford Brookes, Sheffield Hallam, Southampton, Stirling, Ulster, Wolverhampton, York; **No** Cambridge.

GRADUATE DESTINATIONS AND EMPLOYMENT (2011/12 HESA)
Graduates surveyed 4900 **Employed** 2170 **In voluntary employment** 140 **In further study** 1545 **Assumed unemployed** 440

Career note Graduates enter a range of careers. Whilst business, finance and retail areas are popular options, mathematicians also have important roles in the manufacturing industries. Mathematics offers the pleasure of problem-solving, the satisfaction of a rigorous argument and the most widely employable non-vocational degree subject. A student's view: 'Maths trains you to work in the abstract, to think creatively and to come up with concrete conclusions.' These transferable skills are much sought-after by employers. Employment prospects are excellent, with high salaries.

OTHER DEGREE SUBJECTS FOR CONSIDERATION
Accountancy; Actuarial Studies; Astronomy; Astrophysics; Computer Science; Economics; Engineering Sciences; Operational Research; Physics; Statistics.

MEDIA STUDIES

(including **Broadcasting** and **Journalism**; see also **Art and Design (General), Communication Studies/Communication, Computer Courses, Engineering (Acoustics and Sound), Film, Radio, Video and TV Studies, Information Management and Librarianship, Journalism, Photography**)

Intending Media applicants need to check course details carefully since this subject area can involve graphic design, illustration and other art courses as well as the media in the fields of TV, radio and journalism. Courses in Journalism include block and day release, evening/weekend magazine journalism, and photo journalism. Full details can be obtained by referring to www.nctj.com/courses.

Useful websites www.bbc.co.uk/jobs; www.newspapersoc.org.uk; www.ppa.co.uk; careers. thomsonreuters.com; www.nctj.com; www.ipa.co.uk; www.camfoundation.com; www.mediastudies. com.

NB The points totals shown to the left of the institutions are for ease of reference only. It must not be assumed that Tariff points are always used by institutions or that they can be substituted for an offer in grades. The level of an offer is not necessarily indicative of the quality of a course.

Check **Chapter 4** when choosing your university and **Chapter 7** on how to read the subject tables.

COURSE OFFERS INFORMATION

Subject requirements/preferences **GCSE** English and mathematics often required. **AL** No specified subjects required.

Your target offers and examples of courses provided by each institution

340 pts **East Anglia** – AAB–ABB (Transl Media Sp) (IB 32–33 pts)
Leeds – AAB 340 pts (Comms Media) (IB 35 pts)
London (Gold) – AAB–ABB 340–320 pts (Media Comm) (IB 34 pts)
Newcastle – AAB–ABB 340–320 pts (Media Comm Cult St) (IB 34–35 pts)
York – AAB 340 pts (Interact Media) (IB 35 pts)

320 pts **Bournemouth** – 320 pts (Film Prod Cnma) (IB 32 pts)
Cardiff – ABB 320 pts (Jrnl Media Sociol; Jrnl Media Cult St)
Central Lancashire – ABB (Spo Jrnl)
East Anglia – ABB (Media Pol; Transl Media Fr; Media Int Dev; Transl Media Jap; Media St) (IB 32 pts)
Glasgow – ABB 320 pts (Arts Media Inform) (IB 36 pts)
Lancaster – ABB 320 pts (Media Cult St; Film Media St) (IB 32 pts)
Leicester – ABB 320 pts (Comms Media Soty) (IB 32 pts)
Lincoln – 320 pts (Media Prod)
Liverpool – ABB 320 pts (Comm Media) (IB 33 pts)
London (RH) – ABB–ABbb (Media Arts) (IB 34 pts)
Nottingham – ABB (Int Media Comm St; Span Int Media Comms St) (IB 32 pts)
Surrey – ABB (Media Cult Soty) (IB 34 pts)
Sussex – ABB (Media Prac; Media St courses) (IB 34 pts)

300 pts **Aberystwyth** – 300–320 pts (Hist Media; Media Comms) (IB 30–32 pts)
Bournemouth – 300–320 pts (Media Prod)
Brighton – BBB (Media St; Env Media St; Media Engl Lit) (IB 32 pts)
Bristol UWE – 300 pts (Engl Jrnl) (IB 26 pts)
Brunel – BBB 300 pts (Comm Media St; Sociol Media St; Vis Efcts Mth Graph) (IB 32 pts)
Central Lancashire – BBB 300 pts (Media Prod) (IB 26 pts)
Essex – 300–320 pts (Media Cult Soc)
Hertfordshire – 300 pts (Mass Comm; Scrn Cult Media Prac)
Leeds Beckett – 300 pts (Media Comm Cult) (IB 26 pts)
Leicester – BBB (Media Sociol)
Liverpool Hope – 300 pts (Media Comm)
Loughborough – BBB–ABB (Comm Media St; Pub Engl) (IB 32 pts)
Northumbria – 300 pts (Media Jrnl) (IB 26 pts)
Oxford Brookes – BBB (Pub Media) (IB 31 pts)
Swansea – 300 pts (Media St courses; PR Media)

280 pts **Bath Spa** – 280–320 pts (Media Comms) (IB 26 pts)
Birmingham City – BBC 280 pts (Media Comm (Evnt Exhib Ind); Media Comm Jrnl; Media (Mus)) (IB 28 pts)
Bournemouth – 280–300 pts (Dig Media Des; Comm Media) (IB 30–31 pts)
Bristol UWE – 280–320 pts (Media Cult St; Media Jrnl)
Buckingham – BBC–BCC (Jrnl Comm St)
Edge Hill – BBC 280 pts (Media Mus Snd; Engl Media)
Edinburgh Queen Margaret – BBC (Media) (IB 28 pts)
Glasgow Caledonian – BBC (Media Comm) (IB 24 pts)
Gloucestershire – 280–300 pts (Multim Web Des)
Greenwich – 280 pts (Media Comm) (IB 28 pts)
Huddersfield – 280 pts (Adv Media Rel; Media Pop Cult) (IB 28 pts)
Hull – 280–300 pts (Media Cult Soty) (IB 28 pts)
Keele – BBC (Media Comm Cult) (IB 30 pts)

Check **Chapter 4** when choosing your university and **Chapter 7** on how to read the subject tables.

Kingston – 280 pts (Media Cult St)
Leeds Beckett – (Creat Media Tech) (IB 25 pts)
Lincoln – 280 pts (Film TV Jrnl Joint Hons)
London Met – 280 pts (Media St)
Nottingham Trent – 280 pts (Media) (IB 24 pts)
Oxford Brookes – BBC 280 pts (Comm Media Cult) (IB 30 pts)
Plymouth – 280 pts (Geog Media Arts)
Roehampton – 280 pts (Bus Mgt Dig Media) (IB 25 pts)
Salford – 280–320 pts (TV Rad) (IB 31 pts)
Sheffield Hallam – 280 pts (Jrnl; Media)
South Wales – BBC (Media Prod; Perf Media) (IB 25 pts)
Stirling – BBC 280 pts (Euro Film Media) (IB 32 pts)
Suffolk (Univ Campus) – 280 pts (Film Media) (IB 24 pts)
Teesside – 280 pts +interview (Broad Media Prod; Crea Dig Media; Media St; Perf Lv Rec Media)
Ulster – BBC (Media St courses)
260 pts **Bangor** – 260–300 pts (Media St courses)
Cardiff Met (UWIC) – 260 pts (Engl Contemp Media)
Central Lancashire – 240–260 pts (Engl Lang Jrnl)
Chichester – BCC (Media Cult St) (IB 30 pts)
Coventry – BCC 260 pts (Media Prod; Media Comm)
De Montfort – 260 pts (Media Comm; Jrnl) (IB 28 pts)
Derby – 260 pts (Media St; Media Prod)
Edge Hill – 260–280 pts (Media Joint Hons)
Edinburgh Queen Margaret – BCC (PR Media) (IB 28 pts)
Falmouth – 260–300 pts (Jrnl)
Keele – 260–300 pts (Media Comm)
Liverpool John Moores – 260 pts (Int Jrnl; Media Cult Comm) (IB 28 pts)
Manchester Met – 260–280 pts (Dig Media Comm; Dig Media Mark)
Nottingham Trent – 260 pts (Media Joint Hons) (IB 24 pts)
Plymouth – 260 pts (Media Arts) (IB 28 pts)
Sheffield Hallam – 260 pts (PR Media)
Sunderland – 260 pts (Media Prod (TV Rad); Int Jrnl; Media Prod (Vid N Media); Media St (Comb); Media Cult Comm; News Jrnl)
Winchester – 260–300 pts (Jrnl Med St; Media St Psy)
240 pts **Arts London** – 240 pts (Mag Pub; Fash Jrnl (Prt/Broad))
Bangor – 240–260 pts (Jrnl Media St)
Bolton – 240 pts (Media Writ Prod)
Bradford – 240 pts (Media St courses)
Brighton – CCC 240 pts (Media St Sociol/Educ)
Buckingham – CCC 240 pts (Comm Media St; Comm Media Jrnl)
Canterbury Christ Church – CCC 240 pts (Media Comm) (IB 24 pts)
Central Lancashire – 240–260 pts (Film Media; Photo Jrnl)
Chester – 240–280 pts (Media St) (IB 26 pts)
Cumbria – 240 pts (Wldlf Media) (IB 24 pts)
East London – 240 pts (Media Crea Ind; Media St)
Edinburgh Napier – CCC (Dig Media) (IB 27 pts)
Glyndŵr – 240 pts (Broad Jrnl Media Comms; Broad Jrnl Scrn St)
Kingston – 240–280 pts (Media Tech) (IB 26–28 pts)
London South Bank – 240 pts (Media Cult St; Mgt Media St; Prnt Onln Jrnl)
Manchester Met – 240–280 pts (Film Media St; Media Tech) (IB 28 pts)
Northampton – 240–280 pts (Media St courses; Media Prod)
Portsmouth – 240–300 pts (Media St Joint Hons; Sociol Media St)
Robert Gordon – CCC (Media)
Roehampton – 240 pts (Media Cult)

St Mary's – 240 pts (Media Arts) (IB 28 pts)
Sheffield Hallam – 240 pts (Dig Media Prod)
Southampton Solent – 240 pts (Media; Dig Cult Comms; Spo Jrnl; Cult Prod)
Winchester – 240-300 pts (Media Prod) (IB 26-28 pts)
Wolverhampton – CCC (PR)
Worcester – 240-340 pts (Media Cult St) (IB 24 pts)
York St John – 240-280 pts (Media courses)
220 pts **Anglia Ruskin** – 220-260 pts (Media courses) (IB 24 pts)
Creative Arts – 220-240 pts (Media Arts; Spo Jrnl) (IB 24-30 pts)
Falmouth – 220 pts (Dig Media)
Leeds Trinity – 220-260 pts (Engl Media; Media Mark; Media)
St Mark and St John – 220 pts (Media St; Media Prod; Media Wrtg)
200 pts **Bedfordshire** – 200 pts (Media Prod courses; Media Prac (Mass Comm))
Creative Arts – 200 pts (Arts Media) (IB 24-30 pts)
Hull (Coll) – 200 pts (Jrnl Dig Media; Filmm Crea Media Prod; Broad Media)
Leeds Beckett – 200 pts (Broad Media Tech) (IB 24 pts)
Middlesex – 200-240 pts (Media Cult St; Pub Media Cult St; Jrnl Media; Crea Media Writ; Pub Jrnl Media)
Plymouth (CA) – 200 pts (Fash Media Mark)
Portsmouth – 200-280 pts (Dig Media)
Trinity Saint David (Swansea) – 200 pts (Interact Dig Media)
West London – 200 pts (Broad; Media St)
Wolverhampton – 200 pts (Media Cult St; Media Comm St; Film Media Cult St)
180 pts **Farnborough (CT)** – 180-200 pts (Media Prod Mus; Media Prod)
Manchester (Coll) – 180 pts (Actg Media)
Trinity Saint David – 180-300 pts (Media St courses)
160 pts **Abertay** – CC (Media Cult Soty) (IB 26 pts)
Arts London – 160 pts (Media Cult St)
East London – 160 pts (Media Tech)
Peterborough (Reg Coll) – 160 pts (Media)
Ravensbourne – AA-CC (Edit Pst Prod) (IB 28 pts)
South Essex (Coll) – 160 pts (Crea Writ Media)
UHI – CC (Gael Media St)

Alternative offers
See **Chapter 7** and **Appendix 1** for grades/UCAS Tariff points information for the International Baccalaureate, Scottish Highers/Advanced Highers, the Welsh Baccalaureate, the Irish Leaving Certificate, the Cambridge Pre-U Diploma, the Advanced Diploma and the Extended Project.

EXAMPLES OF FOUNDATION DEGREES IN THE SUBJECT FIELD
Bath; Bath Spa; Bedford (Coll); Bedfordshire; Birmingham (UC); Blackpool and Fylde (Coll); Bolton; Bournemouth; Bridgwater (Coll); Brighton; Bristol City (Coll); Bristol UWE; Bucks New; Central Lancashire; Cornwall (Coll); De Montfort; East Riding (Coll); Essex; Exeter (Coll); Falmouth; Glyndŵr; Greenwich; Hertfordshire; Highbury Portsmouth (Coll); Hopwood Hall (Coll); Hull (Coll); Leeds Beckett; Liverpool City (Coll); Llandrillo Cymru (Coll); Manchester (Coll); Neath Port Talbot (Coll); NEW (Coll); Newcastle (Coll); Northbrook (Coll); Norwich City (Coll); Nottingham New (Coll); Plymouth (CA); Sheffield (Coll); Somerset (Coll); South Cheshire (Coll); South Devon (Coll); South Essex (Coll); South Tyneside (Coll); Stockport (Coll); Strathclyde; Suffolk (Univ Campus); Teesside; Truro (Coll); Wigan and Leigh (Coll); Yeovil (Coll); York (Coll).

CHOOSING YOUR COURSE (SEE ALSO CH.1)
Some course features
Bangor The BA in Creative Studies enables students to pursue a variety of related subject areas including creative writing, film studies, theatre studies, media and journalism or to combine modules from these programmes. These subjects are also offered as separate degrees.

Bath Spa The Creative Media Practice course offers a choice of two options from interaction design, digital photography, music technology, media production for TV and radio, PR and marketing for publishing and script-writing for TV and radio. There is also a degree in Media Communication.

Birmingham City Media and Communication courses have specialisms in journalism, media photography, web and new media public relations, radio production and television and music industries. There is also a separate course in Television Technology and Production with a sandwich placement and Multimedia Technology.

Bradford The Media Studies course offers options in several subjects including web, computer games, 3D, animation, film and TV. Courses cover technical, social and cultural aspects.

Brunel A course is offered in Communications and Media Studies with the course focusing on the social aspects of the media and new communications and information technologies. A substantial amount of the course involves practical work. A rigorous and demanding course in Journalism is also offered.

Coventry A course in Media and Communications offers modules in film, television, photography, journalism, public relations and video. There are also courses in Media Production and Journalism.

Creative Arts The Arts and Media degree is interdisciplinary allowing specialisms to be taken from Animation, Digital Film-making, Fine Art and Photography. The course is offered in Farnham.

Universities and colleges teaching quality See www.qaa.ac.uk; http://unistats.direct.gov.uk.

Top research universities and colleges (RAE 2008) See **Communication Studies/Communication**.

Examples of sandwich degree courses Bedfordshire; Birmingham City; Bournemouth; Bradford; Brighton; Brunel; Coventry; De Montfort; Gloucestershire; Greenwich; Hertfordshire; Huddersfield; Kingston; Leeds Beckett; Liverpool John Moores; Manchester Met; Nottingham Trent; Staffordshire; Surrey; Ulster; Worcester.

ADMISSIONS INFORMATION

Number of applicants per place (approx) Bath Spa 4; Birmingham 10; Bournemouth (Interact Media Prod) 24, (Multim Jrnl) 30; Bradford 13; Bristol UWE 20; Canterbury Christ Church 23; Cardiff 11; Cardiff Met (UWIC) 3; Central Lancashire 33; Chichester 6; Creative Arts 3; Cumbria 4; De Montfort 11; East London 27; Falmouth 4; Gloucestershire 25; Greenwich 12; Lincoln 4; London (Gold) 13; London (RH) 11; London South Bank 11; Northampton 4; Northumbria 14; Nottingham Trent 5; Plymouth City (Coll) 33; Portsmouth 5; Sheffield Hallam 56; South Essex (Coll) 10; Southampton Solent (Jrnl) 20, (Media Tech) 6; Strathclyde (Jrnl) 20; Teesside 33; Trinity Saint David (Swansea) 5; West Scotland 6; Westminster 44; Winchester 7.

Advice to applicants and planning the UCAS personal statement Work experience or work shadowing is important. Contact local newspaper offices to meet journalists and to discuss their work. Contact local radio stations and advertising agencies, read newspapers (all types) and be able to describe the different approaches of newspapers. Watch TV coverage of news stories and the way in which the interviewer deals with politicians or members of the public. Give your opinions on the various forms of media. School magazine and/or any published work should be mentioned. A balance of academic and practical skills preferred. Creativity, problem-solving, cultural awareness, communication skills and commitment required. (International students: Fluency in written and spoken English required.) See also **Communication Studies/Communication** and **Appendix 3**.

Misconceptions about this course Birmingham City That Media courses are soft options: they are not! **Cardiff Met (UWIC)** Some applicants believe that the course will automatically lead to a job in the media: it won't. This depends on the student developing other employment skills and experience. **Cumbria** This is not a Media Studies course: it is a highly practical media production course. **Lincoln** (Media Prod) BTEC applicants may think that this is a technology-based course.

Selection interviews Yes Birmingham City, Bournemouth, Creative Arts, East Anglia, London (Gold), London (RH), St Mark and St John, South Wales, Staffordshire, Trinity Saint David (Swansea), West London (group interview), York; **Some** Abertay, Anglia Ruskin, Bath Spa, Brunel, City, Huddersfield, London South Bank, Nottingham Trent, Salford, Sheffield Hallam, Sunderland, Wolverhampton; **No** Cardiff, Cardiff Met (UWIC), Chichester, Nottingham, Portsmouth, South Essex (Coll).

For a quick reference offers calculator, fold out the inside front cover.

Interview advice and questions Past questions include: Which newspapers do you read? Discuss the main differences between the national daily newspapers. Which radio programmes do you listen to each day? Which television programmes do you watch? Should the BBC broadcast advertisements? What do you think are the reasons for the popularity of *EastEnders*? Film or video work, if required, should be edited to a running time of 15 minutes unless otherwise stated. See also **Chapter 6**. **Cardiff Met (UWIC)** What is your favourite area in respect of popular culture? Are you considering taking up the work placement module? If so where would you plan to go? **Cumbria** Role of journalism in society. What is today's main news story? Who is Rupert Murdoch? **Lincoln** Give a written or verbal critique of a media product.

Reasons for rejection (non-academic) No clear commitment (to Broadcast Journalism) plus no evidence of experience (now proving to be essential). Mistaken expectations of the nature of the course. Can't write and doesn't work well in groups. Too specific and narrow areas of media interest, for example, video or script-writing. Lack of knowledge of current affairs. **Cardiff Met (UWIC)** Lack of experience in the field. Application arrived too late.

AFTER-RESULTS ADVICE

Offers to applicants repeating A-levels Same Abertay, Birmingham City, Cardiff, Cardiff Met (UWIC), Chester, Chichester, De Montfort, Huddersfield, Lincoln, Loughborough, Manchester Met, Nottingham Trent, St Mary's, Salford, South Essex (Coll), Staffordshire, Sunderland, Winchester, Wolverhampton.

GRADUATE DESTINATIONS AND EMPLOYMENT (2011/12 HESA)

Graduates surveyed 5390 **Employed** 2515 **In voluntary employment** 230 **In further study** 740 **Assumed unemployed** 700

Career note See **Film, Radio, Video and TV Studies.**

OTHER DEGREE SUBJECTS FOR CONSIDERATION

Advertising; Communication; English; Film, Radio, Video and TV Studies; Journalism; Photography; Public Relations.

MEDICINE

(including **Medical Sciences**; see also **Biological Sciences, Human Sciences/Human Biosciences**)

Medicine is a highly popular choice of degree subject and career. All courses listed below include the same areas of study and training and all lead to a qualification and career in medicine.

Medical schools aim to produce doctors who are clinically competent, who are able to see patients as people and have a holistic and ethical approach (including the ability to understand and manage each patient's case in a family and social context as well as in hospital), who treat patients and colleagues with respect, dignity and sensitivity, are skilled at teamwork and are prepared for continual learning. These aims in several ways reflect the qualities which selectors seek when interviewing applicants. In all cases, close attention will be paid to the confidential report on the UCAS application to judge the applicant's personality, communication skills, academic potential and commitment to a medical career. Methods of teaching may vary slightly, depending on the medical school. To achieve these aims, some medical schools adopt the system of self-directed learning (SDL) in which objectives are set to assess students' progress, and problem-based learning (PBL) which helps students to develop critical thinking and clinical problem-solving skills.

Whilst there is a core curriculum of knowledge, the first three years integrate scientific and clinical experience, and there are fewer formal lectures than before, with more group and individual work. For outstanding students without science A-levels, some pre-medical courses are available. Thereafter, for all, a period of pre-clinical studies leads on to clinical studies. Most medical schools also offer an extra year of study, usually in the middle of the medical degree, to enable students to research a scientific subject leading to an 'intercalated' BSc degree. Additionally, elective periods abroad in the final year can sometimes be taken.

Medical students' and doctors' advice to applicants
'I did not fully appreciate how diverse medicine is as a career. Everyone has their own particular reasons for wishing to pursue it but these will change as you progress through your career. There are many different pathways you can take which makes it all the more exciting... and daunting! Choose your university carefully; in most medical degrees you will only be based at university for the first two years and thereafter you will be in hospitals around the area so choose a city or an area you want to work and live in. Enjoy each aspect of your training and early career; the typical NHS pathway which is laid out in medical school is just one option.'

'The most important qualities for success in my and probably any career are communication, resilience and education. The people with whom you work and your relationships with them are more important than the speciality you practice.'

'Medicine is a career which can open many doors – as a family or hospital doctor, working in Africa treating children with infectious diseases, in a war zone, in a laboratory, in sport, in journalism, and in law. Going on to study law, to specialise in medical law, I have friends who have done all of these things.'

'Get to know what the real working lives of doctors are. The attributes needed to see sick and needy people. The fact that the NHS is a public and not a private organisation and what this means in the changing world of medical knowledge. Some of this is very difficult to learn in the sixth form but periods of work experience will help. In addition to talking to medical students and family friends who are doctors, browse through medical journals and medical websites. Every doctor has had their own individual experiences, good and bad, but the majority would still apply to medicine again if they were 17!'

Applicants for places in Medicine may select only **four** universities or medical schools.

Useful websites www.scicentral.com; www.ipem.ac.uk; www.bmj.com; www.admissionstestingservice.org; www.gmc-uk.org; www.nhscareers.nhs.uk.

NB The points totals shown to the left of the institutions are for ease of reference only. It must not be assumed that Tariff points are always used by institutions or that they can be substituted for an offer in grades. The level of an offer is not necessarily indicative of the quality of a course.

COURSE OFFERS INFORMATION
Subject requirements/preferences **GCSE** In all cases a good spread of science and non-science subjects will be expected at high grades.

Aberdeen English, mathematics, biology, physics or dual award science. Combinations of AB grades expected, especially in sciences.
Birmingham Five GCSEs at A* or A including chemistry, English language and mathematics normally at grade A. Dual science award grade A acceptable as an alternative to physics and biology.
Brighton and Sussex (MS) Mathematics and English at grade B, biology and chemistry.
Bristol Five A/A* grades to include mathematics, English and two sciences.
Cambridge Mathematics, physics, chemistry or dual science award.
Cardiff Four or five A* in nine GCSEs (minimum). English or Welsh at grade B, mathematics at grade B or above, grades AA in dual science or AAA in three sciences.
Dundee Chemistry and biology or human biology essential.
Durham See **Newcastle**.
East Anglia Six GCSE subjects at grade A or above including mathematics, English and two science subjects.
Edinburgh English, mathematics, biology, chemistry or dual science award at grade B or higher.
Glasgow English, chemistry, biology (preferred), mathematics and physics.
Hull York (MS) Six subjects at grades A*–C including English language at grade A or B, English literature at grade A, mathematics at grade B or higher plus chemistry and biology.

Medicine

Consult the Specialist

MPW is one of the UK's best known groups of independent sixth-form colleges. We offer a range of specialist services to those who have chosen a career in Medicine.

Specialist two-year and one-year A level courses

Detailed UCAS advice

"Insight into Medicine" work experience courses

Seminars on applications procedures and interview preparation

Interview training

Mander Portman Woodward

London	020 7835 1355
Birmingham	0121 454 9637
Cambridge	01223 350158

Getting into Medical School by MPW is published by Trotman Publishing

Check **Chapter 4** when choosing your university and **Chapter 7** on how to read the subject tables.

Imperial London Chemistry, biology, physics (or dual science award) plus mathematics and English. At least three subjects are required at grade A, and two subjects at grade B.

Keele Chemistry, physics, biology (dual science award acceptable, grades BB minimum), English language and mathematics at grade B minimum. A broad spread of subjects is expected with a minimum of four at grade A or A*.

Lancaster See **Liverpool**.

Leeds Six subjects at grade B minimum including English, mathematics, chemistry and biology or dual science award.

Leicester English language and sciences (including chemistry) or dual science award.

Liverpool Nine subjects at grades A–C, including dual science (or biology, chemistry and physics), English language and mathematics at grade B minimum.

London (King's) Grade B (minimum) in chemistry, biology and physics (or dual science award), English and mathematics.

London (QM) Six subjects at AB minimum grades including English, mathematics and science subjects.

London (St George's) Typically eight subjects at grade A are required including English language, mathematics and science subjects. Contact the admissions team for a more detailed breakdown of grade requirements.

London (UCL) English and mathematics at grade B minimum plus grade C in a foreign language.

Manchester Seven subjects with five at grades A/A*. Chemistry, biology and physics required at either AS or GCSE grade C minimum, with English and mathematics at grade B minimum.

Newcastle At least five subjects with grades AAAAB to include English, mathematics and either biology, chemistry, physics or dual science award.

Nottingham Six subjects at grade A/A* to include biology, chemistry and physics or dual science award. (Grade A AS physics can compensate for a B at GCSE.)

Oxford Chemistry, mathematics, biology and physics or dual science award acceptable.

Queen's Belfast Chemistry, biology, mathematics and either physics or dual science award.

St Andrews Chemistry, biology, mathematics and physics. If mathematics and biology are not offered at A2 then each must have been passed at grade B or higher. English is required at grade B or higher.

Sheffield At least six subjects at grade A. English, mathematics, chemistry and a science or a dual science award required.

Southampton A minimum of seven subjects at grade A including English, mathematics and dual science award or equivalent. (Widening Access course BM6) Five GCSEs at grade C including English, mathematics and dual science award or equivalent. (Students join the five-year programme on completion of Year Zero.)

AL See **Your target offers and examples of courses provided by each institution** below. Candidates applying for A104 courses at **Bristol**, **Cardiff**, **Dundee**, **East Anglia**, **Edinburgh**, **London (King's)**, **Manchester**, **Sheffield** and **Southampton** are not accepted if they are offering more than one laboratory-based subject (check with university). **London (UCL)** Mathematics and further mathematics will not both be counted towards three AL subjects.

Applicants should note that A-levels in general studies and critical thinking may not be accepted for entry.

Medicine Foundation courses These are designed for students who have demonstrated high academic potential but who have taken non-science subjects or a combination including no more than one of biology, chemistry and physics.

Other requirements: See **Health Requirements** below; DBS clearance is also required.

NB Home and EU-funded students applying for entry to Medicine are required by many universities to sit either the UKCAT or BMAT tests before applying. See **Your target offers and examples of courses provided by each institution** below, **Chapter 5** and **Chapter 6** for further information.

Your target offers and examples of courses provided by each institution

420 pts **Queen's Belfast** – AAAa incl chem +sci/maths +UKCAT (Med 5 yrs) (IB 36 pts HL 666)

410 pts **East Anglia** – AAAb incl biol+sci +UKCAT (Med 5 yrs) (IB 34 pts HL 666)

Edinburgh – AAAb incl chem +maths/sci 410 pts +UKCAT (Med 5/6 yrs) (IB 37 pts HL 766)

Hull York (MS) – AAAb incl chem+biol +UKCAT (Med) (IB 36 pts HL 665)

Imperial London – AAAb incl biol/chem +sci/maths +BMAT (Med) (IB 38 pts HL 665)

Keele – A*ABb–AAAb incl chem+biol +maths/phys (Med) (IB 35 pts HL 665)

Lancaster – AAAb incl chem+biol (Med Srgy) (IB 36 pts HL 666) Application through **Liverpool**. See **Admissions tutors' advice** below

Liverpool – AAAb incl chem+biol (Med 6 yrs) (IB 36 pts HL 666)

London (King's) – AAAb incl chem+biol (Med 5 yrs) (IB 35 pts HL 666)

London (QM) – AAAb incl chem/biol +sci +UKCAT (Med 5 yrs) (IB 38 pts HL 666)

London (St George's) – AAAb–BBCb incl chem+biol +UKCAT (Med 5 yrs) (HL 666)

380 pts **Birmingham** – A*AA–AAA incl chem+biol (Med 5 yrs) (IB 36 pts HL 18 pts)

Cambridge – A*AA incl chem +sci/maths +BMAT (Med 6 yrs) (IB 40–41 pts HL 776)

Exeter – A*AA–AAA +UKCAT (Med) (IB 38–36 pts)

London (UCL) – AAAe incl chem+biol (Med 6 yrs) (IB 38 pts)

Oxford – A*AA incl chem +sci/maths +BMAT (Med 6 yrs) (IB 39 pts HL 766)

Plymouth – A*AA–AAA incl chem +biol/phys +UKCAT (Med Srgy) (IB 38–36 pts)

360 pts **Aberdeen** – AAA chem +1 from biol/maths/phys +UKCAT (Med 5 yrs) (IB 36 pts HL 666 chem)

Brighton and Sussex (MS) – AAA 360 pts +UKCAT (Med 5 yrs) (IB 36 pts HL 6 biol 6 chem)

Bristol – AAA incl chem +biol/phys (Med 5 yrs) (IB 37 pts HL 666)

Cardiff – AAA incl chem/biol +sci +UKCAT (Med 5 yrs) (IB 36 pts HL 18 pts)

Cardiff – AAA (Med 6 yrs) (IB 36 pts HL 18 pts)

Dundee – AAA incl chem+sci +UKCAT (Med 5 yrs; Med 6 yrs incl Pre-Med Year) (IB 37 pts HL 666)

Durham – see **Newcastle** below

Glasgow – AAA incl chem +sci/maths +UKCAT (Med 5 yrs) (IB 36 pts)

Leeds – AAA incl biol+chem +UKCAT (Med 5 yrs) (IB 36 pts HL 6 chem)

Leicester – AAA incl chem +AS biol +UKCAT (Med 5 yrs) (IB 36 pts HL 6 chem 6 biol)

London (King's) – AAA–BBC 360–280 pts (Med Ext Prog 6 yrs) (IB 32 pts)

Manchester – AAA incl chem +sci/maths +UKCAT (Med 5 yrs) (IB 37 pts HL 766)

Newcastle – AAA incl chem/biol +UKCAT (Med Srgy 5 yrs) (IB 38 pts HL 6 chem) Offered through a partnership between **Newcastle** and **Durham** Universities (only Phase I of II available at **Durham**)

Nottingham – AAA incl chem+biol +UKCAT (Med 5 yrs) (IB 36 pts HL 666)

St Andrews – AAA incl chem +sci/maths (Med 5/6 yrs) (IB 38 pts HL 766)

Sheffield – AAA incl chem+sci +UKCAT (Med) (IB 37 pts HL 6)

Sheffield – AAA (Med Fdn Yr) (IB 37 pts HL 6)

Southampton – AAA incl chem+biol +UKCAT (Med 5 yrs) (IB 36 pts HL 18 pts)

340 pts **Manchester** – AAB 340 pts (Med 6 yrs) (IB 35 pts HL 666)

320 pts **East Anglia** – ABB (Med +Fdn Yr) (IB 32 pts)

Alternative offers

See **Chapter 7** and **Appendix 1** for grades/UCAS Tariff points information for the International Baccalaureate, Scottish Highers/Advanced Highers, the Welsh Baccalaureate, the Irish Leaving Certificate, the Cambridge Pre-U Diploma, the Advanced Diploma and the Extended Project.

CHOOSING YOUR COURSE (SEE ALSO CH.1)

Some course features

NB See **Chapter 6** for details of admissions tests to be taken **before** application.

Aberdeen Phase 1 covers the fundamentals of medical sciences followed in Phase 2 by the principles of clinical medicine. Clinical Teaching and Patient contact from Year 1. An intercalated BSc Medical Sciences degree is offered with placements across the Highlands and Islands.

Brighton Brighton and Sussex Medical School students are members of both universities. The course offers an integrated programme of academic and clinical experience with students working with patients from the first term. From Year 3, students are based at the Royal Sussex County Hospital in Brighton. Experience of medical practice in different medical settings in the UK or abroad takes place in Year 4.

Keele The five-year course has five themes, which run through the course: (1) scientific basis of medicine, (2) clinical communication, (3) individual communication and population health, (4) quality and efficiency in healthcare and (5) ethics, personal and professional development. There is also a Health Foundation year.

London (St George's) The MBBS has been designed to enhance the integration between scientific and clinical disciplines and to develop self-directed learning skills.

Newcastle Phase 1 (two years) of the medical course is taken at either Newcastle or Stockton. Students come into contact with patients at the start of their course, being attached to a GP and accompanying them on some of their rounds. Clinical applications are emphasised throughout the course alongside basic sciences. Students not taking science subjects may apply for the pre-medical course. See also **Durham** below.

Oxford The course in Medicine lasts six years. The pre-clinical course lasts three years. This is followed by the clinical course, which is based in the John Radcliffe Hospital. A significant part of this course is examined by continuous assessment.

St Andrews Medical Sciences is a three-year degree course and leads to the ordinary degree of BSc in three years or to an Honours degree in four years. Studies cover molecular biochemistry, human anatomy and human physiology. Half of graduates progress to a clinical place at Manchester University Medical School to follow the three-year clinical course, the remainder have a place at one of the four medical schools in Scotland, almost a third at Edinburgh.

Universities and colleges teaching quality See www.qaa.ac.uk; http://unistats.direct.gov.uk.

Top research universities and colleges (RAE 2008) (Pre-clinical and Human Biological Sciences) Oxford; London (UCL); Manchester; London (QM); London (King's); Bristol; Liverpool; Sussex.

(Hospital-based Clinical subjects) Edinburgh; Cambridge; London (UCL); Oxford; Imperial London; London (King's); Birmingham; London (QM); Aberdeen; Manchester; Newcastle; Southampton; Bristol.

ADMISSIONS INFORMATION

Number of applicants per place (approx) Aberdeen 9; Brighton and Sussex (MS) 10; Bristol (Med) 14, (Pre-Med) 30; Cambridge 6; Cardiff 8; Dundee 7; East Anglia 7; Edinburgh 11; Glasgow 8; Imperial London 7; Leicester 15; Liverpool 8; London (QM) 5; Manchester 7; Newcastle 10; Nottingham 9; St Andrews 8.

Numbers of applicants (a UK **b** EU (non-UK) **c** non-EU **d** mature) Birmingham **a**5 **b**25, (Grad entry) 12; Hull York (MS) **a**130 **b**130 **c**10; Leeds **a**2156 **b**97 **c**352 **d**488; London (King's) **a**311 **b**311 **c**25; London (St George's) **a**3200 **b**250 **c**260 **d**1950; Oxford **a**26% success rate **c**10; Queen's Belfast **a**4 **c**(a small number of places are allocated); Sheffield **a**17 (ave 30 applicants per place for 6yr courses); Cambridge **c**22; London (UCL) **c**24.

Admissions tutors' advice Policies adopted by all medical schools are very similar. However, a brief outline of the information provided by admissions tutors is given below. Further information should be obtained direct from institutions. Applicants wishing to contact medical schools should do so either by letter or by telephone and not by email.

Aberdeen Applicants must take the UKCAT in the year of application. This also applies to those students seeking deferred entry and those who are reapplying. In the past, students with scores between 513 and 776 have been called for interview for 162 places. Applicants to show a knowledge of the core qualities required by doctors and evidence of teamwork and non-academic pursuits. Overseas applicants may be interviewed abroad. Interviews last about 15 minutes. Total intake 152 including 12 international students. Most offers made in March. Points equivalent results not accepted. Re-sits only accepted in exceptional circumstances. International students English language entry requirement (or equivalent): IELTS 7.0. Minimum age on entry 17 years 5 months. Clinical teaching and patient contact in Year 2.

Check **Chapter 4** when choosing your university and **Chapter 7** on how to read the subject tables.

Birmingham Non-academic interests and extra-curricular activities noted in addition to academic factors. General studies not accepted. Interviews last about 15 minutes with three interviewers: a GP, a surgeon and a student. Approximately 1000 called for interview; 25 places for EU students and 12 for graduate entry. 10% take a year off which does not jeopardise the chances of an offer but candidates must be available for interview. Preference for AS candidates with AAAA. Re-sit candidates who failed by a small margin are only considered in exceptional circumstances. Transfers of undergraduates from other medical schools not considered. International applicants must show a good standard of written and spoken English. Second time applicants considered if not previously rejected at interview.

Brighton and Sussex (MS) All applicants required to have grade B in maths and English GCSE. Candidates are interviewed if they have passed the first two stages of assessment (academic and personal statement). Interviews for Medicine are currently held in January, February and March. Re-sit applicants are welcome to apply but only if they have dropped in one grade and one subject (eg AAB). Applicants with lower grades but re-sitting can apply to us once they have re-sat their subjects and obtained AAA. All Year 1 medical school students are guaranteed accommodation as long as they apply by the deadline (some students who live in the local area may not be able to apply for accommodation due to more applicants requiring housing than rooms available). Teaching is 'systems integrated' so students are exposed to the clinical environment from Year 1. Cadaver dissection is also part of the course from Year 1, so students get a real understanding of human anatomy, enhancing their learning experience. As the medical school is small, so are class sizes, meaning that students have a strong relationship with academic and support staff.

Bristol No places are offered without an interview. The top 10% of applicants are called for an interview lasting 15 minutes; the remainder grouped into three categories: 'high reserve', 'hold' and 'unsuccessful' – some from the first two categories will be interviewed. Full details of the interview process are offered on the Bristol website. Widening participation panel considers appropriate candidates, an additional 50 of whom will be interviewed. Criteria for selection: realistic and academic interest in medicine, commitment to helping others, wide range of interests, contribution to school/college activities, personal achievements. Interview criteria: reasons for wanting to study Medicine, awareness of current developments, communication skills, self-confidence, enthusiasm and determination to study, ability to cope with stress, awareness of the content of the course and career. General studies and critical thinking not acceptable. Subject content overlap (eg biology/PE/sports science) not allowed. Deferred entry welcomed (except for A101 (Graduate Entry)) but applicants must be available for interview. Points equivalent results not accepted. International students English language requirement (or equivalent): IELTS 7.5.

Cambridge Most applicants for Medicine at Cambridge have at least three science/mathematics A-levels and some colleges require this or ask for particular A-level subject(s). The standard course is offered to all colleges except Homerton and Hughes Hall. Normally two interviews, of 20 minutes each. Films of interviews on www.cam.ac.uk/interviews/. 80% of applicants are interviewed and tests may be set or school/college essays submitted. Gap Year acceptable but for positive reasons. Clinical studies from Year 4; 50% of students continue at the Cambridge Clinical School (Addenbrooke's Hospital).

Cardiff Admission is determined by a combination of academic performance, non-academic skills, knowledge and completion of the UKCAT test. Great emphasis placed on evidence of a caring nature and exposure to hospital/health environments. Applicant's comment: 'Two interviewers and a 15-minute interview. Mainly questions on "Why Medicine?"' Points-equivalent results not accepted. Clinical studies from Year 1.

Dundee A fully integrated hospital and medical school. Preference given to candidates who achieve the right grades at the first sitting. A system of mini-interviews has been introduced which enable students separate opportunities to sell themselves. Deferred entry acceptable. Clinical attachments in Year 4. World-wide experience in final year electives.

Durham (See also **Newcastle**) The medical course is offered in partnership with Newcastle University. Applicants can apply to the Durham or Newcastle campus. Study is at Queen's Campus, Stockton.

Preference given to applicants with relevant work experience in caring environment, hospital, voluntary capacity or through previous employment. Particular interest in recruiting local students, either school leavers or mature students. Interviews at Stockton with two selectors; may include a written personal qualities assessment test (PQA). Graduate applicants with a 2.2 degree are not accepted even if they possess a master's degree or a PhD. Applicants from non-EU countries must apply to Newcastle where there is a quota of places for overseas students. Clinical contact begins in Year 1.

East Anglia Criteria include academic requirements, capacity to cope with self-directed learning, teamwork, responsibility, motivation. Interview regarded as the acid test; seven stations are used for the interviews, candidates visit each station for one question with six minutes at each station. Two scenario questions (see www.med.uea.ac.uk/mbbs/mbbs application). English entry requirement IELTS 7.5. Clinical experience from Year 1. Re-sits considered if grades of BBB were obtained at the first sitting. Those re-sitting three A-levels require predictions of A*AA, two A-levels A*A, one A-level A*.

Edinburgh All examination grades must be achieved at the first sitting; only in extenuating circumstances will re-sits be considered. Equal weighting given to academic and non-academic criteria. Non-academic criteria score based on personal qualities and skills, evidence of career exploration prior to application, breadth and level of non-academic achievements and interests. Work experience and work shadowing viewed positively but the admissions panel recognise that not all applicants have equal opportunities to gain such experience. Most school-leaving applicants are not interviewed. Graduate and mature applicants may be interviewed; 202 places available, one in seven receive an offer. International applicants not normally called for interview. Clinical experience from Year 1.

Exeter The Medical School admitted its first students in 2013 having previously formed part of the Peninsula Medical School with Plymouth University. Selection procedures include the assessment of UKCAT.

Glasgow General studies is not accepted as a third A-level. Formal work experience is desirable. An interest in caring for others is expected which can be demonstrated through voluntary or paid work in a community setting. Approximately 800 interviews of 15–20 minute duration take place from November to March with two interviewers. Applicants may be assessed against some or all of the following criteria: commitment to medicine, understanding of the core qualities of a doctor, team work/other interests and knowledge of the Glasgow curriculum. Applicants are ranked by UKCAT scores. Scores below the national average (2400–2500) are unlikely to be considered.

Hull York (MS) Students apply to HYMS not to either the University of Hull or York. Students allocated places at Hull or York by ballot for Years 1 and 2. Transfers from other medical schools not accepted. Disabilities listed on UCAS application do not affect the assessment of the application; 550 called for interview, 300 offered places. Interviews of 20 minutes with two people. Article to be read beforehand, with a question to follow. Formally structured interviews exploring academic ability, motivation, understanding of healthcare issues, communication skills, conscientiousness, empathy, tolerance and maturity. Questions are drawn from a bank of possible topics (sample questions available online prior to interview). A-level re-sits not usually accepted. Feedback to unsuccessful candidates after February. Clinical placements from Year 1. Non-EU applicants English language (or equivalent requirement) IELTS 7.5 with at least 7 in each component.

Imperial London 286 places. Fifteen-minute interviews with panel of four or five selectors. Not aimed at being an intimidating experience – an evaluation of motivation, capacity to deal with stress, evidence of working as a leader and team member, ability to multitask, likely contribution to university life, communication skills and maturity. Admissions tutor's comment: 'We look for resourceful men and women with wide interests and accomplishments, a practical concern for others and for those who will make a contribution to the life of the school and hospital.' Results within two weeks. Re-sit candidates must have applied to Imperial School of Medicine previously, have achieved at least CCC and have predictions of AAA in the winter re-sit examinations and have extenuating circumstances to explain previous failure in the referee's statement. Candidates may also write directly to the School. Clinical contact in Year 1.

Check **Chapter 4** when choosing your university and **Chapter 7** on how to read the subject tables.

Keele Keele is no longer in partnership with the Manchester Medical School. All applications are now submitted to Keele. There are 130 places available, 10 for international students (non-EU). There are three entry routes for Medicine: including a Health Foundation Year (A104) for home and international applicants without the science A-levels required for the five-year course (chemistry or biology and one subject from chemistry, biology, mathematics or physics) and with grades of AAB (not including chemistry beyond GCSE) although A-level biology is acceptable with non-science A-levels. Four GCSEs are also required at grades A/A* including English and mathematics at grade C or above. Successful completion of this course gives automatic entry to Year 1 of the five-year Medicine degree; 10 places are available on the graduate entry course for home/EU applicants who enter directly into module 2 of the five-year course. Graduates must offer a 2.1 Honours degree or better in a biomedically related science for entry to this course, although applicants with other backgrounds can be successful with appropriate prior study and preparation for GAMSAT. Re-sit candidates must achieve AAA. English requirement for international applicants is IELTS 7.0.

Lancaster The University delivers the curriculum of the Medical School of Liverpool University, with the academic base at Lancaster University and clinical placements in Lancashire and Cumbria. To apply, use Liverpool University's UCAS code and see www.liv.ac.uk/sme for course and application information.

Leeds UKCAT required. 223 home students plus 20 non-EU students. Admissions tutor's comment: 'Consider your motivation carefully – we do!' Good verbal, non-verbal and presentational skills required. Candidates should: (1) be able to report on some direct experience of what a career in medicine is about; (2) show evidence of social activities on a regular basis (eg, part-time employment, organised community experiences); (3) show evidence of positions of responsibility and interests outside medical and school activities. Disabled students should indicate their disability status on the UCAS form. Gap Years encouraged but candidates must be available for interview; 20% of all applicants interviewed. Points-equivalent results not accepted. International students English language requirement (or equivalent): IELTS 7.5. Re-applications accepted from students who have achieved the right grades. Re-sits only considered in exceptional circumstances and with good supporting evidence; offer AAA. Transfers from other medical schools not encouraged. Clinical practice begins in Year 4.

Leicester Interview lasts 20 minutes with two selectors (one doctor and one final-year medical student; both have had interview training). Interview not an academic test. Selectors each score independently on motivation, communication skills and suitability for a career in medicine. Gap Years acceptable. Re-sits considered only in exceptional circumstances; offer AAA. Transfers from other medical schools not accepted. Clinical work commences in Year 1.

Liverpool In addition to the 374 home/EU places that are available on the A100 Liverpool medical programme, 50 medical places are currently offered at Lancaster University. Students follow the Liverpool curriculum and graduate with a Liverpool degree. 2999 applications were made to Liverpool University (Code L41, course code A105) last year. Evidence of healthcare insight and awareness is necessary. Applicants wishing to take a Gap Year may be considered but applicants must be available for interview. The Liverpool A100 medical programme usually has 24 places available for international students. No international places are available on the Lancaster A105 programme. Under-qualified international students may be able to apply to Liverpool International College prior to placing an application for the Liverpool A100 medical programme. Applicants must meet minimum academic criteria and applications for the medical programme are placed via UCAS in the normal manner. For international students certain minimum language requirements for the course may exist (IELTS of no less than 7.0 in each component).

London (King's) Personal statement a significant factor in selection. Emphasis placed on appreciation of academic, physical and emotional demands of the course, commitment, evidence of working in a caring environment, communication skills and interaction with the general public. Approximately 30% of applicants are called for interview. 25 places for non-EU applicants and all of them are interviewed. Usually interviews are of 15–20 minutes duration with two interviewers. Clinical contact in Year 1.

London (QM) Barts and the London School of Medicine: Personal statement a significant factor in selection. 'You are expected to write your own, with an honest reflection of your strengths and interests and you will be closely questioned on this statement at interview. We don't want people who are simply good at science. High grades are no guarantee of a place.' For interview, applicants are ranked by their UKCAT score – no predetermined scores. Interview of 15–20 minutes. Re-sits only considered in exceptional cases; offer AAAb. Clinical experience from Year 1. 1600 applications are normally received each year. 800 (approx) are interviewed for the 283 places.

London (St George's) Applicants must be taking A-level chemistry and biology (or one to A-level and the other to AS-level). You will be required to complete your A-levels within two years of study and the standard offer is AAA and b in a distinct AS-level. Applicants must have an average grade of A across their top eight GCSEs including English language, maths and double award or the single sciences. Applicants are also required to take the UKCAT test in the year of application. Applicants who meet our A-level and GCSE requirements and achieve our required overall and section scores in UKCAT will be offered an interview. All offers are made post-interview. Applicants are expected to have relevant work experience which is assessed at interview. The English language requirement for international students is IELTS 7.0 with no section less than 6.5. Deferred entry welcome. Medicine (six years, including Foundation year) is for mature non-graduate students only. Medicine (four years, Graduate stream) is for graduates with a 2.2 Hons degree in any discipline. Graduates are not eligible for the five-year Medicine programme. UKCAT selection and overall scores for entry were introduced for the five-year Medicine programme for 2012 onwards.

London (UCL) All candidates are required to take the BMAT. Three selectors interview applicants, each interview lasting 15–20 minutes; 30% of applicants interviewed. Qualities sought include motivation, awareness of scientific and medical issues, ability to express and defend opinions, maturity and individual strengths. Deferred entry for good reason is acceptable. Repeat applications only considered if candidate has previously received and held a firm offer from Royal Free or University College Medical School. Minimum age of entry 18 years. Transfers from other medical schools not accepted. International students may take the University Preparation Certificate for Science and Engineering (UPCSE) which is the minimum entry requirement for entry to Medicine. 24 places for non-EU applicants. Clinical attachments start in Year 3.

Manchester Minimum age of entry 17 years; 380 places for 2700 applicants. Interviews with three selectors last about 15 minutes. Mitigating circumstances regarding the health or disposition of the candidate should appear on the referee's report. If you feel unwell before the interview inform the admissions tutor and the interview will be re-scheduled; pleas of infirmity cannot be accepted after the interview! Candidates should be aware of the advantages and disadvantages of problem-based learning and opinions may be asked. Ethical questions may be raised. Decisions will be made by the end of March. Re-sit offers only made to applicants who received an offer after interview the previous year and who marginally failed to achieve the required grades; increasingly such offers are only made in the light of extenuating circumstances. Second-time applicants should include their previous UCAS number on their statement. Clinical attachments from Year 3.

Newcastle (See also **Durham**) 225 places at Newcastle; 102 places at Durham. Applicants can apply to spend Phases 1 and 2 at either Newcastle or the Durham Stockton campus. Applicants' comments: (Durham): 'Two interviewers and a 25-minute interview. Very relaxed interview. Stockton campus small. Good community spirit but some way from Durham'; (Newcastle): 'I had an interview with two selectors who had a gentle, helpful manner. I didn't feel under pressure but felt stretched.' Retakes not considered except in special circumstances. Deferred entry accepted. Consideration given to candidates who have overcome significant disadvantages (eg caring for parents with ill health). Clinical experience from Year 3.

Nottingham 246 places. Critical thinking and general studies not acceptable. Candidates requesting deferred entry are expected to undertake a constructive year. No offers are made without an interview. Candidates receive preliminary online questionnaire to be completed. Interviews are 15 minutes with two selectors. Re-sit applicants who have previously applied will be reconsidered but only in extenuating circumstances. Deferred entry acceptable. International students English language requirement (or equivalent): IELTS 7.5 (with no less than 7.0 in each element). No transfers accepted from other medical schools. Clinical experience from Year 1. Applicant's comments: 'I had one interview. There were two interviewers: the first asked me questions based on my personal statement, the second asked no scientific questions, focusing on the problems of the NHS and asking how I would deal with certain problems. He finally asked me to convince him why he should offer me a place.'

Oxford Critical thinking and general studies are not acceptable. BMAT required. Biology is recommended at AS-level. 425 applicants called for interview on the basis of academic performance, test score and information on the application form. Ratio of interviewees to places approximately 2.5 to 1. No student admitted without an interview. All colleges use a common set of selection criteria: 26% success rate. Candidate's comment (Lincoln College): 'Two interviewers and two interviews. Questions covered my hobbies and social life, and scientific topics to test my logical train of thought. A great university, but it's not the be-all and end-all if you don't get in.' Clinical experience commences in Year 4.

Plymouth The Plymouth University Peninsula School of Medicine and Dentistry opened for entry in 2013. The typical offers published are not necessarily the threshold for selection for interview. UKCAT must be taken.

Queen's Belfast Majority of applicants are school-leavers; 95% from Northern Ireland. When considering applicants' GCSE performance, the best nine subjects will be scored on the basis of 4 points for an A* and 3 points for an A. Points will also be given or deducted on each UKCAT paper. Offers for re-sitting applicants will be restricted. These applicants will have been expected to have missed their offer by one grade. A proportion of candidates will be called for interview. Interviews last about 15 minutes. A small number of places are allocated to non-EU applicants. Number of places restricted for re-sit applicants who have narrowly missed an offer at Queen's. Clinical experience from Year 1.

St Andrews Medical Science students take a full three-year programme leading to BSc (Hons), followed by clinical medicine at one of its partner medical schools. Interviews last about 20 minutes with two or three selectors. Special attention given to international students and those who achieve qualifications at more than one sitting. As far as possible the interview panel will reflect the gender and ethnic distribution of candidates for interview.

Sheffield Applications processed between October and end of March. Candidates may send additional information concerning extenuating circumstances or health problems via the University's Disrupted Studies form which can be found at: www.shef.ac.uk/undergraduate/apply/applying/disrupted. Interviews last 20 minutes with up to three selectors. A2 re-sits are not accepted. Gap Year acceptable; medicine-related work very helpful. Clinical experience from Year 1. For more information, please see: www.shef.ac.uk/medicine/prospective_ug.

Southampton Only mature, non-graduate applicants are selected for interview. UKCAT required. All applicants should show in their UCAS personal statement and reference that they are (1) self-motivated and have initiative, (2) literate and articulate, (3) able to interact successfully with others, (4) that they have learnt from their experiences with people in health and social care settings. Deferred entry accepted. Candidates who wish to change their year of entry should submit requests before mid-March. Patient contact from Year 1.

Swansea Graduate entry only.

Warwick Graduate entry only.

Advice to applicants and planning the UCAS personal statement (See also **Admissions tutors' advice**) Nearly all universities now require either the UKCAT or BMAT entry tests to be taken before applying for Medicine. Check websites (www.ukcat.ac.uk; www.bmat.org.uk) for details of test dates and test centres and with universities for their requirements. It is essential that you check for the latest information before applying and that you give yourself plenty of time to make arrangements for sitting these tests (see also **Chapter 6**).

Admissions tutors look for certain personal qualities (see Admissions tutors' advice) and these will emerge in your personal statement, at the interview and on your school or college reference. There should be evidence of scientific interest, commitment, enthusiasm, determination, stability, self-motivation, ability to organise your own work, interest in the welfare of others, communication skills, modesty (arrogance and over-confidence could lead to rejection!), breadth of interest, leadership skills, stamina, good physical and mental health.

Some kind of first-hand experience in a medical setting is almost obligatory for those applying for Medicine (see also under Admissions tutors' advice). Depending on your personal contacts in the medical profession, this could include observing operations (for example, orthopaedic surgery), working in hospitals and discussing the career with your GP. Remember that your friends and relatives may have medical conditions that they would be willing to discuss with you – and all this will contribute to your knowledge and show that you are informed and interested. Read medical and scientific magazines and keep up-to-date with important current issues – AIDS, swine 'flu, assisted dying, abortion. Community work, clubs, societies, school and social activities should be mentioned. Show that you have an understanding of the role of health professionals in society and the social factors that influence health and disease. And finally, a comment from one admissions tutor: 'Don't rush around doing things just for your CV. If you are a boring student, be an incredibly well-read boring student! You can play netball, rugby, hockey, make beautiful music and paint with your feet, but if you fail to get the grades you'll be rejected.'

Bristol Deferred places are limited. Late applications may not be accepted.

Misconceptions about this course **Liverpool** Some applicants think that three science subjects at A-level are required to study Medicine – wrong! **London (St George's)** That you should be white, middle class and male: 60% of medical students are now female and 53% of our students are not white.

Selection interviews **Yes** Birmingham, Dundee, East Anglia, Exeter, Oxford (13%), Plymouth; **No** Edinburgh.

Interview advice and questions Questions will vary between applicants, depending on their UCAS statements and their A/AS-level subjects. Questions are likely to relate to A-level specific subjects, general medicine topics and unconnected topics (see also Admissions tutors' advice). The following questions will provide a guide to the range of topics covered in past interviews. Outline the structure of DNA. What is meant by homeostasis? Is a virus a living organism? What has been the most important advance in biology in the last 50 years? What interests you about (i) science, (ii) biology, (iii) chemistry? Why did you choose the particular AS/A-level subjects you are doing? Why do you want to study Medicine/become a doctor? Do you expect people to be grateful? Why do you want to study here? Why should we take you? What do you do to relax? What do you do when you have three or four things to do, and they are all equally urgent? How do you balance work and all the outside activities you do? Do you agree with the concept of Foundation hospitals? What do you think about polyclinics? Do you think NHS doctors and staff should be able to take private patients? If you were in charge of finances for a large health authority, what would be your priorities for funding? If you had to decide between saving the life of a young child and that of an old person, what would you do? Would you treat lung cancer patients who refuse to give up smoking? What do you understand by 'gene therapy'? Can you give any examples? In your opinion what is the most serious cause for concern for the health of the UK? What do you want to do with your medical degree? What do you think the human genome project can offer medicine? Should we pay for donor organs? Where do you see yourself in 15 years' time? What was the last non-technical book you read? What is your favourite piece of classical music? List your top five novels. What is your favourite play? What politician do you admire the most? Who made the most valuable contribution to the 20th century? Why do you think research is important? Why is teamwork important? What do you think about the NHS's problems? Do you think that sport is important? What did you gain from doing work experience in a nursing home? What were the standards like? How does the medical profession deal with social issues? What societies will you join at university? How could you compare your hobby of rowing to medicine? Do you agree that it is difficult to balance the demands of being a doctor with those of starting a family? In doing a medical course, what would you find the most emotionally challenging aspect? How would you cope with emotional strain? Who should have priority for receiving drugs in a flu epidemic/pandemic? How would you deal with the death of a patient? What are stem cells? Why are they controversial? How is cloning done? What constitutes a human being? Describe an egg. How can you measure intelligence? How do we combat genetic diseases? How are genes actually implanted? What do you want to talk about? If you were a cardiothoracic surgeon, would you perform a heart by-pass operation on a smoker? What are the negative aspects of becoming a doctor? At some interviews essays may be set, eg (1) 'A scientific education is a good basis for a medical degree: discuss'; (2) 'Only drugs that are safe and effective should be prescribed to patients: discuss'. Should someone sell their kidney? How would you describe a human to a person from Mars? Should obese people have treatment on the NHS? Occasionally applicants at interview may be given scenarios to discuss (see **East Anglia** under Admissions tutors' advice). See also **Chapter 6**. **Oxford** Tell me about drowning. What do you think of assisted suicide? Would you give a 60-year-old woman IVF treatment? When are people dead?

Reasons for rejection (non-academic) Insufficient vocation demonstrated. No steps taken to gain practical experience relevant to medicine. Doubts as to the ability to cope with the stress of a medical career. Not enough awareness about the career. Lack of knowledge about the course. Applicant appears dull and lacking in enthusiasm and motivation. Lacking a caring, committed attitude towards people. No evidence of broad social, cultural or sporting interests or of teamwork. Poor or lack of communication skills. Arrogance. Over-confident at interview. Unrealistic expectations about being a doctor.

Age at entry Applicants must be 17 years old on 30 September of the year of entry. However, some medical schools stipulate 17 years 6 months, and a small number stipulate 18 years. Those considering entry at 17 would probably be advised to take a Gap Year. **London (St George's)** (Med with Fdn Yr) minimum age of applicants is 21.

Health requirements Medical schools require all students to have their immunity status for hepatitis B, tuberculosis and rubella checked on entry. Offers are usually made subject to satisfactory health screening for hepatitis B. In line with advice from the General Medical Council, students will not be admitted to courses who are found to be e-antigen positive when screened within the first week of the course. Candidates accepting offers should assure themselves of their immunity status.

Mature students Medical schools usually accept a small number of mature students each year. However, several, if not the majority, reject applicants over 30 years of age. Some medical schools accept non-graduates although A-level passes at high grades are usually stipulated. The majority of applicants accepted are likely to be graduates with a first or 2.1 degree. **Birmingham** Maximum age at entry is 30 years. **Bristol** Maximum age at entry is 30 years. **Leeds** Maximum age at entry is 30 years. Applicants should hold the required A-level grades or a high class science degree; 15–20 places. **Southampton** 36 places available, maximum age 40. Applicants with nursing qualifications should hold two grade B A-levels including chemistry. Mature students taking Access courses must achieve 70% in A2 chemistry.

Advice to graduate applicants Graduate applicants are considered by all medical schools. At some medical schools the Graduate Australian Medical Schools Admission Test (GAMSAT) and the Medical Schools Admissions Test (MSAT) are now being used to assess the aptitude of prospective applicants. Applicants at some institutions are selected on the basis of three criteria: (1) an Honours degree at 2.2 or above; (2) the GAMSAT score; (3) performance at interview. All applicants must be EU students. **London (St George's)** Some students think that science graduates are the only ones to do well in GAMSAT: 40% of those on the course do not have a science degree or A-levels; however, work experience is essential.

GRADUATE DESTINATIONS AND EMPLOYMENT (2011/12 HESA)
Clinical Medicine graduates surveyed 4810 **Employed** 4705 **In voluntary employment** 15 **In further study** 70 **Assumed unemployed** 10

Career note Applicants should also bear in mind that while most doctors do work in the NHS, either in hospital services or in general practice, many graduates choose to work in other fields such as public health, pharmacology, the environment, occupational medicine with industrial organisations, the armed services and opportunities abroad.

OTHER DEGREE SUBJECTS FOR CONSIDERATION

Biomedical/Medical Materials Science; Biology; Biotechnology; Clinical Sciences; Dentistry; Dietetics; Genetics; Health Sciences; Immunology; Medical Biochemistry; Medical Engineering; Medical Microbiology; Medical Physics; Medical Product Design; Medical Sciences; Medicinal Chemistry; Midwifery; Nursing; Nutrition; Occupational Therapy; Optometry; Osteopathy; Pharmacology; Pharmacy; Physiology; Physiotherapy; Psychology; Radiography; Speech Sciences; Sports Medicine; Veterinary Medicine; Virology – and Law! (The work of doctors and lawyers is similar: both are required to identify the relevant information – clinical symptoms or legal issues!)

MICROBIOLOGY

(see also **Biological Sciences, Biology, Biotechnology, Genetics**)

Microbiology is a branch of biological science specialising in the study of micro-organisms: bacteria, viruses and fungi. The subject covers the relationship between these organisms and disease and industrial applications such as food and drug production, waste-water treatment and future biochemical uses.

Useful websites www.sgm.ac.uk; www.nature.com/micro; www.microbes.info; www.asm.org; www.microbiologynetwork.com; see also **Biochemistry**, **Biological Sciences** and **Biology**.

NB The points totals shown to the left of the institutions are for ease of reference only. It must not be assumed that Tariff points are always used by institutions or that they can be substituted for an offer in grades. The level of an offer is not necessarily indicative of the quality of a course.

COURSE OFFERS INFORMATION

Subject requirements/preferences **GCSE** English and mathematics and science subjects. **AL** One or two mathematics/science subjects including chemistry and/or biology, required or preferred; grades sometimes specified.

Your target offers and examples of courses provided by each institution

360 pts **Edinburgh** – AAA-ABB 360-320 pts (Dev Cell Biol; Mol Biol) (IB 37-32 pts)

Imperial London – AAA (Microbiol) (IB 38 pts HL 6 biol +chem/maths)

Newcastle – AAA-AAB (Biomed Sci Med Microbiol) (IB 34-35 pts)

Sheffield – AAA-AAB 360-340 pts (Genet Microbiol; Mol Biol; Microbiol; Med Microbiol; Genet Mol Cell Biol) (IB 37-35 pts)

340 pts **Birmingham** – AAB-ABB 340-320 pts (Biol Sci (Microbiol)) (IB 34-35 pts)

Bristol – AAB-ABB 340-320 pts (Cell Mol Med; Path Microbiol; Med Microbiol) (IB 35-33 pts)

Cardiff – AAB-ABB 340-320 pts (Microbiol) (IB 34 pts HL 6 biol chem)

Glasgow – AAB (Mol Cell Biol (Plnt Sci); Microbiol; Mol Cel Biol (Biotech)) (IB 34 pts)

Nottingham – AAB-ABB (Microbiol) (IB 32-34 pts)

Warwick – AAB (Med Microbiol Virol) (IB 36 pts)

York – AAB-ABB (Biotech Microbiol) (IB 35 pts)

320 pts **Aston** – ABB-BBB 320-300 pts (Cell Mol Biol) (IB 33 pts)

East Anglia – ABB incl biol (Microbiol) (IB 32 pts HL 555)

Leeds – ABB-BBB (Med Microbiol; Microbiol Immun; Microbiol Virol; Microbiol) (IB 34-32 pts HL 16-15 pts)

Leicester – ABB (Med Microbiol; Biol Sci courses)

Liverpool – ABB (Microbl Biotech; Microbiol) (IB 33 pts HL 6 biol)

Manchester – AAA-ABB 320-360 pts (Microbiol; Microbiol (Yr Ind); Microbiol Modn Langs) (IB 37-33 pts)

Reading – ABB–AAC incl biol+sci 320 pts (Microbiol) (IB 32 pts)
Strathclyde – ABB (Microbiol; Immun Microbiol) (IB 32 pts)
Surrey – ABB (Microbiol; Microbiol (Med); Fd Sci Microbiol) (IB 34 pts)

300 pts **Aberdeen** – BBB 300 pts (Microbiol)
Aston – ABB–BBB 320–300 pts (Microbiol Immun) (IB 33 pts)
Dundee – BBB (Microbiol) (IB 34 pts)
Heriot-Watt – BBB (Biol Sci (Microbiol)) (IB 27 pts)
Queen's Belfast – BBB/BBCb (Microbiol) (IB 28 pts HL 555)

280 pts **Aberystwyth** – 280–320 pts (Microbiol; Microbiol Zool)
Hertfordshire – 280 pts (Mol Biol Genet)
Huddersfield – BBC 280 pts (Biol (Mol Cell))
Manchester Met – 280 pts (Microbiol Mol Biol) (IB 27 pts)
Nottingham Trent – 280 pts (Microbiol)
Staffordshire – 280 pts (Biol Microbiol)
Stirling – BBC (Cell Biol) (IB 32 pts)

260 pts **Bradford** – 260 pts (Med Microbiol; Med Cell Biol)
Edinburgh Napier – BCC 260 pts (Microbiol Biotech)
Glasgow Caledonian – BCC (Microbiol) (IB 32 pts)

240 pts **East London** – 240 pts incl biol **or** chem min B (Med Microbiol)
Westminster – CCC (Biol Sci (Microbiol)) (IB 26 pts)

200 pts **London South Bank** – 200 pts (Microbiol)
Wolverhampton – 200 pts (App Microbiol)

Alternative offers
See **Chapter 7** and **Appendix 1** for grades/UCAS Tariff points information for the International Baccalaureate, Scottish Highers/Advanced Highers, the Welsh Baccalaureate, the Irish Leaving Certificate, the Cambridge Pre-U Diploma, the Advanced Diploma and the Extended Project.

EXAMPLES OF FOUNDATION DEGREES IN THE SUBJECT FIELD
Petroc; St Helens (Coll); South Devon (Coll); Truro (Coll).

CHOOSING YOUR COURSE (SEE ALSO CH.1)
Some course features
Aston (Microbiol Immun) This course focuses on human and applied biology, human health and welfare. Three- and four-year courses are offered. There is a paid professional placement year.
Cardiff Modules offered in medical microbiology, genetic manipulation, ecology and microbial physiology and biochemistry. There is a professional training year.
Manchester Met Units cover medical microbiology, molecular biology, genetics, biodiversity and micro-organisms. A 12-month placement is offered in Year 3.
Nottingham Special topics in virology, molecular biology, and food and environmental microbiology.

Universities and colleges teaching quality See www.qaa.ac.uk; http://unistats.direct.gov.uk.

Top research universities and colleges (RAE 2008) See **Biological Sciences**.

Examples of sandwich degree courses See also **Biochemistry** and **Biological Sciences**. Aston; Bristol; Cardiff; Leeds; London South Bank; Manchester; Manchester Met; Nottingham Trent; Sheffield Hallam; York.

ADMISSIONS INFORMATION
Number of applicants per place (approx) Aberystwyth 5; Bradford 6; Bristol 5; Cardiff 4; Dundee 5; Leeds 7; Liverpool 3; Nottingham 7; Strathclyde 10; Surrey 4; Wolverhampton 4.

Advice to applicants and planning the UCAS personal statement Relevant experience, particularly for mature students. See **Biological Sciences** and also **Appendix 3**.

Selection interviews **Yes** Bristol, London South Bank, Surrey; **Some** Aberystwyth (mature students only), Cardiff, Leeds, Nottingham, Wolverhampton; **No** Dundee.

Interview advice and questions Examples of past questions include: How much does the country spend on research and on the armed forces? Discuss reproduction in bacteria. What do you particularly like about your study of biology? What would you like to do after your degree? Do you have any strong views on vivisection? Discuss the differences between the courses you have applied for. What important advances have been made in the biological field recently? How would you describe microbiology? Do you know anything about the diseases caused by micro-organisms? What symptoms would be caused by which particular organisms? See also **Chapter 6**.

AFTER-RESULTS ADVICE
Offers to applicants repeating A-levels **Higher** Bristol, Strathclyde, Warwick; **Possibly higher** East Anglia, Nottingham; **Same** Aberystwyth, Anglia Ruskin, Bradford, Cardiff, Leeds, Liverpool, Wolverhampton.

GRADUATE DESTINATIONS AND EMPLOYMENT (2011/12 HESA)
Graduates surveyed 425 **Employed** 155 **In voluntary employment** 0 **In further study** 135 **Assumed unemployed** 55

Career note See **Biology**.

OTHER DEGREE SUBJECTS FOR CONSIDERATION
Animal Sciences; Biochemistry; Biological Sciences; Biology; Biotechnology; Genetics; Medical Sciences; Medicine; Molecular Biology; Pharmacology; Physiology.

MUSIC
(including **Music Technology**; see also **Engineering (Acoustics and Sound)**)

Theory and practice are combined to a greater or lesser extent in most university Music courses and from which about 50% or more of graduates will go on to non-music careers. However, courses are also offered by conservatoires and schools of music where the majority of applicants are aiming to become professional musicians. For these courses the ability to perform on an instrument is more important than academic ability and offers are therefore likely to be lower. See also **Appendix 2**. Some applications are made through the Conservatoires Admissions Service (CUKAS): see **Chapter 6** for details.

Useful websites www.communitymusic.org; www.ism.org; www.roh.org.uk; www.nyo.org.uk; www.cukas.ac.uk.

NB The points totals shown to the left of the institutions are for ease of reference only. It must not be assumed that Tariff points are always used by institutions or that they can be substituted for an offer in grades. The level of an offer is not necessarily indicative of the quality of a course.

COURSE OFFERS INFORMATION
Subject requirements/preferences **GCSE** A foreign language and mathematics may be required. A good range of As and Bs for popular universities. **AL** Music plus an instrumental grade usually required.

Your target offers and examples of courses provided by each institution
380 pts **Cambridge** – A*AA (Mus) (IB 40–41 pts HL 776)
　　　　Imperial London – A*mathsAA (Phys Mus Perf) (IB 39 pts HL 666)
360 pts **Edinburgh** – AAA–ABB 360–320 pts (Maths Mus; Phys Mus; Hist Art Hist Mus)
　　　　　　(IB 37–32 pts)
　　　　London (King's) – AAA (Mus; Ger Mus) (IB 35 pts HL 666 mus)
　　　　Oxford – AAA (Mus) (IB 38–40 pts)
　　　　Southampton – AAA (Maths Mus) (IB 36 pts HL 18 pts)
　　　　Surrey – AAA 360 pts (Mus Snd Rec (Tonmeister)) (IB 37 pts HL 666)

340 pts **Birmingham** – AAA–AAB 340–360 pts (Mus) (IB 36–38 pts)

Brighton – AAB (Dig Mus Snd Arts; Mus Vis Art)

Bristol – AAB–BBB 340–300 pts (Mus) (IB 33–32 pts)

Cardiff – AAB–BBB 340–300 pts +gr 8 theor+prac (Mus courses) (IB 33 pts)

City – AAB 340 pts (Mus)

Durham – AAB 340 pts (Mus) (IB 36 pts)

Glasgow – AAB +gr 8 +audition +interview (Mus; Mus MA) (IB 34 pts)

Lancaster – AAB 340 pts (Mus) (IB 34 pts)

London (RH) – AAB–ABB 340–320 pts (Mus Fr/Ger/Ital/Span; Dr Mus; Mus Phil; Mus Pol St; Phys Mus) (IB 35–34 pts)

Manchester – AAB +gr 8 inst/voice (Mus; Mus Dr) (IB 36–35 pts)

Newcastle – AAB–BBB 340–300 pts (Mus; Folk Trad Mus) (IB 33–35 pts HL 6 mus)

Nottingham – AAB–ABB (Mus) (IB 34 pts)

Southampton – AAB +gr 8 (Mus Mgt Sci; Engl Mus; Phil Mus) (IB 34 pts HL 17 pts)

Surrey – AAB +gr 7 (Mus) (IB 35 pts)

York – AAB–ABB 340–320 pts (Mus) (IB 35–32 pts HL 6 mus)

320 pts **Huddersfield** – ABB (Mus Dr; Mus)

Kent – ABB–BBB incl mus (Mus Tech; Mus; Pop Mus) (IB 33 pts)

Leeds – ABB incl mus (Mus; Mus Joint Hons; Mus (Perf))

Liverpool – ABB 320 pts (Mus/Pop Mus) (IB 33 pts)

London (Gold) – ABB (Mus; Pop Mus; Mus Cmpsn) (IB 32 pts)

Nottingham – ABB (Mus Phil) (IB 32 pts)

Sheffield – ABB (Mus; Mus Joint Hons; Theol Mus) (IB 34 pts)

Southampton – ABB +gr 8 (Mus; Acoust Mus) (IB 32 pts HL 16 pts)

Sussex – ABB incl mus +gr 7 (Mus Inform; Mus) (IB 34 pts)

300 pts **Aberdeen** – BBB 300 pts +gr 8 (Mus St) (IB 32 pts)

Birmingham City – 300 pts (Mus Tech)

Bristol UWE – 300 pts (Crea Mus Tech) (IB 26 pts)

Brunel – BBB incl mus 300 pts (Mus; Perf; Cmpsn; Snc Arts) (IB 32 pts)

Edinburgh – ABC (Mus Tech; Mus) (IB 34 pts HL 654)

Huddersfield – BBB 300 pts (Mus Tech courses)

Leeds Beckett – 300 pts (Mus Tech; Perf; Mus Prod) (IB 26 pts)

London (SOAS) – BBB (Mus Joint Hons) (IB 32 pts HL 554)

Queen's Belfast – BBB (Mus; Mus Tech Snc Art) (IB 32 pts HL 655)

Roehampton – 300–360 pts (P Educ (Mus))

West London – 300 pts (Musl Thea)

280 pts **Bangor** – 280–300 pts (Mus)

Bournemouth – 280–300 pts (Mus Aud Tech) (IB 30–31 pts)

Coventry – BBC 280 pts (Mus Tech) (IB 29 pts)

Cumbria – 280 pts (Dr Perf Musl Thea Perf)

Derby – 280 pts (Mus Tech Prod; Pop Mus Mus Tech)

Edge Hill – BBC 280 pts (Media Mus Snd; Mus Snd Dr)

Gloucestershire – 280–300 pts (Pop Mus; Mus Media Mgt)

Huddersfield – BBC (Mus Jrnl)

Hull – 280–300 pts (Mus) (IB 28 pts)

Manchester Met – 280 pts (Mus; Crea Mus Prod; Pop Mus) (IB 28 pts)

Middlesex – 280 pts (Mus; Mus Bus Arts Mgt; Pop Mus)

Reading – 280 pts (P Ed Mus)

Salford – 280 pts (Mus) (IB 30 pts)

South Wales – BBC 280 pts (Pop Mus; Mus Tech; Crea Snd Mus)

Teesside – 280 pts (Mus Tech)

West London – 280 pts (Mus Tech Pop Mus Perf; Mus Perf Mus Tech)

260 pts **Bangor** – 260–300 pts (Mus Crea Writ; Mus Film St)

Central Lancashire – BCC–BBB 260–300 pts (Mus Prod; Mus Thea)

Chester – 260–300 pts (Pop Mus Perf) (IB 28 pts)

De Montfort – 260 pts (Mus Tech Innov; Mus; Mus Tech Perf)
Hertfordshire – 260 pts (Mus Cmpsn Tech; Mus Tech)
Keele – BCC 260 pts (Mus; Mus Tech)
Kingston – 260–360 pts (Mus Joint Hons; Mus; Crea Mus Tech)
Liverpool Hope – 260–320 pts (Mus)
Liverpool John Moores – 260 pts (Pop Mus St) (IB 28 pts)
Northampton – 260–300 pts (Pop Mus courses)
Oxford Brookes – BCC 260 pts (Mus) (IB 29 pts)
Strathclyde – BCC (App Mus)
Ulster – (Ir Mus)

240 pts **Bath Spa** – 240–300 pts +gr 8 (Mus) (IB 24 pts)
Bishop Grosseteste – 240 pts (App Dr Mus)
Canterbury Christ Church – CCC (Mus; Commer Mus)
Central Lancashire – CCC–BBC 240–280 pts (Mus Prac)
Chester – 240–280 pts (Commer Mus Prod)
Coventry – CCC 240 pts (Mus Perf; Mus Cmpsn) (IB 27 pts)
Edinburgh Napier – BCD 240 pts +gr 8 (Mus; Pop Mus)
Glyndŵr – 240 pts (Mus Tech)
Leeds (CMus) – 240 pts (Mus (Comb); Mus (Jazz); Mus (Pop Mus); Mus (Class Mus); Mus (Prod))
Middlesex – 240 pts (Jazz)
Plymouth – 240 pts (P Mus BEd)
Portsmouth – 240–300 pts (Mus Snd Tech) (IB 28 pts)
Ravensbourne – AA–CC (Mus Prod Media) (IB 28 pts)
RConsvS – 240 pts (Mus BEd) Offered jointly with **Glasgow**
Southampton Solent – 240 pts (Mus Prom; Pop Mus Prod)
Staffordshire – 240–280 pts (Crea Mus Tech; Mus Tech)
Ulster – BCD 240 pts (Dance Mus) (IB 24 pts)
Westminster – CCC (Commer Mus) (IB 26 pts)
West Scotland – CCC (Commer Mus; Mus Tech)

220 pts **Anglia Ruskin** – 220–260 pts (Mus)
Bath Spa – 220–280 pts +gr 8 (Crea Mus Tech)
Blackpool and Fylde (Coll) – 220 pts (Musl Thea)
Chichester – CCD 180–220 pts (Mus) (IB 26 pts)
Creative Arts – 220–240 pts (Mus Jrnl)
Derby – 220–300 pts (Pop Mus Prod Joint Hons)
Falmouth – 220 pts (Pop Mus; Mus; Crea Mus Tech)
Sunderland – 220 pts (Commun Mus; Jazz Pop Commer Mus)
York St John – 220–260 pts (Mus courses)

200 pts **Anglia Ruskin** – 200 pts (Aud Mus Tech)
Bedfordshire – 200 pts (Mus Tech) (IB 24 pts)
Bucks New – 200–240 pts (Aud Mus Prod; Mus Arts Mgt; Mus Mgt Arst Dev)
Doncaster (Coll Univ Centre) – 200 pts (Crea Mus Tech)
East London – 200 pts (Mus Cult (Theor Prod))
Hull (Coll) – 200 pts (Mus Perf; Mus Prod)
London Met – 200–240 pts (Musl Instr)
Plymouth – 200 pts (Mus)
RCMus – CEcc (Mus)
St Mark and St John – 200 pts (Live Mus)
Trinity Saint David (Swansea) – 200–300 pts (Mus Tech)
Wolverhampton – 200 pts (Mus; Mus Pop Mus; Mus Tech)

180 pts **Farnborough (CT)** – 180–200 pts (Media Prod Mus)

160 pts **Colchester (Inst)** – 160 pts (Mus; Musl Thea; Film Mus Sndtrk Prod; Pop Mus)
Grimsby (Univ Centre) – 160 pts (Crea Mus)
Liverpool (LIPA) – 160–280 pts (Mus; Mus Thea Enter Mgt; Snd Tech)

London (Royal Central Sch SpDr) – CC 160 pts (Act (Mus Thea))
Rose Bruford (Coll) – 160–280 pts (Mus Tech; Actr Mushp)
Truro (Coll) – 160 pts (Contemp Wrld Jazz)
UHI – CC (Gael Trad Mus)
100 pts RConsvS – 100 pts (Mus; Scot Mus; Mus Thea)
80 pts Birmingham City – 80 pts (Jazz; Mus) (IB 24 pts)
Guildhall (Sch Mus Dr) – EE (Mus) (IB 24 pts)
Havering (Coll) – contact the College (Contemp Mus Tech)
London (RAcMus) – EE Contact the Academy (Mus BMus)
RNCM – EE 80 pts (Mus)
Royal Welsh (CMusDr) – CC 80 pts +gr 8 principal inst Contact College and apply direct (Mus)
Trinity Laban Consv – EE 80 pts +gr 8 Check with admissions tutor (Mus)
60 pts UHI – D (Pop Mus)

Trinity Laban Consv – +gr 8 Check with admissions tutor (Perf St MMus)

Alternative offers
See **Chapter 7** and **Appendix 1** for grades/UCAS Tariff points information for the International Baccalaureate, Scottish Highers/Advanced Highers, the Welsh Baccalaureate, the Irish Leaving Certificate, the Cambridge Pre-U Diploma, the Advanced Diploma and the Extended Project.

EXAMPLES OF FOUNDATION DEGREES IN THE SUBJECT FIELD
Accrington and Rossendale (Coll); Anglia Ruskin; Bath Spa; Bedford (Coll); Bedfordshire; Bournemouth; Bournemouth and Poole (Coll); Brighton; Brighton and Hove City (Coll); Bucks New; Canterbury Christ Church; Central Lancashire; Chichester; Colchester (Inst); De Montfort; East London; Gateshead (Coll); Gloucestershire; Hull (Coll); Kent; Leeds (CMus); Lincoln; Liverpool City (Coll); Loughborough (Coll); Mid-Cheshire (Coll); Neath Port Talbot (Coll); NEW (Coll); Newcastle (Coll); Northbrook (Coll); Nottingham New (Coll); Petroc; Rotherham (CAT); St Helens (Coll); South Devon (Coll); Staffordshire; Stamford New (Coll); Suffolk (Univ Campus); Sunderland; Sussex; Teesside; Truro (Coll); West London; Westminster; Wolverhampton; Worcester (CT).

CHOOSING YOUR COURSE (SEE ALSO CH.1)
Some course features
Bournemouth The Music and Audio Technology course focuses on the application of hardware and software technologies to create music. There is a 40-week placement in Year 3.
Brighton The course in Music and Visual Art utilises the visual art/music interface with close links between dance, theatre and music. There is also a Digital Music and Sound Arts degree in which music is studied relating to computers and electronic instruments, and a course in Music Production.
Chichester The Music degree has three strands: performance and direction, composing, arranging and improvising, and style and genre. There are also courses in Musical Theatre, Performing Arts, and Commercial Music.
Edinburgh Music is a three-year or four-year Honours course. In each year the curriculum is broadly divided between composition, history and practical studies. Options are introduced in the third year and include electronic music but also cover music technology and acoustics. There is also a BMus course in Music Technology.
Hertfordshire Courses are offered in Music Composition and Technology, Sound Design Technology and Music and Entertainment Industry Management, which has three pathways in studio production, entertainment industry and the classical music industry. There is also a course in Songwriting and Music Production.
Liverpool Hope Music can be studied as a single course or with a large number of combined courses in which students can specialise in popular or classical music. A BA (QTS) is also offered.
St Mark and St John The course in Live Music provides a programme of study focusing on performance technology and media work.

Teesside Music Technology allows students to perform and engineer live performances, set up an internet radio station and to create dub music, sound effects and foley to video and media. Students use the same technology used in the industry and have the chance to undertake exams in the hardware.

Universities and colleges teaching quality See www.qaa.ac.uk; http://unistats.direct.gov.uk.

Top research universities and colleges (RAE 2008) London (RH); Birmingham; Manchester; Southampton; Cambridge; London (King's); Sheffield; Oxford; York; Newcastle; Nottingham.

Examples of sandwich degree courses Birmingham City; Bournemouth; Bristol UWE; Central Lancashire; Coventry; Gloucestershire; Huddersfield; Lancaster; Leeds Beckett; London Met; Oxford Brookes; Portsmouth; Surrey; Teesside.

ADMISSIONS INFORMATION

Number of applicants per place (approx) Anglia Ruskin 5; Bangor 4; Bath Spa 8; Birmingham 8; Bristol 12; Brunel 7; Cambridge 3, (Hom) 4; Cardiff 6; Chichester 4; City 7; Colchester (Inst) 4; Cumbria 7; Durham 5; East Anglia 12; Edinburgh 11; Edinburgh Napier 3; Glasgow 4; Huddersfield 2; Hull 21; Kingston 18; Lancaster 8; Leeds 18; Liverpool 9; Liverpool (LIPA) 12; London (Gold) 7; London (King's) 10; London (RAcMus) 7; London (RH) 7; London (SOAS) 4; London Met 10; Middlesex 23; Newcastle 24; Northampton 3; Northumbria 12; Nottingham 7; Oxford Brookes 12; Queen's Belfast 6; RCMus 10; RConsvS 6; RNCM 8; Roehampton 4; Rose Bruford (Coll) 15; Salford 5; Southampton 5; Strathclyde 15; Surrey 6, (Tonmeister) 12; Trinity Laban Consv 4; Ulster 8; Worcester 8; York 8; York St John 2.

Advice to applicants and planning the UCAS personal statement In addition to your ability and expertise with your chosen musical instrument(s), it is also important to know your composers and to take a critical interest in various kinds of music. Reference should be made to these, visits to concerts listed and any special interests indicated in types of musical activity, for example, opera, ballet. Work with orchestras, choirs and other musical groups should also be included and full details given of any competitions entered and awards obtained. See **Chapter 5** for details of applications for Music courses at conservatoires. **Guildhall (Sch Mus Dr)** International applicants sending extra documentation from overseas must make sure that for Customs purposes they indicate that they will pay any import tax charged. **London (Gold)** We encourage students to bring examples of their written and creative work. **Royal Welsh (CMusDr)** Evidence of performance-related experience, eg youth orchestras, solo work, prizes, scholarships etc. Our course is a conservatoire course as opposed to a more academic university course. We offer a very high standard of performance tuition balanced with academic theory modules. **Surrey** (Snd Rec (Tonmeister)) Demonstration of motivation towards professional sound recording.

Misconceptions about this course Cardiff Some mistakenly think that the BMus scheme is either performance-based or something inferior to the principal music-based degree. **Salford** (Pop Mus Rec) This is not a specialised music technology degree: it is a music degree with specialisation in music technology and production. Specialisation can be significant in Year 3. BTEC Popular Music students must be prepared for the rigours of an academic degree. Some students expect the course to make them famous! **Surrey** Some believe that the Music course is exclusively performance-based (the course includes substantial academic and compositional elements).

Selection interviews Most institutions, plus audition to include a performance of a prepared piece (or pieces) on main instrument. **Yes** Anglia Ruskin, Birmingham City, Cardiff, Doncaster (Coll Univ Centre), Guildhall (Sch Mus Dr), Liverpool (LIPA), Oxford (Mus) 38%; **Some** Bath Spa, Bucks New, Coventry, Staffordshire (Mus Tech), Surrey.

Interview advice and questions See also **Chapter 5** under **Applications for Music Courses at Conservatoires**.

Anglia Ruskin In addition to A-levels, Grade 7 is required (with a good pass, first study) plus Grade 5 minimum keyboard standard. AS-level points are not counted towards the Tariff required for this subject. A demo CD may be required.

Bangor Offer depends on proven ability in historical or compositional fields plus acceptable performance standard. Options include music therapy, recording techniques, jazz.

Bath Spa Some candidates interviewed. Required to perform and sight-read on main instrument, and given aural and critical listening tests. Discussion of previous performing, composing and academic experience. (Crea Mus Tech) Applicants will be required to submit an audio portfolio demonstrating technical and creative skills.

Bristol (Mus Fr/Ger/Ital) No in-depth interviews; candidates invited to Open Days.

Cambridge (St Catharine's) At interview candidates may have to undergo some simple keyboard or aural tests (such as harmonisation of an unseen melody or memorisation of a rhythm). More importantly, they will have to comment on some unseen musical extracts from a stylistic and analytical point of view. Candidates are asked to submit some examples of work before the interview, from the fields of harmony and counterpoint, history and analysis; they are also encouraged to send any other material such as compositions, programme notes or an independent essay on a subject of interest to the candidate. (Taking the STEP examination is not a requirement for admission.) Above all this, though, the main prerequisite for reading Music at St Catharine's is an academic interest in the subject itself.

Canterbury Christ Church Associated Board examinations in two instruments (or one instrument and voice); keyboard competence essential, particularly for the BEd course.

Colchester (Inst) Great stress laid on candidate's ability to communicate love of the subject.

Cumbria Admission by live performance or as a demo. QTS applicants interviewed for teaching suitability. See also **Chapter 6**.

Durham Grade 6 piano (Associated Board), a foreign language (GCSE grade A–C), and A-level music grade B required. **East Anglia** Only unusual and mature candidates are interviewed. Applicants are expected to perform music with insight and show genuine intellectual curiosity about music and its cultural background. At interview candidates will be asked to perform on their principal instrument. Those who play orchestral instruments or sing will also be expected to play simple music on the piano. At interview we look for applicants with proficiency in instrumental or vocal performance (preferably at Grade 8 standard or above), range of experience of music of many types and an intelligent attitude towards discussion.

Edinburgh Napier Most candidates are called for interview, although very well-qualified candidates may be offered a place without interview. All are asked to submit samples of their work. Associated Board Grade 7 on piano is usually expected.

Huddersfield Have an open and inquisitive outlook with regard to all aspects of music from performing to composing, musicology to listening. Candidates auditioned on their principal instrument or voice. They will be asked about playing technique, interpretation and interests.

Hull (Coll) Good instrumental grades can improve chances of an offer and of confirmation in August. Students are not normally required to attend an audition/interview. Decisions will be made according to the information supplied on the UCAS application. Successful applicants will be invited to attend a departmental Open Day. We welcome applications from mature students and those with unconventional qualifications: in such cases an interview may be required.

Kingston Associated Board Grade 8 on main instrument is required, with at least Grade 4 on a keyboard instrument (where this is not the main instrument). Audition and interview may be required. Candidates with non-standard qualifications are interviewed and asked to bring samples of written work.

Lancaster Grade 8 Associated Board required on an instrument or voice and some keyboard proficiency (Grade 6) usually expected. We do not accept candidates without interview. For the Music degree, instrumental or vocal skills equivalent to Grade 8 required. For Music Technology, applicants should hold music theory Grade 5 or be able to demonstrate the ability to read a score. Applicants wishing to take practical studies will need instrumental or vocal skills equivalent to Grade 8.

Leeds Intending students should follow an academic rather than practical-oriented A-level course. The University is experimenting with abandoning the formal interview in favour of small group Open Days for those holding offers made on the UCAS information, to focus on a practical exchange of information relevant to the applicant's decision to accept or reject the offer. Grade 8 Associated Board on an instrument is a normal expectation.

Leeds (CMus) There will be an audition and an essay on music theory.

Liverpool (LIPA) In addition to performing in orchestras etc, give details of any compositions you have completed (the number and styles). Instrumentalists (including vocalists) should describe any performance/gig experience together with any musical instrument grades achieved. (Mus) Candidates should prepare two pieces of contrasting music to play on their chosen instrument. Candidates who have put song-writing/composition as either first or second choice should have a CD of their work to play to the panel. (Snd Tech) Applicants must prepare a critical review of a sound recording of their choice which highlights the technical and production values that they think are the most important. Examples of recorded work they have undertaken should also be available at interview, eg on CD. (Mus Perf Arts) Applicants should have A-levels (or equivalent) and have completed Grade 5 Music Theory before the course commences.

London (Gold) The interview will include an aural discussion of music and the personal interests of the applicant.

London (RAcMus) All candidates are called for audition, and those who are successful are called for a further interview; places are offered later, subject to the minimum GCSE requirements being achieved. (BMus) Applicants sit a 50-minute written paper, and may also be tested on keyboard and aural performance.

London (RH) Candidates are tested with an aural test, a harmony/counterpoint test, a conceptual essay, and a viva at which they are asked questions and asked to perform. On the basis of the results in these tests we make offers. There is a tradition of caring for each individual and we strive to give each applicant a fair hearing. Musicality, a good intellect and real enthusiasm are the qualities we look for.

London (SOAS) Candidates are judged on individual merits. Applicants are expected to have substantial practical experience of musical performance, but not necessarily Western music.

Newcastle We expect a reasonable background knowledge of musical history, basic harmony and counterpoint and keyboard skills of approximately Grade 8 standard; if the main instrument is not piano or organ – Grade 5. While practical skills are important, academic ability is the primary requisite. Practical music or music technology accepted in place of music.

Nottingham A high standard of aural ability is expected. Interviewees take two short written papers, intellectual enquiry and attainment are looked for, together with a good range of knowledge and sense of enterprise. Only borderline/mature students are interviewed, successful applicants are invited to an Open Day.

Nottingham Trent Music students require Grade 6 on two instruments. Candidates submit a marked sample of harmony and/or counterpoint and two marked essays on any areas or aspects of music. Candidates may also submit a portfolio of compositions if they wish, but it is not possible to return any copies. Candidates will take the following tests at interview: (1) A one-hour harmony or counterpoint written test (candidates will not have access to a piano); there is no composition option; (2) A 40-minute aural test in three parts: dictation of a Bach chorale (bass given)/melodic dictation, and identification of errors heard in a two-part piece; (3) Performance of a prepared piece on the candidate's principal instrument or voice (organists, percussionists and candidates requiring an accompanist should inform the Faculty in advance of the interview period); (4) Keyboard skills in three parts: score reading of a string quartet; keyboard harmony; and sight-reading (sight-reading examples will take into account candidates' keyboard proficiency).

RCMus All UK and Eire candidates are required to attend an audition in person but recordings are acceptable from overseas applicants. It must be stressed, however, that personal audition is preferable and those students offered places on the basis of a recorded audition may be required to take a confirmatory audition on arrival. Candidates are required to perform on the principal study instrument as well as undertaking sight-reading, aural tests and paperwork. There is also an interview. Potential scholars sometimes proceed to a second audition, usually on the same day. The academic requirement for the BMus (RCM) course is two A-levels at pass grades. Acceptance is ultimately based on the quality of performance at audition, performing experience and perceived potential as a performer. As a guide, applicants should be of at least Grade 8 distinction standard.

RNCM All applicants are called for audition. Successful applicants proceed to an academic interview which will include aural tests and questions on music theory and history. Student comment: 'A 45-minute interview with a panel of three. Focus was on portfolio of compositions sent in advance. Prior to interview was asked to harmonise a short passage and study an orchestral excerpt followed up at interview. Aural test waived.'

Royal Welsh (CMusDr) All UK and Eire applicants are called to audition in person; overseas candidates may audition by sending a recording. Candidates are required to perform on their sight-reading ability. Candidates who are successful in the audition proceed to interview in which there will be a short aural test. Candidates for the BA (Music) course are required to bring recent examples of harmony, counterpoint and essays.

Surrey (Mus) Applicants may expect to be questioned in the interview about their musical experience, enthusiasm and any particular compositions they have studied. They will also be asked to perform on their first instrument. (Snd Rec (Tonmeister)) Applicants can expect to be questioned about their recording interests and motivation and show an ability to relate A-level scientific knowledge to simple recording equipment. They may be asked to perform on their first instrument.

Trinity Laban Consv Applicants for the BMus degree must attend an audition and show that they have attained a certain level of competence in their principal and second studies, musical subjects and in musical theory. Grade 8 practical and theory can count as one A-level, but not if the second A-level is in music. Overseas applicants may submit a tape recording in the first instance when a place may be offered for one year. Thereafter they will have to undergo a further test. They must also show evidence of good aural perception in musical techniques and musical analysis.

Wolverhampton The audition will involve playing/singing a piece of own-choice music (up to five minutes – no longer). Accompanists may be brought along or the department may be able to provide one if requested in advance. Candidates will be requested to produce a short piece of written work. It would be helpful to see any music certificates and a Record of Achievement if available, together with examples of recent work in music (an essay, harmony, composition etc).

Reasons for rejection (non-academic) Usually academic (auditions, practical, aural/written test). Dull, unenthusiastic students, ignorant about their subject, showing lack of motivation and imagination. **Cambridge** Her harmony was marred by elementary technical errors and her compositions lacked formal and stylistic focus. **London (King's)** Apparent lack of interest, performance not good enough, lack of music history knowledge. Foreign students: language skills inadequate. **Royal Welsh (CMusDr)** Performing/technical ability not of the required standard.

AFTER-RESULTS ADVICE
Offers to applicants repeating A-levels Higher Leeds; **Same** Anglia Ruskin, Bath Spa, Bristol, Cardiff, City, Colchester (Inst), De Montfort, Durham, East Anglia, Guildhall (Sch Mus Dr), Huddersfield, Hull, Kingston, Leeds (CMus), London (RAcMus), London (RH), Nottingham, Rose Bruford (Coll), Royal Welsh (CMusDr), Salford, Staffordshire, Surrey, York, York St John.

GRADUATE DESTINATIONS AND EMPLOYMENT (2011/12 HESA)
Graduates surveyed 4565 **Employed** 1475 **In voluntary employment** 150 **In further study** 1405 **Assumed unemployed** 370

Career note Some graduates go into performance-based careers, many enter the teaching profession and others go into a wide range of careers requiring graduate skills.

OTHER DEGREE SUBJECTS FOR CONSIDERATION
Acoustics; Drama; Musical Theatre; Performance Arts.

NATURAL SCIENCES

(see also **Biological Sciences**)

Natural Sciences degrees allow the student to obtain a broad view of the origins and potential of science in general, and then to focus on one specialist area of scientific study.

Useful websites www.scicentral.com; www.nature.com; see also **Biology**, **Chemistry** and **Physics**.

NB The points totals shown to the left of the institutions are for ease of reference only. It must not be assumed that Tariff points are always used by institutions or that they can be substituted for an offer in grades. The level of an offer is not necessarily indicative of the quality of a course.

COURSE OFFERS INFORMATION

Subject requirements/preferences **GCSE** Strong results, particularly in the sciences. **AL** Science subjects required.

Cambridge (Emmanuel) One AEA science may be required when only two sciences taken; (Peterhouse) STEP may be used as part of conditional offer.

Your target offers and examples of courses provided by each institution
400 pts **London (UCL)** – A*AAe–AAAe (Nat Sci) (IB 38–39 pts HL 766–777)
380 pts **Bath** – A*AA (Nat Sci (St Abrd); Nat Sci) (IB 38 pts HL 766)
   Birmingham – A*AA (Nat Sci; Nat Sci Euro) (IB 36–38 pts)
   Cambridge – A*AA (Nat Sci; Nat Sci (Astro); Nat Sci (Physiol Dev Neuro); Nat Sci (Zool); Nat Sci (Neuro); Nat Sci (Hist Phil Sci); Nat Sci (Bioch); Nat Sci (Biol Biomed Sci); Nat Sci (Chem); Nat Sci (Genet); Nat Sci (Earth Sci); Nat Sci (Mat Sci)) (IB 40–41 pts HL 776)
   Durham – A*AA 380 pts (Nat Sci) (IB 38 pts HL 766–666)
   East Anglia – A*AA (Nat Sci MNatSci; Nat Sci Ind St/Abrd) (IB 35 pts)
   Exeter – A*AA–AAB 380–340 pts (Nat Sci)
360 pts **East Anglia** – AAA (Nat Sci) (IB 34 pts)
   Lancaster – AAA 360 pts (Nat Sci; Nat Sci (N Am)) (IB 36 pts)
   Leeds – AAA (M Nat Sci) (IB 38 pts)
   Leicester – AAA (Nat Sci) (IB 36 pts)
   Nottingham – A*AA (Nat Sci) (IB 36 pts)
220 pts **Liverpool John Moores** – 220 pts (Nat Sci (incl Fdn Yr))

   Open University – contact +44 (0)845 300 6090 **or** www.openuniversity.co.uk/you (Nat Sci)

Alternative offers
See **Chapter 7** and **Appendix 1** for grades/UCAS Tariff points information for the International Baccalaureate, Scottish Highers/Advanced Highers, the Welsh Baccalaureate, the Irish Leaving Certificate, the Cambridge Pre-U Diploma, the Advanced Diploma and the Extended Project.

CHOOSING YOUR COURSE (SEE ALSO CH.1)

Some course features
Bath A flexible range of courses, with opportunity to transfer between the three- and four-year degree programmes and the new undergraduate master's degree. Students can also apply for transfer to a Single Honours programme in Biology, Chemistry or Physics. Optional industrial placement year is also offered.
Cambridge (Nat Sci) Courses focus on the biological and physical sciences with a wide range of final-year specialist subjects from which to choose, including Astrophysics, Chemistry, Geological Sciences, History and Philosophy of Science, Materials Science, Physics or Systems Biology.
Durham (Nat Sci) A very flexible degree programme, with specialisation in a range of subjects, ranging from Anthropology and Astronomy to Earth Sciences, Mathematics, Psychology and Statistics. Students take modules from the Faculties of Arts, Humanities and Social Sciences.
Lancaster (Nat Sci) Two or more science subjects may be chosen. A non-science subject may be studied for a quarter of the course.

Universities and colleges teaching quality See www.qaa.ac.uk; http://unistats.direct.gov.uk.

Top research universities and colleges (RAE 2008) See separate science tables.

Examples of sandwich degree courses Bath; East Anglia.

ADMISSIONS INFORMATION
Number of applicants per place (approx) Bath 6; Birmingham 10; Cambridge 3; Durham 5; Nottingham 7.

Advice to applicants and planning the UCAS personal statement See **Biology**, **Chemistry**, **Physics** and **Appendix 3**.

Selection interviews **Yes** Bath, Cambridge, East Anglia; **No** Birmingham.

Interview advice and questions See also **Chapter 6**. **Cambridge** Questions depend on subject choices and studies at A-level and past questions have included the following: Discuss the setting up of a chemical engineering plant and the probabilities of failure of various components. Questions on the basic principles of physical chemistry, protein structure and functions and physiology. Questions on biological specimens. Comment on the theory of evolution and the story of the Creation in Genesis. What are your weaknesses? Questions on electro-micrographs. What do you talk about with your friends? How would you benefit from a university education? What scientific magazines do you read? Questions on atoms, types of bonding and structures. What are the problems of being tall? What are the differences between metals and non-metals? Why does graphite conduct? Questions on quantum physics and wave mechanics. How could you contribute to life here? What do you see yourself doing in five years' time? If it is common public belief that today's problems, for example industrial pollution, are caused by scientists, why do you wish to become one? Questions on the gyroscopic motion of cycle wheels, the forces on a cycle in motion and the design of mountain bikes. What do you consider will be the most startling scientific development in the future? What do you estimate is the mass of air in this room? If a carrot can grow from one carrot cell, why not a human?

AFTER-RESULTS ADVICE
Offers to applicants repeating A-levels **No** Cambridge.

GRADUATE DESTINATIONS AND EMPLOYMENT (2011/12 HESA)
See **Biology**, **Chemistry**, **Mathematics** and **Physics**.

Career note These courses offer a range of science and in some cases non-scientific subjects, providing students with the flexibility to develop particular interests as they progress through the course.

OTHER DEGREE SUBJECTS FOR CONSIDERATION
Anatomy; Anthropology; Archaeology; Astrophysics; Biochemistry; Biological Sciences; Biology; Chemistry; Earth Sciences; Ecology; Genetics; Geography; Geology; History and Philosophy of Science; Neuroscience; Pharmacology; Physics; Plant Sciences; Psychology; Zoology.

NAVAL ARCHITECTURE
(including **Marine Engineering** and **Ship Science**; see also **Marine/Maritime Studies**)

Professional naval architects or marine engineers are responsible for the design, construction and repair of cruise liners, yachts, submarines, container ships and oil tankers. Ship Science focuses on, for example, vehicles and structures that use the oceans for transport, recreation and energy generation. Courses cover marine structures, transport and operations, design, propulsion and mathematics. Ship design has many similarities to the design of aircraft.

Useful websites www.rina.org.uk; www.strath.ac.uk/na-me; www.naval-architecture.co.uk.

NB The points totals shown to the left of the institutions are for ease of reference only. It must not be assumed that Tariff points are always used by institutions or that they can be substituted for an offer in grades. The level of an offer is not necessarily indicative of the quality of a course.

COURSE OFFERS INFORMATION

Subject requirements/preferences GCSE Grades A–C in mathematics and physics are normally required. **AL** Mathematics and physics usually required.

Your target offers and examples of courses provided by each institution

360 pts Southampton – AAA incl maths phys (Ship Sci (Advncd Mat); Ship Sci (Nvl Archit); Ship Sci (Nvl Eng); Ship Sci (Ycht Sml Crft); Ship Sci; Ship Sci (Eng Mgt)) (IB 36 pts HL 18 pts)

340 pts Newcastle – AAB–ABB 340–320 pts (Mar Tech Sml Crft Tech; Mar Tech Mar Eng) (IB 34–35 pts HL 5 maths phys)

Newcastle – AAB (Mar Tech Mar Eng MEng; Mar Tech Sml Crft Tech MEng; Mar Tech Off Eng MEng) (IB 37 pts HL 5 maths phys)

Strathclyde – AAB (Nvl Archit Mar Eng MEng; Nvl Archit Ocn Eng MEng; Nvl Archit Sml Crft Eng MEng) (IB 36 pts)

320 pts Liverpool John Moores – 320 pts (Mech Mar Eng MEng)

Strathclyde – ABB (Nvl Archit Mar Eng; Nvl Archit Ocn Eng; Nvl Archit Sml Crft Eng) (IB 32 pts)

300 pts Newcastle – BBB–AAB 300–340 pts (Nvl Archit) (IB 32–34 pts HL 5 maths phys)

280 pts Plymouth – 280 pts (Mar Tech) (IB 28 pts)

260 pts Liverpool John Moores – 260 pts (Mech Mar Eng; Naut Sci)

240 pts Southampton Solent – 240 pts (Ycht Des Prod)

200 pts Plymouth – 200 pts (Mar St (Ocn Ycht))

Alternative offers

See **Chapter 7** and **Appendix 1** for grades/UCAS Tariff points information for the International Baccalaureate, Scottish Highers/Advanced Highers, the Welsh Baccalaureate, the Irish Leaving Certificate, the Cambridge Pre-U Diploma, the Advanced Diploma and the Extended Project.

EXAMPLES OF FOUNDATION DEGREES IN THE SUBJECT FIELD

Blackpool and Fylde (Coll); Cornwall (Coll); Liverpool John Moores; Plymouth City (Coll); South Devon (Coll); Southampton Solent.

CHOOSING YOUR COURSE (SEE ALSO CH.1)

Some course features

Newcastle (Mar Tech; Sml Crft Tech; Nvl Archit) All MEng and BEng courses take a common Stage 1 first year and then follow their specialised degree programmes. Transfer is possible between MEng courses and to the Marine Technology BEng degree.

Southampton The course focuses on marine engineering on board ships and other marine structures in collaboration with the Royal Navy.

Strathclyde (Nvl Archit) A broad-based engineering course covering engineering science, flotation and stability, ship and offshore structures design. Topics also include resistance and propulsion, ship structural analysis, marine engineering systems, business and management. Some opportunities for sponsorship and work experience.

Universities and colleges teaching quality See www.qaa.ac.uk; http://unistats.direct.gov.uk.

Top research universities and colleges (RAE 2008) (Naval Architecture and Marine Engineering) Strathclyde.

Examples of sandwich degree courses Plymouth.

ADMISSIONS INFORMATION

Number of applicants per place (approx) Newcastle 9; Southampton 4.

Advice to applicants and planning the UCAS personal statement Special interests in this subject area should be described fully. Visits to shipyards and awareness of ship design from the *Mary Rose* in Portsmouth to modern speedboats should be fully explained and the problems noted. See also **Engineering/Engineering Sciences**, **Marine/Maritime Studies** and **Appendix 3**.

Selection interviews Some Newcastle, Southampton.

Interview advice and questions Because of the highly vocational nature of this subject, applicants will naturally be expected to discuss any work experience and to justify their reasons for choosing the course. See also **Chapter 6**.

AFTER-RESULTS ADVICE
Offers to applicants repeating A-levels Higher Newcastle.

GRADUATE DESTINATIONS AND EMPLOYMENT (2011/12 HESA)
Graduates surveyed 60 **Employed** 35 **In voluntary employment** 0 **In further study** 0 **Assumed unemployed** 10

Career note A small proportion of naval architects work in the shipbuilding and repair industry, others are involved in the construction of oil rigs or may work for ship-owning companies. There are also a number of firms of marine consultants employing naval architects as managers or consultants.

OTHER DEGREE SUBJECTS FOR CONSIDERATION
Aeronautical Engineering; Civil Engineering; Electrical/Electronic Engineering; Geography; Marine Biology; Marine Engineering; Marine/Maritime Studies; Marine Technology; Mechanical Engineering; Oceanography; Physics; Shipping Operations; Transport Management.

NURSING and MIDWIFERY

(including **Paramedic Science**; see also **Biological Sciences, Community Studies/Development, Health Sciences/Studies**)

Abbreviations used in this table A – Adult; C – Child; LD – Learning Disability; MH – Mental Health.

Nursing and Midwifery courses are designed to equip students with the scientific and caring skills demanded by medical science in the 21st century. Courses follow a similar pattern with an introductory programme of study covering clinical skills, nursing practice and the behavioural and social sciences. Thereafter, specialisation starts in adult, child or mental health nursing, or with patients with learning disabilities. Throughout the three-year course students gain extensive clinical experience in hospital wards, clinics, accident and emergency and high-dependency settings. UCAS handles applications for Nursing degree courses. From 2013 nursing became an all-graduate profession.

Useful websites www.scicentral.com; www.nhscareers.nhs.uk; www.nursingtimes.net; see also **Health Sciences/Studies** and **Medicine**.

NB The points totals shown to the left of the institutions are for ease of reference only. It must not be assumed that Tariff points are always used by institutions or that they can be substituted for an offer in grades. The level of an offer is not necessarily indicative of the quality of a course.

COURSE OFFERS INFORMATION
Subject requirements/preferences GCSE English and a science subject. Mathematics required at several universities. **AL** Science subjects required for some courses. **Other** All applicants holding firm offers will require an occupational health check and Disclosure and Barring Service (DBS) clearance and are required to provide documentary evidence that they have not been infected with hepatitis B. (Paramed Sci) Full clean manual UK driving licence with at least a provisional C1 category.

Your target offers and examples of courses provided by each institution

340 pts **Bournemouth** – 340 pts (Midwif)
Bristol UWE – 340 pts (Midwif)
Edinburgh – AAB–BBB 340–300 pts (Nurs St) (IB 34–36 pts HL 555)
Nottingham – AAB (Nurs Sci MNursSci) (IB 34 pts)
Southampton – AAB (Midwif) (IB 34 pts HL 18 pts)

320 pts **Birmingham** – ABB (Nurs A/MH) (IB 34 pts)
Bradford – 320 pts (Midwif St)
Brighton – ABB (Midwif; Nurs A/C/MH)
City – 320 pts (Midwif) (IB 33 pts)
East Anglia – ABB (Midwif) (IB 32 pts)
Manchester – ABB 320 pts (Midwif) (IB 33 pts)
Sheffield Hallam – 320 pts (Midwif)
Surrey – ABB (Midwif; Paramed Prac)
York – ABB (Midwif) (IB 32 pts)

300 pts **Bangor** – 300 pts (Nurs A/C/LD/MH; Midwif)
Birmingham City – BBB 300 pts (Midwif) (IB 36 pts)
Bournemouth – 300 pts (Nurs A/C/LD/MH)
Bristol UWE – 300 pts (Nurs A/C/LD/MH) (IB 24 pts)
Cardiff – BBB 300 pts (Nurs A/C/MH; Midwif) (IB 28 pts)
Cumbria – 300 pts (Midwif)
De Montfort – 300 pts (Midwif)
East Anglia – BBB (Nurs A/C/LD/MH) (IB 31 pts)
Edge Hill – BBB 300 pts (Midwif; Nurs A/C)
Glasgow – BBB (Nurs A/C/LD/MH)
Hertfordshire – 300 pts (Paramed Sci) (IB 28–30 pts)
Huddersfield – BBB (Midwif St; Nurs A/C/LD/MH)
Kingston – BBB (Midwif)
Leeds – BBB (Nurs A/C/LD/MH; Midwif)
Leeds Beckett – (Nurs A/MH)
Liverpool – BBB 300 pts (Nurs) (IB 30 pts)
Liverpool John Moores – 300 pts (Midwif) (IB 26 pts)
London (King's) – BBB (Midwif St Reg; Nurs A/C/MH) (IB 32 pts HL 5 sci)
London South Bank – 300 pts (Midwif)
Manchester Met – 300 pts (Nurs A) (IB 29 pts)
Oxford Brookes – BBB (Midwif)
Plymouth – BBB (Paramed Practnr)
Salford – BBB (Midwif)
South Wales – BBB (Midwif; Nurs A/C/LD/MH)
Southampton – BBB–ABB 300–320 pts (Nurs A/C/MH) (IB 30–32 pts HL 16 pts)
Swansea – BBB 300 pts (Midwif)
West London – 300 pts (Midwif)
Worcester – BBB 300 pts (Midwif; Nurs A/C/MH)
York – BBB (Nurs Prac A/C/LD/MH) (IB 31 pts)

280 pts **Anglia Ruskin** – 280 pts (Midwif) (IB 26 pts)
Birmingham City – 280 pts (Nurs A/C/LD/MH)
Bradford – 280 pts (Nurs A/C/MH)
Central Lancashire – 280 pts (Nurs Pre Reg)
City – 280 pts +interview +IOT test (Nurs A/C/MH)
De Montfort – BBC 280 pts (Nurs A/C)
Glasgow Caledonian – BBC 280 pts (Nurs A/LD/MH)
Greenwich – 280 pts (Midwif)
Liverpool John Moores – 280 pts (Nurs MH) (IB 24 pts)
Manchester – BBC (Nurs A/C/MH) (IB 30 pts)

Northumbria – 280 pts (Nurs A/C/LD/MH; Midwif St)
Nottingham – BBC–BCC (Nurs A/C/LD/MH) (IB 28 pts)
Queen's Belfast – BBC–BCC 280–260 pts (Midwif)
Staffordshire – BBC (Midwif Prac)
Suffolk (Univ Campus) – 280 pts (Midwif)
Swansea – BBC (Nurs A/C/MH)
Ulster – 280 pts (Nurs A/MH)
West London – 280 pts (Nurs A/C/LD/MH)
Wolverhampton – 280 pts (Midwif; Nurs A/C/MH)
260 pts **Brighton** – BCC 260 pts (Paramed Sci) (IB 28 pts)
Canterbury Christ Church – BCC 260 pts (Nurs A/C/MH; Midwif)
Coventry – 260 pts (Midwif)
Edge Hill – BCC 260 pts (Nurs A/C/LD/MH)
Glasgow Caledonian – BCC 260 pts (Nurs St) (IB 24 pts)
Hull – 260 pts (Nurs A/C/LD/MH)
Keele – ABC (Nurs A/C/LD/MH)
Liverpool John Moores – 260 pts (Nurs A) (IB 24 pts)
London South Bank – 260 pts (Nurs A/C/MH)
Northampton – 260–300 pts (Nurs A/C/LD/MH)
Queen's Belfast – BCC–CCD (with relevant subj) **or** BBB–CCC (without relevant subj)
    (Nurs A/C/LD/MH)
Salford – 260–300 pts (Nurs A/C/MH) (IB 25 pts)
Teesside – 260 pts (Midwif)
240 pts **Bedfordshire** – 240 pts (Midwif; Nurs A/C/LD/MH)
Bristol UWE – 240 pts (Paramed Prac)
Bucks New – 240–280 pts (Nurs A/C/MH)
Central Lancashire – 240 pts (Midwif)
Chester – 240–280 pts (Nurs A/C/LD/MH; Midwif) (IB 26 pts)
Coventry – CCC 240 pts (Nurs A/C/LD/MH) (IB 27–28 pts)
Cumbria – 240 pts (Nurs A/LD/MH)
Derby – 240 pts (Nurs A/MH)
Greenwich – 240 pts (Nurs A/C/LD/MH)
Hertfordshire – 240 pts (Midwif; Nurs; Nurs LD Soc Wk) (IB 26–28 pts)
Keele – 240–260 pts (Midwif)
Kingston – 240 pts (Nurs A/C/LD/MH)
Lincoln – CCC 240 pts (Nurs A)
Sheffield Hallam – 240 pts (Nurs St A/C/MH)
Staffordshire – CCC 240 pts (Nurs Prac A/C/MH)
Suffolk (Univ Campus) – 240–280 pts (Nurs A/C/MH)
Teesside – 240 pts +interview (Nurs St A/C/LD/MH)
220 pts **Edinburgh Queen Margaret** – CCD 220 pts (Nurs) (IB 28 pts)
West Scotland – CCD (Midwif)
200 pts **Anglia Ruskin** – 200 pts (Nurs A/C/LD/MH)
Middlesex – 200–300 pts (Midwif; Nurs A/C/MH)
180 pts **Edinburgh Napier** – 180 pts (Nurs A/C/LD/MH; Midwif)
160 pts **Abertay** – CC (Nurs MH)
Dundee – CC (Nurs A/C/MH)
Northampton – CC (Midwif)
Robert Gordon – CC (Nurs A/C/MH; Midwif)
Stirling – CC (Nurs) (IB 28 pts)
West Scotland – CC (Nurs A/MH) (IB 24 pts)
120 pts **Coventry** – (Pre-Hosp Emer Cr)

Open University – contact +44 (0)845 300 6090 **or** www.openuniversity.co.uk/you
    (Nurs Prac)

Check **Chapter 4** when choosing your university and **Chapter 7** on how to read the subject tables.

Alternative offers
See **Chapter 7** and **Appendix 1** for grades/UCAS Tariff points information for the International Baccalaureate, Scottish Highers/Advanced Highers, the Welsh Baccalaureate, the Irish Leaving Certificate, the Cambridge Pre-U Diploma, the Advanced Diploma and the Extended Project.

CHOOSING YOUR COURSE (SEE ALSO CH.1)

Some course features
Anglia Ruskin There is a common element of Nursing for all specialised areas that cover nursing fields in child, adult and mental health. There is also an International Nursing Studies course and a BSc Midwifery degree course.
Bedfordshire Obstetrics, midwifery, the midwife practitioner, women's health, ethics and law are all covered in the Nursing degree. Specialisation is offered in adult, children's and mental health nursing. A Midwifery course is also provided.
Hertfordshire (Paramed Sci) The course runs over four extended academic years and leads to qualifying and registering as a professional paramedic. Theoretical studies are interspersed with clinical practice placements. The third year is a sandwich/practice year when students are paid employees of the London Ambulance Service NHS Trust.
Liverpool The Adult Nursing degree is a three-year course leading to the degree (BNurs), with modules covering physiology, pathophysiology, behavioural sciences, communication skills, clinical skills and curative, rehabilitative and palliative care.
Swansea Nursing students in Wales are paid by a bursary from the NHS Wales Bursary Scheme. It is not means tested. The courses cover adult, child and mental health nursing, prior to which a common Foundation course is offered. There is also a Midwifery degree.

Universities and colleges teaching quality See www.qaa.ac.uk; http://unistats.direct.gov.uk.

Top research universities and colleges (RAE 2008) Manchester; Southampton; Ulster; York; City; Hertfordshire; Leeds; Nottingham; Stirling.

ADMISSIONS INFORMATION

Number of applicants per place (approx) Abertay 10; Anglia Ruskin 10; Bangor 10; Birmingham 8; Birmingham City 15; Bournemouth 9; Brighton 3; Bristol UWE 27; Cardiff 12, (non-EU) 6; Central Lancashire (Midwif) 14; City (Nurs MH) 4, (Nurs C) 8, (Midwif) 5; Cumbria 8; De Montfort 10; Edinburgh Queen Margaret 3; Glasgow Caledonian 12; Glyndŵr 4; Huddersfield (Midwif St) 10; Hull 10; Leeds (Midwif) 12; Liverpool John Moores (Nurs) 5; London (King's) 4; London South Bank 16; Middlesex 10; Northampton 17; Northumbria 16; Nottingham 3; Salford 10, (Midwif) 11; Sheffield Hallam 8; Southampton (Nurs) 15, (Midwif) 25; Staffordshire (Midwif Prac) 10; Surrey 10; Swansea 10; York (Nurs) 8, (Midwif Prac) 2.

Admissions tutors' advice **Essex** Nursing courses are only open to Home/EU students and all eligible students must pass an interview before being made an offer of admission.

Advice to applicants and planning the UCAS personal statement Experience of care work – for example in hospitals, old people's homes, children's homes – is important. Describe what you have done and what you have learned. Read nursing journals in order to be aware of new developments in the treatment of illnesses. Note, in particular, the various needs of patients and the problems they experience. Try to compare different nursing approaches with, for example, children, people with learning disabilities, old people and terminally ill people. If you under-performed at GCSE, give reasons. If you have had work experience or a part-time job, describe how your skills have developed, for example responsibility, communication, team-building, organisational skills. How do you spend your spare time? Explain how your interests help with stress and pressure. See also **Appendix 3**. Admission is subject to eligibility for an NHS bursary. Contact NHS Student Grants Unit, tel 01253 655655.

Misconceptions about this course That Nursing programmes are not demanding. Midwives and nurses don't do shift work and are not involved in travelling! **City** Midwives are only involved at the birth stage and not at the ante-natal and post-natal stages, or in education and support.

Selection interviews Most institutions **Yes** Abertay, Anglia Ruskin, Bangor, Birmingham, Birmingham (UC), Birmingham City, Bournemouth, Brighton, Cardiff, City, Coventry, Dundee, Dundee, East Anglia, Essex, Glyndŵr, Hertfordshire, Hull, Keele, Liverpool John Moores, Nottingham, Salford, Sheffield Hallam, Stirling, Surrey, Swansea, West Scotland, Wolverhampton, York; **Some** Bucks New.

Interview advice and questions Past questions have included: Why do you want to be a nurse? What experience have you had in nursing? What do you think of the nurses' pay situation? Should nurses go on strike? What are your views on abortion? What branch of nursing most interests you? How would you communicate with someone who can't speak English? What is the nurse's role in the community? How should a nurse react in an emergency? How would you cope with telling a patient's relative that the patient was dying? Admissions tutors look for communication skills, team interaction and the applicant's understanding of health/society-related subjects. See also **Chapter 6**. **London South Bank** What do you understand by equal opportunities? **Swansea** What is your perception of the role of the nurse? What qualities do you have that would be good for nursing?

Reasons for rejection (non-academic) Insufficient awareness of the roles and responsibilities of a midwife or nurse. Lack of motivation. Poor communication skills. Lack of awareness of nursing developments through the media. (Detailed knowledge of the NHS or nursing practice not usually required.) Failed medical. Unsatisfactory health record. Not fulfilling the hepatitis B requirements or police check requirements. Poor preparation for the interview. Too shy. Only wants nursing as a means to something else, for example commission in the armed forces. Too many choices on the UCAS application, for example Midwifery, Physiotherapy, Occupational Therapy. No care experience. Some applicants have difficulty with maths – multiplication and division – used in calculating dosage for medicines. **Birmingham** No work experience. **De Montfort** No insight as to nursing as a career or the various branches of nursing. **Swansea** Poor communication skills.

AFTER-RESULTS ADVICE

Offers to applicants repeating A-levels **Higher** Bristol UWE, Cardiff, Hull, Liverpool John Moores (Midwif); **Same** De Montfort, Edinburgh Queen Margaret, Huddersfield, Liverpool John Moores, London South Bank, Salford, Staffordshire, Stirling, Suffolk (Univ Campus), Surrey, Swansea, Wolverhampton; **No** Birmingham City.

GRADUATE DESTINATIONS AND EMPLOYMENT (2011/12 HESA)

Nursing graduates surveyed 19940 **Employed** 14875 **In voluntary employment** 75 **In further study** 1410 **Assumed unemployed** 570

Career note The majority of graduates aim to enter the nursing profession.

OTHER DEGREE SUBJECTS FOR CONSIDERATION

Audiology; Biological Sciences; Biology; Community Studies; Dietetics; Education; Health Studies; Medicine; Nutrition; Occupational Therapy; Optometry; Pharmacology; Pharmacy; Physiotherapy; Podiatry; Psychology; Radiography; Social Policy and Administration; Social Work; Sociology; Speech Therapy; Veterinary Nursing.

NUTRITION

(see also **Dietetics, Food Science/Studies and Technology, Health Sciences/Studies**)

Nutrition attracts a great deal of attention in society and whilst controversy, claim and counter-claim seem to focus daily on the merits and otherwise of food, it is, nevertheless, a scientific study in itself. Courses involve topics relating to diet, health, nutrition and food policy and are designed to prepare students to enter careers as specialists in nutrition and dietetics.

Useful websites www.nutrition.org.uk; www.nutritionsociety.org; see also under **Dietetics**.

NB The points totals shown to the left of the institutions are for ease of reference only. It must not be assumed that Tariff points are always used by institutions or that they can be substituted for an offer in grades. The level of an offer is not necessarily indicative of the quality of a course.

COURSE OFFERS INFORMATION

Subject requirements/preferences GCSE Mathematics and science usually required. **AL** Science subjects required for most courses, biology and/or chemistry preferred.

Your target offers and examples of courses provided by each institution

340 pts **Glasgow** – AAB (Physiol Spo Sci Nutr) (IB 34 pts)
  London (King's) – AAB (Nutr Diet) (IB 35 pts HL 665 chem biol)
  Newcastle – AAB–ABB 340–320 pts (Fd Mark Nutr; Nutr Psy) (IB 34–35 pts)
  Nottingham – AAB–ABB 340–320 pts (Nutr (Diet) MNutr) (IB 32–34 pts)

320 pts **Leeds** – ABB (Fd Sci Nutr; Nutr) (IB 34–32 pts)
  London (King's) – ABB (Nutr) (IB 34 pts)
  Newcastle – ABB 320 pts (Fd Hum Nutr) (IB 34 pts)
  Nottingham – ABB–BBB 320–300 pts (Nutr; Nutr Fd Sci) (IB 30–32 pts)
  Reading – ABB–BBB 320–300 pts (Fd Sci; Nutr Fd Sci; Nutr Fd Consum Sci)
  Surrey – ABB 320 pts (Nutr; Nutr Fd Sci; Nutr Diet) (IB 34 pts)

300 pts **Cardiff Met (UWIC)** – 300 pts (Hum Nutr Diet) (IB 26 pts)
  Greenwich – 300 pts (Hum Nutr)
  Leeds Beckett – 300 pts (Diet; Pbl Hlth (Nutr)) (IB 26 pts)
  Liverpool Hope – 300–320 pts (Hlth Nutr Joint Hons)
  London Met – 300 pts (Diet Nutr)
  Queen's Belfast – BBB 300 pts (Fd Qual Sfty Nutr)

280 pts **Bournemouth** – 280 pts (Nutr) (28 pts)
  Chester – 280–300 pts (Nutr Diet) (IB 28 pts)
  Edge Hill – 280 pts (Nutr Hlth)
  Leeds Trinity – 280 pts (Spo Hlth Exer Nutr; Nutr Fd)
  Manchester Met – 280 pts (Hum Nutr) (IB 28 pts)
  Northumbria – 280 pts (Hum Nutr; Fd Sci Nutr)
  Oxford Brookes – BBC 280 pts (Nutr) (IB 30 pts)
  Plymouth – 280–300 pts (Exer Nutr Hlth; Pblc Hlth Nutr)
  Sheffield Hallam – 280 pts (Fd Nutr; Pblc Hlth Nutr; Nutr Hlth Lfstl)
  Suffolk (Univ Campus) – 280 pts (Nutr Hum Hlth)

260 pts **Bath Spa** – 260–300 pts (Fd Nutr; Hum Nutr)
  Central Lancashire – 260–300 pts (Hum Nutr; Nutr Exer Sci)
  Glasgow Caledonian – BCC incl chem 260 pts (Hum Nutr Diet) (IB 24 pts)
  Hertfordshire – 260 pts (Nutr) (IB 27 pts)
  Huddersfield – BCC 260 pts (Nutr Pblc Hlth; Fd Nutr Hlth)
  Kingston – 260–360 pts (Nutr; Exer Nutr Hlth)
  Liverpool Hope – 260–300 pts (Nutr)
  Liverpool John Moores – 260 pts (Fd Nutr)
  Nottingham Trent – 260 pts (Exer Nutr Hlth)
  Robert Gordon – BCC 260 pts (Nutr Diet) (IB 27 pts)
  South Wales – 260 pts (Nutr Physl Actvt Commun Hlth; Nutr) (IB 28 pts)
  Teesside – 260–280 pts (Fd Nutr)
  Ulster – 260 pts (Hum Nutr)

240 pts **Abertay** – CCC 240 pts (Fd Nutr Hlth)
  Birmingham City – 240 pts (Nutr Sci)
  CAFRE – 240 pts (Fd Des Nutr)
  Cardiff Met (UWIC) – 240 pts (Spo Biomed Nutr)
  Chester – 240–280 pts (Hum Nutr) (IB 26 pts)
  Coventry – CCC 240 pts (Exer Nutr Hlth; Fd Sci Nutr)
  Leeds Trinity – 240–280 pts (Nutr Fd Hlth)

London Met – 240 pts (Hum Nutr)
Robert Gordon – CCC (Nutr)
Roehampton – 240 pts (Nutr Hlth)
St Mary's – 240 pts (Nutr) (IB 28 pts)
Ulster – 240 pts (Fd Nutr)
Worcester – 240–280 pts (Hum Nutr)
220 pts **Harper Adams** – 220–260 pts (Fd Nutr Wlbng)
Westminster – CCD (Hum Nutr; Nutr Exer Sci) (IB 26 pts)
200 pts **London South Bank** – CDD 200 pts (Fd Nutr)
160 pts **Bradford (Coll Univ Centre)** – 160 pts (Soc Nutr Hlth)
Edinburgh Queen Margaret – CC 160 pts (Nutr) (IB 26 pts)

Trinity Saint David – entry is based on individual merit (Hlth Nutr Lfstl)

Alternative offers
See **Chapter 7** and **Appendix 1** for grades/UCAS Tariff points information for the International Baccalaureate, Scottish Highers/Advanced Highers, the Welsh Baccalaureate, the Irish Leaving Certificate, the Cambridge Pre-U Diploma, the Advanced Diploma and the Extended Project.

EXAMPLES OF FOUNDATION DEGREES IN THE SUBJECT FIELD
CAFRE; Truro (Coll).

CHOOSING YOUR COURSE (SEE ALSO CH.1)
Some course features
London (King's) The BSc course is a modular programme with specialised options including diet, disease, obesity, antioxidants and cancer. There is a four-year Nutrition and Dietetics course with clinical placements in Year 2, 3 and 4, leading to qualification as a dietician.
Newcastle (Fd Hum Nutr) Stages 1 and 2 focus on biology and biological chemistry, with an emphasis on nutrition and food science. After a work placement, Stage 3 covers nutrition, health and disease, biotechnology in the food industry, plants as food, and sport and exercise nutrition.
Reading (Nutr Fd Sci) Course is normally four years with a placement year in Year 3.
Sheffield Hallam (Pblc Hlth Nutr) Course includes business elements covering human resources and project management.

Universities and colleges teaching quality See www.qaa.ac.uk; http://unistats.direct.gov.uk.

Top research universities and colleges (RAE 2008) (Nutritional Sciences) See also **Agricultural Sciences/Agriculture**. London (King's).

Examples of sandwich degree courses Cardiff Met (UWIC); Coventry; Glasgow Caledonian; Harper Adams; Huddersfield; Kingston; Leeds Beckett; Lincoln; Manchester Met; Newcastle; Northumbria; Queen's Belfast; Reading; Sheffield Hallam; Surrey; Teesside; Ulster.

ADMISSIONS INFORMATION
Number of applicants per place (approx) Cardiff Met (UWIC) 5; Glasgow Caledonian 8; Liverpool John Moores 10; London (King's) 6; London Met 9; London South Bank 5; Newcastle 5; Nottingham 7; Robert Gordon 4; Surrey 5.

Advice to applicants and planning the UCAS personal statement Information on relevant experience, reasons for wanting to do the degree and careers sought would be useful. See also **Dietetics** and **Appendix 3**. **Surrey** Overseas students not eligible for Nutrition and Dietetics course.

Misconceptions about this course Some applicants do not realise that this is a science course.

Selection interviews **Yes** London Met, London South Bank, Surrey; **Some** Nottingham, Robert Gordon, Roehampton; **No** Liverpool John Moores.

Check **Chapter 4** when choosing your university and **Chapter 7** on how to read the subject tables.

Interview advice and questions Past questions have focused on scientific A-level subjects studied and aspects of subjects enjoyed by the applicants. Questions then arise from answers. Extensive knowledge expected of nutrition as a career and candidates should have talked to people involved in this type of work, for example dietitians. They will also be expected to discuss wider problems such as food supplies in developing countries and nutritional problems resulting from famine. See also **Chapter 6**. **Liverpool John Moores** Interviews are informal. It would be useful for you to bring samples of coursework to the interview.

AFTER-RESULTS ADVICE

Offers to applicants repeating A-levels **Possibly higher** Nottingham; **Same** Liverpool John Moores, Manchester Met, Roehampton, St Mary's, Surrey.

GRADUATE DESTINATIONS AND EMPLOYMENT (2011/12 HESA)

Graduates surveyed 865 **Employed** 440 **In voluntary employment** 30 **In further study** 130 **Assumed unemployed** 70

Career note Nutritionists work in retail, health promotion and sport; others specialise in dietetics.

OTHER DEGREE SUBJECTS FOR CONSIDERATION

Biological Sciences; Biology; Consumer Studies; Dietetics; Food Sciences; Health Studies/Sciences.

OCCUPATIONAL THERAPY

Contrary to common belief, occupational therapy is not an art career although art and craftwork may be involved as a therapeutic exercise. Occupational therapists assess the physical, mental and social needs of ill or disabled people and help them regain lost skills and manage their lives to the best of their circumstances. Most courses include anatomy, physiology, physical rehabilitation, psychology, sociology, mental health and ethics. Selectors look for maturity, initiative, enterprise, tact, sound judgement and organising ability.

Useful websites www.cot.co.uk; www.otdirect.co.uk.

NB The points totals shown to the left of the institutions are for ease of reference only. It must not be assumed that Tariff points are always used by institutions or that they can be substituted for an offer in grades. The level of an offer is not necessarily indicative of the quality of a course.

COURSE OFFERS INFORMATION

Subject requirements/preferences **GCSE** English, mathematics and science grade A–C. **AL** A social science or science subjects required or preferred for most courses. **Other** All applicants need to pass an occupational health check and obtain Disclosure and Barring Service (DBS) clearance.

Your target offers and examples of courses provided by each institution

340 pts **Bristol UWE** – 340 pts (Occ Thera) (IB 28 pts HL 6)
Southampton – AAB incl sci/psy/sociol 340 pts (Occ Thera) (IB 34 pts HL 17 pts)

320 pts **Bournemouth** – 320 pts (Occ Thera) (IB 32 pts HL 555)
Bradford – 320 pts incl 100 pts from sci (Occ Thera) (IB 27 pts)
Cardiff – ABB 320 pts (Occ Thera) (IB 27 pts HL 5)

300 pts **Brunel** – BBB 300 pts (Occ Thera) (IB 32 pts)
East Anglia – BBB 300 pts (Occ Thera) (IB 31 pts HL 655)
Liverpool – BBB 300 pts (Occ Thera) (IB 29 pts HL 555)
London South Bank – BBB 300 pts (Occ Thera) (IB 26 pts)
Northumbria – 300 pts (Occ Thera)
Oxford Brookes – BBB 300 pts (Occ Thera) (IB 32 pts)
Plymouth – 300 pts (Occ Thera) (IB 27 pts)
Salford – BBB 300 pts (Occ Thera) (IB 32 pts)

Health
Sciences

UNIVERSITY OF
Southampton

"I came to Southampton because it is one of the most respected Universities for health sciences. With my degree, I hope to work with injured soldiers in developing world countries. The University offers so many extra-curricular opportunities, there is simply not enough hours in the day. I love the fitness classes at the Jubilee Sports Centre and have kept my first aid certificate up-to-date with the Royal Yachting Association (RYA). I am also on the committee for the University Symphonic Wind Orchestra and play the flute. The library is one of the main attractions of this uni – it is huge. I often go there to work on essays with my friends because there are no distractions and you have all the books you could need."

Lydia Pavia | Occupational Therapy

www.southampton.ac.uk/healthsciences

Ulster – BBB 300 pts +HPAT (Occ Thera) (IB 26 pts)
280 pts **Cumbria** – 280 pts (Occ Thera) (IB 28 pts)
Derby – 280 pts (Occ Thera) (IB 28 pts)
Edinburgh Queen Margaret – BBC 280 pts (Occ Thera) (IB 28 pts)
Huddersfield – 280 pts (Occ Thera)
Northampton – 280–300 pts (Occ Thera) (IB 24 pts)
Sheffield Hallam – 280 pts (Occ Thera)
260 pts **Coventry** – BCC 260 pts (Occ Thera)
Derby – 260–280 pts (Spo Msg Exer Thera Joint Hons)
Robert Gordon – BCC 260 pts (Occ Thera) (IB 27 pts)
York St John – 260 pts (Occ Thera) (IB 24 pts)
240 pts **Canterbury Christ Church** – 240 pts (Occ Thera)
Glasgow Caledonian – CCC 240 pts (Occ Thera) (IB 24 pts)
Teesside – 240–280 pts (Occ Thera) (IB 24 pts)

Brighton – p/t, individual offers may vary, NHS bursaries are available for all courses (Occ Thera)

Alternative offers
See **Chapter 7** and **Appendix 1** for grades/UCAS Tariff points information for the International Baccalaureate, Scottish Highers/Advanced Highers, the Welsh Baccalaureate, the Irish Leaving Certificate, the Cambridge Pre-U Diploma, the Advanced Diploma and the Extended Project.

CHOOSING YOUR COURSE (SEE ALSO CH.1)
Some course features
See also **Health Sciences/Studies**.
Brunel (Occ Thera) Course can be taken for three years full-time or four years part-time.

Check **Chapter 4** when choosing your university and **Chapter 7** on how to read the subject tables.

East Anglia (Occ Thera) Practice placements in hospitals and the community. Advanced units in Year 3 include Context of Practice, Placement and Professional Development.
Liverpool (Occ Thera) Six placements take place throughout the course; 1000 hours required in practice settings for professional registration.

Universities and colleges teaching quality See www.qaa.ac.uk; http://unistats.direct.gov.uk.

ADMISSIONS INFORMATION
Number of applicants per place (approx) Canterbury Christ Church 5; Cardiff 10; Coventry 15; Cumbria 20; Derby 5; East Anglia 5; Edinburgh Queen Margaret 7; Northampton 4; Northumbria 4; Oxford Brookes 12; Robert Gordon 6; Salford 5; Sheffield Hallam 7; Southampton 7; Ulster 13; York St John 5.

Advice to applicants and planning the UCAS personal statement Contact your local hospital and discuss this career with the occupational therapists. Try to obtain work shadowing experience and make notes of your observations. Describe any such visits in full (see also Reasons for rejection (non-academic)). Applicants are expected to have visited two occupational therapy departments, one in a physical or social services setting, one in the mental health field. Good interpersonal skills. Breadth and nature of health-related work experience is important. Also skills, interests (for example, sports, design). Applicants should have a high standard of communication skills and experience of working with people with disabilities. See also **Appendix 3**. **York St John** Contact with the profession essential; very competitive course.

Selection interviews Most institutions. **Yes** Canterbury Christ Church, Coventry, East Anglia, Ulster.

Interview advice and questions Since this is a vocational course, work experience is nearly always essential and applicants are likely to be questioned on the types of work involved and the career. Some universities may use admissions tests: check websites and see **Chapter 6**.

Reasons for rejection (non-academic) Poor communication skills. Lack of knowledge of occupational therapy. Little evidence of working with people. Uncertain about their future career. Lack of maturity. Indecision regarding the profession. **Salford** Failure to function well in groups and inability to perform practical tasks.

AFTER-RESULTS ADVICE
Offers to applicants repeating A-levels **Same** Derby, Salford, York St John.

GRADUATE DESTINATIONS AND EMPLOYMENT (2011/12 HESA)
Career note Occupational therapists (who work mostly in hospital departments) are involved in the rehabilitation of those who have required medical treatment and work with the young, aged and, for example, people with learning difficulties.

OTHER DEGREE SUBJECTS FOR CONSIDERATION
Audiology; Community Studies; Dietetics; Education; Health Studies/Sciences; Nursing; Nutrition; Physiotherapy; Podiatry; Psychology; Radiography; Social Policy and Administration; Social Work; Sociology; Speech Sciences.

OPTOMETRY (OPHTHALMIC OPTICS)
(including **Ophthalmic Dispensing** and **Orthoptics**)

Optometry courses (which are increasingly popular) lead to qualification as an optometrist (previously known as an ophthalmic optician). They provide training in detecting defects and diseases in the eye and in prescribing treatment with, for example, spectacles, contact lenses and other appliances to correct or improve vision. Orthoptics includes the study of general anatomy, physiology and normal child development and leads to a career as an orthoptist. This involves the investigation, diagnosis and treatment of defects of binocular vision and other eye conditions. The main components of degree courses include the study of the eye, the use of diagnostic and measuring equipment and treatment of eye abnormalities. See also **Appendix 3**.

Useful websites www.optical.org; www.orthoptics.org.uk.

NB The points totals shown to the left of the institutions are for ease of reference only. It must not be assumed that Tariff points are always used by institutions or that they can be substituted for an offer in grades. The level of an offer is not necessarily indicative of the quality of a course.

COURSE OFFERS INFORMATION
Subject requirements/preferences **GCSE** Good grades in English and science subjects usually required. **AL** Science subjects required for all Optometry courses. Mathematics usually acceptable.

Your target offers and examples of courses provided by each institution
360 pts **Aston** – AAA incl biol +maths/phys 360 pts (Optom) (IB 34–35 pts HL 665 biol/phys/maths)
         Cardiff – AAA 360 pts (Optom) (IB 34 pts)
         City – AAA 360 pts (Optom) (IB 34 pts)
340 pts **Anglia Ruskin** – AAB 340 pts (Optom) (IB 33 pts HL 6 chem biol phys maths)
         Bradford – AAB 340 pts (Optom) (IB 28 pts)
         Glasgow Caledonian – AAB 340 pts (Optom) (IB 28 pts)
         Manchester – AAB (Optom) (IB 35 pts)
         Plymouth – AAB 340 pts (Optom)
         Ulster – AAB (Optom) (IB 37 pts)
300 pts **Liverpool** – BBB (Orth) (IB 30 pts HL 5 biol)
         Sheffield – BBB 300 pts (Orth) (IB 32 pts)
200 pts **Anglia Ruskin** – 200 pts incl any sci (Oph Disp) (IB 24 pts)
180 pts **City** – 180 pts (Oph Disp)
160 pts **Bradford (Coll Univ Centre)** – CC 160 pts (Oph Disp)
         Glasgow Caledonian – CC 160 pts (Oph Disp) (IB 24 pts)

Alternative offers
See **Chapter 7** and **Appendix 1** for grades/UCAS Tariff points information for the International Baccalaureate, Scottish Highers/Advanced Highers, the Welsh Baccalaureate, the Irish Leaving Certificate, the Cambridge Pre-U Diploma, the Advanced Diploma and the Extended Project.

EXAMPLES OF FOUNDATION DEGREES IN THE SUBJECT FIELD
Anglia Ruskin; City.

CHOOSING YOUR COURSE (SEE ALSO CH.1)
Some course features
Anglia Ruskin The University has forged links with local charities, such as Cam Sight and Guide Dogs, giving students the opportunity to interact with the local community.
Aston The course offers an integration of teaching and professional practice and a hospital placement scheme.
Bradford Placements take place after graduation during the pre-registration year.
Cardiff This is a three-year course after which graduates undertake a one-year pre-registration course.
City Extensive patient contact takes place in Year 3.

Universities and colleges teaching quality See www.qaa.ac.uk; http://unistats.direct.gov.uk.

Top research universities and colleges (RAE 2008) Aston (Optom); City (Biomed Vsn Sci); Cardiff (Optom Vsn Sci).

ADMISSIONS INFORMATION
Number of applicants per place (approx) Anglia Ruskin 12; Aston 7; Bradford 6; Cardiff 13; City 11; Glasgow Caledonian 9.

Numbers of applicants (a UK b EU (non-UK) c non-EU d mature) Anglia Ruskin **a**431 **b**431; Aston **a**700 **b**50 **c**70 **d**10; Bradford **a**600 **b**600 **c**90; Glasgow Caledonian **a**548 **c**23.

Advice to applicants and planning the UCAS personal statement For Optometry courses contact with optometrists is essential, either work shadowing or gaining some work experience. Make notes of your experiences and the work done and report fully on the UCAS application on why the career interests you. See also **Appendix 3**.

Selection interviews Yes Bradford, City; **Some** Anglia Ruskin, Aston, Cardiff; **No** Glasgow Caledonian.

Interview advice and questions Optometry is a competitive subject requiring applicants to have had some work experience on which they will be questioned. See also **Chapter 6**. **Anglia Ruskin** Why will you make a good optometrist? Describe the job.

AFTER-RESULTS ADVICE
Offers to applicants repeating A-levels Higher City; **Possibly higher** Aston; **Same** Anglia Ruskin, Cardiff.

GRADUATE DESTINATIONS AND EMPLOYMENT (2011/12 HESA)
Graduates surveyed 725 **Employed** 515 **In voluntary employment** 10 **In further study** 155 **Assumed unemployed** 20

Career note The great majority of graduates enter private practice either in small businesses or in larger organisations (which have been on the increase in recent years). A small number work in eye hospitals. Orthoptists tend to work in public health and education dealing with children and the elderly.

OTHER DEGREE SUBJECTS FOR CONSIDERATION
Health Studies; Nursing; Occupational Therapy; Physics; Physiotherapy; Radiography; Speech Studies.

PHARMACOLOGY

(including **Toxicology**; see also **Biological Sciences, Health Sciences/Studies**)

Pharmacology is the study of drugs and medicines and courses focus on physiology, biochemistry, toxicology, immunology, microbiology and chemotherapy. Pharmacologists are not qualified to work as pharmacists. Toxicology involves the study of the adverse effects of chemicals on living systems. See also **Appendix 3** under Pharmacology.

Useful websites www.thebts.org; www.bps.ac.uk; www.pharmacology.com.

NB The points totals shown to the left of the institutions are for ease of reference only. It must not be assumed that Tariff points are always used by institutions or that they can be substituted for an offer in grades. The level of an offer is not necessarily indicative of the quality of a course.

COURSE OFFERS INFORMATION
Subject requirements/preferences GCSE English, science and mathematics. **AL** Chemistry and/or biology required for most courses.

Your target offers and examples of courses provided by each institution
380 pts **Cambridge** – A*AA (Nat Sci (Pharmacol)) (IB 40–41 pts HL 776)
   London (UCL) – AAAe–AABe 380–360 pts (Pharmacol) (IB 36–38 pts HL 6 chem +maths/phys/biol)
360 pts **Edinburgh** – AAA–ABB 360–320 pts (Biol Sci (Pharmacol)) (IB 37–32 pts)
   Manchester – AAA–ABB 360–320 pts (Pharmacol (Yr Ind); Pharmacol Physiol (Yr Ind)) (IB 37–33 pts)
   Newcastle – AAA–AAB 360–320 pts (Pharmacol) (IB 34–35 pts HL 5 chem biol)

Southampton – AAA–ABB (Pharmacol) (IB 36–32 pts HL 18–16 pts incl HL 6 chem)

340 pts **Bath** – AAB–ABB (Pharmacol) (IB 34–36 pts HL 666)

Birmingham – ABB 340 pts (Chem Pharmacol) (IB 34–35 pts HL chem)

Bristol – AAB–ABB 340–320 pts (Pharmacol (Yr Ind)) (IB 35 pts HL 666 chem sci)

Cardiff – AAB 340 pts (Med Pharmacol) (IB 34 pts)

Leeds – AAA–ABB incl biol/chem +sci 360–320 pts (Pharmacol) (IB 35–34 pts HL 18–16 pts incl 6 chem/biol +sci)

London (King's) – AAB 340 pts (Pharmacol Mol Genet; Pharmacol) (IB 35 pts HL 665)

Manchester – AAA–AAB (Pharmacol) (IB 37–33 pts)

Nottingham – AAB (Neuro Pharmacol) (IB 34 pts)

320 pts **Dundee** – ABB incl biol chem 320 pts (Pharmacol) (IB 34 pts HL 665)

Glasgow – ABB (Pharmacol) (IB 32 pts)

Leicester – ABB (Biol Sci (Physiol Pharmacol)) (IB 32 pts)

Liverpool – ABB 320 pts (Pharmacol) (IB 33 pts HL 6 chem 5 sci)

Strathclyde – ABB incl chem biol 320 pts (Pharmacol) (IB 32 pts HL6 chem biol)

300 pts **Aberdeen** – BBB (Pharmacol) (IB 30 pts)

Kent – 300 pts (Pharm Physiol)

280 pts **Hertfordshire** – 280 pts (Pharmacol)

Nottingham Trent – 280 pts (Pharmacol)

Portsmouth – BBC 280 pts (Pharmacol) (IB 29 pts HL 665 chem biol sci/maths)

260 pts **Central Lancashire** – BCC 260 pts (Physiol Pharmacol) (IB 25 pts)

Glasgow Caledonian – BCC 260 pts (Pharmacol)

Kingston – 260–280 pts (Pharmacol; Pharmacol Bus)

240 pts **Coventry** – CCC 240 pts (Med Pharmacol Sci)

East London – 240 pts incl chem biol (Pharmacol) (IB 24 pts HL 15 pts)

London Met – 240 pts (Pharmacol) (IB 28 pts)

Westminster – CCC 240 pts (Pharmacol Physiol) (IB 26 pts HL 55 sci)

220 pts **Westminster** – CCD 220 pts (Herb Med) (IB 26 pts HL 55 in 2 sci)

200 pts **Middlesex** – 200–300 pts (Herb Med) (IB 28 pts)

Wolverhampton – 200 pts (Pharmacol) (IB 25 pts)

160 pts **Edinburgh Queen Margaret** – CC 160 pts (App Pharmacol) (IB 26 pts)

Alternative offers

See **Chapter 7** and **Appendix 1** for grades/UCAS Tariff points information for the International Baccalaureate, Scottish Highers/Advanced Highers, the Welsh Baccalaureate, the Irish Leaving Certificate, the Cambridge Pre-U Diploma, the Advanced Diploma and the Extended Project.

CHOOSING YOUR COURSE (SEE ALSO CH.1)

Some course features

Coventry The course in Medical and Pharmacological Sciences focuses on a study of pharmacology and physiology and applications in medicine. It can be taken with a year in professional placement.

Kingston There is an optional sandwich year in full-time employment.

London (King's) A Single Honours degree is offered in Pharmacology. In the first two years the focus is on physiology, biochemistry and pharmacology. In the third year, specialist topics include toxicology, immunology and environmental pharmacology. See also **Biological Sciences**.

Portsmouth The Pharmacology course has a common first year with Biomedical Science. This is a three year full-time course and includes a study of physiology and chemistry to support studies in pharmacology. Overall the course has a biochemical focus towards modern pharmacology with an emphasis on pharmacology in all three years.

Southampton The Pharmacology degree is based on both physiology and biochemistry and looks at the design of drugs and their biological effects. A one-year placement is possible.

Universities and colleges teaching quality See www.qaa.ac.uk; http://unistats.direct.gov.uk.

Examples of sandwich degree courses Bath; Bristol; East London; Kingston; London Met; Manchester; Nottingham Trent; Southampton.

Check **Chapter 4** when choosing your university and **Chapter 7** on how to read the subject tables.

ADMISSIONS INFORMATION

Number of applicants per place (approx) Bath 6; Birmingham 6; Bradford 20; Bristol 8; Cardiff 8; Dundee 5; East London 4; Hertfordshire 10; Leeds 7; Liverpool 5; London (King's) 6; Portsmouth 4; Southampton 8; Strathclyde 10; Wolverhampton 4.

Advice to applicants and planning the UCAS personal statement Contact with the pharmaceutical industry is important in order to be aware of the range of work undertaken. Read pharmaceutical journals (although note that Pharmacology and Pharmacy courses lead to different careers). See also **Pharmacy and Pharmaceutical Sciences**. **Bath** Interests outside A-level studies. Important to produce evidence that there is more to the student than A-level ability. **Bristol** Be aware that a Pharmacology degree is mainly biological rather than chemical although both subjects are important.

Misconceptions about this course Mistaken belief that Pharmacology and Pharmaceutical Sciences is the same as Pharmacy and that a Pharmacology degree will lead to work as a pharmacist.

Selection interviews Yes Bath, Birmingham, Cambridge, Cardiff, Newcastle; **Some** Dundee; **No** Portsmouth.

Interview advice and questions Past questions include: Why do you want to do Pharmacology? Why not Pharmacy? Why not Chemistry? How are pharmacologists employed in industry? What are the issues raised by anti-vivisectionists on animal experimentation? Questions relating to the A-level syllabus in chemistry and biology. See also **Chapter 6**.

Reasons for rejection (non-academic) Confusion between Pharmacology, Pharmacy and Pharmaceutical Sciences. One university rejected two applicants because they had no motivation or understanding of the course (one had A-levels at AAB!). Insurance against rejection for Medicine. Lack of knowledge about pharmacology as a subject.

AFTER-RESULTS ADVICE

Offers to applicants repeating A-levels Higher Bristol, Glasgow, Leeds; **Same** Bath, Bradford, Cardiff, Dundee, Portsmouth.

GRADUATE DESTINATIONS AND EMPLOYMENT (2011/12 HESA)

Pharmacology, Toxicology and Pharmacy graduates surveyed 2690 **Employed** 1935 **In voluntary employment** 35 **In further study** 495 **Assumed unemployed** 95

Career note The majority of pharmacologists work with the large pharmaceutical companies involved in research and development. A small number are employed by the NHS in medical research and clinical trials. Some will eventually diversify and become involved in marketing, sales and advertising.

OTHER DEGREE SUBJECTS FOR CONSIDERATION

Biochemistry; Biological Sciences; Biology; Biotechnology; Chemistry; Life Sciences; Medical Biochemistry; Medicinal Chemistry; Microbiology; Natural Sciences; Pharmaceutical Sciences; Pharmacy; Physiology; Toxicology.

PHARMACY and PHARMACEUTICAL SCIENCES

(including **Herbal Medicine**; see also **Biochemistry, Chemistry, Health Sciences/Studies**)

Pharmacy is the science of medicines, involving research into chemical structures and natural products of possible medicinal value, the development of dosage and the safety testing of products. This table also includes information on courses in Pharmaceutical Science (which should not be confused with Pharmacy) which is a multi-disciplinary subject covering chemistry, biochemistry, pharmacology and medical issues. Pharmaceutical scientists apply their knowledge of science and the biology of disease to the design and delivery of therapeutic agents. Note: All Pharmacy courses leading to MPharm are four years. Only Pharmacy degree courses accredited by the Royal Phamaceutical Society of Great Britain lead to a qualification as a pharmacist. Check prospectuses and websites.

Aston University
Birmingham

School of Life & Health Sciences

Acknowledged as UK-leading with an outstanding reputation for teaching and research. Our excellence in research is integrated into lectures, giving students the distinct advantage of access to the latest trends, thinking, issues and research in their particular field.

Prepare for your future with our range of professionally relevant courses:

- Foundation Degree in Hearing Aid Audiology 2 years full-time with integrated work-based learning
- BSc Healthcare Science (Audiology) 3 years full-time with integrated placements
- BSc Biological Sciences 3 years full-time/4 years full-time with a placement
- BSc Cell and Molecular Biology 3 years full-time/4 years full-time with a placement
- BSc Human Biology 3 years full-time/4 years full-time with a placement
- BSc Microbiology and Immunology 3 years full-time/4 years full-time with a placement
- MBiol Biological Sciences 4 years full-time/5 years fulltime with a placement

- BSc Biomedical Science 3 years full-time/4 years full-time with a placement
- BSc Optometry 3 years full-time
- Masters in Optometry 4 years with an integrated pre-registration year
- Pharmacy – MPharm 4 years full time
- BSc Psychology 3 years full-time/4 years full-time with a placement
- BSc Psychology and Business (Joint Honours) 4 years full-time with a placement
- BSc Psychology and English Language (Joint Honours) 4 years full-time with a placement
- BSc Psychology and Sociology (Joint Honours) 4 years full-time with a placement

We prepare our graduates for professional roles as scientists and practitioners who make a real difference to the communities in which they work and live.

89%
Graduate Employability
A higher proportion than Oxford

Aston University
Birmingham

MBiol Biological Science

Why should you enrol on this programme

This new programme has been designed to give graduates a competitive edge when they apply for positions in Bioscience research in industry or academia. It is an excellent preparation prior to undertaking a PhD.

Key features

> An Enhanced Master's undergraduate programme - students emerge after 4 years with a classified qualification at Master's level. All final year modules are at Master's level (level 7).

> Sixth-month final year practical research project working alongside postgraduate and postdoctoral students in one of Aston's highly-rated research laboratories.

> Strong emphasis on human health and disease and on practical skills training.

> Final year modules are selected from: neurodegenerative disease, obesity and metabolic disorders, stem cell biology, enzyme technology, oxidative stress and inflammatory disease and ABC transporters in health and disease.

> Flexible - transfer to a three-year BSc programme is possible up to the end of year 2.

> Submitted for accreditation by the Society of Biology the professional body for Biologists.

BSc Psychology (Single Honours)

Why study this course

Psychology is a diverse discipline and appropriately trained psychologists are increasingly in demand in both the public and private sectors. At Aston, we offer an engaging and contemporary Psychology curriculum taught by staff who are also internationally recognised research experts. This exciting programme of study is accredited by the British Psychological Society (BPS) and provides students with a thorough grounding in the principles and research methods of psychology. In addition to developing the requisite subject-specific knowledge, there is an emphasis on developing a wide range of analytical and communication skills through the use of innovative learning experiences. Our course has a practical and professional orientation with an option to take a work-based placement year between the second and third years of study, which provides an opportunity to apply developing skills in psychology in a workplace setting.

More about this course

Psychology at Aston is situated within the School of Life and Health Science, which brings together expertise from multiple disciplines that are allied to the health professions. The quality of our facilities, the expertise of our staff and the exciting opportunities for personal development make Aston an ideal place to study Psychology. Our course is divided into core and elective modules over 3 years (or 4 years if students take a placement). Year 1 modules include: abnormal psychology, psychology & the brain, social psychology and cognitive psychology. Year 2 modules include: cognitive neuropsychology, individual differences, language & communication, and developmental psychology. Final year options enable students to specialise in particular topic areas by taking elective modules that typically include: health psychology, psychosis, neuropsychiatric disorders, efficacy of psychotherapy, music & the brain, psychology & work, motivation & emotion, and autism. The third year study also involves completion of a substantial piece of psychological research, conducted in an area of the student's choice with a member of staff with expertise in that area.

Who's this course for

This course is designed for students who want to gain an understanding of human behaviour. It is especially useful for those with a desire to work as a professional psychologist. However, it is also suitable for anyone with a scientific or social scientific background who wants to develop a wide range of analytical and communication skills. Note: studying psychology at A-level is not a prerequisite to studying this subject at degree level. Our Psychology graduates tend to enter careers in business and commerce, caring and social services, teaching and local government among other others. Many of our graduates go on to study for higher degrees at Masters and Doctoral level. This further study, combined with supervised practice, is a prerequisite to working as a professional psychologist. The growth of the service sector puts Psychology graduates at a premium and our graduates have gone on to work in organisations including the Civil Service, the Police Service, local government, clinical services within the NHS, Nestlé, Deloitte and IBM.

University *of*
Hertfordshire

School of
**Life and Medical
Sciences**

The science pioneering the future of healthcare

Pharmacists are the most accessible of all healthcare professionals and represent the integration of fundamental science and patient focused practice. They operate at the forefront of medical innovation – with the design and development of new drugs – and provide daily expert advice to patients on the management and treatment of a variety of medical conditions.

With world-class teaching and advanced facilities led by high impact research programmes, our *MPharm Pharmacy* focuses on the study of science and healthcare. We will provide you with the scientific knowledge, practical skills and professional experience needed to become a technically competent, patient-focused and confident practioner.

You will learn the role of the pharmacist in healthcare and develop an understanding of human health as well as medicines optimisation – so that you may go on to support patients in getting the best outcomes from their treatments.

Become more.

Find out more about this course at:

go.herts.ac.uk/pharmacy

Useful websites www.pharmweb.net; www.rpharms.com; www.chemistanddruggist.co.uk.

NB The points totals shown to the left of the institutions are for ease of reference only. It must not be assumed that Tariff points are always used by institutions or that they can be substituted for an offer in grades. The level of an offer is not necessarily indicative of the quality of a course.

COURSE OFFERS INFORMATION

Subject requirements/preferences GCSE English, mathematics and science subjects. **AL** Chemistry and one or two other sciences required for most courses.

Your target offers and examples of courses provided by each institution

360 pts **Birmingham** – AAA–AAB 360–340 pts (MPharm) (IB 35 pts HL 665 chem sci)
London (King's) – AABe (MPharm) (IB 35 pts HL 665)
London (UCL Sch Pharm) – AAA–AAB 360–340 pts (MPharm) (IB 36–38 pts HL 17–18 pts chem +biol/maths/phys)

340 pts **Aston** – AAB 340 pts (MPharm) (IB 34 pts HL 6 chem +biol/phys 5 maths)
Bath – AAB 340pts (MPharm) (IB 36 pts HL 666 chem +sci/maths)
Cardiff – AAB–ABB (MPharm) (IB 34 pts HL 6 chem +sci/maths)
East Anglia – AAB (MPharm) (IB 33 pts HL 6 chem +sci/maths)
Nottingham – AAB (Pharm MPharm) (IB 34 pts HL 665 chem +sci/maths)
Queen's Belfast – AAB/ABBa (MPharm) (IB 34 pts HL 666)
Reading – AAB–ABB (MPharm) (IB 32–35 pts HL 6 chem)
Strathclyde – AAB (MPharm)
Ulster – AAB (MPharm)

320 pts **Bradford** – 320 pts chem+sci (MPharm) (IB 28 pts HL 666 chem maths biol)
Brighton – ABB (Pharml Cheml Sci; MPharm) (IB 34–36 pts)
Central Lancashire – ABB 320 pts (MPharm) (IB 32 pts)
De Montfort – 320 pts (MPharm) (IB 28 pts HL 6 chem)
Greenwich – ABB (MPharm) (IB 32 pts)
Hertfordshire – 320 pts (MPharm)
Huddersfield – AAB–ABB incl chem+biol 340–320 pts (MPharm) (IB 32 pts HL 665 chem biol maths)
Keele – ABB (MPharm) (IB 32 pts)
Kent – ABB (MPharm) (IB 32 pts)
Loughborough – ABB–BBB 320 pts (Medcnl Pharml Chem) (IB 32–34 pts)
Manchester – ABB–AAA 320–360 pts (MPharm) (IB 33–36 pts HL 665)
Portsmouth – ABB 320 pts (MPharm) (IB 31 pts HL 666 chem sci)
Robert Gordon – ABB incl chem +maths/phys/biol 320 pts (MPharm) (IB 32 pts HL 6 chem 5 sci/maths)
Wolverhampton – 320 pts (MPharm)

300 pts **Greenwich** – 300 pts (Pharml Sci)
Hull – 280–300 pts (Pharml Sci)
Kingston – 300 pts (MPharm)
Leicester – BBB (Pharml Chem) (IB 32 pts HL 5 chem)
Liverpool John Moores – 300–320 pts (Pharm MPharm) (IB 26 pts)
London (QM) – 300 pts (Pharml Chem) (IB 32 pts)
Sunderland – 300–360 pts (MPharm)

280 pts **Arts London** – BBC incl chem+sci 280 pts (Cos Sci)
Central Lancashire – 280 pts (App Biomol Sci)
De Montfort – 280 pts (Pharml Cos Sci)
Hertfordshire – 280 pts (Pharml Sci) (IB 25 pts)

260 pts **Huddersfield** – 260 pts (Pharml Sci)
Kingston – 260 pts (Pharml Sci)
Manchester Met – 260–280 pts (Pharml Chem) (IB 28 pts)
Nottingham Trent – 260 pts (Pharml Medcnl Chem)
South Wales – (Pharml Sci)

Check **Chapter 4** when choosing your university and **Chapter 7** on how to read the subject tables.

240 pts East Anglia – CCC (Pharm Fdn Yr)
London Met – 240 pts incl chem biol (Pharml Sci) (IB 28 pts)
Salford – 240–280 pts (Pharml Sci) (IB 28 pts)
220 pts Westminster – CCD 220 pts (Herb Med) (IB 26 pts HL 55 in 2 sci)
200 pts Wolverhampton – 200 pts incl C chem (Pharml Sci) (IB 25 pts HL 5 chem)

Alternative offers
See **Chapter 7** and **Appendix 1** for grades/UCAS Tariff points information for the International Baccalaureate, Scottish Highers/Advanced Highers, the Welsh Baccalaureate, the Irish Leaving Certificate, the Cambridge Pre-U Diploma, the Advanced Diploma and the Extended Project.

EXAMPLES OF FOUNDATION DEGREES IN THE SUBJECT FIELD
Aston; Birmingham Met (Coll); Kent; (Medway Sch Pharm) Kingston; Preston (Coll); Sunderland City (Coll).

CHOOSING YOUR COURSE (SEE ALSO CH.1)
Some course features
Aston One of the largest pharmacy schools which includes hospital-based clinical teaching.
Brighton (Pharm) Studies include microbiology, clinical pharmacology, pharmacy practice and health psychology reflecting the changing role of the pharmacist.
East Anglia (Pharm) Professional placements begin in Year 1.
Hertfordshire (Pharml Sci) Students not meeting the normal entry requirements can apply for an Extended degree which leads to Year 1 entry.
Keele Hospital, industrial and community placements take place throughout the course.

Universities and colleges teaching quality See www.qaa.ac.uk; http://unistats.direct.gov.uk.

Top research universities and colleges (RAE 2008) Nottingham; Manchester; London (UCL) (Sch Pharm); Bath; Queen's Belfast; East Anglia; London (King's); Strathclyde; Bradford; Cardiff.

Examples of sandwich degree courses Bradford; Coventry; De Montfort; Hertfordshire; Hull.

ADMISSIONS INFORMATION
Number of applicants per place (approx) Aston 10; Bath 6; Bradford 10; Brighton 24 (apply early); Cardiff 5; De Montfort 14; Liverpool John Moores (Pharm) 7; London (King's) 15, (Sch Pharm) 6; Nottingham 8; Portsmouth 20; Robert Gordon 11; Strathclyde 10; Sunderland 20.

Numbers of applicants (a UK **b** EU (non-UK) **c** non-EU **d** mature) Aston **a**1400 **b**100 **c**300 **d**180; Bradford **a**1200 **b**1200 **c**200.

Advice to applicants and planning the UCAS personal statement Work experience and work shadowing with a retail and/or hospital pharmacist is important, and essential for Pharmacy applicants. Read pharmaceutical journals, extend your knowledge of well-known drugs and antibiotics. Read up on the history of drugs. Attend Open Days or careers conferences. See also **Appendix 3**. **Manchester** Students giving preference for Pharmacy are likely to be more successful than those who choose Pharmacy as an alternative to Medicine or Dentistry.

Misconceptions about this course That a degree in Pharmaceutical Science is a qualification leading to a career as a pharmacist. It is not: it is a course which concerns the application of chemical and biomedical science to the design, synthesis and analysis of pharmaceuticals for medicinal purposes. See also **Pharmacology**.

Selection interviews **Yes** Bath, Bradford, Brighton, Cardiff, De Montfort, East Anglia, Keele, Liverpool John Moores, London (UCL Sch Pharm), Manchester, Nottingham, Portsmouth, Reading, Robert Gordon, Strathclyde, Wolverhampton; **Some** Aston.

Interview advice and questions As work experience is essential for Pharmacy applicants, questions are likely to focus on this and what they have discovered. Other relevant questions could include: Why do you want to study Pharmacy? What types of work do pharmacists do? What interests you about the Pharmacy course? What branch of pharmacy do you want to enter? Name a drug – what do you know about it (formula, use etc)? Name a drug from a natural source and its use. Can you think of another way of extracting a drug? Why do fungi destroy bacteria? What is an antibiotic? Can you name one and say how it was discovered? What is insulin? What is its source and function? What is diabetes? What type of insulin is used in its treatment? What is a hormone? What drugs are available over the counter without prescription? What is the formula of aspirin? What is genetic engineering? See also **Chapter 6**. **Bath** Informal and relaxed; 400 approx selected for interview – very few rejected at this stage. **Cardiff** Interviews cover both academic and vocational aspects; candidates must reach a satisfactory level in both areas. **Liverpool John Moores** What are the products of a reaction between an alcohol and a carboxylic acid? **Manchester** Candidates failing to attend interviews will have their applications withdrawn. The majority of applicants are called for interview.

Reasons for rejection (non-academic) Poor communication skills. Poor knowledge of pharmacy and the work of a pharmacist.

AFTER-RESULTS ADVICE
Offers to applicants repeating A-levels Higher Bradford, Cardiff, De Montfort, Liverpool John Moores, London (UCL) (Sch Pharm) AAB, Nottingham (offers rarely made), Portsmouth, Queen's Belfast, Strathclyde; **Possibly higher** Aston, Robert Gordon; **Same** Bath, Brighton, East Anglia, Sunderland, Wolverhampton.

GRADUATE DESTINATIONS AND EMPLOYMENT (2011/12 HESA)
See **Pharmacology**.

Career note The majority of Pharmacy graduates proceed to work in the commercial and retail fields, although opportunities also exist with pharmaceutical companies and in hospital pharmacies. There are also opportunities in agricultural and veterinary pharmacy.

OTHER DEGREE SUBJECTS FOR CONSIDERATION
Biochemistry; Biological Sciences; Biology; Biotechnology; Chemistry; Drug Development; Life Sciences; Medicinal Chemistry; Microbiology; Natural Sciences; Pharmacology; Physiology.

PHILOSOPHY
(see also **Psychology**)

Philosophy is one of the oldest and most fundamental disciplines, which examines the nature of the universe and humanity's place in it. Philosophy seeks to discover the essence of the mind, language and physical reality and discusses the methods used to investigate these topics.

Useful websites www.iep.utm.edu; www.philosophypages.com; www.philosophy.eserver.org; see also **Religious Studies**.

NB The points totals shown to the left of the institutions are for ease of reference only. It must not be assumed that Tariff points are always used by institutions or that they can be substituted for an offer in grades. The level of an offer is not necessarily indicative of the quality of a course.

COURSE OFFERS INFORMATION
Subject requirements/preferences GCSE English and mathematics. A foreign language may be required. **AL** No specific subjects except for joint courses.

Your target offers and examples of courses provided by each institution
430 pts Warwick – A*AAb (PPE) (IB 38 pts)
400 pts London (King's) – A*AAe incl AL fmaths (A*AAa incl AS fmaths) (Maths Phil) (IB 35 pts HL 6 maths)
           Oxford – A*A*A incl maths (Maths Phil) (IB 39 pts)

380 pts **Cambridge** – A*AA (Nat Sci (Hist Phil Sci); Phil) (IB 40-41 pts HL 776)
Durham – A*AA 380 pts (Engl Lit Phil; PPE) (IB 38 pts HL 666)
London (King's) – A*AA +LNAT (Pol Phil Law) (IB 35 pts HL 766)
London (UCL) – AAAe (Phil) (IB 38 pts)
Manchester – A*AA-AAA (Maths Phil) (IB 37 pts HL 18 pts)
Nottingham – A*AA-AAA 380-360 pts (Econ Phil) (IB 38-36 pts)
Oxford – A*AA (Psy Phil Ling) (IB 38-40 pts)
York – A*AA-AAA 380-360 pts (PPE) (IB 37 pts)

360 pts **Bristol** – AAA-AAB 360-340 pts (Phil Econ; Maths Phil; Phil; Phil Theol) (IB 37-35 pts)
Durham – AAA 360 pts (Phil Psy; Phil; Phil Pol) (IB 37 pts)
Edinburgh – AAA-BBB 360-300 pts (Phil; Phil Ling) (IB 40-34 pts)
Exeter – AAA-AAB 360-340 pts (Phil Pol Econ; Phil; PPE) (IB 36-34 pts)
London (King's) – AAA (Phil courses; War St Phil; Fr Phil) (IB 35 pts HL 666)
London LSE – AAA (Phil Econ; Phil Lgc Sci Meth; Pol Phil) (IB 38 pts HL 766)
London NCH – AAA-AAB 340-360 pts (Phil) (IB 37-38 pts HL 77)
Oxford – AAA (PPE; Phil Theol; Phil Modn Langs) (IB 38-40 pts)
St Andrews – AAA-AAB (Phil Scot Hist; Phil courses) (IB 35-38 pts)
Warwick – AAA-AAB (Phil Joint Hons) (IB 38 pts)
York – AAA-AAB (Phys Phil; Phil Pol) (IB 36-35 pts HL 66 maths phys)

340 pts **Birmingham** – AAB-ABB 320-340 pts (Phil) (IB 34-36 pts)
Bristol – AAB-ABB 340-320 pts (Sociol Phil; Phil Modn Lang; Phys Phil) (IB 35-33 pts)
Essex – AAB-ABB (PPE) (IB 33-32 pts)
Glasgow – AAB (Phil) (IB 34 pts)
Lancaster – AAB (PPE; Phil; Phil Relig St; Ling Phil; Maths Phil; Eth Phil Relgn) (IB 35 pts)
Liverpool – AAB-ABB 340-320pts (Phil Joint Hons) (IB 33-35 pts HL 665)
London (Birk) – AAB 340 pts (Phil)
London (King's) – AAB (Relgn Phil Eth) (IB 35 pts HL 665)
London (RH) – AAB-ABB (Mus Phil; Pol Phil Econ; Pol Phil; Phil Joint courses) (IB 35-34 pts)
London (UCL) – AAB-ABB 340-320 pts (Hist Phil Sci) (IB 34-36 pts)
Manchester – AAB (PPE; Theol St Phil Eth) (IB 35 pts)
Newcastle – AAB-ABB 320-340 pts (Phil St Knwl Hum Intr) (IB 32 pts)
Nottingham – AAB (Phil; Phil Theol; Class Civ Phil; Psy Phil; Engl Phil) (IB 34 pts)
Queen's Belfast – AAB 340 pts (PPE) (IB 35 pts HL 666)
Sheffield – AAB (Phil; Pol Phil) (IB 35 pts)
Southampton – AAB (Econ Phil; Phil Hist; Phil Sociol; Phil Pol; Phil Engl; Phil; Film Phil; Phil Maths; Phil Mus) (IB 34 pts HL 17 pts)
Sussex – AAB (Phil) (IB 34-36 pts)
Warwick – AAB 340 pts (Phil) (IB 34 pts HL 66)
York – AAB (Phil; Phil Ling; Engl Phil) (IB 35 pts)

320 pts **Brighton** – ABB (Phil Pol Eth)
Bristol UWE – 320 pts (Phil)
Cardiff – ABB 320 pts (Phil) (IB 33 pts)
Dundee – ABB (Art Phil Contemp Prac) (IB 34 pts)
East Anglia – ABB (PPE; Phil Film St; Phil; Phil Pol; Phil Hist) (IB 32 pts)
Essex – ABB-BBB (Phil; Phil Law; Phil Hist) (IB 32-29 pts)
Kent – ABB (Hist Sci Phil; Phil Joint courses; Phil Soc Psy)
Leeds – ABB (Phil; Phil Joint Hons; Hist Phil Sci courses; Biol Hist Phil Sci)
Liverpool – ABB 320 pts (Phil) (IB 33 pts HL 665)
Manchester – ABB 320 pts (Phil) (IB 34 pts)
Reading – ABB-ACC (Phil courses; Art Phil) (IB 32 pts)
Sheffield – ABB (Theol Mus; Phil Joint Hons) (IB 34 pts)
Swansea – ABB-BBC 320-280 pts (PPE) (IB 33 pts)
Warwick – ABB (Class Civ Phil) (IB 36 pts)

300 pts **Aberdeen** – BBB (Nat Phil (Phys); Phil Hist Art; Phil Joint courses) (IB 32 pts HL 555)
Dundee – BBB (Phil) (IB 30 pts HL 555)

Gloucestershire – 300 pts (Relgn Phil Eth)
Hertfordshire – 300 pts (Phil; Phil Ital)
Hull – 300–340 pts (PPE; Phil; Pol Phil)
Keele – BBB (Phil) (IB 26 pts)
London (Hey) – 300–320 pts (Phil) (IB 30 pts)
Queen's Belfast – BBB (Phil courses) (IB 32 pts HL 655)
Roehampton – 300 pts (Phil)

280 pts **Greenwich** – (Phil Engl Lit; Phil Crea Writ; Phil Hist; Phil Pol; Phil Sociol)
Hull – BBC 280 pts (Psy Phil) (IB 32 pts)
London (Hey) – 280–320 pts (Phil Theol; Phil Relgn Eth)
Manchester Met – 280 pts (Phil Joint Hons; Int Pol Phil) (IB 28 pts)
Newman – 280 pts (Phil Relgn Educ; Phil Relgn Engl)
Oxford Brookes – BBC (Phil)
Stirling – BBC (Phil; PPE) (IB 32 pts)

260 pts **Bath Spa** – 260–300 pts (Relgn Phil Eth) (IB 27 pts)
Central Lancashire – BCC 260 pts (Phil (Comb); Phil) (IB 24 pts)
Dundee – BCC (Euro Phil) (IB 29 pts)
Liverpool Hope – 260–300 pts (Phil Eth)
Nottingham Trent – 260 pts (Phil Joint Hons)
St Mary's – 260 pts (Phil) (IB 28 pts)
Staffordshire – BCC–BB 260 pts (Econ Phil)

240 pts **Bangor** – 240–280 pts (Phil Rel)
Bishop Grosseteste – 240 pts (Theol Eth Soty)
Leeds Trinity – 200–240 pts (Phil Eth Relgn) (IB 24 pts)
Manchester Met – 240–260 pts (Phil) (IB 28 pts)
Staffordshire – 240 pts (Phil Joint Hons)
York St John – 240–280 pts (Relgn Phil Eth) (IB 24 pts)

220 pts **Anglia Ruskin** – 220–260 pts (Phil; Phil Engl Lit)
Northampton – 220–260 pts (Phil; Phil Joint Hons)
Wolverhampton – 220 pts (War St Phil)

200 pts **Wolverhampton** – 200 pts (Law Phil; Phil Sociol; Pol Phil; Relig St Phil)
180 pts **Trinity Saint David** – 180–240 pts (Phil; Phil Joint Hons) (IB 26–28 pts)

Open University – contact +44 (0)845 300 6090 **or** www.openuniversity.co.uk/you
(Phil Psy; PPE)

Alternative offers
See **Chapter 7** and **Appendix 1** for grades/UCAS Tariff points information for the International Baccalaureate, Scottish Highers/Advanced Highers, the Welsh Baccalaureate, the Irish Leaving Certificate, the Cambridge Pre-U Diploma, the Advanced Diploma and the Extended Project.

CHOOSING YOUR COURSE (SEE ALSO CH.1)
Some course features
Exeter A large number of Combined Honours courses are offered in Philosophy including options with modern languages in which a year is spent abroad. Other programmes also allow for a year of study in Europe, North America and Australia.
London (Hey) One of the largest faculties. Philosophy can also be studied with Theology, or Religion and Ethics.
London NCH Twelve modules are taken over three years, including a compulsory dissertation in Year 3. In addition to degree subject modules students study four modules in another degree subject and compulsory core modules in applied ethics, logic and critical thinking to make up the NCH diploma which is awarded alongside a degree.
Manchester Philosophy is a broad course covering the main subject topics such as the philosophy of modern religion, modern political thought, psychology, law and a language. Philosophy is also offered with Politics or Criminology.

Oxford Brookes Philosophy can be studied as a single subject or with a range of joint subjects including Anthropology, Film Studies, Mathematics, Psychology, Sociology and Religion and Theology. **York** A Single Honours and a range of integrated courses can be studied on an 'equal' basis in which Philosophy is taken with English, French, German, History, Linguistics, Sociology, Mathematics and Physics. A Politics, Philosophy and Economics course is also offered. See also **Combined Courses**.

Universities and colleges teaching quality See www.qaa.ac.uk; http://unistats.direct.gov.uk.

Top research universities and colleges (RAE 2008) London (UCL); St Andrews; London (King's); Sheffield; Reading; Cambridge (Hist Phil Sci); London LSE; Oxford; Stirling; Bristol; Essex; London (Birk); Nottingham; Leeds; Middlesex; Edinburgh.

ADMISSIONS INFORMATION

Number of applicants per place (approx) Birmingham 6; Bradford 7; Bristol 19; Cambridge 6; Cardiff 8; Dundee 6; Durham (all courses) 14; East Anglia 6; Hull 19; Kent 9; Lancaster 6; Leeds 10; Liverpool 5; London (Hey) 4; London (King's) 6; London LSE 11; London Met 3; Manchester 10; Middlesex 8; Northampton 3; Nottingham 7; Oxford success rate 44%, (PPE) 29%; Sheffield 6; Southampton 7; Staffordshire 8; Trinity Saint David 4; Warwick 9; York 6.

Advice to applicants and planning the UCAS personal statement Read Bertrand Russell's *Problems of Philosophy*. Refer to any particular aspects of philosophy which interest you (check that these are offered on the courses for which you are applying). Since Philosophy is not a school subject, selectors will expect applicants to have read around the subject. Explain what you know about the nature of studying philosophy. Say what you have read in philosophy and give an example of a philosophical issue that interests you. Universities do not expect applicants to have a wide knowledge of the subject, but evidence that you know what the subject is about is important. **Bristol** Deferred entry considered.

Misconceptions about this course Applicants are sometimes surprised to find what wide-ranging Philosophy courses are offered.

Selection interviews Yes Cambridge, Essex, Lancaster, Leeds, Liverpool, London (Hey), London (UCL), Newcastle, Oxford (Phil Mod Lang) 24%, (PPE) 18%, (Phil Theol) 6%, Southampton, Staffordshire, Trinity Saint David, Warwick; **Some** Bristol, Cardiff, Durham, Hull, London LSE (rare), York; **No** Birmingham, Dundee, East Anglia, Nottingham, Reading.

Interview advice and questions Philosophy is a very wide subject and initially applicants will be asked for their reasons for their choice and their special interests in the subject. Questions in recent years have included: Is there a difference between being tactless and being insensitive? Can you be tactless and thin-skinned? Define the difference between knowledge and belief. Was the vertical distortion of El Greco's paintings a product of a vision defect? What is the point of studying philosophy? What books on philosophy have you read? Discuss the work of a renowned philosopher. What is a philosophical novel? Who has the right to decide your future – yourself or another? What do you want to do with your life? What is a philosophical question? John is your husband, and if John is your husband then necessarily you must be his wife; if you are necessarily his wife then it is not possible that you could not be his wife; so it was impossible for you not to have married him – you were destined for each other. Discuss. What is the difference between a man's entitlements, his deserts and his attributes? What are morals? A good understanding of philosophy is needed for entry to degree courses, and applicants are expected to demonstrate this if they are called to interview. As one admissions tutor stated, 'If you find Bertrand Russell's *Problems of Philosophy* unreadable – don't apply!' See also **Chapter 6**. **Cambridge** If you were to form a government of philosophers what selection process would you use? Is it moral to hook up a psychopath (whose only pleasure is killing) to a really stimulating machine so that he can believe he is in the real world and kill as much as he likes? **Oxford** If you entered a teletransporter and your body was destroyed and instantly recreated on Mars in exactly the same way with all your memories intact etc, would you be the same person? Tutors are not so much concerned with what you know as how you think about it. Evidence required concerning social and political topics and the ability to discuss them critically. (PPE) Is being hungry the same thing as wanting to eat? Why is there not a global government? What do you think of teleport machines? Should there be an intelligence test to decide who should vote? **York** Do human beings have free will? Do we perceive the world as it really is?

Reasons for rejection (non-academic) Evidence of severe psychological disturbance, criminal activity, drug problems (evidence from referees' reports). Lack of knowledge of philosophy. **Oxford** He was not able to explore his thoughts deeply enough or with sufficient centrality. **York** No evidence of having read any philosophical literature.

AFTER-RESULTS ADVICE
Offers to applicants repeating A-levels Higher Bristol (Phil Econ), Essex, Glasgow, Leeds, Warwick; **Same** Birmingham, Bristol, Cardiff, Dundee, Durham, East Anglia, Hull, Liverpool Hope, Newcastle, Nottingham (in some cases), Nottingham Trent, St Mary's, Southampton, Staffordshire, Stirling, Wolverhampton, York; **No** Cambridge.

GRADUATE DESTINATIONS AND EMPLOYMENT (2011/12 HESA)
Graduates surveyed 1785 **Employed** 715 **In voluntary employment** 90 **In further study** 500 **Assumed unemployed** 205

Career note Graduates have a wide range of transferable skills that can lead to employment in many areas, eg management, public administration, publishing, banking and social services.

OTHER DEGREE SUBJECTS FOR CONSIDERATION
Divinity; History and Philosophy of Science; History of Art; Human Sciences; Psychology; Religious Studies; Science; Theology.

PHOTOGRAPHY
(see also **Art and Design (Fine Art), Art and Design (General), Film, Radio, Video and TV Studies, Media Studies**)

Photography courses offer a range of specialised studies involving commercial, industrial and still photography, portraiture and film, digital and video work. Increasingly this subject is featuring in Media courses. See also **Appendix 3**.

Useful websites www.the-aop.org; www.rps.org; www.bjp-online.com.

NB The points totals shown to the left of the institutions are for ease of reference only. It must not be assumed that Tariff points are always used by institutions or that they can be substituted for an offer in grades. The level of an offer is not necessarily indicative of the quality of a course.

COURSE OFFERS INFORMATION
Subject requirements/preferences GCSE Art and/or a portfolio usually required. **AL** One or two subjects may be required, including an art/design or creative subject. Most institutions will make offers on the basis of a portfolio of work.

Your target offers and examples of courses provided by each institution

320 pts	**Bournemouth** – 320 pts (Photo) (IB 32 pts HL 555)
	Brighton – ABB (Photo)
	Glasgow (SA) – ABB (Fn Art (Photo))
	Leeds – ABB (Cnma Photo) (IB 34 pts HL 5 Engl)
300 pts	**Edinburgh (CA)** – BBB 300 pts (Photo) (IB 34 pts HL 555)
	Huddersfield – BBB 300 pts (Photo)
	Leeds Beckett – 300 pts (Photo Jrnl) (IB 24 pts)
	Roehampton – 300 pts (Photo) (IB 25 pts)
	Sheffield Hallam – 300 pts (Photo)
280 pts	**Birmingham City** – 280 pts (Media Comm (Media Photo); Vis Comm (Photo))

Bristol UWE – 280 pts (Photo)
Gloucestershire – 280 pts +interview +portfolio (Photojrnl Doc Photo; Fn Art Photo)
Hertfordshire – 280 pts (Photo)
Kingston – 280 pts (Photo)
Lincoln – 280 pts (Contemp Lns Media)
Manchester Met – 280 pts +portfolio (Photo) (IB 28 pts)
Norwich Arts – BBC 280 pts +interview +portfolio (Photo) (IB 25 pts)
Nottingham Trent – 280 pts (Photo/Photo Euro)
South Wales – (Photo; Doc Photo; Photo Fash Adv)
Suffolk (Univ Campus) – 280 pts (Photo Dig Media; Photo)

260 pts **Bath Spa** – 260 pts incl 100 pts from art/des/photo (Photo) (IB 26 pts)
Bournemouth Arts – BCC 260 pts +portfolio +interview (Photo; Commer Photo)
Coventry – BCC 260 pts (Photo) (IB 28 pts)
De Montfort – 260 pts (Film St Media Comm; Photo Vid)
Derby – 260 pts +portfolio +interview (Photo; Commer Photo) (IB 26 pts)
Falmouth – 260-300 pts +portfolio +interview (Mar Nat Hist Photo; Fash Photo)
      (IB 24 pts)
Southampton Solent – 260 pts (Photo)
Sunderland – 260-300 pts (Photo Comb Hons) (IB 31 pts)

240 pts **Bolton** – 240 pts (Photo)
Bradford – 240 pts (Photo Dig Media)
Canterbury Christ Church – CCC 240 pts (Photo Comb Hons; Photo) (IB 24 pts)
Central Lancashire – 240-260 pts (Photo; Photo Jrnl; Fash Brnd Prom Photo)
Chester – 240-280 pts (Photo; Dig Photo) (IB 26 pts)
Cleveland (CAD) – 240 pts (Photo)
Cumbria – 240 pts (Photo) (IB 30 pts)
Great Yarmouth (Coll) – 240-280 pts +portfolio +interview (Photo Dig Media)
Leeds (CA) – 240 pts (Photo)
London South Bank – 240 pts (Dig Photo)
Northampton – 240-280 pts (Photo Prac)
Plymouth – 240 pts (Photo) (IB 24 pts)
Portsmouth – 240-300 pts incl art/des +portfolio (Photo) (IB 28 pts)
Ravensbourne – AA-CC (Dig Photo) (IB 28 pts)
Salford – 240 pts (Photo)
Staffordshire – CCC 240 pts (Photo; Photojrnl) (IB 24 pts)
Ulster – 240 pts (Photo)
Westminster – CCC (Photo Dig Imag Tech; Clin Photo) (IB 26 pts)

220 pts **Bradford (Coll Univ Centre)** – 220 pts (Photo (Edit Adv Fn Art))
Creative Arts – 220 pts (Photo) (IB 24 pts)
Falmouth – 220 pts +portfolio +interview (Press Edit Photo; Photo)
Sunderland – 220 pts (Photo Vid Dig Imag)

200 pts **Anglia Ruskin** – 200-240 pts (Photo)
Arts London – 200 pts (Photo)
Bedfordshire – 200 pts (Photo Vid Art)
East London – 200 pts (Photo)
Grimsby (Univ Centre) – (Commer Photo)
Hereford (CA) – 200 pts +portfolio +interview (Photo)
Hull (Coll) – 200 pts (Photo)
Middlesex – 200-300 pts (Photo)
Plymouth (CA) – 200 pts (Photo)
Trinity Saint David (Swansea) – 200-360 pts (Photo Arts; Photojrnl)
West London – 200 pts (Photo Dig Imag)
Westminster – BB (Photo Arts) (IB 28 pts)
Wolverhampton – 200 pts (Photo)

180 pts **Farnborough (CT)** – 180 pts (Media Prod Photo)
160 pts **Arts London (CFash)** – 160 pts +portfolio (Fash Photo)
 Blackpool and Fylde (Coll) – 160 pts (Photo)
 Colchester (Inst) – 160 pts (Photo)
 Northbrook (Coll) – 160 pts (Contemp Photo Arts (Prac))
 Robert Gordon – 160 pts (Photo Electron Media) (IB 24 pts)
120 pts **St Helens (Coll)** – 120 pts (Photo)
 Sir Gâr (Coll) – 120 pts +portfolio +interview (Photo)
 80 pts **East Surrey (Coll)** – 80 pts (Dig Photo)
 Stockport (Coll) – 80 pts (Contemp Photo)

Alternative offers
See **Chapter 7** and **Appendix 1** for grades/UCAS Tariff points information for the International Baccalaureate, Scottish Highers/Advanced Highers, the Welsh Baccalaureate, the Irish Leaving Certificate, the Cambridge Pre-U Diploma, the Advanced Diploma and the Extended Project.

EXAMPLES OF FOUNDATION DEGREES IN THE SUBJECT FIELD
Anglia Ruskin; Arts London; Barking and Dagenham (Coll); Bath Spa; Bedfordshire; Blackburn (Coll); Blackpool and Fylde (Coll); Brighton and Hove City (Coll); Bristol City (Coll); Bucks New; Central Nottingham (Coll); Colchester (Inst); Cornwall (Coll); Craven (Coll); Exeter (Coll); Farnborough (CT); Gloucestershire; Greenwich; Hereford (CA); Hertfordshire; Hull (Coll); Kent; Kirklees (Coll); Leeds City (Coll); Leicester (Coll); London Met; Manchester (Coll); Mid-Cheshire (Coll); Myerscough (Coll); Newcastle (Coll); Northbrook (Coll); Nottingham New (Coll); Plymouth (CA); Sheffield (Coll); Stockport (Coll); Truro (Coll); Wakefield (Coll); West London; Westminster City (Coll).

CHOOSING YOUR COURSE (SEE ALSO CH.1)
Some course features
Anglia Ruskin The course offers a broad study of photography without establishing a house style. Experimentation is encouraged.
Kingston The course covers photography in specialist studies covering advertising, architecture, documentary, fashion, interior, publishing and travel.
Nottingham Trent Courses in Photography are offered focusing on Documentary, Art Practice, Fashion or with a year in Europe.
Westminster (Clin Photo) The only full-time degree in clinical photography in the UK, it combines a study of photography and digital imaging with science, anatomy, physiology, biology and clinical practice. Work-based learning in a clinical setting forms a large part of the course.

Universities and colleges teaching quality See www.qaa.ac.uk; http://unistats.direct.gov.uk.

Examples of sandwich degree courses Coventry; Wolverhampton.

ADMISSIONS INFORMATION
Number of applicants per place (approx) Arts London 10; Birmingham City 6; Blackpool and Fylde (Coll) 3; Bournemouth Arts 7; Cleveland (CAD) 2; Derby 20; Edinburgh Napier 33; Falmouth 3; Nottingham Trent 4; Plymouth 2; Plymouth (CA) 7; Portsmouth 4; Staffordshire 3; Stockport (Coll) 6; Trinity Saint David (Swansea) 12.

Advice to applicants and planning the UCAS personal statement Discuss your interest in photography and your knowledge of various aspects of the subject, for example, digital, video, landscape, medical, wildlife and portrait photography. Read photographic journals to keep up-to-date on developments, particularly in photographic technology. You will also need first-hand experience of photography and to be competent in basic skills. See also **Appendix 3**. **Derby** (Non-UK students) Fluency in written and spoken English important. Portfolio of work essential.

Misconceptions about this course Some believe that courses are all practical work with no theory. **Cumbria** They didn't realise the facilities were so good!

Selection interviews Most institutions will interview applicants and expect to see a portfolio of work.

Interview advice and questions Questions relate to the applicant's portfolio of work which, for these courses, is of prime importance. Who are your favourite photographers? What is the most recent exhibition you have attended? Have any leading photographers influenced your work? Questions regarding contemporary photography. Written work sometimes required. See **Chapter 6**.

Reasons for rejection (non-academic) Lack of passion for the subject. Lack of exploration and creativity in practical work. Poorly presented portfolio.

AFTER-RESULTS ADVICE
Offers to applicants repeating A-levels Same Birmingham City, Blackpool and Fylde (Coll), Chester, Cumbria, Manchester Met, Nottingham Trent, Staffordshire.

GRADUATE DESTINATIONS AND EMPLOYMENT (2011/12 HESA)
Cinematics and Photography graduates surveyed 3905 **Employed** 1600 **In voluntary employment** 190 **In further study** 540 **Assumed unemployed** 525

Career note Opportunities for photographers exist in a range of specialisms including advertising and editorial work, fashion, medical, industrial, scientific and technical photography. Some graduates also go into photojournalism and other aspects of the media.

OTHER DEGREE SUBJECTS FOR CONSIDERATION
Art and Design; Digital Animation; Film, Radio, Video and TV Studies; Media Studies; Moving Image; Radiography.

PHYSICAL EDUCATION
(see also Education Studies, Sports Sciences/Studies)

Physical Education courses are very popular and unfortunately restricted in number. Ability in gymnastics or an involvement in sport are obviously important factors.

Useful websites www.afpe.org.uk; www.uksport.gov.uk; see also **Education Studies** and **Teacher Training**.

NB The points totals shown to the left of the institutions are for ease of reference only. It must not be assumed that Tariff points are always used by institutions or that they can be substituted for an offer in grades. The level of an offer is not necessarily indicative of the quality of a course.

COURSE OFFERS INFORMATION
Subject requirements/preferences GCSE English, mathematics and a science. **AL** PE, sports studies and science are preferred subjects and for some courses one of these may be required. Disclosure and Barring Service (DBS) check before starting the course. Declaration of Health usually required.

Your target offers and examples of courses provided by each institution
360 pts **Birmingham** – AAA-ABB 360–320 pts (Spo PE Coach Sci) (IB 35–36 pts)
320 pts **Brighton** – ABB 320 pts (PE) (IB 34 pts)
          Brunel – ABB (Sp Hlth Exer Sci (Spo Dev); PE Youth Spo) (IB 33 pts)
          East Anglia – ABB (PE) (IB 32 pts)
          Edge Hill – 320 pts (PE Sch Spo) (IB 26 pts)
          Sheffield Hallam – 320 pts (PE Sch Spo)
300 pts **Cardiff Met (UWIC)** – 300 pts (Spo PE) (IB 26 pts)
          Edinburgh – BBB 300 pts (PE) (IB 34 pts HL 555)
          Greenwich – 300 pts incl sci (Spo Sci Coach) (IB 24 pts)
          Leeds Beckett – 300 pts (PE courses)

Liverpool John Moores – 300 pts (Spo Dev PE)
280 pts **Greenwich** – 280 pts (PE Spo) (IB 26 pts)
Leeds Beckett – 280 pts (PE Out Educ) (IB 25 pts)
Liverpool John Moores – 280 pts (Educ St PE)
Oxford Brookes – BBC (Spo Coach PE)
Plymouth – (P PE) (IB 26 pts)
St Mark and St John – 280 pts (Coach PE)
Wolverhampton – 280 pts (PE) (IB 25 pts)
Worcester – 280 pts (PE Spo St)
York St John – 280 pts (PE Spo Coach) (IB 24 pts)
260 pts **Bangor** – 260–280 pts (Spo Hlth PE; PE Joint Hons)
Bedfordshire – 260 pts (PE S)
Canterbury Christ Church – 260 pts (PE Spo Exer Sci)
Cardiff Met (UWIC) – 260 pts (Educ St Spo Physl Actvt)
Chichester – BBB–BCC incl PE 260–300 pts (PE Spo Coach) (IB 30 pts)
Newman – 260 pts (Educ Spo St)
Winchester – 260–300 pts (P Educ PE)
240 pts **Bedfordshire** – 240 pts (Spo St) (IB 28–30 pts)
Cumbria – 240 pts (PE)
Glyndŵr – 240–260 pts (Spo Coach)
Leeds Trinity – 240 pts (PE P Spo Dev)
Manchester Met – 240–280 pts (Coach St Spo Dev; PE Spo Ped) (IB 28 pts)
Staffordshire – 240 pts (PE Yth Spo Coach) (IB 24 pts)
220 pts **London Met** – 220 pts (Spo Sci PE) (IB 28 pts)
200 pts **Anglia Ruskin** – 200 pts (Spo Coach PE) (IB 24 pts)
Wolverhampton – 200 pts (Physl Actvt Exer Hlth) (IB 24 pts)
180 pts **Peterborough (Reg Coll)** – 180 pts (Spo Coach PE)
Trinity Saint David – 180–360 pts (PE) (IB 26 pts)

Alternative offers
See **Chapter 7** and **Appendix 1** for grades/UCAS Tariff points information for the International Baccalaureate, Scottish Highers/Advanced Highers, the Welsh Baccalaureate, the Irish Leaving Certificate, the Cambridge Pre-U Diploma, the Advanced Diploma and the Extended Project.

CHOOSING YOUR COURSE (SEE ALSO CH.1)
Some course features
Birmingham (Spo PE Coach Sci) A practical and theoretical programme in sport, physical education and leisure with a placement module in education or the leisure industry.
Chichester (PE Coach) The three-year modular programme focuses on the teaching of physical education and the coaching of sports activities.
East Anglia Options for students to pursue a range of nationally accredited coaching and officiating awards in addition to their formal studies.
Liverpool John Moores Courses are offered for those wanting to train as PE teachers or with specialist studies in sport development and management.
St Mark and St John (Coach PE) Course covers coach and sport education and also leads to a PGCE in PE teaching.

Universities and colleges teaching quality See www.qaa.ac.uk; http://unistats.direct.gov.uk.

Top research universities and colleges (RAE 2008) See **Sports Sciences/Studies**.

ADMISSIONS INFORMATION
Number of applicants per place (approx) Bangor 19; Birmingham 5; Brunel 10; Chichester 5; Edge Hill 40; Leeds Trinity 33; Liverpool John Moores 4; Newman 5; St Mark and St John 18; St Mary's 9; Sheffield Hallam 60; Worcester 31.

Check **Chapter 4** when choosing your university and **Chapter 7** on how to read the subject tables.

Advice to applicants and planning the UCAS personal statement Ability in gymnastics, athletics and all sports and games is important. Full details of these activities should be given on the UCAS application – for example, teams, dates and awards achieved, assisting in extra-curricular activities. Involvement with local sports clubs, health clubs, summer camps, Gap Year. Relevant experience in coaching, teaching, community and youth work. **Liverpool John Moores** Commitment to working with children and a good sports background.

Selection interviews Most institutions. In most cases, applicants will take part in physical education practical tests and games/gymnastics, depending on the course. The results of these tests could affect the level of offers. See also **Chapter 6**.

Interview advice and questions The applicant's interests in physical education will be discussed, with specific questions on, for example, sportsmanship, refereeing, umpiring and coaching. Questions in the past have also included: What qualities should a good netball goal defence possess? How could you encourage a group of children into believing that sport is fun? Do you think that physical education should be compulsory in schools? Why do you think you would make a good teacher? What is the name of the education minister? **Liverpool John Moores** Questions on what the applicant has gained or learned through experiences with children.

Reasons for rejection (non-academic) Poor communication and presentational skills. Relatively poor sporting background or knowledge. Lack of knowledge about the teaching of physical education and the commitment required. Lack of ability in practicalities, for example, gymnastics, dance when relevant. Poor self-presentation. Poor writing skills.

AFTER-RESULTS ADVICE
Offers to applicants repeating A-levels Same Liverpool John Moores, Newman, St Mary's.

GRADUATE DESTINATIONS AND EMPLOYMENT (2011/12 HESA)
See **Sports Sciences/Studies**.

Career note The majority of graduates go into education although, depending on any special interests, they may also go on into the sport and leisure industry.

OTHER DEGREE SUBJECTS FOR CONSIDERATION
Coach Education; Exercise and Fitness; Exercise Physiology; Human Biology; Leisure and Recreation; Physiotherapy; Sport and Exercise Science; Sport Health and Exercise; Sport Studies/Sciences; Sports Coaching; Sports Development; Sports Engineering; Sports Psychology; Sports Therapy.

PHYSICS

(see also **Astronomy and Astrophysics**)

Physics is an increasingly popular subject and a wide variety of courses are available which enables students to follow their own interests and specialisations. Some course options are nanotechnology, medical physics, cosmology, environmental physics and biophysics.

Useful websites www.myphysicscourse.org; www.iop.org; www.physics.org; www.scicentral.com; www.ipem.ac.uk; www.epsrc.ac.uk; jobs.newscientist.com; www.nature.com/physics.

NB The points totals shown to the left of the institutions are for ease of reference only. It must not be assumed that Tariff points are always used by institutions or that they can be substituted for an offer in grades. The level of an offer is not necessarily indicative of the quality of a course.

COURSE OFFERS INFORMATION
Subject requirements/preferences GCSE English, mathematics and science. **AL** Physics and mathematics are required for most courses.

UNIVERSITY *of York*

Department of Physics

Aerial view of campus

THE UNIVERSITY *of York*

Flexible MPhys (4-year) and BSc (3-year) degree programmes

- Friendly, dedicated, accessible and research-active staff
- Beautiful campus environment
- Guaranteed University accommodation for all 1st year students
- Key teaching and research areas include nuclear physics and nuclear astrophysics, fusion and lasers, nanotechnology, magnetic materials, and computational and theoretical physics

New and existing facilities to enhance research-led teaching:

York Plasma Institute: A world-leading interdisciplinary plasma institute for fundamental plasma science and related technology

York-JEOL Nanocentre: An international facility in electron microscopy and lithography specialising in surface physics

AstroCampus: Our redeveloped facilities on campus, co-locating our observatories with our optical, radio and solar telescopes.

Graduate Employment: A key area of concern for many is taken very seriously at York. Currently 80% of our graduates get jobs within 6 months of graduating – the 3rd highest of ANY Physics department (Guardian University Guide 2012).

Equality: We encourage applications from all, regardless of background. We have received an Athena Swan Silver Award and are one of six physics departments to have a Juno Champion status for our achievements with equality for women.

For further information contact:
Email: physics-undergraduate-admissions@york.ac.uk
Web: http://www.york.ac.uk/physics
Phone: (+44) (0)1904 432241

Study Physics at the University of York

The University of York is currently ranked 1st in the UK and 8th in the world (the Times Higher Education 100 under 50, 2012).

Why is it the right place for you to study physics?

We pride ourselves on the quality of the undergraduate experience we offer – as seen in our many satisfied graduates. York has an enviable reputation for having high standards and yet being friendly and welcoming for students from all backgrounds, so anyone has the opportunity to excel.

What can you study?

We have a flexible modular system, offering degrees in Physics, Physics with Astrophysics, Theoretical Physics, Maths and Physics and Physics with Philosophy. All are available as either 3-year BSc and 4-year MPhys, and with an option for a 'year in Europe'. Transfers between degrees are allowed in the 1st year.

How do you study?

We teach via a mix of traditional lectures, small group tutorials, laboratories, workshops and practical sessions, and group and individual projects. All our students carry out an in-depth research project in their final year – often thought to be the best part of the degree!

How can you find out more?

Come along to one of our Open Days, read our undergraduate booklet or visit the website at http://www.york.ac.uk/physics. You can also email any questions to physics-undergraduate-admissions@york.ac.uk.

UNIVERSITY *of York*

University of Salford
MANCHESTER

SCHOOL OF COMPUTING, SCIENCE & ENGINEERING

PhysicSalford
What will you achieve?

At Salford we're taking a different approach to physics, helping you achieve, invent and discover more in life.

By capitalising on the strengths within the University we are able to offer a range of specialised physics degrees that benefit from close links with a wide range of physics employers.

- BSc/MPhys Physics
- BSc/MPhys Physics with Acoustics
- MPhys Physics with studies in North America
- BSc Pure and Applied Physics

The University of Salford campus is just a mile and a half from Manchester city centre, giving you the best of both worlds – a friendly, safe environment but just minutes away from all the fun and opportunities of a big city.

For a Prospectus or to find out more about our Courses, Entry Requirements and Fees:

www.salford.ac.uk/course-finder

T: +44 (0) 161 295 4545
E: cst-enquiries@salford.ac.uk

University of Salford
MANCHESTER

PhysicSalford

Why study Physics?

Physics underpins much in our everyday lives: basic magnetism led to CAT, PET and MRI scanners, photonics led to CDs, LED displays and barcode scanners. In fact much of technology today - mobile phones, solar panels, hydrogen cars, computer technology, music technology and many more - is founded in Physics. As a result physicists are in great demand in almost every walk of life.

Why study Physics at Salford?

The teaching on Salford's Physics degrees is recognised to be of outstanding quality. Courses are informed by the internationally excellent theoretical and applied research undertaken by Physics staff who lead the theoretical and applied research groups of the Materials and Physics Research Centre.

A unique part of the Salford physics degrees is our emphasis on employer engagement.

Professional physicists from employer organisations - like Salford Royal Hospital, the Royal Navy, BDP Acoustics, Atkins Global, and OpTIC Technium - come in to talk about real-life situations of working in industries where physics graduates are sought after. Students are also given problems to solve related to the industry of the guest speaker.

As a Salford physics graduate you will have no shortage of skills. Our teaching methods and physics courses provide you with skills that are relevant in any working environment. As well as being highly numerate, analytical and logical, the chances are that you'll also be a creative thinker - capable of communicating effectively, managing projects and excellent at problem solving and negotiating.

We have excellent facilities on campus: Salford is the birthplace of renowned physicist, James Prescott

Joule and our Joule Physics Laboratories include a purpose built suite of large, open-space teaching laboratories.

Alongside the teaching and facilities, the Salford University Physics Society adds a social dimension to Physics at Salford. The Society organises trips, hosts guest lectures and runs the legendary SUPS Cheese & Wine Evenings. Salford students also get involved in science busking and support on campus events such as the Manchester Science Festival. At Salford you are a physicist from Day 1 of your studies and treated as part of the team.

We run undergraduate courses in **Physics, Physics with Acoustics, Physics with Studies in North America, and Pure and Applied Physics**.

University of Hertfordshire U H

School of
Physics, Astronomy and Mathematics

Where knowledge becomes progress

Images © CERN

Become more.

Find out about our range of courses at:
go.herts.ac.uk/pam-heap

University of Hertfordshire U H

School of
Physics, Astronomy and Mathematics

... Discover how and why

with one of the top ten Schools in the UK*

Physics is one of the most fundamental of all sciences – helping us to better understand the universe through the behaviour of matter, energy and forces – and the catalyst for significant advances that have helped shape modern society. Our School of Physics, Astronomy and Mathematics is home to world-leading research and discoveries, such as:

- Volcanic dust sensors that are helping the Met Office provide vital information on the safety of UK airspace

- Devices for on-the-fly analysis of cloud ice particles to monitor the effects of environmental change

* The Guardian League table 2014

- Approximately 10% of all known planets have been discovered by our astronomers

Study with us and we will provide you with knowledge of the fundamental theories of physics and their application to current research and technology, as well as the opportunity to gain real work experience. With well-developed problem solving abilities and analytical skills, our graduates are highly sought by a range of employers.

Become more.

Find out about our range of courses at:
go.herts.ac.uk/pam-heap

Check **Chapter 4** when choosing your university and **Chapter 7** on how to read the subject tables.

Department of Physics
Durham University

B.Sc. and M.Phys/M.Sci. degrees in Physics, Physics & Astronomy, Theoretical Physics, Mathematics & Physics and Chemistry & Physics

Specialised courses include particle physics, cosmology and photonics

Excellent laboratory facilities include 4 modern telescopes

Supportive college system

Learning based on lectures, tutorials, labs and projects

Internationally renowned research department

http://www.dur.ac.uk/physics
Email: physics.admissions@durham.ac.uk
Tel: +44(0)191 334 3726

Ogden Centre for Fundamental Physics

Your target offers and examples of courses provided by each institution

400 pts **London (King's)** – A*AAa (Maths Phys) (IB 35 pts HL 776 maths phys)

Manchester – A*A*A–A*AA (Phys; Phys Astro) (IB 38–39 pts)

380 pts **Cambridge** – A*AA (Nat Sci (Phys/Physl Sci/Astro)) (IB 40–41 pts HL 776)

Durham – A*AA 380 pts (Phys; Phys Astron; Theor Phys; Nat Sci) (IB 38 pts HL 766 maths phys)

Exeter – A*AA–AAB (Maths Phys) (IB 38–34 pts)

Imperial London – A*mathsAA (Phys; Phys Mus Perf; Phys (Yr Abrd)) (IB 39 pts HL 666)

Lancaster – A*AA 380 pts (Phys Ptcl Phys Cosmo MPhys; Phys Astro Cosmo MPhys; MPhys) (IB 38 pts HL 17 pts)

Nottingham – A*AA–AAA 380–360 pts (Phys; Phys Euro Lang; Phys Theor Phys; Phys Med Phys; Mathem Phys; Phys Theor Astro; Phys Astron) (IB 24 pts HL 665)

Oxford – A*AA (Phys) (IB 38–40 pts)

Warwick – A*AA (Phys; Phys Bus St) (IB 36 pts)

360 pts **Bath** – AAA (Phys; Maths Phys) (IB 36 pts HL 6 maths phys)

Birmingham – AAA (Phys) (IB 34–38 pts)

Cardiff – AAA–ABB 360–320 pts (Phys Astron; Theor Comput Phys; Phys Med Phys; Phys) (IB 32–34 pts HL 6 maths phys)

East Anglia – AAA (Nat Sci) (IB 34 pts)

Edinburgh – AAA–ABB 360–320 pts (Geophys; Geophys Meteor; Phys Meteor; Theor Phys; Phys; Comput Phys; Mathem Phys; Phys Mus) (IB 37–32 pts)

Exeter – AAA–ABB 360–320 pts (Phys; Phys Astro) (IB 36–32 pts)

Lancaster – AAA (Phys; Phys Astro Cosmo; Theor Phys Maths; Phys Ptcl Phys Cosmo) (IB 36 pts HL 16 pts)

Leicester – AAA–AAB (Phys Nanotech) (IB 34 pts)

Liverpool – AAA–ABB (Phys MPhys) (IB 35 pts HL 6 maths phys)

For a quick reference offers calculator, fold out the inside front cover.

Liverpool John Moores – AAA 360 pts (Astro MPhys)

London (King's) – AAA–A*AB (Phys; Phys Theor Phys; Phys Med Apps; Phys Phil) (IB 35 pts HL 666 maths phys)

London (RH) – AAA–AAB (Phys; Theor Phys; Phys Ptcl Phys) (IB 36–35 pts HL 6 maths 6 phys)

London (UCL) – AAA–ABB (Phys; Phys Med Phys; Cheml Phys; Med Phys) (IB 34–38 pts HL 16–18 pts maths phys)

St Andrews – AAA (Phys Photon; Comp Sci Phys; Phys) (IB 38 pts)

Sheffield – AAA (Phys MPhys) (IB 37 pts HL 6 maths 6 phys)

Southampton – AAA (Maths Phys) (IB 36 pts HL 18 pts)

Surrey – AAA 360 pts (Mus Snd Rec (Tonmeister)) (IB 37 pts HL 666)

Swansea – AAA (Phys MPhys; Theor Phys)

York – AAA–AAB (Theor Physics; Phys Phil) (IB 36–35 pts HL 6 maths 6 phys)

340 pts **Bristol** – AAB–ABB 340–320 pts (Phys Astro; Phys Phil; Phys) (IB 35–33 pts HL 6 maths 6 phys)

Cardiff – AAB (Phys MPhys) (IB 32 pts HL 6 maths phys)

Leeds – AAB (Phys; Phys Nanotech; Phys Astro; Theor Phys) (IB 34 pts HL 5 maths phys)

Liverpool – AAB–BBB (Phys Med Apps; Phys; Phys Nucl Sci; Mathem Phys MMath) (IB 33 pts HL 6 maths phys)

London (QM) – AAB–ABB (Astro MSci; Astro; Phys Ptcl Phys; Theor Phys) (IB 30–34 pts HL 6 maths 6 phys)

London (RH) – AAB (Phys Mus) (IB 35 pts)

Loughborough – AAB–ABB (Phys) (IB 34 pts)

Nottingham – AAB (Chem Mol Phys) (IB 34 pts HL 66)

Queen's Belfast – AAB (Phys Astro MSci; Phys MSci; Theor Phys; Phys Med Apps MSci)

Sheffield – AAB (Phys Joint Hons; Theor Phys; Phys BSc; Phys Astro) (IB 35 pts HL 6 maths phys)

Southampton – AAB incl maths phys (Phys Photon; Phys Spc Sci; Phys; Phys Nanotech; Phys Astron) (IB 34 pts HL 17 pts)

Sussex – AAB–ABB (Phys Astro; Phys; Theor Phys) (IB 34 pts HL 5 maths 5 phys)

York – AAB–AAA (Phys; Phys MPhys; Phys Astro; Maths Phys) (IB 36–35 pts)

320 pts **Aberdeen** – ABB (Phys Complex Sys Mdl)

Dundee – ABB (Phys) (IB 32 pts)

East Anglia – ABB incl chem math (Cheml Phys) (IB 32 pts HL 6 chem math)

Glasgow – ABB (Phys Astro; Phys) (IB 32 pts)

Hertfordshire – 320 pts (Phys) (IB 32 pts HL 5 phys maths)

Kent – ABB (Phys)

Leeds – ABB (Chem Phys) (IB 34 pts HL 6 chem)

Leicester – ABB (Phys; Phys Spc Sci Tech; Phys Planet Sci; Phys Astro)

Liverpool – ABB (Geophys (Geol/Phys); Theor Phys; Phys Ocn Clim St) (IB 33 pts)

Loughborough – ABB (Eng Phys; Phys Maths) (IB 34 pts)

Reading – ABB–AAC incl maths phys 320 pts (Env Phys) (IB 32 pts HL 6 maths 5 phys)

Strathclyde – ABB–BBB (Phys) (IB 30–32 pts)

Surrey – ABB (Phys Astron; Phys; Phys Nucl Astro; Phys Sat Tech) (IB 34 pts)

Swansea – ABB (Phys; Phys Nanotech; Phys Spo Sci; Phys Ptcl Phys Cosmo)

300 pts **Aberdeen** – BBB 300 pts (Phys; Nat Phil (Phys))

Heriot-Watt – BBB (Phys courses)

Keele – BBB 300 pts (Phys Comb)

Liverpool John Moores – 300–340 pts (Phys Astron) (IB 24–28 pts)

London (QM) – 300–320 pts (Phys MSci) (IB 32 pts HL 6 maths phys)

Queen's Belfast – BBB (Phys; Phys Med Apps; Phys Astro) (IB 32 pts HL 665 maths phys)

280 pts **Aberystwyth** – 280 pts (Spc Sci Robot; Phys courses) (IB 27 pts)

Central Lancashire – 280–320 pts (Phys)

Hull – BBC–BBB 280–300 pts (Phys; Phys Astro)

Nottingham Trent – 280 pts (Phys; Phys Astro; Phys Nucl Tech)

Salford – 280–300 pts (Phys (St Abrd)) (IB 30 pts HL 5 maths phys)
260 pts **Portsmouth** – 260 pts (App Phys) (IB 28 pts)
Salford – 260–280 pts (Phys; Pure App Phys; Phys Acoust)
240 pts **West Scotland** – CCC (Phys; Phys Nucl Tech) (IB 24 pts)
220 pts **Nottingham Trent** – 220 pts (Phys Foren Apps)

Open University – contact +44 (0)845 300 6090 **or** www.openuniversity.co.uk/you (Physl Sci)

Alternative offers
See **Chapter 7** and **Appendix 1** for grades/UCAS Tariff points information for the International Baccalaureate, Scottish Highers/Advanced Highers, the Welsh Baccalaureate, the Irish Leaving Certificate, the Cambridge Pre-U Diploma, the Advanced Diploma and the Extended Project.

EXAMPLES OF FOUNDATION DEGREES IN THE SUBJECT FIELD
Cardiff; Central Lancashire; Cumbria; Durham; Hull; Keele; Kent; Leeds; Leicester; Liverpool; London (QM); London (RH); Loughborough; Manchester; Nottingham; Nottingham Trent; St Andrews; Salford; Southampton.

CHOOSING YOUR COURSE (SEE ALSO CH.1)
Some course features
Bath After a first year on the Natural Sciences programme or the Mathematics and Physics course it is possible to transfer to Single Honours Physics in Year 2.
Durham Several courses are offered which include Theoretical Physics and Astronomy. Physics can also be taken jointly with seven other subjects and is also offered as part of the Natural Sciences programme.
Kent The Physics course allows considerable flexibility and enables students to defer their choice between Physics and other degree programmes in the Faculty until the end of the first year. Physics can also be studied with Astrophysics and with a year in the USA.
Loughborough An optional year in paid employement is offered either in the UK or abroad.
Warwick A central core of physics and mathematics is taken by all Physics students, ensuring flexibility and freedom of choice in the courses that follow in the second and third years. Mathematics and Physics, and Physics and Business Studies courses are also available.

Universities and colleges teaching quality See www.qaa.ac.uk; http://unistats.direct.gov.uk.

Top research universities and colleges (RAE 2008) Lancaster; Cambridge; Nottingham; St Andrews; Bath; Edinburgh; Durham; Imperial London; Sheffield; London (UCL); Glasgow; Birmingham; Exeter; Sussex.

Examples of sandwich degree courses Bath; Bristol; East Anglia; Edinburgh; Exeter; Glasgow; Hertfordshire; Imperial London; Loughborough; Nottingham Trent; Surrey; West Scotland.

ADMISSIONS INFORMATION
Number of applicants per place (approx) Bath 6; Birmingham 6; Bristol 9; Cardiff 4, (Phys Astron) 6; Dundee 5; Durham 6; Edinburgh 9; Exeter 5; Heriot-Watt 5; Hull 7; Imperial London 3; Kent 8; Lancaster 8; Leeds 7; Leicester 7; Liverpool 4; London (King's) 7; London (QM) 6; London (RH) 9; London (UCL) 6; Loughborough 6; Nottingham 10; Salford 5; Southampton 6; Strathclyde 5; Surrey 5; Swansea 3; Warwick 8; York 5.

Advice to applicants and planning the UCAS personal statement Admissions tutors look for potential, enthusiasm and interest in the subject so interests relating to maths and physics must be mentioned. An awareness of the range of careers in which physics is involved should also be mentioned on the UCAS application together with a demonstration of any particular interests, such as details on a physics or maths book you have read recently (not science fiction!). Make sure to mention if you have attended any courses, summer schools or day conferences on physics and engineering. See also **Appendix 3**. **Bristol** Deferred entry accepted.

Selection interviews **Yes** Aberystwyth, Cambridge, East Anglia, Exeter, Heriot-Watt, Hull, Imperial London, Lancaster, Liverpool, London (QM), London (RH), Loughborough, Oxford (Phys) 24%, (Phys Phil) 20%, Sheffield, Warwick, York; **Some** Cardiff, Durham, Salford; **No** Bath, Birmingham, Dundee, Nottingham, Strathclyde, Surrey, Swansea.

Interview advice and questions Questions will almost certainly focus on those aspects of the physics A/AS-level course which the student enjoys. See also **Chapter 6**. **Bristol** Why Physics? Questions on mechanics, physics and pure maths. Given paper and calculator and questions asked orally; best to take your own calculator. Tutors seek enthusiastic and highly motivated students and the physicist's ability to apply basic principles to unfamiliar situations.

AFTER-RESULTS ADVICE
Offers to applicants repeating A-levels **Higher** Bristol, Glasgow, St Andrews, Warwick; **Possibly higher** Aberystwyth, Hull, Leeds, Loughborough, York; **Same** Birmingham, Cardiff, Dundee, Durham, East Anglia, Exeter, Lancaster, Leicester, Liverpool, Salford, Swansea; **No** Cambridge.

GRADUATE DESTINATIONS AND EMPLOYMENT (2011/12 HESA)
Graduates surveyed 2055 **Employed** 700 **In voluntary employment** 45 **In further study** 880 **Assumed unemployed** 220

Career note Many graduates go into scientific and technical work in the manufacturing industries. However, in recent years, financial work, management and marketing have also attracted many seeking alternative careers.

OTHER DEGREE SUBJECTS FOR CONSIDERATION
Astronomy; Astrophysics; Computer Science; Earth Sciences; Engineering subjects; Geophysics; Materials Science and Metallurgy; Mathematics; Meteorology; Natural Sciences; Oceanography; Optometry; Radiography.

PHYSIOLOGY

(see also **Anatomical Science/Anatomy, Animal Sciences, Psychology**)

Physiology is a study of body function. Courses in this wide-ranging subject will cover the central nervous system, special senses and neuro-muscular mechanisms, and body-regulating systems such as exercise, stress and temperature regulation.

Useful websites www.physoc.org; www.physiology.org; www.bases.org.uk/Physiology; see also **Biological Sciences**.

NB The points totals shown to the left of the institutions are for ease of reference only. It must not be assumed that Tariff points are always used by institutions or that they can be substituted for an offer in grades. The level of an offer is not necessarily indicative of the quality of a course.

COURSE OFFERS INFORMATION
Subject requirements/preferences **GCSE** Science and mathematics at grade A. **AL** Two science subjects are usually required; chemistry and biology are the preferred subjects.

Your target offers and examples of courses provided by each institution

380 pts **Cambridge** – A*AA (Nat Sci (Physiol Dev Neuro)) (IB 40–41 pts HL 776)
360 pts **Edinburgh** – AAA–ABB 360–320 pts (Physiol) (IB 37–32 pts)
        Leeds – AAA–ABB 360–320 pts (Hum Physiol; Spo Sci Physiol) (IB 35–34 pts)
        Manchester – AAA–ABB 360–320 pts (Physiol; Physiol (Yr Ind); Pharmacol Physiol (Yr Ind)) (IB 37–33 pts)
        Newcastle – AAA–AAB incl biol (Physiol Sci) (IB 34–35 pts)
340 pts **Bristol** – AAB (Physiol Sci) (IB 35 pts HL 666 sci)

        Cardiff – AAB–ABB 340–320 pts (Biomed Sci (Physiol)) (IB 34 pts)
        Glasgow – AAB (Physiol Spo Sci; Physiol; Physiol Spo Sci Nutr) (IB 34 pts)
        London (King's) – AAB (Med Physiol) (IB 35 pts)

320 pts **Bristol UWE** – 320 pts (Hlthcr Sci (Lf Sci); Hlthcr Sci (Physiol Sci)) (IB 27 pts)
        Leeds – ABB (Clin Physiol (Cardio))
        Leicester – ABB (Med Physiol) (IB 32 pts)
        Liverpool – ABB (Physiol) (IB 32 pts HL 6 biol)

300 pts **Aberdeen** – BBB (Physiol; Physiol Ind)
        Plymouth – 300 pts (Hlthcr Sci (Physiol Sci)) (IB 28 pts)

280 pts **Manchester Met** – 280 pts (Physiol (Physl Actvt Hlth)) (IB 27 pts)
        Portsmouth – 280 pts (Hum Physiol) (IB 26 pts)
        Ulster – 280 pts (Clin Physiol)

260 pts **Central Lancashire** – BCC 260 pts (Physiol Pharmacol) (IB 25 pts)
        Dundee – BCC (Physiol Sci; Physiol Spo Biomed) (IB 28 pts)
        Edinburgh Napier – BCC (Spo Exer Sci (Exer Physiol))
        Sunderland – 260 pts (Physiol Sci)

240 pts **East London** – 240 pts (Med Physiol)
        Westminster – CCC (Physiol Pharmacol)
        Wolverhampton – 240 pts (Hlthcr Sci (Physiol Sci))

Alternative offers
See **Chapter 7** and **Appendix 1** for grades/UCAS Tariff points information for the International Baccalaureate, Scottish Highers/Advanced Highers, the Welsh Baccalaureate, the Irish Leaving Certificate, the Cambridge Pre-U Diploma, the Advanced Diploma and the Extended Project.

EXAMPLES OF FOUNDATION DEGREES IN THE SUBJECT FIELD
Manchester Met; Westminster.

CHOOSING YOUR COURSE (SEE ALSO CH.1)
Some course features
See also **Biological Sciences**.
Bristol In the first two years Physiology is studied with two other subjects, for example anatomy, pharmacology, psychology, chemistry or biochemistry.
Edinburgh Students are taught through a combination of lectures, tutorials, practical work, problem-based learning and computer-assisted learning. Advanced entry directly into the second year is possible for those with sufficiently high qualifications.
Leeds (Hum Physiol) Course has an optional year in industry or abroad.
Leicester (Med Physiol) Study abroad through the Erasmus scheme is also possible, and a four-year sandwich course is also available.
Newcastle The Biomedical Sciences programme offers seven science subjects, all of which have a common first year. The decision to take Physiology, or any other subject, takes place in Year 2.

Universities and colleges teaching quality See www.qaa.ac.uk; http://unistats.direct.gov.uk.

Top research universities and colleges (RAE 2008) See **Biological Sciences**.

Examples of sandwich degree courses Aberdeen; Cardiff; Leeds; Manchester Met; Ulster; Wolverhampton.

ADMISSIONS INFORMATION
Number of applicants per place (approx) Bristol 6; Cardiff 8; Dundee 5; Leeds 4; Leicester 5; Liverpool 10; London (King's) 5; Newcastle 6.

Advice to applicants and planning the UCAS personal statement See **Anatomical Science/ Anatomy** and **Biological Sciences**.

Selection interviews **Yes** Cambridge, Leeds, Newcastle; **Some** Bristol, Cardiff, Dundee; **No** Leicester.

Interview advice and questions Past questions include: What made you decide to do a Physiology degree? What experimental work have you done connected with physiology? What future career do you have in mind? What is physiology? Why not choose Medicine instead? What practicals do you do at school? See also **Chapter 6**. **Cardiff** Interviewer expects to see outside interests and ability to mix with people as well as an interest in biological sciences.

AFTER-RESULTS ADVICE
Offers to applicants repeating A-levels Higher Bristol, Glasgow, Leeds, Leicester, Newcastle, St Andrews; **Same** Cardiff, Dundee; **No** Cambridge.

GRADUATE DESTINATIONS AND EMPLOYMENT (2011/12 HESA)
See **Anatomical Science/Anatomy**.

Career note See **Biology**.

OTHER DEGREE SUBJECTS FOR CONSIDERATION
Anatomy; Biochemistry; Biological Sciences; Biotechnology; Dentistry; Genetics; Health Studies; Medicine; Microbiology; Nursing; Optometry; Pharmacology; Radiography; Sports Science.

PHYSIOTHERAPY
(see also **Health Sciences/Studies**)

Physiotherapists work as part of a multi-disciplinary team with other health professionals and are involved in the treatment and rehabilitation of patients of all ages and with a wide variety of medical problems. On successful completion of the three-year course, graduates are eligible for State Registration and Membership of the Chartered Society of Physiotherapy.

Useful websites www.csp.org.uk; www.thephysiotherapysite.co.uk; www.nhscareers.nhs.uk; www.physiotherapy.co.uk.

NB The points totals shown to the left of the institutions are for ease of reference only. It must not be assumed that Tariff points are always used by institutions or that they can be substituted for an offer in grades. The level of an offer is not necessarily indicative of the quality of a course.

COURSE OFFERS INFORMATION
Subject requirements/preferences GCSE English, mathematics and science subjects. Many universities stipulate A/B grades in specific subjects. **AL** One or two science subjects are required. **Other** Occupational health check and Disclosure and Barring Service (DBS) clearance.

Your target offers and examples of courses provided by each institution
360 pts Bournemouth – 360 pts (Physio) (IB 33 pts)
       Southampton – AAA incl sci 360 pts (Physio) (IB 36 pts HL 18 pts)
340 pts Birmingham – AAB (Physio) (IB 35–36 pts)
       Bristol UWE – 340 pts (Physio) (IB 28 pts)
       Brunel – AAB 340 pts (Physio) (IB 35 pts HL 6 biol)
       Cardiff – AAB incl biol (Physio) (IB 28 pts)
       Edinburgh Queen Margaret – AAB 340 pts (Physio) (IB 32 pts)
       London (King's) – AAB (Physio) (IB 35 pts HL 665)
       Oxford Brookes – AAB (Physio) (IB 34 pts)
       Plymouth – 340 pts (Physio) (IB 33 pts)
320 pts Bradford – 320 pts (Physio) (IB 27 pts)
       Brighton – ABB (Physio) (IB 34 pts)
       Central Lancashire – ABB (Physio) (IB 30 pts)
       Coventry – ABB incl biol 320 pts (Physio) (IB 34 pts)
       East Anglia – ABB (Physio) (IB 32 pts HL 6 biol)

Hertfordshire – ABB (Physio)
Huddersfield – ABB 320 pts (Physio)
Keele – ABB (Physio) (IB 27 pts)
Kingston – 320 pts (Physio) see under **London (St George's)**
Leeds Beckett – 320 pts (Physio) (IB 27 pts)
Leicester – ABB (Physio) (IB 34 pts)
Liverpool – ABB 320 pts (Physio) (IB 30 pts)
London (St George's) – ABB (Physio)
Manchester Met – ABB 320 pts (Physio) (IB 29 pts)
Northumbria – 320 pts incl 100 pts in hlth sci subj (Physio) (IB 32 pts)
Nottingham – ABB (Physio) (IB 34 pts HL 6 biol)
Salford – ABB (Physio) (IB 32 pts)
Sheffield Hallam – 320 pts (Physio)
York St John – ABB (Physio) (IB 24 pts)
300 pts **Cumbria** – 300 pts (Physio)
East London – 300 pts (Physio) (IB 26 pts)
Glasgow Caledonian – BBB (Physio) (IB 30 pts)
Robert Gordon – BBB (Physio) (IB 32 pts)
Teesside – 300 pts +interview (Physio) (IB 30 pts)
Ulster – BBB +HPAT (Physio) (IB 26 pts)
Worcester – 300–340 pts (Physio) (IB 27 pts)

Alternative offers
See **Chapter 7** and **Appendix 1** for grades/UCAS Tariff points information for the International Baccalaureate, Scottish Highers/Advanced Highers, the Welsh Baccalaureate, the Irish Leaving Certificate, the Cambridge Pre-U Diploma, the Advanced Diploma and the Extended Project.

EXAMPLES OF FOUNDATION DEGREES IN THE SUBJECT FIELD
Edge Hill; Huddersfield; Keele; Salford.

CHOOSING YOUR COURSE (SEE ALSO CH.1)
Some course features
NHS bursaries are available for all Physiotherapy courses.
East London Physiotherapy is available as full-time, or as full-time situated learning where one-third of the course is practice-based and two-thirds are university-based.
Hertfordshire (Physio) One third of the course is spent on practice placements in hospitals and health care units.
Nottingham (Physio) Thirty-two weeks of supervised clinical practice split into eight four-week blocks take place in Years 2 and 3.
Southampton A three-year full-time or four-year part-time course is offered to school leavers.

Universities and colleges teaching quality See www.qaa.ac.uk; http://unistats.direct.gov.uk.

ADMISSIONS INFORMATION
Number of applicants per place (approx) Birmingham 9; Bradford 22; Brighton 30, (overseas) 6; Bristol UWE 12; Brunel 11; Cardiff 17; Coventry 15; East Anglia 14; East London 10; Edinburgh Queen Margaret 11; Glasgow Caledonian 12; Hertfordshire 13; Huddersfield 18; Kingston 9; Liverpool 20; London (King's) 16; Manchester 18; Northumbria 37; Robert Gordon 13; Salford 28; Sheffield Hallam 12; Southampton 36; Teesside 33; Ulster 12.

Advice to applicants and planning the UCAS personal statement Visits to, and work experience in, hospital physiotherapy departments are important although many universities publicly state that this is not necessary. However, with the level of competition for this subject I would regard this as doubtful (see Reasons for rejection). Applicants must demonstrate a clear understanding of the nature of the profession. Give details of voluntary work activities. Take notes of the work done and the different aspects of physiotherapy. Explain your experience fully on the UCAS application. Outside interests and teamwork are considered important. Good communication skills. Observation placement within a physiotherapy department. See also **Appendix 3**. **Coventry** The University of Leicester part-delivers a BSc Physiotherapy degree. This course is a Coventry University degree that has 30 places based at the Leicester campus. Teaching takes place at Leicester and Coventry. Students are admitted by Coventry but live and mostly study at Leicester. **Manchester Met** We need to know why you want to be a physiotherapist. We also look for work shadowing a physiotherapist or work experience in another caring role. Evidence is also required of good communication skills, ability to care for people and of teamwork and leadership. **Salford** Essential for applicants to seek experience in as wide a range of settings as possible.

Misconceptions about this course Some applicants think that physiotherapy has a sports bias.

Selection interviews Most institutions. **Yes** Birmingham, Bradford, Brighton, Brunel, Coventry, East Anglia, East London, Huddersfield, Keele, London (St George's), Nottingham, Robert Gordon, Salford, Sheffield Hallam, Ulster, Ulster; **Some** Cardiff (mature students), Edinburgh Queen Margaret, Kingston, Southampton (mature students).

Interview advice and questions Physiotherapy is one of the most popular courses at present and work experience is very important, if not essential. A sound knowledge of the career, types of treatment used in physiotherapy and some understanding of the possible problems experienced by patients will be expected. Past interview questions include: How does physiotherapy fit into the overall health care system? If one patient was a heavy smoker and the other not, would you treat them the same? What was the most emotionally challenging thing you have ever done? Give an example of teamwork in which you have been involved. Why should we make you an offer? What is chiropractic? What is osteopathy? See also **Chapter 6**.

Reasons for rejection (non-academic) Lack of knowledge of the profession. Failure to convince the interviewers of a reasoned basis for following the profession. Failure to have visited a hospital physiotherapy unit. Lack of awareness of the demands of the course. **Birmingham** Poor communication skills. Lack of career insight. **Bristol UWE** Applicants re-sitting A-levels are not normally considered. **Cardiff** Lack of knowledge of physiotherapy; experience of sports injuries only.

AFTER-RESULTS ADVICE
Offers to applicants repeating A-levels **Higher** Bristol UWE, East Anglia, East London, Glasgow Caledonian, Kingston, Teesside; **Same** Coventry, Edinburgh Queen Margaret, Salford, Southampton.

GRADUATE DESTINATIONS AND EMPLOYMENT (2011/12 HESA)
See **Health Sciences/Studies**.

Career note The professional qualifications gained on graduation enable physiotherapists to seek posts in the NHS where the majority are employed. A small number work in the community health service, particularly in rural areas, whilst others work in residential homes. In addition to private practice, there are also some opportunities in professional sports clubs.

OTHER DEGREE SUBJECTS FOR CONSIDERATION
Anatomy; Audiology; Biological Sciences; Health Studies; Leisure and Recreation; Nursing; Occupational Therapy; Osteopathy; Physical Education; Psychology; Sport Science/Studies.

PLANT SCIENCES
(including **Botany**; see also **Biological Sciences, Biology, Horticulture**)

Plant Sciences cover such areas as plant biochemistry, plant genetics, plant conservation and plant geography. Botany encompasses all aspects of plant science and also other subject areas including agriculture, forestry and horticulture. Botany is basic to these subjects and others including pharmacology and water management. As with other biological sciences, some universities introduce Plant Sciences by way of a common first year with other subjects.

Useful websites www.kew.org; www.anbg.gov.au; www.bsbi.org.uk; www.botany.net; www.botany.org.

NB The points totals shown to the left of the institutions are for ease of reference only. It must not be assumed that Tariff points are always used by institutions or that they can be substituted for an offer in grades. The level of an offer is not necessarily indicative of the quality of a course.

COURSE OFFERS INFORMATION

Subject requirements/preferences **GCSE** Mathematics if not offered at A-level. **AL** One or two science subjects are usually required.

Your target offers and examples of courses provided by each institution
380 pts Cambridge – A*AA (Nat Sci (Plnt Sci)) (IB 40–41 pts HL 776)
360 pts Edinburgh – AAA–ABB 320–360 pts (Plnt Sci) (IB 37–32 pts)
　　　　Manchester – AAA–ABB 360–320 pts (Plnt Sci; Plnt Sci (Yr Ind); Plnt Sci Modn Lang)
　　　　　　(IB 37–33 pts)
　　　　Sheffield – AAA incl biol sci (Plnt Sci MBiolSci) (IB 37 pts)
340 pts Birmingham – AAB–ABB 340–320 pts (Biol Sci (Plnt Biol)) (IB 34–35 pts)
　　　　Glasgow – AAB (Mol Cell Biol (Plnt Sci)) (IB 34 pts)
　　　　Sheffield – AAB incl biol sci (Plnt Sci) (IB 35 pts)
320 pts East Anglia – ABB incl biol (Plnt Sci) (IB 32 pts)
　　　　Nottingham – ABB–BBB 320–300 pts (Plnt Sci) (IB 32–30 pts)
300 pts Aberdeen – BBB (Plnt Soil Sci) (IB 30 pts)
280 pts Aberystwyth – 280–320 pts (Plnt Biol) (IB 28 pts)
260 pts Myerscough (Coll) – 260 pts (Arbor Urb Frsty) (IB 24 pts)
　　　　Worcester – 260–300 pts (Plnt Sci) (IB 24 pts)
240 pts Aberdeen – CCC (Plnt Soil Sci)
　　　　Canterbury Christ Church – 240 pts (Plnt Sci) (IB 24 pts)

Alternative offers
See **Chapter 7** and **Appendix 1** for grades/UCAS Tariff points information for the International Baccalaureate, Scottish Highers/Advanced Highers, the Welsh Baccalaureate, the Irish Leaving Certificate, the Cambridge Pre-U Diploma, the Advanced Diploma and the Extended Project.

CHOOSING YOUR COURSE (SEE ALSO CH.1)

Some course features
See also **Biology** and **Horticulture**.
Aberystwyth (Plant Biol) After a common first year focusing on plant structure, function, physiology and classification, students can tailor their degree scheme through their choice of module options. Field studies in northern Spain and western Ireland are available.
Birmingham Plant Biology is an option in the Biological Sciences programme. Specialisation can take place at the beginning of the course or in Year 2.
Nottingham The course includes a study of the application of plant sciences in the agricultural, biotechnological, horticultural and food industries.

Universities and colleges teaching quality See www.qaa.ac.uk; http://unistats.direct.gov.uk.

Top research universities and colleges (RAE 2008) See **Biological Sciences**.

Examples of sandwich degree courses Glasgow Caledonian; Leeds; Manchester.

ADMISSIONS INFORMATION

Number of applicants per place (approx) Edinburgh 6; Glasgow 4; Nottingham 7; Sheffield 5.

Advice to applicants and planning the UCAS personal statement Visit botanical gardens. See also **Biological Sciences** and **Appendix 4**.

Selection interviews **Yes** Cambridge; **Some** Nottingham.

Interview advice and questions You are likely to be questioned on your biology studies, your reasons for wishing to study Plant Sciences and your ideas about a possible future career. In the past, questions have been asked about Darwin's theory of evolution, photosynthesis and DNA and the value of gardening programmes on TV! See also **Chapter 6**.

AFTER-RESULTS ADVICE
Offers to applicants repeating A-levels **Possibly higher** Nottingham; **Same** Birmingham, Sheffield; **No** Cambridge, Imperial London.

GRADUATE DESTINATIONS AND EMPLOYMENT (2011/12 HESA)
Botany graduates surveyed 45 **Employed** 25 **In voluntary employment** 0 **In further study** 20 **Assumed unemployed** 0

Career note See **Biology** and **Horticulture**.

OTHER DEGREE SUBJECTS FOR CONSIDERATION
Agriculture; Biochemistry; Biological Sciences; Biology; Crop Science (Agronomy); Ecology; Food Science; Forestry; Herbal Medicine; Horticulture; Landscape Architecture; Traditional Chinese Medicine.

PODIATRY (CHIROPODY)

Podiatry is a relatively new term for chiropody and deals with the management of disease and disorders of the ankle and foot. Podiatrists diagnose nail, skin and movement problems, devise treatment plans and carry out treatment for all age groups. Courses lead to state registration, and some work shadowing prior to application is preferred by admissions tutors.

Useful websites www.scpod.org; www.nhscareers.nhs.uk; www.podiatrynetwork.com; www.podiatrytoday.com; www.healthcommunities.com/health-topics/foot-health.shtml.

NB The points totals shown to the left of the institutions are for ease of reference only. It must not be assumed that Tariff points are always used by institutions or that they can be substituted for an offer in grades. The level of an offer is not necessarily indicative of the quality of a course.

COURSE OFFERS INFORMATION
Subject requirements/preferences **GCSE** Mathematics and science subjects. **AL** Biology usually required or preferred. **Other** Hepatitis B, tuberculosis and tetanus immunisation; Disclosure and Barring Service (DBS) clearance (a pre-existing record could prevent a student from participating in the placement component of the course and prevent the student from gaining state registration).

Your target offers and examples of courses provided by each institution
300 pts   **Brighton** – BBB (Pod) (IB 32 pts)
           Huddersfield – BBB 300 pts (Pod) (IB 26 pts)
           Salford – 300 pts (Pod) (IB 27 pts)
           Southampton – BBB (Pod) (IB 30 pts HL 16 pts)
           Ulster – BBB +HPAT (Pod) (IB 26 pts)
280 pts   **Cardiff Met (UWIC)** – 280 pts (Pod) (IB 25 pts)
           East London – 280 pts (Pod Med) (IB 26 pts)
           Northampton – 280–320 pts (Pod) (IB 24 pts)
           Plymouth – 280 pts (Pod) (IB 27 pts)
260 pts   **Glasgow Caledonian** – BCC 260 pts (Pod) (IB 24 pts)
240 pts   **Edinburgh Queen Margaret** – 240 pts (Pod) (IB 26 pts)
220 pts   **Birmingham Met (Coll)** – 220 pts (Pod)
160 pts   **Durham New (Coll)** – 160 pts (Pod)

Check **Chapter 4** when choosing your university and **Chapter 7** on how to read the subject tables.

574 | Podiatry (Chiropody)

Alternative offers
See **Chapter 7** and **Appendix 1** for grades/UCAS Tariff points information for the International Baccalaureate, Scottish Highers/Advanced Highers, the Welsh Baccalaureate, the Irish Leaving Certificate, the Cambridge Pre-U Diploma, the Advanced Diploma and the Extended Project.

EXAMPLES OF FOUNDATION DEGREES IN THE SUBJECT FIELD
Durham New (Coll); Huddersfield.

CHOOSING YOUR COURSE (SEE ALSO CH.1)
Some course features
NHS bursaries are available for all Podiatry courses. See also **Health Sciences/Studies**.
Northampton Students manage their own patient cases during the course.
Plymouth Supervised placements in NHS Trusts from Year 1.
Southampton A modular programme with six units studied in each semester, these include orthopaedic triage, surgery and paediatrics.

Universities and colleges teaching quality See www.qaa.ac.uk; http://unistats.direct.gov.uk.

ADMISSIONS INFORMATION
Number of applicants per place (approx) Birmingham Met (Coll) 4; Cardiff Met (UWIC) 8; Huddersfield 2–3; Northampton 2; Salford 3; Southampton 4.

Advice to applicants and planning the UCAS personal statement Visit a podiatrist's clinic to gain work experience/work shadowing experience. Applicants need the ability to communicate with all age ranges, to work independently, to be resourceful and to possess a focused approach to academic work. Admissions tutors look for evidence of an understanding of podiatry, some work experience, good people skills, and effective communication. Mature applicants must include an academic reference (not an employer reference). See also **Appendix 3**.

Misconceptions about this course **Cardiff Met (UWIC)** Prospective students are often not aware of the demanding requirements of the course: 1000 practical clinical hours augmented by a rigorous academic programme. Applicants are often unaware that whilst the elderly are a significant sub-population of patients with a variety of foot problems, increasingly the role of the podiatrist is the diagnosis and management of biomechanical/developmental disorders as well as the management of the diabetic or rheumatoid patient and those who require surgical intervention for nail problems. **Huddersfield** Many people think that podiatry is limited in its scope of practice to treating toe nails, corns and calluses: FALSE. As professionals, we do treat such pathologies but the scope of practice is much wider. It now includes surgery, biomechanics, sports injuries, treating children and high-risk patients. Because offers are low it is considered an easier course than, for example, Physiotherapy: FALSE. The course is academically demanding in addition to the compulsory clinical requirement.

Selection interviews Most institutions. **Yes** Huddersfield, Southampton, Ulster; **Some** Cardiff Met (UWIC).

Interview advice and questions Past questions include: Have you visited a podiatrist's surgery? What do your friends think about your choice of career? Do you think that being a podiatrist could cause you any physical problems? With which groups of people do podiatrists come into contact? What are your perceptions of the scope of practice of podiatry? What transferable skills do you think you will need? See also **Chapter 6**. **Cardiff Met (UWIC)** What made you consider podiatry as a career? Have you researched your career choice and where did you find the information? What have you discovered and has this altered your original perception of podiatry? What personal characteristics do you think you possess which might be useful for this work? **Southampton** Applicants should show an interest in medical topics. Communication skills are important and an insight into the implications of a career in podiatry.

Reasons for rejection (non-academic) Unconvincing attitude; poor communication and inter-personal skills; lack of motivation; medical condition or physical disabilities which are incompatible with professional practice; no knowledge of chosen profession; lack of work experience.

PODiAtRY

where's the science in that?

The world around us is dominated by science in one way or another, be it **biology** in plants, the human body, **physics** in engineering or communications and **chemistry** in food or DNA research.

Podiatry is no exception....
it's full of science!

For more information on podiatry please visit our website

or contact:

The Society of Chiropodists and Podiatrists

Fellmongers Path, Tower Bridge Road, London SE1 3LY

Telephone: 0207 234 8620 ~ E-mail: enq@scpod.org

www.feetforlife.org

The Society of
Chiropodists and
Podiatrists

Profile: College of Podiatry

The world around us is dominated by science in one way or another, be it biology in plants or the human body, physics in engineering or communications and chemistry in food or DNA research.

Podiatry is no exception . . . it's full of science!

To understand how the lower limb works and to help patients you need to know all sorts about biology, physics and chemistry

Biology

Biology is probably the main science people associate with working in the medical profession. As a podiatrist it's really important to understand the structure of the body as well as how things interact. Podiatrists measure the blood flow in the legs and feet and to do this they have to know exactly how to find the arteries and veins. They can test blood flow in a number of ways by using their hands, ultrasound devices and blood pressure tests.

Treatment of painful or ingrowing toenails is achieved using simple surgical techniques. To do this podiatrists have to give patients injections of anaesthetic, which must be placed accurately near the nerves in the toe. To do the surgery effectively they have to understand the structure of the nail and surrounding tissues. So you can see how important it is to know your anatomy!

Physics

Physics is also important. Podiatrists treat a lot of different patients with biomechanical problems and understanding levers and forces really helps to diagnose the problem and work out how to treat the patient.

Participating in sports puts increased forces through the joints in the legs, which can cause pain and injury. Runners for example can develop foot or leg problems that may need treatment from a podiatrist. Using a treadmill, video equipment and their knowledge a podiatrist can assess the patient, diagnose the problem and potentially provide custom-made insoles that can alter the mechanics of the foot and reduce unwanted forces going through the foot.

Chemistry

Chemistry is also important in podiatry. Chemical reactions are essential for normal body function. Podiatrists need to know how illnesses and medicines may affect different chemical processes in the body to provide appropriate treatment.

Wounds in the skin contain all sorts of biochemicals. Podiatrists must understand what potential interactions there might be with anything they are using to treat a wound that would slow down the healing process. They need to know about different kinds of medication and how they react with the body.

For example understanding chemistry enables a podiatrist to calculate the maximum safe dose of anaesthetic for a patient.

If you would like further information about podiatry training please visit www. careersinpodiatry.com

AFTER-RESULTS ADVICE
Offers to applicants repeating A-levels **Same** Cardiff Met (UWIC), Huddersfield, Salford.

GRADUATE DESTINATIONS AND EMPLOYMENT (2011/12 HESA)
Career note Many state-registered podiatrists are employed by the NHS whilst others work in private practice or commercially run clinics.

OTHER DEGREE SUBJECTS FOR CONSIDERATION
Audiology; Biological Sciences; Health Studies; Nursing; Occupational Therapy; Osteopathy; Physiotherapy.

POLITICS

(including **Government** and **International Politics**; see also **Development Studies, International Relations, Social Sciences/Studies**)

Politics is often described as the study of 'who gets what, where, when and how'. Courses have become increasingly popular in recent years and usually cover the politics and government of the major powers. Because of the variety of degree courses on offer, it is possible to study the politics of almost any country in the world.

Useful websites www.europa.eu; www.gov.uk/government/organisations/foreign-commonwealth-office; www.psa.ac.uk; www.parliament.uk; www.whitehouse.gov; www.amnesty.org; www.gov.uk; www.un.org; www.un.int.

NB The points totals shown to the left of the institutions are for ease of reference only. It must not be assumed that Tariff points are always used by institutions or that they can be substituted for an offer in grades. The level of an offer is not necessarily indicative of the quality of a course.

COURSE OFFERS INFORMATION
Subject requirements/preferences **GCSE** English, mathematics and a foreign language may be required. **AL** No subjects specified; history useful but an arts or social science subject an advantage.

Your target offers and examples of courses provided by each institution
440 pts **Warwick** – A*AAa (Econ Pol Int St) (IB 38 pts HL 6 maths)
430 pts **Warwick** – A*AAb (PPE) (IB 38 pts)
400 pts **London (UCL)** – A*AAe 400 pts (Euro Soc Pol St) (IB 39 pts)
380 pts **Bath** – A*AA incl maths (Econ Pol) (IB 38 pts HL 766)
　　　　　Cambridge – A*AA (Hum Soc Pol Sci (Pol Int Rel); Hum Soc Pol Sci (Assyr Egypt)) (IB 40–41 pts HL 776)
　　　　　Durham – A*AA incl maths 380 pts (PPE) (IB 38 pts HL 666)
　　　　　London (King's) – A*AA +LNAT (Pol Phil Law) (IB 35 pts HL 766)
　　　　　London (UCL) – AAAe 380 pts (Pol E Euro St) (IB 38 pts)
　　　　　York – A*AA–AAA 380–360 pts (PPE) (IB 37 pts)
360 pts **Bath** – AAA (Pol Int Rel) (IB 38 pts HL 666)
　　　　　Bristol – AAA–AAB (Pol Int Rel) (IB 37–35 pts HL 666)
　　　　　Durham – AAA 360 pts (Econ Pol; Pol; Phil Pol) (IB 37 pts)
　　　　　Edinburgh – AAA–BBB 360–300 pts (Pol; Hist Pol; Persn Pol) (IB 42–34 pts)
　　　　　Exeter – AAA–AAB 360–340 pts (Pol Int Rel (Cornwall); Pol; PPE) (IB 36–34 pts)
　　　　　Lancaster – AAA (Hist Pol; Pol (St Abrd)) (IB 36 pts)
　　　　　London (King's) – AAA (Int Pol; War St; Euro Pol) (IB 35 pts HL 666)
　　　　　London (QM) – AAA (Law Pol) (IB 36 pts)
　　　　　London (SOAS) – AAA (Pol) (IB 38 pts HL 766)
　　　　　London LSE – AAA (Gov Hist; Pol Phil; Int Rel; Gov; Gov Econ) (IB 38 pts HL 766)
　　　　　Newcastle – AAA–ABB (Pol Econ; Pol; Gov EU St) (IB 34–37 pts)

Nottingham – AAA (Hist Pol) (IB 36 pts HL 6 hist)
Oxford – AAA (PPE; Hist Pol) (IB 38–40 pts)
Queen's Belfast – AAA/AABa (Law Pol) (IB 34 pts HL 666)
Sussex – AAA–AAB (Law Pol) (IB 35 pts)
Warwick – AAA–AAB (Pol; Pol Joint Hons) (IB 38–36 pts)
York – AAA (Phil Pol) (IB 35 pts)

340 pts Aston – AAB–ABB 340–320 pts (Pol Int Rel) (IB 34–35 pts)
Bristol – AAB–ABB (Pol Modn Lang; Pol Sociol; Soc Plcy Pol) (IB 35–33 pts)
Brunel – AAB–ABB 320–340 pts (Int Pol; Pol Econ; Pol) (IB 35 pts)
Cardiff – AAB 340 pts (Euro Pol Int Rel; Pol; Int Rel Pol)
City – AAB 340 pts (Int Pol) (IB 32 pts)
Essex – AAB–ABB (PPE; Pol) (IB 33–32 pts)
Exeter – A*AA–AAB 380–340 pts (Econ Pol Euro St) (IB 38–34 pts)
Glasgow – AAB (Pol; Pol Joint Hons) (IB 34 pts)
Lancaster – AAB (PPE; Pol Sociol; Pol Int Rel; Pol Relig St; Pol) (IB 35 pts)
Leeds – AAB (Pol Parl St; Pol) (IB 36 pts HL 17 pts)
Liverpool – AAB (Int Pol Plcy; Pol) (IB 35 pts)
London (Gold) – AAB (Int St) (IB 28 pts)
London (King's) – AAB (Pol Int Econ) (IB 36 pts HL 665)
London (RH) – AAB–ABB (Pol Phil; Pol; Mus Pol St; Pol Phil Econ; Econ Pol Int Rel)
(IB 35–34 pts)
London LSE – AAB (Soc Plcy Gov) (IB 37 pts)
Loughborough – AAB (Econ Pol) (IB 36 pts)
Manchester – AAB–ABB (PPE; Econ Pol; Pol Modn Hist; Law Pol; Bus St Pol; Pol Int Rel; Pol
courses) (IB 36–33 pts)
Nottingham – AAB (Pol courses) (IB 36 pts)
Queen's Belfast – AAB 340 pts (PPE) (IB 35 pts HL 666)
Sheffield – AAB (Int Rel Pol; Pol Phil; Pol; Int Pol Scrty St; Hist Pol) (IB 35 pts)
Southampton – AAB–ABB (Pol Fr/Ger; Pol Span/Port Lat Am St; Phil Pol; Modn Hist Pol)
(IB 34 pts HL 17 pts)
Sussex – AAB (Econ Pol; Pol courses) (IB 35 pts)
York – AAB–ABB (Soc Pol Sci; Pol Int Rel; Pol; Engl Pol) (IB 35 pts)

320 pts Aston – ABB (Pol Engl Lang; Pol Soc Plcy; Pol Sociol) (IB 32–34 pts)
Birmingham – ABB (Pol Sci; Int Rel Pol Sci; Pol Econ; Soc Plcy Pol Sci; Euro Pol Soty Econ)
(IB 34 pts)
Brighton – ABB (Phil Pol Eth)
Bristol UWE – 320 pts (Pol)
Cardiff – ABB incl Fr (Pol Dip Etud Pol) (IB 33 pts)
Chichester – ABB–BBC incl hist 320–280 pts (Pol Contemp Hist)
East Anglia – ABB–BBB (PPE; Pol; Media Pol; Pol Sociol; Hist Pol) (IB 32–35 pts)
Essex – ABB–BBB 320–300 pts (Pol Hum Rts) (IB 33–32 pts)
Hull – ABB (Law Pol) (IB 30 pts)
Kent – ABB (Pol; Pol Int Rel; Pol Int Rel (Yr Abrd)) (IB 33 pts)
Kingston – ABB 320 pts (Pol Jrnl) (28 pts)
Leeds – ABB (Chin Pol; Euro Pol Fr/Ger/Ital; Int Dev courses; Pol Port/Russ/Span)
(IB 34 pts)
Leicester – ABB (Pol Econ; Pol) (IB 32 pts)
Liverpool – ABB (Pol Comm St) (IB 33 pts)
London (QM) – ABB (Hist Pol; Pol) (IB 34 pts)
London (RH) – ABB 320 pts (Geog Pol Int Rel) (IB 37 pts HL 666)
Loughborough – ABB–ABC 300–320 pts (Hist Pol; Pol courses) (IB 32–34 pts)
Manchester – ABB (Pol Sociol; Pol Soc Anth) (IB 34 pts)
Newcastle – ABB–BBB 300–320 pts (Pol Sociol) (IB 32 pts)
Northumbria – 320 pts (Pol) (IB 27 pts)
Reading – ABB 320 pts (Pol Int Rel; War Pce Int Rel) (IB 32 pts)

LEEDS METROPOLITAN UNIVERSITY
BA (Hons) Politics

Gain an insight into the fascinating world of politics from political movements, ideologies and theories to wider political participation and engagement. You will study politics in its social context, from domestic politics to international relations.

This course covers issues such as:
• Political activism
• Human rights
• Inequality
• Climate change
• Relations between states and other actors in the international system

All students undertake a voluntary work placement, in the UK or abroad, which aims to increase employability and builds links with key partners including NGOs, MPs, MEPs and Local Councillors.

To find out more visit: **www.leedsmet.ac.uk**

LEEDS METROPOLITAN UNIVERSITY

LEEDS BECKETT UNIVERSITY | From September 2014 Leeds Metropolitan University will become Leeds Beckett University

Sheffield – ABB (Pol Sociol) (IB 33 pts)
Southampton – ABB–BBB (Pol Int Rel; Pol; Pol Econ) (IB 32 pts HL 16 pts)
Strathclyde – ABB (Pol courses) (IB 34 pts)
Surrey – ABB (Pol) (IB 32 pts)
Swansea – ABB–BBC 320–280 pts (PPE) (IB 33 pts)
300 pts **Aberdeen** – BBB (Pol courses; Int Rel courses) (IB 32 pts)
Aberystwyth – 300 pts (Int Pol; Pol St; Euro Pol; Pol courses; Int Pol Third Wrld)
Brighton – BBB (Pol Soc Plcy; Pol Sociol) (IB 32 pts)
Buckingham – BBB 300 pts (Law Pol) (IB 34 pts)
Dundee – BBB (Pol) (IB 30 pts)
Essex – 300–320 pts (Econ Pol) (IB 32–36 pts)
Hertfordshire – 300 pts (Gov Pol)
Huddersfield – BBB 300 pts (Pol; Pol Contemp Hist)
Hull – 300–340 pts (PPE; Pol Int Rel; Pol Phil)
Keele – BBB (Pol) (IB 32 pts)
Lincoln – 300 pts (Pol; Int Rel Pol)
London (Gold) – BBB (Pol)
Northumbria – 300 pts (Hist Pol) (IB 26 pts)
Queen's Belfast – ABB–BBB (Pol Joint Hons)
Surrey – BBB (Int Pol) (IB 32 pts)
Westminster – BBB (Pol) (IB 28 pts)
280 pts **Bradford** – BBC (Pol)
De Montfort – 280 pts (Int Rel Pol; Pol Gov; Pol Sociol)
Greenwich – 280 pts (Phil Pol) (IB 28 pts)
London Met – 280 pts (Pol; Int Rel Pce Cnflct St) (IB 28 pts)
Manchester Met – 280 pts (Int Pol Phil) (IB 28 pts)
Oxford Brookes – BBC (Pol; Int Rel Pol; Econ Pol Int Rel) (IB 31 pts)

Check **Chapter 4** when choosing your university and **Chapter 7** on how to read the subject tables.

Stirling – BBC (Pol; PPE; Pol (Int Pol)) (IB 32 pts)
Swansea – BBC-BBB (Pol; Pol Langs; Pol Comm; Pol Soc Plcy; War Soty) (IB 30 pts)
Winchester – 280-320 pts (Pol Glob St courses) (IB 26 pts)

260 pts **Central Lancashire** – 260-300 pts (Pol courses)
Coventry – BCC (Pol; Pol Hist) (IB 28 pts)
Greenwich – 260 pts (Pol)
Liverpool Hope – 260-320 pts (Pol)
Northampton – 260-280 pts (Pol; Pol Joint Hons)
Nottingham Trent – 260 pts (Pol Hist)
Plymouth – 260 pts (Int Rel Pol) (IB 26 pts)
Sheffield Hallam – 260 pts (Pol)
Sunderland – 260 pts (Pol (Comb))
Ulster – 260-280 pts (Pol) (IB 24 pts)

240 pts **Canterbury Christ Church** – 240 pts (Pol Gov; Pol Glob Gov; Pol)
Chester – 240-280 pts (Pol) (IB 26 pts)
Manchester Met – 240 pts (Pol) (IB 28 pts)
Middlesex – 240 pts (Int Pol) (IB 28 pts)
Nottingham Trent – 240 pts (Pol; Sociol Pol; Pol Int Rel)
Plymouth – 240 pts (Pol Fr; Pol Int Rel) (IB 26 pts)
Portsmouth – 240-300 pts (Pol; Pol Sociol)
Salford – 240-280 pts (Pol; Int Rel Pol) (IB 25 pts)
Westminster – CCC-BCC (Pol (Comb)) (IB 28 pts)
West Scotland – CCC (Pol) (IB 24 pts)
Worcester – 240-340 pts (Pol Ppl Pwr) (IB 24 pts)

220 pts **Kingston** – 220-360 pts (Pol App Econ)
Wolverhampton – 220 pts (Pol Hist)

200 pts **Blackburn (Coll)** – 200 pts (Pol courses)
East London – 200 pts (Int Pol)
Leeds Beckett – 200 pts (Pol) (IB 24 pts)
Wolverhampton – 200 pts (Pol Phil; Sociol Pol)

160 pts **UHI** – CC (Hist Pol)

Open University – contact +44 (0)845 300 6090 **or** www.openuniversity.co.uk/you (PPE)

Alternative offers

See **Chapter 7** and **Appendix 1** for grades/UCAS Tariff points information for the International Baccalaureate, Scottish Highers/Advanced Highers, the Welsh Baccalaureate, the Irish Leaving Certificate, the Cambridge Pre-U Diploma, the Advanced Diploma and the Extended Project.

CHOOSING YOUR COURSE (SEE ALSO CH.1)

Some course features

Bath Politics can be studied alongside Economics, Language and International Relations. (Econ Pol) Option available to spend a year in industry.

Chester The International Development Studies course focuses on socio-economic, political, cultural and environmental aspects, exploring the Third World and comparisons between rich and poor, urban and rural and contemporary and historical. Politics is also offered as a Single or Combined Honours course and covers subjects, such as British government, political thinkers and social policy.

Essex The Department of Government offers a wide range of courses in two main degrees, Politics and International Relations and Politics. A range of specialist options are available covering world politics, democracy and human rights. Twelve other joint courses are also available.

Kent The Department offers two main programmes: Politics and Politics and International Relations, also with French, German and Italian and an optional year in countries including Finland, Japan or the Czech Republic. Other courses include Social Policy, Economics and Politics, Conflict, Peace and Security and Politics and Social Anthropology.

Universities and colleges teaching quality See www.qaa.ac.uk; http://unistats.direct.gov.uk.

Top research universities and colleges (RAE 2008) (Politics and International Studies) Essex; Sheffield; Aberystwyth; Oxford; London LSE; London (UCL); London (SOAS); Sussex (Int Rel); Warwick; Exeter; Nottingham; Manchester; Cambridge.

Examples of sandwich degree courses Aston; Bath; Brunel; Central Lancashire; Coventry; De Montfort; Essex; Lancaster; Loughborough; Middlesex; Nottingham Trent; Oxford Brookes; Plymouth; Surrey.

ADMISSIONS INFORMATION

Number of applicants per place (approx) Aberystwyth 4; Aston 4; Bath 2; Birmingham 6; Bradford 10; Bristol 14; Brunel 5; Buckingham 2; Cardiff 14; Cardiff Met (UWIC) 3; De Montfort 6; Dundee 6; Durham 11; East Anglia 15; Exeter 8; Hull 11, (PPE) 20; Kent 14; Lancaster 14; Leeds 18; Leicester 7; Liverpool 9; Liverpool John Moores 6; London (QM) 10; London (SOAS) 5; London LSE (Gov) 17, (Gov Econ) 10, (Gov Hist) 17; London Met 5; Loughborough 4; Newcastle 9; Northampton 4; Nottingham 5; Nottingham Trent 3; Oxford (PPE) 7; Oxford Brookes 12; Portsmouth 6; Salford 7; Southampton 6; Staffordshire 10; Stirling 9; Swansea 3; Warwick 10; York 6, (PPE) 9.

Advice to applicants and planning the UCAS personal statement Study the workings of government in the UK, Europe and other areas of the world, such as the Middle East, the Far East, America and Russia. Describe visits to the Houses of Commons and Lords and the debates taking place. Attend council meetings – county, town, district, village halls. Describe these visits and agendas. Read current affairs avidly. Be aware of political developments in the major countries and regions of the world including the Middle East, South America, the UK, Europe, USA, China, Korea and Russia. Keep abreast of developments in theatres of war, for example, Afghanistan. Explain your interests in detail. **Aberystwyth** We look for degree candidates with a strong interest in political and social issues and who want to inquire into the way in which the world is organised politically, socially and economically. **Bristol** Deferred entry accepted. **De Montfort** Demonstration of active interest in current affairs and some understanding of how politics affects our daily lives.

Misconceptions about this course **Aberystwyth** Many students believe that they need to study politics at A-level for Politics courses – this is not the case. **Cardiff Met (UWIC)** Some consider that Politics is a narrow subject, only relevant to those who want a political career. **De Montfort** Some applicants believe that a Politics course only covers the mechanics of government and parliament.

Selection interviews **Yes** Cambridge, Durham, Exeter, Hull, Kent, Leeds (Pol Parl St), Liverpool, London (Gold), London South Bank, Oxford, Portsmouth, Sussex; **Some** Aberystwyth, Bath (mature students), Bristol, De Montfort, Dundee, Liverpool John Moores, London (SOAS), London Met, Loughborough, Salford, Surrey, Ulster, Warwick; **No** Birmingham, East Anglia, Essex, Huddersfield, Leicester, London LSE, Nottingham, Reading, Sheffield, Swansea, York (PPE).

Interview advice and questions Questions may stem from A/AS-level studies but applicants will also be expected to be up-to-date in their knowledge and opinions of current events. Questions in recent years have included: What constitutes a 'great power'? What is happening at present in the Labour Party? Define capitalism. What is a political decision? How do opinion polls detract from democracy? Is the European Union a good idea? Why? What are the views of the present government on the European Union? What is a 'spin doctor'? Are politicians hypocrites? See also **Chapter 6**. **De Montfort** Why Politics? What political issues motivate your interests, for example environmentalism, human rights?

AFTER-RESULTS ADVICE

Offers to applicants repeating A-levels **Higher** Essex, Glasgow, Leeds, Newcastle, Nottingham, Warwick, York; **Possibly higher** Hull, Lancaster, Oxford Brookes, Swansea; **Same** Aberystwyth, Birmingham, Bristol, Buckingham, Cardiff Met (UWIC), De Montfort, Dundee, Durham, East Anglia, Lincoln, Liverpool Hope, Liverpool John Moores, London (SOAS), London Met, London South Bank, Loughborough, Nottingham Trent, Portsmouth, Salford, Staffordshire, Stirling, Sussex, Wolverhampton; **No** Cambridge.

GRADUATE DESTINATIONS AND EMPLOYMENT (2011/12 HESA)

Graduates surveyed 4365 **Employed** 2035 **In voluntary employment** 275 **In further study** 1085 **Assumed unemployed** 430

Career note The transferable skills gained in this degree open up a wide range of career opportunities. Graduates seek positions in management, public services and administration and in some cases in political activities.

OTHER DEGREE SUBJECTS FOR CONSIDERATION

Development Studies; Economics; Government; History; International Relations; Public Policy and Administration; Social Policy and Administration; Sociology.

PSYCHOLOGY

(including **Behavioural Science, Cognitive Sciences, Counselling** and **Neuroscience**; see also **Animal Sciences, Biological Sciences, Philosophy, Physiology, Social Sciences/Studies**)

Psychology is a very popular subject, with the number of applications rising by 40,000 in the last 10 years. The study attracts three times more women than men. It covers studies in development, behaviour, perception, memory, language, learning, personality as well as social relationships and abnormal psychology. Psychology is a science and you will be involved in experimentation and statistical analysis. The degree is usually offered as a BSc or a BA course and there are many similarities between them. The differences are in the elective subjects which can be taken in the second and third years. It is not training to enable you to psycho-analyse your friends – psychology is not the same as psychiatry!

To qualify as a chartered psychologist (for which a postgraduate qualification is required) it is necessary to obtain a first degree (or equivalent) qualification which gives eligibility for both Graduate Membership (GM) and the Graduate Basis for Registration (GBR) of the British Psychological Society (BPS). A full list of courses accredited by the British Psychological Society is available on the Society's website www.bps.org.uk. The website also provides careers information and information about all the qualifications needed for careers in the wide-ranging field of psychology. These include Educational, Clinical, Occupational and Forensic Psychology. (See **Appendix 3**.)

Behavioural Science covers the study of animal and human behaviour and offers an overlap between Zoology, Sociology, Psychology and Biological Sciences. Psychology, however, also crosses over into Education, Management Sciences, Human Resource Management, Counselling, Public Relations, Advertising, Artificial Intelligence, Marketing, Retail and Social Studies.

Useful websites www.psychology.org; www.bps.org.uk; www.socialpsychology.org; www.psychcentral. com.

NB The points totals shown to the left of the institutions are for ease of reference only. It must not be assumed that Tariff points are always used by institutions or that they can be substituted for an offer in grades. The level of an offer is not necessarily indicative of the quality of a course.

COURSE OFFERS INFORMATION

Subject requirements/preferences **GCSE** English, mathematics and a science. **AL** A science subject is usually required. Psychology may be accepted as a science subject.

Your target offers and examples of courses provided by each institution
400 pts London (UCL) – A*AAe-AAAe (Psy) (IB 38-39 pts HL 18-19 pts)
380 pts Bath – A*AA (Psy) (IB 38 pts HL 766)
Cambridge – A*AA (Psy Bhv Sci; Nat Sci (Psy)) (IB 40-41 pts HL 776)
Oxford – A*AA (Expmtl Psy; Psy Phil Ling) (IB 38-40 pts)
360 pts Birmingham – AAA-AAB 340-360 pts (Psy) (IB 35-36 pts)
Bristol – AAA-A*AB incl sci/psy/geog (Psy) (IB 37 pts HL 666)

Cardiff – AAA/A*AB–AAB 360 pts (Psy) (IB 36 pts HL 18 pts)
City – AAA 360 pts (Psy) (IB 34 pts)
Durham – AAA 360 pts (Phil Psy; Psy) (IB 37 pts)
Edinburgh – AAA–BBB 360–300 pts (Cog Sci; Cog Sci (Hum)) (IB 37–34 pts)
Exeter – AAA–AAB (Psy; App Psy; Psy Spo Exer Sci) (IB 36–34 pts)
Kent – AAA (App Psy; App Psy Clin Psy) (IB 34 pts)
Manchester – AAA–ABB 360–320 pts (Cog Neuro Psy) (IB 37–33 pts)
Newcastle – AAA–ABB (Psy)
Nottingham – AAA–AAB (Psy; Psy Cog Neuro) (IB 36–34 pts)
St Andrews – AAA (Art Hist Psy; Psy; Geog Psy; Econ Psy; Comp Sci Psy)
Surrey – AAA (Psy) (IB 34 pts)
Sussex – AAA–AAB 360–340 pts (Psy Am St) (IB 35 pts)
York – AAA–AAB (Psy) (IB 35–36 pts)
340 pts Bangor – 340–280 pts (Psy; Psy Clin Hlth Psy; Psy Neuropsy; Psy Chld Lang Dev; Spo Exer Psy)
Bristol UWE – 340 pts (Psy courses) (IB 28 pts)
Brunel – AAB–ABB 340–320 pts (Psy courses) (IB 35 pts)
Durham – AAB 340 pts (Psy App) (IB 36 pts)
Edinburgh – AAB (Psy)
Glasgow – AAB (Psy) (IB 34 pts)
Kent – AAB (Psy Clin Psy; Soc Psy; Psy; Psy St Euro) (IB 34 pts)
Lancaster – AAB (Psy; Ling Psy; Psy Stats) (IB 35 pts)
Leeds – AAB (Psy) (IB 35 pts)
Leicester – AAB (Psy; Psy Cog Neuro)
Liverpool – AAB–ABB (Psy) (IB 34 pts)
London (Gold) – AAB–ABB (Psy) (IB 34 pts)
Loughborough – AAB–ABB (Soc Psy; Psy) (IB 34–36 pts)
Manchester – AAB (Psy) (IB 36–33 pts)
Newcastle – AAB (Biol Psy; Nutr Psy)
Nottingham – AAB (Psy Phil) (IB 34 pts HL 665)
Reading – AAB–ABB (Psy; Psy Biol; Art Psy)
Sheffield – AAB (Psy) (IB 35 pts)
Southampton – AAB (Psy; App Soc Sci (Crimin Psy St); Educ St Psy) (IB 34 pts HL 17 pts)
Strathclyde – AAB (Econ Psy)
Sussex – AAA–AAB (Psy; Psy Cog Sci; Psy Neuro; Psy Sociol) (IB 35 pts)
Swansea – AAB–ABB (Psy) (IB 33–34 pts)
Warwick – AAB (Psy) (IB 36 pts)
320 pts Aston – ABB–AAB 320–340 pts (Psy; Psy Engl Lang; Psy Sociol)
Bournemouth – 320 pts (Spo Psy Coach Sci; Psy)
Bristol UWE – 320 pts (Crimin Psy)
East Anglia – ABB (Psy) (IB 32 pts)
Glasgow Caledonian – ABB 320 pts (Psy)
Greenwich – 320 pts (Psy)
Kent – ABB (Phil Soc Psy)
Leicester – ABB (Psy Sociol)
Liverpool John Moores – 320–280 pts (App Spo Psy; Foren Psy Crim Just)
London (Birk) – ABB 320 pts (Psy)
London (QM) – ABB (Psy)
Northumbria – 320 pts (Psy)
Oxford Brookes – ABB (Psy) (IB 33 pts)
Portsmouth – 320 pts (Psy) (IB 30 pts)
Queen's Belfast – ABB/BBBb (Psy)
Strathclyde – ABB (Psy) (IB 34 pts)
Sussex – AAB–ABB (Neuro Cog Sci) (IB 34 pts)
York – ABB (Sociol Soc Psy) (IB 34 pts)

Check **Chapter 4** when choosing your university and **Chapter 7** on how to read the subject tables.

Join now as a Subscriber

The British Psychological Society is the representative body for psychology and psychologists in the UK. We are responsible for the development, promotion and application of psychology for the public good.

As a Subscriber you can:

- Receive full online access to *The Psychologist*, our monthly magazine;
- Keep up-to-date with the latest developments affecting psychology;
- Contribute to our discussion groups;
- Attend our events to find out more about a career in psychology;
- Benefit from high street discounts.

Find out more and to join online

www.bps.org.uk/join

Why choose a BPS accredited degree?

Accreditation is a mark of quality, studying an accredited degree in psychology can be the first step towards becoming a psychologist, but it will also give you valuable skills that can be used in a variety of sectors such as education, business, health and the media.

Studying an accredited psychology degree gives you eligibility for Graduate Basis for Chartered Membership (GBC).

GBC is required to train to become a Chartered psychologist.

For more information about accreditation and to see which courses are accredited visit **www.bps.org.uk/accreditation**

Student membership

Once you're studying an accredited undergraduate degree, membership will broaden your appreciation and understanding of psychology, and open up a network of like-minded students, academics and professionals, not to mention future opportunities.

For more information on Student membership visit **www.bps.org.uk/student**

The British
Psychological Society

Study psychology at the University of Greenwich

There are many great reasons to choose to study these programmes at the University of Greenwich, including:

- The majority of research is rated of an internationally excellent standard
- Our students are very satisfied – 91% of 2013 graduates were satisfied overall with their course*
- You will be taught by a team of highly qualified, committed academics
- We have high employment rates – 90% of our students are in employment or postgraduate education, 6 months after graduating*
- You will enjoy an attractive campus university experience only 20 minutes from central London

*Unistats

What some of our students have to say:

Since being accepted on the BSc Hons Psychology programme, active encouragement from my tutors has already led to real and valuable experience within the discipline, which, I am confident, will help make a career within psychology a very real possibility.

Studying at such an open and relaxed campus has also allowed me to meet a diverse range of people, many of whom have now become friends; some are fellow students, others are lecturers who show a genuine interest in helping students reach their potential. As areas of focus range from psychological research methods to neuroscience, the programme is as varied as it is challenging and should appeal to anyone interested in human behaviour, the brain, and thought processes.

Ross Friday,
BSc Hons Psychology

Studying at the University of Greenwich has been very rewarding, and has helped me develop professionally and personally. Lectures and seminars are interactive with opportunities to ask questions and debate topics. The course leaders are always happy to help and give advice; they all seemed very passionate about their jobs and have a genuine interest in teaching. One of the things I enjoyed most was working as a research assistant because I could put into practice what I learned in my research methods course as well as gaining new skills and valuable experience.

The campus has great facilities, a fantastic library as well as lots of green spaces where you can enjoy the wonderful surroundings. I highly recommend the University of Greenwich to anyone wishing to study psychology or psychology with counselling.

Andreea Maigut,
BSc Hons Psychology with Counselling

Entry requirements: 320 UCAS points from at A-Levels and/or BTEC (40 points of which can come from AS Level)

School of
Life and Medical Sciences

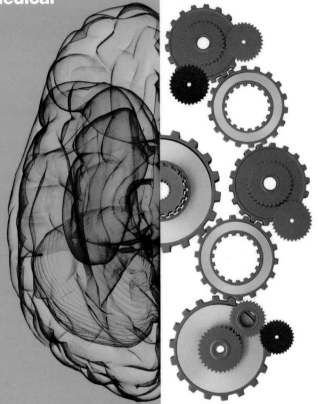

Explore the science of mind and behaviour

The human mind is as complex as it is remarkable and to fully understand the relationship between the way it works and how people think and behave, you will need to develop both theoretical knowledge and a range of practical skills. Our *BSc (Hons) Psychology* provides a strong grounding in all major areas of the subject and will also help you apply your learning to the real concerns of people of all ages and backgrounds.

Accredited by the British Psychological Society, this course combines coverage of core topics in Psychology with a range of specialist, applied optional courses. Taught within one of the largest

Psychology departments in the UK, you will have access to well-equipped laboratories, excellent computing facilities and staff who are actively engaged in significant and highly regarded research.

Studying in this stimulating and supportive environment, renowned for both its academic excellence and practical approach, will prepare you for employment or postgraduate study.

Become more.

Find out more about this course at:

go.herts.ac.uk/psychology

THINK PSYCHOLOGY
THINK BANGOR

PRIFYSGOL
BANGOR
UNIVERSITY

"The School of Psychology at Bangor is producing some of the best quality psychology graduates in the UK". – External Examiners Report

Bangor has an unusual combination of qualities, which make our department uniquely well positioned to offer undergraduates an exceptional learning experience and a degree which carries with it the reputation of an exceptional department.

What makes Bangor Unique?

- One of only 5 departments in the UK to be ranked in the top 20 by The Times 2014 League table for Student Satisfaction, Research Quality and Graduate Prospects
- Established in 1963 Bangor Psychology is one of the oldest and largest in the UK with over 1100 students
- Our world-class research focused academics are involved in undergraduate teaching, which is lead by a research active Teaching Team who focus on delivering the undergraduate programmes. This dual emphasis provides students with a skill set that is second to none and a degree which carries with it our worldwide research reputation
- We have developed sophisticated systems that ensure our students achieve their full potential in a department that combines excellence with accessibility.
- We have a large number of laboratories including a research dedicated 3T fMRI scanner.

Psychology gives students an excellent mix of key skills and access to a varied range of professions, flexibility which is very valuable in today's economic climate and Bangor University, with the School of Psychology in the vanguard, has been at the forefront of the drive to embed employability into academically rigorous degrees.

Entry Requirements

Our normal offers are in the range of 340-280 points. General Studies/Key Skills are not accepted and applicants are strongly preferred to have at least 1 relevant science A level (Maths, Biology, Human Biology, Physics, Chemistry, Statistics, Psychology, Science) GCSE Maths & English are required. Applications from those with other qualifications are welcomed.

Undergraduate Courses

BSc Psychology
BSc Psychology with Clinical & Health
BSc Psychology with Neuropsychology
BSc Psychology with Child & Language Development
BSc Psychology and Business*

What's Bangor Like?

Bangor is situated on the north Wales coast between the mountains of Snowdonia and the sea, making it one of the most attractive university towns in the UK. Bangor has a reputation as a multi-cultural, multi-lingual, safe and friendly city, which hosts over 11,000 students drawn from across the globe.

If you require any further information, please do not hesitate to contact us.

*subject to validation

Contact us for more information:
School of Psychology, Bangor University, Gwynedd LL57 2AS **t.** +44(0)1248 382629
 e. psychology@bangor.ac.uk   @PsychBangor www.bangor.ac.uk/psychology

300 pts   **Aberdeen** – BBB 300 pts (Psy; Neuro Psy) (IB 32 pts)
Aberystwyth – 300 pts (Psy Crimin) (IB 30 pts)
Bolton – 300 pts (Psy; Cnslg Psy; Crimin Foren Psy) (IB 26 pts)
Brighton – BBB (App Psy Sociol; App Psy Crimin) (IB 32 pts)
Buckingham – BBB 300 pts (Mark Psy; Psy Span; Psy)
Central Lancashire – 260–300 pts (Psy) (IB 25–28 pts)
Chichester – 300 pts (Psy) (IB 32 pts)
Coventry – BBB (Psy; Spo Psy) (IB 28 pts)
De Montfort – 300 pts (Psy; Psy Crimin; Educ St Psy)
Derby – 300–260 pts (Psy)
Edge Hill – BBB 300 pts (Psy) (IB 26 pts)
Essex – 300–320 pts (Psy) (IB 29 pts)
Heriot-Watt – BBB (Psy courses)
Huddersfield – BBB 300 pts (Psy; Psy Crimin; Psy Cnslg)
Keele – 300–320 pts (App Psy; Neuro Psy)
Lincoln – 300 pts (Psy; Psy Chld St)
London (Hey) – 300–320 pts (Phil) (IB 30 pts)
London (RH) – 300–320 pts (Psy)
London Met – 300 pts (Psy)
Manchester Met – BBB–BBC (Psy; Psy Sp Path) (IB 30 pts)
Middlesex – 300 pts (Psy HR Mgt; Psy Comb courses)
Roehampton – 300 pts (Psy Cnslg; Psy Hlth)
Sheffield Hallam – 300 pts (Psy)
West London – 300 pts (Psy; Psy Crimin/Cnslg Theor)
Westminster – BBB (Psy) (IB 32 pts)

280 pts **Aberystwyth** – 280 pts (Psy) (IB 27 pts)
Bath Spa – 280–300 pts (Psy Comb Hons)
Birmingham City – 280 pts (Psy)
Cardiff Met (UWIC) – 280 pts (Psy)
Gloucestershire – 280–300 pts (Educ St Psy)
Hertfordshire – 280 pts (Psy)
Hull – BBC 280 pts (Psy; Psy Crimin; Psy Spo Sci; Psy Phil)
Leeds Beckett – 280 pts (Crimin Psy; Psy Soc) (IB 25 pts)
Leeds Trinity – (Psy; Foren Psy)
Lincoln – 280 pts (Bus Mark)
Liverpool John Moores – 280 pts (Crimin Psy) (IB 29 pts)
Loughborough – BBC 280–300 pts (Ergon (Hum Fact Des)) (IB 30–32 pts)
Manchester Met – 280–300 pts (Psy Sociol; Psy Spo Exer) (IB 30 pts)
Newman – 280 pts (Psy)
Northampton – 280–320 pts (Psy courses)
Nottingham Trent – 280 pts (Psy)
Portsmouth – 280 pts (Mark Psy) (IB 29 pts)
Roehampton – 280–340 pts (Psy)
Salford – 280 pts (Psy) (IB 27 pts)
Sheffield Hallam – 280 pts (Crimin Psy; Psy Sociol)
South Wales – 280 pts (App Psy; Dev Psy; Psy)
Staffordshire – 280 pts (Psy Crimin)
Stirling – BBC (Psy) (IB 32 pts)
Ulster – 280–300 pts (Dr Psy; Psy courses)
Worcester – 280 pts (Hlth Psy; Psy)
York St John – 280 pts (Psy) (IB 24 pts)
260 pts **BPP** – 260 pts (Psy; Law Psy)
Bradford – 260 pts (Psy; Psy Crimin)
Canterbury Christ Church – BCC 260 pts (Psy)
Central Lancashire – 260–300 pts (Spo Psy; Neuropsy)
Chester – 260–300 pts (Psy courses) (IB 28 pts)
Coventry – BCC 260 pts (Sociol Psy)
Derby – 260–280 pts (Spo Psy Joint Hons)
Dundee – BCC (Psy) (IB 29 pts)
Edinburgh Napier – BCC 260 pts (Psy; Psy Sociol)
Edinburgh Queen Margaret – 260 pts (Psy; Hlth Psy)
Glyndŵr – 260 pts (Psy)
Greenwich – 260 pts (Crimin Crim Psy)
Kingston – 260 pts (Psy) (IB 30 pts)
Leeds Beckett – 260 pts (Psy courses) (IB 24 pts HL 6 sci)
Liverpool Hope – 260–300 pts (Psy; Psy Comb Hons)
Liverpool John Moores – 260–300 pts (App Psy) (IB 25 pts)
London South Bank – 260 pts (Psy Clin Psy; Psy; Psy Chld Dev)
Northampton – 260–300 pts (Mark Psy)
Nottingham Trent – 260 pts (Law Psy)
St Mary's – 260 pts (Psy) (IB 28 pts)
Salford – 260 pts (Psy St Cnslg St) (IB 27 pts)
Sheffield Hallam – 260 pts (Educ Psy Cnslg)
South Wales – 260 pts (Psy Cnslg St)
Sunderland – 260 pts (Psy (Comb); Psy; Psy Cnslg)
Teesside – 260 pts (Psy Crimin; Psy; Foren Psy; Psy Cnslg)
Winchester – 260–300 pts (Media St Psy)
240 pts **Anglia Ruskin** – 240 pts (Psy)
Bath Spa – 240–300 pts (Psy)

Check **Chapter 4** when choosing your university and **Chapter 7** on how to read the subject tables.

Bedfordshire – 240 pts (Psy) (IB 24 pts)
Bradford – 240 pts (Psy Mgt) (IB 24 pts)
Bucks New – 240–280 pts (Psy Crimin)
Central Lancashire – 240–300 pts (Cross-Cult Psy; Foren Psy; Hlth Psy) (IB 25–28 pts)
Chester – 240–280 pts (Cnslg Sk) (IB 26 pts)
Derby – 240 pts (Crea Expr Thera (Dance/Dr/Mus/Art))
Farnborough (CT) – BCD 240 pts (Psy Mark; Psy Crimin)
Glasgow Caledonian – CCC 240 pts (Psy Interact Enter)
Oldham (Univ Campus) – 240 pts (Psy St)
Portsmouth – 240–300 pts (Sociol Psy)
Southampton Solent – 240 pts (Psy)
Southampton Solent – 240 pts (Psy (Hlth Psy)) (IB 24 pts)
Suffolk (Univ Campus) – 240–280 pts (Psy Sociol; Psy Bus Mgt; Psy Yth St)
West Scotland – CCC (Psy) (IB 24 pts)

220 pts Anglia Ruskin – 220 pts (Psy Crimin)
Edinburgh Queen Margaret – CCD 220 pts (Psy Sociol) (IB 26 pts)
Kent – CCD (Autsm St)
Nottingham Trent – 220 pts (Psy Educ Dev; Ely Yrs Psy Educ; Psy Spec Incl Educ)
Plymouth – 220–300 pts (App Psy; Psy; Psy Sociol)
Wolverhampton – 220–240 pts (Psy; Cnslg Psy)

200 pts Bedfordshire – 200 pts (App Psy; Hlth Psy; Psy (Crim Bhv))
Blackburn (Coll) – 200 pts +interview (App Psy (Cnslg Hlth))
Bradford (Coll Univ Centre) – 200 pts (Cnslg Psy Commun Set)
Bucks New – 200–280 pts (Psy)
Cumbria – 200 pts (App Psy)
East London – 200 pts (Psy; Dev Psy; Foren Psy)
Glyndŵr – 200 pts (Foren Sci Crim Just)
Peterborough (Reg Coll) – 200 pts (Psysoc St)
Staffordshire – 200–280 pts (Psy; Foren Psy)
Trinity Saint David (Swansea) – 200 pts (Cnslg St Educ St; Educ St Psy)

180 pts Abertay – (Foren Psy; Psy; Psy Cnslg)
Bradford – 180–220 pts (Psy Sociol)
Trinity Saint David – 180–360 pts (Psy)
Trinity Saint David (Swansea) – 180 pts (Cnslg Dr; Cnslg St Psy)
UHI – BC (Psy)
West Anglia (Coll) – 180 pts (Psysoc St)

160 pts Abertay – CC 160 pts (Foren Psychobiol) (IB 26 pts)
Norwich City (Coll) – 160 pts (Engl Psy Soc; Psy Sociol)

120 pts Colchester (Inst) – 120 pts (Cnslg St)
Grimsby (Univ Centre) – 120 pts (App Psy)

Open University – contact +44 (0)845 300 6090 **or** www.openuniversity.co.uk/you (Psy; Soc Sci Psy St)

Alternative offers

See **Chapter 7** and **Appendix 1** for grades/UCAS Tariff points information for the International Baccalaureate, Scottish Highers/Advanced Highers, the Welsh Baccalaureate, the Irish Leaving Certificate, the Cambridge Pre-U Diploma, the Advanced Diploma and the Extended Project.

EXAMPLES OF FOUNDATION DEGREES IN THE SUBJECT FIELD

Bedford (Coll); Bedfordshire; Cornwall (Coll); Duchy (Coll); East London; Glyndŵr; Middlesex; Petroc; South Devon (Coll); Truro (Coll).

CHOOSING YOUR COURSE (SEE ALSO CH.1)

Some course features

Bangor A leading psychology department with courses which include clinical and health psychology, neuropsychology and child and language development.

Kent Psychology, Social Psychology, and Applied Psychology courses provide a broad base from which to specialise. Clinical psychology features largely in some programmes. Psychology can be taken with Law, Anthropology and Sociology.

Kingston Psychology is offered as part of the modular course with a choice of some 10 other subjects including languages (French or Spanish), Criminology, Journalism and Creative Writing.

Liverpool Hope The BSc Psychology Single Honours degree confers eligibility for registration with the British Psychological Society. There is also a Sport Psychology degree. Combined courses are also offered.

Loughborough (Ergonomics) This practical course centres on providing solutions to improve the ways in which people interact with their technical and social environment, for example by finding out how aircraft can be made more safe, by designing workplaces to be more efficient. Students acquire a broad understanding of human stucture, function and behaviour and spend the third year on a relevant industrial placement.

Universities and colleges teaching quality See www.qaa.ac.uk; http://unistats.direct.gov.uk.

Top research universities and colleges (RAE 2008) Cambridge; Oxford; Birmingham; London (UCL); London (Birk); Cardiff; St Andrews; London (RH); York; Glasgow; Bangor.

Examples of sandwich degree courses Aston; Bath; Bedfordshire; Bournemouth; Bristol UWE; Brunel; Cardiff; Coventry; De Montfort; Hertfordshire; Huddersfield; Kent; Lancaster; Loughborough; Middlesex; Newcastle; Nottingham Trent; Surrey; Ulster; Westminster.

ADMISSIONS INFORMATION

Number of applicants per place (approx) Abertay 5; Aston 6; Bangor 5; Bath 10; Bath Spa 10; Birmingham 9; Bolton 5; Bournemouth 4; Bradford 2; Bristol 17; Bristol UWE 12; Brunel 20; Buckingham 1; Cardiff 10; Cardiff Met (UWIC) 5; Central Lancashire 13; Chester 20; City 6; Coventry 7; De Montfort 10; Derby 6; Dundee 6; Durham 20; East Anglia (Psysoc St) 6; Edinburgh Napier 6; Exeter 14; Glasgow Caledonian 15; Gloucestershire 50; Greenwich 8; Hertfordshire 22; Huddersfield 3; Hull 14; Kent 15; Lancaster 20; Leeds 12; Leeds Trinity 13; Leicester 6; Liverpool 21; Liverpool John Moores 8; London (RH) 10; London (UCL) 18; London LSE 14; London South Bank 7; Loughborough 8; Manchester Met 27, (Psy p/t) 2; Middlesex 10; Newcastle 20; Newman 3; Northampton 4; Northumbria 2; Nottingham 9; Nottingham Trent 3; Oxford Brookes 29; Plymouth 5; Portsmouth 10; Roehampton 7; Salford 4; Sheffield 12; Sheffield Hallam 10; Southampton 30; Staffordshire 6; Stirling 9; Surrey 10; Sussex 5; Swansea 7; Teesside 10; Warwick 13; Westminster 6; Worcester 9; York 9; York St John 3.

Numbers of applicants (a UK b EU (non-UK) c non-EU d mature) Aston a800 b100 c70 d90; Bristol a1421 b1421 c91 d156; Derby a407 b152 c5; Leeds a1758 b36 c37 d165; London (UCL) a1500 c250; Manchester Met a14 b14 c14 d14; Trinity Saint David (Swansea) a800 b800 c50.

Advice to applicants and planning the UCAS personal statement Psychology is heavily over-subscribed so prepare well in advance by choosing suitable AS and A-level subjects. Contact the Education and Social Services departments in your local authority office to arrange meetings with psychologists to gain a knowledge of the work. Make notes during those meetings and of any work experience gained and describe these fully on the UCAS application. Reference to introductory reading in psychology is important (many students have a distorted image of it). Demonstrate your interest in psychology through, for example, voluntary or other work experience. See also **Appendix 3**.

Bristol General scientific interests are important. Only consider this course if you have some aptitude and liking for scientific study (either in biological or physical sciences). Deferred entry accepted.

Leeds One A-level subject must be taken from psychology, geography, maths, chemistry, physics or biology.

Check **Chapter 4** when choosing your university and **Chapter 7** on how to read the subject tables.

Misconceptions about this course Some believe a Psychology course will train them as therapists or counsellors – it will not. **Bath** They think that they are going to learn about themselves. **Birmingham** Some applicants underestimate the scientific nature of the course. **Exeter** It's scientific! **Lincoln** Applicants should be aware that this is a science-based course. Academic psychology is an empirical science requiring research methodologies and statistical analysis. **Reading** Not all applicants are aware that it is a science-based course and are surprised at the high science and statistics content. **Sussex** Applicants should note that the BSc course is not harder than the BA course. Many students mistakenly believe that psychology consists of counselling and that there is no maths. Psychology is a science. **York** Some students think psychology means Freud which it hasn't done for 50 years or more. They do not realise that psychology is a science in the same vein as biology, chemistry or physics. Only 20% of Psychology graduates become professional psychologists. This involves taking a postgraduate degree in a specialist area of psychology.

Selection interviews Yes Birmingham, Brunel, Cambridge, Durham, Exeter, Glyndŵr, London (QM), London South Bank, Middlesex, Northampton, Oxford (Exp Psy) 24%, (Psy Phil) 20%, Oxford Brookes, Plymouth, Reading; **Some** Anglia Ruskin, Aston, Bangor, Bolton, Bristol, Cardiff, Derby (non-standard applications), East Anglia, Glasgow Caledonian, Leeds (mature students), London (UCL) (300 out of 1500 applicants), London Met, Nottingham Trent (non-standard applications), Roehampton, Salford, South Wales, Southampton, Sunderland, Swansea; **No** Buckingham, Chichester, Dundee, Essex, Huddersfield, Keele, Leeds Trinity, Leicester, Liverpool John Moores, Newcastle, Nottingham, Surrey, York.

Interview advice and questions Although some applicants will have studied the subject at A-level and will have a broad understanding of its coverage, it is still essential to have gained some work experience or to have discussed the career with a professional psychologist. Questions will focus on this and in previous years they have included: What have you read about psychology? What do you expect to gain by studying psychology? What are your parents' and teachers' views on your choice of subject? Are you interested in any particular branch of the subject? Is psychology an art or a science? Do you think you are well suited to this course? Why? Do you think it is possible that if we learn enough about the functioning of the brain we can create a computer that is functionally the same? What is counselling? Is it necessary? Know the differences between the various branches of psychology and discuss any specific interests, for example, in clinical, occupational, educational, criminal psychology and cognitive, neuro-, social or physiological psychology. What influences young children's food choices? What stereotypes do we have of people with mental illness? See also **Chapter 6**. **Bangor** Each application is treated individually and considered on its own merits. **Oxford** Ability to evaluate evidence and to have the capacity for logical and creative thinking.

Reasons for rejection (non-academic) Lack of background reading and lack of awareness of psychology; poor communication skills; misunderstanding of what is involved in a degree course. Poor personal statement. Poor grades, especially in GCSE maths. **Exeter** Competition for places – we can select those with exceptional grades. **Surrey** Inarticulate. **Warwick** (BSc) Lack of science background.

AFTER-RESULTS ADVICE
Offers to applicants repeating A-levels Higher Birmingham, City, Loughborough, Newcastle, Portsmouth, Southampton, Swansea, Warwick, York; **Possibly higher** Aston, Northampton; **Same** Aston (Comb Hons), Bangor, Bolton, Brunel, Cardiff, Cardiff Met (UWIC), Chester, Derby, Dundee, Durham, East Anglia, Huddersfield, Hull, Lincoln, Liverpool Hope, Liverpool John Moores, London (RH), London South Bank, Manchester Met, Newman, Nottingham, Nottingham Trent, Oxford Brookes, Roehampton, Salford, Sheffield Hallam, Staffordshire, Stirling, Suffolk (Univ Campus), Sunderland, Surrey, Ulster, West London, Wolverhampton, York St John; **No** Cambridge.

GRADUATE DESTINATIONS AND EMPLOYMENT (2011/12 HESA)
Graduates surveyed 11015 **Employed** 4650 **In voluntary employment** 450 **In further study** 2650 **Assumed unemployed** 835

Career note Clinical, educational and occupational psychology are the three main specialist careers for graduate psychologists, all involving further study. Ergonomics, human–computer interaction, marketing, public relations, human resource management, advertising, the social services, the prison and rehabilitation services also provide alternative career routes.

OTHER DEGREE SUBJECTS FOR CONSIDERATION

Anthropology; Behavioural Science; Cognitive Sciences; Education; Health Studies; Neuroscience; Sociology

RADIOGRAPHY

(including **Medical Imaging** and **Radiotherapy**; see also **Health Sciences/Studies**)

Many institutions offer both Diagnostic and Therapeutic Radiography but applicants should check this, and course entry requirements, before applying. Information on courses is also available from the Society of Radiographers (see **Appendix 3**). Diagnostic Radiography is the demonstration on film (or other imaging materials) of the position and structure of the body's organs using radiation or other imaging media. Therapeutic Radiography is the planning and administration of treatment for patients suffering from malignant and non-malignant disease using different forms of radiation. Courses lead to state registration.

Useful websites www.sor.org; www.radiographycareers.co.uk; www.nhscareers.nhs.uk.

NB The points totals shown to the left of the institutions are for ease of reference only. It must not be assumed that Tariff points are always used by institutions or that they can be substituted for an offer in grades. The level of an offer is not necessarily indicative of the quality of a course.

COURSE OFFERS INFORMATION

Subject requirements/preferences **GCSE** Five subjects including English, mathematics and a science subject (usually at one sitting). **AL** One or two sciences required; mathematics may be acceptable. (Radiothera) One science subject required for some courses. Psychology may not be considered a science subject at some institutions. **Other** Applicants required to have an occupational health check and a Disclosure and Barring Service (DBS) clearance. Visit to, or work experience in, a hospital imaging department often required/expected.

Your target offers and examples of courses provided by each institution

340 pts **Exeter** – AAB–BBC (Med Imag (Diag Radiog)) (IB 34–28 pts)
320 pts **Bradford** – 320 pts (Diag Radiog) (IB 27 pts)
        City – 320 pts (Radiog (Radiothera Onc); Radiog (Diag Imag)) (IB 33 pts)
        Leeds – ABB incl sci (Radiog (Diag)) (IB 34 pts)
        Sheffield Hallam – 320 pts (Diag Radiog)
300 pts **Bangor** – 300 pts (Diag Radiog Imag) (IB 28 pts)
        Birmingham City – BBB 300 pts (Radiothera; Diag Radiog) (IB 26 pts)
        Bristol UWE – 300 pts (Diag Imag; Radiothera Onc) (IB 26 pts)
        Cardiff – BBB 300 pts (Diag Radiog Imag) (IB 26 pts)
        Cumbria – 300 pts (Radiog (Diag)) (IB 28 pts)
        Derby – 300 pts (Diag Radiog)
        Hertfordshire – 300 pts (Radiothera Onc; Diag Radiog Imag) (IB 24–26 pts)
        Liverpool – BBB (Diag Radiog; Radiothera) (IB 30 pts)
        London (St George's) – 300 pts (Diag Radiog; Ther Radiog)
        Portsmouth – 300 pts (Diag Radiog; Ther Radiog)
        Salford – 300 pts (Diag Radiog) (IB 26 pts)
        Ulster – BBB +HPAT (Radiog (Diag/Ther)) (IB 25 pts)
280 pts **Cardiff** – BBC 280 pts (Radiother Onc)
        London South Bank – 280–300 pts (Diag Radiog; Thera Radiog)
        Sheffield Hallam – 280 pts (Radiothera Onc)

Check **Chapter 4** when choosing your university and **Chapter 7** on how to read the subject tables.

      Suffolk (Univ Campus) – 280 pts (Diag Radiog; Radiothera Onc)
260 pts **Canterbury Christ Church** – BCC 260 pts (Diag Radiog) (IB 24 pts)
      Glasgow Caledonian – BCC (Rdtn Onc Sci; Diag Imag Sci)
      Robert Gordon – BCC (Diag Radiog) (IB 27 pts)
      Teesside – 260–300 pts +interview (Diag Radiog) (IB 24 pts)
240 pts **Edinburgh Queen Margaret** – CCC 240 pts (Diag Radiog; Ther Radiog) (IB 26 pts)

Alternative offers
See **Chapter 7** and **Appendix 1** for grades/UCAS Tariff points information for the International Baccalaureate, Scottish Highers/Advanced Highers, the Welsh Baccalaureate, the Irish Leaving Certificate, the Cambridge Pre-U Diploma, the Advanced Diploma and the Extended Project.

CHOOSING YOUR COURSE (SEE ALSO CH.1)
Some course features
Cardiff The year is divided into seven academic and seven clinical blocks. Placements are in radiography departments throughout south Wales.
City Radiography and Oncology and Radiography (Diagnostic Imaging) are offered.
Cumbria Fifty-four weeks of clinical placements in the three-year course are spent in hospitals in northern England. Students' preferences are taken into account.
Exeter (Med Imag (Diag Radiog)) This is a specialist course leading to a career as a diagnostic radiographer.
Portsmouth There is a seven-week exchange programme working in hospitals in Hong Kong.

Universities and colleges teaching quality See www.qaa.ac.uk; http://unistats.direct.gov.uk.

ADMISSIONS INFORMATION
Number of applicants per place (approx) Birmingham City (Radiothera) 8; Bradford 8; Cardiff 3; Derby 6; Glasgow Caledonian 7; Hertfordshire (Diag Radiog Imag) 8; Leeds 10; Liverpool 13; London (St George's) 7; London South Bank 9; Portsmouth 10; Robert Gordon 5; Salford 10; Sheffield Hallam 8, (Radiothera Onc) 3; Southampton 5; Suffolk (Univ Campus) 3; Teesside 10.

Advice to applicants and planning the UCAS personal statement Contacts with radiographers and visits to the radiography departments of hospitals should be discussed in full on the UCAS application. See also **Appendix 3**. **Birmingham City** Evidence needed of a visit to at least one imaging department or oncology (radiotherapy) department before completing the UCAS application. Evidence of good research into the career. **Liverpool** Choice between therapeutic and diagnostic pathways should be made before applying. **Salford** Selectors look for evidence of communication skills, teamwork, work experience in public areas.

Misconceptions about this course There is often confusion between radiotherapy and diagnostic imaging and between diagnostic and therapeutic radiography.

Selection interviews Yes Bangor, Birmingham City, Canterbury Christ Church, Cardiff, City, Derby, Edinburgh Queen Margaret, Exeter, Hertfordshire, London (St George's), London South Bank, Portsmouth, Salford, Sheffield Hallam.

Interview advice and questions All applicants should have discussed this career with a radiographer and visited a hospital radiography department. Questions follow from these contacts. Where does radiography fit into the overall health care system? See also **Chapter 6**.

Reasons for rejection (non-academic) Lack of interest in people. Poor communication skills. Occasionally students may be unsuitable for the clinical environment, for example, they express a fear of blood and needles; poor grasp of radiography as a career. Unable to meet criteria for employment in the NHS, for example, health factors, criminal convictions, severe disabilities.

AFTER-RESULTS ADVICE
Offers to applicants repeating A-levels Higher London (St George's); **Same** Derby, Salford.

GRADUATE DESTINATIONS AND EMPLOYMENT (2011/12 HESA)
See **Health Science/Studies**.

Career note Most radiographers work in the NHS in hospital radiography departments undertaking diagnostic or therapeutic treatment. Others work in private healthcare.

OTHER DEGREE SUBJECTS FOR CONSIDERATION
Audiology; Forensic Engineering; Health Studies; Medical Physics; Nursing; Occupational Therapy; Physics; Podiatry; Speech Sciences.

RELIGIOUS STUDIES

(including **Biblical Studies**, **Divinity**, **Islamic Studies**, **Jewish Studies** and **Theology**)

The subject content of these courses varies and students should check prospectuses carefully. They are not intended as training courses for ministry; an adherence to a particular religious denomination is not a necessary qualification for entry. Islamic Studies focuses on a faith which has much in common with Christianity and Judaism, is the second largest religion in the world, extending from Africa to the East Indies, and is focused on the Middle East.

Useful websites www.guardian.co.uk/religion; www.cwmission.org; www.miraclestudies.net; www. academicinfo.net/religindex.html; www.theologywebsite.com; www.jewishstudies.org; www. jewishstudies.virtualave.net; www.jewfaq.org; www.virtualreligion.net; www.jis.oxfordjournals.org.

NB The points totals shown to the left of the institutions are for ease of reference only. It must not be assumed that Tariff points are always used by institutions or that they can be substituted for an offer in grades. The level of an offer is not necessarily indicative of the quality of a course.

COURSE OFFERS INFORMATION
Subject requirements/preferences **GCSE** English and mathematics. For teacher training, English and mathematics and science. **AL** Religious studies or theology may be required or preferred for some courses.

Your target offers and examples of courses provided by each institution
380 pts **Cambridge** – A*AA (Theol Relig St) (IB 40–41 pts HL 776)
360 pts **Durham** – AAA 360 pts (Phil Theol) (IB 37 pts)
      Edinburgh – AAA-BBB (Islam St) (IB 37–34 pts)
      Oxford – AAA (Phil Theol; Theol Relgn; Theol Orntl St) (IB 38–40 pts)
      St Andrews – AAA (Bib St; Theol St; Theol; Bib St Engl; Heb courses) (IB 36–38 pts)
340 pts **Cardiff** – AAB 340 pts (Maths Relig St) (IB 33 pts)
      Durham – AAB 340 pts (Theol; Theol (Int St)) (IB 36 pts)
      Edinburgh – AAB-BBB (Relig St) (IB 36–34 pts)
      Exeter – AAB-BBB (Theol courses) (IB 34–29 pts)
      Lancaster – AAB (Phil Relig St; Relig St; Pol Relig St; Relig St Sociol) (IB 35 pts)
      London (King's) – AAB (Relgn Pol Soty; Theol; Relgn Phil Eth) (IB 35 pts HL 665)
      London (SOAS) – AAB (Islam St) (IB 36 pts HL 666)
      London (UCL) – ABBe (Jew Hist) (IB 34 pts HL 16 pts)
      Manchester – AAB-BBB 300–340 pts (St Relgn Theol) (IB 36–31 pts)
      Sheffield – AAB (Bib Lit Engl) (IB 35 pts)
320 pts **Birmingham** – ABB (Theol Relgn) (IB 34 pts)
      Bristol – ABB (Relgn Theol) (IB 33 pts HL 665)
      Cardiff – AAB-BBB (Relig Theol St; Sociol Relig St) (IB 28–36 pts)
      Edinburgh – ABB (Div Class) (IB 36 pts)
      Glasgow – ABB (Theol Relig St) (IB 36 pts)
      Leeds – ABB (Islam St; Theol Relig St; Russ Civ Theol Relig St)
      London (SOAS) – ABB (St Relgns) (IB 34 pts HL 555)

Nottingham – ABB (Theol; Engl Theol) (IB 32 pts)
Roehampton – 320 pts (Theol Rel St) (IB 25 pts)
Sheffield – ABB (Relgn Theol Bib; Relgn Theol Bib Ling) (IB 33 pts)
Stranmillis (UC) – ABB +interview (Relig St Educ)

300 pts **Aberdeen** – BBB (Theol; Div; Relig St) (IB 30 pts)
Cardiff – BBB (Relig St Span/Ital) (IB 26 pts)
Chichester – BBB-BCC (Theol Relgn) (IB 30 pts)
Gloucestershire – 300 pts (Relgn Phil Eth)
Kent – BBB (Relig St)
Queen's Belfast – BBB/BBCb (Theol) (IB 29 pts)
Trinity Saint David – 220–300 pts (Theol; Theol Relig St; Relig St Islam St) (IB 26 pts)

280 pts **Huddersfield** – BBC 280 pts (Relgn Educ)
Hull – 280–320 pts (Phil Relgn; Hisp St Relgn Joint Hons)
London (Hey) – 280–320 pts (Ab Relgn; St Relgn; Div; Theol; Phil Theol; Phil Relgn Eth)
Newman – 280 pts (Phil Relgn Educ; Phil Relgn Engl)
Oxford Brookes – BBC (Relgn Theol)
Stirling – BBC (Relgn) (IB 32 pts)

260 pts **Bath Spa** – 260–300 pts (Relgn Phil Eth; St Relgn Comb courses)
Edge Hill – 260 pts (Relig Educ QTS)
Hull – 260–340 pts (Relgn Joint courses) (IB 28–30 pts)
Islamic Advanced St (Coll) – BCC 260 pts (Islam St) (IB 32 pts)
Liverpool Hope – 260 pts (Theol Relig St)
Newman – 260 pts (Theol)
South Wales – 260 pts (Relig St) (IB 24 pts)
Winchester – 260–300 pts (Theol Relig St)

240 pts **Bangor** – 240–280 pts (Phil Rel)
Bishop Grosseteste – 240 pts (Theol Eth Soty)
Canterbury Christ Church – 240 pts (Theol; Relig St)
Chester – 240–280 pts (Relig St; Theol Relig St; Theol)
Leeds Trinity – 200–240 pts (Phil Eth Relgn) (IB 24 pts)
St Mary's – 240 pts (Theol Relig St) (IB 28 pts)
York St John – 240–280 pts (Theol Relig St; Relgn Phil Eth) (IB 24 pts)

200 pts **Central Lancashire** – 200–300 pts (Relgn Cult Soty (Comb))
Cumbria – 200 pts (Relig St) (IB 28 pts)
Leeds Trinity – 200–240 pts (Relig St; Theol) (IB 24 pts)
Wolverhampton – 200 pts (Relig St Sociol; Relig St Phil; Relig St courses) (IB 24 pts)

160 pts **UHI** – CC (Theol St)

140 pts **Islamic Advanced St (Coll)** – 140–220 pts (Mslm Cult Civ) (IB 32 pts)

Alternative offers

See **Chapter 7** and **Appendix 1** for grades/UCAS Tariff points information for the International Baccalaureate, Scottish Highers/Advanced Highers, the Welsh Baccalaureate, the Irish Leaving Certificate, the Cambridge Pre-U Diploma, the Advanced Diploma and the Extended Project.

CHOOSING YOUR COURSE (SEE ALSO CH.1)

Some course features

Birmingham (Theol) The course covers Christianity, Islam, Judaism, Sikhism, Hinduism and other contemporary spiritualities.

Durham (Theol) The course combines aspects of philosophy, history and social sciences and includes a detailed study of the Old and New Testaments.

Edinburgh MA and Honours and BA General degrees are offered in Religious Studies and Divinity. There is also a Bachelor of Divinity course equipping students for the ordained ministry.

Lancaster (Relig St) A distinguished course offering core and optional modules approaching religion from theological, sociological, anthropological, psychological and philosophical perspectives. The main studies include Judaism, Christianity, Islam, Hinduism, Buddhism and philosophy.

Sheffield (Bib Lit Eng) The only course in England looking at the development of the Bible and its place in contemporary society, politics, art, film, literature and music.

Universities and colleges teaching quality See www.qaa.ac.uk; http://unistats.direct.gov.uk.

Top research universities and colleges (RAE 2008) (Theology, Divinity and Religious Studies) Durham; Aberdeen; Cambridge; Oxford; London (UCL); Manchester; Sheffield; Edinburgh; Nottingham.

ADMISSIONS INFORMATION

Number of applicants per place (approx) Bangor 5; Birmingham 4; Bristol 9; Cambridge 2; Chichester 6; Cumbria 12; Durham 6; Edinburgh 3; Exeter 7; Glasgow 4; Hull 10; Kent 13; Lancaster 6; Leeds 4; Leeds Trinity 4; Liverpool Hope 6; London (Hey) 4; London (King's) 6; Middlesex 4; Newman 2; Nottingham 10; Sheffield 7; Trinity Saint David 7; Winchester 6; York St John 2.

Advice to applicants and planning the UCAS personal statement An awareness of the differences between the main religions is important as is any special research you have done to help you decide on your preferred courses. Interests in the religious art and architecture of various periods and styles should be noted. Applicants should have an open-minded approach to studying a diverse range of religious traditions. **Bristol** Deferred entry accepted.

Misconceptions about this course Some students think that you must be religious to study Theology – in fact, people of all faiths and none study the subject. A study of religions is not Christian theology. **Leeds** Some applicants are not aware of the breadth of the subject. We offer modules covering New Testament, Christian theology, Islamic studies, Hinduism, Buddhism, Sikhism, Christian ethics, sociology of religion. **Newman** That the Theology course only concentrates on the Christian/Catholic religions – all major religions are covered.

Selection interviews **Yes** Cambridge, Hull, Lancaster, London (Hey), Oxford (Theol) 38%, Oxford Brookes, Trinity Saint David, Winchester; **Some** Bristol, Cardiff, Durham, Leeds, London (SOAS); **No** Birmingham, Chester, Chichester, Edinburgh, Glasgow, Leeds Trinity, Nottingham, Sheffield.

Interview advice and questions Past questions have included: Why do you want to study Theology/Biblical Studies/Religious Studies? What do you hope to do after obtaining your degree? Questions relating to the A-level syllabus. Questions on current theological topics. Do you have any strong religious convictions? Do you think that your religious beliefs will be changed at the end of the course? Why did you choose Religious Studies rather than Biblical Studies? How would you explain the miracles to a 10-year-old? (BEd course). Do you agree with the National Lottery? How do you think you can apply theology to your career? See also **Chapter 6**. **Cambridge** There is a Christian priest who regularly visits India and converted to a Hindu priest. When he is in England he still practises as a Christian priest. What problems might this pose? Do you believe we should eradicate Christmas on the basis that it offends other religious groups? **Oxford** The ability to defend one's opinions and willingness to engage in a lively dialogue are both important.

Reasons for rejection (non-academic) Students not attending Open Days may be rejected. Too religiously conservative. Failure to interact. Lack of motivation to study a subject which goes beyond A-level. **Cardiff** Insufficiently open to an academic study of religion.

AFTER-RESULTS ADVICE

Offers to applicants repeating A-levels **Higher** Hull, Manchester, St Andrews; **Possibly higher** Cambridge (Hom); **Same** Bangor, Birmingham, Cardiff, Chester, Durham, Glasgow, Greenwich, Lancaster, Leeds, Liverpool Hope, London (SOAS), Nottingham, St Mary's, Sheffield, Stirling, Trinity Saint David, Winchester, Wolverhampton, York St John; **No** Cambridge.

GRADUATE DESTINATIONS AND EMPLOYMENT (2011/12 HESA)
Theology and Religious Studies graduates surveyed 1990 **Employed** 740 **In voluntary employment** 175 **In further study** 615 **Assumed unemployed** 110

Career note Although a small number of graduates may regard these courses as a preparation for entry to religious orders, the great majority enter other careers, with teaching particularly popular.

OTHER DEGREE SUBJECTS FOR CONSIDERATION

Community Studies; Education; History; Philosophy; Psychology; Social Policy and Administration; Social Work.

RETAIL MANAGEMENT

(see also **Business and Management Courses, Business and Management Courses (International and European), Business and Management Courses (Specialised), Marketing**)

This subject attracts a large number of applicants each year and it is necessary to have work experience before applying. The work itself varies depending on the type of retail outlet. After completing their courses graduates in a large department store will be involved in different aspects of the business, for example supervising shop assistants, warehouse and packing staff. They could also receive special training in the sales of particular goods, for example food and drink, clothing, furniture. Subsequently there may be opportunities to become buyers. In more specialised shops, for example shoes, fashion and food, graduates are likely to work only with these products, with opportunities to reach senior management.

Useful websites www.brc.org.uk; www.retailweek.com; www.theretailbulletin.com; www.retailcareers.co.uk; www.retailchoice.com; www.nrf.com.

NB The points totals shown to the left of the institutions are for ease of reference only. It must not be assumed that Tariff points are always used by institutions or that they can be substituted for an offer in grades. The level of an offer is not necessarily indicative of the quality of a course.

COURSE OFFERS INFORMATION

Subject requirements/preferences GCSE English and mathematics at grade C or above. **AL** No subjects specified.

Your target offers and examples of courses provided by each institution

360 pts **Loughborough** – AAA–AAB (Rtl Mark Mgt) (IB 36 pts)
340 pts **Manchester** – AAB 340 pts (Fash Tex Rtl; Des Mgt Fash Rtl) (IB 35 pts)
320 pts **Surrey** – ABB (Bus Rtl Mgt) (IB 34 pts)
300 pts **Brighton** – BBB (Rtl Mgt) (IB 32 pts)
        Heriot-Watt – BBB (Fash Mark Rtl) (IB 28 pts)
        Westminster – BBB 300 pts (Bus Mgt (Rtl); Bus St Rtl) (IB 28 pts)
280 pts **Birmingham City** – 280 pts (Fash Rtl Mgt) (IB 28 pts)
        Cardiff Met (UWIC) – 280 pts (Mark Mgt)
        De Montfort – 280 pts (Rtl Mgt) (IB 28 pts)
        Manchester Met – 280 pts (Rtl Mark Mgt) (IB 28 pts)
        Stirling – BBC (Rtl Mark) (IB 32 pts)
260 pts **Central Lancashire** – BBB–BCC 260–300 pts (Rtl Mgt (Buy/Fash/Mark)) (IB 26 pts)
        De Montfort – 260 pts (Fash Buy)
240 pts **Bournemouth** – 240–280 pts (Rtl Mgt) (IB 26–30 pts)
        Glasgow Caledonian – CCC 240 pts (Int Rtl Mark) (IB 24 pts)

Alternative offers

See **Chapter 7** and **Appendix 1** for grades/UCAS Tariff points information for the International Baccalaureate, Scottish Highers/Advanced Highers, the Welsh Baccalaureate, the Irish Leaving Certificate, the Cambridge Pre-U Diploma, the Advanced Diploma and the Extended Project.

EXAMPLES OF FOUNDATION DEGREES IN THE SUBJECT FIELD
Arts London; Blackburn (Coll); Blackpool and Fylde (Coll); East London; Grimsby (Univ Centre); Hull (Coll); Leeds City (Coll); Llandrillo Cymru (Coll); Manchester Met; Norwich City (Coll); Wolverhampton; Worcester.

CHOOSING YOUR COURSE (SEE ALSO CH.1)
Some course features
Birmingham City (Fash Rtl Mgt) The course focuses on the global fashion industry and design management. It includes fabric sourcing, pattern cutting and manufacturing, and fashion forecasting.
Bournemouth (Rtl Mgt) The course has paid industrial placements and overseas opportunities.
Loughborough (Rtl Mark Mgt) This four-year sandwich course includes a placement year leading to a Diploma in Professional Studies. Retailers are closely involved throughout and provide lectures, case studies, skills workshops and company visits.
Surrey (Rtl Mgt) A long-established course with an optional placement year.

Universities and colleges teaching quality See www.qaa.ac.uk; http://unistats.direct.gov.uk.

Examples of sandwich degree courses Birmingham City; Bournemouth; Brighton; Central Lancashire; De Montfort; Manchester Met; Surrey; Westminster.

ADMISSIONS INFORMATION
Number of applicants per place (approx) See also **Business and Management Courses**.
Bournemouth 8; Manchester Met 10.

Advice to applicants and planning the UCAS personal statement See also **Business and Management Courses**. **Manchester Met** (Rtl Mark Mgt) Evidence of working with people or voluntary work experience (department unable to assist with sponsorships).

Misconceptions about this course See **Business and Management Courses**.

Selection interviews **Yes** Birmingham City.

Interview advice and questions See **Business and Management Courses**.

Reasons for rejection (non-academic) See **Business and Management Courses**.

GRADUATE DESTINATIONS AND EMPLOYMENT (2011/12 HESA)
See **Business and Management Courses**.

Career note Majority of graduates work in business involved in marketing and retail work. Employment options include brand design, product management, advertising, PR, sales and account management.

OTHER DEGREE SUBJECTS FOR CONSIDERATION
Business Studies; Consumer Sciences/Studies; E-Commerce; Human Resource Management; Psychology; Supply Chain Management.

RUSSIAN and EAST EUROPEAN STUDIES

(including **Bulgarian, Croatian, Czech, Finnish, Georgian, Hungarian, Polish, Romanian, Russian** and **Serbian**; see also **European Studies, Languages**)

East European Studies cover a wide range of the less popular language courses and should be considered by anyone with a love of and gift for languages. Many natural linguists often devote themselves to one of the popular European languages studied up to A-level, when their language skills could be extended to the more unusual languages, thereby increasing their future career opportunities.

Useful websites www.basees.org.uk; www.iol.org.uk; www.bbc.co.uk/languages; www.languageadvantage.com; www.languagematters.co.uk; www.cilt.org.uk.

NB The points totals shown to the left of the institutions are for ease of reference only. It must not be assumed that Tariff points are always used by institutions or that they can be substituted for an offer in grades. The level of an offer is not necessarily indicative of the quality of a course.

COURSE OFFERS INFORMATION

Subject requirements/preferences GCSE A foreign language. **AL** One or two modern languages may be stipulated.

Your target offers and examples of courses provided by each institution

380 pts Cambridge – A*AA 380 pts (Modn Mediev Lang) (IB 40–41 pts HL 776)

360 pts Durham – AAA (Russ) (IB 37 pts)

Edinburgh – AAA–BBB 360–300 pts (Russ St) (IB 37–34 pts)

London (UCL) – AABe–ABBe (Russ St; Bulg/Czech/Hung/Polh/Romn/Slovak E Euro; Russ Hist) (IB 34–36 pts)

Manchester – AAA (Russ Jap IPML) (IB 37 pts)

Oxford – AAA (Modn Langs (Russ +2nd Lang); Euro Mid E Langs (Cz/Russ); Russ) (IB 38–40 pts)

St Andrews – AAA–AAB (Russ courses) (IB 38–35 pts)

340 pts Bath – AAB–ABB (Russ Pol) (IB 36–34 pts)

Exeter – AAB–ABB 340 pts (Russ) (IB 34–32 pts)

Glasgow – AAB (Russ; Cnt E Euro St) (IB 34 pts)

Manchester – AAB–BBB 300–340 pts (Russ St; Russ Jap; Russ Chin) (IB 31–36 pts)

320 pts Bath – ABB–AAA 320–360 pts (Modn Langs Euro St; Russ courses) (IB 34–36 pts)

Birmingham – AAB–ABB (Russ St courses)

Bristol – ABB–BBB (Russ; Russ (Cz/Port)) (IB 32–33 pts)

Leeds – ABB (Russ Civ Theol Relig St; Russ Advnc/Bgn Span; Russ Advnc/Sociol; Russ Advnc/Bgn)

London (QM) – ABB–BBB 300–320 pts (Fr/Ger/Russ Dr) (IB 34 pts)

Nottingham – ABB (Russ courses; Engl Russ; Hisp St Russ; Hist Russ; Engl E Euro Cult St; Engl Serb/Cro) (IB 32 pts)

Sheffield – AAB–ABB 320–340 pts (Russ St; Russ St Joint Hons)

300 pts London (QM) – BBB 300 pts (Russ; Russ Bus Mgt) (IB 32 pts)

Nottingham – ABC–BBB (Serb/Cro St) (IB 30 pts)

Alternative offers

See **Chapter 7** and **Appendix 1** for grades/UCAS Tariff points information for the International Baccalaureate, Scottish Highers/Advanced Highers, the Welsh Baccalaureate, the Irish Leaving Certificate, the Cambridge Pre-U Diploma, the Advanced Diploma and the Extended Project.

CHOOSING YOUR COURSE (SEE ALSO CH.1)

Some course features

See also **Languages**.

Durham Russian is only offered as one of two or three other subjects in the Combined Honours course.

Edinburgh The Russian Studies course covers language, literature, art, film, and music.

Glasgow At all levels language tuition is given by Russian native language speakers.

Nottingham Beginners' courses are offered in Russian which can also be combined with another subject taken from the very wide range available, from Serbo-Croat to Contemporary Chinese Studies.

Universities and colleges teaching quality See www.qaa.ac.uk; http://unistats.direct.gov.uk.

Top research universities and colleges (RAE 2008) (Russian, Slavonic and East European languages) Manchester; Oxford; Sheffield; Cambridge; Bristol; Nottingham; Exeter.

ADMISSIONS INFORMATION

Number of applicants per place (approx) Birmingham 3; Bristol 7; Durham 7; Leeds 3; London (UCL) (E Euro St Bulg) 1; Nottingham 5.

Advice to applicants and planning the UCAS personal statement Visits to Eastern Europe should be mentioned, supported by your special reasons for wishing to study the language. A knowledge of the cultural, economic and political scene could be important. Fluent English important for non-UK students. Evidence of wide reading, travel and residence abroad. See also **Appendix 3** under Languages.

Selection interviews Yes Cambridge, London (UCL), Oxford; **Some** Durham; **No** Exeter, Nottingham.

Interview advice and questions Since many applicants will not have taken Russian at A-level, questions often focus on their reasons for choosing a Russian degree, and their knowledge of, and interest in, Russia. Those taking A-level Russian are likely to be questioned on the course and on any reading done outside A-level work. East European Studies applicants will need to show some knowledge of their chosen country/countries and any specific reasons why they wish to follow the course. See also **Chapter 6**. **Leeds** See **Languages**.

Reasons for rejection (non-academic) Lack of perceived commitment for a demanding *ab initio* subject.

AFTER-RESULTS ADVICE

Offers to applicants repeating A-levels Higher Bristol, Glasgow, Leeds, St Andrews; **Same** Durham; **No** Cambridge.

GRADUATE DESTINATIONS AND EMPLOYMENT (2011/12 HESA)

Graduates surveyed 145 **Employed** 50 **In voluntary employment** 5 **In further study** 35 **Assumed unemployed** 25

Career note See **Languages**.

OTHER DEGREE SUBJECTS FOR CONSIDERATION

Economics; European Studies; International Relations; Linguistics; Politics; other languages.

SCANDINAVIAN STUDIES

(see also **Languages**)

Scandinavian Studies provides students who enjoy languages with the opportunity to extend their language expertise to learn a modern Scandinavian language – Danish, Norwegian or Swedish – from beginner's level to Honours level in four years, including a year in Scandinavia. The three languages are very similar to each other and a knowledge of one makes it possible to access easily the literature and cultures of the other two. Viking Studies includes Old Norse, runology and archaeology.

Useful websites www.cilt.org.uk; www.iol.org.uk; www.bbc.co.uk/languages; www.languageadvantage.com; www.languagematters.co.uk; www.scandinaviahouse.org; www.scandinavianstudy.org.

NB The points totals shown to the left of the institutions are for ease of reference only. It must not be assumed that Tariff points are always used by institutions or that they can be substituted for an offer in grades. The level of an offer is not necessarily indicative of the quality of a course.

COURSE OFFERS INFORMATION

Subject requirements/preferences GCSE Foreign language preferred for all courses. **AL** A modern language may be required.

Your target offers and examples of courses provided by each institution
380 pts Cambridge – A*AA (A-Sxn Nrs Celt) (IB 40–41 pts HL 776)
360 pts Edinburgh – AAA–BBB 360–300 pts (Scand St (Dan Norw Swed)) (IB 37–34 pts HL 555)
340 pts London (UCL) – ABBe (Vkg St; Ice; Scand St) (IB 34 pts)
320 pts Nottingham – ABB (Vkg St) (IB 32 pts HL 5 Engl)

Alternative offers
See **Chapter 7** and **Appendix 1** for grades/UCAS Tariff points information for the International Baccalaureate, Scottish Highers/Advanced Highers, the Welsh Baccalaureate, the Irish Leaving Certificate, the Cambridge Pre-U Diploma, the Advanced Diploma and the Extended Project.

CHOOSING YOUR COURSE (SEE ALSO CH.1)
Some course features
See also **Languages**.
Cambridge (A-Sxn Nrs Celt) Old Norse is offered as part of this degree.
Edinburgh Beginners are provided with a concentrated course in the spoken and written language of their choice from Danish, Norwegian or Swedish. Year 3 is spent in a university or working in one of the Scandinavian countries.
London (UCL) Danish, Norwegian and Swedish are taught from scratch on the Scandinavian Studies courses. Icelandic and one other Scandinavian language are taught on the Icelandic course. No prior knowledge of the languages is required.

Universities and colleges teaching quality See www.qaa.ac.uk; http://unistats.direct.gov.uk.

Top research universities and colleges (RAE 2008) See **German**.

ADMISSIONS INFORMATION
Number of applicants per place (approx) London (UCL) 3.

Advice to applicants and planning the UCAS personal statement Visits to Scandinavian countries could be the source of an interest in studying these languages. You should also be aware of cultural, political, geographical and economic aspects of Scandinavian countries. Knowledge of these should be shown in your statement.

Selection interviews **Yes** Cambridge.

Interview advice and questions Applicants in the past have been questioned on why they have chosen this subject area, on their visits to Scandinavia and on their knowledge of the country/ countries and their people. Future career plans are likely to be discussed. See also **Chapter 6**.

Reasons for rejection (non-academic) One applicant didn't know the difference between a noun and a verb.

AFTER-RESULTS ADVICE
Offers to applicants repeating A-levels **No** Cambridge.

GRADUATE DESTINATIONS AND EMPLOYMENT (2011/12 HESA)
See **Languages**.

Career note See **Languages**.

OTHER DEGREE SUBJECTS FOR CONSIDERATION
Archaeology; European History/Studies; History; other modern languages, including, for example, Russian and East European languages.

SOCIAL and PUBLIC POLICY and ADMINISTRATION

(see also **Community Studies/Development, Social Work, Sociology**)

Social Policy is a multi-disciplinary degree that combines elements from sociology, political science, social and economic history, economics, cultural studies and philosophy. It is a study of the needs of society and how best to provide such services as education, housing, health and welfare services.

Useful websites www.local.gov.uk; www.swap.ac.uk.

NB The points totals shown to the left of the institutions are for ease of reference only. It must not be assumed that Tariff points are always used by institutions or that they can be substituted for an offer in grades. The level of an offer is not necessarily indicative of the quality of a course.

COURSE OFFERS INFORMATION

Subject requirements/preferences GCSE English and mathematics normally required. **AL** No subjects specified.

Your target offers and examples of courses provided by each institution

380 pts **Cambridge** – A*AA 380 pts (Hum Soc Pol Sci (Assyr Egypt); Hum Soc Pol Sci (Pol Int Rel))
　　　　(IB 40–41 pts HL 776)
　　　　Durham – A*AA 380 pts (Comb Hons Soc Sci) (IB 38 pts)

340 pts **Bath** – AAB–BBB (Soc Plcy courses) (IB 32–35 pts)
　　　　Bristol – AAB (Soc Plcy Pol) (IB 35 pts)
　　　　Durham – AAB 340 pts (Anth Soty) (IB 36 pts)
　　　　Edinburgh – AAB–BBB 340–300 pts (Soc Plcy courses) (IB 36–34 pts)
　　　　Glasgow – AAB (Pblc Plcy) (IB 34 pts)
　　　　London LSE – AAB (Soc Plcy Econ; Soc Plcy Crimin; Soc Plcy; Soc Plcy Gov; Soc Pol Sociol)
　　　　(IB 37 pts)

320 pts **Aston** – ABB (Pol Soc Plcy; Bus Mgt Pblc Plcy) (IB 32–34 pts)
　　　　Birmingham – ABB (Plan Soc Plcy) (IB 34 pts)
　　　　Bristol – ABB–BBB 320–300 pts (Soc Plcy Sociol; Soc Plcy) (IB 33–32 pts)
　　　　Cardiff – ABB 320 pts (Crimin Soc Plcy) (IB 32 pts)
　　　　Kent – ABB (Soc Plcy) (IB 34 pts)
　　　　Leeds – ABB (Interd Soc Pol Sociol; Soc Plcy courses)
　　　　Nottingham – ABB (Sociol Soc Pol) (IB 32 pts)
　　　　Sheffield – ABB (Soc Plcy Crimin) (IB 34 pts)
　　　　Southampton – ABB (Sociol Soc Plcy)

300 pts **Aston** – BBB–ABB 300–320 pts (Sociol Soc Pol) (IB 32–34 pts)
　　　　Birmingham – BBB (Soc Plcy) (IB 32 pts)
　　　　Brighton – BBB (Crimin Soc Plcy; Pol Soc Plcy) (IB 32 pts)
　　　　Cardiff – BBB 300 pts (Educ Soc Plcy; Soc Plcy Sociol)
　　　　Lincoln – 300 pts (Crimin Soc Plcy)
　　　　Liverpool – BBB (Sociol Soc Plcy) (IB 30 pts)
　　　　London (Gold) – BBB (Econ Pol Pblc Plcy) (IB 35 pts HL 666)
　　　　Loughborough – BBB–ABC 300 pts (Crimin Soc Plcy) (IB 32 pts)
　　　　Nottingham – BBB (Soc Wk) (IB 30 pts)
　　　　Queen's Belfast – BBB (Soc Plcy courses)
　　　　Sheffield – BBB (Soc Plcy Sociol) (IB 32 pts)
　　　　Swansea – BBB (Soc Plcy; Crimin Soc Plcy) (IB 36–32 pts)
　　　　York – BBB (Soc Plcy) (IB 30 pts)

280 pts **Bournemouth** – 280 pts (Sociol Soc Plcy) (IB 30 pts)
　　　　London Met – 280 pts (Hlth Soc Plcy; Sociol Soc Plcy)

      Manchester Met – 280 pts (Pblc Serv; PR Dig Comms Mgt) (IB 28 pts)
      Salford – 280 pts (Soc Plcy) (IB 24 pts)
      Stirling – BBC 280 pts (Sociol Soc Plcy) (IB 32 pts)

260 pts **Central Lancashire** – 260–300 pts (Soc Plcy (Comb))
      Liverpool Hope – 260–300 pts (Soc Plcy courses)
      Ulster – 260 pts (Soc Plcy)

240 pts **Bangor** – 240–280 pts (Soc Plcy Joint Hons; Sociol Soc Pol)
      Lincoln – 240 pts (Soc Plcy)
      Llandrillo Cymru (Coll) – 240 pts (Pblc Soc Plcy)
      West Scotland – CCC (Soc Plcy; Occ Sfty Hlth) (IB 24 pts)

200 pts **Anglia Ruskin** – 200 pts (Soc Plcy) (IB 24 pts)
      Wolverhampton – 200–220 pts (Soc Plcy courses)

      Open University – contact +44 (0)845 300 6090 **or** www.openuniversity.co.uk/you (Soc Plcy Sociol)

Alternative offers

See **Chapter 7** and **Appendix 1** for grades/UCAS Tariff points information for the International Baccalaureate, Scottish Highers/Advanced Highers, the Welsh Baccalaureate, the Irish Leaving Certificate, the Cambridge Pre-U Diploma, the Advanced Diploma and the Extended Project.

EXAMPLES OF FOUNDATION DEGREES IN THE SUBJECT FIELD

Accrington and Rossendale (Coll); Bradford; City; Grimsby (Univ Centre); Hull (Coll); St Helens (Coll); Sunderland; Worcester.

CHOOSING YOUR COURSE (SEE ALSO CH.1)

Some course features

Anglia Ruskin (Soc Plcy courses) In addition to an optional semester abroad in Year 2 there is also an internship module in which students can gain vocational experience with an organisation.

Aston Social Policy courses are offered with work placements.

Cambridge The course in Human, Social and Political Sciences offers a variety of subjects covering politics, sociology, anthropology or archaeology. Specialist subjects are chosen in Year 2.

Kent (Soc Plcy) Course has an option to study Sociology or Criminology in Year 1.

London LSE (Soc Plcy) An outside option of special interest to the student is taken in each year of the course. A module in social psychology is offered for students taking courses in Social Policy and Criminology.

Sheffield (Soc Plcy Crimin) There is a Year Abroad scheme where students can spend time in the USA and Australia.

Universities and colleges teaching quality See www.qaa.ac.uk; http://unistats.direct.gov.uk.

Top research universities and colleges (RAE 2008) See **Social Work**.

Examples of sandwich degree courses Aston; Bath.

ADMISSIONS INFORMATION

Number of applicants per place (approx) Aston 8; Bangor 6; Bath 6; Birmingham 5; Bristol 3; Cardiff 4; Central Lancashire 6; Kent 5; Leeds 10; London LSE (Soc Plcy) 4, (Soc Plcy Sociol) 8, (Soc Plcy Econ) 7, (Soc Plcy Gov) 14; Loughborough 5; Manchester Met 4; Nottingham 3; Southampton 6; Stirling 11; Swansea 6; York 3.

Advice to applicants and planning the UCAS personal statement Careers in public and social administration are covered by this subject; consequently a good knowledge of these occupations and contacts with the social services should be discussed fully on your UCAS application. Gain work experience if possible. (See **Appendix 3** for contact details of some relevant organisations.) **Aston** The course is specially tailored for students aiming for careers in NHS management, the civil service and local government. **Bangor** Ability to communicate and work in a group. **Bristol** Deferred entry accepted. **York** Work experience, including voluntary work relevant to social policy.

Misconceptions about this course York Some applicants imagine that the course is vocational and leads directly to social work – it does not. Graduates in this field are well placed for a wide range of careers.

Selection interviews Yes London LSE, Swansea; **Some** Anglia Ruskin, Bangor, Bath (mature students), Cardiff, Kent, Leeds (mature students), Loughborough, Salford, Southampton, York; **No** Birmingham, Nottingham.

Interview advice and questions Past questions have included: What relevance has history to social administration? What do you understand by 'public policy'? What advantage do you think studying social science gives when working in policy fields? How could the image of public management of services be improved? Applicants should be fully aware of the content and the differences between all the courses on offer, why they want to study Social Policy and their career objectives. See also **Chapter 6**.

Reasons for rejection (non-academic) Some universities require attendance when they invite applicants to Open Days (check). Lack of awareness of current social issues. See also **Social Work**. **Bath** Applicant really wanted Business Studies: evidence that teacher, careers adviser or parents are pushing the applicant into the subject or higher education.

AFTER-RESULTS ADVICE
Offers to applicants repeating A-levels Higher Glasgow, Leeds; **Same** Anglia Ruskin, Bangor, Bath, Birmingham, Brighton, Cardiff, Loughborough, Salford, Southampton, York.

GRADUATE DESTINATIONS AND EMPLOYMENT (2011/12 HESA)
Social Policy graduates surveyed 1610 **Employed** 825 **In voluntary employment** 45 **In further study** 340 **Assumed unemployed** 120

Career note See **Social Sciences/Studies**.

OTHER DEGREE SUBJECTS FOR CONSIDERATION
Behavioural Science; Community Studies; Criminology; Economic and Social History; Economics; Education; Government; Health Studies; Human Resource Management; Law; Politics; Psychology; Social Work; Sociology; Women's Studies.

SOCIAL SCIENCES/STUDIES

(including **Combined Social Sciences, Criminology, Criminal Justice, Human Rights** and **Police Studies**; see also **Combined Courses, Education Studies, Health Sciences/Studies, Law, Politics, Psychology, Teacher Training**)

Most Social Sciences/Studies courses take a broad view of aspects of society, for example, economics, politics, history, social psychology and urban studies. Applied Social Studies usually focuses on practical and theoretical preparation for a career in social work. These courses are particularly popular with mature students and some universities and colleges offer shortened degree courses for those with relevant work experience.

Useful websites www.csv.org.uk; www.intute.ac.uk.

NB The points totals shown to the left of the institutions are for ease of reference only. It must not be assumed that Tariff points are always used by institutions or that they can be substituted for an offer in grades. The level of an offer is not necessarily indicative of the quality of a course.

COURSE OFFERS INFORMATION
Subject requirements/preferences GCSE Usually English and mathematics; a science may be required. **AL** No subjects specified. **Other** A Disclosure and Barring Service (DBS) check and relevant work experience required for some courses.

Your target offers and examples of courses provided by each institution

380 pts **Durham** – A*AA 380 pts (Comb Hons Soc Sci) (IB 38 pts)

Exeter – A*AA-AAB 380-340 pts (Flex Comb Hons (Crimin)) (IB 38-34 pts)

360 pts **Lancaster** – AAA (Law Crimin) (IB 36 pts HL 16 pts)

Manchester – AAA-ABB 360-320 pts (Biol Sci Soty) (IB 37-33 pts)

340 pts **Bath** – AAB-BBB 340-300 pts (Soc Sci) (IB 32-35 pts HL 555)

Cardiff – AAB (Crimin) (IB 34 pts)

Durham – AAB 340 pts (Crimin) (IB 36 pts)

Lancaster – AAB (Crimin) (IB 35 pts)

Leeds – AAB (Crim Just Crimin) (IB 36 pts)

London (UCL) – AAB-ABB 340-320 pts (Sci Soc) (IB 34-36 pts)

London LSE – AAB (Soc Plcy Crimin) (IB 37 pts)

Southampton – AAB (App Soc Sci (Crimin Psy St); App Soc Sci) (IB 34 pts HL 17 pts)

Surrey – AAB (Law Crimin) (IB 35 pts)

York – AAB-ABB (Soc Pol Sci) (IB 35 pts)

320 pts **Aberystwyth** – ABB 320 pts (Hum Rts)

Brighton – ABB (Hum (War Cnflct Modnty)) (IB 34 pts)

Bristol UWE – 320 pts (Crimin Psy; Crimin Joint Hons)

Cardiff – ABB 320 pts (Crimin Soc Plcy; Crimin Sociol; Soc Sci) (IB 32 pts)

City – ABB 320 pts (Crimin Sociol) (IB 33 pts)

Essex – ABB-BBB 320-300 pts (Crimin; Hum Rts courses; Sociol Crimin; Law Hum Rts (LLB)) (IB 32-30 pts)

Kent – ABB 280-300 pts (Crimin; Crimin Joint Hons)

Leicester – ABB (Crimin) (IB 32 pts)

Liverpool – ABB (Crimin) (IB 33 pts)

Liverpool John Moores – 320 pts (Foren Psy Crim Just) (IB 33 pts)

Manchester – ABB (Crimin; Soc Anth Crimin; Law Crimin)

Queen's Belfast – ABB-BBBb (Crimin)

Sheffield – ABB (Soc Plcy Crimin) (IB 34 pts)

Southampton – ABB (App Soc Sci (Crimin); App Soc Sci (Anth)) (IB 32 pts HL 16 pts)

Surrey – ABB (Crimin Sociol) (IB 34 pts)

300 pts **Birmingham** – BBB (Soc Pol Crim Plcg Commun Just) (IB 32 pts)

Bolton – 300 pts (Crimin Foren Psy) (IB 26 pts)

Brighton – BBB (App Psy Crimin; Soc Sci; Crimin Soc Plcy; Crimin Sociol) (IB 32 pts)

Cardiff – BBB 300 pts (Crimin Educ) (IB 32-34 pts)

Central Lancashire – BBB (Law Hum Rts (LLB))

Greenwich – 300 pts (Foren Sci Crim)

Huddersfield – BBB 300 pts (Psy Crimin)

Keele – BBB 300 pts (Crimin) (IB 32 pts)

Kent – BBB (Crim Just St) (IB 33 pts)

Lincoln – 300 pts (Crimin; Crimin Soc Plcy)

Liverpool John Moores – 300 pts (Law Crim Just) (IB 30 pts)

London (Birk) – BBB 300 pts (Crimin Crim Just)

London (RH) – BBB (Crimin Sociol)

Loughborough – BBB-ABC 300 pts (Crimin Soc Plcy) (IB 32 pts)

Northumbria – 300 pts (Crimin) (IB 26 pts)

Stranmillis (UC) – BBB (Ely Chld St)

Ulster – 300 pts (Crimin Crim Just)

West London – 300 pts (Psy Crimin/Cnslg Theor)

York – BBB (App Soc Sci (Chld Yng Ppl/Crm); Crim Just; App Soc Sci) (IB 31 pts)

280 pts **Aberystwyth** – 280 pts (Crimin) (IB 28 pts)

Birmingham City – 280 pts (Crimin courses; Crimin Plcg)

Central Lancashire – 280-320 pts (Plcg Crim Invstg)

De Montfort – 280 pts (Sociol; Law Hum Rts Soc Just)

Derby – 280 pts (Foren Sci Crimin)

Edge Hill – BBC 280 pts (Crimin Crim Just)
Gloucestershire – 280–300 pts (Crimin)
Huddersfield – 280 pts (Crimin)
Hull – BBC 280 pts (Psy Crimin)
Kent – BBC (Soc Sci) (IB 33 pts)
Kingston – 280–320 pts (Crimin courses)
Leeds Beckett – 280 pts (Crimin; Crimin Psy; Psy Soc) (IB 25 pts)
Liverpool John Moores – 280 pts (Crimin; Crim Just; Crimin Psy) (IB 29 pts)
London Met – 280 pts (Soc Sci)
Manchester Met – 280 pts (Crm St; Crimin; Crimin Joint Hons)
Northumbria – 280 pts (Crimin Foren Sci)
Nottingham Trent – 280 pts (Crimin; Law Crimin)
Roehampton – 280 pts (Crimin) (IB 25 pts)
Salford – 280–240 pts (Crimin; Crimin Cult St)
Sheffield Hallam – 280 pts (Crimin; Crimin Sociol; Crimin Psy; Spo Dev Coach)
South Wales – BBC (Plcg Sci; Crimin)
Staffordshire – 280 pts (Psy Crimin; Plcg Crim Invstg)
Stirling – BBC (Crimin Joint Hons) (IB 32 pts)
Suffolk (Univ Campus) – 280 pts (Crimin; Crimin Yth St; Sociol Crimin)
Teesside – 280–300 pts (Crim Scn Sci)
Westminster – BBC (Crim Just)
Winchester – 280–320 pts (Crimin) (IB 26 pts)
260 pts **Bradford** – 260 pts (Psy Crimin)
Central Lancashire – 260–300 pts (BSL Df St; Crimin Comb courses)
Chester – 260–300 pts (Law Jrnl/Crimin) (IB 28 pts)
Coventry – BCC 260 pts (Crimin) (IB 28 pts)
De Montfort – 260 pts (App Crimin; App Crimin Foren Sci)
Derby – 260 pts (App Crimin)
Edinburgh Napier – BCC 260 pts (Soc Sci; Crimin)
Greenwich – 260 pts (Crimin; Crimin Crim Psy)
Hull – 260–300 pts (Crimin)
Liverpool Hope – 260–320 pts (Crimin)
Liverpool John Moores – 260 pts (Crimin Sociol) (IB 27 pts)
London (Birk) – BCC 260 pts (Soc Sci)
London Met – 260 pts (Crimin)
Middlesex – 260 pts (Crimin (Plcg); Crimin courses)
Northampton – 260–280 pts (Crimin)
Nottingham Trent – 260 pts (Comm Soty)
Plymouth – 260–300 pts (Crimin Crim Just St)
Sheffield Hallam – 260 pts (App Soc Sci)
South Wales – (Crimin Crim Just)
Sunderland – 260 pts (Crimin)
Teesside – 260 pts (Psy Crimin)
West London – 260 pys (Crimin)
Westminster – BCC/BB (Soc Sci) (IB 28 pts)
245 pts **Glasgow Caledonian** – CCC 245 pts (Soc Sci (Crimin); Soc Sci)
240 pts **Bangor** – 240–280 pts (Crimin Crim Just)
Bradford – 240 pts (App Crim Just St)
Bucks New – 240–300 pts (Plcg St)
Canterbury Christ Church – 240 pts (App Crimin; Plcg St)
Chester – 240–280 pts (Crimin) (IB 26 pts)
Cornwall (Coll) – (Soc Sci Comb)
East London – (Crimin Crim Just)
Farnborough (CT) – BCD 240 pts (Psy Crimin)
Glyndŵr – 240 pts (Crimin Crim Just)

Check **Chapter 4** when choosing your university and **Chapter 7** on how to read the subject tables.

Kingston – 240–360 pts (Hum Rts)
Lincoln – 240 pts (Soc Sci)
London South Bank – CCC 240 pts (Crimin)
Portsmouth – 240–300 pts (Crimin Crim Just)
Robert Gordon – CCC (App Soc Sci)
Southampton Solent – 240 pts (Crimin; Crim Invstg Psy)
Teesside – 240 pts (Crimin courses; Crim Invstg)
West Scotland – CCC (Soc Sci courses)

220 pts **Abertay** – CCD (Plcg Scrty)
Anglia Ruskin – 220–260 pts (Crimin courses) (IB 24 pts)
Bishop Grosseteste – 220 pts (Ely Chld St courses)
Peterborough (Reg Coll) – 220 pts (Crimin)

200 pts **Bedfordshire** – 200 pts (Crimin; App Soc St)
Blackburn (Coll) – 200 pts (Soc Sci)
Bucks New – 200–240 pts (Crimin) (IB 24 pts)
Cumbria – 200 pts (Soc Sci Crimin; Crimin Law; Plcg Invstg Crimin)
Doncaster (Coll Univ Centre) – 200 pts (App Soc Sci; Crim Just)
Huddersfield – 200 pts (Soc Sci)
Middlesex – 200–280 pts (Yth Just)
Wolverhampton – 200 pts (Crimin Crim Just; Crimin; Foren Sci Crimin; Plcg)

180 pts **West Scotland** – BC (Crim Just) (IB 24 pts)
160 pts **Abertay** – CC 160 pts (Soc Sci; Crimin St)
Accrington and Rossendale (Coll) – 160 pts (Hlth App Soc St)
Bolton – (Plcg St)
Central Lancashire – 160 pts (Plcg)
London (Gold) – CC (App Soc Sci Commun Dev Yth Wk)
Norwich City (Coll) – 160 pts (Engl Psy Soc)
South Essex (Coll) – 160 pts (Soc St)
Trinity Saint David (Swansea) – 160 pts (Pblc Serv)

60 pts **UHI** – D (Soc Sci)

Open University – contact +44 (0)845 300 6090 **or** www.openuniversity.co.uk/you (Crimin Psy St; Soc Sci Econ; Soc Sci Geog; Soc Sci Media St; Soc Sci Pol; Soc Sci Psy St)

Alternative offers
See **Chapter 7** and **Appendix 1** for grades/UCAS Tariff points information for the International Baccalaureate, Scottish Highers/Advanced Highers, the Welsh Baccalaureate, the Irish Leaving Certificate, the Cambridge Pre-U Diploma, the Advanced Diploma and the Extended Project.

EXAMPLES OF FOUNDATION DEGREES IN THE SUBJECT FIELD
See also **Social and Public Policy and Administration**. Winchester.

CHOOSING YOUR COURSE (SEE ALSO CH.1)
Some course features
Brighton Options to select areas of applied social science in such fields as criminology, politics and psychology. Foreign exchanges are offered in France, Spain, Sweden and USA.
Central Lancashire Degree courses in Criminology, Deaf Studies and joint British Sign Language, Human Rights and Social Policy are offered on the Combined Honours and joint programmes. The University offers a unit degree scheme that includes courses from economics, psychology and sociology.
Huddersfield There are courses in Criminology, Health and Community Studies and Youth and Community Work. A three-year course is also offered leading to a degree and a Diploma in Social Work.

Universities and colleges teaching quality See www.qaa.ac.uk; http://unistats.direct.gov.uk.

Top research universities and colleges (RAE 2008) See **Social Work**.

Examples of sandwich degree courses Bath; Coventry; De Montfort; Middlesex; Portsmouth; Surrey; Teesside.

ADMISSIONS INFORMATION
Number of applicants per place (approx) Abertay 1; Bangor 2; Bath 6; Bradford 15; Cornwall (Coll) 2; Coventry 7; Cumbria 4; De Montfort 1; Durham 3; East London 10; Edge Hill 5; Edinburgh 12; Glasgow Caledonian 9; Hull 5; Kingston 5; Leicester (Crimin) 9; Liverpool 13; London (King's) 5; London LSE 14; London South Bank 3; Manchester Met 10; Middlesex 26; Northampton 5; Nottingham Trent 2; Portsmouth 3; Roehampton 6; Salford 12; Sheffield Hallam 7; Southampton 6; Staffordshire 2; Sunderland 11; Swansea 8; West Scotland 5; Westminster 14; Winchester 3; York 5.

Advice to applicants and planning the UCAS personal statement The Social Sciences/Studies subject area covers several topics. Focus on these (or some of these) and state your main areas of interest, outlining your work experience, personal goals and motivation to follow the course. Show your interest in current affairs and especially in social issues and government policies.

Misconceptions about this course **Cornwall (Coll)** That students transfer to Plymouth at the end of Year 1: this is a three-year course in Cornwall.

Selection interviews **Yes** Anglia Ruskin, Bangor, Birmingham, Birmingham City, Coventry, Cumbria, Doncaster (Coll Univ Centre), Edge Hill, Essex, Glasgow Caledonian, Hull, Kingston, London South Bank, Nottingham Trent, Oxford, Roehampton, Salford, Sunderland, West London, West Scotland; **Some** Abertay, Bath (mature students), Cornwall (Coll), East London, Robert Gordon, South Wales, Staffordshire, Westminster, Winchester; **No** Durham, York.

Interview advice and questions Past questions have included: Define democracy. What is the role of the Church in nationalistic aspirations? Does today's government listen to its people? Questions on current affairs. How would you change the running of your school? What are the faults of the Labour Party/Conservative Party? Do you agree with the National Lottery? Is money from the National Lottery well spent? Give examples of how the social services have failed. What is your understanding of the social origins of problems? See also **Chapter 6**.

Reasons for rejection (non-academic) Stated preference for other institutions. Incompetence in answering questions.

AFTER-RESULTS ADVICE
Offers to applicants repeating A-levels **Higher** Essex, Glasgow, Swansea; **Possibly higher** Salford; **Same** Abertay, Anglia Ruskin, Bangor, Bradford, Chester, Cornwall (Coll), Coventry, Cumbria, Durham, East Anglia, Gloucestershire, Leeds, Liverpool, London Met, London South Bank, Manchester Met, Nottingham Trent, Roehampton, Sheffield Hallam, Staffordshire, Stirling, Winchester, Wolverhampton.

GRADUATE DESTINATIONS AND EMPLOYMENT (2011/12 HESA)
See **Law**, **Politics** and **Psychology**

Career note Graduates find careers in all aspects of social provision, for example health services, welfare agencies such as housing departments, the probation service, police forces, the prison service, personnel work and residential care and other careers not necessarily linked with their degree subjects.

OTHER DEGREE SUBJECTS FOR CONSIDERATION
Business Studies; Community Studies; Economics; Education; Geography; Government; Health Studies; Law; Politics; Psychology; Public Administration; Social Policy; Social Work; Sociology; Urban Studies.

SOCIAL WORK

(see also **Community Studies/Development, Social and Public Policy and Administration**)

Social Work courses (which lead to careers in social work) have similarities to those in Applied Social Studies, Social Policy and Administration, Community Studies and Health Studies. If you are offered a place on a Social Work course which leads to registration as a social worker, you must undergo the Disclosure and Barring Service (DBS) check. You will also have to provide health information and certification. Check for full details of training and careers in social work with the General Social Care Council (see **Appendix 3**). Students from England receive full payment of fees and student bursaries from the General Social Care Council.

Useful websites www.swap.ac.uk; www.ageuk.org.uk; www.samaritans.org; www.ccwales.org.uk; www.sssc.uk.com; www.niscc.info.

NB The points totals shown to the left of the institutions are for ease of reference only. It must not be assumed that Tariff points are always used by institutions or that they can be substituted for an offer in grades. The level of an offer is not necessarily indicative of the quality of a course.

COURSE OFFERS INFORMATION

Subject requirements/preferences GCSE English and mathematics usually required. **AL** No subjects specified. **Other** Disclosure and Barring Service (DBS) check and an occupational health check required. Check also with universities for applicant minimum age requirements.

Your target offers and examples of courses provided by each institution

340 pts Edinburgh – AAB–BBB 340–300 pts (Soc Wk) (IB 34–36 pts)
320 pts Bath – ABB–BBB 320–300 pts (Soc Wk App Soc St) (IB 32–34 pts)
Birmingham – ABB (Soc Wk) (IB 32–34 pts)
Brighton – ABB (Soc Wk) (IB 34 pts)
Lancaster – ABB (Soc Wk) (IB 32 pts)
Queen's Belfast – ABB (Soc Wk)
Sussex – ABB (Chld Yth Theor Prac; Soc Wk) (IB 34 pts)
300 pts Bournemouth – BBB (Soc Wk) (IB 31 pts)
Bristol UWE – BBB (Soc Wk) (IB 26 pts)
Brunel – BBB 300 pts (Soc Wk) (IB 32 pts)
Coventry – BBB 300 pts (Soc Wk)
De Montfort – 300 pts (Soc Wk)
East Anglia – BBB (Soc Wk) (IB 31 pts)
Huddersfield – BBB (Soc Wk)
Leeds – BBB (Soc Wk)
Leeds Beckett – +interview (Soc Wk) (IB 26 pts)
Liverpool Hope – 300–320 pts (Soc Wk)
Nottingham – BBB (Soc Wk) (IB 30 pts)
Salford – 300 pts (Soc Wk St) (IB 27 pts)
Strathclyde – BBB (Soc Wk) (IB 28 pts)
Ulster – BBB 300 pts (Soc Wk)
York – BBB (Soc Wk) (IB 30 pts)
280 pts Birmingham City – 280 pts (Soc Wk)
Bucks New – 240–280 pts (Soc Wk)
Chichester – (Charity Dev) (IB 30 pts)
East London – 280 pts (Soc Wk)
Edge Hill – 280 pts (Soc Wk)
Gloucestershire – 280–300 pts (Soc Wk)
Hull – 280 pts (Soc Wk)
Kent – BBC (Soc Wk) (IB 33 pts)
Kingston – 280 pts (Soc Wk)
Lincoln – 280 pts (Soc Wk)

Social Work | 613

Liverpool John Moores – 280 pts (Soc Wk) (IB 25 pts)
London (Gold) – BBC (Soc Wk) (IB 32 pts)
London Met – 280 pts (Soc Wk)
Manchester Met – 280–300 pts (Soc Wk) (IB 29 pts)
Middlesex – BBC 280 pts (Soc Wk)
Newman – (Wk Chld Yng Ppl Fmly)
Northampton – 260–280 pts (Soc Wk)
Northumbria – 280 pts (Soc Wk)
Nottingham Trent – 280 pts (Soc Wk)
Oxford Brookes – BBC (Soc Wk)
Portsmouth – (Soc Wk)
Sheffield Hallam – (Soc Wk)
South Wales – 280 pts (Soc Wk)
Stirling – BBC (Soc Wk) (IB 32 pts)
Suffolk (Univ Campus) – 280 pts (Soc Wk)

260 pts Bradford – 260 pts (Soc Wk)
Derby – 260 pts (Soc Wk (App))
Glyndŵr – 260–300 pts (Soc Wk)
Greenwich – 260 pts (Soc Wk)
Hertfordshire – 260 pts (Soc Wk)
Keele – BCC (Soc Wk) (IB 26–28 pts)
Liverpool John Moores – 260 pts (Hlth Soc Cr Fmly Indiv Comm)
Northampton – 260–300 pts (Soc Cr courses)
Sunderland – 260–360 pts (Soc Wk)
Swansea – BCC (Soc Wk)
Wiltshire (Coll) – 260 pts (Soc Wk)
Winchester – 260–300 pts (Soc Wk) (IB 26 pts)
Wolverhampton – 260 pts (Soc Wk)

240 pts Anglia Ruskin – 240 pts (Soc Wk)
Bedfordshire – 240 pts (Soc Wk; Hlth Soc Cr)
Canterbury Christ Church – 240 pts (Soc Wk) (IB 24 pts)
Cardiff Met (UWIC) – 240 pts (Soc Wk; Hlth Soc Cr)
Central Lancashire – 240 pts (Soc Wk)
Chester – 240–280 pts (Soc Wk) (IB 26 pts)
Chichester – 240 pts (Soc Wk) (IB 30 pts)
Cumbria – 240 pts (Soc Wk)
Dundee – AB–CCC (Soc Wk)
Glasgow Caledonian – CCC 240 pts (Soc Wk) (IB 24 pts)
Havering (Coll) – 240 pts (Soc Wk)
Liverpool City (Coll) – (Soc Wk)
London South Bank – 200–240 pts (Soc Wk)
Manchester Met – 240–280 pts (Chld Yth St; Soc Cr)
NEW (Coll) – 240 pts (Soc Wk)
Norwich City (Coll) – 240 pts (App Soc Wk)
Robert Gordon – CCC 240 pts (Soc Wk)
South Wales – 240 pts (Yth Commun Wk)
Southampton Solent – 240 pts (Soc Wk)
Stockport (Coll) – 240–280 pts (Soc Wk)
Teesside – 240 pts +interview (Soc Wk)

230 pts Plymouth – 230 pts (Soc Wk)
220 pts Nottingham Trent – 220 pts (Yth St)
St Mark and St John – 220 pts (Chld PE; Hlth Soc Wlf)
West Scotland – CCD (Soc Wk)
Winchester – 220–260 pts (Hlth Commun Soc Cr St)
200 pts Bradford (Coll Univ Centre) – 200 pts (Soc Wk)

       Cumbria – 200 pts (Wkg Chld Fam)
       Derby – 200 pts (App Commun Yth Wk)
       Doncaster (Coll Univ Centre) – 200 pts (Ely Chld St)
       Leeds Trinity – 200–240 pts (Wkg Chld Yng Ppl Fmly)
       St Mark and St John – 200 pts (Yth Commun Wk)
       West London – 200 pts (Soc Wk)
180 pts **St Mark and St John** – 180 pts (Wrkg Chld Yng Ppl; Ely Chld Educ; Commun Dev; Chld Welf
         Soty; Chld Yng Ppl)
       Staffordshire – 180–260 pts (Soc Wk)
160 pts **Bradford (Coll Univ Centre)** – 160 pts +DBS check (Erly Yrs Prac)
       Colchester (Inst) – 160 pts (Ely Yrs; Hlth Soc Cr)
       Durham New (Coll) – 160 pts (Soc Wk)
       London (Gold) – CC (App Soc Sci Commun Dev Yth Wk)

       Open University – contact +44 (0)845 300 6090 **or** www.openuniversity.co.uk/you (Soc Wk)

Alternative offers
See **Chapter 7** and **Appendix 1** for grades/UCAS Tariff points information for the International Baccalaureate, Scottish Highers/Advanced Highers, the Welsh Baccalaureate, the Irish Leaving Certificate, the Cambridge Pre-U Diploma, the Advanced Diploma and the Extended Project.

EXAMPLES OF FOUNDATION DEGREES IN THE SUBJECT FIELD
See also **Social and Public Policy and Administration**. Central Lancashire; Cornwall (Coll); London Met; St Mark and St John; Somerset (Coll); Sunderland; Worcester.

CHOOSING YOUR COURSE (SEE ALSO CH.1)
Some course features
Brunel Placements are in Years 1, 2 and 3. Students undertake 30 days placement in the first year, 70 in the second year and 100 in the final year.
Coventry The course covers law, human growth and development, communication skills and partnership working.
East Anglia (Soc Wk) 200 days spent on placements with social work agencies.
Edinburgh Years 1 and 2 of the course cover the history and development of social work while Years 3 and 4 look at the context and complexity of practice. Placements are available.
Sussex In the Social Work degree, 170 days of placement take place in Years 2 and 3.

Universities and colleges teaching quality See www.qaa.ac.uk; http://unistats.direct.gov.uk.

Top research universities and colleges (RAE 2008) (Social Work and Social Policy and Administration) London LSE; Bath; Leeds; Kent; Edinburgh; York; City; Oxford; Sheffield; Lancaster; Keele; Birmingham; London South Bank; Nottingham Trent; Sussex.

ADMISSIONS INFORMATION
Number of applicants per place (approx) Bangor 8; Bath 8; Birmingham 13; Bradford 10; Coventry 22; Dundee 6; London Met 27; Northampton 7; Nottingham Trent 6; Sheffield Hallam 4; Southampton 10; Staffordshire 3.

Advice to applicants and planning the UCAS personal statement The statement should show motivation for social work, relevant work experience, awareness of the demands of social work and give relevant personal information, for example disabilities. Awareness of the origins of personal and family difficulties, commitment to anti-discriminatory practice. Most applicants for these courses will have significant experience of a statutory care agency or voluntary/private organisation providing a social work or social care service. See also **Social and Public Policy and Administration** and **Appendix 4**.

Selection interviews Yes Anglia Ruskin, Birmingham, Birmingham City, Bradford, Brunel, Canterbury Christ Church, Chichester, Coventry, East Anglia, Edinburgh, Glyndŵr, Hull, Keele, Kent, Liverpool Hope,

Nottingham, Nottingham Trent, Portsmouth, Robert Gordon, Salford, Sheffield Hallam, Staffordshire, West London, West Scotland, Winchester, Wolverhampton, York; **Some** Cardiff Met (UWIC), Dundee, Liverpool John Moores.

Interview advice and questions What qualities are needed to be a social worker? What use do you think you will be to society as a social worker? Why should money be spent on prison offenders? Your younger brother is playing truant and mixing with bad company. Your parents don't know. What would you do? See also **Social and Public Policy and Administration** and **Chapter 6**.

Reasons for rejection (non-academic) Criminal convictions.

AFTER-RESULTS ADVICE
Offers to applicants repeating A-levels Same Bangor, Lincoln, Liverpool Hope, Salford City (Coll), Staffordshire, Suffolk (Univ Campus), Wolverhampton.

GRADUATE DESTINATIONS AND EMPLOYMENT (2011/12 HESA)
Graduates surveyed 9865 **Employed** 5170 **In voluntary employment** 120 **In further study** 1985 **Assumed unemployed** 575

Career note See **Social Sciences/Studies**.

OTHER DEGREE SUBJECTS FOR CONSIDERATION
Community Studies; Conductive Education; Criminology; Economics; Education; Health Studies; Law; Psychology; Public Sector Management and Administration; Social Policy; Sociology; Youth Studies.

SOCIOLOGY
(see also **Anthropology, Social and Public Policy and Administration**)

Sociology is the study of social organisation, social structures, systems, institutions and practices. Courses are likely to include the meaning and structure of, for example, race, ethnicity and gender, industrial behaviour, crime and deviance, health and illness. **NB** Sociology is not a training course for social workers, although some graduates take additional qualifications to qualify in social work.

Useful websites www.britsoc.co.uk; www.asanet.org; www.sociology.org.uk; www.sociology.org.

NB The points totals shown to the left of the institutions are for ease of reference only. It must not be assumed that Tariff points are always used by institutions or that they can be substituted for an offer in grades. The level of an offer is not necessarily indicative of the quality of a course.

COURSE OFFERS INFORMATION
Subject requirements/preferences GCSE English and mathematics usually required. **AL** No subjects specified.

Your target offers and examples of courses provided by each institution
380 pts **Cambridge** – A*AA (Hum Soc Pol Sci (Sociol)) (IB 40–41 pts HL 766–777)
     Warwick – AABc (Law Sociol) (IB 36 pts)
360 pts **Edinburgh** – AAA–BBB 360–300 pts (Sociol; Sociol Soc Econ Hist) (IB 37–34 pts HL 666–555)
340 pts **Bath** – AAB–BBB 340–300 pts (Sociol) (IB 32–35 pts)
     Bristol – AAB–ABB 340–320 pts (Sociol Phil; Pol Sociol) (IB 35–33 pts)
     Durham – AAB 340 pts (Sociol) (IB 36 pts)
     Lancaster – AAB (Film Socio; Pol Sociol; Relig St Sociol) (IB 35 pts)
     London LSE – AAB (Soc Pol Sociol) (IB 37 pts)
     Manchester – AAB (Bus St Sociol; Econ Sociol) (IB 35 pts)
     Southampton – AAB (Phil Sociol) (IB 34 pts HL 17 pts)
     Sussex – AAA–AAB (Psy Sociol) (IB 35 pts)
     Warwick – AAB (Sociol) (IB 36 pts)

320 pts **Aston** – ABB–AAB (Pol Sociol; Psy Sociol) (IB 32–34 pts)
Birmingham – ABB (Sociol; Soc Plcy Pol Sci) (IB 32–34 pts)
Bristol – ABB–BBB 320–300 pts (Soc Plcy Sociol; Sociol) (IB 33–32 pts)
Brunel – ABB 320 pts (Anth Sociol) (IB 33–35 pts)
Cardiff – ABB 320 pts (Sociol; Sociol Relig St; Sociol Welsh; Jrnl Media Sociol) (IB 32 pts)
City – ABB (Sociol) (IB 33 pts)
Durham – ABB 320 pts (Sociol Law)
Essex – ABB–BBB 320–300 pts (Sociol; Sociol Mgt; Sociol Crimin; Sociol Hum Rts; Sociol Soc Anth) (IB 32–30 pts)
Exeter – ABB–BBB (Sociol; Sociol Joint Hons)
Glasgow – ABB (Sociol) (IB 36 pts)
Kent – ABB (Sociol; Sociol (Yr Abrd)) (IB 34 pts)
Lancaster – ABB (Sociol; Crimin Sociol) (IB 32 pts)
Leeds – ABB (Sociol; Interd Soc Pol Sociol; Russ Advnc/Sociol)
Leicester – ABB (Psy Sociol)
London LSE – ABB (Sociol) (IB 37 pts)
Manchester – ABB (Pol Sociol) (IB 34 pts)
Nottingham – ABB (Film TV St Cult Sociol; Sociol; Sociol Soc Plcy) (IB 32 pts)
Sheffield – ABB (Engl Lang Sociol; Sociol Bus Mgt; Pol Sociol) (IB 33 pts)
Southampton – ABB (Sociol; Sociol Soc Plcy)
Surrey – ABB–BBB (Sociol)
Sussex – ABB–BBB (Sociol) (IB 32 pts)
York – ABB (Sociol; Sociol Soc Psy; Sociol Educ) (IB 34 pts)

300 pts **Aberdeen** – BBB (Sociol)
Aston – BBB 300 pts (Sociol courses) (IB 33 pts)
Brighton – BBB (Sociol; Crimin Sociol; App Psy Sociol; Pol Sociol; Sociol Soc Plcy) (IB 32 pts)
Brunel – BBB 300 pts (Sociol Media St) (IB 32 pts)
Cardiff – BBB 300 pts (Educ Sociol) (IB 32 pts)
City – BBB 300 pts (Sociol Psy) (IB 32 pts)
Greenwich – 300 pts (Sociol)
Keele – BBB (Sociol) (IB 32 pts)
Leicester – BBB (Sociol) (IB 28–30 pts)
Liverpool – BBB (Sociol; Crimin Sociol) (IB 30 pts)
London (Gold) – BBB (Sociol) (IB 28 pts)
Loughborough – BBB–ABB 300–320 pts (Sociol) (IB 32 pts)
Manchester – BBB (Sociol) (IB 32 pts)
Newcastle – BBB (Sociol) (IB 32 pts)
Northumbria – 300 pts (Sociol)
Queen's Belfast – BBB (Sociol courses)
Sheffield – BBB (Soc Plcy Sociol) (IB 32 pts)

280 pts **Birmingham City** – 280 pts (Sociol; Sociol Crimin; Sociol Psy) (IB 26 pts)
Bournemouth – 280 pts (Sociol courses)
Brighton – BBC (Sociol Soc Hist) (IB 30 pts)
Bristol UWE – (Sociol) (IB 28 pts)
De Montfort – 280 pts (Sociol; Pol Sociol)
Edge Hill – 280 pts (Sociol; Hist Sociol)
Gloucestershire – 280 pts (Sociol)
Greenwich – 280 pts (Phil Socio) (IB 28 pts)
Huddersfield – 280 pts (Sociol)
Hull – 280–320 pts (Sociol; Soc Anth Sociol)
Kingston – 280 pts (Sociol)
Leeds Beckett – 280 pts (Sociol) (IB 25 pts)
London Met – 280 pts (Sociol)

Manchester Met – 280–300 pts (Psy Sociol) (IB 30 pts)
Oxford Brookes – BBC (Sociol) (IB 31 pts)
Roehampton – 280 pts (Sociol)
Sheffield Hallam – 280 pts (Sociol; Psy Sociol)
South Wales – 280 pts (Sociol Educ; Sociol Crimin) (IB 25 pts)
Stirling – BBC 280 pts (Sociol Soc Plcy) (IB 32 pts)
Suffolk (Univ Campus) – 280 pts (Sociol Yth St; Sociol Crimin)
Westminster – BBC (Sociol) (IB 28 pts)
Winchester – 280–320 pts (Sociol) (IB 26 pts)

260 pts **Bath Spa** – 260–300 pts (Sociol Comb courses)
Coventry – BCC 260 pts (Sociol; Sociol Psy; Sociol Crimin)
Derby – 260–300 pts (Sociol Joint Hons)
Edinburgh Napier – BCC 260 pts (Psy Sociol)
Hull – 260–300 pts (Sociol Film St)
Liverpool John Moores – 260 pts (Crimin Sociol; Sociol)
Manchester Met – 260 pts (Sociol) (IB 28 pts)
Nottingham Trent – 260 pts (Sociol)
Plymouth – 260–300 pts (Sociol)
St Mary's – 260 pts (Sociol) (IB 28 pts)
Sunderland – 260 pts (Sociol)
Ulster – 260–280 pts (Sociol) (IB 24 pts)

240 pts **Bangor** – 240–280 pts (Sociol; Sociol Soc Pol) (IB 28 pts)
Bath Spa – 240–280 pts (Sociol)
Bradford – (Sociol)
Brighton – CCC 240 pts (Media St Sociol/Educ)
Canterbury Christ Church – 240 pts (Sociol) (IB 24 pts)
Central Lancashire – 240–300 pts (Sociol)
Chester – 240–280 pts (Sociol) (IB 26 pts)
London South Bank – 240 pts (Sociol)
Northampton – 240–280 pts (Sociol)
Nottingham Trent – 240 pts (Sociol Pol)
Portsmouth – 240–300 pts (Sociol; Sociol Media St; Sociol Psy; Pol Sociol)
Salford – 240 pts (Sociol) (IB 29 pts)
Staffordshire – 240–200 pts (Sociol)
Suffolk (Univ Campus) – 240–280 pts (Psy Sociol)
Ulster – CCC 240 pts (Sociol Ir) (IB 24 pts HL 12 pts)
West Scotland – CCC 240 pts (Sociol) (IB 24 pts)

220 pts **Anglia Ruskin** – 220–260 pts (Sociol)
Bangor – 220–260 pts (Sociol; Sociol Joint Hons) (IB 24 pts)
Derby – 220 pts (Sociol)
Edinburgh Queen Margaret – CCD 220 pts (Psy Sociol) (IB 26 pts)
Plymouth – 220–300 pts (Psy Sociol)
Teesside – 220 pts (Sociol)
Worcester – 220–260 pts (Sociol)

200 pts **Blackburn (Coll)** – 200 pts (Sociol courses)
East London – 200 pts (Sociol)
Middlesex – 200–280 pts (Sociol)
Peterborough (Reg Coll) – 200 pts (Sociol)
Wolverhampton – 200 pts (Sociol; Sociol Pol; Phil Sociol; Relig St Sociol)

180 pts **Bedfordshire** – 180–220 pts (Crimin Sociol)
Bradford – 180–220 pts (Psy Sociol)
West Anglia (Coll) – 180 pts (Psysoc St; Sociol Engl Lit)

160 pts **Abertay** – CC 160 pts (Sociol)

120 pts **Anglia Ruskin** – DD (Sociol Engl)

Check **Chapter 4** when choosing your university and **Chapter 7** on how to read the subject tables.

Alternative offers
See **Chapter 7** and **Appendix 1** for grades/UCAS Tariff points information for the International
Baccalaureate, Scottish Highers/Advanced Highers, the Welsh Baccalaureate, the Irish
Leaving Certificate, the Cambridge Pre-U Diploma, the Advanced Diploma and the Extended
Project.

EXAMPLES OF FOUNDATION DEGREES IN THE SUBJECT FIELD
South Devon (Coll).

CHOOSING YOUR COURSE (SEE ALSO CH.1)
Some course features
Bristol In the first year of the Sociology course students choose two additional subjects from the
Faculties of Social Sciences and the Arts. There are joint programmes combining with Philosophy,
Social Policy and Theology. Sociology can also be taken with study abroad.
Edinburgh Sociology, the discipline which examines the relationship between individuals and society,
is offered as a Single Honours course or with Social Anthropology, Politics, South Asian Studies or
Economic History.
Kent A Single Honours course is offered. In Part II, core courses are taken, including social analysis
and research practices in sociology, as well as optional third-year courses such as the sociology of
politics, education, food, work, gender and the family.
Leeds In the first year of the Sociology degree social, intellectual and cultural trends in contemporary
society are studied together with study and research skills. Central problems in sociology and social
policy form the core subjects in Year 2, and in Year 3 options are taken from a wide range of topics
from which students are asked to choose three for further research.
London LSE The degree comprises 12 modules: six compulsory and six optional. A module in social
psychology is offered for students taking courses in Sociology.

Universities and colleges teaching quality See www.qaa.ac.uk; http://unistats.direct.gov.uk.

Top research universities and colleges (RAE 2008) Manchester; Essex; London (Gold); York;
Lancaster; Surrey; Edinburgh; Warwick; Cardiff; Exeter; Oxford; Cambridge.

Examples of sandwich degree courses Aston; Bath; Bristol UWE; Brunel; Coventry; Middlesex;
Plymouth; Surrey.

ADMISSIONS INFORMATION
Number of applicants per place (approx) Aston 8; Bangor 1; Bath 7; Birmingham 8; Birmingham
City 12; Bristol 8; Brunel 24; Cardiff 5; Cardiff Met (UWIC) 4; City 11; Durham 13; East Anglia 15; East
London 8; Exeter 5; Gloucestershire 8; Greenwich 5; Hull 11; Kent 10; Kingston 9; Lancaster 12; Leeds
14; Leicester 4; Liverpool 9; Liverpool John Moores 10; London (Gold) 5; London LSE 10; London Met
3; Loughborough 10; Northampton 3; Northumbria 18; Nottingham 7; Plymouth 9; Portsmouth 12;
Roehampton 4; Sheffield Hallam 7; Southampton 4; Staffordshire 10; Sunderland 5; Surrey 6; Warwick
20; Worcester 5; York 5.

Advice to applicants and planning the UCAS personal statement Show your ability to
communicate and work as part of a group and your curiosity about issues such as social conflict and
social change between social groups. Discuss your interests in sociology on the personal statement.
Demonstrate an intellectual curiosity about sociology and social problems. See also **Social Sciences/
Studies**. **Bristol** Deferred entry accepted.

Misconceptions about this course Some applicants believe that all sociologists want to become
social workers. **Birmingham** Students with an interest in crime and deviance may be disappointed
that we do not offer modules in this area. **London Met** That it is the stamping ground of student
activists and has no relevance to the real world.

Selection interviews **Yes** Birmingham City, Brunel, Cambridge, City, Derby, Durham, East London,
Lancaster, Liverpool, London (Gold), Newcastle; **Some** Anglia Ruskin, Aston, Bath (mature applicants),
Bath Spa, Cardiff, Exeter, Hull, Kent, Leeds, Leicester, London Met, Loughborough, Nottingham Trent,

Salford, Sheffield Hallam, Southampton, Staffordshire; **No** Birmingham, Bristol, Essex, Liverpool John Moores, Nottingham, Portsmouth, St Mary's, Surrey, Warwick, York.

Interview advice and questions Past questions have included: Why do you want to study Sociology? What books have you read on the subject? How do you see the role of women changing in the next 20 years? See also **Chapter 6**. **London Met** Questions will focus on existing level of interest in the subject and the applicant's expectations about studying.

Reasons for rejection (non-academic) Evidence of difficulty with written work. Non-attendance at Open Days (find out from your universities if your attendance will affect their offers). 'In the middle of an interview for Sociology a student asked us if we could interview him for Sports Studies instead!' See also **Social and Public Policy and Administration**. **Durham** No evidence of awareness of what the course involves. **London Met** References which indicated that the individual would not be able to work effectively within a diverse student group; concern that the applicant had not put any serious thought into the choice of subject for study.

AFTER-RESULTS ADVICE
Offers to applicants repeating A-levels Higher Brunel, East London, Essex, Glasgow, Hull, Newcastle, Nottingham Trent, Warwick, York; **Possibly higher** Leeds, Liverpool, Portsmouth; **Same** Aston, Bangor, Bath, Birmingham, Birmingham City, Bristol, Cardiff, Coventry, Derby, Durham, Gloucestershire, Kingston, Lancaster, Liverpool John Moores, London Met, Loughborough, Northumbria, Roehampton, St Mary's, Salford, Sheffield Hallam, Southampton, Staffordshire; **No** Cambridge.

GRADUATE DESTINATIONS AND EMPLOYMENT (2011/12 HESA)
Graduates surveyed 1610 **Employed** 825 **In voluntary employment** 225 **In further study** 340 **Assumed unemployed** 120

Career note See **Social Sciences/Studies**.

OTHER DEGREE SUBJECTS FOR CONSIDERATION
Anthropology; Economic and Social History; Economics; Education; Geography; Government; Health Studies; History; Law; Politics; Psychology; Social Policy; Social Work.

SPANISH

(including **Hispanic Studies** and **Portuguese**; see also **Languages, Latin American Studies**)

Spanish can be studied by focusing on the language and literature of Spain. Broader courses in Hispanic Studies (see also **Latin American Studies**) are available which also include Portuguese and Latin American studies. See also **Appendix 3** under Languages.

Useful websites www.donquijote.co.uk; www.europa.eu; www.cilt.org.uk; www.iol.org.uk; www.bbc. co.uk/languages; www.languageadvantage.com; www.languagematters.co.uk; www.studyspanish. com; www.spanishlanguageguide.com; see also **Latin American Studies**.

NB The points totals shown to the left of the institutions are for ease of reference only. It must not be assumed that Tariff points are always used by institutions or that they can be substituted for an offer in grades. The level of an offer is not necessarily indicative of the quality of a course.

COURSE OFFERS INFORMATION
Subject requirements/preferences GCSE English, mathematics or science and a foreign language. **AL** Spanish required for most courses.

Your target offers and examples of courses provided by each institution
380 pts **Cambridge** – A*AA 380 pts (Modn Mediev Lang) (IB 40–41 pts HL 776)
Imperial London – A*AA–AAA (Chem Fr/Ger/Span Sci) (IB 38 pts HL 7 chem 6 maths)

London (UCL) – AAAe–ABBe 380–340 pts (Modn Lang) (IB 34–38 pts)

Warwick – AABc (Hist Lit Cult Am) (IB 36 pts)

360 pts **Bath** – AAA (Int Mgt Modn Langs (Span)) (IB 37 pts HL 6 Span)

Edinburgh – AAA 360 pts (Int Bus Fr/Ger/Span) (IB 37 pts HL 666–555)

London (King's) – AAA–AAB 360–340 pts (Euro St (Fr/Ger/Span)) (IB 33–35 pts)

London (UCL) – AABe (Span Lat Am St) (IB 36 pts)

Oxford – AAA (Port courses; Span courses) (IB 38–40 pts)

St Andrews – AAA (Maths Span; Mgt Span) (IB 36–38 pts)

Southampton – AAA (Maths Fr/Ger/Span) (IB 36 pts HL 18 pts)

340 pts **Aston** – AAB–ABB 340–320 pts (Int Bus Fr/Ger/Span) (IB 34 pts HL 665)

Birmingham – AAB (Hisp St Hist; Engl Lit Hisp St) (IB 36 pts)

Durham – AAB 340 pts (Span)

East Anglia – AAB (Modn Lang Span) (IB 33 pts)

Exeter – AAB–ABB (Span) (IB 32–29 pts)

Glasgow – AAB (Hisp St) (IB 34 pts)

Lancaster – AAB (Span St) (IB 32 pts)

Leeds – AAB (Russ Advnc/Bgn Span) (IB 35 pts)

London (King's) – AAB (Fr Hisp St; Hisp St) (IB 35 pts)

London (RH) – AAB–ABB 340–320 pts (Mgt Fr/Ger/Ital/Span) (IB 35–34 pts)

Manchester – AAB–ABB (Span Port Lat Am St; Span courses) (IB 33–37 pts)

Nottingham – AAB (Mgt St Fr/Ger/Span) (IB 34 pts)

St Andrews – AAB (Span courses) (IB 35 pts)

Southampton – AAB–ABB (Span Lat Am St; Film Fr/Ger/Span; Engl Fr/Ger/Span; Pol Span/
Port Lat Am St; Span courses) (IB 34 pts HL 17 pts)

Surrey – AAB (Span courses)

Sussex – AAB–BBB (Dr St Span) (IB 34–36 pts)

York – AAB–ABB (Fr Sp Lang; Span courses) (IB 34 pts)

320 pts **Aston** – ABB–BBB 320 pts (Span Comb Hons) (IB 32 pts)

Bath – ABB–AAA 320–360 pts (Modn Langs Euro St) (IB 34–36 pts)

Birmingham – AAB–ABB (Hisp St; Span Hist Art) (IB 36–34 pts)

Bristol – ABB–BBC (Span; Hisp St) (IB 35–30 pts)

Cardiff – ABB 320 pts (Span) (IB 30 pts)

Dundee – ABB 320 pts (Law Lang) (IB 32 pts)

East Anglia – AAB–ABB (Transl Media Sp; Fr Span Lang Mgt St (4 yrs); Span Lang Mgt St;
Span Int Dev St; Span Film TV) (IB 32–33 pts)

Essex – ABB–BBB 320–300 pts (Lat Am St courses) (IB 32–30 pts)

Glasgow – ABB (Span) (IB 36 pts)

Lancaster – ABB (Span St Geog) (IB 32 pts)

Leeds – ABB (Span; Span Port Lat Am St) (IB 34 pts HL 16 pts)

Liverpool – ABB–BBB (Span)

London (RH) – ABB–BBB (Span Fr/Ger/Ital; Span; Span courses)

Nottingham – ABB 320 pts (Film TV Hisp St; Span Int Media Comms St; Hisp St) (IB 32 pts)

Sheffield – ABB (Hisp St) (IB 34 pts HL 6 Span)

Strathclyde – ABB (Span courses)

Sussex – ABB–AAB (Span courses) (IB 34–35 pts)

Warwick – ABB 320 pts (Hisp St) (IB 34 pts HL 6 modn lang)

300 pts **Aberdeen** – BBB (Span)

Buckingham – BBB–BBC (Mark Span; Psy Span) (IB 34 pts)

Dundee – BBB (Span courses) (IB 30 pts)

East Anglia – BBB–BBC (Span Int Dev St)

Essex – ABB–BBB 300–320 pts (Span St Modn Langs) (IB 32–30 pts)

Heriot-Watt – BBB (Maths Span; Span App Lang St) (IB 28 pts)

Hertfordshire – 300 pts (Mark Span)

Liverpool – BBB (Hisp St Ital) (IB 30 pts)

London (QM) – BBB–AAB 300–340 pts (Hisp St; Hisp St courses) (IB 32–34 pts HL 5 lang)
Nottingham – BBB (Engl Span) (IB 26 pts)
Plymouth – 300 pts (Engl Span) (IB 26 pts)
Queen's Belfast – BBB/BBCb (Span St; Span Port St)
Salford – 300 pts (Span courses)
Swansea – BBB (Span Leg St; Span Comp Sci)

280 pts **Aberystwyth** – 280–320 pts (Span courses)
Hull – 280–300 pts (Span; Fr/Ger/Ital/Span Hist)
Leeds Beckett – (Lang St)
Oxford Brookes – BBC 280 pts (Span (Minor Comb)) (IB 31 pts)
Roehampton – 280–320 pts (Span)
Salford – 320–280 pts (Modn Lang Transl Interp St (Fr/Ger/Port/Span))
Stirling – BBC (Span Lat Am St) (IB 32 pts)
Swansea – BBC (Span) (IB 30 pts)

260 pts **Central Lancashire** – 260–300 pts (Span Int Bus)
Coventry – BBC–BCC 260–280 pts (Span; Span Bus; Span Int Rel) (IB 28 pts)
Greenwich – 260 pts (Span)
London (Birk) – 260–300 pts (Span courses)
London Met – 260 pts (Span Lat Am St)
Manchester Met – 260–280 pts (Ling Lang (Fr/Ger/Ital/Span); Span St) (IB 28 pts)
Middlesex – 260 pts (Bus Mgt Fr/Ger/Ital/Span)
Nottingham Trent – 260 pts (Span Joint Hons)
Sunderland – 260 pts (Span (Comb))
Ulster – 260 pts (Span courses)
Westminster – BCC (Transl St (Span); Span courses) (IB 28 pts)

240 pts **Bangor** – 240–260 pts (Span courses)
Chester – 240–280 pts (Span courses) (IB 26 pts)
Euro Bus Sch London – 240 pts (Int Bus Span)
Kingston – 240–320 pts (Span courses) (IB 25–27 pts)
Middlesex – 240 pts (Int Tour Mgt Span)
Plymouth – 240 pts (Int Bus Span) (IB 24 pts)
Ulster – CCC–BBC 240–280 pts (Bus St Fr/Ger/Span) (IB 24 pts)

200 pts **Portsmouth** – 200–280 pts (Span St; Span Lat Am St) (IB 28 pts)

80 pts **London (Birk)** – p/t, for under 21s (over 21s varies) (Modn Langs Euro St (Fr, Ger, Jap, Port, Span))

Alternative offers
See **Chapter 7** and **Appendix 1** for grades/UCAS Tariff points information for the International Baccalaureate, the Scottish Highers/Advanced Highers, the Welsh Baccalaureate, the Irish Leaving Certificate, the Cambridge Pre-U Diploma, the Advanced Diploma and the Extended Project.

CHOOSING YOUR COURSE (SEE ALSO CH.1)
Some course features
East Anglia For particularly able students, Spanish courses are offered over three years, not the usual four-year course.
Heriot-Watt Spanish can be taken with Interpreting and Translating, International Management and Teaching English to Speakers of Other Languages.
London (King's) The University offers a very wide range of courses covering Hispanic, Portuguese and Brazilian Studies.
London Met There is an Open Language programme offered to students to continue a study of a preferred language irrespective of their chosen degree course (see also **Languages**).
Warwick (Hist Lit Cult Ams) A four-year interdisciplinary course, with the third year spent at a university in the Americas. Spanish language is taught throughout, with beginners following an introductory course in Year 1, and students with A-level Spanish taking one more advanced course. There are opportunities to study Spanish American literature as poetry.

Universities and colleges teaching quality See www.qaa.ac.uk; http://unistats.direct.gov.uk.

Top research universities and colleges (RAE 2008) (Iberian and Latin American languages) Nottingham; Cambridge; London (King's) (Port); London (Birk); Durham; London (QM); Leeds; St Andrews; Newcastle; Queen's Belfast.

ADMISSIONS INFORMATION
Number of applicants per place (approx) Birmingham 9; Bristol 7; Cardiff 3; Exeter 5; Hull 14; Leeds 10; Liverpool 3; London (King's) 6; London (QM) 5; London (UCL) 6; Middlesex 2; Newcastle 12; Nottingham 7; Portsmouth 4; Salford 5.

Advice to applicants and planning the UCAS personal statement Visits to Spanish-speaking countries should be discussed. Study the geography, culture, literature and politics of Spain (or Portugal) and discuss your interests in full. Further information could be obtained from embassies in London. See also **Appendix 3** under Languages.

Selection interviews **Yes** Cambridge, Hull, London (UCL), Oxford, Southampton; **Some** Cardiff, Leeds, London (QM), London (RH), Nottingham, Roehampton, Swansea.

Interview advice and questions Candidates offering A-level Spanish are likely to be questioned on their A-level work, their reasons for wanting to take the subject and on their knowledge of Spain and its people. Interest in Spain is important for all applicants. Student comment: 'Mostly questions about the literature I had read and I was given a poem and asked questions on it.' Questions were asked in the target language. 'There were two interviewers for the Spanish interview; they did their best to trip me up and to make me think under pressure by asking aggressive questions.' See **Chapter 6**.

AFTER-RESULTS ADVICE
Offers to applicants repeating A-levels **Higher** Glasgow, Leeds; **Same** Cardiff, Chester, Hull, Liverpool, London (RH), Newcastle, Nottingham, Roehampton, Swansea; **No** Cambridge.

GRADUATE DESTINATIONS AND EMPLOYMENT (2011/12 HESA)
Spanish Studies graduates surveyed 1090 **Employed** 495 **In voluntary employment** 35 **In further study** 230 **Assumed unemployed** 75

Career note See **Languages**.

OTHER DEGREE SUBJECTS FOR CONSIDERATION
International Business Studies; Latin American Studies; Linguistics; see other language tables.

SPEECH PATHOLOGY/SCIENCES/THERAPY

(including **Deaf Studies** and **Phonetics**; see also **Communication Studies/Communication, Health Sciences/Studies**)

Speech Pathology/Sciences/Therapy is the study of speech defects caused by accident, disease or psychological trauma. These can include failure to develop communication at the usual age, voice disorders, physical and learning disabilities and stammering. Courses lead to qualification as a speech therapist. This is one of many medical courses. See also **Medicine** and **Appendix 3**.

Useful websites www.rcslt.org; www.speechteach.co.uk; www.asha.org.

NB The points totals shown to the left of the institutions are for ease of reference only. It must not be assumed that Tariff points are always used by institutions or that they can be substituted for an offer in grades. The level of an offer is not necessarily indicative of the quality of a course.

COURSE OFFERS INFORMATION

Subject requirements/preferences **GCSE** English language, modern foreign language and biology/ dual award science at grade B or above. **AL** At least one science subject; biology may be stipulated, psychology and English language may be preferred. **Other** Disclosure and Barring Service (DBS) and occupational health checks essential for speech sciences/speech therapy applicants.

Your target offers and examples of courses provided by each institution

380 pts **City** – A*AA 380 pts (Sp Lang Thera) (IB 35 pts HL 555)
340 pts **East Anglia** – AAB (Sp Lang Thera) (IB 33 pts HL 666)
  Edinburgh Queen Margaret – AAB 340 pts (Sp Lang Thera) (IB 32 pts)
  Manchester – AAB (Sp Lang Thera) (IB 35 pts)
  Newcastle – AAB (Sp Lang Sci) (IB 35 pts)
  Reading – AAB (Sp Lang Thera) (IB 35 pts)
320 pts **Leeds Beckett** – ABB 320 pts (Sp Lang Thera) (IB 27 pts HL 555)
  St Mark and St John – ABB 320 pts (Sp Lang Thera)
  Sheffield – ABB (Sp Lang Sci) (IB 34 pts)
  Strathclyde – ABB (Sp Lang Path) (IB 32 pts)
300 pts **Birmingham City** – 300 pts (Sp Lang Thera) (IB 36 pts)
  Cardiff Met (UWIC) – BBB 300 pts (Sp Lang Thera) (IB 25 pts)
  De Montfort – BBB 300 pts (Hum Comm (Sp Lang Thera)) (IB 30 pts)
  Manchester Met – BBB (Sp Path Thera) (IB 30 pts)
  St Mark and St John – 300 pts (Sp Sci)
  Ulster – BBB +HPAT (Sp Lang Thera)

Alternative offers

See **Chapter 7** and **Appendix 1** for grades/UCAS Tariff points information for the International Baccalaureate, Scottish Highers/Advanced Highers, the Welsh Baccalaureate, the Irish Leaving Certificate, the Cambridge Pre-U Diploma, the Advanced Diploma and the Extended Project.

EXAMPLES OF FOUNDATION DEGREES IN THE SUBJECT FIELD

Portsmouth.

CHOOSING YOUR COURSE (SEE ALSO CH.1)

Some course features
Cardiff Met (UWIC) Course includes a module in bilingual studies which focuses on the needs of multicultural and multilingual groups.
Manchester Met Placements are once weekly or in an eight-week block and may be anywhere in the Manchester region, so temporary accommodation may be needed.
Reading (Sp Lang Thera) Clinics are run on campus in collaboration with the local authority. The course involves the use of computer-assisted analyses of language.
Sheffield (Sp Sci) Course leads to qualification as a speech therapist. (Hum Comm Sci) Focuses on the use of speech and language and how the process fails, for example in autism and dyslexia, but is not a professional qualification in speech therapy.

Universities and colleges teaching quality See www.qaa.ac.uk; http://unistats.direct.gov.uk.

Top research universities and colleges (RAE 2008) (Language and Communication Science) City.

ADMISSIONS INFORMATION

Number of applicants per place (approx) Birmingham City 28; Cardiff Met (UWIC) 10; City 16; De Montfort 5; Edinburgh Queen Margaret 12; London (UCL) 9; Manchester 13; Manchester Met 21; Newcastle 23.

Advice to applicants and planning the UCAS personal statement Contact with speech therapists and visits to their clinics are an essential part of the preparation for this career. Discuss your contacts in full, giving details of any work experience or work shadowing you have done and your interest in helping people to communicate, showing evidence of good 'people skills'. See also **Appendix 3** and

Chapter 6. Manchester Selectors look for some practical experience with individuals who have communication or swallowing difficulties. (International students) Good English required because of placement periods.

Misconceptions about this course Some students fail to differentiate between speech therapy, occupational therapy and physiotherapy. They do not realise that to study speech and language therapy there are academic demands, including the study of linguistics, psychology, medical sciences and clinical dynamics, so the course is intensive. **Cardiff Met (UWIC)** Some are under the impression that good grades are not necessary, that it is an easy option and one has to speak with a standard pronunciation.

Selection interviews Yes Birmingham City, East Anglia, Edinburgh Queen Margaret, Manchester Met, St Mark and St John, Sheffield, Ulster; **No** De Montfort.

Interview advice and questions Have you visited a speech and language therapy clinic? What did you see there? What made you want to become a speech therapist? What type of speech problems are there? What type of person would make a good speech therapist? Interviews often include an ear test (test of listening ability). See also **Chapter 6. Cardiff Met (UWIC)** Interviewees must demonstrate an insight into communication problems and explain how one speech sound is produced.

Reasons for rejection (non-academic) Insufficient knowledge of speech and language therapy. Lack of maturity. Poor communication skills. Written language problems.

AFTER-RESULTS ADVICE
Offers to applicants repeating A-levels Higher Birmingham City, Cardiff Met (UWIC); **Possibly higher** Manchester Met; **Same** City, De Montfort, Newcastle.

GRADUATE DESTINATIONS AND EMPLOYMENT (2011/12 HESA)
Career note Speech therapists work mainly in NHS clinics, some work in hospitals and others in special schools or units for the mentally or physically handicapped. The demand for speech therapists is high.

OTHER DEGREE SUBJECTS FOR CONSIDERATION
Audiology; Communication Studies; Deaf Studies; Education; Health Studies; Linguistics; Psychology.

SPORTS SCIENCES/STUDIES
(see also Leisure and Recreation Management/Studies, Physical Education)

In addition to the theory and practice of many different sporting activities, Sports Sciences/Studies courses also cover the psychological aspects of sports and of sports business administration. The geography, economics and sociology of recreation may also be included. The England and Wales Cricket Board has introduced the Universities Centres of Cricketing Excellence scheme (UCCE). Details can be obtained from the following centres of excellence: Cambridge Centre www.mccuniversities.org/cambridge; Cardiff/Glamorgan Centre www.mccuniversities.org/cardiff-glamorgan; Durham Centre www.mccuniversities.org/durham; Leeds/Bradford Centre www.mccuniversities.org/leeds-bradford; Loughborough Centre www.mccuniversities.org/loughborough; Oxford Centre www.mccuniversities.org/oxford. See also **Appendix 3**.

Useful websites www.uksport.gov.uk; www.laureus.com; www.wsff.org.uk; www.sta.co.uk; www.sportscotland.org.uk; www.thebapa.org.uk; www.planet-science.com.

NB The points totals shown to the left of the institutions are for ease of reference only. It must not be assumed that Tariff points are always used by institutions or that they can be substituted for an offer in grades. The level of an offer is not necessarily indicative of the quality of a course.

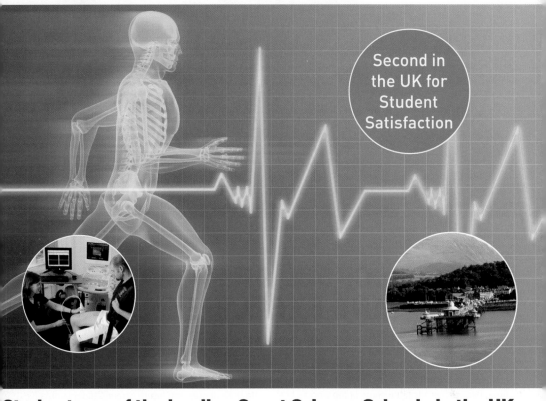

PRIFYSGOL
BANGOR
UNIVERSITY

SCHOOL OF SPORT, HEALTH AND EXERCISE SCIENCES

The School of Sport, Health and Exercise Sciences (SHES) has a 35-year track record of providing high-calibre undergraduate degrees. During this time, Bangor has attracted some of the world's best teaching and research staff who have contributed to the development of one of the UK's truly excellent degree programmes. Ranked **2nd in the UK** for student satisfaction – GPA score 4.4 out of 5 (Complete University Guide 2014).

Learn from the best and be inspired – The School's Extremes Research Group is rapidly gaining a reputation for leading the field of high altitude and extreme physiology and the Institute for the Psychology of Elite Performance (IPEP) is uniquely placed to integrate lessons learnt from business, sport and the military to enhance performance. All this research is directly applicable to the School's undergraduate programmes. For example, students undertaking the Sport Science (Outdoor Activities) degree have the opportunity to put theory into practice in an Expedition module run by staff from the Extremes Research Group and the expertise of IPEP researchers has been instrumental in developing the Sport and Exercise Psychology degree.

Go further with your Bangor degree – All students undertake an Advanced Employability module which offers the opportunity to develop skills relevant to their degree and future career. Students obtain qualifications and complete work experience that is aligned to their post-degree aspirations. This ensures that individuals graduate not only with a degree of the highest calibre but with a CV full of transferable skills that enables them to excel in today's competitive job mark. In addition, Bangor University's Careers and Employability Service is recognised nationally as being one of the most active careers services in the UK.

Sport Science by the sea – The University's location between the mountains of Snowdonia and the Menai Strait and Anglesey – one of the prime university locations in the UK – provides an excellent opportunity for students to enhance their academic work – life balance. The School encourages students to become actively involved in life outside the lecture hall, including joining the many clubs and societies on offer and taking advantage of the surrounding countryside. Free membership of all student clubs and societies is a unique aspect of the Bangor experience.

www.bangor.ac.uk/sport

University *of* Hertfordshire

UH

School of
Life and Medical Sciences

Today's insight – tomorrow's success

With a long and successful reputation for providing a variety of sports focused degrees, we will equip you with up-to-the-minute knowledge in some of the newest and fastest growing subjects. You will learn within state-of-the-art facilities through a winning combination of theory, practice and applied research.

Our expert and research active staff will help you to develop the in-depth knowledge essential to your chosen area – from anatomy, physiology, nutrition and psychology to sports coaching, development and management, injury and rehabilitation. We will also provide you with opportunities to apply your knowledge and gain invaluable real experience via work placements and study abroad.

With excellent graduate employment levels and student satisfaction scores, our range of courses will allow you to specialise in your area of interest. These include:

- BSc (Hons) Sports Studies
- BSc (Hons) Sports and Exercise Science
- BSc (Hons) Hons Sports Therapy

Become more.

Find out more about our range of courses at:

go.herts.ac.uk/sports

COURSE OFFERS INFORMATION

Subject requirements/preferences GCSE English, mathematics and, often, a science subject. **AL** Science required for Sport Science courses. PE required for some Sport Studies courses. **Other** Disclosure and Barring Service (DBS) disclosure required for many courses. Evidence of commitment to sport.

Your target offers and examples of courses provided by each institution

360 pts **Bath** – AAA (Spo Exer Sci) (IB 36 pts)
Birmingham – AAA-AAB 360-340 pts (Spo Exer Sci) (IB 35-36 pts)
Leeds – AAA-ABB 320-360 pts (Spo Exer Sci; Spo Sci Physiol) (IB 35-34 pts HL 18-16 pts)
Loughborough – AAA (Spo Exer Sci) (IB 36 pts)

340 pts **Bangor** – 340-320 pts (Spo Exer Psy) (IB 28 pts)
Bath – AAB (Spo Soc Sci) (IB 35 pts)
Birmingham – AAB (Spo Mat Sci) (IB 35 pts)
Durham – AAB 340 pts (Spo Exer Physl Act) (IB 36 pts)
Exeter – AAB-ABB 320-340 pts (Exer Spo Sci) (IB 34-32 pts)
Glasgow – AAB (Physiol Spo Sci; Physiol Spo Sci Nutr) (IB 34 pts)
Loughborough – AAB (Spo Sci Mgt; Engl Spo Sci; Geog Spo Sci; Spo Soc Sci) (IB 34-36 pts)

320 pts **Bangor** – 320-260 pts (Spo Sci; Spo Hlth PE; Spo Hlth Exer Sci; Spo Sci (Out Act); Spo Sci (PE))
Birmingham – AAB-ABB 320-340 pts (App Glf Mgt St) (IB 34-35 pts)
Bournemouth – 320 pts (Spo Mgt)
Brighton – ABB (Spo Exer Sci; Spo Coach) (IB 34 pts)
Brunel – ABB 320 pts (Spo Hlth Exer Sci (Coach); Spo Hlth Exer Sci (Spo Dev); Spo Hlth Exer Sci; Spo Hlth Exer Sci (Hum Perf)) (IB 33 pts)
Cardiff Met (UWIC) – 320 pts (Spo Exer Sci; Spo Condit Rehab Msg)
Central Lancashire – ABB-BBC (Spo Jrnl) (IB 32 pts)
Kent – ABB (Spo Thera; Spo Sci) (IB 33 pts)
Lincoln – 320 pts (Spo Exer Sci)
Loughborough – ABB (Spo Mgt) (IB 32 pts)
Nottingham Trent – 320 pts (Spo Exer Sci)
Portsmouth – 280-320 pts (Spo Exer Sci) (IB 28 pts)
Swansea – ABB (Phys Spo Sci)
Ulster – ABB (Spo Sci; Spo Exer Sci)

300 pts **Aberdeen** – BBB (Spo Exer Sci; Spo St (Exer Hlth)) (IB 32 pts)
Brighton – BBB 300 pts (Spo Jrnl) (IB 32 pts)
Cardiff Met (UWIC) – 300 pts (Spo PE) (IB 26 pts)
Coventry – BBB 300 pts (Spo Psy) (IB 28 pts)
Dundee – AAB (Spo Biomed) (IB 30 pts)
Essex – 300-340 pts (Spo Exer Sci) (IB 30-28 pts)
Gloucestershire – 300 pts (Spo Dev)
Greenwich – (Spo Sci; Spo Sci Coach)
Huddersfield – BBB 300 pts (Spo Prom Mark)
Kent – BBB (Spo Exer Mgt; Spo Exer Hlth) (IB 33 pts)
Leeds Beckett – 300 pts (Spo courses) (IB 26 pts)
Nottingham Trent – 300 pts (Spo Sci Mgt; Coach Spo Sci) (IB 28 pts)
Sheffield Hallam – 300 pts (Spo Exer Sci; Spo Coach; Physl Actvt Spo Hlth)
Strathclyde – BBB (Spo Physl Actvt) (IB 32 pts)
Swansea – BBB 300 pts (Spo Sci)

280 pts **Aberystwyth** – 280 pts (Spo Exer Sci) (IB 24 pts)
Bournemouth – 280-320 pts (Spo Dev Coach Sci) (IB 30-32 pts)
Bristol UWE – 280-340 pts (Spo Bus Mgt; Spo Thera Rehab)
Central Lancashire – 280-300 pts (Spo Thera; Spo Sci)
East London – 280 pts (Spo Jrnl)

Edge Hill – 280 pts (Spo Thera; Spo Dev; Spo Exer Sci; Spo St)
Edinburgh – BBC 280 pts (App Spo Sci) (IB 33 pts)
Gloucestershire – 280–300 pts (Spo Thera; Spo Sci; Spo Educ)
Hertfordshire – (Spo Exer Sci; Spo St)
Huddersfield – BBC (Spo Jrnl) (IB 28 pts)
Hull – 280 pts (Spo Exer Sci; Psy Spo Sci)
Leeds Beckett – 280 pts (Spo Mark; Spo Physl Actv Hlth) (IB 24–25 pts)
Leeds Trinity – 240–280 pts (Spo Jrnl; Spo Hlth Exer Nutr)
Liverpool John Moores – 280–320 pts (Spo Exer Sci; Sci Ftbl; Coach Dev)
Manchester Met – 280–300 pts (Psy Spo Exer; Spo Mgt; Spo Exer Sci) (IB 28 pts)
Middlesex – 280 pts (Spo Exer Rehab) (IB 28 pts)
Newman – 280 pts (Spo St) (IB 26 pts)
Northumbria – 280–300 pts (Spo Mgt) (IB 25 pts)
Nottingham Trent – 280 pts (Spo Sci Maths)
Oxford Brookes – BBC (Spo Exer Sci) (IB 30 pts)
Portsmouth – 280 pts (Spo Mgt Bus Comm) (IB 25 pts)
Sheffield Hallam – 280 pts (Spo Tech)
South Wales – BBC 280 pts (Spo St; Spo Dev; Spo Psy; Spo Exer Sci; Spo St; Ftbl Coach Perf; Rgby Coach Perf) (IB 25 pts)
Stirling – BBC (Spo St; Exer Sci) (IB 32 pts)
UCFB – 280–300 pts (Spo Bus courses)
Worcester – 280 pts (Spo St; Spo Bus Mgt; Spo Thera) (IB 25–28 pts)
Writtle (Coll) – 280 pts (Spo Exer Perf courses) (IB 24 pts)

260 pts **Birmingham (UC)** – (Spo Thera)
Central Lancashire – 260–300 pts (Spo Psy)
Chester – 260–300 pts (Spo Sci courses; Spo Jrnl; Spo Exer Sci courses) (IB 28 pts)
Chichester – BCC 260–300 pts (Spo courses) (IB 28 pts)
Coventry – BCC (Spo Mark; Spo Mgt; Spo Thera) (IB 28 pts)
Derby – 260–280 pts (Spo Exer Sci; Spo Coach Joint Hons; Spo Dev Joint Hons; Spo Msg Exer Thera Joint Hons; Spo Psy Joint Hons)
Edinburgh – BCC 260 pts (Spo Recr Mgt) (IB 32 pts)
Edinburgh Napier – BCC (Spo Exer Sci (Exer Physiol))
Glasgow Caledonian – BCC (Spo Mgt)
Glyndŵr – 260 pts (Spo Exer Sci)
Kingston – 260–360 pts (Spo Analys Coach)
Liverpool Hope – 260–300 pts (Spo St; Spo Psy) (IB 26 pts)
Northampton – 260–300 pts (Spo St courses)
St Mary's – 260 pts (Spo Sci)
Sheffield Hallam – 260 pts (Spo Bus Mgt)
Sunderland – 260 pts (Spo Exer Dev; Spo Exer Sci; Spo St; Spo Coach; Spo (Comb))
Teesside – 260 pts (Spo Thera; Spo Exer (App Spo Sci); Spo Exer (Coach Sci); Spo Dev; Spo Exer (App Exer Sci); Spo Exer (Spo St))
Ulster – 260 pts (Spo Tech) (IB 24 pts)
Winchester – 260–300 pts (Spo Coach Dev; Spo Mgt)

240 pts **Bedfordshire** – 240 pts (Spo St) (IB 28–30 pts)
Birmingham (UC) – (Spo Mgt)
Bolton – (Spo Exer Sci)
Canterbury Christ Church – 240 pts (Spo Exer Sci courses)
Central Lancashire – 240–280 pts (Spo Evnt Mgt; Advntr Spo Sci)
Cumbria – 240 pts (Spo Exer Thera; Spo St (Spo Physl Actvt Dev); Spo Exer Sci; Coach Spo Dev)
Derby – 240 pts (Spo Exer St)
East London – (Spo Exer Sci; Spo Dev)
Edinburgh Napier – 240–260 pts (Spo Tech; Spo Exer Sci courses)
Glyndŵr – 240–260 pts (Spo Coach)

Hull – 240–280 pts (Spo Coach Perf; Spo Rehab)
Leeds Trinity – 240–280 pts (Spo Psy) (IB 24 pts)
Manchester Met – 240–280 pts (Spo Mark Mgt; Spo Dev; Coach St; Coach St Spo Dev) (IB 28 pts)
Nottingham Trent – 240 pts (Eqn Spo Sci) (IB 29 pts)
Robert Gordon – CCC 240 pts (App Spo Exer Sci) (IB 26 pts)
Roehampton – 240–280 pts (Spo Sci; Spo Exer Sci)
St Mark and St John – 240 pts (Spo Thera; App Spo Sci Coach)
St Mary's – 240 pts (Spo Coach Sci; Spo Rehab; Strg Condit Sci) (IB 28 pts)
Salford – 240–280 pts (Spo Sci)
Southampton Solent – 240 pts (Spo St Bus)
Staffordshire – 240 pts (Spo St; Spo Exer Sci)
West Scotland – CCC (Spo Exer Sci; Spo Jrnl) (IB 24 pts)
Wolverhampton – (Spo Coach; Spo St)

220 pts **Kingston** – 220–360 pts (Spo Sci)
London Met – 220 pts (Spo Sci)
Myerscough (Coll) – 220 pts (Spotrf Sci Mgt)
St Mark and St John – 220 pts (Spo Dev; Out Advntr Educ)
Warwickshire (Coll) – 220 pts (Eqn Hum Spo Sci)
York St John – 220–260 pts (Spo Soty Dev; Spo Sci Perf Condit; Spo Sci Injry Mgt)

200 pts **Anglia Ruskin** – 200 pts (Spo Sci) (IB 24 pts)
Bedfordshire – (Ftbl St; Spo Jrnl)
Bishop Burton (Coll) – 200 pts (Spo Coach Dev Fit)
Bucks New – 200–240 pts (Spo Mgt Ftbl St)
Chester – 200–240 pts IB 24 pts (Spo Dev)
Doncaster (Coll Univ Centre) – 200 pts (Spo Fit Hlth Sci)
Farnborough (CT) – 200 pts (Spo Sci (Hum Perf))
London South Bank – (Spo Exer Sci)
Middlesex – 200–300 pts (Spo Exer Sci)
South Essex (Coll) – 200 pts (Spo St) (IB 24 pts)
Suffolk (Univ Campus) – 200–240 pts (Spo Exer Sci)
Wolverhampton – (Spo Mgt)

180 pts **Lincoln (Coll)** – (Golf Sci Dev)
Trinity Saint David – 180–360 pts (Hlth Exer Spo St) (IB 26 pts)

160 pts **Abertay** – CC 160 pts (Spo Exer)
Trinity Saint David (Swansea) – 160 pts (Spo Mgt)

140 pts **Sir Gâr (Coll)** – 140 pts (Spo Coach Perf)

120 pts **Colchester (Inst)** – 120 pts (Mgt Spo)

Alternative offers

See **Chapter 7** and **Appendix 1** for grades/UCAS Tariff points information for the International Baccalaureate, Scottish Highers/Advanced Highers, the Welsh Baccalaureate, the Irish Leaving Certificate, the Cambridge Pre-U Diploma, the Advanced Diploma and the Extended Project.

EXAMPLES OF FOUNDATION DEGREES IN THE SUBJECT FIELD

Accrington and Rossendale (Coll); Anglia Ruskin; Arts London; Barnet and Southgate (Coll); Bath; Bedford (Coll); Bedfordshire; Birmingham (UC); Bishop Burton (Coll); Blackburn (Coll); Blackpool and Fylde (Coll); Bolton; Bournemouth; Brighton; Bristol UWE; Central Lancashire; Central Nottingham (Coll); Chichester; Colchester (Inst); Cornwall (Coll); Cumbria; Dearne Valley (Coll); Duchy (Coll); Durham New (Coll); East Riding (Coll); Easton Otley (Coll); Exeter (Coll); Farnborough (CT); Gloucestershire; Greenwich; Grimsby (Univ Centre); Hertfordshire; Hopwood Hall (Coll); Hull (Coll); Kingston (Coll); Leeds City (Coll); Leeds Beckett; Lincoln (Coll); Llandrillo Cymru (Coll); London Met; London South Bank; Loughborough (Coll); Macclesfield (Coll); Manchester (Coll); Mid-Cheshire (Coll); Middlesex; Myerscough (Coll); Nescot; Newcastle (Coll); North Lindsey (Coll); Northampton; Norwich City (Coll); Oxford Brookes; Pembrokeshire (Coll); Petroc; Plumpton (Coll); Plymouth; Roehampton;

St Mark and St John; St Mary's; Sheffield (Coll); Sir Gâr (Coll); South Cheshire (Coll); Staffordshire; Stamford New (Coll); Suffolk (Univ Campus); Swindon (Coll); Tameside (Coll); Teesside; Tottenham Hotspur (Fdn); Truro (Coll); Wakefield (Coll); Warwickshire (Coll); West Cheshire (Coll); Wigan and Leigh (Coll); Wolverhampton; Worcester (CT); York (Coll).

CHOOSING YOUR COURSE (SEE ALSO CH.1)

Some course features

Birmingham (Spo Mat Sci) This course focuses on the design and materials used in the manufacture of sports equipment. Research placements are offered during summer vacations.

Brighton (Spo Jrnl) A placement project takes place in the final year. The course is accredited by the National Council for the Training of Journalists.

Brunel After a common first year, students select their preferred specialisation in administration, coaching, exercise and fitness, physical education or a multi-disciplinary route.

Leeds (Spo Sci Physiol) The course covers various medical issues involved in sport such as drugs, the biochemistry of exercise, and the physiology of elite performance. There is an opportunity to gain coaching qualifications.

Loughborough The University has a national and international reputation in sport, leisure management and physical education.

Middlesex (Spo Exer Rehab) The course involves the study of human anatomy and physiology, disabilities of the physically active, the progression of and precautions against injuries.

Universities and colleges teaching quality See www.qaa.ac.uk; http://unistats.direct.gov.uk.

Top research universities and colleges (RAE 2008) (Sports-related studies) Birmingham; Loughborough; Bristol; Liverpool John Moores; Stirling; Bath; Leeds Beckett; Brunel; Bangor; Exeter; Leeds.

Examples of sandwich degree courses Bath; Bournemouth; Brighton; Brunel; Cardiff Met (UWIC); Central Lancashire; Chichester; Coventry; Gloucestershire; Hertfordshire; Huddersfield; Kingston; Leeds; Leeds Beckett; Loughborough; Manchester Met; Nottingham Trent; Plymouth; Salford; Sheffield Hallam; Sunderland; Trinity Saint David (Swansea); Ulster.

ADMISSIONS INFORMATION

Number of applicants per place (approx) Aberystwyth 5; Bangor 15; Bath (Coach Educ Spo Dev) 8; Birmingham 7; Brunel 6; Canterbury Christ Church 30; Cardiff Met (UWIC) 10; Chichester 4; Cumbria 14, (Spo St) 6; Durham 6; Edinburgh 11; Exeter 23; Gloucestershire 8; Kingston 13; Leeds 25; Leeds Trinity 35; Liverpool John Moores 4; Loughborough 20; Manchester Met 16; Northampton 4; Northumbria 30; Nottingham Trent 8; Portsmouth 12; Roehampton 8; St Mary's 4; Salford 30; Sheffield Hallam 7; South Essex (Coll) 1; Southampton 8; Staffordshire 12; Stirling 10; Strathclyde 28; Sunderland 2; Swansea 6; Teesside 15; Winchester 5; Wolverhampton 4; Worcester 10; York St John 4.

Advice to applicants and planning the UCAS personal statement See also **Physical Education** and **Appendix 3**. **Cardiff Met (UWIC)** A strong personal statement required which clearly identifies current performance profile and indicates a balanced lifestyle. **Salford** Previous experience in a sporting environment will be noted. Previous study is preferred in biology/human biology, physics, chemistry, physical education/sports studies. Psychology is preferred. (Coach Sci) For these courses applicants must have proven coaching skills to gain a place. (Spo Sci) These are laboratory-based courses examining the physical stress of sport on the human body. A sound scientific aptitude is required. Although professional sporting qualifications and high level practical experience cannot take the place of scientific entry qualifications, they will be considered in any borderline applicants holding a conditional offer. Comment on any coaching or competitive experience.

Misconceptions about this course **Bath** (Spo Exer Sci) This is not a sports course with a high component of practical sport: it is a science programme with minimal practical sport. (Coach Educ Spo Dev) This is not necessarily a course for elite athletes. **Birmingham** (App Glf Mgt St) Applicants do not appreciate the academic depth required across key areas (it is, in a sense, a multiple Honours course – business management, sports science, coaching theory, materials science). **Sheffield Hallam**

(Spo Tech) Some applicants expect an engineering course! **Swansea** (Spo Sci) Applicants underestimate the quantity of maths on the course. Many applicants are uncertain about the differences between Sports Studies and Sports Science.

Selection interviews **Yes** Essex, Leeds, Nottingham Trent, Sheffield Hallam, Stirling, West Scotland; **Some** Anglia Ruskin, Bath, Cardiff Met (UWIC), Chichester, Cumbria, Derby, Durham, East Anglia, Leeds Trinity, Liverpool John Moores, Roehampton, St Mary's, Salford, Sheffield Hallam, Staffordshire, Wolverhampton; **No** Birmingham, Edinburgh.

Interview advice and questions Applicants' interests in sport and their sporting activities are likely to be discussed at length. Past questions include: How do you strike a balance between sport and academic work? How many, and which, sports do you coach? For how long? Have you devised your own coaching programme? What age range do you coach? Do you coach unsupervised? See also **Chapter 6**. **Loughborough** A high level of sporting achievement is expected

Reasons for rejection (non-academic) Not genuinely interested in outdoor activities. Poor sporting background or knowledge. Personal appearance. Inability to apply their science to their specialist sport. Illiteracy. Using the course as a second option to physiotherapy. Arrogance. Expectation that they will be playing sport all day. When the course is explained to them some applicants realise that a more arts-based course would be more appropriate.

AFTER-RESULTS ADVICE
Offers to applicants repeating A-levels **Higher** Swansea; **Same** Cardiff Met (UWIC), Chichester, Derby, Dundee, Lincoln, Liverpool John Moores, Loughborough, Plymouth, Roehampton, St Mary's, Salford, Sheffield Hallam, Staffordshire, Stirling, Sunderland, Winchester, Wolverhampton, York St John.

GRADUATE DESTINATIONS AND EMPLOYMENT (2011/12 HESA)
Graduates surveyed 8460 **Employed** 3650 **In voluntary employment** 255 **In further study** 2160 **Assumed unemployed** 470

Career note Career options include sport development, coaching, teaching, outdoor centres, sports equipment development, sales, recreation management and professional sport.

OTHER DEGREE SUBJECTS FOR CONSIDERATION
Anatomy; Biology; Human Movement Studies; Leisure and Recreation Management; Nutrition; Physical Education; Physiology; Physiotherapy; Sports Equipment Product Design.

STATISTICS
(see also **Economics, Mathematics**)

Statistics has mathematical underpinnings but is primarily concerned with the collection, interpretation and analysis of data. Statistics are used to analyse and solve problems in a wide range of areas, particularly in the scientific, business, government and public services.

Useful websites www.rss.org.uk; www.statistics.gov.uk.

NB The points totals shown to the left of the institutions are for ease of reference only. It must not be assumed that Tariff points are always used by institutions or that they can be substituted for an offer in grades. The level of an offer is not necessarily indicative of the quality of a course.

COURSE OFFERS INFORMATION
Subject requirements/preferences **GCSE** English and mathematics. **AL** Mathematics required for all courses.

Your target offers and examples of courses provided by each institution
400 pts **Imperial London** – A*A*A (Maths Stats; Maths Stats Fin; Maths Optim Stats) (IB 39 pts HL 7 maths)

London (UCL) – A*AAe-AAAe (Stats Sci; Stats Mgt Bus; Stats; Stats Econ Fin) (IB 38–39 pts HL 18–19 pts 7 maths)

Oxford – A*A*A (Maths Stats) (IB 39 pts HL 7 maths)

380 pts **Bath** – A*AA (Stats) (IB 39 pts HL 6 maths)

Warwick – A*AA (MORSE (Act Fin Maths)) (IB 37 pts HL 7 maths)

360 pts **Birmingham** – AAA incl maths (Mathem Econ Stats) (IB 36–38 pts HL 6 maths)

City – AAA 360 pts (Mathem Sci Stats) (IB 32 pts)

Edinburgh – AAA-ABB 360-320 pts (Maths Stats) (IB 37-32 pts)

Glasgow – AAA-A*AB (Fin Stats) (IB 36 pts)

Lancaster – AAA (Stats; Stats (St Abrd)) (IB 36 pts)

Leeds – AAA-A*AB (Maths Stats) (IB 35 pts HL 6 maths)

London (QM) – 360 pts (Maths Stats MSci) (IB 34 pts HL 6 maths)

London LSE – AAA (Stats Fin; Bus Maths Stats) (IB 38 pts)

Manchester – A*AA-AAA (Maths Stats) (IB 37 pts HL 6 maths)

Queen's Belfast – A*AB-AAA (Maths Stats OR MSci) (IB 34 pts)

St Andrews – AAA (Stats) (IB 36 pts)

Southampton – AAA (Maths OR Stats Econ; Maths Stats) (IB 36 pts)

York – AAA (Maths Stats)

340 pts **Cardiff** – AAB 340 pts (Maths OR Stats) (IB 33 pts)

East Anglia – A maths AB (Bus Stats) (IB 32 pts HL 6 maths)

Glasgow – AAB (Stats) (IB 34 pts)

Lancaster – AAB (Psy Stats) (IB 35 pts)

London (QM) – 340 pts (Maths Stats) (IB 34 pts HL 6 maths)

Newcastle – AAB (Maths Stats; Stats Mgt; Stats) (IB 34-36 pts HL 6 maths)

Surrey – AAB 340 pts (Maths Stats) (IB 35 pts)

320 pts **Aberystwyth** – 280-320 pts (App Maths PMaths) (IB 28 pts)

Brunel – ABB 320 pts (Maths Stats Mgt) (IB 33 pts)

Heriot-Watt – ABB (Comb St (Stats); Stats Modl)

Kent – ABB (Maths Stats) (IB 33 pts)

Liverpool – ABB (Maths Stats) (IB 33 pts HL 6 maths)

London (RH) – ABB (Maths Stats) (IB 33 pts HL 6 maths)

Plymouth – 320 pts (Maths Stats) (IB 30 pts)

Queen's Belfast – ABB (Maths Stats OR) (IB 33 pts)

Reading – 320-340 pts (Maths App Stats; Maths Stats Comput Maths)

300 pts **Bristol UWE** – 300 pts (Stats) (IB 26-28 pts)

Greenwich – 300 pts (Stats) (IB 25 pts)

Strathclyde – BBB (Maths Stats Econ; Maths Stats) (IB 32 pts)

280 pts **Kingston** – 280 pts (Act Maths Stats; Stats Bus)

Staffordshire – 280 pts (Maths Stats) (IB 24 pts)

260 pts **Portsmouth** – 260-300 pts (Maths Stats) (IB 26 pts)

240 pts **Coventry** – CCC 240 pts (Maths Stats) (IB 27 pts)

200 pts **London Met** – 200 pts (Maths Stats) (IB 28 pts)

80 pts **London (Birk)** – p/t, for under 21s (over 21s varies) (Maths Stats; Stats Econ; Stats Mgt)

Alternative offers

See **Chapter 7** and **Appendix 1** for grades/UCAS Tariff points information for the International Baccalaureate, Scottish Highers/Advanced Highers, the Welsh Baccalaureate, the Irish Leaving Certificate, the Cambridge Pre-U Diploma, the Advanced Diploma and the Extended Project.

CHOOSING YOUR COURSE (SEE ALSO CH.1)

Some course features

Birmingham (Math Econ Stats) An integrated course covering the study of economics from a mathematical perspective including IT and computer skills.

Kingston (Maths Stats courses) An optional professional placement year is offered to students.

Warwick (MORSE) Course has a statistics specialisation in Years 3 and 4 of the BSc and MMORSE courses.

Universities and colleges teaching quality See www.qaa.ac.uk; http://unistats.direct.gov.uk.

Top research universities and colleges (RAE 2008) (Statistics and Operational Research) Oxford; Imperial London; Bristol; Warwick; Leeds; Kent; Southampton; Lancaster.

Examples of sandwich degree courses Bath; Bristol UWE; Brunel; Cardiff; Coventry; Kent; Kingston; Portsmouth; Reading; Staffordshire; Surrey.

ADMISSIONS INFORMATION
Number of applicants per place (approx) Bath 10; Coventry 3; East London 3; Heriot-Watt 6; Lancaster 11; Liverpool John Moores 6; London (UCL) 9; London LSE 9; Newcastle 5; Southampton 10; York 5.

Advice to applicants and planning the UCAS personal statement Love mathematics, don't expect an easy life. See also **Mathematics** and **Appendix 3**.

Selection interviews Yes Bath, Birmingham, Liverpool, London (UCL), Newcastle; **Some** East Anglia, Greenwich; **No** Reading.

Interview advice and questions Questions could be asked on your A-level syllabus (particularly in mathematics). Applicants' knowledge of statistics and their interest in the subject are likely to be tested, together with their awareness of the application of statistics in commerce and industry. See also **Chapter 6**.

AFTER-RESULTS ADVICE
Offers to applicants repeating A-levels Higher Kent, Leeds, Liverpool, Liverpool John Moores, Newcastle, **Same** Birmingham.

GRADUATE DESTINATIONS AND EMPLOYMENT (2011/12 HESA)
Graduates surveyed 335 **Employed** 175 **In voluntary employment** 5 **In further study** 90 **Assumed unemployed** 25

Career note See **Mathematics**.

OTHER DEGREE SUBJECTS FOR CONSIDERATION
Accountancy; Actuarial Sciences; Business Information Technology; Business Studies; Computer Science; Economics; Financial Services; Mathematical Studies; Mathematics.

SURVEYING

(including **Building** and **Quantity Surveying** and **Property Management/Development. For Financial Investment in Property see under Finance**; see also **Agricultural Sciences/Agriculture, Building and Construction, Housing, Town and Country Planning**)

Surveying covers a very diverse range of careers and courses and following a Royal Institution of Chartered Surveyors (RICS) accredited course is the accepted way to become a Chartered Surveyor. There are three main specialisms, which involve the Built Environment (Building Surveying, Project Management and Quantity Surveying); Land Surveying (Rural, Planning, Environmental, Minerals and Waste Management); Property Surveying (Commercial and Residential Property and Valuation, Facilities Management, Arts and Antiques). Student membership of the RICS is possible. Not all the courses listed below receive RICS accreditation; check with the university or college prior to applying.

Useful websites www.rics.org/ru/join/student; www.cstt.org.uk.

REAL ESTATE AND CONSTRUCTION

A firm foundation for a long-lasting and rewarding career

OXFORD
BROOKES
UNIVERSITY

The Department of Real Estate and Construction at Oxford Brookes University is one of the largest of its kind in the UK and has offered programmes in real estate and construction for more than four decades.

The department's undergraduate and postgraduate programmes are consistently ranked as excellent in both student surveys and independent quality assessments.

The aim is to prepare students for rewarding careers through strong links with industry and staff whose teaching is underpinned by professional/consultancy work. Graduates are highly sought after both nationally and internationally.

Construction Project Management BSc (Hons)

Quantity Surveying and Commercial Management BSc (Hons)

Real Estate Management BSc (Hons)

/OBUrealestateconstruction

@OBU_REC

query@brookes.ac.uk

tde.bz/rec-heap

NB The points totals shown to the left of the institutions are for ease of reference only. It must not be assumed that Tariff points are always used by institutions or that they can be substituted for an offer in grades. The level of an offer is not necessarily indicative of the quality of a course.

COURSE OFFERS INFORMATION

Subject requirements/preferences GCSE English and mathematics grade A–C. **AL** No subjects specified; mathematics useful.

Your target offers and examples of courses provided by each institution

380 pts **Cambridge** – A*AA (Lnd Econ) (IB 40–41 pts HL 776)

340 pts **Reading** – AAB (Rl Est)

320 pts **Newcastle** – ABB–BBB 320–300 pts (Surv Map Sci) (IB 32–34 pts HL 5 maths)
Northumbria – 320 pts (Plan Rl Est Dev)
Oxford Brookes – ABB–BBB 320–300 pts (Rl Est Mgt) (IB 32–33 pts)
Reading – ABB/AAC 320 pts (Bld Surv; Quant Surv) (IB 32 pts)
Ulster – 320 pts (Quant Surv)

300 pts **Aberdeen** – BBB (Rl Est Mgt)
Brighton – BBB 300 pts (Bld Surv) (IB 32 pts)
Bristol UWE – 300 pts (Bld Surv; Rl Est)
Heriot-Watt – BBB 300 pts (Plan Prop Dev)
Kingston – 300 pts (Rl Est Mgt; Prop Plan Dev)
Loughborough – 300 pts (Commer Mgt Quant Surv) (IB 32 pts)
Northumbria – 300 pts (Bld Surv; Quant Surv)
Plymouth – BBB 300 pts (Bld Surv Env; Ocn Explor) (IB 28–30 pts)
Ulster – 300 pts (Bld Surv) (IB 25–32 pts)

285 pts **Glasgow Caledonian** – 285 pts (Bld Surv)

Check **Chapter 4** when choosing your university and **Chapter 7** on how to read the subject tables.

Manage your future with undergraduate study at Ulster...

Fees only £6000 for GB Students

Top 20 University for UCAS applications

Largest University on the island of Ireland

Professional Accreditation

Housing Management

Apply Now!

Professional Education for a Professional Future

adbe.ulster.ac.uk

study.ulster.ac.uk

University of ULSTER

Your future, make it happen

HOUSING MANAGEMENT AT ULSTER

BSc Hons

Have you considered studying Housing Management at Ulster? The university is based in Belfast, the most student friendly city in the UK, with some of the best value student accommodation, a vibrant nightlife and only one hour away from most major cities in Great Britain.

Are you concerned with the overall well-being of society, the economy and the environment? Are you interested in Sustainability, Social Policy, Planning and Regeneration?

Yes? Then come and study Housing Management at Ulster.

Housing management takes many forms, from giving advice to homeless people on how they can go about getting a house, to collecting rents, assessing repairs on a house, allocating houses to tenants and even to running a multi-million pound organisation responsible for thousands of houses in one area.

There have been many changes in the housing sector over the last few years - growing owner occupation, the rise in homelessness and repossessions, the increasing importance of housing associations, the growth of tenant managed housing and recently, a recognition that housing professionals need to work with other public services to regenerate the communities in which people live.

The overall aim of the course is to produce graduates with the skills and knowledge to pursue a career in housing and other linked areas of activity to a high professional standard. The course will show how housing management affects the individual in society, and how a grounding in the built environment can be used to encourage a critical understanding of housing needs and the formulation and implementation of policy. By means of research, practical placements and dialogue with practitioners, the course aims to improve professional practice and in doing so, serve the needs of the community.

Students completing the degree will be exempt from the academic requirements for professional membership of the Chartered Institute of Housing and are therefore eligible for positions in the housing profession.

On completion of the programme, professionals are prepared for a career in an environment encompassing the administrative, financial and technical aspects of housing, in local authorities and other public sector housing organisations, housing associations and private sector housing organisations.

Northern Ireland has the largest social housing provision in Western Europe and changes to local government make it the perfect place to study Housing Management in the UK.

Visit **study.ulster.ac.uk** for more information including entry requirements.

We hope to see you on the Housing Management course at Ulster soon.

University of ULSTER

Your future, make it happen

UCAS
BSc Hons Housing Management   K450

280 pts **Birmingham City** – 280 pts (Quant Surv; Rl Est Mgt; Bld Surv)
Bristol UWE – 280 pts (Quant Surv Commer Mgt; Prop Inv Mgt) (IB 24–28 pts)
Kingston – 280–300 pts (Bld Surv; Art Mark)
Leeds Beckett – 280 pts (Bld Surv; Quant Surv) (IB 25 pts)
Northumbria – 280 pts (Commer Quant Surv) (IB 25 pts)
Nottingham Trent – 280 pts (Rl Est; Bld Surv; Quant Surv Constr Commer Mgt)
Oxford Brookes – BBC–BCC 280–260 pts (Quant Surv Commer Mgt; Cnstr Proj Mgt; Plan Prop Dev) (IB 30–31 pts)
Royal Agricultural Univ – 280–300 pts (Prop Agncy Mgt)
Sheffield Hallam – BBC 280 pts (Bld Surv; Quant Surv)
Westminster – BBC 280 pts (Bld Surv; Quant Surv; Bus Prop; Rl Est) (IB 26–28 pts)
270 pts **Anglia Ruskin** – 270 pts (Bld Surv; Quant Surv; Rl Est Mgt)
Glasgow Caledonian – 270 pts (Quant Surv)
Liverpool John Moores – 270 pts (Quant Surv; Rl Est Mgt courses; Bld Surv)
Portsmouth – 270–300 pts (Prop Dev; Quant Surv)
260 pts **Coventry** – BCC 260 pts (Bld Surv) (IB 29 pts)
Greenwich – 260 pts (Quant Surv)
Salford – 260–300 pts (Bld Surv; Quant Surv)
South Wales – BCC (Quant Surv Commer Mgt))
240 pts **Bolton** – 240 pts (Bld Surv Prop Mgt)
Central Lancashire – 240 pts (Quant Surv; Bld Surv)
Coventry – 240 pts (Quant Surv Commer Mgt)
East London – 240 pts (Civ Eng Surv Surv Map Sci; Surv Map Sci)
Edinburgh Napier – CCC 240 pts (Prop Dev Val; Quant Surv)
Harper Adams – CCC–BCC 240–260 pts (Rur Prop Mgt)
Nottingham Trent – 240 pts (Quant Surv) (IB 28 pts)
Plymouth – 240 pts (Env Constr Surv) (IB 24 pts)
Robert Gordon – CCC–BBB 240–300 pts (Surv (Quant Surv))
Wolverhampton – CCC (Bld Surv) (IB 26 pts)
230 pts **CEM** – 230 pts (Bld Serv Quant Surv; Bld Surv; Est Mgt; Quant Surv)
220 pts **Derby** – 220–300 pts (Prop Dev Joint Hons)
London South Bank – 220 pts (Commer Mgt (Quant Surv); Bld Surv)
200 pts **Wolverhampton** – 200 pts (Quant Surv)
160 pts **Trinity Saint David (Swansea)** – 160 pts (Quant Surv)

Alternative offers
See **Chapter 7** and **Appendix 1** for grades/UCAS Tariff points information for the International Baccalaureate, Scottish Highers/Advanced Highers, the Welsh Baccalaureate, the Irish Leaving Certificate, the Cambridge Pre-U Diploma, the Advanced Diploma and the Extended Project.

EXAMPLES OF FOUNDATION DEGREES IN THE SUBJECT FIELD
Bolton.

CHOOSING YOUR COURSE (SEE ALSO CH.1)
Some course features
Anglia Ruskin (Quant Surv) The course shares many common themes with the Building Surveying course but also focuses on management practice, project management and procurement.
Kingston (Prop Plan Dev) The course involves the study of economics, law and business.
Loughborough (Commer Mgt Quant Surv) Accredited by the RICS. Sponsorship is a condition of entry to the course. All suitable applicants are interviewed by the sponsors.
Northumbria (Bld Surv) The course focuses on buildings in use, looking at maintenance, alteration, repair, refurbishment and restoration of existing buildings and also new buildings.
Portsmouth (Prop Dev) A study of small housing to large major property development projects. The final year involves fieldwork in Europe studying major built environment projects.

For a quick reference offers calculator, fold out the inside front cover.

Robert Gordon Common first years for Building and Quantity Surveying students who make a final choice of subject at the beginning of Year 2. This is a feature of other universities, eg Edinburgh Napier.

Universities and colleges teaching quality See www.qaa.ac.uk; http://unistats.direct.gov.uk. Check on RICS accreditation.

Examples of sandwich degree courses Bristol UWE; Central Lancashire; Coventry; Glasgow Caledonian; Kingston; Leeds Beckett; Liverpool John Moores; London South Bank; Loughborough; Northampton; Northumbria; Nottingham Trent; Oxford Brookes; Sheffield Hallam; Ulster; Wolverhampton.

ADMISSIONS INFORMATION

Number of applicants per place (approx) Anglia Ruskin 2; Birmingham City 4; Cambridge 3; Edinburgh Napier 12; Glasgow Caledonian 3; Glyndŵr 3; Greenwich 8; Harper Adams 4; Kingston (Quant Surv) 1, (Prop) 22; Liverpool John Moores (Quant Surv) 10, (Prop) 15; London South Bank 2; Loughborough 9; Northumbria (Quant Surv) 17, (Prop) 17; Nottingham Trent (Quant Surv) 10, (Prop) 3; Oxford Brookes (Quant Surv) 4, (Prop) 5; Portsmouth 5; Robert Gordon 5; Royal Agricultural Univ 3; Salford (Quant Surv) 6, (Prop) 3; Sheffield Hallam (Quant Surv) 7, (Prop) 5; Westminster 10; Wolverhampton 6.

Admissions tutors' advice **Nottingham Trent** Candidates should demonstrate that they have researched the employment opportunities in the property and construction sectors.

Advice to applicants and planning the UCAS personal statement Surveyors work with architects and builders as well as in their own consultancies dealing with commercial and residential property. Work experience with various firms is strongly recommended depending on the type of surveying speciality preferred. Read surveying magazines. **Cambridge** Statements should be customised to the overall interests of students, not to the Land Economy Tripos specifically. **Oxford Brookes** Apply early. Applicants should be reflective. We are looking for at least 50%–60% of the personal statement to cover issues surrounding why they want to do the course, what motivates them about the subject, how they have developed their interest, how their A-levels have helped them and what they have gained from any work experience. Extra-curricular activities are useful but should not dominate the statement.

Misconceptions about this course Students underestimate the need for numerical competence.

Selection interviews **Yes** Birmingham City, Cambridge, Glasgow Caledonian, Harper Adams, Heriot-Watt, Kingston, Loughborough, Oxford Brookes, Royal Agricultural Univ, South Wales, Ulster; **Some** Anglia Ruskin, East London, Robert Gordon, Salford; **No** Edinburgh Napier, Liverpool John Moores, Nottingham Trent.

Interview advice and questions What types of work are undertaken by surveyors? How do you qualify? What did you learn on your work experience? See also **Chapter 6**. **Cambridge** (Land Econ) Questions on subsidies and the euro and economics. Who owns London? How important is the modern day church in town planning? How important are natural resources to a country? Is it more important to focus on poverty at home or abroad? Is the environment a bigger crisis than poverty? Do you think that getting involved with poverty abroad is interfering with others 'freedoms'? (The questions were based on information given in the personal statement.) Students sit a thinking test and a written exam. **Oxford Brookes** Interviews for applicants who are likely to be offered a place. Telephone interviews for those who cannot attend. Group exercise at interview. No offers without an interview.

Reasons for rejection (non-academic) Inability to communicate. Lack of motivation. Indecisiveness about reasons for choosing the course. **Loughborough** Applicants more suited to a practical type of course rather than an academic one. **Nottingham Trent** Incoherent and badly written application forms.

Check **Chapter 4** when choosing your university and **Chapter 7** on how to read the subject tables.

AFTER-RESULTS ADVICE

Offers to applicants repeating A-levels **Higher** Bolton, Nottingham Trent; **Possibly higher** Liverpool John Moores; **Same** Abertay, Coventry, Edinburgh Napier, Oxford Brookes, Portsmouth, Robert Gordon, Salford.

GRADUATE DESTINATIONS AND EMPLOYMENT (2011/12 HESA)

Career note See **Building and Construction**.

OTHER DEGREE SUBJECTS FOR CONSIDERATION

Architecture; Building and Construction; Civil Engineering; Estate Management; Town Planning; Urban Studies.

TEACHER TRAINING

(see also **Education Studies, Social Sciences/Studies**)

Abbreviations used in this table: ITE – Initial Teacher Education; ITT – Initial Teacher Training; P – Primary Teaching; QTS – Qualified Teacher Status; S – Secondary Teaching; STQ – Scottish Teaching Qualification.

Teacher training courses are offered in the following subject areas: Art and Design (P); Biology (P S); Business Studies (S); Chemistry (P S); Childhood (P); Computer Education (P); Creative and Performing Arts (P); Dance (P S); Design and Technology (P S); Drama (P S); English (P S); Environmental Science (P S); Environmental Studies (P); French (P S); General Primary; Geography (P S); History (P S); Maths (P S); Music (P S); Physical Education/Movement Studies (P S); Religious Studies (P); Science (P S); Sociology (P); Textile Design (P); Welsh (P).

For further information on teaching as a career see websites below and **Appendix 3** for contact details. Over 50 taster courses are offered each year to those considering teaching as a career. Early Childhood Studies has been introduced in recent years by a number of universities. The courses focus on child development, from birth to eight years of age, and the provision of education for children and their families. It is a multi-disciplinary subject and can cover social problems and legal and psychological issues. Note that many institutions listed below also offer one-year Postgraduate Certificate in Education (PGCE) courses which qualify graduates to teach other subjects.

Useful websites www.gtcs.org.uk; www.gttr.ac.uk; teachertrainingcymru.org; www.education.gov.uk.

NB The points totals shown to the left of the institutions are for ease of reference only. It must not be assumed that Tariff points are always used by institutions or that they can be substituted for an offer in grades. The level of an offer is not necessarily indicative of the quality of a course.

COURSE OFFERS INFORMATION

Subject requirements/preferences See **Education Studies**.

Your target offers and examples of courses provided by each institution
360 pts **Loughborough** – AAA–AAB (Maths Maths Educ) (IB 36 pts)
340 pts **Stranmillis (UC)** – AAB (P Educ)
　　　　Strathclyde – ABB (Chem Teach) (IB 34 pts)
320 pts **Bristol UWE** – 320 pts (P ITE; P Educ BA ITT)
　　　　Durham – ABB 320 pts (P Educ) (IB 34 pts)
　　　　Edge Hill – 320 pts (P/S Educ courses)
　　　　Essex – ABB–BBB (Maths S Teach)
　　　　Stranmillis (UC) – ABB +interview (Relig St Educ)
　　　　Strathclyde – ABB (Chem Teach; P Educ)

300 pts **Aberdeen** – BBB 300 pts (P Educ) (IB 30 pts)
Birmingham City – 300 pts (Educ P QTS)
Brighton – BBB (P Educ) (IB 32 pts)
Canterbury Christ Church – 300 pts (P Educ QTS)
Chichester – BBB (P Educ Teach) (IB 30 pts)
Glasgow – BBB (Relig Phil Educ; Educ P QTS) (IB 32 pts)
Hertfordshire – 300 pts (Educ P BEd QTS)
Liverpool Hope – 300–320 pts (P Educ QTS)
Liverpool John Moores – 300 pts (P Educ)
Middlesex – 300 pts (P Educ QTS)
Roehampton – 300–360 pts (P Educ QTS; P Educ (Mus); P Educ (Maths))
Sheffield Hallam – 300 pts (P Educ)
Sunderland – 300 pts (P Educ)
Winchester – 300–340 pts (P Educ Geog)
Worcester – 300 pts (P ITE)
York St John – 300 pts (Educ P)

280 pts **Bishop Grosseteste** – 280 pts (P Educ BA QTS)
Canterbury Christ Church – 280 pts (Maths Educ QTS)
Chester – 280–300 pts (Teach Trg P Ely Yrs QTS) (IB 28 pts)
Chichester – BBC (Maths Teach KS 2+3) (IB 28 pts)
Cumbria – 280 pts (P Educ BA QTS; Ely Yrs Educ QTS)
Derby – 280 pts (Educ BEd)
Gloucestershire – 280 pts (P Educ BEd QTS)
Liverpool John Moores – 280–300 pts (Educ St (P))
London (RAc Dance) – 280 pts (Ballet Educ)
Manchester Met – BBC (P Ed) (IB 29 pts)
Newman – 280 pts (P Educ Arts QTS)
Northampton – 280–320 pts (Ely Yrs Educ QTS; P Educ QTS)
Northumbria – 280 pts (P Teach; Educ P)
Nottingham Trent – BBC (P Educ QTS)
Oxford Brookes – BBC (P Teach Educ) (IB 30 pts)
Plymouth – (P PE) (IB 26 pts)
Reading – 280 pts (P Educ courses)
St Mark and St John – 280 pts (S Educ PE QTS)
South Wales – 280 pts (P Teach St BA QTS; S Teach Des Tech)
West Scotland – BBC (Educ)
Winchester – 280–340 pts (P Educ QTS)
Wolverhampton – 280 pts (P BEd)

260 pts **Bedfordshire** – 260 pts (PE S)
Cardiff Met (UWIC) – 260 pts (S Educ QTS)
Edge Hill – 260 pts (Relig Educ QTS)
Hull – 260 pts (Educ P)
Leeds Beckett – 260 pts (P Educ; Ely Yrs Educ QTS) (IB 24 pts)
London Met – 260 pts (Educ P)
Reading – 260–300 pts (Chem Educ)
St Mary's – 260 pts (P Educ) (IB 28 pts)
West Scotland – BCC–CDDd (P Educ)
Winchester – 260–300 pts (Educ P) (IB 24 pts)

240 pts **Bangor** – 240 pts (P Educ QTS)
Bedfordshire – 240 pts (P Educ BEd QTS)
Huddersfield – CCC (Ely Yrs)
Kingston – 240 pts (P Teach QTS)
Leeds Trinity – 240–260 pts (S PE)
Nottingham Trent – 240 pts (S Des Tech Educ)

Check **Chapter 4** when choosing your university and **Chapter 7** on how to read the subject tables.

Plymouth – 240 pts (P Teach BEd; P Mus BEd)
RConsvS – 240 pts (Mus BEd) offered jointly with **Glasgow**
St Mark and St John – 240 pts (P Educ QTS)
Stirling – CCD–BCC (Educ (P); Educ (S))
220 pts **Dundee** – AB–CCC (P Educ)
Nottingham Trent – 220 pts (S Physl Sci Educ)
St Mark and St John – 220 pts (Spec Educ Nds)
200 pts **Bangor** – 200–240 pts (Des Tech (S Educ) QTS)
Canterbury Christ Church – 200 pts (P Educ Modn Lang)
Greenwich – 200 pts (Educ P BA QTS)
Leeds Trinity – 200 pts (Educ)
Sheffield Hallam – 200–240 pts (Des Tech Educ QTS)
Wolverhampton – 200–260 pts (Educ P)
York St John – 200–220 pts (Educ St)
180 pts **Trinity Saint David** – 180–360 pts (P Educ St) (IB 26 pts)
80 pts **UHI** – C (Ely Educ Chldcr)

Alternative offers
See **Chapter 7** and **Appendix 1** for grades/UCAS Tariff points information for the International Baccalaureate, Scottish Highers/Advanced Highers, the Welsh Baccalaureate, the Irish Leaving Certificate, the Cambridge Pre-U Diploma, the Advanced Diploma and the Extended Project.

EXAMPLES OF FOUNDATION DEGREES IN THE SUBJECT FIELD
Bath Spa; Bishop Grosseteste; Blackpool and Fylde (Coll); Bradford (Coll Univ Centre); Bristol UWE; Carshalton (Coll); Cornwall (Coll); Cumbria; Gloucestershire; Greenwich; Havering (Coll); Kingston; Manchester Met; Mid-Cheshire (Coll); Middlesex; Nottingham New (Coll); St Mark and St John; South Cheshire (Coll); Truro (Coll); Worcester.

CHOOSING YOUR COURSE (SEE ALSO CH.1)
Some course features
Bristol UWE (P ITE) This course offers students the opportunity to develop within work-based settings through teaching experiences during their time at university. The University is currently developing new models of partnership to give students as much experience as possible before graduation; see the website for details.
Chichester Primary teacher training, and postgraduate courses in Primary and Secondary Education.
Cumbria In addition to Primary and Secondary Education courses with specialist options ICT, English, Maths and RE, there are also several options covering outdoor education and leadership.
Durham Education Studies is offered with specialist subjects chosen from English, Geography, History, Music and Primary teaching.
Glasgow (Educ P QTS) A four-year course that leads to a master's Diploma in Education offering the chance to study abroad. Graduates of this course are eligible for one year's induction experience in a Scottish primary school.
Hull BA Primary Teaching covers Sciences, English, and Mathematics; there are also courses in Education with Early Childhood Studies, Social Inclusion and Special Needs, or in Education and Society.
Liverpool Hope Education Studies plus the option to take primary teaching courses with specialisation in a range of subjects.
Liverpool John Moores Early Years and Primary Education courses are offered and also Outdoor Education, Education Studies and Sport Development and Physical Education.
Loughborough (Maths Maths Educ) This course offers a substantial study of mathematics alongside the option to research and study the psychological and sociological demands of teaching.
Middlesex Education Studies can be taken with a National Curriculum subject as a route to a PGCE in Primary or Secondary Education.
Plymouth General Primary courses are offered in Art and Design, Early Childhood Studies, English,

Digital Literacy, Mathematics, Music, Physical Education and Science. There is also a course in Steiner Waldorf Education. Some experience abroad is possible in Canada, Africa, Spain and the USA.
Roehampton (P Educ QTS) School-based learning is offered in every year of this degree, with students spending a minimum of 24 weeks in school across the three-year course. Students will also have the opportunity to specialise in a subject they are particularly interested in alongside general studies.

Universities and colleges teaching quality See www.qaa.ac.uk; http://unistats.direct.gov.uk.

Top research universities and colleges (RAE 2008) See www.tda.gov.uk (England); www.shefc.ac.uk (Scotland); www.elwa.org.uk (Wales); www.unistats.com. Manchester Met; Durham; Stirling.

ADMISSIONS INFORMATION

Number of applicants per place (approx) Bangor 5; Bishop Grosseteste 12; Bristol UWE 20; Canterbury Christ Church 15; Cardiff Met (UWIC) 3; Chester 25; Cumbria 5; Derby 13; Dundee 5; Durham 8; Edge Hill 17; Gloucestershire 20; Gloucestershire Greenwich 3; Hull 7; Kingston 9; Liverpool Hope 5; Liverpool John Moores 3; Manchester Met 23, (Maths) 4; Middlesex 7; Newman (S Engl) 3, (Theol) 3, (Ely Yrs) 5, (Biol) 7, (Geog) 3, (PE) 6, (Sci) 1; Northampton 7; Northumbria 8; Nottingham Trent 11; Oxford Brookes 6; Plymouth 14; Roehampton 6; St Mark and St John 5; St Mary's 19; Sheffield Hallam 7, (PE) 60; Strathclyde 7; Trinity Saint David 10; West Scotland 7; Winchester 4; Wolverhampton 4; Worcester 21, (Engl) 51.

Advice to applicants and planning the UCAS personal statement Any application for teacher training courses requires candidates to have experience of observation in schools and with children relevant to the choice of age range. Describe what you have learned from this. Any work with young people should be described in detail, indicating any problems which you may have seen which children create for the teacher. Applicants are strongly advised to have had some teaching practice prior to interview and should give evidence of time spent in a primary or secondary school and give an analysis of activity undertaken with children. Give details of music qualifications, if any. Admissions tutors look for precise, succinct, well-reasoned, well-written statements (no mistakes!). All applicants for Initial Teacher Training (ITT) courses in England leading to Qualified Teacher Status must register provisionally with the General Teaching Council for England. Check with www.gtce.org.uk for full details. See also **Chapter 6**.

Selection interviews Check all institutions. It is a requirement that all candidates for teacher training are interviewed. **Yes** Bangor, Bishop Grosseteste, Bristol UWE, Cardiff Met (UWIC), Derby, Dundee, Durham, Kingston, Liverpool John Moores, Manchester Met, Newman, Nottingham Trent, Oxford Brookes, Plymouth, Roehampton, St Mark and St John, West Scotland, Winchester, Worcester, York St John; **Some** Birmingham City.

Interview advice and questions Questions invariably focus on why you want to teach and your experiences in the classroom. In some cases you may be asked to write an essay on these topics. Questions in the past have included: What do you think are important issues in education at present? Discussion of course work will take place for Art applicants. **Derby** Applicants are asked about an aspect of education. **Liverpool John Moores** Discussion regarding any experience the applicant has had with children.

Reasons for rejection (non-academic) Unable to meet the requirements of written standard English. Ungrammatical personal statements. Lack of research about teaching at primary or secondary levels. Lack of experience in schools. Insufficient experience of working with people; tendency to be racist.

AFTER-RESULTS ADVICE

Offers to applicants repeating A-levels **Higher** Oxford Brookes; **Possibly higher** Cumbria; **Same** Bangor, Bishop Grosseteste, Brighton, Canterbury Christ Church, Chester, Derby, Dundee, Durham, Liverpool Hope, Liverpool John Moores, Manchester Met, Newman, Northumbria, Nottingham Trent, Roehampton, St Mark and St John, St Mary's, Stirling, Sunderland, UHI, Winchester, Wolverhampton, Worcester, York St John; **No** Kingston.

Check **Chapter 4** when choosing your university and **Chapter 7** on how to read the subject tables.

GRADUATE DESTINATIONS AND EMPLOYMENT (2011/12 HESA)
Graduates surveyed 13535 **Employed** 9425 **In voluntary employment** 80 **In further study** 1110
Assumed unemployed 440

Career note See **Education Studies**.

OTHER DEGREE SUBJECTS FOR CONSIDERATION
Education Studies; Psychology; Social Policy; Social Sciences; Social Work.

TOURISM and TRAVEL

(see also **Business and Management Courses, Business and Management Courses (International
and European), Business and Management Courses (Specialised), Hospitality and Event
Management, Leisure and Recreation Management/Studies**)

Tourism and Travel courses are popular; some are combined with Hospitality Management which
provides students with specialisms in two areas. Courses involve business studies and a detailed
study of tourism and travel. Industrial placements are frequently involved and language options are
often included. See also **Appendix 3**.

Useful websites www.wttc.org; www.abta.com; www.thebapa.org.uk.

*NB The points totals shown to the left of the institutions are for ease of reference only. It must not
be assumed that Tariff points are always used by institutions or that they can be substituted for an
offer in grades. The level of an offer is not necessarily indicative of the quality of a course.*

COURSE OFFERS INFORMATION
Subject requirements/preferences **GCSE** English and mathematics required. **AL** No subjects
specified.

Your target offers and examples of courses provided by each institution
360 pts **Exeter** – AAA–AAB 360–340 pts (Mgt Tour) (IB 36–33 pts)
320 pts **Strathclyde** – ABB 320 pts (Mgt Hspty Tour) (IB 33 pts)
　　　　　Surrey – ABB (Tour Mgt; Int Hspty Tour Mgt) (IB 34 pts)
300 pts **Brighton** – BBB (Int Tour Mgt) (IB 32 pts)
　　　　　Bristol UWE – 300 pts (Tour Mgt)
　　　　　Kent – BBB (Bus St (Tour)) (IB 33 pts HL 14 pts)
　　　　　Northumbria – 300 pts (Bus Tour Mgt; Trav Tour Mgt) (IB 26 pts)
280 pts **East London** – 280 pts (Int Tour Mgt)
　　　　　Greenwich – 280 pts (Tour Mgt)
　　　　　Hertfordshire – 280 pts (Int Tour Mgt; Tour Mgt Lang; Tour Mgt)
　　　　　Leeds Beckett – 280 pts (Int Tour Mgt) (IB 25 pts)
　　　　　Lincoln – 280 pts (Int Tour Mgt)
　　　　　Manchester Met – 280 pts (Tour Mgt) (IB 28 pts)
　　　　　Sheffield Hallam – 280 pts (Evnts Mgt Tour; Int Htl Mgt; Tour Mgt (Int); Tour Hspty Bus Mgt
　　　　　　　(Int))
　　　　　Suffolk (Univ Campus) – 280 pts (Tour Mgt)
　　　　　Ulster – BBC 280 pts (Int Htl Tour Mgt)
　　　　　Westminster – BBC 280 pts (Tour Plan) (IB 28 pts)
260 pts **Aberystwyth** – 260 pts (Tour Mgt) (IB 28 pts)
　　　　　Bolton – 260 pts (Int Tour Mgt)
　　　　　Bournemouth – 260–300 pts (Tour Mgt)
　　　　　Coventry – 260 pts (Strat Tour Hspty Mgt)
　　　　　Derby – 260 pts (Tour Mgt)

Edinburgh Queen Margaret – BCC 260 pts (Hspty Tour Mgt)
Glasgow Caledonian – BCC 260 pts (Bus (Tour))
Gloucestershire – 260 pts (Tour Mgt)
Hull – 260 pts (Tour Mgt; Int Tour Mgt)
Liverpool Hope – 260–300 pts (Tour)
Liverpool John Moores – 260 pts (Tour Leis Mgt)
SRUC – BCC (Actvt Tour Mgt)
Staffordshire – 260 pts (Tour Mgt)
Sunderland – 260 pts (Int Tour Hspty Mgt; Tour (Comb); Tour Mgt)
Ulster – 260–280 pts (Int Trav Tour Mgt; Int Trav Tour St Langs)
Westminster – 260–280 pts (Tour Bus) (IB 26 pts)

240 pts **Birmingham City** – 240–260 pts (Advntr Tour Mgt; Intl Tour Mgt; Tour Bus Mgt)
Bishop Grosseteste – 240 pts (Tour)
Canterbury Christ Church – 240 pts (Tour Leis St; Tour Mgt) (IB 24 pts)
Cardiff Met (UWIC) – 240 pts (Tour Mgt courses; Int Tour Hspty Mgt)
Central Lancashire – 240–280 pts (Int Tour Mgt)
Chester – 240–280 pts (Tour) (IB 26 pts)
Chichester – CCC–BCD 240 pts (Tour Mgt) (IB 28 pts)
Edinburgh Napier – 240 pts (Tour Mgt; Tour Entre Mgt; Tour Mgt HR Mgt)
Hertfordshire – 240 pts (Tour Joint Hons)
London Met – 240 pts (Int Tour Mgt; Tour Trav Mgt)
London South Bank – 240 pts (Tour Hspty Leis Mgt)
Middlesex – (Int Tour Mgt)
Plymouth – 240 pts (Cru Mgt; Tour Mgt; Bus Tour; Int Tour Mgt)
Robert Gordon – CCC (Int Tour Mgt) (IB 26 pts)
Salford – 240–280 pts (Tour Mgt; Leis Tour Mgt)
Southampton Solent – 240 pts (Cru Ind Mgt)
York St John – 240–300 pts (Tour Mgt; Tour Mgt Mark)

220 pts **Portsmouth** – 220 pts (Hspty Mgt Tour)
St Mary's – 220 pts (Tour; Tour Mgt) (IB 28 pts)
Southampton Solent – 220 pts (Tour Mgt; Int Tour Mgt)

200 pts **Anglia Ruskin** – 200–240 pts (Tour Mgt)
Bedfordshire – 200 pts (Trav Tour; Int Tour Mgt)
Birmingham (UC) – 200 pts (Tour Bus Mgt; Int Tour Mgt; Advntr Tour Mgt)
Blackpool and Fylde (Coll) – 200 pts (Int Rsrt Tour Mgt)
Bucks New – 200–240 pts (Tour courses)
West London – 200 pts (Trav Tour Mgt)
Wolverhampton – 200 pts (Tour Mgt)
York St John – 200 pts (Int Tour Mgt)

160 pts **Trinity Saint David (Swansea)** – 160 pts (Int Trav Tour Mgt; Tour Mgt)
UHI – CC 160 pts (Advntr Tour Mgt)

120 pts **Grimsby (Univ Centre)** – 120–240 pts (Tour Bus Mgt)
Llandrillo Cymru (Coll) – 120 pts (Mgt Trav Tour)

80 pts **UHI** – C–A 80–140 pts (Tour Hosp Mgt)

Alternative offers
See **Chapter 7** and **Appendix 1** for grades/UCAS Tariff points information for the International Baccalaureate, Scottish Highers/Advanced Highers, the Welsh Baccalaureate, the Irish Leaving Certificate, the Cambridge Pre-U Diploma, the Advanced Diploma and the Extended Project.

EXAMPLES OF FOUNDATION DEGREES IN THE SUBJECT FIELD
Arts London (CComm); Bath Spa; Birmingham (UC); Bishop Burton (Coll); Blackpool and Fylde (Coll); Bournemouth and Poole (Coll); Brighton and Hove City (Coll); Central Lancashire; Chichester; Cornwall

(Coll); Craven (Coll); Dearne Valley (Coll); Durham New (Coll); Ealing, Hammersmith and West London (Coll); East Surrey (Coll); Edge Hill; Grimsby (Univ Centre); Guildford (Coll); Highbury Portsmouth (Coll); Hull (Coll); Liverpool City (Coll); Mid-Cheshire (Coll); Newcastle (Coll); Norwich City (Coll); Nottingham New (Coll); South Cheshire (Coll); South Devon (Coll); Sunderland; Teesside; Tyne Met (Coll); West London; Westminster Kingsway (Coll); Worcester; Worcester (CT).

CHOOSING YOUR COURSE (SEE ALSO CH.1)
Some course features
Bristol UWE The course covers business and management activities, general tourism, international tourism, event and festival management. There is also a placement year in the industry.
Exeter The course has a vocational emphasis preparing students for careers in business and management. Students have the opportunity to study abroad or to spend their third year on an industrial placement. Students can study up to 30 credits per year outside of their chosen course so long as any necessary prerequisites have been completed.
Plymouth (Cru Mgt) The course covers hospitality and tourism topics and is operated in conjunction with P&O Cruises. There are 30 places available and all applicants are interviewed.
Southampton Solent Courses are offered in Cruise Management, International Tourism, Event Management with Sport and Tourism Management.
West London In addition to airline travel the course includes modules in retail travel, attractions management, inclusive tour operations and transport management.

Universities and colleges teaching quality See www.qaa.ac.uk; http://unistats.direct.gov.uk.

Examples of sandwich degree courses Bedfordshire; Birmingham (UC); Bournemouth; Brighton; Bristol UWE; Cardiff Met (UWIC); Central Lancashire; Chichester; Coventry; Gloucestershire; Greenwich; Hertfordshire; Huddersfield; Leeds Beckett; Liverpool John Moores; Llandrillo Cymru (Coll); London Met; Manchester Met; Middlesex; Northumbria; Plymouth; Portsmouth; Salford; Sheffield Hallam; South Cheshire (Coll); Staffordshire; Sunderland; Surrey; Trinity Saint David (Swansea); Ulster; Wolverhampton.

ADMISSIONS INFORMATION
Number of applicants per place (approx) Aberystwyth 3; Birmingham (UC) 10; Bournemouth 16; Derby 4; Liverpool John Moores 10; Northumbria 6; Sheffield Hallam 12; Sunderland 2.

Advice to applicants and planning the UCAS personal statement Work experience in the travel and tourism industry is important – in agencies, in the airline industry or hotels. This work should be described in detail. Any experience with people in sales work, dealing with the public – their problems and complaints – should also be included. Travel should be outlined, detailing places visited. Genuine interest in travel, diverse cultures and people. Good communication skills required. See also **Appendix 3**.

Misconceptions about this course Wolverhampton Some applicants are uncertain whether or not to take a Business Management course instead of Tourism Management. They should be aware that the latter will equip them with a tourism-specific knowledge of business.

Selection interviews Yes Brighton, Derby; **Some** Anglia Ruskin, Lincoln, Salford, Sunderland; **No** Liverpool John Moores, Surrey.

Interview advice and questions Past questions have included: What problems have you experienced when travelling? Questions on places visited. Experiences of air, rail and sea travel. What is marketing? What special qualities do you have that will be of use in the travel industry? See also **Chapter 6**.

Reasons for rejection (non-academic) Wolverhampton English language competence.

AFTER-RESULTS ADVICE
Offers to applicants repeating A-levels Same Anglia Ruskin, Birmingham (UC), Chester, Derby, Lincoln, Liverpool John Moores, Manchester Met, Northumbria, St Mary's, Salford, Wolverhampton.

For a quick reference offers calculator, fold out the inside front cover.

GRADUATE DESTINATIONS AND EMPLOYMENT (2011/12 HESA)
See **Hospitality and Event Management**.

Career note See **Business and Management Courses**.

OTHER DEGREE SUBJECTS FOR CONSIDERATION
Airline and Airport Management; Business Studies; Events Management; Heritage Management; Hospitality Management; Leisure and Recreation Management; Travel Management.

TOWN and COUNTRY PLANNING

(including **Environmental Planning** and **Urban Studies**; see also **Development Studies, Environmental Sciences/Studies, Housing, Surveying, Transport Management and Planning**)

Town and Country Planning courses are very similar and some lead to qualification or part of a qualification as a member of the Royal Town Planning Institute (RTPI). Further information from the RTPI (see **Appendix 3**).

Useful websites www.rtpi.org.uk; www.townplanningreview.lupjournals.org.

NB The points totals shown to the left of the institutions are for ease of reference only. It must not be assumed that Tariff points are always used by institutions or that they can be substituted for an offer in grades. The level of an offer is not necessarily indicative of the quality of a course.

COURSE OFFERS INFORMATION
Subject requirements/preferences **GCSE** English and mathematics required. **AL** Geography may be specified.

Your target offers and examples of courses provided by each institution
380 pts **Cambridge** – A*AA (Lnd Econ) (IB 40–41 pts HL 776)
360 pts **London (UCL)** – AABe (Plan Rl Est) (IB 37 pts)
340 pts **Cardiff** – AAB–ABB 340–320 pts (Geog (Hum) Plan)
       London (UCL) – ABBe (Urb St; Urb Plan Des Mgt) (IB 32 pts)
       London LSE – AAB (Env Dev) (IB 37 pts HL 666)
       Reading – AAB (Rl Est Plan Dev; Rl Est)
320 pts **Birmingham** – ABB (Plan Econ; Geog Urb Reg Plan; Plan Soc Plcy) (IB 32–34 pts)
       Cardiff – ABB–BBB 320–300 pts (Cty Reg Plan) (IB 32 pts)
       Liverpool – ABB (Twn Reg Plan) (IB 33 pts)
       Newcastle – ABB–BBC 320–280 pts (Plan)
       Northumbria – 320 pts (Plan Rl Est Dev)
       Sheffield – ABB (Urb St; Geog Plan; Urb St Plan)
300 pts **Dundee** – BBB (Twn Reg Plan) (IB 30 pts HL 555)
       Heriot-Watt – BBB (Urb Plan Prop Dev)
       Leeds Beckett – 300 pts (Hum Geog Plan) (IB 26 pts)
       Liverpool – BBB (Env Plan; Urb Regn Plan) (IB 31 pts)
       Manchester – BBB (Twn Cntry Plan MTCP; Twn Cntry Plan BA; Env Mgt)
       Queen's Belfast – BBB/BBCb (Env Plan)
280 pts **Birmingham City** – 280 pts (Plan Env Dev)
       Bristol UWE – 280 pts (Twn Cntry Plan)
       Nottingham Trent – 280 pts (Plan Dev)
       Oxford Brookes – BBC (City Reg Plan; Plan Prop Dev) (IB 31 pts)
       Sheffield Hallam – 280 pts incl geog (Geog Plan)
       Westminster – BBC (Prop Plan) (IB 26 pts)

240 pts **Canterbury Christ Church** – 240 pts (Urb Reg St)
London South Bank – CCC 240 pts (Urb Env Plan)

Alternative offers
See **Chapter 7** and **Appendix 1** for grades/UCAS Tariff points information for the International Baccalaureate, Scottish Highers/Advanced Highers, the Welsh Baccalaureate, the Irish Leaving Certificate, the Cambridge Pre-U Diploma, the Advanced Diploma and the Extended Project.

EXAMPLES OF FOUNDATION DEGREES IN THE SUBJECT FIELD
Anglia Ruskin; Birmingham City; Blackburn (Coll); Derby; Glyndŵr; Grimsby (Univ Centre); Middlesex; Northampton; Royal Agricultural Univ.

CHOOSING YOUR COURSE (SEE ALSO CH.1)
Some course features
Birmingham Urban and Regional Planning is offered combined with Geography. A joint degree in Planning is offered with Economics or Social Policy and a programme in Spatial Planning and Business Management is also available.
Oxford Brookes Two degrees, Planning and Property Development, and City and Regional Planning, are offered as Single Honours courses. The former is accredited by the RTPI when combined with the postgraduate diploma in Planning and the post-graduation Assessment of Professional Competence.
Sheffield Hallam An Urban and Environmental Planning degree is offered with options to specialise in regeneration, environment and conservation and design. A course in Geography and Planning is also available.

Universities and colleges teaching quality See www.qaa.ac.uk; http://unistats.direct.gov.uk.

Plan and Develop your future with undergraduate study at Ulster...

Fees only £6000 for GB Students

Top 20 University for UCAS applications

Largest University on the island of Ireland

Professional Accreditation

Planning and Property Development

Property Investment, Appraisal and Development

Professional Education for a Professional Future

adbe.ulster.ac.uk

study.ulster.ac.uk

University of ULSTER

Your future, make it happen

PLAN AND DEVELOP YOUR FUTURE AT ULSTER

BSc Hons / MSci

Have you considered studying Planning or Property Development at Ulster? The university is based in Belfast, the most student friendly city in the UK, with some of the best value student accommodation, a vibrant nightlife and only one hour away from most major cities in Great Britain. The School of the Built Environment offers courses in planning, property, appraisal and development.

Would you like to help shape policies to tackle climate change and combat global warming? Would you like to contribute to the creation of self-sufficient, sustainable communities and shrink our ecological footprint?

Yes? Then come and study Planning & Property Development (PPD) at Ulster.

'The MSci PPD degree is an exciting course which allows you to develop an array of skills and knowledge on a wide range of topics relating to the built environment. Through individual research and practical group studies, the course offers an exceptional base to pursue individual interests in relation to the built environment, sustainability and regeneration. The Planning and Property Development course provides a suitable base upon which to build a professional career, through the completion of projects which are special to particular communities and realistic in their objectives."

Colleen Quinn (Graduate from MSci Planning and Property Development)

With a focus on understanding the conditions necessary to make development happen, and using the island of Ireland as a laboratory for learning e.g. through case studies, the course, accredited by RICS and RTPI, prepares graduates for careers across the world.

The Property Investment, Appraisal and Development (PIAD) degree is the premier property academic programme on the Island of Ireland. The School of the Built Environment at the University of Ulster has been educating graduates for the real estate profession since the early 1980's and is highly regarded by the surveying profession.

The degree is accredited by the international professional body, the Royal Institution of Chartered Surveyors (RICS) and this accreditation can help in attaining professional chartered status upon successful graduation and completion of the RICS Assessment of Professional Competencies (APC). The Property course is the only course within the School of the Built Environment which offers 3 distinct APC pathways to RICS membership, namely Commercial Property, Residential and Valuation.

The opportunities in real estate at international, national and local levels remain vast and diverse offering potentially attractive prospects for young and enthusiastic surveyors wishing to operate in a challenging and dynamic profession.

Visit **study.ulster.ac.uk** for more information including entry requirements.

We hope to see you on a planning or property course at Ulster soon.

UCAS

MSci Planning and Property Development	KK42
BSc Hons Property Investment, Appraisal and Development	K291

University of ULSTER

Your future, make it happen

Top research universities and colleges (RAE 2008) Sheffield; Cardiff; Newcastle; Leeds; Reading; Manchester; London (UCL).

Examples of sandwich degree courses Birmingham City; Cardiff; Northumbria; Nottingham Trent; Sheffield Hallam.

ADMISSIONS INFORMATION

Number of applicants per place (approx) Birmingham 2; Birmingham City 6; Bristol UWE 6; Cardiff 6; Dundee 5; London (UCL) 6; London South Bank 3; Newcastle 9; Oxford Brookes 3; Sheffield Hallam 6.

Advice to applicants and planning the UCAS personal statement Visit your local planning office and discuss the career with planners. Know plans and proposed developments in your area and any objections to them. Study the history of town planning worldwide and the development of new towns in the UK during the 20th century, for example Bournville, Milton Keynes, Port Sunlight, Welwyn Garden City, Cumbernauld, and the advantages and disadvantages which became apparent. See also **Appendix 3**. **Oxford Brookes** See **Surveying**.

Selection interviews **Yes** London (UCL), London South Bank, Newcastle, Oxford Brookes; **Some** Birmingham City, Cardiff; **No** Dundee.

Interview advice and questions Since Town and Country Planning courses are vocational, work experience in a planning office is relevant and questions are likely to be asked on the type of work done and the problems faced by planners. Questions in recent years have included: If you were re-planning your home county for the future, what points would you consider? How are statistics used in urban planning? How do you think the problem of inner cities can be solved? Have you visited your local planning office? See also **Chapter 6**.

Reasons for rejection (non-academic) Lack of commitment to study for a professional qualification in Town Planning.

AFTER-RESULTS ADVICE

Offers to applicants repeating A-levels **Higher** Bristol UWE, Newcastle; **Same** Birmingham City, Cardiff, Dundee, London South Bank, Oxford Brookes.

GRADUATE DESTINATIONS AND EMPLOYMENT (2011/12 HESA)

Planning (urban, rural and regional) graduates surveyed 1060 **Employed** 635 **In voluntary employment** 25 **In further study** 210 **Assumed unemployed** 75

Career note Town Planning graduates have a choice of career options within local authority planning offices. In addition to working on individual projects on urban development, they will also be involved in advising, co-ordinating and adjudicating in disputes and appeals. Planners also work closely with economists, surveyors and sociologists and their skills open up a wide range of other careers.

OTHER DEGREE SUBJECTS FOR CONSIDERATION

Architecture; Countryside Management; Environmental Studies; Geography; Heritage Management; Housing; Land Economy; Property; Public Administration; Real Estate; Sociology; Surveying; Transport Management.

TRANSPORT MANAGEMENT and PLANNING

(including **Logistics**, **Transport Design** and **Supply Chain Management**; see also **Engineering/ Engineering Sciences**, **Town and Country Planning**)

Transport Management and Planning is a specialised branch of business studies with many applications on land, sea and air. It is not as popular as the less specialised Business Studies courses but is just as relevant and will provide the student with an excellent introduction to management and its problems.

Useful websites www.cilt-international.com; www.transportweb.com; www.nats.aero; www.ciltuk. org.uk.

NB The points totals shown to the left of the institutions are for ease of reference only. It must not be assumed that Tariff points are always used by institutions or that they can be substituted for an offer in grades. The level of an offer is not necessarily indicative of the quality of a course.

COURSE OFFERS INFORMATION

Subject requirements/preferences **GCSE** English and mathematics required. **AL** No subjects specified.

Birmingham GCSE Mathematics grade B required.

Your target offers and examples of courses provided by each institution

340 pts   **Cardiff** – AAB 340 pts (Bus Mgt (Log Ops)) (IB 35 pts)
      Leeds – AAB incl geog (Geog Trans Plan) (IB 35 pts)
320 pts   **Aston** – ABB–BBB 320–300 pts (Trans Mgt; Log Mgt) (IB 32 pts)
300 pts   **Coventry** – BBB 300 pts (Avn Mgt) (IB 29 pts)
      Northumbria – 300 pts (Bus Log Sply Chn Mgt; Trans Des)
      Ulster – 300 pts incl BB (Trans Plan)
280 pts   **Greenwich** – 280 pts (Bus Log Trans Mgt)
      Loughborough – 280 pts (Trans Bus Mgt; Air Trans Mgt) (IB 30 pts)
260 pts   **Coventry** – BCC 260 pts (Auto Trans Des)
      Edinburgh Napier – 260 pts (Trans Mgt)
      Huddersfield – BCC 260 pts (Air Trans Log Mgt; Trans Log Mgt)
      Liverpool John Moores – 260 pts (Mgt Trans Log)
      West London – 260 pts (Airln Airpt Mgt)
240 pts   **Bucks New** – 240–280 pts (Air Trans Plt Trg)
      Plymouth – 240 pts (Cru Mgt) (IB 24 pts)
      Southampton Solent – 240 pts (Cru Ind Mgt)
      Staffordshire – CCC 240 pts (Trans Des)
200 pts   **Bucks New** – 200–240 pts (Airln Airpt Mgt; Airln Mgt; Airpt Mgt)
      Plymouth – 200 pts (Mar St (Navig Marit Sci)) (IB 28 pts)
120 pts   **Trinity Saint David (Swansea)** – 120–160 pts (Log Sply Chn Mgt)

Alternative offers

See **Chapter 7** and **Appendix 1** for grades/UCAS Tariff points information for the International Baccalaureate, Scottish Highers/Advanced Highers, the Welsh Baccalaureate, the Irish Leaving Certificate, the Cambridge Pre-U Diploma, the Advanced Diploma and the Extended Project.

EXAMPLES OF FOUNDATION DEGREES IN THE SUBJECT FIELD

Greenwich; Liverpool John Moores; West London.

CHOOSING YOUR COURSE (SEE ALSO CH.1)

Some course features

Aston (Log Mgt) This is a business course focusing on the supply chain and distribution industry. There is a four-year course involving paid professional experience.

Bucks New (Air Trans Plt Trg) Students who fail to achieve any of the pilot training modules have the option to transfer to Transport with Pilot Training or Airline and Airport Management.

Cardiff All Business Management courses share a common first year so there is a relative amount of flexibility in their structure. Students may apply to transfer programme at the end of their first year. The logistics and operations specialism offers a 20 week work placement in organisations such as

Admiral, Arriva Trains, Deloitte, HSBC, Network Rail, Proxima and Welsh Water. There is also the opportunity to spend time abroad.

Liverpool John Moores (Mgt Trans Log) The course is accredited by the Chartered Institute of Logistics and Transport; there is an option for a placement/sandwich year in industry.

Loughborough (Trans Bus Mgt; Air Trans Mgt) Courses include a year in industry. French, German and Spanish modules can be selected.

Plymouth (Cru Mgt) The course focuses on the study of cruise tourism and the management of cruise operations. There is an optional year on a cruise ship.

Universities and colleges teaching quality See www.qaa.ac.uk; http://unistats.direct.gov.uk.

Examples of sandwich degree courses Aston; Coventry; Huddersfield; Liverpool John Moores; Loughborough; Plymouth.

ADMISSIONS INFORMATION
Number of applicants per place (approx) Aston 5; Coventry 5; Huddersfield 5; Loughborough 11.

Advice to applicants and planning the UCAS personal statement Air, sea, road and rail transport are the main specialist areas. Contacts with those involved and work experience or work shadowing should be described in full. See also **Appendix 3**.

Selection interviews **Yes** Loughborough, Plymouth; **Some** Aston, Bucks New; **No** Huddersfield, Loughborough.

Interview advice and questions Some knowledge of the transport industry (land, sea and air) is likely to be important at interview. Reading around the subject is also important, as are any contacts with management staff in the industries. Past questions have included: What developments are taking place to reduce the number of cars on the roads? What transport problems are there in your own locality? How did you travel to your interview? What problems did you encounter? How could they have been overcome? See also **Chapter 6**.

AFTER-RESULTS ADVICE
Offers to applicants repeating A-levels **Same** Aston.

GRADUATE DESTINATIONS AND EMPLOYMENT (2011/12 HESA)
Career note Many graduates will aim for openings linked with specialisms in their degree courses. These could cover air, rail, sea, bus or freight transport in which they will be involved in the management and control of operations as well as marketing and financial operations.

OTHER DEGREE SUBJECTS FOR CONSIDERATION
Air Transport Engineering; Civil Engineering; Environmental Studies; Logistics; Marine Transport; Town and Country Planning; Urban Studies.

VETERINARY SCIENCE/MEDICINE

(including **Bioveterinary Sciences** and **Veterinary Nursing**; see also **Animal Sciences**)

Veterinary Medicine/Science degrees enable students to acquire the professional skills and experience to qualify as veterinary surgeons. Courses follow the same pattern and combine a rigorous scientific training with practical experience. The demand for these courses is considerable (see below) and work experience is essential prior to application. Graduate entry programmes provide a route to qualifying as a vet to graduates with good degrees in specified subjects. See also **Appendix 3**.

Veterinary Nursing Honours degree courses combine both the academic learning and the nursing training required by the Royal College of Veterinary Surgeons, and can also include practice management. Foundation degrees in Veterinary Nursing are more widely available. Bioveterinary Sciences are usually three-year full-time BSc degree courses focusing on animal biology, management and disease but do not qualify graduates to work as vets. For places in Veterinary Science/Medicine, applicants may select only four universities. Applicants to the University of Cambridge Veterinary School and the Royal Veterinary College, University of London are required to sit the BioMedical Admissions Test (BMAT) (see **Chapter 6**).

Useful websites www.rcvs.org.uk; www.admissionstestingservice.org; www.bvna.org.uk; www.spvs. org.uk.

NB The points totals shown to the left of the institutions are for ease of reference only. It must not be assumed that Tariff points are always used by institutions or that they can be substituted for an offer in grades. The level of an offer is not necessarily indicative of the quality of a course.

COURSE OFFERS INFORMATION
Subject requirements/preferences GCSE (Vet Sci/Med) Grade B English, mathematics, physics, dual science if not at A-level. **AL** (Vet Sci/Med) See offers below. (Vet Nurs) Biology and another science may be required. **Other** Work experience essential for Veterinary Science/Medicine and Veterinary Nursing courses and preferred for other courses: check requirements. Health checks may be required.

Bristol (Vet Sci/Med) Grade A in five or six GCSE subjects. Grade A or B in GCSE physics.
Glasgow (Vet Sci/Med) Grade A or B in GCSE physics.
Liverpool (Vet Sci/Med) GCSE English, mathematics, physics, dual science grade B if not at A-level. (Vet Nurs) Five GCSE subjects including English and two sciences.

Your target offers and examples of courses provided by each institution
410 pts **Liverpool** – AAAb (Vet Sci) (IB 36 pts HL 666)
380 pts **Cambridge** – A*AA incl 3 AL sci +BMAT (Vet Med) (IB 40–42 pts)
360 pts **Bristol** – AAA incl chem+biol 360 pts (Vet Sci) (IB 37 pts HL 666)
         Edinburgh – AAA incl chem+biol +maths/phys 360 pts (Vet Med) (IB 36 pts)
         London (RVC) – AAA–AAB incl chem+biol +BMAT (Vet Med)
340 pts **Bristol** – AAB (Vet Sci incl Pre-Vet Yr) (IB 35 pts HL 666)
         Glasgow – A*AA incl chem+biol (Vet Med Srgy) (IB 36 pts)
         Nottingham – AAB (Vet Med Srgy; Vet Med +Prelim Yr) (IB 36 pts)
         Surrey – AAB (Vet Biosci) (IB 35 pts)
320 pts **Liverpool** – ABB incl biol sci (Biovet Sci) (IB 32 pts HL 6 biol 5 sci)
300 pts **Glasgow** – BBB incl chem+biol (Vet Biosci) (IB 32 pts)
         London (RVC) – BBB incl chem +maths/phys/biol 300 pts BMAT reqd for Merit Scholarship
            (Biovet Sci 3 yrs)
280 pts **Bristol** – BBC incl biol+chem at BB (Vet Nurs Biovet Sci) (IB 30 pts HL 655)
         Lincoln – 280 pts incl biol (Biovet Sci)
260 pts **Harper Adams** – BBB–AAA 260–300 pts (Vet Nurs Prac Mgt; Biovet Sci)
240 pts **Edinburgh Napier** – CCC 240 pts (Vet Nurs)
         London (RVC) – BCD (Vet Nurs)
         London (RVC) – CCC incl chem+biol (Vet Gateway prog 1 yr)
         Middlesex – 240 pts (Vet Nurs)
220 pts **West Anglia (Coll)** – 220 pts (Vet Nurs App Anim Bhv)
200 pts **Myerscough (Coll)** – 200 pts (Vet Nurs)
160 pts **Bristol UWE** – 160 pts incl biol (Vet Nurs Sci) (IB 26 pts)
         Warwickshire (Coll) – 160 pts (Vet Nurs)

Alternative offers
See **Chapter 7** and **Appendix 1** for grades/UCAS Tariff points information for the International Baccalaureate, Scottish Highers/Advanced Highers, the Welsh Baccalaureate, the Irish Leaving Certificate, the Cambridge Pre-U Diploma, the Advanced Diploma and the Extended Project.

EXAMPLES OF FOUNDATION DEGREES IN THE SUBJECT FIELD

Askham Bryan (Coll); Brighton; Bristol UWE; Duchy (Coll); Easton Otley (Coll); Greenwich; Harper Adams; Nottingham Trent; Plumpton (Coll); Warwickshire (Coll); West Anglia (Coll).

CHOOSING YOUR COURSE (SEE ALSO CH.1)

Some course features

Author's note Veterinary Science/Medicine is an intensely competitive subject and, as in the case of Medicine, one or two offers and three rejections are not uncommon. As a result, the Royal College of Veterinary Surgeons has raised a number of points which are relevant to applicants and advisers.

1　Every candidate for a Veterinary Medicine/Science degree course should be advised to spend a suitable period with a veterinarian in practice.
2　A period spent in veterinary work may reveal a hitherto unsuspected allergy or sensitivity following contact with various animals.
3　Potential applicants should be under no illusions about the difficulty of the task they have set themselves: at least five applicants for every available place, with no likelihood of places being increased at the present time.
4　There are so many candidates who can produce the necessary level of scholastic attainment that other considerations have to be taken into account in making the choice. In most cases, the number of GCSE grade As will be crucial. This is current practice. Headteachers' reports and details of applicants' interests, activities and background are very relevant and are taken fully into consideration; applicants are reminded to include details of periods of time spent with veterinary surgeons.
5　Any applicant who has not received an offer but who achieves the grades required for admission ought to get in touch, as soon as the results are known, with the schools and enquire about the prospects of entry at the Clearing stage. All courses cover the same subject topics.

Bristol UWE The degree in Veterinary Nursing Science includes 70 weeks of work placement and leads to the RCVS qualification. This course and that of the Foundation Veterinary Nursing Science take place at Hartpury College, Gloucester.

Edinburgh The curriculum of the Veterinary Medicine course falls into interrelated main parts. The pre-clinical part covers the biology and chemistry of the animal body, and the foundation clinical studies part deals with the surgery, diagnostic imaging, anaesthesia and pharmacology.

London (RVC) (Vet Gateway) (entry grades CCC) Course guarantees a place on the five-year Veterinary Medicine programme. Applicants require chemistry and biology and any other subject at A-level (except general studies) and there are other conditions for eligibility (see www.rvc.ac.uk). (BSc Biovet Sci 3 yr) Course does not qualify graduates to practise as veterinary surgeons. There is also a six-year Veterinary Medicine Combined course.

Nottingham The course which involves the Preliminary Year is for students without the required science qualifications but who have high academic achievement in non-science or vocational subjects. Successful completion of the course enables direct entry into Year 1 of the five-year course.

Surrey The degree in Veterinary Biosciences focuses on animal health and disease. There are opportunities for professional placements.

Universities and colleges teaching quality See www.qaa.ac.uk; http://unistats.direct.gov.uk.

Top research universities and colleges (RAE 2008) See **Agricultural Sciences/Agriculture**.

Examples of sandwich degree courses Bristol UWE; Harper Adams.

ADMISSIONS INFORMATION

Number of applicants per place (approx) Bristol (Vet Sci) 12, (Vet Nurs Biovet Sci) 6; Cambridge 5; Edinburgh 17; Glasgow 20; Liverpool 12; London (RVC) 5; Nottingham 11.

Numbers of applicants (a UK b EU (non-UK) c non-EU d mature) London (RVC) a759 b71 c156 d172.

Advice to applicants and planning the UCAS personal statement Applicants for Veterinary Science must limit their choices to four universities and submit their applications by 15 October. They may add one alternative course. Work experience is almost always essential so discuss this in full, giving information about the size and type of practice and the type of work in which you were involved. See also **Appendix 3. Bristol** Six weeks of work experience including two weeks in a veterinary practice, one week lambing and one week on a dairy farm. **Cambridge** Work experience expected. **Edinburgh** Competition for places is intense: 72 places are available and only one in seven applicants will receive an offer. The strongest candidates are interviewed and are normally required to take with them an additional reference outlining recent work experience with large and small animals; examples include dairy or lambing experience, kennels or catteries, or an abattoir visit. **Glasgow** A minimum of two weeks in a veterinary practice plus experience of work on a dairy farm, working at a stables, assisting at lambing, work at a cattery or kennels and if possible a visit to an abattoir. Additional experience at a zoo or wildlife park. **Liverpool** The selection process involves three areas: academic ability to cope with the course; knowledge of vocational aspects of veterinary science acquired through work experience in veterinary practice and six further weeks of experience working with animals; personal attributes that demonstrate responsibility and self-motivation. **London (RVC)** Six weeks' hands-on experience needed: two weeks in a veterinary practice, and two weeks in another animal environment, for example riding school, zoo, kennels. **Nottingham** Six weeks (minimum) of work experience required and preferably one day at an abattoir.

Misconceptions about this course Bristol UWE (Vet Nurs Sci) Students think that the degree qualifies them as veterinary nurses but in fact RCVS assessment/training is additional. **Liverpool** (Biovet Sci) Some applicants think that the course allows students to transfer to Veterinary Science: it does not.

Selection interviews (Vet Sci and Vet Nurs) All institutions **Some** Surrey (Vet Biosci).

Interview advice and questions Past questions have included: Why do you want to be a vet? Have you visited a veterinary practice? What did you see? Do you think there should be a Vet National Health Service? What are your views on vivisection? What are your views on intensive factory farming? How can you justify thousands of pounds of taxpayers' money being spent on training you to be a vet when it could be used to train a civil engineer? When would you feel it your responsibility to tell battery hen farmers that they were being cruel to their livestock? What are your views on vegetarians? How does aspirin stop pain? Why does it only work for a certain length of time? Do you eat beef? Outline the bovine TB problem. Questions on A-level science syllabus. See also **Chapter 6. Glasgow** Applicants complete a questionnaire prior to interview. Questions cover experience with animals, reasons for choice of career, animal welfare, teamwork, work experience, stressful situations.

Reasons for rejection (non-academic) Failure to demonstrate motivation. Lack of basic knowledge or understanding of ethical and animal issues.

AFTER-RESULTS ADVICE
Offers to applicants repeating A-levels Higher London (RVC); **Same** Bristol UWE (Vet Nurs Sci), Liverpool; **No** Cambridge, Edinburgh, Glasgow.

GRADUATE DESTINATIONS AND EMPLOYMENT (2011/12 HESA)
Graduates surveyed 475 **Employed** 400 **In voluntary employment** 15 **In further study** 15 **Assumed unemployed** 30

Career note Over 80% of veterinary surgeons work in private practice with the remainder involved in research in universities, government-financed research departments and in firms linked with farming, foodstuff manufacturers and pharmaceutical companies.

OTHER DEGREE SUBJECTS FOR CONSIDERATION
Agricultural Science; Agriculture; Animal Sciences; Biological Sciences; Biology; Dentistry; Equine Dental Science; Equine Management; Equine Studies; Medicine; Zoology.

ZOOLOGY

(including **Animal Biology**; see also **Agricultural Sciences/Agriculture, Animal Sciences, Biological Sciences, Biology**)

Zoology courses have a biological science foundation and could cover animal ecology, marine and fisheries biology, animal population, development and behaviour and, on some courses, wildlife management and fisheries.

Useful websites www.biaza.org.uk; live.sob.netxtra.net; www.zsl.org; www.academicinfo.net/zoo.html.

NB The points totals shown to the left of the institutions are for ease of reference only. It must not be assumed that Tariff points are always used by institutions or that they can be substituted for an offer in grades. The level of an offer is not necessarily indicative of the quality of a course.

COURSE OFFERS INFORMATION

Subject requirements/preferences GCSE English and science/mathematics required or preferred. **AL** One or two sciences will be required.

Your target offers and examples of courses provided by each institution

380 pts **Cambridge** – A*AA (Nat Sci (Zool)) (IB 40–41 pts HL 776)
360 pts **Edinburgh** – AAA–ABB 360–320 pts (Biol Sci (Zool)) (IB 37–32 pts)
Exeter – AAA–ABB 360–340 pts (Zool courses) (IB 34 pts)
Imperial London – AAA incl chem +sci/maths 360 pts (Zool) (IB 38 pts HL 66)
Manchester – AAA–ABB 360–320 pts (Zool; Zool Modn Lang; Zool (Yr Ind)) (IB 37–33 pts)
Sheffield – AAA incl biol+sci (Zool MBiol) (IB 37 pts)
Southampton – AAA–ABB 360–320 pts (Zool) (IB 36–32 pts HL 18–16 pts)
340 pts **Birmingham** – AAB–ABB 320–340 pts (Biol Sci (Zool)) (IB 32–34 pts)
Bristol – AAB incl at least 2 sci/maths 340 pts (Zool) (IB 35 pts HL 666)
Cardiff – AAB–ABB 340–320 pts (Zool) (IB 34 pts HL 5 biol chem)
Glasgow – AAB 340 pts (Anim Biol) (IB 34 pts)
Leeds – AAB 340 pts (Zool) (IB 36–32 pts HL 16–15 pts)
Newcastle – AAB–ABB (Zool; Mar Zool) (IB 34–35 pts)
Nottingham – AAB–ABB (Zool) (IB 32–34 pts)
Roehampton – 340 pts (Zool)
St Andrews – AAB (Zool) (IB 32 pts)
Sheffield – AAB incl biol+sci (Zool BSc) (IB 35 pts)
320 pts **Glasgow** – ABB (Zool) (IB 32 pts)
Leicester – ABB (Biol Sci (Zool)) (IB 32 pts)
Liverpool – ABB incl biol +sci/maths (Zool) (IB 33 pts HL 6 biol)
London (QM) – ABB 320 pts (Zool) (IB 34 pts)
Swansea – ABB (Zool) (IB 33 pts)
300 pts **Aberdeen** – BBB incl maths/sci (Zool) (IB 28 pts)
London (RH) – 300–320 pts (Zool) (IB 34 pts)
Queen's Belfast – BBB incl biol (Zool) (IB 28 pts HL 555)
Reading – BBB–ABC (Zool)
South Wales – BBB (Int Wldlf Biol) (IB 28 pts)
280 pts **Aberystwyth** – 280–320 pts (Zool; Microbiol Zool)
Bangor – 280–320 pts (Mar Biol Zool)
Hull – 280–300 pts (Aqua Zool; Zool)
Lincoln – (Zool)
260 pts **Bangor** – 260–320 pts (Zool; Zool Cons; Mar Vert Zool; Zool Mar Zool)
Derby – 260 pts (Zool)
Liverpool John Moores – 260–300 pts (Zool) (IB 25 pts)

Manchester Met – 260–280 pts (Wldlf Biol) (IB 27 pts)
Northampton – 260–280 pts (Wldlf Cons) (IB 24 pts)
Nottingham Trent – 260 pts (Zoo Biol)
240 pts **Anglia Ruskin** – 240 pts (Zool)
Salford – (Zool)
West Scotland – CCC incl sci (App Biosci Zool)

Alternative offers
See **Chapter 7** and **Appendix 1** for grades/UCAS Tariff points information for the International Baccalaureate, Scottish Highers/Advanced Highers, the Welsh Baccalaureate, the Irish Leaving Certificate, the Cambridge Pre-U Diploma, the Advanced Diploma and the Extended Project.

EXAMPLES OF FOUNDATION DEGREES IN THE SUBJECT FIELD
See also **Animal Sciences**. Cornwall (Coll); Glyndŵr; Greenwich; Leeds City (Coll); Nottingham Trent.

CHOOSING YOUR COURSE (SEE ALSO CH.1)
Some course features
See also **Biological Sciences**.
Anglia Ruskin (Zool) Study in the USA is an option for one semester.
Edinburgh Zoology is a specialist study as in many Biological Science degrees.
Hull (Aqua Zool) Course focuses on the interface between land and water and expands on the animal biology aspects of marine and freshwater biology.

Universities and colleges teaching quality See www.qaa.ac.uk; http://unistats.direct.gov.uk.

Examples of sandwich degree courses Cardiff; Leeds; Liverpool John Moores; Manchester; Nottingham Trent.

ADMISSIONS INFORMATION
Number of applicants per place (approx) Aberystwyth 8; Bangor 3; Bristol 13; Cardiff 8; Leeds 7; Liverpool John Moores 6; London (RH) 6; Newcastle 15; Nottingham 6; Southampton 7; Swansea 6.

Advice to applicants and planning the UCAS personal statement Interests in animals should be described, together with any first-hand experience gained. Visits to zoos, farms, fish farms etc and field courses attended should be described, together with any special points of interest you noted.

Selection interviews **Yes** Hull, London (RH), Newcastle; **Some** Derby, Roehampton, Southampton; **No** Cardiff, Liverpool, Swansea.

Interview advice and questions Past questions have included: Why do you want to study Zoology? What career do you hope to follow on graduation? Specimens may be given to identify. Questions usually asked on the A-level subjects. See also **Chapter 6**.

AFTER-RESULTS ADVICE
Offers to applicants repeating A-levels **Higher** Bristol, Hull, Leeds, Swansea; **Same** Aberystwyth, Bangor, Cardiff, Derby, Liverpool, Liverpool John Moores, London (RH), Roehampton, Swansea.

GRADUATE DESTINATIONS AND EMPLOYMENT (2011/12 HESA)
Graduates surveyed 970 **Employed** 330 **In voluntary employment** 55 **In further study** 275 **Assumed unemployed** 100

Career note See **Biology**.

OTHER DEGREE SUBJECTS FOR CONSIDERATION
Animal Ecology; Animal Sciences; Aquaculture; Biological Sciences; Biology; Ecology; Fisheries Management; Marine Biology; Parasitology; Veterinary Science; Wildlife Management.

INFORMATION FOR INTERNATIONAL STUDENTS

The choice of a subject to study (from over 50,000 degree courses) and of a university or college (from more than 300 institutions) is a major task for students living in the UK. For overseas and EU applicants it is even greater, and the decisions that have to be made need much careful planning, preferably beginning two years before the start of the course. **NB** Beware that there are some private institutions offering bogus degrees: check www.ucas.com to ensure your university and college choices are legitimate.

APPLICATIONS AND THE POINTS-BASED IMMIGRATION SYSTEM

In addition to submitting your application through UCAS (see **Chapter 5**) a Points-based Immigration System is now in operation for overseas students. The main features of this system include:

- **Confirmation of Acceptance for Studies (CAS) number** When you accept an offer the institution will send you a CAS number which you will need to include on your visa application.
- **Maintenance** Students will need to show that they are able to pay for the first year's tuition fees, plus £800 per month for accommodation and living expenses. Additional funds and regulations apply for those bringing dependants into the UK.
- **Proof of qualifications** Your visa letter will list all the qualifications that you submitted to obtain your university place and original proof will be required of these qualifications when submitting your visa application. These documents will be checked by the Home Office. Any fraudulent documents will result in your visa application being rejected and a possible ban from entering the UK for 10 years.
- **Attendance** Once you have started your course, your attendance will be monitored. Non-attending students will be reported to the UK Border Agency.

Full details can be obtained from www.ukcisa.org.uk.

SELECTION, ADMISSION AND FINANCE

The first reason for making early contact with your preferred institution is to check their requirements for your chosen subject and their selection policies for overseas applicants. For example, for all Art and some Architecture courses you will have to present a portfolio of work or slides. For Music courses your application often will have to be accompanied by a recording you have made of your playing or singing and, in many cases, a personal audition will be necessary. Attendance at an interview in this country is compulsory for some universities and for some courses. At other institutions the interview may take place either in the UK or with a university or college representative in your own country.

The ability to speak and write good English is essential and many institutions require evidence of competence, for example scores from the International English Language Testing System (IELTS) or from the Test of English as a Foreign Language (TOEFL) (see www.ielts.org and www.ets.org/toefl). For some institutions you may have to send examples of your written work. Each institution provides information about its English language entry requirements and a summary of this is given for each university listed below. International students should note that the recommended threshold for minimum English language requirements is IELTS 6.5–7.0. Recent research indicates that students with a lower score may have difficulty in dealing with their course.

In the next chapter you will find a directory of universities and colleges in the UK, together with their contact details. Most universities and colleges in the UK have an overseas student adviser who can advise you on these and other points you need to consider, such as passports, visas, entry certificates, evidence of financial support, medical certificates, medical insurance, and the numbers of overseas students in the university from your own country. All these details are very important and need to be considered at the same time as choosing your course and institution.

The subject tables in **Chapter 8** provide a comprehensive picture of courses on offer and of comparative entry levels. However, before making an application, other factors should be considered such as English language entry requirements (see above), the availability of English language teaching, living costs, tuition fees and any scholarships or other awards which might be offered. Detailed information about these can be obtained from the international offices in each university or college, from British higher education fairs throughout the world and from the British Council offices abroad and from websites: see www.britishcouncil.org; www.education.org.

Below is a brief summary of the arrangements made by each university in the UK for international students aiming to take a full-time degree programme. The information is presented as follows:

- Institution.
- International student numbers.
- English language entry requirements for degree programmes shown in either IELTS, TOEFL or occasionally CEFR scores. These vary between universities and courses. For the IELTS, scores can range from 5.5 to 7.5, and for the TOEFL computer-based test, scores can range from a minimum of 213; for the written TOEFL the usual minimum entry level is 5.0. For CEFR, students should reach a level of at least B2. For full details contact the university or college.
- Arrangements for English tuition.
- International Foundation courses.
- Annual tuition fees (approximate) for full-time undergraduate degree courses. Tuition fees also usually include fees for examinations and graduation. These figures are approximate and are subject to change each year. EU students pay 'home student' fees, except for those from the Channel Islands and the Isle of Man; students from the British Overseas Territories are now treated as home students for fee purposes at universities and other institutions of higher education.
- Annual living costs. These are also approximate and represent the costs for a single student over the year. The living costs shown cover university accommodation (usually guaranteed for the first year only), food, books, clothing and travel in the UK, but not travel to or from the UK. (Costs are likely to rise year by year in line with the rate of inflation in the UK, currently around 3% per year.) Overseas students are normally permitted to take part-time work for a period of up to 20 hours per week.
- Scholarships and awards for non-EU students (most universities offer awards for EU students).

UNIVERSITY INFORMATION AND FEES FOR UNDERGRADUATE INTERNATIONAL STUDENTS

From 2012 the UK Government introduced an increase in tuition fees that will affect the fees charged for courses for non-EU/international students. Intending applicants should therefore check university websites before applying. **The fees published below (unless otherwise stated) are those being charged to students in 2013/14 (check websites for 2015/16 fees).**

Aberdeen Approximately 14% of students come from 120 nationalities. *English language entry requirement (or equivalent):* IELTS 6.0; Medicine 7.0. Four-week English course available in August before the start of the academic year. *Fees:* £12,000–£15,000; Clinical Medicine £26,500. *Living costs:* £650–£800 per month.

Abertay About 10% of the student population are international students. *English language entry requirement (or equivalent):* IELTS 6.0 (no band less than 5.5). Pre-sessional English course available, also full-time English course September to May and free English tuition throughout degree course. *Fees:* £10,250–£12,650. *Living costs:* £6000–£7000.

Aberystwyth International students make up approximately 7% of the undergraduate student population. *English language entry requirement (or equivalent):* IELTS 6.5 to 7. Full-time tuition in English available. *Fees:* Arts and Social Science subjects £9750, Science subjects £10,750. *Living costs:* £6000–£7000. International scholarships are available.

Anglia Ruskin Twenty-one per cent of the student population are international students. *English language entry requirement (or equivalent):* IELTS 5.5. A one-year International Foundation programme available. *Fees:* Arts subjects £9800; Science subjects £10,300. Scholarships available. *Living costs:* £8450.

Arts London A large number of international students. *English language entry requirement (or equivalent):* IELTS 6.5. Courses in Fashion Promotion, Acting, Directing require IELTS 7.5. Language Centre courses in academic English for 12, 24, 34 or 36 weeks. *Fees:* £13,800. *Living costs:* £1000 per month. Scholarships and bursaries available.

Arts London (Central St Martins CAD) *Fees:* £13,800; Acting £18,256; Drama £16,389; Theatre Practice £17,066.

Aston Over 1000 international students from over 120 countries, with 15% of the total student population from overseas. International Orientation programme at the beginning of the academic year. *English language entry requirement (or equivalent):* IELTS 6.0–6.5. International Foundation programme offered as a bridge to the degree courses. Pre-sessional English classes also available of five and 10 weeks' duration. *Fees:* Non-Science programmes £12,500; Social Science and Computing courses £13,500; Engineering and Science courses £15,500. *Living costs:* £800 per month. Scholarships offered, including bursaries for Engineering and Science subjects.

Bangor Around 20% of the student population come from 115 countries worldwide. *English language entry requirement (or equivalent):* IELTS 6.0. Pre-study English course available starting September, January or April depending on level of English proficiency, leads to International Foundation course. One-month or two-month courses before commencement of degree course also offered. *Fees:* Arts, Social Sciences and Education £11,000; Bangor Business School courses £11,500; Law £11,000; Science, Engineering and Health Studies £12,800. *Living costs:* Lower cost of living than many other UK cities. International entrance scholarships available.

Bath Over 1500 international students from around 100 countries. *English language entry requirement (or equivalent):* IELTS 6.0–7.0. *Fees:* £10,750–£17,400. *Living costs:* £8500–£9500. Scholarships, bursaries and awards available.

Bath Spa Students from 40 countries. *English language entry requirement (or equivalent):* IELTS 6.0 for subjects supported by the Undergraduate Course for International Students (UCIS). Foundation courses available for students below this score. *Fees:* £10,535; BA Tourism and Management £11,270. *Living costs:* £8000–£8500.

Bedfordshire Over 3000 EU and international students. *English language entry requirement (or equivalent):* IELTS 6.0. General English programmes are offered, including a summer school. *Fees:* £9600. *Living costs:* £6500–£7500.

Birmingham Over 4000 international students from 152 countries. *English language entry requirement (or equivalent):* IELTS 6.0, 6.5 or 7.0, depending on programme of study. Six-, 10- and 20-week English language programmes available, depending on language proficiency, ranging from IELTS 4.5 to 5.5. *Fees:* Non-laboratory subjects £11,700–£12,900; Laboratory subjects £15,150; Clinical Medicine £27,500. *Living costs:* £12,140–£16,000; Clinical Medicine £28,100. Awards are offered by some subject departments including all Engineering subjects, Computer Science, Earth Sciences, Law, and Psychology.

Birmingham (UC) There are 1100 students from 65 countries. Specific entry requirements for each country are found on the University website. *English language entry requirement (or equivalent):* IELTS 6.0, min 5.5. *Fees:* £8800.

Birmingham City Large number of international students. *English language entry requirement (or equivalent):* IELTS 6.0. Pre-sessional language courses and in-session language support. Orientation programme for all students. *Fees:* Non-Science courses £10,100; Laboratory-based courses £11,300; Conservatoire/Acting courses £14,600. *Living costs:* £6000–£7000. Music bursaries.

Bolton There are 623 international students from 79 countries represented. *English language entry requirement (or equivalent):* IELTS 6.0. Courses start in September, some in January. Pre-sessional and in-session English tuition plus Access and Foundation programmes available in Business Management and Engineering. *Fees:* £9900. *Living costs:* £7000–£8000.

Bournemouth A large number of international students. *English language entry requirement (or equivalent):* IELTS 6.0. Preparatory English programme offered, starting in January, April or July depending on applicant's level of English (entry IELTS 4.5/5.0/5.5). Several language schools in the town (see www.englishuk.com.uk or www.baselt.org.uk). Pre-sessional study skills programme also offered. *Fees:* £9500–£11,500. *Living costs:* £680–£750 per month. Some subject awards available.

Bournemouth Arts *Fees:* £12,510.

Bradford Over 100 countries represented (22%). *English language entry requirement (or equivalent):* IELTS 6.0. Some students may be admitted to Year 2, depending on qualifications. *Fees:* Science and Engineering courses £13,100; Management/Social Science/Media courses £11,000. *Living costs:* £6000–£8500. Ten scholarships to cover the duration of the course.

Brighton Some 1400 international students from over 100 countries. *English language entry requirement (or equivalent):* IELTS 6.0 (or 5.5 for less linguistically demanding subjects). New four-year degree programme (UK4) includes preparatory year. *Fees:* £10,900–£12,900; Medicine £24,860. *Living costs:* £7000–£8000. Fixed fees possible. Merit scholarships for students from Norway and some countries in the Far East and Africa.

Brighton and Sussex (MS) *Fees:* £16,200.

Bristol Approximately 1500 students from over 100 countries. *English language entry requirement (or equivalent):* IELTS 6.5 (possibly lower for some Science and Engineering subjects). *Fees:* Arts subjects £14,750; Science subjects £17,750; Clinical subjects £33,000. *Living costs:* £6700–£10,000. Some bursaries and scholarships for one year from some subject departments including Dentistry, Law, Medicine and Veterinary Science.

Bristol UWE More than 1750 international students. *English language entry requirement (or equivalent):* IELTS 6.0. English language preparatory and pre-sessional courses offered. English modules can also be taken throughout your degree. *Fees:* £10,750. *Living costs:* £6500–£9000. Some partial fee scholarships are available in Computing, Mathematics and Engineering, and Law scholarships for students from the Far East, South Africa, the West Indies and North America.

Brunel More than 2000 international students from over 110 countries. *English language entry requirement (or equivalent):* IELTS 6.0 for Science/Technology courses, 7.0 for Law, 6.5 for other subjects. English language tuition offered during and before the course but only to improve existing skills. *Fees:* £13,000–£16,000. *Living costs:* £2065 per term. Twenty bursaries offered.

Buckingham Eighty nationalities represented at this small university. *English language entry requirement (or equivalent):* IELTS 6.0. English test for applicants without English as first language (Accountancy, Business courses, Communication Studies, English, History, Politics). *Fees:* Check with the University. *Living costs:* £8000–£9000. Tuition-fee discount for students from the Bahamas, Bulgaria and India. Some scholarships for students from the Far East, Russia and Eastern Europe.

Bucks New Around 7.5% of the student population are international students coming from 50 countries. *English language entry requirement (or equivalent):* IELTS 6.0. *Fees:* £9500. *Living costs:* £6000–£7000.

Cambridge Over 1000 international undergraduate students. *English language entry requirement (or equivalent):* IELTS 7.0 overall, with minimum of 6.0 in each element. TOEFL (written) 600 (minimum) and at least 5.0 in TOEFL test of written English. *Fees:* Tuition fees range between £13,662 and £33,069, depending on the course studied. See www.study.cam.ac.uk/undergraduate/international/finance/ index.html#tuition for more details. College fees vary between Colleges but are normally between £4500 and £5500 per year. *Living costs:* £8450. Information relating to fees and finance for international students is available online: www.study.cam.ac.uk/undergraduate/international/finance.

Canterbury Christ Church International students from 80 countries. *English language entry requirement (or equivalent):* IELTS 6.0. *Fees:* £9710. *Living costs:* £9000.

Cardiff Over 3500 international students from 100 countries. *English language entry requirement (or equivalent):* IELTS 6.0–7.0. Comprehensive selection of pre-sessional language courses from three weeks to nine months. Induction course for all students. International Foundation courses for Business, Law, Engineering, Computer Science and Health and Life Sciences. *Fees:* Arts courses £13,500–£18,000;

Clinical courses £29,800. *Living costs:* £830 per month. Law scholarships offered on the basis of academic merit.

Cardiff Met (UWIC) The University has over 800 international students enrolled from 120 different countries. *English language entry requirement (or equivalent):* IELTS 4.5 minimum. *Fees:* £9700. *Living costs:* £5500–£6500.

Central Lancashire Large international student population (2000) from many countries. *English language entry requirement (or equivalent):* IELTS 6.0. Competence in written and spoken English required on application. *Fees:* £10,950–£11,950. *Living costs:* £6000–£7000.

Chester *English language entry requirement (or equivalent):* IELTS 6.0. International Foundation year available for Business Studies students. *Fees:* £10,700. *Living costs:* £7200.

Chichester International students from several countries. *English language entry requirement (or equivalent):* IELTS 6.0 or 5.5 if taking a joint degree with International English Studies. *Fees:* £9660–£11,025. *Living costs:* £7000–£8000.

City A large international community with students from over 160 countries. *English language entry requirement (or equivalent):* IELTS 6.0 (6.5 for Business, Law and Journalism). August and September pre-sessional English language courses, and in-session English workshops. International Foundation programmes in Law, Business, Engineering and Management. *Fees:* £10,000–£13,000. *Living costs:* £10,500–£12,500. Scholarships available for applicants for Actuarial Science, Engineering (Cypriot applicants only) and Law.

Coventry About 2500 international students. *English language entry requirement (or equivalent):* IELTS 6.0. *Fees:* £10,080–£12,000. *Living costs:* £6000–£7000. Scholarships available.

Creative Arts *Fees:* £11,140. *Living costs:* £7500–£10,000.

Cumbria *English language entry requirement (or equivalent):* IELTS 6.0. *Fees:* £9960–£14,965.

De Montfort Over 1000 international students from more than 100 countries. *English language entry requirement (or equivalent):* IELTS 6.5 (lower for some faculties). In-session English tuition in some degree courses. One-year International Foundation Certificate courses in Business and Law. Orientation programme in September for all students. *Fees:* Classroom-based £10,250; Laboratory-based £10,750. *Living costs:* £8500–£9500. Some scholarships for overseas students.

Derby Students from 70 countries. *English language entry requirement (or equivalent):* IELTS 6.0. Courses offered to those needing tuition in English language. Foundation courses (£5200) and pre-sessional intensive English tuition (£2000) offered, and also language support whilst studying for degree. *Fees:* £9700. *Living costs:* £5000–£6000. International scholarships available for applicants from some countries in the Far East.

Dundee Students from 83 countries. *English language entry requirement (or equivalent):* IELTS 6.0. Foundation courses in English and for Business and Art and Design courses. *Fees:* College of Arts and Social Sciences programmes £10,200 with the exception of Architecture £12,000; Pre-Clinical Medicine £18,750; Clinical Medicine £28,750; Pre-Clinical Dentistry £18,060; Clinical Dentistry £27,606; College of Art, Science and Engineering all programmes £12,750 with the exceptions of Civil Engineering £14,850; Mathematics £12,250; Mechanical/Electrical Engineering/Physics/Renewable Energy £13,850; Art and Design £11,850. *Living costs:* £6500–£7500. Some awards for overseas students in Accountancy, Art and Design, Arts and Social Sciences, Law and Science and Engineering.

Durham Some 1600 international students from over 120 countries. *English language entry requirement (or equivalent):* IELTS 6.5. Three-day induction programme before the start of the academic year. Intensive English language course is provided if standard of English does not meet the required level. *Fees:* Classroom-based £14,000; Laboratory-based £17,900.

East Anglia Over 2000 international students from 120 countries. *English language entry requirement (or equivalent):* IELTS 6.0 (higher for some courses). Four, eight and 12-week pre-sessional courses in English and tuition during degree courses. *Fees:* Classroom-based subjects £12,300; Laboratory-based subjects £14,900; Medicine £27,500. *Living costs:* £6500–£7500. Scholarships available including awards, based on academic merit, cover part of the cost of tuition fees.

East London About 3300 international students from 120 countries. *English language entry requirement (or equivalent):* IELTS 6.0. One-year full-time preparatory English course available. *Fees:* Architecture £12,420; Physiotherapy £14,040; other programmes £9900. *Living costs:* £1000 per month.

Edge Hill There is a small number of international students. *English language entry requirement (or equivalent):* IELTS 6.5. *Fees:* £10,800. *Living costs:* £5000–£6000 per year.

Edinburgh Some 4000 international students from 120 countries. *English language entry requirement (or equivalent):* IELTS 6.0–6.5. English language support. *Fees:* £13,300–£17,500. *Living costs:* £800 per month. Merit-based scholarships available, as well as specific scholarships for students from Africa or the Indian subcontinent.

Edinburgh Napier Approximately 4000 international students. *English language entry requirement (or equivalent):* IELTS 6.0 overall with no component below 5.5. English language programmes in September and January; English language support through Foundation programmes. *Fees:* Classroom-based £9690; Laboratory-based £11,250. *Living costs:* £800 per month.

Edinburgh Queen Margaret Some 400 international students from 50 countries. *English language entry requirement (or equivalent):* IELTS 5.5. *Fees:* £10,170–£12,090. *Living costs:* £5400. Some partial scholarships for self-funding students.

Essex International students from over 135 countries. *English language entry requirement (or equivalent):* IELTS 6.0–6.5. English language courses available before entry to degree course. *Fees:* Laboratory-based courses in Biological Sciences, Health and Human Sciences and Psychology £13,500; all other full-time undergraduate degrees £11,500. *Living costs:* £6000–£9000. A comprehensive package of scholarships and busaries is available. See www.essex.ac.uk/studentfinance.

Exeter Around 4000 international students from 130 countries. *English language entry requirement (or equivalent):* IELTS 6.5–7.0. The full-time Foundation programmes combine academic study, intensive English language teaching and study skills to prepare for entry into the first year of a degree. The INTO University of Exeter Centre offers pathways in Business Management, Accounting, Humanities, Law and Social Science, Economics, Finance and Management, Engineering, Mathematics and Physical Sciences and Biomedical, Life and Environmental Sciences. The full-time International Diploma programmes offer high-quality preparation for entry into the second year of a bachelor's degree at the University of Exeter, combining intensive English language teaching with a first-year degree level syllabus. Full-time six and 11 week intensive summer pre-sessional English language programmes are available commencing in June and July at the INTO University of Exeter Centre. *Fees:* Accounting £16,000; Arts, Humanities, Social Science (including Business and Law), Mathematics, Geography £14,500; Combined Honours programmes that combine a science and a non-science subject £15,500; Medicine £17,000 (Years 1 and 2), £29,000 (Years 3, 4 and 5); Science and Engineering (including Psychology and Sport Sciences) £17,000. *Living costs:* £7200–£9600. A range of scholarships and awards are available. Further information is available at www.exeter.ac.uk/studying/funding/prospective.

Falmouth *Fees:* £10,900.

Glasgow Over 2000 international students. *English language entry requirement (or equivalent):* IELTS 6.5 (higher for some courses). The English as a Foreign Language Unit offers intensive five-week pre-sessional language courses in a Foundation programme covering English language and study skills. *Fees:* Arts and Social Science programmes £13,000; Engineering, Science, College of Medical, Veterinary and Life Sciences programmes £16,500; Clinical courses £30,000. *Living costs:* £6000–£7500. Fee-waiver scholarships and automatic Fourth Year scholarships available (not for Dentistry, Medicine or Veterinary Science).

Glasgow Caledonian Students from 70 countries. *English language entry requirement (or equivalent):* IELTS 6.0. English language programmes available. *Fees:* £10,200–£14,500. *Living costs:* £800 per month.

Gloucestershire *English language entry requirement (or equivalent):* IELTS 5.5. English language support and mentor scheme with other international students. *Fees:* £10,200. *Living costs:* £5396–£6346 for nine months.

Glyndŵr The University welcomes students from Europe and worldwide. *English language entry requirement (or equivalent):* IELTS 6.0. *Fees:* £8950. *Living costs:* £7500.

Greenwich Over 4900 international students (including those from European countries). *English language entry requirement (or equivalent):* IELTS 6.0. Pre-sessional English courses, Access and International Foundation programmes. *Fees:* £10,100. *Living costs:* £9500–£10,500. Scholarships open to applicants from 25 countries.

Harper Adams *Fees:* £9650.

Heriot-Watt Twenty-three per cent of the student population comes from over 90 countries. *English language entry requirement (or equivalent):* IELTS 6.0. Several English language courses are offered; these range in length depending on students' requirements. *Fees:* Laboratory-based Science and Engineering courses £15,490; Non-laboratory-based courses £12,280. *Living costs:* £800 per month. Some international scholarships are available.

Hertfordshire Students from over 90 countries are at present studying at the University. *English language entry requirement (or equivalent):* IELTS 6.0. English language tuition is offered in the one-year International Foundation course, in a course for the Foundation Certificate in English for Academic Purposes, and in a pre-sessional intensive English course held during the summer months. *Fees:* Classroom-based courses £10,100; Laboratory-based courses £10,600. *Living costs:* £600 per month.

Huddersfield International students from over 80 countries. English language courses available and a one-year International Foundation course in English language with options in Business, Computing, Engineering, Mathematics and Music. Students guaranteed entry to Huddersfield courses on completion. *English language entry requirement (or equivalent):* 6.0. *Fees:* £11,500; Computing, Engineering and Science £12,500. *Living costs:* £6500–£7500.

Hull Ten per cent of students are from outside the EU. *English language entry requirement (or equivalent):* IELTS 6.0. English summer study programmes available. *Fees:* Non-Science programmes £12,000; Science programmes £14,400. *Living costs:* £6500–£8500. Excellent overseas scholarship provisions depending on the chosen subject and the student's country of origin.

Hull York (MS) *Fees:* £25,420.

ifs (UC) *Fees:* £10,500.

Imperial London Some 5000 international students from over 110 countries. *English language entry requirement (or equivalent):* IELTS 6.5–7.0. *Fees:* Engineering £25,000; Medicine £39,150; Medicine Non-clinical £27,500; Natural Science £25,000. *Living costs:* £1000 per month. Scholarships available.

Keele Large number of overseas students. *English language entry requirement (or equivalent):* IELTS 6.0–6.5. English language summer school before the start of degree course. International Foundation year degree programmes (entry IELTS 4.5). *Fees:* £10,500–£12,500; Medicine £21,000–£24,000. *Living costs:* £284 per week. Some bursaries valued at £1300 per annum.

Kent About 25% of the student population are from overseas. *English language entry requirement (or equivalent):* IELTS 5.5. Foundation programmes (entry IELTS 5.0) offered to prepare students for Arts, Business, Science, Engineering and Law courses. Non-degree courses also offered for one year or less. *Fees:* Non-laboratory £12,030; Laboratory £14,360; International Foundation Programme £11,250. *Living costs:* £7000–£13,000.

Kingston More than 2000 international students from over 70 countries. *English language entry requirement (or equivalent):* IELTS 6.5. Foundation level Science and Technology courses. Pre-sessional English language courses and free English support during degree studies. *Fees:* £10,750–£12,350. *Living costs:* £1000 per month.

Lancaster Twenty per cent of student population from over 100 countries. *English language entry requirement (or equivalent):* IELTS 5.5–6.0. Pre-sessional and in-session English language courses cover reading, writing, listening and speaking skills. *Fees:* £14,250. *Living costs:* £7000–£8000.

Leeds Approximately 4000 students from outside the UK. *English language entry requirement (or equivalent):* IELTS 6.0. *Fees:* £12,900–£14,800; Science/Engineering £16,200; Clinical Dentistry/Medicine £18,450–£30,700. *Living costs:* £7000–£9000.

Leeds Beckett Over 2500 international students from 110 countries. *English language entry requirement (or equivalent):* IELTS 6.0 (IELTS 4.0 or 5.0 for the International Foundation programme, starting September or February). Also general English courses. *Fees:* £9500. *Living costs:* £8000–£9000.

Leeds Trinity *Fees:* £9300.

Leicester Fourteen per cent of full-time students are from outside the UK. *English language entry requirement (or equivalent):* IELTS 6.0 (IELTS 6.5 for Law, Medicine, Arts and Social Science programmes, 5.5 for the Foundation year). English language preparatory programmes and on-going support Foundation programme. *Fees:* £13,395–£16,525; Clinical Medicine £30,820. *Living costs:* £680–£730 per month.

Lincoln Over 2000 students from more than 40 countries. *English language entry requirement (or equivalent):* IELTS 6.0. *Fees:* £11,798–£13,648. *Living costs:* £7800–£9000.

Liverpool Approximately 3800 international (non EU) students from over 120 countries in the first year for undergraduate and postgraduate programmes. *English language entry requirement (or equivalent):* Science and Engineering: IELTS 6.0, min 5.5 in each component. Environment and Planning, Urban Regeneration and Planning and MPlan Town and Regional Planning: IELTS 6.5, min 5.5 in each component. Humanities and Social Sciences and Health and Life Sciences (excluding Clinical Medicine and Dentistry): IELTS 6.5, min 5.5 in each component. Biological Sciences: IELTS 6.0, min 5.5 in each component. Clinical Medicine and Dentistry: IELTS 7.0, min 7.0 in each component. *Fees:* £12,750–£15,700; Dentistry, Medicine £23,700; Veterinary Science £23,000. Further information on international student fees can be viewed at: http://www.liv.ac.uk/study/international/money-and-scholarships/undergraduate-fees/ *Living costs:* £5000–£6000. Scholarships available, including special awards for students from Hong Kong and Singapore.

Liverpool Hope Approximately 700 international students. *English language entry requirement (or equivalent):* IELTS 6.0. Language courses available. *Fees:* £9000. *Living costs:* £7000–£8000.

Liverpool John Moores A large number of overseas students. *English language entry requirement (or equivalent):* IELTS 6.0. Pre-sessional and in-session English tuition available. *Fees:* £9000–£12,040. *Living costs:* £7200.

London (Birk) *Fees:* BA Modern Language degrees £11,334; other BA, BSc and LLB £11,925.

London (Gold) Some 1500 overseas students. *English language entry requirement (or equivalent):* IELTS 6.5; IELTS 5.5 for Extension degrees and IELTS 5.0 for entry to the one-year Foundation course. Certificate course in Language and Contemporary Culture or pre-sessional programmes available. *Fees:* £11,700–£15,000. *Living costs:* £1000 per month.

London (Hey) *English language entry requirement (or equivalent):* IELTS 6.0. *Fees:* £10,000. *Living costs:* £1000 per month.

London (Inst Ed) *Fees:* £13,410.

London (Inst Paris) *Fees:* £12,600.

London (King's) A large number of international students (20%). *English language entry requirement (or equivalent):* IELTS 6.5 for Engineering, Nursing, Science courses; 7.0 for Dentistry, Law, Medicine, Physiotherapy; 7.5 for Humanities, Social Sciences. Pre-sessional summer courses and a one-year Foundation course available. *Fees:* Classroom-based £15,000; Laboratory-based £19,000; Clinically based subjects £35,000. *Living costs:* £1000 per month. Awards available.

London (QM) Large number of international students (20%). *English language entry requirement (or equivalent):* IELTS 6.5. International Foundation course covering English language tuition and specialist courses in Business, Management, Economics, Mathematics, Spanish, Geography and European Studies. The course guarantees progression to linked degree courses including Law. *Fees:* Classroom-based subjects £12,750; Laboratory-based subjects £15,500; Dentistry and Medicine £19,400–£29,600. *Living costs:* £1000 per month.

London (RH) Twenty percent of students from over 120 countries. *English language entry requirement (or equivalent):* IELTS 4.0–5.5 for English language programmes. Ten-month Foundation course with studies in English language and introduction to specialist studies in a range of degree subjects. *Fees:* £12,600–£14,250. *Living costs:* £1000 per month.

London (RVC) About 110 international students. *Fees:* £12,240–£25,000. *Living costs:* £1000 per month.

London (St George's) There are a variety of courses that international and non-EU students can apply to. Full details on entry requirements for each individual course is available on the University website. *English language entry requirement (or equivalent):* A language level of at least CEFR C1. *Fees:* Physiotherapy/Radiography £13,500; Pre-clinical £18,630; MBBS £32,663. *Living costs:* £1000.

London (SOAS) Large number of international students (30%). *English language entry requirement (or equivalent):* IELTS 7.0. A one-year foundation programme and English language courses available with an entry requirement of IELTS 4.0. Three-day International Students' Orientation programme. *Fees:* £14,590. *Living costs:* £1000 per month.

London (UCL) Some 7000 students (34% of the total student body) are from countries outside the UK. *English language entry requirement (or equivalent):* Science and Engineering IELTS 6.5; Arts courses 7.0; Speech Science and Law 7.5. *Fees:* Arts, Social Sciences, Humanities £14,750; Science/Engineering £17,000–£19,500; Medicine £29,000. *Living costs:* £1000 per month.

London (UCL Sch Pharm) Approximately 20% of the student body are international students. *English language entry requirement (or equivalent):* IELTS 6.5. *Fees:* £16,500. *Living costs:* £1000 per month.

London LSE Approximately 5500 international students represent 150 countries. *English language entry requirement (or equivalent):* IELTS 7.0. Test of English as a Foreign Language (TOEFL) with a minimum score of 627 in the paper test including 5.5 in writing and 50 in TSE, or 107 in the internet-based test with a minimum of 25 out of 30 in each of the four skills. All English tests should include a speaking test. *Fees:* £16,392. *Living costs:* £1000 per month.

London Met Over 4000 students from 147 countries. *English language entry requirement (or equivalent):* IELTS 5.5. One-year International Foundation programme (IELTS entry requirement 4.5). Full range of English courses. *Fees:* £9000.

London NCH *English language entry requirement (or equivalent):* students must be fully competent in English and if English is not your first language, NCH may require you to take a test in English language such as IELTS or TOEFL. All students must submit a piece of written work to apply. *Fees:* Contact the college. *Living costs:* £1000 per month.

London South Bank Approximately 2500 international students, including 1300 from the EU. *English language entry requirement (or equivalent):* IELTS 6.0. Pre-study English course and a University Foundation course for overseas students. *Fees:* From £10,000. *Living costs:* £1000 per month.

Loughborough Some 1000 undergraduate students from outside the UK. *English language entry requirement (or equivalent):* IELTS 6.5 with a minimum of 6.0 in all sub-tests. Special pre-sessional courses offered by the Student Support Centre. *Fees:* £13,750–£17,300. *Living costs:* £4500–£9000, depending on type of accommodation and facilities.

Manchester A high proportion of international students from over 180 countries. *English language entry requirement (or equivalent):* IELTS 6.0–7.5, depending on the high linguistic demands of courses, for example Law, Management and Medicine. Foundation Year programme in Informatics, Engineering, Science and Biological Sciences. English language courses are also offered. *Fees:* £14,000–£18,000; Clinical Medicine £32,000. *Living costs:* £8600 for 40 weeks. Some scholarships and bursaries are available.

Manchester Met A large number of international students. *English language entry requirement (or equivalent):* IELTS 6.0. English language courses in January, April and July. *Fees:* £11,000; Business £10,250; Physiotherapy £12,500; Architecture £18,000. *Living costs:* £7800.

Middlesex International students from 30 countries around the world. *English language entry requirement (or equivalent):* IELTS 6.0. Foundation course (IELTS entry requirement 4.5). Extended English language course from September to July. International summer school. *Fees:* £10,700. *Living costs:* £1000 per month.

Newcastle Over 2500 students from outside the UK. *English language entry requirement (or equivalent):* IELTS 6.5 (7.0 for English, Law and Medicine). English language support and Foundation programmes in Arts and Social Sciences, Business and Finance, Computing, Science and Engineering. *Fees:* £12,075–£15,490; Medicine £15,490–£28,670. About 30% of students entering university in 2014/15 will benefit from financial support by way of scholarships and fee discounts. *Living costs:* £8000 for nine months.

Northampton Over 700 students from over 100 countries. *English language entry requirement (or equivalent):* IELTS 6.0. English language courses available. *Fees:* £9750; Occupational Therapy/Podiatry £10,750. *Living costs:* £5400–£6400.

Northumbria Approximately 2500 international students from over 80 countries. *English language entry requirement (or equivalent):* IELTS 5.5–6.5. English language and Foundation courses. *Fees:* £10,700–£12,700. *Living costs:* £7500–£8500. Country scholarships for students from over 15 countries; some merit-based course scholarships.

Norwich Arts Approximately 650 international students. *English language entry requirements (or equivalent):* IELTS 6.0 (with a minimum of 5.5 in all sections). English language study and pre-course training offered with the International Foundation course. *Fees:* £12,000.

Nottingham Students from over 150 countries. *English language entry requirement (or equivalent):* IELTS 6.0–6.5 (7.5 for Medicine). *Fees:* £12,830–£16,510; Medicine £17,400 (Years 1 and 2), £30,240 (Years 3, 4 and 5). *Living costs:* £12,110–£25,690. Scholarships for siblings and Science applicants.

Nottingham Trent Large number of overseas students. *English language entry requirement (or equivalent):* IELTS 6.5. English language courses (19, 10 and five weeks) available. *Fees:* £11,500–£12,000. *Living costs:* £7500–£8500. Discounted overseas fees for some applicants for Art and Design courses.

Open University Courses are open to students throughout the world with study online or with educational partners. Tutorial support is by telephone, fax, computer conferencing or email. *Fees:* Non-EU students' fees vary depending on type of course.

Oxford Students from 140 countries (one third of the student body). *English language entry requirement (or equivalent):* IELTS 7.0 (minimum), TOEFL 600 (275 in the computer-based TOEFL). *Fees:* £14,415–£21,220. *Living costs:* £7500–£8500. University and college scholarships and awards are available.

Oxford Brookes Large number of international students. *English language entry requirement (or equivalent):* IELTS scores for Engineering and Construction 5.5; for Business, Social Sciences, Computing and Humanities 6.0; for Law and Psychology 6.5. Large number of English language support courses from two weeks to two years offered by the Centre for English Language Studies. *Fees:* £11,900–£12,400. *Living costs:* £990 per month. Engineering scholarships and family awards.

Plymouth *English language entry requirement (or equivalent):* IELTS 6.0–6.5. 'English for University' courses available with IELTS entry requirement of 4.5. *Fees:* £10,500. *Living costs:* £6500–£7500. Scholarships for applicants from Malaysia.

Portsmouth Students from over 100 countries. *English language entry requirement (or equivalent):* IELTS 6.0 (5.5 for Foundation-level study). Induction, academic skills and language courses available. *Fees:* £11,000–£12,500. Check with the University.

Queen's Belfast Over 60 countries represented by 2400 international students. *English language entry requirement (or equivalent):* IELTS 6.0–6.5. Special English language summer schools and pre-university language courses are provided, also weekly language courses. Three-day orientation programme held before the start of the academic year. *Fees:* £11,500–£28,720. *Living costs:* £600 per month. Awards available.

Reading Over 3000 students from 125 countries. *English language entry requirement (or equivalent):* IELTS 6.5–7.0. International Foundation programme offering English language tuition and specialist studies in a choice of 14 subjects. Other pre-sessional English courses offered. *Fees:* £12,600–£15,000. *Living costs:* £6500–£8500. Some scholarships offered.

Robert Gordon Approximately 500 international students from over 50 countries. *English language entry requirement (or equivalent):* IELTS 6.0. Pre-entry English programme requirement IELTS 5.0 or above. *Fees:* £9500–£11,800. *Living costs:* £5000–£6000. Partial scholarship scheme.

Roehampton *English language entry requirement (or equivalent):* IELTS 5.5–6.0. *Fees:* £11,500. *Living costs:* £7500–£8500.

Royal Agricultural Univ Over 1100 international students from over 40 different countries. *English language entry requirement (or equivalent):* IELTS 6.0. Pre-entry English programme requirements IELTS 5.0. *Fees:* £10,000. *Living costs:* £6000–£8000.

St Andrews 26% of students are from overseas. *English language entry requirement (or equivalent):* IELTS 6.5. Pre-entry English and study skills programmes and Foundation courses specialising in Arts, Science or Social Science subjects. *Fees:* £15,460; Medicine £23,540. *Living costs:* £7500–£8500. Scholarships available.

St Mark and St John IELTS 6.0. *Fees:* £9400–£10,350.

Salford Some 1500 international students. *English language entry requirement (or equivalent):* IELTS 6.0. English study programmes and a very comprehensive International Foundation year. *Fees:* £8000–£12,540. *Living costs:* £7200.

Sheffield Over 3700 international students. *English language entry requirement (or equivalent):* IELTS 6.0. Preparatory English courses (one–nine months) and an international summer school with English classes. *Fees:* £13,390–£17,470; Clinical Medicine £17,470 (Year 3 onwards £31,580). *Living costs:* £800 per month. Scholarships available for applicants from Africa and the Far East, for siblings and alumni.

Sheffield Hallam Over 80 countries represented by 3000 international students. *English language entry requirement (or equivalent):* IELTS 6.0. English language tuition available on four, eight and 12-week courses (£810, £1700 and £2200 respectively and IELTS entry requirement 4.5). *Fees:* £10,680–£11,880. *Living costs:* £7000–£8000.

South Wales IELTS from 5.0. Pre-sessional course offered in English with course lengths of between five and 20 weeks depending on the applicant's proficiency. An International Foundation Programme is also offered. *Fees:* £8950–£11,300. *Living costs:* £5500–£6500.

Southampton Over 2000 international students. *English language entry requirement (or equivalent):* IELTS 6.0–6.5. English courses offered and also an International Foundation course covering Arts, Humanities, Social Sciences and Law. *Fees:* £13,200–£16,320; Clinical Medicine £31,500. *Living costs:* £7500–£8500. Awards available in Computer Science, Electronics, Law, Mathematics and Science.

Southampton Solent Students from over 50 countries. *English language entry requirement (or equivalent):* IELTS 6.0. Induction programme and language tuition available. *Fees:* £9785–£10,300. *Living costs:* £8000.

Staffordshire Students from over 70 countries. *English language entry requirement (or equivalent):* IELTS 5.5–6.0. English tuition available. *Fees:* £9875. *Living costs:* £7000.

Stirling Thirteen per cent of the student population are overseas students from 70 nationalities. *English language entry requirement (or equivalent):* IELTS 6.0. English language tuition available. *Fees:* £10,750–£12,900. *Living costs:* £5000–£6000. Some scholarships are available. Please see www.stir.ac.uk/scholarships.

Strathclyde Students from 90 countries. *English language entry requirement (or equivalent):* IELTS 6.5. Pre-entry and pre-sessional English tuition available. *Fees:* £10,200–£14,800. *Living costs:* £7500–£8500.

Sunderland A large number of international students. *English language entry requirement (or equivalent):* IELTS 5.5–6.0. English language tuition available. *Fees:* £9000. *Living costs:* £500 per month.

Surrey A large international community with 43% from the Far East. *English language entry requirement (or equivalent):* IELTS 6.0. English language courses and summer courses offered. *Fees:* £12,130–£15,160. *Living costs:* £7000–£8000. Scholarships and bursaries offered, including awards for students on Civil Engineering courses.

Sussex More than 2500 international students. *English language entry requirement (or equivalent):* IELTS 6.5. English language and study skills courses available. International Foundation courses offered, covering English language tuition and a choice from Humanities, Law, Media Studies, Social Sciences and Cultural Studies and Science and Technology. *Fees:* £13,000–£16,200; Medicine £24,860. *Living costs:* £840–£1010 per month. Forty international scholarships.

Swansea Students from over 100 countries. *English language entry requirement (or equivalent):* IELTS 6.0. Pre-sessional English language courses available and on-going support during degree courses. *Fees:* £10,500–£13,500. *Living costs:* £6000–£7000. Some overseas scholarships and prizes.

Teesside Students from over 75 countries. *English language entry requirement (or equivalent):* IELTS 6.5 for Law, English and Humanities, 5.5 for Engineering, Science, Technology and Computing courses and 6.0 for all other courses. Free English courses available throughout the year while following degree programmes. International summer school available. *Fees:* £10,450. *Living costs:* £6500.

Trinity Saint David International students are well represented at the University. More information can be found on the international student section of the website, www.trinitysaintdavid.ac.uk/en/international/aboutus or by contacting the international office internationalcc@trinitysaintdavid.ac.uk. *English language entry requirement (or equivalent):* IELTS 6.0. International Foundation programme. Accommodation possible for each year at university. *Fees:* £9000. *Living costs:* £6500–£7500.

Trinity Saint David (Swansea) *English language entry requirement (or equivalent):* IELTS 6.5. *Fees:* £9000. *Living costs:* £5500–£6500.

UHI *English language entry requirement (or equivalent):* IELTS 6.0; minimum 5.5 in all four components. *Fees:* £8244–£9786. *Living costs:* Check with the University.

Ulster Students from over 40 countries. *English language entry requirement (or equivalent):* IELTS 5.5. *Fees:* £9500. *Living costs:* £6000–£7000.

Univ Law *Fees:* £7500–£10,500.

Warwick Over 3500 international students. *English language entry requirement (or equivalent):* IELTS 6.0 for Science courses, 6.5 for Arts courses, 6.5 for MORSE courses, and 7.0 for Social Studies and Business courses. English support available. *Fees:* £14,420–£18,390; Medicine £16,840–£29,340. *Living costs:* £6500–£7500. More than 20 awards available for overseas students.

West London A large number of international students. *English language entry requirement (or equivalent):* IELTS 5.0 for the International Foundation programme and 5.5 for undergraduate courses. English language support available and also pre-sessional courses. *Fees:* £9350. *Living costs:* £1000 per month.

West Scotland Over 1100 international students. *English language entry requirement (or equivalent):* IELTS 6.0. English language Foundation course available. *Fees:* £10,500. *Living costs:* £8244–£9786. Some first-year scholarships are available. See www.uws.ac.uk/international-students/applications.

Westminster Students from 148 countries (51% Asian). *English language entry requirement (or equivalent):* IELTS 6.0. International Foundation certificate courses available focusing on the Built Environment, Mathematics and Computing or Social Sciences and Literature. *Fees:* £11,750. *Living costs:* £1000 per month.

Winchester Some 150 international students from 30 countries. *English language entry requirement (or equivalent):* IELTS 6.0. Language courses available. *Fees:* £10,500–£11,000. *Living costs:* £7500–£8500.

Wolverhampton A large number (2500) of international students from over 100 countries. *English language entry requirement (or equivalent):* IELTS 6.0. English courses available over one or two months or longer. International student programme. *Fees:* £10,420. *Living costs:* £7200. Twenty Scholarships for Excellence offered.

Worcester *English language entry requirement (or equivalent):* IELTS 6.0. *Fees:* Check with the University. *Living costs:* £6000–£6500.

York Fifteen per cent of students from outside the UK. *English language entry requirement (or equivalent):* IELTS 6.0. Six-month and pre-sessional English language courses. Intensive vacation courses. *Fees:* £12,720–£16,540; Medicine £24,080. *Living costs:* £7800. Several scholarships for overseas students.

York St John *English language entry requirement (or equivalent):* IELTS 6.0 (three-year degree course or four-year course including Foundation year). *Fees:* £9000; Occupational Therapy/Physiotherapy £11,500. *Living costs:* £7900–£8600.

BRITISH OVERSEAS TERRITORIES STUDENTS

Students from British Overseas Territories are now treated as home students for fee purposes at universities and other institutions of higher education in the UK. The territories to which this policy applies are:

British Overseas Territories Anguilla, Bermuda, British Antarctic Territory, British Indian Ocean Territory, British Virgin Islands, Cayman Islands, Falkland Islands, Montserrat, Pitcairn Islands, South Georgia and the South Sandwich Islands, St Helena and its Dependencies, Turks and Caicos Islands.

Overseas Territories of other EU member states Greenland, Faroe Islands (Denmark), Netherlands Antilles (Bonaire, Curacao, Saba, St Eustatius, St Marten), Aruba (Netherlands), New Caledonia, French Polynesia, Wallis and Futura, Mayotte, St Pierre et Miquelon (France).

SECTION 1: UNIVERSITIES

Listed below are universities in the United Kingdom that offer degree and diploma courses at higher education level. Applications to these institutions are submitted through UCAS except for part-time courses, private universities and colleges, and further education courses. For current information refer to the websites shown and also to www.ucas.com for a comprehensive list of degree and diploma courses (see **Appendix 4**).

Aberdeen This is a city-centre university on Scotland's east coast. (University of Aberdeen, Students Admissions and School Leavers, University Office, King's College, Aberdeen, Scotland AB24 3FX. Tel 01224 272090; www.abdn.ac.uk)

Abertay The University has a modern city-centre campus and a range of courses with an applied, practical focus. (Abertay University, Student Recruitment Office, Kydd Building, Dundee, Scotland DD1 1HG. Tel 01382 308000; www.abertay.ac.uk)

Aberystwyth This is a coastal university with an attractive campus. (Aberystwyth University, Undergraduate Admissions Office, Student Welcome Centre, Penglais Campus, Aberystwyth, Wales SY23 3FB. Tel 01970 622021; www.aber.ac.uk)

Anglia Ruskin The University has main campuses in Cambridge and Chelmsford and partner colleges throughout East Anglia. (Anglia Ruskin University, Bishop Hall Lane, Chelmsford, England CM1 1SQ. Tel 01245 686868; www.anglia.ac.uk)

Arts London Six distinctive and distinguished colleges make up University of the Arts London: Camberwell College of Arts, Central Saint Martins College of Arts and Design, Chelsea College of Art and Design, London College of Communication, London College of Fashion, and Wimbledon College of Art. The Colleges offer the University's 20,000 students a diverse range of courses at all levels from foundation and undergraduate to postgraduate and research. (University of the Arts London, 272 High Holborn, London, England WC1V 7EY. Tel 020 7514 6000; www.arts.ac.uk)

Aston This University has a green campus in the centre of Birmingham with academic, sporting and social activities on site. (Aston University, The Registry (Admissions), Aston Triangle, Birmingham, England B4 7ET. Tel 0121 204 4444; www.aston.ac.uk)

Bangor The University has a central site in Bangor on the Menai Straits with partner institutions (including the Welsh College of Horticulture) throughout North Wales. (Bangor University, The Student Recruitment Unit, Bangor, Wales LL57 2DG. Tel 01248 382017; www.bangor.ac.uk)

Bath The University is on a rural campus one mile from the centre of Bath, with partner colleges in Bath, Swindon and Wiltshire. (University of Bath, Claverton Down, Bath, England BA2 7AY. Tel 01225 383019; www.bath.ac.uk)

Bath Spa This University was created in 2005 and is located on two campuses near Bath, with partner colleges in Wiltshire. (Bath Spa University, Admissions Office, Newton Park, Newton St Loe, Bath, England BA2 9BN. Tel 01225 875875; www.bathspa.ac.uk)

Bedfordshire The University was formed in August 2006 from the merger of Luton University and the Bedford campus of De Montfort University. The main campus is in the centre of Luton, with two campuses in Bedford, and four partner colleges. (University of Bedfordshire, The Admissions Office, University Square, Luton, England LU1 3JU. Tel 01234 400400; www.beds.ac.uk)

Birmingham This is a 'red-brick' university at Edgbaston to the south of the city, with a second campus at Selly Oak. (University of Birmingham, Edgbaston, Birmingham, England B15 2TT. Tel 0121 415 8900; www.birmingham.ac.uk)

Birmingham (UC) A specialist institution offering courses in Hospitality, Tourism and allied studies. (University College Birmingham, Summer Row, Birmingham, England B3 1JB. Tel 0121 604 1000; www.ucb.ac.uk)

Birmingham City Part-time evening courses are offered for mature students wishing to read for first and higher degrees. Courses are offered in the Faculties of Arts, Science, Social Science and Continuing Education. (Birmingham City University, City North Campus, Birmingham, England B42 2SU. Tel 0121 331 5000; www.bcu.ac.uk)

Bishop Grosseteste A Church of England foundation offering Single and Joint Honours courses in Childhood Studies, Drama, Education, English and Theology and Ethics. (Bishop Grosseteste University, Longdales Road, Lincoln, England LN1 3DY. Tel 01522 527347; www.bishopg.ac.uk)

Bolton The University was granted university status in 2005 and is based at Deane Campus, close to the town centre. The University has been a higher education provider since 1982 and can trace its roots back to the first mechanical institutes. It was the third in the country, opening in 1824. (University of Bolton, Recruitment and Admissions, Deane Road, Bolton, England BL3 5AB. Tel 01204 900600; www.bolton.ac.uk)

Bournemouth The University site is in a large coastal resort, with partner colleges in the region also offering courses. (Bournemouth University, Talbot Campus, Fern Barrow, Poole, England BH12 5BB. Tel 01202 961916; www.bournemouth.ac.uk)

Bournemouth Arts Arts University Bournemouth (formerly The Arts University College at Bournemouth) was established in 1885 as a specialist institution in art, design, media and performance. (Arts University Bournemouth, Wallisdown, Poole, England BH12 5HH. Tel 01202 533011; www.aub.ac.uk)

BPP Campuses in Birmingham, London and Manchester. (BPP University, 6th Floor Boulton House, Chorlton Street, Manchester, England M1 3HY. Tel 0330 060 3100; www.bpp.com)

Bradford The University's main campus is close to the city centre, with the School of Management two miles away. (University of Bradford, Course Enquiries Office, Richmond Road, Bradford, England BD7 1DP. Tel 0800 073 1255; www.bradford.ac.uk)

Brighton Situated on the south coast, the University has five campuses in Brighton, Eastbourne and Hastings. University-validated courses are offered at several partner colleges. (University of Brighton, The Registry (Admissions), Mithras House, Lewes Road, Brighton, England BN2 4AT. Tel 01273 600900; www.brighton.ac.uk)

Brighton and Sussex (MS) BSMS is a small medical school, based in Falmer, approximately five miles away from the centre of Brighton. There is frequent public transport from central Brighton to both sites, with 24-hour buses running seven days a week. (Brighton and Sussex Medical School, BSMS Admissions, University of Sussex, Brighton, England BN1 9PX. Tel 01273 643528; www.bsms.ac.uk)

Bristol A world-renowned university, one of the most popular in the UK. This is a city university with halls of residence in Stoke Bishop and Clifton. (University of Bristol, Senate House, Tyndall Avenue, Bristol, England BS8 1TH. Tel 0117 928 9000; www.bristol.ac.uk)

Bristol UWE The University has four campuses in and around Bristol with an associate Faculty at Hartpury, and regional centres in Bath, Gloucestershire and Swindon. It also has links with the Bristol Old Vic Theatre School and the Royal West of England Academy. (University of the West of England, Bristol, Admissions Office, Frenchay Campus, Coldharbour Lane, Bristol, England BS16 1QY. Tel 0117 965 6261; www.uwe.ac.uk)

Brunel The University has a compact campus to the west of London at Uxbridge. (Brunel University, Admissions Office, Uxbridge, England UB8 3PH. Tel 01895 265265; www.brunel.ac.uk)

Buckingham A small independent university, it has two sites within the town some 40 miles north of London offering two-year (eight-term) degrees. (University of Buckingham, Admissions Office, Hunter Street, Buckingham, England MK18 1EG. Tel 01280 814080; www.buckingham.ac.uk)

Bucks New It has two campuses in High Wycombe and one at Chalfont St Giles, and links with partner colleges; two of which are UCFB (Burnley and Wembley) offering football courses. (Buckinghamshire New University, Admissions, Queen Alexandra Road, High Wycombe, England HP11 2JZ. Tel 0800 056 5660; www.bucks.ac.uk)

Cambridge The University has 29 undergraduate Colleges located throughout the city: Christ's, Churchill, Clare, Corpus Christi, Downing, Emmanuel, Fitzwilliam, Girton, Gonville and Caius, Homerton, Hughes Hall (mature students only), Jesus, King's, Lucy Cavendish (mature, female students only), Magdalene, Murray Edwards (female students only), Newnham (female students only), Pembroke, Peterhouse, Queens', Robinson, St Catharine's, St Edmund's (mature students only), St John's, Selwyn, Sidney Sussex, Trinity, Trinity Hall, and Wolfson (mature students only). (University of Cambridge, Cambridge Admissions Office, Fitzwilliam House, 32 Trumpington Street, Cambridge, England CB2 1QY. Tel 01223 337733; www.cam.ac.uk)

Canterbury Christ Church The University was created in 2005 with the main campus located near Canterbury city centre and campuses also at Broadstairs, Medway University Centre and Folkestone. The University is the third highest in England for student employability. (Canterbury Christ Church University, Admissions, North Holmes Road, Canterbury, England CT1 1QU. Tel 01227 782900; www.canterbury.ac.uk)

Cardiff The main (Cathays Park) campus of the University is located in the city centre, with the Heath Park campus a mile to the south. (Cardiff University, Admissions, MacKenzie House, 30–36 Newport Road, Cardiff, Wales CF10 3XQ. Tel 029 2087 4000; www.cardiff.ac.uk)

Cardiff Met (UWIC) Cardiff Metropolitan University (formerly UWIC) sits in the heart of the capital and is made up of five academic schools: Cardiff School of Art and Design, Cardiff School of Education, Cardiff School of Health Sciences, Cardiff School of Management and Cardiff School of Sport. (Cardiff Metropolitan University, Llandaff Campus, Western Avenue, Cardiff, Wales CF5 2YB. Tel 029 2041 6044; Admissions Enquiries 029 2041 6010; www.cardiffmet.ac.uk)

Central Lancashire The University is located on a small campus close to Preston city centre. Single and Joint Honours are offered with subjects either studied equally or weighted towards one subject in a 75/25 split. (University of Central Lancashire, Admissions Office, Preston, England PR1 2HE. Tel 01772 201201; www.uclan.ac.uk)

Chester The University was formed in 2005 and is located on a campus in Chester with a second campus in Warrington and three partner colleges. (University of Chester, Undergraduate Admissions, Parkgate Road, Chester, England CH1 4BJ. Tel 01244 512528; www.chester.ac.uk)

Chichester One of the UK's smallest universities with just over 5500 students. Campuses are situated in Chichester and Bognor Regis. (University of Chichester, Admissions, Bishop Otter Campus, College Lane, Chichester, England PO19 6PE. Tel 01243 816002; www.chi.ac.uk)

City The University is situated in central London, with Nursing and Midwifery courses located at St Bartholomew's Hospital. (City University London, Undergraduate Admissions Office, Northampton Square, London, England EC1V 0HB. Tel 020 7040 5060; www.city.ac.uk)

Coventry The University has a 33-acre campus in Coventry and a number of teaching centres throughout the city with courses offered in several partner colleges. (Coventry University, The Student Centre, 1 Gulson Road, Coventry, England CV1 2JH. Tel 024 7615 2222; www.coventry.ac.uk)

Creative Arts The University has five colleges: three in Kent (Canterbury, Maidstone and Rochester) and two in Surrey (Epsom and Farnham). (University for the Creative Arts, Enquiries Service, Falkner Road, Farnham, England GU9 7DS. Tel 01252 892960; www.ucreative.ac.uk)

Cumbria This University was founded in 2007 by the merger of three institutions: Cumbria Institute of the Arts, St Martin's College and University of Central Lancashire's Cumbria site (including the campus at Newton Rigg). The University of Cumbria's four campuses are located at Carlisle Fusehill Street, Carlisle Brampton Road, Lancaster and Ambleside and it also has sites at Energus Workington, Newton Rigg College Penrith, Tower Hamlets London and Furness College Barrow-in-Furness. (University of Cumbria, Fusehill Street, Carlisle, Cumbria, England CA1 2HH. Tel 0845 606 1144; www.cumbria.ac.uk)

De Montfort The University has two sites in Leicester and nine associated colleges. (De Montfort University, Students Admissions, The Gateway, Leicester, England LE1 9BH. Tel 0116 255 1551; www.dmu.ac.uk)

Derby The University has two campuses: one close to Derby city centre and the second at Buxton. (University of Derby, Admissions, Kedleston Road, Derby, England DE22 1GB. Tel 01332 591167; www.derby.ac.uk)

Dundee A city-centre campus, with the Medical School and School of Nursing located at Ninewells Hospital to the west of the city. (University of Dundee, Admissions and Student Recruitment, Nethergate, Dundee, Scotland DD1 4HN. Tel 01382 383838; www.dundee.ac.uk)

Durham The University has 15 colleges admitting undergraduates, split between the main site in Durham city and on the Queen's campus, Stockton. Durham city colleges: Collingwood, Grey, Hatfield, Josephine Butler, St Aidan's, St Chad's, St Cuthbert's, St Hild and St Bede, St John's, St Mary's, Trevelyan, University, Van Mildert. Stockton colleges: John Snow, Stephenson. Durham University is the third oldest university in England. Undergraduate students have access to teaching by world experts, award-winning study facilities, extensive collections of books and learning resources and a unique collegiate system offering a distinctive student experience. (Durham University, The Palatine Centre, Stockton Road, Durham, England DH1 3LE. Tel 0191 334 6128; www.dur.ac.uk)

East Anglia The University is set in parkland close to Norwich. (University of East Anglia, Admissions Office, Norwich Research Park, Norwich, England NR4 7TJ. Tel 01603 591515; www.uea.ac.uk)

East London The University has campuses in London at Stratford and Docklands. Courses are also offered at several colleges in Greater London. (University of East London, Docklands Campus, 4–6 University Way, London, England E16 2RD. Tel 020 8223 3333; www.uel.ac.uk)

Edge Hill The University is situated on a spacious campus in Ormskirk near Liverpool and offers a wide range of three-year degrees. (Edge Hill University, St Helens Road, Ormskirk, England L39 4QP. Tel 01695 575171; www.edgehill.ac.uk)

Edinburgh The University's Central Area is located on the south side of the city centre. The King's Buildings (the main science and engineering campus), Medical School and Vet School are all to the south of the city centre, within easy travelling distance. (Edinburgh University, Old College, South Bridge, Edinburgh, Scotland EH8 9YL. Tel 0131 650 1000; www.ed.ac.uk)

Edinburgh Napier The University has three main campuses in Edinburgh: the Business School is based in Craiglockhart Campus, the Faculty of Engineering, Computing and Creative Industries is based at Merchiston Campus and the Faculty of Health Life and Social Sciences is based at Sighthill Campus. (Edinburgh Napier University, Information Office, Craiglockart Campus, Edinburgh, Scotland EH14 1DJ. Tel 0845 520 3050; www.napier.ac.uk)

Edinburgh Queen Margaret This new university (2007) is located on a new, purpose-built campus on the Firth of Forth, east of Edinburgh, with student accommodation on site. (Queen Margaret University, Edinburgh, The Admissions Office, Queen Margaret University Drive, Musselburgh, Edinburgh, Scotland EH21 6UU. Tel 0131 474 0000; www.qmu.ac.uk)

Essex The University has a parkland campus two miles from Colchester. The University and the South Essex College Partnership also provide degree schemes at the new Southend campus. (University of Essex, Undergraduate Admissions, Wivenhoe Park, Colchester, England CO4 3SQ. Tel 01206 873666; www.essex.ac.uk)

Exeter The University has two sites in Exeter: the Streatham campus is the largest, and the St Luke's campus is a mile away. A third campus (the Cornwall campus) is situated at Penryn near Falmouth in Cornwall. (University of Exeter, Admissions Office, 8th Floor, Laver Building, North Park Road, Exeter, England EX4 4QE. Tel 0844 620 0012; www.exeter.ac.uk)

Falmouth Falmouth University specialises in arts-based subjects and is split between two campuses at Falmouth and Penryn. (Falmouth University, Admissions Office, Woodlane, Falmouth, England TR11 4RH. Tel 01326 213730; www.falmouth.ac.uk)

Glamorgan The University of Glamorgan and the University of Wales, Newport merged in 2013 to create the University of South Wales. Please see **South Wales** for more information.

Glasgow The University has three campuses: two on the outskirts of Glasgow and one on the Crichton campus at Dumfries. Glasgow School of Art and the Scottish Agricultural College in Ayr are associated institutions. (University of Glasgow, Recruitment and International Office, 71 Southpark Avenue, Glasgow, Scotland G12 8QQ. Tel 0141 330 2000; www.gla.ac.uk)

Glasgow Caledonian The University has a city-centre campus. (Glasgow Caledonian University, Cowcaddens Road, Glasgow, Scotland G4 0BA. Tel 0141 331 3334; www.gcu.ac.uk)

Gloucestershire Three campuses in Cheltenham and one in Gloucester form the University. It also has partner colleges in Gloucestershire, Herefordshire, Wiltshire and Worcestershire. Many students are home-based. (University of Gloucestershire, Admissions Office, The Park, Cheltenham, England GL50 2RH. Tel 0844 801 0001; www.glos.ac.uk)

Glyndŵr This is a new university (2008), formerly North East Wales IHE, and is situated in Wrexham town centre. (Glyndŵr University, Mold Road, Wrexham, Wales LL11 2AW. Tel 01978 293439; www.glyndwr.ac.uk)

Greenwich The main campus of the University is at Greenwich, a second is at Avery Hill in south London and a third is at Medway at Chatham Maritime, Kent. There are also partner colleges in east London and Kent. (University of Greenwich, Old Royal Naval College, Park Row, London, England SE10 9LS. Tel 020 8331 9000; www.gre.ac.uk)

Harper Adams A specialist institution offering courses in Agriculture and allied subjects. (Harper Adams University, Admissions Office, Newport, England TF10 8NB. Tel 01952 815000; www.harper-adams.ac.uk)

Heriot-Watt The University has a large parkland campus seven miles west of Edinburgh and a second campus in the Scottish Borders at Galashiels 35 miles to the south. (Heriot-Watt University, Admissions Unit, Edinburgh Campus, Edinburgh, Scotland EH14 4AS. Tel 0131 449 5111; www.hw.ac.uk)

Hertfordshire The University has two campuses in Hatfield. Courses are also offered through a consortium of four Hertfordshire colleges and the University has links with all Hertfordshire further education colleges. (University of Hertfordshire, University Admissions Service, College Lane, Hatfield, England AL10 9AB. Tel 01707 284800; www.herts.ac.uk)

Huddersfield This is a town-centre university with University Centres at Barnsley and Oldham and links to colleges of further education throughout the north of England. (University of Huddersfield, Admissions Office, Queensgate, Huddersfield, England HD1 3DH. Tel 01484 473969; www.hud.ac.uk)

Hull The main campus is in Hull, two miles from the city centre, with a smaller campus at Scarborough. (University of Hull, Admissions Service, Cottingham Road, Hull, England HU6 7RX. Tel 01482 466100; www.hull.ac.uk)

Hull York (MS) The Medical School is a partnership between the Universities of Hull and York, with teaching facilities on the main campuses of both universities. (Hull York Medical School, Admissions Office, University of York, Heslington, York, England YO10 5DD. Tel 0870 124 5500; www.hyms.ac.uk)

ifs (UC) The **ifs** *University College* is a registered charity, incorporated by Royal Charter and has a remit to provide the financial services industry with a skilled and competent workforce while also promoting a better understanding of finance amongst consumers. The **ifs** has a heritage in the provision of financial education spanning 130 years. (**ifs** *University College*, 8th Floor, Peninsular House, 36 Monument Street, London, England EC3R 8LJ. Tel 01227 829499; www.ifslearning.ac.uk)

Imperial London The College became an independent university, separate from the University of London, in 2007. The central site is in South Kensington. Medicine is based mainly at St Mary's Hospital, Paddington, Charing Cross Hospital and Hammersmith Hospital. (Imperial College London, Registry, Level 3 Sherfield Building, South Kensington Campus, London, England SW7 2AZ. Tel 020 7589 5111; www.imperial.ac.uk)

Keele This is a small university on a green campus five miles from Stoke-on-Trent. (Keele University, Academic Registry, Keele, England ST5 5BG. Tel 01782 734005; www.keele.ac.uk)

Kent The University is a leading research-led university in the south-east of England. It has two main campuses in Canterbury and Medway, with two associate colleges (South Kent College, Mid-Kent College) and is the lead sponsor of Brompton Academy. (University of Kent, Enrolment Management Services, The Registry, Canterbury, England CT2 7NZ. Tel 01227 827272; www.kent.ac.uk)

Kingston With four campuses in and around the town and 10 partner colleges, the University has easy access to London. (Kingston University, River House, 53–57 High Street, Kingston upon Thames, England KT1 1LQ. Tel 0844 855 2177; www.kingston.ac.uk)

Lancaster The University has a parkland site three miles south of Lancaster city centre. It is collegiate with each student being a member of one of the eight colleges. (Lancaster University, Undergraduate Admissions Office, Bailrigg, Lancaster, England LA1 4YW. Tel 01524 592028; www.lancaster.ac.uk)

Leeds The University is sited on a campus in the centre of the city. (University of Leeds, Undergraduate Admissions Office, Leeds, England LS2 9JT. Tel 0113 343 3999; www.leeds.ac.uk)

Leeds Beckett The University (formerly Leeds Metropolitan) has two campuses, one in the city and a second in Headingley on the outskirts of Leeds, and partner colleges throughout the region. (Leeds Beckett University, City Campus, Leeds, England LS1 3HE. Tel 0113 812 3113; www.leedsmet.ac.uk)

Leeds Trinity Originally established as a Catholic teacher training college, now offering a wide range of courses. (Leeds Trinity University, Student Enquiries Office, Brownberrie Lane, Horsforth, Leeds, England LS18 5HD. Tel 0113 283 7100; www.leedstrinity.ac.uk)

Leicester The compact campus is located on the southern edge of the city. (University of Leicester, Admissions Office, University Road, Leicester, England LE1 7RH. Tel 0116 252 2522; www.le.ac.uk)

Lincoln The Brayford and Cathedral campuses are in the city, with the Riseholme Park campus some five miles away. There is also a campus in Hull and associated colleges in Lincolnshire. (University of Lincoln, Academic Registry, Brayford Pool, Lincoln, England LN6 7TS. Tel 01522 886644; www.lincoln.ac.uk)

Liverpool The University has a large city-centre campus. (University of Liverpool, Student Recruitment and Admissions Office, Foundation Building, Brownlow Hill, Liverpool, England L69 7ZX. Tel 0151 794 5927; www.liv.ac.uk)

Liverpool Hope Liverpool Hope University has two campuses: one four miles from the city centre, the other a brisk walk from the city centre. Liverpool is a vibrant student city offering plenty of cultural, sporting, musical and social opportunities to students. (Liverpool Hope University, Admissions Office, Hope Park, Liverpool, England L16 9JD. Tel 0151 291 3000; www.hope.ac.uk)

Liverpool John Moores Liverpool John Moores University is a thriving, vibrant university located at the heart of Liverpool, consisting of three large campuses. (Liverpool John Moores University, Kingsway House, 2nd Floor, Hatton Garden, Liverpool, England L3 2AJ. Tel 0151 231 5090; www.ljmu.ac.uk)

London (Birk) The College is situated in Bloomsbury in the London University precinct and provides part-time and evening higher-education courses. (Birkbeck, University of London, Malet Street, London, England WC1E 7HX. Tel 020 7631 6000; www.bbk.ac.uk)

London (Gold) The College is located on a single campus in south-east London. (Goldsmiths, University of London, New Cross, London, England SE14 6NW. Tel 020 7919 7171; www.gold.ac.uk)

London (Hey) The College is on a site in central London, offering specialist studies in Philosophy or Theology. (Heythrop College, University of London, Registry, Kensington Square, London, England W8 5HN. Tel 020 7795 6600; www.heythrop.ac.uk)

London (Inst Ed) (Institute of Education, University of London, 20 Bedford Way, London, England WC1H 0AL. Tel 020 7612 6000; www.ioe.ac.uk)

London (Inst Paris) The Institute's Department of French Studies and Comparative Studies is located in central Paris and operates in partnership with Queen Mary and Royal Holloway, University of London.

(University of London Institute in Paris, 9–11 rue de Constantine, 75340, Paris, France Cedex 07. Tel +33 (0) 1 44 11 73 83/76; www.ulip.lon.ac.uk)

London (King's) The College has campuses in central and south London (Strand, Waterloo and London Bridge) and includes the School of Medicine, the Dental Institute and the School of Biomedical and Health Sciences. (King's College, University of London, Enquiries, Strand, London, England WC2R 2LS. Tel 020 7836 5454; www.kcl.ac.uk)

London (QM) There is a city campus in the East End of London. (Queen Mary, University of London, Admissions Office, Mile End Road, London, England E1 4NS. Tel 020 7882 5511; www.qmul. ac.uk)

London (RH) There is a large campus with halls of residence situated at Egham, 19 miles west of central London and three miles from Windsor. (Royal Holloway, University of London, Egham Hill, Egham, England TW20 0EX. Tel 01784 434455; www.rhul.ac.uk)

London (RVC) The College has campuses in London and Hertfordshire. (Royal Veterinary College, University of London, Royal College Street, London, England NW1 0TU. Tel 020 7468 5147; www.rvc. ac.uk)

London (St George's) Located on a compact site in south-west London, St George's is a specialist health sciences university, having extensive links with many hospitals and practices, and also with Kingston University and Royal Holloway London. (St George's, University of London, Cranmer Terrace, London, England SW17 0RE. Tel 020 8672 9944; www.sgul.ac.uk)

London (SOAS) The School of Oriental and African Studies (SOAS) is a college of the University of London and the only higher education institution in the UK specialising in the study of Asia, Africa and the Near and Middle East. (School of Oriental and African Studies, University of London, Thornhaugh Street, Russell Square, London, England WC1H 0XG. Tel 020 7637 2388; www.soas.ac.uk)

London (UCL) The College is located in Bloomsbury in the London University precinct. (University College London, University of London, Gower Street, London, England WC1E 6BT. Tel 020 7679 2000; www.ucl. ac.uk)

London (UCL Sch Pharm) The School has a central London site close to the London University precinct. (UCL School of Pharmacy, University of London, 29–39 Brunswick Square, London, England WC1N 1AX. Tel 020 7753 5831; www.ucl.ac.uk/pharmacy)

London LSE The School is located in the heart of London and specialises in the whole range of social science subjects (from Economics, Politics and Law to Sociology, Accounting and Finance). (London School of Economics and Political Science, Undergraduate Admissions Office, Houghton Street, London, England WC2A 2AE. Tel 020 7955 7125; www.lse.ac.uk)

London Met The University has two campuses: one in north London (with the largest (new) science laboratory in Europe) and one in the City, and several partner colleges. (London Metropolitan University, Admissions Office, 166–220 Holloway Road, London, England N7 8DB. Tel 020 7133 4200; www. londonmet.ac.uk)

London NCH NCH is an independent university college, centrally located in Bloomsbury, which is dedicated to providing high academic experience. (New College of the Humanities, 19 Bedford Square, London, England WC1B 3HH. Tel 020 7637 4550; www.nchum.org)

London Regent's The University has now been established as the UK's second private university offering a range of degree courses to the 4500 students based at it's central London location in Regent's Park. (Regent's University London, Inner Circle, Regent's Park, London, England NW1 4NS. Tel 020 7487 7700; www.regents.ac.uk)

London South Bank The main campus of the University is in Southwark on the south bank of the Thames in London. Other campuses are at Whipps Cross in east London and at Havering in Essex. (London South Bank University, Admissions Office, 90 London Road, London, England SE1 6LN. Tel 0800 923 8888; www.lsbu.ac.uk)

Loughborough On a large rural single-site campus, the University is a mile from the town centre. (Loughborough University, Undergraduate Admissions Office, Loughborough, England LE11 3TU. Tel 01509 263171; www.lboro.ac.uk)

Manchester The University has a large precinct one mile south of the city centre. The University of Manchester has a long tradition of excellence in higher education. (University of Manchester, Student Recruitment and Admissions, Rutherford Building, Oxford Road, Manchester, England M13 9PL. Tel 0161 275 2077; www.manchester.ac.uk)

Manchester Met The University has five sites in Manchester and one in Cheshire. It offers a wide choice of vocational and non-vocational courses, the former with industrial and commercial placements. (Manchester Metropolitan University, Admissions Office, All Saints Building, All Saints, Manchester, England M15 6BH. Tel 0161 247 2000; www.mmu.ac.uk)

Middlesex This is a multi-campus university in north London with associate colleges in the region. (Middlesex University, Hendon Campus, The Burroughs, London, England NW4 4BT. Tel 020 8411 5555; www.mdx.ac.uk)

Newcastle The University has a single campus in the city centre. (Newcastle University, Admissions Office, 6 Kensington Terrace, Newcastle-upon-Tyne, England NE1 7RU. Tel 0191 222 6000; www.ncl.ac.uk)

Newman This Catholic foundation offers a wide range of courses to undergraduates of all religions. (Newman University, Admissions Registrar, Genners Lane, Bartley Green, Birmingham, England B32 3NT. Tel 0121 476 1181; www.newman.ac.uk)

Newport The University of Glamorgan and the University of Wales, Newport merged in 2013 to create the University of South Wales. Please see **South Wales** for more information.

Northampton The University (created in 2005) has two campuses close to the town centre. (University of Northampton, Admissions Office, Park Campus, Boughton Green Road, Northampton, England NN2 7AL. Tel 0800 358 2232; www.northampton.ac.uk)

Northumbria The University has two campuses in and around Newcastle. (Northumbria University, Ellison Place, Newcastle-upon-Tyne, England NE1 8ST. Tel 0191 243 7420; www.northumbria.ac.uk)

Norwich Arts Courses focus on Art and Design and Media Studies (Norwich University of the Arts, Admissions, Francis House, 3–7 Redwell Street, Norwich, England NR2 4SN. Tel 01603 610561; www.nua.ac.uk)

Nottingham This is a large, campus university to the west of the city with a second campus two miles from the city centre, and a third at Sutton Bonington for the new School of Veterinary Science and Medicine, 10 miles south of University Park. (University of Nottingham, University Park, Nottingham, England NG7 2RD. Tel 0115 951 5559; www.nottingham.ac.uk)

Nottingham Trent The University has three campuses: City site, in the centre of Nottingham, Clifton and Brackenhurst. The Clifton campus of the University is four miles from Nottingham city centre and caters for Education, Humanities and Science, whilst Brackenhurst, near Southwell, focuses on land-based subjects. (Nottingham Trent University, Registry Admissions, Dryden Centre, Burton Street, Nottingham, England NG1 4BU. Tel 0115 941 8418; www.ntu.ac.uk)

Open University This is the UK's largest university for part-time and distance-learning higher education, providing support for students who must be aged over 18 years. Application and registration is made direct to the OU, and not through UCAS (at present). (Open University, Walton Hall, Milton Keynes, England MK7 6AA. Tel 0845 300 6090; www.open.ac.uk)

Oxford The University has 30 colleges and five private halls admitting undergraduates. Colleges: Balliol, Brasenose, Christ Church, Corpus Christi, Exeter, Harris Manchester (mature students only), Hertford, Jesus, Keble, Lady Margaret Hall, Lincoln, Magdalen, Mansfield, Merton, New, Oriel, Pembroke, St Anne's, St Catherine's, St Edmund Hall, St Hilda's, St Hugh's, St John's, St Peter's, Somerville, Queen's, Trinity, University, Wadham, Worcester. Permanent Private Halls: Blackfriars, Regent's Park College, St Benet's

Hall, St Stephen's House, Wycliffe. Whilst many universities offer reduced fees or bursaries, Oxford provides both in addition to generous support to those on a family income of less than £16,000. (University of Oxford, Undergraduate Admissions Office, University Offices, Wellington Square, Oxford, England OX1 2JD. Tel 01865 288000; www.ox.ac.uk)

Oxford Brookes The University has three main campuses in and around Oxford. (Oxford Brookes University, Admissions Office, Headington Campus, Gipsy Lane, Oxford, England OX3 0BP. Tel 01865 484848; www.brookes.ac.uk)

Peninsula (MS) From 2013 new students are studying for University of Exeter or Plymouth University degrees. Please see these institutions for more information.

Plymouth The University has two main campuses: one in Plymouth and a second, the Peninsula Allied Health Centre, is four miles north of the main campus. Courses are also offered at eight partner colleges. (University of Plymouth, Central Admissions, Drake Circus, Plymouth, England PL4 8AA. Tel 01752 585858; www.plymouth.ac.uk)

Portsmouth The main campus of the University is close to the town centre; courses are also taught at colleges in Hampshire and Surrey. (University of Portsmouth, Academic Registry, University House, Winston Churchill Avenue, Portsmouth, England PO1 2UP. Tel 023 9284 8484; www.port.ac.uk)

Queen's Belfast The University has a large campus in the south of the city. (Queen's University Belfast, Admissions Service, University Road, Belfast, Northern Ireland BT7 1NN. Tel 028 9024 5133; www.qub.ac.uk)

Reading Situated on 320 acres of landscaped parkland, the campus won the Green Flag Award in 2011 as the highest-rated university campus in the Scheme's national People's Choice Awards. There are three campuses in the University, with the main (Whiteknights) on a rural campus at the edge of the city, and two others within walking distance. Foundation degrees are taught at two partner colleges. (University of Reading, Student Recruitment Office, PO Box 217, Reading, England RG6 6AH. Tel 0118 378 8619; www.rdg.ac.uk)

Richmond (Am Int Univ) Richmond, The American International University in London, is an independent, not-for-profit, international, liberal arts and professional studies university established in 1972. It educates a multi-cultural student body in the American liberal arts tradition. (Richmond, The American International University in London, Queen's Road, Richmond-upon-Thames, England TW10 6JP. Tel 020 8332 8200; www.richmond.ac.uk)

Robert Gordon The University has two campuses in and near Aberdeen city centre. (Robert Gordon University, Admissions Office, Administration Building, Schoolhill, Aberdeen, Scotland AB10 1FR. Tel 01224 262728; www.rgu.ac.uk)

Roehampton Roehampton, London's only campus university, is located in south-west London, close to Richmond Park, and has four colleges: Digby Stuart, Froebel, Southlands and Whitelands. (Roehampton University, Enquiries Office, Erasmus House, Roehampton Lane, London, England SW15 5PU. Tel 020 8392 3000; www.roehampton.ac.uk)

St Andrews Founded in 1413, and the third oldest university in the English-speaking world, this is a town-centre university on the east coast of Scotland. (University of St Andrews, Admissions Application Centre, St Katherine's West, 16 The Scores, St Andrews, Scotland KY16 9AJ. Tel 01334 462150; www.st-andrews.ac.uk)

St Mark and St John A teacher training institution by tradition but now offering a range of courses. (University of St Mark and St John, Admissions Office, Derriford Road, Plymouth, England PL6 8BH. Tel 01752 636890; www.marjon.ac.uk)

St Mary's A small, picturesque university located between Richmond and Kingston-on-Thames in south-west London. Combined courses offer two subjects in Year 1, a major/minor choice in Year 2 and the final degree subject in Year 3. Originally founded for the training of teachers it now offers a wide range of additional subjects for its 3700 full-time students. (St Mary's University Twickenham,

Registry, Waldegrave Road, Strawberry Hill, Twickenham, England TW1 4SX. Tel 020 8240 4000; www. smuc.ac.uk)

Salford This is a city-centre campus university. All courses are taught in the central campus, except for Midwifery which is taught at Bury and Nursing which is at Eccles. (University of Salford, Admissions Officer, The Crescent, Salford, England M5 4WT. Tel 0161 295 4545; www.salford.ac.uk)

Sheffield The University campus is close to Sheffield's city centre. (University of Sheffield, Western Bank, Sheffield, England S10 2TN. Tel 0114 222 2000; www.shef.ac.uk)

Sheffield Hallam The University has two campuses: one in the city centre, and the second two miles away. (Sheffield Hallam University, Admissions Office, City Campus, Howard Street, Sheffield, England S1 1WB. Tel 0114 225 5555; www.shu.ac.uk)

South Wales The University of South Wales was formed by the merger of the University of Glamorgan and the University of Wales, Newport. (University of South Wales, Treforest Campus, Pontypridd, Wales CF37 1DL. Tel 0845 576 7778; www.southwales.ac.uk)

Southampton The University has five main campuses in Southampton and Winchester. (University of Southampton, University Road, Southampton, England SO17 1BJ. Tel 023 8059 5000; www.southampton. ac.uk)

Southampton Solent Southampton Solent University first became a university in 2005 but has a well-established background in higher education which can be traced back to 1856. Situated close to Southampton city centre, the University has two partner colleges. (Southampton Solent University, Student Recruitment, East Park Terrace, Southampton, England SO14 0YN. Tel 023 8031 9039; www. solent.ac.uk)

Staffordshire The University has campuses at Stafford, Stoke, Lichfield, Shrewsbury and several regional colleges. (Staffordshire University, Admissions, C117 Cadman Building, College Road, Stoke-on-Trent, England ST4 2DE. Tel 01782 294400; www.staffs.ac.uk)

Stirling A campus-based university close to the centre of Stirling. (University of Stirling, UG Admissions Office, Stirling, Scotland FK9 4LA. Tel 01786 467044; www.stir.ac.uk)

Strathclyde The University's main campus is in Glasgow city centre, with the Jordanhill campus to the west of the city. (University of Strathclyde, 16 Richmond Street, Glasgow, Scotland G1 1XQ. Tel 0141 552 4400; www.strath.ac.uk)

Sunderland The main campus of the University is in Sunderland city centre, with the Sir Tom Cowie campus across the river accommodating the Business School and Informatics Centre. (University of Sunderland, Edinburgh Building, City Campus, Chester Road, Sunderland, England SR1 3SD. Tel 0191 515 3154; www.sunderland.ac.uk)

Surrey The University has a modern campus a mile from Guildford city centre. Some Foundation-year teaching takes place in local colleges. (University of Surrey, Stag Hill, Guildford, England GU2 7XH. Tel 01483 300800; www.surrey.ac.uk)

Sussex The University has a single-site campus four miles from Brighton. (University of Sussex, Student Recruitment Services, Sussex House, Falmer, Brighton, England BN1 9RH. Tel 01273 876787; www.sussex. ac.uk)

Swansea The University is situated in a parkland campus outside Swansea. (Swansea University, Admissions, Singleton Park, Swansea, Wales SA2 8PP. Tel 01792 205678; www.swan.ac.uk)

Teesside This is a city-centre university, with its campus in Middlesbrough. It has links with colleges in the region. (Teesside University, Admissions Office, Middlesbrough, England TS1 3BA. Tel 01642 218121; www.tees.ac.uk)

Trinity Saint David This university was created by the merger of the University of Wales, Lampeter, Trinity University College Carmarthen and, more recently, Swansea Metropolitan, with courses run in all locations.

(Trinity Saint David, University of Wales, Academic Registry, Lampeter, Wales SA48 7ED. Tel Carmarthen 01267 676767; Lampeter 01570 422351; Swansea 07192 481000; www.trinitysaintdavid.ac.uk)

Trinity Saint David (Swansea) Formerly Swansea Metropolitan, this University merged with Trinity Saint David in 2013 and is situated in the centre of Swansea. (Trinity Saint David (Swansea), Admissions Office, Mount Pleasant Campus, Swansea, Wales SA1 6ED. Tel 01792 481000; www.trinitysaintdavid.ac.uk)

UHI The University of the Highlands and Islands is based on a partnership of colleges and research centres. Courses are offered thoughout Scotland at various centres including Argyll, Lews Castle, Moray, Perth, Orkney and Shetland. (University of the Highlands and Islands, Course Information Unit, Executive Office, Ness Walk, Inverness, Scotland IV3 5SQ. Tel 01463 279000; www.uhi.ac.uk)

Ulster The University has four campuses: Belfast, Coleraine, Jordanstown, and Magee in Londonderry. (University of Ulster, Belfast Campus, York Street, Belfast, Northern Ireland BT15 1ED. Tel 028 701 23456; www.ulster.ac.uk)

Univ Law (formally the College of Law) The University offers specialised law courses across the country with centres in Birmingham, Bristol, Chester, Guildford, London, Manchester and York. (University of Law, Braboeuf Manor, St Catherines, Guildford, England GU3 1HA. Tel 0800 289997; www.law.ac.uk)

Warwick The University has a single-site campus situated three miles outside Coventry. (University of Warwick, Student Admissions Office, Coventry, England CV4 7AL. Tel 024 7652 3723; www.warwick.ac.uk)

West London (formerly Thames Valley University) The University has campuses at Ealing, Reading, Slough and Brentford, and links with four sites in west London and associated colleges. (University of West London, Learning Advice Centre, St Mary's Road, London, England W5 5RF. Tel 0800 036 8888; www.uwl.ac.uk)

West Scotland This university was formed in 2007 from the merger of the University of Paisley and Bell College. There are four campuses: Paisley, Ayr, Hamilton and Dumfries. UWS, which is unique due to its geographical spread, provides local university access for over 30% of Scotland's population. (University of the West of Scotland, Admissions Office, High Street, Paisley, Scotland PA1 2BE. Tel 0141 849 4101; www.uws.ac.uk)

Westminster The University has four campuses (Cavendish, Marylebone and Regent in central London and Harrow) and associated colleges including the British Academy of New Music. (University of Westminster, 309 Regent Street, London, England W1B 2HW. Tel 020 7915 5511; www.westminster.ac.uk)

Winchester A university close to the centre of Winchester with additional sites in Basingstoke and Bournemouth. (University of Winchester, Course Enquiries, West Hill, Winchester, England SO22 4NR. Tel 01962 827234; www.winchester.ac.uk)

Wolverhampton The University has two campuses in Wolverhampton and others in Walsall and Telford. (University of Wolverhampton, Wulfruna Street, Wolverhampton, England WV1 1LY. Tel 0800 953 3222; www.wlv.ac.uk)

Worcester This new university (2005) is located on a campus a short distance from Worcester city centre. (University of Worcester, Admissions Office, Henwick Grove, Worcester, England WR2 6AJ. Tel 01905 855111; www.worcester.ac.uk)

York The University has a landscaped campus on the outskirts of York and a smaller central site, the beautiful medieval King's Manor in the city centre. The University aims to select not only students who have the ability and motivation to benefit from the programmes they intend to follow but also students who will make a contribution to University life. (University of York, Admissions and School Liaison, Heslington, York, England YO10 5DD. Tel 01904 320000; www.york.ac.uk)

York St John The University is based on an award-winning campus in the centre of York with almost 6000 students studying a wide range of subjects. (York St John University, Lord Mayor's Walk, York, England YO31 7EX. Tel 01904 624624; www.yorksj.ac.uk)

SECTION 2: UNIVERSITY COLLEGES, INSTITUTES, AND SPECIALIST COLLEGES OF AGRICULTURE AND HORTICULTURE, ART, DANCE, DRAMA, MUSIC, OSTEOPATHY AND SPEECH

University colleges and institutes provide undergraduate and postgraduate courses in a wide range of subjects and are university-sector institutions. While many universities and university colleges offer courses in art, design, music, drama, agriculture, horticulture and courses connected to the land-based industries, the specialist colleges listed below provide courses at many levels, often part-time, in these separate fields.

It is important that you read prospectuses and check websites carefully and go to Open Days to find out as much as you can about these colleges and about their courses which interest you. Applications for full-time courses at the institutions listed below are through UCAS.

Abbreviations used below A = Art and Design; **Ag** = Agriculture, Animals and Land-related courses; **C** = Communication; **D** = Drama, Performing and Theatre Arts; **Da** = Dance; **F** = Fashion; **H** = Horticulture and Landscape-related courses; **M** = Music.

Academy of Live and Recorded Arts (ALRA) Studio 24, Royal Victoria Patriotic Building, John Archer Way, London, England SW18 3SX. Tel 020 8870 6475; www.alra.co.uk [**D**]

Anglo-European College of Chiropractic 13–15 Parkwood Road, Bournemouth, England BH5 2DF. Tel 01202 436200; www.aecc.ac.uk

Anniesland College Hatfield Campus, 19 Hatfield Drive, Glasgow, Scotland G12 0YE. Tel 0141 272 9000; www.anniesland.ac.uk

Architectural Association School of Architecture 36 Bedford Square, London, England WC1B 3ES. Tel 020 7887 4051; www.aaschool.ac.uk

Arts Educational Schools London Cone Ripman House, 14 Bath Road, London, England W4 1LY. Tel 020 8987 6666; www.artsed.co.uk [**A**]

Askham Bryan College Askham Bryan, York, England YO23 3FR. Tel 01904 772277; www.askham-bryan.ac.uk [**Ag**]

Berkshire College of Agriculture Hall Place, Burchetts Green, Maidenhead, England SL6 6QR. Tel 01628 824444; www.bca.ac.uk [**Ag**]

Bishop Burton College Learner Services, York Road, Bishop Burton, England HU17 8QG. Tel 01964 553000; www.bishopburton.ac.uk [**Ag**]

Bristol Old Vic Theatre School Bristol Old Vic Theatre School is an affiliate of the Conservatoire for Dance and Drama and is an Associate School of the University of the West of England. 2 Downside Road, Clifton, Bristol, England BS8 2XF. Tel 0117 973 3535; www.oldvic.ac.uk [**D**]

British College of Osteopathic Medicine Lief House, 120–122 Finchley Road, London, England NW3 5HR. Tel 020 7435 6464; www.bcom.ac.uk

British School of Osteopathy 275 Borough High Street, London, England SE1 1JE. Tel 020 7407 0222; Student Admissions 020 7089 5316; www.bso.ac.uk

Camberwell College of Art, University of the Arts London Peckham Road, London, England SE5 8UF. Tel 020 7514 6302; www.arts.ac.uk/camberwell [**A**]

Capel Manor College Administrative Office, Bullsmore Lane, Enfield, England EN1 4RQ. Tel 0845 612 2122; www.capel.ac.uk [**H**]

Cavendish College London 35–37 Alfred Place, London, England WC1E 7DP. Tel 0800 881 5232; www.theeducators.com/cavendish

Central Saint Martins College of Art and Design, University of the Arts London 1 Granary Square, King's Cross, London, England N1C 4AA. Tel 020 7514 7023; www.arts.ac.uk/csm [**A**]

Chelsea College of Art and Design, University of the Arts London 16 John Islip Street, London, England SW1P 4JU. Tel 020 7514 7751; www.arts.ac.uk/chelsea [**A**]

City and Guilds of London Art School 124 Kennington Park Road, London, England SE11 4DJ. Tel 020 7735 2306; www.cityandguildsartschool.ac.uk [**A**]

City College Norwich Ipswich Road, Norwich, England NR2 2LJ. Tel 01603 773311; www.ccn.ac.uk [**A**]

Cleveland College of Art and Design Green Lane, Linthorpe, Middlesbrough, England TS5 7RJ. Tel 01642 288000; www.ccad.ac.uk [**A**]

Colchester Institute Course Enquiries, Sheepen Road, Colchester, England CO3 3LL. Tel 01206 712000; www.colchester.ac.uk

College of Agriculture, Food and Rural Enterprise (CAFRE) Greenmount Campus, 45 Tirgracy Road, Antrim, Northern Ireland BT41 4PS. Tel 0800 028 4291; www.cafre.ac.uk [**Ag**]

College of Estate Management Whiteknights, Reading, England RG6 6AW. Tel 0800 019 9697; www.cem.ac.uk

Courtauld Institute of Art, University of London The Courtauld Institute of Art is one of the world's leading centres for the study of the history and conservation of art and architecture, and its gallery houses one of Britain's best-loved collections. Based at Somerset House, The Courtauld is an independent college of the University of London. Somerset House, Strand, London, England WC2R 0RN. Tel 020 7848 2645; www.courtauld.ac.uk [**A**]

Drama Centre London (part of Central St Martin's, University of the Arts London). Saffron House, 10 Back Hill, London, England EC1R 5LQ. Tel 020 7514 8760; Auditions 020 7514 7156 or 020 7514 8769; www.csm.arts.ac.uk/drama [**D**]

East 15 Acting School Hatfields, Rectory Lane, Loughton, England IG10 3RY. Tel 020 8508 5983; www.east15.ac.uk [**D**]

Edinburgh College of Art Academic Registry, Lauriston Place, Edinburgh, Scotland EH3 9DF. Tel 0131 651 5800; www.ed.ac.uk/eca [**A**]

European School of Osteopathy Boxley House, The Street, Boxley, Maidstone, England ME14 3DZ. Tel 01622 671558; www.eso.ac.uk

Glasgow School of Art 167 Renfrew Street, Glasgow, Scotland G3 6RQ. Tel 0141 353 4500; www.gsa.ac.uk [**A**]

Gray's School of Art, Robert Gordon University Garthdee Road, Aberdeen, Scotland AB10 7QD. Tel 01224 262728; www.rgu.ac.uk/grays [**A**]

Guildford School of Acting, GSA Conservatoire Stag Hill Campus, Guildford, England GU2 7XH. Tel 01483 684052; www.conservatoire.org [**D**]

Guildhall School of Music and Drama Silk Street, London, England EC2Y 8DT. Tel 020 7628 2571; www.gsmd.ac.uk [**M**]

Hartpury College Hartpury House, Hartpury, England GL19 3BE. Tel 01452 702345; www.hartpury.ac.uk [**Ag**]

Heatherley School of Fine Art 75 Lots Road, London, England SW10 0RN. Tel 020 7351 4190; www.heatherleys.org [**A**]

Hereford College of Arts Folly Lane, Hereford, England HR1 1LT. Tel 01432 273359; www.hca.ac.uk [**A**]

Leeds College of Art Blenheim Walk, Leeds, England LS2 9AQ. Tel 0113 202 8000; www.leeds-art.ac.uk [**A**]

Leeds College of Music 3 Quarry Hill, Leeds, England LS2 7PD. Tel 0113 222 3416; www.lcm.ac.uk [**M**]

Liverpool Institute for Performing Arts The Liverpool Institute of Performing Arts provides courses in Acting, Community Drama, Dance, Music, Theatre and Entertainment Management, Sound Technology,

Theatre and Performance Design, and Theatre and Performance Technology. For the past four years LIPA has traced 85% of each year group who have graduated, of these an average 93% are in work with 82% working in the performing arts. Mount Street, Liverpool, England L1 9HF. Tel 0151 330 3000; www.lipa.ac.uk [**D**]

London Academy of Music and Dramatic Art 155 Talgarth Road, London, England W14 9DA. Tel 020 8834 0500; www.lamda.org.uk [**M**]

London College of Communication, University of the Arts London Elephant and Castle, London, England SE1 6SB. Tel 020 7514 6599; www.arts.ac.uk/lcc [**C**]

London College of Fashion, University of the Arts London 20 John Princes Street, London, England W1G 0BJ. Tel 020 7514 7563; www.arts.ac.uk/fashion [**F**]

Mountview Academy of Theatre Arts Mountview is situated in Wood Green, in the Borough of Haringey, north London; home of Alexandra Palace. It is well placed for easy access to West End theatres, fringe theatres and London nightlife. Founded in 1945, Mountview offers extensive and stimulating training for those interested in pursuing a performance, directing or technical theatre career. Ralph Richardson Memorial Studio, Kingfisher Place, Clarendon Road, London, England N22 6XF. Tel 020 8881 2201; www.mountview.org.uk [**D**]

Myerscough College Six miles north of Preston, Myerscough College is a higher and further education college dating back to the 19th century. It specialises in education and training for the land-based and sports industries, offering more than 20 different subjects. Myerscough Hall, St Michael's Road, Bilsborrow, Preston, England PR3 0RY. Tel 01995 642211; www.myerscough.ac.uk [**Ag**]

Northern School of Contemporary Dance 98 Chapeltown Road, Leeds, England LS7 4BH. Tel 0113 219 3000; www.nscd.ac.uk [**Da**]

Northop College (part of Coleg Cambria) Holywell Road, Northop, Wales CH7 6AA. Tel 01352 841000; www.cambria.ac.uk [**H**]

Plymouth College of Art Tavistock Place, Plymouth, England PL4 8AT. Tel 01752 203434; www.plymouthart.ac.uk [**A**]

Ravensbourne 6 Penrose Way, London, England SE10 0EW. Tel 020 3040 3500; www.rave.ac.uk [**C**]

Reaseheath College Reaseheath, Nantwich, England CW5 6DF. Tel 01270 625131; HE Enquiries 01270 613284; www.reaseheath.ac.uk [**Ag**]

Rose Bruford College Lamorbey Park Campus, Burnt Oak Lane, Sidcup, England DA15 9DF. Tel 020 8308 2600; www.bruford.ac.uk [**D**]

Royal Academy of Dance 36 Battersea Square, London, England SW11 3RA. Tel 020 7326 8000; www.rad.org.uk [**Da**]

Royal Academy of Dramatic Art (RADA) 62–64 Gower Street, London, England WC1E 6ED. Tel 020 7636 7076; www.rada.ac.uk [**D**]

Royal Academy of Music, University of London This is Britain's senior conservatoire, founded in 1822. Marylebone Road, London, England NW1 5HT. Tel 020 7873 7373; www.ram.ac.uk [**M**]

Royal Ballet School 46 Floral Street, London, England WC2E 9DA. Tel 020 7836 8899; www.royal-ballet-school.org.uk [**Da**]

Royal Central School of Speech and Drama The School's main campus is at the Embassy Theatre, 15 minutes by Underground from Central London. Royal Central School of Speech and Drama, Eton Avenue, London, England NW3 3HY. Tel 020 7722 8183; www.cssd.ac.uk [**D**]

Royal College of Music Prince Consort Road, London, England SW7 2BS. Tel 020 7591 4300; www.rcm.ac.uk [**M**]

Royal Conservatoire of Scotland (formerly Royal Scottish Academy of Music and Drama) 100 Renfrew Street, Glasgow, Scotland G2 3DB. Tel 0141 332 4101; www.rcs.ac.uk [**M**]

Royal Northern College of Music 124 Oxford Road, Manchester, England M13 9RD. Tel 0161 907 5200; www.rncm.ac.uk [**M**]

Royal Welsh College of Music and Drama Castle Grounds, Cathays Park, Cardiff, Wales CF10 3ER. Tel 029 2039 1361; www.rwcmd.ac.uk [**M**]

Ruskin School of Drawing and Fine Art 74 High Street, Oxford, England OX1 4BG. Tel 01865 276940; www.ruskin-sch.ox.ac.uk [**A**]

Scotland's Rural College Student Recruitment and Admissions Office, SAC Riverside Campus, University Avenue, Ayr, Scotland KA8 0SR. Tel 0800 269453; www.sruc.ac.uk [**Ag**]

Slade School of Fine Art, University College London Part of UCL, The Slade School of Fine Art is concerned with contemporary art and the practice, history and theories that inform it. Gower Street, London, England WC1E 6BT. Tel 020 7679 2313; www.ucl.ac.uk/slade [**A**]

Sparsholt College Hampshire Westley Lane, Sparsholt, Winchester, England SO21 2NF. Tel 01962 776441; www.sparsholt.ac.uk [**H**]

Stranmillis University College Academic Registry, Stranmillis Road, Belfast, Northern Ireland BT9 5DY. Tel 028 9038 1271; www.stran.ac.uk

Trinity Laban Conservatoire of Music and Dance Creekside, London, England SE8 3DZ. Tel 020 8691 8600; www.trinitylaban.ac.uk [**M**]

University Campus Suffolk Admissions Office, Waterfront Building, Neptune Quay, Ipswich, England IP4 1QJ. Tel 01473 338000; www.ucs.ac.uk

University College of Football Business (partner college of Bucks New University) Campuses in Burnley and Wembley. Burnley Football Club, Turf Moor, Harry Potts Way, Burnley, England BB10 4BX. Tel 0843 208 2222; www.ucfb.com

Wimbledon College of Art, University of the Arts London Merton Hall Road, London, England SW19 3QA. Tel 020 7514 9641; www.wimbledon.arts.ac.uk [**A**]

Winchester School of Art, University of Southampton Park Avenue, Winchester, England SO23 8DL. Tel 023 8059 7141; www.wsa.soton.ac.uk [**A**]

Writtle College Lordship Road, Chelmsford, England CM1 3RR. Tel 01245 424200; www.writtle.ac.uk [**H**]

SECTION 3: UNIVERSITY CENTRES, FURTHER EDUCATION AND OTHER COLLEGES OFFERING HIGHER EDUCATION COURSES

Changes are taking place fast in this sector, with the merger of colleges and the introduction in 2009 of University Centres. These are linked to further education colleges and to one or more universities, and provide Foundation and Honours degree courses (often part-time) and sometimes postgraduate qualifications.

The following colleges appear under various subject headings in the tables in **Chapter 8** and are in UCAS for some of their courses. See prospectuses and websites for application details.

University Centres

Barony College SRUC Barony Campus, Parkgate, Dumfries, Scotland DG1 3NE. Tel 01387 860251; www.barony.ac.uk

Blackburn College Feilden Street, Blackburn, England BB2 1LH. Tel 01254 55144; Student Hotline 01254 292929; www.blackburn.ac.uk

Bradford College University Centre Admissions Office, Great Horton Road, Bradford, England BD7 1AY. Tel 01274 433333; www.bradfordcollege.ac.uk

College of West Anglia King's Lynn Centre, Tennyson Avenue, King's Lynn, Norfolk, England PE30 2QW. Tel 01553 761144; www.cwa.ac.uk

Doncaster College and University Centre High Melton, Doncaster, England DN5 7SZ. Tel 0800 358 7474; www.don.ac.uk

University Campus Oldham Cromwell Street, Oldham, England OL1 1BB. Tel 0161 334 8800; www.uco. oldham.ac.uk

University Centre Folkestone Mill Bay, Folkestone, England CT20 1JG. Tel 01227 782900; www. canterbury.ac.uk/AboutUs/Findus/Folkestone.aspx

University Centre Grimsby Nuns Corner, Laceby Road, Grimsby, England DN34 5BQ. Tel 0800 315002; www.grimsby.ac.uk

University Centre Milton Keynes 200 Silbury Boulevard, Milton Keynes, England MK9 1LT. Tel 01908 688223; www.mkcollege.ac.uk

University Centre Yeovil 91 Preston Road, Yeovil, England BA20 2DN. Tel 01935 845454; www.ucy. ac.uk

Other Further Education Colleges

Abingdon and Witney College Abingdon Campus, Wootton Road, Abingdon, England OX14 1GG. Tel 01235 555585; www.abingdon-witney.ac.uk

Accrington and Rossendale College Broad Oak Campus, Broad Oak Road, Accrington, England BB5 2AW. Tel 01254 389933; Information and Care 01254 354354; www.accross.ac.uk

Andover College Charlton Road, Andover, England SP10 1EJ. Tel 01264 360000; www.andover.ac.uk

Angus College Keptie Road, Arbroath, Scotland DD11 3EA. Tel 01241 432600; www.angus.ac.uk

Argyll College (UHI partner college – see Section 1) West Bay, Dunoon, Scotland PA23 7HP. Tel 0845 230 9969; www.argyll.uhi.ac.uk

Aylesbury College Oxford Road, Aylesbury, England HP21 8PD. Tel 01296 588588; www.aylesbury.ac.uk

Ayrshire College Dam Park, Ayr, Scotland KA8 0EU. Tel 0300 303 0303; www.ayrcoll.ac.uk

Banff and Buchan College Main Campus, Henderson Road, Fraserburgh, Scotland AB43 9GA. Tel 01346 586100; www.banff-buchan.ac.uk

Barking and Dagenham College Rush Green Campus, Dagenham Road, Romford, England RM7 0XU. Tel 020 8090 3020; www.barkingdagenhamcollege.ac.uk

Barnet and Southgate College Wood Street, Barnet, England EN5 4AZ. Tel 020 8266 4000; www. barnetsouthgate.ac.uk

Barnfield College New Bedford Road Campus, New Bedford Road, Luton, England LU2 7BF. Tel 01582 569569; http://college.barnfield.ac.uk

Barnsley College Church Street, Barnsley, England S70 2AN. Tel 01226 216165; www.barnsley.ac.uk

Basingstoke College of Technology Worting Road, Basingstoke, England RG21 8TN. Tel 01256 306237; www.bcot.ac.uk

Bedford College Cauldwell Street, Bedford, England MK42 9AH. Tel 01234 291000; www.bedford.ac.uk

Bexley College Tower Road, Belvedere, England DA17 6JA. Tel 01322 442331; www.bexley.ac.uk

Bicton College East Budleigh, Budleigh Salterton, England EX9 7BY. Tel 01395 562400; www.bicton. ac.uk

Birmingham Metropolitan College (incorporating Matthew Boulton College of Further and Higher Education and Sutton Coldfield College) Jennens Road, Birmingham, England B4 7PS. Tel 0845 155 0101; www.bmetc.ac.uk

Bishop Auckland College Woodhouse Lane, Bishop Auckland, England DL14 6JZ. Tel 01388 443000; www.bacoll.ac.uk

Blackpool and The Fylde College Ashfield Road, Bispham, Blackpool, England FY2 0HB. Tel 01253 504343; www.blackpool.ac.uk

Borders College Head Office, Scottish Borders Campus, Nether Road, Galashiels, Scotland TD1 3HE. Tel 01896 662600; www.borderscollege.ac.uk

Boston College Skirbeck Road, Boston, England PE21 6JF. Tel 01205 365701; www.boston.ac.uk

Bournemouth and Poole College Customer Enquiry Centre, North Road, Poole, England BH14 0LS. Tel 01202 205205; www.thecollege.co.uk

Bournville College Longbridge Lane, Longbridge, Birmingham, England B31 2AJ. Tel 0121 477 1300; www.bournville.ac.uk

Bracknell and Wokingham College College Information Centre, Church Road, Bracknell, England RG12 1DJ. Tel 0845 330 3343; www.bracknell.ac.uk

Bridgend College Cowbridge Road, Bridgend, Wales CF31 3DF. Tel 01656 302302; www.bridgend.ac.uk

Bridgwater College Bath Road, Bridgwater, England TA6 4PZ. Tel 01278 455464; www.bridgwater.ac.uk

Brockenhurst College Lyndhurst Road, Brockenhurst, England SO42 7ZE. Tel 01590 625555; www.brock.ac.uk

Bromley College of Further and Higher Education Rookery Lane, Bromley, England BR2 8HE. Tel 020 8295 7000; www.bromley.ac.uk

Brooklands College Weybridge Campus, Heath Road, Weybridge, England KT13 8TT. Tel 01932 797797; www.brooklands.ac.uk

Brooksby Melton College Melton Mowbray Campus, Ashfordby Road, Melton Mowbray, England LE13 0HJ. Tel 01664 850850; www.brooksbymelton.ac.uk

Burnley College Princess Way, Burnley, England BB12 0AN. Tel 01282 733373; Student Services 01282 733333; www.burnley.ac.uk

Burton College Student Services, Lichfield Street, Burton-on-Trent, England DE14 3RL. Tel 01283 494400; www.burton-college.ac.uk

Bury College Woodbury Centre, Market Street, Bury, England BL9 0BG. Tel 0161 280 8280; www.burycollege.ac.uk

Buxton and Leek College Part of University of Derby, the college has campuses in Leek, Buxton and on the main campus of the university. Stockwell Street, Leek, England ST13 6DP. Tel 0800 074 0099; www.blc.ac.uk

Calderdale College Francis Street, Halifax, England HX1 3UZ. Tel 01422 399399; www.calderdale.ac.uk

Cambridge Regional College Kings Hedges Road, Cambridge, England CB4 2QT. Tel 01223 418200; www.camre.ac.uk

Canterbury College New Dover Road, Canterbury, England CT1 3AJ. Tel 01227 811111; Learning Advice/ Courses 01227 811188; www.cant-col.ac.uk

Carlisle College Information Unit, Victoria Place, Carlisle, England CA1 1HS. Tel 01228 822700; www.carlisle.ac.uk

Carmel College Prescot Road, St Helens, England WA10 3AG. Tel 01744 452200; www.carmel.ac.uk

Carnegie College (formerly Lauder College) Pittsburgh Road, Halbeath, Dunfermline, Scotland KY11 8DY. Tel 0844 248 0155; www.carnegiecollege.ac.uk

Carshalton College Nightingale Road, Carshalton, England SM5 2EJ. Tel 020 8544 4444; www.carshalton. ac.uk

CECOS London College 59 Crompton Road, London, England N1 2YT. Tel 020 7359 3316; www.cecos. co.uk

Central Bedfordshire College (formerly Dunstable College) Kingsway, Dunstable, England LU5 4HG. Tel 0845 355 2525; www.centralbeds.ac.uk

Central College Nottingham A multi-campus college, with 11 locations across the city of Nottingham. Jesse Boot Avenue, Science Park, University Boulevard, Nottingham, England NG7 2RU. Tel 0115 914 6414; www.centralnottingham.ac.uk

Chelmsford College 102 Moulsham Street, Chelmsford, England CM2 0JQ. Tel 01245 265611; www. chelmsford.ac.uk

Chesterfield College Infirmary Road, Chesterfield, England S41 7NG. Tel 01246 500500; www.chesterfield. ac.uk

Chichester College Westgate Fields, Chichester, England PO19 1SB. Tel 01243 786321; www.chichester. ac.uk

City and Islington College The Marlborough Building, 383 Holloway Road, London, England N7 0RN. Tel 020 7700 9200; www.candi.ac.uk

City College Brighton and Hove Pelham Street, Brighton, England BN1 4FA. Tel 01273 667788; Course Advisers 01273 667759; www.ccb.ac.uk

City College Coventry Swanswell Centre, 50 Swanswell Street, Coventry, England CV1 5DG. Tel 024 7679 1000; Course Information 024 7679 1627; www.covcollege.ac.uk

City College Plymouth (formerly Plymouth College of Further Education) Kings Road, Devonport, Plymouth, England PL1 5QG. Tel 01752 305300; www.cityplym.ac.uk

City of Bath College Student Advice Centre, Avon St, Bath, England BA1 1UP. Tel 01225 312191; www. citybathcoll.ac.uk

City of Bristol College Ashley Down Road, Bristol, England BS7 9BU. Tel 0117 312 5000; www.cityofbristol. ac.uk

City of Glasgow College (formed in 2010 from a merger between Glasgow Nautical College, Glasgow Metropolitan and College of Commerce) 60 North Hanover Street, Glasgow, Scotland G1 2BP. Tel 0141 566 6222; www.cityofglasgowcollege.ac.uk

City of Liverpool College Bankfield Road, Liverpool, England L13 0BQ. Tel 0151 252 3000; www.liv-coll. ac.uk

City of Sunderland College Bede Centre, Durham Road, Sunderland, England SR3 4AH. Tel 0191 511 6000; HE Admissions 0191 511 6260; www.sunderlandcollege.ac.uk

City of Westminster College Paddington Green Campus, London, England W2 1NB. Tel 020 7723 8826; www.cwc.ac.uk

City of Wolverhampton College Paget Road Campus, Paget Road, Wolverhampton, England WV6 0DU. Tel 01902 836000; www.wolvcoll.ac.uk

Cliff College Calver, Hope Valley, Derbyshire, England S32 3XG. Tel 01246 584202; www.cliffcollege. ac.uk

Clydebank College College Square, Queens' Quay, Clydebank, Scotland G81 1BF. Tel 0141 951 7400; www.clydebank.ac.uk

Coatbridge College Kildonan Street, Coatbridge, Scotland ML5 3LS. Tel 01236 436000; www.coatbridge. ac.uk

Coleg Llandrillo Cymru Llandudno Road, Rhos-on-Sea, Wales LL28 4HZ. Tel 01492 546666; www. llandrillo.ac.uk

Coleg Menai Ffriddoedd Road, Bangor, Gwynedd, Wales LL57 2TP. Tel 01248 370125; www.menai.ac. uk

Coleg Sir Gâr Graig Campus, Sandy Road, Pwll, Wales SA15 4DN. Tel 01554 748000; www.colegsirgar. ac.uk

College of Haringey, Enfield and North East London (formed in 2009 from a merger between Enfield College and the College of North East London) Enfield Centre, 73 Hertford Road, Enfield, England EN3 5HA. Tel 020 8442 3103; www.conel.ac.uk

College of North West London Willesden Centre, Dudden Hill Lane, London, England NW10 2XD. Tel 020 8208 5000; Course Information 020 8208 5050; www.cnwl.ac.uk

College Ystrad Mynach Twyn Road, Ystrad Mynach, Hengoed, Wales CF82 7XR. Tel 01443 816888; www. ystrad-mynach.ac.uk

Cornwall College Camborne Campus, Trevenson Road, Pool, Redruth, England TR15 3RD. Tel 01209 616161; www.cornwall.ac.uk

Craven College High Street, Skipton, England BD23 1JY. Tel 01756 708001; www.craven-college.ac.uk

Croydon College College Road, Croydon, England CR9 1DX. Tel 020 8760 5934; www.croydon.ac.uk

Cumbernauld College Town Centre, Cumbernauld, Glasgow, Scotland G67 1HU. Tel 01236 731811; www. cumbernauld.ac.uk

Darlington College Central Park, Haughton Road, Darlington, England DL1 1DR. Tel 01325 503030; www. darlington.ac.uk

Dearne Valley College Manvers Park, Wath-upon-Dearne, Rotherham, England S63 7EW. Tel 01709 513355; www.dearne-coll.ac.uk

Derby College Prince Charles Avenue, Mackworth, Derby, England DE22 4LR. Tel 0800 028 0289; Course Enquiries 01332 387473; www.derby-college.ac.uk

Derwentside College Consett Campus, Front Street, Consett, England DH8 5EE. Tel 01207 585900; www. derwentside.ac.uk

Duchy College Rosewarne Campus, Camborne, England TR14 0AB. Tel 01209 722100; www.duchy.ac. uk

Dudley College The Broadway, Dudley, England DY1 4AS. Tel 01384 363000; Course Enquiries 01384 363363; www.dudleycol.ac.uk

Dumfries and Galloway College College Gate, Bankend Road, Dumfries, Scotland DG1 4FD. Tel 01387 734059; www.dumgal.ac.uk

Dundee College Kingsway Campus, Old Glamis Road, Dundee, Scotland DD3 8LE. Tel 01382 834834; Student Services 01382 834844; www.dundeecollege.ac.uk

Ealing, Hammersmith and West London College The Green, London, England W5 5EW. Tel 0800 980 2175; www.wlc.ac.uk

East Berkshire College Langley Campus, Station Road, Langley, England SL3 8BY. Tel 0845 373 2500; www.eastberks.ac.uk

East Durham College Houghall Campus, Houghall, England DH1 3SG. Tel 0191 375 4700; www. eastdurham.ac.uk

East Kent College Ramsgate Road, Broadstairs, England CT10 1PN. Tel 01843 605040; Admissions 01843 605049; www.eastkent.ac.uk

East Riding College Beverley Campus, Gallows Lane, Beverley, England HU17 7DT. Tel 0845 120 0037; www.eastridingcollege.ac.uk

East Surrey College Gatton Point, London Road, Redhill, England RH1 2JT. Tel 01737 788445; www.esc.ac.uk

Eastleigh College Chestnut Avenue, Eastleigh, England SO50 5FS. Tel 023 8091 1299; www.eastleigh.ac.uk

Easton and Otley College Easton, Norwich, England NR9 5DX. Tel 01603 731200; www.eastonotley.ac.uk

Edinburgh College Granton Campus, 350 West Granton Road, Edinburgh, Scotland EH5 1QE. Tel 0131 669 4400; www.edinburghcollege.ac.uk

Edinburgh's Telford College Now part of Edinburgh College. Granton Campus, 350 West Granton Road, Edinburgh, Scotland EH5 1QE. Tel 0131 669 4400; www.edinburghcollege.ac.uk

European Business School Admissions Department, Regent's College, Regent's Park, Inner Circle, London, England NW1 4NS. Tel 020 7487 7505; www.regents.ac.uk/about/schools/european-business-school-london

Exeter College Hele Road, Exeter, England EX4 4JS. Tel 01392 400500; www.exe-coll.ac.uk

Fareham College Bishopsfield Road, Fareham, England PO14 1NH. Tel 01329 815200; www.fareham.ac.uk

Farnborough College of Technology Boundary Road, Farnborough, England GU14 6SB. Tel 01252 407040; www.farn-ct.ac.uk

Fife College St Brycedale Campus, St Brycedale Avenue, Kirkcaldy, Scotland KY1 1EX. Tel 01592 223400; www.fife.ac.uk

Filton College Now part of South Gloucestershire and Stroud College. Filton Avenue, Filton, England BS34 7AT. Tel 0117 931 2121; www.filton.ac.uk

Forth Valley College Falkirk Campus, Grangemouth Road, Falkirk, Scotland FK2 9AD. Tel 0845 634 4444; www.forthvalley.ac.uk

Furness College Channelside, Barrow-in-Furness, England LA14 2PJ. Tel 01229 825017; www.furness.ac.uk

Gateshead College Baltic Campus, Baltic Business Quarter, Quarryfield Road, Gateshead, England NE8 3BE. Tel 0191 490 2246; www.gateshead.ac.uk

Glasgow Clyde College Mosspark Drive, Glasgow, Scotland G52 3AY. Tel 0141 272 3333; www.cardonald.ac.uk

Gloucestershire College Gloucester Campus, Llanthony Road, Gloucester, England GL2 5JQ. Tel 0845 155 2020; www.gloscol.ac.uk

Gower College Swansea (Coleg Abertawe; now part of Gower College Swansea) Tycoch Campus, Tycoch Road, Swansea, Wales SA2 9EB. Tel 01792 284000; www.gowercollegeswansea.ac.uk

Grantham College Stonebridge Road, Grantham, England NG31 9AP. Tel 01476 400200; Course Information 0800 052 1577; www.grantham.ac.uk

Great Yarmouth College Suffolk Road, Southtown, Great Yarmouth, England NR31 0ED. Tel 01493 655261; www.gyc.ac.uk

Greenwich School of Management Meridian House, Royal Hill, London, England SE10 8RD. Tel 020 8516 7800; http://gsm.org.uk

Guildford College Stoke Park Campus, Stoke Road, Guildford, England GU1 1EZ. Tel 01483 448500; www.guildford.ac.uk

Hackney Community College Shoreditch Campus, Falkirk Street, London, England N1 6HQ. Tel 020 7613 9123; www.tcch.ac.uk

Hadlow College Hadlow College, Hadlow, Tonbridge, England TN11 0AL. Tel 0500 551434; www.hadlow.ac.uk

Halesowen College Whittingham Road, Halesowen, England B63 3NA. Tel 0121 602 7777; www.halesowen.ac.uk

Harlow College Velizy Avenue, Harlow, England CM20 3EZ. Tel 01279 868000; www.harlow-college.ac.uk

Harrow College Harrow on the Hill Campus, Lowlands Road, Harrow, England HA1 3AQ. Tel 020 8909 6000; www.harrow.ac.uk

Hartlepool College of Further Education Stockton Street, Hartlepool, England TS24 7NT. Tel 01429 295000; www.hartlepoolfe.ac.uk

Havering College Ardleigh Green Road, Hornchurch, England RM11 2LL. Tel 01708 455011; Course Information 01708 462801; www.havering-college.ac.uk

Henley College Coventry Henley Road, Bell Green, Coventry, England CV2 1ED. Tel 024 7662 6300; www.henley-cov.ac.uk

Herefordshire and Ludlow College Folly Lane, Hereford, England HR1 1LS. Tel 0800 032 1986; www.hlcollege.ac.uk

Hertford Regional College Ware Centre, Scotts Road, Ware, England SG12 9JF. Tel 01992 411400; www.hrc.ac.uk

Highbury College Portsmouth Tudor Crescent, Portsmouth, England PO6 2SA. Tel 023 9238 3131; www.highbury.ac.uk

Highland Theological College (UHI partner college – see Section 1) High Street, Dingwall, Scotland IV15 9HA. Tel 01349 780000; www.htc.uhi.ac.uk

Hillcroft College South Bank, Surbiton, England KT6 6DF. Tel 020 8399 2688; www.hillcroft.ac.uk

Hopwood Hall College Rochdale Campus, St Mary's Gate, Rochdale, England OL12 6RY. Tel 01706 345346; www.hopwood.ac.uk

Hugh Baird College Balliol Road, Bootle, England L20 7EW. Tel 0151 353 4444; www.hughbaird.ac.uk

Hull College The Queen's Gardens Centre, Wilberforce Drive, Hull, England HU1 3DG. Tel 01482 598744; www.hull-college.ac.uk

Huntingdonshire Regional College California Road, Huntingdon, England PE29 1BL. Tel 01480 379100; www.huntingdon.ac.uk

Islamic College for Advanced Studies 133 High Road, London, England NW10 2SW. Tel 020 8451 9993; www.islamic-college.ac.uk

Isle of Wight College Medina Way, Newport, Isle of Wight, England PO30 5TA. Tel 01983 526631; www.iwcollege.ac.uk

James Watt College Finnart Street, Greenock, Scotland PA16 8HF. Tel 01475 724433; www.jameswatt.ac.uk

Jewel and Esk College (now part of Edinburgh College) Edinburgh Campus, 24 Milton Road East, Edinburgh, Scotland EH15 2PP. Tel 0131 334 7000; Information Services 0131 334 7163; www.jec.ac.uk

K College Brook Street, Tonbridge, England TN9 2PW. Tel 0845 207 8220; www.kcollege.ac.uk

Kaplan Holborn College 179–191 Borough High St, London, England SE1 1HR. Tel 020 3642 1999; www.holborncollege.ac.uk

Kendal College Milnthorpe Road, Kendal, England LA9 5AY. Tel 01539 814700; www.kendal.ac.uk

Kensington College of Business Wesley House, 4 Wild Court, London, England WC2B 4AU. Tel 020 7404 6330; www.kensingtoncoll.ac.uk

Kidderminster College Market Street, Kidderminster, England DY10 1AB. Tel 01562 512025; www.kidderminster.ac.uk

Kilmarnock College Holehouse Road, Kilmarnock, Scotland KA3 7AT. Tel 01563 523501; www.kilmarnock.ac.uk

Kingston College Kingston Hall Road, Kingston upon Thames, England KT1 2AQ. Tel 020 8546 2151; www.kingston-college.ac.uk

Kingston Maurward College Kingston Maurward, Dorchester, England DT2 8PY. Tel 01305 215000; Course Enquiries 01305 215215; www.kmc.ac.uk

Kirklees College (formerly Dewsbury College) Information Office, Waterfront Quarter, Manchester Road, Huddersfield, England HD1 3HH. Tel 01484 437000; Course Enquiries 01484 437070; www.kirkleescollege.ac.uk

Knowsley Community College Rupert Road, Roby, Kirkby, England L36 9TD. Tel 0845 155 1055; www.knowsleycollege.ac.uk

Lakes College, West Cumbria Hallwood Road, Lillyhall Business Park, Workington, England CA14 4JN. Tel 01946 839300; www.lcwc.ac.uk

Lambeth College 45 Clapham Common South Side, London, England SW4 9BL. Tel 020 7501 5010; Course Information 020 7501 5000; www.lambethcollege.ac.uk

Lancaster and Morecambe College Morecambe Road, Lancaster, England LA1 2TY. Tel 01524 66215; www.lmc.ac.uk

Langside College 50 Prospecthill Road, Glasgow, Scotland G42 9LB. Tel 0141 272 3636; www.langside.ac.uk

Lansdowne College 40–44 Bark Place, London, England W2 4AT. Tel 020 7616 4400; www.lansdownecollege.com

Leeds City College Thomas Danby Campus, Roundhay Road, Leeds, England LS7 3BG. Tel 0113 386 1996; Course Enquiries 0113 386 1997; www.leedscitycollege.ac.uk

Leeds College of Building North Street, Leeds, England LS2 7QT. Tel 0113 222 6000; www.lcb.ac.uk

Leicester College Freemen's Park Campus, Aylestone Road, Leicester, England LE2 7LW. Tel 0116 224 2240; www.leicestercollege.ac.uk

Leo Baeck College The Sternberg Centre, 80 East End Road, London, England N3 2SY. Tel 020 8349 5600; www.lbc.ac.uk

Lewisham College Lewisham Way, London, England SE4 1UT. Tel 020 8692 0353; Course Enquiries 0800 834545; www.lewisham.ac.uk

Lews Castle College (UHI partner college – see Section 1) Castle Grounds, Stornoway, Isle of Lewis, Scotland HS2 0XR. Tel 01851 770000; www.lews.uhi.ac.uk

Lincoln College Monks Road, Lincoln, England LN2 5HQ. Tel 01522 876000; www.lincolncollege.ac.uk

London College of Business and Computing Millennium Place, 206 Cambridge Heath Road, London, England E2 9NQ. Tel 020 8983 4193; www.lcbc.com

London School of Commerce Chaucer House, White Hart Yard, London, England SE1 1NX. Tel 020 7357 0077; www.lsclondon.co.uk

Loughborough College Radmoor Road, Loughborough, England LE11 3BT. Tel 01509 618375; www.loucoll.ac.uk

Macclesfield College Park Lane, Macclesfield, England SK11 8LF. Tel 01625 410002; www.macclesfield.ac.uk

Mid-Cheshire College Hartford Campus, Chester Road, Northwich, England CW8 1LJ. Tel 01606 74444; www.midchesh.ac.uk

Middlesbrough College Dock Street, Middlesbrough, England TS2 1AD. Tel 01642 333333; www.mbro.ac.uk

Mid-Kent College Medway Campus, Medway Road, Gillingham, England ME7 1FN. Tel 01634 402020; www.midkent.ac.uk

Milton Keynes College Chaffron Way Campus, Woughton Campus West, Leadenhall, Milton Keynes, England MK6 5LP. Tel 01908 684444; www.mkcollege.ac.uk

Moray College (UHI partner college – see Section 1) Moray Street, Elgin, Scotland IV30 1JJ. Tel 01343 576000; Course Enquiries 0845 272 3600; www.moray.uhi.ac.uk

Moulton College West Street, Moulton, England NN3 7RR. Tel 01604 491131; www.moulton.ac.uk

Nazarene Theological College Dene Road, Didsbury, Manchester, England M20 2GU. Tel 0161 445 3063; www.nazarene.ac.uk

Neath Port Talbot College Dwr-y-Felin Road, Neath, Wales SA10 7RF. Tel 01639 648000; www.nptcgroup.ac.uk

Nelson and Colne College Reedyford Site, Scotland Road, Nelson, England BB9 7YT. Tel 01282 440272; www.nelson.ac.uk

Nescot, North East Surrey College of Technology Reigate Road, Ewell, Epsom, England KT17 3DS. Tel 020 8394 3038; www.nescot.ac.uk

New College Durham Framwellgate Moor Campus, Durham, England DH1 5ES. Tel 0191 375 4000; www.newcollegedurham.ac.uk

New College Nottingham The Adams Building, Stoney Street, Nottingham, England NG1 1NG. Tel 01159 100100; www.ncn.ac.uk

New College Stamford Drift Road, Stamford, England PE9 1XA. Tel 01780 484300; www.stamford.ac.uk

New College Swindon New College Drive, Swindon, England SN3 1AH. Tel 01793 611470; www.newcollege.ac.uk

New College Telford King Street, Wellington, Telford, England TF1 1NY. Tel 01952 641892; www.nct.ac.uk

Newbury College Monks Lane, Newbury, England RG14 7TD. Tel 01635 845000; www.newbury-college.ac.uk

Newcastle College Rye Hill Campus, Scotswood Road, Newcastle-upon-Tyne, England NE4 7SA. Tel 0191 200 4000; www.ncl-coll.ac.uk

Newcastle-under-Lyme College Knutton Lane, Newcastle-under-Lyme, England ST5 2GB. Tel 01782 254254; www.nulc.ac.uk

Newham College of Further Education East Ham Campus, High Street South, London, England E6 6ER. Tel 020 8257 4446; www.newham.ac.uk

North Atlantic Fisheries College (UHI partner college – see Section 1) NAFC Marine Centre, Port Arthur, Scalloway, Scotland ZE1 0UN. Tel 01595 772000; www.nafc.ac.uk

North East Scotland College Gallowgate Centre, Gallowgate, Aberdeen, Scotland AB25 1BN. Tel 01224 612000; Information and Booking Centre 01224 612330; www.nescol.ac.uk

North East Worcestershire College Redditch Campus, Peakman Street, Redditch, England B98 8DW. Tel 01527 570020; www.ne-worcs.ac.uk

North Glasgow College 123 Flemington Street, Springburn, Glasgow, Scotland G21 4TD. Tel 0141 630 5000; www.northglasgowcollege.ac.uk

North Hertfordshire College Monkswood Way, Stevenage, England SG1 1LA. Tel 01462 424242; www.nhc.ac.uk

North Highland College (UHI partner college – see Section 1) Ormlie Road, Thurso, Scotland KW14 7EE. Tel 01847 889000; www.northhighland.ac.uk

North Lindsey College Kingsway, Scunthorpe, England DN17 1AJ. Tel 01724 281111; www.northlindsey.ac.uk

North Nottinghamshire College Carlton Road, Worksop, England S81 7HP. Tel 01909 504504; Student Services 01909 504500; www.nnotts-col.ac.uk

North Warwickshire and Hinckley College Nuneaton Campus, Hinckley Road, Nuneaton, England CV11 6BH. Tel 024 7624 3000; www.nwhc.ac.uk

North West Kent College Oakfield Lane, Dartford, England DA1 2JT. Tel 0800 074 1447; www.nwkcollege.ac.uk

Northampton College Booth Lane, Northampton, England NN3 3RF. Tel 0845 300 4401; www.northamptoncollege.ac.uk

Northbrook College, Sussex West Durrington Campus, Littlehampton Road, Worthing, England BN12 6NU. Tel 0845 155 6060; www.northbrook.ac.uk

Northern Regional College (formerly North East Institute of Further and Higher Education) Ballymena Campus, Trostan Avenue Building, Ballymena, Northern Ireland BT43 7BN. Tel 028 2563 6221; www.nrc.ac.uk

Northumberland College College Road, Ashington, England NE63 9RG. Tel 01670 841200; www.northumberland.ac.uk

Norton Radstock College South Hill Park, Radstock, England BA3 3RW. Tel 01761 433161; www.nortcoll.ac.uk

Oaklands College, St Albans Smallford Campus, Hatfield Road, St Albans, England AL4 0JA. Tel 01727 737000; www.oaklands.ac.uk

Oatridge College Ecclesmachan, Broxburn, Scotland EH52 6NH. Tel 01506 864800; www.oatridge.ac.uk

Orkney College (UHI partner college – see Section 1) East Road, Kirkwall, Scotland KW15 1LX. Tel 01856 569000; www.orkney.uhi.ac.uk

Otley College Otley, Ipswich, England IP6 9NE. Tel 01473 785543; www.otleycollege.ac.uk

Oxford and Cherwell Valley College Banbury Campus, Broughton Road, Banbury, Oxford, England OX16 9QA. Tel 01865 550550; www.ocvc.ac.uk

Pembrokeshire College (Coleg Sir Benfro) Merlins Bridge, Haverfordwest, Wales SA61 1SZ. Tel 01437 753000; Freephone 0800 977 6788; www.pembrokeshire.ac.uk

Perth College (UHI partner college – see Section 1) Crieff Road, Perth, Scotland PH1 2NX. Tel 0845 270 1177; www.perth.uhi.ac.uk

Peterborough Regional College Park Crescent, Peterborough, England PE1 4DZ. Tel 0845 872 8722; www.peterborough.ac.uk

Petroc Old Sticklepath Hill, Sticklepath, Barnstaple, England EX31 2BQ. Tel 01271 345291; www.petroc.ac.uk

Plumpton College Ditchling Road, Near Lewes, England BN7 3AE. Tel 01273 890454; www.plumpton.ac.uk

Portsmouth College Tangier Road, Copnor, Portsmouth, England PO3 6PZ. Tel 023 9266 7521; www.portsmouth-college.ac.uk

Preston College Fulwood Campus, St Vincent's Road, Preston, England PR2 8UR. Tel 01772 225000; www.preston.ac.uk

Redbridge College Little Heath, Barley Lane, Romford, England RM6 4XT. Tel 020 8548 7400; www.redbridge-college.ac.uk

Redcar and Cleveland College Corporation Road, Redcar, England TS10 1EZ. Tel 01642 473132; www.cleveland.ac.uk

Reid Kerr College Admission Unit, Renfrew Road, Paisley, Scotland PA3 4DR. Tel 0800 052 7343; www.reidkerr.ac.uk

Richmond-upon-Thames College Egerton Road, Twickenham, England TW2 7SJ. Tel 020 8607 8000; Courses Information Unit 020 8607 8306; www.rutc.ac.uk

Riverside College Halton Kingsway Campus, Kingsway, Widnes, England WA8 7QQ. Tel 0151 257 2800; www.riversidecollege.ac.uk

Rotherham College of Arts and Technology Town Centre Campus, Eastwood Lane, Rotherham, England S65 1EG. Tel 01709 722777; www.rotherham.ac.uk

Royal National College for the Blind College Road, Hereford, England HR1 1EB. Tel 01432 265725; www.rncb.ac.uk

Runshaw College Langdale Road, Leyland, England PR25 3DQ. Tel 01772 622677; www.runshaw.ac.uk

Ruskin College Ruskin Hall, Dunstan Road, Old Headington, Oxford, England OX3 9BZ. Tel 01865 759600; www.ruskin.ac.uk

Sabhal Mòr Ostaig (UHI partner college – see Section 1) ACC, Sleat, Scotland IV44 8RQ. Tel 01471 888000; www.smo.uhi.ac.uk

St Helens College Water Street, St Helens, England WA10 1PP. Tel 0800 996699; www.sthelens.ac.uk

Salford City College Worsley Campus, Walkden Road, Worsley, England M28 7QD. Tel 0161 631 5000; www.salfordcc.ac.uk

Sandwell College Central Campus, 1 Spon Lane, West Bromwich, England B70 6AW. Tel 0800 622006; www.sandwell.ac.uk

School of Audio Engineering Institute Head Office, Littlemore Park, Armstrong Road, Oxford, England OX4 4FY. Tel 020 7923 9159; uk.sae.edu

Scottish Association for Marine Science (UHI partner college – see Section 1) Scottish Marine Institute, Oban, Argyll, Scotland PA37 1QA. Tel 01631 559000; www.sams.ac.uk

Selby College Abbot's Road, Selby, England YO8 8AT. Tel 01757 211000; www.selby.ac.uk

Sheffield College Granville Road, Sheffield, England S2 2RL. Tel 0114 260 2600; www.sheffcol.ac.uk

Shetland College (UHI partner college – see Section 1) Gremista, Lerwick, Scotland ZE1 0PX. Tel 01595 771000; www.shetland.uhi.ac.uk

Shrewsbury College of Arts and Technology London Road, Shrewsbury, England SY2 6PR. Tel 01743 342342; www.shrewsbury.ac.uk

Shuttleworth College Old Warden Park, Biggleswade, England SG18 9DX. Tel 01767 626222; www.shuttleworth.ac.uk

Solihull College Blossomfield Campus, Blossomfield Road, Solihull, England B91 1SB. Tel 0121 678 7000; www.solihull.ac.uk

Somerset College Wellington Road, Taunton, England TA1 5AX. Tel 01823 366331; www.somerset.ac.uk

South and City College Birmingham Digbeth Campus, High Street Deritend, Digbeth, England B5 5SU. Tel 0800 111 6311; www.sccb.ac.uk

South Cheshire College Dane Bank Avenue, Crewe, England CW2 8AB. Tel 01270 654654; www.s-cheshire.ac.uk

South Devon College Vantage Point, Long Road, Paignton, England TQ4 7EJ. Tel 01803 540540; www.southdevon.ac.uk

South Downs College College Road, Waterlooville, England PO7 8AA. Tel 023 9279 7979; www.southdowns.ac.uk

South Essex College (formerly South East Essex College; merged in January 2010 with Thurrock and Basildon College) Nethermayne, Basildon, England SS16 5NN. Tel 0845 521 2345; www.southessex.ac.uk

South Gloucestershire and Stroud College Stratford Road, Stroud, England GL5 4AH. Tel 0800 056 7253; www.sgscol.ac.uk

South Lanarkshire College College Way, East Kilbride, Scotland G75 0NE. Tel 01355 807780; www.south-lanarkshire-college.ac.uk

South Leicestershire College South Wigston Campus, Blaby Road, South Wigston, England LE18 4PH. Tel 0116 264 3535; www.slcollege.ac.uk

South Staffordshire College Cannock Campus, Crown House, Beecroft Road, Cannock, England WS11 1JP. Tel 0300 456 2424; www.southstaffs.ac.uk

South Thames College Wandsworth High Street, London, England SW18 2PP. Tel 020 8918 7777; www.south-thames.ac.uk

South Tyneside College Westoe Campus, St George's Avenue, South Shields, England NE34 6ET. Tel 0191 427 3500; www.stc.ac.uk

Southampton City College St Mary Street, Southampton, England SO14 1AR. Tel 023 8048 4848; www.southampton-city.ac.uk

Southern Regional College (formerly Upper Bann Institute) Portadown Campus, 36–44 Lurgan Road, Portadown, Craigavon, Northern Ireland BT63 5BL. Tel 028 3839 7777; www.src.ac.uk

Southport College Mornington Road, Southport, England PR9 0TT. Tel 01704 500606; www.southport-college.ac.uk

Southwark College (now part of Lewisham College) Waterloo Centre, The Cut, London, England SE1 8LE. Tel 020 7815 1500; www.lewisham.ac.uk

Stafford College Earl Street, Stafford, England ST16 2QR. Tel 01785 223800; www.staffordcoll.ac.uk

Staffordshire University Regional Federation Partnerships Office, E200 Cadman Building, College Road, Stoke-on-Trent, England ST4 2DE. Tel 01782 353517; www.staffs.ac.uk

Stephenson College Thornborough Road, Coalville, England LE67 3TN. Tel 01530 836136; www.stephensoncoll.ac.uk

Stevenson College Edinburgh (now part of Edinburgh College) Sighthill, Bankhead Avenue, Edinburgh, Scotland EH11 4DE. Tel 0131 669 4400; www.stevenson.ac.uk

Stockport College Town Centre Campus, Wellington Road South, Stockport, England SK1 3UQ. Tel 0161 958 3100; www.stockport.ac.uk

Stockton Riverside College Harvard Avenue, Stockton-on-Tees, England TS17 6FB. Tel 01642 865400; www.stockton.ac.uk

Stoke-on-Trent College Cauldon Campus, Stoke Road, Shelton, Stoke-on-Trent, England ST4 2DG. Tel 01782 208208; www.stokecoll.ac.uk

Stourbridge College Hagley Road Centre, Hagley Road, Stourbridge, England DY8 1QU. Tel 01384 344344; www.stourbridge.ac.uk

Stow College 43 Shamrock Street, Glasgow, Scotland G4 9LD. Tel 0844 249 8585; www.stow.ac.uk

Stratford-upon-Avon College The Willows North, Alcester Road, Stratford-upon-Avon, England CV37 9QR. Tel 01789 266245; www.stratford.ac.uk

Strode College Church Road, Street, England BA16 0AB. Tel 01458 844400; www.strode-college.ac.uk

Strode's College High Street, Egham, England TW20 9DR. Tel 01784 437506; www.strodes.ac.uk

Sussex Coast College Hastings (formerly Hastings College of Art and Technology) Station Plaza Campus, Station Approach, Hastings, England TN34 1BA. Tel 01424 442222; www.sussexcoast.ac.uk

Sussex Downs College EVOC (Eastbourne Campus), Cross Levels Way, Eastbourne, England BN21 2UF. Tel 01323 637637; www.sussexdowns.ac.uk

Swindon College North Star Campus, North Star Avenue, Swindon, England SN2 1DY. Tel 0800 731 2250; www.swindon-college.ac.uk

Tameside College Beaufort Road, Ashton-under-Lyne, England OL6 6NX. Tel 0161 908 6600; www.tameside.ac.uk

Telford College of Arts and Technology Haybridge Road, Wellington, Telford, England TF1 2NP. Tel 01952 642200; www.tcat.ac.uk

The London College UCK Kensington Campus, Victoria Gardens, London, England W11 3PE. Tel 020 7243 4000; www.lcuck.ac.uk

The Manchester College (formerly Manchester College of Art and Technology and City College Manchester) Ashton Old Road, Openshaw, Manchester, England M11 2WH. Tel 0161 909 6655; www.themanchestercollege.ac.uk

The Oldham College Rochdale Road, Oldham, England OL9 6AA. Tel 0800 269480; www.oldham.ac.uk

Tottenham Hotspur Foundation Tottenham Hotspur Foundation, Bill Nicholson Way, 748 High Road, London, England N17 0AP. Tel 020 8365 5138; www.tottenhamhotspur.com/foundation

Totton College Water Lane, Totton, England SO40 3ZX. Tel 023 8087 4874; www.totton.ac.uk

Trafford College Talbot Road Campus, Talbot Road, Stretford, England M32 0XH. Tel 0161 886 7000; www.trafford.ac.uk

Tresham College of Further and Higher Education Kettering Campus, Windmill Avenue, Kettering, England NN15 6ER. Tel 0845 658 8990; www.tresham.ac.uk

Truro College College Road, Truro, England TR1 3XX. Tel 01872 267000; www.truro-penwith.ac.uk

Tyne Metropolitan College Battle Hill Drive, Wallsend, England NE28 9NL. Tel 0191 229 5000; www.tynemet.ac.uk

Uxbridge College Park Road, Uxbridge, England UB8 1NQ. Tel 01895 853333; www.uxbridge.ac.uk

Wakefield College Margaret Street, Wakefield, England WF1 2DH. Tel 01924 789111; www.wakefield.ac.uk

Walford and North Shropshire College Oswestry Campus, Shrewsbury Road, Oswestry, England SY11 4QB. Tel 01691 688000; www.wnsc.ac.uk

Walsall College Wisemore Campus, Littleton Street West, Walsall, England WS2 8ES. Tel 01922 657000; www.walsallcollege.ac.uk

Waltham Forest College Forest Road, Walthamstow, London, England E17 4JB. Tel 020 8501 8501; www.waltham.ac.uk

Warrington Collegiate Winwick Road, Warrington, England WA2 8QA. Tel 01925 494494; www.warrington.ac.uk

Warwickshire College Leamington Centre, Warwick New Road, Leamington Spa, England CV32 5JE. Tel 01926 318000; www.warwickshire.ac.uk

West Cheshire College Chester Campus, Eaton Road, Handbridge, Chester, England CH4 7ER. Tel 01244 656555; www.west-cheshire.ac.uk

West Herts College Watford Campus, Hempstead Road, Watford, England WD17 3EZ. Tel 01923 812000; www.westherts.ac.uk

West Highland College (formed from a merger between Lochaber and Skye and Wester Ross College; UHI partner college – see Section 1) Carmichael Way, Fort William, Scotland PH33 6FF. Tel 01379 874000; www.whc.uhi.ac.uk

West Lothian College Almondvale Crescent, Livingston, Scotland EH54 7EP. Tel 01506 418181; www.west-lothian.ac.uk

West Nottinghamshire College Derby Road, Mansfield, England NG18 5BH. Tel 0808 100 3626; www.wnc.ac.uk

West Suffolk College Out Risbygate, Bury St Edmunds, England IP33 3RL. Tel 01284 701301; www.westsuffolkcollege.ac.uk

West Thames College London Road, Isleworth, England TW7 4HS. Tel 020 8326 2000; www.west-thames.ac.uk

Westminster Kingsway College St James's Park Centre, Castle Lane, London, England SW1E 6DR. Tel 0870 060 9800; www.westking.ac.uk

Weston College Knightstone Campus, Weston College, Knightstone Road, Weston-super-Mare, England BS23 2AL. Tel 01934 411411; www.weston.ac.uk

Weymouth College Cranford Avenue, Weymouth, England DT4 7LQ. Tel 01305 761100; Course Applications 0870 060 9800/1; www.weymouth.ac.uk

Wigan and Leigh College Parsons Walk, Wigan, England WN1 1RU. Tel 01942 761600; www.wigan-leigh.ac.uk

Wiltshire College Chippenham Campus, Cocklebury Road, Chippenham, England SN15 3QD. Tel 01249 464644; www.wiltshire.ac.uk

Wirral Metropolitan College Conway Park Campus, Europa Boulevard, Conway Park, Birkenhead, England CH41 4NT. Tel 0151 551 7777; www.wmc.ac.uk

Worcester College of Technology Deansway, Worcester, England WR1 2JF. Tel 01905 725555; www.wortech.ac.uk

Yeovil College Mudford Road, Yeovil, England BA21 4DR. Tel 01935 423921; www.yeovil.ac.uk

York College Sim Balk Lane, York, England YO23 2BB. Tel 01904 770400; www.yorkcollege.ac.uk

Yorkshire Coast College Lady Edith's Drive, Scarborough, England YO12 5RN. Tel 01723 372105; www.yorkshirecoastcollege.ac.uk

APPENDIX 1 UCAS 2015 ENTRY TARIFF POINTS TABLES

GCE A/AS-LEVELS • SCOTTISH HIGHERS/ADVANCED HIGHERS • WELSH BACCALAUREATE • IRISH LEAVING CERTIFICATE • INTERNATIONAL BACCALAUREATE DIPLOMA • CAMBRIDGE PRE-U • PROGRESSION AND ADVANCED DIPLOMA • EXTENDED PROJECT • MUSIC EXAMINATIONS

GCE A/AS-Levels

Grade					Tariff points
GCE and AVCE Double Award	A-level with additional AS (9 units)	GCE A-level and AVCE	GCE AS Double Award	GCE AS and AS VCE	
A*A*					280
A*A					260
AA					240
AB					220
BB	A*A				200
BC	AA				180
	AB				170
CC					160
	BB				150
CD	BC	A*			140
DD	CC	A	AA		120
	CD		AB		110
DE		B	BB		100
	DD		BC		90
EE	DE	C	CC		80
			CD		70
	EE	D	DD	A	60
			DE	B	50
		E	EE	C	40
				D	30
				E	20

Scottish Highers/Advanced Highers

Grade	Higher	Advanced Higher
A	80	130
B	65	110
C	50	90
D	36	72

Welsh Baccalaureate Core

Grade	Tariff points
Pass	120

NB Core points awarded only to candidates obtaining the Welsh Baccalaureate Advanced Diploma

Irish Leaving Certificate

Grade		Tariff points
Higher	Ordinary	
A1		90
A2		77
B1		71
B2		64
B3		58
C1		52
C2		45
C3	A1	39
D1		33
D2	A2	26
D3	B1	20
	B2	14
	B3	7

IB Diploma

IB Diploma points	Tariff points
45	720
44	698
43	676
42	654
41	632
40	611
39	589
38	567
37	545
36	523
35	501
34	479
33	457
32	435
31	413
30	392
29	370
28	348
27	326
26	304
25	282
24	260

Cambridge Pre-U

Grade	Principal subject	Global perspectives and research	Short course
D1	To be confirmed	To be confirmed	To be confirmed
D2	145	140	To be confirmed
D3	130	126	60
M1	115	112	53
M2	101	98	46
M3	87	84	39
P1	73	70	32
P2	59	56	26
P3	46	42	20

Progression Diploma

Grade	Tariff points
A*	350
A	300
B	250
C	200
D	150
E	100

NB The Advanced Diploma = Progression Diploma plus Additional and Specialist Learning (ASL)

Extended Project – Stand alone

Grade	Tariff points
A*	70
A	60
B	50
C	40
D	30
E	20

Points cannot be counted if taken as part of Progression/Advanced Diploma.

Music examinations

Practical			Theory			Tariff points
Grade 8	Grade 7	Grade 6	Grade 8	Grade 7	Grade 6	
D						75
M						70
	D					60
P	M					55
		D				45
	P	M				40
			D			30
		P	M			25
			P	D		20
				M	D	15
				P	M	10
					P	5

Additional points will be awarded for music examinations from the Associated Board of the Royal Schools of Music (ABRSM), the Guildhall School of Music and Drama, the London College of Music Examinations (LCMM) and Trinity College of Music (music examinations at grades 6, 7, 8 (D=Distinction; M=Merit; P=Pass))

NB Full acknowledgement is made to UCAS for this information. For further details of all qualifications awarded UCAS Tariff points see www.ucas.com/how-it-all-works/explore-your-options/entry-requirements/tariff-tables. Note that the Tariff is constantly updated and new qualifications are introduced each year.

Universities in the UK accept a range of international qualifications and those which normally satisfy the minimum general entrance requirements are listed below. However, the specific levels of achievement or grades required for entry to degree courses with international qualifications will vary, depending on the popularity of the university or college and the chosen degree programme. The subject tables in **Chapter 8** provide a guide to the levels of entry to courses although direct comparisons between A-level grades and international qualifications are not always possible except for the three European examinations listed at the end of this Appendix. Students not holding the required qualifications should consider taking an International Foundation course.

International students whose mother tongue is not English and/or who have not studied for their secondary education in English will be required to pass an English test such as IELTS (International English Language Testing System) or TOEFL (the Test of English as a Foreign Language). Entry requirements vary between universities and courses. For the IELTS, scores can range from 5.5 to 7.5, for the TOEFL computer-based test scores can range from a minimum of 213, and for the TOEFL written test the minimum entry score is 5.0 (see www.ielts.org and www.ets.org/toefl).

Algeria Baccalaureate de l'Enseignement Secondaire
Argentina Completion of Year One of Licenciado/Professional Title
Australia Completion of Year 12 certificates
Austria Reifazeugnis/Maturazeugnis
Bahrain Two-year diploma or associate degree
Bangladesh Bachelor of Arts, Science and Commerce
Belgium Certificat d'Enseignement Secondaire Superieur
Bermuda Diploma of Arts and Science
Bosnia-Herzegovina Secondary School Leaving Diploma
Brazil Completion of Ensino Medio and a good pass in the Vestibular
Brunei Brunei GCE A-level
Bulgaria Diploma za Zavarshino Sredno Obrazovanie (Diploma of Completed Secondary Education)
Canada Completion of Grade 12 secondary/high school certificate or equivalent
Chile Completion of secondary education and a good pass in the Prueba de Seleccion Universitaria (formerly Prueba de Conocimientos Especificos)
China Completion of one year of a Bachelor degree from a recognised university with good grades
Croatia Matura (Secondary school leaving diploma)
Cyprus Apolytirion/Lise Bitirme Diploma with good grades
Czech Republic Vysvedceni o Maturitni Zkousce/Maturita
Denmark Studentereksamen (HF), (HHX), (HTX)
Egypt Completion of year one of a Bachelor degree or two-year Diploma
Finland Ylioppilastutkinoto/Studentexamen (Matriculation certificate)
France French Baccalaureate
Gambia West African Senior Secondary Certificate Exam (WASSCE) Advanced Level
Georgia Successful completion of Year One of a Bachelor degree
Germany Abitur
Ghana West African Senior Secondary Certificate Exam (WASSCE)/A-levels
Greece Apolytirion of Eniaio Lykeio (previously Apolytirion of Lykeio)
Hong Kong A-levels/HKALE
Hungary Erettsegi/Matura
Iceland Studentsprof

India High grades from Standard XII School Leaving examinations from certain examination boards
Ireland Irish Leaving Certificate Higher Level
Israel Bagrut
Italy Diploma Conseguito con l'Esame di Stato (formerly the Diploma di Matura) with good grades
Japan Upper Secondary School leaving diploma/Kotogakko Sotsugyo Shomeisho plus Foundation year
Kenya Cambridge Overseas Higher School Certificate
Lebanon Lebanese Baccalaureate plus Foundation year
Malaysia Sijil Tinggi Persekolahan Malaysia (STPM, Malaysia Higher School Certificate)
Mauritius Cambridge Overseas Higher School Certificate or A-levels
Mexico Bachillerato plus Foundation year
Netherlands Voorbereidend Wetenschappelijk Onderwijs (VWO)
Nigeria Successful completion of year one of a Bachelor degree
Norway Diploma of a completed 3-year course of upper secondary education
Pakistan Bachelor degree
Poland Matura/Swiadectwo Dojrzalosci
Portugal Diploma de Ensino Secundario
Russian Federation Diploma of completed Specialised Secondary Education or successful completion of first year of Bakalav
Saudi Arabia Successful completion of first year of a Bachelor degree
Serbia and Montenegro Matura
Singapore Polytechnic Diploma or A-levels
South Korea Junior College Diploma
Spain Curso de Orientacion Universitaria (COU) with good grades
Sri Lanka A-levels
Sweden Fullstandigt Slutbetyg fran Gymnasieskolan
Taiwan Senior High school Diploma
Thailand Successful completion of year one of a Bachelor degree
Turkey Devlet Lise Diplomasi (State High School Diploma) with good grades
Uganda Uganda Advanced Certificate of Education (UACE) or East African Advanced Certificate of Education
Ukraine Successful completion of year one of Bakakavre
USA Good grades from the High School Graduation Diploma with SAT and/or APT

COMPARISONS BETWEEN A-LEVEL GRADES AND THE FOLLOWING EUROPEAN EXAMINATIONS

A-level grades	AAA	AAB	ABB	BBB	BBC	BCC
European Baccalaureate	85%	80%	75%	70%	65%	60%
French Baccalaureate	16 Bien	15 Bien	14 Bien	13 Assez Bien	12 Assez Bien	11 Assez Bien
German Abitur	1.0–1.2	1.3–1.4	1.5–1.8	1.9–2.1	2.2–2.4	2.5–2.7

Professional associations vary in size and function and many offer examinations to provide members with vocational qualifications. However, many of the larger bodies do not conduct examinations but accept evidence provided by the satisfactory completion of appropriate degree and diploma courses. When applying for courses in vocational subjects, therefore, it is important to check whether your chosen course is accredited by a professional association, since membership of such bodies is usually necessary for progression in your chosen career after graduation.

Information about careers, which you can use as background information for your UCAS application, can be obtained from the organisations below listed under the subject table headings used in **Chapter 8**. Full details of professional associations, their examinations and the degree courses accredited by them are published in *British Qualifications* (see **Appendix 4**).

Some additional organisations that can provide useful careers-related information are listed below under the subject table headings and other sources of relevant information are indicated in the subject tables of **Chapter 8** and in **Appendix 4**.

Accountancy/Accounting
Association of Accounting Technicians www.aat.org.uk
Association of International Accountants www.aiaworldwide.com
Chartered Accountants Ireland www.charteredaccountants.ie
Chartered Institute of Internal Auditors www.iia.org.uk
Chartered Institute of Management Accountants www.cimaglobal.com
Chartered Institute of Public Finance and Accountancy www.cipfa.org
Chartered Institute of Taxation www.tax.org.uk
Institute of Accounting Technicians in Ireland www.accountingtechniciansireland.ie
Institute of Chartered Accountants in England and Wales www.icaew.com
Institute of Chartered Accountants of Scotland www.icas.org.uk
Institute of Financial Accountants www.ifa.org.uk
The Global Body for Professional Accountants www.accaglobal.com

Actuarial Science/Studies
Institute and Faculty of Actuaries www.actuaries.org.uk

Agricultural Sciences/Agriculture
Royal Agricultural Society of England www.rase.org.uk

Animal Sciences
British Horse Society www.bhs.org.uk
British Society of Animal Science www.bsas.org.uk

Anthropology
Association of Social Anthropologists of the UK and Commonwealth www.theasa.org
Royal Anthropological Institute www.therai.org.uk

Archaeology
Council for British Archaeology www.archaeologyuk.org
Institute for Archaeologists www.archaeologists.net

Architecture
Chartered Institute of Architectural Technologists www.ciat.org.uk
Royal Incorporation of Architects in Scotland www.rias.org.uk
Royal Institute of British Architects www.architecture.com

Art and Design
Arts Council England www.artscouncil.org.uk
Association of Illustrators www.theaoi.com
Association of Photographers www.the-aop.org
British Association of Art Therapists www.baat.org
British Association of Paintings Conservator-Restorers www.bapcr.org.uk
British Institute of Professional Photography www.bipp.com
Chartered Society of Designers www.csd.org.uk
Craft Council www.craftscouncil.org.uk
Design Council www.designcouncil.org.uk
Institute of Conservation www.icon.org.uk
Institute of Professional Goldsmiths www.ipgold.
National Society for Education in Art and Design www.nsead.org
Royal British Society of Sculptors www.rbs.org.uk
Scottish Arts Council www.creativescotland.com
Textile Institute www.texi.org

Astronomy/Astrophysics
Royal Astronomical Society www.ras.org.uk

Biochemistry (see also Chemistry)
Association for Clinical Biochemistry and Laboratory Medicine www.acb.org.uk
Biochemical Society www.biochemistry.org
British Society for Immunology http://bsi.immunology.org

Biological Sciences/Biology
British Society for Genetic Medicine www.bsgm.org.uk
Genetics Society www.genetics.org.uk
Institute of Biomedical Science www.ibms.org
Society of Biology www.societyofbiology.org

Building
Chartered Institute of Building www.ciob.org
Chartered Institution of Building Services Engineers www.cibse.org
Construction Industry Training Board (CITB) www.citb.co.uk

Business Courses
Chartered Institute of Personnel and Development www.cipd.co.uk
Chartered Institute of Public Relations www.cipr.co.uk
Chartered Management Institute www.managers.org.uk
Communication, Advertising and Marketing Education Foundation (CAM Foundation)
     www.camfoundation.com
Department for Business, Innovation, and Skills www.bis.gov.uk
Institute of Administrative Management www.instam.org
Institute of Chartered Secretaries and Administrators www.icsa.org.uk
Institute of Consulting www.iconsulting.org.uk
Institute of Export www.export.org.uk
Institute of Practitioners in Advertising www.ipa.co.uk
Institute of Sales and Marketing Management www.ismm.co.uk
Skills CFA www.skillscfa.org

Chemistry
Institute of Nanotechnology www.nano.org.uk
Royal Society of Chemistry www.rsc.org

Computer Courses
BCS The Chartered Institute for IT www.bcs.org
Institute for the Management of Information Systems www.imis.org.uk
Institution of Analysts and Programmers www.iap.org.uk
Learning and Performance Institute www.learningandperformanceinstitute.com

Consumer Studies/Sciences
Trading Standards Institute www.tradingstandards.gov.uk

Dance
Council for Dance Education and Training www.cdet.org.uk

Dentistry
British Association of Dental Nurses www.badn.org.uk
British Association of Dental Therapists www.badt.org.uk
British Dental Association www.bda.org
British Society of Dental Hygiene and Therapy www.bsdht.org.uk
Dental Laboratories Association www.dla.org.uk
Dental Technologists Association www.dta-uk.org
General Dental Council www.gdc-uk.org

Dietetics
British Dietetic Association www.bda.uk.com

Drama
Equity www.equity.org.uk
Society of British Theatre Designers www.theatredesign.org.uk

Economics
Royal Economic Society www.res.org.uk

Education and Teacher Training
Department for Education www.education.gov.uk
General Teaching Council for Northern Ireland www.gtcni.org.uk
General Teaching Council for Scotland www.gtcs.org.uk
General Teaching Council for Wales www.gtcw.org.uk

Engineering/Engineering Sciences
Energy Institute www.energyinst.org.uk
Engineering Council UK www.engc.org.uk
Institute for Manufacturing www.ifm.eng.cam.ac.uk
Institute of Acoustics www.ioa.org.uk
Institute of Marine Engineering, Science and Technology www.imarest.org
Institution of Agricultural Engineers www.iagre.org
Institution of Civil Engineers www.ice.org.uk
Institution of Engineering Designers www.ied.org.uk
Institution of Engineering and Technology www.theiet.org
Institution of Mechanical Engineers www.imeche.org
Nuclear Institute www.nuclearinst.com
Royal Aeronautical Society www.aerosociety.com

Environmental Science/Studies
Chartered Institute of Ecology and Environmental Management www.cieem.net
Chartered Institute of Environmental Health www.cieh.org
Chartered Institution of Wastes Management www.ciwm.co.uk
Chartered Institution of Water and Environmental Management www.ciwem.org
Environment Agency www.environment-agency.gov.uk
Institution of Environmental Sciences www.ies-uk.org.uk
Institution of Occupational Safety and Health www.iosh.co.uk
Royal Environmental Health Institute of Scotland www.rehis.com
Society for the Environment www.socenv.org.uk

Film, Radio, Video and TV Studies
British Film Institute www.bfi.org.uk
Skillset (National Training Organisation for broadcast, film, video and multimedia) www.skillset.org

Finance (including Banking and Insurance)
Chartered Banker www.charteredbanker.com
Chartered Institute of Loss Adjusters www.cila.co.uk
Chartered Insurance Institute www.cii.co.uk
Chartered Institute for Securities and Investment www.cisi.org
Financial and Legal Skills Partnership www.financialskillspartnership.org.uk
Institute of Financial Services www.ifslearning.ac.uk
Personal Finance Society www.thepfs.org

Food Science/Studies and Technology
Institute of Food Science and Technology www.ifst.org
Society of Food Hygiene and Technology www.sofht.co.uk

Forensic Science
Forensic Science Society www.forensic-science-society.org

Forestry
Institute of Chartered Foresters www.charteredforesters.org
Wood Technology Society www.iwsc.org.uk
Royal Forestry Society www.rfs.org.uk

Geography
British Cartographic Society www.cartography.org.uk
Royal Geographical Society www.rgs.org
Royal Meteorological Society www.rmets.org

Geology/Geological Sciences
Geological Society www.geolsoc.org.uk

Health Sciences/Studies
British Academy of Audiology www.baaudiology.org
British and Irish Orthoptic Society www.orthoptics.org.uk
British Association of Prosthetists and Orthotists www.bapo.com
British Chiropractic Association www.chiropractic-uk.co.uk
British Occupational Hygiene Society www.bohs.org
British Osteopathic Association www.osteopathy.org
General Osteopathic Council www.osteopathy.org.uk
Institute for Complementary and Natural Medicine www.icnm.org.uk
Institution of Occupational Safety and Health www.iosh.co.uk
Society of Homeopaths www.homeopathy-soh.org

History
Royal Historical Society www.royalhistoricalsociety.org

Horticulture
Institute of Horticulture www.horticulture.org.uk

Hospitality and Hotel Management
Institute of Hospitality www.instituteofhospitality.org
People 1st www.people1st.co.uk

Housing
Chartered Institute of Housing www.cih.org

Human Resource Management
Chartered Institute of Personnel and Development www.cipd.co.uk

Information Management
Association for Information Management www.aslib.co.uk
Chartered Institute of Library and Information Professionals www.cilip.org.uk

Landscape Architecture
Landscape Institute www.landscapeinstitute.org.uk

Languages
Chartered Institute of Linguists www.iol.org.uk
Institute of Translation and Interpreting www.iti.org.uk

Law
Bar Council www.barcouncil.org.uk
Chartered Institute of Legal Executives www.cilex.org.uk
Faculty of Advocates www.advocates.org.uk
Law Society of England and Wales www.lawsociety.org.uk
Law Society of Northern Ireland www.lawsoc-ni.org
Law Society of Scotland www.lawscot.org.uk

Leisure and Recreation Management/Studies
Chartered Institute for the Management of Sport and Physical Activity www.cimspa.co.uk

Linguistics
British Association for Applied Linguistics www.baal.org.uk
Royal College of Speech and Language Therapists www.rcslt.org

Marine/Maritime Studies
Nautical Institute www.nautinst.org

Marketing
Chartered Institute of Marketing www.cim.co.uk
Institute of Sales and Marketing Management www.ismm.co.uk

Materials Science/Metallurgy
Institute of Materials, Minerals and Mining www.iom3.org

Mathematics
Council for Mathematical Sciences www.cms.ac.uk

Institute of Mathematics and its Applications www.ima.org.uk
London Mathematical Society www.lms.ac.uk
Mathematical Association www.m-a.org.uk

Media Studies

British Broadcasting Corporation www.bbc.co.uk/careers/home
National Council for the Training of Journalists www.nctj.com
Skillset (National training organisation for broadcast, film, video and multimedia) www.skillset.org
Society for Editors and Proofreaders www.sfep.org.uk
Society of Authors www.societyofauthors.org

Medicine

British Medical Association www.bma.org.uk
General Medical Council www.gmc-uk.org
Institute for Complementary and Natural Medicine www.icnm.org.uk

Microbiology (see also Biological Sciences/Biology)

Society for General Microbiology www.sgm.ac.uk

Music

Incorporated Society of Musicians www.ism.org
Institute of Musical Instrument Technology www.imit.org.uk

Naval Architecture

Royal Institution of Naval Architects www.rina.org.uk

Nursing and Midwifery

Community Practitioners' and Health Visitors' Association www.unitetheunion.org/cphva
Health and Social Care in Northern Ireland www.hscni.net
Nursing and Midwifery Council www.nmc-uk.org
Royal College of Midwives www.rcm.org.uk
Royal College of Nursing www.rcn.org.uk

Nutrition (see Dietetics)

Occupational Therapy

British Association/College of Occupational Therapists www.cot.co.uk

Optometry

Association of British Dispensing Opticians www.abdo.org.uk
British and Irish Orthoptic Society www.orthoptics.org.uk
College of Optometrists www.college-optometrists.org
General Optical Council www.optical.org

Pharmacology

British Toxicology Society www.thebts.org
Royal Pharmaceutical Society of Great Britain www.rpharms.com

Pharmacy

Royal Pharmaceutical Society of Great Britain www.rpharms.com

Photography

Association of Photographers www.the-aop.org
British Institute of Professional Photography www.bipp.com
Royal Photographic Society www.rps.org

Physical Education (*see* **Education and Teacher Training** *and* **Sports Sciences/Studies**)

Physics
Institute of Physics www.iop.org
Institute of Physics and Engineering in Medicine www.ipem.ac.uk

Physiotherapy
Association of Chartered Physiotherapists in Animal Therapy www.acpat.org
Chartered Society of Physiotherapy www.csp.org.uk

Plant Sciences (*see* **Biological Sciences/Biology**)

Podiatry
Society of Chiropodists and Podiatrists www.scpod.org

Property Management/Development
Chartered Institute of Building www.ciob.org
Chartered Surveyors Training Trust www.cstt.org.uk
National Association of Estate Agents www.naea.co.uk
Royal Institution of Chartered Surveyors www.rics.org

Psychology
British Psychological Society www.bps.org.uk

Public Relations
Chartered Institute of Public Relations www.cipr.co.uk

Quantity Surveying
Chartered Institute of Building www.ciob.org
Royal Institution of Chartered Surveyors www.rics.org

Radiography
Society and College of Radiographers www.sor.org

Social Work
Care Council for Wales www.ccwales.org.uk
Health and Care Professions Council www.hpc-uk.org
Northern Ireland Social Care Council www.niscc.info
Scottish Social Services Council www.sssc.uk.com

Sociology
British Sociological Association www.britsoc.co.uk

Speech Pathology/Sciences/Therapy
Royal College of Speech and Language Therapists www.rcslt.org

Sports Sciences/Studies
British Association of Sport and Exercise Sciences www.bases.org.uk
Chartered Institute for the Management of Sport and Physical Activity www.cimspa.co.uk
English Institute of Sport www.eis2win.co.uk
Scottish Institute of Sport www.sisport.com
Society of Sports Therapists www.society-of-sports-therapists.org
Sport England www.sportengland.org
Sport Scotland www.sportscotland.org.uk
Sport Wales www.sportwales.org.uk

Sports Institute Northern Ireland www.sini.co.uk
UK Sport www.uksport.gov.uk

Statistics
Royal Statistical Society www.rss.org.uk

Tourism and Travel
Institute of Travel and Tourism www.itt.co.uk

Town and Country Planning
Royal Town Planning Institute www.rtpi.org.uk

Transport Management and Planning
Chartered Institute of Logistics and Transport www.ciltuk.org.uk

Veterinary Science/Medicine/Nursing
Association of Chartered Physiotherapists in Animal Therapy www.acpat.org
British Veterinary Nursing Association www.bvna.org.uk
Royal College of Veterinary Surgeons www.rcvs.org.uk
Royal Veterinary College www.rvc.ac.uk

Zoology
Royal Entomological Society www.royensoc.co.uk
Zoological Society of London www.zsl.org

APPENDIX 4
BOOKLIST AND USEFUL WEBSITES

Unless otherwise stated, the publications in this list are all available from Trotman Publishing

STANDARD REFERENCE BOOKS
British Qualifications 2014, 44th edition, Kogan Page
British Vocational Qualifications, 13th edition, Kogan Page

OTHER BOOKS AND RESOURCES
Choosing Your Degree Course & University, 14th edition, Brian Heap
Cut the Cost of Uni, Gwenda Thomas
Destinations of Leavers from Higher Education 2011/13, Higher Education Statistics Agency Services
    (available from HESA)
Getting into course guides: Art & Design Courses, Business & Economics Courses, Dental School,
    Engineering Courses, Law, Medical School, Nursing & Midwifery, Oxford & Cambridge, Pharmacy
    and Pharmacology Courses, Physiotherapy Courses, Psychology Courses, Veterinary School
A Guide to Uni Life, Lucy Tobin
How to Complete Your UCAS Application: 2015 Entry
Insiders' Guide to Applying to University, 2nd edition, Karla Fitzhugh
Studying Abroad 2015, Cerys Evans
Studying and Learning at University, Alan Pritchard, Sage Study Skills Series
Studying in the UK, Cerys Evans
The Times Good University Guide 2014, John O'Leary, Times Books
University Scholarships, Awards and Bursaries, 8th edition, Brian Heap
Which Uni? Find the Best University for You, Karla Fitzhugh
Working in Accountancy, Sherridan Hughes
Working in Law, Charlie Phillips
Working in the City, Mike Poole
Working in Engineering, Tony Price
Working in Science, Tracy Johnson
Working in Teaching, Alan Newland
Your Gap Year, 7th edition, Susan Griffith, Crimson Publishing

USEFUL WEBSITES
Education, course and applications information
www.gov.uk/browse/education
www.britishcouncil.org/erasmus
www.hesa.ac.uk
www.opendays.com (information on university and college Open Days)
http://unistats.direct.gov.uk (official information from UK universities and colleges for comparing courses)
www.ucas.com
www.disabilityrightsuk.org

Careers information
www.army.mod.uk/join
www.careerseurope.co.uk
www.connexions-live.com
www.tomorrowsengineers.org.uk

www.insidecareers.co.uk
www.isco.org.uk
www.milkround.com
www.nhscareers.nhs.uk
www.prospects.ac.uk
www.socialworkandcarejobs.com
www.trotman.co.uk

Gap Years
www.gapyear.com
www.gap-year.com
www.yini.org.uk (Year in Industry)

Study overseas
www.acu.ac.uk
www.fulbright.org.uk
www.allaboutcollege.com

COURSE INDEX

INDEX OF ADVERTISERS